HANDBOOK OF MEDICAL AND PSYCHOLOGICAL HYPNOSIS

Gary R. Elkins, PhD, ABPP, ABPH, is the author of *Relief From Hot Flashes: The Natural, Drug-Free Program to Reduce Hot Flashes, Improve Sleep, and Ease Stress,* and the groundbreaking publication *Hypnotic Relaxation Therapy: Principles and Applications*, a training manual in hypnosis for health care providers. He is the associate editor of the *International Journal of Clinical and Experimental Hypnosis* and *BCM Complementary and Alternative Medicine,* and consulting editor of *Psychology of Consciousness: Theory, Research, and Practice.* Dr. Elkins is a professor of psychology and neuroscience at Baylor University, where he is the director of the Mind–Body Medicine Research Laboratory. Dr. Elkins is also a clinical professor at the Texas A&M University Health Science Center. He maintains a private practice in clinical psychology with specialization in clinical health psychology, behavioral medicine, and hypnotherapy. Dr. Elkins has board certification from the American Board of Professional Psychology (ABPP) and the American Board of Psychological Hypnosis (ABPH). He is a past president of the American Society of Clinical Hypnosis, Society of Psychological Hypnosis, and the American Board of Psychological Hypnosis. He is the 2014–2017 president of the Society for Clinical and Experimental Hypnosis. With over 40 years of experience in hypnosis and 100 publications, he conducts an ongoing program of research into the use of hypnotherapy and mind–body interventions. He is a nationally and internationally recognized speaker on hypnosis and topics such as complementary and alternative medicine, psychotherapy, pain management, sleep problems, hot flashes, and mind–body interventions in health care.

HANDBOOK OF MEDICAL AND PSYCHOLOGICAL HYPNOSIS
Foundations, Applications, and Professional Issues

Gary R. Elkins, PhD, ABPP, ABPH

SPRINGER PUBLISHING COMPANY
NEW YORK

Springer Publishing Company, LLC
11 West 42nd Street
New York, NY 10036
www.springerpub.com

Acquisitions Editor: Stephanie Drew
Compositor: Exeter Premedia Services Private Ltd.

ISBN: 9780826124869
e-book ISBN: 9780826124876

16 17 18 19 20 / 5 4 3 2 1

The author and the publisher of this Work have made every effort to use sources believed to be reliable to provide information that is accurate and compatible with the standards generally accepted at the time of publication. The author and publisher shall not be liable for any special, consequential, or exemplary damages resulting, in whole or in part, from the readers' use of, or reliance on, the information contained in this book. The publisher has no responsibility for the persistence or accuracy of URLs for external or third-party Internet websites referred to in this publication and does not guarantee that any content on such websites is, or will remain, accurate or appropriate.

Library of Congress Cataloging-in-Publication Data

Names: Elkins, Gary Ray, 1952- , editor.
Title: Handbook of medical and psychological hypnosis: foundations,
   applications, and professional issues / [edited by] Gary R. Elkins.
Description: New York, NY: Springer Publishing Company, LLC, [2017] |
   Includes bibliographical references and index.
Identifiers: LCCN 2016013692| ISBN 9780826124869 | ISBN 9780826124876 (e-book)
Subjects: | MESH: Hypnosis—methods
Classification: LCC RC495 | NLM WM 415 | DDC 615.8/512—dc23
LC record available at https://lccn.loc.gov/2016013692

Printed in the United States of America by McNaughton and Gunn.

In loving memory of my father and mother, Billy Ray Elkins and Jewel Dean Elkins, who gave me everything I needed; I wish I had listened to them more.

In memory of my father-in-law, Zeverino Gutierrez, who taught me to always consult the right book—sometimes the Bible and sometimes Popular Mechanics.

To my wife, Guillerma Gamez Elkins, who is the guiding light of faith and love for our family.

Contents

III. PSYCHOLOGICAL APPLICATIONS

IV. PROFESSIONAL ISSUES

Contributors

Assen Alladin, PhD
Cumming School of Medicine
University of Calgary
Calgary, Alberta, Canada

David Alter, PhD, ABPP, ABPH, FACHP
Institute for Brain-Behavior Integration
Minnetonka, Minnesota

Ran D. Anbar, MD, FAAP
Professor Emerita of Pediatrics and Medicine
SUNY Upstate Medical University
Center Point Medicine
La Jolla, California

Philip R. Appel, PhD
Assistant Professor, Department of
    Rehabilitation Medicine
Georgetown University
Director, Psychological Services
MedStar National Rehabilitation Network
Washington, DC

Arreed Franz Barabasz, EdD, PhD, ABPP
Editor, *International Journal of Clinical and
    Experimental Hypnosis*
Washington State University
Pullman, Washington

Marianne Barabasz, EdD
Washington State University
Pullman, Washington

Debra Barton, RN, PhD, AOCN, FAAN
University of Michigan School of Nursing
Ann Arbor, Michigan

Juliette Bowers, PsyD
Federal Medical Center
Lexington, Kentucky

Roland A. Carlstedt, PhD, ABSP, BCIA
Research Associate, McLean Hospital
    Developmental Biopsychiatry Research Program
Research Associate in Psychology, Harvard
    Medical School, Department of Psychiatry
Chairman and Chief Sport Psychologist, American
    Board of Sport Psychology
Boston, Massachusetts

Consuelo Casula, PhD
Private Practice, Psychologist and
    Psychotherapist
Milan, Italy

Robin Chapman, PsyD, ABPP
St. Thomas Community Health Center
New Orleans, Louisiana

Ciara Christensen, PhD
St. Luke's Clinic, Behavioral Health Services
Twin Falls, Idaho

Maren Cordi, PhD
Division of Cognitive Biopsychology and
    Methods
University of Fribourg
Fribourg, Switzerland

Lauren Koep Crawshaw, PsyD
South Texas VA Medical Center
San Antonio, Texas

Carolyn Daitch, PhD, LP, FMPA, FASCH
Director, Center for the Treatment of Anxiety
    Disorders
Farmington Hills, Michigan

Giuseppe De Benedittis, MD, PhD
University of Milan
Milan, Italy

Flavio G. Di Leone, MD
School of Psychiatry of the Department of
    Neurology and Psychiatry
Policlinico Umberto I Hospital
Rome, Italy

E. Thomas Dowd, PhD, ABPP
Rainier Behavioral Health
Tacoma, Washington

Gary Elkins, PhD, ABPP, ABPH
Baylor University
Waco, Texas

Betty Alice Erickson, MS, LPC, LMFT
Private Practice, Psychotherapy
Dallas, Texas

Benedicto A. Fernandes, MD
University of Illinois School of Medicine
Peoria, Illinois

Gabor Filo, DDS
Private Practice, Dentistry
Hamilton, Ontario, Canada

Claire Frederick, MD
Private Practice, Psychiatry
Tahoe City, California

Ashley Gartner, PsyD
The Ludden Group, P.C.
Rockwall, Texas

Carol Ginandes, PhD, ABPP
Assistant Professor of Psychology, Harvard
    Medical School
Private Practice
Watertown, Massachusetts

David Godot, PsyD
Private Practice, Psychologist
Los Angeles, California

Katalin Gombos, PhD
Szent Janos Hospital and North-Buda
    Unified Hospitals
Budapest, Hungary

Ashley Goodman, DDS
Private Practice, Dentistry
San Diego, California

Joseph P. Green, PhD
The Ohio State University, Lima
Lima, Ohio

Daniel Handel, MD
Denver Health Medical Center
University of Colorado School of Medicine
Denver, Colorado

Michael Heap, BSc, MSc, PhD, C. Psychol,
    MSc in Forensic Psychology
University of Sheffield
Sheffield, England

Kimberly Hickman, MSCP
Baylor University
Waco, Texas

Adam Iglesias, PhD
Private Practice, Licensed Psychologist
Palm Beach Gardens, Florida

Alex Iglesias, PhD
Private Practice, Psychology and Psychotherapy
Palm Beach Gardens, Florida

Edit Jakubovits, PhD
Semmelweis University
Budapest, Hungary

Mark Jensen, PhD
University of Washington
Harborview Medical Center
Seattle, Washington

Aimee Johnson, PhD
Wake Forest School of Medicine
Winston-Salem, North Carolina

Alisa Johnson, BA
Baylor University
Waco, Texas

Pamela Kaiser, PhD, CPNP, CNS
Co-Founder & Co-Director, National Pediatric
    Hypnosis Training Institute
Private Practice, Psychotherapy, Children and Teens
Menlo Park, California

Zoltán Kekecs, PhD
Imperial College–London
London, England

Cassie Kendrick, PsyD
Private Practice, Clinical Psychology
Woodway, Texas

Carol Kershaw, EdD
Milton Erickson Institute of Houston
Houston, Texas

Irving Kirsch, PhD
Program in Placebo Studies & Therapeutic
    Encounter (PiPS)
Beth Israel Deaconess Medical Center/Harvard
    Medical School
Boston, Massachusetts

John Klocek, PhD
Baylor University
Waco, Texas

Richard P. Kluft, MD, PhD
Private Practice
Bala Cynwyd, Pennsylvania

Daniel P. Kohen, MD, FAAP, ABMH
Partners-in-Healing of Minneapolis
Minnetonka, Minnesota

Mathieu Landry, BSc
McGill University
Montreal, Quebec, Canada

Elvira Lang, MD, FSIR, FSCEH
Comfort Talk®, LLC
Brookline, Massachusetts

Jeffrey E. Lazarus, MD, FAAP
Private Practice, Pediatrics
Menlo Park, California

Alexander A. Levitan, MD, MPH, ABMH
Private Practice, Internal Medicine/Medical
    Oncology
New Brighton, Minnesota

Camillo Loriedo, MD, PhD
Professor of Psychiatry, University of Rome
    School of Medicine
President, Italian Society of Hypnosis
Past-President, International Society of Hypnosis
Rome, Italy

Steven Jay Lynn, PhD, ABPP (Clinical, Forensic)
Professor, Department of Psychology
Binghamton University
Binghamton, New York

Joseph Meyerson, MA
Tel Aviv University
Tel Aviv, Israel

Yesenia Mosca, BA
Baylor University
Waco, Texas

Donald Moss, PhD
Dean, College of Integrative Medicine and
    Health Sciences
Saybrook University
Oakland, California

Thomas F. Nagy, PhD
Independent Practice in Psychology
Adjunct Clinical Associate Professor, Department
    of Psychiatry and Behavioral Sciences
Stanford Medical School
Palo Alto, California

Nicholas Olendzki, MSCP
Baylor University
Waco, Texas

Karen Olness, MD
Professor Emerita of Pediatrics, Global Health
    and Diseases
Case Western Reserve University
Cleveland, Ohio

Olafur S. Palsson, PsyD
Professor of Medicine
University of North Carolina at Chapel Hill
Chapel Hill, North Carolina

Ronald J. Pekala, PhD
Private Practice, West Chester, Pennsylvania &
    Coatesville Veterans Administration Medical
    Center
Coatesville, Pennsylvania

Michelle Perfect, PhD
University of Arizona
Tucson, Arizona

Burkhard Peter, PhD Dipl Psych
MEG-Stiftung and Ludwig Maximilians
   University of Munich
München, Germany

Björn Rasch, Prof. Dr. Rer. Nat.
Division of Cognitive Biopsychology and
   Methods
University of Fribourg
Fribourg, Switzerland

Amir Raz, PhD, ABPH
Canada Research Chair in the Cognitive
   Neuroscience of Attention
Department of Psychiatry at McGill University
Senior Investigator in the Lady Davis Institute
   for Medical Research of the Jewish General
   Hospital
Montreal, Quebec, Canada

Pamela Sadler, PhD, C Psych
Associate Professor, Department of
   Psychology
Wilfrid Laurier University
Waterloo, Ontario, Canada

Marty Sapp, EdD
University of Wisconsin-Milwaukee
Milwaukee, Wisconsin

Philip D. Shenefelt, MD
Professor, Dermatology and Cutaneous
   Surgery
University of South Florida
Tampa, Florida

Dan Short, PhD
Director, Phoenix Institute of Ericksonian
   Therapy
Scottsdale, Arizona

Jim Sliwinski, PhD
Finlandia University
Hancock, Michigan

Sharon Spiegel, PhD
Private Practice, Clinical Psychology
Bethesda, Maryland

Linda Thomson, PhD, MSN, APRN,
   ABMH, ABHN
Hypnosis for Health and Healing
Ludlow, Vermont

Moshe S. Torem, MD
Chief Integrative Medicine, Akron General
   Medical Center
Professor of Psychiatry, Northeast Ohio
   Medical University
Akron, Ohio

Graham F. Wagstaff, PhD
University of Liverpool
Liverpool, England

Thomas W. Wall, PhD, ABPP, ABPH
Seattle Pacific University
Seattle, Washington

Anette Werner, PhD, Midwife, Master
   of Health Science
Assistant Professor, Institute of Clinical Research
University of Southern Denmark
Odense M, Denmark

Jacqueline M. Wheatcroft, PhD
University of Liverpool
Liverpool, England

Eric Willmarth, PhD
Saybrook University
San Francisco, California

Erik Woody, PhD
University of Waterloo
Waterloo, Ontario, Canada

Yimin Yu, MSCP
Baylor University
Waco, Texas

Foreword

Hypnotherapy is the use of clinical hypnosis to treat medical and psychological disorders and enhance health and well-being. The broad applications of hypnosis in medicine and psychotherapy require clinicians to have a vast amount of knowledge and training in the requisite methods and skills. This *Handbook of Medical and Psychological Hypnosis: Foundations, Applications, and Professional Issues* provides the depth of knowledge needed by a provider of hypnotherapy. It is a book for practitioners—psychologists, physicians, psychotherapists, clinical social workers, marriage and family therapists, mental health counselors, nurses, dentists, chiropractors, and acupuncturists. As competency in hypnotherapy requires lifelong learning, this book fills this role by providing the foundational knowledge needed by the beginner and the depth of clinical wisdom and skills used by experienced clinicians.

Handbook of Medical and Psychological Hypnosis: Foundations, Applications, and Professional Issues is destined to become *the* essential companion to courses and workshops on clinical hypnosis. It begins with thorough coverage of the material typically found in introductory workshops on clinical hypnosis and then moves to more advanced topics such as the theories, approaches, empirical research, and the many hypnotic therapeutic interventions. The reader will learn about both the empirical basis of hypnosis and the practical "how-to" techniques that are necessary to conduct hypnotic inductions, intervene with hypnotic suggestions, and pursue the highest levels of professional practice. The superior quality of this book is not surprising given that Dr. Elkins is internationally known and has served as president of the American Society of Clinical Hypnosis, the Society for Clinical and Experimental Hypnosis, and the Society for Psychological Hypnosis, where

he has organized multiple workshops and written on the most widely accepted standards of training in clinical hypnosis.

Every clinician who utilizes hypnosis in his or her practice and every student who is learning hypnosis will want to have this comprehensive desk reference on the bookshelf. The book provides the reader with the major approaches to hypnotherapy—hypnotic relaxation, cognitive, Ericksonian, hypnoanalysis, and ego-state therapy—with each topic written by the leaders in the field. In addition, this book gives physicians, dentists, and therapists a resource to expand and improve their practice with all the major applications of hypnosis in health care. With 75 chapters and contributions from an equally large number of the world's most expert researchers and hypnotherapists in the field, it represents the largest, most comprehensive, and up-to-date textbook on clinical hypnosis yet to be assembled. This comprehensive reference is an invaluable book for anyone engaged in providing hypnotherapy to his or her patients and clients.

The chapters on medical applications address over 30 topics and problems in which hypnotherapy may be integrated into effective practice. There are chapters on asthma, bone fractures, chronic pain, dental applications, enuresis, fibromyalgia, headaches, hypertension, irritable bowel syndrome, obstetrical care, menopausal symptoms (hot flashes), nail biting, nausea associated with chemotherapy, acute pain management, procedural pain, palliative care, Parkinson's disease, pediatrics, pre-surgery anesthesia, Raynaud's syndrome, rehabilitation, skin disorders, warts, spasmodic torticollis, surgery, vocal cord dysfunction, stress, and autoimmune disorders.

Behavioral health professionals, including psychotherapists, psychiatrists, and psychologists, now have a reference for the multiple applications of hypnosis in psychotherapy and health psychology. Chapters on psychological applications include: addictions and relapse prevention, affect regulation, anger management, anxiety in children and adults, bereavement, conversion disorder, depression, eating disorders, ego strengthening, fear of flying, marital communication, obesity and weight loss, posttraumatic stress disorder, sexual self-image, sleep, smoking cessation, sports performance, and stress management. There are also chapters on forensic interviewing with hypnosis, flow and peak experiences, and mindfulness and hypnosis.

In addition to its wealth of hypnotic information, this book is a tremendous resource for self-study and practice. Each of the chapters on the applications of hypnosis includes a discussion of the empirical clinical trials and the contemporary knowledge about hypnosis, case studies, and transcripts or techniques. The chapters on applications are written to give the reader examples of hypnotic transcripts—what clinicians actually say during hypnotic inductions and hypnotherapy sessions. This provides the reader with the highly useful resource of hypnotic verbalizations and ideas for formulating hypnotic suggestions for treatment of specific problems. The transcripts are provided as examples—not to be applied in cookbook fashion, but as foundations for individualized hypnotic interventions for each patient.

Professional issues are also addressed in this book and include in-depth discussions on certification in clinical hypnosis and ethical considerations. Also incorporated is an extremely useful chapter on the precautions of hypnosis in patient care. It is noteworthy that this one-of-a-kind book clearly integrates relevant research throughout and provides a resource of information on contemporary research in medical and psychological hypnosis.

This book is a perfect companion to clinical workshops and courses in hypnosis. I can speak to this personally, as in my case, after having completed the training in introductory and intermediate clinical hypnosis, I became interested in the use of hypnosis to boost the immune system; increase wound healing; decrease anxiety, stress, or tension; and address specific problems including high blood pressure, insomnia, headaches, and low back pain, as well as help my clients with smoking cessation. However, I quickly became aware of the need for an authoritative text where I could find relevant research and practical guidance on how to best treat these problems. *Handbook of Medical and Psychological Hypnosis* fills this need and precisely provides this resource.

The credentials of and respect for Dr. Elkins make this book an authoritative contribution to our field. Dr. Elkins is a professor of Psychology and Neuroscience who has become one of the leaders in the field of clinical hypnosis. He is a brilliant scholar and a master clinician who has served as president of several hypnosis organizations, led hundreds of hypnosis workshops, and taught thousands of professionals about clinical hypnosis. Dr. Elkins has made contributions to almost every area of hypnosis—ranging from defining hypnosis, to developing a scale to measure hypnotizability (the Elkins Hypnotizability Scale), to teaching and conducting clinical research into innovative applications of hypnosis such as in the relief of hot flashes and optimization of hypnosis to improve sleep and ease stress. His Mind-Body Medicine Research Laboratory at Baylor University is focused specifically on hypnosis research and has been continually funded by the National Institutes of Health. His clinical knowledge, scientific expertise, and exceptional breadth of knowledge are reflected in this book that is destined to be a classic in the field.

In this book, Dr. Elkins has brought together the finest clinicians and academicians from around the world to contribute their respective expertise and clinical skills. This was a very large undertaking that required many hours of writing, dedication, and a great commitment on the part of Dr. Elkins, as well as the many chapter contributors. We can be grateful for this massive work. The result is that we now have a magnificent resource for the practice of hypnotherapy.

Maximilian Muenke, MD
Chief, Medical Genetics Branch
Director, NIH Medical Genetics and Genomic
 Medicine Residency and Fellowship Program
National Institute of Human Genome Research
 National Institutes of Health, Bethesda,
 Maryland
Approved Consultant in Clinical Hypnosis
 American Society of Clinical Hypnosis
Member, Society for Clinical and
 Experimental Hypnosis

Preface

Hypnosis has a wide range of uses in the treatment of medical and psychological conditions. Further, there is an increasing body of research that supports hypnotic interventions in psychotherapy and health care. In the United States, the National Institutes of Health has supported numerous clinical trials of psychological interventions that utilize relaxation, suggestion, imagery, and various forms of self-hypnosis. Considerable evidence now exists to show that mind–body interventions, including hypnosis, can be of great benefit in the treatment of disorders ranging from chronic pain, anxiety, and stress to coping with medical procedures, irritable bowel syndrome, menopausal symptoms such as hot flashes, and sleep problems, just to name a few. Given the mounting evidence for hypnosis, health care professionals are increasingly challenged to take a more integrative approach and learn about hypnosis as a primary therapy or as an adjunct to other psychotherapy approaches. This book provides a comprehensive resource for students and professionals in the helping professions to learn about hypnosis and its many applications.

Hypnosis is generally understood as a state of consciousness involving focused attention and reduced peripheral awareness in which there is an enhanced capacity for response to suggestion (Elkins, Barabasz, Council, & Spiegel, 2015). In clinical practice, hypnosis generally involves an induction procedure with suggestions for focusing attention, followed by suggestions for relaxation and a hypnotic state. The hypnotic state is sometimes referred to as a trance state and is characterized by attentive concentration and reduction in judgmental critical thinking. As a result, during a hypnotic state, a person may be more receptive to positive suggestions. While a formal hypnotic induction is often used in hypnotherapy, a hypnotic state may occur naturally, such as becoming absorbed in reading, daydreaming, or becoming engrossed in a fascinating movie. In some ways, a hypnotic state may be compared with meditation or other relaxation-based methods that involve an inward focusing of attention and calmness (Stewart, 2005). Both meditation and hypnosis may be self-guided (self-hypnosis) and a state of meditation may be understood as hypnosis, depending on the state achieved. However, hypnotherapy differs from meditation in that hypnotic suggestions may vary a great deal and are intentionally goal-directed. Hypnotic suggestions may involve mental imagery, direct suggestion, or indirect suggestions using stories or metaphors. Much of the skill in using hypnosis depends upon the ability to achieve a hypnotic state and individualize hypnotic suggestions to achieve a desired effect.

The first section of this book—*Foundations of Medical and Psychological Hypnosis*—includes much of the information that might be covered in a basic level workshop on hypnosis. While hypnotic methods of inducing a state of consciousness and therapeutic suggestions have been used for centuries, the early history of hypnosis begins with the Austrian physician Franz Anton Mesmer, who developed a thriving practice in Vienna and later in Paris in the late 1700s. The term *hypnosis* was introduced by a Scottish physician, James Braid, during the early 1800s, in which it was recognized that the hypnotic state is different from sleep but involves concentrated attention and absorption. The rise of scientific research into hypnosis began following World War II, during which time there was a need for effective psychological interventions for pain management and treatment of posttraumatic stress. Ernest Hilgard and his research team at Stanford University conducted numerous studies and developed scales for measurement of hypnotizability. Many of the currently used clinical methods of hypnotic suggestion were introduced by

Milton Erickson, MD (1901–1980). Milton Erickson was a psychiatrist and leading practitioner of hypnotherapy who developed many innovative methods of hypnotic induction and intervention. During the late 1940s and early 1950s, the present day hypnosis societies were established, including the Society for Clinical and Experimental Hypnosis, followed by the American Society of Hypnosis, the European Society of Hypnosis, and the International Society of Hypnosis.

Also covered in the Foundations section are the theories of hypnosis, hypnotizability, neurophysiology, and clinical methods for presenting hypnosis to patients and formulating hypnotic suggestions. While the mechanisms of hypnosis are not yet fully known, the reader should carefully read this section to develop a fuller understanding of hypnosis and hypnotic inductions.

The Foundations section of the book also introduces the major approaches. Hypnosis may be integrated with cognitive behavioral or psychodynamic therapy. In addition, there are several systems that are more specific to hypnotherapy. These include approaches such as Ericksonian therapy (based on the methods of Milton Erickson, MD) and ego-state therapy (based upon the methods of Jack Watkins, PhD). This also includes the theory and principles of hypnotic relaxation therapy, as developed in my clinical practice and the Mind-Body Medicine Research Laboratory at Baylor University. Each of these systems includes some conceptualization of hypnotic inductions and consideration of unconscious processes in the therapeutic process. The reader will find this section to be very useful, as it provides an understanding of the rich and complex nature of hypnotic interventions to change cognitions, facilitate insight, relieve symptoms, change behavior, and develop coping skills.

The second section of the book is the largest, as it covers the *Medical Applications*. This section provides a ready reference for clinicians to help deal with most problems for which evidence exists on the use of hypnosis in clinical practice. Many chapters in the Medical Applications section are organized with the following components:

- Introduction (description of the problem, prevalence, symptoms, etc.)
- Evidence (relevant research)
- Case example
- Technique or transcript
- Summary or clinical tips, and so on.

Medical Applications are presented in alphabetical order and include 34 chapters covering both adult and child applications. Each chapter provides a review of existing empirical evidence as well as clinical technique. Transcripts are provided as an example of hypnotic intervention; however, it is generally understood that hypnosis is individualized based upon the needs of each patient.

The *Psychological Applications* section comprises 22 chapters on a range of topics from addictions and relapse prevention to treatment of anxieties and stress management. Most of the chapters in this section include case examples of hypnosis in therapy, transcripts, as well as guidance on how hypnosis can be most effectively used in clinical practice.

The last section of the book covers *Professional Issues* in the practice of hypnosis. This section is intended for clinical practitioners as well as researchers. Topics include ethical practice, placebo effects, and information on certification and specialty boards in medical and psychological hypnosis (i.e., the American Board of Psychological Hypnosis, American Board of Medical Hypnosis, American Board of Dental Hypnosis, American Hypnosis Board for Clinical Social Work, and American Board of Hypnosis in Nursing). Precautions regarding the use of hypnosis are also presented. Hypnosis can be a very powerful and effective tool when used by a skilled clinician. However, like a scalpel, its effectiveness depends largely upon the expertise of the practitioner. It is important for the skilled clinician to know both when to use hypnosis and when to *not* use hypnosis.

Finally, research methods in medical and psychological hypnosis are presented. Research into clinical hypnosis and empirical evidence continues to expand. This includes well-designed randomized clinical trials as well as research into the psychological and physiological mechanisms that may be involved in hypnotic responding. Critical evaluation of evidence is important to know how to best use the evolving body of knowledge about hypnosis. Also, researchers must develop sophisticated methods to study hypnosis and related mind–body therapies to determine the effective components and further applications.

HOW TO USE THIS BOOK

This book was written for several purposes. It was written to fill the gap between hypnosis clinical practice and research; provide foundational knowledge about hypnosis theory and practice; and serve as a desk reference on a range of medical and psychological applications as well as professional issues. It is a comprehensive text and may be used in graduate study in training programs for physicians, psychologists, psychotherapists, and other health care providers.

The clinician should use this book to identify the theory and clinical techniques useful in presenting hypnosis, structuring hypnotic inductions, and formulating hypnotic suggestions. Practitioners will find a wealth of information on the theories and techniques of hypnotic interventions, which may be integrated with other therapeutic approaches or, in some cases, used alone.

Learning hypnotherapy is a process that requires practice as well as reading. This book can be used to gain the essential knowledge about hypnosis for development of clinical skills. It is important to refine skills through practice and mentorship. This book may be used in conjunction with workshops, training programs, course work, and clinical supervision. Readers are encouraged to seek out appropriate training with skilled teachers such as may be found in professional organizations. Clinical skill is built through practice and the process of supervision and counsel. The same is true in regard to clinical skill in hypnosis. The use of hypnosis should be consistent with both the needs of the patient and the professional's area of expertise. It is always the case that one should restrict one's use of hypnosis to areas in which the individual has expertise and appropriate certification.

As a desk reference, this book can be used as a resource by clinicians who may be treating patients with a variety of presenting problems. It is not uncommon that hypnosis is sometimes considered for especially complex cases. This book provides a reference for most uses of hypnosis such as pain management, psychophysiological symptoms, smoking cessation, weight loss, and stress, as well as rare or challenging problems such as conversion disorder and spasmodic torticollis. Also, innovative uses of hypnosis are identified such as for facilitating marital communication, forensic interviewing, mindfulness, and improvement of slow-wave sleep.

Becoming an expert in clinical and experimental hypnosis requires lifelong learning. This book is designed to be a key resource to facilitate that process.

Gary R. Elkins, PhD, ABPP, ABPH
Professor and Director, Mind-Body Medicine
   Research Laboratory
Baylor University

REFERENCES

Elkins, G., Barabasz, A., Council, J., & Spiegel, D. (2015). Advancing research and practice: The revised APA Division 30 definition of hypnosis. *International Journal of Clinical and Experimental Hypnosis, 63*(1), 1–9.

Stewart, J. (2005). Hypnosis in contemporary medicine. *Mayo Clinic Proceedings, 80*(4), 511–524.

Acknowledgments

The vision for this book has been with me for many years, as I have served as the president of several organizations (American Society of Clinical Hypnosis, Society of Psychological Hypnosis, and Society for Clinical and Experimental Hypnosis) and conducted workshops and research in clinical hypnosis for most of my professional career. I began to envision a work that would be comprehensive, draw upon the most highly recognized experts in hypnosis, integrate research and clinical practice, and provide a much-needed contemporary handbook on medical and psychological hypnosis. I knew that such a book would be a large undertaking and would depend on the contributions of many. It seemed like an overwhelming task. It was through my consultation with Stephanie Drew at Springer Publishing Company that this vision began to become a reality. I want to first thank Ms. Stephanie Drew and Ms. Mindy Chen for their support and guidance throughout this process. I could not imagine a more favorable place to publish than Springer Publishing Company.

Many of my colleagues and friends agreed to share their knowledge and wrote chapters for this book; all provided their best work. These individuals are the authors of the 75 chapters contained in this book. I am deeply grateful to each of them—too numerous to list here, but thankfully they are all identified in the contributors listing. Those who contributed were selected from around the world based upon their expertise, excellence in teaching and writing, or their research (in many cases, all three). Please refer to each chapter as an acknowledgment of them.

I also want to recognize the leadership and members of the International Society of Hypnosis, Society for Clinical and Experimental Hypnosis, Canadian Society of Clinical Hypnosis, European Society of Hypnosis, and American Society of Hypnosis for their contributions and training. Most of the contributors are members of one or more of these societies. In my experience of some 40-plus years as a clinical health psychologist and clinician/researcher, the very best clinicians and teachers I have known are found in these professional hypnosis organizations. Seriously, they are the best.

In addition, the Department of Psychology and Neuroscience at Baylor University and our department chair, Dr. Charles Weaver, have provided me with an incredibly supportive and stimulating environment in which to live and work. At Baylor University, I have been privileged to mentor doctoral students, teach clinical psychology, be given space and resources to conduct hypnosis research, and offered the opportunity to collaborate with colleagues and hospitals. It is the finest institution and faculty to be found anywhere.

This is my opportunity to express a special "thank you" to the wonderful students, postdoctoral fellows, and staff in the Mind-Body Medicine Research Laboratory at Baylor. Especially, I am appreciative of Nicole O'Guinn for reading and providing very helpful edits to the references and chapters. I thank Mackenzie Kallemeyn and Vicki Patterson, who also read and provided suggestions for edits to the references and many chapters. Each of them provided much time, effort, and thoughtfulness for which I am very appreciative. I hope they were able to benefit from reading these chapters as they continue their professional education and careers.

I want to also express my heartfelt gratitude to my wife, Guillerma, for her support, encouragement, and excellent Italian Cream Cake! Both she and her cake gave me the strength I needed in preparing this manuscript. She is without compare, beautiful and strong in body, mind, and spirit.

Foundations of Medical and Psychological Hypnosis

SECTION

I

History of Medical and Psychological Hypnosis

John Klocek

The topic of hypnosis and its use in medical and clinical settings is one that, seemingly more often than not, quickly elicits a demonstratively expressed opinion among medical and mental health practitioners, scientists, and observers. These opinions are delivered with widely varied degrees of actual knowledge and understanding about hypnosis, its uses, and its history. The current text is designed to provide a comprehensive resource to those seeking a more substantive understanding of hypnosis and its uses—both established and emerging. As with any field, essential to this knowledge base is an awareness of history. An understanding of the people and the forces that guided and shaped the development of hypnosis provides an important context to the current state of research, application, and dissemination of hypnosis as a clinical tool in a variety of medical and clinical settings. It also helps us understand why, despite a history that can be traced back more than 250 years, the thoughts and opinions about the utility and validity of hypnosis remain so varied today.

The history of the utilization of hypnosis in medical and clinical settings by European practitioners can be clearly traced to the late 1700s, though the history of hypnosis and forms of hypnosis extend much further into the past and into many different regions and cultures. As others have detailed, the histories of numerous cultures from diverse areas of the world describe the use of hypnotic or trance-like states for social, religious, and medical reasons (e.g., Thomason, 2010; Winkelman, 1986). As a full history of hypnosis is beyond the scope of a single chapter, we confine ourselves to a brief description of the history of the study and application of hypnosis in Western (European) medicine. While at times drawing on traditions and practices from many areas of the world and diverse cultural traditions, it is this branch of the history of hypnosis that provides the context important for the understanding of the application and research of hypnosis in Western medicine today.

EARLY HISTORY AND DEVELOPMENT

Hypnosis has its origin in mesmerism (Bramwell, 1903). In the late 1700s, the Viennese physician Anton Mesmer began to use "mesmerism" in medical settings for the treatment of a wide range of medical problems. Based on his theory that the human body was subject to the same tidal forces affected by the planets, he believed that cures for a wide range of medical problems could be effected by using magnets to help redistribute a "magnetic fluid" through suggestion and moving magnets across the patron's body. However, as noted by Hammond (2013), Mesmer appears to have derived a number of his central ideas and practices from other individuals. For example, as early as the late 1600s, the English physician Maxwell theorized that magnetic medicine could be beneficial in aiding the treatment of diseases attributable to insufficient levels of a universal spirit (Hammond, 2013). Mesmer, with a flair for the dramatic, frequently utilized theatrical music, magnets, and other props in the delivery of his treatment. Despite the documented successes of his treatments, it may have been the theatrical elements and reluctance to subject his treatments to controlled trials (Hammond, 2013) that drew the ire of the medical community and the authorities in Vienna. Alienated in Vienna, Mesmer moved to Paris and resumed his practice (Hammond, 2013). Once again, his treatment successes brought great acclaim and renewed scrutiny. This eventually resulted in the formation of the

Franklin Commission by King Louis XVI to study mesmerism (Elkins, 2014). The commission's report in 1784 dismissed mesmerism as trickery and Mesmer himself as a charlatan, resulting in a substantial decline in the application and research concerned with mesmerism in Paris. Thomas Jefferson went so far as to seek the barring of mesmerism from the United States. The ripples of the strength with which Mesmer was dismissed by the Franklin report likely echoes today. Nevertheless, other physicians, taken with the success of the treatments, continued to apply and systematically study mesmerism and hypnosis.

John Elliotson, often remembered as an early adopter of the stethoscope within his medical practice, was a forward-looking physician who passionately pursued emerging advances in medical care (Bramwell, 1903). Following his exposure to mesmerism in the 1830s by a visiting physician, Elliotson initiated his own research into its application at University College in London. Bramwell (1903) notes that based on initial successes he experienced, Elliotson pursued his growing interest in mesmerism with much "zeal." He thus alienated colleagues and ran afoul of the hospital's official opposition to mesmerism, resulting in his resignation from the hospital. Nevertheless, he continued as a strong proponent of the approach in cases he thought it suitable (he continued to treat patients utilizing the more conventional methods of the time), giving talks encouraging the dispassionate and scientific study of the phenomenon. Elliotson published a journal—*Zoist*—detailing work in the area from 1843 through 1855 (Bramwell, 1903).

James Esdaile, a Scottish contemporary of Elliotson, began using mesmeric-like approaches (Edmonston, 1986) while employed as a physician by the East India Company in India. He began the use of hypnosis in surgical settings in the mid-1800s, presenting over 100 successful cases to the government. He was subsequently placed in charge of a small hospital in Calcutta for the purposes of further application and study of his work. Though regularly attacked in the Indian medical journals, he continued the use of hypnosis in surgery. Esdaile performed over 300 significant and thousands of minor surgeries with little to no pain in an era that preceded pharmacological anesthesia (Bramwell, 1903). He left India in 1851, returning to Scotland where he successfully introduced mesmeric approaches in surgery and continued to advocate for the use of hypnosis as a useful approach to anesthesia for surgical procedures (Hammond, 2013).

BEGINNINGS OF MODERN HYPNOSIS

To this point, the study of hypnosis had been primarily an accumulation of successful case studies. As medicine increasingly turned to systematic and rigorous scientific methodology to establish the basis for medical practice, there was a need for hypnosis to be defined and studied with similar rigor.

James Braid began to fill this need following his first exposure to mesmerism in 1841. He authored a series of papers in which he described experiments he conducted investigating mesmerism. Based on his findings that the effects of mesmerism were more related to sleeplike states and not related to magnetism, he asserted that a new term—*hypnosis*—was in order (Hammond, 2013). He also repeatedly asserted that the powerful phenomenon of hypnosis had a physiological and psychological basis and should thus be used only by physicians (Bramwell, 1903). Braid stripped away most of the trappings utilized in original mesmeric approaches and instructed patients primarily in eye fixation techniques (Elkins, 2014; Hammond, 2013). Braid died before he could publish his planned follow-up works to his initial work in hypnosis (Bramwell, 1903).

The French physician Ambroise-Auguste Liebeault began serious study of hypnosis in 1860, and in 1864, settling into a small country practice in Nancy, France, he emphasized the use of hypnosis as a method of treating various ailments (Hammond, 2013). Liebeault practiced in a rural setting and devoted his practice to the poor—whom he often treated for free (Bramwell, 1903). In his description of first-person observations of Liebeault's work, Bramwell (1903) describes the use of suggestion for the negation of morbid symptoms as well as the maintenance of conditions, which support general good health and functioning. Liebeault also developed a friendship and collaboration with Hippolyte Bernheim through the successful treatment of a patient who had not benefitted from 6 months of treatment for sciatica by Bernheim (Bramwell, 1903). Initially quite skeptical, Bernheim visited Liebeault at Nancy. He started to observe Liebeault's work and soon became an ardent supporter and collaborator. The publishing of their work, which emphasized the psychological factors associated with hypnosis, coincided with the emerging utilization of hypnosis for psychiatric patients (Elkins, 2014).

One of the individuals most readily associated with the application of hypnosis to clinical psychiatric settings was the French neurologist Jean-Martin Charcot. Based on his initial work with patients at a mental hospital for women, he erroneously came to believe that hypnosis was a form of hysteria. Accordingly, Charcot believed that hypnosis could only be induced in those individuals who were physiologically predisposed to hysteria (Hammond, 2013). This physiologically based hypothesis of hypnosis differed markedly from the factors proposed to influence the response to hypnosis by Liebeault and Bernheim during the 1870s and 1880s—a period of significant growth for hypnosis in Europe.

The application of hypnosis in clinical psychiatric settings continued to be at the fore in the latter part of the 19th century. Pierre Janet, for example, further developed and made extensive use of hypnosis in clinical psychiatric settings. Janet proposed the dissociation of the unconscious as a defense mechanism and believed that the deeper an individual moved into hypnosis, the more accessible the unconscious became (Elkins, 2014; Hammond, 2013). Janet's work with hypnosis in psychotherapy had a strong influence on his contemporaries and is still influential in the treatment of dissociative and conversion disorders (Hammond, 2013).

Josef Breuer and Sigmund Freud, two contemporaries of Janet, further advanced the use of hypnosis in clinical psychiatric settings. Breuer, a physician from Vienna, utilized hypnosis in his treatment of hysterical reactions by encouraging patients to discuss the bases for their ailments while hypnotized. Freud, also a Viennese physician, became enamored of hypnosis and spent time studying with both Charcot at Salpêtrière and with Bernheim at Nancy (Hammond, 2013). Breuer and he became friends and collaborators while Freud was engaged in the initial development of his theory of the unconscious and the application of that theory to the treatment of hysterical patients. Although Freud ceased crediting Janet's influence as early as 1896,

he cited the influence of Janet in his early work with hypnosis to access the subconscious (Elkins, 2014; Hammond, 2013). Following the death of Charcot in 1893 and Freud's increasing influence and reliance on free association in psychiatric treatment, the use of hypnosis in clinical psychiatric settings followed a similar decline as that in the research and in the use of hypnosis in medical settings.

MODERN HYPNOSIS

The confluence of increased rigor in research, creative application of hypnotic interventions in medical and clinical psychiatric settings, and an increasing interest in and acceptance of integrated approaches to health care (e.g., Baum, Perry, & Tarbell, 2004) resulted in tremendous growth in the study and application of hypnosis in the 20th century. Stewart (2005), for example, provides a review of more than 100 clinical trials of hypnosis in the treatment of acute and chronic pain, and applications in allergy medicine, dermatology, gastroenterology, hematology, hypertension, neurology, obesity, obstetrics, oncology, pulmonary medicine, rheumatology, surgery, and urology published between 1966 and 2004. Elkins (2014) provides a sampling of published applications of hypnosis in similar areas as well as in the management of stress, anxiety, depression, and posttraumatic stress disorder.

The work of Clark Hull in the late 1920s and early 1930s helped end the decline seen after Charcot's death and the popularity of Freud's methods of free association (Elkins, 2014). Hull was a rigorous scientist who came to psychology after carefully studying the field and determining that it was "a true natural science" and that its primary laws would ultimately be expressible quantitatively (Beach, 1959, p. 7). Though perhaps best known for his work in learning and behavior theory, he engaged in a 10-year systematic study of hypnosis and suggestibility, which culminated in the book *Hypnosis and Suggestibility: An Experimental Approach* (1933).

The use of hypnosis was also evident in psychiatric treatment during and following World War I and World War II. For example, the film *Let There Be Light* (1946) documents the use of hypnosis and suggestion enhanced by the use of sodium pentothal in the treatment of hysterical paralysis and what is now known to be posttraumatic stress disorder in American soldiers following World War II.

Following World War II, an interest in the further study and application of hypnosis in medical and clinical settings emerged. The late 1950s saw the formation of a number of organizations dedicated to the scientific study of hypnosis including the American Society of Clinical Hypnosis and the International Society of Hypnosis. The development of these organizations was paralleled by the development of a number of academically based laboratories dedicated to the scientific study of hypnosis and its potential applications (Elkins, 2014). The rigor with which these organizations and laboratories sought to study hypnosis mirrored the increasing scientific rigor emerging in the study of psychiatry and psychology.

Ernest Hilgard founded the Laboratory of Hypnosis Research at Stanford University in the 1950s. Hilgard and his collaborator, Andre Weitzenhoffer, took the stand that a standard measure of hypnosis was essential to understanding hypnosis, its applicability, and its utility (Elkins, 2014). The subsequent development of the Stanford Hypnotic Susceptibility Scale (Weitzenhoffer & Hilgard, 1959) marked the first effort to develop an empirically validated measure of hypnosis and hypnotizability and provided the basis to evaluate previously advanced theories regarding hypnosis and hypnotizability. Around the same time, Martin Orne founded the Hypnosis Research Project at the Massachusetts Mental Health Center. His research into hypnosis, which continued when he moved his laboratory to the University of Pennsylvania in 1964, also emphasized the importance of the ability to reliably and validly measure hypnotizibility (Elkins, 2014). For example, Orne published a carefully constructed series of experiments to address the competing interpretations of hypnosis as the hypnotic subject's desire to play the role of a hypnotized individual, a marked increase in suggestibility (Hull, 1933), or a less well-defined "altered state of consciousness" (Orne, 1959, p. 277). While the paper does indeed advance the understanding of the nature of hypnosis, Orne (1959) concludes that "until an invariant index of hypnosis can be established, such a diagnosis must be confirmed by the subject's report of alterations in his experience, since the real focus of hypnosis appears to lie in the subjective experience of trance" (p. 298). Such attention to the rigor of the research investigating hypnosis may have contributed to the series of statements acknowledging the acceptance of the utility of hypnosis by the British Medical Association (1956), the American Medical Association (1958), and the American Psychiatric Association (1961) that appeared soon afterward (Stewart, 2005).

In clinical settings, the American psychiatrist Milton Erickson was busily applying the use of hypnosis in novel ways to the practice of psychotherapy (Stewart, 2005). He was also a founding member of the American Society for Clinical Hypnosis and a prolific author who published over 100 articles. Of perhaps particular note was the creativity he utilized in carefully tailoring hypnotic interventions to the specific needs and characteristics of the patients he treated (Elkins, 2014).

Not surprisingly, the proliferation of research and application of hypnosis in medical and clinical settings led to the need for a definition of hypnosis that would allow for a more well-defined common language. In 1994, the Society of Psychological Hypnosis (Division 30 of the American Psychological Association) published a definition of hypnosis. Almost immediately, the definition was criticized on a number of fronts that included being too long, including specific conditions for which hypnosis might be useful, and being theoretically biased and limited (Elkins, Barabasz, Council, & Spiegel, 2015). Accordingly, a revised definition of hypnosis was published in 2003. It, too, met with criticism. It is in this context that Elkins and colleagues (Elkins et al., 2015), in conjunction with Division 30 (Society of Psychological Hypnosis) of the American Psychological Association, put forward a definition of hypnosis intended to provide a common point of reference for clinicians and researchers, while simultaneously allowing for varied perspectives, theories, and hypotheses to be included. The resulting definition of hypnosis, "a state of consciousness involving focused attention and reduced peripheral awareness characterized by an enhanced capacity for response to suggestion" (Elkins et al., 2015, p. 6), is the culmination of over 250 years of development—and the starting point for the evaluation and advancement of the work detailed in the subsequent pages.

The history of hypnosis in medical and clinical settings provides an excellent example of the importance of understanding the historical context in which a particular clinical approach was developed. The history of hypnosis is long, complex, and essential to understanding the current state of knowledge, application, and research of hypnosis in medical and clinical settings.

REFERENCES

Baum, A., Perry, N. W., & Tarbell, S. (2004). The development of psychology as a health science. In T. J. Boll, R. G. Frank, A. Baum, & J. L. Wallender (Eds.), *Handbook of clinical health psychology* (Vol. 3, pp. 9–28). Washington, DC: American Psychological Association. doi:10.1037/11590-001

Beach, F. A. (1959). *Clark Leonard Hull: A biographical memoir*. Washington, DC: National Academy of Sciences.

Bramwell, J. M. (1903). *Hypnotism: It's history, practice, and theory*. Philadelphia, PA: J. B. Lippincott.

Edmonston, W. E. (1986). *The induction of hypnosis*. New York, NY: Wiley.

Elkins, G. (2014). *Hypnotic relaxation therapy principles and applications*. New York, NY: Springer Publishing Company.

Elkins, G. R., Barabasz, A. F., Council, J. R., & Spiegel, D. (2015). Advancing research and practice: The revised APA Division 30 definition of hypnosis. *International Journal of Clinical and Experimental Hypnosis, 63*(1), 1–9. doi:10.1080/00207144.2014.961870

Hammond, D. C. (2013). A review of the history of hypnosis through the late 19th century. *American Journal of Clinical Hypnosis, 56*(2), 174–191.

Hull, L. C. (1933). *Hypnosis and suggestibility: An experimental approach*. New York, NY: Appleton-Century.

Orne, M. T. (1959). The nature of hypnosis: Artifact and essence. *Journal of Abnormal and Social Psychology, 58*(3), 277–299.

Stewart, J. H. (2005). Hypnosis in contemporary medicine. *Mayo Clinic Proceedings, 80*(4), 511–524. doi:10.4065/80.4.511

Thomason, T. (2010). The role of altered states of consciousness in Native American healing. *Journal of Rural Community Psychology, 13*(1). Retrieved from http://works.bepress.com/timothy_thomason/10

Weitzenhoffer, A. M., & Hilgard, E. R. (1959). *Stanford hypnotic susceptibility scales, forms A & B*. Palo Alto, CA: Consulting Psychologists Press.

Winkelman, M. (1986). Trance states: A theoretical model and cross-cultural analysis. *Ethos, 14*, 174–203.

Theories of Hypnosis

Michael Heap

2

CHAPTER

An appropriate starting point for a review of theories of hypnosis is to ask the question, "What observations require an explanation when hypnosis is said to be taking place?" Hence, it is useful to begin with a description of what the participants in the context labeled "hypnosis" actually do. For reasons that become apparent later, when the role of the induction procedure is discussed, there is an argument for including in this description the participants' understanding that what is taking place is "hypnosis." Further than this, we may say: "Hypnosis is a process in which one person, designated the hypnotist, offers suggestions to another person, designated the subject, for imaginative experiences entailing alterations in perception, memory and action" (Kihlström, 2008, p. 21).

If this were all, there would be little need for a theory that explains what is observed. What is missing is how the subject responds. Hence, the earlier definition goes on to say: "These experiences are associated with a degree of subjective conviction bordering on delusion, and an experienced involuntariness bordering on compulsion" (Kihlström, 2008, p. 21).

It is the nature of these reported experiences—the sense of reality and effortlessness (i.e., they are not the outcome of some conscious process or strategy)—that requires explanation.

Of course, a theory of hypnosis must account for far more than this—the intercorrelations in subjects' responsiveness to suggestions across a range of modalities and cognitive processes; the variation in the proportion of people who respond to different types of suggestion; the consistency of a person's hypnotic suggestibility over many years; the factors that account for why some people are more suggestible than others; and so forth. Let us, however, stay with the two key characteristics, namely, the sense of reality and the apparent involuntariness of the subject's response.

HYPNOSIS: THE TRADITIONAL MODEL

What may be termed the *traditional model* for accounting for these phenomena rests on the assumption that to respond in the previous manner, subjects must first experience an altered state of consciousness or "trance," one property of which is heightened suggestibility. To attain this state, they must undergo a hypnotic induction. Typically, the hypnotist encourages the subject to narrow the attention onto just one stimulus, image, or idea and repeatedly informs the subject that he or she is becoming relaxed, tired, drowsy, and sleepy. Various suggestions may then be given, some requiring deeper levels of trance than others. Not all subjects can achieve these; hence, a subject's trance depth is signaled by the suggestions to which he or she is responsive following the induction. The subject finally awakens from the hypnotic state when instructed by the hypnotist.

Hypersuggestibility is not the only property that has historically been claimed for the hypnotic trance. Other alleged properties have included hyperobedience or automatism, profound insensibility to pain, ability to perform superhuman or even supernatural feats, hypermnesia (the ability to recall accurate details of even remote events in one's life), extreme literalism, and facilitated communication with the unconscious mind.

HYPNOSIS: CONTEMPORARY PERSPECTIVES

It is fair to say that the more ambitious claims concerning the hypnotic trance listed earlier have not withstood the test of experimental scrutiny. A little more could be said about spontaneous insensibility to pain, but not here. Spontaneous amnesia of any significance is uncommon; it is not unknown but it is usually reversible and not currently regarded as a definitive property of hypnosis (see Mazzoni, Heap, & Scoboria, 2010). Access to unconscious processes is still claimed by clinical practitioners; more about this is discussed later.

More than this, however, it is not only the claimed properties of the hypnotic state that have come under scrutiny; its very existence has been questioned by many researchers and theoreticians. Indeed, throughout most of the second half of the past century, the theoretical landscape of hypnosis was dominated by the "state versus nonstate" controversy or, more technically, "special process" versus "socio-cognitive" (Lynn & Rhue, 1991).

Socio-Cognitive Theories of Hypnosis

Socio-cognitive theories attempt to explain hypnotic phenomena in terms of normal cognitive and social psychological processes such as imagery (Hull, 1933), role enactment (Sarbin & Coe, 1972), compliance (Wagstaff, 1981), response expectancy (Kirsch, 1991), and various combinations of these (e.g., Barber, Spanos, & Chaves, 1974; Spanos, 1991). The hypnotic subject is perceived as actively deploying his or her available skills—which may include deception—to create the experiences and responses suggested by the hypnotist. Such theories do not rely on the concept of a special state of consciousness resulting from the prior administration of an induction procedure.

Except in instances where deception, simulation, or compliance are the predominant psychological mechanisms at work, advocates of these approaches do not as a rule deny the subjective accounts of the reality of the suggested experiences and their seemingly involuntary or automatic nature. However, it is proposed that although hypnotic subjects are strategically active in creating the suggested responses, the context and the instructions provided by the hypnotist predispose them to interpret their experiences and behavior as involuntary and "happening to them" (see, e.g., Lynn, Kirsch, & Hallquist, 2008, and the discrepancy-attribution theory of Barnier, Dienes, & Mitchell, 2008, in the following text).

Particularly influential in advocating the case for a socio-cognitive understanding of hypnosis

was the late Nicholas Spanos. Essentially, Spanos (see, e.g., Gorassini, 1999, 2004; Spanos, 1991) considered that the key factors underlying responsiveness to hypnotic suggestion are the subjects' attitudes and expectations about hypnosis and their interpretation of the requirements of the hypnotic interaction. First, subjects who approach hypnosis with positive expectations about the experience, unhindered by misgivings such as loss of will and self-control, are more likely to respond to the hypnotist's suggestions than those with negative expectations. Second, suggestible participants are those who "strategically enact" the behavior and experiences required by the hypnotic suggestion, including the requirement to experience the response as though it were happening involuntarily.

Somewhat at odds with this theory is that hypnotic suggestibility scores, as measured by standard scales, tend to be highly consistent over time, although the correlation between these scores and major personality traits and cognitive abilities is at best marginal (see, e.g., Laurence, Beaulieu-Prévost, & du Chéné, 2008). The high consistency of scores was demonstrated by Piccione, Hilgard, and Zimbardo (1989) by following experimental volunteers over a 25-year period, and a study of twins by Morgan (1973) indicated that an individual's hypnotic suggestibility may, at least in part, be genetically determined (see also Horton & Crawford, 2004; Ray, 2007).

However, if Spanos is correct, then it should be possible to enhance an individual's suggestibility by encouraging positive expectations about the hypnotic experience, dispelling any misconceptions and anxieties, and coaching the subject in ways of strategically enacting the targeted behavior or experience. Accordingly, Spanos and his colleagues devised a set of procedures, the Carleton Skill Training Program (Gorassini, 2004; Gorassini & Spanos, 1999), intended to achieve these effects. They report significant and lasting enhancement in the participants' measured suggestibility, although other studies report only transient changes (see Laurence et al., 2008, for an overview of this controversy). An obvious criticism of this procedure is that it may simply be teaching participants one way of responding to hypnotic suggestions, but this is not how untrained "naturally suggestible" subjects respond.

In keeping with the socio-cognitive stance is the more recent discrepancy-attribution theory developed by Barnier et al. (2008). This draws on the work on memory attributions and illusions by Whittlesea and Williams (2001a, 2001b). Briefly, this theory proposes that hypnotic procedures facilitate the subject's experience of the suggested responses. Even though this effect may be quite marginal, it is unexpected (it "takes the subject by surprise"), and the subject is then inclined to attribute this to a lack of control and/or the reality of the experience.

Modern accounts that contrast with the previously described socio-cognitive perspective have been termed *special process theories* and typically posit the operation of some form of dissociation in the perceptual-cognitive-behavioral network as a key feature of "the hypnotic state." Before examining these, it is apposite to review some key experimental findings.

Suggestion: Implicit and Explicit Effects

A theory of hypnosis must acknowledge that responsive subjects are genuine in their insistence that they are not deliberately enacting the suggested behavior or adopting a conscious strategy to create the experience; the effects appear to them as real and effortless. Over the years, investigations have revealed another recurrent aspect of hypnotic responding.

Consider first the suggestion of a negative hallucination. In a series of investigations, Orne (1959, 1962) gave hypnotic subjects the suggestion that when they opened their eyes they would not see the chair in front of them. Some responsive subjects reported not seeing the chair; yet when they were asked to stand up and walk forward, they avoided the chair. On the other hand, subjects who were asked to *pretend* that they were deeply hypnotized were more likely to collide with the chair. In another experiment, subjects who were able to "hallucinate" a person sitting opposite them in a real chair were also able to describe parts of the chair, which would normally have been obscured by its occupant. Simulators were more inclined to deny being able to do this. Finally, Orne (1972) described how he age-regressed a subject to a period in his life when he was only able to speak and understand German; when asked several times in English whether he understood English (using a different phraseology each time) he replied, "*Nein.*" (More common is the observation that age-regressed subjects respond

without difficulty to questions and instructions that, in reality, they would not have understood at the age to which they are regressed.) Orne called this phenomenon *trance logic*.

Trance logic and the associated experimental demonstrations have drawn criticism both on methodological and theoretical grounds (see Lynn & Rhue, 1991; Wagstaff, 1981); it is not typical of all hypnotically suggestible subjects and may be evident in nonhypnotic contexts (Sheehan, 1986). Nevertheless, it exemplifies a theme that has emerged from investigations of suggested experiences over a range of modalities. An instance of this is suggested deafness for one's own voice. Subjects who indicate that, in response to this suggestion, they are unable to hear their voice nevertheless show the usual speech disruption with delayed auditory feedback, whereby their speech output is played back to them with a slight delay (Barber & Calverley, 1964). It has been similarly demonstrated that visual information that is apparently unperceived by hypnotically blind subjects can still influence later performance on cognitive tasks (Bryant & McConkey, 1989). Finally, in response to suggestions of posthypnotic amnesia for material such as lists of words, explicit memory (i.e., conscious recall) is impaired but not implicit memory. The "forgotten" material still has the potential to interfere with the recall of a word list presented earlier that is not included in the amnesia suggestion (Coe, Basden, Basden, & Graham, 1976). Indeed, the target material is manifest in a range of indices of implicit memory such as word associations and the completion of word fragments. This is now a well-established finding (Mazzoni et al., 2010).

The Theory of Dissociated Experience

These results suggest that when responding to such suggestions, responsive subjects may be able to inhibit from consciousness perceptual and cognitive experiences to which they nevertheless respond implicitly (Kihlström, 2014). Hence, one process that may account for the realistic and involuntary nature of their experience is some kind of dissociative or inhibitory mechanism operating within the perceptual-cognitive-behavioral network.

The concept of "dissocation" forms the basis of the highly influential "neo-dissociation theory" developed by Ernest Hilgard (1986). The dissociation mechanism in this case is to be construed as a normal function, as manifested when, for instance, one assigns attentional priority to particular activities or experiences while automatically engaging in other activities or being unaware of other experiences potentially available to consciousness. Examples are driving a car while holding a conversation with a passenger (at times concentrating on one while automatically and successfully executing the other) and not being aware of pain while attending to an emergency. Responsive subjects may be able to manipulate this mechanism in accordance with the requirements of the hypnotist's suggestions. Thus, when responding, say, to an arm levitation suggestion, the subject is conscious that the arm is rising but the intention and effort of lifting it is now outside of his or her awareness; the arm thus appears to him or her to be moving "on its own." Or when responding to a suggestion of glove anesthesia, the subject withdraws attention from the experience of pain, but the intention and associated cognitive effort are again, unlike in other circumstances, outside of awareness.

Hilgard's theory goes much further than the description in the preceding text and makes the ambitious proposal that cognitive activity and experience that is not consciously expressed during hypnosis is still accessible by a form of dual consciousness. One method of demonstrating this in the laboratory is the "hidden observer" effect (Hilgard, 1986). For example, during hypnotic analgesia the experimenter suggests that a hidden or "unhypnotized" part of the mind is aware of the pain and can give the true pain ratings "out of awareness," say in writing or by pressing numbered keys. These ratings are indeed much higher than those elicited when the hypnotic subject is asked directly. Similar experiments have been performed on hypnoamnesia, hypnotically suggested deafness, and ideomotor responding. Hilgard used the term *amnesic barrier* to describe the separation between this "unhypnotized" part—the "executive ego"—and the various cognitive structures associated with the suggested responses.

Neo-dissociation theory and, in particular, the idea of the hidden observer have proved attractive for many practitioners of hypnosis, notably those for whom the process of dissociation and constructs such as ego states are fundamental to their therapeutic approaches. It also provides a basis for some commonly used hypnoanalytical methods such as ideomotor finger signaling. However, it remains

a topic of some controversy; for example, Spanos and Hewitt (1980) and Spanos, Gwynn, and Stam (1983) demonstrated that "hidden observers" can be suggested that report a *higher* level of pain (see the special issue of *Contemporary Hypnosis* [Naish, 2005], and the review by Bayne, 2007).

If the hidden observer is a genuine dual consciousness phenomenon, then it is only demonstrable in a minority of individuals, even with high suggestibility (Laurence & Perry, 1981). Nevertheless, the criticisms still leave intact the idea that some form of dissociative mechanism is deployed when subjects respond positively to hypnotic suggestions.

The Theory of Dissociated Control

Following on from Hilgard's neo-dissociation theory, other dissociative models of hypnotic responding have made use of the distinction between activity that is habitual and automatic, as in familiar contexts, and activity that requires a greater degree of "executive" control and monitoring, such as executing an unfamiliar or complex task.

Along these lines, a major theoretical development in the 1990s is the "dissociated control" theory of Woody and Bowers (1994; see also Jamieson & Woody, 2007; Woody & Sadler, 2008). This relies more extensively than Hilgard's model on existing neuropsychological ideas concerning the nature of controlled and automatic behavior, notably the theory of executive functioning developed by Norman and Shallice (1986). Briefly, this theory proposes that in routine situations, thinking and behaving are controlled by low-level cognitive control networks or schemata. Schemata are automatically cued by stimuli in the individual's internal and external environment, and for routine and well-learned activities, the appropriate schema is selected by a low-level process termed *contention scheduling*. However, in unusual or nonroutine contexts, in which the usual schemata do not apply (e.g., driving an unfamiliar car) or their triggers are not present, a higher level executive process, termed the *supervisory attentional system* (SAS), comes into play to exert control over contention scheduling, exciting and inhibiting schemata according to the requirements of the specific context. This is associated with a sense of effort and volition unlike activities that are triggered automatically at the level of contention scheduling.

According to the model of dissociated control, as a result of the hypnotic induction, the influence of the subject's executive control system (the SAS) on schema selection is weakened and he or she accordingly responds to the hypnotist's suggestions in a genuinely automatic and involuntary manner. Thus, as opposed to *dissociated experience* as posited by Hilgard, we have *dissociated control*: The subject's executive control functions are suppressed and in effect surrendered to the hypnotist by the process of hypnotic induction.

A criticism of the theory of dissociated control has been that it has difficulty explaining novel and complex hypnotic responding (Kirsch & Lynn, 1998). Also, if the hypnotist "assumes the role of the SAS," how does the theory account for self-hypnosis in which subjects and patients are taught, for example, to experience ideomotor responses such as arm levitation or to diminish their experience of pain by themselves? A similar problem arises with posthypnotic suggestion. In this case, the subject has been alerted from "the hypnotic state" yet responds in a seemingly automatic manner to the agreed cue, even when the hypnotist is not present and the subject has returned to his or her everyday environment. What the underlying mechanism for this is in terms of dissociated control (or other special-state models) is unclear.

In fact, there is evidence that responding to suggestion, including posthypnotic suggestion, does require cognitive effort; hence, the experience of involuntariness reported by subjects may be a misattribution on their part (see recent research by Tobis & Kihlström, 2010; Wyzenbeek & Bryant, 2012). This is consistent with the socio-cognitive position (Kirsch & Lynn, 1999; but see Woody & Bowers, 1994, for their interpretation).

Recently, Jamieson and Woody (2007) have proposed modifications to the dissociated control theory that posit a failure of the normal process of executive *monitoring* that modifies executive control activity in response to feedback (see also Woody & Sadler, 2008).

The Cold Control Theory

A recent development that is consistent with dissociated experience theory is the cold control theory of Dienes and Perner (2007). Unlike Hilgard's

model, this does not make strong assumptions about dual consciousness. However, it draws on Hilgard's work and that of Norman and Shallice (1986) as well as ideas concerning the nature of consciousness developed by Rosenthal (2005). The last-mentioned author distinguishes between first- and second-order mental states or thoughts and proposes that consciousness of any mental state (first order) is not possible without awareness of being in that mental state (second order). As an illustration, it can be demonstrated that some patients with a lesion in the visual cortex may be unaware of stimuli in part of their visual field and may yet choose the correct response in a forced choice recognition experiment. They are "seeing" yet "not conscious of seeing." Similarly, during hypnosis, responsive subjects exercise executive control by forming the intention to respond to a suggestion (a first-order thought) but not the second-order thought "I am intending to do this." The second-order thought may then be "I am *not* intending to do this." Thus, the response is felt to be involuntary and the experience real. According to the theory, preparing the subject for hypnosis creates the expectation of unintentionality; otherwise, no strong assumptions are made about the existence of a hypnotic state.

THE ROLE OF THE HYPNOTIC INDUCTION IN DISSOCIATIVE AND SOCIO-COGNITIVE THEORIES

In his account of his neo-dissociation theory, Hilgard emphasized the importance of the hypnotic induction and regarded it as a means of preparing the subject for the suggestions to follow—that is, "to produce a readiness for dissociative experiences," which he appears to equate with "the hypnotic state" (Hilgard, 1986, p. 226; see Kirsch, 2011, for a discussion of Hilgard's position on this). In the case of Woody and Bowers's theory, the hypnotic state resulting from the induction is associated with inhibition of executive control; as this is considered to be located in the prefrontal cortex, the hypnotized person can be compared with someone with impaired functioning in that part of the brain.

Laboratory studies have in fact revealed that, following the usual induction procedure, suggestibility scores are overall only moderately higher than when no induction is administered and for some subjects there is no increase and even a decrease (Kirsch & Braffman, 1999). Moreover, when the traditional induction is replaced by "task motivational instructions" or an "alert–active" induction (suggestions of increasing awareness, alertness, and energy, and sometimes substitution of the chair or couch with an exercise bicycle), ingestion of a "hypnosis pill," or inhalation of a (inert) "hypnosis gas," the same increase in suggestibility is found (Baker & Kirsch, 1993; Bányai & Hilgard, 1976; Barber & Calverley, 1963; Glass & Barber, 1961). Hence, at least as far as suggestibility is concerned, the role of the hypnotic induction may simply be to enhance both the subjects' commitment to engage in the suggestions to follow and their expectations of a positive response. Thus, the hypnotist is free to choose from a range of procedures, so long as the subject is explicitly informed, or makes the inference, that a hypnotic induction is being carried out (Gandhi & Oakley, 2005; Wagstaff, 2014). None of this is compatible with the idea that the hypnotic induction places the subject in a special neurophysiological state in which he or she remains until "alerted."

THEORIES OF HYPNOSIS: CONSENSUS AND INTEGRATION

As has been noted, what I have termed the traditional understanding of hypnosis, outlined at the beginning of this chapter, has been the subject of much laboratory investigation over the past 50 years or so. As a result of this, a number of more comprehensive theories of hypnosis have been proposed, the most challenging of which have been broadly labeled "socio-cognitive." Examination of the theoretical landscape around 25 years ago (Lynn & Rhue, 1991) reveals how wide the divergence between these and the "special process" theories had reached and how intense the debate had become between the various protagonists.

Since then, greater agreement has emerged as to the likely theoretical underpinnings of hypnosis. Importantly, the need to account for the reality of the subjects' suggested experiences and their reported involuntary nature has been more firmly acknowledged. To this end, we have witnessed the emergence of a set of theoretical models that are grounded in contemporary cognitive neuroscience and which posit some form of dissociation or inhibition in the perceptual-cognitive-behavioral process that accounts for the responsive subject's experience. The fate of executive control during hypnosis is of particular focus. These theories appear now to offer greater opportunity for exchange of ideas with existing socio-cognitive models (Kirsch & Lynn, 1998; Lynn & Green, 2011). One outcome of these developments, especially due to socio-cognitive researchers, has been the displacement of the trance concept and the induction from their pivotal roles. Thus, the center of gravity of theorizing has moved decisively over to the two remaining components, suggestion and suggestibility. However, while it is fair to say that there is presently no indication that there exists a unique neurophysiological "signature" of hypnosis that is invariant over the range of hypnotic responding (Burgess, 2007; Nash & Barnier, 2008; Wagstaff, 2014), many theorists continue to insist on the integrity of "the hypnotic state" and its explanatory status. Some resolution of these opposing viewpoints can be facilitated by acknowledging the following:

- First, as Wagstaff (2014) notes (see also Barber, 1999), it may still be the case that, following an induction (especially the relaxation/sleep type), *some* subjects experience a trance-like state, but this is not a prerequisite of hypnotic responding.
- Second, whatever one's theoretical position, it may still be meaningful to assert that the hypnotic subject who is responding to a suggestion of profound changes in the way he or she is experiencing the world is *ipso facto* "in an altered state of consciousness."
- Third, there is evidence that the "state of readiness and expectation" that the induction promotes, as envisaged by socio-cognitive theorists, may itself have identifiable neurophysiological correlates (McGeown, Mazzoni, Venneri, & Kirsch, 2009).

Is a "hypnotic state" resulting from the induction procedure a necessary component of dissociation theories? As was noted earlier, the cold control theory of dissociative experience does not explicitly require this. But without the idea of a hypnotic state, how would we conceptualize the distinction between hypnosis and suggestion? For further discussion of this important issue, the reader is referred to Wagstaff (2014).

Another sign of consensus is the recognition that no single process can account for successful responding to a hypnotic suggestion. Hypnosis is a complex interaction between the hypnotist and the subject, and the context and subjects may deploy a range of cognitive skills to achieve the suggested effects. Expectancy and the perceived demands—implicit and explicit—of the context remain important components of any explanatory account of the behavior and experience of the subject. Observe, for example, the qualitative differences in the responses and reports of hypnotic subjects in the clinic, the laboratory, the training course, and, most dramatically, the stage show, in which the participants are required to respond in a highly visible, flamboyant manner for the entertainment of the audience (Heap, 2000).

Is it trite to say that brain-imaging research mainly informs us about the response to suggestions of people (often students selected for their extreme level of suggestibility) who are participating in a highly refined scientific experiment and who are enclosed in a brain-scanning machine? Whatever the answer, there are limitations to any reductionist approach that attempts to account for a phenomenon as complex and multilayered as hypnosis. Theories that integrate research findings at all levels—social, cognitive, behavioral, and neurophysiological—are likely to prove the most useful (cf. Brown & Oakley, 2007).

Related to the previous discussion is the acknowledgment that hypnotic suggestibility is not a unitary trait. As in the case of IQ, identical ratings on a scale may arise from quite different score profiles. Indeed, a full account of the processes underlying suggestibility has yet to be achieved, one difficulty being the lack of a strong correlation between suggestibility scores and other important traits and cognitive dispositions (Laurence et al., 2008).

THEORIES OF HYPNOSIS: THEIR RELEVANCE TO CLINICAL HYPNOSIS

So far in this chapter, clinical hypnosis has barely had a mention. Yet, until well into the 20th century, the study of hypnosis and its antecedent, mesmerism, was dominated by professionals in the fields of medicine and psychiatry who were most interested in the presumed psychopathological manifestations and clinical applications. These practitioners adhered to the traditional model: The hypnotist places the subject in a trance state, which has unusual psychological properties including hypersuggestibility.

Particularly since the middle of the past century, the investigation and understanding of hypnosis has increasingly become the domain of experimental psychologists and neuroscientists. Academic research and theory is now mainly focused on applying existing ideas from neuroscience to understanding how normal individuals are able to respond successfully to suggestions that bring about temporary but often quite profound changes in their experience and behavior and why others respond less markedly if at all. As a result, the earlier claimed properties of the "hypnotic state" have been discounted or called into question, and many theoreticians and experimentalists now reject it altogether as an explanatory construct.

Where does this leave clinical hypnosis? I suggest that hypnosis as currently conceived by experimentalists and theoreticians is now rather different from that conceived by clinicians and therapists (Heap, 2011). That is, clinical hypnosis is now only partially informed by experimental hypnosis. This conclusion is particularly apposite when considering multisession psychotherapeutic applications (as opposed, for example, to single-session interventions for helping patients cope with painful or anxiety-provoking medical or dental procedures). It is clear that, for their purposes, clinicians continue to adhere to traditional assumptions about hypnosis: As a result of the induction and deepening procedure, the patient enters a trance state that of itself has beneficial properties, notably mental and physical relaxation and facilitated access to unconscious processes. In addition, the patient is rendered more amenable to the ministrations and suggestions provided by the therapist, which are able to bring about permanent beneficial changes in how the patient experiences and responds to his or her everyday life. However, with some exceptions, such as the control and management of pain, current research in the laboratory, and the direction in which theorizing has been proceeding, do not immediately indicate that hypnosis can have such profound and enduring effects. Indeed, one very telling observation is the weakness and unreliability of any relationship between the benefits of clinical hypnosis and the hypnotic suggestibility of the patients as measured by scales developed in the laboratory (Montgomery, Schnur, & David, 2011).

We are not without examples of theoretical approaches to hypnosis that are informed by its clinical applications (Lankton & Matthews, 2010; Nash, 2008). However, my opinion is that we need a much more open discussion between the parties concerned—the clinicians, the experimentalists, and the theoreticians—and a greater willingness on their part to acknowledge their differences. None of this is to deny the value of clinical hypnosis, but perhaps this field now requires a more coherent theoretical formulation along with more experimental investigations that directly test its underlying assumptions.

REFERENCES

Baker, S. L., & Kirsch, I. (1993). Hypnotic and placebo analgesia: Order effects and the placebo label. *Contemporary Hypnosis, 10*, 117–126.

Bányai, E. I., & Hilgard, E. R. (1976). A comparison of active-alert hypnotic induction with traditional relaxation induction. *Journal of Abnormal Psychology, 85*(2), 218–224.

Barber, T. X. (1999). A comprehensive three-dimensional theory of hypnosis. In I. Kirsch, A. Capafons, E. Cardeña-Buelna, & S. Amigó (Eds.), *Clinical hypnosis and self-regulation: Cognitive-behavioral perspectives* (pp. 21–48). Washington, DC: American Psychological Association.

Barber, T. X., & Calverley, D. S. (1963). Toward a theory of hypnotic behavior: Effects on suggestibility of task motivating instructions and attitudes toward hypnosis. *Journal of Abnormal and Social Psychology, 67*(6), 557–565.

Barber, T. X., & Calverley, D. S. (1964). Experimental studies in "hypnotic" behaviour: Suggested deafness evaluated by delayed auditory feedback. *British Journal of Psychology (London, England: 1953), 55*, 439–446.

Barber, T. X., Spanos, N. P., & Chaves, J. F. (1974). *Hypnosis, imagination and human potentialities.* New York, NY: Pergamon Press.

Barnier, A. J., Dienes, Z., & Mitchell, C. J. (2008). How hypnosis happens: New cognitive theories of hypnotic responding. In M. R. Nash & A. J. Barnier (Eds.), *The Oxford handbook of hypnosis* (pp. 141–177). Oxford, UK: Oxford University Press. doi:10.1093/oxfordhb/9780198570097.001.0001

Bayne, T. (2007). Hypnosis and the unity of consciousness. In G. Jamieson (Ed.), *Hypnosis and conscious states: The cognitive neuroscience perspective* (pp. 93–109). Oxford, UK: Oxford University Press.

Brown, R. J., & Oakley, D. A. (2007). An integrative cognitive model of hypnosis and high hypnotisability. In M. Heap, R. J. Brown, & D. A. Oakley (Eds.), *The highly hypnotisable person* (pp. 152–186). London, UK: Brunner-Routledge.

Bryant, R. A., & McConkey, K. M. (1989). Hypnotic blindness, awareness, and attribution. *Journal of Abnormal Psychology, 98*(4), 443–447.

Burgess, A. (2007). On the contribution of neurophysiology to hypnotic research: Current state and future directions. In G. Jamieson (Ed.), *Hypnosis and conscious states: The cognitive neuroscience perspective* (pp. 195–219). Oxford, UK: Oxford University Press.

Coe, W. C., Basden, B., Basden, D., & Graham, C. (1976). Posthypnotic amnesia: Suggestions of an active process in dissociative phenomena. *Journal of Abnormal Psychology, 85*(5), 455–458.

Dienes, Z., & Perner, J. (2007). The cold control theory of hypnosis. In G. Jamieson (Ed.), *Hypnosis and conscious states: The cognitive neuroscience perspective* (pp. 293–314). Oxford, UK: Oxford University Press.

Gandhi, B., & Oakley, D. A. (2005). Does hypnosis by any other name smell as sweet? The efficacy of "hypnotic" inductions depends on the label "hypnosis." *Consciousness and Cognition, 14*(2), 304–315. doi:10.1016/j.concog.2004.12.004

Glass, L. B., & Barber, T. X. (1961). A note on hypnotic behavior, the definition of the situation, and the placebo-effect. *Journal of Nervous and Mental Disease, 132*, 539–541.

Gorassini, D. R. (1999). Hypnotic responsiveness: A cognitive-behavioral analysis of self-deception. In I. Kirsch, A. Capafons, S. Amigó, & E. Cardeña (Eds.), *Clinical hypnosis and self-regulation therapy: A cognitive-behavioral perspective* (pp. 73–103). Washington, DC: American Psychological Association. doi:10.1037/10282-003

Gorassini, D. R. (2004). Enhancing hypnozability. In M. Heap, R. J. Brown, & D. A. Oakley (Eds.), *The highly hypnotisable person* (pp. 213–239). London, UK: Brunner-Routledge.

Gorassini, D. R., & Spanos, N. P. (1999). The Carleton Skill Training Program for Modifying Hypnotic Suggestibility: Original version and variations. In I. Kirsch, A. Capafons, E. Cardeña-Buelna, & S. Amigó (Eds.), *Clinical hypnosis and self-regulation: Cognitive-behavioural perspectives* (pp. 141–177). Washington, DC: American Psychological Association. doi:10.1037/10282-006

Heap, M. (2000). The alleged dangers of stage hypnosis. *Contemporary Hypnosis, 17*, 117–126.

Heap, M. (2011). Does clinical hypnosis have anything to do with experimental hypnosis? *Journal of Mind-Body Regulation, 1*, 17–30.

Hilgard, E. R. (1986). *Divided consciousness: Multiple controls in human thought and action* (expanded ed.). New York, NY: Wiley.

Horton, J. E., & Crawford, H. J. (2004). Neurophysiological and genetic determinants of high hypnotisability. In M. Heap, R. J. Brown, & D. A. Oakley (Eds.), *The highly hypnotisable person* (pp. 133–151). London, UK: Brunner-Routledge.

Hull, C. (1933). *Hypnosis and suggestibility*. New York, NY: Appleton Century Crofts.

Jamieson, G. A., & Woody, E. Z. (2007). Dissociated control as a paradigm for cognitive neuroscience research and theorizing in hypnosis. In G. A. Jamieson (Ed.), *Hypnosis and conscious states: The cognitive neuroscience perspective* (pp. 111–129). Oxford, UK: Oxford University Press.

Kihlström, J. F. (2008). The domain of hypnosis, revisited. In M. R. Nash & A. J. Barnier (Eds.), *The Oxford handbook of hypnosis* (pp. 21–52). Oxford, UK: Oxford University Press.

Kihlström, J. F. (2014). Hypnosis and cognition. *Psychology of Consciousness: Theory, Research, and Practice, 1*, 139–152.

Kirsch, I. (1991). The social learning theory of hypnosis. In S. J. Lynn & J. W. Rhue (Eds.), *Theories of hypnosis: Current models and perspectives* (pp. 439–465). New York, NY: Guilford Press.

Kirsch, I. (2011). The altered state issue; dead or alive? *International Journal of Clinical and Experimental Hypnosis, 59*(3), 350–362. doi:10.1080/00207144.2011.570681

Kirsch, I., & Braffman, W. (1999). Correlates of hypnotisability: The first empirical study. *Contemporary Hypnosis, 16*, 224–230.

Kirsch, I., & Lynn, S. J. (1998). Dissociation theories of hypnosis. *Psychological Bulletin, 123*(1), 100–115.

Kirsch, I., & Lynn, S. J. (1999). Hypnotic involuntariness and the automaticity of everyday life. In I. Kirsch, A. Capafons, E. Cardeña-Buelna, & S. Amigó (Eds.), *Clinical hypnosis and self-regulation: Cognitive-behavioral perspectives* (pp. 49–72). Washington, DC: American Psychological Association.

Lankton, S. R., & Matthews, W. J. (2010). An Ericksonian model of clinical hypnosis. In S. J. Lynn, J. W. Rhue, & I. Kirsch (Eds.), *Handbook of clinical hypnosis* (pp. 209–237). Washington, DC: American Psychological Association.

Laurence, J.-R., Beaulieu-Prévost, D., & du Chéné, T. (2008). Measuring and understanding individual differences in hypnotisability. In M. R. Nash & A. J. Barnier (Eds.), *The Oxford handbook of hypnosis* (pp. 225–253). Oxford, UK: Oxford University Press.

Laurence, J. R., & Perry, C. (1981). The "hidden observer" phenomenon in hypnosis: Some additional findings. *Journal of Abnormal Psychology, 90*(4), 334–344.

Lynn, S. J., & Green, J. P. (2011). The sociocognitive and dissociation theories of hypnosis: Toward a rapprochement. *International Journal of Clinical and Experimental Hypnosis, 59*(3), 277–293. doi:10.1080/00207144.2011.570652

Lynn, S. J., Kirsch, I., & Hallquist, M. N. (2008). Social cognitive theories of hypnosis. In M. R. Nash & A. J. Barnier (Eds.), *The Oxford handbook of hypnosis* (pp. 111–139). Oxford, UK: Oxford University Press. doi:10.1093/oxfordhb/9780198570097.013.0005

Lynn, S. J., & Rhue, J. W. (1991). *Theories of hypnosis: Current models and perspectives*. New York, NY: Guilford Press.

Mazzoni, G., Heap, M., & Scoboria, A. (2010). Hypnosis and memory: Theory, laboratory research and applications. In S. J. Lynn, J. W. Rhue, & I. Kirsch (Eds.), *Handbook of clinical hypnosis* (pp. 709–741). Washington DC: American Psychological Association.

McGeown, W. J., Mazzoni, G., Venneri, A., & Kirsch, I. (2009). Hypnotic induction decreases anterior default mode activity. *Consciousness and Cognition, 18*(4), 848–855. doi:10.1016/j.concog.2009.09.001

Montgomery, G. H., Schnur, J. B., & David, D. (2011). The impact of hypnotic suggestibility in clinical care settings. *The International Journal of Clinical and Experimental Hypnosis, 59*(3), 294–309. doi:10.1080/00207144.2011.570656

Morgan, A. H. (1973). The heritability of hypnotic susceptibility in twins. *Journal of Abnormal Psychology, 82*(1), 55–61.

Naish, P. L. N. (2005). On the inevitability of finding hypnosis-simulator equivalence. *Contemporary Hypnosis, 22*(3), 154–157.

Nash, M. R. (2008). A psychoanalytic theory of hypnosis: A clinically informed approach. In M. R. Nash & A. J. Barnier (Eds.), *The Oxford handbook of hypnosis* (pp. 201–222). Oxford, UK: Oxford University Press. doi:10.1093/oxfordhb/9780198570097.013.0008

Nash, M. R., & Barnier, A. J. (Eds.). (2008). *The Oxford handbook of hypnosis* (pp. 201–222). Oxford, UK: Oxford University Press.

Norman, D. A., & Shallice, T. (1986). Attention to action: Willed and automatic control of behaviour. In R. J. Davidson, G. E. Schwartz, & D. Shapiro (Eds.), *Consciousness and self-regulation* (Vol. 4, pp. 1–18). New York, NY: Plenum Press.

Orne, M. T. (1959). The nature of hypnosis: Artifact and essence. *Journal of Abnormal Psychology, 58*(3), 277–299.

Orne, M. T. (1962). Hypnotically induced hallucinations. In L. J. West (Ed.), *Hallucinations* (pp. 211–219). New York, NY: Grune and Stratton.

Orne, M. T. (1972). On the simulating subject as a quasi-control in hypnosis research: What, why and how? In E. Fromm & R. E. Shor (Eds.), *Hypnosis: Research developments and perspectives*. Chicago, IL: Aldine-Atherton.

Piccione, C., Hilgard, E. R., & Zimbardo, P. G. (1989). On the stability of measured hypnotizability over a 25-year period. *Journal of Personality and Social Psychology, 56*(2), 289–295.

Ray, W. J. (2007). The experience of agency and hypnosis from an evolutionary perspective. In G. Jamieson (Ed.), *Hypnosis and conscious states: The cognitive neuroscience perspective* (pp. 224–240). Oxford, UK: Oxford University Press.

Rosenthal, D. (2005). *Consciousness and mind*. Oxford, UK: Oxford University Press.

Sarbin, T. R., & Coe, W. C. (1972). *Hypnosis: A social psychological analysis of influence communication*. New York, NY: Holt, Rinehart & Winston.

Sheehan, P. W. (1986). An individual difference account of hypnosis. In P. L. N. Naish (Ed.), *What is hypnosis? Current theories and research*. Philadelphia, PA: Open University Press.

Spanos, N. P. (1991). A sociocognitive approach to hypnosis. In S. J. Lynn & J. W. Rhue (Eds.), *Theories of hypnosis: Current models and perspectives* (pp. 324–361). New York, NY: Guilford Press.

Spanos, N. P., Gwynn, M. I., & Stam, H. J. (1983). Instructional demands and ratings of overt and hidden pain during hypnotic analgesia. *Journal of Abnormal Psychology, 92*(4), 479–488.

Spanos, N. P., & Hewitt, E. C. (1980). The hidden observer in hypnotic analgesia: Discovery or experimental creation? *Journal of Personality and Social Psychology, 39*(6), 1201–1214.

Tobis, I. P., & Kihlström, J. F. (2010). Allocation of attentional resources in posthypnotic suggestion. *International Journal of Clinical and Experimental Hypnosis, 58*(4), 367–382. doi:10.1080/00207144.2010.499330

Wagstaff, G. F. (1981). *Hypnosis, compliance and belief*. Brighton, Sussex: Harvester Press.

Wagstaff, G. F. (2014). On the centrality of the concept of an altered state to definitions of hypnosis. *Journal of Mind-Body Regulation, 2*, 90–108. Retrieved from http://mbr.journalhosting.ucalgary.ca/mbr/index.php/mbr/article/view/525

Whittlesea, B. W. A., & Williams, L. D. (2001a). The discrepancy-attribution hypothesis: I. The heuristic basis of feelings of familiarity. *Journal of Experimental Psychology: Learning, Memory, & Cognition, 27*, 3–13.

Whittlesea, B. W. A., & Williams, L. D. (2001b). The discrepancy-attribution hypothesis: II. Expectation, uncertainty, surprise, and feelings of familiarity. *Journal of Experimental Psychology: Learning, Memory, & Cognition, 27*, 14–33.

Woody, E. Z., & Bowers, K. S. (1994). A frontal assault on dissociative control. In S. J. Lynn & J. W. Rhue (Eds.), *Dissociation: Clinical and theoretical perspectives* (pp. 52–79). New York, NY: Guilford Press.

Woody, E. Z., & Sadler, P. (2008). Dissociation theories of hypnosis. In M. R. Nash & A. J. Barnier (Eds.), *The Oxford handbook of hypnosis* (pp. 81–110). Oxford, UK: Oxford University Press. doi:10.1093/oxfordhb/9780198570097.013.0004

Wyzenbeek, M., & Bryant, R. A. (2012). The cognitive demands of hypnotic response. *International Journal of Clinical and Experimental Hypnosis, 60*(1), 67–80. doi:10.1080/00207144.2011.622197

Neurophysiology of Hypnosis

Mathieu Landry and Amir Raz

Advances in neuroimaging and electrophysiology provide new ways to explore the intricacies of the living human brain (Dolan, 2008; Jacobs & Kahana, 2010). These developments have increased the expectation that neuroscience can elucidate some of the most fundamental questions about the human mind (Choudhury & Slaby, 2011). Hypnosis is part and parcel of this ongoing trend (Oakley & Halligan, 2009, 2013; Raz, 2011a). However, after more than two decades of imaging the hypnotized brain, studies have yet to deliver a reliable neurobiological model of hypnosis (Landry & Raz, 2015). One central obstacle pertains to the inherent complexity of hypnotic phenomena, which emerge from the interaction of multiple factors (Nash & Barnier, 2008). Three factors play a central role in the efficacy of the hypnotic response: interindividual differences in hypnotizability or susceptibility to suggestion, the induction procedure, and the type and content of the (post) hypnotic suggestions (Figure 3.1; Mazzoni, Venneri, McGeown, & Kirsch, 2013; Oakley & Halligan, 2010). This chapter delves into the neuroscience of hypnosis by focusing on these central components. Accordingly, here we examine and summarize neuroimaging and electrophysiological assays of hypnotizability, hypnotic induction, and (post) hypnotic suggestions.

Three conclusions follow from our brief appraisal. First, hypnotic phenomena seem to engage frontal areas of the human brain. In particular, hypnosis involves regions implicated in mental alertness, executive control, top-down regulation, and monitoring processes. Second, hypnosis induces global changes in neural connectivity patterns—in other words, hypnosis emerges from complex brain dynamics. Third, research highlights the ability of (post)hypnotic suggestions to selectively engage relevant brain regions. This aspect underscores the precision of suggestion to target and influence specific perceptual, cognitive, or motor processes.

INTERINDIVIDUAL VARIABILITY

Individuals respond differently to suggestion (Piccione, Hilgard, & Zimbardo, 1989). Researchers typically differentiate highly hypnotizable individuals (HHIs) from low hypnotizable individuals (LHIs) using standardized scales that measure hypnotizability (Heap, Brown, & Oakley, 2004; Laurence, Beaulieu-Prévost, & Du Chéné, 2008). HHIs are distinct in that they possess mental abilities that allow them to produce reliable hypnotic responses to challenging suggestions. However, few psychological and neurobiological correlates predict hypnotizability (Lichtenberg, Bachner-Melman, Ebstein, & Crawford, 2004; Raz, 2005; Tellegen & Atkinson, 1974). The absence of a unique reliable correlate implies that hypnotizability represents a multifactorial sociocognitive construct. Beyond the dichotomy that differentiates HHIs from LHIs, research on hypnotizability reveals that HHIs rarely represent a homogeneous group. Indeed, heterogeneity across HHIs suggests that this group may comprise various subcategories (McConkey & Barnier, 2004; Terhune, Cardeña, & Lindgren, 2011a, 2011b). Certain researchers propose that such variability in hypnosis reflects individual differences in cognitive styles, wherein successful hypnotic responses rely on specific ways to process suggestions and implement cognitive strategies (Barnier, Cox, & McConkey, 2014; Laurence et al., 2008).

At the brain level, hypnotizability correlates with greater brain volume in certain frontal lobe areas (see Figure 3.2; Horton, Crawford, Harrington, & Downs, 2004; Huber, Lui, Duzzi, Pagnoni, &

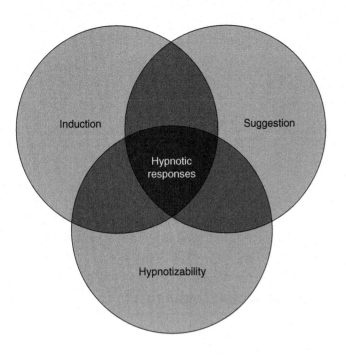

FIGURE 3.1 The hypnotic response is located at the confluence of three central factors: interindividual variability in hypnotizability, the induction procedure, and the content of hypnotic suggestions.

Porro, 2014). Neurocognitive functions associated with these brain regions therefore likely influence hypnotizability. Functional investigations further emphasize these observations. Functional connectivity evaluates the level of synchronicity between distant brain regions to uncover neural networks (Friston, 2011). Functional connectivity assumes that concurrent neural activity between areas reflects neural networks. Consistent with structural evidence, studies reveal functional differences between HHIs and LHIs (Hoeft et al., 2012; Huber et al., 2014). Specifically, HHIs show higher connectivity between the dorsolateral prefrontal cortex (DLPFC) and the anterior cingulate cortex (ACC; Figure 3.2). Evidence therefore indicates that structural and functional differences of the frontal brain relate to hypnotizability.

Additional findings further emphasize the role of the DLPFC in hypnotizability. Repeated transcranial magnetic stimulation (rTMS) represents an experimental technique that allows researchers to induce a short-lived neural dysfunction of the targeted brain region, thereby producing so-called virtual brain lesions (Pascual-Leone, 1999; Raz & Wolfson, 2010). Cognitive neuroscientists often employ this approach to verify whether the targeted region is necessary for a specific perceptual, cognitive, or motor function (Friston, 2011). A recent study used rTMS to demonstrate that transient dysfunction of the DLPFC increases hypnotizability (Dienes & Hutton, 2013). These observations supplement aforementioned findings on the role of the frontal brain in hypnosis and allude to a causal relationship between frontal neurocognitive functions and hypnotizability. They also hint that altered functioning of the prefrontal cortex influences the reliability of the hypnotic response (Crawford & Gruzelier, 1992). However, despite the importance of this finding, neuropsychological observations with neurological patients hardly yield comparable results (Kihlström, Glisky, McGovern, Rapcsak, & Mennemeier, 2013). Further examination is therefore necessary to better understand the role of the DLPFC in hypnotizability.

The frontal areas identified across triangulate investigations usually converge on executive control, top-down regulation, and monitoring processes (e.g., Nee et al., 2013; Shenhav, Botvinick, & Cohen, 2013). These observations are consistent with executive control theories of hypnosis and intimate that interindividual variability in hypnotic response mainly reflects differences in functions of the frontal lobe. Accordingly, variation in the implementation of attentional and executive neurocognitive routines putatively explains the spectrum of hypnotizability.

INDUCTION

Hypnotic inductions typically aim to induce a heightened level of attentional focus (Maldonado & Spiegel, 2008). Similar to being deeply immersed in a book or a movie, this mental plane of intense absorption steers attention away from irrelevant thoughts and sensory events, while simultaneously increasing focus toward the suggestions. The phenomenology of hypnosis frequently includes deep feelings of relaxation alongside a sensation of mental absorption (Cardeña, Jönsson, Terhune, & Marcusson-Clavertz, 2013). Consistent with this account, the hypnotic induction recruits brain regions implicated in the regulation of attention and mental alertness. In particular, neuroimaging reveals that complex thalamocortical signal changes correlate with increased feelings of mental

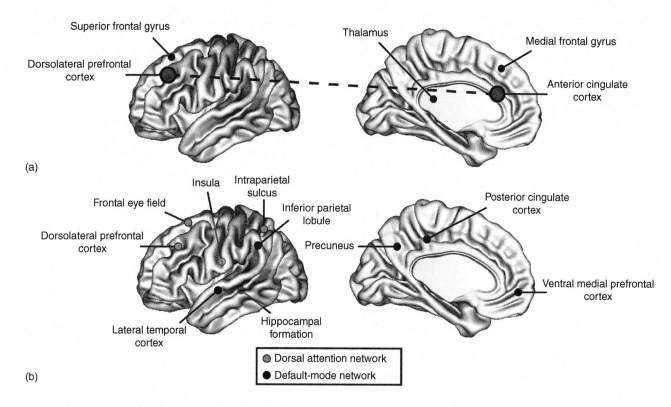

FIGURE 3.2 (a). Structural imaging of hypnotizability reports significant differences in brain volume for the superior and medial frontal gyri in HHIs compared with LHIs. Also, numerous reports document findings related to the connection between the DLPFC and the ACC, as well as specific thalamocortical dynamics. These effects relate to hypnotizability and hypnotic induction. **(b).** Hypnotic induction disengages the default mode network, which comprises the lateral temporal cortex, the hippocampal formation, the inferior parietal lobule, the precuneus, the posterior cingulate cortex, and the ventral medial prefrontal cortex, and engages the dorsal attention network, which comprises the DLPFC, the frontal eye field, the insula, and the intraparietal sulcus.

ACC, anterior cingulate cortex; DLPFC, dorsolateral prefrontal cortex; HHI, highly hypnotizable individual.

absorption and relaxation following an induction (Rainville, Hofbauer, Bushnell, Duncan, & Price, 2002). This type of neural dynamic colors the intricacies of hypnotic planes, wherein greater attentional focus and enhanced mental effort often parallel subjective feelings of relaxation—"the effortless effort."

During resting-state imaging, researchers examine brain activity in the near absence of concurrent experimental factors, that is, at rest. This approach aims to uncover brain networks by assessing functional connectivity among brain regions (de Luca, Beckmann, de Stefano, Matthews, & Smith, 2006). Using this experimental approach, resting-state investigations of hypnosis have focused mainly on two such brain networks: the default mode network and the prefrontal attention network (see Figure 3.2; Deeley et al., 2012; Demertzi et al., 2011; McGeown, Mazzoni, Venneri, & Kirsch, 2009). The default network comprises several cortical midline

structures and typically relates to introspection, mind wandering, and spontaneous cognition (Buckner, Andrews Hanna, & Schacter, 2008; Mason et al., 2007; Smallwood & Schooler, 2015). The induction procedure links to a reduction in default network activity, which proposes that this hypnotic procedure reduces introspection and spontaneous cognition. This neural pattern joins a concurrent engagement of the prefrontal attention network (Raz & Buhle, 2006). The simultaneous reduction in default network activity and increase in attention network activity could therefore reflect a marked reduction in spontaneous cognition and increased attention focus in anticipation of upcoming instructions. According to this view, a heightened level of response preparation involves the recruitment of the alerting network and facilitates the subsequent production of hypnotic responses to suggestion (Kirsch, 1997). Consistent with this interpretation, the induction procedure instigates increased neural

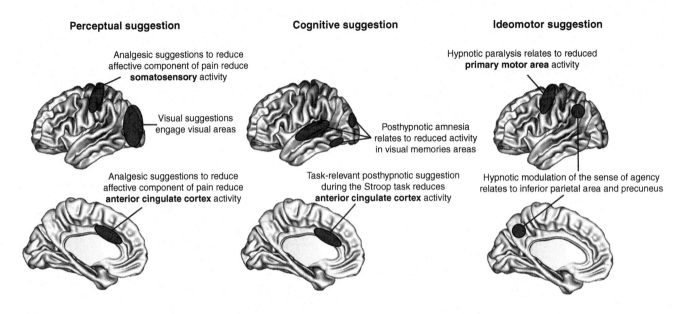

FIGURE 3.3 Suggestion alters neural activity in corresponding brain regions. Perceptual suggestions alter sensory and perceptual brain networks; cognitive suggestions alter brain networks related to cognitive processes; and ideomotor suggestions alter brain networks involved in the planning, production, and monitoring of action.

activity during hypnotic response (McGeown et al., 2012). Induction-related increases in mental alertness and focused attention thus appear to act as hypnotic facilitators (Lifshitz & Raz, 2012).

Despite increased attention, hypnotic inductions without task-specific suggestion typically relate to poor performance, for example, in the context of the Stroop paradigm (e.g., Jamieson & Sheehan, 2004). According to dissociation theorists, a disconnect between executive and supervisory processes during hypnosis may account for this impairment (Woody & Farvolden, 1998; Woody & Sadler, 2008). This interruption thus hinders cognitive control and prevents flexible adjustment of attention, for example, in the Stroop color-naming task (Terhune, Cardeña, & Lindgren, 2011c). At the neural level, distinct activation profiles of the DLPFC and ACC index this decoupling of executive control and monitoring processes (see Figure 3.2; Egner, Jamieson, & Gruzelier, 2005). Moreover, concurrent desynchronized oscillatory patterns between these brain regions likely denote a breakdown in cortical communication, whereas reduced frontoparietal synchronized activity relates to experiences of dissociation (Terhune et al., 2011a). Hence, dissociation theorists view the induction procedure as altering functional connectivity between anterior and posterior areas implicated in higher order cognitive processes.

Electrophysiological studies of hypnotic induction reveal general fluctuations in neural activity. These changes denote reduced synchronicity among cerebral regions. Specifically, HHIs show less phase synchronization over the frontal areas following a hypnotic induction (Baghdadi & Nasrabadi, 2012). They also exhibit distinct global neural oscillatory patterns (de Pascalis, 2007; Fingelkurts, Fingelkurts, Kallio, & Revonsuo, 2007). These neurophysiological oscillations occur alongside induction instructions, marked by a general boost in neural activity near the end of the induction procedure (Hinterberger, Schöner, & Halsband, 2011). These results not only underscore widespread induction-related neural patterns but also demonstrate how stepwise induction procedures encompass various brain dynamics. The ACC could be involved in such global brain changes (Tang, Rothbart, & Posner, 2012). Overall, hypnotic inductions relate to global oscillatory patterns across many brain networks. Neural fluctuations enable the coordination of brain networks as well as the emergence of complex brain functions (Buzsaki, 2006). Therefore, hypnotic modulations of neural alternations underlie the effect of induction over higher cognitive functions.

Several phenomenological experiences often accompany hypnotic induction (Cardeña, 2005). Because multiple facets of hypnosis primarily surface subjectively, methodological frameworks that combine measures of brain activity and subjective reports provide vital information frequently obviated by the prevalent experimental approaches in cognitive neuroscience (Cusumano & Raz, 2014; Lifshitz, Cusumano, & Raz, 2013). Neurophenomenological investigations of hypnosis document that several subjective dimensions of hypnosis correspond to specific neurophysiological fluctuations (Cardeña et al., 2013). For example, self-perceived hypnotic depth relates to particular synchronized neural patterns. These results further validate the authenticity of self-reported phenomenological experience during hypnosis. Yet, matching widespread neural dynamics to specific subjective experience remains a challenge and induction-related neural fluctuations are difficult to interpret.

In summary, brain imaging of hypnotic induction relates to complex neural dynamics that include the alerting and executive networks. These neural patterns parallel enhanced mental absorption. Concomitant decreased default mode network activity in HHIs proposes that the hypnotic induction also reduces introspection and the generation of internal thoughts. These findings therefore support the notion that HHIs respond to the induction procedure by engaging attention in anticipation of an upcoming suggestion and disengaging it from irrelevant thoughts and sensory events. Furthermore, altered brain connectivity is congruent with the idea that induction-related attention phenomena decouple executive control from monitoring processes (Brown & Oakley, 2004). Electrophysiological investigations have identified neural dynamics that match these dissociation patterns (Lee et al., 2007). Under this lens, fluctuations in brain connectivity seem to subserve various conscious experiences during hypnosis.

SUGGESTION

In hypnosis, suggestions are communicable representations in the form of verbal statements capable of yielding a perceptual, cognitive, or motor response (Halligan & Oakley, 2014). Previous studies document the wide range of suggestion-related effects (Michael, Garry, & Kirsch, 2012). Critically, these studies also report that reliable hypnotic responses to suggestion scantily require a formal induction procedure (Mazzoni et al., 2009;

Raz, Kirsch, Pollard, & Nitkin-Kaner, 2006). Findings from studies using brain imaging corroborate these notions (McGeown et al., 2012). A reliable hypnotic response even in the absence of an induction procedure may well capture the centrality of hypnotic responsiveness.

Consistent with top-down views of hypnosis (Raz, 2011b), suggestion-related hypnotic phenomena involve a wide spectrum of frontal activation patterns (Landry & Raz, 2015). Hypnotic suggestions notably relate to the prefrontal and anterior cingulate cortices. Responses to suggestion, moreover, exert their actions through frontal neurocognitive functions (Rainville, Hofbauer, et al., 1999). However, isolating the neural mechanisms of hypnotic responses remains a challenging enterprise because suggestion-related frontal activations vary across studies. This heterogeneity of frontal patterns likely stems from a combination of factors: the content of the suggestion, the quality of the interaction with the operator, interindividual variability, and contextual considerations. Consequently, the recruitment of frontal executive functions and top-down regulation processes during the hypnotic response may well denote inter- and intraindividual cognitive strategies (McConkey & Barnier, 2004).

The domain of (post)hypnotic suggestions includes a broad collection of perceptual, cognitive, and ideomotor phenomena (Woody & Sadler, 2008). Neuroimaging appears to validate these effects at the brain level (see Figure 3.3; del Casale et al., 2012; Kihlström, 2013). However, these studies only show that hypnotic suggestion can selectively modulate corresponding cortical areas and that these effects are consistent with first-person reports. In this manner, neuroimaging of hypnotic response to suggestion validates the potential of hypnosis to reliably act upon targeted aspects of emotion, cognition, thought, and action. Box 3.1 summarizes a few neurophysiological observations related to these different domains of suggestion.

The heterogeneity of neural patterns across the different types of suggestion proposes that brain processes combine in various ways to yield a wide range of hypnotic phenomena. The content of suggestions thus represents a prominent component of hypnosis that compels researchers and clinicians to pay close attention to the way they formulate their instructions (Spiegel & Barabasz, 1988). Even

---

BOX 3.1 SUMMARY OF HYPNOTIC SUGGESTIONS AND RELATED NEUROPHYSIOLOGICAL OBSERVATIONS

Perceptual Suggestion. Suggestions intended to alter visual perception engage the visual areas (see Figure 3.3; Kosslyn, Thompson, Costantini-Ferrando, Alpert, & Spiegel, 2000; McGeown et al., 2012). Electrophysiological findings intimate that such altered visual perception reflects early modulations of sensory processing (Koivisto, Kirjanen, Revonsuo, & Kallio, 2013). Hypnotic analgesia also engages the corresponding brain areas, wherein this type of suggestion modulates the pain neuromatrix (Jensen & Patterson, 2014). Critically, evidence demonstrates that different suggestions for analgesia can influence distinct aspects of pain perception, as well as their neural correlates (see Figure 3.3; Hofbauer, Rainville, Duncan, & Bushnell, 2001; Rainville, Carrier, Hofbauer, Bushnell, & Duncan, 1999; Rainville, Duncan, Price, Carrier, & Bushnell, 1997). Specifically, suggestions intended to suppress affective dimensions of nociception (i.e., the unpleasant aspects of pain perception) relate to reduced activity in the ACC, whereas suggestions intended to suppress pain intensity (i.e., the sensory quality of pain perception) modulate neural activity in the sensory brain area. Overall, evidence confirms that hypnotic responses to perceptual suggestions involve modulations of perceptual and sensory brain networks.

    Cognitive Suggestion. We previously described how induction alone yields poor Stroop performances in HHIs. In contrast, task-relevant suggestions can produce the opposite effect and improve performance (Lifshitz, Aubert Bonn, Fischer, Kashem, & Raz, 2013; Raz, Shapiro, Fan, & Posner, 2002). Indeed, carefully crafted suggestion to impair reading ability causes significant improvement in the Stroop task for HHIs. Moreover, the Stroop paradigm relates to increased ACC activity, which likely reflects cognitive interference triggered by a task-irrelevant automatic response (Shenhav et al., 2013). Hypnotic suggestions for alexia also suppress this characteristic neural response of the Stroop task (see Figure 3.3; Raz, Fan, & Posner, 2005). These behavioral and neuroimaging observations demonstrate how posthypnotic suggestions can assist top-down regulation processes to appropriately manage cognitive conflict and effectively override ballistic processes. These results sharply contrast with performance on the Stroop task following an induction alone. This distinction highlights essential psychological facets of hypnotic inductions and suggestions: whereas the induction alone corresponds to an inability to self-initiate a reliable task-relevant strategy, hypnotic suggestions actually foster a steadfast response through efficient top-down stratagems (Egner & Raz, 2007). Evidence therefore demonstrates the effectiveness of cognitive suggestions to heighten executive control.

    Neuroimaging studies of posthypnotic amnesia likewise document distinct neural responses (see Figure 3.3; Allen, Iacono, Laravuso, & Dunn, 1995; Mendelsohn, Chalamish, Solomonovich, & Dudai, 2008). These reports notably isolate cortical networks implicated in memory retrieval processes. These results are therefore consistent with the notion that posthypnotic amnesia mainly results from retrieval deficits (Kihlström, 1997). Importantly, again evidence supports the idea that suggestions target corresponding brain processes.

    Ideomotor Suggestions. Ideomotor suggestions alter the preparation, execution, and monitoring of actions (Cojan et al., 2009). This type of suggestion thus influences the production of specific movements (e.g., Halligan, Athwal, Oakley, & Frackowiak, 2000) and the inherent sense of agency that typically accompanies voluntary movements (i.e., the feeling of control over one's actions; Blakemore, Oakley, & Frith, 2003). Hypnotic paralysis recruits distinct neural circuits than feigned paralysis, which underlines the neural specificity of the hypnotic response to ideomotor suggestions from mere simulation (Cojan et al., 2009; Ward, Oakley, Frackowiak, & Halligan, 2003). Hypnotic paralysis also affects primary motor activity, yet hardly perturbs preparatory motor activity (see Figure 3.3; Cojan et al., 2009; Deeley et al., 2013). Hence, action inhibition during paralysis occurs late in the chain of the ideomotor hierarchy. Altered feelings of agency during hypnosis refer to a diminished sense of control during the production of actions (Polito, Barnier, Woody, & Connors, 2014). These distortions of the self notably relate to areas involved in action monitoring such as the precuneus, inferior parietal area, and the cerebellum (Blakemore et al., 2003; Deeley et al., 2014). These observations provide meaningful information concerning the neural substrates of agency.

---

minute differences in the formatting of suggestions may cause distinct neural responses (Barabasz et al., 1999). Nonetheless, beyond this variability, these findings highlight the ability of suggestions to selectively engage specific brain networks that correspond to the content of these instructions. The neuroscience of hypnosis therefore demonstrates how hypnosis can target specific perceptual, cognitive, or ideomotor processes (Landry, Appourchaux, & Raz, 2014).

CONCLUSION

Hypnotic phenomena index an interaction among many psychosocial factors. Three prominent factors tower: interindividual variability in hypnotizability, the induction procedure, and the content of hypnotic suggestions (Mazzoni et al., 2013; Oakley & Halligan, 2010). In this chapter, we briefly discussed neuroscientific evidence related to these factors. For example, we showed how numerous findings attest to the centrality of the frontal brain in hypnosis. These observations implicate neural networks related to mental alertness, executive control, top-down regulation, and cognitive monitoring. In particular, evidence shows that hypnotizability, a psychological trait, relates to structural and functional specificities, likely coded within the frontal brain. Studies also report that the induction procedure recruits central nodes of the control networks involved in mobilizing attention. This neural response may reflect a form of mental preparation, perhaps a strategy, to produce a fitting hypnotic response. Moreover, neuroimaging of hypnosis denotes altered connectivity patterns between anterior and posterior areas, thereby supporting dissociation views of hypnosis. Finally, evidence confirms the efficacy of hypnotic suggestions to reliably engage focal brain networks. Overall, ongoing investigations concerning the neural correlates of hypnosis afford researchers and clinicians better scientific understanding regarding the underlying brain mechanisms that subserve hypnotic phenomena. Such findings deliver a reliable framework that contributes to the development of a general theory of hypnosis.

REFERENCES

Allen, J. J., Iacono, W. G., Laravuso, J. J., & Dunn, L. A. (1995). An event-related potential investigation of posthypnotic recognition amnesia. *Journal of Abnormal Psychology*, 104(3), 421.

Baghdadi, G., & Nasrabadi, A. M. (2012). EEG phase synchronization during hypnosis induction. *Journal of Medical Engineering & Technology*, 36(4), 222–229. doi:10.3109/03091902.2012.668262

Barabasz, A., Barabasz, M., Jensen, S., Calvin, S., Trevisan, M., & Warner, D. (1999). Cortical event-related potentials show the structure of hypnotic suggestions is crucial. *International Journal of Clinical and Experimental Hypnosis*, 47(1), 5–22. doi:10.1080/00207149908410019

Barnier, A. J., Cox, R. E., & McConkey, K. M. (2014). The province of "highs": The high hypnotizable person in the science of hypnosis and in psychological science. *Psychology of Consciousness: Theory, Research, and Practice*, 1(2), 168–183.

Blakemore, S. J., Oakley, D. A., & Frith, C. D. (2003). Delusions of alien control in the normal brain. *Neuropsychologia*, 41(8), 1058–1067.

Brown, R. J., & Oakley, D. A. (2004). An integrative cognitive theory of hypnosis and high hypnotizability. In R. J. Brown & D. A. Oakley (Eds.), *High hypnotizability: Theoretical, experimental and clinical perspectives* (pp. 152–186). New York, NY: Brunner-Routledge.

Buckner, R. L., Andrews-Hanna, J. R., & Schacter, D. L. (2008). The brain's default network. *Annals of the New York Academy of Sciences*, 1124(1), 1–38. doi:10.1196/annals.1440.011

Buzsaki, G. (2006). *Rhythms of the brain* New York, NY. Oxford University Press.

Cardeña, E. (2005). The phenomenology of deep hypnosis: Quiescent and physically active. *International Journal of Clinical and Experimental Hypnosis*, 53(1), 37–59. doi:10.1080/00207140490914234

Cardeña, E., Jönsson, P., Terhune, D. B., & Marcusson-Clavertz, D. (2013). The neurophenomenology of neutral hypnosis. *Cortex; a Journal Devoted to the Study of the Nervous System and Behavior*, 49(2), 375–385. doi:10.1016/j.cortex.2012.04.001

Choudhury, S., & Slaby, J. (2011). *Critical neuroscience: A handbook of the social and cultural contexts of neuroscience*. Oxford, UK: John Wiley & Sons.

Cojan, Y., Waber, L., Schwartz, S., Rossier, L., Forster, A., & Vuilleumier, P. (2009). The brain under self-control: Modulation of inhibitory and monitoring cortical networks during hypnotic paralysis. *Neuron*, 62(6), 862–875. doi:10.1016/j.neuron.2009.05.021

Crawford, H. J., & Gruzelier, J. H. (1992). A midstream view of the neuropsychophysiology of hypnosis: Recent research and future directions. In E. Fromm & M. R. Nash (Eds.), *Contemporary hypnosis research* (pp. 227–266). New York, NY: Guilford Press.

Cusumano, E. P., & Raz, A. (2014). Harnessing psychoanalytical methods for a phenomenological neuroscience. *Frontiers in Psychology*, 5(334). doi:10.3389/fpsyg.2014.00334

de Luca, M., Beckmann, C. F., de Stefano, N., Matthews, P. M., & Smith, S. M. (2006). fMRI resting state networks define distinct modes of long-distance interactions in the human brain. *NeuroImage*, 29(4), 1359–1367. doi:10.1016/j.neuroimage.2005.08.035

de Pascalis, V. (2007). Phase-ordered gamma oscillations and the modulation of hypnotic experience. In G. A. Jamieson (Ed.), *Hypnosis and conscious states: The cognitive neuroscience perspective* (pp. 67–89). New York, NY: Oxford University Press.

Deeley, Q., Oakley, D. A., Toone, B., Bell, V., Walsh, E., Marquand, A. F., . . . Halligan, P. W. (2013). The functional anatomy of suggested limb paralysis. *Cortex; a Journal Devoted to the Study of the Nervous System and Behavior*, 49(2), 411–422. doi:10.1016/j.cortex.2012.09.016

Deeley, Q., Oakley, D. A., Toone, B., Giampietro, V., Brammer, M. J., Williams, S. C., & Halligan, P. W. (2012). Modulating the default mode network using hypnosis. *International Journal of Clinical and Experimental Hypnosis*, 60(2), 206–228. doi:10.1080/00207144.2012.648070

Deeley, Q., Oakley, D. A., Walsh, E., Bell, V., Mehta, M. A., & Halligan, P. W. (2014). Modelling psychiatric and cultural possession phenomena with suggestion and fMRI. *Cortex; a Journal Devoted to the Study of the Nervous System and Behavior, 53*, 107–119. doi:10.1016/j.cortex.2014.01.004

del Casale, A., Ferracuti, S., Rapinesi, C., Serata, D., Sani, G., Savoja, V., . . . Girardi, P. (2012). Neurocognition under hypnosis: Findings from recent functional neuroimaging studies. *International Journal of Clinical and Experimental Hypnosis, 60*(3), 286–317.

Demertzi, A., Soddu, A., Faymonville, M. E., Bahri, M. A., Gosseries, O., Vanhaudenhuyse, A., . . . Laureys, S. (2011). Hypnotic modulation of resting state fMRI default mode and extrinsic network connectivity. *Progress in Brain Research, 193*, 309–322. doi:10.1016/B978-0-444-53839-0.00020-X

Dienes, Z., & Hutton, S. (2013). Understanding hypnosis metacognitively: rTMS applied to left DLPFC increases hypnotic suggestibility. *Cortex; a Journal Devoted to the Study of the Nervous System and Behavior, 49*(2), 386–392. doi:10.1016/j.cortex.2012.07.009

Dolan, R. J. (2008). Neuroimaging of cognition: Past, present, and future. *Neuron, 60*(3), 496–502. doi:10.1016/j.neuron.2008.10.038

Egner, T., Jamieson, G., & Gruzelier, J. (2005). Hypnosis decouples cognitive control from conflict monitoring processes of the frontal lobe. *NeuroImage, 27*(4), 969–978. doi:10.1016/j.neuroimage.2005.05.002

Egner, T., & Raz, A. (2007). Cognitive control processes and hypnosis. In G. A. Jamieson (Ed.), *Hypnosis and conscious states: The cognitive neuroscience perspective* (pp. 29–50). New York, NY: Oxford University Press.

Fingelkurts, A. A., Fingelkurts, A. A., Kallio, S., & Revonsuo, A. (2007). Cortex functional connectivity as a neurophysiological correlate of hypnosis: An EEG case study. *Neuropsychologia, 45*(7), 1452–1462. doi:10.1016/j.neuropsychologia.2006.11.018

Friston, K. J. (2011). Functional and effective connectivity: A review. *Brain Connectivity, 1*(1), 13–36. doi:10.1089/brain.2011.0008

Halligan, P. W., Athwal, B. S., Oakley, D. A., & Frackowiak, R. S. (2000). Imaging hypnotic paralysis: Implications for conversion hysteria. *The Lancet, 355*(9208), 986–987.

Halligan, P. W., & Oakley, D. A. (2014). Hypnosis and beyond: Exploring the broader domain of suggestion. *Psychology of Consciousness: Theory, Research, and Practice, 1*(2), 105.

Heap, M., Brown, R. J., & Oakley, D. A. (2004). *The highly hypnotizable person: Theoretical, experimental and clinical issues.* London, UK: Routledge.

Hinterberger, TT., Schöner, J., & Halsband, U. (2011). Analysis of electrophysiological state patterns and changes during hypnosis induction. *International Journal of Clinical and Experimental Hypnosis, 59*(2), 165–179. doi:10.1080/00207144.2011.546188

Hoeft, F., Gabrieli, J. D., Whitfield-Gabrieli, S., Haas, B. W., Bammer, R., Menon, V., & Spiegel, D. (2012). Functional brain basis of hypnotizability. *Archives of General Psychiatry, 69*(10), 1064–1072. doi:10.1001/archgenpsychiatry.2011.2190

Hofbauer, R. K., Rainville, P., Duncan, G. H., & Bushnell, M. C. (2001). Cortical representation of the sensory dimension of pain. *Journal of Neurophysiology, 86*(1), 402–411.

Horton, J. E., Crawford, H. J., Harrington, G., & Downs, J. H. (2004). Increased anterior corpus callosum size associated positively with hypnotizability and the ability to control pain. *Brain: A Journal of Neurology, 127*(Pt. 8), 1741–1747. doi:10.1093/brain/awh196

Huber, A., Lui, F., Duzzi, D., Pagnoni, G., & Porro, C. A. (2014). Structural and functional cerebral correlates of hypnotic suggestibility. *PloS One, 9*(3), e93187. doi:10.1371/journal.pone.0093187

Jacobs, J., & Kahana, M. J. (2010). Direct brain recordings fuel advances in cognitive electrophysiology. *Trends in Cognitive Sciences, 14*(4), 162–171. doi:10.1016/j.tics.2010.01.005

Jamieson, G. A., & Sheehan, P. W. (2004). An empirical test of Woody and Bowers's dissociated-control theory of hypnosis. *International Journal of Clinical and Experimental Hypnosis, 52*(3), 232–249. doi:10.1080/0020714049052349

Jensen, M. P., & Patterson, D. R. (2014). Hypnotic approaches for chronic pain management: Clinical implications of recent research findings. *The American Psychologist, 69*(2), 167. doi:10.1037/a0035644

Kihlström, J. F. (1997). Hypnosis, memory and amnesia. *Philosophical Transactions of the Royal Society B-Biological Sciences, 352*(1362), 1727–1732.

Kihlström, J. F. (2013). Neuro-hypnotism: Prospects for hypnosis and neuroscience. *Cortex; a Journal Devoted to the Study of the Nervous System and Behavior, 49*(2), 365–374. doi:10.1016/j.cortex.2012.05.016

Kihlström, J. F., Glisky, M. L., McGovern, S., Rapcsak, S. Z., & Mennemeier, M. S. (2013). Hypnosis in the right hemisphere. *Cortex; a Journal Devoted to the Study of the Nervous System and Behavior, 49*(2), 393–399. doi:10.1016/j.cortex.2012.04.018

Kirsch, I. (1997). Response expectancy theory and application: A decennial review. *Applied and Preventive Psychology, 6*(2), 69–79.

Koivisto, M., Kirjanen, S., Revonsuo, A., & Kallio, S. (2013). A preconscious neural mechanism of hypnotically altered colors: A double case study. *PloS One, 8*(8), e70900. doi:10.1371/journal.pone.0070900

Kosslyn, S. M., Thompson, W. L., Costantini-Ferrando, M. F., Alpert, N. M., & Spiegel, D. (2000). Hypnotic visual illusion alters color processing in the brain.

American Journal of Psychiatry, 157(8), 1279–1284. doi:10.1176/appi.ajp.157.8.1279

Landry, M., Appourchaux, K., & Raz, A. (2014). Elucidating unconscious processing with instrumental hypnosis. *Frontiers in Psychology, 5*. doi:10.3389/fpsyg.2014.00785

Landry, M., & Raz, A. (2015). Hypnosis and imaging of the living brain. *American Journal of Clinical Hypnosis, 57*(3), 285–313. doi:10.1080/00029157.2014.978496

Laurence, J.-R., Beaulieu-Prévost, D., & Du Chéné, T. (2008). Measuring and understanding individual differences in hypnotizability. In A. J. Barnier & M. R. Nash (Eds.), *The Oxford handbook of hypnosis: Theory, research, and practice*. New York, NY: Oxford University Press.

Lee, J.-S., Spiegel, D., Kim, S.-B., Lee, J.-H., Kim, S.-I., Yang, B.-H., & Nam, J.-H. (2007). Fractal analysis of EEG in hypnosis and its relationship with hypnotizability. *International Journal of Clinical and Experimental Hypnosis, 55*(1), 14–31.

Lichtenberg, P., Bachner-Melman, R., Ebstein, R. P., & Crawford, H. J. (2004). Hypnotic susceptibility: Multidimensional relationships with Cloninger's Tridimensional Personality Questionnaire, COMT polymorphisms, absorption, and attentional characteristics. *International Journal of Clinical and Experimental Hypnosis, 52*(1), 47–72. doi:10.1076/iceh.52.1.47.23922

Lifshitz, M., Aubert Bonn, N., Fischer, A., Kashem, I. F., & Raz, A. (2013). Using suggestion to modulate automatic processes: From Stroop to McGurk and beyond. *Cortex, 49*(2), 463–473. doi:10.1016/j.cortex.2012.08.007

Lifshitz, M., Cusumano, E. P., & Raz, A. (2013). Hypnosis as neurophenomenology. *Frontiers in Human Neuroscience, 7*. doi:10.3389/fnhum.2013.00469

Lifshitz, M., & Raz, A. (2012). Hypnosis and meditation: Vehicles of attention and suggestion. *Journal of Mind–Body Regulation, 2*(1), 3–11.

Maldonado, J. R., & Spiegel, D. (2008). *Hypnosis psychiatry* (pp. 1982–2026). Chichester, UK: John Wiley & Sons.

Mason, M. F., Norton, M. I., van Horn, J. D., Wegner, D. M., Grafton, S. T., & Macrae, C. N. (2007). Wandering minds: The default network and stimulus-independent thought. *Science, 315*(5810), 393–395. doi:10.1126/science.1131295

Mazzoni, G., Rotriquenz, E., Carvalho, C., Vannucci, M., Roberts, K., & Kirsch, I. (2009). Suggested visual hallucinations in and out of hypnosis. *Consciousness and Cognition, 18*(2), 494–499. doi:10.1016/j.concog.2009.02.002

Mazzoni, G., Venneri, A., McGeown, W. J., & Kirsch, I. (2013). Neuroimaging resolution of the altered state hypothesis. *Cortex; a Journal Devoted to the Study of the Nervous System and Behavior, 49*(2), 400–410. doi:10.1016/j.cortex.2012.08.005

McConkey, K. M., & Barnier, A. J. (2004). High hypnotisability: Unity and diversity in behaviour and experience. In M. Heap, R. J. Brown, & D. A. Oakley (Eds.), *The highly hypnotizable person: Theoretical, experimental and clinical issues* (pp. 61–84). New York, NY: Routledge.

McGeown, W. J., Mazzoni, G., Venneri, A., & Kirsch, I. (2009). Hypnotic induction decreases anterior default mode activity. *Consciousness and Cognition, 18*(4), 848–855. doi:10.1016/j.concog.2009.09.001

McGeown, W. J., Venneri, A., Kirsch, I., Nocetti, L., Roberts, K., Foan, L., & Mazzoni, G. (2012). Suggested visual hallucination without hypnosis enhances activity in visual areas of the brain. *Consciousness and Cognition, 21*(1), 100–116. doi:10.1016/j.concog.2011.10.015

Mendelsohn, A., Chalamish, Y., Solomonovich, A., & Dudai, Y. (2008). Mesmerizing memories: Brain substrates of episodic memory suppression in posthypnotic amnesia. *Neuron, 57*(1), 159–170. doi:10.1016/j.neuron.2007.11.022

Michael, R. B., Garry, M., & Kirsch, I. (2012). Suggestion, cognition, and behavior. *Current Directions in Psychological Science, 21*(3), 151–156.

Nash, M. R., & Barnier, A. J. (2008). *The Oxford handbook of hypnosis: Theory, research and practice*. New York, NY: Oxford University Press.

Nee, D. E., Brown, J. W., Askren, M. K., Berman, M. G., Demiralp, E., Krawitz, A., & Jonides, J. (2013). A meta-analysis of executive components of working memory. *Cerebral Cortex (New York, NY: 1991), 23*(2), 264–282. doi:10.1093/cercor/bhs007

Oakley, D. A., & Halligan, P. W. (2009). Hypnotic suggestion and cognitive neuroscience. *Trends in Cognitive Sciences, 13*(6), 264–270.

Oakley, D. A., & Halligan, P. W. (2010). Psychophysiological foundations of hypnosis and suggestion. In J. W. Rhue, S. J. Lynn, & I. Kirsch (Eds.), *Handbook of clinical hypnosis* (pp. 79–177). Washington, DC: American Psychological Association.

Oakley, D. A., & Halligan, P. W. (2013). Hypnotic suggestion: Opportunities for cognitive neuroscience. *Nature Reviews. Neuroscience, 14*(8), 565–576. doi:10.1038/nrn3538

Pascual-Leone, A., Bartres-Fazf, D., & Keenan, J. P. (1999). Transcranial magnetic stimulation: Studying the brain-behaviour relationship by induction of "virtual lesions." *Philosophical Transactions of the Royal Society of London, Series B: Biological Sciences, 354*(1387), 1229–1238.

Piccione, C., Hilgard, E. R., & Zimbardo, P. G. (1989). On the degree of stability of measured hypnotizability over a 25-year period. *Journal of Personality and Social Psychology, 56*(2), 289–295.

Polito, V., Barnier, A. J., Woody, E. Z., & Connors, M. H. (2014). Measuring agency change across the domain of hypnosis. *Psychology of Consciousness: Theory, Research, and Practice, 1*(1), 3.

Rainville, P., Carrier, B., Hofbauer, R. K., Bushnell, M. C., & Duncan, G. H. (1999). Dissociation of sensory and affective dimensions of pain using hypnotic modulation. *Pain, 82*(2), 159–171.

Rainville, P., Duncan, G. H., Price, D. D., Carrier, B., & Bushnell, M. C. (1997). Pain affect encoded in human anterior cingulate but not somatosensory cortex. *Science, 277*(5328), 968–971.

Rainville, P., Hofbauer, R. K., Bushnell, M. C., Duncan, G. H., & Price, D. D. (2002). Hypnosis modulates activity in brain structures involved in the regulation of consciousness. *Journal of Cognitive Neuroscience, 14*(6), 887–901. doi:10.1162/089892902760191117

Rainville, P., Hofbauer, R. K., Paus, T., Duncan, G. H., Bushnell, M. C., & Price, D. D. (1999). Cerebral mechanisms of hypnotic induction and suggestion. *Journal of Cognitive Neuroscience, 11*(1), 110–125.

Raz, A. (2005). Attention and hypnosis: Neural substrates and genetic associations of two converging processes. *International Journal of Clinical and Experimental Hypnosis, 53*(3), 237–258. doi:10.1080/00207140590961295

Raz, A. (2011a). Does neuroimaging of suggestion elucidate hypnotic trance? *International Journal of Clinical and Experimental Hypnosis, 59*(3), 363–377. doi:10.1080/00207144.2011.570682

Raz, A. (2011b). Hypnosis: A twilight zone of the top-down variety. *Trends in Cognitive Sciences, 15*(12), 555–557.

Raz, A., & Buhle, J. (2006). Typologies of attentional networks. *Nature Reviews: Neuroscience, 7*(5), 367–379. doi:10.1038/nrn1903

Raz, A., Fan, J., & Posner, M. I. (2005). Hypnotic suggestion reduces conflict in the human brain. *Proceedings of the National Academy of Sciences of the United States, 102*(28), 9978–9983.

Raz, A., Kirsch, I., Pollard, J., & Nitkin-Kaner, Y. (2006). Suggestion reduces the Stroop effect. *Psychological Science, 17*(2), 91–95. doi:10.1111/j.1467-9280.2006.01669.x

Raz, A., Shapiro, T., Fan, J., & Posner, M. I. (2002). Hypnotic suggestion and the modulation of Stroop interference. *Archives of General Psychiatry, 59*(12), 1155–1161.

Raz, A., & Wolfson, J. B. (2010). From dynamic lesions to brain imaging of behavioral lesions: Alloying the gold of psychoanalysis with the copper of suggestion. *Neuropsychoanalysis: An Interdisciplinary Journal for Psychoanalysis and the Neurosciences, 12*(1), 5–18.

Shenhav, A., Botvinick, M. M., & Cohen, J. D. (2013). The expected value of control: An integrative theory of anterior cingulate cortex function. *Neuron, 79*(2), 217–240. doi:10.1016/j.neuron.2013.07.007

Smallwood, J., & Schooler, J. W. (2015). The science of mind wandering: Empirically navigating the stream of consciousness. *Annual Review of Psychology, 66*, 487–518. doi:10.1146/annurev-psych-010814-015331

Spiegel, D., & Barabasz, A. F. (1988). Effects of hypnotic instructions on P300 event-related-potential amplitudes: Research and clinical implications. *American Journal of Clinical Hypnosis, 31*(1), 11–17. doi:10.1080/00029157.1988.10402762

Tang, Y. Y., Rothbart, M. K., & Posner, M. I. (2012). Neural correlates of establishing, maintaining, and switching brain states. *Trends in Cognitive Sciences, 16*(6), 330–337. doi:10.1016/j.tics.2012.05.001

Tellegen, A., & Atkinson, G. (1974). Openness to absorbing and self-altering experiences ("absorption"), a trait related to hypnotic susceptibility. *Journal of Abnormal Psychology, 83*(3), 268.

Terhune, D. B., Cardeña, E., & Lindgren, M. (2011a). Differential frontal parietal phase synchrony during hypnosis as a function of hypnotic suggestibility. *Psychophysiology, 48*(10), 1444–1447.

Terhune, D. B., Cardeña, E., & Lindgren, M. (2011b). Dissociative tendencies and individual differences in high hypnotic suggestibility. *Cognitive Neuropsychiatry, 16*(2), 113–135.

Terhune, D. B., Cardeña, E., & Lindgren, M. (2011c). Dissociated control as a signature of typological variability in high hypnotic suggestibility. *Consciousness and Cognition, 20*(3), 727–736.

Ward, N. S., Oakley, D. A., Frackowiak, R. S., & Halligan, P. W. (2003). Differential brain activations during intentionally simulated and subjectively experienced paralysis. *Cognitive Neuropsychiatry, 8*(4), 295–312. doi:10.1080/13546800344000200

Woody, E., & Farvolden, P. (1998). Dissociation in hypnosis and frontal executive function. *American Journal of Clinical Hypnosis, 40*(3), 206–216. doi:10.1080/00029157.1998.10403427

Woody, E. Z., & Sadler, P. (2008). Dissociation theories of hypnosis. In M. R. Nash & A. J. Barnier (Eds.), *The Oxford handbook of hypnosis* (pp. 81–110). Oxford, UK: Oxford University Press.

Presenting Hypnosis to Patients

Joseph Meyerson

Hypnosis is a special word to which patients attribute contradictory meanings and expectations. On the one hand, hypnosis seems to invite a person to set out on an enchanting journey of self-exploration, self-healing, and self-empowerment along the yellow brick road escorted by the Wizard of Oz (the hypnotherapist). On the other hand, hypnosis threatens participants with a loss of their grasp on reality, a weakening of their self-control, and a sense of being operated and manipulated by a wicked sorcerer (the hypnotherapist). When first introduced to hypnosis, patients often bring with them this mixture of amazement and fear. Based on the assumption that appropriate expectations are a very important element in the effective implementation of hypnosis, the way in which hypnosis is presented to patients is crucial for maximizing therapeutic results and minimizing complications (Benham, Woody, Wilson, & Nash, 2006; Kirsch, 2011). Appropriate preparation for hypnosis sessions must take into consideration patients' motivation to be treated using hypnosis, the problem to be treated, the hypnotherapist's model and the field of hypnosis implementation, patients' attitudes toward and expectations from hypnosis and the hypnotherapist, and patients' cultural baggage concerning hypnosis (the myth of hypnosis).

PATIENTS' MOTIVATIONS FOR SEEKING TREATMENT THROUGH HYPNOSIS

Patients have diverse motivations for considering hypnosis as a treatment modality. Some consider it to be a last resort after previous unsuccessful attempts at treatment. Some see it as an effective adjunct treatment to conventional therapy. Some are driven by the positive results they have seen in relatives or friends who have undergone hypnosis. And some are attracted to hypnotic therapies

by misconceptions and unrealistic expectations. It is also important to mention patients who are brought to hypnotherapists by proxy motivators, such as friends and family members. Each of these motivations must be addressed accordingly. I usually consider motivational issues during preliminary telephone conversations, which can help in initial advance screening. These conversations should include simple questions such as, "How did you handle this problem previously?," "What caused you to decide to seek help from me?," and "What caused you to decide that hypnosis would be useful for you?" Such questions can help a therapist discover patients' motivations and act accordingly. In this initial stage of treatment, adjusting patients' motivations and expectations of hypnosis and the hypnotherapist are very important. The rule of thumb is to use this telephone screening to educate patients and/or to refer those motivated by major misconceptions concerning hypnosis to other treatment modalities. Among these misconceptions is the belief that hypnosis is a lie detector that can help a patient know all about his spouse's infidelities, or the notion that hypnosis is a one-session treatment that can change someone's personality or chronic health problems dramatically and forever. Generally speaking, during the first contact with patients, it is obligatory to give them a realistic picture of hypnosis while at the same time arousing their hope, involvement, and curiosity.

PROBLEM TO BE TREATED AND THERAPEUTIC MODEL OF HYPNOSIS IMPLEMENTATION

Professionals who use hypnosis in their clinical practice acknowledge that hypnosis is characterized by numerous levels and dimensions. It is impractical, and even impossible, to provide patients with all the data we have today concerning hypnosis.

Erickson's "seeding" techniques (Battino, 2005) can serve as a good guiding principle in presenting hypnosis to patients based on the problems that need to be treated. As a rule, patients seeking psychotherapeutic help should be informed about the relevant accessing and regulating aspects of hypnosis that can be manifested with regard to behaviors, thoughts, memories, emotions, associations, fantasies, and other mental elements. Patients with physiological difficulties should be educated of the possibilities that hypnotized subjects can uncover and use to become more sensitive to and purposefully influence autonomic physiological processes that are usually beyond conscious control. Patients with psychosomatic disorders should be told about the dissociative qualities of hypnosis that may help them differentiate somatic soreness from somatoform expressions of emotional conflicts and problems and learn to handle each of these accordingly.

The model of therapeutic integration of hypnosis in clinical practice can also play a role in introducing hypnosis to the patient. We can usually identify four major clinical models in the field of contemporary hypnotherapy (Meyerson, 2012). One of the best known models is the classical, script-oriented suggestibility model, in which hypnosis aims at reducing patients' analytical and critical thinking and at increasing their acceptance of the therapist's therapeutic suggestions (Allen, 2004; Gafner, 2010). Another perspective on hypnosis implementation is the eclectic, or adjunct, and tool-oriented use of hypnosis, which offers the therapist grounded in different theoretical orientations (e.g., behavioristic, dynamic, existential) the option to import instruments and insights from parallel clinical and theoretical orientations under the umbrella of hypnosis (Heap, 2012; Kroger, 2007). The third common clinical perspective is the "magnifying glass" orientation, which sees hypnosis as a magnifier of familiar techniques and processes (Green, Barabasz, Barrett, & Montgomery, 2005). Finally, the integrative model, which this author commonly adopts in his clinical work, relates to hypnosis as a basic and natural process that is essential for self-healing and can serve as an infrastructure for any therapeutic procedure regardless of the theoretical orientation and professional specialization of the professional using it (Alladin, 2008; Erickson, Rossi, & Rossi, 1976; Voit & DeLaney, 2004). Explaining and presenting the working model to patients in simple and clear language, and telling patients what they can expect from the hypnotherapeutic process, will increase patient cooperation and dramatically reduce resistance and complications.

Finally, the therapist must clearly delineate the borders of his expertise in hypnosis, not only for ethical reasons but also in order to help patients develop appropriate expectations and desired results from the therapeutic process. For instance, patients seeking treatment for dental phobia sometimes covertly expect to be treated for all phobic reactions disrupting their lives. Those patients should be guided to expect that the treatment will be oriented specifically toward future dental interactions with the goal of converting them to relatively safe experiences (Meyerson & Uziel, 2014).

As for referrals from other psychotherapists, for reasons of professional responsibility and concern for patient well-being, this author usually does not accept patients for hypnotic psychotherapy if they are undergoing psychotherapy with a psychotherapist who does not use hypnosis. This is especially true if the referral was intended merely for specific and seemingly focused interventions ("only to treat this phobic reaction"; "only to refresh memories from past traumatic experience"; "only to help with converting insights to actions"). From the author's point of view, a hypnotic psychotherapist is like a surgeon and cannot be responsible only for opening the abdominal cavity using the scalpel of hypnosis and at the same time not take responsibility for the operation as a whole.

PATIENTS' ATTITUDES TO AND EXPECTATIONS OF HYPNOSIS AND THE HYPNOTHERAPIST

Patients' attitudes toward and expectations from hypnosis and the hypnotherapist are usually derived from several basic sources: personal and interpersonal experiences, large group or local/national events, and the historical–cultural–mythical arena (Meyerson, 2014). Positive attitudes can usually be used as a powerful therapeutic impetus but should be realistically grounded and adapted to the current therapist's hypnotherapeutic methods and take the patient's present circumstances into account.

Problematic expectations that develop on the personal and interpersonal levels are usually caused by previous negative or unprofessional experiences with hypnosis or hypnosis-like experiences, such as meditation, guided imagination, and stage hypnosis (Battino, 2007). Such expectations also can be acquired by proxy and based on stories told by relatives, friends, or acquaintances. Information from the theater, books, movies, or other sources can also affect these misconceptions acquired on the personal and interpersonal levels (Barrett, 2006; Pintar & Lynn, 2008). Local large groups or national false beliefs about hypnosis usually emerge from fabled and well-known events entrenched in the local/national memory (Kleinhauz, Dreyfuss, Beran, Goldberg, & Azikri, 1979; Meyerson, 2014). Cultural and mythical elements influencing public views of hypnosis can be partially attributed to the historical roots of modern hypnosis. Pioneers, such as Mesmer, Braid, and Charcot, have developed and used applications and theories and have created an appropriate platform for such historically rooted impressions (for review, see Rosenfeld, 2008). Some of the cultural–mythical elements responsible for misconceptions about hypnosis seem to also serve as symbolic descriptions of hypnosis and of trance phenomena. Moreover, as proposed by French structural anthropologist and myth researcher Claude Lévi-Strauss, these descriptions may function as popular science that enables humans to understand abstract things about the world around them (e.g., hypnosis) on an observable and sensible level (Lévi-Strauss, 1966; Segal, 2004).

In preparing patients for their first hypnosis session, modern hypnotherapists strive to change patients' misconceptions concerning hypnosis that are usually related to apprehensions about losing autonomous and intended functioning (Yapko, 1994, 2012). The clinician can usually relieve these worries through rational and apparently scientific explanations using everyday examples and stories from the recent and ancient history of hypnosis (Capafons et al., 2005). This approach is even more effective when verified by helping patients try hypnosis on themselves using short and safe exercises (Voit & DeLaney, 2004). Before the first hypnosis session, the author finds it very useful to tell the patient the following: "During this hypnosis session you are free to remember, to be aware of the process and to emerge from hypnosis independently whenever you wish, simply by opening your eyes."

This hypnoeducational approach is effective in negating misconceptions rooted on the personal, interpersonal, and local/national levels. Nevertheless, cultural–mythical elements must be treated by the complementary approach of remythification of the hypnosis myth (Meyerson, 2014).

REMYTHIFICATION OF THE HYPNOSIS MYTH

According to the hypnosis myth, hypnosis is a very powerful and dangerous enterprise with almost miraculous short-term consequences that can be devastating in the long run. The myth depicts the hypnotherapist as cruel and manipulative and the hypnotized patient as weak, dependent, and defenseless. This myth has been reinforced in movies, novels, and plays, and is sometimes exploited and empowered by stage shows demonstrating hypnosis (Barrett, 2006). Social scientist Judith Pintar states in her in-depth study of the history of hypnosis and the hypnosis myth that the popular view of hypnosis has remained almost unchanged for at least the last three centuries despite demystification efforts by the scientific community of hypnotherapists during this period. According to Erickson's "utilization" strategy, the mythical elements of these persistent sociocultural misconceptions concerning hypnosis in contemporary society must be treated not by eliminating the myth, but rather by renewing it through a process known as *remythification* (Meyerson, 2014). This process involves strengthening the positive, useful, and constructive elements of the myth and reducing its negative, non-useful, and incongruent elements. Taking into account the cultural–anthropological view of leading myth researchers such as Barthes (1972) and Lévi-Strauss (1966), we can conclude that even today contemporary society needs mythical explanations of complex phenomena like hypnosis, and that myths constantly mutate and are reformulated based on social needs. If in the modern society of the 20th century clinicians and leaders in the field of hypnosis employed demystification and scientific orientation in the remythification of hypnosis, the cultural needs for relativism, authenticity, and spirituality in the postmodern society of the 21st century dictate that we must reestablish the remythification process. We can do this by examining the dichotomies, multilevel and multilateral explanations in theoretical, empirical, and clinical approaches to hypnosis and hypnotherapy (Lynn, Rhue, & Kirsch, 2010; Nash & Barnier, 2008) utilizing mythical and culturally influenced patterns.

PRACTICAL CONSIDERATIONS

Contemporary hypnotherapists formulating a new contemporary myth narrative during initial patient interviews must not to be afraid to refer to hypnosis as a "trance state." Even though distinctions between the "conscious" and the "unconscious" parts of the mind as well as "left brain–right brain" terminology are not strictly scientifically based and are still the subject of academic debate, hypnotherapists must not hesitate to use these distinctions for explaining hypnosis (Lilienfeld, Lynn, Ruscio, & Beyerstein, 2009; Raz, Schwartzman, & Guindi, 2008). Metaphorical and poetic language grounded in the patient's experiences and values can be useful as well.

To demonstrate and clarify this proposed process of remythification for dealing with the hypnosis myth, I use the question–answer format used elsewhere (for the full version, see Meyerson, 2014). Dialectically phrased answers to questions can serve as proper remythification tools. Generally speaking, answering patients' questions is a very effective way of informing them about hypnosis and dealing with misconceptions and myths. Questions typical of patients troubled by control issues are as follows:

Q: "Isn't hypnosis a powerful way of controlling people?"

A: "*Although hypnosis is not about control, a special kind of alliance is certainly formed between the hypnotherapist and the person hypnotized. Each individual involved in the hypnotic process is more attuned to the other and also to himself*" (Meyerson, 2014, p. 387).

Q: "Can one do or say anything contrary to one's will while under hypnosis?"

A: "*Hypnosis cannot force you to do or to say anything against your core values, but humans have diverse and, at times, contrasting wills. During hypnotherapy, the will that guides you to improved health and enhanced wellbeing can be heard more clearly, and even be empowered.*"

Patients also have questions regarding the long-term outcomes of hypnotic interventions, such as the following:

Q: "Is hypnosis a dangerous procedure?"

Such questions can provide the therapist further opportunities for remythification.

A: "*Hypnosis is a powerful therapeutic instrument and in the hands of an experienced clinician can do a great deal of good. So, as with anything, it is important to choose the right person for the right job*" (Meyerson, 2014, p. 387).

CONCLUSION

Although hypnosis is considered to be a natural everyday phenomenon, it, at the same time, constitutes a powerful and potent therapeutic entity. Bearing this in mind, in this chapter I have proposed that the preparation of patients for hypnotic procedures should not be taken lightly. Appropriate patient screening based on the motivations for seeking hypnotherapy, the patient's problems and needs, the therapist's area of expertise, and the model of hypnosis implementation is ethically required, and should be considered the point of departure for the preparation phase. Patients' attitudes toward and expectations from hypnosis and from the hypnotherapist should be examined and considered using proper explanations that take into account personal, interpersonal, and large group experiences. Finally, deeply rooted mythical aspects and misconceptions should be treated using remythification strategies.

In summary, adequate explanations supported by demonstrations and a remythification approach to patients' sociocultural baggage can save a lot of time in preparing for hypnotherapy by preventing complications, reducing resistance, and helping to make the hypnotherapeutic process more effective, satisfying, and fascinating for both the hypnotherapist and the patient.

REFERENCES

Alladin, A. (2008). *Cognitive hypnotherapy*. Chichester, UK: John Wiley & Sons.

Allen, R. P. (2004). *Scripts and strategies in hypnotherapy: The complete works.* Carmarthen, Wales; Williston, VT: Crown House Publishing.

Barrett, D. (2006). Hypnosis in film and television. *American Journal of Clinical Hypnosis, 49*(1), 13–30. doi:10.1080/00029157.2006.10401549

Barthes, R. (1972). *Mythologies* (Lavers, A. Trans.). London, UK: Farrar, Straus and Giroux.

Battino, R. (2007). *Guided imagery: Psychotherapy and healing through the mind-body connection.* Bancyfelin, Carmarthen, UK: Crown House Publishing.

Battino, T. L. S. R. (2005). *Ericksonian approaches: A comprehensive manual* (2nd ed.). Bancyfelin, Carmarthen, UK: Crown House Publishing.

Benham, G., Woody, E. Z., Wilson, K. S., & Nash, M. R. (2006). Expect the unexpected: Ability, attitude, and responsiveness to hypnosis. *Journal of Personality and Social Psychology, 91*(2), 342–350. doi:10.1037/0022-3514.91.2.342

Capafons, A., Cabañas, S., Alarcón, A., Espejo, B., Mendoza, M. E., Chaves, J. F., & Monje, A. (2005). Effects of different types of preparatory information on attitudes toward hypnosis. *Contemporary Hypnosis, 22*(2), 67–76. doi:10.1002/ch.25

Erickson, M. H., Rossi, S. I., & Rossi, E. L. (1976). *Hypnotic realities: The induction of clinical hypnosis and forms of indirect suggestion.* North Stratford, NH: Irvington Publishing Inc.

Gafner, G. (2010). *Techniques of hypnotic induction* (1st ed.). Carmarthen, Wales: Crown House Publishing.

Green, J. P., Barabasz, A. F., Barrett, D., & Montgomery, G. H. (2005). Forging ahead: The 2003 APA Division 30 definition of hypnosis. *International Journal of Clinical and Experimental Hypnosis, 53*(3), 259–264. doi:10.1080/00207140590961321

Heap, M. (2012). *Hypnotherapy: A handbook.* New York, NY: McGraw-Hill International.

Kirsch, I. (2011). The altered state issue: Dead or alive? *International Journal of Clinical and Experimental Hypnosis, 59*(3), 350–362. doi:10.1080/00207144.2011.570681

Kleinhauz, M., Dreyfuss, D. A., Beran, B., Goldberg, T., & Azikri, D. (1979). Some after-effects of stage hypnosis: A case study of psychopathological manifestations. *International Journal of Clinical and Experimental Hypnosis, 27*(3), 219–226. doi:10.1080/00207147908407563

Kroger, W. S. (2007). *Clinical & experimental hypnosis: In medicine, dentistry, and psychology* (2 Har/DVD). Philadelphia, PA: Lippincott Williams & Wilkins.

Lévi-Strauss, C. (1966). *The savage mind.* Chicago, IL: University of Chicago Press.

Lilienfeld, S. O., Lynn, S. J., Ruscio, J., & Beyerstein, B. L. (2009). *50 great myths of popular psychology: Shattering widespread misconceptions about human behavior* (1st ed.). West Sussex, UK: Wiley-Blackwell.

Lynn, S. J., Rhue, J. W., & Kirsch, I. (2010). *Handbook of clinical hypnosis* (2nd ed.). Washington, DC: American Psychological Association.

Meyerson, J. (2012). *Hypnotic psychotherapy.* Presented at the Hypnosis in Clinical, Medical and Rehabilitative Psychology, Tel Aviv.

Meyerson, J. (2014). The myth of hypnosis: The need for remythification. *International Journal of Clinical and Experimental Hypnosis, 62*(3), 378–393. doi:10.1080/00207144.2014.901090

Meyerson, J., & Uziel, N. (2014). Application of hypno-dissociative strategies during dental treatment of patients with severe dental phobia. *International Journal of Clinical and Experimental Hypnosis, 62*(2), 179–187. doi:10.1080/00207144.2014.869129

Nash., M. R., & Barnier., A. J. (2008). *The Oxford handbook of hypnosis.* New York, NY: Oxford University Press.

Pintar, J., & Lynn, S. J. (2008). *Hypnosis.* Oxford, UK: Wiley-Blackwell.

Raz, A., Schwartzman, D., & Guindi, D. (2008). Hemihypnosis, hypnosis, and the importance of knowing right from trend. *American Journal of Clinical Hypnosis, 51*(2), 201–208. doi:10.1080/00029157.2008.10401665

Rosenfeld, S. M. (2008). *A critical history of hypnotism: The unauthorized story.* Bloomington, IN: Xlibris.

Segal, R. A. (2004). *Myth: A very short introduction.* New York, NY: Oxford University Press.

Voit, R., & DeLaney, M. (2004). *Hypnosis in clinical practice: Steps for mastering hypnotherapy.* New York, NY: Routledge.

Yapko, M. D. (1994). *Essentials of hypnosis* (1st ed.). New York, NY: Routledge.

Yapko, M. D. (2012). *Trancework: An introduction to the practice of clinical hypnosis* (4th ed.). New York, NY: Routledge.

Hypnotizability

Erik Woody and Pamela Sadler

Some years ago, one of the authors was standing in line waiting to give a brief presentation about his research to a classroom of students. To pass the time, the colleague in front of him, a new faculty member, turned and asked, "What are you interested in?" When the author replied, "Hypnosis," the colleague stepped back with a look of incredulity. He explained that he and his wife, who were open-minded and genuinely interested, had recently tried hypnosis, but none of the suggestions had any perceivable effect on either of them. From this experience, he had concluded that hypnosis was a "total fraud."

Other individuals' responses to hypnosis are often quite the opposite of this. University-based hypnosis researchers can readily identify so-called hypnotic virtuosos because they repeatedly attain perfect scores on scales of hypnotizability. Years ago, Kenneth Bowers invited the students in his lab to invent a series of special, very difficult suggestions to try in a demonstration session with such a hypnotic virtuoso. This virtuoso was able to enact all of the special suggestions, even extremely difficult ones. For example, one suggestion involved a bottle of very strong ammonia, of which none of the students was able to take a whiff without an involuntary backward jerk of the head. Their idea was to ask the virtuoso to sniff the bottle to experience the smell of chocolate and see if the head jerk occurred. In the session, the virtuoso reported the bottle smelled like chocolate, without any head jerk, whereupon Ken improvised and said, "Well, of course, but what *kind* of chocolate?" In response, the virtuoso snorted vigorously and repeatedly at the bottle (as Ken tried to pry it out of his hand to keep him from hurting himself), eventually announcing his discovery with a big smile: "A Hershey bar!"

These examples illustrate the huge spectrum of individual differences in people's responsiveness to hypnosis, which range from the inability to experience even simple suggestions that most people readily pass, at one end, to the capacity for far-reaching changes in the experience of reality, at the other. This wide range of individual differences was evident from the earliest days of investigations into hypnosis (Dixon & Laurence, 1992; Laurence, Beaulieu-Prévost, & du Chéné, 2008) and continues to be one of the most fundamental, well-established facts about it. A widely used term to refer to these crucial differences is *hypnotizability*, but other terms are also used synonymously, such as *hypnotic susceptibility, hypnotic suggestibility,* and *hypnotic responsiveness.*

In a clinical treatment context, the importance of hypnotizability is closely akin to the importance of individual differences in response to other treatments (for example, medications), the appreciation of which is crucial for high-quality health care. To illustrate, the foregoing two individuals would need to be handled quite differently by a hypnotherapist and would likely present very different possibilities for approaches to intervention.

MEASUREMENT AND CONCEPTION OF HYPNOTIZABILITY

Boring (1923) famously offered the following definition of intelligence: "Intelligence is what is measured by intelligence tests." In a similar vein, one might be tempted to say, "Hypnotizability is what is measured by hypnosis scales." This statement would be appropriate in two ways. First, to a considerable extent, the development of hypnosis scales was strongly influenced by the operational and psychometric approach advanced in work to measure intelligence. Second, as we shall see, the currently prevailing conception of hypnotizability is largely a reflection of the way in which it is measured by hypnosis scales.

The crucial phase of development of hypnosis scales was the work of Weitzenhoffer and Hilgard in the late 1950s and early 1960s. They took what may be termed a *work sample approach* (Woody & Barnier, 2008). Rather than attempting to predict hypnotic responsiveness with, say, a set of underlying basic factors (e.g., personality, cognitive, or neuropsychological), in the work sample approach, test developers attempt to measure as directly as possible what they want to know. To apply this approach to hypnosis, we simply put individuals in a standardized hypnotic circumstance by providing a standardized induction, give them a predetermined series of suggestions, and measure how they respond. Typically, the individual's score is the total number of suggestions to which he or she responded successfully. Consistent with the adage that the best predictor of behavior is past behavior, this index of hypnotizability may be used to predict how the individual will respond to hypnosis in the future.

The most influential hypnosis scales developed by Weitzenhoffer and Hilgard (1959, 1962) are two alternate forms consisting mainly of relatively easy suggestions, the Stanford Hypnotic Susceptibility Scales, Forms A and B (SHSS:A and SHSS:B), and a further scale designed to follow up testing on the SHSS:A or SHSS:B by giving more emphasis to relatively difficult suggestions, the Stanford Hypnotic Susceptibility Scale, Form C (SHSS:C). Kihlström (2008) pointed out that the SHSS:C has come to be widely regarded as the gold standard of hypnosis scales. Each of these scales consists of an induction and a dozen suggestions, designed to be administered by a hypnotist to an individual subject. Because group administration of hypnosis scales is far more efficient for conducting research, Shor and Orne (1962) developed a format of the SHSS:A suitable for group testing, the Harvard Group Scale of Hypnotic Susceptibility, Form A (HGSHS:A). The HGSHS:A has been, by far, the most widely used hypnosis scale worldwide. Similarly, Bowers (1993, 1998) developed a version of the SHSS:C suitable for testing in small groups, the Waterloo-Stanford Group Scale of Hypnotic Susceptibility, Form C (WSGC), which has also been used extensively in hypnosis research.

Hypnosis produces a number of potentially important subjective effects that can be measured, including feelings of hypnotic depth (Field, 1965), transferential phenomena like archaic involvement (Nash & Spinler, 1989), and other phenomenological states (Pekala, 1991). However, there is fairly wide agreement that a key subjective effect of hypnosis is an alteration of the sense of agency, such that when the hypnotic subject carries out a suggestion, it feels as if it is happening on its own, extravolitionally. Terms used to denote this experience include the *classic suggestion effect* (Weitzenhoffer, 1974, 1980) and *involuntariness* (Bowers, 1981). Like other subjective phenomena in hypnosis, the sense of agency can be measured through self-report scales (Polito, Barnier, & Woody, 2013; Polito, Barnier, Woody, & Connors, 2014).

Somewhat surprisingly, given the importance of subjective phenomena in hypnosis, the scoring of the most widely used hypnosis scales does not make use of self-report of subjective effects at all. Instead, in these scales, each suggestion is typically scored based on observable behavior—for example, whether the hypnotic subject's arm lowers visibly in response to the suggestion that it is becoming heavier. The working assumption is that these behavioral effects are usually allied to accompanying changes in the sense of agency (Bowers, 1981). Although Weitzenhoffer (1997) eventually came to regret the narrow focus in the hypnosis scales on observable behavior, Weitzenhoffer and Hilgard's original decision to anchor the scoring of hypnosis scales in observable behaviors very likely contributed to the credibility of these scales with social scientists more generally (i.e., hypnosis is not just "in the head").

Hundreds of research studies using the SHSS:A, SHSS:C, HGSHS:A, and WSGC have established some important, widely accepted findings about hypnotizability (Woody & Barnier, 2008):

- *Consistent individual differences*—People who are good at enacting one type of hypnotic suggestion also tend to be good at enacting other types of hypnotic suggestion. Factor analysis of hypnosis scale data consistently yields multiple factors, suggesting the existence of distinguishable, relatively specific abilities that affect response to some kinds of suggestions more than others (Balthazard & Woody, 1985). However, these factors intercorrelate strongly, indicating the presence of an underlying, *g*-like, general ability common to all hypnotic responses.

- *Difficulty spectrum relating suggestions to ability levels*—Hypnotic suggestions differ considerably in their level of difficulty, from easy suggestions that most people can pass, like arm lowering, to difficult ones that only a minority can pass, like hallucinations. In addition, this difficulty spectrum maps closely onto ability levels, such that only people high in hypnotizability are likely to pass difficult hypnotic suggestions.
- *Bell-shaped distribution*—Across the general population, levels of hypnotizability are reasonably bell shaped, or normally distributed. A relatively small proportion of people are very unresponsive to hypnosis, no matter how easy the suggestions are; and likewise only a small proportion of people are hypnotic virtuosos, able to pass virtually all suggestions, even very difficult ones. A large proportion of people occupy the middle of the distribution, in a band of moderate levels of hypnotizability.
- *High stability over time*—Hypnotizability is a trait that is very stable over time. Individual differences in hypnotizability remain consistent even over a period of a quarter of a century (Piccione, Hilgard, & Zimbardo, 1989).
- *Distinct from other kinds of suggestibility*—Hypnotizability is quite distinct from other, everyday types of suggestibility, such as persuasibility, interrogative suggestibility (the tendency to be affected by leading questions), placebo responsiveness, and conformity (Tasso & Pérez, 2008).

In essence, using hypnosis scales, we estimate people's levels of hypnotizability by putting them in a hypnotic circumstance and administering a series of hypnotic suggestions to see how they respond. The resulting construct of "hypnotizability" can seem frustratingly circular (akin to explaining responsible behavior by referring to the trait of "conscientiousness"). Readers may wonder whether, instead, there is a way to anticipate people's levels of hypnotizability prior to ever submitting them to hypnosis—that is, by using personality, attentional, or cognitive traits measured outside of hypnosis. An intriguing example is the personality trait of absorption (Tellegen & Atkinson, 1974), which may be briefly defined as the tendency to show a highly focused style of attention in everyday life (hence resembling hypnosis). Although the search for nonhypnotic correlates of hypnotizability is a flourishing area of research, which offers the prospect of a deeper understanding of what hypnotizability is, it is fair to say that so far, no such correlates have proven to be sufficiently strongly related to hypnotizability to substitute for its measurement using a hypnosis scale. Practically speaking, if we want to know how hypnotizable people are, we cannot guess accurately from other information; instead, we need to hypnotize them and see how they respond.

USE OF HYPNOSIS SCALES IN RESEARCH

Hypnosis scales are the foundation for laboratory research on hypnosis, and published laboratory research on hypnosis virtually always uses them (Woody & Barnier, 2008). By far, the most commonly used paradigm is to use hypnosis scales to preselect individuals for participation in a subsequent experiment. Indeed, the highest quality procedure involves pretesting on two successive hypnosis scales. Specifically, the HGSHS:A is administered in a large group setting (e.g., a lecture classroom), and then the highest scorers (scoring, say, 9–12 on the 12-point hypnosis scale) and the lowest scorers (scoring, say, 0–3) are selected out for further testing. These selected individuals are then either individually administered the SHSS:C or administered the WSGC in groups of up to about a dozen. The people who consistently score high on both hypnosis scales are identified as "high hypnotizable," and the people who consistently score low on both scales as "low hypnotizable." The individuals so selected comprise the two subject groups for participation in the subsequent experiment.

It is possible, and fairly common, to preselect high and low groups based on the administration of only a single hypnosis scale (e.g., the HGSHS:A), although this is considered to be a less desirable method. Testing with two hypnosis scales has some clear advantages: The second testing confirms the high or low hypnotizable status of each participant, so that we are more confident each is a bona fide member of the high or low hypnotizable subject groups; and participants gain some experience with hypnosis, such that their performance can reach a plateau, or characteristic level, prior to the experiment. Finally, it is also possible to use the hypnosis scales to select out a middle group, with a moderate level of hypnotizability; however, this is done infrequently.

Using hypnosis scales to preselect participants yields some advantages of enormous practical importance for laboratory research on hypnosis. First, focusing attention on those who are genuinely responsive to hypnosis, the high hypnotizable group, greatly increases the statistical power of the experiment. For example, say we want to compare two different types of hypnotic suggestion for analgesia: suggestions including counterpain imagery versus suggestions with no imagery (Hargadon, Bowers, & Woody, 1995). If we were to run these two experimental conditions using unselected participants, the within-condition variance in both conditions would be very high, reflecting the huge individual differences in people's response to hypnotic suggestions (e.g., many participants might experience virtually no analgesia in either condition). These within-condition differences would go into the error term and work against our being able to show any difference between the two types of suggestion. In contrast, the responses of preselected high hypnotizable participants will tend to be far more homogeneous, making us much more confident about the detection of between-condition differences.

A second, related advantage of using hypnosis scales to preselect participants is that it enables us to study relatively unusual or rare hypnotic phenomena—namely, ones obtainable in only a small minority of the general population, like hypnotic hallucinations or delusions. For this purpose, our subject group may be defined as those who not only consistently score high on hypnosis scales but also pass the suggestions of the relevant type on the hypnosis scales (e.g., suggestions of hallucinations to select subjects for an experiment on hypnotic hallucinations, or suggestions of amnesia to select subjects for an experiment on hypnotic manipulation of memory). It is also possible to supplement the hypnosis scales with a further, specialized assessment of the particular type of hypnotic response to be targeted in the experiment, to further ensure that the subjects selected for the experiment are capable of producing the behavior to be studied (e.g., Szechtman, Woody, Bowers, & Nahmias, 1998). For example, this kind of carefully targeted subject selection may be especially important for neuroimaging studies, the

success of which depends crucially on homogeneity of response across the participants within any condition.

A third advantage of using hypnosis scales to preselect participants for laboratory studies is that the low hypnotizable individuals can serve as a valuable control group. If the phenomenon being studied is truly hypnotic, the low hypnotizable group should generally not show it, providing an important contrast with the high hypnotizable group. This contrast helps to ensure that results obtained in the experiment are not attributable to demand effects, wherein participants are simply acting the way they think they are supposed to be acting.

The widespread practice of preselection using hypnosis scales also has some potentially important disadvantages. First, because including people scoring in the middle range of the distribution of hypnotizability would afford relatively little boost in statistical power, these moderate hypnotizable individuals are very often not run at all in hypnosis experiments. The irony for clinicians is that this middle range of the hypnotizability distribution is where most of their patients would lie, rather than at the extremes. Thus, it might be argued that, at least to some extent, laboratory studies of hypnosis may not be eliciting the responses that clinicians would typically encounter. For any given phenomenon, we may lack information about whether, in their responses, individuals moderate in hypnotizability are similar to low hypnotizables, similar to high hypnotizables, in between, or quite different from both.

Second, preselection using hypnosis scales tacitly but very strongly reinforces an important underlying assumption that hypnotizability is all one thing—in other words, that there is only one underlying ability at work, and that the differences between people in response to hypnosis reflect their standing on this one ability. In contrast, there is considerable evidence that hypnotizability is actually multidimensional, consisting of multiple distinguishable abilities (Woody, Bowers, & Oakman, 1992; Woody & McConkey, 2003). In principle, multidimensionality complicates the interpretation of experiments contrasting high versus low hypnotizables. For example, the lows may tend to lack a type of ability that the moderates and highs have, and the highs may tend to possess another type of ability that the moderates and lows lack, so that the high versus low comparison would actually be quite complex. To date, there has been little work using a multidimensional conception of hypnotizability to predict and explain hypnotic behavior; readers intrigued by this possibility are encouraged to look at Woody, Barnier, and McConkey (2005) and the last two sections (pp. 267–278) of Woody and Barnier (2008).

A related possibility is that there may be distinct types of responding to hypnosis—in other words, even among those highly responsive to hypnosis, individuals may enact the same hypnotic suggestion in different ways, using different underlying processes (McConkey, Glisky, & Kihlström, 1989; Sheehan & McConkey, 1982). For example, Barber (1999) proposed that there are three distinct types of individuals who are hypnotically responsive: those whose hypnotic responses are chiefly due to their high motivation and positive set; those who are fantasy-prone and use imaginative processes in hypnosis; and those for whom hypnosis elicits dissociative processes that block material from awareness. At present, hypnosis scales do not provide this kind of process differentiation at all. Nonetheless, for a clinician, knowing how a patient goes about enacting a hypnotic suggestion (e.g., whether through mental imagery or dissociative processes) could obviously be of considerable importance in helping him or her to optimize the usefulness of the intervention. Although typological conceptions of hypnotizability have not yet had much impact, they are currently an important area of research (e.g., Terhune & Cardeña, 2010).

USE OF HYPNOSIS SCALES IN CLINICAL PRACTICE

The attitudes of clinicians toward hypnosis scales tend to be strikingly different from those of hypnosis researchers. At the convention of the Society for Clinical and Experimental Hypnosis (SCEH) a few years ago, a speaker began his keynote address by asking for a show of hands of those who at least occasionally used hypnosis scales in their clinical work. Out of an audience of about 50 clinicians, only two hands went up (including that of one of the present authors). The speaker, a strongly clinically oriented researcher, was visibly taken aback. As this anecdote indicates, clinicians, unlike hypnosis researchers, typically show little or no interest in the use of hypnosis scales in their work.

It is possible to make a case that clinicians should be far more interested in the use of hypnosis scales. At the same SCEH conference, Edward Frischholz commented to one of the present authors, "How are we ever going to make any scientific progress if we can't convince clinicians to use hypnosis scales?" Ed's statement, which may seem puzzling at first blush, implies that hypnosis scales are the necessary foundation for the scientific advancement of clinical hypnosis. Previously, Kenneth Bowers argued very forcefully for this point of view, which he stated in a form one of the authors (Woody, 1997) has dubbed the Bowers Doctrine (Bowers, 1982, p. 6; see also Bowers, 1984): "An effect is not a classic suggestion effect [that is, a genuine hypnotic effect] unless it is correlated with hypnotic ability as standardly assessed." Woody and Barnier (2008, p. 258) explicated this pithy statement as follows:

> The idea is that individual differences, as measured by the standardized scales, should be the touchstone for true hypnotic phenomena. There are lots of experimental and treatment effects that we might be tempted to call hypnotic. But ones that turn out not to be associated with hypnotizability should be regarded as nonspecific effects, not part of the essence of hypnosis.

In short, unless clinicians administer hypnosis scales to their clients, aggregate data over many cases, and evaluate the correlation of the hypnotizability scores with treatment outcomes, we cannot find out whether the treatment effects are truly hypnotic or attributable to other, nonspecific factors. As we have previously commented, "Without this information, hypnotherapy seems wide open to the criticism that it may be an assortment of nonspecific effects masquerading under an exotic label" (Sadler & Woody, 2010, p. 163).

Based partly on this reasoning, we wholeheartedly recommend that clinicians use hypnosis scales in their hypnotherapeutic work. In addition to providing important information about the patient's level of hypnotizability, the administration of a hypnosis scale can serve other purposes, such as introducing and normalizing hypnosis in a relatively nonthreatening way. Patients' behavioral responses, on which their scale score is based, can readily be supplemented by a postadministration discussion of their co-occurring subjective experiences, which provides useful information about the process/typology issues mentioned earlier. Sadler and Woody (2010, pp. 168–171) present a case study, which illustrates how we embed the administration of a hypnosis scale into therapy and make use of the results in tailoring hypnotic interventions.

Despite this recommendation, it has to be admitted that the hypnosis scales in widespread use by hypnosis researchers are somewhat awkward to use in clinical practice and not particularly well tuned to the needs of clinicians. They are arguably too long (i.e., time-consuming); they tend to overemphasize motor effects of little relevance to most therapy, rather than changes in cognition and emotion of greater relevance; and, with their purely behavioral scoring, they do not provide important information about the client's subjective experiences. Previous attempts to develop shorter hypnosis scales for use by clinicians have not been particularly successful (e.g., Hilgard, Crawford, & Wert, 1979; Morgan & Hilgard, 1978–1979). However, a clinical hypnotizability scale recently developed by Elkins (2014), the Elkins Hypnotizability Scale (EHS), appears to address the foregoing issues sensibly and is well worth consideration.

CONCLUSION

The wide range of individual differences in response to hypnotic suggestions, termed hypnotizability, is one of the most important and best established facts about hypnosis. The measurement of hypnotizability through standardized hypnosis scales has provided the foundation of modern hypnosis research but has had relatively little impact on clinical practice. We hope that the present chapter, possibly together with the advancement of more clinically useful scales, will encourage clinicians to include a standardized hypnosis scale as part of their hypnotherapy work. The resulting data would hold much promise for illuminating the effects of hypnosis in clinical practice and contributing ultimately to a better scientific understanding of hypnosis.

REFERENCES

Balthazard, C. G., & Woody, E. Z. (1985). The "stuff" of hypnotic performance: A review of psychometric approaches. *Psychological Bulletin, 98*(2), 283–296.

Barber, T. X. (1999). A comprehensive three-dimensional theory of hypnosis. In I. Kirsch, A. Capafons, E. Cardena-Buelna, & S. Amigo (Eds.), *Clinical hypnosis and self-regulation: Cognitive-behavioural perspectives* (pp. 21–48). Washington, DC: American Psychological Association. doi:10.1037/10282-001

Boring, E. (1923). Intelligence as the tests test it. *New Republic, 35,* 35–37.

Bowers, K. S. (1981). Do the Stanford scales tap the "classic suggestion effect"? *International Journal of Clinical and Experimental Hypnosis, 29*(1), 42–53.

Bowers, K. S. (1982, August). *Suggestion and subtle control.* Paper presented at the 90th annual meeting of the American Psychological Association, Washington, DC.

Bowers, K. S. (1984). Hypnosis. In N. S. Endler & J. M. Hunt (Eds.), *Personality and behavior disorders* (2nd ed. , Vol. 1, pp. 439–475). New York, NY: Wiley.

Bowers, K. S. (1993). The Waterloo-Stanford Group C (WSGC) scale of hypnotic susceptibility: Normative and comparative data. *International Journal of Clinical and Experimental Hypnosis, 41*(1), 35–46.

Bowers, K. S. (1998). Waterloo-Stanford Group Scale of Hypnotic Susceptibility, Form C: Manual and response booklet. *International Journal of Clinical and Experimental Hypnosis, 46*(3), 250–268.

Dixon, M., & Laurence, J.-R. (1992). Two hundred years of hypnosis research: Questions resolved? Questions unanswered! In E. Fromm & M. Nash (Eds.), *Contemporary hypnosis research* (pp. 34–66). New York, NY: Guilford Press.

Elkins, G. (2014). *Hypnotic relaxation therapy.* New York, NY: Springer Publishing Company.

Field, P. B. (1965). An inventory scale of hypnotic depth. *International Journal of Clinical and Experimental Hypnosis, 13*(4), 238–249.

Hargadon, R., Bowers, K. S., & Woody, E. Z. (1995). Does counter-pain imagery mediate hypnotic analgesia? *Journal of Abnormal Psychology, 104*(3), 508–516.

Hilgard, E. R., Crawford, H. J., & Wert, A. (1979). The Stanford Hypnotic Arm Levitation Induction and Test (SHALIT): A six minute hypnotic induction and measurement scale. *International Journal of Clinical and Experimental Hypnosis, 27*(2), 111–124.

Kihlström, J. F. (2008). The domain of hypnosis, revisited. In M. R. Nash & A. J. Barnier (Eds.), *The Oxford handbook of hypnosis: Theory, research and practice* (pp. 21–52). Oxford, UK: Oxford University Press.

Laurence, J.-R., Beaulieu-Prévost, D., & du Chéné, T. (2008). Measuring and understanding individual differences in hypnotizability. In M. R. Nash & A. J. Barnier (Eds.), *The Oxford handbook of hypnosis: Theory, research and practice* (pp. 225–253). Oxford, UK: Oxford University Press.

McConkey, K. M., Glisky, M. L., & Kihlström, J. F. (1989). Individual differences among hypnotic virtuosos: A case comparison. *Australian Journal of Clinical and Experimental Hypnosis*, 17, 131–140.

Morgan, A. H., & Hilgard, J. R. (1978–1979). The Stanford Hypnotic Clinical Scale for adults. *American Journal of Clinical Hypnosis*, 21(2–3), 134–147.

Nash, M. R., & Spinler, D. (1989). Hypnosis and transference: A measure of archaic involvement. *International Journal of Clinical and Experimental Hypnosis*, 37(2), 129–144.

Pekala, R. J. (1991). *The Phenomenology of Consciousness Inventory (PCI)*. West Chester, PA: Mid-Atlantic Educational Institute.

Piccione, C., Hilgard, E. R., & Zimbardo, P. G. (1989). On the degree of stability of measured hypnotizability over a 25-year period. *Journal of Personality and Social Psychology*, 56(2), 289–295.

Polito, V., Barnier, A. J., & Woody, E. Z. (2013). Developing the Sense of Agency Rating Scale (SOARS): An empirical measure of agency disruption in hypnosis. *Consciousness and cognition*, 22(3), 684–696.

Polito, V., Barnier, A. J., Woody, E., & Connors, M. J. (2014). Measuring agency across domains of hypnosis. *Psychology of Consciousness: Theory, Research, and Practice*, 1(1), 3–19.

Sadler, P., & Woody, E. (2010). Dissociation in hypnosis: Theoretical frameworks and psychotherapeutic implications. In J. W. Rhue, S. J. Lynn, & I. Kirsch (Eds.), *Handbook of clinical hypnosis* (2nd ed., pp. 151–268). Washington, DC: American Psychological Association.

Sheehan, P. W., & McConkey, K. M. (1982). *Hypnosis and experience: The exploration of phenomena and process*. Hillsdale, NJ: Lawrence Erlbaum.

Shor, R. E., & Orne, E. C. (1962). *The Harvard Group Scale of Hypnotic Susceptibility, Form A*. Palo Alto, CA: Consulting Psychologists Press.

Szechtman, H., Woody, E., Bowers, K. S., & Nahmias, C. (1998). Where the imaginal appears real: A PET study of auditory hallucinations. *Proceedings of the National Academy of Sciences*, 95(4), 1956–1960. doi:10.1073/pnas.95.4.1956

Tasso, A. F., & Pérez, N. A. (2008). Parsing everyday suggestibility: What does it tell us about hypnosis? In M. R. Nash & A. J. Barnier (Eds.), *The Oxford handbook of hypnosis* (pp. 283–309). Oxford, UK: Oxford University Press. doi:10.1093/oxfordhb/9780198570097.013.0011

Tellegen, A., & Atkinson, G. (1974). Openness to absorbing and self-altering experiences ("absorption"), a trait related to hypnotic susceptibility. *Journal of Abnormal Psychology*, 83(3), 268–277.

Terhune, D. B., & Cardeña, E. (2010). Differential patterns of spontaneous experiential response to a hypnotic induction: A latent profile analysis. *Consciousness and Cognition*, 19(4), 1140–1150.

Weitzenhoffer, A. M. (1974). When is an "instruction" an instruction? *International Journal of Clinical and Experimental Hypnosis*, 22(3), 258–269.

Weitzenhoffer, A. M. (1980). Hypnotic susceptibility revisited. *American Journal of Clinical Hypnosis*, 22(3), 130–134.

Weitzenhoffer, A. M. (1997). Hypnotic susceptibility: A personal and historical note regarding the development and naming of the Stanford scales. *International Journal of Clinical and Experimental Hypnosis*, 45(2), 126–143.

Weitzenhoffer, A. M., & Hilgard, E. R. (1959). *Stanford Hypnotic Susceptibility Scale, Forms A and B*. Palo Alto, CA: Consulting Psychologists Press.

Weitzenhoffer, A. M., & Hilgard, E. R. (1962). *Stanford Hypnotic Susceptibility Scale, Form C*. Palo Alto, CA: Consulting Psychologists Press.

Woody, E. Z. (1997). Have the hypnotic susceptibility scales outlived their usefulness? *International Journal of Clinical and Experimental Hypnosis*, 45(3), 226–238.

Woody, E. Z., & Barnier, A. J. (2008). Hypnosis scales for the twenty-first century: What do we need and how should we use them? In M. R. Nash & A. J. Barnier (Eds.), *The Oxford handbook of hypnosis* (pp. 255–281). Oxford, UK: Oxford University Press. doi:10.1093/oxfordhb/9780198570097.013.0010

Woody, E. Z., Barnier, A. J., & McConkey, K. M. (2005). Multiple hypnotizabilities: Differentiating the building blocks of hypnotic response. *Psychological Assessment*, 17(2), 200–211.

Woody, E. Z., Bowers, K. S., & Oakman, J. M. (1992). A conceptual analysis of hypnotic responsiveness: Experience, individual differences, and context. In *Contemporary hypnosis research* (pp. 3–33). New York, NY: Guilford Press.

Woody, E. Z., & McConkey, K. M. (2003). What we don't know about the brain and hypnosis, but need to: A view from the Buckhorn Inn. *International Journal of Clinical and Experimental Hypnosis*, 51(3), 309–338.

Laws and Principles of Hypnotic Inductions

Consuelo Casula

Becoming experts in hypnosis involves finding the combination that opens the heart and the mind of the patient through creating a context of effective communication (Zeig, 2006). The hypnotherapist learns to choose the verbal and nonverbal communication most suitable for each patient in order to send therapeutic messages that resonate and evoke the desired effects.

Becoming experts in hypnosis involves creative integration of the therapist's psychological competence and ability to build and maintain rapport with each patient, after awakening his or her motivation, collaboration, and commitment (Gilligan, 1987; Kane & Olness, 2004). Thus, the therapist chooses the right timing (*kairòs*) and different types of inductions and suggestions.

In order to reinforce the effectiveness of selected hypnotic suggestions, the hypnotist respects basic principles and follows laws. Even in the field of hypnosis, the elevation of principles to the status of "laws" has taken place after experts verified their utility and efficacy in their practice. Principles are the source of the law, while laws enrich principles, and both are always evolving, influencing, and reinforcing each other in practice.

Some of these laws and principles are well known and attributed to the authors who formulated them, such as Emile Coué or Dabney Ewin, among others (Coué, 2008; Ewin, 2009). Several textbooks cover various laws and principles, presenting them as general rules whose validity is reinforced pragmatically by their positive effect, without a precise author (Hammond, 1990).

Each hypnotherapist has a repertoire of inductions repeatedly used, but every time is like the first time. Actually, it is the first time because when the hypnotherapist and subject meet, they create a relationship that did not exist before, and they influence each other.

Hypnotic inductions can be learned through the books that illustrate them. It is, however, much more complex to select, in real time, what to say and the best suggestion to give to a specific patient. This choice leads to eliciting motivation, gaining acceptance, building confidence, and protecting collaboration (Lang & Laser, 2009). To create rapport during induction, the hypnotist combines learned inductions with mindfulness of the moment while calibrating the unique human being before him or her, on that specific day, with that specific need or goal.

The aim in writing this chapter is to present some of the many laws and principles that are known in the literature as tools of the hypnotic therapist's everyday practice. There are two premises to this chapter: (a) Hypnosis is a natural phenomenon based on human beings with a conscious and unconscious mind, and (b) trance is an altered state of awareness that exists on a continuum. Trance is at one end of a continuum of experiential involvement (Gilligan, 1987). It is not an artificial state separate from other physiological and psychological experiences, and it does not work like an on/off switch.

HYPNOSIS AS A NATURAL PHENOMENON

Trance is a natural capacity of any subject. This natural capacity implies that the unconscious potential of each individual can be enhanced to stimulate attitudinal changes. The premise that trance represents one end of a continuum of experiential involvement implies that the hypnotist accepts responsibility for (a) securing and maintaining intentional absorption, (b) accessing and developing unconscious processes, and (c) bypassing and diminishing the power of the conscious processes (Gilligan, 1987).

While formal instructions of an induction may appear deceivingly simple, eliciting trance in reality requires motivating the subject to its use and depends on the setting where it occurs. In a *clinical* setting, the main motivation for the patient is to be helped, to improve and change some dysfunctional behavior, thoughts, or attitudes; in a *laboratory* setting, the motivation of the subject can be curiosity, experiencing something new, contributing to a research project, or learning; and in a *demonstration* setting, the motivation for the subject is usually learning by doing instead of observing or listening (Kane & Olness, 2004). In general, the subject is taught and expected to rely on his or her own unconscious and to learn that his or her unconscious can initiate nonvolitional behaviors without the control of his or her conscious mind. I would like to underline that the clinical setting is where laws and principles presented in this article are applied.

As a natural phenomenon, hypnosis contains those laws of nature that we take for granted and that instead we should be fully aware of when we practice hypnosis (Hadot, 2004). During practice, it is helpful to keep in mind that (a) in nature, there is constant change. "The only thing that never changes is change itself" is a quote attributed to the philosopher Heraclitus. (b) Everything is different; every animal, plant, flower, blade of grass, and person is unique. (c) Nature loves to keep secrets; many things are still unknown and they reside in the mystery of nature. This is one of the reasons why we continue searching for answers, exploring the unknown, and staying curious and open to a world full of new possibilities.

Respecting those natural laws helps the hypnotist to recognize and accept the subject's uniqueness, encourage his or her changes, and discover hidden resources. One of the natural mysteries is the unconscious, which helps to reveal some deep secrets or unexplored areas through dream analysis and through hypnosis. Hypnosis is considered the royal road to the unconscious.

Thus, the task of the hypnotist is to recognize the uniqueness of the subject, activate the rich hidden potential of his or her unconscious, promote the changes that are most useful in that moment, and use the client's own resources. Besides being a natural phenomenon, hypnosis is intra- and interpersonal.

HYPNOSIS AS AN INTRAPERSONAL PHENOMENON

Everyone has his or her own trance, like an inner dialogue or visual imagination. The intrapersonal trance follows the laws of perceived reality, subjective interpretation, and expectancy.

The Law of Perceived Reality

The law of perceived reality attests that each individual has a subjective, not objective, experience of reality. Since we cannot know the external world as it is, we create an internal representation of it, a personal map based on the process of selection, generalization, and distortion (Bandler & Grinder, 1975). When we forget that "the map is not the territory" (Korzybski, 1958), we deceive ourselves that our own inner map is the external reality and act as if this belief were a fact (Bateson, 1972).

The Law of Subjective Interpretation

The process of creating our own maps following a subjective interpretation of the perceived reality can be simplistically divided into two opposing categories. Some people give an optimistic interpretation of what happens to them; they cultivate a positive and resilient attitude, learn from mistakes, and transform problems into challenges and destiny into choice, with the attitude "I can" or "It is possible." Others have a pessimistic attitude and tend to think they are unfortunate, unworthy, incompetent, and inadequate and that their effort is useless because they will not get what they aspire to, with the attitude "I cannot" or "It is not possible." Of course, there are also persons without polar thinking and able to see the pros and cons of their life.

The Law of Expectancy

The subject who strongly believes he or she is responsible for his or her own success unconsciously recognizes, utilizes, or creates favorable circumstances leading to success. She or he takes advantage of conditions as opportunities and initiates the steps necessary to succeed. Using positive mental expectancy based on a strong belief that the world is a place full of opportunities and it is worthwhile to give it a try, the subject creates a mental image of success—thus, everything seems to go smoothly. These subjects expect good things to happen; with this attitude, they ignore the bad and strengthen the good. They vividly imagine themselves successful and they create their own destiny.

On the other hand, the person who conceives life as hard, difficult, and full of negative experiences and who sees himself or herself as unfortunate or as a failure will find more difficulties than opportunities and might create traps for himself or herself, places to stumble and fall. These mechanisms are also known as the "self-fulfilling prophecy," discovered by the sociologist Robert K. Merton. The self-fulfilling prophecy is holding a *false* conception, which elicits behavior that makes the false belief come *true* (Merton, 1948).

Practicing these laws and principles helps the hypnotist to remember that when patients narrate their story, they are creating it, showing their blurred or clear lenses, their rose-colored or dark thoughts, and their rigid or flexible attitude (White, 2007; White & Epston, 1990). For these reasons, when we listen to patients' narrations, we look to understanding their way of creating meaning of events, their attributional style, and their positive or negative approach.

In particular, during a therapy session, it is important to understand if subjects are more problem and past oriented or solution and future oriented; if they tend to give positive or negative attribution; if they are constructive or destructive; and if their mind is focused on what to do to achieve goals rather than be absolutely sure that they will never succeed in achieving what they want.

On the other hand, hypnosis helps the subject to test reality, assess the feasibility of a change she or he wants, and to be prepared to take the necessary steps to achieve the goal with awakened resources.

HYPNOSIS AS AN INTERPERSONAL PHENOMENON

Hypnosis is also an interpersonal phenomenon based on the relationship between a hypnotist and a subject. It is empathic involvement with one another (Yapko, 2011). This kind of relationship needs to be built on trust, confidence, and collaboration, which constitute the foundation for a therapeutic alliance. During the beginning of the relationship with the subject, the hypnotist knows that she or he has to be careful in order to build and maintain rapport through the respect of laws and principles such as the principles of collaboration, individualization, and utilization.

The Principle of Collaboration

Building and maintaining a therapeutic alliance is important in any kind of psychotherapy and mandatory for hypnosis and hypnotherapy. Without reciprocal trust, confidence, and collaboration, it is difficult to create the climate that facilitates the elicitation and utilization of trance (Gilligan, 1987).

Hypnosis and trance induction do not contain the inner or intrinsic power of hypnotizability; rather, they are the result of a relationship built on the collaboration principle of a therapeutic alliance.

During the therapeutic conversation, the therapist builds a positive environment that helps the patient feel welcome in a safe place with the necessary comfort to awaken the dormant resources and to elicit the hidden potentiality.

The safe place created externally by the therapeutic alliance can also be evoked internally, inviting the subject to find his or her inner *safe* place. The safe place can become the *serenity* place—the *happy, creative, recovering, healthy, laughing* place or the *true refuge*, according to the circumstances and needs of the subject (Ewin, 2009; Hammond, 1990). In this case, the hypnotist elicits positive expectations that the problem will be solved naturally, spontaneously, and automatically. The subject who feels the comfort of being in an external and internal safe place recovers his or her confidence and trust, easily relaxes, and better collaborates with the therapist for his or her own well-being. The rapport is reinforced by Erickson's principles of individualization and utilization.

The Principles of Individualization and Utilization

Erickson's principle of individualization asserts that the more the hypnotist is able to recognize and ratify the uniqueness of the subject, the more the subject feels welcomed and accepted for who she or he is; thereby, the collaboration is reinforced.

This principle states that each subject is unique and special, that each human being has his or her idiosyncratic qualities, memories and dreams, and needs and desires. This reminds the hypnotist that the value of an induction is commensurate with its plasticity, its ability to stimulate the mind of the subject by creating new forms of thoughts that are the result of mutual flexible adaptation between the mind of the hypnotist and the mind of the subject. The special interpersonal phenomenon created by hypnosis is based on building and maintaining rapport.

The Principle of Building and Maintaining Rapport

Hypnosis is an elegant and effective form of multilevel communication, whether verbal or nonverbal, and hypnotists are masters of the art of listening, observing, and speaking. While listening, these clinicians concentrate attention on the words selected, the metaphors chosen, and the patient's style of communication. They also carefully observe the minimal cues and the inevitable accompaniment of nonverbal communication, especially checking if it is congruent with the content of the message.

The Principle of Listening and Observing

During the initial conversation, the hypnotist collects information about the subject by listening to the content and observing his or her nonverbal and paraverbal communication, words and phrases, idiosyncratic posture, body and hand movements, and voice modulation. In particular, the hypnotist observes breathing patterns, facial expressions, eye blink rate, gesticulation, and vocal intonation patterns such as tone, tempo, timber, volume, pauses, and sighs.

This initial phase of carefully listening to and observing the style of communication of the subject gives the hypnotist necessary information regarding his or her relational style—passive, aggressive, manipulative, or assertive—his or her representational systems and predicates—visual, auditory, or kinesthetic—as well as his or her attitude toward the problem or the solution.

While listening to and observing the subject's communication patterns, the hypnotist might ask open and nonspecific questions as well as invite the subject to define terms experientially (Yapko, 2012), to be more precise, more descriptive, and less interpretative, or to clarify what is vague or ambiguous. This helps the hypnotist to better understand the inner map of the patient's world and to use his or her language as much as sensibly possible.

Once the rapport is established, the trust gained, the collaboration obtained, and the seed sown, the phenomenon of hypnosis can happen smoothly. At this point, the hypnotist moves from the (apparently) normal therapeutic conversation, producing the trance induction with the principle of acceptance of the interactive trance and the consent of suggestion acceptability. In addition, the hypnotist paces the patient's rate of breathing, slows down his or her speed, makes appropriate pauses, lowers the volume, and uses a calming rhythm, thus inducing and eliciting calm, relaxation, and confidence.

The Principle of Pacing and Leading

During the initial phase of the induction, the hypnotist can follow the *pace and lead* method, pacing what the subject is experiencing and leading to a therapeutic goal.

"You are seated in front of me (pace)*, your feet on the ground* (pace)*, listening to my voice* (pace)*, and you start realizing that you are beginning to relax* (lead)*, so that you are ready to start the discovery of what is relevant for you"* (motivation).

The initial phase of the trance induction is important because it nurtures the motivation and the collaboration of the subject. For this reason, the hypnotist follows the principle of pacing, leading, and creating a climate of acceptance and a "yes set."

The Principle of Acceptance and Yes Set

The yes set is evoked by pacing patient behavior and by using truisms, which are simple undeniable facts and universal truths so evident that they cannot be denied. Once the yes set has been established, the hypnotist elicits a positive acceptance of the work that will be done together, thus ratifying trust and collaboration.

At this initial stage, it is also important to use a sequence of truisms to generate an accepting attitude.

"Many times you have felt that your curiosity makes you open to exploring new things." "Everyone has experienced that when we are engaged in interesting activities time passes quickly." "It is part of human experience to adjust our body when we want to listen carefully."

These kinds of truisms can be useful when the subject is ready to accept the suggestion to enter the trance.

Creating a yes set of acceptance of what will come out from the trance work motivates the subject toward a goal. The principle of collaboration emphasizes that the hypnotist works with the subject within an interaction based on a collaborative teaching/learning attitude, which requires readiness, concentration, and eagerness to obtain something.

"I don't know whether you prefer to close your eyes when your eyelids are tired or you are already ready to gently close your eyes because you are curious about what your unconscious is going to show you."

In practical terms this means that, when working with hypnosis, the therapist should repeatedly motivate the subject by giving the reasons for what she or he is asked to do, thereby helping the subject achieve a goal during the session as proof that she or he can achieve other goals after the session.

The Principle of Confirmation of Suggestion Acceptability

After the subject is in a trance state, the hypnotherapist can follow the principle of confirmation of suggestion acceptability and track the subject's acceptability by direct questions such as

"Are you feeling good?" "Is it okay for you?" "Do you like the feeling of lightness of your hands?" "Would that be alright with you?"

The hypnotherapist can also ask for unconscious signaling such as

"Give me a sign when your unconscious mind is ready to consider this idea." "You can nod your head when you have found what you were looking for." "You can smile when you are satisfied with what you have found." "You can spontaneously let your yes finger move up" (Cheek, 1994; Ewin & Eimer, 2006).

The Principle of Trance Ratification

Once the subject is in trance, the hypnotist is very careful to observe his or her minimal cues and to encourage, reinforce, and compliment any positive response, even the smallest one. During this phase, the hypnotist follows the principle of trance ratification to persuade the subject of the power and inner potentialities of his or her unconscious mind.

The principle of trance ratification indicates the importance of naming the hypnotic phenomena that occur spontaneously during the session in order to persuade the subject that the trance is a natural phenomenon. Providing and calling attention to experiences that demonstrate to the subject that something is happening in his or her body and mind avolitionally gives the subject the awareness that hypnosis is a different, natural, and powerful state.

"Now that your breath is calm and regular, it is easy for you to feel the small movements of your fingers as if they were telling you something important."

A refractionation method can also be used to lead the subject into a trance, have him or her come out of the trance and talk for a while, then go back into the trance, then come out and talk some more, and continue going back and forth. This oscillating method helps to deepen the trance to the desired level, reinforcing each return to the trance by telling the subject she or he is doing an excellent job.

The Principle of Positive Reinforcement

The principle of positive reinforcement proposes using simple words such as *good, that's right, you're doing well, everything is going well*, and *excellent* as well as emotional vocal expressions such as "hmmm," "aha," "wow," and "hmm."

Once the trance is ratified, the hypnotist proceeds with the principle of interspersing and embedding suggestions (Bandler & Grinder, 1975; Lankton & Lankton, 1983; Haley, 1973).

For example,

"While you go deeper and deeper into relaxation, you notice that new ideas come gently to your mind, awakening your curiosity to explore these new ideas with an open heart and mind."

The Principle of Binding Ratifying Experience to Desired Goal

After trance ratification, confirmation of suggestion acceptability, and positive reinforcements, the hypnotist can follow the principle of binding ratifying experience to the desired goal, thus increasing the sense of self-efficacy and confidence in inner resources, such as

"When you are aware that you have found what you were looking for, just take a deep breath and find the right time to come back here bringing with you helpful knowledge."

"Now that you have noticed that your unconscious mind has already given you some important answers, you realize the power of your unconscious mind, so that using this power of your mind you can now start thinking that you can also reach what you want."

All laws and principles presented so far are reinforced by the use of positive language.

The Principle of Positive Language

When the hypnotist moves the subject to the stage of trance through formal induction, she or he changes her or his verbal and nonverbal communication. Usually the voice becomes softer, the rhythm slower, the breathing more regular, the body rather still, with essential movements to emphasize significant words. The words are selected with conscious precision and care for their implications in order to favor positive suggestions and avoid ambiguity, doubt, or negativity.

When the hypnotist notices that the subject is ready for the induction, she or he can change her

or his way of talking and invite the patient to adopt the posture that facilitates trance, using sentences like

"Now take a comfortable and dignified posture, with both feet flat on the floor, your back resting on the chair, and your hands on your thighs, so that when you are ready you can let your eyelids gently close so as to allow yourself to concentrate attention internally."

While the hypnotist talks, he or she paces the subject's breathing and posture, delivering suggestions on exhaling and pausing during inhaling, and does not use words that imply failure, such as *try*, or doubt, such as *maybe*, or uncertainty, such as *if*. Usually, the hypnotist uses the present tense or immediate future and positive language and structure, such as *"Soon you will begin to feel more relaxed . . . so that you realize that you are ready to. . . ."*

In general, hypnotists tend to use positive suggestions rather than negative, such as *"Now you feel more calm"* rather than *"less tense."* Imperatives are stated positively, such as *"Remember a positive memory"* rather than *"Don't think about a negative memory,"* respecting the principle that the unconscious is based on experiences and does not know the meaning of "no." We know the opposite effect of the command *"Don't think about a pink panther."* We know that each word has evocative power.

Hypnotherapists usually individualize the induction to fit the subject's needs, utilizing the interests, beliefs, habits, and modes of expression and thinking of the subject to create motivational statements such as

"Since x happened, then y happens; while x happens, then y happens; when x happens, then y happens; after x happened, then y happens."

"When you remember that time when you were able to overcome that difficulty, you recognize that specific resource you had then that can help you again in this moment of your life."

During an induction, the therapist usually states the desired end result, without details of how it is to be reached, using the process of creative imagination, employing the principle that a visual image of the desired effect makes suggestions more powerful.

"Look at your face and see your smiling expression after passing the exam, feel the satisfaction for what you have achieved and hear your voice celebrating it."

Hypnosis is a form of art, and, as all forms of art, it is based on the principle of selection. When this principle is not respected, there is a risk of losing the attention of the subject and the effectiveness of the message. The intervention becomes ineffective when the subject has the impression that the hypnotist follows a mechanical, worn-out, and withered script. For this reason, it is also important to practice the law of parsimony, the principle of repetition, and the carrot effect.

The Principle of Repetition

When we find the best suggestion, instead of diluting it with weaker ones, we can apply the principle of repetition. This principle indicates the efficacy of replicating two or three suggestions three to four times, no more. It is advisable to begin with a small suggestion and build on it, giving adequate time for the effect to take place.

The Carrot Effect

Another way to reinforce collaboration and motivation to go toward an interesting goal is through the carrot effect. Instead of pushing the subject away from a negative position, the hypnotist uses the carrot effect to encourage him or her to desire reaching an aim, imagining vividly the positive consequences of this achievement. The carrot effect can be combined with another principle called seeding or priming. Seeding is the process of anticipating something that will occur later, preparing the ground for that to happen and paving the subject's receptivity (Zeig, 2006).

"When you are at home and think about what you have discovered today, you will realize that this discovery leads to other stimulating discoveries."

All the previous laws and principles connected with positive hypnotic language are reinforced by their timeliness. *Kairòs* in Greek means the accuracy of timing, neither too early nor too late.

The Principle of Timeliness (*Kairòs*)

Experience teaches hypnotists that the most interesting suggestions, the most appropriate metaphors, or reframing can be ineffective if uttered when the subject is not ready, is unreceptive, or is distant. The art of waiting for the right moment requires the ability to be patient until the subject's maximum receptivity is reached.

"I remember the case of a patient of mine whose eyes filled with tears when I asked her if she was aware of how generous she had been. At that point I asked her to close her eyes, feel the emotion that brought tears into her eyes, and welcome all the memories connected with that feeling."

Choosing the right time for the induction, the suggestion, or the metaphor is something that hypnotherapists learn by doing and by calibrating the patient's feedback, both verbal and nonverbal.

Recognizing the right moment to say something or to remain silent is important for every psychotherapist and it is crucial for the hypnotist. Eliciting a trance when the subject is ready to enter it, giving a suggestion when the subject is receptive, and stimulating a trance phenomenon when the patient is anticipating it are expressions of the art of timeliness. In contrast, when we try to push the subject to do what we want, we lose rapport and credibility.

The Principle of Building a Response Set Gradually

The principle of timeliness reminds the hypnotist to be permissive concerning time, thus giving subjects the time they need to enter a trance state, to deepen it, and to respond to suggestions.

In fact, it is important for the hypnotist to build a response set gradually and follow the principle of successive approximation. This principle suggests giving patients time to develop the response, without pressure for an immediate answer, but showing trust and confidence that when the patient is ready, the answer will arrive, at the right moment for the patient, not for the therapist.

"Soon you will sense a lightness starting to develop in that hand . . . and you can begin to wonder just

when this sense of lightness will extend the light-ness to your arm."

No hurry is required, no rush is needed. On the contrary, the hypnotist can reassure the subject by telling him or her *"You have all the time you need to complete the work you are doing right now."* And when the phrase "right now" is pronounced with particular emphasis, after a significant pause, the patient might perceive it as an embedded command: *"Complete . . . right now."*

The Law of Parsimony

The law of parsimony invites the hypnotist to be simple, to keep his or her suggestions easy to follow.

This law reminds the hypnotist to use the fewest words possible, to be incisive through being concise and precise. It is not helpful or efficacious to overwhelm patients with too many words, suggestions, or metaphors. When we submerge patients with too many words or ideas, we water down and impoverish the meaning to be conveyed. Dabney Ewin (2009) reminds us of the efficacy of 10 words, following Emile Coué's famous sentence to be repeated like a mantra 20 times twice a day: "Every day, in every way, I am getting better and better."

The Law of Concentrated Attention

Coué says, "Whenever attention is concentrated on an idea over and over again, it spontaneously tends to realize itself." This law is based on the principle of hypnosis as an altered state where the subject is focused on his or her inner world to reinforce hidden potentialities and awaken dormant resources.

Any induction usually starts by inviting the subject to concentrate his or her attention on something either external—such as a fixed point, a pendulum, or his or her hands—or internal—such as one's own breathing, heartbeat, or inner sensation in any part of the body. At this point, the hypnotist can ask the subject to move attention to the goal she or he wants to reach.

"What you are seeing with your inner sight keeps you concentrated until you find what you are looking for."

Through the patient's concentrated attention, the therapist helps him or her to focus on something important to explore, to discover, and to understand. These suggestions are usually well received, thanks to the trust and rapport already created between the patient and therapist.

Once the trance state has been obtained, the therapist sends his or her suggestions to capture the patient's attention and repeats them as often as necessary. Through repetition, attention becomes focused and its ideas magnified in their effect. In this way, therapeutic messages are emphasized.

"Now that you are relaxed, you notice you are ready to focus your attention inside of you to explore what you need to explore right now. . . . Stay there all the time you need, focus your attention on what is really relevant for you here and now."

Ewin's Law

Another important aspect of timeless regard is when to be permissive or authoritarian. It is also pertinent to understand when to convey the most important suggestion and at what level of trance. The sensitivity and the experience of the hypnotist signals the right time to send a permissive suggestion or an authoritarian command. Usually, a permissive style and indirectness are more appreciated with lighter trances, while authoritative and direct suggestions are well accepted in a deeper trance when rapport and collaboration are consolidated and the client is trustful, committed, and motivated.

Regarding the right time to invite the patient to "go deeper and deeper," Dabney Ewin asserts that "a patient tends to go as deep as s/he needs to go to solve a problem. A patient tends to stay as light as necessary to protect him/herself." And Milton Erickson proposed that it is better to convey the most important suggestions toward the end of a trance, after approximately 20 minutes of trance, supposedly when it has reached the deepest level.

Having presented laws and principles governing the relationship between subject and hypnotist, I now present the three Coué's laws that are connected with the trance itself. These laws were first formulated around the beginning of the past century by Emile Coué (1857–1926), the father of autosuggestion and of the placebo effect.

The Law of Dominant Effect

The law of dominant effect states that the strongest emotion will always win. When fear of failure, for instance, is stronger than the desire to succeed, the subject is deprived of the energy necessary for success, and is instead immobilized by fear. When the subject is under the dominant effect of fear, the hypnotist can elicit cognitive and epistemic emotions, such as curiosity or doubt. With curiosity, the patient temporarily suspends impediments and mentally goes toward what is now considered reachable. With doubt, the subject puts aside the presumption of failure and confronts the veracity of his or her convictions, so he or she becomes open to explore different options.

"Follow your creative imagination until you discover that you already know what to do to solve that problem."

Since hypnosis strategically utilizes mechanisms that naturally alleviate anxiety—silence, pauses, breathing rate, paraverbal reinforcements, and positive communication—it helps to put aside the intellectual activity that might disturb the unconscious process. It also reinforces the effortless quality of the unconscious. When we facilitate the patient to reduce her or his anxiety through hypnosis, symptoms maintained by anxiety diminish or disappear or, at least, are better controlled. Generally, the process of induction and deepening relieves anxiety and elicits calm, which can be reinforced with therapeutic healing, ego-strengthening messages, and progressive relaxation (Elkins, 2014).

"While you are exploring your inner sensations, you are also discovering something new, something that opens your heart and mind."

The intensity of a suggestion is proportional to the emotion that accompanies it. An idea affects the unconscious weakly if it is not accompanied by excitement, enthusiasm, and hope. Negative thoughts and emotions can capture attention. Negative ideas stick to our minds because of the powerful emotions attached to them, especially the emotion of fear or anger. Hypnosis offers several techniques to elicit strong positive emotions, such as symbolic and guided imagery, among others. Symbolic imagery techniques are particularly

helpful in working through problems like guilt, anger, and fear, while guided imagery techniques are more apt for enhancing insight, self-understanding, and self-exploration (Casula, 1997; Casula, 2002).

In patients with low self-esteem, ego-strengthening suggestions are particularly useful to modify underlying limiting assumptions and negative internal dialogue. It can also be useful to elicit age regression to the time before the arousal of anxiety. Other techniques are helpful to empower the subject and elicit his or her resilience (Casula, 2011; Short, Erickson, & Erickson-Klein, 2005).

"Now that you come from the future of that traumatic past experience you can recognize that you have learned something that you could not learn otherwise."

Since a strong emotion triumphs over and replaces a weaker one, the hypnotist can facilitate systematic desensitization and mentally rehearse coping successfully with these emotions, offering a "corrective emotional experience." The corrective emotional experience helps the person to repair the past traumas with recent learnings and to change old patterns no longer needed with new patterns that are more effective.

I remember the case of a young woman with a phobia about fireworks. During an induction, I worked on the difference between being frightened and being afraid. I asked her to go back to the first time when she felt fear of fireworks. She went back to when she was a child. She was walking with her grandmother when they heard the unexpected explosion of a firecracker. Without explanation, her grandmother grabbed her by the hand and ran. This memory helped her to understand that she had been conditioned by her grandmother's fear of bombs during the war. She then realized that firecrackers make a sudden frightening noise and that fireworks are expected and can be fascinating.

Alternately, the hypnotist can use irreverent strategies to elicit different emotions, selecting the most appropriate one for the situation, enhancing visualization, and giving posthypnotic suggestions to encourage behavioral responses to the positive imagined situation (Cecchin, Lane, & Ray, 2003).

> I remember the case of a young woman, an only child, who, in one month, had lost her parents. Missing them, she expressed a desire to reach them, threatening suicide. In an irreverent manner, I asked her why she hated her parents so much. Once I had captured her attention, I told her: "If you kill yourself, you will kill your parents. If you die, you bring with you all the traces of your parents, and they will die forever with you. If you live a good life, you are the living proof that you had good parents and they will prolong their life through yours."

For this reason, it is important to consider patients' negative emotions and beliefs as something that follows the natural law of change. Fright is a fast and short emotion that gives the information that we might face a danger and helps us to be vigilant. It changes quickly when we discover the risk is over and we feel relief. Or if we realize that we are in danger, we prepare ourselves to face fright with a fight, flight, or freeze response. We defend ourselves by transforming fright into action.

> I remember the case of a woman who developed fibromyalgia when her son was struggling against a serious illness. Currently, her son is past danger, but his mother is not. I suggested to her that now that the danger is over, her fear could also disappear and give room to relief, gratitude, and serenity.

Nothing lasts forever, not even the strongest emotion. Everything changes. Patients in trance can question and confront their emotions or thoughts with a reality test, and then let them go, realizing that thoughts are only thoughts and emotions are only emotions. It is also important to help patients to cultivate positive emotions toward success so that any limiting feelings do not overcome the positive ones. Despite the fact that some level of doubt and fear protects us, optimism, hope, and faith should be predominant, if we do not want negative emotions to overrule empowering thoughts or good intentions.

The Law of Reversed Effect

This law asserts that the harder you try, the less you will succeed. We have experienced the truth of this statement on many occasions of our personal and professional daily lives. The law of reversed effect (also known as the law of reversed effort) underlines that the more one wants to achieve something through will, determination, and conscious effort, the less unconscious collaboration there is.

Everyone has a conscious and an unconscious state of mind. Our conscious minds are designed to make decisions and enjoy experiences, while our unconscious minds internalize a series of complex procedures to transform them into automatic habits. The conscious and unconscious mind have different functions; conscious effort and willpower reside in our conscious mind, while creativity and imagination reside in our unconscious mind. When conscious and unconscious mind are in conflict, the unconscious mind prevails; when they are in agreement, each of them reinforces the other. When will and imagination are in conflict, imagination wins with the help of creativity, flexibility, and future pacing elicited by hypnosis.

The law of reversed effect inspires a covert hypnosis technique, offering an elegant way to distract the conscious mind, thus awakening the unconscious mind and, paradoxically, persuading someone to accept an idea by suggesting the opposite to him or her.

> I remember the case of a university student who struggled to prepare for an exam, sure that he would not pass it. I agreed with him, telling him that his struggle was useless and unnecessary and that it would be better for him to leave the University and open an Italian bar in Acapulco. The more serious I was in suggesting this idea, the more he found good reasons to convince me that he would pass the exam and finish his University degree.

The notion of reversed effect is that the harder one consciously tries to do something, forcing himself or herself, the harder it becomes to achieve because the wrong part of our mind is being used. In the field of clinical hypnosis, this law reminds us to make suggestions looking for a physiological response from the subject, eliciting creative imagination and moving the patient from the problem to the solution. Suggestions aim at replacing negative beliefs with positive beneficial ones; thus, the subject responds to those beliefs accordingly.

"You can listen to the silence of the room that finally allows you to listen to your inner voice that whispers . . . I love you, you are worthy, you deserve, you can."

When the patient is ready to open his or her mind and heart to imagination, it will be easier to accept positive suggestions. The correct way to attain change is to use the mind's own change processes, thus eliciting creative visualization and emotional association:

"Now go into your future and see that you have solved your problem and have already realized your goal, and observe all the changes in your personal and professional life." (de Shazer, 1994)

In this way the therapist creates suggestions that the patient can use, free of the tension caused by too much effort and with an accompanying sense that things can be easily accomplished.

"You realize that from now on you are supported by your strong belief that you have all the resources you need to achieve what you want, let your unconscious mind help you, guide you, support you."

When the subject is prone to imagining things easier than he or she had thought, he or she is also ready to take the first step without wrestling with his or her willpower. This attitude focuses upon the goal and allows the mind to intuitively find its own means to achieving that goal, breaking it down into steps and stages, facilitating the mind's ability to work out solutions naturally.

In many cases, the effort to change an undesirable habit may actually serve to reinforce the habit. Practice has shown that the best way to break a bad habit is to form a clear mental image of the desired end result and to practice without effort toward reaching that goal. Instead of trying hard by conscious effort and willpower to change undesirable habits, it is more efficacious to simply let the subject relax. Once relaxed, the subject mentally pictures himself or herself as he or she wants to be and allows the new habit patterns to form automatically, reinforcing them through the repetition. Once the new

habit pattern has been installed or imprinted, it will automatically strengthen itself with each repetition and each successful performance.

Hypnosis inductions and suggestions can help the subject to realize that reality might be different from what was perceived and lead the subject to gain openness, flexibility, and creativity.

The Law of Autosuggestion

Emile Coué stated, "I have never cured anyone in my life. All I do is show people how they can cure themselves." Many hypnotists say that they have never hypnotized anyone and have only helped a subject to enter his or her own trance. Even in hypnosis, every subject has the freedom to accept or refuse suggestions, especially if any of them is too different or distant from her or his belief. The more powerful the suggestion is, the faster it becomes an autosuggestion. The subject then repeats it within himself or herself and adopts it as a new way of thinking, feeling, and acting.

I remember the case of a young woman who didn't want to accept the offer from her firm to resign at once with 24 months of her salary because she was afraid of not being able to find another job. After several months of therapy, she decided to accept the offer and when I asked her what helped her to decide, she told me that she kept repeating in her mind one of my suggestions:

"We live in a world full of uncertainty, ambiguity, and complexity. The only certainty you have is that you have two legs, two arms, and a brain, and you can always find a job."

All the laws and principles presented so far are founded on the basic assumption that hypnosis is a natural phenomenon and it is both intra- and interpersonal (Zeig, 1982). To elicit a trance in the subject, the hypnotist has to remember that every suggestion is autosuggestion. This is the primary reason why it is so important to observe and listen carefully to the subject, to notice the multiple manifestations of his or her verbal and nonverbal communication, and to reinforce the positive in order to counteract the subject's own negative suggestions.

THE PRACTICE OF LAWS AND PRINCIPLES

The implementation of the laws and principles of induction allows hypnotists to acquire elegance and effectiveness in their results. The elegance of the hypnotist is enabled by the rapport built and maintained through careful and skillful listening and observing, pacing and leading, a yes set of acceptance, confirmation of suggestions, acceptability, trance ratification, positive reinforcement, and binding the avolitional experience to the desired goal.

The efficacy of the hypnotist is enabled by the use of positive and parsimonious language, *nothing in excess,* reinforced by the repetition of the most effective suggestion and by the timeliness of building a response set gradually, as well as selection of the degree of depth of the trance according to the patient's needs.

Becoming experts in hypnosis involves being aware that the learned application of these laws and principles becomes intrinsically embodied in the hypnotist's way of conveying therapeutic messages both to the subject's conscious and unconscious mind while eliciting avolitional experiences and responsiveness. The expert hypnotist follows the natural flow of the continuum phenomenon from intrapersonal trance—where the law of perceived reality, subjective interpretation, and expectancy are dominant—to interpersonal trance, where it is necessary to follow the principles of collaboration, individualization, and utilization of what the subject brings.

The practical application of these laws and principles are substantiated and reinforced by the three most important Coué laws. Following the laws of concentrated attention, dominant effect, and reversed effect gives us the flexible solidity of a master who knows that all he or she has learned about the theory is now in his or her mind and heart, in his or her conscious and unconscious mind.

ACKNOWLEDGMENTS

The author gratefully acknowledges the materials provided by, and the informative conversations with, Julie Linden, PhD, culled from her work teaching the principles and laws of hypnosis.

REFERENCES

Bandler, R., & Grinder, J. (1975). *Patterns of the hypnotic techniques of Milton H. Erickson* (Vol. 1). Cupertino, CA: Meta Publication.

Bateson, G. (1972). *Steps to an ecology of mind.* Chicago, IL: University of Chicago Press.

Casula, C. (1997). A guided imagery: The seven rooms hypnos. *Swedish Journal of Hypnosis in Psychotherapy and Psychosomatic Medicine and the Journal of European Society of Hypnosis in Psychotherapy and Psychosomatic Medicine, XXIV*(3), 116–121.

Casula, C. (2002). *Giardinieri, principesse, porcospini. Metafore per l'evoluzione personale e professionale.* Milano: Franco Angeli.

Casula, C. (2011). *La forza della vulnerabilità. Utilizzare la resilienza per superare le avversità.* Milano: Franco Angeli.

Cecchin, G., Lane, G., & Ray, W. A. (2003). *Irriverenza. Una strategia di sopravvivenza per i terapeuti.* Milano: Franco Angeli.

Cheek, D. B. (1994). *Hypnosis: The application of ideomotor techniques.* Boston, MA: Allyn & Bacon.

Coué, E. (2008, December 26). *Encyclopedia britannica online.*

de Shazer, S. (1994). *Words were originally magic.* New York, NY: W. W. Norton.

Elkins, G. (2014). *Hypnotic relaxation therapy: Principles and applications.* New York, NY: Springer Publishing Company.

Ewin, D. (2009). *101 Things I wish I'd known when I started using hypnosis.* Williston, VT: Crown House Publishing.

Ewin, D. M., & Eimer, B. N. (2006). *Ideomotor signals for rapid hypnoanalysis. A how to manual.* Springfield, IL: Charles C. Thomas.

Gilligan, S. (1987). *Therapeutic trances: The cooperative principle in Ericksonian hypnotherapy.* New York, NY: Brunner/Mazel.

Hadot, P. (2004). *Il velo di Iside. Storia dell'idea di natura.* Torino: Einaudi.

Haley, J. (1973). *Uncommon therapy. The psychiatric techniques of Milton H. Erickson, M.D.* New York, NY: W. W. Norton.

Hammond, D. C. (1990). *Handbook of hypnotic suggestions and metaphors.* New York, NY: W. W. Norton.

Kane, S., & Olness, K. (Eds.). (2004). *The art of therapeutic communication: The collected works of Kay F. Thompson.* Williston, VT: Crown House Publishing.

Korzybski, A. (1958). *Science and sanity: An introduction to non-Aristotelian systems and general semantics* (4th ed.). Lakeville, CT: International Non-Aristotelian Library Pub.

Lang, E., & Laser, E. (2009). Patient sedation without medication. Rapid rapport and quick hypnotic techniques. *Academic Radiology, 17*(12), 1585–1586.

Lankton, S. R., & Lankton, C. H. (1983). *The answer within: A clinical framework for Ericksonian hypnotherapy.* New York, NY: Brunner Mazel.

Merton, R. K. (1948). The self-fulfilling prophecy. *The Antioch Review, 8*(2), 193–210.

Short, D., Erickson, B. A., & Erickson-Klein, R. (2005). *Hope and resiliency: Understanding the psychotherapeutic strategies of Milton Erickson, M.D.* Bancyfelin, Carmarthen, UK: Crown House Publishing.

White, M. (2007). *Maps of narrative practice.* New York, NY: W. W. Norton.

White, M., & Epston, D. (1990). *Narrative means to therapeutic ends.* New York, NY: W. W. Norton.

Yapko, M. D. (2011). *Mindfulness and hypnosis: The power of suggestion to transform experience.* New York, NY: W. W. Norton.

Yapko, M. D. (2012). *Trancework. An introduction to the practice of clinical hypnosis* (4th ed.). New York, NY: Routledge.

Zeig, J. K. (1982). *Ericksonian approaches to hypnosis and psychotherapy.* New York, NY: Brunner-Mazel.

Zeig, J. K. (Eds.). (2006). *Confluence: The selected papers of Jeffrey K. Zeig* (Vol. 1). Phoenix, AZ: Zeig, Tucker & Theisen.

Formulating Hypnotic Suggestions

David Godot

7

C H A P T E R

In considering how to formulate "hypnotic" suggestions, it is useful to first begin to think about the nature and construction of suggestions outside of the hypnotic context. For our purposes, I propose that a suggestion is any manner of transmitting your intention into another person's behavior or experience.

For example, if I intend for you to walk into my office and sit down, I might enjoin you to do so in a variety of ways. I might simply give you directions: "Come into my office and sit down." However, the authoritarian nature of this suggestion would only be appropriate within a limited number of culturally defined settings. I would be more likely to frame my intention as a question or an invitation: "Please come in" or "Why don't you come in?" Rather than telling you to sit down, I might offer you the gift of a seat: "Please have a seat" or even "Make yourself comfortable." All of these suggestions are a means of communicating the same intention, but the manner in which the intention is suggested creates and maintains a particular frame for the relationship. In some cases, I may not make any verbal utterance at all regarding your entering my office and sitting down, but might simply move one hand outward and downward in a gesture of invitation. If our relationship is well enough established that we already share a mutual intention for you to come in and sit down upon arrival at my office door, then it may be that no suggestion is necessary—we can discuss other things while our shared intention is carried out *naturally and automatically*.

Now suppose I see you looking unhappy and want to make you feel better—so I intend to change your affective state. If I simply enjoin you to smile, you might comply momentarily, but since smiling is mostly the outward result of the internal processes we refer to as happiness, any compliance will usually produce only superficial and transient

changes in your affective state. I might therefore instead suggest that you directly alter your affect by saying something like "Don't be sad" or "Be happy." However, since most people tend to experience their affective state as being outside of their conscious control, this suggestion may further highlight your apparent lack of control—thereby increasing your experience of unhappiness. In order to achieve meaningful affective change, a new state must be elicited. I might do this by telling you a joke (distraction), by drawing your attention to some positive aspect of your present situation (distortion), or by asking you to recall the time we took a hot air balloon ride together (dissociation; Frischholz, 2010).

In a therapeutic interaction, the patient and clinician typically share a mutual intention to alter some condition of the patient's existence. However, no matter how motivated the patient, a particular set of more specific intentions must become a part of the experience in order for the transaction to be a success. The clinician constructs a "treatment" that consists of a series of specific intentions that the patient must manifest—in the form of consent at the very least, and in many cases as self-directed action. For example, if a patient presents to his or her physician with a sore throat, the physician may instruct the patient to submit to a throat swab, to come in for a follow-up appointment, to visit the pharmacy, and to remember to take an antibiotic capsule each morning for 7 days. A psychologist treating a phobia may suggest that the patient participate in a series of graded exposures despite the immediate discomfort of doing so. If the patient does not respond to these treatment suggestions, the patient might maintain the more general intention of getting better, but not take any particular actions that would lead the patient to experience positive results. Clinicians are therefore tasked with stoking their patients' *expectancy* and *motivation* for the specific interventions they prescribe.

At this point, it becomes important to note that each patient, and each person, holds multiple and often conflicting motivations based on his or her particular configuration of values, beliefs, and resources. Furthermore, these motivations and their resulting intentions are not always available to us as conscious understandings. We have all had the experience of behaving in some unusual or undesirable way and then asking ourselves, "Why did I do that?" Or of performing some action more effectively than we imagined ourselves capable of.

The primary distinction between hypnotic and nonhypnotic styles of suggestion is that a hypnotic suggestion is explicitly intended to stimulate motivation from outside the level of conscious awareness—so that the desired intentions will be carried out without any need for the suggestion's recipient to pay attention to them happening or to exert any effort in causing them to happen. The suggested phenomena can then occur *naturally and automatically*.

For example, you breathe automatically. If you do not think about breathing all day long, nevertheless, not a single minute will go by in which you fail to draw and expel breath. However, suppose your pattern of breathing is somewhat disordered—perhaps you habitually draw shallow and rapid breaths without even noticing that you are doing so. Because this pattern of breathing can have profound effects on other aspects of your physiology, it may be desirable to change it. But you do not maintain your pattern of breathing at a conscious level. So while you may be able to temporarily exert your intention to breathe more slowly and deeply, as soon as you are distracted by something else, your breath will tend to more or less return to its previous pace and speed. Gradually, through practice, you might hope that your unconscious pattern of breathing will be altered, so that you can at last begin to enjoy discovering yourself breathing in a relaxed way *naturally and automatically throughout the day*. Whereas nonhypnotic suggestions call for the initiation or maintenance of activities that are consciously chosen and will generally only become habitual through much focus and repetition, hypnotic suggestions aim to directly influence the automatic, unconscious processes that effect physiology, habits, attitudes, and beliefs.

PRINCIPLES OF HYPNOTIC SUGGESTION

From this previous discussion, I offer that the most basic principle of formulating hypnotic suggestions is to structure and administer them in a manner that consistently promotes automaticity. Zeig (2014) elegantly describes this as "gift-wrapping"—your intention for the patient is wrapped up in language that associates the patient to the types of emotional, mental, social, and physiological possibilities that can facilitate its realization without the need for intentional responding. In this way, a *response set* is established, in which a particular type of response is potentiated through repeated activation. The basic components of this gift-wrapping are *truisms, conjunctions, contingencies*, and *dissociated language*.

A *truism* is simply a statement that the patient can readily observe to be true. Because things that are already true do not require any action, they can be used to promote a stance of passive observation while artfully guiding attention, offering suggestions, and ratifying the trance (Erickson, Rossi, & Rossi, 1976). For example: At this moment, you are reading the words on this page; and some part of you is able to make sense out of these words automatically; and you can notice the changes in your awareness as that process continues on its own. Those three statements drew your attention first to the fact of reading words on a page, then to the essentially unconscious nature of this aspect of your present activity, and then to the reality that shifting your attention has altered your awareness. Because each of those statements is essentially indisputable, they yield no resistance. And yet each has the effect of guiding your focus to increasingly internal, unconscious processes.

Conjunctions and *contingencies* are the parts of speech that allow us to string together these suggestive truths so as to lead the patient into various response sets. Because we desire to minimize conscious analysis and resistance, it is helpful to frame each suggestion as a natural outgrowth of the last. Consider the following series of suggestions: "Continue reading this chapter. Feel relaxed. Be fascinated. Learn the material deeply." Each suggestion is a new command for you to evaluate—you must orient yourself toward their meaning and then decide whether you want to obey them. I can make it much easier for you to experience a relaxed feeling of deep learning by framing these suggestions as truisms, linking them together, and making them contingent upon something that you are already doing (which is reading the chapter.) So, *as you continue reading this chapter, you can relax into a feeling of fascination about how deeply you can learn*. I have not told you to relax and learn deeply, I have just reminded you that you can do so when you are feeling fascinated. And you really can.

The use of *dissociated language* is a natural outgrowth of these principles. If I am working with you hypnotically, I do not want *you* (the conscious self that you identify as) to do anything other than *notice and observe* what is *happening to you*. I do not want you to feel the weight of responsibility for producing learning—how would you go about doing that anyway? Learning is something that just happens when the conditions are right, and those conditions are attention, interest, and relevance. So why not *just allow those eyes to continue absorbing this chapter deeply, as you attend to the feeling of fascination about the deep learning that is beginning to take place inside of you.*

You can really begin to notice the manner in which this chapter is written. The information is being provided on two levels simultaneously, so that you can begin to feel as though the ability to formulate these suggestions is building up within you naturally, and then later on you can return to the beginning of this chapter and read it over, to gain the conscious knowledge of exactly *how* you have become able to formulate the artful suggestions you will have begun to find yourself using in practice, naturally and automatically.

Now, let us translate these principles into a clinical situation. If I want to induce hypnotic (avolitional) eye closure, I cannot just tell the patient to close his or her eyes, because that will induce a nonhypnotic (volitional) eye closure. But I can build up an involuntary somatic response set by suggesting that a dissociated eye closure will be contingent upon something that is already happening and connecting it with other current phenomena. In the following example, I will denote truisms as (t), conjunctions as (cj), contingencies as (cg), and dissociated language as (d):

Each time you breathe out (cg), **you can notice the sense of heaviness as your body moves gently downward** (t). *And* (cj) *as you continue to attend to those sensations* (cg), **you can experience that feeling of heaviness more deeply** (t), *filling up more and more of your body with that gentle, pleasant feeling. And*

(cj) *as that heaviness continues to develop* (cg), **you can notice the heaviness in your arms** (t), **you can notice the heaviness in your head** (t), **you can notice the heaviness in your eyes** (t). *And* (cj) *as those eyes* (d) **become heavier and heavier, you can feel them wanting to close** (t). *And* (cj) *as those eyes* (d) **begin to blink more frequently and more slowly** (cg), *it may begin to feel like an awful lot of work trying to keep them open* (t). *And* (cg) **you can enjoy a certain feeling of relief** (t) *when you finally* (cg) *allow them to close tightly* (d) *and go into a deep hypnotic trance* (cj).

What we have done there is to utilize the characteristics of the ongoing, automatic process of breathing to gradually build up a response set for avolitional sensations and muscle movements. Each time a person breathes out, the shoulders, chest, back, and neck all tend to settle downward—you can notice it in your own pattern of breathing right now. And because any sensation a person attends to will tend to get stronger, it is a truism to draw focus to the manner in which attention alters the somatic experience. Now, any part of the human body has physical weight that is subject to gravity, so if I draw your attention to the heaviness of your arms or head, it will always be true that you can notice those sensations. The same forces affect the eyelids, but to a much lesser degree—however, the subject is now tuned in to those types of sensations, and so will be able to become aware of the heaviness of the eyelids in a way the subject might not usually be prone to. It is also true to say that a person can feel his or her eyes wanting to close, because eyes are always closing on their own in order to blink. But we create a contingency here: *As the eyes begin to blink more frequently and slowly, it may feel like work to keep them open*. Because we have not put any particular time frame on the development of frequent and slow eye blinks, this cannot contradict the subject's experience—since, if the phenomenon has not happened yet, it *can begin* to happen, or can even be perceived to happen without any objective change. And our contingency demands that whenever that happens, it will feel like work to keep them open. Since nobody likes to do unnecessary work, it can legitimately feel like a relief to allow them to close tightly—note the dissociative language: It is not a relief to *close them tightly*, but rather to *allow them to close tightly*. This is the culmination of our involuntary somatic response set—eye closure that is experienced as automatic and involuntary. This is, in itself, a hypnotic phenomenon, and so at this point, we can feel confident that hypnosis is occurring. And because we know that, we can use a simple conjunction to connect the existing hypnotic phenomenon with the idea that hypnosis is occurring (*"and go into a deep hypnotic trance,"*) essentially asking the patient's conscious mind to go away (Where is a hypnotic trance? How does one go there?) and accept that a trance state now exists. So there we have a complete hypnotic induction built up from nothing but these four basic principles: truisms, conjunctions, contingencies, and dissociated language.

GUIDELINES FOR FORMULATING HYPNOTIC SUGGESTIONS

In 1923, the French pharmacist Émile Coué laid out four laws of suggestion, which continue to be of great value to the modern practitioner.

The Law of Concentrated Attention

An idea tends to realize itself, within the limits of possibility. The more attention is focused on an idea, the more powerful it becomes. Therefore, desirable ideas should be accentuated and repeated, while undesirable ideas are minimized. Repetition is an important aspect of hypnotic suggestion for this reason—through repetition, the subject is given time to experience multiple aspects of a suggestion, its corollaries, and its implications, and so to concentrate their attention on their associations to the suggested actions. While classical hypnotists tended to simply repeat suggestions verbatim over and over, it is now generally considered preferable to repeat important suggestions a number of times in different ways, so as to play a more direct role in conjuring these important associations (Hammond, 1990; Zeig, 2014). This type of repetition will usually begin with more indirect forms of suggestion, such as metaphor, seeding, and embedded commands (which is reviewed later on in this chapter), and gradually progress to more direct suggestions.

The Law of Reversed Effort

If a person fears that he cannot do something, the harder he tries, the less he is able. This is a natural

extension of the Law of Concentrated Attention; the more a person struggles against an idea, the more powerful it becomes—because an idea tends to realize itself the more it is attended to. It is therefore desirable to frame suggestions in a present tense and with a positive structure (Hammond, 1990; Yapko, 2003). For example, note the effects that the following suggestions have on you as you read them:

"Now clear your mind of any anxiety you have about being able to employ these techniques in your work. Put aside any memories of times you tried other techniques and failed miserably, and allow yourself to forget about the intense feelings of inadequacy that have often seemed to plague you in new endeavors. From now on you will no longer experience anxiety, and in the future you will find that you will no longer be troubled by a fear of failure."

Compare your response to those well-meaning but horrifically negative suggestions with the following:

"Now allow your body to relax, as you just go back in your mind and remember how incredible you felt the first time you realized that you really are capable of helping people in a profound and important way. Maybe it was early on in your training, as your apprehension was replaced with the thrill of getting to put all those new ideas into practice. Or it might have been more recently, as you have been able to take a step back from all the pressure and realize just how far you've come. And as you now begin to really feel your growing understanding of the nature of hypnotic suggestion, you may notice that familiar feeling of confidence and passion stirring inside you now."

I often use Pascal's example of a balance beam, as cited by Coué (Coué, 1923). Most people would have little trouble walking the length of a 20-foot balance beam if it were lain out on the floor. But if we suspended the same beam 1,500 feet above ground, who among us would trust ourselves to walk it? The increased danger of falling creates a context in which it feels very important to succeed, and so we exert greater conscious effort. But our conscious efforts only undermine the real active principle within us, and so have a reversed effect. A talented acrobat does not accomplish impressive feats through the conscious effort of overcoming the sheer difficulty of them, but through an effort-less reliance on what has already been learned at an unconscious level. Just as you and I do not consciously manipulate the muscles in our legs as we walk—skillful actions must be effected by *unconscious* processes, due to the limitations of conscious attention. They therefore cannot be *done*, they must be *allowed to happen*.

The Law of Auxiliary Emotion

The intensity of a suggestion is proportional to the emotion that accompanies it. Negative ideas easily become fixed in our subconscious minds because of the powerful emotions attached to them. A single frightful event often precipitates a phobia that can last a lifetime if left untreated. Therefore, we can strengthen positive suggestions by connecting them with powerful emotions, and we can banish negative suggestions by diffusing the emotions associated with them.

For example, in the treatment of trauma, I routinely guide my patients to reexperience their traumatic events from a dissociated perspective, in which they are insulated from the emotions that previously gave the memory its power. In my experience, this type of dissociated exposure treatment is dramatically more effective than traditional exposure-based trauma therapy, because it explicitly and rapidly severs the connection between the traumatic memory and the emotions it has been associated with. Patients can then be guided, through simple cognitive interventions, to develop new emotional associations, such as strength in having survived and security in knowing that even though it seemed terrible at the time, they made it through okay. Since the outcome is now known, they no longer have any need to be afraid of what will happen (Ewin, 2009).

The Law of Dominant Effect

When the will and the imagination are at odds, the imagination invariably wins. A contest between conscious and unconscious processes is no contest at all. I have talked with hundreds of addicts who decided firmly and resolutely that they would never go near a drug again, only to find themselves using at the very earliest opportunity. They know the results will be terrible, but they *imagine* getting high. As Ewin (2009) observes, phobics can be totally convinced of the safety of traveling in an elevator, but if they still *imagine* there is danger, they will be taking the stairs.

This same principle can be used to elicit effects that are otherwise outside of conscious control. As Hammond (1990) points out, it would be extremely difficult to consciously will a physiological phenomenon such as sexual arousal, orgasm, perspiration, or salivation. But now remember the last time you sliced into a ripe, juicy lemon and smelled that crisp fragrance wafting up as the acidic juice ran out over your fingers. And as you lick that intense, sour juice off your fingers, you can feel your lips pucker as the flavor spreads out across your tongue. And just by imagining this, your mouth begins to salivate naturally and automatically. For this reason, it is better to focus on activating the imagination and eliciting internal states and resources, rather than appealing directly to the conscious will.

Likewise, resistant patients can often nevertheless be afforded effective treatment by avoiding the seemingly inescapable battle of wills altogether, and instead engaging their imaginations in processes that mirror the therapeutic processes you wish to effect. This can be accomplished through the use of stories, metaphors, and symbolic interventions.

GUIDELINES FOR ADMINISTERING HYPNOTIC SUGGESTIONS

Earlier in this chapter, I introduced the idea of structuring suggestions to **establish hypnotic response sets**—rather than simply suggesting isolated hypnotic responses—and this idea bears repeating. The amount of time that it can take to cultivate a good, automatic, hypnotic response varies widely based on the personal characteristics of the patient, situational and relational factors, and the subject's internal state at the time the suggestions are being administered. By way of example, let me suggest right now as you are reading, that you take a quick break and relax your whole body before reading on.

This relatively accessible autonomic response might have taken you a short time, a long time, or you might have decided it was too much effort to be worth doing at all. And your degree of success will have been determined by your mindset, degree of motivation, ambient stress level, and current surroundings. I did not walk you into the state of relaxation. I did not break it down for you into manageable pieces by advising you to attend first to one part of the body and then to another, noticing the sensations in each, breathing into them, and gradually allowing them to let go of their tension and tightness. First allowing a foot to relax, and then a leg, and gradually up along the length of your spine. In other words, I asked for a complex autonomic response without first establishing a response set that made it easy for you to produce that response.

Some patients will be extremely receptive to your suggestions, motivated to respond, imaginative, and high in innate hypnotic susceptibility, and those patients will tend to respond well regardless of how much care you have taken to gift-wrap the experience for them. But I suggest you assume that those patient factors (which are entirely outside your control) may not be present. And you can get into the habit of thinking not only about what you want patients to do, but how you can help them access the internal resources and imaginative associations that will lead them to *naturally and automatically* find themselves doing those things. You want to structure the experience for them in such a way as to make the desired response the most natural response.

Let us take arm levitation as another example. Suppose I suggest to you: *"Your hand is getting lighter and lighter now, and will soon begin to float upward."* This suggestion does a fine job of asking for a feeling of lightness and the beginning of levitation, but it does not establish the associations that make it likely that this will happen. As a result, highly hypnotizable individuals may respond well to it *because they are naturally prone to arranging their imaginative power in a way that facilitates this type of responding.* But the vast majority of individuals will struggle to experience what you are asking them to experience. Worse, they may experience their lack of response as a failure, and conclude that hypnosis cannot help them. You want to be sure to take the time to set your patients up for success. Spiegel and Spiegel's (2004, p. 58) excellent Hypnotic Induction Profile provides a very straightforward and directive example of building a response set for arm levitation:

"Imagine a feeling of floating, floating right down through the chair. There will be something pleasant and welcome about this sensation of floating. And as you concentrate on this floating, I am going to concentrate on your left arm and hand.

In a while, I am going to stroke the middle finger of your left hand, and after I do so, you will develop movement sensations in that finger. Then the movement sensations will spread, causing your left hand to feel really light and buoyant, and you will let it float upward."

The subject's conscious mind is occupied with an imaginative somatosensory task (a feeling of floating), and advised that something else *that the subject does not need to concentrate on* will be taking place involving the left arm and hand. It is explained that when the subject's finger is stroked, her or she will develop *movement sensations* in that finger, and that as those sensations spread a feeling of lightness will develop that causes the hand to rise. After these suggestions are administered, the sensory signal they describe is provided by the practitioner, in the form of gentle downward pressure on the middle finger and then up along the arm. This downward pressure tends to produce a slight, corrective upward movement (or movement sensation) in the finger and arm, making this suggestion a truism. This stroke of the finger is continued up along the arm toward the elbow, which ratifies the suggestion that the movement sensations will spread. A feeling of lightness and buoyancy is made contingent upon the spreading of those movement sensations, and the subject is given instructions on how he or she can respond to that involuntary sense of lightness—by *allowing* the hand to float upward. By building up the response set in this way, even individuals with relatively low innate hypnotizability are often able to experience some degree of success.

Additionally, it is important to *give clients time to develop responses.* Just as there is a large degree of variability in the amount of time and care required to establish a successful response set, so too is there variability in the time it may take for an individual to produce a particular response. In fact, the less hypnotically gifted a person is, the more time it will tend to take for the person to manifest a suggested phenomenon (Spiegel & Spiegel, 2004). In many cases, the feeling that a suggestion is "not working" is simply a result of impatience and inexperience; all that may be needed is to demonstrate positive expectancy by waiting patiently for the subject to develop the suggested response. You can begin to feel more and more comfortable with silence.

In other cases, you may find that only partial responses are elicited, which must be encouraged and reinforced as the desired response is gradually approximated (Hammond, 1990). No matter what happens, it is important to **frame the patient's responses as successes** regardless of whether they match up with your expectations, because doing so maintains the sense that the patient does not need to consciously attend to or criticize what is happening. The more ego-involved a patient becomes in the hypnotic process, the more difficult it will be for the patient to manifest fully automatic responses. An anxious patient who feels like he or she is not doing hypnosis right will no more be able to manifest a good arm levitation than be able to walk across a balance beam 1,500 feet in the air. I like to think about this aspect of a hypnotist's work as being like the supervillain who responds to everything with the pleasure of a mastermind whose incomprehensibly intricate scheme is playing out exactly according to plan. No matter what happens, the villain exclaims "Yesss . . . that's riiiiight!"

In a recent workshop practice session, one of the participants seemed unable to experience arm levitation. Each member of her practice group took a turn trying to induce the phenomenon, and the more they tried the more resistant that arm became. And so I encouraged and reinforced the resistant response by saying to her,

"You're doing much better than you think you're doing at experiencing hypnosis . . . did you know that? And that arm is doing much better than you think it's doing at experiencing hypnosis. Because the more you've focused on that arm, and all the feelings that you think it's been supposed to have been having, that arm just keeps getting heavier and heavier, doesn't it? That's right. And the more you want that arm to raise up into the air, I'll bet it just gets more and more difficult to lift it, because of that uncontrollable feeling of heaviness. As if the arm were made of a big, heavy chunk of solid lead. So heavy it could sink to the bottom of the ocean. I wonder whether that arm has already gotten so heavy that you wouldn't even be able to lift it if you tried. Isn't that right? I wonder what it would feel like if you were to just try to lift that arm now."

The subject responded by unsuccessfully attempting to lift the arm in question, causing it to fall off

her lap and hang limply over the side of the chair. She could have experienced her lack of arm levitation as a failure and left thinking she was no good at hypnosis. Instead, she left with the quite correct sense that she had successfully experienced a fairly powerful ideomotor hypnotic phenomenon.

FORMS OF HYPNOTIC SUGGESTION

The more direct, or overt, a suggestion is, the more easily it can be understood and integrated into the patient's response pattern. However, it can also be more readily subjected to conscious evaluation and criticism, and so may more readily evoke existing performance anxiety or defensiveness. Therefore, the degree of directness or indirectness that is appropriate may vary moment by moment, based on the type of suggestion being offered and the pattern of responding the patient is currently exhibiting (Yapko, 2003).

In most situations, it is desirable to repeat a given suggestion several times in different forms, generally moving from more indirect to more direct. So to induce age regression, I might first recount a story about my own childhood, then mention a number of truisms related to some particular period of childhood, then use a couple of indirect suggestions about going back to that time, before making a number of direct suggestions about the types of specific experiences I would like the patient to have. This builds up a clear pattern of associations (a response set) that makes it easy for the patient to accomplish the direct suggestions I will ultimately administer.

Direct Suggestion

Let us begin by using the principles discussed so far to generate some fairly direct suggestions for a variety of hypnotic phenomena, psychological effects, and medical effects. You may notice that these suggestions are not squarely focused on the desired phenomena themselves, but rather on the cognitive processes and imaginative associations that might facilitate those phenomena:

- *Negative hallucination:* **"There is no one here in the room now except you and I. And if you looked around, we are the only two people you would have to see, because there's no sense having to see people who aren't there."**

- *Age regression*: *"Now go back in your memory, and remember when you first learned all the letters of the alphabet. The way it feels to hold that large pencil in your little hand."*
- *Time distortion*: *"We all have times when time seems to be moving very slowly, barely moving at all. And you can experience each minute as if it were an hour."*
- *Anxiety relief*: *"And as you think of that old trigger for anxiety, you'll notice how strongly you can see yourself practicing this new ability to just relax and play with challenging situations. So you can really see how that same old trigger for anxiety is now becoming a trigger for joy and fun."*
- *Behavioral activation for depression*: *"The more you begin to notice that depressed feeling coming on, the more urgently you'll feel compelled to get up and begin to exercise."*
- *Analgesia*: *"Now imagine that area being filled with a cool blue feeling like an ice pack that soothes the discomfort. So that those uncomfortable feelings just fade off into the background."*
- *Anesthesia*: *"You can imagine that that hand doesn't even really belong to you. Like it belongs to someone else and isn't even really a part of you. And you already know that you can't feel anything that happens to my hand—Why would you? It's not your hand, so you can't feel it. And as you look at that hand, there isn't any reason for you to notice any feeling at all."*

Indirect Suggestion

Indirect suggestions are *implied* suggestions, and these can occur in either hypnotic or nonhypnotic situations. I started this chapter talking about various ways that I might invite you into my office. Among the examples were a couple of fairly innocent-looking questions that Bandler and Grinder (1975) described as **conversational postulates**: "Would you like to come in?" or "Why don't you come in?" In each case, the suggestion to *come in* is embedded within a question that is not likely to be answered as a question. If I asked you whether you wanted to come in and you replied "yes" without moving from the hallway, it would be a very unusual interaction. And yet, framing my suggestion as a question makes it seem more polite—because I am

explicitly giving you an option, even though it is an option you already had.

Now we can take that simple conversational principle and apply it quite hypnotically. By adding in the basic ingredients of hypnotic suggestion—truisms, conjunctions, contingencies, and dissociated language—hypnotic suggestions can be offered that are similarly soft and polite. I might ask you "Would you like to sit down and relax?" or "Why don't you begin by closing your eyes and going into a nice trance?" Maybe I am wondering, "Would it be alright for those eyes to begin to close as you inhale deeply?" or "Can you imagine the feeling of your eyes beginning to close?"

In the pages that follow, we consider a number of increasingly indirect forms of suggestion, most of which were developed and described by Milton H. Erickson, MD. It is important to note, as Erickson, Rossi, and Rossi (1976, p. 312) suggested:

> These hypnotic forms are all merely descriptive labels of different aspects of suggestion; they need not function independently of each other. . . . In fact, the art of formulating suggestions is to utilize as many of these mutually reinforcing forms as possible in close proximity.

As you may already be starting to realize, you can craft extremely interesting and powerful suggestions by weaving together a few very simple principles of hypnotic communication. Let us return to **truisms** for a moment to deepen our understanding of communication. We previously examined truisms that were observably true, but there are also many things that we know to be true internally, and things that are true for everyone. Consider the following sequence of truisms that draws focus to a number of universal experiences in order to build up a sleepy/dreamy response set:

- *"We've all had times when we weren't quite awake, and weren't quite asleep."*
- *"And you already know how to <u>fall asleep</u>, even if sometimes it can be difficult to remember."*
- *"Most people find that when they're not thinking about how tired they are, that's when they're most likely to <u>just drift off.</u>"*
- *"And there have been times when you didn't even realize you weren't paying attention, until*

your mind had already drifted a long way off into a daydream."

- *"And when people daydream, the outside world seems to disappear—they just go inside and find what's most important to them in this moment."*

Now, **presuppositions** are statements that assume something to be true. To tell a patient, "I'm not sure you're *all the way* in a trance *yet*" presupposes that he or she will end up *all the way* in a trance; the only question is whether it has already happened. Care must be taken not to engage the subject's tendency for critical reasoning when using presuppositions this way, as it would be very easy to presuppose something too far outside the subject's current belief system to be rapidly accepted without conscious reflection. For example, I might ask you: "How hilarious will it be when you start sending me Christmas cards, seemingly out of nowhere?" There is a chance you might *add me to your Christmas card list this year* so you can enjoy being a part of this great hypnosis in-joke. You might even find yourself laughing about it the next time you are standing in a greeting card aisle looking for a card. On the other hand, I might have broken rapport with you to some extent (i.e., engaged your critical conscious mind—*Is this guy trying to get me to do something weird?*).

Presuppositions and truisms can be used together very powerfully for this reason (Zeig, 2014). Suppose I want to induce a state of relaxation. Some truisms related to this are *"You can relax; a part of you knows how to relax; there have been times when you've felt unusually relaxed."* Because these statements are all true, we can safely presuppose them in ways that evoke more desirable and more automatic responses:

- *"You can fully enjoy relaxing"*—relaxation is presupposed; the only question is how fully you'll be able to enjoy it.
- *"You can enjoy allowing your body to relax very slowly"*—this complex presupposition takes it for granted that your body will relax, calling into question whether you will enjoy it and how slowly it can happen.
- *"I'm not sure if you realize that a part of you knows how to relax quickly and completely"*—relaxation is taken for granted, focusing instead on which part does the relaxing, how quickly

and completely it will do so, and whether you are aware of it.

- *"A part of you already knows that you can choose to relax yourself"*—it is assumed that you can relax; you are only left to wonder which part is able to make the decision to do so.
- *"Your mind can begin to dwell on those times in the past when you've felt unusually relaxed"*—it is presupposed that you can relax, and that there have been times when you were unusually relaxed, and the question is how fully you can inhabit those memories now.

Now just imagine stringing those presupposed truisms together with some conjunctions, contingencies, and dissociated language to create a smooth, multifaceted hypnotic suggestion:

"Take a moment to fully enjoy the feeling of allowing your body to relax completely now, just allowing that to happen very slowly. And I'm not sure if you realize that a part of you knows just exactly how slowly or quickly to choose to allow that body to fully relax. And as each part of the body is relaxing now at just the right pace and speed, your mind can begin to dwell on those times in the past when you've felt unusually relaxed."

■ **Embedded Commands**

By altering the tone and tempo with which a suggestion is delivered, certain words and phrases can become implicit commands. Take, for example, the truism, *"A part of you already knows how to . . . relax your body completely."* A slight pause and change of inflection turns *relax your body completely* into a clear and direct command that is not likely to be perceived as such on a conscious level, provided it is delivered in a smooth and natural manner. Zeig (2014) notes that it is generally more effective to *underemphasize* embedded commands, rather than *overemphasize* them, as underemphasis delineates them from the rest of the dialogue just as clearly, while being much less likely to be consciously perceived as a direct suggestion.

Some discussion about pacing in general might be helpful to you now as you consider beginning to employ embedded commands in your hypnotic speech. Speaking more slowly, and allowing some space . . . and time . . . to pass between . . . these ideas . . . provides more and more . . . opportunity . . . to . . . *go inside* . . . and really *begin to discover* . . . the inner significance . . . of all the things . . . *you're learning now* . . . and allow, *your unconscious* . . . to apply these new understandings . . . in ways that will surprise and delight . . . your conscious mind.

In addition to allowing the patient's mind more time to find internal associations for each phrase, speaking more slowly and deliberately also allows you as a practitioner more time to track the associations you are cultivating and build more intentional associative momentum. Once you have established a good hypnotic tone and tempo, you will find there are endless opportunities to embed commands within the therapeutic dialogue. For example, you can begin building a hypnotic response set before you have officially begun "doing" hypnosis, by embedding commands within the early discussions about what to expect during the hypnosis session.

Hypnotic suggestions can be embedded in quotations to especially good effect, because the suggestion is delivered as though from a hypothetical third party who need not be resisted. For example: *"My friend John experienced a deeper hypnotic trance than anyone I ever knew. And when I asked him how to <u>go into a really deep trance</u>, he told me, '<u>pay careful attention to that very slight buzz of electricity as the top eyelid meets the bottom one</u>.' "*

■ Not Knowing, Not Doing

As we have discussed, the nature of hypnotic suggestion is that we are asking our patients not to do things, but rather to allow those things to happen. We are asking them not to know things, but rather to allow those things to be known. Erickson, Rossi, and Rossi (1976, p. 23) note,

> Most people do not know that most mental processes are autonomous. . . . It comes as a pleasant surprise when they relax and find that associations, sensations, perceptions, movements, and mental mechanisms can proceed quite on their own. This autonomous flow of undirected experience is a simple way of defining trance.

Suggestions of the following form can therefore be highly effective in eliciting trance:

"You can just continue sitting there, and you don't even have to hold yourself up, because your body just stays comfortably in its place. And you can continue to hear the sound of my voice without even bothering to listen, because your unconscious mind will just inevitably absorb what's going on. And you don't have to make any kind of effort at all . . . you don't even have to hold your eyes open. And you can sleep without dreaming, and you can dream without remembering the dream."

■ Binds and Double Binds

A bind is a suggestion that provides a free, conscious choice between two comparable alternatives, where each alternative facilitates the patient's movement toward the desired response. Some examples:

- Would you prefer to go into a trance gradually, or more rapidly?
- Would you prefer to experience hypnosis in the chair, or on the sofa?
- Would you like to decide on an affirmation before going into trance, or while you're already in trance?

A double bind, on the other hand, offers a choice between alternatives that cannot be consciously produced. The subject must wait for an unconscious response to manifest itself before the subject can know the outcome. Following are some example suggestions for a variety of hypnotic phenomena:

- *Relaxation*: *"And what part of your body begins to feel the most comfortable?"*
- *Arm levitation*: *"Do you first notice that feeling of lightness starting in the fingers, or in the back of the hand? Or does it begin with the wrist moving upward?"*
- *Anesthesia*: *"Is that anesthesia progressing quickly, or slowly?"*
- *Negative auditory hallucination*: *"You can just be aware of the sound of my voice, or you can simply ignore everything else."*

- *Time distortion*: *"Time may seem to be passing very quickly, or you may simply be unaware of its passing."*
- *Restriction of blood flow*: *"You might notice a particular sensation as the blood stops flowing into that area, or you might simply be aware of a reduced ability to bleed without being fully sure of how you know."*

■ Conscious–Unconscious Double Binds

The more resistant or anxious a patient is, the more useful it may become to draw an explicit distinction between conscious and unconscious processes as they are occurring (Erickson, Rossi, & Rossi, 1976). The conscious–unconscious double bind offers unconscious alternatives in a way that offers education about the nature of hypnotic processing (Lankton & Lankton, 1983) such as

- *Ideomotor signaling*: *"We've all had the experience of not even realizing that our head is nodding yes or shaking no. And if your unconscious mind is ready to begin looking for solutions to this problem, then your head can begin to nod yes whether or not you're even aware of it. And if it needs more time to prepare, then you may or may not feel it as your head gently shakes no."*
- *Problem solving*: *"Your unconscious mind can continue to work on this problem after you leave. And you might or might not be aware, consciously, that this process is taking place until the solution emerges unexpectedly into consciousness."*
- *Panic attacks*: *"If you didn't notice you were feeling anxious, you wouldn't have to panic about it. Isn't that right? And so you can begin to realize the need to panic only after your unconscious mind has found a solution for the anxiety, or you can consciously work out those solutions before noticing any feelings of panic."*

■ Dissociative Double Binds

This type of bind provides two alternatives, neither of which can be responded to without an act of dissociation. This type of suggestion creates a disorienting effect, because the dissociative statements offered essentially cannot be understood consciously. Therefore, a tendency toward cognitive dissociation is elicited by merely trying to understand what has been said. These statements are easier to compose than they are to parse, so let us work on building some from the ground up.

Suppose my intention is to induce or deepen a trance state in a subject who is consciously critical of his or her ability to experience trance. I might want to begin building a response set by discussing the fact that everyone goes to sleep and dreams, and we have all had the experience of drifting off into a daydream. Now, I will write two dissociative statements that each presuppose that a trance will be experienced. In the first, I will offer the opportunity to continue feeling consciously awake even as trance is experienced: *"You can dream you're awake, even while you're in trance."* And to complete the double bind, I will offer the reverse opportunity, which would be to actually remain awake while nevertheless experiencing trance: *"Or, you can <u>feel as if you are in trance</u>, even while awake."*

Let us craft another, aimed at eliciting somatic dissociation. As before, we will create two dissociative statements that each presuppose the desired experience—in this case a dissociation between the conscious mind and the somatic experiences of the body. So, in the first statement, we will suggest that a person can be mentally awake while the body sleeps, and in the second, we will offer that the body can be awake but without being a part of awareness:

"You can allow your mind to awaken while the body remains asleep, or you can develop a recognition that the body is awake, without needing to have any experience of that awakeness or of that body."

CONCLUSION

Each of us uses language every day without really being aware of how we are doing it. You simply trust your unconscious mind to translate your intentions into spoken words, and then allow those words to emerge. And your style of speech evolves over time—there have been periods of time when you acquired new words or phrases, or when a familiar phrasing became more common in your vernacular. Your rhythm and intonation change based on the environment that you are in, the people you are around, and the subject at hand. And I really do not know whether you will first begin to employ the suggestive strategies outlined in this chapter consciously and deliberately, gradually acquiring new habits of speech, or whether you will first discover yourself using a new, more effective style of suggestion with your patients, only to go back later and really study and refine that change. What I do know is that the more comfortable and familiar these forms of hypnotic suggestion become, the easier it will be for you to experience success. And you can begin to develop that comfort and familiarity now, by spending a very interesting and enjoyable period of time completing the exercises that follow.

First, review this list of hypnotic phenomena. For each one, write out two or three distinct ways you might go about building up and then activating a response set for it. Write each suggestion in a complete form that includes some truisms, conjunctions, contingencies, and dissociated language as well as some indirect suggestions and some direct suggestions:

- Catalepsy
- Levitation
- Analgesia
- Anesthesia
- Amnesia
- Hypermnesia
- Time distortion
- Age regression
- Age progression
- Positive hallucination
- Negative hallucination
- Dissociation

Next, generate a list of six or eight hypnotic effects that you want to be able to reliably elicit in your patients. For example, any clinician will want to be able to elicit states of relaxation, motivation, comfort, and trust. A psychotherapist will want suggestions to address common ailments such as anxiety, panic, insomnia, nightmares, sadness, anhedonia, and self-worth. A physician will want suggestions for common complaints such as headache, muscle ache, gastrointestinal distress, needle phobia, and so on. Once you have developed this list, use it to complete these exercises again, crafting for each item two or three complete suggestions that elicit and then activate a response set for your desired outcome.

As you spend this time engaging your imagination in the process of formulating hypnotic suggestions, it will become increasingly natural and automatic for you to do so in your practice. And as you re-read this chapter, you will become increasingly aware of the forms of hypnotic suggestion demonstrated throughout.

REFERENCES

Bandler, R., & Grinder, J. (1975). *Patterns of the hypnotic techniques of Milton H. Erickson, MD* (Vol. 1). Cupertino, CA: Meta Publications.

Coué, É. (1923). *How to practice suggestion & autosuggestion.* New York, NY: American Library Service.

Erickson, M. H., Rossi, E. L., & Rossi, S. I. (1976). *Hypnotic realities: The induction of clinical hypnosis and forms of indirect suggestion.* New York, NY: Irvington Publishers.

Ewin, D. M. (2009). *101 things I wish I'd known when I started using hypnosis.* Bancyfelin, Wales: Crown House Publishing.

Frischholz, E. J. (2010, October 9). Uses of hypnosis in the treatment of pain: The 3-D approach. Presentation to the Chicago Society of Clinical Hypnosis.

Hammond, D. C. (Ed.). (1990). *Handbook of hypnotic suggestions and metaphors.* New York, NY: W. W. Norton.

Lankton, S. R., & Lankton, C. H. (1983). *The answer within: A clinical framework of Ericksonian hypnotherapy.* New York, NY: Brunner/Mazel.

Spiegel, H., & Spiegel, D. (2004). *Trance and treatment: Clinical uses of hypnosis* (2nd ed.). Arlington, VA: American Psychiatric Publishing.

Yapko, M. D. (2003). *Trancework: An introduction to the practice of clinical hypnosis* (3rd ed.). New York, NY: Routledge.

Zeig, J. K. (2014). *The induction of hypnosis: An Ericksonian elicitation approach.* Phoenix, AZ: The Milton H. Erickson Foundation Press.

Hypnotic Phenomena and Deepening Techniques

Arreed Franz Barabasz and Marianne Barabasz

The phenomena that are associated with the applications of hypnosis are evident to both researchers and practitioners. Hypnotic phenomena can include subjective changes as well as behavioral responses to each suggestion. While there are many aspects to hypnotic phenomena, this chapter includes descriptions of two of the more profound types of phenomena that can be elicited with hypnosis, keys to successful hypnotic inductions, a technique to help resistant patients respond to hypnosis, and effective deepening protocols. The techniques provided have been found to elicit hypnotic responses beyond what might be predicted by hypnotizability scale scores (Barabasz & Watkins, 2005).

- *Dissociation phenomenon.* One of the profound phenomena is illustrated by the following example. Milton Erickson asked a student, already hypnotized by Ernest Hilgard, to hold up his right arm. Erickson held the arm gently in the upraised position while explaining that he was lowering the upraised hand and arm. Upon letting go of the still upraised hand, he touched the student's lap, as if still holding his hand, to indicate that the hand was now resting in his lap. To validate that the student volunteer was hallucinating the hand on his lap, Erickson encouraged him to place his left hand over his right hand on his lap and to hold it there. Erickson then pinched the hand of the upright arm with great intensity using his fingernails. "Observing no apparent response to the painful pinch, he calmly inquired as to whether the subject had just felt anything. There was no mention of anesthesia, or any expected performance. The student casually reported he felt nothing. How could he feel something in the hand that was,

as he knew it, somewhere else" (Barabasz & Watkins, 2005, p. 53)?

- *Delusion phenomenon.* Another of these phenomena is the delusion phenomenon. Since clinical delusions in psychological conditions are difficult to study because of comorbidity variables, psychologists have turned to hypnosis to create a credible, reversible delusion. Barnier and her colleagues used hypnosis to re-create mirrored self-misidentification, a delusional belief that the person the subject sees in a mirror is a stranger (Barnier, Cox, Connors, Langdon & Coltheart, 2011). This delusion was exhibited by a patient with dementia who claimed he saw a stranger when he looked at his reflection in the mirror. Staring at his reflection, he stated, "He looks like me but I think you can distinguish it's not me . . . he's got a personality himself." When the experimenter stood next to the patient so both reflections were visible, the patient identified the experimenter but was still unable to identify himself. Using high hypnotizable normal subjects, Barnier's study showed that given a hypnotic suggestion to see a stranger in the mirror, subjects described seeing a stranger with physical characteristics different than their own. Remarkably, despite the fact that the subjects' beliefs about seeing a stranger were clearly false, they easily came up with sensible reasons to explain the stranger's presence, as did the genuine patients. In hypnosis research, subjects remained resilient in their delusional beliefs despite "clinically inspired challenges."

Voluntary behaviors can be carried out without hypnosis, using methods ranging from mere suggestion to simple directions to role-playing by the subject to please the hypnotist. However, veridical hypnosis is required to obtain more complex or difficult suggested changes to perception such as the two presented earlier. When such changes are produced by hypnosis, as measured by the Elkins Hypnotizability Scale (EHS) hallucination and dissociation items, they can be surprising to the subject because they are so dramatically convincing of the potency of hypnosis compared with simple motoric responses such as the EHS arm immobilization and arm levitation items (Elkins, 2014).

One of the most common applications of the alteration of perception phenomenon is for the relief of pain (Barabasz & Barabasz, 1989). Hypnosis is now recognized as evidence based for pain management (Jensen, 2011; Patterson, 2010) for extremely painful medical procedures such as burn debridement and surgery without anesthetics. Blocking pain stimuli is also routine in the interventional radiology clinic at Harvard Medical School (Lang & Rosen, 2002).

It is quite amazing to the lay observer to hear a hypnotist say to his or her subject, "When I count up to five, you will be wide awake, alert, and you will no longer have the headache, which has been troubling you." The subject emerges smiling and reports, "It doesn't hurt now." Has the pain really stopped? Does it make any difference that the physiological marker of pain may still be present? As Jack Hilgard (1992) pointed out, pain is what hurts and when the hurt is gone, the pain is gone. Even though a pain is initiated organically in some part of the body, the subject must "receive" it at a higher level of brain function before one feels the hurt (Hilgard, 1992). As in the Milton Erickson example earlier, if it is dissociated from perceptual centers, one does not sense the pain.

A new posttraumatic stress disorder (PTSD) treatment uses the alteration of pain perception to help reveal key psychological cues to be integrated in the abreactive hypnotic reconstruction of the trauma. The single session of 5 to 6 hours is evidence based and manualized (Barabasz, Barabasz, Christensen, French, & Watkins, 2013; Christensen, Barabasz, & Barabasz, 2013). The ego state harboring the trauma may only reveal itself through the body, either kinesthetically or by a psychosomatic symptom. Hypnosis is used to increase the discomfort to demonstrate that the patient can influence its perception and then be relieved. Such pains can often reveal the linkage between the discomfort and the trauma. Once

the linkage is revealed, it can be used as a stimulus in the reconstructed "reliving" of the trauma event critical to the curative abreactive phase.

The ability of hypnotized subjects to exhibit unusual behaviors, which transcend apparent normal limits of function, has never ceased to amaze the average person who observes it for the first time. "Even experienced clinicians and researchers, who have become accustomed to observing certain responses to hypnosis and view reactions not normally obtainable in un-hypnotized individuals, frequently re-experience a sense of awe" (Barabasz & Watkins, 2005, pp. 27–28).

The phenomena described in the preceding text are examples of the dramatic effects that can be elicited by hypnosis. However, such responses can only occur when subjects and patients are experiencing the hypnotic state with a level of depth sufficient for the demands of the suggestion. One of the common problems is that there is far too much assumption about depth currently in the hypnosis field among both researchers and clinicians. Throughout my 40+ years in the field, I have seen acclaimed experts charge ahead to offer up hypnotic suggestions without the slightest attempt to ensure that the poor subject, whether of low, average, or high hypnotizability, is actually experiencing hypnosis. There should be no surprise as to why a subject failed to respond to the suggestion if hypnotic depth needed for the task was less than adequate. Too often, a recorded induction is played or a protocol read with no systematic clinical assessment of the subject's responses to the induction instructions. This often elicits only responses that can be wrought by mere suggestion and social influence rather than a genuine hypnotic responding.

KEYS TO SUCCESSFUL HYPNOTIC INDUCTIONS

The following describes hypnotic induction elements necessary to maximize hypnotic responding and lays the foundation for enhancement of hypnotic depth.

As described in Barabasz and Watkins (2005), the *preparatory phase* consists of descriptions of hypnotic responding, which are embedded in the hypnotic induction. The preparatory phase is entirely future tense oriented. Wording may include suggestions such as *"Your eyelids will become heavier and heavier and you will want to close your eyes, eventually your eyes will be so tired you __will__ close them—it __will__ become impossible to keep them open, the pressure of your hand resting on your leg __will__ become less and less—that hand __will__ become lighter and lighter*" (the word "that" is used to facilitate dissociation of the hand from the person; from an analytical view [Watkins & Barabasz, 2008], this implies that the hand becomes "object energized" instead of remaining "ego energized"). *"Eventually, __it will__ begin to rise, to lift on its own. You may notice that you __will__ get an increase in salivation as you go into hypnosis, some people have that response, you might too, its just one of those perfectly normal responses some people have at this stage, maybe you __will__ have it too, maybe not, but all of the time __you will__ __become__ more and more calm"* (or more alert, if an alert induction is preferred for the response anticipated; these are specific responses indicating what __will__ be felt, rather than a call for relaxation). The key element of the preparatory phase is that when suggesting responses in the future tense, you are protected from loss of rapport if there is no behavioral evidence of them displayed by the subject yet. Patience is also essential. I once took nearly an hour to evoke levitation of the patient's hand of just a couple of inches. However, once accomplished, the response to the induction became so profound that future hypnotic rapport was assured. Deep rapid inductions became the norm for this patient, which helped to facilitate dramatic therapeutic gains and lasting positive life changes.

The *transition phase* consists of descriptions of hypnotic responding as you observe them (Barabasz & Watkins, 2005, p. 122). The induction shifts to using the present tense. Subjects' concentration becomes effortless as they begin to dissociate and become unaware of all but the hypnotic activity. Moving on to this phase prematurely is a recipe for failure to achieve veridical hypnosis. This failure is the most common induction mistake I have witnessed not only by those in training but by established experts in the field. Remarkably, you may obtain an apparent positive response, but if you have moved to this stage without confirmation or the suggested response in the preparatory phase, it may only represent some sort of simple social compliance. You might, for example, achieve simple relaxation at best (in contrast to genuine hypnotic relaxation) or simple effortful nonhypnotic responses to easy suggestions (Elkins, 2014). Such effortful responses are those that could be evoked

without hypnosis per se. Those who still cling to the socio-cognitive belief that hypnosis is nothing more than an artifact of social influence and non-hypnotic suggestibility sometimes literally tell their subjects to "try as hard as you can" or "just try harder" (references omitted to protect the guilty). To obtain veridical hypnotic responses, initiate the transition phase only when you have in reality observed the patient's responses suggested in the preparatory phase. As you become experienced and mindful of the phases of hypnosis, you will learn to observe your patient more closely as you will be less preoccupied with carrying out the specifics of the induction procedure. As a result, you will be able to use these subtle clinical observations of hypnotic response in the transition phase, regardless of whether you suggested them in the earlier phase because our patients and research subjects frequently repeat their own idiosyncratic responses in the process of entering hypnosis. Wording typical of the transition phase might be as follows (upon noticing eye flutter): *"Your eyes are beginning to flutter, they may close soon"*; then as the eyes close for an instant, say, *"There the eyes closed, yes, so much more comfortable closed than open."*

The *hypnotic rapport phase* (Barabasz & Watkins, 2005, pp. 122–123) constitutes the true hypnotic experience where the patient's responses to hypnotic suggestions are perceived to be automatic (involuntary) and effortless. There is a shift toward primary process (Barabasz & Christensen, 2006; Fromm, 1992) where one maintains some aspects of secondary process where vigilance and defenses relax (Barabasz, 1982). Rapport phase wording involves whatever is required by the clinical demands of the situation or the research protocol. Hypnotic deepening as well as depth checks should correspond to the difficulty of the hypnotic response required.

Confidence and belief in the hypnotic modality are also critical. Consider, for a moment, that the patient is regressed at least to some degree. Why would you expect to be trusted to use hypnosis in therapy any further if you were thought to be unsure of yourself or to have no understanding that the hypnotic state is real (Elkins, Barabasz, Council & Spiegel, 2015)? No practitioner, no matter how clever, can resonate with a patient while trying to hide disbelief in the reality of the modality he or she is attempting to use. To obtain difficult responses to hypnotic suggestions (pain relief, surgery without anesthesia, amnesia, trauma resolution, etc.), you must absolutely expect it to work. As the late Bruner "Fig" Newton explained (2000), "You must know it will work."

Once the rapport phase is established, develop a series of graded hypnotic suggestions. Do not interrupt the process by calling for simple voluntary behaviors. In the rapport phase, the subject is capable of true hypnotic phenomena including (a) increased suggestibility, (b) attentional redistribution (if told to listen only to your voice, all else will be effortlessly ignored), (c) no desire to make plans; the here and now is all that he or she will focus on, (d) a reduction in reality testing where reality distortions are readily accepted (may uncritically accept hallucinated experiences such as petting an imaginary rabbit), (e) responding with posthypnotic amnesia when so instructed as well as restoration of what has transpired by posthypnotic signal, and (f) the ability to readily enact unusual roles when instructed to do so such as reenacting behaviors characteristic of an earlier age or reconstruction or "reliving" of a significant prior event (age regression).

HELPING RESISTANT CLIENTS

The nature of true hypnotic responding is that things "happen" to the subject, apparently without his or her conscious control or "willing" it. Let us begin with the experience of an involuntary automatic action, which can be demonstrated by the Kohnstamm phenomenon (Barabasz & Watkins, 2005). Students of hypnosis as well as our patients can experience this phenomenon, if only to acquaint themselves more intimately with the kind of feeling one has when hypnotized and responding to suggestions.

The Kohnstamm Protocol

"Please stand near the wall with your shoulder 90° to it, your feet about a foot from the wall. Push the back of your hand against the wall; push it hard against the wall. Don't lean your body toward the wall. Just stand erect and push the back of the hand against the wall. Push hard, harder, still harder. Now, please continue this for an entire minute if you can. A minute will seem like a long time while you are doing this."

The practitioner/experimenter announces 15-second intervals. Each time, he or she continues to urge subjects to push harder with all their strength against the wall with the back of the hand.

At the end of 1 minute, the instruction is given, "Now turn and face me." To the great astonishment of the subject, the arm will slowly rise as if automatically. Of course, the phenomenon is not a hypnotic effect but is based on muscle fatigue. By tiring one set of muscles in the arm, the opposing muscles simply contract and lift the arm. While this is not hypnosis, the experience is close to that felt by those who are responding to hypnotic suggestions in the trance state. The concept of automaticity (dissociation) is conveyed. Something is happening to them; they are not doing anything. Unfortunately, the Kohnstamm demonstration is insufficient by itself to overcome the defenses of the resistant client.

Protocol for Barabasz's Induction for Resistant Patients

This "Verbal-Non-Verbal Dissociation technique" (Barabasz & Watkins, 2005, pp. 159–162) builds upon the Kohnstamm phenomenon. It is worth attempting even with those who have scored in the lowest ranges of the hypnotizability tests. In a small, but significant, number of cases, it overcomes underlying resistance to hypnosis, which may be due to variables other than lack of innate hypnotizability.

"If you're ready, please stand with your left (or right) shoulder about a foot from the wall, here let me help [show him or her how to stand in the correct proximity to the wall consistent with the basic Kohnstamm protocol in the preceding text]. *OKAY, please just simply press the back of your hand against the wall, just your hand not your body, pretty much as hard as you can press it against the wall. Are you pressing hard now?* [Presumably the subject says yes.] *GOOD, press a little harder if you can. This takes a whole minute but you can do it.* [Watch a clock behind subject, noting the second hand, yet at the same time, for the entire minute, maintain constant contact with the subject's eyes. This is eased by focusing on the subject's nose bridge.] *GOOD, that's already 30 seconds, just 30 more seconds to go, just keep pressing and pressing that hand harder*

and harder against the wall, pressing, pressing, pressing as hard as you can! The rest of your body can be calm and at ease, but keep <u>that</u> hand pressing against the wall. Feel it pushing harder. Just keep pressing harder. Now just 10 seconds to go, keep that hand pressing against the wall, real hard now. Almost there [at about 10 seconds remaining]. GOOD, now just step away from the wall." [<u>Say nothing more to the subject now</u> but continue staring directly at the subject's nose bridge. As he or she moves away from the wall, use your peripheral vision to note the hand-rising effect produced by the Kohnstamm phenomenon. At the same time, change your focus to looking directly behind the patient while subtly leading and mirroring the subject's arm float by lifting your own arm. Focusing behind the patient's head, shifting from looking into his or her eyes (bridge of nose) helps to further distract conscious processing of the arm levitation as you will be perceived as looking through the patient. Be sure to lift the opposite arm as that used by the subject, so you are providing a mirrorlike image to the subject as part of your nonverbal hypnotic induction cue.]

<u>Now say</u> *"<u>Your</u> arm is just floating up by itself! <u>It</u> can relax too and be calm. As it goes down, you too, <u>will</u> go down into a deep pleasant hypnotic calmness, and when <u>the arm</u> is all the way down, your eyes can close too. Please try to keep them open until your arm is so calmly down, down, down, and you are seated in that chair behind you. Please try not to go any deeper into hypnosis until you are in the chair."*

Once the arm is all the way down, the subject is seated, and the eyes are closed, you may proceed to test hypnotic suggestions, deepening, your research protocol, or the planned therapeutic intervention. The entire procedure requires a few practice trials to assure it will flow with calm confidence. You must exude the confidence that you know these suggested reactions will happen despite the fact that you may be surprised yourself with the expectation that a known resistant subject will actually respond. Contrary to notions promulgated by some research reports, neither the subject's negative expectations nor your expectation, based on the low hypnotizability score or other beliefs about

the subject, will have much effect on the outcome of the induction (Tome-Pires, Ludena, & Pires, 2015). Proficiency confidence is but one feature that separates the more effective practitioner using hypnosis from the one who is limited to reliance on easily elicited hypnotic talents such as mundane responses to suggestion rather than helping the patient unleash veridical hypnotic dissociative capacities.

HYPNOTIC DEEPENING

Obvious to even the most casual observer is that to respond to suggestions of varying difficulty requires varying levels of hypnotic depth. Little hypnotic depth, with little if any dissociation, would be needed to obtain responses to easy suggestions where social–psychologial variables could play the key role without any difficulty (responses to suggestions of calmness, easing up, letting go) in contrast to the level of depth needed for the adaptive dissociation essential for painless surgery without an anesthetic. Elkins (2014) explains and graphs the concept of adaptive dissociation where true hypnotic responding (requiring some depth) arises from the experiential/unconscious and responses are experienced as involuntary (automatic). Complementing Elkins' elegant description, Watkins and Barabasz (2005) graphed the levels of ego participation required across the hypnotic depth continuum.

As explained in greater detail elsewhere (Barabasz & Watkins, 2005), the matter of hypnotic involvement is one of degree. A person is neither in nor out of a hypnotic state; one experiences hypnosis lightly, significantly, or deeply. The hypnotic induction may be best understood as a continuous process, starting with the first responses to hypnotic suggestion and gradually developing into increasingly profound focused involvement in the trance state. Hypnotizability tests, such as the EHS and the various Stanford scales, appear to measure not only the ability of an individual to be hypnotized but also the "depth" to which it is possible to hypnotize that person. The point, lost on many who employ hypnosis in research but also clinically, is that the depth adequate to achieve the suggested response is not automatically manifested the moment a person is exposed to a hypnotic induction or self-hypnotic experience (Kahn & Fromm, 1992).

DEEPENING PROTOCOLS

Floating and Revolving in a Cloud

After the initial hypnotic induction has been accomplished, ask the subject to imagine that he or she is floating in a soft, fluffy cloud. Ask the subject to raise a finger if feeling as if in that fluffy cloud. *"Feeling the soft cloud, wrapped all around like a fleecy blanket."* This often begins the deepening process by encouraging a regression to infantile fantasies.

Next, extend the "floating in a cloud" instruction by drawing attention to potential kinesthetic and vestibular sensations.

"You are floating in this soft safe cloud high above the Earth. You can see the tiny houses below you. If you are picturing the tiny houses, raise a finger. You feel a great sense of strength and peace. It seems now as if you are revolving around and around in that cloud so that first you see the Earth below you. [Often if the involvement is becoming automatic the subject may raise a finger to confirm the perception without being asked to do so.] *Feel yourself rotating backwards so that it is now behind you. Now you are turning so that it is above you. Now, it is in front of you. And you continue floating over backwards, around and around and around. The Earth continues to change as it is below you, behind you, above you, in front of you. Below- Behind- Above-In front. Around and around and around"* (Barabasz & Watkins, 2005, p. 198).

This deepening technique can be kept up for some time as the individual feels himself or herself rotating around and around as oriented by the place of the Earth "far below."

Revolving Wheels

The majority of patients react to this extension of the initial induction by entering their most profoundly deepened state.

"Now you are lying on a grassy slope away from city hassles out in the country. You notice in front of you a large old-fashioned wagon wheel. Do you see it now? Just raise a finger when you do. The wagon wheel is so close and so large that it almost fills your entire field of vision. You stare at it, you are taken by the size of the huge hub, the thick wood spokes, and the old iron rim around the outside edge. If you look closely at this iron rim, you will notice that there are points of light in it imbedded as if they were tiny light bulbs. Do you see the points of light? Just raise a finger. In fact, there are seven such points of light evenly spaced around the rim of the wheel. Can you see the points of light—flecks of shiny metal in the rusty old rim? [Once a finger rises, proceed.] *Now look at each point of light: The first. The second. The third. The fourth. The fifth. The sixth. And the seventh. Now focus your eyes on that seventh tiny point of light on the rim of the wheel. As you stare at it, the wheel begins slowly to revolve. It is as if your staring at it is making it move by itself. It is turning very slowly around and around and you are continuing to focus your eyes on that seventh point of light as it goes with the wheel around and around and around. It seems as if there is a voice also coming from the wheel that keeps saying over and over again, 'Deeper, deeper, deeper.' And as the wheel turns and you follow that seventh point of light with your eyes, it goes around and around and around, and the voice keeps saying 'deeper, deeper, deeper.' Around and around and around. Deeper, deeper, deeper."*

"The wheel is turning faster and faster [often a finger raises to confirm here but it is normally no longer important to ask for it]. *It is going around, and around and around, and the voice keeps saying 'deeper, deeper, deeper.' It is getting harder and harder to keep focusing on the seventh light on that spinning wheel, which is going around and around and around with the voice saying 'deeper, deeper, deeper!'"*

"The wheel is spinning so fast around and around and around that the spokes blur. And you can hardly keep focusing on the seventh point of light. It's going so fast that all seven lights blend into a fiery ring of light around the outside rim of the wagon wheel, which is spinning around and

around and around. And the voice with it is saying 'deeper, deeper, deeper.'"

"And now it seems as if you are slowly retreating back from the wheel, or as if it is moving back and away from you, and you can see a second spinning wheel coming into the field of view. Now there are two spinning wheels with fiery rings of light around their rims going around and around and around. And two voices saying, 'deeper, deeper, deeper.'"

"The wheels are now getting smaller and another light comes into your field of view. There are now three spinning wheels going around and around and around and three voices saying, 'deeper, deeper, deeper.'"

"They move away from you so that a fourth, then a fifth, and then a sixth wheel comes into view. Six spinning wheels going around and around and around and a half dozen voices softly saying, 'deeper, deeper, deeper.'"

"As they move away from you, even more wheels come into view, seven, eight, nine, ten, eleven, twelve spinning fiery rings and a dozen voices very softly saying, 'deeper, deeper, deeper.'"

"Now they are moving so far away into space that it seems like a hundred tiny spinning wheels of light are going around and around and around, miles and miles from you and hundreds of tiny voices are softly whispering, 'deeper, deeper, deeper, deeper, deeper.'"

"And the tiny rings of light are slowly fading away, and the whispering voices are getting so soft you can hardly hear them as they say, 'deeper, deeper, deeper, deeper.' And finally, all the light is gone and all the voices are gone, and there is nothing left but a great soft warm darkness that fills your entire world, and you feel deeply at peace with the whole universe."

As you read the induction to your patient, your voice should gradually go through various changes to convey the changing perceptions. At first, while describing the wheel as it begins to turn, your voice should be strong, to convey complete confidence, yet slowly paced. As more

wheels appear, the rate of speech/words per minute should gradually increase, "around and around and around." And as the voices decrease in number, drop the pitch until at the end you are saying "deeper, deeper, deeper, deeper" very rapidly but very softly. Finally, the induction ends in a soft, warm, and darkened image much like the origins of our life in the womb. This deepening technique frequently facilitates hypnotic regression to the point where the patient loses nearly all secondary processing capacity for the duration of the induction. It can be a truly remarkable effect, so be prepared rather than surprised—it is a routine effect of this type of deepening induction.

A few patients simply cannot respond at all to the revolving wheels protocol (Barabasz & Watkins, 2005, p. 200). Others report that they were annoyed by the slow development of the fantasy. As always, check the subject's reactions to it after alertness is complete. A small but significant number of subjects enter a state so deep that after about the third wheel they become completely amnesic to the later developments. This is a powerful effect of the induction; patients should be reassured that it is "normal" or "routine" to mitigate any anxieties if they occur.

Finally, when reading research as well as clinical reports, one is wise to evaluate them with the recognition that enthusiastic clinicians often overevaluate their accomplishments using hypnosis, while overly critical experimenters sometimes using only scripted inductions administered by inexperienced university students may simply have failed to elicit the phenomena. Nonetheless, even the most critical and rigorous of us in the field generally agree that regardless of what hypnosis is, unusual alterations in behavior, perception, affect, and cognition can be achieved by means of it, if attention is paid to the induction process and deepening has been accomplished when appropriate.

REFERENCES

Barabasz, A., Barabasz, M., Christensen, C., French, B., & Watkins, J. G. (2013). Efficacy of single-session abreactive ego state therapy for combat stress injury, PTSD, and ASD. *International Journal of Clinical and Experimental Hypnosis, 61*(1), 1–19.

Barabasz, A., & Christensen, C. (2006). Age regression: Tailored vs scripted inductions. *American Journal of Clinical Hypnosis*, 48(4), 251–261.

Barabasz, A., & Watkins, J. G. (2005). *The hypnotherapeutic techniques* (2nd ed.). New York, NY: Brunner-Rutledge.

Barabasz, A. F. (1982). Restricted environmental stimulation and the enhancement of hypnotizability: Pain, EEG alpha, skin conductance and temperature responses. *International Journal of Clinical and Experimental Hypnosis*, 30(2), 147–166.

Barabasz, A. F., & Barabasz, M. (1989). Effect of restricted environmental stimulation: Enhancement of hypnotizability for experimental and chronic pain control. *International Journal of Clinical and Experimental Hypnosis*, 37(3), 217–231.

Barnier, A. J., Cox, R. E., Connors, M., Langdon, R., & Coltheart, M. (2010). A stranger in the looking glass: Developing and challenging a hypnotic mirrored-self misidentification delusion. *International Journal of Clinical and Experimental Hypnosis*, 59(1), 1–26.

Christensen, C., Barabasz, A., & Barabasz, M. (2013). Efficacy of abreactive ego state therapy for PTSD: Trauma resolution, depression, and anxiety. *International Journal of Clinical and Experimental Hypnosis*, 61(1), 20–37.

Elkins, G. (2014). *Hypnotic relaxation therapy; principles and applications*. New York, NY: Springer Publishing Company.

Elkins, G. R., Barabasz, A. F., Council, J. R., & Spiegel, D. (2015). Advancing research and practice: The revised APA Division 30 definition of hypnosis. *International Journal of Clinical and Experimental Hypnosis*, 63(1), 1–9.

Fromm, E. (1992). An ego-psychological theory of hypnosis. In E. Fromm & M. Nash (Eds.), *Contemporary hypnosis research* (pp. 131–148). New York, NY: Guilford Press.

Hilgard, E. (1992). Dissociation and theories of hypnosis. In E. Fromm & M. Nash (Eds.), *Contemporary hypnosis research* (pp. 69–101). New York, NY: Guilford Press.

Jensen, M. P. (2011). *Hypnosis for chronic pain management: Workbook*. NewYork, NY. Oxford University Press.

Kahn, S., & Fromm, E. (1992). Self hypnosis, personality and the experiential method. In E. Fromm & M. Nash (Eds.), *Contemporary hypnosis research* (pp. 69–101). New York, NY: Guilford Press.

Lang, E. V., & Rosen, M. P. (2002). Case analysis of adjunct hypnosis with sedation during outpatient interventional radiologic procedures. *Radiology*, 222(2), 375–382.

Newton, B. (2000, Oct. 25–29). Is your hypnosis what you think it is? Workshop presented at the 51st Annual Workshops and Scientific Program of the Society for Clinical and Experimental Hypnosis, Seattle.

Patterson, D. R. (2010). *Hypnosis for pain control*. Washington, DC: American Psychological Association.

Tome-Pires, C., Ludena, M. A., & Pires, C. (2015). Expectancies and hypnotic responsiveness: Experimental design flaw revealed. *International Journal of Clinical and Experimental Hypnosis*, 63(2), 129–143.

Watkins, J. G., & Barabasz, A. (2008). *Advanced hypnotherapy: Hypnodynamic techniques*. New York, NY: Routledge.

Resistance: Solving Problems During Hypnotic Inductions

Dan Short

This chapter offers a scientific perspective on the variety of problems that might emerge between a patient and practitioner during hypnotic induction. I hesitate to use the word *resistance* because of its implication that failure in therapy is always the fault of the patient. This term has also become associated with highly speculative assumptions of unconscious sabotage. Using a broader problem-solving perspective, this chapter focuses attention on all members of the dyad to better determine which actions, emotions, or beliefs are interfering with desired outcomes.

Clinical hypnosis is essentially a cooperative endeavor, in which the priming of unconscious associations combines with the creation of a deep expectation that therapeutic change will occur. With this definition, it is apparent that effective hypnotic problem solving remains balanced upon a fulcrum of trust and voluntary consent. This differentiates clinical hypnosis from hypnosis used by entertainers, by cult recruiters (Hassan, 2012), or by Central Intelligence Agency (CIA) interrogators (Ross, 2007). When writing about the subject of resistance in clinical hypnosis, Weitzenhoffer (1989) warned that above all else, "a subject should be willing to be hypnotized, have confidence and trust in the hypnotist, and have a readiness for inner changes, especially changes implemented by an outer agent" (p. 140). For these reasons, expert practitioners seek confirmation that the patient wants to be hypnotized or has a continuing desire to be hypnotized. According to Christenson (1958),

> It will be found, even with experienced subjects, that if they are not in the mood to be hypnotized, there is no point in going further. . . . In fact, it is best to concede to the new subject that if he does not wish to be hypnotized, he cannot be forced. (p. 38)

When the patient feels invited to participate in a process that is permissive, collaborative, and founded on a respect for his or her goals, there is a decreased likelihood that problems will occur (Fromm, 1980).

FEAR

Experts agree that fear is one of the most common reasons for resistance to induction (Frauman, Lynn, & Brentar, 1993; Weizenhoffer, 1989; Yapko, 2013) and the most common fear is of the hypnotic state itself. For those who have never experienced hypnosis or have only seen it demonstrated in comedy clubs, the prospect of being hypnotized may induce panic. Such individuals may fear losing control, revealing embarrassing secrets, developing excessive dependency, or having to comply with the practitioner's every command. Confidence can be increased by offering the patient the option of maintaining full awareness and control over his or her actions, including the ability to open the eyes or lift a finger to stop the induction. Another possibility is to offer the option of "waking hypnosis," so that the patient can keep his or her eyes open, or the option of limiting the scope of the trance to one small part of the patient's body, such as a hand or an arm (Short, Erickson, & Erickson-Klein, 2005), which is easily accomplished using ideomotor signaling or other suggestions for automatic responses that the patient can observe. Another piecemeal approach is to invite the patient to close her eyes and merely imagine what trance will be like, what the practitioner might do to improve the experience, and what suggestions will be most helpful to achieve her goals. This exercise often reveals fears and misconceptions that inhibit full participation (Frauman, Lynn, & Brentar, 1993). Dedicating some time to this type of preinduction activity helps prepare the patient with the information needed to set his or her mind at ease. It also defines the situation as one in which the patient is an important contributor with power to alter the course of events, if necessary.

Another common fear is the fear of failure. This fear may be felt by the patient, the practitioner, or both. Patients who have tried almost every other method of treatment, without success, may verbalize their doubt that they can go into trance or they may try to avoid failure by seeking to delay the procedure. Performance anxiety is likely to escalate with pressure, for instance, if the patient gets the idea that trance induction is a test of whether therapy, as a whole, will succeed. It is important to honor all of the patient's requests, for instance, stopping the induction if the patient does not feel ready. If this occurs, the therapy can be temporarily shifted to another form of treatment, such as counseling, and returning to hypnosis at a later time. Confidence can also be increased by having hypnotic responding modeled for the patient, a strategy that dates back to Liebault's work in Nancy, France.

For the practitioner, it is important to be able to tolerate fear of failure and to accept the possibility of making small mistakes. Other fears that interfere with a confident induction procedure include the practitioner's fear of power, fear of the unexpected, or fear of disapproval from others. Ironically, overfocusing on the nuances of hypnotic induction or the depth of trance tends to increase anxiety while distracting attention from the more important question of how hypnosis is going to support the needs and goals of the patient. For these reasons, it is advisable not to worry about the intricacies of a technique or to become overly concerned with flawless execution. As long as patients know that the clinician is entirely focused on their well-being, they are generally forgiving of small mistakes and just as eager to see treatment methods succeed.

PROBLEMATIC EXPECTATIONS

As with fearful feelings, unrealistic expectations of what will occur during hypnosis (e.g., the loss of all awareness, a complete amnesia for the experience, or the loss of all volitional control) should be addressed prior to induction so that unfulfilled expectancies do not result in the patient inferring that he or she cannot be hypnotized (Overholser, 1988). Failure to correct erroneous beliefs often results in the patient declaring, "I must not have been hypnotized. I heard every word you said!" If magical expectations are not addressed, it is less likely that the patient will be able to recognize or appreciate small gains achieved during trance.

Before induction, it is important to carefully assess the patient's history of hypnotic experiences and subsequent attitudes. Relevant details include patients' perceptions of how deeply they were hypnotized, whether the experience was enjoyable, how the patients responded to various suggestions, what was most helpful or what was not helpful, and what sensations were experienced (Frauman, Lynn, & Brentar, 1993). This knowledge enables the practitioner to select inductions and hypnotic techniques that are compatible with the patient's expectancies. Experienced practitioners have long known that if a subject truly believes a method will hypnotize him, then a surprisingly wide variety of methods can serve as effective induction (Weitzenhoffer, 1989). During the first hypnotic session, it is advisable to allow the patient to succeed with easy suggestions, such as imagery, changes in skin temperature, and psychomotor movement, before moving to more complex experiences such as glove anesthesia, positive or negative hallucinations, and hypnotic amnesia. Success with early responsiveness to suggestion strengthens expectations, thereby ensuring greater responsiveness to subsequent suggestions (Kirsch, 1990).

Ironically, a problem can be defined as any discrepancy between what is expected and what is occurring. Thus, the more flexible and open-minded the practitioner, the fewer the problems that are likely to be encountered. Perhaps the most common problematic expectation held by practitioners of hypnosis is that a favored induction technique should work equally well with all patients. However, dating back to the earliest research on hypnosis, luminaries such as Bernheim (1889/1947) and Janet (1925) have argued that methods, which work very well with some subjects, may not work equally well with others, and that even those who have responded well to a particular technique may prefer a different technique on a different occasion.

Also, both the therapist and patient should have realistic expectations for the experience of hypnosis. For example, expectations such as that hypnosis requires absolute compliance to be effective can be problematic. Realistic expectations come from recognizing that the hypnotic state does not involve sleep or a loss of consciousness. According to Erickson (1948), "Hypnosis does not change the person, nor does it alter his past experiential life. It serves to permit him to learn more about himself and to express himself more adequately" (p. 514). And as stated by Wolberg (1948), "It has many values; but it does have limitations in terms of the individual's existing motivations and his capacities for change. Therapeutic failures occur with hypnosis as with any other form of therapy" (p. 418).

MISCOMMUNICATION

Perhaps one of the most hapless problems that can occur during hypnotic induction is that of *miscommunication*. In some instances, the patient is trying to cooperate but does not understand what the practitioner is requesting, because the suggestion was either too vague or stated in too narrow terms. During trance, suggestions should be simple and repeated more than once. The more complicated a suggestion, the more difficult it will be for the patient to carry it out. Another possibility is that the patient is responding in a very literal and circumscribed manner. For instance, a patient who is told to watch her arm levitate may watch a hallucinated arm movement without any physical changes to the position of her arm. Or a person who is told to "feel more and more sleepy" may not close his eyes until being told specifically to do so. This is especially likely to happen during hypnosis with children (Short, 1999). It would be a serious mistake to interpret these behaviors as unconscious resistance when what is actually occurring is unexpected compliance with a miscommunication by the practitioner. For these reasons, suggestions should be brief, precise, and worded as close as possible to the known habits and thoughts of the patient, thereby reducing the likelihood of miscommunication.

Because communication works best as a two-way street, it is helpful to invite the patient to talk during trance induction so that you have a better understanding of his or her subjective experiences and emerging hypnotic realities. Similarly, increased observation results in greater sensitivity to the needs of the patient and increased responsiveness. When seeking to understand an individual's emotional experience, it is particularly important to study the movements of the eyes and face, which yield more information than spoken language (Ekman, 2003; Hess, 1965). A sudden look of concern may indicate problems with word choice. For instance, some patients will respond violently to the idea of being "hypnotized" but they do not mind the thought of "going into a trance" just as some patients are terrified of being labeled as "crazy" but do not mind being identified as "mentally ill" (Short, Erickson, & Erickson-Klien, 2005). The primary solution for any problem with communication is to gather more information with the hope of increasing empathic understanding.

POWER STRUGGLES

According to Erickson (1956), apparent resistance is often no more than an unconscious test of the hypnotherapist's willingness to meet patients halfway rather than forcing them to act entirely in accord with his ideas. Similarly, Christenson (1958) noted that some patients are more resistant to hypnotic induction during the second attempt than on the first, a temporary condition that disappears once they demonstrate that they can resist the process, if they wish. Orne (1965) points out that hypnosis can increase problems of countertransference, leading to a power struggle as the practitioner seeks to gratify his or her needs rather than the needs of the patient. If the patient has a history of being harshly dominated by others, then an unfortunate transference–countertransference dynamic is likely to result in a failure to go into trance or a failure to awaken. Because the practitioner is not likely to recognize his or her unconscious needs, evidence of a two-way power struggle is more easily identified through the patient's reactions. For example, if the patient begins to tense up as the practitioner offers suggestions for relaxation, then that patient's needs should be given more careful consideration. Other subtle indicators of an emerging power struggle include a loud cough or the patient needing to blow his nose just as each suggestion is spoken, as well as any other behavior that interrupts the process and demonstrates that the suggestions have failed to produce their intended effect. Under these conditions, the practitioner needs to find a way to increase the patient's ability to act independently and in accord with his or her personal will.

In response to the problem of power struggles, Erickson (1958, p. 92) developed "permissive suggestion." He illustrated this technique with a sample dialogue, filled with options:

"Shortly your right hand, or it may be your left hand, will begin to lift up, or it may press down, or it may not move at all, but we will wait to see just what happens. Maybe the thumb will be first, or you may feel something happening in your little finger, but the really important thing is not whether your hand lifts up or presses down or just remains still; rather, it is your ability to sense fully whatever feelings may develop in your hand."

Anytime a person feels trapped in a situation that threatens loss of control, the instinctual response is to resist. No sensible person wishes to surrender basic rights and personal freedoms, such as the right to talk or not talk, the right to keep one's eyes open, the right to listen or not listen, the right to sit or stand, and the right to refuse external manipulation. With this in mind, the practitioner uses permissive suggestion, asking leading questions such as *"Would you like to go into trance now or later? . . . Would you like to go into trance standing up or sitting?"* or offering options, such as *"You can listen to my voice or replace it with the sound of your own inner wisdom."* When there is obvious concern for the freedom and needs of the patient, power struggles are less likely to emerge. Even more importantly, as stated by Fromm (1980, p. 426),

The clinical objective is to strengthen patient autonomy and self-pride in mastering a problem situation. This process begins with an induction procedure that permits the patient to decide how and when he or she will manifest the various phenomena of hypnosis.

AMBIVALENCE

Clinical ambivalence is defined as a discrepancy between deliberate intention and automatic behaviors, resulting in self-contradictory actions. It is an approach–avoid conflict that remains hidden beneath conscious awareness. For instance, a request for hypnosis from a patient who subsequently seeks to dominate the conversation, never allowing any time for the practitioner to respond as requested, is a sign of ambivalence. Erickson (1958) believed that the very fact that a patient requests hypnosis and then offers resistance indicates a state of ambivalence. Haley (1958) observed such a situation when an individual from the audience stood with crossed arms and challenged Erickson to hypnotize him. Erickson invited the participant to join him on the lecture platform, asked him to sit down, and then said to him, "I want you to stay awake, wider and wider awake, wider and wider awake." At that point, the subject closed his eyes and entered into a hypnotic sleep state.

When dealing with the problem of resistance, Erickson often talked of "displacing" and "discharging" the resistance. Though he did not specify the circumstances in which this approach is needed, he listed numerous case examples, each containing indications of ambivalence. For example, one such patient announced that he wanted to be treated with hypnosis but then insisted that he could not be hypnotized (Erickson, Rossi, & Rossi, 1976, p. 221). This seemingly paradoxical position represents a contradictory attitude not only to hypnosis but to the whole of therapy; otherwise, the patient would have requested a form of therapy that he thought would work well. For this reason, Erickson's problem solving was not limited to the process of induction but to the patient's responsiveness to therapy as a whole.

With this particular patient, Erickson commented that there were three additional chairs in the office and that if hypnosis were attempted in each of these chairs, the induction would probably fail more times than it succeeded. After trying three chairs, unsuccessfully, the patient was readily hypnotized in the fourth chair. Though this process might seem mysterious, the core principle is fairly simple. If the patient is ambivalent, it means that he wishes to have hypnosis fail and he wishes to have it succeed. Thus, the practitioner needs to provide some opportunity for failure and at least one opportunity for success (remember the man from the audience; he "failed" to keep his eyes open). When offering posthypnotic suggestions to such a patient, it would be reasonable to expect that some of the suggestions will fail. Using Erickson's method, the resistance is dealt with first, so the resistance is "used up and discharged." Once the need for failure is addressed, the patient is nicely positioned to end with a success experience.

As with every other method described in this chapter, it should not be assumed that the induction is the only place where this type of problem will be encountered. The patient may be highly ambivalent about a large number of things, including trusting others, making changes to behavior, or whether or not to remain in therapy. When the practitioner understands the process of disambiguation (Short, 2014), then presumably refractory patients readily cooperate as their needs are met and their goals achieved.

CONCLUSION

Before ending this discussion, it is important to note that the principles discussed in this chapter have application not only to hypnotic induction but to the whole of any therapeutic endeavor. As stated by Bates (1993), "Patients' fears, ambivalences, and dynamic conflicts influence their responses to hypnotic treatment, as do considerations such as secondary gain" (pp. 25–26). When considering the broader interpersonal dynamics that surround therapy, it is helpful to recognize that the preconditions for the induction of hypnosis are very similar to the preconditions required for a successful therapeutic relationship (Orne & Dinges, 1989). As argued by Zeig (2014), the lessons learned from differences in response to the induction procedure can provide valuable information for planning the course of treatment and for avoiding costly ruptures to the overall therapeutic alliance.

Even when the initial induction proceeds with relative ease, there are certain circumstances in which successful trance induction is a problem. For example, prepsychotic patients have been known to decompensate during hypnosis (Gill & Brenman, 1959) as well as those with a paranoid level of resistance to being manipulated or controlled (Orne, 1965; Speigel, 1978). A procedure that produces alterations in conscious awareness

is also risky with those who perceive themselves as victims of sudden, intrusive, and unwanted intimacy (Frauman, Lynn, & Brentar, 1993). This brings us back to the central thesis of the opening section, which is that clinical hypnosis should always be built on a solid base of trust and voluntary consent. The practitioner who assumes an overly rigid, authoritarian, coercive, or insensitive stance toward the patient will understandably encounter problems with induction (Fromm, 1980; Lazar & Dempster, 1984; Yapko, 2013). The expert hypnotherapist has an expectation of discovery and a curiosity about the patient's reality. When the practitioner is flexible, caring, and openminded, there is a greater likelihood of success with hypnotic inductions and therapy as a whole.

REFERENCES

Bates, B. L. (1993). Individual differences in response to hypnosis. In J. Rhue, S. Lynn, & I. Kirsch (Eds.), *Handbook of clinical hypnosis*. Washington, DC: American Psychological Association.

Bernheim, H. (1889/1947). *Suggestive therapeutics: A treatise on the nature and uses of hypnotism*. New York, NY: London Book Company.

Christenson, J. (1958). *Dynamics in hypnotic induction*. New York, NY: Macmillan.

Ekman, P. (2003). *Emotions revealed: Recognizing faces and feelings to improve communication and emotional life*. New York, NY: Times Books.

Erickson, M. (1948). Hypnotic psychotherapy. *The Medical Clinics of North America, 32*, 571–583.

Erickson, M. (1956). Deep hypnosis and its induction. In L. M. LeCron (Ed.), *Experimental hypnosis* (pp. 70–114). New York, NY: Macmillan.

Erickson, M., Rossi, E., & Rossi, S. (1976). *Hypnotic realities: The induction of clinical hypnosis and forms of indirect suggestion*. London, UK: Irvington Publishers.

Frauman, D., Lynn, S., & Brentar, J. (1993). *Prevention and therapeutic management of "negative effects" in hypnotherapy*. Washington, DC: American Psychological Association.

Fromm, E. (1980). Values in hypnotherapy. *Psychotherapy: Theory, Research and Practice, 17*, 425–430.

Gill, M., & Brenman, M. (1959). *Hypnosis and related states: Psychoanalytic studies in regression*. Madison, CT: International University Press.

Haley, J. (1958). An interactional explanation of hypnosis. *American Journal of Clinical Hypnosis, 1*, 41–57.

Hassan, S. (2012). *Freedom of mind: Helping loved ones leave controlling people, cults, and beliefs.* Newton, MA: Freedom of Mind Press.

Hess, E. H. (1965). Attitude and pupil size. *Scientific American, 212,* 46–54.

Janet, P. (1925). *Psychological healing: A historical and clinical study.* London, UK: G. Allen & Unwin.

Kirsch, I. (1990). *Changing expectations: A key to effective psychotherapy.* Pacific Grove, CA: Brooks/ Cole.

Lazar, B. S., & Dempster, C. R. (1984). Operator variables in successful hypnotherapy. *International Journal of Clinical and Experimental Hypnosis, 32*(1), 28–40.

Orne, M. T. (1965). Undesirable effects of hypnosis: The determinants and management. *International Journal of Clinical and Experimental Hypnosis, 13*(4), 226–237.

Orne, M., & Dinges, D. (1989). *Comprehensive textbook of psychiatry.* Baltimore, MD: Lippincott Williams & Wilkins.

Overholser, J. (1988). Applied psychological hypnosis: Management of problematic situations. *Professional Psychology: Research and Practice, 19,* 409–415.

Ross, C. A. (2007). Ethics of CIA and military contracting by psychiatrists and psychologists. *Ethical Human Psychology and Psychiatry, 9,* 25–34.

Short, D. (1999). *Hypnosis and children: Analysis of theory and research.* Philadelphia, PA: Brunner/ Mazel.

Short, D. (2014). The blood and guts of experiential psychotherapy. *Psychotherapy in Australia, 21,* 68–75.

Short, D., Erickson, B. A., & Erickson-Klein, R. (2005). *Hope & resiliency: Understanding the psychotherapeutic strategies of Milton H. Erickson, M.D.* London, UK: Crown House.

Speigel, H. (1978). *Trance and treatment.* New York, NY: Basic Books.

Weitzenhoffer, A. M. (1989). *The practice of hypnotism.* New York, NY: Wiley.

Wolberg, L. R. (1948). *Medical hypnosis.* New York, NY: Grune & Stratton.

Yapko, M. D. (2013). *Essentials of hypnosis.* New York, NY: Routledge.

Zeig, J. K. (2014). *The induction of hypnosis: An Ericksonian approach.* Phoenix, AZ: The Milton H. Erickson Foundation Press.

Hypnotic Relaxation Therapy

Gary Elkins

There is an ever-expanding body of knowledge about hypnosis and support for the utilization of hypnotic inductions, therapeutic suggestions, metaphors, and teaching patients how to use self-hypnosis. Further, clinical research has begun to provide greater clarity on the components that contribute to the effectiveness of hypnotic interventions in clinical practice. However, since the term *hypnotherapy* has existed for many years, it has, over time, taken on different meanings for different individuals. Therefore, there is a need for specificity in regard to the methods and theoretical conceptualization of hypnosis in therapy. Specificity allows for study of the mechanisms of hypnosis and ultimately contributes to optimizing hypnosis within the context of therapy.

In response to this need, I identified the term *hypnotic relaxation therapy* (HRT) to signify the particular theoretical conceptualization and underlying principles for hypnotherapy that are discussed in this chapter (Elkins, 2014). HRT arose from my over 40 years of clinical practice as well as from an ongoing program of research into clinical trials of hypnosis and its essentials and mechanisms. My early work with hypnosis was primarily within a psychotherapy practice for the treatment of behavioral health problems. The value of hypnosis is undeniable and there are many case reports and well-designed studies that attest to the fact that hypnosis can be used in a manner to relieve pain, decrease anxiety, change behavior, help people cope with medical procedures (Hammond, 1990), and even reduce hot flashes and improve the physiology of sleep. However, as my research program grew, it became apparent that there was a need to develop a system of hypnotherapy that would clearly define essential components, specify what constitutes a hypnotic relaxation induction, and formulate theoretical perspectives on related concepts such as the unconscious mind and the role of hypnotizability in understanding response to hypnotic interventions. In developing the principles and therapy, I chose the term *hypnotic relaxation therapy* because it is relatively free from the negative historical connotations of "hypnosis" and it more accurately identifies the approach used in clinical practice as well as research in which suggestions for relaxation are used for therapeutic effect. Also, I have found that some patients prefer the term *hypnotic relaxation therapy* as it is most reflective of their experience of using hypnotic relaxation inductions and self-hypnosis that includes focusing of attention, imagery, and a relaxed state to achieve therapeutic goals.

HRT is founded on an evidence-based approach to professional practice. In this regard, the methods of HRT should be considered to be dynamic rather than fixed. The methods are founded upon a desire to utilize "what works." Clinical research is essential to determine the efficacy of interventions, the mechanisms of effects, and the source of discovery at its best (Lynn, Kirsch, Barabasz, Cardena, & Patterson, 2000). Methods that are shown to be effective are integrated and methods that research shows to be ineffective are modified or abandoned. The skilled clinician should be familiar with all of the factors that contribute to clinical competence: relevant research, cultural factors, competent assessment, and clinical skills in achieving a positive therapeutic relationship (Levant, 2005) as well as the methods of HRT. Also, the use of HRT should be limited to one's expertise and areas of specialization and broad knowledge of medical and psychological problems.

In this chapter, I present the theoretical basis of HRT, the meaning and relevance of therapeutic relaxation, the foundational principles, HRT in practice, and a sample transcript of a hypnotic relaxation induction. Also, there is quite a bit of research to support the idea that individual differences in hypnotic abilities exist. However, there is also evidence that clearly indicates that even persons in the low range of hypnotizability can benefit from hypnosis. It may be that individuals in the lower range may require more sessions or that hypnotic interventions may need to be modified to optimize hypnotic responding (such as in combination with other nonhypnotic methods). This has important implications for how HRT is applied and the number of sessions required for a person to achieve therapeutic effects. Measurement of hypnotizability can be a very valuable, but not always necessary, tool for the clinician using HRT. The Elkins Hypnotizability Scale (EHS; Elkins, 2014) was developed for ease of administration by the clinician, time efficiency, and relevance to clinical practice and is discussed in this chapter. We first consider the hypnotic state as an outcome of the process of a hypnotic relaxation induction.

THE HYPNOTIC STATE

The identification of the hypnotic state is fundamental to clinical practice as well as for research into the experiential nature of hypnosis (Fromm, 1987). Hypnosis has been described as a state of mind of focused attention and one in which critical thinking is decreased such that hypnotic suggestions can be more easily accepted and experienced (Spiegel, Greenleaf, & Spiegel, 2000). The state of focused attention and increased receptivity to therapeutic suggestions are developed within a cooperative relationship between the patient and therapist. Thus, hypnosis is defined as a state (Nash, 2005) that can be achieved through the process of a hypnotic induction or through naturally occurring experiences (Barabasz, 2005).

A contemporary definition of hypnosis is "A state of consciousness involving focused attention and reduced peripheral awareness characterized by an enhanced capacity for response to suggestion" (Elkins, Barabasz, Council, & Spiegel, 2015). This concise definition simply identifies the object of interest (hypnosis) and its characteristics. The definition provides a basis for identifying the hypnotic state and, at the same time, allows for alternative theories of the mechanisms as well as inquiries as to whether the hypnotic state may be similar to other states (i.e., meditative, mindfulness, yoga) or unique to hypnosis. Past research

demonstrated a distinct pattern of neurophysiological changes in the brain associated with a hypnotic state, especially in highly suggestible participants (McGeown, Mazzoni, Venneri, & Kirsch, 2009). Neutral hypnosis (without specific suggestions for certain hypnotic phenomena) activates the default mode network including the medial frontal gyrus and anterior cingulate cortex. Related to the default nextwork (Rainville, Hofbauer, Bushnell, Duncan, & Price, 2002), hypnosis has been experimentally shown to reduce sympathetic nervous system activation (Kekecs, Szekely, & Varga, 2016). Posthypnotic induction changes are further evidenced on EEG by an increase of theta and alpha frequency band power in frontal regions, suggesting an increase in activity of the brain's attentional systems (Jamieson & Burgess, 2014), and a whole-brain increase of beta and gamma frequency band power, suggesting decreased neural effort and increased relaxation overall (Cardeña, Jönsson, Terhune, & Marcusson-Clavertz, 2013).

THERAPEUTIC RELAXATION

In clinical practice, hypnotic interventions very often utilize suggestions for eye closure and directly suggest or imply that the hypnotic state can be enhanced with relaxation. The accumulated clinical research provides persuasive evidence that relaxation-based interventions (including hypnosis) have therapeutic benefit. It is an important fact that most investigations and empirical trials of hypnosis have utilized relaxation-based inductions and suggestions. Therefore, HRT emphasizes the use of relaxation-based induction and relaxation (mental and physical experiences are integrated into treatment). Hypnotic relaxation and suggestion have been used in the treatment of disorders such as irritable bowel syndrome (Galovski & Blanchard, 1998; Palsson, Turner, & Whitehead, 2006; Prior, Colgan, & Whorwell, 1990), hot flashes (Elkins et al., 2008; Elkins, 2014), and dermatological disorders (Spanos, Stenstrom, & Johnson, 1988; Spanos, Williams, & Gwynn, 1990), Moreover, hypnotic relaxation and suggestions have been effectively used to induce analgesia and reduce pain during medical procedures (Lang et al., 2000). Hypnotic relaxation may moderate the effects of stress on immunity (Kiecolt-Glaser,

Marucha, Atkinson, & Glaser, 2001). It has also been used with favorable results in the treatment of several mental health conditions including chronic depressive syndromes and posttraumatic stress disorder (Bryant, Creamer, O'Donnell, Silove, & McFarlane, 2008).

Hypnosis using relaxation-based inductions has been shown to have a broad range of applications. Relaxation-based inductions have been shown to be of benefit for general pain management (Brown & Hammond, 2007; Hawkins, 2001; Montgomery, DuHamel, & Redd, 2000) and improving recovery from pain-related procedures (Montgomery, David, Winkel, Silverstein, & Bovbjerg, 2002; Patterson & Ptacek, 1997). Hypnotic relaxation–based interventions have also been studied in cancer-related pain (Elkins, Cheung, Marcus, Palamara, & Rajab, 2004; Néron & Stephenson, 2007), tension and migraine headaches (Olness, MacDonald, & Uden, 1987), labor length and labor pain (Brown & Hammond, 2007), and procedural pain and anxiety (Elkins, Marcus, Bates, Cook, & Rajab, 2006; Enqvist, Björklund, Engman, & Jakobsson, 1997).

Hypnosis with suggestions for mental and physical relaxation along with other suggestions can provide a large analgesic effect for many types of pain and meets the criteria for "well-established treatments." Patterson and Jenson (2003) and Elkins, Jensen, and Patterson (2007) found in recent reviews of the literature that hypnotic relaxation-based interventions for pain relief were found to be superior to placebo for both acute and chronic pain.

It is, however, noteworthy that the hypnotic state is not completely dependent upon relaxation. The hypnotic state of focused attention, absorption, and increased response to suggestion can be achieved during active states. For example, long-distance runners, athletes, musicians, and artists may enter a hypnotic state while eyes are open. One study of "active–alert" hypnosis involved individuals riding a stationary bicycle while receiving hypnotic induction to achieve a hypnotic state (Bányai & Hilgard, 1976). It was shown that hypnotic states can be achieved without relaxation. It is simply that relaxation can be therapeutically beneficial in the treatment of medical and psychological problems. It is no coincidence that many psychological treatments such as systemic desensitization, mental imagery, exposure-based cognitive behavioral therapy, mindfulness stress reduction, and behavioral stress management use suggestions for relaxation akin to hypnotic relaxation intervention. In comparison to methods such as progressive muscle relaxation, HRT may have some advantages as there is an emphasis on both physical and mental relaxation when using HRT.

COMPONENTS OF THE RESPONSE TO HYPNOTIC SUGGESTION

While hypnosis may be defined as "a state of consciousness involving focused attention and reduced peripheral awareness characterized by an enhanced capacity for response to suggestion" (Elkins et al., 2015), it is important to recognize that in the clinical setting, responses to hypnotic suggestions are multiply determined. There are a number of factors that can affect an individual's response to hypnotic suggestion.

Certainly, hypnotizability is an important factor. An individual must have the capacity for achieving a hypnotic state in order to respond to hypnotic inductions. The concept of *dissociation* may explain at least part of the shift to a state of consciousness in which critical thinking is decreased and internal imagery becomes a primary "reality" for the patient in a hypnotic state. The concept of dissociation may be thought of as reflective of psychopathology, such as in dissociative states such as fugue states or dissociative identity disorder. However, it is known that most people who are hypnotizable do not suffer from any of these dissociative disorders. Therefore, it is reasonable to think of dissociation as having a normal or adaptive connotation.

The concept of *adaptive dissociation* is central to HRT. Responses to hypnotic suggestions are affected by a mixture of social–psychological factors and adaptive dissociation. Social–psychological factors refer to processes such as cognitive expectancies (Kirsch, 1985), the context in which a hypnotic induction is completed (Elkins, 2014), and the motivation of the patient (Braffman & Kirsch, 1999). These are powerful factors and individuals who are highly motivated, have a positive expectancy, and have received a hypnotic induction within a professional setting are more likely to cooperate and be able to respond to certain hypnotic suggestions (Kirsch & Lynn, 1998). These factors are important in psychotherapy in general (Kirsch, 1990) and are highly relevant to the adaptive dissociation theory of hypnotic responding.

However, at the heart of hypnotic responding is the concept that the individual is able to enter a hypnotic state, sometimes referred to as a "trance state," in which responses are experienced as automatic, involuntary, and outside of voluntary control. When this occurs, the individual has achieved a degree of dissociation in which conscious control is suspended to a degree and unconscious processes are more dominant in directing responses. Thus, behaviors or feelings that are usually outside of conscious, voluntary control can be achieved. During a hypnotic induction, the patient may be encouraged to "let go" of conscious control, to "not try," and to simply allow responses to occur. In this way, the patient becomes, to a greater or lesser degree, an observer of his or her own thoughts, feelings, and behaviors. Thus, hypnotic responding is a mixture of voluntary/cooperative behavior and involuntary/dissociative behavior. This may be illustrated in Figure 10.1 in which, during a deeper hypnotic state, there is a shift from voluntary/social–psychological factors to involuntary/dissociative factors. Since this process is adaptive (allows the patient to enter a deeper hypnotic state) and collaborative in the clinical context, it is referred to as an adaptive dissociation theory of hypnotic responding (Figure 10.1).

Essentially, the depth of trance refers to the degree to which the individual is able to shift awareness to achieve dissociation and access the unconscious system. As this occurs, responses arise more from the unconscious and are experienced as automatic or involuntary. The deeper the hypnotic state, the more the dissociation is achieved and responses are perceived as occurring involuntarily.

In the hypnotic state, the experiential/unconscious system assumes executive control. Within the adaptive dissociation theory of hypnotic responding, dissociation has a positive function in that it facilitates patients' ability to achieve their goals.

Therefore, adaptive dissociation refers to an individual's ability to achieve a shift in executive control such that there is greater access to the unconscious processes, and responses that occur are beyond simple voluntary effort or role-playing. Responses that are considered "easy" are ones that most people can respond. Easy responses are those that are primarily dependent upon cooperation and voluntary responding (such as suggestions for one to close the eyes or lower an outstretched arm). "Difficult" responses are those that require dissociation to achieve and are involuntarily experienced (such as suggestions for analgesia during major surgery, positive hallucinations in response to hypnotic suggestion, and, to a degree, posthypnotic amnesia). Responses to more difficult hypnotic suggestions are most likely associated with brain alterations from normal waking consciousness.

The social–psychological components of hypnotic responding may blend into dissociative abilities so that in a practical sense, the response to a particular hypnotic suggestion may be a mixture of social–psychological factors and depth of the hypnotic state. The skilled clinician can recognize and utilize all of the components toward the desired therapeutic effect. I now turn attention to the primary principles of HRT as it relates to clinical practice.

HRT ASSUMES ALL COMMUNICATION IS PROCESSED, IN VARYING DEGREES, WITHIN BOTH CONSCIOUS AND UNCONSCIOUS AWARENESS

Central to HRT is the assumption that humans have both a conscious and an unconscious mind. Conscious awareness refers to our capacity to be aware of our external environment, to think rationally and critically, to utilize logic to guide our actions, to engage in abstract thinking, and to exert conscious effort in approaching tasks. The conscious mind is of great benefit and can lead to effective problem solving, scientific analysis, and objective consideration of facts.

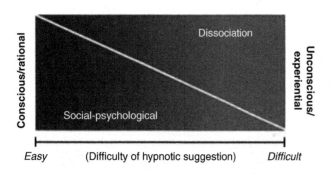

FIGURE 10.1 Adaptive dissociation and hypnotic response.

The unconscious mind also exists but operates in a very different manner. The unconscious is conceptualized as an *experiential system* (Epstein, 1994). The unconscious mind, from the perspective of HRT, is an experiential system that operates automatically and effortlessly. The unconscious mind is emotionally driven, outcome oriented, and is more influenced by experience rather than logic. The language of the unconscious mind is that of images, metaphors, narratives, gut feelings, and direct suggestions. It is slower to change in comparison to the conscious mind and has a very powerful effect on our emotions, physiology, and behavior.

From the perspective of HRT, the conscious and unconscious minds are conceptualized from a social–psychological perspective, specifically Cognitive-Experiential Theory (Epstein & Pacini, 1999). This is a *dual process theory* in which it is assumed that all information is processed at both the conscious and unconscious levels of awareness. However, during a hypnotic state, unconscious processes/the experiential system is more available for influence and the language of the unconscious may be used in formulating hypnotic suggestions (i.e., imagery, metaphors, stories, emotional implications, as well as direct suggestion).

The cognitive–experiential unconscious is quite different from the psychoanalytic unconscious and from the cognitive unconscious (Kihlström, 1990). The psychoanalytic unconscious may be considered the first wave of thinking about the unconscious, emphasizing primary process thinking, the id, and psychodynamics. The second wave of thinking about the unconscious may be referred to as the *cognitive unconscious,* which is devoid of the prior psychoanalytic theories. However, a limitation of the cognitive unconscious is that it did not very well account for the emotionally driven nature of unconscious processes and did not fully differentiate it from the conscious mind.

The third wave of thinking about the unconscious (Epstein, 1973, 1990, 1994, 2003; Epstein & Pacini, 1999) formulates the unconscious as more comprehensive, uniquely operational, and distinct from the conscious mind. During both everyday consciousness and a hypnotic state, information is processed about operations both within and outside of conscious awareness (Hilgard, 1974, 1977); however, it is during hypnosis that unconscious processes are more operational. Table 10.1

TABLE 10.1

COMPARISON OF THE UNCONSCIOUS/EXPERIENTIAL AND CONSCIOUS/RATIONAL SYSTEMS	
Experiential System	**Rational System**
1. Holistic	1. Analytic
2. Emotionally driven	2. Logically driven
3. Outcome oriented	3. Process oriented
4. Influenced by "vibes"/gut feelings	4. Influenced by conscious appraisals
5. Perception is influenced by concrete images, metaphors, and narratives	5. Perception is influenced by abstract symbols, words, and numbers
6. Rapid information processing	6. Slow information processing
7. Slower to change	7. Changes more rapidly
8. Operates automatically, effortless	8. Operates through conscious effort
9. Understanding comes through experience	9. Understanding comes through logic and evidence

provides a representation of the difference and functioning of the unconscious/experiential mind and the conscious/rational mind.

It can be seen that the experiential/unconscious mind is an experiential system that is influenced by images and stories, and is responsive to the emotional content of interventions. In this regard, HRT is best thought of as an experiential therapy. The language of the unconscious includes narratives, stories, feelings, images, vibes, and multilevel communication (Lankton & Lankton, 1983). The focus of HRT is to provide the patient with healing experiences and those healing experiences are created by words and images that are primarily processed by the unconscious mind and utilize the language of the experiential unconscious.

HRT IS MOST EFFECTIVE WITHIN A POSITIVE THERAPEUTIC RELATIONSHIP

Rapport and a positive therapeutic relationship are essential to achieve an optimal response to HRT in the context of psychotherapy or medical procedures. The hypnotherapeutic relationship is collaborative and involves a relationship of trust and confidence. The interests and goals of the patient should be discussed and valued. The common factors associated with therapeutic communication should be utilized (Frank & Frank, 1993; Wampold, 2001). These include a

1. Bond of trust between the hypnotherapist and patient
2. Safe space and time in which a hypnotic induction can be provided
3. Mutual understanding of the presenting problem
4. Hypnotherapeutic plan that is acceptable to the patient
5. Hypnotic intervention that provides acceptable options for overcoming specific difficulties

Prior to initiating a hypnotic induction, the patient should be given information about HRT and any misconceptions about hypnosis should be discussed. The therapist should convey unconditional positive regard and seek to proceed at a pace that is acceptable to the patient. The process of hypnotic induction should be described to the patient and any preferences for induction methods or imagery should be elicited. The cultural and personal background of the patient should be carefully considered and hypnotic interventions modified accordingly. This process of establishing a positive hypnotherapeutic relationship is ongoing and may require several sessions before proceeding to a formal or informal hypnotic induction. If the therapist perceives hesitancy or if the patient expresses a lack of trust, then engaging in a hypnotic induction is best delayed until a positive therapeutic relationship has been established.

A positive relationship is important in most psychotherapy approaches but is especially important in hypnotic interventions. Experiencing hypnosis in the therapeutic context, the patient purposely achieves a hypnotic state in which critical judgment is set aside and hypnotic suggestions are accepted uncritically to a greater or lesser degree. Even the process of asking a patient to close the eyes during a hypnotic induction involves a certain degree of trust and confidence in the hypnotherapist. Establishing a positive therapeutic relationship can be beneficial in reducing resistance and enhancing benefits from HRT.

HRT IS DIRECTED TOWARD EMPOWERING THE PATIENT

During the process of HRT, the symptoms that are presented by the patient are addressed. The relief of symptoms can be empowering for many patients. It is important to keep in mind that the patient's goals and aims for therapy are of primary importance. The patient should be treated with deep respect at all times and the entire hypnotherapy process should be directed toward enhancing the patient's well-being and personal goal achievement. HRT is experiential; therefore, the patient is both receiving hypnotic suggestions and learning the experience of hypnotic relaxation.

Empowering the patient may also involve teaching self-hypnosis. As the patient becomes more familiar with hypnotic relaxation, he or she is able to enter a hypnotic state more quickly. It may be very helpful to make audio recordings of HRT sessions such that the patient can practice hypnotic relaxation at home and reinforce therapeutic suggestions. At other times, it may be very helpful to formally teach patients self-hypnosis. This process is best practiced in session and may be supplemented with audio recordings. The patient may be provided with an outline of the steps for practice of self-hypnosis. An example of self-hypnosis instructions that may be provided within the context of HRT is as follows:

Ten Steps for Self-Hypnosis (Adapted From Elkins, 2014)

1. Roll eyes upward and focus your attention on a particular spot or object.
2. Take a deep breath of air and, as you exhale, allow your eyelids to gently close.
3. Now, focus on your breathing and with each breath of air you breathe out, relax. Allow your body and mind to become more relaxed.
4. Now, allow the relaxation, mental and physical, to become more complete. A wave of relaxation spreads from the top of your head down to your feet.
5. Now, allow one part of your mind to drift to a calm and pleasant place, a place where you are safe and feel secure, calm, and at ease. Go to that place now, where you find more comfort.

6. Now, as you are there . . . deepen this hypnotic relaxation . . . going even deeper, relaxed. Not only deeply <u>physically relaxed</u> but also <u>emotionally relaxed</u>, calm, more at peace, and more at ease. And <u>mentally calm and relaxed</u>, relaxed within your thoughts and feelings and physically deeply relaxed and comfortable.
7. And you are there, in that pleasant place, so relaxed that you notice every good thing that is there.
8. And remaining more relaxed and at ease, feeling more in control of your feelings and allowing a feeling of well-being to be experienced . . . a feeling of self-acceptance and calmness.
9. Now, go even a little deeper, relax . . . deepen the hypnotic relaxation even more now. Head, neck, arms, back, chest, stomach, legs and feet, completely relaxed and comfortable, releasing every worry and every tension now.
10. And now gently and easily return to conscious alertness, taking your own time and at your own pace, in a way that pleases you.

Teaching patients self-hypnosis can have added benefits as the hypnotic state may provide a method to reduce stress, sleep better, or cope with problems. Self-hypnosis can enhance treatment effects and be utilized as a "homework assignment" when integrated within the overall process of HRT.

HRT SESSIONS ARE GOAL DIRECTED

Within HRT, hypnotic suggestions are designed to achieve specific goals. As such, hypnotic suggestions can vary a great deal depending upon the desired effect. Suggestions may be given for relaxation, warmth, analgesia, coolness, calmness, or insight, just to name a few. Specific suggestions are worded toward achieving specific effects. For example, in the treatment of menopausal symptoms such as hot flashes, suggestions are given for feelings of coolness. This may involve images such as walking down a mountain path on a cool or snowy day or feeling a cool breeze on the beach. The response is to perceive coolness and alter both psychological and physiological responses.

Suggestions for warmth would generally be contraindicated for individuals suffering from hot

flashes; however, patients with chronic pain conditions such as chronic back pain or fibromyalgia may benefit from mental imagery and suggestions to achieve feelings of warmth in a painful area such as the lower back or shoulders. Hypnotic suggestions to achieve warmth may include images such as sitting in warm water or feelings of the warmth of sunshine on the back and shoulders.

Developing highly effective, goal-directed hypnotic suggestions requires planning and creativity on the part of the therapist. Formulating hypnotic suggestions should consider the physiology of the symptom, experiential aspects of the problem, and preferences and culture of the patient. This also requires the therapist to structure sessions toward session goals and overall goals. It can be helpful to use rating scales to determine progress in goal achievement and ways to modify hypnotic suggestions as needed.

HRT RECOGNIZES INDIVIDUAL DIFFERENCES IN HYPNOTIZABILITY EXIST

Hypnotizability refers to "an individual's ability to experience suggested alterations in physiology, sensations, emotions, thoughts, or behavior during hypnosis" (Elkins et al., 2015). In the past, terms such as *hypnotic susceptibility* have been used. However, the ability to respond to hypnotic suggestions is best considered as a talent or characteristic within the individual. This emphasizes that the response to suggestion is reflective of the patient's ability and openness to suggestion and the therapy process.

There have been numerous studies that have shown that the distribution of hypnotizability follows a normal curve with a small percentage of people in the low range and a small percentage of people in the high range and most in the midrange of hypnotizability. Estimates are that about 10% of adults are highly hypnotizable (Hilgard, 1965) and a slightly lower number are in the low range. Hypnotizability is a relatively stable trait that can be accurately measured over time. The correlation between initial assessments and reassessment 20 years later was found to be .71 (Piccione, Hilgard, & Zimbardo, 1989), reflecting a high degree of stability in hypnotizability. Recognizing that there are individual differences in hypnotic abilities can give useful information to the therapist. The EHS was developed to assess hypnotizability in both research and clinical practice.

The EHS (Elkins, 2014) was developed in accordance with the following criteria: (a) pleasantness; (b) time efficiency; (c) reliability and validity to assess low, moderate, high, and very high hypnotizables; and (d) ease of use in both clinical and laboratory settings. The EHS has been shown to have very good test–retest reliability (Cronbach's $\alpha = .849$) and convergent validity (correlation with the Stanford Hypnotic Susceptibility Scale–Form C, $r = .821$, $p < .001$; Elkins, 2014).

The EHS consists of 12 items. The administration of the scale involves a standardized hypnotic relaxation induction. The hypnotic induction is followed by deepening suggestions and then hypnotic suggestions of increasing difficulty (from easy to difficult). The items on the EHS consist of a series of hypnotic suggestions for experiences ranging from simple motor responses to more involved imagery and posthypnotic amnesia. A total score (ranging from 0 to 12) is obtained from the EHS, with a higher score indicating a higher level of hypnotic responsiveness. The items of the EHS are as follows:

EHS 1 (subjective arm heaviness)

EHS 2 (arm immobility)

EHS 3 (subjective arm lightness)

EHS 4 (arm levitation)

EHS 5 (elbow lift)

EHS 6 (clear imagery)

EHS 7 (dissociation experience)

EHS 8 (faint rose smell)

EHS 9 (distinct rose smell)

EHS 10 (vague visual hallucination)

EHS 11 (distinct visual hallucination)

EHS 12 (posthypnotic amnesia)

The full EHS protocol presentation is beyond the page limitations of this chapter; however, the scale and administration protocol along with scoring criteria have been previously published (Elkins, 2014). The administration of the EHS is pleasant and may be utilized to facilitate an initial hypnotic induction as well as to provide an indication of hypnotizability in a given patient.

HRT USES A VARIETY OF METHODS FOR HYPNOTIC INDUCTION, SUGGESTION, AND FACILITATING THERAPEUTIC EXPERIENCES

Hypnotic inductions generally involve a focus of attention. However, the focus of attention may be on an object, a feeling, a thought, or even a focus on breathing. In addition, hypnotic suggestions may be formulated in a variety of ways. For some patients, suggestions may be formulated in a directive manner while, for others, more permissive suggestions may be more effective. Given the experiential nature of HRT, hypnotic suggestions may be formulated as images, stories, narratives, or metaphors. The hypnotherapist should be mindful that hypnotic suggestions can be facilitated through sound and quality of voice as well as through nonverbal cues and gestures. Creativity and skill in delivery of hypnotic suggestions is as important as the specific wording or transcript that may be used.

HRT IS BOTH STRUCTURED AND INDIVIDUALIZED

HRT generally progresses through several phases. The initial sessions are devoted to completing a case formulation, assessing hypnotizability, developing a positive therapeutic relationship, and orienting the patient to the process of hypnosis in therapy. Also, in the initial sessions, goals are identified and, when possible, rating scales are selected to measure progress in goal achievement. Rating scales can involve simple visual analog ratings (i.e., 0–100 numeric scales) or brief psychometric measures such as the Psychological Distress Profile (Elkins & Johnson, 2015). The first hypnotic relaxation induction may be via administration of the

EHS or follow a structured transcript to introduce hypnotic relaxation and therapeutic suggestions.

The focus of the second stage of HRT involves increasing individualization of hypnotic suggestions and intervention. This involves review of the patient's experiences and progress and individual preferences. The hypnotherapist should conduct posthypnotic inquiry to gather as many details as necessary to achieve a good understanding of the patient's individual responses and preferences for mental imagery and suggestion. The process of individualization also involves suggestions to achieve specific goals as may be identified in the hypnotherapy process.

The third phase of HRT involves continued individualization of the specific hypnotic suggestions and also involves teaching self-hypnosis. Initially, the patient may be provided with audio recordings of sessions for home practice. This is particularly useful when the patient presents with a symptom that can be modified through self-practice of hypnotic relaxation. Examples include problems such as pain, poor sleep, fears or anxieties, and hot flashes. As the patient learns self-hypnosis, the process of hypnotic relaxation may be applied to other areas of the patient's life as may be appropriate.

The last phase of HRT is focused upon ways of maintaining treatment gains. This may involve "booster sessions" or other plans for follow-up. The patient may gain greater insight during HRT, and a final focus of treatment may involve a sense of closure to old issues or problems.

HRT IS INTEGRATIVE

HRT may be utilized as a primary treatment modality; however, it is most often integrated with other evidence-based interventions such as cognitive behavioral therapy. HRT sessions generally involve a hypnotic induction, but the overall therapy process is likely to include interventions such as cognitive restructuring, insight-oriented psychotherapy, and behavioral interventions. HRT is integrated with other modalities to achieve the goals for each session as well as overall treatment goals.

For example, HRT might be integrated with supportive counseling, marital counseling, lifestyle analysis, or exploring underlying unconscious issues. HRT can be integrated with biofeedback, relaxation training, mindfulness, or other methods of stress management. In the treatment of sleep disturbance, for instance, HRT may be integrated with sleep hygiene instructions, sleep restriction therapy, or sleep medications.

HRT MAY BE DIRECTED TOWARD DEVELOPING COPING SKILLS, SYMPTOM RELIEF, FACILITATING INSIGHT, OR RELAPSE PREVENTION

There are four broadly defined uses of HRT. First, HRT can be effectively used in the development of coping skills. As HRT involves therapeutic relaxation, it can be applied to reduce anxiety, to manage stress, and to calm the mind. Like mindfulness practice, persons who are skilled in the use of hypnotic relaxation can increase their awareness of their feelings and learn to maintain a more calm state even in the face of daily hassles and difficult circumstances.

Second, HRT can be used for symptom alteration or symptom reduction. When HRT is used for symptom alteration, hypnotic suggestions are especially designed either to modify the experience of the symptom or to alter the physiology that underlies it. In the case of pain, suggestions may be given to alter the experience of pain such that it changes in sensation. Pain may be suggested to become smaller, of shorter duration, less intense, or replaced with another sensation such as warmth or tingling. Suggestions can also be given for the patient to ignore the symptom such that the perception of pain "fades into the background" of conscious awareness. Posthypnotic suggestions are usually used when symptom alteration is a primary goal.

A third use of HRT is to facilitate insight. Hypnotic relaxation inductions involve a hypnotic state in which conscious defenses are lowered and unconscious processes may become more available. Direct suggestions for insight may be given or hypnoprojective methods may be utilized to gain greater insight into symptoms. For example, suggestions to visualize a box or a trunk in which some important information may be contained may be utilized to allow the patient to project feelings or other awareness onto material that emerges from looking into the imaginary box or trunk.

Fourth, HRT can be used to assist with relapse prevention. This may involve the regular practice of hypnotic relaxation techniques or self-hypnosis on an ongoing basis even after formal therapy sessions end. HRT used in combination with posthypnotic suggestions can help maintain relapse prevention. Also, as noted earlier, HRT can be integrated with other nonhypnotic methods such as bibliotherapy, group therapy, or supportive counseling to maintain gains that are already achieved in therapy.

HRT USES A BIO-PSYCHO-SOCIAL FORMULATION IN CASE FORMULATION AND TREATMENT PLANNING

Case conceptualization in HRT considers the whole person: past history, physical and medical history, psychological factors, social environment, mental status, and experiential (unconscious) representations of the presenting problem or symptom. Case formulation involves conducting a detailed history and constructing a list of problems and strengths. It involves gathering sufficient information or conducting tests to arrive at an accurate diagnosis. The specific components of case formulation and treatment planning involve

- *History of presenting problem:* The history of the presenting problem can help clarify the dynamics in the case and set goals for resolution of the presenting symptom or problem.
- *Timeline and key events:* The timeline and key events in the person's life are reviewed toward greater understanding of factors that contribute to the patient's worldview and issues that may need to be resolved.
- *Physical factors:* Physical causes of symptoms should be evaluated and medical referral considered if appropriate. Symptoms such as anxiety and pain can have physical causes that should be ruled out or evaluated as the history dictates.
- *Psychological factors:* Contributing psychological factors may be determined by a skillful clinical interview. Also, psychological testing is often considered in order to determine the nature and intensity of psychological factors.
- *Social environment:* Often, symptoms and problems can only be understood in the context of the patient's social environment. This can include cultural factors as well as the patient's extended home, work, or family structure and environment.
- *Mental status:* A mental status examination should be conducted to determine the patient's present mental and emotional functioning and cognitive status and to rule out any serious psychopathology that may be a contraindication to hypnosis.
- *Strengths and weaknesses:* It is usually helpful to make a list of the patient's areas of strengths and weaknesses. Strengths can be a source of focus and utilized to build upon strategies for interventions.
- *Diagnosis:* An accurate diagnosis is essential for effective treatment planning. Accurate diagnosis can also provide guidance for an overall treatment plan and integration of HRT with other psychological or medical therapies.
- *Hypnotic experience and ability:* It is usually very helpful to obtain an estimate of the patient's hypnotizability. This may be accomplished through formal assessment such as administration of the EHS or through informal means during the ongoing process of monitoring response to HRT sessions.
- *Experiential representations:* Consistent with the theory of HRT that all information is processed at both conscious and unconscious levels of awareness, identifying how the presenting problem is represented within the unconscious/experiential system is a highly useful aspect of HRT case formulation. The patient's experiential representation of his or her symptom or problem is likely to come more to the surface during hypnotic relaxation induction with specific suggestions for imagery of the symptom. It is likely that the patient's symptoms can be represented in some symbolic or narrative form or as an image. The existence of the unconscious mind, that is, the experiential system should be discussed with the patient. This discussion can include questions to explore possible experiential representations of problems or symptoms. For example, the following questions may be useful in exploration symptoms:

1. *"Can you imagine the symptom as a shape, color, animal, or object?"*

2. *"Have you ever had a dream about the symptom; how was the symptom represented in the dream? Was it represented in any symbolic manner?"*

3. *"Does there seem to be any emotion associated with the symptom? Does it ever bring to your awareness feeling angry, fearful, or calm?"*

4. *"Can you imagine any way that the symptom could change to become either better or worse? How would it change if it got better?"*

The information is used in the case conceptualization and can provide very useful guidance in forming specific hypnotic suggestions to be used in HRT in subsequent sessions.

BECOMING A CLINICIAN SKILLED IN HYPNOTIC RELAXATION THERAPY

Becoming skilled in HRT takes considerable study and practice. Attending workshops can be very useful, as can reading and remaining current on the ever-expanding literature on clinical research into hypnosis as well as other psychological and medical therapies. When utilized by a skilled clinician, HRT is a powerful tool that can be used with creativity and effectiveness. The following provides a transcript of an HRT induction that includes some areas where individualized suggestions may be inserted to meet the needs of particular patients seen in clinical settings.

HYPNOTIC RELAXATION INDUCTION WITH INDIVIDUALIZATION (ADAPTED FROM ELKINS, 2014)

Focusing of Attention

"All hypnotic inductions begin with a focus of attention . . . and for our purposes today . . . you can settle into the chair where you are sitting . . . and when you are ready to begin to enter a comfortable hypnotic state . . . closing your eyes . . . as the eye lids close . . . focusing your attention on your breathing . . . and notice the feelings that go along with breathing in and breathing out . . . notice the coolness of the air in your nostrils as you breathe

in . . . and the feeling of letting go . . . as you breathe out . . . soon becoming more and more relaxed . . . somehow each breath of air seems to take you into a deeper and more relaxed state . . . where you can accomplish the things you wish to accomplish today. . . ."*

Initial Suggestions for Relaxation

"And allowing the relaxation to come to you, easily and naturally. . . . At times you may think of the word relax as you breathe out . . . and yet at other times, the relaxation just becomes more complete without your having to do anything at all . . . just noticing relaxation . . . more and more . . . your forehead relaxes . . . your neck . . . your jaw . . . goes limp and so relaxed . . . your shoulders . . . your back . . . and this profound relaxation . . . now . . . can spread into your arms . . . they become limp and heavy . . . the hands relax . . . back and stomach relax . . . legs become relaxed and limp . . . even your toes and feet become more and more calm . . . more and more . . . relaxed . . . as you drift into a deeper hypnotic state. . . ."

Encouraging Fading of the Generalized Reality Orientation

". . . And as this occurs . . . other things begin to fade into the background . . . awareness of calmness . . . and . . . changes in sensations naturally occur. . . . At times you may notice a heaviness in your arms and legs . . . and . . . at other times . . . it may change into a floating or rocking sensation . . . as if you were just floating in space . . . and as this occurs, the relaxation becomes a little deeper . . . blood pressure may become a little less . . . heart rate a little slower . . . be aware of your own inner experience . . . as other things fade into the background . . . more . . . and more."

Deepening Suggestions

"And it is possible to go into an even deeper hypnotic state . . . the deeper the relaxation . . . the better the response. . . . Letting go . . . and finding

that as I count the numbers from 10 to 1 it is possible to become so deeply absorbed in this experience . . . the hypnotic state becomes deeper and deeper. . . .

10 . . . allowing a wave of good relaxation to come to you . . . it spreads across your forehead . . . across your face . . . letting go of all tension . . . drifting deeper . . .

9 . . . a relaxation that now spreads across your shoulders. . . . They slump . . . any tension that has remained . . . just begins to drift away . . . and is replaced with comfort . . . calmness . . .

8 . . . the kind of calm relaxed feeling you experienced before on a pleasant day . . . a day at Fort Parker State Park . . . a place where you feel safe and secure . . . a place where it is possible to feel at ease . . . as you go there with a part of your mind . . . noticing everything that is there on this particular day . . . perhaps you are sitting outside . . . so that you can look out . . . and see the lake . . . the peaceful water . . . the surface of the water is calm . . . and it is that time of day . . . when it is peaceful . . . perhaps evening time . . . and notice all the beautiful colors across the sky . . . as the sun is setting . . .

7 . . . and take a deep breath of air and go even deeper . . . more relaxed, more calm . . .

6 . . . and the tension just flows out of you . . . as if it were all flowing out of the bottoms of your feet. . . . The shoulders slump . . . the arms become limp . . . even the fingers of each hand are limp and so deeply relaxed . . .

5 . . . the muscles of the back . . . and stomach relax . . . breathing becomes easier . . . so calming . . . as you look out on the lake . . . drifting into a deeper hypnotic state . . .

4 . . . legs relax . . . your right leg becomes limp and comfortable . . . the left leg . . . so relaxed . . . no tension . . . no stress . . . drifting deeper . . .

3 . . . going deeper as the relaxation becomes more complete . . . feet become very deeply relaxed. . . . They are limp . . . and all the

tension . . . any that has remained drifts away . . . flowing out the bottoms of your feet . . .

2 . . . and notice the calmness . . . almost there . . .

1 . . . so deeply relaxed."

Setting the Overall Session Goal

". . . And within this relaxed state it is possible to achieve greater control . . . this symptom can become less and less . . . today . . . it soon becomes less and less. . . ." [Here individualized imagery may be suggested based upon the patient's needs and preferences.]

Mental Imagery and Dissociation

"So that . . . your mind can drift to other times and places where you have found comfort . . . real comfort . . . no tension . . . no stress . . . no headache . . . so that as you hear my voice . . . a part of your mind can take you to a pleasant place [Here individualized imagery may be suggested based upon the patient's needs and preferences.] *. . . a part of your mind . . . remembers the comfort that you experienced . . . there . . . and so you do go there again . . . a good place to be . . . nodding your head when you are there . . . very good. . . . and it is a pleasant day . . . are you there? . . . Nodding your head yes as you are . . . very good . . . and as you notice the tingly feeling . . . and the symptom becomes less and less* [Here individualized imagery may be suggested based upon the patient's needs and preferences.] *. . . and as you notice this . . . nodding your head yes . . . very good . . . it becomes less and less . . . like a sound that has been too loud . . . and it becomes softer and softer . . . like soft gentle music . . . the soft gentle sound of the waves coming in on the shore and going back out . . . each wave takes you to deeper comfort . . . more control . . . no stress . . . no headache . . . so calm. . . ."* [Here individualized imagery may be suggested based upon the patient's needs and preferences.]

Reinforcement of Response

" . . . And you have done very well today . . . and taking from this experience . . . from this

experience of hypnotic relaxation . . . whatever you need . . . to achieve and continue to achieve the control . . . you have done very well. . . ."

Posthypnotic Suggestion

"And in the future . . . you will find . . . that each time you experience this hypnotic relaxation . . . it will be possible to go to your pleasant place [Here individualized imagery may be suggested based upon the patient's needs and preferences.] *. . . or wherever you need to go . . . and find comfort . . . and as you do . . . headaches will become less and less . . . less frequent . . . less severe . . . and this will be a pleasant experience . . . so that headaches . . . more and more become a distant memory . . . that fades into the background. . . ."*

Alerting

"Now . . . in a moment . . . returning to conscious alertness . . . normal sensations return to your arms . . . your legs . . . returning to conscious alertness in your own time and pace . . . soon your eyelids can open . . . when you are ready for them to open . . . and as they do open . . . returning . . . all the way . . . back to conscious alertness . . . in your own time and pace as I count from 1 to 4. . . . 1. . . . 2. . . . 3. . . . 4. . . ."

Posthypnotic Inquiry

After obtaining the second rating of the target symptom, the hypnotherapist should ask the patient about his or her experience during the session in order to determine any additional or alternative preferences for mental imagery.

"Between now and next week, would you please continue to practice with either the CD from the first session or the one today? Good. When you practice, remember that you just need a time and place where you will not be interrupted; and a place where you can either sit with good support for your head, neck, and shoulders, or lay down. It is important that you aim for daily practice. It can be whatever time of the day that works best for you. For example, continuing to practice in the evening or before you go to sleep is fine for some of the times. However, please practice at other times

also so that you get the full benefit. Please also notice any experience during your practice that may be helpful to let me know about. Just as you did today, notice any images, feelings, or memories that occur as you practice. I am interested in the details of your experience and what helps you the most."

CONCLUSION

In summary, HRT is a particular system or approach to hypnotherapy. It involves a careful case formulation and treatment planning that capitalizes on the evolving body of empirical evidence for hypnotic relaxation interventions and psychotherapy. It is both structured and individualized and considers that all information is processed at both the conscious (rational) and unconscious (experiential) levels of awareness. It is a highly integrative therapy that may be directed toward the development of coping skills, symptom relief/alteration, facilitating insight, or relapse prevention. Assessment of hypnotizability is considered an important tool, as individual differences in hypnotic abilities exist and therapy can be modified to adjust to these individual differences. Adaptive dissociation theory integrates consideration of both social–psychological factors and dissociation as relevant in response to specific hypnotic suggestions. HRT is most effective within a positive therapeutic relationship and in consideration of the patient's experiential representations of his or her problems or symptoms. The goal of HRT is to empower the patient, and teaching self-hypnosis is often a part of the overall HRT intervention strategy. HRT is an experiential therapy that may complement other evidence-based therapies. The methods used in HRT vary a great deal and continue to expand as knowledge about hypnosis continues to become more sophisticated and well established.

REFERENCES

Bányai, E. I., & Hilgard, E. R. (1976). A comparison of active-alert hypnotic induction with traditional relaxation induction. *Journal of Abnormal Psychology, 85*(2), 218–224.

Barabasz, A. F. (2005). Whither spontaneous hypnosis: A critical issue for practitioners and researchers. *American Journal of Clinical Hypnosis*, 48(2-3), 91–97. doi:10.1080/00029157.2005.10401501

Braffman, W., & Kirsch, I. (1999). Imaginative suggestibility and hypnotizability: An empirical analysis. *Journal of Personality and Social Psychology*, 77(3), 578–587.

Brown, D. C., & Hammond, C. D. (2007). Evidence-based clinical hypnosis in obstetrics, labor and delivery and preterm labor. *International Journal of Clinical and Experimental Hypnosis*, 55(3), 355–371.

Bryant, R. A., Creamer, M., O'Donnell, M., Silove, D., & McFarlane, A. C. (2008). A multisite study of initial respiration rate and heart rate as predictors of posttraumatic stress disorder. *Journal of Clinical Psychiatry*, 6(11), 1694–1701.

Cardeña, E., Jönsson, P., Terhune, D. B., & Marcusson-Clavertz, D. (2013). The neurophenomenology of neutral hypnosis. *Cortex*, 49(2), 375–385. doi:10.1016/j.cortex.2012.04.001

Elkins, G. (2014). *Hypnotic relaxation therapy: Principles and applications*. New York, NY: Springer Publishing Company.

Elkins, G. R., Barabasz, A. F., Council, J. R., & Spiegel, D. (2015). Advancing research and practice: The revised APA Division 30 definition of hypnosis. *American Journal of Clinical Hypnosis*, 57(4), 378–385.

Elkins, G. R., Cheung, A., Marcus, J., Palamara, L., & Rajab, H. (2004). Hypnosis to reduce pain in cancer survivors with advanced disease: A prospective study. *Journal of Cancer Integrative Medicine*, 2(4), 167–172.

Elkins, G., Jensen, M. P., & Patterson, D. R. (2007). Hypnotherapy for the management of chronic pain. *International Journal of Clinical and Experimental Hypnosis*, 55(3), 275–287.

Elkins, G., & Johnson, A. (2015). *Psychological distress profile*. Menlo Park, CA: Mind Garden.

Elkins, G., Marcus, J., Bates, J., Rajab, M., & Cook, T. (2006). Intensive hypnotherapy for smoking cessation: A prospective study. *International Journal of Clinical and Experimental Hypnosis*, 54(3), 303–315. doi:10.1080/00207140600689512

Elkins, G., Marcus, J., Stearns, V., Perfect, M., Rajab, M. H., Ruud, C., . . . Keith, T. (2008). Randomized trial of a hypnosis intervention for treatment of hot flashes among breast cancer survivors. *Journal of Clinical Oncology: Official Journal of the American Society of Clinical Oncology*, 26(31), 5022–5026. doi:10.1200/JCO.2008.16.6389

Enqvist, B., Björklund, C., Engman, M., & Jakobsson, J. (1997). Preoperative hypnosis reduces postoperative vomiting after surgery of the breasts: A prospective, randomized and blinded study. *Acta Anaesthesiologica Scandinavica*, 41(8), 1028–1032.

Epstein, S. (1973). The self-concept revisited, or a theory of a theory. *The American Psychologist*, 28(5), 404–416.

Epstein, S. (1990). Cognitive-experiential self-theory. In L. Pervin (Ed.), *Handbook of personality: Theory and research* (pp. 165–192). New York, NY: Guilford Press.

Epstein, S. (1994). Integration of the cognitive and the psychodynamic unconscious. *The American Psychologist*, 49(8), 709–724.

Epstein, S. (2003). Cognitive-experiential self-theory of personality. In I. B. Weiner (Ed.), *Handbook of psychology* (pp. 159–184). Hoboken, NJ: John Wiley & Sons.

Epstein, S., & Pacini, R. (1999). Some basic issues regarding dual-process theories from the perspective of cognitive-experiential self-theory. In S. Chaiken & Y. Trope (Ed.), *Dual-process theories in social psychology* (pp. 462–482). New York, NY: Guilford Press.

Frank, J. D., & Frank, J. B. (1993). *Persuasion and healing: A comparative study of psychotherapy* (3rd ed.). Baltimore, MD: Johns Hopkins University Press.

Fromm, E. (1987). Significant developments in clinical hypnosis during the past 25 years. *International Journal of Clinical and Experimental Hypnosis*, 35(4), 215–230.

Galovski, T. E., & Blanchard, E. B. (1998). Treatment of irritable bowel syndrome with hypnotherapy. *Applied Psychophysiological Biofeedback*, 23(4), 219–232.

Hammond, D. C. (1990). *Handbook of hypnotic suggestions and metaphors*. New York, NY: W. W. Norton.

Hawkins, R. M. F. (2001). A systematic meta-review of hypnosis as an empirically supported treatment for pain. *Pain Reviews*, 8(2), 47–73.

Hilgard, E. R. (1965). *Hypnotic susceptibility*. New York, NY: Harcourt, Brace & Jovanovich.

Hilgard, E. R. (1974). Toward a neo-dissociation theory: Multiple cognitive controls in human functioning. *Perspectives in Biology and Medicine*, 17(3), 301–316.

Hilgard, E. R. (1977). *Divided consciousness: Multiple controls in human thought and action*. New York, NY: Wiley.

Jamieson, G. A., & Burgess, A. P. (2014). Hypnotic induction is followed by state-like changes in the organization of EEG functional connectivity in the theta and beta frequency bands in high-hypnotically susceptible individuals. *Frontiers in Human Neuroscience*, 8(210). doi:10.3389/fnhum.2014.00528

Kekecs, Z., Szekely, A., & Varga, K. (2016). Alterations in electrodermal activity and cardiac parasympathetic tone during hypnosis. *Psychophysiology*, 53(2), 268–277.

Kiecolt-Glaser, J. K., Marucha, P. T., Atkinson, C., & Glaser, R. (2001). Hypnosis as a modulator of cellular immune dysregulation during acute stress. *Journal of Consulting and Clinical Psychology*, 69(4), 674–682.

Kihlström, J. F. (1990). The psychological unconscious. In L. Pervin (Ed.), *Handbook of personality: Theory and research* (pp. 445–464). New York, NY: Guilford Press.

Kirsch, I. (1985). Response expectancy as a determinant of experience and behavior. *American Psychologist, 40*, 1189–1202.

Kirsch, I. (1990). *Changing expectations: A key to effective psychotherapy*. Pacific Grove, CA: Brooks/Cole.

Kirsch, I., &Lynn, S. J. (1998). Dissociation theories of hypnosis. *Psychological Bulletin, 223*, 100–115.

Lang, E. V., Benotsch, E. G., Fick, L. J., Lutgendorf, S., Berbaum, M. L., Berbaum, K. S., & Spiegel, D. (2000). Adjunctive non-pharmacological analgesia for invasive medical procedures: A randomized trial. *The Lancet, 355*(9214), 1486–1490.

Lankton, S., & Lankton, C. (1983). *The answer within: A clinical framework of Ericksonian hypnotherapy*. New York, NY: Brunner Mazel.

Levant, R. (2005). *Report of the 2005 Presidential Task Force on Evidence-Based Practice. American Psychological Association Evidence Based Practice Final Report*, 1–28.

Lynn, S. J., Kirsch, I., Barabasz, A., Cardeña, E., & Patterson, D. (2000). Hypnosis as an empirically supported clinical intervention: The state of the evidence and a look to the future. *International Journal of Clinical and Experimental Hypnosis, 48*(2), 239–259.

McGeown, W. J., Mazzoni, G., Venneri, A., & Kirsch, I. (2009). Hypnotic induction decreases anterior default mode activity. *Consciousness and Cognition, 18*, 848–855.

Montgomery, G. H., David, D., Winkel, G., Silverstein, J. H., & Bovbjerg, D. H. (2002). The effectiveness of adjunctive hypnosis with surgical patients: A meta-analysis. *Anesthesia and Analgesia, 94*(6), 1639–1645.

Montgomery, G. H., DuHamel, K. N., & Redd, W. H. (2000). A meta-analysis of hypnotically induced analgesia: How effective is hypnosis? *International Journal of Clinical Hypnosis, 48*(2), 138–153.

Nash, M. R. (2005). The importance of being earnest when crafting definitions: Science and scientism are not the same thing. *International Journal of Clinical and Experimental Hypnosis, 53*(3), 265–280.

Néron, S., & Stephenson, R. (2007). Effectiveness of hypnotherapy with cancer patients' trajectory: Emesis, acute pain, and analgesia and anxiolysis in procedures. *International Journal of Clinical and Experimental Hypnosis, 55*(3), 336–354.

Olness, K., MacDonald, J. T., & Uden, D. L. (1987). Comparison of self-hypnosis and propranolol in the treatment of juvenile classic migraine. *Pediatrics, 79*(4), 593–597.

Palsson, O. S., Turner, M. J., & Whitehead, W. E. (2006). Hypnosis home treatment for irritable bowel syndrome: A pilot study. *International Journal of Clinical and Experimental Hypnosis, 54*(1), 85–99.

Patterson, D. R., & Jensen, M. P. (2003). Hypnosis and clinical pain. *Psychological Bulletin, 129*, 495–521.

Patterson, D. R., & Ptacek, J. T. (1997). Baseline pain as a moderator of hypnotic analgesia for burn injury treatment. *Journal of Consulting and Clinical Psychology, 65*(1), 60–67.

Piccione, C., Hilgard, E. R., & Zimbardo, P. G. (1989). On the degree of stability of measured hypnotizability over a 25-year period. *Journal of Personality and Social Psychology, 56*(2), 289–295.

Prior, A., Colgan, S. M., & Whorwell, P. J. (1990). Changes in rectal sensitivity after hypnotherapy in patients with irritable bowel syndromes. *Gut, 31*(8), 896–898. doi:10.1136/gut.31.8.896

Rainville, P., Hofbauer, R. K., Bushnell, M. C., Duncan, G. H., & Price, D. D. (2002). Hypnosis modulates activity in brain structures involved in the regulation of consciousness. *Journal of Cognitive Neuroscience, 14*(6), 887–901. doi:10.1162/089892902760191117

Spanos, N. P., Stenstrom, R. J., & Johnson, J. C. (1988). Hypnosis, placebo, and suggestion in the treatment of warts. *Psychosomatic Medicine, 50*(3), 245–260.

Spanos, N. P., Williams, V., & Gwynn, M. I. (1990). Effects of hypnotic, placebo, and salicylic acid treatments on wart regression. *Psychosomatic Medicine, 52*(1), 109–114.

Spiegel, H., Greenleaf, M., & Spiegel, D. (2000). Hypnosis. In B. J. Sadock & V. A. Sadock (Eds.), *Kaplan and Sadock's comprehensive textbook of psychiatry* (7th ed., Vol. 2, pp. 2138–2146). Philadelphia, PA: Lippincott Williams & Wilkins.

Wampold, B. E. (2001). *The great psychotherapy debate: Models, methods, and findings*. Mahwah, NJ: Lawrence Erlbaum.

Cognitive Hypnotherapy

Assen Alladin

Traditionally, hypnotherapy, as an adjunctive therapy, has been combined with other psychotherapies. However, the blending has not always been driven by a coherent theory of integration; it has vacillated from being very systematic to being outright idiosyncratic (Alladin & Amundson, 2011). This chapter describes cognitive hypnotherapy (CH), a model of integrative hypnotherapy that provides an evidence-based framework for combining clinical practice and research. CH combines hypnotherapy with cognitive behavioral therapy (CBT) in the management of emotional disorders. In this model of clinical practice, assimilation of techniques is based on case formulation and empirical findings. This blended version of clinical practice meets the criteria for an assimilative model of integrated psychotherapy, which is considered the latest and the best integrative psychotherapy model for synthesizing both theory and empirical findings (Gold & Stricker, 2006). Moreover, it provides an *additive design* for studying the effect of hypnosis when it is combined with other psychotherapies. Furthermore, this chapter takes a *transdiagnostic* approach to understanding and treating emotional disorders (e.g., Barlow, 2002). Because various emotional disorders (e.g., anxiety and depression) share similar pathophysiological pathways, a unified treatment protocol is described to address the factors that underlie all emotional disorders, rather than focusing on techniques targeted at disorder-specific symptoms (e.g., panic attacks in panic disorder, excessive worry in generalized anxiety disorder). Before describing the treatment components of CH, the definition of emotional disorders is explored and the effectiveness of CH as an integrative therapy is briefly reviewed.

EMOTIONAL DISORDERS AS A TRANSDIAGNOSTIC SYNDROME

Emotional disorders refer to a spectrum of psychological conditions, such as anxiety, depression, dissociation, somatization, and trauma-related problems. A person with an emotional disorder is characterized by a tendency to experience precipitous increases in negative affect in response to environmental stimuli, and to interpret the subsequent experience as being harmful (Andrews, 1990, 1996; Brown & Barlow, 2009; Payne, Ellard, Farchione, Fairholme, & Barlow, 2014; Sauer-Zavala et al., 2012). The unification of emotional disorders as a transdiagnostic syndrome is based on findings from recent research, which suggest that (a) various emotional disorders share similar etiological pathways or pathophysiological processes in the genesis and presentation of symptoms; (b) there are high rates of comorbidity amongst emotional disorders (Wilamowska et al., 2010); and (c) psychological treatments targeting a specific emotional disorder often lead to improvements in comorbid disorders (Barlow et al., 2011; Brown, Antony, & Barlow, 1995; Tsao, Lewin, & Craske, 1998; Tsao, Mystkowski, Zucker, & Craske, 2002).

Barlow (1991, 2000, 2002; Suarez, Bennett, Goldstein, & Barlow, 2009), in his *triple vulnerability theory*, has described in detail how a set of vulnerabilities or diatheses can interact to produce anxiety disorders or related emotional disorders. The triple vulnerability theory incorporates three sets of predisposition that interact to produce symptoms: (a) a generalized biological vulnerability, (b) a generalized psychological vulnerability, and (c) a specific psychological vulnerability emerging from early learning. Much of the research on generalized biological and psychological vulnerabilities has focused on the core temperamental dimension of *neuroticism* (also labeled *negative affect, behavioral inhibition,* or *trait anxiety*), which is an enduring tendency to experience negative affect (Brown, Chorpita, & Barlow, 1998; Gershuny & Sher, 1998; Kasch, Rottenberg, Arnow, & Gotlib, 2002; Watson, Clark, & Carey, 1988). A generalized biological vulnerability involves nonspecific genetic contributions to the development of neuroticism. Early life experiences that contribute to a generalized psychological vulnerability, or diathesis, consist of negative, particularly unpredictable or uncontrollable, events. This diathesis in turn leads to the development of neuroticism later on in life. The contribution of these three predisposing factors in the manifestation of symptoms of generalized anxiety disorder (GAD) and major depressive disorder (MDD) can be illustrated by the case of Fred (discussed later in his chapter). Whenever Fred got stressed out, he would experience heightened negative reactivity (due to his biological predisposition) and would immediately begin to catastrophize about his symptoms (psychological vulnerability), convinced that he would not be able to deal with the discomfort and embarrassment (lack of confidence based on childhood emotional injuries). Consequently, he would present symptoms of either GAD or MDD, depending on the interpretation and perceived consequences of his negative reactivity and affect.

Barlow et al. (2011), based on evidence that psychological treatments targeted at a specific emotional disorder often lead to improvements in comorbid disorders (Brown et al., 1995; Tsao et al., 1998; Tsao et al., 2002), developed a *unified protocol* (UP) for transdiagnostic treatment of emotional disorders. UP is a cognitive behavioral intervention specifically developed to treat anxiety, depression, and dissociative, somatoform, and trauma-related disorders (Sauer-Zavala et al., 2012). However, the overall aim of UP is not to address disorder-specific symptoms (e.g., panic attacks in panic disorder, excessive worry in generalized anxiety disorder), but the factors that underlie all emotional disorders, such as neuroticism. Preliminary data support the hypothesis that treatment targeted at common underlying factors decrease symptoms across various emotional disorders (Ellard, Fairholme, Boisseau, Farchione, & Barlow, 2010; Payne et al., 2014).

Specifically, UP targets heightened negative reactivity to emotions by identifying maladaptive responses to emotions and developing more effective strategies to manage these experiences (Ellard et al., 2010). To achieve these goals, UP uses seven separate, but interrelated, treatment modules:

1. Motivational interview
2. Psychoeducation about adaptive functions of emotions
3. Learning skills to relate to negative emotions as they occur, including increasing present-focused awareness and acceptance of emotions
4. Cognitive flexibility with consequences of emotions
5. Attention to behaviors that may function to avoid emotions
6. Attending to internal experience
7. Exposure to in vivo exercises

These strategies implemented by UP practitioners are distilled from decades of research on effective cognitive and behavioral treatments for anxiety and mood disorders (see Barlow, 2002) and from more recent findings on adaptive emotion regulation (e.g., Campbell-Sills, Barlow, Brown, & Hofmann, 2006). The central tenet across all these treatment modules is to help patients with emotional disorders cultivate reduced negative reactivity to emotions. This is achieved by teaching patients skills to effectively manage and regulate their negative emotions as they occur (Sauer-Zavala et al., 2012). The goals of CH described in this chapter are not different from those of UP.

EFFECTIVENESS OF CH WITH EMOTIONAL DISORDERS

Indirectly, CH as an integrated psychotherapy has evolved as a transdiagnostic psychological treatment of emotional disorders. Although it was not specifically devised as a unified treatment protocol for emotional disorders, the main goals of CH involved (a) helping patients reduce their reactivity to internal and external cues, and (b) teaching them skills to regulate their affect. This chapter adopts a unified approach to treating emotional disorders. Some of the intervention modules described somewhat vary from UP (e.g., UP does not use hypnosis), but the treatment goals are similar.

CH is a major evidence-based submodality of modern hypnotherapy. It gained greater impetus since the publication of the influential meta-analysis by Kirsch, Montgomery, and Sapirstein (1995), which clearly proved that the addition of hypnosis to CBT substantially enhances treatment outcomes. More recently, the additive effect of CH has been demonstrated with a variety of conditions, including anxiety disorders (Golden, 2012), acute stress disorder (Bryant, Moulds, Guthrie, & Nixon, 2005), bulimia nervosa (Barabasz, 2012), chronic pain (Elkins, Johnson, & Fisher, 2012; Jensen, 2013), depression (Alladin & Alibhai, 2007), insomnia (Graci & Hardie, 2007), migraine headache (Hammond, 2007), posttraumatic stress disorder (Lynn & Cardeña, 2007), psychosomatic disorders (Flammer & Alladin, 2007), and somatoform disorders (Alladin, 2008; Moene, Spinhoven, Hoogduin, & Van Dyck, 2003). Moreover, as previously mentioned, CH is recognized as an integrative model of psychotherapy (Alladin, 2008, 2012; Alladin & Amundson, 2011). Although hypnotherapy has not been directly tested as a unified treatment for emotional disorders, some disorder-specific studies clearly indicate its positive impact on comorbid disorders. For example, Alladin and Alibhai (2007), in their CH trial with depression, found the treatment to produce significant reduction in both anxiety and depression scores. Dobbin, Maxwell, and Elton (2009) found self-hypnosis to be effective in the management of depression among primary care patients with depression. Similarly, Barabasz, Barabasz, Christensen, French, and Watkins (2013) and Christensen, Barabasz, and Barabasz (2013) found ego-state therapy targeted at posttraumatic stress disorder to be effective in reducing symptoms of depression. Before describing the components of CH in the management of emotional disorders, the case of Fred is briefly reported.

Case of Fred

This case is a condensed version of a case study described by Alladin (2015). Some salient details of the case are used here to illustrate some of the techniques that are utilized by CH therapists in the management of emotional disorders. Fred was referred to the author by his psychiatrist for psychological treatment. He had a long history of chronic "anxiety" and "depression" and he had been followed up by a psychiatrist for over 10 years. Fred was a 54-year-old team leader at a highly successful, multinational electronic company. By training, Fred was an electrical engineer, but for the past 5 years he had been holding a very senior position as a project manager. Initially, Fred was very excited about his promotion, but gradually lost interest in his job and lacked motivation to go to work, as he constantly questioned whether he was qualified for the job, or whether he would be able to deliver what his boss expected of him. He became preoccupied with the prospect of being laid off, although there was no indication for such a worry, and he started to ruminate about the negative consequences of losing his job. Consequently, he developed clinical symptoms of anxiety and depression. He had difficulty falling and staying asleep at night. He felt nervous, anxious, restless, and at times depressed. He found it very difficult to relax or unwind. At times, he got so anxious, overwhelmed, or panicky that he could not cope with his job; hence, on two occasions it necessitated short-term admission to the psychiatric unit of the local general hospital. He was followed up by his psychiatrist as an outpatient, mainly for monitoring his response to antidepressant medication. He was referred for psychological treatment as his psychiatrist considered individual psychotherapy an important component of the treatment. There was a positive history of anxiety and depression in the maternal side of his family.

Fred had been married for over 25 years. His wife, a lawyer by profession, had given up her job to be more supportive to her husband and her two daughters, who were at the university. He was brought up in a "commercial family." His father was a successful businessman, dominant, charismatic, a "natural leader," and well-respected in the community. Because of his very busy life, Fred's father was detached from the family, but not unsupportive. Fred described himself as being the "total opposite" to his father. He described his mother as being passive, "an ordinary housewife," and not very knowledgeable about the world. He had two older sisters, who were both married and living in the same town as his parents.

CH AS UNIFIED TREATMENT FOR EMOTIONAL DISORDERS

The major components of CH as a unified treatment for emotional disorders are briefly described here. For a more detailed description of the stages and the components of CH, refer to Alladin (1994, 2007, 2008, 2012, 2015). CH generally consists of 20 weekly sessions, which can be expanded or modified according to the patient's clinical needs, areas of concern, and severity of presenting symptoms. CH for emotional disorders can be broadly divided into two separate, but overlapping, phases of treatment. The first phase, mainly consisting of hypnotherapy and CBT, is targeted at symptoms management. The second phase, if needed, focuses on uncovering and healing the underlying cause of the emotional disorder. For some patients, the initial phase of the therapy may be sufficient, while for others it serves as a preparation for more complex therapy of exploring the roots of the emotional disorder. The first phase of the treatment usually consists of hypnotherapy and CBT. The second phase of CH involves deep hypnotherapy strategies (e.g., affect bridge, split screen technique) for uncovering and healing the wounded self.

Case Formulation and Therapeutic Alliance

Before starting therapy, it is good clinical practice for the therapist to take a detailed clinical history to formulate the diagnosis and identify the essential psychological, physiological, and social aspects of the patient's difficulties. CH case conceptualization underlines the role of cognitive distortions, negative self-instructions, irrational automatic thoughts and beliefs, schemas, and negative ruminations or negative self-hypnosis (NSH) in the understanding of the patient's emotional disorder. An efficient way of obtaining this information within the context of CH is to take a case formulation approach as described by Alladin (2007, 2008). A case formulation approach allows the clinician to tailor a nomothetic (general) treatment protocol, derived from randomized clinical trials, to the needs of the individual (idiographic) patient. Moreover,

therapeutic alliance is vitally important in psychotherapy (Norcross, 2002) as all effective psychotherapy is predicated on the establishment of a safe, secure, and solid therapeutic alliance (Wolfe, 2005). Some clinicians, on the other hand, have argued that therapeutic alliance is "necessary but insufficient" for change (e.g., Beck, Rush, Shaw, & Emery, 1979). Nevertheless, a patient who feels disrespected or uncomfortable with his or her therapist is more likely to discontinue therapy, while a patient with strong therapeutic alliance may persevere with the difficult work of change.

Hypnotherapy for Symptom Management

In the first phase of CH, hypnotherapy is specifically targeted at symptoms management. The hypnotherapy components include (a) relaxation training; (b) demonstration of the power of the mind over the body; (c) ego strengthening; (d) expansion of awareness; (e) modulation and regulation of symptoms; (f) self-hypnosis training; (g) positive mood induction; and (h) posthypnotic suggestions (PHS).

■ Relaxation Training

One of the major reasons for using hypnosis with emotional disorders is to cultivate the *relaxation response*. The relaxation response can be defined as a set of integrated physiological mechanisms and "adjustments" that are elicited when an individual engages in a repetitive mental or physical activity and passively ignores distracting thoughts (Esch, Fricchione, & Stefano, 2003). Patients with emotional disorders experience high levels of tension, nervousness, and steep physiological reactivity (e.g., Beck & Emery, 1985, 2005; Clark & Beck, 2010). Even patients with depression experience high levels of anxiety either due to comorbid anxiety (Dozois & Westra, 2004) or a lack of confidence in their abilities to effectively handle life challenges. For these reasons, patients with depression often derive significant benefit from simply learning to relax (Dobbin, Maxwell, & Elton, 2009). There is extensive evidence that relaxation alone, or in combination with other therapies, is beneficial to both normal and multiple clinical populations, including emotional disorders (Elkins, 2014; Walsh, 2011). Relaxation training appears to be well suited for the treatment of diffuse anxieties (Borkovec & Weerts, 1976) and it represents one of the most-used nonpharmacological approaches in anxiety management worldwide (Barrows & Jacobs, 2002), both as a bona fide anxiolytic treatment in itself (Öst, 1987) or as an adjunct to more complex therapies, such as systematic desensitization (Goldfried, 1971) and CBT (Beck & Emery, 1985, 2005; Clark & Beck, 2010). For decades, relaxation training has been shown to attain many of the same benefits as benzodiazepines, but without the side-effect profile of medication (Stahl & Moore, 2013).

Various hypnotic induction techniques can be utilized to induce relaxation. The author often uses the *relaxation with counting method* adapted from Gibbons (1979; see Alladin, 2007) for inducing and deepening hypnosis, as this technique is easily adapted for self-hypnosis training. As Fred was experiencing high levels of tension, nervousness, irritation, and felt on edge most of the time, he found the relaxation induced by hypnosis very calming and comforting. The relaxation response (feeling calm and fully relaxed) coupled with a sense of detachment—while he was aware of his worries, but not involved with the content or meanings of his worries—served as an experiential strategy to desensitize his anxiety-related worries.

Demonstration of the Power of the Mind

To further empower Fred and to ratify the credibility of hypnotherapy, eye and body catalepsies were induced in the second hypnotherapy session. Fred was very intrigued that he could not open his eyes or get out of the reclining chair. The cataleptic demonstration in the therapy session provides a powerful procedure for reducing skepticism about hypnosis, fostering positive expectancy, and instilling confidence in patients with emotional disorders that they can tap into their personal resources to deal with their symptoms. Based on findings from *third-wave* CBTs (e.g., Hayes, 2004; Hayes, Luoma, Bond, Masuda, & Lillis, 2006; Linehan, 1993), CH places less emphasis on "controlling," "blocking," or "suppressing" symptoms. Instead, therapists teach their patients to examine and change their relationship with their internal experience and their cognitive activities, rather than trying to control their thoughts or emotions (Butler, Fennell, & Hackman, 2008). There is abundant

research evidence that suggests that it is not only ineffective to try to intentionally control private events (e.g., Clark, 2005; Wegner, 1994; Wilson, Lindsey, & Schooler, 2000), but such attempts produce extremely paradoxical responses (e.g., Campbell-Sills et al., 2006; Morita, 1998). In addition, hypnosis offers a powerful means for producing *syncretic cognition* (Alladin, 2006, 2007), which consists of a mixture of cognitive, somatic, perceptual, physiological, visceral, and kinesthetic changes. Hypnotic induction and modulation of syncretic cognition offers patients with emotional disorders direct and compelling evidence that they can alter their subjective experience. Most importantly, the ability to produce novel and diverse experiences can arouse in them a sense of hope that negative affect can be managed.

Ego Strengthening

Ego-strengthening suggestions are offered to patients with emotional disorders to promote confidence and self-efficacy. While in deep hypnotic trance, patients are encouraged to visualize acquiring the skill of "letting go" and not cogitating with their symptoms while feeling anxious or depressed. The following sample of ego-strengthening suggestions were offered to Fred:

"As a result of this treatment and as a result of listening to your Self-Hypnosis CD, every day you will feel calmer and much more relaxed."

"Although you are aware of your concerns and your worries, you will be able to put everything on hold and let go. This shows that you can relax and let go even if you are aware of everything. You don't need to empty your mind to be able to relax."

After the first hypnotherapy session, patients are given a Self-Hypnosis CD to listen to at home as homework (see under "Self-Hypnosis Training" for further details).

Expansion of Awareness

Patients with emotional disorders tend to be preoccupied with negative affect and the consequences of their symptoms (Papageorgiou & Wells, 2004), resulting in a narrowing down of their range of experience. Neisser (1967) viewed marked constriction in the range of behaviors and self-attributions as characteristic of psychopathology. Hypnosis renders a powerful vehicle for expanding awareness and amplifying positive experience. This can be achieved by using Brown and Fromm's (1990) technique of *enhancing affective experience and its expression* (hereafter referred as "awareness expansion"). While Fred was in a deep hypnotic trance, he was directed to focus his attention on the relaxation response and then guided to focus on his feelings and sensations:

"You have now become so deeply relaxed that you begin to feel a beautiful sensation of peace and tranquility, relaxation and calm, following all over your mind and body. Giving you such a pleasant, and such a soothing sensation all over your mind and body, that you feel completely relaxed, totally relaxed, both mentally and physically. And yet you are aware of everything, you are aware of all the sound and noise around you, you are aware of your thoughts and your imagination, and yet you feel so relaxed, so calm and so peaceful. This shows that you have the ability to relax, the ability to let go, and the ability to put everything on hold."

"Now you can become aware of all the good feelings you are experiencing. You feel calm, peaceful, relaxed, and very, very comfortable. You may also become aware of feeling heavy, light, or detached, or distancing away from everything, becoming more and more detached, distancing away from everything, drifting into a deep, deep hypnotic state."

From the expansion of awareness training, patients discover that they have the ability to relax and the capacity to experience different feelings and sensations. Fred was surprised that he could put things on hold, that is, although he was aware of his worries, uncertainties, and fears, he was able to detach from anticipatory concerns. With practice he was able to relax and experience different contextual feelings, albeit while aware of his concerns and worries. He also discovered that he had the talent to produce, amplify, and express a variety of positive feelings and experiences. The induction of such positive syncretic experience gives patients with emotional disorders the confidence that they could learn to "flow" with their emotions, distress, and concerns.

To help patients become further disengaged from their worries and negative reactivity, they are introduced to *imaginal exposure therapy* (Wolpe, 1958; Wolpe & Lazarus, 1966), which is considered to be an important component of CH for emotional disorders (Golden, 2012). While in deep hypnosis, the patients are directed to focus on their worries, uncertainties, and reactivity. Then they are instructed to utilize their self-hypnosis skills to relax and calm down whenever they experience any anxiety or depression associated with their recurring thoughts and worries. In other words, the goal is not to control their symptoms; the focus is on learning to tolerate their distress.

Here is a sample of suggestions used with Fred to help him get engaged in the imaginal exposure.

"When I count from one to five, by the time you hear me say "five," you will begin to feel whatever emotion or reaction that is associated with any worrying thought or uncertainty that crosses your mind."

Once he felt the negative emotion, he was instructed to amplify the affect associated with the thought or uncertainty. Facing the worries can be quite emotionally evocative for some patients with emotional disorders. It is therefore important for the therapist to gently encourage the patient to continue to face the worries as this will help the patient learn to tolerate the distress associated with worries. Moreover, by "staying" with the worries, the patient learns to generate strategies for coping with distress.

"When I count slowly from one to five, as I count you will begin to experience the anxious feelings more and more intensely, so that when I reach the count of five, at the count of five you will feel the full reaction as strongly as you can bear in ONE . . . TWO . . . THREE . . . FOUR . . . FIVE. Now notice what you feel and you can describe it to me."

Fred was then advised to utilize his self-hypnosis skill to cope with the anxious feeling or fearful reaction.

"Now, imagine using your self-hypnosis skill to deal with the anxious reaction. Now you have

the ability to relax and to put things on hold, you can let go and calm down even if the worrying thoughts come into your mind. You don't have to control your anxiety; just try to calm down and distance away from your thoughts just as you do when you practice self-hypnosis."

After several rounds of repetition of this set of suggestions, Fred was able to relax completely while being aware of his worries and uncertainties. As previously mentioned, based on findings from acceptance and mindfulness-based therapies (AMBT), the focus of the exposure therapy is not to control the symptoms of emotional disorders, but to teach patients techniques to deal with their symptoms, or learn to *surf over* it (Alladin, 2014a, 2014b, 2015). Recent research findings indicate that fears, anxiety, and depression are partly generated by overly rigid attempts to avoid the emotional experience of fear and anxiety (e.g., Butler et al., 2008; Greeson & Brantley, 2009; Roemer, Williston, Eustis, & Orsillo, 2013). The toleration of fear, anxiety, and depression is therefore considered a critical component in the psychological treatment of emotional disorders. Hence, the goal of exposure therapy should not be on immediate reduction of negative emotion, but rather on learning to tolerate distress and discomfort. The mental rehearsal in trance provides patients a safe milieu to learn to face their worrying thoughts and associated reactivity, rather than catastrophizing or cogitating about them. Fred indicated that he learned to tolerate his worrying thoughts and discovered that "staying with the anxiety was not as bad" as he thought.

The awareness expansion training is found to be particularly effective with patients with emotional disorders whose current symptoms are dominated by depressive moods. Hypnotic expansion and amplification of experience in depression (a) bring underlying emotions into awareness; (b) create awareness of various feelings; (c) intensify positive affect; (d) enhance "discovered" affect; (e) induce positive moods; and (f) increase motivation for change (Brown & Fromm, 1990, pp. 322–324). This technique not only disrupts the depressive cycle, it also helps to develop *antidepressive pathways* (Alladin, 2007). Moreover, positive associations (opposite of maladaptive dissociations), produced by forward projection, can also be utilized to produce "an alternative subjective reality" that helps patients with depression "feel better"

(Yapko, 1992, p. 134). For detailed descriptions of how to produce positive associations in patients with depression, see Yapko (1992, pp. 144–163) and Edgette and Edgette (1995, pp. 145–158).

■ Ego Strengthening

Ego-strengthening suggestions are utilized in hypnotherapy to increase self-esteem and self-efficacy. Bandura (1977) provided experimental evidence that self-efficacy, the expectation and confidence of being able to cope successfully with various situations, is one of the key elements in the effective treatment of psychological disorders. Individuals with a sense of high self-efficacy perceive themselves as being in control of themselves. If patients with emotional disorders can be instructed to view themselves as self-efficacious, they may then be able to perceive the future as more hopeful.

A popular method for increasing self-efficacy within the hypnotherapeutic context is to provide ego-strengthening suggestions to patients while they are in a deep hypnotic trance. The goals of ego-strengthening suggestions are to reduce anxiety and depression, and to gradually restore the patient's self-confidence in his or her ability to cope effectively with problems and distress (Hartland, 1971). Alladin (2008, pp. 247–249) has provided a list of generalized ego-strengthening suggestions that can be routinely used in hypnotherapy with a variety of medical and psychological conditions. However, when working with patients with emotional disorders, it is important to craft ego-strengthening suggestions in such a way that they appear credible and logical to the patients. For example, rather than globally stating "every day you will feel better," it is advisable to suggest:

"As a result of this treatment and as a result of listening to your Self-Hypnosis CD everyday, you will learn new skills to deal with your difficulties and distress, and as a result you will begin to feel better."

This set of suggestions not only sounds logical, improvement becomes contingent on continuing with the therapy and practicing with the Self-Hypnosis CD daily (Alladin, 1994, 2006, 2007, 2012). As previously mentioned, at the termination of the first hypnosis session, the patient is given a Self-Hypnosis CD to listen to at home everyday as home work.

■ Posthypnotic Suggestions

PHS are routinely delivered during hypnotherapy to counter problem behaviors, negative emotions, dysfunctional cognitions, NSH, and negative self-affirmations. As discussed in the context of triple theory, patients with emotional disorders are predisposed to reflexively ruminate with negative self-suggestions, particularly after experiencing a negative affect (e.g., "I will not be able to cope"). This can be regarded as a form of NHS or PHS, which maintains the anxious or depressive cycle. To break this reflexive pattern of thinking, it is important to counter the NSH. The following is an example of a set of PHS provided by Alladin (2006, p. 162) for countering NSH:

"While you are in an upsetting situation, you will become more aware of how to deal with it rather than focusing on your emotional reaction."

Yapko (2003) points out that PHSs serve as a necessary part of the therapeutic process if the patient is to carry out new possibilities into future experiences based on the hypnosis session.

■ Self-Hypnosis Training

Apart from learning to relax, the self-hypnosis component of CH is also devised to create positive affect and counter NSH. At the end of the first hypnotherapy session, the patient is provided with an audio CD that contains (a) a relaxation and counting method for induction and deepening of hypnosis; (b) expansion of awareness (aware of internal and external stimuli); (c) ego-strengthening suggestions; and (d) PHSs. The homework assignment of listening to the Self-Hypnosis CD daily offers continuity of treatment between sessions and creates a setting for the patient to learn self-hypnosis.

To further consolidate their skill of generalizing self-hypnosis to real-life situations, patients with emotional disorders are introduced to the *clenched fist technique* (Stein, 1963). The clenching of the dominant fist serves as an anchor for the elicitation of the relaxation response. The fist as an anchor is easily established during a hypnotic trance. When the patient is in a deep trance state, he or she is advised to become aware of the profound relaxation as well as the feeling of confidence and self-control.

Then the patient is instructed to make a fist with the preferred hand, followed by these suggestions:

"From now on, whenever you wish to feel just as you are feeling now, all you have to do is to clench your preferred fist and anchor your mind to this experience. Moreover, from now on, whenever you feel anxious, you can tame the feeling by clenching your fist and anchoring your mind to this experience . . . and with practice you will get better and better at it."

The anchoring technique is experientially ratified by hypnotic imaginal rehearsal training and reinforced by PHSs. Most patients find the clenched fist technique concrete and "portable," and easily applied in a variety of anxiety-provoking situations. However, clenching of the fist may not serve as an appropriate anchor for some patients as it may conjure anger or aggression. In such a case, pressing of the thumb against the little finger (in same preferred hand) may be more appropriate.

■ Positive Mood Induction

Nolen-Hoeksema (2004) and Papageorgiou and Wells (2004) found patients with anxiety and depression to be preoccupied with repetitive catastrophic thoughts and negative images called *ruminations*. Ruminations can easily become obsessional in nature and further sensitize the anxiety and depressive neuropathways, thus impeding therapeutic progress and symptomatic relief (Monroe & Harkness, 2005; Post, 1992). To counter negative ruminations and to prevent kindling of maladaptive neuropathways, the *positive mood induction* technique is used in CH (Alladin, 1994, 2006, 2007, 2012).

The positive mood induction technique involves systematic focusing on positive experiences. The patient is encouraged to make a list of 10 to 15 pleasant or positive experiences and then to focus on the list, one item at a time, for about 30 seconds, three to four times a day. The technique is initially practiced (with three items from the list) in hypnosis in the therapist's office. When in hypnosis, the patient is instructed to focus on one of the positive experiences from his or her list, which is then amplified with suggestions from the therapist. This technique is similar to the awareness expansion training described earlier. However, to develop antianxiety or antidepressive neuropathways, more emphasis is placed on producing somatosensory changes and concomitant physiological changes, rather than merely focusing on affective experience. The procedure is repeated with at least three positive experiences from the patient's list. PHSs are provided so that the patient will be able to reexperience positive mood easily while practicing with the list at home. To consolidate the technique and to activate positive kindling, the patient is encouraged to practice with the list of positive experiences at home three to four times a day.

Cognitive Behavioral Therapy

CBT is the most widely studied psychosocial treatment for emotional disorders. A vast number of controlled trials have consistently demonstrated CBT to be effective in the reduction of acute symptoms of anxiety and depression, and its effect has been found to be comparable to pharmacological treatment (e.g., Butler, Chapman, Forman, & Beck, 2006; Clark & Beck, 2010; Iddon & Grant, 2013). However, most treatment trials have targeted specific disorders such as anxiety, depression, PTSD, and so on, rather than focusing on a unified treatment protocol. As the general cognitive behavioral theories of psychopathology are predicated on the notion that errors in information processing (i.e., cognitive distortions) lead to negative beliefs and distressing symptoms, they can be easily applied to emotional disorders. The central basis of the cognitive theories of emotional disorders is the formation of dysfunctional schemas (i.e., attitudes and assumptions) generated from previous experience, which may lay dormant until they are activated by thematic events. As previously discussed, negative early experience is one of the three predispositions identified by the triple theory of emotional disorders (e.g., Barlow, 2002). Impelled by such predisposition, patients with emotional disorders are inclined to interpret negative reactivity to environmental stimuli as being harmful (e.g., Payne et al., 2014). Therefore, teaching these patients to recognize and examine their negative beliefs and information-processing proclivities has been found to produce relief from their symptoms, and enable them to cope more effectively with life's challenges (e.g., Clark & Beck, 2010; Ellard et al., 2010; Payne et al., 2014).

Furthermore, the process of cognitive distortion in patients with emotional disorders can be regarded as a form of NSH, which can be easily modified by hypnotherapy (e.g., Alladin, 2007, 2008; Araoz, 1981, 1985). Although cognitive behavioral theories of emotional disorders do not make direct reference to hypnosis or dissociation in the formation of symptoms, their description of the patient's preoccupation with cognitive distortions can be regarded as a form of NSH. The following observation of a patient with depression recorded by Beck et al. (1979) captures this element.

> In milder depressions the patient is generally able to view his negative thoughts with some objectivity. As the depression worsens, his thinking becomes increasingly dominated by negative ideas . . . and [he or she] may find it enormously difficult to concentrate on external stimuli . . . or engage in voluntary activities . . . the idiosyncratic cognitive organization has become autonomous . . . [so] that the individual is unresponsive to changes in his immediate environment. (p.13)

This patient's negative rumination and consequent dysphoric responses can be considered analogous to the concepts of NSH and deep trance state, respectively. Yapko (1992, 1997) also views the negative affect produced by cognitive distortions in patients with depression to be a form of symptomatic trance.

In the treatment of emotional disorders, CBT is used to help patients recognize and modify their cognitive distortions through the use of evidence and applications of logic. CBT uses some very well-known and tested reason-based models for interventions such as Socratic logic-based dialogues and Aristotle's method of collecting and categorizing information about the world (Leahy, 2003). As CBT techniques are well described elsewhere (see Beck, 1995), they are not described in detail here. For a detailed description of the sequential progression of CBT within the CH framework, see Alladin (1994, 2007, 2008, 2012). Within the CH perspective, CBT is viewed as a conscious strategy for countering NSH in order to circumvent the negative affect or the symptomatic trance state (Yapko, 1992). The CBT component of CH for this purpose can be extended over four to six sessions. However, the actual number of CBT sessions is determined by the needs of the patient and the severity of the presenting symptoms. The following CBT transcript adapted from Alladin

(2008, pp. 107–110) illustrates how Roger, who had PTSD, was guided to reevaluate and change his maladaptive belief of the world ("The world is unsafe") that stemmed from his traumatic experience (saw many innocent people killed and maimed in a war zone).

Therapist: *Roger, what do you mean by "the world is unsafe"?*

Roger: *You can't go out there, you may get killed.*

Therapist: *What do you mean by "out there"?*

Roger: *Well, you can't go out in the street without getting killed or mugged.*

Therapist: *So, let me get it right what you are saying. You believe that if you go out in the street, you will either get killed or mugged.*

Roger: *Certainly.*

Therapist: *How much do you believe in the belief that you will get shot or mugged when you go out in the street?*

Roger: *Totally, one hundred percent.*

Therapist: *What kind of a thinking error is this?*

Roger: *All-or-nothing thinking, magnification, and I'm overgeneralizing.*

(This transcript is from Roger's third session of CBT. From his previous sessions of CBT and homework assignments, Roger was well versed in the types of cognitive distortions anxious people ruminate with, as described by Burns [1999]).

Therapist: *So you are aware that your thinking is inaccurate.*

Roger: *Yes, but I can't help it. I know I live in a fairly safe neighborhood, but my mind keeps going back to East Europe. I get confused. My mind keeps going back as if I'm still there. It's so crazy.*

Therapist: *Do you see the connection between your thinking and your negative reaction?*

Roger: *Yes, it's so dumb. Whenever I think of going out, I think of the dangerous situations we faced in East Europe, people getting shot, arrested, and blown up. But this is so dumb, I know I am not going to get attacked or shot going to the store in Canada.*

Therapist: *So your thinking gets confused. When you think of going out to the local store you think you are in East Europe.*

Roger: *Yes, but I can't help it.*

Therapist: *Having the thoughts that you are in East Europe and exposed to dangers are not intentional on your part. You don't think this way on purpose. As a result of your traumatic experiences, your mind has developed many associations with the fearful and dangerous situations you were in. Also, you learned to think automatically about danger, even in situations where there is no danger. Does this make sense to you?*

Roger: *Yes, but how do I get out of this?*

Therapist: *As we talked before, we use disputation or reasoning. Suppose you are thinking of going to the store and the thought crosses your mind that you will be mugged or shot. How would you reason with this statement?*

Roger: *I can remind myself that I'm not in East Europe, my assignment is over. I am at home now, and this is a safe environment.*

Therapist: *That's excellent. You have to separate "then" from "now." You have to reason that you are in a safe environment now, even if your thinking keeps going back to East Europe.*

Roger: *I guess I always knew my thinking was wrong, but the feelings are so real that you begin to go along with your feeling, rather than thinking with your head. Funny, this is what cops are taught to do.*

Therapist: *What kind of a thinking error is this, when you are thinking with your feeling?*

Roger: *Emotional reasoning. You are right, I need to use my head more than my feeling.*

Therapist: *That's right, you have to continue to assess the link between your thinking and your feeling. Try to identity the cognitive distortion and then reason with it.*

As a result of this session Roger was able to modify his maladaptive beliefs and, consequently, he started to venture out more often and to different places.

HYPNOSIS-AIDED SYSTEMATIC DESENSITIZATION

Although imaginal exposure can be helpful in building confidence to deal with avoidance behaviors, some patients may still feel very anxious to face real anxiety-provoking situations. One of the ways to overcome this obstacle is to use *systematic desensitization* (SD) as a preparation before introducing patients to *exposure in vivo* (Golden, 2012). SD, also known as *counterconditioning*, is a common evidence-based behavioral technique based on classical conditioning (Farris & Jouriles, 1993). This technique involves pairing two stimuli that elicit incompatible responses (e.g., anxiety and relaxation). In SD, a person with anxiety is gradually exposed to an anxiety-provoking object or situation while learning to be relaxed. In the framework of CH, the relaxation component of SD is replaced by hypnosis; hence, this treatment approach is referred to as *hypnosis-aided systematic desensitization* (HASD) (Iglesias, Iglesias, & Iglesias, 2014). A number of reports in the literature support the effectiveness of combining hypnosis with SD in the treatment of specific phobias (e.g., Glick, 1970). Normally a hierarchy of anxiety—consisting of a list of situations or objects, ranked from least feared to most feared—is constructed before starting SD. Moreover, each fearful situation is self-rated in terms of *subjective units of discomfort* (SUD) on a 0 to 100 scale (0 representing no fear and 100 standing for the worst/maximum fear).

While feeling very relaxed in deep hypnosis, the patient is asked to imagine each hierarchy of fear in turn, starting with the lowest item in the hierarchy. The patient is instructed to focus on the target situation until the SUD level goes down to 0. It is important for the patient to master one hierarchy, that is, be able to imagine the target situation without any anxiety before moving on to the next item in the hierarchy. Failure to master a situation from the hierarchy may produce resistance to work with the next item, which is likely to be more anxiety provoking (higher SUD level). Usually, after several sessions of SD patients feel confident to progress on to gradual exposure in vivo.

Gradual in Vivo Exposure Therapy

Exposure in vivo is a key component of CBT for overcoming avoidance behaviors. It has also been found to be efficacious with a variety of anxiety disorders (Follette & Smith, 2005) and it is considered to be the gold standard treatment for agoraphobia (Chambless, 1985; Hazlett-Stevens, 2006). Exposure in vivo is designed to help patients with emotional disorders confront fearful situations, memories, and images in a therapeutic manner. It involves a step-by-step approach to conquering anxiety or distress elicited by certain specific situations or objects. The patient draws on his or her relaxation skills, self-hypnosis, and cognitive coping strategies to manage the discomfort associated with the successive exposure steps. Usually the same hierarchy of fear/anxiety/distress used for SD is utilized for the graded in vivo desensitization procedure.

Healing Self-Wounds

Once a patient achieves some measure of control over his or her symptoms from either hypnotherapy or CBT (or a combination of both), the therapist has to make a decision about the next step of intervention. For those patients who improved and believe that they have met their goals, the therapy is considered complete and it is duly terminated. Those patients who wish to explore the roots of their emotional disorder are enrolled in the next phase of therapy, which consists of accessing and healing the self-wounds.

Hypnotherapy provides an array of methods for uncovering and restructuring unconscious causes or roots of emotional disorders (Alladin, 2012, 2013a, 2014b, 2015; Brown & Fromm, 1986; Ewin & Eimer, 2006; Watkins, 1971; Watkins & Barabasz, 2008). Some of the most common hypnotic techniques for accessing tacit self-wounds include (a) direct suggestions; (b) hypnotic age regression; (c) affect bridge; and (d) hypnotic exploration. Once the origin of self-wounds is uncovered and the implicit meaning of the symptoms is figured out, the therapy normally segues into healing the emotional injury. Some of the hypnotic strategies used for healing emotional hurt include (a) cognitive restructuring under hypnosis; (b) editing and deleting the "unconscious file"; (c) the split screen technique; and (d) the empty chair technique. For the present purpose, the affect bridge, the split screen, and the empty chair techniques will be described and illustrated by the case of Fred.

After 10 sessions of CBT and hypnotherapy, Fred noticed significant improvement in his affect. He felt less anxious, depressed, and worried, and he was less preoccupied with uncertainties about his future. Nevertheless, he still had some anxieties and depression, and felt the need to produce "deep changes" inside him. He was interested to explore the root causes of his fears, worries, and the tendency to catastrophize. He was also interested in knowing why he felt insecure, lacked confidence, and doubted his abilities at work. The next segment of therapy thus involved in-depth hypnotherapy and consisted of accessing and healing the wounded self or emotional injuries (Alladin, 2013b, 2014a, 2014b, 2015; Wolfe, 2005, 2006).

Elicitation of Self-Wounds

To explore any underlying self-wounds that might have been connected with Fred's emotional problems, the affect bridge technique was used. The feeling of anxiety that he experienced while he was worried about being laid off from his job was used as a bridge to elicit his first anxiety attack. While feeling very anxious, he remembered the first anxiety attack he had when he was 16 years old. It was during his father's 50th birthday party. The party was held at his home and most of the guests were his father's close friends and business partners. While Fred was having a casual conversation with one of his father's friends, the person commented: "You are not like your father. You appear to be very quiet and shy. You should be like your father, look how smart and popular he is." Fred felt embarrassed, hurt, flustered, confused, and so overwhelmed that he had to run out of the house, and he waited for all the guests to leave before he could come into the house. Since Fred was about 12 years old, he became aware that he was shy, reserved, and lacked confidence. Gradually, he became very conscious that he lacked confidence and, on several occasions, he cried for not being like his father. Subsequently, he concluded that he was weak, inferior, and "not good enough for anything." The comments from his father's friend confirmed his negative beliefs (i.e., he is no good as he could not be like his father) and caused further injury to his already wounded self (sense of inadequacy). Fred's pathological worry thus served as a blanket to suppress his feelings of inadequacy and self-doubt.

To compensate for his sense of inadequacy, Fred got involved in sports and academia. He did not do very well in sports, which further reinforced his belief that he was not good enough. He did quite well academically, and without much difficulty he graduated with honors in electrical engineering. Because of his good grades and outstanding internship performance, Fred was very easily able to secure a job as an electrical engineer in a large electronics company. He worked diligently, for which he was rewarded with several promotions. Unfortunately, Fred started to worry about "everything," began to doubt himself rather than focusing on his achievements, and started to cogitate with his symptoms, gradually presenting symptoms of depression and GAD.

From the uncovering work, it was formulated that Fred's emotional disorder was connected to his emotional injuries, resulting in the formation of negative self-schemas and the maintenance of his symptoms (see Alladin, 2013b). The next segment of hypnotherapy was therefore targeted on detoxifying the meaning of his anxiety, depression, and worries.

DETOXIFICATION OF MEANING OF ANXIETY, DEPRESSION, AND WORRY

The split screen technique (Alladin, 2008; Cardeña, Maldonado, van der Hart, & Spiegel, 2000; Lynn & Cardeña, 2007; Spiegel, 1981) was used to help Fred detoxify the meaning of his anxiety, depression, and worry. This hypnotic strategy utilizes the "adult ego state" to assist the "weak ego state" in dealing with distress-provoking situations. It also unites the two "ego states" to work together as a team when the Self is threatened, rather than splitting from each other when stressed out. The following therapy transcript adapted from Alladin (2015) illustrates how the split screen technique was used with Fred to help him deal with the toxic meaning of his emotional disorder. The transcript began while Fred was in a deep hypnotic trance.

Therapist: *Now I would like you to imagine sitting in front of a large TV or cinema screen, which is vertically split in two halves, consisting of a right side and a left side. Can you imagine this?*

Fred: [He raised his "YES" finger. Ideomotor signals were already set up—raising his right index finger represented "YES" and raising his left index finger indicated "NO."]

Therapist: *Imagine that the right side of the screen is lighting up as if it's ready to project an image. Imagine yourself being projected on the right side of the screen, just as you are now. Feeling very relaxed, very comfortable, in complete control, and aware of everything. And now become aware of the things you have achieved, things that you are proud of. Do you feel these good feelings?*

Fred: [After a moment, his YES finger went up.]

Therapist: *That's very good. Do you feel the sense of achievement?*

Fred: [The YES finger went up.]

Therapist: *Are you thinking about your achievement related to having been promoted to team leader in your company? (Fred had disclosed this information to the therapist in previous sessions.)*

Fred: [The YES finger went up.]

Therapist: *Just focus on the good feelings and become aware that you made it to this senior position despite your anxiety and depression. This proves to you that you have a strong side, a successful side, a side that can rescue you from difficulties and help you to succeed. We are going to call this part of you the "adult side" or your "adult ego state." Is that acceptable to you?*

Fred: [He raised his YES finger.]

Therapist: *Leave this side of yourself on the right side of the screen and imagine yourself being projected on the left side of the screen now. On the left side of the screen, imagine yourself being in a situation that causes anxiety or depression for you. Can you imagine this?*

Fred: [His YES finger went up.]

Therapist: *Now become aware of all the feelings that you are experiencing. Don't be afraid to let all the negative feelings come over you, because soon we will show you how to deal with them. Become aware of all the physical sensations that you are feeling. Become aware of all the thoughts that are going through your mind and become aware of your behaviors. Can you feel these?*

Fred: [The YES finger went up.]

Therapist: *Become aware of the whole experience and we are going to call this part of you the "weak part of you" or the "child ego state" as we discussed before. Is this acceptable to you?*

Fred: [The YES finger went up.]

Therapist: *Now imagine, your adult ego state is stepping out from the right side to the left side of the screen. Can you imagine this?*

Fred: [He raised his YES finger.]

Therapist: *Imagine that your adult ego state is reassuring your child ego state. He is telling your child ego state not to be afraid because he is here to help him out and guide him to deal with his fears, worries, and depression. From now on, the child part of you doesn't have to handle difficulties on his own, he can work as a team with the adult part of you. Imagine that the strong part of you is telling the weak part of you that in therapy he has learned many strategies for dealing with anxiety and depression that he can teach you. Imagine he is demonstrating to the weak part of you how to relax, how to let go, and how to reason with fearful, depressing, and worrying thoughts. Continue to imagine this until you feel the weak part of you feels reassured and now knows what to do when feeling upset or distressed. Imagine that your weak part feels protected and empowered knowing that he is not alone, he can get help from the adult ego state whenever the need arises. The weak part also realizes that the strong part is a part of your Self and so is the strong part of your Self. So from now on you both can work as a team. Is this acceptable to you?*

Fred: [The YES finger went up.]

Fred found the split screen technique very helpful. It reminded him of the strategies that he had learned in therapy, and it served as a useful mental rehearsal training for coping with his emotional difficulties.

Differentiating Between Accurate and Inaccurate Self-Views

Driven by self-wounds, patients with emotional disorders develop very negative self-views about themselves, the world, and the future (e.g., "It will be unbearable if I get nervous or embarrassed") (Alladin, 2013b, 2014a, 2015; Beck et al., 1979; Bowlby, 1973; Wolfe, 2005, 2006). It is thus important to help patients with emotional disorders differentiate between their painful self-views that are based on facts and those that are based on inaccurate opinions. Although Fred was never undermined or put down by his father, it was his own perception about himself in comparison to his father that led to his painful self-views. Because he did not possess his father's characteristics, Fred concluded he was inferior, inadequate, weak, and not deserving of respect from others. These cognitive distortions were confirmed by his father's friend at his father's birthday party. The painful views of his "self" created a feeling and experience that he would not be able to cope with the vicissitudes of life. He also came to believe that exposure of his self-wounds, either to himself or to others, would produce overwhelming embarrassment, shame, and humiliation, which he desperately wanted to avoid. Because the rigors and realities of everyday living are unavoidable, Fred developed maladaptive coping strategies, such as behavioral avoidance, excessive worries, rumination with cognitive distortions, and preoccupation with his symptoms to protect himself from facing situations that were perceived to produce distressing affect. Unfortunately, these indirect strategies did not minimize his distress; instead, they reinforced his painful core beliefs about his self. Moreover, these strategies kept Fred away from facing his fears and self-wounds head-on, resulting in the perpetuation of his symptoms. Furthermore, in response to the initial anxiety, Fred got into the habit of *cogitating* about being anxious or depressed; consequently, he became *anxious for feeling anxious*; and *depressed for feeling depressed.*

From the uncovering procedure, it emerged that Fred had a major conflict regarding his self. His "idealized self" was to be like his father, but his "real self" contrasted with his father's attributes and achievements. Not being able to achieve his idealized self was unbearable and totally unacceptable to him. He was terrified of exposing his weakness to others. He was thus determined to project his idealized self to others. His "what ifs" or worries represented self-doubts of whether he would be able to project and sustain his ideal self in challenging situations. The next component of the experiential hypnotherapy thus consisted of helping Fred acknowledge and accept his real self. The empty chair technique, which is a Gestalt therapy role-playing strategy (Perls, Hefferline, & Goodman, 1951; Woldt & Toman, 2005) for reducing intrapersonal or interpersonal conflicts (Nichols & Schwartz, 2008), was used to help Fred accept his real self. In this procedure, while in deep hypnosis, Fred was directed to talk to his father, whom he imagined sitting in an empty chair in the therapist's office, across from him. By imagining his father sitting in the empty chair in the safety of the therapy situation, Fred was able to express various strong feelings about himself and his father that he had been harboring inside him since he was a teenager. This procedure consisted of two interrelated parts. During the first part of the procedure, Fred talked to his father, while his father was silent. In the second part, the father spoke to Fred and then they both talked to each other in turn.

By engaging in the empty-chair work, and with the support and direction from the therapist, Fred was able to express his strong, both negative and positive, feelings toward his father. He told his father in great detail everything he admired and respected about him. He then told his father that he wanted to be like him, but was not able to. Fred became very upset and started to cry loudly; he could not contain his tears when he started telling his father how painful it was for him that he could not be strong, charismatic, and successful like him. He described how painful it was for him to hear people comment that he was not like his father. Even in sports and at school he was not in the top 10. He expressed in detail how embarrassing, humiliating, and painful it was for him to hear from people that he was not as good as his father. It was even more painful for him to realize that he would never be like his father, nor be as successful as him. He saw himself as a failure. He also expressed to his father that he was very hurt and angry because he (father) did not spend much time with him while he was growing up, and never got involved in his schooling or sports activities.

In the next segment of the empty-chair work, Fred imagined his father talking to him (he talked for his father) after he disclosed his pain, distress, and disappointment to him. His "father" (father in parentheses represents Fred talking for his father) told Fred that he could not be like him as they were both different individuals. Father felt flattered that his son thought so highly of him and wanted to be like him. If his son did not happen to be like him, it did not mean he was a failure or a weak person. In fact, father felt relieved that his son was not in the same line of business as him because it was so challenging and demanding, including being less attentive to his family, in order to be a successful business man. Father expressed envy at his son, that is, his son had the opportunity to go to university and study to become an electrical engineer, while he never had the opportunity to go to the university; since he graduated from high school he had been working nonstop.

The next part of the therapy session involved both Fred and father talking to each other in turn.

Fred: *Why you never told me I am a failure?*

Father: *I did not know you thought that you were a failure. I did not know that you wanted to be like me.*

Fred: *You should have known this because you are my father. You should have looked after me and supported me when I was upset.*

Father: *I did not know that you were upset and I did not know what you were thinking.*

With prompting from the therapist, father apologized to Fred, who realized that he was expecting his father to read his mind (cognitive distortion). He realized that this was an unrealistic expectation. Then father described Fred's achievement in detail (which was minimized by Fred) in terms of his sports activities and his performance at university. He emphasized how well Fred did during his internship, which helped him secure a job as an electrical engineer in a very well-known international company. He also pointed out how well Fred did at his job that he was promoted to team leader. Moreover, father described the positive aspect of Fred's household and immediate family.

In addition to the empty chair technique, as homework, Fred was encouraged to write down a full description of his ideal self in terms of personality attributes, education, occupation, achievements, and family life. He had to repeat the same with his real self and then compare the two profiles, highlighting the differences, the similarities, and the tenability of the real self in comparison to his ideal self. Finally, he had to decide whether the real self was acceptable to him, although it did not measure up to his ideal self.

The empty chair conversation helped Fred (a) realize that his ideal self was constructed by a set of cognitive distortions; (b) his father was not responsible for his emotional injury; (c) not achieving his ideal self did not mean he was a failure; (d) his father did not perceive him to be a failure; (e) people would not consider him to be a failure if he did not reach the ideal self; and (f) he could live a "normal life" satisfactorily with his real self.

Fred showed very good response to CH. The therapy helped him identify the explicit and the implicit nature of his anxiety, as well as the roots of his wounded self. While behavioral and cognitive strategies helped him symptomatically, the hypnotherapy, by virtue of its phenomenological nature, made the therapy experiential and thus more meaningful to him. He found the hypnotic exploration technique very helpful in accessing and healing his self-wounds. The empty chair and the split screen techniques permitted him to accept his real self. As therapy progressed, Fred was less worried about the future and cogitated less about his anxiety and depression. At work, he felt more relaxed and worried less about losing his job.

CONCLUSION

This chapter described a unified treatment protocol for emotional disorders. CH provides a variety of treatment interventions for emotional disorders distilled from decades of research on effective cognitive, behavioral, and hypnotherapeutic treatments for anxiety, mood, and trauma-based disorders. Based on case formulation, the therapist can choose the "best-fit" strategies for each individual patient with an emotional disorder. The number of sessions and the sequence of the stages of CH are determined by the clinical needs of each individual patient. However, the central tenet across all these treatment strategies is to help patients with emotional disorders cultivate reduced negative reactivity to emotions and distress-provoking situations.

This is achieved by teaching patients skills to effectively manage and regulate their negative emotions as they occur (Sauer-Zavala et al., 2012). The goals of CH are not different from those of UP as described by Barlow and colleagues. There is preliminary evidence that the UP is effective with emotional disorders. It is hoped that research in the future will provide further support for the unified treatment of emotional disorders. It is also hoped that CH for emotional disorders will be validated.

REFERENCES

Alladin, A. (1994). Cognitive hypnotherapy with depression. *Journal of Cognitive Psychotherapy: An International Quarterly*, 8(4), 275–288.

Alladin, A. (2006). *The clinical use of hypnosis with cognitive behavior therapy: A practitioner's casebook.* New York, NY: Springer Publishing Company.

Alladin, A. (2007). *Handbook of cognitive hypnotherapy for depression: An evidence-based approach.* Philadelphia, PA: Lippincott Williams & Wilkins.

Alladin, A. (2008). *Cognitive hypnotherapy: An integrated approach to treatment of emotional disorders.* Chichester, West Sussex: John Wiley & Sons.

Alladin, A. (2012). Cognitive hypnotherapy for major depressive disorder. *American Journal of Clinical Hypnosis*, 54(4), 275–293. doi:10.1080/00029157.2012.654527

Alladin, A. (2013a). Healing the wounded self: Combining hypnotherapy with ego state therapy. *American Journal of Clinical Hypnosis*, 56, 3–22.

Alladin, A. (2013b). The power of belief and expectancy in understanding and management of depression. *American Journal of Clinical Hypnosis*, 55, 249–271.

Alladin, A. (2014a). Mindfulness-based hypnosis: Blending science, beliefs, and wisdoms to catalyze healing. *American Journal of Clinical Hypnosis*, 56(3), 285–302.

Alladin, A. (2014b). The wounded self: A new approach to understanding and treating anxiety disorders. *American Journal of Clinical Hypnosis*, 56(4), 368–388.

Alladin, A. (2015). *Integrative CBT for anxiety disorders: An evidence-based approach to enhancing cognitive behavioral therapy with mindfulness and hypnotherapy.* Chester, UK: Wiley.

Alladin, A., & Alibhai, A. (2007). Cognitive hypnotherapy for depression: An empirical investigation. *International Journal of Clinical and Experimental Hypnosis*, 55(2), 147–166. doi:10.1080/00207140601177897

Alladin, A., & Amundson, J. (2011). Cognitive hypnotherapy as an assimilative model of therapy. *Contemporary Hypnosis and Integrative Therapy*, 28, 17–45.

Andrews, G. (1990). Classification of neurotic disorders. *Journal of the Royal Society of Medicine*, 83(10), 606–607.

Andrews, G. (1996). *Comorbidity in neurotic disorders: The similarities are more important than the difference.* New York, NY: Guilford Press.

Araoz, D. L. (1981). Negative self-hypnosis. *Journal of Contemporary Psychotherapy*, 12, 45–52.

Araoz, D. L. (1985). *The new hypnosis.* New York, NY: Brunner/Mazel.

Bandura, A. (1977). Self-efficacy: Toward a unifying theory of behavioural change. *Psychological Review*, 84(2), 191–215.

Barabasz, A., Barabasz, M., Christensen, C., French, B., & Watkins, J. G. (2013). Efficacy of single-session abreactive ego state therapy for combat stress injury, PTSD, and ASD. *International Journal of Clinical and Experimental Hypnosis*, 61(1), 1–19. doi:10.1080/00207144.2013.729377

Barabasz, M. (2012). Cognitive hypnotherapy with bulimia. *American Journal of Clinical Hypnosis*, 54(4), 353–364. doi:10.1080/00029157.2012.658122

Barlow, D. H. (1991). Disorders of emotion. *Psychological Inquiry*, 2, 58–71.

Barlow, D. H. (2000). Unravelling the mysteries of anxiety and its disorders from the perspective of emotion theory. *The American Psychologist*, 55(11), 1247–1263.

Barlow, D. H. (2002). *Anxiety and its disorders: The nature and treatment of anxiety and panic.* New York, NY: Guilford Press.

Barlow, D. H., Ellard, K. K., Fairholme, C. P., Farchione, T. J., Boisseau, C. L., Allen, L. B., & Ehrenreich-May, J. T. (2011). *The unified protocol for transdiagnostic treatment of emotional disorders: Client workbook.* New York, NY: Oxford University Press.

Barrows, K. A., & Jacobs, B. P. (2002). Mind-body medicine: An introduction and review of the literature. *The Medical Clinics of North America*, 86(1), 11–31.

Beck, A. T., & Emery, G. (1985). *Anxiety disorders and phobias: A cognitive perspective.* New York, NY: Basic Books.

Beck, A. T., & Emery, G. (2005). *Anxiety disorders and phobias: A cognitive perspective.* New York, NY: Basic Books.

Beck, A. T., Rush, A. J., Shaw, B. F., & Emery, G. (1979). *Cognitive therapy of depression.* New York, NY: Guilford Press.

Beck, J. (1995). *Cognitive therapy: Basics and beyond.* New York, NY: Guilford Press.

Borkovec, T. D., & Weerts, T. C. (1976). Effects of progressive relaxation on sleep disturbance: An electroencephalographic evaluation. *Psychosomatic Medicine, 38*(3), 173–180.

Bowlby, J. (1973). *Separation: Anxiety and anger.* New York, NY: Basic Books.

Brown, D. P., & Fromm, E. (1986). *Hypnotherapy and hypnoanalysis.* Hillsdale, NJ: Erlbaum Lawrence.

Brown, D. P., & Fromm, E. (1990). *Hypnotic suggestions and metaphors.* New York, NY: W. W. Norton.

Brown, T. A., Antony, M. M., & Barlow, D. H. (1995). Diagnostic comorbidity in panic disorder: Effect on treatment outcome and course of comorbid diagnoses following treatment. *Journal of Consulting and Clinical Psychology, 63*(3), 408–418.

Brown, T. A., & Barlow, D. H. (2009). A proposal for a dimensional classification system based on the shared features of the *DSM-IV* anxiety and mood disorders: Implications for assessment and treatment. *Psychological Assessment, 12,* 256–271.

Brown, T. A., Chorpita, B. F., & Barlow, D. H. (1998). Structural relationships among dimensions of the *DSM-IV* anxiety and mood disorders and dimensions of negative affect, positive affect, and autonomic arousal. *Journal of Abnormal Psychology, 107*(2), 179–192.

Bryant, R. A., Moulds, M. L., Guthrie, R. M., & Nixon, R. (2005). The additive benefit of hypnosis and cognitive-behavioral therapy in treating acute stress disorder. *Journal of Consulting and Clinical Psychology, 73*(2), 334–340. doi:10.1037/0022-006X.73.2.334

Burns, D. D. (1999). *Feeling good: The new mood therapy.* New York, NY: Avon Books.

Butler, A. C., Chapman, J. E., Forman, E. M., & Beck, A. T. (2006). The empirical status of cognitive behaviour therapy: A review of meta-analyses. *Clinical Psychology Review, 26*(1), 17–31. doi:10.1016/j.cpr.2005.07.003

Butler, G., Fennell, M., & Hackman, A. (2008). *Cognitive-behavioral therapy for anxiety disorders: Mastering clinical challenges.* New York, NY: Guilford Press.

Campbell-Sills, L., Barlow, D. H., Brown, T. A., & Hofmann, S. G. (2006). Acceptability and suppression of negative emotion in anxiety and mood disorders. *Emotion, 6*(4), 587–595. doi:10.1037/1528-3542.6.4.587

Cardeña, E., Maldonado, J., van der Hart, O., & Spiegel, D. (2000). Hypnosis. In E. Foa, T. Keane, & M. Friedman (Eds.), *Effective treatment for PTSD* (pp. 247–279). New York, NY: Guilford Press.

Chambless, D. L. (1985). Agoraphobia. In M. Hersen & A. Bellack (Eds.), *Handbook of clinical behavior therapy with adults* (pp. 49–87). New York, NY: Plenum Press.

Christensen, C., Barabasz, A., & Barabasz, M. (2013). Efficacy of abreactive ego state therapy for PTSD: Trauma, resolution, depression and anxiety.

International Journal of Clinical and Experimental Hypnosis, 61(1), 20–37. doi:10.1080/00207144.2013.729386

Clark, D. A., & Beck, A. T. (2010). *Cognitive therapy of anxiety disorders: Science and practice.* New York, NY: Guilford Press.

Clark, L. A. (2005). Temperament as a unifying basis for personality and psychopathology. *Journal of Abnormal Psychology, 114*(4), 505–521. doi:10.1037/0021-843X.114.4.505

Dobbin, A., Maxwell, M., & Elton, R. (2009). A benchmarked feasibility study of a self-hypnosis treatment for depression in primary care. *International Journal of Clinical and Experimental Hypnosis, 57*(3), 293–318. doi:10.1080/00207140902881221

Dozois, D. J., & Westra, H. A. (2004). *The prevention of anxiety and depression: Theory, research, and practice.* Washington, DC: American Psychological Association.

Edgette, J. H., & Edgette, J. S. (1995). *The handbook of hypnotic phenomena in psychotherapy.* New York, NY: Brunner/Mazel.

Elkins, G. (2014). *Hypnotic relaxation therapy: Principles and applications.* New York, NY: Springer Publishing Company.

Elkins, G., Johnson, A., & Fisher, W. (2012). Cognitive hypnotherapy for pain management. *American Journal of Clinical Hypnosis, 54*(4), 294–310. doi:10.1080/00029157.2011.654284

Ellard, K. K., Fairholme, C. P., Boisseau, C. L., Farchione, T., & Barlow, D. H. (2010). Unified protocol for the transdiagnostic treatment of emotional disorders: Protocol development and initial outcome data. *Cognitive and Behavioral Practice, 17,* 88–101.

Esch, T., Fricchione, G., & Stefano, G. (2003). Use of relaxation response in stress-related diseases. *Medical Science Monitor, 9*(2), 23–34.

Ewin, D. M., & Eimer, B. N. (2006). *Ideomotor signals for rapid hypnoanalysis: A how-to manual.* Springfield, IL: Charles C. Thomas.

Farris, A. M., & Jouriles, E. N. (1993). *Handbook of behaviour therapy in the psychiatric setting.* New York, NY: Plenum Press.

Flammer, E., & Alladin, A. (2007). The efficacy of hypnotherapy in the treatment of psychosomatic disorders: Meta-analytical evidence. *International Journal of Clinical and Experimental Hypnosis, 55*(3), 251–274. doi:10.1080/00207140701338696

Follette, V. M., & Smith, A. A. (2005). *Encyclopedia of cognitive behavior therapy.* New York, NY: Springer Publishing Company.

Gershuny, B. S., & Sher, K. J. (1998). The relation between personality and anxiety: Findings from a 3-year prospective study. *Journal of Abnormal Psychology, 107*(2), 252–262.

Gibbons, D. E. (1979). *Applied hypnosis and hyperempiria.* New York, NY: Plenum Press.

Glick, B. S. (1970). Conditioning therapy with phobic patients: Success and failure. *American Journal of Psychotherapy*, 24(1), 92–101.

Gold, J. R., & Stricker, G. (2006). *A casebook of psychotherapy integration*. Washington, DC: American Psychological Association.

Golden, W. L. (2012). Cognitive hypnotherapy for anxiety disorders. *American Journal of Clinical Hypnosis*, 54(4), 263–274. doi:10.1080/00029157.2011.650333

Goldfried, M. R. (1971). Systematic desensitization as training in self-control. *Journal of Consulting and Clinical Psychology*, 37(2), 228–234.

Graci, G. M., & Hardie, J. C. (2007). Evidence-based hypnotherapy for the management of sleep disorders. *International Journal of Clinical and Experimental Hypnosis*, 55(3), 288–302. doi:10.1080/00207140701338662

Greeson, J., & Brantley, J. (2009). *Mindfulness and anxiety disorders: Developing a wise relationship with the inner experience of fear*. New York, NY: Springer Publishing Company.

Hammond, D. C. (2007). Review of the efficacy of clinical hypnosis with headaches and migraines. *International Journal of Clinical and Experimental Hypnosis*, 55(2), 207–219. doi:10.1080/00207140601177921

Hartland, J. (1971). *Medical and dental hypnosis and its clinical applications*. London, UK: Bailliere Tindall.

Hayes, S. C. (2004). Acceptance and commitment therapy, relational frame theory, and the third wave of behavioral and cognitive therapies. *Behavior Therapy*, 35, 639–665.

Hayes, S. C., Luoma, J. B., Bond, F. W., Masuda, A., & Lillis, J. (2006). Acceptance and commitment therapy: Model, processes, and outcomes. *Behaviour Research and Therapy*, 44(1), 1–25. doi:10.1016/j.brat.2005.06.006

Hazlett-Stevens, H. (2006). *Practitioner's guide to evidence-based psychotherapy*. New York, NY: Springer Publishing Company.

Iddon, J. L., & Grant, L. (2013). Behavioral and cognitive treatment interventions in depression: An analysis of the evidence base. *Open Journal of Depression*, 2(2), 11–15.

Iglesias, A., Iglesias, A., & Iglesias, A. (2013). I-95 phobia treated with hypnotic systematic desensitization: A case report. *American Journal of Clinical Hypnosis*, 56(2), 143–151.

Jensen, M. P. (2013). *Hypnosis for chronic pain management*. New York, NY: Oxford University Press.

Kasch, K. L., Rottenberg, J., Arnow, B. A., & Gotlib, I. H. (2002). Behavioral activation and inhibition systems and the severity and course of depression. *Journal of Abnormal Psychology*, 111(4), 589–597.

Kirsch, I., Montgomery, G., & Sapirstein, G. (1995). Hypnosis as an adjunct to cognitive-behavioral psychotherapy: A meta-analysis. *Journal of Consulting and Clinical Psychology*, 63(2), 214–220.

Leahy, R. L. (2003). *Cognitive therapy techniques: A practitioner's guide*. New York, NY: Guilford Press.

Linehan, M. M. (1993). *Cognitive behavioral treatment of borderline personality disorder*. New York, NY: Guilford Press.

Lynn, S. J., & Cardeña, E. (2007). Hypnosis and the treatment of posttraumatic conditions: An evidence-based approach. *International Journal of Clinical and Experimental Hypnosis*, 55(2), 167–188. doi:10.1080/00207140601177905

Moene, F. C., Spinhoven, P., Hoogduin, K. A., & van Dyck, R. (2003). A randomized controlled clinical trial of a hypnosis-based treatment for patients with conversion disorder, motor type. *International Journal of Clinical and Experimental Hypnosis*, 51(1), 29–50. doi:10.1076/iceh.51.1.29.14067

Monroe, S. M., & Harkness, K. L. (2005). Life stress, the "kindling" hypothesis, and recurrence of depression: Considerations from life stress perspectives. *Psychological Review*, 112(2), 417–445. doi:10.1037/0033-295X.112.2.417

Morita, S. (1998). *Morita therapy and the true nature of anxiety-based disorders*. Albany, NY: State University of New York Press.

Neisser, U. (1967). *Cognitive psychology*. New York, NY: Psychology Press.

Nichols, M. P., & Schwartz, R. C. (2008). *Family therapy: Concepts and methods*. New York, NY: Pearson Education.

Nolen-Hoeksema, S. (2004). *Abnormal psychology*. New York, NY: McGraw-Hill Companies.

Norcross, J. C. (2002). *Psychotherapy relationships that work: Therapist contributions and responsiveness to patient needs*. New York, NY: Oxford University Press.

Öst, L. G. (1987). Applied relaxation: Description of a coping technique and review of controlled studies. *Behaviour Research and Therapy*, 25(5), 397–409.

Papageorgiou, C., & Wells, A. (2004). *Depressive rumination: Nature, theory and treatment*. Chichester, UK: John Wiley & Sons.

Payne, L. A., Ellard, K. K., Farchione, T. J., Fairholme, C. P., & Barlow, D. H. (2014). *Clinical handbook of psychological disorders: A step-by-step treatment manual*. New York, NY: Guilford Press.

Perls, F. S., Hefferline, R., & Goodman, P. (1951). *Gestalt therapy*. New York, NY: Dell.

Post, R. M. (1992). Transduction of psychosocial stress into the neurobiology of recurrent affective disorder. *American Journal of Psychiatry*, 149(8), 999–1010. doi:10.1176/ajp.149.8.999

Roemer, L., Williston, S. K., Eustis, E. H., & Orsillo, S. M. (2013). Mindfulness and acceptance-based behavioral therapies for anxiety disorders. *Current Psychiatry Reports*, 15, 1–10.

Sauer-Zavala, S., Boswell, J. F., Gallagher, M. W., Bentley, K. H., Ametaj, A., & Barlow, D. H. (2012). The role of negative affectivity and negative reactivity to emotions in predicting outcomes in the unified protocol for the transdiagnostic treatment of emotional disorders. *Behavior Research and Therapy, 50,* 551–557.

Spiegel, D. (1981). Vietnam grief work using hypnosis. *American Journal of Clinical Hypnosis, 24*(1), 33–40. doi:10.1080/00029157.1981.10403281

Stahl, S. M., & Moore, B. A. (2013). *Anxiety disorders: A guide for integrating psychopharmacology and psychotherapy.* New York, NY: Routledge.

Stein, C. (1963). Clenched-fist as a hypnobehavioral procedure. *American Journal of Clinical Hypnosis, 2,* 113–119.

Suarez, L., Bennett, S. M., Goldstein, C., & Barlow, D. H. (2009). *Handbook of anxiety and the anxiety disorders.* New York, NY: Oxford University Press.

Tsao, J. C., Lewin, M. R., & Craske, M. G. (1998). The effects of cognitive-behavior therapy for panic disorders on comorbid conditions. *Journal of Anxiety Disorders, 12*(4), 357–371.

Tsao, J. C., Mystkowski, J. L., Zucker, B. G., & Craske, M. G. (2002). Effects of cognitive-behavior therapy for panic disorder on cormorbid conditions: Replication and extension. *Behavior Therapy, 33,* 493–509.

Walsh, R. (2011). Lifestyle and mental health. *American Psychologist, 66*(7), 579–592. doi:10.1037/a0021769

Watkins, J. G. (1971). The affect bridge: A hypnoanalytic technique. *International Journal of Clinical and Experimental Hypnosis, 19*(1), 21–27. doi:10.1080/00207147108407148

Watkins, J. G., & Barabasz, A. F. (2008). *Advanced hypnotherapy: Hypnodynamic techniques.* New York, NY: Routledge.

Watson, D., Clark, L. A., & Carey, G. (1988). Positive and negative affectivity and their relation to anxiety and depressive disorders. *Journal of Abnormal Psychology, 97*(3), 346–353.

Wegner, D. M. (1994). Ironic processes of mental control. *Psychological Review, 101*(1), 34–52.

Wilamowska, Z. A., Thompson-Hollands, J., Fairholme, C. P., Ellard, K. K., Farchione, T. J., & Barlow, D. H. (2010). Conceptual background, development, and preliminary data from the unified protocol for transdiagnostic treatment of emotional disorders. *Depression and Anxiety, 27*(10), 882–890. doi:10.1002/da.20735

Wilson, T. D., Lindsey, S., & Schooler, T. Y. (2000). A model of dual attitudes. *Psychological Review, 107*(1), 101–126.

Woldt, A. L., & Toman, S. M. (2005). *Gestalt therapy: History, theory, and practice.* Thousand Oaks, CA: Sage Publications.

Wolfe, B. E. (2005). *Understanding and treating anxiety disorders: An integrative approach to healing the wounded self.* Washington, DC: American Psychological Association.

Wolfe, B. E. (2006). *A casebook of psychotherapy integration.* Washington, DC: American Psychological Association.

Wolpe, J. (1958). *Psychotherapy by reciprocal inhibition.* Stanford, CA: Stanford University Press.

Wolpe, J., & Lazarus, A. A. (1966). *Behavior therapy techniques.* Oxford, UK: Pergamon.

Yapko, M. D. (1992). *Hypnosis and the treatment of depressions: Strategies for change.* New York, NY: Brunner/Mazel.

Yapko, M. D. (1997). *Breaking the patterns of depression.* New York, NY: Random House/ Doubleday.

Yapko, M. D. (2003). *Trancework: An introduction to the practice of clinical hypnosis.* New York, NY: Brunner-Routledge.

Ericksonian Hypnotherapy

Betty Alice Erickson

Ericksonian hypnotherapy, like its originator Milton H. Erickson, MD, is profoundly simple, yet simply profound. An explanation of either or both winds through trails of common sense, seemingly contradictory statements, wise multilayered interventions and more indefinable auras of the conscious and unconscious, as well as hypnotic connections even felt by observers.

Arguably the most famous hypnotist of the 20th century, Erickson spent most of his professional life reestablishing the validity of hypnosis for medical, dental, and psychotherapy professionals. Almost single-handedly he revolutionized its paradigm and lived to see his contributions accepted so thoroughly that many people today do not realize—or remember—when hypnosis was different. Over the years, science, with its increased capacity to measure brain functions, has validated much of his work. However, some of the premises still cannot be defined fully or validated due to a lack of ability to measure or codify them objectively.

A standard definition of "Ericksonian hypnosis" is difficult. Multilevel and flexible, it is patient-centered, using whatever is effective for that instance and patient. Often indirect and informal, it can produce a hypnotic state naturally by ostensibly ordinary conversation. Frequently very permissive, it also can be very direct and authoritative. It is different yet inclusive of "standard" schools of hypnosis. Probably the best definition is that it is an overall approach to the complex phenomenon of hypnosis more than it is a separate entity.

Considering some of the characteristics of the man behind these changes and advances in hypnosis provides a framework for better understanding the fundamentals of his work. However, Erickson's real contribution to hypnosis and psychotherapy, with which hypnosis is inextricably intertwined, is virtually impossible to convey fully in print. One of its values is that it is so multileveled, so individualized, so complex, yet so simple, that observing, studying, and practicing are the most effective ways of appreciating its intricacies.

EARLY BACKGROUND

As a boy, young Milton learned about hypnosis through an advertisement in a popular magazine. His younger sister Bertha was his first subject. Working with her convinced him that hypnosis was beyond his limited expertise, so he decided to wait until he was in college to study it. In 1923, as an undergraduate at the University of Wisconsin, he saw Professor Clark Hull demonstrating hypnosis and knew he was ready to learn more. After that class, he began practicing self-hypnosis and working not only with the demonstration subject but with every other willing person he could find, including friends, fellow students, and family members.

He took extensive notes, which he presented to Dr. Hull the next year. The two men disagreed— Erickson was not enthusiastic about authoritative and highly structured approaches; Hull very much preferred those. However, Hull did construct a semester-long class in hypnosis including both men's points of view. He was most definitely the professor, but he used some of Erickson's work in that class. They never did agree on fundamental ideas, but Erickson maintained respect for Hull's scholarship and dedication to science.

He also recognized similarities between them. Raised on Midwestern farms, both were used to hard work. Both had suffered bouts of infantile paralysis as young men; while Erickson's was much more severe, neither recovered full movement. Both considered themselves scientists.

At this point, Erickson was inspired to continue studying hypnosis and decided to add what he thought, rather than continuing the path others were taking. He never abandoned that goal.

After graduation in 1928, with both an MD and an MA in psychology, Erickson did his medical internship at the Colorado Institute for the Criminally Insane. There he was forbidden by terms of his contract even to mention the term *hypnosis*. Obviously, this was long before any psychotropic drugs; Erickson never forgot the many lessons he learned there about true mental illness. He then continued to work at increasingly important positions in various mental hospitals for decades. It was during this time that he began his significant research into hypnosis.

After a severe attack of "serum sickness," a life-threatening reaction to an anti-tetanus vaccine in 1948, he moved to Arizona. After a year of recuperation and a year working at Arizona State Hospital, he shifted to private practice. He preferred the more flexible schedule and looked forward to having students. His health remained precarious for the rest of his life. Now it is recognized that he also suffered from post-polio syndrome, but at the time, it was diagnosed as another strand of the three known types of infantile paralysis.

TEACHING

Most of Erickson's students wanted to understand his approach to psychotherapy; however, his innovative psychotherapeutic methods could not be separated from his work in hypnosis. Among those early students was Jay Haley, referred by Erickson's long-time friend, Gregory Bateson, who had founded the Bateson Project to study communicative aspects of schizophrenia. Haley became an early proponent of Erickson's work and the two maintained their friendship for decades.

Bateson also referred Raymond Birdwhistell, PhD, an American anthropologist who founded kinesics and also was formulating his theory that well over half of communication was kinetic rather than verbal. The mutual influence of Birdwhistell and Erickson can only be surmised, but over several years, the two had many lengthy conversations.

When the Palo Alto Mental Research Institute (MRI) was later established, John Weakland, Paul Watzlawick, Richard Fisch, and others came to Arizona to learn more. Erickson and his union of psychotherapy and hypnosis still influence MRI's work as well as many other therapy systems.

Erickson's major goal remained to bring the use of hypnosis into the hands of qualified professionals as the powerful tool he knew it was. Evident of his interweaving of psychology and hypnosis, and perhaps directly springing from his work with the talented people of the Palo Alto group, was the founding of the American Society of Clinical Hypnosis (ASCH) in 1957. This grew from "The Seminars on Hypnosis," which had taught primarily physicians and dentists to use hypnosis effectively in their practices during the early 1950s.

One of the specific goals in forming ASCH was that nonacademicians, primarily practicing clinical psychologists, and social workers have a professional organization for hypnosis. Erickson and several colleagues dedicated significant profits from seminars to the new society. He became its founding president and remained editor of the ASCH journal for 10 years.

RESEARCH

A great deal of Erickson's early professional life was spent on scientific research. He always regarded himself as a scientist interested mainly in hypnotic phenomena. He published over 200 professional articles, most based on that work. Many experiments were carefully done to explore mind–body connections. The list of topics is eclectic and extensive; he worked with and then published about virtually every problem he encountered in his lifelong practice as a psychiatrist.

A cursory overview includes such wide-ranging topics as chronic pain, control of bleeding, Tourette's syndrome, enuresis, cancer, end-of-life pain and treatment, weight gain and loss, headaches, time distortion, placebo responses, even sneezing patterns, possible dreaming in an infant, and breast enlargement in a teenager, as well as complex and lengthy work with an aphasic stroke victim.

Nothing was out of range for his intellectual curiosity. A student doubted hypnotic age regression and skeptically remarked that knowing the name of the day for a given date in a previous year was merely a numerical calculation. Erickson and his mathematician son, Allan H. Erickson, who was then teaching college algebra classes, devised an experiment to show the ease or difficulty in doing this. Repeating somewhat a study Erickson did decades earlier with psychotic patients, the two men formulated two problems for 40 college algebra students. The results in this experiment were similar to the older study. It is complicated and difficult to quickly and correctly calculate the day of the week for a given past date—even for college students in an algebra class (Erickson & Erickson, 2010).

I will summarize one published case from the subject's point of view. As a child, I had severe amblyopia. Patching my strong eye, treatment still used today, was not very effective—and I hated it. Corrective eye muscle surgery was scheduled, but canceled when I caught chicken pox. Erickson, not highly in favor of the surgery to begin with, decided to teach me to overcome my "lazy" eye. To succeed, he had to emphasize the visual processing of the weaker left eye, which my brain had learned to ignore to avoid blurry and double vision. He had to teach my "lazy" eye to be more active in seeing so my brain would use that information effectively.

He decided to "shut off" my right eye so my left eye would be forced to work harder—he was going to "patch" the strong right eye using hypnosis. I was only 8 years old, so the method had to intrigue me or I would view it as a trial and undoubtedly would not cooperate fully. I disliked my frequent eye examinations and was not too fond of the doctor. Erickson asked if I wanted to learn how to fool the doctor. In retrospect, clearly, he set up an informal trance with that question; more than half a century later, I still smile thinking of how I fooled the doctor, whose name I do not even remember.

Sitting in front of a mirror, I first imagined gazing far away with one eye and then the other. Then I watched, using a mirror, how my pupils responded when I thought about looking at bright or dim lights with one eye while the other did not see anything. Next I learned to "look at the sun" in my mind, with only one eye while the other one looked at darkness. Doing that, I got to see a very large difference in the size of my pupils. I played with these concepts all summer, almost every afternoon, and often with Erickson beside me. My goal was to fool the eye doctor; his was to increase my sight by "reprogramming" my left eye to be more

active and my brain to use input from both eyes rather than just the stronger one.

At my next exam, my eye doctor was visibly concerned as my pupils contracted and expanded at random intervals. I was delighted. When I told the ophthalmologist I was doing it on purpose, he did not believe me. Then I triumphantly got to show him. The next time I saw him, he asked me to do it again, and I did.

This was a success from every aspect, certainly from my perspective. My sight improved in my left eye; further, it has not deteriorated. Even now, virtually every eye doctor remarks how well my eyes are balanced despite much poorer vision in my left eye.

POSTHYPNOTIC SUGGESTIONS

Erickson believed posthypnotic suggestions, as well as all other suggestions or interactions in trance, had to be agreeable to the conscious. Even though the conscious mind is often bypassed in hypnosis, it continues to have this amount of monitoring.

One of Erickson's favorite posthypnotic suggestions when psychotherapeutic work had been done was *"And some things can be left in the unconscious where they can really help you"* (his emphasis). That ambiguous suggestion is only beneficial.

Martin Orne, MD, PhD, who later became a well-known hypnosis researcher, studied with Erickson for a summer in the mid-1950s. I was often his practice subject. Once in a demonstration, he asked me to remove my watch as a posthypnotic suggestion. When he wove the "signal" word into conversation, I touched my watch but did not remove it.

Orne later asked why I had not followed his posthypnotic suggestion, which I did not consciously remember. I responded I had felt like taking off my watch but I did not think it respectful. It did not fit with my idea of a demonstration subject; I should not distract the audience's attention by removing my wristwatch.

Later, as a college student, in a deep trance in front of a large number of physicians, I stood and announced to a man in the back of the room that he had called me by the wrong name. I then sat back down with no regard for his embarrassment, apology, or even that Erickson then had to "repair" the situation.

I remembered the incorrect name and my actions, but not what happened afterward, so I asked Erickson. He used it to explain that a healthy subject is protective of a sense of self even in a deep trance. Even in a trance, the conscious mind monitors. That was not enough reassurance for me. It seemed strange I would interrupt a demonstration, let alone embarrass a man who had merely called me by the wrong name, a common mistake. Erickson laughed and said that was precisely why I had done what I had.

My double name is frequently changed to a more common one. Being called the wrong name has always annoyed me; as a young teenager, I had begun to introduce myself using only the first half. Erickson called me by my complete first name and the man made a common error in his question. In a trance, my more childlike unconscious defended me.

I still did not believe that my embarrassing an unknown man in a group of his peers was all right. Erickson reminded me I had been willing to embarrass Martin Orne, whom I considered a friend, when I refused a harmless posthypnotic suggestion simply because it did not fit with my idea of my task. Names are very important. I was not going to let anyone, even or especially a stranger, call me by an annoyingly wrong name.

He added that he should have corrected the man immediately; he knew it annoyed me. From now on, he added, he would. My double name continued to be a problem in demonstrations, and Erickson always corrected the error.

Orne continued investigating whether subjects could be hypnotized into doing behaviors not consciously acceptable. Erickson continued his belief they would not. The two remained friends and respectful of the other's work until Erickson's death.

CONCEPTS

One of Erickson's most notable contributions to hypnosis was redefinition of it as a cocreated relationship between people and not what is done to someone by another person. This is now such an accepted belief about hypnosis that most people do not even remember that it was Erickson's concept and originally not widely accepted.

He described hypnotic trance many times, in many ways. It was "an altered state of consciousness" (Erickson & Rossi, 1981). There were no scientific ways to measure it. Also, it was "giving all attention to certain stimuli or certain aspects of a stimulus complex" (Erickson, 1944) as well as "a marked receptiveness to ideas and understandings and an increased willingness to respond either positively or negatively to those ideas" (Erickson & Rossi, 1980).

Other times, he said it was the kind of reality that exists in dreams and compared it to a child's confusion about if a dream was actually reality. Internal processes were more important than his words; he wanted his voice to be merely a background to the subject's own reality (Erickson & Rossi, 1979).

Erickson also said it to be a focused beam of attention, usually directed inward, bypassing conscious defenses and accessing unconscious or forgotten resources while excluding extraneous stimuli.

CONSCIOUS AND UNCONSCIOUS

Erickson repeated endlessly that the conscious and the unconscious are two separate systems and parts of the different levels of awareness and understanding that people have (Havens, 1989). Conventional wisdom calls it "listening to our gut."

Hypnosis speaks from and to the unconscious, which Erickson believed to be benign and similar to a small child—happy, enthusiastic, curious, loving and sharing, and excited and joyful, often in a childlike way. He taught that a healthy adult is in touch with the part of the unconscious that finds joy in mundane pleasures—cool ice cream on a hot day or the excitement of a puppy's wagging tail. This allows us all to experience unexpected wonders—a double rainbow or a hummingbird hovering over a flower. He strongly believed in, modeled, and taught about keeping delight and joy in life.

CATALEPSY

Catalepsy is another sign of a trance. Erickson once explained that people could hold their eight-pound heads up, erect, for hours at a time because they knew how to balance their neck muscles perfectly. Catalepsy allows people to balance their muscles perfectly in ways that cannot be done consciously. In a trance, people also become unaware of their outstretched arm just as we are unaware of holding our heads erect. Fatigue is not anticipated, tired muscles are automatically adjusted, and the effort is not regarded as difficult.

Erickson enjoyed teaching his patients catalepsy, particularly hand levitation. It validated trance and gave subjects a way of recreating their trance by remembering how it felt when their hand lifted seemingly by itself.

He utilized people's common responses to enhance catalepsy. When he lifted a subject's hand, he would hold his palm flat with his thumb and four fingers almost hanging loose. He would press his thumb on one side of the wrist with the four fingers firmly on the opposite side. As the induction would continue, he would gradually lessen the pressure of the fingers while keeping the pressure of the thumb firm.

As he continued to talk, he used his voice as yet another tool; as he talked about the lightness the person could feel, almost unnoticeably his fingers would slip off the wrist, one by one, while the pressure of his thumb remained. The hand and forearm were being "held up" solely by the thumb pressing on one side of the wrist. Slipping into the trance felt natural.

ECONOMY

Hypnosis is an economy of communicating as well as of understanding behavior even though, and perhaps because, the unconscious is highly literal. Deliberate movements are lessened—a single nod conveys yes. Verbal responses are limited to what is asked. Erickson often asked, "Will you tell me your name?" In a waking state, even in a light trance where the conscious is more active, the question is answered with the person's name. In a deeper trance, subjects typically nod their heads, indicating yes they will. They are not asked, however, so they do not give their name.

He said repeatedly, especially in his later years, that the most powerful way to create a hypnotic trance with another person is that the hypnotist be in a trance himself and have an air of delighted expectation that the other would join him. This is true whether it is a formally induced trance or a conversational one.

PAIN

Over years, the ability of hypnosis to manage pain became even more important to him. He used self-hypnosis consistently, especially in his later years, to manage the chronic and acute pain he felt from muscle spasms as a result of post-polio syndrome. He published on this; he taught most of his children and some of his older grandchildren to use self-hypnosis for pain management.

CHILDBIRTH

All over the world and for centuries, women have had babies with minimal suffering. Part of this is based on necessity, clearly. It is a luxury to have a clean hospital bed and a physician and nurses at hand for any emergency. However, a normal childbirth was planned by nature to be reasonably quick and with little pain.

My mother used hypnosis for the birth of her children, as I did for my children. My mother had read the precursor to Grantly Dick-Read's (1942) *Childbirth Without Fear* and I read the newer version. Erickson did not focus on lessening pain; he used Dick-Read's terminology to redefine it and then added curiosity and time distortion. Women could perceive each contraction as lasting but a few seconds, and times between as long enough to "catch a quick but restful nap." Additionally, he gave a combination of facts, questions, and distractions. We all know that everything in nature is different—each leaf, each fingerprint, even each snowflake, although whether anyone has ever examined them all is unknown. If you stand at the edge of the ocean and watch the waves, each one is different. A bigger one is almost always followed by several smaller ones. The same could be true of each contraction. . . . You could wonder if the next would be larger or smaller.

While Erickson was in the delivery room for my mother's first children, he relied on her expertise for the later ones. He did teach me and then announced I could do it without any more help. My children were born in military hospitals, where there is sometimes a cookie-cutter approach. My obstetrician, weary of my continued requests to bypass the routine spinal anesthesia for hypnosis, finally announced I could use hypnosis only if I was trained by Milton Erickson. I was, so I did. Later, he even asked me to run a group for his other patients.

UNCONSCIOUS

In Erickson's explanation of the unconscious, he stated:

> Underneath the diversified nature of the consciously organized aspects of the personality, the unconscious talks in a language which has a remarkable uniformity; further, that language has laws so constant that the unconscious of one individual is better equipped to understand the unconscious of another than the conscious aspects of the personality of either. (Erickson & Kubie, 1940)

He spent a lot of time refining his definitions of the unconscious. Over the years, they, like his definition of hypnosis, became so accepted that it is often forgotten they first came from Erickson. I believe he would think that was the best outcome possible.

We all know a lot more than we realize. Erickson believed that knowledge was stored in people's unconscious minds. Specifically in reference to hypnosis, he said people "have had a lifetime of experience in which talking is done at a conscious level and have no realization that talking is possible at a purely unconscious level of awareness" (Erickson, 1952). He wove understandings of the unconscious mind into easy-to-understand examples. We all know how many swallows of water are necessary to quench thirst well before the water has had a chance to be absorbed—and we know, without consciously knowing how we know, that we need more on a hot summer's day than we do during the cold winter.

The unconscious also tries to help us, sometimes in a childlike way. We all know people who will explain that their morbid obesity keeps people away. Sometimes it is very useful to our adult self; we know how to manage pain—we have seen a bruise on our body without any conscious knowledge of how it occurred. We all remember something that we think we have forgotten, when something reminds us, or even when we put it aside to "remember later." "Sleeping on an idea" is in the common vernacular.

One of hypnosis's greatest attributes is accessing the vast amount of knowledge we have that we do not consciously know we have. From this comes Erickson's oft-quoted remark to trust the unconscious. However, even with Erickson's fervent belief in the power of the unconscious, he knew that, as Michael Yapko, PhD, so wisely added, "But sometimes, the conscious gets in the way."

CHANGES FROM HYPNOSIS

Erickson believed it was generally fruitless to take away behaviors from patients or even alter them, even if they were used incorrectly. His philosophical stance was "expand perspectives." Conversational hypnosis allowed these changes because the person heard with more than the conscious mind.

Even with the oft-referenced examples of the institutionalized man who believed he was Jesus, the couple with enuresis, or the African Violet Lady, Erickson did not attempt to change behaviors. He merely indicated another happier, more productive choice. He gave the man the idea that his "blessing" motions were similar to the motions Jesus made as a carpenter sanding wood. A great shift was built on that undeniable, albeit psychotic truth. The young couple had to decide if they would participate in "an experiment" to receive free treatment. It genuinely was an experiment as Erickson had never tried that approach before. With the depressed African Violet Lady, he made a seemingly offhand suggestion, appealing to several aspects of her, perhaps only unconsciously known, finer desires and suggested a fitting way to interweave those in her life.

People typically hear only that which fits within their established paradigm of life. Expanded viewpoints give more options. Virtually all people want to live happy, independent, and productive lives.

MULTILEVEL COMMUNICATION

All language and virtually all communication have several levels. Erickson told Ernest Rossi, "From my childhood on, I practiced talking on two or three levels" (Erickson & Rossi, 1981). We are all experts at understanding multiple meanings even if we do not always consciously recognize how or even that we have done it. Erickson made a life study of it, pointing out the importance of really observing, rather than merely looking, with common examples. We have all not noticed when a man shaves off his mustache or a teenager's braces are removed. Erickson always did.

A wife can say, "I'm not mad, why would you think I was mad at you?" The husband knows she is angry and wants something from him. We attribute that to the tone of voice, context, and the kinetics of communication. Our unconscious recognizes she said "mad" twice and added "at you"; both are unnecessary emphasis. This is a very simple example quantifying multilevel communication.

Communication also falls prey to meanings people already have. People believe their experiences are like those of other people and we all do have common experiences. However, "a couple of drinks at bedtime" has no real meaning without knowing how big the glass is. The simple word *snag* means different things to a lumberjack, someone with a new sweater, a manicurist, and a company looking at their production process.

Our unconscious has a better ability to understand real meanings. Conventional wisdom tells us: "Listen to your gut." Well-trained police officers, physicians, and certainly con artists have these abilities honed to a sharp point. They calculate their responses by understanding cues that the "normal" person would never notice, let alone factor into a reaction. These are simple examples of awareness of multilevel communication sharpened by experience, discussion with more knowledgeable people, thoughtful reflection, and acceptance of our personal abilities and goals.

Knowledge is available from our unconscious mind any time we need it; we do not have to know it consciously. People commonly say in emergency situations, "I just went into automatic mode!"

Erickson also knew feelings spring from the unconscious, which "behaves in accord with its own code of behavior" as he said in a presentation to ASCH in 1966. People not only vigorously defend feelings but they are usually fond of them. The most appealing language to anyone is connected with personal feelings, spoken or not, conscious or not. Strengthening the eye muscles of a child to avoid surgery is a goal virtually incomprehensible to the child. The lure of playing a parent-sanctioned trick on a disliked grown-up is irresistible.

Erickson did not recognize "resistance"—he saw it as not using the correct language to aim the patient in his own direction in a way that most pleased and benefited him.

INDUCTIONS

"An Hypnotic Technique for Resistant Patients: The Patient, the Technique and Its Rationale and Field Experiments" includes a transcript of an induction for an angry and uncooperative patient (Erickson, 1964). Here he indicates that a hypnotic induction is simply a communication of ideas and the fostering of different thoughts within the subject.

Hypnotic inductions are the result of the processes and understandings already existing within the subject himself. These processes are elicited by the hypnotist as he communicates effectively. What the hypnotist does, Erickson indicates, is to provide a means to stimulate and arouse the subject's past conscious and unconscious learning. As Erickson concludes the article: "One primarily meets the patient's needs on the terms he himself proposes; and then one fixates the patient's attention, through adequate respect for and utilization of his method of presenting his problem to his own inner processes of mental function."

A phrase he used in so many inductions—"You can see your hand as though it isn't even yours"—is a multilayered expansion of self-perceptions. "You can" reinforces trust in the subject's abilities and recognizes independence, as "can" is not an order. For some, perhaps many, it can also reference the children's tale of *The Little Engine That Could* where the little engine triumphed because he thought he could. "As though" is an indirect dissociation giving the information that dissociation is a skill and all skills can be valuable. It also sets a framework for future pain management.

Sometimes he would add, " . . .*but you know it is yours and you can even wiggle those fingers, if you want. . . . "* This supports independence, ensures control, and enhances the dissociation and trance by using "those" instead of the more usual "your." The personal pronoun "yours" is in juxtaposition with the indefinite pronoun "those" serving as an adjective. Subjects often smile as they wiggle their fingers, so finding pleasure in self and unexpected places is reinforced. It also provides another opportunity to recognize success. The hypnotist can say with a happy smile, "That's right!" as Erickson so often did. Even with closed eyes, people hear a smile and know the hypnotist is joining in that pleasure. Working with hypnosis, Erickson rarely, if ever, praised with any phrase other than "That's right," said with a happy smile and clear emphasis. Spoken words such as "Good" or "Wonderful" can easily be heard by the childlike unconscious as judgmental.

PSYCHOTHERAPY

With the amount of scientific research he published, Erickson was always a bit surprised, especially in his later years, to be more widely recognized for psychotherapeutic work. His goal to expand and legitimize hypnosis had never changed. Most of his hypnotic work included some form of psychotherapy and all psychotherapy included some amount of hypnosis, so it became more and more difficult to differentiate the two and sort out the differences.

Additionally, he eschewed psychological theories, believing that the physiological and psychological differences and the vastly different experiences and interpretations that people had were far too varied to be fit within any theory. That did not affect his knowledge that people definitely had many commonalities.

In his later years, defining hypnosis became even more complex because he moved almost exclusively to conversational inductions. Was that really hypnosis? Was it merely intense conversation with the client focusing on what Erickson said? Did Erickson believe he had induced a useful hypnotic trance with no techniques? Could that even be done by merely telling a story? What were the intellectual underpinnings of even considering this as hypnosis?

BACKGROUND

A marked receptiveness to ideas and understandings and an increased willingness to respond either positively or negatively to those ideas at this time, the closest thing to a biography is *Milton H. Erickson, M.D.: An American Healer*, published in 2006 (Erickson, Keeney, & Keeney, 2006). Erickson's time spent growing up on a farm remained a basic premise of his life philosophy. He never lost the ethic of hard work or of the many life lessons that farm life teaches. One favorite adage was: "If you sow enough seeds, some of them will sprout—especially if you don't keep pulling them up to check on them."

Even as a youngster, he was interested in the ways that people thought and how they would use whatever was available. For years, he got up very early when new snow had fallen and tramped a path through it to the mile-distant school. Some parts would be straight, whereas other parts were wandering, even circular. Sometimes it would be well trodden; other times, he would make just one set of footprints.

Then he would race home, do his morning chores, run back, and hide to watch the other students walking to school. He wanted to see just how circuitous or how faint he could make the path before others would break their own way through the snow. Sometimes he would join them and see just how easily they would follow the longer path if they were distracted by conversation. He learned how indirect he could be, before people ignored his path to their goal, as well as how much diversion it took to distract people into following a more indirect route.

It is easy to see more of the beginnings of his hypnotic psychotherapy with oft-told tales of his boyhood behaviors that illustrate deep understandings that carried over into his life's work. Two are used here.

First, Erickson was amused at his father's unsuccessful efforts at pulling an unwilling calf from bright daylight into the darker barn. His annoyed father told him to try it himself, and young Milton stepped up to the calf standing stubbornly at the entrance and yanked her tail. She immediately bolted forward into the barn.

The second was when a lost and unfamiliar-looking horse suddenly appeared at the family farm. No one knew to whom the horse belonged.

As the adults tried to figure out a solution, Erickson vanished with the horse. When he returned, he announced he had returned it to the owner. Asked how he knew where the horse lived, the young boy replied he did not. But he knew the horse knew. So he got on its back and kept the horse focused on moving rather than grazing on the tempting grass along the way.

The messages are clear—work with resistance, rather than against it; keep focused on the solution, the assets of the other, even if they are not immediately or easily recognized. And those are just a few.

Bedridden and totally paralyzed with infantile paralysis at 17, Erickson amused himself by listening to footsteps outside his house. First, he would try to figure out if it was a man or a woman and how old the person was. After entry into the house, he would listen to the conversation to guess what the person really wanted—merely sociability, information, or a favor. If it were something more than just a friendly visit, who would be the first to say it directly? He never stopped listening to people carefully, realizing that what is not said is very often far more important than what is not.

From his paralysis, he learned to explore and believe in the power of the brain–body connection, the beginning of his understanding of neural plasticity. He first moved by remembering how it felt to move his toe and his thumb. He often said he sometimes did not know if he was moving his finger or if he was just remembering how it felt. Whichever it was, it did not matter.

One day, placed in his rocking chair and unable to see out the window while his family worked in the fields, he tried to remember how it felt when he rocked his chair. As he focused on remembering to remember exactly how it felt, the chair moved slightly. And he literally, and figuratively, moved forward from that.

He learned to walk, first on crutches, by examining his baby sister as she began to stand and then walk unaided. He broke the task down into minute movements—just exactly how was weight shifted? What was then required? This division of complex learning into small discrete tasks occurred in the very early 1920s, long before educational theories began promoting that idea.

In the fall, he asked for his wheelchair to be put at the edge of a harvested field. When his family was out of sight, he would fall out of his chair so he could crawl over the harvested stubble as far as he could manage. He always knew if he was not seated in his chair when his mother returned, she would not allow him to be wheeled to the edge of the fields again. He made it back every time, knowing this great and painful effort was the best hope for the life he wanted. Although he walked with a cane his entire life, he was always pleased he was out of a wheelchair until the last 10 years of his life.

He realized one change leads naturally to another—like laws of physics, each physical change or new behavior opens onto a reaction, another behavior—even if they are not equal and opposite. Changes create different arenas; building and expanding on those can not only be easier, but each step gives its own reward.

DEFINITION OF NORMAL

During World War II, Erickson spent years giving psychiatric evaluations to young men who had passed their physical exams and appeared at his door clad only in a towel. Erickson carefully arranged his room—the examinee's chair at a slightly awkward angle, so face-to-face contact required the man to shift his upper body. Smoking was very common, even encouraged, and cigarettes, matches, and an ashtray were placed invitingly, but out of convenient reach on the desk. Then he watched the men as each entered.

"Good" signs were if the young man sat down without moving the chair, turned to face Erickson, and waited for a cigarette to be offered. "Bad" signs were if the man repositioned his chair without asking or did not make an effort to face Erickson when he was seated. Most of those who did that also reached out for a cigarette. Jay Haley often said, with a smile, that was the beginning of brief therapy.

The rest of his life, Erickson talked about the two most important things he had learned. First was an even bigger respect for the spirit of mankind—thousands of young men passed though his office, almost all wanting to convince the doctor they were good candidates to risk their lives for their country. The second was the vast range of normal. People could be raised with enormous differences in values, likes, and perceptions, in so many different cultural ways. Yet they were fine people. That may have been where he formed one of his therapeutic and personal guidelines: Behaviors that did not harm other human beings and did not use them for personal gain, without their considered consent, were normal and acceptable.

Erickson's wife and frequent collaborator, Elizabeth Moore Erickson, and this author developed "Erickson's Ten Rules of Life" in the early 1990s in an attempt to codify some of the basic premises of his work—the common sense, which is sometimes forgotten, especially in the complexities of psychotherapy. Included are aphorisms such as that life itself is hard work, unfair, and contains suffering and pain. However, the law of averages is usually correct. What is in your heart really governs how you live more than what is in your head. What we receive in life depends on merit but also good luck or bad luck or a combination of the two. Erickson said the last "rule" over and over: "Life was made for amateurs and we're all amateurs at it." This one sentence demonstrates common sense, humility, and wisdom, in truthful phrasing, but in a way we do not often think about.

NATURALISTIC–CONVERSATIONALIST HYPNOSIS IN PSYCHOTHERAPY

As he aged, Erickson became more and more interested in informal trances; they have the same attributes as formal trances, are easier to create, and we are all used to them. Just the words *"Once upon a time, a long time ago, in a faraway kingdom lived a handsome prince"* creates an inward beam of attention as the listener settles back to hear about a beautiful princess and maybe a dragon, but definitely a happy ending. That expectation, from the listener's own past, and openness to it creates a naturalistic trance, where the induction, body, and even the intent can be more indirect. The whole trance can become exactly what the subject wants for his unconscious needs. As the subject is creating his own state, resistance is effectively gone.

Such trances can be as effective as more formal ones. Jay Haley wrote about Erickson conversing with one of his children who had just fallen, jammed his tooth into his gum, and severely cut his lip (Haley, 1986). First, Erickson agreed with the

little boy and repeated that the cut really must hurt a lot. Not only did the unexpected and, for most people, counterintuitive remarks get the child's attention, but Erickson's credibility was immediately established. It **did** hurt a lot.

The amount and color of the blood was admired and the boy began considering his bleeding not as an alarming loss, but as a remarkable tribute to the quality of it. This different perspective was interesting as well as filled with self-praise, because he had created that blood.

Eventually, the boy trotted off to the emergency room, washcloth held tightly to his cut, mirror in his hand, to demand more stitches than his older sister had accumulated. Validation of the severity of the injury, redefining of the blood loss as a chance to admire its richness, then curiosity over whether compression would be strong enough to stop the blood flow focused on what was more pleasing than pain and powerlessness. Adding competition with his older sister's stitches would be enticing to any younger brother. Additionally, it gave him a feeling of control—he could demand the doctor give him more stitches, which ensured he would be a cooperative patient, certainly the adults' goal.

Hypnosis was never mentioned, but features of a hypnotic trance were certainly present. There is still some debate whether trance can be definitively determined even with input from science. I am not sure what Erickson believed, but his beliefs are not relevant today, decades after his death. What is relevant, then and now, is that Erickson was interested in results—not necessarily in what the results were called—thinking, good luck, concentration, or hypnosis.

He had already spent much time researching how people could make physiological changes, could manage pain, and could promote healing more rapidly from surgery and other wounds with hypnosis (Erickson, 1980). When Martin Orne spent time with Erickson, one of his goals was to define exactly what Erickson considered hypnosis to be. A subset was to become more familiar with objective signs of hypnosis and devise a way that might help Orne define it more clearly.

Over the next several weeks, this author's task was to be in a hypnotic trance without Orne noticing. We engaged in ordinary activities, walks, and conversations. To my delight, Martin, a semiprofessional magician, entertained me with many feats of what truly seemed like magic. At intervals, we both wrote down our experiences.

At the end of summer, they discussed observations of objective signs of a trance. It turned out to be much more difficult than either expected. Interactions such as laughing and conversation were common in my self-reported trances; Orne expressed surprise and even doubt, while I was very certain I had been in a trance.

With only one subject, this was very far from scientific research. It was merely a teaching experience—actually for us all. Over time, the results of their curiosity and certainly the notebooks have been lost. Both Erickson and Orne confirmed what I already felt—it was very difficult to draw clear boundaries between a waking state and a hypnotic trance . . . even for the subject.

EXPANSION OF PERSPECTIVES

In a trance, the unconscious hears on multiple levels—conscious defenses are bypassed. This one concept covers an enormous area of Erickson's hypnotic and therapeutic work. A broadening of views always gives options. With options, people have choices and independence, a primary joy in life. An intriguing new thought engages people in themselves; the inward focus creates trance—there can be no resistance. No one told them anything, asked them to think or behave differently. Trust in the person is clear.

Erickson also used the notion that unexpected interruption of ordinary behavior tends to produce an immediate trance as the listener reorients and reprocesses for a cogent response. Once he and I were disagreeing about whether all behaviors and abilities were learned or could be part of the brain's hardwiring. Finally, he fixed his eyes on me and asked intently but with a curious tone, "Do you believe in Beethoven?"

"Of course, I believe in Beethoven! What kind of a question is that?"

With great intensity, he responded: "Beethoven wrote 'Ode to Joy,' late in his life when he was deaf. Is that teachable?"

My immediate change in thinking might have also occurred in conversation. However, the sudden switch in topic, which was still related to our discussion, required me to focus inward and then understand on a wider level. He did not tell me anything; he just "made" me ask myself my own question.

OBSERVATION

Erickson was always fascinated by how people unknowingly communicated so much about themselves. Once, he had a beautifully dressed and carefully coiffed new appointment walk in the office—fluffy ruffled blouse, well-fitting skirt, long dangling earrings, and very high heels. Seated in the chair closest to Erickson, leaning closely toward him, the prospective patient talked about how futile the search for an adequate psychiatrist had been. Erickson was almost the last on the list. Glancing down, carefully brushing a piece of lint off the shoulder nearest Erickson, the patient leaned closer. With legs crossed, foot jiggling, there was a nervous wait for Erickson's response. Erickson gazed intently at his new patient and asked, "How long have you been wearing women's clothing?" The man leaned back and said, "You are the right psychiatrist."

After the patient was successfully discharged, Erickson told this story many times, complete with the gesture of brushing lint off a shoulder. Rarely did anyone recognize the patient was a cross-dresser.

There are clues even in a print version. Nowhere was a pronoun used. When a careful but somewhat awkward construction is used for anything, something is probably being concealed. There are also usually reasons for unnecessary, distracting details. A fluffy ruffled blouse conceals a male Adam's apple. Women walk differently than men—cross their legs differently. Finally, this story is in the section about the importance of observation.

Telling it, Erickson was able to demonstrate the lint-brushing gesture. Women brush lint from their shoulders with their arm angled out to make room for their breasts; men reach directly across their chest.

The first time I heard this, I asked, "What would you have done if the patient had been a woman?" He responded, "Then she would have thought I was asking a strange question as psychiatrists do and responded, 'Oh, about 16, I don't know.'" I continued: "What if he didn't want you to know?" Erickson merely replied, "He challenged me, so he did."

STORYTELLING

Erickson experimented endlessly to see just how easily trances could be induced. As a young man, he practiced on us children with games and storytelling. A favorite was the continuing tale of a frog, "White Tummy—and that was his name because he had a green back and a white tummy and White Tummy lived on a big green lily pad. . . ." The reader can infer the beginning of a story-induced trance with even those few words.

Even babies were not exempt. He would look into their eyes, with outstretched forefinger, saying slowly but intently, "Bumble-bee, bumble-bee. . . ." He would pause, then "Bzzz" slowly, moving his finger closer. With a final "Bzzz," still looking in the child's eyes, he would smile and tickle the tummy. When I first saw him doing this with my son, I asked what he was doing. "Teaching him to go into a self-induced hypnotic trance where his memories become real and experiential to him." He intently looked at David, my year-old son, and slowly raised an extended forefinger. David burst into laughter holding his hands over his tummy. It was not an anticipatory laugh; the sensation was obviously real. Without that intense trance-inducing gaze and slow movement, the boy would have merely looked at the forefinger and waited for something else.

Conversational trances are easily induced by stories. The subject hears the story content but can also easily hear the message within. From the Bible to Aesop's fables to Grandma sitting us on her lap, we are used to learning from stories.

Many of Erickson's stories had similar messages, but details were tailored for the listener. All were told in the same way. Steve Lankton, LCSW, DAHB, one of Erickson's students and renowned in his own right as an author, hypnotist, and therapist, reviewed Jane Parson-Fein's newly released DVD of Erickson's actual teaching. One long induction, overtly demonstrating various trance phenomena, told stories about life and its variety—seasons of the year, seeds, and new plants at the arboretum. He talked about the mysteries of migration: salmon hatching in streams, going to the sea to mature, and then returning home, and about baby kangaroos at the zoo. The trance was actually aimed at and was successful in preventing the subject's carefully planned suicide, even though a nonsuicidal listener would not hear that message.

Lankton noted the pace of Erickson's voice was about half the rate of normal speech. A listener has difficulty focusing solely on the words and information in the story. Minds wander, while the unconscious hears the underlying meaning. The careful looseness of construction lets people retrieve their own personal associations. Then they often believe Erickson is talking directly to them (Lankton, 2015).

Probably the quality most overlooked in Erickson's work was his very genuine caring and compassion for his patients. That feeling, the feeling of love, is impossible to measure scientifically. Less than 200 years have passed since the discovery of x-rays, which allowed us to see bones in our living bodies. Now we routinely monitor the electrical currents produced by in our brains through EEG recordings and fMRI. The future often brings credibility to things that were impossible to support scientifically just a few years previously.

The importance of caring is illustrated by one of Erickson's cases quoted often: Joe, the florist. Joe was dying painfully; his goal was to have less pain, less medication so he could interact with his family more coherently. Erickson says he was

> most dubious about achieving any kind of success with Joe since, in addition to his physical condition, there were definite evidences of toxic reactions to excessive medication. Despite the author's unfavorable view of possibilities, there was one thing of which he could be confident. He could keep his doubts to himself and he could let Joe know by manner, tone of voice, by everything said, that the author was genuinely interested in him, was genuinely desirous of helping him. If even that little could be communicated to Joe, it should be of some comfort, however small, to Joe and to the family members and to the nurses within listening. (Erickson, 1966)

I was then living close to Joe's home. When Erickson left on a lengthy teaching trip, he asked me to call and then to visit Joe; he had told both Joe and his wife that he was going to do that. I was not aware of how desperately ill Joe was but when I called, I was welcomed and invited to come see him. Upon arrival, Joe's wife told me merely to sit with him and talk "gently about garden plants" and to touch his hand while I talked. I was with him for about 20 minutes; Joe lay motionless, but I knew he was hearing me.

Afterward, his wife and I shared cups of tea. She told me Erickson had kept "her Joe" alive and enjoying life. Joe felt Erickson cared for him, cared about him, and "had love in his heart." That made Joe want to have more of his family and of life, and he did. She wanted me to thank Erickson and tell him what she said.

Perhaps sometime in the future, we will be able scientifically to measure the powerful feelings of love and caring just as surely as we can feel them today. When we reach that goal, then we can scientifically assess the true healing power of it. And I do not think Erickson will be surprised.

Erickson's legacy of redefinition of hypnosis in scientific research, in the seamless melding of hypnosis with psychotherapy, in the demonstration of the validity of conversational trances, and in his clarity about differences between and usefulness of conscious and unconscious minds is lasting, well established, accepted, and taught by many all over the world.

I believe he would also want to be remembered as a person who changed the face of hypnosis and psychotherapy by caring deeply and compassionately about people and their long-term welfare and by being unafraid of letting them know that.

For comprehensive overviews of Milton H. Erickson's work, I recommend:

"In the Room With Milton H. Erickson, M.D." Six DVDs of Milton Erickson teaching, complete with subtitles. Bound transcript also available at Jane Parsons-Fein's website: Pfti.org

The Wisdom of Milton H. Erickson; The Complete Volume by Ronald A. Havens, Crown House Publishing, Norwalk CT.

The Complete Works of Milton Erickson, a 16-volume set, edited by Ernest Rossi, R. Erickson-Klein, & K. Rossi, The Milton H. Erickson Foundation Press, Phoenix, AZ.

Uncommon Therapy by Jay Haley, Grunne & Stratton, New York, NY.

Collected Papers of Milton H. Erickson, M.D., a 4-volume set, edited by Ernest Rossi, Halstead Press; John Wiley & Sons, Inc., New York, NY.

REFERENCES

Dick-Read, G. (1942). *Childbirth without fear*. London, UK: Pinter & Martin.

Erickson, B. A., Keeney, B., & Keeney, B. P. (2006). *Milton H. Erickson, M.D.: An American healer*. Sedgwick, MN: Leete's Island Books.

Erickson, M. H. (1944). An experimental investigation of the hypnotic subject's apparent ability to become unaware of stimuli. *Journal of General Psychology, 31*(2), 191–212. doi:10.1080/00221309.1944.10543188

Erickson, M. H. (1952). *A lecture by Milton H. Erickson, Los Angles, June 25* [Audio Recording No. CD/EMH.52.6.25].(Phoenix, AZ: Milton H. Erickson Foundation Archives).

Erickson, M. H. (1964). A hypnotic technique for resistant patients: The patient, the technique, and its rationale, and field experiments. *American Journal Clinical Hypnosis, 7*(1), 8–32.

Erickson, M. H. (1980). *Hypnosis in obstetrics*. In E. Rossi (Ed.), *Collected papers of Milton H. Erickson, M.D.* New York, NY: Irving Publishing.

Erickson, M. H., & Rossi, E. L. (1980). *Investigation of psychodynamic processes: The collected papers of Milton H. Erickson on hypnosis*. New York, NY: Irvington.

Erickson, M. H., & Rossi, E. L. (1981). *Experiencing hypnosis: Therapeutic approaches to altered states*. New York, NY: Irvington.

Erickson, M. H. (1966). The interspersal hypnotic technique for symptom correction and pain control. *American Journal of Clinical Hypnosis, 8*(3), 198–209. doi:10.1080/00029157.1966.10402492

Erickson, M. H., & Erickson, A. H. (2010). Past weekday determination in hypnotic and waking states. In E. Rossi, R. Erickson-Klein, & K. Rossi (Eds.), *The collected works of Milton H. Erickson* (pp. 89–95). Phoenix, AZ: The Milton H. Erickson Foundation Press.

Erickson, M. H., & Kubie, L. S. (1940). The translation of the cryptic automatic writing of one hypnotic subject by another in a trance-like dissociated state. *Psychoanalytic Quarterly, 9*, 51–63.

Erickson, M. H., & Rossi, E. L. (1979). *Hypnotherapy: An exploratory case book*. New York, NY: Irvington.

Haley, J. (1986). *Uncommon therapy: The psychiatric techniques of Milton H. Erickson, M.D.* New York, NY: W. W. Norton.

Havens, R. (1989). *The wisdom of Milton H. Erickson: Hypnosis and hypnotherapy*. St. Paul, MN: Paragon House.

Lankton, S. R. (2015). *Review of* In Room With Milton H. Erickson, M.D. [Review of the DVD *In Room With Milton H. Erickson*, produced by Jane Parsons-Fein, 2014.]

Hypnosis From a Psychoanalytic Perspective

Thomas W. Wall

It is the intent of this chapter to bring together the postmodern psychoanalytic perspective for both contemporary models of psychodynamic thought and hypnosis and the relational variables as they relate to hypnosis from this perspective. While there is no clear or agreed-upon current psychoanalytic model of hypnosis, hopefully this chapter will serve as an impetus for further exploration within this theoretical frame of reference.

The focus includes a brief historical discussion of hypnosis from early analytic formulations to more current models that include contemporary dimensions of more evidence-based psychoanalytic thought. In addition, reference is made to object relations, neuroscience, and attachment theory. This is followed by a review of five relational variables, the meaning of which has evolved over time. These variables have special application for the hypnotically trained practitioner as sources of understanding and knowledge about our patients from an intersubjective perspective.

The relationship between hypnosis and psychoanalytic/psychodynamic thought dates back to Freud and Breuer's book, *Studies on Hysteria*, (1957/1895). Their collabokration involved the use of hypnosis in treating hysterical symptomology. Their approaches utilized hypnosis from somewhat different perspectives and have been regarded as the first use of hypnosis as an "instrument" for a more scientific investigation of the mind. Breuer emphasized a dissociated state described as a "hypnoidal state" and emphasized catharsis and abreaction. He used hypnosis in an effort to regress the patient back to the original experience and the associated "strangulated affects" carried in the memory of the original experience. These affects were cut off from consciousness. Through hypnosis, the affects associated with the original experience were made conscious and "discharged" or abreacted.

For Freud, the original instrument for treatment was hypnotic suggestion. As noted in his introduction (p. xvii):

> If there were also *unconscious* mental processes, some special instrument was clearly required. The obvious instrument for this purpose was hypnotic suggestion—hypnotic suggestion used, not for directly therapeutic purposes, but to persuade the patient to produce material from the unconscious region of the mind.

Freud used hypnosis in the case of Frau Emmy Von N., who suffered from severe animal phobias. He noted she was relatively easy to hypnotize. He employed the use of the cathartic method with her for the first time. He explained in the "Preliminary Communication" (Freud, 1893) which begins the case histories, "We regard hysterical symptoms as the effects and residues of excitations which have acted upon the nervous system as traumas." Later, he opined that therapeutic success on the whole was considerable, but it was not a lasting one. Throughout the text, Freud developed/discovered new ideas regarding early psychoanalytic theory and practice. For instance, he learned that a precipitating factor in hysteria could be psychological as well as physical. When psychological, the etiologies of the symptoms were not remembered by the patient or available to conscious memory. This led him to the concept of *repression*, a defense of unconscious forgetting of a threatening or disturbing experience. He later observed that the repression produced an unconscious resistance primarily due to distressing effects of fright, anxiety, or shame, among others. He concluded that recollection alone of these affects or working through the associated affect does not necessarily produce a favorable result. In addition, Freud introduced the concept of *transference* for the first time, defining it as a "false connection." Edelstein (1981) references an incident in which Freud used hypnosis with a female patient who suddenly awoke and threw her arms around him. From this, he thought he understood the "mysterious element" behind hypnosis (transference), and "in order to exclude it, it was necessary to abandon hypnosis." Fromm and Nash (1997, p. 11) explain that Freud later revised his definition of *hypnosis* as "the influencing of a person by means of the transference phenomena."

Eventually, Freud abandoned the use of hypnosis altogether due to a number of reasons including the "mysterious element," and in part due to the patient's *resistance* to the treatment or lack of cooperation in his or her own treatment. Also, as noted earlier, the effects of the treatment were not necessarily lasting. Due to Freud's abandonment of hypnosis and a stubborn adherence to his instinctual drive-based theory along with the many who followed his theoretical perspective, with few exceptions hypnosis was not written about within the psychoanalytic literature. Notable exceptions were Wolberg (1945), Kline (1958), Gill and Brenman (1961), Schneck (1965), Barnett (1981), and Watkins (1992), as well as others who continued to explore the use of hypnosis within a broad psychodynamic framework. Kline (1955, p. 80) noted, "The efficacy of hypnosis, as a definitive therapeutic procedure in itself, is not related to hypnosis as much as it is related to the use of hypnosis within the framework of a knowledge of psychodynamics and of related behavioral science." Kline's comment foresaw the future direction of both psychoanalytic thought and the use of hypnosis within this framework.

Gill and Brenman (1961, pp. xix–xx) in their book, *Hypnosis and Related States: Psychoanalytic Studies in Regression*, offer a bridge between the transference-based explanations of hypnosis and a "state of altered ego-functioning" by arguing that the "regressive process of hypnosis is more than a transference phenomenon and can be initiated either by sensory-motor-ideational deprivation or by the stimulation of an archaic relationship to the hypnotist." This was a shift in theory that included both transference-based explanations of hypnosis and a dissociative perspective. For many years, various authors argued for transference-based explanations of hypnosis that were primarily based on a one-person

psychology. Less attention was placed on the therapeutic relationship/therapeutic alliance and more on technique and theory from a drive-based model. It was a change in theory associated with Hartman and the ego psychologists that allowed hypnosis to be considered as more than a transference phenomenon. He emphasized the ego as a structure in its own right not tied exclusively to instinctual processes as Freud and others postulated. He proposed conflict-free ego functions. The emphasis was on primary autonomy including defense, adaptation, reality testing, and affect regulation. This allowed Gill and Brenman (1961) to expand the "regressive process of hypnosis" to include external influence on the sensory-motor-ideational experience of the patient as well as retaining the transference explanation. In effect, this opened the door for "postmodernism," which is an umbrella term referring to a shift from a one-person psychology to a two-person psychology. That is, the therapist is no longer seen as the objective observer. The observer is also the observed. Loewenthal and Snell (2003, p. 1) have proposed that postmodern thinking "underlies the importance of putting the other (the client/patient) first, and it emphasizes the inter-subjective, what can emerge 'in the in-between.'" Elsewhere, they make the point that "language is never static, but always changing . . . that our words and gestures are cultural, personal and inter-subjective *acts*" (p. 1). In support of this notion, the intersubjective approach of Stolorow and Lachmann (1985), emphasize that the mind does not exist in isolation. They view transference not as a regression or biologically determined drive but in interactional terms between patient and therapist as an expression of striving to organize experience and create meaning. Winnicott (1971) elaborated the idea of "potential space or transitional space" in terms of intersubjectivity by noting the duality that something can have an independent objective existence and at the same time is self-created, that is, is endowed with personal or illusory meaning. (I elaborate this notion later in relation to the hypnotic experience.) Greenberg and Mitchel (1983), in their classic text, *Object Relations in Psychoanalytic Theory*, note the focus of therapy is not on the patient; rather, the interactive field seeks to establish connection with the other, preserve relational ties, and differentiate the therapist from the other. This suggests that transference is unique to the patient–therapist pair and is coconstructed within the interactional field. The view is that we are object seeking/relationally seeking rather than drive discharging and that the primary goal of the ego/self is to achieve and maintain object relatedness/object attachment. They proposed that who we are is embedded within a matrix of relationships and that the mind is composed of relational configurations. Moreover, they suggest we struggle to maintain our object ties while simultaneously trying to differentiate ourselves from them. Early psychoanalytic explanations of hypnosis were based on a one-person model, while more contemporary theories are based on a two-person codetermined model.

Parallel to this perspective, hypnosis went through a similar developmental phase. As late as 1991, Chase and Chase reiterated that hypnosis was viewed as direct or indirect suggestion, primarily a transference phenomenon. They proposed an integrated approach toward hypnosis in which transference served the function of allowing cooperation with the induction process for the purpose of invoking a topographic regression (a regression in function). This in turn led to a readiness for dissociation, defined as a "universal ego capacity for holding different ideas, affects, and memories simultaneously in different levels of awareness" (Chase & Chase, 1991). They note that a topographical regression "is brought about by reducing the reality oriented ego functions which in turn reduce the level of conscious awareness and the general reality orientation of the ego" (Chase & Chase, 1991, p. 516). In some ways, this is similar to Gill and Bren man's (1961) explanation of hypnosis that includes both transference and dissociation as key elements, though not necessarily from a two-person model.

In a thoughtful way, Fromm (1987) chronicles the significant developments in hypnosis in the past 25 years. She discusses new treatment approaches such as hypnoanalysis for psychotic disorders, certain personality disorders, posttraumatic stress disorder (PTSD), and various somatic disorders. She notes that various hypnotic techniques have been influenced by the changes in psychoanalytic methods derived from object relations and self theories. The history of hypnosis has primarily involved direct and indirect suggestion. She notes the significant role imagery plays for therapeutic purposes in various applications of hypnosis. In this regard, Sandler (1990, pp. 874–875) also has written "Internal objects can be regarded as the structural basis for the fantasies which provide very necessary

feelings connected with the experience of the *presence* of the object." That is, internal objects have the capacity to create, through the fantasy of the individual, the quality of the "presence" of the object. This adds support for Fromm's view noting the role imagery plays in more contemporary and expanded uses of hypnosis in treatment.

Today, the emphasis on transference issues and what they reveal within the dyad are focused on developing and maintaining an effective therapeutic alliance. Geller and Porges (2014, p. 178) have noted, "Effective therapeutic work is only possible when the client feels safe and secure in the therapy setting." To this end, they have developed the concept that therapeutic presence is central to positive change for clients in psychotherapy and that "differential therapeutic outcomes may only be minimally attributed to specific techniques" (Geller & Porges, 2014, p. 178). They have defined *therapeutic presence* to include therapists "being fully in the moment on several concurrently occurring dimensions, including physical, emotional, cognitive, and relational" (Geller & Porges, 2014, p. 178). They have posited four significant variables:

> being grounded and in contact with one's integrated and healthy self; being open, receptive to, and immersed in what is poignant in the moment; having a larger sense of spaciousness and expansion of awareness and perception; and having the intention of being with and for the client in service of their healing process. (p. 179)

They have offered the opinion that "therapists' presence invites the client to feel 'met' and understood, as well as safe enough to become present within their own experience, and in relationship with their therapist, allowing for deeper therapeutic work to occur" (p. 179). The practitioner trained in both psychodynamic approaches to therapy and hypnosis appreciates the importance of "being present in the moment" and following the suggestion by Geller and Proges in the quote in the preceding text. From the hypnosis literature, this links to what Baker (2000) has described as essentially the same position.

The interaction effect may well be the mechanism for the therapeutic action of hypnosis. It is not what the hypnotist does, which is critical. It is how the dyad construes and experiences how they are together that seems most evocative and evolutionary. (p. 65)

THEORETICAL CONSTRUCTS

With this overview of the evolution of psychoanalytic methods and the co-occuring changes in our understanding of what constitutes the hypnotic experience, it will be important to look at the evidence supporting each. Wachtel (2010) has made a distinction between "evidence-based practice" and treatments as "empirically validated." He has argued for the importance of focusing on the principles and process that are the basis for effective therapeutic work and not treatments, per se. He notes the work of Rosen and Davidson (2003, p. 306), "Any authoritative body representing the science of psychology should work toward the identification of empirically supported principles of change." For a review of the efficacy of hypnosis, see Mendoza and Capafons (2009) who has provided a literature review in this regard. Another study by Landholt and Milling (2011) has provided excellent support for the efficacy of hypnosis for labor and delivery pain. Their conclusion is, "Hypnosis tends to outperform standard medical care and interventions that are non-hypnotic in nature in relieving pain" (p. 1029). It is beyond the scope of this chapter to review the many references that support Wachtel's focus, noting principles of change as they relate to hypnotic interventions.

There is a growing body of research to support "empirically supported" psychodynamic therapies. The reader is referred to Smit et al. (2012) and Levy and Ablon (2009) for an excellent review of the literature. Shedler's (2010, p. 98) review, "The Efficacy of Psychodynamic Therapy," is a comprehensive review of the empirical evidence "that patients who receive psychodynamic therapy not only maintain therapeutic gains, but continue to improve over time." He has noted seven features that reliably distinguish psychodynamic therapy from other therapies.

These therapies are "focusing on affect and the expression of emotion," "exploration of attempts to avoid distressing thoughts and feelings," "identification of recurring themes and patterns," a "developmental focus" exploring early experiences and the way the past influences the present, "focus on interpersonal relations," "focus on the therapy relationship," and "exploring fantasy life" (Schedler, 2010, pp. 99–100). The therapist trained psychodynamically with advanced training in hypnosis would use these therapy variables, focusing on both assessment and the development of treatment goals as codetermined in the treatment relationship. In this regard, Schedler (2010, p. 100) notes that "this material is a rich source of information about how the person views self and others, interprets and makes sense of experience, and interferes with a potential capacity to find greater enjoyment and meaning in life." Cortina (2010), writing about the future of psychodynamic psychotherapy, proposed basic concepts similar to Schedler's. Under developmental processes, he noted the importance of attachment theory and the work of John Bolby and Mary Ainsworth and her colleagues. Their work has contributed to the notion of secure and insecure attachment and the development of an internal working model. In addition, he noted the importance of "implicit relational knowing" or procedural knowing that is "unconscious not because it is repressed, but because sub-symbolic processes of information cannot be retrieved consciously." Siegel (1999, p. 72) has proposed that "mental models" are the basic components of implicit memory: "forming mental models is the essential manner in which the brain learns from the past and directly influences the present and shapes future actions."

From the hypnosis literature, Diamond, (1986) delineated a number of processes the hypnotically trained psychodynamic therapist focuses on. These are similar to those of the nonhypnotically trained clinician, in addition to those mentioned by Schedler and others. Diamond (1986, p. 239) noted a "focus on subtleties of communication" involving the exchange of information with respect to unconscious communication. Subtleties of communication suggest an appreciation to attend to and respond to unconscious mental processes in the "language" specific to each hemisphere. From the neuroscience literature, Schore (2012, p. 5) has noted, "It is now clear that psychotherapeutic changes in conscious cognition alone, without changes in emotion processing, are limited." Bromberg (2011, p. 126), referencing the change from a one-person to a two-person psychology, has proposed three clinical shifts related to this conceptual change: "a shift from the primacy of content to the primacy of context; a shift from the primacy of cognition to the primacy of affect; and a shift away from (but not yet an abandonment) of technique."

Schore (2012, p. 7) has proposed the importance and delineated the functions of the right hemisphere. He has described the highest human functions—"stress regulation, intersubjectivity, humor, empathy, compassion, morality, and creativity—all of which are right brain functions. I am also suggesting an expanded capacity for right and not left brain processing lies at the core of clinical expertise." This is an important notion, as hypnosis has often been regarded as involving a shift from left- to right-brain processing. Clearly, the therapeutic relationship and much of what constitutes hypnotic interventions are an effort to quiet the left brain and promote a dissociative state that involves communication from left brain to right brain. McGilchrist (2009, p. 176) has noted:

> I believe that the representation of the two hemispheres is not equal, and that while both contribute to our knowledge of the world, which therefore needs to be synthesized, one hemisphere, the right hemisphere, has precedence, in that it understands that knowledge that the other comes to have, and is alone able to synthesize what both know into a useable whole.

What makes this important for the health care professional trained in the uses of hypnosis is attention to the nonlanguage aspects of therapeutic work and their importance in treatment. The perception of voices and the prosodic elements of speech, gestures, body postures, facial expressions, somatic experiences, and others are characterized by a general pattern of right hemispheric functional asymmetry. These contribute to the formation and ongoing development of the therapeutic relationship and those variables cited earlier such as the empathic capacity, mindfulness, and the focus on intersubjectivity.

THE ARCHITECTURE OF RELATIONAL VARIABLES

With this orientation and associated theoretical constructs, it will be important to review the

relational variables that the psychodynamically and hypnotically trained practitioners use for both assessment and treatment as they arise in the interaction field for both. The relational variables are the therapeutic alliance, transference, countertransference, projective identification, and the use of transitional experience. As we look at these relational dimensions, it is important to appreciate how they inform us about our patients and ourselves and aid in the development of appropriate treatment approaches.

Therapeutic Alliance

It is well documented that a good therapeutic relationship correlates with a positive treatment outcome. It is also a consistent observation that the patient's subjective evaluation of the relationship, rather than specific therapist interventions, has the most impact on treatment outcome. Hovarth and Symonds (1991) summarized 15 years of research and concluded that the quality of the alliance, given variations in definition, is the most robust predictor of outcome in psychotherapy. Parallel to this in the hypnosis literature is Baker's quote noted earlier regarding how the dyad "construes and experiences how they are together" that is most important.

The therapeutic alliance is the *reality* of the relationship and depends on the capacity of both to see each other in reality as separate beings, with the capacity to observe one's projections on the therapist. The alliance is the framework against which transference projections are identified, understood, and worked through. In other words, it is the patient's experience of "them together" that correlates most positively with therapeutic outcome. It involves the interactive experience of responsiveness, attunement, and attachment. It involves a willingness to enter the patient's emotional space. Allen et al. (1996, p. 259) have focused on "patient collaboration" as a key facet of the therapeutic alliance. In addition, they have noted, "Our findings reflect the extent to which the patient and therapist are jointly engaged in the process of *making psychological meaning of significant material.*" They have further argued from an insight-oriented perspective that the value is not just confined to the content of interpretive work, but is the "*process of fostering the patient's capacity for reflection.*"

All psychotherapy and hypnotic work depends on the quality of the therapeutic alliance. All of the relational variables involved in the treatment process rest on the established relationship as the foundation on which treatment is coconstructed. Markin (2014, p. 331) has noted the importance of the question, "What kind of relationship does my client need to get better, not just what do I need to do to my client to make him or her better?" It has been argued that the quality of the alliance, measured in different ways, is a powerful predictor of treatment outcome. In this regard, the capacity to utilize hypnotic treatment or capacity for hypnotizability is dependent on the capacity to engage in light-to-moderate states of dissociation, defined as the capacity to perform two tasks simultaneously, called parallel processing, as in the observing ego and the experiencing ego. Said another way, hypnotizability is the capacity to alter one's conscious experience while being in a relationship that feels safe and secure enough to allow one to participate in an induction procedure to promote a dissociative experience. This means the patient's relational capacity to form an attachment and work meaningfully within that attachment is part of the assessment process for both psychotherapy and hypnosis. Numerous authors have made the point for the consistent observation that the client's subjective evaluation of the relationship, rather than the therapist's actual behavior, has the most impact on therapy outcome. I would argue that it is both the subjective evaluation of the patient and therapist's evaluation of the relationship that are most crucial to a successful outcome.

Transference

Transference is an essential relational variable for all psychodynamic treatment approaches. Its value lies in understanding and appreciating the nature of the therapeutic relationship and its importance as a source of informing us about how our patients experience us and/or the therapeutic relationship. One of the earliest discussions of transference appears in *Studies on Hysteria* (Breuer & Freud, 1895). Freud referred to transference as a "false connection" whereby the patient transfers unconscious ideas about figures from the past onto the person of the physician. Transference has been defined in various ways. For example, it has been defined as the unconscious, intrapsychic, affective experience largely determined by previous significant attachment relationships. Levy and Scala (2012, p. 392) have defined *transference* as a "tendency in which representational aspects of important and formative relationships (such as parents and siblings) can be both consciously experienced and/or unconsciously ascribed to other relationships." For a discussion of the evidence for the concept of transference, see Luborsky et al. (1985) and, more recently, Levy and Scala (2012).

Transference has been viewed through many lenses. For example, it has been seen as a form of regression, displacement, projection, distortion, and as an organizing activity. The latter is associated with Stolorow and Lachman (1985), who argued for transference as an organizing activity because it is general enough and sufficiently inclusive to embrace multiple dimensions. They proposed "transference, not as a biologically determined tendency to repeat the past, ad infinitum, for its own sake, but rather as the expression of a universal psychological striving to *organize experience and construct meanings*" (p. 27; italics added).

In 1949, Donald Hebb proposed that neurons, which fire together at one time, tend to fire together in the future, or neurons that fire together wire together. This is the basis of neural association that functionally links the activity of neurons. Siegel (1999) has proposed that memory is based on the binding together of various neuronal activation patterns. This is how the neural net remembers. Transference becomes possible through the activation of neural patterns associatively linked to our internal working model developed through interactions with primary caregivers. Transference can be evoked by how the therapist is experienced by the patient as this relates to the associational activation of the neural net. This is not the past–past, but the present–past. What is experienced and labeled as the past is "alive" in the present in some way as a dynamic in the present. Schore (2014, p. 390) has noted that "acting at levels beneath conscious awareness, this internal working model is accessed to perceive, appraise, and regulate social-emotional information and guide action in familiar and especially novel interpersonal environments." Mental models are the basic components of implicit memory (Siegel, 1999). He has noted that we "filter our interactions with others through the lenses of mental models created from patterns of experiences in the past." In this way, transference is activated by associatively linking the present relational experience to past relational experiences developed from the implicit learning derived from the internal working model.

From a hypnotic perspective, transference elements either evoked by the therapist or developed over time through the patient's experience of the therapeutic relationship are important to the ongoing assessment process and developing a treatment approach unique to the individual. Transference is primarily an unconscious expression from implicit memory as opposed to conscious or explicit memory. As Schore and others have noted, these implicit elements form part of our subjective sense of ourselves. In this regard, as they have noted, we act, feel, and imagine without recognition of the influence of past experience on our present sense of reality. Said another way, Shuren and Grafman (2002, p. 918) have proposed that the "right hemisphere holds representations of emotional states associated with events experienced by the individual." When the individual encounters a familiar scenario, "representations of past emotional experiences are retrieved from the right hemisphere and are incorporated into the reasoning process." This is important; as the nature of the therapeutic alliance is developed, it will be influenced by these past emotional experiences. Hence, attention to these transference elements are important as they can influence the development of the alliance either positively or negatively and ultimately the success of the treatment. For example, trust of the therapist using hypnosis, feeling safe and secure in the attachment, and being aware of how one is being perceived and experienced are examples of possible transference elements to be appreciated.

Countertransference

In 1910, Freud wrote about countertransference in a paper entitled *The Future Prospects of Psychoanalytic Therapy*. He focused on the analyst's transference, that is, displaced feelings, conflicts, and wishes, onto the patient. He proposed that the analyst should recognize and *overcome* his or her countertransference (italics added). He saw it as an impediment and disruptive to the process of therapy. With a few exceptions, little was written about countertransference between the periods of 1910 and 1948. Tansey and Burke (1989) labeled this period "four decades of silence"

in terms of significant writings on countertransference. In 1950, Paula Heimann, in a landmark paper, *"On Countertransference,"* described the treatment relationship between two persons as characterized by strong feelings in both participants. She made the important contribution that countertransference should refer to all the feelings the therapist has for the patient. She stated, "The analyst's unconscious understands that of his patient on a much deeper and more accurate level than the analyst's conscious." Moreover, she noted, "This is the most dynamic way in which his patient's voice reaches him" (Heimann, 1950, p. 82). She proposed that by attending to the feelings aroused in the therapist with his patient's associations and behavior, the therapist is best able to be reached by the patient's voice. The evolution of countertransference moved from originally being thought of as an obstacle to treatment ("to be overcome"), later viewed as potentially neurotic with possible therapeutic value, to being recognized as an instrument or normative phenomena to be appreciated and used to enhance understanding of the therapist–patient interaction. Moreover, following Heimann's thoughts, attending to one's internal subjective experiences as images, thoughts, and feelings as possible communications from the patient's right brain, the "patient's voice" is able to reach the therapist's right brain on a deeper level than conscious communication.

It has been argued that emotional attunement is fundamentally left brain to right brain. Siegel (1999, p. 88) has noted, "Attunement involves alignment of states of mind in moments of engagement, during which affect is communicated with facial expression, vocalizations, body gestures, and eye contact." That is, attunement supports Schore's notion that "transference-countertransference transactions represent nonconscious nonverbal right brain-mind-body-communications" (Schore, 2012, p. 41). This supports the importance of the therapist attending to more than the acoustic data. Thoughts, feelings, and images that spontaneously come into the therapist's awareness are a source of reverie or intuition as a possible communication to the therapist's right brain. The communication of feeling states between the patient's and therapist's right brains can be described as "intersubjectivity." This again suggests the importance of the therapist attending to his or her own internal experience of the patient as a source of communication and information. For example, in listening to a patient describe her history of abuse, I began to get the image of the Pieta statue on display in the Vatican of Mary holding Christ. I thought this was curious at first and began to wonder what the patient was trying to relay to me about her self-experience. Was the image related to something about a mother holding a child and offering comfort? Was the patient trying to communicate something about her suffering that activated an image in me related to several possible meanings? Other possible meanings crossed my mind, but after containing the image over time, I eventually decided aspects of both were important. The notion of seeking comfort and wanting me to be a source of comfort, given the apparent extent of her suffering, seemed most relevant. While I never directly shared the image of the statue with her, I was able to reflect about the importance and need for comfort. My reflection included an appreciation for and acknowledgment of the degree of her emotional distress, that is, her long-standing sufferance. Attention to countertransference thoughts, feelings, and images are important sources for the patient's voice to reach the therapist/hypnotist as communication from right brain to right brain. Dorpat (2001, p. 450) noted, "Intuitions, images, and emotions derived primarily from the primary process system provide an immediate and prereflective awareness of our vital relations with both ourselves and others." The current themes in psychodynamic psychotherapy as Shedler (2010) has proposed are "affect and expression of emotion," the "exploration of attempts to avoid distressing thoughts and feelings," and attending to development issues as reflections of one's internal working model, that is, the importance of past early experiences with caregivers and how this influences our relationship experiences in the present. By attending to our ongoing countertransference experiences as important sources of information about our patients, the alliance relationship, and ourselves, we have an "instrument" to aid in our ongoing efforts to help the patient feel felt.

Projective Identification

Projective identification is related to countertransference and was first identified by Melanie Kline in 1946. She argued that projective identification was the basis of many anxiety situations

and was considered a primitive defense against anxiety through the concept of splitting. Splitting was viewed as a biologically determined mode of managing danger as an unconscious way to create safety by distancing the "endangered" from the "endangering." The projection was understood as an effort, in fantasy or interpersonally, to remove the internal danger by locating the danger outside of oneself. Ogden (1979, p. 1) has explained that

> projective identification is a concept that addresses the way in which feeling-states corresponding to the unconscious fantasies of one person (the projector) are engendered in and processed by another person (the recipient), that is, the way in which one person makes use of another person to experience and contain an aspect of himself.

Projection differs from projective identifications. In projection, the person feels a psychological distance from the object, whereas in projective identification, "the person experiences a feeling of oneness with the recipient with regard to the expelled feeling, idea, or self-representation" (Ogden, 1979, p. 34). This process is similar to that of a patient who interacts with the therapist in a way that puts pressure to act in a "role-responsive" fashion consistent with the internal dynamics of the patient. A former patient entered treatment with significant problems in her interpersonal relationship. She was referred for possible use of hypnosis and psychotherapy. The initial sessions began with significant criticisms of the office location, the decorations, the presence of leather chairs, and on it went. Each session contained some criticisms that were somewhat difficult to explore as to their meaning. Over time, I began to feel somewhat angry at the interaction and had fantasies of expelling her from the treatment. On reflection, this seemed to possibly be an example of projective identification developing between us. As I became aware of wanting to "get rid of her" through a referral, I began to speculate if there was a relationship between what I was feeling and possibly what she felt as a child growing up in a very problematic family. At a point in the treatment, I speculated as to a possible relationship between what was occurring between her early family experiences and our interaction. I wondered if she was trying to tell me what it felt like growing up (i.e., that she often felt unwanted or rejected).

As tears formed in her eyes, we had a very important moment between us as she acknowledged often feeling unwanted or disconnected primarily from her mother and, to some extent, her father.

Ogden (1979) identified a three-part process as to the mechanism of projective identification. The first step involves an aspect of the self projectively disavowed by unconsciously placing it in someone else. Second, the projector exerts interpersonal pressure to coerce the other person to experience or unconsciously identify with what has been projected. And third, the recipient of the projection processes and contains the projected contents, leading to an eventual reintrojection of him or her by the patient in a modified form. They are then reclaimed or reintegrated (Ogden, 1979, p. 9). A number of possible purposes have been identified for projective identification, for example, as a defense to distance from an unwanted part or affect; as a communication to make oneself understood by pressure on the therapist to experience feelings like one's own; and as a pathway for psychological change through reintrojection of the projection after it is modified by the containment of the therapist based on the evolving therapeutic work.

Projective identification is an important relational variable for the psychodynamically trained therapist who is also trained in the uses of hypnosis. The following is a clinical example that informed the therapeutic suggestions using hypnosis derived from an experience of projective identification with a young resident surgeon. In essence, the intake interviews revealed a history of significant academic achievement and training as a capable and gifted physician. Family history revealed parents more involved in their own world rather than as nurturing or very involved parents. The patient felt like his parents expected high achievement and yet they seemed unable to be emotionally supportive and expressive, acknowledging his successes. As I listened to his narrative, I had the fantasy of being his father. I became aware of my pride in his efforts and wondered how he felt about his academic performance and current resident experience. He described his mentor as being somewhat like his father in that he lacked significant emotional support for his mentee. It appeared I was the one in the relational matrix having warm prideful feelings. I thought these feelings were on "the wrong side of the room"—in me, not him. Following

Ogden, these feelings needed to be contained until they could be reintroduced in some way to provide an opportunity for reintegration of these feelings in him. Being aware of Sandler's (1990) writings about the structure of internal objects, that "internal objects have the capacity to create through the fantasy life of the individual, the quality of a 'presence' of the object," I began using imagery hypnotically to create a fantasy of being in a surgical suite. The patient was instructed to observe the clock in the surgical suite and see the face of his father smiling and nodding at him and to notice what he was feeling as he experienced this. His eyes misted as a clear emotional moment and communication that misted my eyes. The goal was to begin the establishment of pride and appreciation within him for all he had accomplished academically and medically. What ensued from this was an emotional discussion for both of us, given my fantasy of being his father and his fantasy of reconnecting with feelings as the son of an approving father that he could begin to internalize. One of the characteristics of transitional objects is the symbolic representation of the absent other. The hypnotic experience repeated several times hopefully provided a pathway to change through experiencing his disavowed feelings into a more stable sense of self or reintegration of these feelings in support of enhanced self-esteem.

Transitional Experience

The last variable is both a relational variable and a way to think about the hypnotic experience. It draws on the work of a British analyst, Donald Winnicott. One of his most important contributions to object relations theory was the idea of transitional objects and what he later called transitional space. This is the intermediate area between fantasy and reality or the true object and the symbolic object. The transitional object is not an internal or subjective object and it is not merely an external object. It is a combination of both. Transitional phenomena belong to the intermediate area of experience to which inner reality and external life both contribute. Winnicott (1971) used the concept of *transitional experience* to describe the process through which individuals develop the capacity to infuse external objective experience with subjective, personal meaning; to develop a sense of agency; and to develop the capacity to represent experience in a subjective and symbolic form. Winnicott called early transitional objects the child's first *illusion*. Illusion is used in the healthy sense that can lead to the ability to pretend and the willingness to suspend disbelief. It is in the transitional space that imagination can develop. In unconscious fantasy, a dog is a dog, whereas in imagination, there is a layering of symbolic meanings. Understanding the meaning of one's experience is possible only when one thing can stand for another without being the other. The capacity to distinguish the symbol from the symbolized is the achievement of subjectivity. Baker (2000, p. 59) has emphasized the "relational matrix of hypnosis" and has suggested "that hypnotic experience is itself a kind of transitional phenomenon, as consciousness progresses across varying areas of focused awareness and internal absorption while maintaining a simultaneous connection to external reality and the presence of the therapist." In this context, the therapist develops the meaning of the transitional experience from the agreed goals of the treatment. The therapist serves a containing or holding function within the context of the therapeutic alliance and is attuned to both his or her own and the patient's experience.

A clinical example of transitional experience and attunement of the symbol and the symbolized occurred when a patient, referred for hypnosis, remained silent during the initial three appointments. On the fourth appointment, she was quite late, detained in significant traffic. She said there was nothing she could do but wait for the traffic to clear. I wondered to myself if, on another level, she was saying something about our relationship. Separating the symbol (the real traffic) from the symbolized (her silence), I asked if she needed me to be patient until she could clear her "internal traffic" to allow us to begin exploring the reasons for her referral as part of beginning our relationship. She thanked me and remained somewhat silent for the remainder of the hour. This was an example of attunement and acceptance of her silence. In effect, I contained the silence till she was ready to engage, which she eventually did.

In hypnosis, as in psychotherapy, empathy or mindfulness is a psychological process that occurs within the context of dialectic between being and not being the other. Thus, in the intermediate space, empathy becomes playing with an idea of being the other while knowing at the same time that one is not. This is the space for reflection between the symbol and the symbolized. This is the space where one thing stands for another in a way that can be thought about and understood. This is the space where "bridge traffic" can be understood as a symbol for internal traffic. Intermediate space is also called metaphoric space. The psychodynamic therapist doing therapy along with hypnotic interventions serves the transitional function of linking feelings with words, objective experiences with mental images, body sensations with mental images, and the present with the past, all of which support internal integration.

What I want to propose is the conceptual usefulness of transitional or intermediate space as where the hypnotic experience most likely occurs. This is the area between fantasy/imagination/metaphor and reality. One measure of hypnotizability would involve the capacity to distinguish between the symbol and the symbolized and be absorbed in this intermediate space. The subject shifts the awareness through focused attention, reduction of the generalized reality orientation, and being absorbed while maintaining some connection to external reality. It is the therapist who codirects, contains the experience, and gives meaning to the transitional experience. In 1959, Orne proposed a similar idea using the term *trance logic* to account for what occurs in the subjective experience of the patient or the transitional space where inner reality and external life both contribute. Trance logic was defined as the ability to tolerate logical inconsistencies. Ogden, Winnicott, and Orne use different language to describe a similar conceptual phenomenon that involves the capacity to distinguish the symbol from the symbolized. From this perspective, hypnosis can be thought of as combining and creatively using the transitional or metaphoric space where both internal reality and external life come together in the service of the goals of treatment.

CASE EXAMPLE

This section concludes with a brief case example of how the relational variables contributed to initially working with the patient and ultimately deciding the appropriate hypnotic suggestions. The patient was referred for psychotherapy and possible hypnosis. To preserve the identity of the patient, certain liberties have been taken to alter essential facts while preserving the essence of the treatment.

Miss G, a retired physician, was referred for significant issues of anxiety and some depression. The anxiety seemed somewhat pervasive and intermittent in her life for many years. Currently, it significantly interfered in the quality of her retirement. Her history revealed a woman who was steadfast in her desire to be a physician over the desires of her parents for her future. While she seemed proud of her decision, I wondered what meaning this disparity between her desires and those of her parents might have for our relationship. From the alliance/transference perspective, were there experiences in her history to assist me with the question about the kind of relationship she would need? From a transference point of view, what factors in her history might influence our relationship and/or our work together? Would there be some relationship between her parental experience of nonacceptance of her choice of a profession and how the past might influence the present? I speculated that at a preconscious level, she might have concerns as to my support for and appreciation of her decision or fear that I might be critical or judgmental "like they were." Was this a contributor to her anxiety? Was her anxiety in any way related to her early attachment figures? This led to our first hypnotic intervention. I had her review a series of patient relationships that were important and satisfying to her and had her notice the feelings associated with each. I offered the thought that these could become a source of pride and reinforce the validity of her original decision to be a physician. I offered her, as one goal of development, the eventual formation of a more secure sense of self and self-efficacy. In addition, I offered the suggestion that the empathy she showed her patients she could also offer herself, that is, having a sense of compassion for all her education and training and her years as a physician. This seemed to resonate with her and deepen our relationship.

Now that she was retired, I wondered if there was some loss of identity from Dr. G to Ms. G. Given that she "fought hard" to maintain her decision raised the question for me of whether her current anxieties might be exacerbated by this loss. My countertransference was quite positive with my sense that she truly had a heart like the lion received in the Wizard of Oz. I thought the tenacity of her decision to be a physician suggested good

ego strength/resilience in the face of parental opposition. Her experience with many of her patients was the living proof inside her that she chose the correct path. Her experience could trump an old fear. These thoughts were offered to establish our relationship and provide suggestions that hopefully promoted greater self-acceptance. Indirectly, I hoped this included my acceptance of her decision and the belief that she was a good physician.

After one of the hypnotic sessions, she revealed "having killed a patient at one time." We explored this over the next several sessions. I wondered if this added to the source of her anxiety and was interpreted in some way as meaning she made the wrong decision and her parents were right. The patient in question was in the intensive care unit (ICU) and not expected to live, given the diagnosis and the extent of the disease process. He asked her if she could give him a medication to ease his discomfort and suffering. She gave him a medication for anxiety for which he expressed his appreciation.

She later left the hospital, returning to her quarters for a much-needed brief rest. When she later returned to see the patient in the ICU, she was informed he died within the past hour. She concluded that she "likely killed him." This hospital met to discuss the case in their Morbidity and Mortality Conference and she refused to attend. She felt they would arrive at the conclusion she feared, that she had a part in the death. The hospital did not implicate her although she maintained her fear/anxiety that her actions were involved in the patient's death. Hypnotically, I encouraged her to go back to this memory and describe her experience. She reported feeling almost overwhelmed with compassion for this person. I suggested that she gave the patient a gift, her understanding and compassion, by reducing his suffering. I asked her to focus on the face of the patient and describe what she saw. His look was one of gratitude. I suggested from her description of his facial expression, *"You have heard and understood me and allowed me to experience less suffering."* In short, he gave you a gift as well in his response to you. There was an exchange of "gifts" with her emotional investment in him and his response of appreciation for her. What seemed to resonate with her was having a different way of holding/containing this experience with the compassion and the love one is able to communicate through acts of kindness and compassion. Over the next several weeks, she reported sleeping better and felt the anxiety decreasing significantly.

In this abbreviated discussion, it is the relational variables that are important and informative in developing the therapeutic alliance; being sensitive to possible transference issues; noting one's countertransference experiences throughout the treatment; considering projective identification as part of the experience of the patient; and working within the intersubjectivity of the relationship. Paraphrasing Baker, cited earlier, it is how the relationship is construed or interpreted and experienced by both, as that is of greater importance than what the hypnotist does.

As stated in the beginning of this chapter, the intent was to bring together a postmodern psychoanalytic perspective for contemporary models of psychodynamic thought and hypnosis. No one theory "owns" in any complete sense either psychodynamic/psychoanalytic theory or hypnosis. It is my hope the reader will find utility in further exploration of concepts to further inform his or her clinical work.

REFERENCES

Allen, J. G., Coyne, L., Colson, D. B., Horwitz, L., Gabbard, G. O., Frieswyk, S. H., & Newson, G. (1996). Patterns of therapist interventions associated with patient collaboration. *Psychotherapy: Theory, Research, Practice, and Training*, 33(2), 254–261. doi:10.1037/0033-3204.33.2.254

Baker, E. L. (2000). Reflections on the hypnotic relationship: Projective identification, containment, and attunement. *International Journal of Clinical and Experimental Hypnosis*, 48(1), 56–69. doi:10.1080/00207140008410361

Barnett, E. (1981). *Analytical hypnotherapy–principles and practice*. Kingston, Ontario: Junica Publishing Company Limited.

Breuer, J., & Freud, S. (1957/1895). *Studies on hysteria*. New York, NY: Basic Books.

Bromberg, P. M. (2011). *The shadow of the tsunami: And the growth of the relational mind*. New York, NY: Routledge.

Chase, J. S., & Chase, L. S. (1991). Hypnosis revisited: Towards an integrated approach. *International Review of Psychoanalysis*, 18, 513–526.

Cortina, M. (2010). The future of psychodynamic psychotherapy. *Psychiatry*, 73(1), 43-56.

Diamond, M. (1986). Hypnotically augmented psychotherapy: The unique contributions of the hypnotically trained clinician. *American Journal of Clinical Hypnosis*, 28(4), 238-247.

Dorpat, T. L. (2001). Primary process communication. *Psychoanalytic Inquiry*, 21(3), 448–463. doi:10.1080/07351692109348946

Edelstein, G. (1981). *Trauma, trance, and transformation*. New York, NY: Brunner/Mazel.

Freud, S. (1966). Sketches for the 'preliminary communication' of 1893. In *The Standard Edition of the Complete Psychological Works of Sigmund Freud* (Vol. 1). Pre-Psycho-Analytic Publications and Unpublished Drafts 1966

Freud, S. (1910). The future prospects of psychoanalytic therapy. *Standard Edition*, 11, 3–55.

Fromm, E. (1987). Significant developments in clinical hypnosis during the past 25 years. *International Journal of Clinical and Experimental Hypnosis*, 35(4), 215–230. doi:10.1080/00207148708416056

Fromm, E., & Nash, M. (1997). *Psychoanalysis and hypnosis*. Madison, WI: International University Press.

Geller, S. M., & Porges, S. W. (2014). Therapeutic presence: Neurophysiological mechanisms mediating feeling safe in therapeutic relationships. *Journal of Psychotherapy Integration*, 24(3), 178–192. doi:10.1037/a0037511

Gill, M., & Brenman, M. (1961). *Hypnosis and related states: Psychoanatytic studies in regression*. New York, NY: International Universities Press.

Greenberg, J., & Mitchell, M. (1983). *Object relations in psychoanalytic theory*. Cambridge, MA: Harvard University Press.

Hebb, D. O. (1949). *The organization of behavior: A neuropsychological theory*. New York, NY: Wiley.

Heimann, P. (1950). On countertransference. *International Journal of Psychoanalysis*, 31, 81–84.

Hovarth, A. O., & Symonds, B. D. (1991). Relation between working alliance and outcome in psychotherapy: A meta-analysis. *Journal of Counseling Psychology*, 38, 139–149.

Kline, M. (1946). *Developments on psycho-analysis*. London, UK: Hogarth Press.

Kline, M. (1955). *Hypnodynamic psychology*. New York, NY: The Julian Press.

Kline, M. (1958). *Freud and hypnosis: The interaction of psychodynamics and hypnosis*. New York, NY: Julian Press.

Landholt, A., & Milling, L. (2011). The efficacy of hypnosis as an intervention for labor and delivery pain. *Clinical Psychology Review*, 6, 1022–1031.

Levy, R., & Ablon, J. (2009). *Handbook of evidence-based psychodynamic psychotherapy*. Totowa, NJ: Humana Press. doi:10.1037/a0029371

Levy, K. N., & Scala, J. W. (2012). Transference interpretations, and transference focused psychotherapies. *Psychotherapy*, 49(3), 391–403. doi:10.1037/a0029371

Loewenthal, D., & Snell, R. (2003). *Post-modernism for psychotherapists*. New York, NY: Brunner-Routledge.

Luborsky, L., Mellon, J., van Ravenswaay, P., Childress, A. R., Cohen, K. D., Hole, A. V., & Alexander, K. A. (1985). A verification of Freud's grandest clinical hypothesis: The transference. *Clinical Psychology Review*, 3, 231–246.

Markin, R. D. (2014). Toward common identity for relationally oriented clinicians: A place to hang one's hat. *Psychotherapy*, 51(3), 327–333. doi:10.1037/a0037093

McGilchrist, I. (2009). *The master and his emissary*. New Haven, CT: Yale University Press.

Ogden, T. H. (1979). *Projective identification & psychotherapeutic technique*. New York, NY: Jason Aronson.

Orne, M. T. (1959). The nature of hypnosis: Artifact or essence. *Journal of Abnormal and Social Psychology*, 58(3), 277–299. doi:10.1037/h0046128

Rosen, G. M., & Davison, G. C. (2003). Psychology should list empirically supported principles of change (ESPs) and not credential trademarked therapies or other treatment packages. *Behavior Modification*, 27(2), 300-312.

Sandler, J. (1990). On internal object relations. *Journal of the American Psychoanalytic Association*, 38(4), 859–880. doi:10.1177/000306519003800401

Schneck, J. (1965). *Principles and practice of hypnoanalysis*. Springfield, IL: Charles C. Thomas.

Schore, A. (2012). *The science of the art of psychotherapy*. New York, NY: W. W. Norton.

Score, A. (2014). The right brain as dominant in psychotherapy. *Psychotherapy: Theory, Research & Practice*, 51(3), 388-397.

Shedler, J. (2010). The efficacy of psychodynamic psychotherapy. *American Psychologist*, 65(2), 98-109.

Shuren, J. E., & Grafman, J. (2002). The neurology of reasoning. *Archives of Neurology*, 59(6), 916–919.

Siegel, D. (1999). *The developing mind–toward a neurobiology of interpersonal experience*. New York, NY: Guilford Press.

Smit, Y., Huibers, M. J., Ioannidis, J. P., van Dyck, R., van Tilburg, W., & Arntz, A. (2012). The effectiveness of long-term psychoanalytic psychotherap–a meta-analysis of randomized controlled trials. *Clinical Psychology Review*, 32(2), 81–92. doi:10.1016/j.cpr.2011.11.003

Stolorow, R. D., & Lachmann, F. M. (1985). Transference: The future of an illusion. *The Annual of Psychoanalysis*, 12(13), 19–37.

Tansey, M., & Burke, W. (1989). *Understanding countertransference, from projective identification to empathy*. Hillsdale, NJ: Analytic Press.

Wachtel, P. (2010). Beyond "ests"–problematic assumptions in the pursuit of evidenced-based practice. *Psychoanalytic Psychology*, 3(6), 251–272.

Watkins, J. (1992). *Hypnoanalytic techniques*. New York, NY: Irvington Publishers.

Winnicott, D. (1971). *Transitional objects and transitional phenomena: In playing and reality*. New York, NY: Basic Books.

Wolberg, L. (1945). *Hypnoanalysis*. New York, NY: Grune and Stratton.

Ego-State Therapy

Claire Frederick

The emergence of ego-state therapy as a hypno-analytic therapy and a psychotherapeutic modality is a significant chapter in the history of hypnosis. Ego-state therapy is based on the view of the mind as polypsychic (Ellenberger, 1970), that is, composed of multiple aspects or parts (Watkins, 1978, 1993; Watkins & Barabasz, 2008). They based their work on Federn's (1928, 1952) theory that ego states, or parts of the personality, are formed during normal human development. They also used Federn's (1928, 1952) energy theories to explain the relationship of these parts to one another, to the self, and to the world. Although some factors intrinsic to their method (Hidden Observer Phenomena; Hilgard, 1973, 1977) have been scrutinized for possibly sourcing unreliable material based on therapist demand and unconscious patient manipulations (Lynn, 2001; Lynn, Maré, Kvaal, Segal, & Sivec, 1994) or simply being based on incomplete or incorrectly focused data (Frischholz, 2001; Woody & McConkey, 2003), a steady accumulation of experimental data and theory suggests scientific underpinnings for this therapeutic method. They come from several areas that include hypnosis (Hilgard, 1973, 1977), child development studies (Harter, 1988; Harter, Bresnick, Bouchey, & Whitsell, 1997), and neurophysiology (Gazzaniga, 1995; Ornstein, 1987; Rainville, Carrier, Hofbauer, Bushnell, & Duncan, 1999; Rainville, Hofbauer, Bushnell, Duncan, & Price, 2002; Reinders et al., 2003; Siegel, 1999). For example, Siegel (1999, pp. 229–230) observed that the kinds of personality clusters often seen in adult pathologies can be seen in children who are developing normally.

> We have multiple and varied "selves," which are needed to carry out the diverse activities of our lives. . . . As we can see, both developmental studies and cognitive science appear to suggest

that we have many selves. Within a specialized "self" or "self-state," as we are now defining it, there is cohesion in the moment and continuity across time.

There were several reasons for the spread of this new approach into the 21st century (Frederick, 2005). The Watkinses were indefatigable in conducting increasing numbers of national and international workshops (Steckler, 1989). Moreover, a number of colleagues (Barabasz, 2013; Frederick, 2005; Frederick & McNeal, 1999; Ginandes, 2002, 2006; Hartman, 1995, 2002; Morton, 2001, Morton & Frederick, 1997; Phillips, 2000; Phillips & Frederick; 1995) integrated ego-state therapy with a number of bedrock areas of psychotherapy such as phase-oriented treatment, developmental repair, the transference/countertransference field, posttraumatic stress reactions, Ericksonian approaches, and conscious–unconscious complementarity. Also, ego-state therapy emerged at a time when trauma pathology and the dissociative disorders were emerging from historical obscurity (Ellenberger, 1970) into topics of relevant, even compelling, clinical focus (Ross, 1989; van der Kolk, 1986). Finally, ego-state therapy spread because of its essential compatibility with many other therapeutic modalities. Ego-state therapy is not a stand-alone therapy (Frederick, 2005). Once ego states are activated, one or more therapeutic orientations or modalities must guide the therapeutic work with the parts. Ego-state therapy is compatible with all therapeutic orientations including cognitive behavioral and psychodynamic, the energy therapies (Gallo, 2004), eye movement desensitization and reprocessing (EMDR), and social reconstruction therapies (Feinstein & Krippner, 2006).

Ego-state therapy has been hailed by many clinicians as a way of working more intimately and more deeply with components (also conceptualized as energies or aspects) of the human personality in order to bring about symptom relief and significant personality changes. Fragmentation of personality can result from severe trauma or the effects of cumulative trauma such as childhood abuse, rape, assault, physical injuries, natural disasters, or trauma caused by war. Ego-state therapy can help with healing and promote functional well-being.

EVIDENCE–BASED STUDIES AND OTHER RESEARCH ISSUES

Ego-state therapy has a very sparse evidence base and has research problems similar to psychodynamically oriented psychotherapies (Miller, Luborsky, Barber, & Docherty, 1993) and hypnotically facilitated therapies in general (Fromm & Nash, 1992). However, the dominant evidence-based paradigm may not necessarily be sufficient to evaluate the usefulness of ego-state therapy. Hageman and Frederick (2009; 2014) have undertaken an in-depth examination of research issues pertaining to ego-state therapy. They emphasized potential conflicts inherent in favoring both evidence-based and phenomenological research in hypnosis and ego-state therapy. Frederick (2005, p. 350) had suggested earlier that the research future of ego-state therapy "may well rest on its becoming the object of several different types of research (neurophysiological, individual case studies, traditional group studies) that will examine both efficacy and effectiveness issues." Hageman and Frederick (2009, 2014) observed that several kinds of research could be done within the field of ego-state therapy. Among them were evidence-based, effectiveness, psychophysiological, and phenomenological studies. They reviewed the philosophy of science supportive of these efforts and the shifts in opinion about what actually constitutes a scientific study. They believed that ego-state therapy often was viewed as producing positive results because it had been subjected to many phenomenological studies (Giorgi & Giorgi, 2003; Husserl, 1977, 1960; Merleau-Ponty, 1962; Sartre, 2012, 1970) by clinicians who had not been recognized or identified as such. Phenomenological studies had resulted, over the years, in the introduction of numerous agreed-upon criteria into the standards of care both for ego-state therapy and for hypnotically facilitated therapies in general. They called for an end to the research model wars, and like Osoweic (2014), for a more integrated approach to research. Hageman and

Frederick (2014) viewed research factions in conflict as being very much like a dysfunctional internal family in need of healing.

Recently, ego-state therapy has been shown to have as strong an evidence base for certain war veterans diagnosed with posttraumatic stress disorder (PTSD; American Psychiatric Association [APA] 2013) with memories of their traumatic experiences. Further, several studies have indicated that Ego-state therapy may be as successful as other evidence-based therapies (Barabasz, 2013; Barabasz et al., 2013; Christensen, Barabasz, & Barabasz, 2013). There is now manualized treatment based on this work available for this population (Barabasz, Barabasz, & Watkins, 2011). There remain significant problems in evidence-based research for ego-state therapy. Among them are population selection, comorbidities, and the frequent, and often confusing to researchers, combination of ego-state therapy with other psychotherapies.

In this chapter, the reader has an opportunity to review clinical presentations of ego-state problems and the diagnosis of ego-state pathology, methods for clinical activation of ego states, how ego-state therapy is conducted, and the goals and principles of ego-state therapy. We also visit some of the very real practical and ethical issues related to the kinds of qualifications that are necessary for therapists to be able to do consistently safe and clinically rewarding ego-state therapy.

HOW EGO STATES HARM AND HOW THEY HELP

Clinical Case Example: Greta I

Greta was raised in a harshly demanding family from rural Holland. She divorced her abusive husband once her children were grown. Greta was actively seeking dating partners online, and each relationship featured early sexual intimacy with troubled, immature, quasi-abusive men. A part of Greta's personality presented as a sad 4-year-old child craving loving, intense closeness. This part suffered when Greta was not sexually active with a dating partner. Such relationships mitigated the distress she experienced when she was alone. This aspect of her personality pushed her into unwise dating decisions and undesirable companionship. Greta was frustrated with her behavior because she said, "I know better." This was true, as other aspects of her personality experienced shame over these behaviors and had clarity that they were not good for her.

The presence of a notable sense of self-division is one of the signs that ego-state pathology may be present. Patients may report, "What I am doing is just not me." The "strange" behaviors and their consequences can be quite painful. Among them are self-destructive behaviors, mind–body problems, antisocial activities, and sexual problems. How does this come about?

> An ego state may be defined as an organized system of behavior and experience whose elements are bound together by some common principle, and which is separated from other such states by a boundary that is more or less permeable. (Watkins & Watkins, 1997, p. 25)

It is useful to think of ego states as being separated from one another by something that can be viewed in an imaginary and metaphorical sense as a semipermeable membrane. These states or personality parts can be conceptualized as existing on a spectrum. The stronger or "thicker" the boundaries that separate them from other ego states, the less they are able to communicate and work collaboratively. Some degree of separation is associated with clinical issues such as depression, obsessive compulsive and other anxiety disorders, eating disorders, and compulsive sexual behaviors. Greater separation among ego states is present with PTSD, dissociative disorders such as dissociative fugue state, conversion disorders (APA, 2013), and unspecified dissociative disorders, often referred to as dissociative disorders not otherwise specified (DDNOS; APA, 2000). The most extreme degrees of separation among ego states is found in dissociative identity disorder (DID; APA, 2013), formerly known as multiple personality disorder. In this condition, hypnosis is not needed for ego-state activation, and the ego states are referred to as "alters" (Figure14.1).

In the healthy or integrated condition, the ego states share mental content and act cooperatively much as a healthy family does. Ego-state therapy is adaptational. It is axiomatic that "every ego state has come to help" (Frederick, 2005, p. 351). Every ego state is formed in an attempt to help the greater personality. Greta's child ego state was trying to help her find a secure base in order to heal her anxious, insecure attachment pattern. Her need for a secure base was perceived as a desperate one by deep levels

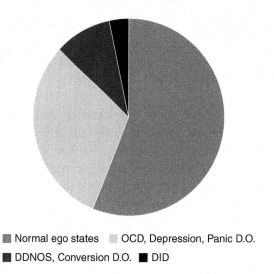

■ Normal ego states   OCD, Depression, Panic D.O.
■ DDNOS, Conversion D.O.   ■ DID

FIGURE 14.1 Increasing separation of ego states.

of Greta's mind, and the child part was trying to help through desperate measures. Other dynamics related to trauma also may have contributed to the Little Girl's development. Ego-state formation takes place in order to meet human needs as we live our lives. The causes for ego-state formation are

1. **Cultural adaptation.** Children require different personality energies for different activities, tasks, and relationships in their lives.
2. **Introjection.** As we form our identities, we take in aspects of our parents and other significant adults and events in our lives.
3. **Trauma.** Children must be able to survive traumatic experience without resorting to psychosis or suicide. Ego-state formation is a creative alternative.
4. **Inadequate caregiver attachment behavior.** Frederick (2005) added this category to the Watkinses' (Watkins & Watkins, 1997) original causative factors for ego-state formation.

PATHOLOGICAL PRESENTATIONS OF EGO STATES: MAKING THE DIAGNOSIS

Clinical Case Example: Greta II

I observed Greta's mood states switching rapidly. A confident, cognitively functional Greta could change dramatically into a persona in great distress when a boyfriend failed to call on time. Greta's tone of voice, vocabulary, and body posture were quite different when the Little Girl became activated. Greta was aware of some of these changes. She told me that she believed she had gone crazy.

Frederick (2005) has emphasized that exploration for ego-state pathology should only take place within the patient's complete medical and psychological evaluation. Psychoses as well as certain organic illnesses such as temporal lobe epilepsy, brain lesions, and metabolic difficulties, among a host of other medical problems, can mimic ego-state problems. Ego-state diagnostic explorations, "must always be embedded within sound medical and psychological practice" (Frederick, 2005, p. 363).

There are several ways ego-state problems may present (Frederick, 2005):

1. **Ego-dystonia.** When the therapist hears, "It just isn't like me at all," there should be a pursuit of the material in greater detail (Frederick, 2005, p. 365).
2. **Unusual or unexplained affect.** Affect that is inappropriate or simply unusual, amplified, constricted, absent, or unexplained can signal ego-state problems.
3. **Unusual or unexplained somatic experiences.** These include a variety of pain syndromes and mysterious physical symptoms.
4. **Unusual or unexplained experiences within fantasy life.** These include repetitive horror shows or recurring presentations of images such as abstract designs (Frederick & Phillips, 1996).
5. **The language of "parts."** "A part of me wants to do thus-and-so; while another part of me wants to do something completely different."
6. **Feelings of self-division.** This can cause patients to perceive themselves as the battlefields upon which internal struggles or wars are waged.
7. **The feeling of craziness.** For many patients, manifestations of dividedness are signs that they are crazy.
8. **Exaggerated "self-talk"** or actual internal chatter.
9. **Observed unusual behaviors.** These include tics or other bodily movements, interferences with vocal productions, changes in the body's position and tonality, and unusual facial expressions.
10. **Refractoriness to treatment.** This causes patients with ego-state problems to keep trying to find therapists who can help them.
11. **Positive diagnostic ego-state exploration.**

PSYCHOEDUCATION AND THE INFORMED CONSENT

The informed consent for ego-state therapy, like the informed consent for hypnosis, is done always outside of trance. However, it can be useful to repeat them when the patient is in the trance state as this allows the therapist to communicate with all the parts (see "Clinical Case Example: Greta III" for a sample script). Ego-state therapy–informed consents are always educational. They can take place over several sessions, and they always offer alternative therapies and choices if the patient is not a candidate for or rejects ego-state therapy.

How Do You Explore?

Suggestions that could implant ideas of specific parts experiences rather than reveal what is already there are not practically or ethically acceptable. The therapist must steer between unhelpful denial of parts experiences and suggestions or exaggerations that incite the patient's imagination to create false experiences to meet supposed therapist expectations. Not every patient is a candidate for ego-state therapy, and it is important not to "box in" any patient into a theoretical model.

Clinical Case Example: Greta III

Greta was prepared for her first ego-state exploration with psychoeducation.

"There are many ways to look at the human personality. One way that I find useful, and I believe that in a very real sense is the way things are, is to think of the human personality as composed of parts, and being very much like a family inside. We like to think, and we usually think, of ourselves as being undivided. Yet, if you consider it, you realize that you may be more like a diamond or another jewel that has many facets. Each one reflects something different. Each one is an intrinsic and important part of the jewel . . . you probably experience

things very differently when you're at work from when you're at a party or visiting your family. Yet, every one of the parts of you is 'you.' It's possible that the mind is very much like the body. The body needs differentiation, specialization, and parts. The heart does not do the same thing that the brain does. Yet, we need them both. It's important for you to realize that every personality part has come to help. Even those that may be connected with symptoms are in some way trying to be helpful. When personality energies or parts, or aspects of the self, don't get along, when they're not cooperating and working together, often when one of them goes off all on its own, symptoms can develop. It's possible, not necessarily so at all, but possible, that the problems that brought you here could be part of some difficulty within your own internal family of selves."
(Frederick, 2005, p. 368)

Greta and I discussed the concepts raised. Then Greta was helped to enter trance and invited to find/create a very peaceful place where a group or a family could get together. When she signaled that she had done this, I (CF) said:

"I would like to invite the part of [Greta's] . . . personality to come into the space that . . . she has prepared. It's all right if no parts come in, or if there are no parts to come in. Also, the act of entering the space does not commit the parts to do anything, to be anything, or to say anything. We will also understand if there are some parts who have decided to wait before we find out about them. It's just a way for us to begin to get to know you, and again, it's okay if no parts come in."
(Frederick, 2005, p. 372).

Before Greta left trance, I thanked the parts for showing up and extended my understanding to any parts that may not have shown up for their own reasons. Once she was dehypnotized, Greta reported on her experience. She had seen several child parts, a weeping adult, a very angry teenager, and a shadowy figure of indeterminate age and sex. She identified one of the child parts as the Little Girl who pushed her to relationships with immature and difficult men.

The technique I used with Greta was an imagery technique, my variation of techniques used by Watkins and Watkins (1997).

There are several ways to activate ego states:

1. **Indirect talking through** is the first and most preparatory approach to ego-state communication to the ego state. It contains many psychoeducational elements. Phillips and Frederick (1995) suggest that the talking through can also embed messages of hope, strength, and capability on an unconscious level.

2. **Direct talking through** is an approach that specifically addresses a particular ego state. For example:
I believe that that part of you that sends you preoccupations and impulses to have sadomasochistic is trying to help you in some way. You told me that the people who abused you often said that that was the only way you could get love. Remember, they told you that your parents didn't love you. I wonder if the part that wants you to go out and get that rough and humiliating sex isn't really looking for love, deep love, the kind that every kid needs (Frederick, 2005, p. 372).

3. **Calling out ego states** for direct verbal interaction can be done with formal hypnotic trance. This kind of script may be helpful:
I wonder if there is a part of X (the patient) that knows something about (name the symptom). If there is such a part, I would like to have the opportunity to get to know you better. If you wish, you can just speak to me through X's lips (Frederick, 2005, p. 372).

4. **Imagery techniques.** Helen Watkins (Watkins & Watkins, 1997) invited ego states to sit at a Round Table. With his Dissociative Table Technique, Frasier (2003) also used a table. Frederick (2005) uses a less structured imagery invitation that is purposefully broad, explicitly informs parts that they do not have to interact should they appear, and accommodates for failure of parts to show up.

5. **Ideomotor exploration** is recommended strongly for beginners in ego-state therapy. It has the built-in safeguard of placing the control of what happens directly with the patient's unconscious mind. A slow safe respectful dialogue can be established to discover whether there is a part that knows about a particular problem, whether the part would be willing to communicate, and, if it is not willing, what might need to happen in order for future conversation to take place.

6. **Affect and somatic activations.** These activation methods focus on what the patient is feeling

emotionally or sensing in the body when a specific problem is broached. Further exploration into affects, perceptions, thoughts, and so forth can follow.

7. **Externalization techniques.** Helen Watkins (Watkins & Watkins, 1997) often demonstrated ego states in subjects with her variation of a Gestalt chair technique (Fagan et al., 1974). Automatic writing, soft sculpture, drawing, and doodling also can be pathways to ego-state activation.

WORKING THERAPEUTICALLY WITH EGO STATES

The Goals of Ego-State Therapy

■ **Clinical Case Example: Greta IV**

Greta's early reaction to the child part that plunged her into bad relationships was to ask me to get rid of the part. I explained this could not be our goal. "This child is a part of you. She is trying to help you in her own way. She is important because every part of you is important." I explained that one of our goals was to help this part develop feelings of safety and security and to progress developmentally. I used this occasion to explain the goals of ego-state therapy. I also began to help Greta develop some ideas about the enormity of the distress the Little Girl felt. It would be necessary for her to work on increasing both empathy and alliances with this part of her personality.

The goal of ego-state therapy is integration, an ongoing organization of mind characterized by communication and harmony among the parts. Ego-state therapy has been described as a combination of family therapy and individual therapy (Watkins & Watkins, 1997). Individual parts, like Greta's Little Girl, may need psychotherapeutic work for attachment repair and repair of other developmental deficits before they are able to work harmoniously with other parts. Like some of Greta's parts, many ego states may require help processing trauma material. In therapy, all of Greta's parts were guided into a cooperative model and helped to live in an increasingly caring inner environment they themselves created.

The therapist's primary goal is to form therapeutic alliances with every part. These alliances serve as models for the alliances the parts will have with one another, just as the therapist's empathy for the parts becomes a model for the empathy the parts will develop. The therapist becomes a cheerleader for helping parts become less narcissistic and works persistently to promote communication and empathy within the internal family. The therapist also encourages parts to begin to work on tasks together. Some important goals in the progress of ego-state therapy are

1. Communication
2. Human rights. Democracy must prevail. Every part is just as important as every other part
3. Promotion of healing alliances among ego states
4. Ego strengthening and symptom management
5. Attachment and separation–individuation repair
6. Other developmental repair such as repair of cognitive errors, affect containment and modulation, the establishment of object constancy
7. Resolution of trauma issues without retraumatization

Any therapeutic technique that can be used with an individual patient can be used with an ego state. However, ego-state therapy must take place within the framework of phase-oriented treatment. Janet (1889; 1919) introduced phase-oriented treatment as essential for the treatment of trauma. Janet's model was supplanted over time (Ellenberger, 1970) and then rediscovered by Horowitz (1973). It is now the standard of care for trauma therapy, and several models are currently in use (Brown & Fromm, 1986; Courtois, 1988; Herman, 1992; McCann & Pearlman, 1990; Phillips & Frederick, 1995). Conducting treatment in phases or stages allows us to stabilize patients. There are several reasons why this is essential. One is that the treatment process should never inflict unnecessary pain. Another is that unwise exposure to trauma material can retraumatize and destabilize patients and place them into a vicious circle of retraumatization, excessive dependency, increased vulnerability to retraumatization, and even spontaneous abreaction. Also, patients need enough affective and cognitive function to be able to participate in the therapeutic process. Stabilization whenever needed throughout the course of treatment promotes function as opposed to stagnation. Phillips and Frederick's model (1995) was created specifically for hypnotically facilitated treatment. Like

Janet (van der Hart, Brown, & Turco, 1990), they use hypnosis to facilitate each phase of treatment. Their model, the SARI model, is a four-stage model.

Stage I. Safety and Stabilization

This stage features physical and psychological safety and stability. It emphasizes good boundaries, ego strengthening, the initiation of therapeutic alliances, symptom reduction, and developmental repair.

■ Clinical Case Example: Greta IV

Greta learned to use self-hypnosis to access conflict-free resources such as the powerful center core energies, inner strength (Frederick & McNeal, 1999), and inner wisdom (Frederick & McNeal, 1999; Krakauer, 2001, 2006), as well as to interact with her ideal parents (Brown, 2011). Although I had to do a great deal of coaching and reminding, she learned to meet with her ideal parents on a regular basis. Eventually, Greta was able to activate these resources intermittently when she experienced distress. She began to have intermittent experiences of a secure base and of having some control over her life. Both her anxiety attacks and fears decreased.

Stage II. Accessing Trauma Material

Trauma material can be accessed in a number of ways. One often described in the hypnotic literature is abreaction (Phillips & Frederick, 1995). The concept of abreaction was voiced initially by Freud in 1893 (Akhtar, 2009). It is related to the theory of catharsis, which was well described by Aristotle (Rhys-Roberts & Bywater, 1984). Abreaction is a cathartic process in which affect connected with trauma material is relived and discharged sufficiently to free the patient from many of the trauma bonds with which it was associated. The idea is that once this psychological abscess has been lanced, healing can take place.

Watkins and Watkins used and advocated full-blown abreactions to access and reprocess trauma material, and Christensen, Barabasz, and Barabasz (2013) have demonstrated the efficacy of such an approach with war veterans who present with memories of their traumata. John G. Watkins (1949) had had extensive experience treating World War II veterans successfully with hypnotically facilitated abreaction. The Watkinses' comfort and success with abreactions also was related to the nature of their practices. They were academics, and they frequently did intensive therapeutic work on extended weekends. Often, they were not bound by the usual schedule pattern of most practicing clinicians, and they were able to allow abreactions to play out to complete extinction and to give healing corrective experiences within prolonged time frames seldom available in usual practice frameworks.

Within most contemporary clinical settings, trauma material is accessed through many avenues including memory material, dreams, parapraxes, and artistic productions. Memory itself is never precise, and any efforts to access trauma has to be done within the framework that there is a difference between historical or factual truth and narrative (patient's own subjective) truth (Herman, 1992; Phillips & Frederick, 1995). Hypnosis can be used to access abreactions in installments (fractionated abreactions; Kluft, 1989). Contemporary clinical ego-state therapy much more commonly utilizes the intersubjective therapeutic relationship, ego strengthening, developmental repair, and partial or fractionated abreaction (Courtois, 1988; Courtois & Ford, 2009; Frederick, 2005; Frederick & McNeal, 1999; Phillips & Frederick, 1995). The goal is not catharsis, but rather to reduce "the discrepancy between current concepts and enduring schemata" (Horowitz, 1974, p. 771).

Stage III. Reassociation, Reworking

This stage focuses on corrective emotional experiences (Alexander & French, 1946), reassociation of previously dissociated material, further developmental work, additional corrections of cognitive errors, new expressiveness, and the development of new external resources such as new relationships, activities, vocations, and avocations.

Stage IV: Integration

In this stage, dissociated material is reintegrated into the personality, and the ego states become integrated. They enter into a dynamic and seamless arrangement of internal harmony, cooperation, and continuing coconsciousness.

INTEGRATION IN EGO-STATE THERAPY

Clinical Case Example: Greta

Eventually, Greta was able to form working relationships with the other parts of her personality. The shadowy part, she discovered, was associated with depression and self-destructive thoughts. Some of the parts began to join her regular visitations to her ideal parents and were able to utilize inner strength and other center core phenomena. They communicated with one another, and some of them began to work on specific tasks together. At first, these tasks took place only in Greta's imagination. For example, several parts worked in an imaginary garden together. Subsequently, they worked on Greta's external garden cooperatively.

Greta's ego states were moving in the direction of integration. As they got to know one another better and developed greater empathy for one another, they would share eventually their subjective selves: their fears, wishes, dreams, and desires. Integration would be present when that coconsciousness had become a continuous phenomenon, and they worked together in harmony. None of the parts would go away as Greta had wished initially for the Little Girl. Instead, they would have undergone some degree of transformation in order to be able to achieve the state of integration. In Greta's case, both developmental repair and trauma resolution with individual ego states would be necessary. Ego-state therapists begin working toward integration at the very beginning of treatment. They seed hope for a future with such harmony, use metaphors such as that of peace following a long war, and utilize the language of integration whenever it is appropriately possible. Integration is, indeed, the great prize of treatment because it is essential for both healthy relationships and successful child-rearing.

Who Is Qualified to Practice Ego-State Therapy?

Just as not every patient is a candidate for ego-state therapy, so also every therapist is not destined to become an ego-state therapist. Numerous factors such as theoretical base, temperament, hypnotic talents, and comfort with imagery and personification are relevant to one's choice and ability to do this kind of work. All ego-state therapists are also hypnotherapists, and the qualities described as essential for good hypnotherapists by Diamond (1984, 1986, 1987) and also those described by Frederick and McNeal (1999) are also required.

Because some of the concepts of ego-state therapy and other polypsychic therapies permeate the environment of psychotherapeutic practice, because this therapeutic modality can be quite useful with complex cases, and because its theory and practice may seem deceptively simple, it is widely practiced. However, a compelling question, both practical and ethical, is whether there are standards of competence and of training for ego-state therapy. Adequate training is essential, and such standards exist and are the subject of frequent evaluation and review. There are two bodies that monitor standards, evaluate performance, and certify therapists in ego-state therapy. Ego State Therapy International (2011), founded in 2011, has created standards of training for certification in ego-state therapy. Qualified professionals who use hypnosis must first be qualified in their own fields and specialties. Since ego-state therapy is a psychotherapeutic modality, it follows that those who practice it should be trained and licensed psychotherapists. Because trauma plays such an important role in the development of symptoms, practitioners will also have in-depth training in the field of trauma and dissociation, such as formal training with the International Society of Trauma and Dissociation. Because ego-state therapy always involves the use of hypnosis and advanced hypnotic techniques, such a practitioner must have advanced hypnosis training and supervision. In-depth knowledge of numerous contiguous areas is required. These include multiple psychological systems, resource activation, ego strengthening, attachment repair, other structural developmental repair, eating disorders, anxiety disorders, and dreams and dreaming. These are not frivolous requirements. The extensive working familiarity and knowledge allows the qualified ego-state therapist to respond therapeutically to the wide variety of complex issues that reside in the patient population.

The Foundation for Ego State Therapy (FEST, 2009) has been slower in its development. It is in the process of creating standards under the guidance of a broad representation of ego-state therapy and ego-state therapy-related experts. FEST (2009) has established criteria for certification that includes a master's degree and appropriate licensure, the equivalent of 24 hours of hypnosis training from a recognized institute of higher learning or professional hypnosis society, at least 24 hours of training in the fundamentals of ego-state therapy, at least 16 hours of training at the intermediate level, completion of at least 30 hours of advanced training in ego-state therapy, and completion and documentation of at least 30 hours of clinical consultation with senior faculty.

In 2012, a 36-hour program was approved for certification by the Ontario Division of the Canadian Society of Clinical Hypnosis and the University of Toronto, and recently the board of the New England Society of Clinical Hypnosis has approved a program for ego-state therapy certification. Although models for certification continue to be subjects of active discussion in the ego-state therapy community and may vary with geography and time frames, it is clear that there are standards that cannot be ignored. The era of the "wild" ego-state therapist has ended on practical, ethical, and, now, legal bases.

CONCLUSION

This chapter has followed ego-state therapy from its beginnings as a hypnoanalytic therapy to its expansion into a widely practiced therapeutic modality, with standards for training and competence that include a very large knowledge base within psychotherapy. Ego-state issues affect many behaviors and phenomena in health care patients that might be otherwise inexplicable. This chapter describes the nature of ego states and of their configurations in health and distress. It has used a series of clinical vignettes to show how ego-state pathology manifests itself, how it is diagnosed, and how it is treated safely within a phase-oriented strategy. Its purpose is to acquaint the reader with the field of ego-state therapy. Psychotherapists who find it interesting may learn more about it, and clinicians who will not practice it will be more informed about ego-state problems that exist among their patients.

REFERENCES

Akhtar, S. (2009). *Comprehensive dictionary of psychoanalysis*. London, UK: Karnac Books.

Alexander, F. G., & French, T. M. (1946). *Psychoanalytic therapy: Principles and applications*. New York, NY: Ronald.

American Psychiatric Association. (2000). *Diagnostic and statistical manual of mental disorders*. Washington, DC: American Psychiatric Press.

American Psychiatric Association. (2013). *Diagnostic and statistical manual of mental disorders*. Washington, DC: American Psychiatric Press.

Barabasz, A. (2013). Evidence-based abreactive ego state therapy for PTSD. *American Journal of Clinical Hypnosis, 56*, 54–65. doi:10.1080/00029157.2013.770384

Barabasz, A. F., Barabasz, M., & Watkins, J. G. (2011). Single-session manualized ego state therapy for combat stress injury, PTSD and ASD. *International Journal of Clinical and Experimental Hypnosis, 59*(4), 379–391.

Barabasz, A. F., Barabasz, M., Christensen, C., French, B., & Watkins, J. G. (2013). Efficacy of single-session abreactive ego state therapy for combat stress injury, PTSD, and ASD. *International Journal of Clinical and Experimental Hypnosis, 61*(1), 1–19.

Brown, D. P. (2011). *How to treat attachment pathology*. Presented at the meeting of New England Society of Clinical Hypnosis Newton Wellesley Hospital, Newton, MA.

Brown, D. P., & Fromm, E. (1986). *Hypnotherapy and hypnoanalysis*. Hillsdale, NJ: Lawrence Erlbaum.

Christensen, C., Brown, P., & Turco, R. (1990). A placebo controlled test of the effects of single session ego state therapy for PTSD. *International Journal of Clinical and Experimental Hypnosis, 61*, 20–37.

Courtois, C. A. (1988). *Healing the incest wound: Adult survivors in therapy*. New York, NY: W. W. Norton.

Courtois, C. A., & Ford, J. D. (2009). *Treating complex traumatic stress disorders (adults): Scientific foundations and therapeutic models*. New York, NY: The Guilford Press.

Diamond, M. J. (1984). It takes two to tango: Some thoughts on the neglected importance of the hypnotist in an interactive hypnotherapeutic relationship. *American Journal of Clinical Hypnosis, 27*(1), 3–13.

Diamond, M. J. (1986). Hypnotically augmented psychotherapy: The unique contributions of the hypnotically trained clinician. *American Journal of Clinical Hypnosis, 28*(4), 238–247.

Diamond, M. J. (1987). The interactional basis of the hypnotic experience: On the relational dimensions of hypnosis. *International Journal of Clinical and Experimental Hypnosis, 35*(2), 95–115.

Ego State Therapy International. (2011). Retrieved from http://egostateinternational.com

Ellenberger, H. F. (1970). *The discovery of the unconscious*. New York, NY: Basic Books, Inc.

Fagan, J., Lauver, D., Smith, S., Deloach, S., Katz, M., & Wood, E. (1974). Critical Incidents in the Empty Chair. *Counseling Psychologist, 4*(4), 33–42.

Federn, P. (1928). Narcissism in the structure of the ego. *International Journal of Psychoanalysis*, 9, 401–419.

Federn, P. (1952). *Ego psychology and the psychoses*. New York, NY: Basic Books.

Feinstein, D., & Krippner, S. (2006). *The mythic path: Discovering the guiding stories of your past creating a vision for your future*. Santa Rosa, CA: Energy Psychology Press/Elite Books.

Fraser, G. A. (2003). Fraser's "Dissociative Table Technique" revised, revised: A strategy for working with ego states in Dissociative Disorders and Ego State Therapy. *Journal of Trauma and Dissociation*, 4(4), 5–28. doi:10.1300/J229v04_02

Frederick, C. (2005). Selected topics in ego state therapy. *International Journal of Clinical and Experimental Hypnosis*, 53(4), 339–428.

Frederick, C., & McNeal, S. (1999). *Inner strengths: Contemporary psychotherapy and hypnosis for ego-strengthening*. New York, NY: Routledge.

Frederick, C., & Phillips, M. (1996). Decoding mystifying signals: Translating symbolic communications of elusive ego-states. *American Journal of Clinical Hypnosis*, 38, 87–96.

Frischholz, E. J. (2001). Different perspectives on informed consent and clinical hypnosis. *American Journal of Clinical Hypnosis*, 43(3–4), 323–328.

Fromm, E., & Nash, M. (1992). *Contemporary hypnosis research*. New York, NY: Guilford Press.

Gallo, F. (2004). *Energy psychology: Explorations on the interface of energy, cognition, behavior, and health*. Boca Raton, FL: CRC Press.

Gazzaniga, M. S. (1995, March). *Consciousness is an instinct*. Presented at the meeting of the American Society of Clinical Hypnosis. San Diego, CA.

Ginandes, C. (2002). Extended, strategic therapy for recalcitrant mind–body healing. *American Journal of Clinical Hypnosis*, 45(2), 91–102.

Ginandes, C. (2006). Six players on the inner stage: Using ego state therapy with the medically ill. *International Journal of Clinical and Experimental Hypnosis*, 54(2), 113–129.

Giorgi, A., & Giorgi, B. (2003). The descriptive phenomenological psychological method. In P. Camic, J. Rhodes, & L. Yardley (Eds.), *Qualitative research in psychology: Expanding perspectives in methodology and design* (pp. 243–273). Washington, DC: American Psychological Association.

Hageman, J. H., & Frederick, C. (2009). *Ego state therapy: The need for credible research*. Presented at the Meeting of Society for Clinical and Experimental Hypnosis Annual Conference, Reno, Nevada.

Hageman, J. H., & Frederick, C. (2014). Phenomeno-logical and evidence based research in ego state therapy: Recognized and unrecognized successes and future directions. *American Journal of Clinical Hypnosis*, 56(1), 66–85.

Harter, S. (1988). Developmental processes in the construction of the self. In T. Yawkey & J. Johnson (Eds.), *Integrative processes and socialization* (pp. 45–78). Hillsdale, NJ: Lawrence Erlbaum.

Hartman, W. (1995). *Ego state therapy with sexually traumatized children*. Pretoria: Kagiso.

Hartman, W. (2002). Ego state therapy—then and now: Towards a naturalistic utilization approach, a tribute to John. *Swedish Journal of Hypnosis in Psychotherapy and Psychosomatic Medicine*, 39, 52-58

Herman, J. L. (1992). *Trauma and recovery*. New York, NY: Basic Books.

Hilgard, E. R. (1973). A neodissociation interpretation of pain reduction in hypnosis. *Psychological Review*, 80(5), 396–411.

Hilgard, E. R. (1977). *Divided consciousness multiple controls in human thought and action*. New York, NY: Wiley.

Horowitz, L. (1974). *Clinical prediction in psychotherapy*. New York, NY: Jason Aronson.

Horowitz, M. J. (1973). Phase oriented treatment of stress response syndromes. *American Journal of Psychotherapy*, 27(4), 506–515.

Horowitz, M. J. (1976). *Stress response systems*. Northvale, NJ: Jason Aronson.

Husserl, E. (1960). *The Cartesian meditations: An introduction to phenomenology*. The Hague, Netherlands: Martinus Nijhoff.

Husserl, E. (1977). *Logical investigations*. London, UK: Routledge & Kegan Paul.

Janet, P. (1919). *Psychological healing: A historical and clinical study*. New York, NY: Arne.

Janet., P. (1889). *L'autisme psychologique [Psychological sutomatism]*. Paris, France: Feliz Alcan.

Kluft, R. P. (1989). Playing for time: Temporizing techniques in the treatment of multiple personality disorder. *American Journal of Clinical Hypnosis*, 32(2), 90–98.

Krakauer, S. Y. (2001). *Treating dissociative disorder: The power of the collective heart*. Ann Arbor, MI: Edwards Brothers.

Krakauer, S. Y. (2006). The two-part film technique: Empowering dissociative clients to alter cognitive distortions and maladaptive behaviors. *Journal of Trauma & Dissociation: The Official Journal of the International Society for the Study of Dissociation (ISSD)*, 7(2), 39–67.

Lynn, S. J. (2001). Hypnosis, the hidden observer, and the not-so-hidden consent. *American Journal of Clinical Hypnosis*, 43(3–4), 291–292.

Lynn, S. J., Maré, C., Kvaal, S., Segal, D., & Sivec, H. (1994). The hidden observer, hypnotic trains, and age regression: Clinical implications. *American Journal of Clinical Hypnosis*, 37(2), 130–142. doi.org/10.1080/00 029157.1994.10403125.

McCann, I. L., & Pearlman, L. A. (1990). *Psychological trauma and the adult survivor. Theory, therapy, and transformation.* New York, NY: Brunner/Mazel.

Merleau-Ponty, M. (1962). *Phenomenology of perception.* New York, NY: Humanities Press.

Miller, N. E., Luborsky, L., Barber, J. P., & Docherty, J. P. (1993). *Psychodynamic treatment research: A handbook for clinical practice.* New York, NY: Basic Books.

Morton, P. A. (2001). Ego state therapy in female reproductive issues. *Hypnos, 27*(3), 124–131.

Morton, P., & Frederick, C. (1997). Intrapsychic transitional space: A resource for integration in hypnotherapy. *Hypnos, 24,* 32–41.

Ornstein, R. (1987). *Multimind: A new way to look at human behavior.* New York, NY: Houghton Mifflin.

Osoweic, D. A. (2014). Philosophy of science and the emerging paradigm: Implications for hypnosis. *American Journal of Clinical Hypnosis, 56*(3), 216–233.

Phillips, M. (2000). *Finding the energy to heal: How EMDR, hypnosis, TFT, imagery, and body-focused therapy can help restore mind-body health.* New York, NY: W. W. Norton.

Phillips, M., & Frederick, C. (1995). *Healing the divided self: Clinical and Ericksonian hypnotherapy for dissociative and post-traumatic conditions.* New York, NY: W. W. Norton.

Rainville, P., Carrier, B., Hofbauer, R. K., Bushnell, M. C., & Duncan, G. H. (1999). Dissociation of sensory and affective dimensions of pain using hypnotic modulation. *Pain, 182,* 159–171.

Rainville, P., Hofbauer, R. K., Bushnell, M. C., Duncan, G. H., & Price, D. D. (2002). Hypnosis modulates activity in brain structures involved in the regulation of consciousness. *Journal of Cognitive Neuroscience, 14*(6), 887–901.

Reinders, A. A., Nijenhuis, E. R., Paans, A. M., Korf, J., Willemsen, A. T., & den Boer, J. A. (2003). One brain, two selves. *NeuroImage, 20*(4), 2119–2125.

Rhys-Roberts, W., & Bywater, I. (1984). *The rhetorics and poetics of Aristotle.* New York, NY: The Modern Library.

Ross, C. J. (1989). *Multiple personality disorder.* New York, NY: John Wiley & Sons.

Sartre, J. (1970). Intentionality: A fundamental ideal of Husserl's phenomenology. *Journal of the British Society for Phenomenology, 1,* 4–5. doi.org/10.1080/00071773.1970.11006118.

Sartre, J. P. (2012). *The imagination.* New York, NY: Routledge.

Siegel, D. J. (1999). *The developing mind: Toward a neurobiology of interpersonal experience.* New York, NY: Guilford Press.

Steckler, J. (1989). A workshop with John and Helen Watkins. *Trauma and Recovery,* 25–26.

The Foundation for Ego State Therapy (FEST). (2009). Unpublished document.

Van der Hart, O., Brown, P., & Turco, R. (1990). Hypnotherapy for Traumatic Grief: Janetian and Modern Approaches Integrated. *American Journal of Clinical Hypnosis, 32,* 263–271. doi:10.1080/00029157.2013.770384.

Van der Hart, O., Brown, P., & Turco, R. (1990). Hypnotherapy for Traumatic Grief: Janetian and Modern Approaches Integrated. *American Journal of Clinical Hypnosis, 32,* 263–271. doi:10.1080/00029157.2013.770384

Van der Kolk, B. A. (1986). *Psychological trauma.* Washington, DC: American Psychiatric Press.

Watkins, H. H. (1978). *Ego-state therapy.* New York, NY: Human Sciences Press.

Watkins, H. H. (1993). Ego-state therapy: An overview. *American Journal of Clinical Hypnosis, 35*(4), 232–240. doi.org/10.1080/00029157.1993.10403014.

Watkins, J. G. (1949). *Hypnotherapy of war neuroses.* New York, NY: Ronald Press.

Watkins, J. G., & Barabasz, A. F. (2008). *Advanced hypnotherapy: Hypnodynamic techniques.* New York, NY: Routledge.

Watkins, J. G., & Watkins, H. H. (1976). *Hypnoanalytic ego-state therapy.* American Academy of Psychotherapists Tape Library Audio tape no. 97, Orlando, FL.

Woody, E. Z., & McConkey, K. M. (2003). What we don't know about the brain and hypnosis but need to: The view from Buckhorn Inn. *International Journal of Clinical and Experimental Hypnosis, 51*(3), 309–338. doi.org/10.1076/iceh.51.3.309.15523.

Medical Applications

Asthma

Ran D. Anbar

Asthma is considered to be a chronic inflammatory disease of the airways that affects more than 25 million people, including more than 7 million children, in the United States (NHIS, 2011). The airway inflammation predisposes the airways to become hyperreactive, constrict, and develop swelling in reaction to various stimuli. This leads to episodic limitations of air flow and difficulty with breathing that are at least partially reversible (Cohn, Elias, & Chupp, 2004). Patients with allergies are more prone to developing asthma (Huss et al., 2001). Viral infections are among the most common triggers of asthma flare-ups and may even predispose people to the development of asthma (Sigurs, Bjarnason, Sigurbergsson, & Kjellman, 2000). The morbidity of asthma includes missed school days and workdays, in order to undergo evaluation and therapy, and decreased quality of life, as patients may have poor exercise tolerance, poor sleep quality, and the need to avoid certain environments. There is also an increased risk of mortality (Adams et al., 2006; Graham, Blaiss, Bayliss, Espindle, & Ware, 2000; Hallstrand, Curtis, Aitken, & Sullivan, 2003).

Asthma is treated with a combination of anti-inflammatory ("controller") and bronchodilator ("rescue") medications that typically are inhaled (O'Byrne & Parameswaran, 2006). It is well recognized that the management of asthma can be complicated by several medical factors such as allergies (Halonen, Stern, Wright, Taussig, & Martinez, 1997), gastroesophageal reflux (Avidan, Sonnenberg, Schnell, & Sontag, 2001; Kiljander, Salomaa, Hietanen, & Terho, 1999), and chronic sinusitis (Guerra, Sherrill, Martinez, & Barbee, 2002). Patients with asthma and their health care providers also are well aware that environmental exposures such as cigarette smoke, air pollution, or other small particulate airborne matter that are irritating to the lungs when they are inhaled can trigger asthma (Malo, Lemière, Gautrin, & Labrecque, 2004; Strachan & Cook, 1998). However, many providers do not address the possibility that asthma can be triggered by emotional factors such as anxiety, depression, anger, and even excitement about a happy event (Busse et al., 1995; Sandberg et al., 2000). The lack of attention paid to the emotional issues that affect patients with asthma may be related to lack of knowledge regarding how to recognize symptoms suggestive of emotional factors at play, or clinicians' inability to provide patients with appropriate care for their mental health needs (Anbar & Hall, 2012). Ironically, a large proportion of patients who are referred to asthma care specialists because their respiratory symptoms are inadequately controlled with medical therapy suffer from symptoms that are triggered by stress (Anbar & Geisler, 2005; Seear, Wensley, & West, 2005).

Thus, the hallmark symptoms of asthma, including cough, wheeze, and shortness of breath, can all be triggered by psychological stressors. Furthermore, when a patient or even another health care provider reports "wheezing" as a symptom, it is essential to verify that this represents classical wheezing. Classical wheezing can be defined as a high-pitched whistling sound localized to the lower airways that occurs primarily with exhalation (Weinberger & Abu-Hasan, 2007). In contrast, a lower pitched inspiratory sound localized to the upper airway or throat, often mistaken for "wheezing," actually is characteristic of an upper airway obstruction, which, in a patient with asthma, is most commonly caused by vocal cord dysfunction (VCD). Interestingly, VCD typically is triggered by psychological factors. Sometimes, patients or parents even apply "wheezing" as a descriptor of a noise emanating from the nose, which is not reflective of any lung problem. In this setting, anxiety about the nasal "wheezing" can contribute to the perception that the patient's asthma is inadequately controlled.

Such anxiety may cause or exacerbate the patient's asthma symptoms (Baron & Marcotte, 1994; ten Thoren & Petermann, 2000). Finally, it should be kept in mind that a significant number of patients who do not respond to asthma therapy have been misdiagnosed with asthma (Weinberger & Abu-Hasan, 2007). The most common diagnoses in this setting include

1. Anxiety that has led to the development of shortness of breath
2. VCD independent of asthma that causes difficulty in association with inhalation, inspiratory stridor that may be incorrectly termed as "wheezing," and even occasional coughing
3. Habit cough that presents as a loud, harsh, and disruptive cough that typically resolves once patients are asleep

It is notable that all three of the aforementioned diagnoses are amenable to treatment with hypnosis.

RESEARCH

In multiple case reports, hypnosis has been reported to have beneficial effects on the subjective aspects of asthma, which include symptom frequency and severity, coping with asthma-specific fears, managing acute attacks, and frequency of medication use and health visits (Brown, 2007). Hypnosis may also be efficacious for decreasing airway obstruction and stabilizing airway hyper-responsiveness in some individuals (Aronoff, Aronoff, & Peck, 1975; Ben-Zvi, Spohn, Young, & Kattan, 1982; Fernandez, 1993). Some case reports have suggested that the use of hypnosis can be associated with dramatic improvements in asthma symptoms (Anbar, 2003; Anbar & Sachdeva, 2011). Notably, as these observations were made in an uncontrolled context, it cannot be concluded that hypnosis was a key intervention but rather that randomized studies of hypnosis in the treatment of asthma are indicated.

Only a few such studies of hypnosis in patients with asthma have been reported over the past five decades. A randomized study of 25 children with asthma showed no significant effect of four weekly hypnosis sessions on the patients' forced expiratory volume in one second (FEV_1) or daily symptom scores (Smith & Burns, 1960). In a study of 62 asthma patients who were randomized to receive three different hypnosis protocols or a control intervention at three different sites, patients who were taught to use hypnosis reported less wheezing and bronchodilator use, but no significant changes in pulmonary function were documented (Maher-Loughnan, Mason, Macdonald, & Fry, 1962). However, in a multicenter yearlong trial, 252 children and adults with moderate and severe asthma were randomized to receive monthly hypnosis sessions and daily self-hypnosis or to a control group in which patients used daily relaxation and were taught breathing exercises. Hypnosis was associated with an increase in FEV_1 of 4.3% ($p < 0.05$). There was no significant difference between the groups in their incidence of wheezing or medication use (British Tuberculosis Association, 1968).

In another randomized controlled study of 39 adults with mild-to-moderate asthma, patients who were highly skilled in hypnosis (high hypnotizable) demonstrated a significant reduction in reactivity to methacholine challenge testing (PC_{20} 9.1 vs. 15.9, $p < 0.01$) and decreased chronic bronchodilator use (26% reduction, $p < 0.05$), as well as decreased subjective scores for nocturnal symptoms (62%, $p < 0.05$), wheeze (53%, $p < 0.01$), and activity limitation (40%, $p < 0.01$). In contrast, patients who did not use hypnosis well (low hypnotizable) or were in the control group demonstrated no significant changes in these parameters (Ewer & Stewart, 1986).

In the only pediatric controlled trial that has been reported to date, 28 patients were divided into four groups (hypnosis, suggestion only, attention only, and a nonintervention control group). At 1-month, 6-month, and 2-year follow-ups, no significant differences emerged between groups on physiological measures of pulmonary function. Children taught to use self-hypnotic techniques had a significantly larger reduction in wheezing as compared with the control group (52% vs. 35%, $p < 0.05$). Also, these children reported fewer emergency room visits and fewer missed school days relative to the control and suggestion groups but not compared to the attention group (Kohen, 1995). These results should be interpreted with caution due to the small sample size.

As is described in the remainder of this chapter, there are many ways in which hypnosis might be applied in the treatment of asthma (Anbar, 2014). Thus, some of the variability in outcome of the described studies and reports regarding the use of hypnosis for asthma likely is related in part to the different hypnotic approaches that were offered. Furthermore, when used clinically, hypnosis is most effective when suggestions are made based on the interests, motivation, and abilities of individual patients (Anbar, 2007). Thus, experimental studies that employ uniform protocols for the management of asthma with hypnosis likely underestimate the effectiveness of clinical hypnosis. Given the small number of studies of hypnosis for asthma, more randomized, controlled studies of hypnosis and asthma would be helpful. Such studies would benefit from the use of larger patient populations and flexible hypnosis protocols that allow for individualizing the hypnosis experience. As is true for all medical illnesses for which hypnosis is offered, it is essential that the patient's illness be managed medically with concurrent application of hypnosis therapy (Anbar & Hall, 2012).

CASE EXAMPLE

A 13-year-old patient reported that his asthma often was triggered when he became angry or sad. For example, he sometimes had to leave the room to use his rescue inhaler during the middle of altercations with his 17-year-old brother who picked on him. He explained that frequently he had been experiencing cough and shortness of breath on mornings when he had an important test at school. Sometimes, he said that he awakened at night as a result of a nightmare and felt as if he could not breathe. In those instances, he would awaken his mother and ask to use his rescue inhaler.

The patient was offered an opportunity to learn how to use hypnosis to become calmer, so that he would have better control of his body's reactions during stressful situations. The patient was eager to learn such a technique and was provided instructions similar to those presented in the following text (Anbar, Sugarman, & Wester, 2013). The phrasing was delivered in a soft voice with many pauses that allowed the clinician to observe the patient's physical reactions. A month after he learned to calm himself with hypnosis, the patient reported that he used it on a regular basis and felt much calmer overall. He said that he was able to

remain calmer and his asthma no longer was triggered during interactions with his brother or in relation to school tests. He reported that he had had no recent nightmares.

TRANSCRIPT: HYPNOSIS FOR ASTHMA SYMPTOMS

"Imagine a favorite, safe place, which you would enjoy visiting. It can be a place you have been to, would like to go to, or even an imaginary place. Let me know when you have this place in mind. . . . Now, imagine what you might see there. What colors might you see? Are there people there? Are there sights there that make you happy? Now, what might you hear there? Is it silent? Are there sounds of nature? Talking? Music? What might you smell? Fragrance? Perfume? Salty air? Fresh air? If you touch something, what would it feel like? Soft? Smooth? Rough? Wet? And if there is something to eat or drink there, imagine what it might taste like. Is it salty? Sour? Sweet? Notice how the more you imagine your different senses the more relaxed you can become, and the more real the experience can become."

Now I am going to talk to you about relaxing even more. You can start by relaxing your forehead. That's right. Now, let that comfortable feeling of relaxation pass into the muscles around your eyes. Your eyes can be open or closed, whichever is more comfortable for you. Now, let the relaxation spread to your cheeks. And jaw. Sometimes, it helps to open the mouth a bit in order to allow the jaw to become very relaxed. Now, let the relaxation spread to your neck. Your shoulders. Your arms. And your hands. Very good. Now, take in a deep breath, and let it out slowly. Notice how your chest relaxes as you do that. Now, take in another deep breath, let it out slowly, and notice how your belly relaxes as you do that. Excellent. Now, let the relaxation spread. To your back. Your legs. And your feet. That's right. Notice how relaxed you have become. How peaceful, and calm, and content, and serene, and tranquil, and in control, and comfortable you can be. Very relaxed, very calm, and very comfortable. Your breathing can be easy and comfortable. That's right.

This can be a great feeling, right? This is a feeling you can achieve anytime you want to just by imagining returning to your relaxing place. Let me know when you are ready to come back in a few moments by raising your hand, or nodding. Very good. Now, before you come back, you might tell yourself four things. First, congratulate yourself for your excellent imagination and ability to relax. Remind yourself to practice your hypnosis skills every day for at least 2 weeks so that you can become very good with its use. Hypnosis is a mind–body skill. The more you practice it, the better you become. Next, remind yourself that whenever you want to relax, you can go back to your favorite place in your imagination. Finally, right now your mind is open to good suggestions. You can tell yourself good things. And the more you tell these to yourself, the more they come true. For example, you might tell yourself, I like how I feel now and I want to feel this way for the rest of the day. I am going to do well on my tests in school. I am going to remain calm and have fun the next time I interact with my friends. [The clinician can suggest specific affirmations based on the patient's interests and experiences.] *And once you are done telling yourself all the good things you need to hear, once the time is right, and you'll know exactly when that time is; then come back. Formal example (often useful with adults, and applicable especially to patients who are deeply absorbed in the hypnotic experience): Now I am going to count from 1 to 5. The higher I count the more alert you can become. The more you will be able to feel the chair in which you are sitting, and the floor beneath your feet. That's right. 1 . . . 2. . . . You can sit up straighter . . . 3. . . . More alert . . . 4. . . . Your eyes can start to open . . . 5. . . . You can open your eyes, and look around you.*"

ADDITIONAL TECHNIQUES

There are several additional hypnotic techniques that can be useful in the treatment of patients with asthma, including those that are described in the following text. Patients can be taught to use some of these techniques through self-hypnosis on an as-needed basis.

Imagery Specific to Symptoms

Patients can be coached to open their constricted airways through realistic or creative imagery. Especially for patients who are going to use realistic images, it can be helpful to show drawings or photographs of constricted airways in contrast to images of airways that are open.

"When your asthma is bothering you, imagine seeing the airways as constricted, and in your mind's eye open them. Notice how your body follows that imagery and helps you feel better. Imagine your asthma medication entering your lungs and attaching to the muscles that surround your airways. Imagine that the medication massages the muscles until they relax and allow your airways to open. Imagine the air you inhale to be warm, clean, and humid, just like you might encounter in a tropical rain forest. Notice that as you breathe in that wonderful air, your breathing can become more and more comfortable. If a boa constrictor tightened itself around your lungs, how do you think you might convince it to loosen its grip? Perhaps offer it an enticing meal? Scare it with a more fearsome creature? How does it feel once the boa leaves?"

Breathing Techniques

Breathing retraining can help improve asthma symptoms and pulmonary function (Holloway & Ram, 2004) and thus can be helpful when included within a hypnotic intervention.

Breathing primarily with expansion of the diaphragm as opposed to through the use of thoracic muscles helps expand the lungs better and thus enhances the effectiveness of breathing, which can help patients feel more relaxed (Barker, Jones, O'Connell & Everard, 2013). Such breathing can be taught with the following instructions:

"Imagine a sailboat at the bottom of your sternum. Notice how when you inhale, the rowboat can rise, and when you exhale, the sailboat can fall. Good. Focus on that sailboat as you breathe comfortably, and notice how you can feel better and breathe more easily. . . . Inhale slowly through your nose for a count of 4, hold your breath for a count of 5, and exhale slowly through your mouth for a count of 7. Repeat this cycle 10 times. Notice

how much more relaxed you become as your breathing control improves."

Breathing through the nose helps humidify, warm, and clean the inhaled air and thus is less likely to irritate hyperreactive airways. Holding the breath allows for better expansion of the lungs. Exhaling slowly helps resolve anxiety-associated hyperventilation.

Subconscious Exploration

When asthma symptoms result from psychological stressors that are expressed through somatic symptoms, subconscious exploration with the aid of a clinician can sometimes help patients come to a better self-understanding regarding their psychological triggers (Anbar & Linden, 2010). This can help formulate ways of addressing such stressors more effectively.

Before engaging the subconscious through hypnosis, it is helpful to discuss the patient's understanding of the role of the subconscious (Anbar, 2008). A clinically useful definition of the subconscious is *"The part of your mind of which you are often unaware."* A patient also can be told,

"When you do things without thinking about them, this is an example of the subconscious in action. The subconscious shows you dreams while you sleep. Sometimes, when you are about to do something wrong, you may hear a small voice in the back of your head that cautions you. Many people call that 'the conscience,' but even this can be thought of as emanating from the subconscious."

The "inner advisor" technique allows the subconscious to interact with the patient through an imagined figure (Hammond, 1990). For example,

"Imagine yourself in your comfortable place. Look around for a house or another structure with a door that you may not have noticed before. Once you find it, let me know. That's right. Now, knock on the door and when it opens, you will meet your inner advisor. Perhaps it will be a person, animal, or thing. Once you meet your advisor, ask if it would be all right to ask him or her some questions."

Once the inner advisor is identified, a discussion can ensue with the advisor through questions posed by the clinician or even the patient. An advantage of this technique is that the advisor can answer in full sentences, although oftentimes the answer is short and concrete. A disadvantage is that the patient is aware of the answers since he or she verbalizes them, and therefore the subconscious may choose not to share information that could be upsetting to the patient.

Rehearsal

Some patients benefit from imagined rehearsal of their hypnosis techniques.

"Imagine yourself in a situation during which you often develop your asthma symptoms, such as when you are around something to which you are allergic, or when you are taking a test in school. Now, imagine using your relaxation sign in that situation, and notice how your breathing can remain easy and comfortable."

Other patients are willing to experience their respiratory symptoms in order to learn the extent of their mastery of their illness (Tal & Miklich, 1976).

"Imagine a situation in which your asthma starts bothering you, and allow yourself to feel your airways constricting. Notice how your breathing can become more labored. Let your breathing worsen as much as you feel comfortable, and when you are ready to help yourself feel better, use your relaxation sign. Notice how rapidly you can feel better. Now you know that you can be in much better charge of your asthma."

Age Regression

Respiratory symptoms sometimes develop as a result of stressful early life experiences (Yonas, Lange, & Celedón, 2012). For example, psychosocial stress, a near-drowning episode, choking on food during infancy, or an allergic reaction may be related to development of long-term breathing issues. Some clinicians believe that even difficulty with breathing associated with birth experiences can lead to the development of asthma (Dabney Ewin, personal communication). Patients affected by such events can improve with the use of clinician-guided hypnotic regression techniques (Hammond, 1990). Hypnotic regression may be beneficial even in the absence of an actual triggering event, as learning to deal with an imagined triggering event can serve as a metaphor for mastery of asthma.

Hypnotic regression instructions can be given in many ways including through initially teaching a patient to use a relaxation sign and ideomotor signaling (as in the preceding text).

"Have your subconscious take you back to the very first time when you experienced breathing difficulties. Perhaps this was a time when you were scared for your life because it felt as if you would be unable to breathe again. Your subconscious will signal to me with the 'yes' finger when you find yourself at that time again. . . . Very good. Now, teach your younger self to employ the relaxation sign, and tell yourself you can breathe again. You survived and felt good again. Go ahead and exhale, and breathe comfortably. . . . Now, allow your subconscious to bring you back to the present, and it will let you know when you have returned by signaling with the 'yes' finger. Very good. You may be surprised by how much better your asthma now has become."

CONCLUSION

Asthma is one of the most common diseases in the Western world. In the early 20th century, it was considered as one of the "Holy Seven" psychosomatic disorders (Anbar & Hall, 2012) and thus was thought to be amenable to psychological therapy. However, by the late 20th century, medical scientists had characterized it as a chronic inflammatory disease and the focus of its treatment had shifted toward medical therapy directed at the underlying physiological abnormalities. In the early 21st century, we have become more aware that psychological abnormalities can both predispose to and be the result of asthma. Thus, optimal treatment of asthma requires concurrent attention to its physiological and psychological manifestations. As a psychological therapy, hypnosis appears to provide an effective, efficient tool for the treatment of asthma as well as some of its associated common comorbidities including anxiety and VCD.

REFERENCES

Adams, R. J., Wilson, D. H., Taylor, A. W., Daly, A., Tursan d'Espaignet, E., Dal Grande, E., & Ruffin, R. E. (2006). Coexistent chronic conditions and asthma quality of life: A population-based study. *Chest, 129*(2), 285–291.

Anbar, R. D. (2003). Self-hypnosis for anxiety associated with severe asthma: A case report. *BMC Pediatrics, 22,* 3–7.

Anbar, R. D. (2007). User friendly hypnosis as an adjunct for treatment of habit cough: A case report. *American Journal of Clinical Hypnosis, 50*(2), 171–176.

Anbar, R. D. (2008). Subconscious guided therapy with hypnosis. *American Journal of Clinical Hypnosis, 50*(4), 323–334.

Anbar, R. D. (2014). Hypnosis for treatment of functional symptoms in children. In R. D. Anbar (Ed.), *Functional symptoms in pediatric disease: A clinical guide* (pp. 305–318). New York, NY: Springer Publishing Company.

Anbar, R. D., & Geisler, S. C. (2005). Identification of children who may benefit from self-hypnosis at a pediatric pulmonary center. *BMC Pediatrics, 5*(1), 6.

Anbar, R. D., & Hall, H. R. (2012). What is a functional respiratory disorder? In R. Anbar (Ed.), *Functional respiratory disorders: When respiratory symptoms do not respond to pulmonary treatment* (pp. 3–17). New York, NY: Humana Press.

Anbar, R. D., & Linden, J. H. (2010). Understanding dissociation and insight in the treatment of shortness of breath with hypnosis: A case study. *American Journal of Clinical Hypnosis, 52*(4), 263–273.

Anbar, R. D., & Sachdeva, S. (2011). Treatment of psychological factors in a child with difficult asthma: A case report. *American Journal of Clinical Hypnosis, 54*(1), 47–55.

Anbar, R. D., Sugarman, L., & Wester, W. (2013). Hypnosis for children with chronic disease. In *Therapeutic hypnosis with children and adolescents* (pp. 403–431). Bethel, CT: Crown House Publishing.

Aronoff, G. M., Aronoff, S., & Peck, L. W. (1975). Hypnotherapy in the treatment of bronchial asthma. *Annals of Allergy, 34*(6), 356–362.

Avidan, B., Sonnenberg, A., Schnell, T. G., & Sontag, S. J. (2001). Temporal associations between coughing or wheezing and acid reflux in asthmatics. *Gut, 49*(6), 767–772.

Barker, N. J., Jones, M., O'Connell, N. E., & Everard, M. L. (2013). Breathing exercises for dysfunctional breathing/hyperventilation syndrome in children. *Cochrane Database of Systematic Reviews, 12.*

Baron, C., & Marcotte, J. E. (1994). Role of panic attacks in the intractability of asthma in children. *Pediatrics, 94*(1), 108–110.

Ben-Zvi, Z., Spohn, W. A., Young, S. H., & Kattan, M. (1982). Hypnosis for exercise-induced asthma. *American Review of Respiratory Disease, 25*(4), 392–395.

British Tuberculosis Association. (1968). Hypnosis for asthma–a controlled trial: A report to the research committee of the British Tuberculosis Association. *British Medical Journal, 4*(5623), 71–76.

Brown, D. (2007). Evidence-based hypnotherapy for asthma: A critical review. *International Journal of Clinical and Experimental Hypnosis, 55*(2), 220–249.

Busse, W. W., Kiecolt-Glaser, J. K., Coe, C., Martin, R. J., Weiss, S. T., & Parker, S. R. (1995). Stress and asthma. *American Journal of Respiratory and Critical Care Medicine, 151*(1), 249–252.

Cohn, L., Elias, J. A., & Chupp, G. L. (2004). Asthma: Mechanisms of disease persistence and progression. *Annual Review of Immunology, 22*, 789–815.

Ewer, T. C., & Stewart, D. E. (1986). Improvement in bronchial hyper-responsiveness in patients with moderate asthma, after treatment with a hypnotic technique: A randomized controlled trial. *British Medical Journal (Clinical Research ed.), 293*(6555), 1129–1132.

Fernandez, O. F. (1993). Hypnosis: Its use in acute attacks of bronchial asthma. *Hypnos, 20*, 236–245.

Graham, D. M., Blaiss, M. S., Bayliss, M. S., Espindle, D. M., & Ware, J. E. (2000). Impact of changes in asthma severity on health-related quality of life in pediatric and adult asthma patients: Results from the asthma outcomes monitoring system. *Allergy and Asthma Proceedings: The Official Journal of Regional and State Allergy Societies, 21*(3), 151–158.

Guerra, S., Sherrill, D. L., Martinez, F. D., & Barbee, R. A. (2002). Rhinitis as an independent risk factor for adult-onset asthma. *Journal of Allergy and Clinical Immunology, 109*(3), 419–425.

Hallstrand, T. S., Curtis, J. R., Aitken, M. L., & Sullivan, S. D. (2003). Quality of life in adolescents with mild asthma. *Pediatric Pulmonology, 36*(6), 536–543.

Halonen, M., Stern, D. A., Wright, A. L., Taussig, L. M., & Martinez, F. D. (1997). Alternaria as a major allergen for asthma in children raised in a desert environment. *American Journal of Respiratory and Critical Care Medicine, 155*(4), 1356–1361.

Hammond, D. C. (1990). *Handbook of hypnotic suggestions and metaphors*. New York, NY: W. W. Norton.

Holloway, E., & Ram, F. S. (2004). Breathing exercises for asthma. *Cochrane Database Systematic Reviews, 10*.

Huss, K., Adkinson, N. F., Eggleston, P. A., Dawson, C., Van Natta, M. L., & Hamilton, R. G. (2001). House dust mite and cockroach exposure are strong risk factors for positive allergy skin test responses in the Childhood Asthma Management Program. *Journal of Allergy and Clinical Immunology, 107*(1), 48–54.

Kiljander, T. O., Salomaa, E. R., Hietanen, E. K., & Terho, E. O. (1999). Gastro esophageal reflux in asthmatics: A double-blind, placebo-controlled crossover study with omeprazole. *Chest, 116*(5), 1257–1264.

Kohen, D. P. (1995). Relaxation/mental imagery (self-hypnosis) for childhood asthma: Behavioral outcomes in a prospective, controlled study. *Hypnos, 22*, 132–144.

Maher-Loughnan, G. P., Mason, A. A., Macdonald, N., & Fry, L. (1962). Controlled trial of hypnosis in the symptomatic treatment of asthma. *British Medical Journal, 2*(5301), 371–376.

Malo, J. L., Lemière, C., Gautrin, D., & Labrecque, M. (2004). Occupational asthma. *Current Opinion in Pulmonary Medicine, 10*(1), 57–61.

National Health Interview Survey (NHIS). (2011). Hyattsville, MD: National Center for Health Statistics (NCHS), Centers for Disease Control and Prevention. Retrieved from http://www.cdc.gov/asthma/nhis/2011/data.htm

O'Byrne, P. M., & Parameswaran, K. (2006). Pharmacological management of mild or moderate persistent asthma. *The Lancet, 368*(9537), 794–803.

Sandberg, S., Paton, J. Y., Ahola, S., McCann, D. C., McGuinness, D., Hillary, C. R., & Oja, H. (2000). The role of acute and chronic stress in asthma attacks in children. *The Lancet, 356*(9234), 982–987.

Seear, M., Wensley, D., & West, N. (2005). How accurate is the diagnosis of exercise induced asthma among Vancouver schoolchildren? *Archives of Disease in Childhood, 90*(9), 898–902.

Sigurs, N., Bjarnason, R., Sigurbergsson, F., & Kjellman, B. (2000). Respiratory syncytial virus bronchiolitis in infancy is an important risk factor for asthma and allergy at age 7. *American Journal of Respiratory and Critical Care Medicine, 161*(5), 1501–1507.

Smith, J. M., & Burns, C. L. (1960). The treatment of asthmatic children by hypnotic suggestion. *British Journal of Diseases of the Chest, 54*, 78–91.

Strachan, D. P., & Cook, D. G. (1998). Health effects of passive smoking, parental smoking and childhood asthma: Longitudinal and case-control studies. *Thorax, 53*(3), 204–212.

Tal, A., & Miklich, D. R. (1976). Emotionally induced decreases in pulmonary flow rates in asthmatic children. *Psychosomatic Medicine, 38*(3), 190–200.

ten Thoren, C., & Petermann, F. (2000). Reviewing asthma and anxiety. *Respiratory Medicine, 94*(5), 409–415.

Weinberger, M., & Abu-Hasan, M. (2007). Pseudo-asthma: When cough, wheezing, and dyspnea are not asthma. *Pediatrics, 120*(4), 855–864.

Yonas, M. A., Lange, N. E., & Celedón, J. C. (2012). Psychosocial stress and asthma morbidity. *Current Opinion in Allergy and Clinical Immunology, 12*(2), 202–210.

Autoimmune Disorders

Moshe S. Torem

The past several decades of medical research have brought a deeper and wider understanding of the immune system and its role in maintaining health and preventing the onset of disease (Kumar, Kawai, & Akira, 2011). The immune system is designed, among its other functions, to identify and destroy foreign invading disease-causing organisms and viruses. However, when the immune system misidentifies the antigens on our own cells as antigens of foreign organisms such as bacteria, viruses, or fungi, the immune system attacks these cells with the purpose of protecting the integrity and health of the living organism as a whole. The process of this attack may produce inflammation and an autoimmune disease. The following diseases have so far been identified as involving an autoimmune mechanism: acute rheumatic fever, Addison's disease, ankylosing spondylitis, antiphospholipid syndrome, autoimmune alopecia, autoimmune hemolytic anemia, autoimmune polyglandular syndrome, autoimmune thrombocytopenic purpura, Behcet's syndrome, celiac disease or sprue, chronic fatigue immune dysfunction syndrome, dermatitis herpetiformis, dermatomyositis, diabetes mellitus type I, diffuse scleroderma, fibromyalgia syndrome, Goodpasture's syndrome, Graves' disease, Guillain-Barre syndrome, Hashimoto's thyroiditis, Henoch-Schonlein purpura, autoimmune hepatitis, immune-mediated infertility, insulin-resistant diabetes mellitus, lupus erythematosus, microscopic polyangiitis, multiple sclerosis, myasthenia gravis, pemphigus foliaceus, pemphigus vulgaris, pernicious anemia, polyarteritis nodosa, polymyalgia rheumatica, polymyositis/dermatomyositis, psoriasis, psoriatic arthritis, Reiter's syndrome, relapsing polychondritis, rheumatoid arthritis, Sjogren's syndrome, stiff-man syndrome, sympathetic ophthalmia, systemic lupus erythematosus, systemic necrotizing vasculitis, vitiligo, and Wegener's granulomatosis.

Walsh and Rau (2000) pointed out that autoimmune diseases are in fact a leading cause of death among young and middle-aged women in the United States. The prevalence of autoimmune diseases in American women is about 5% (Jacobsen, Gange, Rose, & Graham, 1997).

Typical autoimmune diseases have a remitting–relapsing course. Following the first episode of the disease, many patients spontaneously enter into a remission. The purpose of all treatments currently available is to accomplish these goals: to shorten the time of the acute phase and to reduce the intensity of the inflammation and symptoms involved with this acute phase of the disease. The first treatment goal is to get the patient into a full remission as soon as possible. The second goal of treatment is to keep patients in a remission as long as possible, ideally for the rest of their lives.

Mind–body approaches to enhance the achievement of the goals, mentioned in the preceding text, in treatment are based on the research discoveries in the field of psychoneuroimmunology over the past 40 years. The field of psychoneuroimmunology postulates that the central nervous system and the immune system communicate with each other on a regular basis. Ader and Nicholas Cohen (1975, 1981, 1982, 1985) and Ader (2000) have shown through ingenious experimental design studies how the central nervous system influences the functions of the immune system. Later, Dantzer (2001) and, separately, Vollmer-Conna (2001) postulated that illness behavior associated with an acute infection may in fact be the result of a communication between the immune system and the brain, which is adaptive for the organism's recovery and overall survival. Life events such as losses involving the emotions of grief, sadness, and depression typically produce a suppression of the immune system and compromise its ability to quickly mobilize a defensive response to pathogenic bacteria, viruses, or fungi (Ipsa, Devi, & Ravindra, 2014; Kiecolt-Glaser & Glaser, 2002). On the other hand, it is well known that optimism, exuberance, joy, laughter, proper nutrition, restorative nocturnal sleep, and effective stress management skills enhance the functioning of the immune system as pointed out by Cousins (1976), Rossi (1993), Dreher (1995), Ravicz (2000), Charnetski and Brennan (2001), Klasing (2007), and Lange, Dimitrov, and Born (2010).

EVIDENCE (RELEVANT RESEARCH)

Recent studies have shown that nearly all antigens in human cells can generate autoimmunity (Baranzini, 2013). However, the body has developed various mechanisms that have induced tolerance of our immune system to such antigens. Specific immune system mechanisms ensuring tolerance to cells and tissues of one's self appear during the development of B cells. This happens in the bone marrow where B cells are generated, followed by the migration of these B cells to peripheral tissues. Some B cells go through the thymus gland and get specialized for specific functions. These specialized cells are called "T cells." There are two types of T cells: T helper cells that help the B cells in producing antibodies that attack and destroy the invading pathogenic organisms (bacteria, viruses, fungi, etc.) and T suppressor cells that are designed to reign in the B cells and the T helper cells when they become too aggressive. It is postulated that one mechanism that operates in the development of autoimmune disorders involves an immune system, which has lost its natural balance either by weakening of the T suppressor cells' response or by an overproduction of B cells and T helper cells, which may be involved in producing antibodies that mistakenly attack the organism's own cells and tissues, failing to identify them as part of its own self organism. It is still unclear why certain types of tissues are selected to be attacked and other tissues are spared.

George F. Solomon (1981; Solomon, Amkraut, & Kasper, 1974; Solomon, Levine, & Kraft, 1968; Solomon & Moss, 1964) of Stanford University was the first American scientist who studied the interaction between the mind and the immune system. Solomon was working in the 1960s treating patients with rheumatoid arthritis and he observed that these patients would typically enter into a relapse during stressful times in their lives. He hypothesized that the immune system must be somehow triggered to attack the patient's joints during times of stress. He then hypothesized that our immune system must be very sensitive to stress and responsive to emotions and thoughts.

In the 1970s, the psychologist Robert Ader and his colleague, immunologist Nicholas Cohen, both from the University of Rochester School of Medicine, managed to conduct an ingenious set of experiments in mice whereby they were able to demonstrate behavioral conditioning of immune system responses. A group of mice where given an injection of the immune suppressant drug Cytoxan. This was coupled with an exposure to saccharin-sweetened water, which the mice drank. After feeding the mice with sweet water, the suppression of the immune response was demonstrated even when 14 days later, the mice were given an injection of saline coupled with an exposure to saccharin-sweetened water. An injection of saline alone without the exposure of sweetened water did not produce the same immune system suppression (Ader & Cohen, 1975). Later, Ader and Cohen (1981, 1982, 1985) studied a group of rats that had lupus erythematosus. Ader was able to condition the rats to reduce their immune system aggressiveness toward their own cells. The results were an impressive reduction in the rats' symptoms of acute lupus inflammation. Several years later, Olness and Ader (1992) was able to use this model in helping a young girl suffering from lupus by conditioning her immune system to be suppressed and cutting the planned chemotherapy treatments from 12 to six, achieving a significant clinical improvement that lasted for over 5 years.

It is understood today that the brain affects the immune system by secreting neurotransmitters and hormones that activate specific receptors on the surface of T and B lymphocytes. This activates certain intracellular mechanisms that either suppress or enhance their activity as cells of the immune system response. Some have referred to these specific molecules that are secreted by the central nervous system, which affect the immune system, as neuroimmunotransmitters.

The brain's connection with the immune system is believed to be mediated through the limbic-hypothalamic-pituitary pathway. The immune system responds through the secretion of hormones and other specific chemicals that act as neuroimmunotransmitters. Thereby, these hormones deliver specific messages from the central nervous system to the immune system. Later, Booth and Ashbridge (1993) proposed that the immune system and the nervous system are an integrated entity with a common goal of establishing and maintaining a self-identity of living organisms.

THE ROLE OF HYPNOSIS

Brown and Fromm (1987, p. 145) stated that the treatment of autoimmune diseases by psychological means was largely undeveloped. They described a treatment protocol similar to that used with cancer patients.

> The clinician begins by teaching the patient to self monitor the vicissitudes of the autoimmune symptoms. The patient keeps daily records of the symptoms, noting daily activities and subjectively rating the level of tension. The therapist helps the patient uncover the relationship between stressful situations and the exacerbation of symptoms.

In the next step, the patient is taught a variety of ways to reduce the effects of stress on the mind and body. These methods involve nonhypnotic relaxation as described by Achterberg and Lawlis (1980) and Benson (1975, 1979, 1984, 1996) and also hypnotic relaxation techniques as described by Millikin (1964).

In cases of rheumatoid arthritis, an outbreak of symptoms is often preceded by an increase in muscle tension as reported by Gottschalk, Serota, and Shapiro (1950). Cheek and LeCron (1968) reported that reducing emotional intrapsychic conflicts associated with one's health and illness can be worked through with hypnotherapy, thus reducing the severity of an acute attack and promoting the process of remission. Bowers and Kelly (1979) believed that any application of hypnotherapy that improves the patient's overall health and well-being may contribute to a positive effect on healthy regulation of the immune system. Achterberg, McGraw, and Lawlis (1981) stated that relaxation training and regular practice of muscle relaxation may have a prophylactic effect in postponing and possibly preventing the acute relapse of symptoms in rheumatoid arthritis. Brown and Fromm (1987)

reported that a variety of hypnotherapeutic procedures can be used to enhance patients' well-being, positive emotional state, self-efficacy, and quality of life to better cope with their illness.

Pain and discomfort that are associated with autoimmune diseases can be alleviated with hypnotherapy with good results as reported by Van Pelt (1961), Millikin (1964), Crasilneck and Hall (1975), Smith and Balaban (1983), and Torem (2007).

Earnest Rossi (1986, 1990, 1993; Rossi & Cheek, 1988) reported on the various mechanisms by which the mind communicates with the immune system and how the use of hypnosis may help as a therapeutic aid in the recovery of patients suffering from autoimmune disorders. According to Rossi, when patients shift into a state of hypnosis, they can communicate with the unconscious mind and speak directly to tissues and cells by using the language of imagery with all five senses. In addition, other well-known methods such as cognitive reframing, relabeling, and reorganizing the mind–body communication can be utilized to benefit patients and promote healing (Torem, 2007).

Laidlaw, Booth, and Large (1996) showed that 32 of 38 experimental participants were able to reduce wheal size following a hypnotic suggestion to do so. Kiecolt-Glaser and her colleagues (Kiecolt-Glaser, Marucha, Atkinson, & Glaser, 2001; Kiecolt-Glaser, McGuire, Robles, & Glaser, 2002) have shown that hypnosis can be used as a modulator of cellular immune dysregulation. Brigham-Davis (1994) reported on the therapeutic use of imagery in patients suffering from systemic lupus erythematosus, scleroderma, rheumatoid arthritis, multiple sclerosis, amyotrophic lateral sclerosis, chronic fatigue immune dysfunction syndrome, fibromyalgia, and myasthenia gravis. Brigham-Davis's strategy was to help patients view their immune system as a friendly, loving, and protective organ within their body. Brigham-Davis emphasized the crucial importance of a balance in the immune system between T helper cells and T suppressor cells as necessary for optimal functioning of the immune system.

In my experience practicing in the field of mind–body integrative medicine, I have used hypnosis and guided imagery in a variety of clinical settings and with many patients suffering from a wide spectrum of disease entities. My work with patients who have suffered from autoimmune disorders was significant in my own development as a therapist and healer. One of the hallmarks of many patients suffering from autoimmune disorders is the cyclical nature of their disease. It typically cycles from remission to relapse and then again into a remission. When I first treated a patient in an acute state of lupus erythematosus, I made the prediction that the patient would in fact get better. In fact, what happened was that this patient went into a remission and believed that it was the hypnotic intervention that produced this remission, and so did I. Our mutual belief may have in fact enhanced the results of the intervention. However, the cyclical nature of autoimmune disorders was obviously an important factor that contributed to a successful outcome.

The following is a list of interventions that can be enhanced by using hypnosis in patients with autoimmune disorders: mind–body relaxation, ego strengthening, ego-state therapy, relabeling, reframing, restructuring, "back from the future" age progression, end result focus enhancement, and therapeutic metaphors with symbolic guided imagery (Torem, 1987, 1992a, 1992b, 1993, 2007).

Generally, I start with the simplest intervention and gradually build up to the more complex interventions. Exceptions can be made for patients who have experience in practicing self-hypnosis or meditation. Another important element is to match the therapeutic intervention with the patient's personality/temperament and what has particularly worked well for him or her in the past. Moreover, it is important to conduct a comprehensive interview with patients focused on not only gathering detailed information on how the symptoms evolved and what precipitated the recent relapse but also obtaining detailed information on the patients' expectations from the use of hypnosis in their therapy and how they imagine themselves being healed from their autoimmune disorder and how they see themselves achieving a life-long remission. Obtaining this information is vitally important in designing a therapeutic plan that will be compatible with the patient's inherent personality traits and expectations for a successful, reasonable outcome of treatment.

CASE EXAMPLE—RHEUMATOID ARTHRITIS

J. was a 25-year-old single woman who had been diagnosed with rheumatoid arthritis as a teenager. By the age of 25, she already had several relapses followed by spontaneous remissions. At one time, she was treated with corticosteroids and the side effects caused her to gain over 30 pounds of body weight, which she disliked. She came to my office referred by another patient with the goal of "doing anything, even hypnosis to get me into remission as long as I don't have to take steroids again." I performed the Hypnotic Induction Profile (HIP; Spiegel, 1973, 1977). Her score was 4 with an intact profile. She learned to use self-hypnosis quickly and effectively by focusing on the ocean beach scene imagery to achieve a state of calmness and activate the relaxation response.

We continued discussing what she wanted to accomplish and she simply said, "To get back into a remission as quickly as possible." Smiling, she added, "and . . . stay there for the rest of my life." She already had experienced previous remissions, some of them spontaneous without any specific medical treatment.

We proceeded with a dialogue on what it was like to enter into a remission in the past. She described in detail how the pain and swelling in her joints were relieved and how she was able to move around flexibly without any discomfort. She loved to swim and went into detail describing her skills of floating in the waters of the ocean and swimming pool. She then described how much she enjoyed her brief sessions in the whirlpool right after a lap in the swimming pool of her gym. We then proceeded by asking her to enter into a state of self-hypnotic trance, focusing on the ocean beach scene imagery and experiencing it with all five senses. This was done using interactive imagery whereby she verbalized her experiences on the ocean beach of her choice.

We then proceeded by using future-focused imagery, utilizing the "back from the future" technique (Torem, 1992a, 2006). The focus was not only in achieving the experience of returning to optimal functioning of her physical mobility and other activities but also on gaining a new sense of healthy balance in her life on a mind–body–spirit continuum. She was then asked to internalize these experiences with members of her family and friends, internalizing the experience with all five senses (visual, auditory, tactile, olfactory, and gustatory) as well as internalizing feelings of joy, love, and mastery, having achieved a healthy balance of activities in day-to-day living. When she was guided out of the hypnotic state, she reported with a smile that she already felt better and that her joints felt more flexible, free, and limber. She reported that she had to consciously think about the pain and focus on it to recognize if it was still present.

Four weeks later, she came to the office for a follow-up visit and stated with a smile on her face that she was now back in remission as pronounced by her rheumatologist. Her goal now was to stay in remission for "the rest of my life." She was instructed to continue to practice self-hypnosis with guided imagery focused on activating the relaxation response on a daily basis. In addition, we discussed a variety of skills she was to learn and practice in her daily living to improve her effective communication in social settings: being assertive, having a clearer picture of her values, and noting align-ingher daily living to be compatible with these values. We also discussed her goal of including spirituality in her daily life by becoming more authentic in her friendships and establishing a sense of meaning and connection with a higher power. Follow-up visits at 3 months, 6 months, and 9 months found her in a stable healthy remission, continuing to practice self-hypnosis and guided imagery.

TECHNIQUE OR TRANSCRIPT

The following transcript includes specific wording to the patient designed to induce a state of hypnosis with suggestions for calmness and relaxation first in a preferred imagery setting. It is then followed by specific imagery and suggestions to induce a remission in the patient's autoimmune disorder relapse. Ask the patient to sit in a comfortable chair and body position. Then, say the following:

"Please go ahead and take a deep breath . . . and as you exhale, let your eyelids close and let your body float. . . . Keep on breathing comfortably in and out at your own pace [I match the words in and out with the patient's actual breathing, saying the word "in" when the patient inhales and saying the word "out" when the patient exhales.] *. . . as you continue to sit here . . . breathing comfortably in and out . . . with each breath that you take . . . as you inhale, in comes the calmness . . . and as you exhale . . . out goes the stress and the tension. . . . As you listen to my voice and focus on the*

words, you may know that you were born with a deeply endowed wisdom for creative imagination . . . which you already have used on your own to escape and detach yourself from difficult and stressful situations at home and at school. . . . As we discussed before, you may wish to take a special trip to the ocean beach . . . as a way to relax and recharge your batteries . . . and gain a new perspective. . . . Allow yourself now, if you wish, to experience your special ocean beach. . . . It is a beautiful day in early summer [the season is chosen by the patient in the prehypnotic discussion] *. . . the temperature is comfortably warm, just right, the way you like it. . . . The sky is clear and blue . . . as you look at the sky, you wonder to yourself . . . with awe at the endless depth of the blue sky. . . . You look at the ocean, and you can wonder on the similarity and differences . . . between the color of the sky and the color of the ocean. . . . You look at the two as they merge together at the horizon, far, far away. . . . Now take a look at the ocean again and notice the waves as they are breaking and receding, white and foamy in rhythm. Look at the beach and notice the color of the sand . . . is it yellow? . . . is it white? . . . is it gray? . . . or perhaps a blend of two or three of these colors. . . . You may look around and notice . . . can you see any seagulls floating up and down with the currents of the air? . . . Can you see some of them diving down into the waters of the ocean to catch their fish? . . . If you look closely, you may see some of the seagulls are standing together . . . in a group on the beach at a distance . . . basking in the sun. . . . As you zoom in closer . . . you may wonder at the color of their beaks . . . are they white, gray, or orange in color? . . . Some may be standing on only one foot, and others on both feet . . . some have orange-colored feet and others have gray feet. . . . Isn't it interesting how much variability there is in nature, and yet all these seagulls are healthy and normal? . . . And now, you may wish to experience your special ocean beach with your sense of hearing. . . . Listen to the sounds of the waves as they are breaking and receding in rhythm . . . the surf of the ocean is so predictable and calming. . . . Listen to the seagulls . . . can you hear their special chatter as they communicate with each other? . . . And now, you may wish to proceed by experiencing this ocean beach with your sense of touch. . . . Allow yourself to touch the dry sand with your bare feet . . . notice the sensation of the sand under* *your feet, over your feet, and between your toes. . . . Notice the sand as it is soft, dry, and comfortably warm. . . . Allow yourself, if you wish, to be playful about it . . . you may even touch the sand with your hands and fingers. . . . You may now proceed by taking a walk on the sand toward the waters of the ocean. . . . Notice as you get close to the waters of the ocean . . . the waves are breaking on the beach. . . . Notice how the sand becomes moist, not as dry and more firm, not as soft and more cool, not as warm as the dry sand. . . . Isn't that change interesting in the sensation you experience under your feet? . . . If you wish, you may now allow yourself to be touched by the waters of the ocean where the waves are breaking on the beach. . . . Notice the sensation of wetness and coolness on your feet touched by the waters of a breaking wave. . . . Compare it to the rest of your body that is exposed to the sun . . . where you experience the sensation of dryness and warmth from the sun rays touching your skin. . . . Notice the contrast of sensations, wetness and coolness on your feet compared with a dry, warm sensation on the rest of your skin touched by rays of the sun. . . . You may keep on walking gently on the beach . . . and as you do, notice the breeze of clean and fresh ocean air touching your face and your hair. . . . And as we move on, you may now experience the ocean beach with your sense of smell. . . . Take a deep, deep breath through your nose, and as you do, inhale this fresh, clean ocean air . . . notice the unique scent of a blend of aromas combining the smell of seaweeds, fish, salt, and much, much more than that . . . which is unique to ocean beaches. . . . And as you keep on walking . . . gently and comfortably . . . on the beach, you may now experience your ocean beach with your sense of taste. . . . Allow yourself, if you wish, to touch your lips with your tongue . . . as you do, you may notice the special salty taste on your lips so typical of ocean beaches. . . . Now that you have experienced your special ocean beach with all of your five senses . . . you may find yourself a nice comfortable spot either in the shade under a beach umbrella . . . or in the sun sitting comfortably and looking at the ocean . . . seeing the waves breaking and receding in eternal rhythm . . . watching the seagulls soaring and floating in the air. . . . Notice the sensation of inner calmness, tranquility, and peace . . . and remember that you can do this exercise on your own. . . . Any time you wish to take*

a break in a safe place where you can close your eyes safely . . . you can visit this ocean beach and recharge your batteries for calmness, tranquility, and peace. . . . The more you do this exercise, the easier and easier it becomes for you . . . and the more it has a lasting effect of calmness on your mind, body, spirit, and soul. . . . As you continue to practice this exercise on your own every day . . . in every way you are getting better and better . . . healthier and healthier; stronger and stronger . . . your mind becomes more clear, your thoughts are more focused . . . your feelings are more positive . . . you find yourself using this gift to ease yourself into natural sleep at night . . . you find yourself smiling spontaneously, knowing that you have this special gift of hypnotic imagery that always stays with you . . . and you can shift your focus and visit your beach where it is safe. . . . And now . . . whenever you are ready . . . we can count back from 3 to 1 . . . and you can return from the ocean beach back to this office . . . and as you do, you bring back with you these wonderful gifts and memories of calmness, inner peace, tranquility, and new hope. . . . And now let's count together. At the count of 3, you get ready to shift gears into the regular state of consciousness . . . at the count of 2, your look up with your eyes while you keep your eyelids closed . . . go ahead and do so now, and at the count of 1, you let your eyelids open . . . that's right . . . notice your eyes come back to focus . . . you become fully alert and awake right here in this office. . . . You are ready to assume all the regular functions of day-to-day living in the most adaptive and healthy way. . . ."

Now ask the patient to guide herself into a state of self-hypnosis by reexperiencing her special ocean beach and thereby reactivating the relaxation response. Once the patient has reached this special hypnotic state, proceed with the following words:

"As you are sitting in the chair, go ahead and put yourself in a comfortable position . . . take a deep, deep breath . . . and as you exhale slowly, go ahead and guide yourself into this special meditative state of calmness and tranquility. . . . And when you are ready, open a new channel of concentration whereby you experience yourself in the future . . . you have now achieved a full remission from rheumatoid arthritis. . . . Your joints are comfortable, flexible, and limber. . . . Experience

yourself walking easily and comfortably on your favorite beach. . . . The sun is shining. . . . The sky is blue. . . . The sand is dry and comfortably warm. . . . You experience a sense of calmness, energy, and health. . . . Take in these experiences on a conscious and unconscious level. . . . The visual sights . . . the sounds of the waves and the seagulls . . . the comfortably warm sensations of the dry sand . . . the special scent of the ocean beach . . . and the salty taste on your lips. . . . Combine this with your new inner sense of achieving health and comfort in your life. . . . Combine it with your new sense of mastery in practicing the skills of effectively managing the stresses of daily living. . . . You have achieved balance in your life between work, family, and leisure activities. . . . You now take time to rest. . . . You have learned to listen to your body and respect the signals from your body. . . . Your immune system has learned to successfully identify all the healthy cells in your body as part of the self and is now dedicated to protect these cells and it has gained new wisdom and knowledge differentiating between the cells of your own body [that are all labeled with the initials of your name] *and the antigens on the surface of foreign cells from viruses and pathogenic bacteria. . . . Now, take in all these experiences and your accomplishments and bring them back from the future to the present as special gifts that will continue and stay with you every day for the rest of your life. . . . When you are ready, we can now together count back from 3 to 1 . . . at the count of 3, get ready to shift gears to the regular state of consciousness, here and now in my office on* [today's date]. *. . . At the count of 2, you look up with your eyes, while your eyelids are still closed, . . . and at the count of 1, you let your eyelids slowly open, your eyes come back to focus, you become fully alert and awake . . . back to the regular state of consciousness oriented and ready to engage in the activities of daily living in an adaptive and healthy way."*

CONCLUSION

For centuries, Western allopathic medicine has believed that the immune system is a separate and independent system within the human body that is not connected to the central nervous system. However, thousands of research studies that have been done over the past 40 years have now provided us with a body of scientific data that has confirmed that the immune system and the central nervous system communicate with each other on a regular basis and are not independent of each other. Autoimmune diseases are characterized by cyclical relapses and remissions resulting from impairment in the immune system whereby cells of one's own immune system attack certain cells and tissues within one's own body, misidentifying them as cells of foreign organisms. This chapter was aimed at showing how this knowledge can be realized in the treatment of people with autoimmune disorders. The use of hypnosis and imagery create a special opportunity to affect the immune system in ways that enhance a quicker resolution of an acute relapse of an autoimmune disorder and promote the patient's progress into a state of remission. The case example presented illustrated the use of a variety of therapeutic techniques with healing imagery that were enhanced by the use of hypnosis.

Future research is needed with the use of control groups and the inclusion of placebo to determine whether this effect can be produced with a large population and for how long the positive effect can be sustained. The great benefit of such an approach is that it has relatively few undesirable side effects and that the potential benefits far outweigh any potential risks.

REFERENCES

Achterberg, J. A., & Lawlis, G. F. (1980). Rheumatoid arthritis: A psychological perspective. In J. Achterberg & G. Lawlis (Eds.), *Bridges of the bodymind. Behavioral approaches to healthcare* (pp. 255–305). Champaign, IL: Institute for Personality and Ability Testing.

Achterberg, J., McGraw, P., & Lawlis, G. F. (1981). Rheumatoid arthritis: A study of relaxation and temperature biofeedback as an adjunctive therapy. *Biofeedback and Self-Regulation, 6*(2), 207–223.

Ader, R. (2000). On the development of psychoneuroimmunology. *European Journal of Pharmacology, 405*(1-3), 167–176.

Ader, R., & Cohen, N. (1975). Behaviorally conditioned immunosuppression. *Psychosomatic Medicine, 37*(4), 333–340.

Ader, R., & Cohen, N. (1981). Conditioned immunopharmacologic responses. In R. Adler (Ed.), *Psychoneuroimmunology*. New York, NY: Academic Press.

Ader, R., & Cohen, N. (1982). Behaviorally conditioned immunosuppression and murine systemic lupus erythematosus. *Science, 215*(4539), 1534–1536.

Ader, R., & Cohen, N. (1985). CNS-immune interactions: Conditioning phenomena, brain and behavioral sciences. *Behavioral and Brain Sciences, 8*(03), 379–426. doi:10.1017/S0140525X00000765

Baranzini, S. E. (2013). Autoimmune disorders. In G. Ginsberg & H. Willard (Eds.), *Genomic and personalized medicine* (pp. 822–838). Burlington, MA: Academic Press-Elsevier.

Benson, H. (1975). *The relaxation response*. New York, NY: William Morrow.

Benson, H. (1979). *The mind/body effect*. New York, NY: Simon & Schuster.

Benson, H. (1984). *Beyond the relaxation response*. New York, NY: Times Books.

Benson, H. (1996). *Timeless healing: The power and biology of belief*. New York, NY: Scribner.

Booth, R. J., & Ashbridge, K. R. (1993). A fresh look at the relationship between the psyche and the immune system. *Teleological Coherence and Harmony of Purpose, 9*, 4–23.

Bowers, K. S., & Kelly, P. (1979). Stress, disease, psychotherapy and hypnosis. *Journal of Abnormal Psychology, 88*(5), 490–505.

Brigham-Davis, D. (1994). *Imagery for getting well: Clinical applications of behavioral medicine* (pp. 343–354). New York, NY: W. W. Norton.

Brown, D. P., & Fromm, E. (1987). *Hypnosis & behavioral medicine*. Hillsdale, NJ: Lawrence Erlbaum.

Charnetski, C. J., & Brennan, F. X. (2001). *Feeling good is good for you. How pleasure can boost your immune system and lengthen your life*. New York, NY: Rodale.

Cheek, D. B., & LeCron, L. M. (1968). *Clinical hypnotherapy*. New York, NY: Grune & Stratton.

Cousins, N. (1976). Anatomy of an illness. *New England Journal of Medicine, 295*(26), 1458–1463.

Crasilneck, T. L., & Hall, J. A. (1975). *Clinical hypnosis: Principles and applications*. New York, NY: Grune & Stratton.

Dantzer, R. (2001). Cytokine-induced sickness behavior: Where do we stand? *Brain, Behavior, and Immunity, 15*(1), 7–24.

Dreher, H. (1995). *The immune power personality*. New York, NY: Penguin Group.

Gottschalk, L. A., Serota, H. M., & Shapiro, L. B. (1950). Psychologic conflict and neuromuscular tension: Preliminary report and a method, as applied to rheumatoid arthritis. *Psychosomatic Medicine, 12*(5), 315–319.

Ipsa, S., Devi, M. P., & Ravindra, S. V. (2014). Dysregulating our immunity!!! *Stress TMU Journal of Dentistry, 1*, 10–13.

Jacobson, D. L., Gange, S. J., Rose, N. R., & Graham, N. M. (1997). Epidemiology and estimated population burden of selected autoimmune disease in the United States. *Clinical Immunology and Immunopathology, 84*(3), 223–243.

Kiecolt-Glaser, J. K., & Glaser, R. (2002). Depression and immune function: Central pathways to morbidity and mortality. *Journal of Psychosomatic Research, 53*(4), 873–876.

Kiecolot-Glaser, J. K., Marucha, P. T., Atkinson, C., & Glaser, R. (2001). Hypnosis as a modulator of cellular immune dysregulation during acute stress. *Journal of Clinical Psychology, 69*, 674–682.

Kiecolt-Glaser, J. K., McGuire, L., Robles, T. F., & Glaser, R. (2002). Psychoneuroimmunology and psychosomatic medicine: Back to the future. *Psychosomatic Medicine, 64*(1), 15–28.

Klasing, K. C. (2007). Nutrition and the immune system. *British Poultry Science, 48*(5), 525–537.

Kumar, H., Kawai, T., & Akira, S. (2011). Pathogen recognition the innate immune system. *International Reviews of Immunology, 30*(1), 16–34.

Laidlaw, T. M., Booth, R. J., & Large, R. G. (1996). Reduction in skin reactions to histamine after a hypnotic procedure. *Psychosomatic Medicine, 58*(3), 242–248.

Lange, T., Dimitrov, S., & Born, J. (2010). Effects of sleep and circadian rhythm on the human immune system. *Annals of the New York Academy of Sciences, 1193*, 48–59.

Millikin, L. A. (1964). Arthritis and Raynaud's syndromes: As psychosomatic problems sucessfully treated with hypnotheraphy. *British Journal of Medical Hypnotism, 15*, 37–44.

Olness, K., & Ader, R. (1992). Conditioning as an adjunct in the pharmachotherapy of lupus erythematosus. *Journal of Developmental and Behavioral Pediatrics, 13*(2), 124–125.

Ravicz, S. (2000). *Thriving with your autoimmune disorder*. Oakland, CA: New Harbinger Publications.

Rossi, E. L. (1986). *The psychobiology of mind-body healing*. New York, NY: W. W. Norton.

Rossi, E. L. (1990). From mind to molecule: More than a metaphor. In J. Zeig & S. Gilligan (Eds.), *Brief therapy myths, methods, and metaphors*. New York, NY: Brunner/Mazel.

Rossi, E. L. (1993). *The psychobiology of mind-body healing* (Revisition ed.). New York, NY: W. W Norton.

Rossi, E. L., & Cheek, D. B. (1988). *Mind-body therapy*. New York, NY: W. W. Norton.

Smith, S. J., & Balaban, A. B. (1983). A multidimensional approach to pain relief: Case report of a patient with systemic lupus erythematosus. *The International Journal of Clinical and Experimental Hypnosis, 31*(2), 72–81.

Solomon, G. F. (1981). Emotional and personality factors in the onset and course of autoimmune disease. In R. Ader (Eds.), *Psychoneuroimmunology*. New York, NY: Academic Press.

Solomon, G. F., Amkraut, A. A., & Kasper, P. (1974). Immunity, emotions and stress. *Annals of Clinical Research*, 6(6), 313–322.

Solomon, G. F., Levine, S., & Kraft, J. K. (1968). Early experience and immunity. *Nature*, 220(5169), 821–822.

Solomon, G. F., & Moss, R. H. (1964). Emotions, immunity and disease: A speculative theoretical integration. *Archives of General Psychiatry*, 11, 657–674.

Spiegel, H. (1973). *Manual for hypnotic induction profile: Eye-roll levitation method*. New York, NY: Soni Medica.

Spiegel, H. (1977). The Hypnotic Induction Profile: A review of its development. *Annals of the New York Academy of Sciences*, 296, 129–142.

Torem, M. S. (1987). Hypnosis in the treatment of depression. In W. Wester (Ed.), *Clinical hypnosis a case management approach* (pp. 288–301). Cincinnati, OH: Behavioral Science Center.

Torem, M. S. (1992a). Back from the future: A powerful age-progression technique. *American Journal of Clinical Hypnosis*, 35(2), 81–88.

Torem, M. S. (1992b). Therapeutic imagery enhanced by hypnosis. *Psychiatric Medicine*, 10(4), 1–12.

Torem, M. S. (1993). Therapeutic writing as a form of ego-state therapy. *American Journal of Clinical Hypnosis*, 35(4), 267–276.

Torem, M. S. (2006). Treating depression: A remedy from the future. In M. Yapko (Ed.), *Hypnosis and treating depression: Applications in clinical practice* (pp. 97–119). New York, NY: Routledge.

Torem, M. S. (2007). Mind-body hypnotic imagery in the treatment of auto-immune disorders. *American Journal of Clinical Hypnosis*, 50(2), 157–170.

Van Pelt, S. J. (1961). Hypnotism, "rheumatism" and fibrositis. *British Journal of Medical Hypnotism*, 12, 19–21.

Vollmer-Conna, U. (2001). Acute sickness behavior: An immune system-to-brain communication? *Psychological Medicine*, 31(5), 761–767.

Walsh, S. J., & Rau, L. M. (2000). Autoimmune diseases: A leading cause of death among young and middle-aged women in the United States. *American Journal of Public Health*, 90(9), 1463–1466.

Bone Fractures

Carol Ginandes

Although, at first glance, using hypnosis to accelerate healing bone fractures may strike the reader as far-fetched, this chapter discusses a randomized controlled trial to test that possibility (Ginandes & Rosenthal, 1999). Hypnosis was chosen as an adjunctive treatment for fracture healing not for its clinical utility per se, since simple fractures, not requiring surgery, generally heal themselves with orthopedic care and cast immobilization during a normative course of repair (Frost, 1989). Rather, the goal of the study was to see if this previously untested application of hypnosis could confirm the hypothesis that hypnosis can exert measurable effects on tissue healing.

Since the study procedures and outcomes have been described elsewhere in detail (Ginandes & Rosenthal, 1999), they are summarized only briefly in this chapter. Participants had all sustained a nondisplaced malleolar (ankle) fracture, did not require surgery, and were instead treated with cast immobilization and usual orthopedic care. Half of the sample was randomized to receive an adjunctive, multisession hypnotic intervention designed to speed fracture healing and recovery. The results, garnered from orthopedic and radiological data assessments, showed trends toward faster healing in the hypnotic intervention group. The most intriguing finding was the observation of a significantly greater degree of fracture edge healing, as seen in the radiographs, of the hypnotic group: At 6 weeks after fracture, their fractures had the appearance of being 8.5 weeks healed.

The more relevant clinical focus for this chapter, however, is on the hypnotic intervention administered. Since bone fracture healing had not been previously tested with hypnosis, the study's principal investigator, the author of this chapter, created the study intervention protocol for the trial. The text of the hypnosis protocol has not been published in print, and its length makes it prohibitive to include within this chapter. However, a discussion of the conceptual approach underlying the development of the protocol as a "phase-oriented, biologically paced intervention" (Ginandes, 2002; Ginandes, 2005b) and its thematic components, along with illustrative excerpts of content, may be informative. In addition, an adapted version of the study protocol, published in audio format by the author as "Rapid Recovery From Injury" (Ginandes, 2005a), may serve as a resource for closer study and more general clinical use.

BACKGROUND AND RESEARCH

As evidenced by this volume, a wide array of adjunctive, functional applications of medical hypnosis has been shown to moderate symptoms and the ability to withstand uncomfortable and/or anxiety-producing conditions and procedures (Kroger, 2008; Pinnell & Covino, 2000; Wobst, 2007). However, the distinction between the hypnotic facilitation of "functional healing" to help patients generally feel better and tolerate procedures with greater comfort and "structural healing," that is, the hypnotic stimulation of tissue change itself, is a significant one. Despite the magnitude of functional, medical applications that have been documented, there have been few randomized clinical trials exploring the potential use of hypnosis for accelerating structural healing.

A significant precursor to this line of inquiry was what was perhaps the first "trial" of the efficacy of medical hypnosis in both functional and structural effects, in the 1840s, in India, when James Esdaile documented surgical procedures performed in the field prior to the introduction of chemical anesthesia and antiseptic sterilization. There he made the astoundingly prescient observation that those patients requiring surgical amputation who underwent "mesmeric passes" to induce a kind of catatonia during surgery experienced "insensibility to pain," fewer infections, and lower rates of mortality than their nonhypnotically treated counterparts (Esdaile, 1957).

Although a review of the medical hypnosis literature is beyond the scope of this chapter, it is pertinent to highlight that, in the past two decades, there has been an impressive proliferation of applications of adjunctive medical hypnosis in the surgical domain, with such efforts targeting preparation for surgery, diminishing procedural anxiety, limiting intraoperative blood loss, maintaining systemic homeostasis, and moderating postoperative pain (Blankfield, 1991; Ginandes, Brooks, Sando, Jones, & Aker, 2003; Lang et al., 2000; Montgomery, DuHamel, & Redd, 2000).

However, applications of hypnosis used expressly for tissue healing continue to be underutilized, with the exception of impressive case reports from the domain of dermatology, which have documented hypnotically accelerating the healing of severe burns by attenuating the size and depth of the burn and moderating the usual course of edema and inflammatory progression (Ewin, 1978; Margolis, Domangue, Ehleben, & Shrier, 1983; Moore & Kaplan, 1983; Patterson, Goldberg, & Ehde, 1996). Other significant reports of the hypnotic mediation of the course of cutaneous conditions include the large amount of literature on a wart removal (Ewin, 1992) and the amelioration of various dermatological diseases including psoriasis, eczema, herpes simplex, and so forth (Shenefelt, 2000). Although these hypnotic effects on dermatological conditions have been noted to have accelerated tissue healing as a line of formal research, testing these observations has been handicapped by methodological limitations such as lack of randomization, support for hypnosis research trials, and adequate control groups for comparisons in controlled trials.

RANDOMIZED CONTROLLED STUDY: USING HYPNOSIS TO ACCELERATE BONE FRACTURE HEALING

The randomized controlled pilot study of bone fracture healing (Ginandes & Rosenthal, 1999)

was conducted to explore just this intriguing question: Could a targeted hypnotic intervention not only measurably augment functional recovery but also accelerate anatomical tissue healing per se? To test the hypothesis with an example of normative physical healing, the study cohort selected was a homogeneous, healthy, young adult sample with a nondisplaced malleolar (ankle) fracture that could generate both clinical as well as objective radiographic data (Frost, 1989). Since the pilot study took place in New England, icy winter weather provided an opportunity to accrue 12 study subjects, recruited from the orthopedic emergency room, who had had the unfortunate accident of sustaining such an injury. Screening excluded participants requiring surgical intervention as well as those with any behaviors that would slow healing (such as smoking) or confounding illnesses such as diabetes and other systemic illnesses. All study subjects received standard orthopedic care at 1 (within 48 hours), 3, 6, 9, and 12 weeks after the fracture injury; these included physical examinations, cast immobilization, routine serial x-rays, and measures related to pain assessment and ankle function. Those participants who were randomized to the treatment group ($n = 6$) also received a scripted hypnotic intervention over six hour-long meetings with the study hypnotherapist, in addition to audiotapes for at-home practice. The study radiologist, who had no contact with study participants and who was blind to group assignment, assessed all of the study participants' radiographs and compared them to a single normative set of radiographs of the study fracture. Through this comparison, he scored the relative amounts of healing of two observed features, fracture edge and fracture line, for each study subject at each data point during the first 12 weeks after fracture. The scored data of these radiographic outcomes revealed the notable difference in fracture edge healing at 6 weeks, with the hypnosis group's fractures resembling 8.5 weeks of healing. In addition, all of the orthopedic data showed similar trends toward faster healing in the hypnosis group through the ninth week, with lower self-reported pain through 6 weeks and greater recovery of ankle mobility and the functional ability to descend stairs (Ginandes & Rosenthal, 1999).

METHODOLOGY

Design of the Hypnotic Intervention: A "Phase-Oriented, Biologically Paced Protocol"

The conceptual template that guided the creation of the study intervention to augment bone fracture healing is the author's model that is called a "phase-oriented, biologically-paced protocol" (Ginandes 2002; Ginandes, 2005b; Ginandes & Rosenthal, 1999). In general, a scripted hypnotic intervention, whether consisting of simple or elaborate, direct or indirect suggestions pertaining to the clinical condition in question is often conceived of and administered as a unitary intervention at a discrete point in time. This approach typically front-loads the delivery of a battery of hypnotic suggestions pertaining to different symptoms and phases of a condition in one or two sessions. The pertinent suggestions or variations of them may be repeated, and, in standard approaches, hypnotic-deepening techniques are utilized to enhance their absorption. Posthypnotic suggestions are provided to generalize to behaviors after the fact (Hammond, 1990; Yapko, 2012).

By way of contrast, the fracture-healing study protocol was presented in six, hour-long sessions beginning within hours of the injury and continuing through the first 12 weeks of fracture repair. In six progressive, stage-oriented sessions, the hypnotic content addressed the normative stages of fracture healing, with emphasis on the healing process and an acceleration of the time frame (Ginandes & Rosenthal, 1999).

This design format was utilized because in the case of a physiologically complex process of bodily healing that proceeds over weeks or months in a phasic manner, many conditions are not sufficiently impacted by a unitary set of hypnotic suggestions (Ginandes, 2002). The stimulation of physiological changes on the cellular level may require more of a comprehensive input to the mind–body interface than is typically needed for changes in psycho-behavioral functioning (Ginandes, 1994; Rossi, 1993).

Such a phase-oriented intervention can be delivered through in vivo contact, audio presentation, or, ideally, as was the case in the fracture-healing study, a combination of both. With an in-person administration, it is recommended that an audio recording of each stage of the intervention be provided to the patient after the session with the directive to listen to it repeatedly between sessions and to log daily compliance behavior. The promise of exchanging the current audio recording for a different one at the next visit, as the patient makes "healing progress," is motivating.

Although it is desirable, in general, for hypnotic suggestions to be personalized for a specific patient in a way that will resonate with his or her unique cognitive and emotional makeup, it is difficult to integrate this approach into a standardized research protocol designed for uniform administration across study subjects. However, the generous use of an open-ended suggestion format in which the patient supplies his or her own inner content to a structured query and is invited to discard or modify any specific suggestions can help personalize the material (Yapko, 1986, 2012). Incorporating both direct and indirect suggestions and using multimodal imagery to address different representational systems will help to capture the absorption and processing styles of various individuals.

To plan a hypnotic protocol to administer over several sessions, the clinician needs to become familiar with the normative stages and phases of the course of healing in question. The goal is for the content to provide an immersive, changing set of healing suggestions that target the tasks and goals of the physiological phase operative at that particular time in the healing process (Ginandes & Rosenthal, 1999; Ginandes, 2002). Thus, the fracture study protocol began to address the sequential tasks of bone fracture healing and general recovery as soon as possible after the injury and progressed throughout the first three months of normative fracture repair. The intervention began in the initial "fracture phase" (also called "inflammatory" or "reactive") and continued through the early "reparative phase" (also called "granulation phase"). For the "modeling/remodeling phase" (Einhorn, 1998; Frost, 1989), which, de facto, extended beyond the study time frame, further suggestions were seeded to anticipate successful longer term bone remodeling and comprehensive rehabilitation.

Within the first hours of the fracture, hypnotic suggestions targeted the moderation of the rapid onset of physical symptoms: pain, swelling, and inflammation. The emotional shock and attendant feelings of distress in response to a sudden bodily trauma were also addressed with suggestions focused on alleviation of the anxiety, anger, blame, helplessness, and depression that an accidental injury evokes.

Beginning about 2 to 3 weeks after fracture, as the "reparative phase" elicited the cleanup and removal of cellular debris from the site, the creation of cartilage and bony callus, and the beginning of lamellar bone formation, hypnotic suggestions were tailored to stimulate accelerated, healthy bone proliferation on the cellular level. For the subsequent "remodeling phase" (beginning about 4 weeks after fracture and continuing over several months), characterized by the ongoing development of compact bone and the recovery of mobility and weight bearing, mental rehearsal strategies targeted the future pacing of comprehensive rehabilitation and the projected long-term remodeling of strong, permanent replacement bone at the fracture site.

THEMATIC CONTENT OF THE "PHASE-ORIENTED, BIOLOGICALLY PACED PROTOCOL"

Since the text transcript of the six sessions of hypnotic content, delivered over the 12-week duration of the study time frame, cannot be included here, the reader wanting a comprehensive sense of the intervention is referred to the audio version, which was adapted from the study intervention to address healing not only from bone fractures but also from a variety of other injuries (Ginandes, 2005a).

FOUR SUGGESTION STRATEGIES

What follows is a discussion of the conceptual approach to the cumulative suggestions embedded in the study protocol as well as some adapted, sample phrases. Four categories of suggestion strategies provided the structure for the intervention: general suggestions for whole body/mind healing seeded throughout the protocol, "biological resource retrieval," cultivating emotional coping responses to an injury, and targeting healing tasks at different stages of the healing process.

General Suggestions for Whole Body/Mind Healing

These were interspersed throughout the protocol in all phases. The following topical themes describe them.

■ Systemic Normalization and "Body Wisdom"

Suggestions for the reestablishment of systemic homeostasis after the injury were reiterated. These were verbalized in a presumptive suggestion format and communicated that although the patient did not know the precise biological details of how bone fractures are healed, his or her body could be trusted to direct a normal course of healing:

". . . So comforting to know that your body/mind knows exactly what it needs to do on the cellular level to repair and renew your body. . . . And you can allow your body to heal itself through and through in the best possible fashion. . . ."

■ Accelerating the Course of Organic Healing

In a "biologically paced, phase-oriented protocol," suggestions pertaining to both the end goals and the intermediate steps are designed to keep pace with the normative phases of physiological recovery. Several imagery techniques focused on stimulating site-specific cellular repair are utilized: metaphors of healing, consultation with the body part, and "pseudoscientific instruments" such as a "laser-healing machine" (Ginandes, 1994). However, the outcome effect may be greater if such suggestions target an *accelerated course* of organic healing in that time frame (Gianandes, 2002; Ginandes & Rosenthal, 1999). For example, *". . . Now that you are injured, it's time to begin healing yourself. . . watching a time-lapse movie . . . perhaps even speeding up the progress. . . ."*

"Biological Resource Retrieval"

This strategy, developed by the author, called "biological age regression" or "biological resource retrieval" (Ginandes, 2005a; Ginandes & Rosenthal, 1999), refers to the hypnotic elicitation of somatic memory of physiological development from earlier life phases. Just as with the resource retrieval of psychological material, somatic resource states can be retrieved, anchored, and called upon to stimulate present and future healing. For example, in the bone fracture protocol, the subjects were guided hypnotically to recall, in a multisensory memory experience, that time from childhood when *"those bones were growing so quickly, so strongly . . . day by day"* in order to tap into the physiological orchestration of growth factors from that era.

Cultivating Emotional Coping Responses

Another critical component is therapeutic attunement to the variety and sequential course of emotional responses that are evoked by physical injury or incapacitation. The resulting loss of functioning, daily routine, and self-image, even for a limited duration, as is the case with simple bone fracture healing, is an internal stressor that, if left unattended, may delay recovery and even cellular healing (Godbout & Glaser, 2006). Thus, the intervention focused suggestions on helping the patient gain an understanding of the range of normal emotional reactions and, through the cumulative acquisition of a self-hypnosis skill set, the development of a sense of agency and empowerment despite a debilitating injury. Future anticipation of recovery of the normal self, but perhaps *"even stronger"* both physically and emotionally, ratified the ego-strengthening suggestion. An abbreviated example follows.

CASE EXAMPLE

One of the study subjects was a 35-year-old woman who was randomized to the hypnosis treatment. Having recently emigrated from a Balkan country, she had been working two jobs as a health care aide in order to afford to bring her family to the United States. When she had the misfortune of slipping on an icy curbstone, she fractured not only her ankle but also her sense of self-reliance. Unable to drive or go to work for the duration, she became depressed and vocally blamed herself for the accidental injury. The emotionally focused suggestions in the hypnosis intervention helped her understand and process her feelings as a normative response to her impairment and helped her to avoid a slide into a clinical depression.

Phase-Oriented Suggestions Targeting Healing Tasks

In this section, all of the text examples are suggestion phrases adapted from the protocol intervention (Ginandes, 1994; Ginandes, 2005a). Since they have been extracted from much longer suggestion sections that flesh out the sequential content, the examples that are provided in the following text cannot be used as stand-alone scripts. They are offered simply as phrases illustrating some of the topical content sequentially embedded in the matrix of the extended protocol.

■ Days 1–14 After Injury ("Fracture, Reactive, Inflammatory Phase")

Suggestions: Psychoeducation About Hypnosis, Suggestions for Trance Training, Inductions for Settling in, Seeding Comfort, Site Transfer of Comfort Sensations, Begin/Accelerate Healing Process, Reduce Inflammation and Swelling, Metaphorical Story, Emotional Containment in a "Worry Box," "Healing Waters Imagery," Deep Rest to Enhance Cellular Healing.

". . . Breathing easily, knowing you are tending to your healing now . . . the oxygen dispersing its reparative nutrients throughout your body . . . a definite sense of relief flowing in. . . . Those hands . . . warmth, coolness, a pleasant numbness . . . which sensation is most comforting to place on that injured area now . . . to flow into and through . . . wrapping that ankle in your healing intention . . . now that you have gotten medical attention for that injury, you don't need that alarm bell . . . turning down the volume way, way down . . . your body/ mind knows exactly what it needs to do on the cellular level to repair and renew your body now . . . just imagine what will happen now if you give it a little extra help . . . and as she headed to the emergency room, she immediately shifted into trance and began to speak to the nerves and the skin . . . permeated by a deep cooling soothing sensation through and through . . . transported to just the right areas of tissue for cleansing and rebuilding tissue there. Soothing away any inflammation or swelling. . . . When people get injured, they may have many feelings about what happened to them . . . sad, fearful, even helpless when they have been hurt . . . even blame themselves for what happened, even an

accident . . . as strange as it seems to be angry with yourself when you are already hurting, . . . useful to put some of these feelings aside or tone them down . . . a place to go ahead and put away any negative feelings, or thoughts, or ruminations about your injury that are not helpful to your healing process for now . . . clear your head and heart space to make room for more soothing, comforting healing feelings that will speed your recovery . . . settling into a warm tub is a very soothing experience . . . at just the right temperature . . . wash away any remaining soreness . . . perhaps you will feel that area that was injured regaining mobility, strength, and flexibility over time . . . seeds planted beneath the surface in rich soil can sprout and grow strong and healthy . . . the body can settle into a profoundly powerful state of comfortable relaxation in order to restore itself . . . you can just rest and let your body heal beautifully. . . ."

■ Weeks 2–3 After Injury ("Reparative Phase" Begins)

Suggestions: Healing "Key Words," Clear Residual Inflammation, Future Pace Recovery, "Targeting Site-Specific Cellular Repair" With an "Imaginary Laser-Healing Machine" "Power Nap" to Consolidate Healing (Ginandes, 1994).

". . . Breathing in and saying the word 'heal.' Then as you breathe out, say the word 'clear'. . . clear out any inflammation from that tissue that is being replaced or rebuilt with the infinite healing wisdom of your body/mind . . . making way for healthy new tissue . . . cartilage, bone, and blood vessels . . . all work together to bridge the fracture site . . . create your own laser light–healing machine now for yourself . . . in a good position to emit a healing beam . . . in and around and through the area being healed . . . just the right intensity focused . . . to stimulate the cellular process of repair and recovery . . . notice whether the color and intensity of the light changes as you progress along in your process toward complete recovery. . . ."

■ Weeks 3–5 After Injury ("Remodeling, Rehabilitation Phase" Begins)

Suggestions: Enhance Control With the "Comfort Meter," Metaphor of "Springtime in Your Body," Key Word "Strengthen," "Biological Age Regression," "Healing Potion" (Ginandes, 1994).

". . . Set your comfort meter to just the right level of ease . . . have you ever noticed how green and bright and healthy the new shoots at the ends of an evergreen bush start coming in the spring? . . . Bones grow themselves anew from the inside out . . . you know how as kids we are told to drink milk and eat certain healthy foods to build strong bones . . . playing and moving and flexing, those bones and muscles develop more and more strength . . . have a pleasant inner glimpse of some children playing now . . . using their bodies to grow strong and flexible . . . special healing potion now flows through your body into every, muscle, ligament, bone, organ, into every single cell, those bones growing anew . . . like building a bridge, the engineers know all about the materials they are using, how to support the weight and the span required. . . ."

■ Five Weeks After Injury ("Remodeling," "Rehabilitation Phase" Continues)

Suggestions: Time Travel Progression, "Top of Your Game," Senior Rehabilitation Story, Future Pacing Cast Removal, Balance and Strength, Generalization of Skills, Power Nap Consolidation.

". . . Your own time travel machine or just see your continued healing on that inner video screen . . . in many different ways whether that be renovating or decorating a living space, or remodeling or modeling something artistically . . . ever had the chance to use clay and make things into new shapes with clay? . . . your body knows exactly how to remodel that bone of yours as . . . gradually, consistently being replaced with strong permanent bone . . . that is as strong, new, and useful as that original bone . . . how the Greek columns have stood the test of time and eternity . . . getting back on your feet . . . to see/feel yourself one, two, three weeks from now strongly walking, moving, carrying . . . just the right pace . . . flexing and climbing and perhaps even dancing, playing tennis, whatever it is . . . more and more as you recover . . . rotating easily, flexing as before and perhaps even a little more . . . a see-saw perfectly horizontally balanced on the center point, both

sides at equal angles . . . doing their job of supporting you equally . . . when it's time to stand on your own two feet . . . with more strength . . . more firm confidence than you had imagined possible . . . becoming healthy and strong inside and out . . . at any time in your life . . . the day when it will be time for the cast to come off . . . your body will have been ready for some time, inwardly growing strong and healthy . . . strong and confident, the injury a thing of the past . . . triumphant you will feel as you look back over your remarkable journey of healing . . . aware in your own way of how very far you have come, on many different levels of healing since the time of your injury . . . many blessings woven into the fabric of this very special time period in your life, learnings and healings that you will treasure . . . and realize how powerful your healing thoughts have been. . . ."

CONCLUSION

The goal of the study was to test the hypothesis that a hypnotic intervention could measurably accelerate the normal course of structural healing of a nondisplaced ankle fracture in comparison with usual orthopedic care only. The results, which corroborated this intriguing proposition at pilot levels of significance, served as an important stepping-stone along the relatively uncharted path of hypnotically facilitated tissue healing.

In a subsequent collaborative study, the author tested this hypothesis again in a randomized controlled trial with postsurgical wound healing. One experimental group received a hypnotic intervention designed to accelerate incision healing, an additional control group received supportive attention without hypnosis, and the third group received usual care only. In this trial, results were significant as well, with greater objectively observed tissue (incision) healing at weeks 1 and 7 after surgery in the hypnotic intervention group (Ginandes et al., 2003).

Both studies provided the opportunity to create a "phase-oriented, biologically paced" hypnotic intervention protocol to accelerate somatic healing. In this line of research, hypnotically accelerated structural healing, many more studies will be needed to clarify the exact mechanisms by which hypnotic healing suggestions can be translated into such beneficial physical changes.

After both trials testing hypnotically accelerated healing showed significant findings, the author recorded two adapted audio versions of the intervention protocols in order to make them available to those seeking to use hypnosis to accelerate healing from an injury or a surgery (Ginandes, 2005a, 2006). A serendipitous chance to test the utility of the injury-healing program soon came by way of a medical colleague who had sustained a traumatic fall.

CASE EXAMPLE: PELVIC FRACTURE

A 73-year-old female medical professional suffered a pelvic fracture after slipping and falling down a steep, icy set of four entry stairs. The fracture was shown, on x-ray, to be nondisplaced and did not require surgery. However, such pelvic fractures can be life-threatening as they often entail internal bleeding and complications, and the healing is generally a long and painful course (Dyer & Vrahas, 2006). As fate would have it, the patient, a colleague, was familiar with the bone fracture study and was quickly able to obtain a copy of the audio program. She used it daily at least once and often more frequently throughout the first few weeks after her injury. For her 6-week follow-up, she was referred to consult with an orthopedist who was a recognized expert in pelvic fractures. He carefully reviewed her clinical presentation and all of her serial radiographs. In a later conversation with the author, the patient reported the orthopedist's comments as follows: "It looks as though you have healed faster than anyone of any age and in perfect alignment! What have you been doing?"

ACKNOWLEDGMENTS

Funding/support: The fracture-healing hypnosis trial was supported by award number R21RR0906 from the National Institutes of Health (NIH) through the Office of Alternative Medicine (now called the National Center for Complementary and Alternative Medicine).

REFERENCES

Blankfield, R. P. (1991). Suggestion, relaxation, and hypnosis as adjuncts in the care of surgery patients: A review of the literature. *American Journal of Clinical Hypnosis, 33*(3), 172–186.

Dyer, G. S., & Vrahas, M. S. (2006). Review of the pathophysiology and acute management of hemorrhage in pelvic fracture. *Injury, 37*(7), 602–613.

Einhorn, T. A. (1998). The cell and molecular biology of fracture healing. *Clinical Orthopaedics and Related Research, 355S*, S7–S21.

Esdaile, J. (1957). *Hypnosis in medicine and surgery*. New York, NY: Institute for Researchin Hypnosis and the Julian Press (original publication, 1850).

Ewin, D. M. (1978). *Hypnosis at its bicentennial*. New York, NY: Springer Publishing Company.

Ewin, D. M. (1992). Hypnotherapy for warts (verruca vulgaris): 41 consecutive cases with 33 cures. *American Journal of Clinical Hypnosis, 35*(1), 1–10.

Frost, H. M. (1989). The biology of fracture healing: An overview for clinicians. *Clinical Orthopedics and Related Research, 248*, 283–293.

Ginandes, C. (1994, December). Harnessing the healing unconscious: Hypnotic strategies for enhanced healing master class. *Sixth Annual International Conference on the Psychology of Health, Immunity and Disease, National Institute for the Clinical Applications of Behavioral Medicine*, Hilton Head, South Carolina.

Ginandes, C. (2002). Extended, strategic therapy for recalcitrant mind/body healing: An integrative model. *American Journal of Clinical Hypnosis, 45*(2), 91–102.

Ginandes, C. (2005a). *Rapid recovery from injury* [Audio CD]. Cincinnati, Ohio: Health Journeys.

Ginandes, C. (2005b). The strategic integration of hypnosis and CBT for the treatment of mind/body conditions. *Clinical Use of Hypnosis in Cognitive Behavior Therapy: A Practitioner's Casebook*, 243–245.

Ginandes, C. (2006). *Smooth surgery, rapid recovery: A systematic hypnotic approach* [Audio CD]. Dallas, TX: The Hypnosis Network.

Ginandes, C., Brooks, P., Sando, W., Jones, C., & Aker, J. (2003). Can medical hypnosis accelerate post-surgical wound healing? Results of a clinical trial. *American Journal of Clinical Hypnosis, 45*(4), 333–351.

Ginandes, C. S., & Rosenthal, D. I. (1999). Using hypnosis to accelerate the healing of bone fractures: A randomized controlled pilot study. *Alternative Therapies in Health and Medicine, 5*(2), 67–75.

Godbout, J. P., & Glaser, R. (2006). Stress-induced immune dysregulation: Implications for wound healing, infectious disease and cancer. *Journal of Neuroimmune Pharmacology: The Official Journal of the Society on NeuroImmune Pharmacology, 1*(4), 421–427.

Hammond, D. C. (Ed.). (1990). *Handbook of hypnotic suggestions and metaphors*. New York, NY: W. W. Norton.

Kroger, W. S. (2008). *Clinical and experimental hypnosis in medicine, dentistry, and psychology*. Philadelphia, PA: Lippincott Williams & Wilkins.

Lang, E. V., Benotsch, E. G., Fick, L. J., Lutgendorf, S., Berbaum, M. L., Berbaum, K. S., . . . Spiegel, D. (2000). Adjunctive non-pharmacological analgesia for invasive medical procedures: A randomised trial. *The Lancet, 355*(9214), 1486–1490.

Margolis, C. G., Domangue, B. B., Ehleben, C., & Shrier, L. (1983). Hypnosis in the early treatment of burns: A pilot study. *American Journal of Clinical Hypnosis, 26*(1), 9–15.

Montgomery, G. H., DuHamel, K. N., & Redd, W. H. (2000). A meta-analysis of hypnotically induced analgesia: How effective is hypnosis? *International Journal of Clinical and Experimental Hypnosis, 48*(2), 138–153.

Moore, L. E., & Kaplan, J. Z. (1983). Hypnotically accelerated burn wound healing. *American Journal of Clinical Hypnosis, 26*(1), 16–19.

Patterson, D. R., Goldberg, M. L., & Ehde, D. M. (1996). Hypnosis in the treatment of patients with severe burns. *American Journal of Clinical Hypnosis, 38*(3), 200–212.

Pinnell, C. M., & Covino, N. A. (2000). Empirical findings on the use of hypnosis in medicine: A critical review. *International Journal of Clinical and Experimental Hypnosis, 48*(2), 170–194.

Rossi, E. L. (1993). *The psychobiology of mind-body healing: New concepts of therapeutic hypnosis*. New York, NY: W. W. Norton.

Shenefelt, P. D. (2000). Hypnosis in dermatology. *Archives of Dermatology, 136*(3), 393–399.

Wobst, A. H. (2007). Hypnosis and surgery: Past, present, and future. *Anesthesia and Analgesia, 104*(5), 1199–1208.

Yapko, M. D. (1986). Hypnotic and strategic interventions in the treatment of anorexia nervosa. *American Journal of Clinical Hypnosis, 28*(4), 224–232.

Yapko, M. D. (2012). *Trancework: An introduction to the practice of clinical hypnosis* (4th ed.). London, UK: Routledge.

Cancer-Related Fatigue

Kimberly Hickman, Debra Barton, and Gary Elkins

Cancer-related fatigue (CRF) has long been recognized as one of the most difficult symptoms to manage during cancer treatment, and it remains one of the most common unrelieved symptoms (Jacobsen, Donovan, Vadaparampil, & Small, 2007) following chemotherapy, radiation, or surgery. Fatigue, which has been described as a sense of tiredness that cannot be alleviated by sleep or rest, plays a significant role in the quality of life associated with cancer and cancer treatment because of its interference with daily functioning (Mock et al., 2000; Morrow, Shelke, Roscoe, Hickok, & Mustian, 2005; Prue, Rankin, Allen, Gracey, & Cramp, 2006; Stone & Minton, 2008; Watson & Mock, 2004). Fatigue accounts for substantial levels of disability and contributes greatly to the overall burden of illness, as it may disrupt physical, mental, and social functioning as well as psychosocial adjustment (Curt et al., 2000; Prue et al., 2006; Stone & Minton, 2008). Hypnosis may help to improve a cancer survivor's fatigue levels by inducing a hypnotic state and giving suggestions for increased energy and vitality. These suggestions can be to increase strength and positivity or to create an expectancy to have these experiences in the future.

RESEARCH

In a systematic review of CRF occurrence in patients undergoing chemo- or radiotherapy, Prue and colleagues (2006) determined prevalence rates to vary from 39% to above 90%. Further, for a number of persons, fatigue persists well beyond treatment's end. For example, significant or severe fatigue has been reported in 19% to 38% of survivors (e.g., Servaes, van der Werf, Prins, Verhagen, & Bleijenberg, 2001; Servaes, Verhagen, & Bleijenberg, 2002), and some degree of fatigue has been reported in as high as 82% of lung cancer survivors (Okuyama et al., 2001). Reports estimate that approximately 30% to 38% of cancer survivors suffer from persistent and severe CRF and this fatigue can persist 5 to 10 years after diagnosis (Bower et al., 2006) and up to 5 years after treatment (Bower et al., 2000; Minton & Stone, 2008; Servaes, Verhagen, & Bleijenberg, 2002).

Despite the widespread occurrence of CRF, few randomized controlled trials have examined the effects of available treatments (pharmacological or nonpharmacological), and there is limited evidence to support available interventions (Mock, 2004). Current treatments for fatigue include pharmacological therapies, psychoeducation, psychotherapy, and exercise (Escalante, 2003; Jacobsen, Donovan, Vadaparampil, & Small, 2007).

With regard to pharmacological agents, research has been limited, and there remains a lack of consensus regarding the best treatment for CRF. A systematic review of the available pharmacological treatments by Minton and colleagues (2008) demonstrated limited support for methylphenidate and somewhat more substantial support for the use of hematopoietic agents for anemic patients. Of the two trials examining methylphenidate's use, only one demonstrated superiority over placebo, and more recent research remains inconclusive (Minton, Richardson, Sharpe, Hotoph, & Stone, 2011; Moraska et al., 2010). Further, methylphenidate has significant addiction potential and poses the risk of typical side effects associated with psychostimulants (e.g., nervousness, decreased appetite, insomnia). Additionally, with regard to the use of hematopoietic agents, CRF is not entirely explained by anemia (Minton, Richardson, Sharpe, Hotopf, & Stone, 2008), and the effectiveness of these agents is limited depending upon hemoglobin levels. Further, possible side effects of these medications, such as thromboembolic events, make their routine use somewhat unreasonable, particularly in a vulnerable patient population.

With regard to nonpharmacological interventions, evidence is also limited but supports the use of exercise and, to a lesser degree, psychotherapy in the management of CRF (Cramp & Daniel, 2008; Jacobsen et al., 2007; Lawrence, 2004). However, inconsistent methodologies complicate study replication and aggregation of data across studies. Attention Restoration Theory (ART; Kaplan, 1995, 2001) has suggested that attentional fatigue may be reduced through exposure to nature. Research demonstrates that attentional fatigue experienced by cancer patients is reduced by exposure to nature that is individualized (Cimprich, 1992; Cimprich & Ronis, 2003). For example, some persons may prefer walking outside along a trail while others may prefer sitting near a river or lake.

Preliminary research has examined the use of hypnotherapy to address CRF (Jensen et al., 2012; Montgomery et al., 2009). Hypnotic relaxation therapy (Elkins, 2013) is a mind–body intervention that has been used in treating symptoms related to cancer and cancer treatment, such as pain (e.g., Elkins et al., 2004; Montgomery, Weltz, Seltz, & Bovbjerg, 2002; Tomé-Pires & Miró, 2012), nausea and vomiting (Richardson et al., 2007), and hot flashes (Elkins et al., 2008). Additionally, hypnotic relaxation and mental imagery has shown some preliminary promise as an intervention to address CRF (Jensen et al., 2012; Montgomery et al., 2009). However, to date, the research is limited and the effect of relaxation alone on relieving fatigue has had little effect.

CASE EXAMPLE

A 74-year-old female breast cancer survivor presented with fatigue that had emerged during cancer treatment and had not subsided for over 1 year. The woman cited concerns as tiring easily throughout the day and becoming increasingly irritable as she experienced decreased energy. She noted that she would often need to eat quickly to help with irritability and fatigue. She stated that although she slept well and exercised three times a week, chemotherapy and radiation had left her feeling chronically tired and fatigued. On measures assessing for past, current, and predicted future fatigue levels, she demonstrated clinically significant ratings of fatigue. Following the intake session, five sessions of hypnosis were conducted to help decrease CRF. Sessions included a relaxation-based hypnotic induction with suggestions for increased energy, individualized and awe-inspiring natural imagery, and encouragement for the practice of self-hypnosis between sessions.

The following is a sample of a script that may be included over a multisession treatment such as for the client mentioned in the preceding text.

TRANSCRIPT

It is important to begin the session by reviewing what will be covered during the session and preview future sessions. Information regarding hypnosis, including common myths and misconceptions, may be discussed. It will likely be helpful to ask for information regarding personalized awe-inspiring natural imagery as a way to incorporate personal preferences into hypnotic suggestions. The hypnotic induction involves a focus of attention, suggestions for relaxation, mental imagery for increased energy, and posthypnotic suggestions for decreased fatigue. The following edited transcript provides an example of the hypnotic relaxation intervention.

"Calm . . . and peaceful. A peaceful feeling . . . within yourself. Now, soon finding that you will be able to experience being outside, in nature, in particular places . . . where you experience the beauty and restorative energy of nature such as mountains, streams, watching clouds, and oceans. . . . As I give you suggestions to experience being in nature, you will be able to experience all

of the images, sounds, feelings, and sensations that I suggest.

Now, first you will be able to experience being in the mountains . . . as you notice your breathing . . . as I count three breaths . . . at the third breath, you will be able to see and experience beautiful mountains . . . with high peaks . . . on a warm pleasant day. . . . All right . . . take a relaxing breath of air . . . 1 . . . good . . . another breath of air . . . 2 . . . good . . . and soon you will be in the mountains . . . a third breath . . . 3 . . . good . . . now . . . seeing mountains . . . you are high in the mountains . . . it is a beautiful place . . . the air is crisp and fresh . . . notice the trees around you . . . really look at them . . . tall trees . . . green fir trees . . . pine trees . . . their branches reach up to the sky . . . and the sky is blue . . . there are white puffy clouds drifting across the sky . . . stop for a moment . . . and just watch the clouds, gently drift across the sky . . . it is pleasant here . . . it is quite enough to hear the sound of the wind as it drifts through the trees. . . .

. . . And soon walking down a mountain path . . . see this path before you . . . as you begin to walk down this mountain path . . . feeling better and better . . . more energy . . . and a sense of fascination . . . what will you see or discover today? As you walk down the path . . . there are the trees . . . and look, there are flowers . . . beautiful mountain flowers . . . see the colors . . . stop and carefully look . . . a butterfly going from flower to flower . . . watch with a sense of fascination at the natural beauty . . . the colors . . . watch the butterfly . . . and breathe the fresh, good air . . . and as you go on further . . . this path follows a little stream.

A little stream goes through the mountains . . . the path goes along the stream . . . the water is clear, crystal clear . . . it is clean and cool and good. Watch and hear the sound out of the water as it flows over the rocks and stones . . . it is a pleasant sound . . . a good sound . . . and the water flows into pools and little waterfalls . . . ahead is a pool of water . . . stop and look at the water . . . do you see any fish . . . trout in the stream? Any in the pool of water? It's a very pleasant place, a safe place. The path is following a little stream . . . the water is crystal clear . . . very beautiful . . . a lovely

place to be. Follow this path; it will take you to a waterfall . . . a beautiful waterfall . . . you can see this waterfall up ahead . . . and somehow you're drawn to it. Now you're surrounded by nature. Trees and grass . . . water . . . birds in the trees. As you go closer to this waterfall, there's a place to sit . . . a rock, a place to sit . . . you can watch the waterfall.

Now follow this path further . . . it will take you to another place that is fascinating and inspiring . . . as you go on further . . . ahead there is a little clearing . . . a place where you can look out on the vast beauty of the mountains. . . .

You are now high in the mountains . . . beautiful mountains . . . and this clearing leads you to a place . . . a very scenic place . . . you are at the edge of the clearing and you can look far out and see the range of mountains for miles and miles in the distance . . . see the colors . . . see the clouds . . . feel the wind . . . and notice your feelings . . . here there is a sense of awe . . . just looking and watching . . . there! There is an eagle flying across the sky . . . a beautiful eagle . . . watch it . . . one of God's creatures . . . it floats on the wind . . . going to its nest . . . awe-inspiring . . . beautiful . . . and restoring of energy, body, mind, and soul . . . energy. . . .

Within this hypnotic state . . . your mind remembers sights and sounds . . . of nature. Now soon finding that the scenes of nature can change further . . . now soon . . . being near an ocean . . . walking along a beautiful beach. And within your own experience . . . your thoughts can drift to such a place. As I describe being near a beautiful beach . . . you can feel as if you are . . . there . . . near a beautiful beach. Able to see the sand . . . and hear the sound of the ocean. A part of your mind remembers the sound . . . of waves as they come in on a sandy beach . . . and the images now can change . . . so that you can see a beautiful beach before you. A place where you can see the waves coming in . . . on this beautiful beach.

Looking out . . . across the ocean . . . and you can see a long way in the distance . . . you might see sailboats in the distance . . . or see seabirds, *seagulls . . . along the shore . . . it's a pleasant day . . . a warm day . . . but just pleasantly warm. There is a breeze, a sea breeze . . . and you might enjoy going for a walk . . . just walking along the beach . . . as you look out across the beach . . . and as you can see the waves come in. The areas where the sand is cool and wet . . . as the waves come in. And notice whether you're wearing shoes . . . or if your feet are bare as you begin to walk . . . along the shoreline of this beach . . . this beautiful beach. Each step you take . . . begin to feel better and better . . . more energy . . . a positive feeling . . . a positive feeling within yourself . . . as you walk along the beach . . . any feelings of fatigue become less and less. Experiencing nature . . . a sense of fascination, interest, awe, and enjoyment.*

And . . . as you are there, somehow a source of energy begins to come to you . . . greater vitality . . . greater energy . . . filling you. Strength in your muscles . . . strength in your arms . . . and a positive optimistic attitude . . . seeing things in a positive way . . . more at peace within yourself . . . looking forward to the future . . . a feeling that things are just as they need to be . . . feeling that in the big picture everything's going to be all right.

A good feeling about yourself. Good feelings about everything around you now. Peaceful and calm. Any fatigue drifts away as you notice this optimism. As you feel calm . . . there's no stress . . . no worries.

You will find as you continue to experience hypnotic relaxation that you will sleep very well. Each night when you go to sleep or you take a nap . . . you will find it to be very refreshing. When you awaken, you will notice vitality and energy. You will begin to feel better day by day, as stress is reduced . . . as you find an optimistic attitude and feelings within yourself . . . and as you become more aware of nature around you.

You will find the energy to exercise as is appropriate for you . . . whether that is gentle stretching, going for a walk, or whatever activity or exercise is right and best for you. You will have the energy . . . to do the things that you really wish

to do. As this occurs, you will feel better . . . and better. In looking forward to these things occurring . . . as now you just drift . . . deeper, relaxed. A safe and secure feeling . . . the kind of feeling that you could have being at home . . . perhaps safe and secure in your own bed . . . the kind of sleep that's possible when you feel safe and comfortable . . . even if it's raining, gently raining outside.

At such a time . . . feeling safe and secure is so important. Even seeing the glimpses of lightning far in the distance . . . as you can hear a gentle rain . . . and let every muscle relax. Your thoughts can drift . . . filled with positive feelings, good feelings that become more and more as you relax deeper, and deeper. You will find that whether now, or later, whichever is right for you, when you are alert you will find more energy . . . as if you've gotten a good rest . . . and reenergized.

As I begin to count some more numbers now . . . these numbers can serve as a cue to return to conscious alertness. Or, if you prefer to drift into sleep, the numbers can serve in that manner as well. Whatever is best . . . whatever is right for you . . . at this particular time . . . as I count the numbers . . . from 1 to 4. 1 . . . 2 . . . 3 . . . and 4. . . . Very good."

CONCLUSION

CRF is a significant problem as it affects the lives of millions of cancer survivors. The impact of CRF is devastating, and there is a pressing need for safe and effective interventions. Although standard care usually involves recommendations for exercise or medications, many patients cannot or do not exercise; medications are not especially effective and cause problematic side effects for many patients.

Hypnosis is one potential alternative that seems promising in the treatment of CRF. Hypnotherapy is a safe, nonpharmacological treatment that has shown considerable promise as a method of addressing cancer-related symptoms, and research demonstrates that hypnosis can be integrated into treatment programs for cancer patients and survivors (e.g., Elkins et al., 2004; Elkins et al., 2008; Montgomery et al., 2007). Data have also shown hypnosis to be effective in addressing symptoms related to cancer and cancer treatment, including decreasing nausea (e.g., Vickers & Cassileth, 2001) and pain (e.g., Elkins et al., 2004; Elkins & Handel, 2001; Montgomery et al., 2002; Montgomery et al., 2007; Vickers & Cassileth, 2001), reducing chemotherapy-induced menopausal hot flashes (e.g., Elkins et al., 2008; Younus, Simpson, Collins, & Wang, 2003), and improving immune function and survival (e.g. Gruzelier, 2002; Spiegel, Kraemer, Bloom, & Gottheil, 1989). Further research is needed to build upon the existing literature to validate the utility of using hypnosis to reduce CRF.

CLINICAL SUMMARY

- Hypnosis sessions should be structured around individualized natural imagery. Ask clients about relaxing imagery and tailor sessions around their needs.
- Hypnotic suggestions should incorporate suggestions for increased energy, increased muscle strength, increased optimism, and increased vitality. Posthypnotic suggestions are encouraged to increase the effectiveness of the induction.
- Psychological barriers such as personality disorders and psychosis should be assessed before attempting to enter a hypnotic trance state.

REFERENCES

Bower, J. E., Ganz, P. A., Desmond, K. A., Bernaards, C., Rowland, J. H., Meyerowitz, B. E., & Belin, T. R. (2006). Fatigue in long-term carcinoma survivors: A longitudinal investigation. *Cancer*, 106(4), 751–758.

Bower, J. E., Ganz, P. A., Desmond, K. A., Rowland, J. H., Meyerowitz, B. E., & Belin, T. R. (2000). Fatigue in cancer survivors: Occurrence, correlates, and impact on quality of life. *Journal of Clinical Oncology: Official Journal of the American Society of Clinical Oncology*, 18(4), 743–753.

Cimprich, B. (1992). Attentional fatigue following cancer surgery. *Research in Nursing & Health*, 15(3), 199–207.

Cimprich, B., & Ronis, D. L. (2003). An environmental intervention to restore attention in women with newly diagnosed cancer. *Cancer Nursing*, 26(4), 284–292.

Curt, G. A. (2001). Fatigue in cancer. *British Medical Journal (Clinical Research Ed.)*, 322(7302), 1560. doi:10.1136/bmj.322.7302.1560

Curt, G. A., Breitbart, W., Cella, D., Groopman, J. E., Horning, S. J., Itri, L. M., . . . Vogelzang, N. J. (2000). Completed impact of cancer-related fatigue on the lives of patients: New findings from the fatigue coalition. *The Oncologist*, 5(5), 353–360.

Elkins, G. R. (2013). *Hypnotic relaxation therapy: Principles and applications*. New York, NY: Springer Publishing Company.

Elkins, G. R., & Handel, D. H. (2001). Clinical hypnosis: An essential in the "tool kit" for family practice. *Clinics in Family Practice*, 3(1), 113–126.

Elkins, G. R., Marcus, J. D., Palamara, L., Cheung, A., Young, R., & Rajab, H. (2004). Hypnosis to reduce pain in cancer survivors with advanced disease: A prospective study. *Journal of Cancer Integrative Medicine*, 2(4), 167–172.

Elkins, G., Marcus, J., Stearns, V., Perfect, M., Rajab, M. H., Ruud, C., . . . Keith, T. (2008). Randomized trial of a hypnosis intervention for treatment of hot flashes among cancer survivors. *Journal of Clinical Oncology: Official Journal of the American Society of Clinical Oncology*, 26(31), 5022–5026.

Escalante, C. P. (2003). Treatment of cancer-related fatigue: An update. *Supportive Care in Cancer: Official Journal of the Multinational Association of Supportive Care in Cancer*, 11(2), 79–83.

Gruzelier, J. H. (2002). A review of the impact of hypnosis, relaxation, guided imagery and individual differences on aspects of immunity and health. *Stress*, 5(2), 147–163.

Jacobsen, P. B., Donovan, K. A., Vadaparampil, S. T., & Small, B. J. (2007). Systematic review and meta-analysis of psychological and activity-based interventions for cancer-related fatigue. *Health Psychology: Official Journal of the Division of Health Psychology, American Psychological Association*, 26(6), 660–667.

Jensen, M. P., Gralow, J. R., Braden, A., Gertz, K. J., Fann, J. R., & Syrjala, K. L. (2012). Hypnosis for symptom management in women with cancer: A pilot study. *International Journal of Clinical and Experimental Hypnosis*, 60(2), 135–159.

Kaplan, S. (1995). The restorative benefits of nature: Toward an integrative framework. *Journal of Environmental Psychology*, 15(3), 169–182.

Kaplan, S. (2001). Meditation, restoration, and the management of mental fatigue. *Environment and Behavior*, 33(4), 480–506.

Lawrence, D. P. (2004). Evidence report on the occurrence, assessment, and treatment of fatigue in cancer patients. *Journal of the National Cancer Institute Monographs, 2004*(32), 40–50.

Minton, O., Richardson, A., Sharpe, M., Hotopf, M., & Stone, P. (2008). A systematic review and meta-analysis of the pharmacological treatment of cancer-related fatigue. *Journal of the National Cancer Institute, 100*(16), 1155–1166.

Minton, O., Richardson, A., Sharpe, M., Hotopf, M., & Stone, P. C. (2011). Psychostimulants for the management of cancer-related fatigue: A systematic review and meta-analysis. *Journal of Pain and Symptom Management, 41*(4), 761–767.

Minton, O., & Stone, P. (2008). How common is fatigue in disease-free cancer survivors? A systematic review of the literature. *Breast Cancer Research and Treatment, 112*(1), 5–13.

Mock, V. (2004). Evidence-based treatment for cancer-related fatigue. *Journal of the National Cancer Institute. Monographs, 32*(32), 112–118.

Mock, V., Atkinson, A., Barsevick, A., Cella, D., Cimprich, B., Cleeland, C., . . . Stahl, C. (2000). NCCN practice guidelines for cancer-related fatigue. *Oncology, 14*(11A), 151–161.

Montgomery, G. H., Bovbjerg, D. H., Schnur, J. B., David, D., Goldfarb, A., Weltz, C. R., . . . Silverstein, J. H. (2007). A randomized clinical trial of a brief hypnosis intervention to control side effects in surgery patients. *Journal of the National Cancer Institute, 99*(17), 1304–1312.

Montgomery, G. H., Kangas, M., David, D., Hallquist, M. N., Green, S., Bovbjerg, D. H., & Schnur, J. B. (2009). Fatigue during cancer radiotherapy: An initial randomized study of cognitive behavioral therapy plus hypnosis. *Health Psychology: Official Journal of the Division of Health Psychology, American Psychological Association, 28*(3), 317–322.

Montgomery, G. H., Weltz, C. R., Seltz, M., & Bovbjerg, D. H. (2002). Brief presurgery hypnosis reduces distress and pain in excisional biopsy patients. *International Journal of Clinical and Experimental Hypnosis, 50*(1), 17–32.

Moraska, A. R., Sood, A., Dakhil, S. R., Sloan, J. A., Barton, D., Atherton, P. J., . . . Loprinzi, C. L. (2010). Phase III, randomized, double-blind, placebo-controlled study of long-acting methylphenidate for cancer-related fatigue: North Central Cancer Treatment Group NCCTG-N05C7 trial. *Journal of Clinical Oncology: Official Journal of the American Society of Clinical Oncology, 28*(23), 3673–3679.

Morrow, G. R., Shelke, A. R., Roscoe, J. A., Hickok, J. T., & Mustian, K. (2005). Management of cancer-related fatigue. *Cancer Investigation, 23*(3), 229–239.

Okuyama, T., Tanaka, K., Akechi, T., Kugaya, A., Okamura, H., Nishiwaki, Y., . . . Uchitomi, Y. (2001). Fatigue in ambulatory patients with advanced lung cancer: Prevalence, correlated factors, and screening. *Journal of Pain and Symptom Management, 22*(1), 554–564.

Prue, G., Rankin, J., Allen, J., Gracey, J., & Cramp, F. (2006). Cancer-related fatigue: A critical appraisal. *European Journal of Cancer (Oxford, England: 1990), 42*(7), 846–863.

Richardson, J., Smith, J. E., McCall, G., Richardson, A., Pilkington, K., & Kirsch, I. (2007). Hypnosis for nausea and vomiting in cancer chemotherapy: A systematic review of the research evidence. *European Journal of Cancer Care, 16*(5), 402–412.

Servaes, P., van der Werf, S., Prins, J., Verhagen, S., & Bleijenberg, G. (2001). Fatigue in disease-free cancer patients compared with fatigue in patients with chronic fatigue syndrome. *Supportive Care in Cancer, 9*(1), 11–17.

Servaes, P., Verhagen, S., & Bleijenberg, G. (2002). Determinants of chronic fatigue in disease-free cancer patients: A cross-sectional study. *Annals of Oncology: Official Journal of the European Society for Medical Oncology/ESMO, 13*(4), 589–598.

Spiegel, D., Kraemer, H., Bloom, J., & Gottheil, E. (1989). Effect of psychosocial treatment on survival of patients with metastatic cancer. *The Lancet, 334*(8668), 888–891.

Stewart, J. H. (2005). Hypnosis in contemporary medicine. *Mayo Clinic Proceedings, 80*(4), 511–524.

Stone, P. C., & Minton, O. (2008). Cancer-related fatigue. *European Journal of Cancer (Oxford, England: 1990), 44*(8), 1097–1104.

Tomé-Pires, C., & Miró, J. (2012). Hypnosis for the management of chronic and cancer procedure-related pain in children. *International Journal of Clinical and Experimental Hypnosis, 60*(4), 432–457.

Vickers, A. J., & Cassileth, B. R. (2001). Unconventional therapies for cancer and cancer-related symptoms. *The Lancet. Oncology, 2*(4), 226–232.

Watson, T., & Mock, V. (2004). Exercise as an intervention for cancer-related fatigue. *Physical Therapy, 84*(8), 736–742.

Younus, J., Simpson, I., Collins, A., & Wang, X. (2003). Mind control of menopause. *Women's Health Issues: Official Publication of the Jacobs Institute of Women's Health, 13*(2), 74–78.

Cataract Eye Surgery: Preparation for Eye Surgery Assisted by Positive Therapeutic Suggestions

Edit Jakubovits, Zoltán Kekecs, and Katalin Gombos

Cataract removal is one of the most commonly performed surgical procedures worldwide (Taylor, 2000). Most people experience some extent of anxiety in the perioperative period of their cataract surgery; elderly patients and patients with high trait anxiety are the most affected (Hadjistavropoulos, Snider, & Hadjistavropoulos, 2001; Nijkamp et al., 2004).

In most surgical procedures, patients tend to seek out information about the operation. However, a high percentage of patients who are about to undergo cataract surgery tend to avoid patient education, usually because they think it would be anxiety provoking for them (O'Malley, Newmark, Rothman, & Strassman, 1989). Yet, previous studies show that providing information on the cataract surgery procedure and the experience of undergoing the procedure have various benefits, such as lower overall anxiety, increased patient satisfaction, and better understanding of the procedure and risks, which is critical for informed consent (Pager, 2005; Ramos, de Matos, Branquinho, & Pereira, 2011). For these reasons, it is important to provide information to patients in a non-anxiety-provoking way.

A good way of doing this is using positive therapeutic suggestions (Kekecs & Varga, 2013). Prior studies have shown that using positive suggestions before and during ophthalmic surgery can increase the subjective well-being of the patient and can also result in higher satisfaction with the surgery for the patient and for the operating doctor as well (Cruise, Chung, Yogendran, & Little, 1997; John & Parrino, 1983). The authors of this chapter also

performed a randomized controlled trial involving 84 participants (suggestion group $N = 34$, control group $N = 50$) to assess the effectiveness of therapeutic suggestion in the preparation of patients for their cataract surgery (Kekecs, Jakubovits, Varga, & Gombos, 2014). In this study, patients in the suggestion group prepared for their cataract surgery using a tape containing information about the operation and positive therapeutic suggestions. We found that these patients were calmer in the perioperative period and were more cooperative during the procedure, according to the surgeon (blind to group allocation), compared with the control group. Data of this study also suggest that heart rate was lowered during surgery in the suggestion group (although this latter result is not statistically significant when using Bonferroni correction for multiple statistical tests).

In the following section, we provide a description of the suggestion script used in the study to explain the rationale of the particular suggestions and metaphors used.

The suggestion script was developed by a hypnotherapist (E. J., first author) in close cooperation with the eye surgeon (K. G., third author) performing the operations in the study. Patients got the audiotaped suggestions 2 to 4 weeks before their surgery and were encouraged to listen to the recording at least twice a week, the last time being on the night before the operation. The number of home practice sessions might be associated with the extent of the intervention's effects. The final script was read and taped by the eye surgeon. This is important because this way, the voice of the operating doctor can associate with the positive experiences and the relaxation response evoked by the tape, which can help the patient to evoke the same experiences again during surgery.

The main goal of the script is to reduce the fear of the unknown by providing information about the surgery. Information about the operation is always provided in conjunction with positive suggestions. Another important objective is to offer a relaxation technique to the patients, which will help them to overcome fear and anxiety in the perioperative period. This is achieved by focusing on the breathing and using the safe place technique. One of the reasons for providing the tape prior to the day of the surgery is to give the patients enough time to practice this relaxation technique so that they are proficient in using it by the time of the operation. The third major theme of the suggestion script is to facilitate letting go of the old lens and accepting the new artificial one. This is achieved by directing awareness to breathing (exhalation—letting go, inhalation—letting in) and also by a few thoughts of farewell to the old lens that is to be replaced by the surgery. Assisting this work of mourning may lead to a faster healing process and a smoother consolidation of the new lens.

The setting and scene of eye surgery can be utilized well to support relaxation and hypnosis. For example, the patient has to stare at the brilliant light of the microscope during the whole procedure, which is ideal to focus attention and to induce a hypnotic state. Induction by focusing on a light source originated from Braid, who himself performed hundreds of eye surgeries in his time (Bramwell, 1896). Aside from using the light of the microscope as an induction tool, metaphors of a healing light can be built around this bright light as well. The supine position and the monotone sound of the phacoemulsification machine can also be utilized to support the relaxation and the trance state.

The following script is a newer version of the script used in our study, revised based on therapist and patient experiences (Varga, 2011a, 2011b; Varga & Diószeghy, 2001).

SUGGESTION SCRIPT FOR PREPARATION FOR CATARACT SURGERY

"Greetings! I'm . . . [the therapist introduces himself/herself here. If the operating doctor is reading

the script, he or she can also tell that he or she will perform the surgery]. *You will hear my voice on this recording that is approximately 20 minutes long. This relaxation tape is a preparation for your eye surgery. Its purpose is to make sure that the time you spend in the operating room will be comfortable and that you will have a swift recovery.*

Please listen to this recording at least twice a week 2 weeks prior to the operation, and please listen to this tape on the evening before the surgery by all means!

If you can imagine or experience what I'm saying, that's wonderful, but it's just as useful if you just listen to my suggestions. You can listen to the tape while sitting or lying down, whichever is more comfortable. For this short period, make sure that you are in a calm and quiet place and ask others to respect this as well. You should also turn off your phone. Of course if a situation occurs that unconditionally requires you to act, you will be instantly alert and be able to do as necessary.

If you are prepared, I'd like you to position yourself comfortably and just listen with all your ears. You can let your eyes close; this way you can pay more attention inward and to my words. Comfortably. . . . Now you can close your eyes . . . that's right. You will be able to rest comfortably during the surgery as well because we will help you, so that your eye will be in just the right spot even in this relaxed state.

I'd like you to know that every medical intervention and support is only a possibility. The real healing is done from the inside, by your own body. You can contribute to the success greatly by letting your body accept this external support. The fact that you are listening to this recording already shows that you want to do everything possible for your healing. I'd like to ask you now to concentrate strongly on my words and just follow what I'm saying, so that I can help you relax.

I'd like you to pay attention to your breathing. Just breathe at your own pace, as it feels alright. Notice that the air you take in is slightly cooler, . . . on exhalation, it's a bit warmer. Observe that on inhalation, your chest is rising, expanding. On exhalation, it subsides. Inhalation at your own pace: Fresh air fills the lungs . . . exhalation: The worn-out air leaves . . . inhalation: Oxygen flows in . . . exhalation: The carbon dioxide vacates your body, leaving free space for the fresh air, the fresh oxygen. Just observe your breathing at your own pace further! That's right! . . . While you pay attention so intensely, your body is getting fresher and fresher, your thoughts are getting clearer. You can listen to my words more and more easily as well. Just observe the flow of air further! That's right. Exhalation . . . and inhalation. . . . Letting go . . . and letting in. . . .

I'm curious whether you have noticed, that while you observe your breathing this way, with every breath, tension is decreased in your body. It is completely natural to be a little more tense preparing for a surgery, even when you know how much easier your life will be after it. This little tension might even have helped you, so that you are now able to focus on this surgery exclusively and prepare for it. Yet, now you can let go of this tension together with the used air. You don't need it anymore. . . . Exhalation . . . you are calmer and calmer. . . . Inhalation . . . fresh air and calmness flows in . . . exhalation, let go of the remaining tension with it . . . inhalation . . . you are calmer and calmer while you do this. . . . Wonderful!

I'm curious if it occurred to you that our outflowing carbon dioxide nourishes the plants and we get oxygen produced by the plants back in return. This oxygen refreshes and replenishes our body when we inhale. Nature cleans and transforms the exhaled carbon dioxide . . . so that we are able to receive it in the form of oxygen. . . . The endless cycle of life! What a great cooperation . . . with every breath you can feel the love of nature more and more. . . . You probably have a favorite place, which fills you with strength, so that you can experience this strength, this safety even more. . . . You almost breathe together with nature now . . . in safety . . . calmly . . . with joy. . . . Exhalation . . . and inhalation . . . at your own pace. . . . Letting go . . . and letting in . . . the body knows this, and your mind also starts to grasp this more and more, and it gets refreshed, and relaxed . . . lets go and lets in . . . something new that helps . . . and now a wonderful new light appears . . . maybe the sun shines through the

trees brilliantly . . . maybe it is really like healing sunlight, as it gets brighter and brighter, maybe golden, . . . maybe it has some other color. Perhaps it's just a feeling that you are more and more relaxed, perhaps it's just pleasing to listen to what I'm saying. That's right . . . and that color, that calmness . . . is really safe. Just let the sunshine in. Just let it fill up your whole body.

Now that you are this relaxed and you can concentrate on my words even more, I'll tell you what exactly will happen in the operating room. Of course, there may be some deviation from this, but you will accept those just as calmly and loosely as you now listen to my words, my voice. [This is an important step, to ensure that even if something goes differently during the operation, the patient can still remain calm. If the operating doctor reads this, she can add]: *"My voice will be calming to you as well when we meet in the operating room."*

So now, please listen to me! When you arrive in the forefront of the operating room, you'll get a number of eye drops. One of them helps your pupil to dilate; this way it'll be easier for us to see through the operated area. You'll get anesthetizing eye drops too. It'll be good to know that with every drop, your pupil will get more and more dilated and your eye will get more and more anesthetized as long as it's needed for the surgery. When you get the eye drops, you can reinforce these feelings by saying this to yourself: 'With every drop, my pupil gets wider and wider, and my eye gets more and more anesthetized as long as it's needed for the surgery. My eyes will feel good and comfortable after the surgery as well.'

Before the operation, your eye will be cleaned with a disinfectant solution. People tend to feel this a little cool. What will it feel like for you? You might imagine this is like a pleasant cool breeze that washes away not only bacteria but the remaining tension too. At this point, some people imagine their favorite place in nature, where this pleasant cool breeze gently refreshes and relaxes the eye and the whole face. You are in a favorable position, because you have already imagined this beautiful and safe place, where you breathe together with nature and let tension be taken by the wind. After this, for the sake of cleanliness, we will cover you with sterile sheets and we will fixate the operated area with an adhesive foil. At this point, it helps for most people to imagine their favorite place and to notice that they breathe together with nature. It will feel good to immerse in an experience that fills you with strength. I can also imagine that you will be able to relax with your own unique method, to mobilize your inner imaginative world for your healing, while we are working on that eye from the outside. We can cooperate brilliantly this way. We need this cooperation so that you can follow our requests with ease during surgery. If you need anything, you can ask even during the operation, because the most important thing for us is that you feel as good as possible. We can operate more safely, swiftly, and precisely this way. For some people, it is helpful to rehearse the method I advised for relaxation. So I'll tell you once again how you can practice this method of relaxation and how you can easily recall it during surgery to assist the operation:

Just start to observe the flow of the air! Just breathe at your own pace, as it suits you. Notice that the air you take in is slightly cooler . . . , on exhalation, it's a bit warmer. Observe that on inhalation, your chest is rising, expanding. On exhalation, it subsides. . . . Inhalation at your own pace: Fresh air fills the lungs . . . exhalation: The used air leaves. . . . Inhalation: Oxygen flows in . . . exhalation: The carbon dioxide vacates your body, leaving free space for the fresh air, the fresh oxygen. Just observe your breathing at your own pace further! That's right! Nature cleans and transforms the exhaled carbon dioxide . . . so that we can receive it in a new form, as oxygen. . . . The endless cycle of life! What a great cooperation. . . . With every breath, you can experience the love of nature more and more. . . . You probably have a favorite place, which fills you with strength . . . so that you can experience this strength, this safety even more. . . . You almost breathe together with nature now . . . in safety . . . calmly . . . with joy. . . . Exhalation . . . and inhalation . . . at your own pace. . . . Letting go . . . and letting in . . . the body knows this, and your mind also starts to grasp this more and more. And it gets refreshed, and relaxed . . . lets go and lets in . . . something new that helps . . . and now a wonderful new light appears . . . maybe the sun shines through the trees brilliantly . . . maybe it is really like healing sunlight, as it gets brighter and brighter, maybe

golden, . . . maybe it has some other color. Perhaps it's just a feeling that you are more and more relaxed, perhaps it's just pleasing to listen to what I'm saying. That's right . . . and that color, that calmness . . . is really safe. Just let the sunshine in. Just let it slowly fill your whole body.

The light of the microscope that lights up the operated area will shine into your eye and will intensify this whole experience. Just let your eye into this light courageously! [Say this last sentence in a resolute tone.] *And meanwhile, your breathing gets calmer and calmer . . . it's easier and easier to focus on what I'm saying . . . only the things that I say directly to you matter, every other noise fades farther and farther away and helps you maintain your concentration. Just breathe at your own pace, as it pleases you, just observe . . . exhalation . . . letting go . . .inhalation . . . letting in . . . at your own pace . . . it gets brighter and brighter . . . more and more secure . . . and calm . . . calmer and calmer. . . . Just observe how your eye relaxes, how does it feel?*

Slowly, this healing light fills the lens and the lens capsule in which there is the cloudy, hardened lens core . . . and it helps the surgery to go smoothly and successfully. The eye is more and more relaxed, it follows my instructions even more easily. Calmly and securely. Just allow it, just let it in . . . , we help you so that your eye can remain in just the right spot even in this relaxed state. Just let your eye into the light comfortably! We supplement your blinking through the surgery. From time to time, we moisturize your eye from the outside so that you can relax in safety and concentrate on the calming images of your healing. The core of the lens is dissolved by the ultrasound equipment, and the flowing fluid cleans the area as the operation progresses . . . exhalation . . . and inhalation . . . letting go . . . and letting in. . . . The refreshing air flows, healing flows, the cleansing fluid flows. The lights get clearer as well, maybe you can already see shapes . . . just observe. The refreshing air flows, healing flows, the cleansing fluid flows, the lights get clearer. The healing energy flows and gets to every place where it is needed. It reaches your eye as well. Letting go . . . and letting in . . . the body knows this, and your mind also starts to grasp this more and more, and it gets refreshed, and relaxed . . . lets go and lets in . . . something new that helps . . . and this beautiful light . . . as the lens gets clearer, as the sun shines through the trees brilliantly . . . maybe it is really like healing sunlight, as it gets brighter and brighter, maybe golden . . . maybe it has some other color. Perhaps it's just a feeling that you are more and more relaxed, perhaps it's just pleasing to listen to what I'm saying. Very good. . . . And that color, that calmness . . . is really secure. Just let the sunshine in. Just let it slowly fill your whole body.

I'm curious if it had occurred to you how long this old lens has served you. Now it has changed. It got tired and hard. It's time to let it go while we acknowledge its past servitude. Maybe it saw things that were painful or that hurt you. Now, go on and just allow these feelings to be purified too. . . . Let them into the light . . . let everything be cleaned that needs to. How reassuring it is to know that we can implant a new tissue-friendly lens. That there is an opportunity to use these safe things that can adjust to the human body. Just observe the breathing . . . at your own pace . . . just allow it . . . just observe. . . . Exhalation: I let the old go into the light . . . inhalation: I let the new in . . . , the breathing . . . the lens . . . easy, . . . easier and easier . . . more and more secure. . . .

The operation slowly comes to an end. We remove the supporting tools and the sheets. Just take a deep breath, and exhale! That's right! You got through the procedure, and started to go on the way toward healing. While they put the bandage on your eye, I'd like you to remember what I'm saying now: When you get out of the operating room, back to your normal daily life, you will be able to wear the bandage easily while it's needed. It's only there to protect your eye from external influences and to provide safety after the operation. Whatever you feel under the bandage shows that you have started on the path of healing. You know that the eye is cleaned by tears. Maybe the watering of your eye will temporarily intensify, because the eye cleans itself this way. Just let this happen. This is only temporary, and it is part of the healing process. Most people handle this well and it stops after a while. I'd like you to know that we are available if you need any assistance. We have effective modern medication at our disposal. When you are examined

on the day after the surgery, the bandages will be removed [or *"I will examine you"* and *"I will remove the bandages,"* if the operating doctor is reading the script and she will do the examination]. *It will be comfortable for your eye that you'll wear sunglasses for a period of time, until it is no longer necessary. This intervention is so safe that people can usually go back entirely to their usual business after a few days.*

Now we are finished with the exercise. Simply take a deep breath, and open your eyes! Go back to your usual world, full with energy and rich with experiences. The relaxation exercise has ended. Have a good day."

CONTRAINDICATIONS

Detailed description of the steps of surgery can evoke prior surgical experiences. Used in a controlled environment, this technique might help patients who have unprocessed traumatic experience from a prior surgery to resolve these traumas. However, unsupervised recall of these memories might be counterproductive. Thus, for such clients, it is contraindicated to use audio-recorded suggestions alone for surgical preparation. In these cases, it might be better to do in-person therapist-delivered intervention to have better control over the resolution of the trauma.

EXPERIENCES OF CLIENTS

The intervention can have extra benefits in addition to those encountered in the upcoming surgery; as an example, it can provide psychosocial and physical support for elderly patients who live alone in the weeks of preparation for surgery. For example, a patient in our study reported: "I got refreshed physically and mentally after listening to the recording in the evenings."

Other quotes from clients: "I concentrated intently during the surgery, and sighed in my solitude. I respired steadily. I knew what was coming, and everything happened accordingly." "When they lay me on the operating table, everything was natural, and I wasn't upset. When I analyzed this in a hindsight, I realized that this was because of the pleasant voice of my doctor, which I listened to before." "During the surgery, I remembered what she told me on the recording, and I followed it. For example, that I should think of something nice, or that I should pay attention to my breathing. It helped me to calm down." "I was a bit anxious before the surgery, but the lovely voice of the doctor set me at ease. I knew that I will be able to follow her instructions."

REFERENCES

Bramwell, J. M. (1896). James Braid, surgeon and hypnotist. *Brain*, *19*(1), 90–116.

Cruise, C. J., Chung, F., Yogendran, S., & Little, D. (1997). Music increases satisfaction in elderly outpatients undergoing cataract surgery. *Canadian Journal of Anaesthesia = Journal Canadien d'anesthéSie*, *44*(1), 43–48. doi:10.1007/BF03014323

Hadjistavropoulos, H. D., Snider, B. S., & Hadjistavropoulos, T. (2001). Anxiety in older persons waiting for cataract surgery: Investigating the contributing factors. *Canadian Journal on Aging/La Revue Canadienne Du Vieillissement*, *20*(1), 97–112.

John, M. E., & Parrino, J. P. (1983). Practical hypnotic suggestion in ophthalmic surgery. *American Journal of Ophthalmology*, *96*(4), 540–542.

Kekecs, Z., & Varga, K. (2013). Positive suggestion techniques in somatic medicine: A review of the empirical studies. *Interventional Medicine & Applied Science*, *5*(3), 101–111. doi:10.1556/IMAS.5.2013.3.2

Kekecs, Z., Jakubovits, E., Varga, K., & Gombos, K. (2014). Effects of patient education and therapeutic suggestions on cataract surgery patients: A randomized controlled clinical trial. *Patient Education and Counseling*, *94*(1), 116–122. doi:10.1016/j.pec.2013.09.019

Nijkamp, M. D., Kenens, C. A., Dijker, A. J., Ruiter, R. A., Hiddema, F., & Nuijts, R. M. (2004). Determinants of surgery related anxiety in cataract patients. *British Journal of Ophthalmology*, *88*(10), 1310–1314. doi:10.1136/bjo.2003.037788

O'Malley, T. P., Newmark, T. S., Rothman, M. I., & Strassman, H. D. (1989). Emotional aspects of cataract surgery. *International Journal of Psychiatry in Medicine*, *19*(1), 85–89.

Pager, C. K. (2005). Randomised controlled trial of preoperative information to improve satisfaction with cataract surgery. *British Journal of Ophthalmology*, *89*(1), 10–13. doi:10.1136/bjo.2004.048637

Ramos, M. L., de Matos, M. G., Branquinho, C., & Pereira, L. M. (2011). Helping patients in cataract peri-and post-surgery: A simple intervention addressing anxiety. *International Journal of Nursing and Midwifery*, *3*(7), 76–80.

Taylor, H. R. (2000). Cataract: How much surgery do we have to do? *British Journal of Ophthalmology*, *84*(1), 1–2.

Varga, K. (Ed.). (2011a). *Beyond the words: Communication and suggestion in medical practice.* New York, NY: Nova Science Publishers.

Varga, K. (2011b). Suggestions–Step by step. In K. Varga (Ed.), *Beyond the words. Communication and suggestion in medical practice* (pp. 413–421). New York, NY: Nova Science Publishers.

Varga, K., & Diószeghy, C. (2001). *Hűtésbefizetés, avagy szuggesztiók alkalmazása az orvosi gyakorlatban (application of suggestions in medical practice).* Budapest: Pólya kiadó.

Cystic Fibrosis

Ran D. Anbar

20

CHAPTER

Cystic fibrosis (CF) causes the body to produce thick secretions that lead to damage of the respiratory, gastrointestinal, and reproductive systems. Symptoms of CF can include cough, shortness of breath, pneumonia, chronic sinusitis, abdominal pain, malnutrition, and infertility. The damage caused by CF in the lungs is so severe that the disease is life-shortening. Many patients require lung transplantation in order to survive. Unfortunately, the average patient undergoing transplantation only lives an additional 5 years. Fortunately, due to many new therapies developed during the past five decades, the average life expectancy for these patients has increased from less than 10 years to 37 years (Cystic Fibrosis Foundation, 2014b; Meyers & Anbar, 2012; Mogayzel & Flume, 2010).

CF is the most common fatal hereditary disorder among Caucasians. It affects approximately 30,000 Americans and an additional 40,000 people worldwide. CF is an autosomal recessive disorder, which means that when both parents carry a CF mutation, each of their children has a 25% chance of developing the disease. In the United States, about 1 in 25 Caucasians is a carrier of a CF mutation, and approximately 1 out of every 3,200 individuals has CF (Cystic Fibrosis Foundation, 2014a).

Treatment of CF requires multiple daily therapies, including nebulized medications and inhaled puffers, as well as several oral medications to help with breathing and digestion, supplement nutrition, and treat infections. Some patients require the use of a feeding tube that is inserted through their skin into their stomach (gastrostomy tube). Additionally, patients typically are asked to perform chest physiotherapy for 30 to 60 minutes daily to loosen secretions from the lungs. All told, daily therapy for CF may take 2 hours or more. Further, it is recommended that patients be evaluated at a CF care center at least four times yearly. As the disease progresses, patients develop respiratory

exacerbations that can require up to several weeks of intravenous antibiotics every year. Also, patients can develop significant gastrointestinal and endocrine problems such as bowel obstruction, liver disease, pancreatitis, and diabetes. As a result of the treatment burden of this chronic illness, many patients struggle to adhere to their prescribed therapeutic regimen (Kettler, Sawyer, Winefield, & Greville, 2002; Smith & Wood, 2007).

As patients become older, they contend with many psychosocial stressors related to CF, including its progressive and ultimately terminal nature; stress within their families related to their illness; difficulties with integrating their self-care needs within their school, work, and social life; and deciding with whom they want to share that they are affected by the disease (Meyers & Anbar, 2012).

RESEARCH

There are few reports in the literature regarding the use of hypnosis in patients with CF. Belsky and Khanna (1994) reported a small controlled trial of 12 children with CF. They used self-hypnosis to affect both psychological and physiological aspects of their disease. Use of hypnosis was associated with a reduction in anxiety as well as an increase in peak expiratory flow rates.

In a case series of 49 patients with CF who agreed to use self-hypnosis for help with their disease, 86% were successful at achieving their predetermined goals. Such goals included relaxation, relief of procedural pain, headaches, medication palatability, and other symptoms associated with their disease. Not one patient experienced worsening of symptoms(Anbar, 2000). Although the clinician did not necessarily encourage continuous use of hypnosis, nearly half of these patients continued to use hypnosis as a self-help tool an average of 4 years later. The most common reasons for their ongoing use of hypnosis involved the achievement of relaxation or alleviation of discomfort associated with procedural pain (Anbar, 2003). In another case series, after being taught how to use self-hypnosis to help augment the effectiveness of their chest physiotherapy, four out of seven patients reported that they continued to use this technique at home on a regular basis (Anbar, 2014).

The effectiveness of clinical hypnosis is enhanced greatly through the use of a patient-centered approach, as demonstrated in the case example in the following text. Such an approach should be integrated into health care broadly as part of standard medical care. The following clinical encounter occurred in the setting of a subspecialty medical center.

CASE EXAMPLE

A 13-year-old boy was accompanied by his parents for his first visit to our CF center. They had been told by their pediatrician 2 days earlier that the patient's sweat test was diagnostic for CF. As frequently occurs these days before the first appointment, the family had read about the disease on the Internet. The patient's mother was tearful as she explained she was very upset after finding out about the average age of survival.

"Every person is different," I began, in order to reassure her. "Your son probably has a milder form of the disease, so he can do better than average. We have very good therapies, and are developing new ones. Also, you should know that we are coming closer to finding a cure for CF, and I think he will do well until the cure comes."

I introduced the family in detail to how CF affects various organ systems and answered their questions. "It's perfectly all right if you don't remember what I have told you," I reassured them. "We will provide similar information in writing and in a video. We can also go over it all again during future visits." I asked the patient what he thought about what was being said. He leaned his head on his right hand and replied, "I'm taking it in. I can't change it. But I'm OK." "Are you ready for me to discuss with you the kinds of therapies we can use?" "Yes," he answered.

"The therapies for CF target the organs that are affected by the disease," I explained. "For the lungs we have a number of therapies. Some of these are recommended and the others are suggested. You get to decide which therapies you want to do, because this is your disease."

"There are various therapies you can use to help your lungs," I continued. "It is recommended that you inhale nebulized dornase alfa, which helps thin your airway mucus, and you might also want to use nebulized salt water, which will help you cough. In this way the secretions will be cleared better from your lungs. You might even want to learn how to use hypnosis as a way of clearing your lungs. I have a number of patients who found this to be very useful."

"For your gut, I will prescribe enzymes that you should take before every meal and snack in order to help digest your food. Do you have any questions?" He shook his head. "So, which of these therapies will you choose to use?" "Well, first of all I want to learn hypnosis," he answered. "How about the other therapies?" I asked. "I'll do all of them," he smiled. "But hypnosis seems very cool."

While asking about this young man's interests, I learned that he was a videographer and that he hoped to become a film director. He had already posted a number of skillful videos on the Internet. "I just had an idea!" I exclaimed. "Maybe you could document some of your experiences with CF. For example, today, you can go home and video record your thoughts about everything that has transpired. Hopefully, this is the only day in your life when you will have been diagnosed with a serious illness. Maybe you could use what you record now as part of a future movie." My patient seemed quite enthused. "I have some ideas already," he said thoughtfully. "This is really great. Thank you!"

That evening, my patient videotaped his thoughts and said he looked forward to videotaping his first encounters with the various therapies he had been prescribed.

Two years later, the patient continued to do very well. He was very adherent to his therapies and his state of health was excellent. He did develop some shortness of breath related to anxiety, which resolved with the aid of counseling and use of hypnosis that were provided at our CF center. The anxiety related to his feeling that he was wasting his time participating in recreational activities, whereas he needed to focus more on his academic and career ambitions. He was offered the reframe that allowing his mind to relax during recreational activities provided him a chance to "recharge" and therefore be better prepared for, and more likely to achieve, his goals.

Thus, this case demonstrates that the use of a patient-centered approach shaped the experience of this patient and his family, as they formed their impression of a very serious illness, and helped the patient integrate hypnosis more easily into his self-care. Instead of dealing with predominant feelings of grief and trepidation, they began creating a base upon which to build mastery over the illness and an appreciation of the opportunities it would bring.

TECHNIQUES: HYPNOSIS APPLICATIONS FOR PEOPLE WITH CF

Because patients with CF are prone to the development of both medical and psychological complications of their illness, a symptom may be the result of physiological or psychological dysregulation. In many cases, both factors contribute to the presentation. It is therefore essential that the application of hypnosis for a patient with CF be done concurrently with the provision of appropriate medical assessment and treatment. Thus, only patients who are receiving medical care for their CF at an accredited CF care center should be considered for any of the following possible applications of hypnosis. Notably, providing concurrent medical and psychological therapy, as illustrated in this chapter, allows amelioration of symptoms that are influenced by psychological effects and may be associated with a reduction in necessary medical therapy (Anbar & Hall, 2012). Each hypnosis application example listed in the following text includes a *noncomprehensive* list of common medical issues that might be assessed before or in conjunction with hypnosis therapy. All of the applications assume the patient has been taught how to achieve a state of relaxation using hypnosis.

Anxiety: Brief examples of medical considerations: Assess whether any of the patient's medications might be contributing to the presentation of anxiety, such as use of beta-agonists, montelukast, or corticosteroids (inhaled and systemic). Assess whether the patient is sleeping adequately, as poor sleep can be associated with increased anxiety (Mattewal & Subramanian, 2009).

While a patient is experiencing a calm state in hypnosis, the patient can rehearse the application of an anchoring gesture ("relaxation sign") that can trigger calmness. Patients find it easier to select a gesture (such as crossing their fingers or making a fist) before starting hypnosis.

"Now that you feel comfortable in hypnosis, make your relaxation sign and tell yourself: From now on, whenever I want to become this relaxed, I can make my sign, and immediately my mind and body will become this calm, even when I am not doing hypnosis."

When the patient realerts after hypnosis, the experience can be validated by suggesting the patient employ the anchoring gesture and observe the associated relaxation response. *"Whenever you become stressed you can use your sign, and in this way you can maintain an improved sense of calm throughout the day."*

Shortness of breath: Shortness of breath is a subjective feeling that can arise as a result of many factors including a worsening lung condition, cardiac problems, lack of physical conditioning, and anxiety (Homnick, 2012). Identification of the cause of shortness of breath allows for the application of an appropriate therapy. Symptoms suggestive of a psychological trigger of shortness of breath include a complaint of difficulty with inhalation, inspiratory noise, and anxiety-related symptoms such as dizziness, shakiness, palpitations, and paresthesia that can cause tingling or numbness in the extremities (Anbar & Geisler, 2005). Hypnosis for shortness of breath can utilize suggestions for relaxation and stress reduction. A patient can be asked to describe the appearance of his or her lungs both when experiencing shortness of breath and when breathing normally.

"To resolve your shortness of breath, imagine that your lungs are changing in appearance from abnormal to normal."

Need for chest physiotherapy: Ongoing chest physiotherapy is essential for the maintenance of good health in patients with CF. The clinician should review whether the currently prescribed physiotherapy regimen is the most compatible with the patient's lifestyle among the various available alternatives (Rand, Hill, & Prasad, 2013). Also, it is often helpful to encourage patient adherence to prescribed chest physiotherapy techniques in addition to the employment of hypnosis to augment the effectiveness of the physiotherapy. Once in hypnosis, a patient can be coached:

"Pick a small imaginary character who can help clear your lungs by entering your airways. Let me know when you've done so. Now, imagine the character removing sputum from one lung lobe at a time. Let me know when you've done that. [Patients often will cough vigorously while using this imagery for 3–10 minutes.] *Good. Now, imagine your character spraying hypertonic saline into one lobe at a time, and let me know when you've done that.* [This suggestion should only be used with patients who have experienced use of hypertonic saline.] *Great job! Finally, imagine your character photographing your airways in order to verify whether they are sufficiently clean. Then, have it clear any remaining sputum."* (Anbar, 2014)

Abdominal pain: Before introducing hypnosis, it is important to assure that the patient is taking enzymes before each meal and snack. Assessment should include determining if there is evidence of gastrointestinal malabsorption, chronic constipation, distal intestinal obstructive syndrome, gastroesophageal reflux, gastritis, celiac disease, pancreatitis, or even inflammatory bowel disease (Gelfond & Borowitz, 2013). Once these factors are addressed, hypnosis may be used to reduce abdominal pain. While in hypnosis, a patient can be coached to imagine changing the color of his or her abdomen from one that represents discomfort (e.g., red) to one that represents the abdominal appearance when it is comfortable (e.g., blue). Permit the patient to choose his or her own colors. *"Allow the color to change from red to blue, and notice how your abdomen can feel better as you do this."*

Gastroesophageal reflux: Before introducing hypnosis for gastroesophageal reflux medical considerations, include a review of the patient's medications and diet for possible triggers of the reflux. Consider medical conditions including celiac disease, diabetic gastroparesis, and medication side effects that can present with symptoms that mimic reflux. When appropriate, treat with

anti-reflux medications (Gelfond & Borowitz, 2013). A sample hypnosis approach includes suggestions for the control of reflux symptoms: *"When you feel your reflux symptoms, imagine a soft waterfall in your food pipe. Notice how you can feel better as the water washes down your food."*

Adherence: Medical considerations in regard to adherence include questions such as the following: Are there aversive medication side effects or unpleasant taste, which the patient has not mentioned? Are there psychosocial issues that preclude adherence to prescribed therapies, such as lack of money, time, or social support? Does the patient have a psychological condition such as attention deficit disorder, depression, or oppositional defiant disorder that interferes with adherence (Smith & Wood, 2007)?

Hypnosis can be used to foster adherence to taking medications as prescribed. While in hypnosis, a patient can be coached to imagine that he or she needs to unlock the mouth with a pancreatic enzyme in order to be able to open it to eat (Anbar, 2000). A patient who dislikes the taste of an inhaled medication can be coached to change the taste.

"Imagine seeing your favorite food. Imagine how it smells, its texture, and how it tastes when you eat it. While you inhale your medication, imagine you are smelling and tasting your favorite food." (Anbar, 2002)

When nonadherence is the result of a feeling of hopelessness, a patient can be helped through the visualization of a better future.

"Imagine how much better you will feel and how active you will be able to be once you remain adherent to all of your therapies." (Anbar & Murthy, 2010)

CONCLUSION

People with CF face many challenges directly and indirectly related to their chronic illness. Teaching them self-coping skills such as hypnosis is associated with a significant improvement of their quality of life and is empowering to the patients.

REFERENCES

Anbar, R. D. (2000). Self-hypnosis for patients with cystic fibrosis. *Pediatric Pulmonology, 30*(6), 461–465.

Anbar, R. D. (2002). You don't like the taste of your medication? *Clinical Pediatrics, 41*(3), 197–198.

Anbar, R. D. (2003). Perspectives of patients with cystic fibrosis regarding the long-term utility of hypnosis (abstract). *Pediatric Pulmonology Supplement, 25,* 267.

Anbar, R. D. (2014). Self-hypnosis as a complementary airway clearance technique in patients with cystic fibrosis (abstract). *American Journal of Respiratory and Critical Care Medicine, 189,* A4682.

Anbar, R. D., & Geisler, S. C. (2005). Identification of children who may benefit from self-hypnosis at a pediatric pulmonary center. *BMC Pediatrics, 5*(1), 6. doi:10.1186/1471-2431-5-6

Anbar, R. D., & Hall, H. R. (2012). What is a functional respiratory disorder? In R. Anbar (Ed.), *Functional respiratory disorders: When respiratory symptoms do not respond to pulmonary treatment* (pp. 3–17). New York, NY: Humana Press. doi:10.1007/978-1-61779-857-3_1

Anbar, R. D., & Murthy, V. V. (2010). Reestablishment of hope as an intervention for a patient with cystic fibrosis awaiting lung transplantation. *Journal of Alternative and Complementary Medicine, 16*(9), 1007–1010. doi:10.1089/acm.2010.0107

Belsky, J., & Khanna, P. (1994). The effects of self-hypnosis for children with cystic fibrosis: A pilot study. *American Journal of Clinical Hypnosis, 36*(4), 282–292. doi:10.1080/00029157.1994.10403088

Cystic Fibrosis Foundation. (2014a). *About cystic fibrosis: Frequently asked questions.* Retrieved from http://www.cff.org/AboutCF/Faqs

Cystic Fibrosis Foundation. (2014b). Patient registry 2013 annual data report. Retrieved from http://www.cff.org

Gelfond, D., & Borowitz, D. (2013). Gastrointestinal complications of cystic fibrosis. *Clinical Gastroenterology and Hepatology: The Official Clinical Practice Journal of the American Gastroenterological Association, 11*(4), 333–342. doi:10.1016/j.cgh.2012.11.006

Homnick, D. N. (2012). Dyspnea. In R. Anbar (Ed.), *Functional respiratory disorders: When respiratory symptoms do not respond to pulmonary treatment* (pp. 67–87). New York, NY: Humana Press. doi:10.1007/978-1-61779-857-3_4

Kettler, L. J., Sawyer, S. M., Winefield, H. R., & Greville, H. W. (2002). Determinants of adherence in adults with cystic fibrosis. *Thorax, 57*(5), 459–464. doi.org/10.1136/thorax.57.5.459 .

Mattewal, A., & Subramanian, S. (2009). Sleep disturbances in cystic fibrosis. *Current Respiratory Medicine Reviews, 5*(4), 230–232. doi:10.2174/157339809790112401

Meyers, D. G., & Anbar, R. D. (2012). Functional aspects of an organic respiratory disorder: Cystic fibrosis. In R. Anbar (Ed.), *Functional respiratory disorders: When respiratory symptoms do not respond to pulmonary treatment* (pp. 19–47). New York, NY: Humana Press. doi:10.1007/978-1-61779-857-3_2

Mogayzel, P. J., & Flume, P. A. (2010). Update in cystic fibrosis 2009. *American Journal of Respiratory and Critical Care Medicine, 181*(6), 539–544. doi:10.1164/rccm.200912-1943UP

Rand, S., Hill, L., & Prasad, S. A. (2013). Physiotherapy in cystic fibrosis: Optimising techniques to improve outcomes. *Pediatric Respiratory Reviews, 14*(4), 263–269. doi:10.1016/j.prrv.2012.08.006

Smith, B. A., & Wood, B. L. (2007). Psychological factors affecting disease activity in children and adolescents with cystic fibrosis: Medical adherence as a mediator. *Current Opinion in Pediatrics, 19*(5), 553–558. doi:10.1097/MOP.0b013e3282ef480a

Dental Applications

Ashley Goodman and Gabor Filo

Hypnosis as an analgesic and anesthetic has had a long history of application in dentistry. In March 1952, the American Hypnodontic Society formally defined *hypnodontics* as: "That science which deals with the study and application of controlled suggestion and/or hypnosis as applied to dentistry; it is that science which teaches the patient to use his or her innate abilities in order to make him or her more amenable to various dental procedures" (Moss, 1952). While in today's dental world it is rarely employed as a sole anesthetic, hypnosis can be a very important adjunctive or alternative method for managing pain and anxiety. Also, occasionally, patients do present with medical concerns or psychological ones in which they would prefer to, or must, avoid chemical anesthesia of any sort. As in all aspects of clinical interventions, careful patient selection is important. In the use of hypnosis to manage dental pain or anxiety, this may include assessment of mental status and determination of hypnotizability.

Another application of hypnosis in dentistry is in the control of gagging. Gagging, or retching, which is a more apt descriptor of the experience, is a hindrance to both patient and dentist. Hypnosis has been used successfully to control it. Hypnosis and its core paradigm, principles, and techniques offer the dental clinician a method by which patients may experience more comfort and tolerate dental procedures better.

Also, hypnosis may be of benefit in treatment of bruxism. Bruxism is a complex dental problem that falls within the domains of psychological issues, purely dentition-related ones, and sleep disorders. From the dental perspective, it is usually addressed from the constellation of temporomandibular disorders. Hypnosis has been applied to aspects of bruxism by many practitioners. The applications proposed by Erickson (Rossi & Ryan, 1985) and Somer (1997), for example, are concurrent with the state of science at the time and from the perspective of the particular practitioner. The clinician's art requires that the correct diagnosis be determined to apply the best hypnotic intervention. As the science expands, bruxism as a part of disordered sleep—specifically apnea—may be best utilized as in denture adaptation. Namely, it should be used to help the patient accept and adapt to his or her continuous positive airway pressure (CPAP) machines or his or her mandibular advancement appliances. It would be foolhardy, if not lethal, to remove or constrain the symptom of bruxing. If physiological etiologies have been ruled out by appropriate examination and diagnosis, then the psychological aspect may be addressed. Whether this falls into the dental scope of practice is jurisdictionally determined.

Hemorrhage control is one of the more impressive aspects of hypnodontics. One of the authors of this chapter (GF), some 30 years ago, had a patient with a tooth that had perforated into the alveolus. he had dental fear issues, we had used hypnosis to give him control. The author asked him to turn off the bleeding at the height of the alveolar crest, like a spigot. Amazingly, the clot formed as requested and in much faster time than anticipated. If the author had ever had doubts, this eliminated them. Saliva control is similar and can be had by appropriate imagery and metaphor. As physiological control goes, it is less dramatic than the control of bleeding.

Also, hypnosis has been used with habit management in children and adults. These include negative ones—such as digit sucking addressed by Erickson, bruxism, the chewing of foreign objects—to motivating a positive one (which must surely be a genetic trait) of flossing (Clarke, 1997; Kelly, 1990; Rossi & Ryan, 1985).

Patient management, from the dentist and staff perspective, is critical. The paradigm in most locales is a single dentist, multiple auxiliaries, or

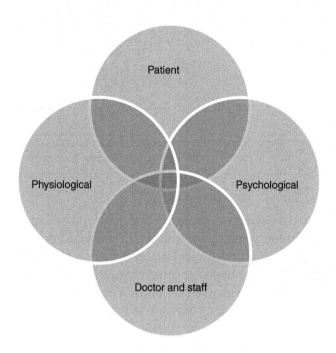

FIGURE 21.1 Integrative physiological and psychological domains in dental care.

small multiclinician clinics. Although there are hospital dental clinics, they are not prevalent. Thus, besides being direct patient care facilities, the average dental clinic is also a small business regardless of whether the funding for care is fee for service or some variant of an insurance-provider program. Time is leveraged by utilizing a variety of auxiliaries alongside the doctor to mitigate the ever-increasing overheads associated with running dental facilities. There is an integration of both psychological and physiological domains associated with pain, and these are relevant to both the patient and the doctor and medical staff. As Figure 21.1 indicates, there is an overlap of the domains. The most important feature of this diagram is the inseparability of the domains—the mind–body whole applies to all of the people in the dental interaction and the interaction is a constant flux. It is an ebb and flow of mutual influence.

RESEARCH

Dental anxiety, fear, and phobia studies show patient avoidance in the general populace range from 10% to 40% depending on the study. A Canadian study evaluating the need for

dental general anesthesia demonstrated 9.8% of the respondents (out of 1,100 surveyed) had some fear, while 5.5% had severe fear (Chanpong, Haas, & Locker, 2005). This encompasses the mildly trepidatious to the white knucklers. These states of anxiety have both negative physiological and psychological consequences.

Neutral hypnosis without any goal-directed suggestions has been shown to have positive benefits. Jensen et al. (2006) found that this included an increase in positive affect ("increased relaxation," "well-being," "acceptance," and a "better attitude"), decreased negative affect (stress, anxiety, and depression), social benefits, increased energy, satisfaction that therapy could be provided at home, surprise at how easy self-hypnosis was, significant positive impact on life (increased self-awareness, provided meditation practice, follow-up calls helpful, increased focus, "all natural"), and lowered blood pressure. Improved sleep and a ". . . profound implication in every aspect of my life" were also noted in their small-scale study. They also noted pain reduction, an increased sense of control over pain, and a sense of having a new option or tool for pain management.

Casiglia and coworkers denoted a cardioprotective feature of hypnosis in dental anesthesia. Trigeminal pain, as they state, is associated with vasodilation and bradycardia, which can be mitigated with hypnosis (Casiglia et al., 2012). Hence, it has value in the prevention and mitigation of syncope (Frost, 1959).

Eitner and coworkers used a novel audio pillow with recorded hypnotherapy instructions and music for anxiolysis during dental implant surgery. They found the results promising (Eitner, Sokol, Wichmann, Bauer, & Engels, 2011). Further study of recorded hypnotic tapes during oral and maxillofacial surgery by Hermes and coworkers found that hypnosis, with good patient compliance, was reliable and standardizable (Hermes, Truebger, Hakim, & Sieg, 2005).

Pedodontic applications of hypnosis have also received attention. A literature search ended with the equivocal conclusion that the research was wanting, but "the advantages of using hypnotic elements and hypnosis in pediatric dentistry are evident" (Peretz, Bercovich, & Blumer, 2013). Huet's group concluded that hypnosis is certainly effective for anxiety and dental anesthesia with children (Huet, Lucas-Polomeni, Robert, Sixou, & Wodey, 2011). Adinolfi and Gava came to the supportive conclusion that "children who receive self-hypnosis trainings achieve significantly greater improvements in their physical health, quality of life, and self-esteem" (Adinolfi & Gava, 2013).

DiClementi, Deffenbaugh, and Jackson (2007) attempted to determine whether hypnotizability, absorption, and negative cognitions could be used as prognosticators of dental anxiety. They found them to be predictors of dental anxiety and that hypnosis may be of benefit to some, but not all, patients (DiClementi et al., 2007).

This finding was consistent with the research by Hilgard and Hilgard (1975) and the following generalities about reducing pain with hypnotic suggestions in the laboratory and clinical settings:

- Pain can be diminished with hypnotic suggestions of analgesia.
- The degree of reduction correlates to the measured hypnotic susceptibility.
- Highly hypnotizable subjects can reduce pain more in hypnosis than in the waking state with suggestion alone.
- For very low hypnotizable subjects, hypnotic suggestions are akin to placebo.
- Hypnotic suggestions are applicable to many painful conditions.

CASE STUDY

Bob, a 48-year-old Caucasian male, was referred to the practice by an otolaryngologist. At the time of referral, he had a massive right-sided facial cellulitis for which he was to spend a week in the hospital receiving intravenous antibiotic therapy. He had a history of dental avoidance that had caught up to him with the abscessing of tooth 13 (the upper right cuspid [Federation Dentaire Internationale tooth coding is used throughout]). His reasons for using hypnosis as a modality were threefold: first, he wished to avoid pain; second, he considered the needle as painful as dental treatment; and finally, he wished to "control the flight or fight response to dental procedures." Bob was reluctantly open to the use of a local anesthetic as an adjunct.

Intraoral examination revealed a mutilated dentition with bilateral posterior edentulism (tooth loss). Four teeth had apical pathology, while three of these were only root stumps. Bob had generalized periodontitis (gum disease) and decay in his remaining teeth. The presented dental treatment plan consisted of root canal therapy, a buildup and crown for tooth 13, extraction of the root stumps, root planing and scaling to restore some health to his gums, and seven restorations. Following specialty periodontal treatment, partial dentures would replace the missing posteriors.

Hypnosis intervention was accomplished in three sessions with an audio recording being made of each session. At the second session, arm levitation was employed for induction. He was also introduced to analgesia/anesthesia for trance ratification. Both of these techniques were chosen to validate to Bob that he was able to control his physiology. During the third session, which was also his first dental treatment appointment, ego strengthening was given along with posthypnotic suggestions for healing and comfort.

We accomplished, in one very long appointment, root canal therapy on tooth 13, all his restorations, and the extraction of the three root stumps. All of this occurred uneventfully, as did his posttreatment period. Bob has been a good ongoing continuing care patient since. He consistently utilizes self-hypnosis at all his appointments.

TRANSCRIPTS

Relaxing a patient begins the moment the patient enters the office. The décor should be muted and welcoming (earth tones), rather than sensory-stimulating, such as bold reds and oranges. An open reception area is preferred where patients may be greeted by a pleasant first-impression receptionist with a smile and inviting tone. In addition, the dental nurse should greet and escort the patient to the treatment area, which should afford the patient his or her privacy while still imparting a feeling of openness, comfort, and cleanliness. Suggestions for relaxation during hypnosis are usually provided.

"With each slow deep breath, you might feel wave upon wave of comfort, relaxation, and security

rise from the bottoms of your feet . . . to your knees, waist, tummy, chest . . . along your arms to the very tips of your fingers. All the muscles in your neck, allowing your head to comfortably balance, as the muscles in your face relax . . . totally. Wave upon wave of a very comfortable, relaxing, and secure feeling as you allow your mind to take leave of your body as though you were in a wonderful dream drawing your mind to a place that is your own, comfortable, relaxing, and very secure. Enjoy."

"Shortly we will be returning to the present, but you will remember this as a very pleasant, comfortable, relaxing, and secure experience; one that you will want to return to. You will associate this feeling with being in the comfortable treatment chair and will automatically return to this comfortable, relaxing, and secure feeling by sitting in the treatment chair; taking a few slow, deep breaths; allowing your eyes to close; and setting your mind free to return to your dreamlike place and feelings of comfort, relaxation, and security.

Method	Comment
Have the patient take a deep breath and close his or her eyes. The patient is asked to "pretend" that the eyelids are so heavy that he or she is unable to open them. "They just won't work!" When the patient is certain of this, he or she should "try." When failure sets in, ask the patient to relax the eyes and open them. Repeat three times in fair succession. Each time have relaxation doubling or tripling; mention may be made of the increased comfort. Last time, let the eyes remain closed and move on. . . . Test degree of physical relaxation by lifting the patient's hand a few inches and dropping it.	Automatic relaxation with exhalation. This is the beginning of an eyelid catalepsy. A challenge that will fail to reinforce the process. Fractionation to ensure depth. Once the process has started, all suggestions deepen. Hand should fall into lap without effort.
Next request the patient to count out loud backward from 100. With each number double the relaxation and comfort. At the number 98, forget the numbers. If the patient has not forgotten, then have him or her "turn off the lights" or "clean them off a blackboard."	Further deepening. Eliciting amnesia further intensifies trance. You can ask the patient to verbalize the answer, let him or her know he or she can speak when queried.
Let the patient know that you are going to stroke the back of his or her hand three times. With each stroke, the patient's relaxation doubles as he or she notes a change in the feeling of the hand. Mention that the sensation will become more profound with each stroke. Suggestions of numbness, like making a snowball bare handed, are useful.	The beginnings of glove anesthesia. Intensification of the anesthesia. Any metaphor including injection of a local anesthetic may work if there are no contraindications (e.g., needle phobic or allergy to local anesthetic).
Ask the patient to "remain just as he or she is and open the eyes." Have the patient compare both of his or her hands. In the old days, a needle would be inserted into the back of the hand with the glove anesthesia; today, a pinch is used to ratify the anesthesia. Have the patient close his or her eyes.	Eliciting eyes open trance. Dissociation pointed out. Trance and anesthesia ratification.
Ask the patient, "If you have experienced physical relaxation, do you wish to experience mental relaxation as well'?" Once an affirmative is received, accompany the patient on an elevator going down three floors to the basement of relaxation. Once there in the basement, the doors can open to a "safe room." The patient can be realerted using whatever method is comfortable.	Permission and suggestion of deeper state possibility— eliciting anticipation. Deepening. Arriving at Esdaile coma, or somnambular or plenary trance. Counting out is good to ensure full alerting.

Right now, it is time to return to the present on the count of three; one . . . two . . . three."

Hypnosis may also be used to facilitate analgesia as was done in Bob's case report in the previous section. An outline of this method and commentary is provided as it should be adapted to an individual patient's needs and preferences. The elegance of the method is its versatility and adaptability—the clinician's imagination is the only limiting factor. The preceding table (adapted from the originator, Dr. Dave Elman) provides methods of intervention and commentary. Dave Elman's induction has been mentioned in both case studies. Rather than relating the entire script verbatim, the framework is described and parsed.

Central to providing the most meaningful suggestions for the patient is, naturally, the dental professional's ability to obtain a good history, especially concerning those events that may have been the precipitant of the gagging episodes, and providing follow-up positive reinforcement for success.

Progressive desensitization along with hypnosis is a valuable tool for gaggers. While gagging often relates to an inability to tolerate dentures (Barsby, 1994), we often receive referrals from orthodontic offices that have difficulty taking impressions for study models, usually on children. Children are the easiest patients to treat with hypnosis due to their vivid imaginations and ability to concentrate (Kohen & Olness, 2011) reaching an apex of suggestibility around 9 years of age, with a gradual decline until age 15 through the early 20s when there is a leveling off. Progressive desensitization (PD) is made into a game where the children are provided a small baggie of alginate impression material, some tongue blades (mixing sticks), and appropriate disposable impression trays. A light trance is brought on with progressive relaxation with the parents' consent. Just a small amount of mixed alginate is placed in the maxillary anterior tray. The tray is held and controlled by the child with the dentist merely directing the child's hand by holding the wrist, along with providing some distracting banter; this may include placing a special spoon with warm ice cream in the mouth but stating it is not to be swallowed. The dentist assists the child in removing the impression tray

with a great deal of positive reinforcement as to how well he or she did as the child is brought back to the present (realerting). Instructions are given to practice at home with continuing positive reinforcement as just a bit more alginate is placed from the anterior back, taking care not to overload the tray. The child and parent return to the office in a week and a working impression is taken while assisting the child to hold the tray. Sometimes, the first attempt at the office becomes "practice" if insufficient for the working model. The unpoured impressions are packed up in a baggie with a moist paper towel to be delivered by the patient immediately to the orthodontics office where continuing positive reinforcement is provided.

CONCLUSION

Hypnosis has many applications in dentistry with adults and children. Research is generally supportive of the use of hypnosis for managing pain, reducing anxiety, managing gagging, and performing other applications in dentistry. In addition, the use of hypnosis includes careful use of language, both during hypnosis and during informal interaction. In dentistry, perhaps the aim, as is often stated by many, is to become hypnotic. This means to be aware of the factors in a patient encounter and respond appropriately. Thus, formal hypnosis is usually replaced by hypnotic technique in the course of communication.

Listen to the "representational mode" used by the patient and communicate back in the same mode. The most common modes are (a) visual—I see what you mean; (b) auditory—I hear what you're saying; and (c) kinesthetic—I feel that I understand you. However, words comprise only approximately 7% of interpersonal communication. Voice inflexion and tonality comprise 56% and body language another 37%. Coining suggestions as positives rather than negative concepts will enhance the subject's response. Eliminate the word *try*. Delivery of suggestions is more inclusive than merely the content of the suggestion—it includes pace and expression, rhythm, repetition, alliteration, and assonance. There is the choice between authoritarian and permissive suggestions that may be implications, questions, yes sets, embedded suggestions, and illusions of choice—the double bind, to superficially enumerate the possibilities (Simons, 2007). Hypnosis may be provided by the dentist or a psychologist (or other health care professional with hypnosis expertise) and may be included in the dental patient management and treatment referral team.

REFERENCES

Adinolfi, B., & Gava, N. (2013). Controlled outcome studies of child clinical hypnosis. *Acta Biomedica: Atenei Parmensis, 84*(2), 94–97.

Barsby, M. J. (1994). Hypnosis in the management of "gagging" and intolerance to dentures. *British Dental Journal, 176*(3), 97–102.

Brown, D. C. (2009). *Advances in the use of hypnosis for medicine, dentistry and pain prevention/management.* Bethel, CT: Crown House Publishing.

Casiglia, E., Tikhonoff, V., Giordano, N., Andreatta, E., Regaldo, G., Tosello, M. T., . . . Facco, E. (2012). Measured outcomes with hypnosis as an experimental tool in a cardiovascular physiology laboratory. *International Journal of Clinical and Experimental Hypnosis, 60*(2), 241–261.

Chanpong, B., Haas, D. A., & Locker, D. (2005). Need and demand for sedation or general anesthesia in dentistry: A national survey of the Canadian population. *Anesthesia Progress, 52*(1), 3–11.

Clarke, J. H. (1997). The role of hypnosis in treating bruxism. In M. Mershtedt (Ed.), *Hypnosis in dentistry, hypnosis international monographs 3* (pp. 79–85). Munich: M. E. G. Stiftung.

DiClementi, J. D., Deffenbaugh, J., & Jackson, D. (2007). Hypnotizability, absorption and negative cognitions as predictors of dental anxiety: Two pilot studies. *Journal of the American Dental Association (1939), 138*(9), 1242–1250.

Eitner, S., Sokol, B., Wichmann, M., Bauer, J., & Engels, D. (2011). Clinical use of a novel audio pillow with recorded hypnotherapy instructions and music for anxiolysis during dental implant surgery: A prospective study. *International Journal of Clinical and Experimental Hypnosis, 59*(2), 180–197.

Eli, I. (1992). *Oral psychophysiology stress, pain, and behaviour in dental care.* Boca Raton, FL: CRC Press.

Frost, T. W. (1959). *Hypnosis in general dental practice.* Chicago, IL: Year Book Publishers.

Hermes, D., Truebger, D., Hakim, S. G., & Sieg, P. (2005). Tape recorded hypnosis in oral and maxillofacial surgery-basics and first clinical experience. *Journal of Cranio-Maxillo-Facial Surgery:*

Official Publication of the European Association for Cranio-Maxillo-Facial Surgery, 33(2), 123–129.

Hilgard, E., & Hilgard, J. (1994). *Hypnosis in the Relief of Pain.* Los Altos, CA: William Kaufmann.

Holden, A. (2012). The art of suggestion: The use of hypnosis in dentistry. *British Dental Journal, 212*(11), 549–551.

Huet, A., Lucas-Polomeni, M. M., Robert, J. C., Sixou, J. L., & Wodey, E. (2011). Hypnosis and dental anesthesia in children: A prospective controlled study. *International Journal of Clinical and Experimental Hypnosis, 59*(4), 424–440.

Jensen, M. P., Mcarthur, K. D., Barber, J., Hanley, M. A., Engel, J. M., Romano, J. M., . . . Patterson, D. R. (2006). Satisfaction with, and the beneficial side effects of, hypnotic analgesia. *International Journal of Clinical and Experimental Hypnosis, 54*(4), 432–447. doi:10.1080/00207140600856798

Kelly, K. A. (1990). Suggestions to promote flossing. In C. D. Hammond (Ed.), *Handbook of hypnotic suggestions and metaphors* (p. 185). New York, NY: W. W. Norton.

Kohen, D., & Olness, K. (2011). *Hypnosis and hypnotherapy with children* (4th ed.). New York, NY: Routledge.

Kohen, D., & Olness, K. (2011). *Hypnosis and hypnotherapy with children* (4th ed.). New York, NY: Routledge.

Landa, J. S. (1953). *The dynamics of psychosomatic dentistry.* Brooklyn, NY: Dental Items of Interest Publishing.

Lang, E. (2009). *Patient dedation without medication rapid rapport and quick hypnotic techniques.* Victoria, BC: Trafford Publishing.

McDonald, A. E. (1949). *Psychosomatics and hypnotism in dentistry.* New Orleans, LA: Andrew McDonald.

Merstedt, M. (1997). *Hypnosis in dentistry hypnosis international monographs 3.* Munich: M. E. G. Stiftung.

Moss, A. A. (1952). *Hypnodontics or hypnotism in dentistry.* Brooklyn, NY: Dental Items of Interest Publishing.

Mostofsky, D. F. (2006). *Behavioral dentistry.* Ames, IA: Blackwell Munksgaard.

Peretz, B., Bercovich, R., & Blumer, S. (2013). Using elements of hypnosis prior to or during pediatric dental treatment. *Pediatric Dentistry, 35*(1), 33–36.

Rossi, E. L., & Ryan, M. O. (1985). *Life reframing in hypnosis by Milton H. Erickson.* New York, NY: Irvington Publishers.

Ryan, E. J. (1946). *Psychobiologic foundations in dentistry.* Springfield, IL: Charles C. Thomas.

Shaw, S. I. (1958). *Clinical applications of hypnosis in dentistry.* Philadelphia, PA: W. B. Saunders.

Simons, D. P. (2007). *Hypnosis and communication in dental practice*. New Malden, Surrey: Quintessence Publishing.

Simpson, R., Goepferd, S., Ogesen, R., & Zach, G. (1985). *Hypnosis in dentistry: A handbook for clinincal use*. Springfield, IL: Charles C. Thomas.

Somer, E. (1997). Hypnobehavioral and hypnodynamic interventions in temporomandibular disorders. In M. Mehrstedt (Ed.), *Hypnosis in dentistry hypnosis international monographs 3* (pp. 87–98). Munich: M. E. G. Stiftung.

Wannemueller, A., Joehren, P., Haug, S., Hatting, M., Elsesser, K., & Sartory, G. (2011). A practice-based comparison of brief cognitive behavioural treatment, two kinds of hypnosis and general anaesthesia in dental phobia. *Psychotherapy and Psychosomatics*, *80*(3), 159–165. doi: 10.1159/000320977.

Diabetes Mellitus

Michelle Perfect

Diabetes mellitus is a cluster of metabolic disorders attributable to glucose (blood sugars in the body) dysregulation. Diagnosis of diabetes is based on lab results in duplicate of hemoglobin A1c (HbA1c) greater than or equal to 6.5%, or a fasting glucose test value of 126 mg/dL (Chiang, Kirkman, Laffel, & Peters, 2014; Kumar, Gupta, & Feldman, 2015).

Type 1 diabetes mellitus (T1DM) is an autoimmune disorder that destroys the beta cells in the pancreas. This destruction leads to the body's inability to produce insulin, a hormone that is needed to regulate blood glucose (sugars). Symptoms that often appear upon onset of diabetes include frequent urination, polyuria, excessive thirst, weight loss, and elevated glucose levels (Chiang et al., 2014). For onset in childhood, these symptoms often present rapidly, whereas in adults, symptoms appear more gradually (Chiang et al., 2014). Although not always, it is typically diagnosed in childhood.

Type 2 diabetes mellitus (T2DM) is attributable to incremental deficits in insulin production leading to insulin resistance. Although it is sometimes difficult to discern if a child has T1DM or T2DM, one of the diagnostic indicators is positive glutamic acid decarboxylase or insulinoma-associated antibodies (Dabelea et al., 2014; Kumar et al., 2015). Approximately 85% of individuals with T1DM are positive for these antibodies. Although there are many with T1DM who are not positive, the prevalence of T1DM is just under 2 children per every 1,000. In an epidemiological study, Caucasian youth had the highest rates of diabetes, with approximately 2.55 children diagnosed per 1,000. These rates show a significant increase over a 10-year period. These rates correspond to roughly 78,000 children domestically and internationally being diagnosed with T1DM each year (Dabelea et al., 2014). In adults, approximately 15,000 are diagnosed annually in the United States (Juvenile Diabetes Research Foundation, n.d.).

T2DM is increasing in children, but the rates are still lower than T1DM. For instance, Dabelea et al. (2014) reported that the prevalence was 0.49 children per 1,000 diagnosed with T2DM. The rates are higher in older adolescents.

DIABETES MANAGEMENT

The crux of diabetes management is regulating glucose (blood sugars) in the body. All individuals with T1DM require exogenous insulin coupled with dietary regulation and physical activity. They must monitor their sugars and count carbohydrate intake to determine how much additional insulin should be administered (Perfect & Jaramillo, 2012). More frequent blood glucose monitoring has been found to predict lower HbA1c values (Bui, Perlman, & Daneman, 2005). Individuals with T2DM may take insulin, but they typically take oral medication to reduce insulin resistance. The focus is also on weight management, including diet and exercise. Assessment and monitoring of those with diabetes should include accessing resources, evaluating mental health concerns, and glucose monitoring. Treatment should be individualized and address any areas of concern identified through the screening.

The need to address psychosocial factors associated with diabetes is also supported by literature. Accordingly, prevalence data suggest that as many as one third to one half of adolescents diagnosed with diabetes experience a variety of mental health problems, which is considerably higher than the general population (Blanz, Rensch-Riemann, Fritz-Sigmund, & Schmidt, 1993; Kovacs, Goldston, Obrosky, & Bonar, 1997; Kovacs, Mukerji, Iyengar, & Drash, 1996; Kovacs, Obrosky, Goldston, & Drash, 1997; Northam, Matthews, Anderson, Cameron, & Werther, 2005; Reynolds

& Helgeson, 2011). In the absence of adequate treatment, these symptoms persist or worsen as they transition into adulthood (Bryden, Dunger, Mayou, Peveler, & Neil, 2003).

Although there is currently no evidence-based guidelines regarding sleep as part of diabetes management, research has also shown that short sleep duration, inconsistent sleep, less time in deep sleep, and sleep-disordered breathing each predict higher glucose levels in youth with T1DM (Perfect, 2014; Perfect et al., 2012; Villa et al., 2000). Further, sleep insufficiency is a risk factor for developing T2DM, and sleep disturbances relate to poorer glucose regulation (Knutson, Ryden, Mander, & Cauter, 2006). Thus, sleep should be evaluated and, if found to be a problem, targeted accordingly.

As for T2DM, some individuals also take insulin, but the primary treatment is medication to assist with insulin productivity, diet, and exercise. Overweight status, particularly obesity, both increases the risk of T2DM and contributes to comorbidities. Further, it has been noted that randomized clinical trials have demonstrated that lifestyle interventions coupled with medication can mitigate the chances of being diagnosed with T2DM as well.

HYPNOSIS AND DIABETES

Several aspects of diabetes management, including weight control, stress management, exercise, and sleep hygiene, have their own body of research or anecdotal clinical evidence to support hypnosis as a component of targeting these areas of health and wellness. Thus, this chapter briefly summarizes each to demonstrate the potential components that hypnosis may address for individuals with diabetes. For purposes of this chapter, we adopt the updated definition of hypnosis: "A state of consciousness involving focused attention and reduced peripheral awareness characterized by an enhanced capacity for response to suggestion" (Elkins, Barabasz, Council, & Spiegel, 2015, p. 6). Such a definition works well for individuals with diabetes for several reasons. First, diabetes is a chronic medical condition that involves considerable self-care. Blood glucose monitoring, medication administration, and lifestyle behaviors, such as physical activity, diet,

and sleep, are all components of diabetes management that require time, attention, motivation, and consistency.

Compliance and Motivation

Management of diabetes is, in part, developmental in that through early adolescence, parents considerably oversee and monitor children's diabetes. As youth move into adolescence, their compliance declines. The downward shift in compliance levels is partly due to the increased autonomy afforded to them and the expectations of independence. There are also competing interests, such as wanting to fit in with their peers and missing important class time. Adolescents often perceive that family members and health care providers pressure them (Croom et al., 2011). Thus, including hypnosis as part of a wellness package may allow the adolescent to feel more in control and be more open to suggestions by these adults. Accordingly, in a small study (n = 7), adolescents participated in a hypnotic intervention that involved both clinician-induced hypnosis and self-hypnosis to increase compliance in testing, medication usage, and dietary intake. The authors utilized hypnosis to empower the adolescents and give them a sense of security and control (Ratner, Gross, Casas, & Castells, 1990).

Stress Management

In addition to the developmental changes in diabetes management, individuals across the life span with diabetes have been found to have significantly more stress than those without a chronic medical condition (Lloyd, Smith, & Weinger, 2005). Further, stress both in subjective reporting as well as physiological markers, such as cortisol levels, have been linked with poorer coping and sleep in individuals with diabetes (Perfect, Elkins, Lyle-Lahroud, & Posey, 2010). Thus, interventions that aim to increase diabetes self-care often target psychosocial factors and stress management. With regard to stress management, hypnotic relaxation may allow the individual to feel in control or confident in his or her own abilities (Diment, 1991). The impact of hypnosis on these areas is important because self-mastery and optimistic attitudes relate to lower glucose levels (Perfect & Jaramillo, 2012). It may also reduce anxieties related to diabetes, such as risk of blood sugars going too low or fear of the needle (Diment, 1991).

Weight Control and Eating Behaviors

Several authors have addressed the potential for hypnosis to assist with weight loss for youth who are overweight or obese (Elkins & Perfect, 2008; Xu & Cardeña, 2007). Although there are limited data for hypnosis as the exclusive intervention to target weight loss (Stewart, 2005), when included in tandem with behavioral management techniques (e.g., covert modeling, self-control and monitoring) and cognitive behavioral therapy, some studies have found additional and sustained weight loss among individuals in the condition that included hypnotic suggestions (Barabasz & Spiegel, 1989; Bolocofsky, Spinler, & Coulthard-Morris, 1985; Bornstein & Devine, 1980; Davis & Dawson, 1980). One study supported the importance of individualizing hypnotic suggestions rather than using a generic script (Barabasz & Spiegel, 1989). Further, studies support that hypnosis as a coping tool to deal with stress may contribute to weight loss rather than suggestion tied to food (Stradling, Roberts, Wilson, & Lovelock, 1998). A major limitation is that recent empirical studies are lacking, and more recent data as to the effectiveness of hypnosis as an adjunct to medical and therapeutic interventions are needed.

CASE EXAMPLE

Given the preliminary research support and anecdotal evidence for hypnosis for compliance and motivation, stress management, and weight control, hypnotic relaxation has the potential to effectively augment current treatments in diabetes management (Perfect & Elkins, 2010). "Jessica" is a 13-year-old Caucasian adolescent girl with a history of T1DM, first diagnosed when she was 8 years old. Her body mass index was at the 90th percentile and her pretreatment HbA1C was 9.8%. She received daily insulin via a pump. At the start of treatment, her glucose levels averaged 250, but often reached as high as 350. She had been hospitalized for ketoacidosis three months earlier and had ketones in her urine two weeks prior to

coming in for treatment. She denied experimenting with drugs or alcohol.

Jessica lived with both biological parents. Jessica experienced stress in school work and although she identified a best friend, she noted that she wished she would be invited to more events and outings with peers. She had difficulties with sleep, averaging only 7.5 hours of sleep per night. She typically went to bed by 11 p.m., but woke up at 6 a.m. for school on school nights and midnight to 8 a.m. or 8:30 a.m. on nonschool nights. She indicated she fell asleep right away when she did go to sleep.

Jessica had some difficulty with eating bouts, but not to an excessive degree. She ate when she was stressed. She and her mom reported that she "forgot" to test blood sugars after she ate the additional food and therefore did not adjust her insulin to accommodate increased carbohydrate-rich foods. She did not engage in frequent or rigorous physical activities because she felt self-conscious and reported not enjoying exercise.

Baseline data included a one-week sleep diary, an actigraphy (accelerometer worn on the wrist that measures sleep–wake activity), and the Perceived Stress Scale (PSS; Cohen, Kamarck, & Mermelstein, 1983). The diary indicated that Jessica slept an average of 7.3 hours, whereas the actigraphy showed 6.7 hours, which is less than the recommended 9 or more hours for adolescents. Her sleep efficiency (number of minutes reported sleeping divided by the total number of minutes reported in bed) was 89%, which was considered to be adequate. Average sleep onset latency (the time it takes to fall asleep; SOL) was 14.0 minutes. Her PSS score was 29 (out of a possible 40); higher scores indicate more stress.

Jessica's treatment plan included goals to regularly and consistently manage her diabetes, make healthy food choices, decrease levels of stress as evidenced by decreased scores on the PSS, and increase sleep duration as reflected in her and her mom's self-report. A combination of cognitive behavioral therapy with hypnotic relaxation (Perfect & Elkins, 2010) was the primary modality. As part of the stress management—to foster positive expectancies and self-esteem and empower Jessica to self-monitor her own diabetes—hypnotic relaxation was employed. Thus, the focus of the case for this chapter is the components of hypnosis, rather than the complete intervention.

Jessica was asked to sit in a recliner and focus her attention on a spot on the wall (*focusing attention*). Suggestions were given that she could become more relaxed and that she could imagine "a wave of relaxation" spreading from her head down to her feet (*suggestions for relaxation*). She was instructed to "let her eyelids close" as she relaxed her body (*eye closure*). Initial imagery to facilitate a deeper state of relaxation included a description of her walking down a staircase and "with each step going deeper, relaxed" (*fading of the generalized reality orientation* and *deepening suggestions*). There was also the suggestion that she imagine herself sinking into the cushions of a chair on a warm summer day and to feel the sensations associated with the heat of the sun and the breeze (*mental imagery*).

Jessica was then provided with suggestions for alerting, and was given time to come out of the hypnotic induction at her own pace (*alerting*). She was asked to describe images that she perceived as relaxing. She reported that she could envision a large movie theater, climbing down steps and smelling the butter of the popcorn and hearing the crunch of people eating. Jessica was provided with a tape with a hypnotic relaxation induction. She was also provided with a *posthypnotic suggestion* that her stress would be reduced and she would be able to remember to check her blood sugars with daily practice of hypnosis.

During the next session, Jessica reported that she was using hypnosis daily right before going to sleep and that she and her mom had set a bedtime of 10 p.m. She still was able to fall asleep right away. To foster a more individualized approach, the same framework was used, but this time, the suggestions included Jessica walking down the stairs into a movie theater, with each step becoming deeper relaxed. She was asked to imagine the fragrance of the popcorn. It was suggested that she feel a floating sensation as she sat on a chair in the theater that reclined slightly and to notice the gentle rocking of the chair (*mental imagery* and *dissociation*). At the end of the session, Jessica and her mom were given instructions on self-hypnosis and encouraged to practice hypnosis without using the tape.

During the next session, the focus was on monitoring blood sugars and barriers to compliance. Jessica had increased her blood sugar checks from twice a day to consistently four or five times. Cognitive behavioral approaches were incorporated to counter some distorted thinking related to "I am the only one who has to do this," "It is not fair,"

"I will never be able to be like normal teenagers." As part of the effort to change her way of thinking, the hypnotic induction included suggestions about eating and self-care, such as "each day you will take good care of yourself by managing your diabetes.... Even now visualize and see in your mind remembering and following the doctors' instructions about when to check and how to use your insulin—having a feeling of accomplishment and control as you care for yourself." In consultation with the diabetes educator and considering her own personal goals, suggestions for better food choices were also provided.

TRANSCRIPT

An example of the type of hypnotic suggestions for addressing the behaviors related to good management of diabetes is provided.

"You will find that you are making good choices about foods. You will enjoy taking care of yourself by having a good breakfast of protein and fruit. You will be able to reach your goal of resisting urges to eat salty foods and sweets in between meals and you will be satisfied with less fatty and sugary foods at meals."

CONCLUSION

Jessica completed a total of four sessions and two phone call check-ins over a two-month period. Her stress levels did decrease (PSS score from 29 to 19) and sleep duration on both the diary and actigraphy increased by 37 and 29 minutes, respectively. Hypnosis can be a very beneficial adjunctive treatment for patients with diabetes. Targets for hypnotic intervention include dietary changes, improved sleep, weight control and motivation, compliance with medical treatments, and stress management.

REFERENCES

Barabasz, M., & Spiegel, D. (1989). Hypnotizability and weight loss in obese subjects. *International Journal of Eating Disorders, 8*(3), 335–341. doi:10.1002/1098-108X(198905)8:3<335::AID-EAT2260080309>3.0.CO;2-O

Blanz, B. J., Rensch-Riemann, B. S., Fritz-Sigmund, D. I., & Schmidt, M. H. (1993). IDDM is a risk factor for adolescent psychiatric disorders. *Diabetes Care*, *16*(12), 1579–1587.

Bolocofsky, D. N., Spinler, D., & Coulthard-Morris, L. (1985). Effectiveness of hypnosis as an adjunct to behavioral weight management. *Journal of Clinical Psychology*, *41*(1), 35–40.

Bornstein, P. H., & Devine, D. A. (1980). Covert modeling-hypnosis in the treatment of obesity. *Psychotherapy: Theory, Research & Practice*, *17*(3), 272–276. doi:10.1037/h0085922

Bryden, K. S., Dunger, D. B., Mayou, R. A., Peveler, R. C., & Neil, H. A. (2003). Poor prognosis of young adults with type 1 diabetes: A longitudinal study. *Diabetes Care*, *26*(4), 1052–1057.

Bui, H., Perlman, K., & Daneman, D. (2005). *Self-monitoring of blood glucose in children and teens with diabetes*. Pediatric Diabetes, 6(1), 50–62. doi:10.1111/j.1399-543X.2005.00095.x

Chiang, J. L., Kirkman, M. S., Laffel, L. M., & Peters, A. L., Type 1 Diabetes Sourcebook Authors. (2014). Type 1 diabetes through the life span: A position statement of the American Diabetes Association. *Diabetes Care*, *37*(7), 2034–2054. doi:10.2337/dc14-1140

Cohen, S., Kamarck, T., & Mermelstein, R. (1983). A global measure of perceived stress. *Journal of Health and Social Behavior*, *24*(4), 385–396.

Croom, A., Wiebe, D. J., Berg, C. A., Lindsay, R., Donaldson, D., Foster, C., . . . Swinyard, M. T. (2011). Adolescent and parent perceptions of patient-centered communication while managing type 1 diabetes. *Journal of Pediatric Psychology*, *36*(2), 206–215.

Dabelea, D., Mayer-Davis, E. J., Saydah, S., Imperatore, G., Linder, B., Divers, J., & Hamman, R. F. (2014). Prevalence of type 1 and type 2 diabetes among children and adolescents from 2001 to 2009. *Journal of the American Medical Association*, *311*(17), 1778–1786. doi:10.1001/jama.2014.3201

Davis, S., & Dawson, J. G. (1980). Hypnotherapy for weight control. *Psychological Reports*, *46*(1), 311–314. doi:10.2466/pr0.1980.46.1.311

Diment, A. D. (1991). Uses of hypnosis in diabetes-related stress management counseling. *Australian Journal of Clinical & Experimental Hypnosis*, *19*, 97–101.

Elkins, G. R., Barabasz, A. F., Council, J. R., & Spiegel, D. (2015). Advancing research and practice: The revised APA Division 30 definition of hypnosis. *International Journal of Clinical Experimental Hypnosis*, *53*, 1–9.

Elkins, G., & Perfect, M. (2008). Hypnosis and health-compromising behaviors. In M. Nash & A. Barnier (Eds.), *Oxford handbook of clinical hypnosis*. Oxford: Oxford University Press. doi:10.1093/oxfordhb/9780198570097.013.0023

Juvenile Diabetes Research Foundation. (n.d.). *Type 1 diabetes facts*. Retrieved from http://jdrf.org/about-jdrf/fact-sheets/type-1-diabetes-facts

Knutson, K. L., Ryden, A. M., Mander, B. A., & Cauter, E. V. (2006). Role of sleep duration and quality in the risk and severity of type 2 diabetes mellitus. *Archives of Internal Medicine*, *166*, 1768–1774.

Kovacs, M., Goldston, D., Obrosky, D. S., & Bonar, L. K. (1997). Psychiatric disorders in youths with IDDM: Rates and risk factors. *Diabetes Care*, *20*, 36–44.

Kovacs, M., Mukerji, P., Iyengar, S., & Drash, A. (1996). Psychiatric disorder and metabolic control among youths with IDDM: A longitudinal study. *Diabetes Care*, *19*, 318–323.

Kovacs, M., Obrosky, D. S., Goldston, D., & Drash, A. (1997). Major depressive disorder in youths with IDDM: A controlled prospective study of course and outcome. *Diabetes Care*, *20*, 45–51.

Kumar, R. B., Gupta, M., & Feldman, B. J. (2015). The development of next-generation screening and diagnostic platforms will change diabetes care. *Expert Review of Molecular Diagnostics*, *15*(3), 20, 291–294

Lloyd, C., Smith, J., & Weinger, K. (2005). Stress and diabetes: A review of the links. *Diabetes Spectrum*, *18*, 121–127. doi:10.2337/diaspect.18.2.121

Northam, E. A., Matthews, L. K., Anderson, P. J., Cameron, F. J., & Werther, G. A. (2005). Psychiatric morbidity and health outcome in type 1 diabetes—Perspectives from a prospective longitudinal study. *Diabetic Medicine*, *22*(2), 152–157.

Perfect, M. M. (2014). The relations of sleep and glucose to school performance in youth with type I diabetes. *Journal of Applied School Psychology*, *30*(1), 7–28.

Perfect, M. M., & Elkins, G. R. (2010). Cognitive behavioral therapy and hypnotic relaxation to treat sleep problems in adolescents with diabetes. *Journal of Clinical Psychology*, *66*, 1205–1215. doi:10.1002/jclp.20732

Perfect, M. M., Elkins, G. R., Lyle-Lahroud, T., & Posey, J. R. (2010). Stress and sleep quality among individuals with diabetes. *Stress and Health*, *26*, 61–74. doi:10.1002/smi.1262

Perfect, M. M., & Jaramillo, E. (2012). Relations between resiliency, diabetes-related quality of life, and disease markers to school-related outcomes in adolescents with diabetes. *School Psychology Quarterly*, *27*, 29–40. doi:10.1037/a0027984

Perfect, M. M., Patel, P. G., Scott, R. E., Wheeler, M. D., Patel, C., Griffin, K., . . . Quan, S. F. (2012). Sleep, glucose, and daytime functioning in youth with type 1 diabetes. *Sleep*, *35*(1), 81–88.

Ratner, H., Gross, L., Casas, J., & Castells, S. (1990). A hypnotherapeutic approach to the improvement of compliance in adolescent diabetics. *American Journal of Clinical Hypnosis*, *32*, 154–159.

Reynolds, K. A., & Helgeson, V. S. (2011). Children with diabetes compared to peers: Depressed? Distressed? A meta-analytic review. *Annual Behavioral Medicine*, *42*, 29–41.

Stewart, J. (2005). Hypnosis in contemporary medicine. *Mayo Clinic Proceedings*, *80*(4), 511–524.

Stradling, J., Roberts, D., Wilson, A., & Lovelock, F. (1998). Controlled trial of hypnotherapy for weight loss in patients with obstructive sleep apnea. *International Journal of Obesity Related Metabolic Disorders, 22,* 278–281.

Villa, M. P., Multari, G., Montesano, M., Pagani, J., Cervoni, M., Midulla, F., . . . Ronchetti, R. (2000). Sleep apnea in children with diabetes mellitus: Effect of glycemic control. *Diabetologia, 43*(6), 696–702.

Xu, Y., & Cardeña, E. (2007). Hypnosis as an adjunct therapy in the management of diabetes. *International Journal of Clinical and Experimental Hypnosis, 56*(1), 63–72.

Dysphagia

David Alter

Doors can be defined by their two primary surfaces. One surface faces the space interior to the door's inside edge. The door's other surface is oriented to the great beyond that lies exterior to the outer edge. Like a door, the human oral cavity, including the mouth, tongue, lips, teeth, cheeks, palate, and epiglottis, constitutes an important boundary actively regulating the relationship between our inner and outer worlds.

Similarly to the boundary defining the perimeter of our cells, what passes back and forth across the boundary, and how the passage occurs, partly defines both the cell's and a person's overall health. Life-sustaining food makes its way across this portal in one direction, passing into our esophagus on its journey to providing nourishment to our cells. Life-sustaining air moves back and forth through the oral gate in a never-ending rhythm that defines the beginning and ending moments of our lives. Carried by our breath and moving in the opposite direction to the flow of food move the sounds of life—language—that convey everything from our loftiest ideas and aspirations to our romantic yearnings to our basest impulses. Those articulated sounds are projected out into the world by coordinated movements of tissues of the oral cavity and lungs.

The world that exists on the interior of our oral cavity is an evolutionary engineering wonder that serves many functions. Like many engineering marvels, occasionally things go wrong. *Dysphagia* is the term for all manner of swallowing difficulties that can arise in spite of the mouth's wondrous design. As this chapter highlights, swallowing difficulties can arise from multiple sources: neural injury, as in stroke or cerebral palsy; inflammatory processes such as eosinophilia, which causes swelling and swallowing difficulties; gastroesophageal reflux disease (GERD) that ladles strong stomach acids into and up the esophagus, burning those tissues

and causing a cascade of problems, including swallowing difficulties; or more commonly a range of conditions strongly associated with anxiety-spectrum concerns and acquired psychophysiological habits that impact acid production levels and muscle contraction patterns ranging from elevated background muscle tension levels to muscle spasticity in key oral structures that affect swallowing. The latter are often described as *functional esophageal disorders* (Galmiche et al., 2006). Regardless of the source of the dysphagia, incorporation of clinical hypnosis into a treatment plan can significantly enhance the effectiveness of the treatment process.

Let's review the major functions served by the mouth. Doing so can begin to seed the reader's mind with a variety of associations that can evolve into therapeutic metaphors and clinical strategies useful in treating particular clients and their specific dysphagic conditions. The mouth serves as a protective boundary, preventing all manner of foreign objects from gaining entry to our lungs or digestive tract. It engages in a marvelous pas de deux with our nasal passages so that scent, temperature, texture, and taste combine to make what we eat flavorful and enjoyable, or notify us quickly if what the oral cavity holds is rancid or otherwise distasteful, or even dangerous. The lips, cheeks, teeth, gums, palate, and tongue coordinate their actions to allow us to transform ideas into audible expressions that connect us, one to another, through verbal or nonverbal language in support of our fundamental social nature.

Kay F. Thompson, an important dentist and hypnosis pioneer, recognized the central role of the mouth in setting the stage for the development of many physical and psychological ailments. She called the mouth the "emotional learning center of the body" (Thompson, 2004). She contended that the oral cavity is crucial for the "lifetime development of the individual" (Thompson, 2004). Over the course of an individual's life, various traumatic experiences invade this sacred sanctum and show up later in one guise or another, with dysphagia being but one form among many (Klinger & Strang, 1987).

Arguably the most important function served by the mouth and its various structures is where the transformation of foodstuff into life-sustaining molecules that are absorbed into our body through the lumen of our gut takes its first important step. The process of chewing our food and preparing it for swallowing is among the most overlearned habits we develop. Within hours of birth we are already at work learning to coordinate the lips, tongue, cheeks, and the process of respiration so that we can ingest breast milk. Newborns enter the world primed for nursing because they have been practicing even more fundamental neuromotor aspects of swallowing for months. Studies show that in utero, fetuses have already begun swallowing amniotic fluid by the 18th to 24th weeks of gestation (Arvedson, 2006). The exercise of this ongoing intrauterine swallowing behavior aids in the maturation of the fetal gastrointestinal tract. Moreover, there are strong associations between infants who develop swallowing difficulties and a higher subsequent incidence of inhibited growth rates, undernourishment, pulmonary disorders (e.g., bronchiectasis), generally compromised physical health, and increased incidence of subsequent expressive language disorders in children and adolescents. Mathisen, Worrall, Masel, Wall, and Shepherd (1999) described how swallowing difficulties are associated with disruption to the normal mother–infant bonding, thereby setting the stage for a range of potential attachment-related difficulties involving the growing infant later on (Mathisen et al., 1999). Theorists from Freud to Wilbur have linked the mouth and our experiences while seeking to master its functions to the ultimate form of our lifelong psychological development (Salkind, 2004; Wilbur, 1996).

DYSPHAGIA'S SCOPE

According to a survey of adult primary-care patients, the prevalence of dysphagia in the general population is surprisingly high, running approximately 23% (Wilkins, Gillies, Thomas, & Wagner, 2007). The study found the gender ratio for reported symptoms was approximately 80% for women and 20% for men. Among infants and young children, the prevalence is more than 50% in those born with various congenital structural, neurological, and neuromuscular abnormalities, while the overall prevalence among all infants is 25%. Approximately 1 million people are diagnosed with the condition annually, while approximately 15 million people are affected by some form of swallowing dysregulation at any given time (Dysphagia Fact Sheet, n.d.).

The distribution of those affected by dysphagia is bimodal. Infants and children born with cleft palate, cerebral palsy, or other neurodevelopmental conditions represent one of the modes, while generally older adults who have suffered stroke, head/neck cancers, Parkinson's disease, amyotrophic lateral sclerosis (ALS), and, increasingly, those with Alzheimer's disease combine to constitute the second general population spike. The presence of dysphagia represents a significant mortality risk. It is often the originating cause of aspiration pneumonia, which is the fifth leading cause of death among adults age 65 or older. As the greying of the U.S. population continues with the aging of the baby-boomer generation, the prevalence of dysphagia and dysphagia-related conditions can be expected to increase.

THIS SWALLOW ISN'T IN CAPISTRANO

There is limited literature highlighting the beneficial role that hypnosis serves in the specific treatment of dysphagia across the age span. However, the established benefit of hypnosis with anxiety-spectrum concerns (Elkins, 1984; Nash, 2009; Sugarman, Garrison, & Willford, 2013), as well as the psychophysiological aspects of different neuromuscular conditions (de Benedittis, 1996; Spankus & Freeman, 1962), would seemingly make the use of hypnosis in treating individuals with dysphagia an obvious resource. Moreover, with regard to irritable bowel syndrome, a more common condition often involving no clear-cut organic cause, hypnosis has been established as the single most-effective clinical intervention (Kearney & Chang, 2008; Lindfors et al., 2012; Palsson et al., 2002).

Yet, as is often the case, the published literature on the effectiveness of hypnosis in treating conditions such as dysphagia falls far short of the frequency with which unpublished case reports attest to its underappreciated and underutilized potential for achieving positive clinical outcomes.

Absent, ineffective, or uncoordinated sympathetic/parasympathetic innervation of swallowing muscles was recognized as playing a role in dysphagia early in the 20th century. For nearly 100 years, the use of clinical hypnosis to facilitate muscle relaxation or reestablish an effective peristaltic wave was recognized as beneficial to sufferers of dysphagia (Magonet, 1961). Clinical hypnosis has been successfully incorporated into the treatment of dysphagia associated with cancer (Kopel & Quinn, 1996); in rapidly reversing, in a pediatric office setting, an acquired, but misdirected, self-protective swallowing habit developed by a 9-year-old who had choked on his food (Elinoff, 1991); in treating aspects of neuromuscular dysregulation in an individual with multiple sclerosis (Dane, 1996); in addressing the complex psychophysiology of gagging and vomiting in a 10-year-old with pill-swallowing fears (Lagrone, 2011); and in reversing a dysphagic pattern coupled with emesis established over 20 years that threatened to erode tooth enamel to the degree that full dental replacement of the client's teeth loomed, as described in the following case report.

CASE STUDY

Marching to the Sergeant's Beat

Bill, a 45-year-old single man, was referred for a health psychology consultation by his gastroenterologist. Bill's presenting concern involved difficulty swallowing his food comfortably as it was almost immediately accompanied by a sense of esophageal constriction and then, beginning about 10 minutes later, repeated episodes of vomiting into the back of his throat what he had just recently eaten. Over the 23 years that had passed since he first developed this behavior while in boot camp in the Army, he had learned to swallow back down the partially digested food he had regurgitated, which was often accompanied by fairly large, unchewed bits of food.

When asked why he opted to seek therapy at this point in time, he indicated he was about to have to undergo major dental surgery to replace his teeth. The corrosive stomach acid in which he had continuously bathed his teeth had significantly degraded his tooth enamel. He said it was too expensive a habit to maintain and he wondered whether the referral to me could offer him effective alternatives as "nothing else has worked so far." Moreover, as is often the case with these presenting concerns, multiple workups and procedures, as well as a slew of prescribed medications, had failed to eliminate the problem or even identify an organic cause. Quite commonly, clients with these concerns add considerable diagnostic frustration to the list of presenting concerns when repeatedly told "there is nothing wrong with you that we can find" in spite of daily experiences with disruptive symptoms. Often, that frustration can be channeled in the direction of therapeutic motivation. This is especially so when it is aligned with activation of the client's internal resources and oriented toward positive therapeutic change through the use of hypnosis.

The initial assessment explored his history for evidence of clinical levels of anxiety or depression. None were found. Evidence of functional benefits associated with the onset and/or maintenance of the problem (e.g., being excused from aspects of his military service responsibilities while in the service) was lacking. It was evident he had become quite habituated to the presence of this symptom pattern. He seemingly accepted its inevitability with a curious but understandable passivity born of more than two decades of thrice-daily behavioral conditioning with emesis following meals. There was evidence of a mildly slowed stomach emptying pattern but not to the degree that the specter of gastroparesis was raised. Apparently, he had always been a rather slow eater, suggesting slowed stomach emptying had long been present but without clinical consequences as long as he ate quite slowly. The gastroenterologist did not conclude that the reduced stomach motility had any significant current role in generating the client's symptom pattern. Similarly, no evidence of esophageal reflux was found, nor were there signs of structural anomalies or evidence of compromised swallowing based upon barium swallow studies.

Careful questioning of the details surrounding the development of the behavior ultimately led him to casually recall how all recruits would follow their sergeants into the mess halls where they would wolf down their food as quickly as possible because, as soon as the sergeant pushed his tray away, *everyone* was done eating. To exit the mess hall late was to invite all sorts of unpleasantries on the slowpoke and his fellow grunts. The motivation and even necessity of "binge eating" was clear. While Bill learned very quickly to eat fast, his stomach never accepted military protocol. He recalled simply "swallowing" the expectation to stuff his mouth even as he unwittingly experienced a quiet revolt in his stomach, which would periodically send back boluses of food into his mouth for the next several hours. Bill learned to simply swallow the regurgitated food back down, working to avoid having this unpleasant problem become noticeable to anyone else at any time. Following his military service, he maintained the acquired habit of excessively rapid eating even though his outer life was no longer regulated by the rigid and stern expectations of his drill sergeant.

Undoing and Redoing

"Isn't it interesting how we can sometimes forget to remember what we once knew how to do so naturally, and how we later learned to do something new that was not as useful as what we knew before?" So began the naturalistic induction that oriented Bill toward a regressive experience that took him back to the time in his life before the problem began. Drawing upon techniques of Milton Erickson, the session utilized regression to memories of acquisition of early developmental milestones. Bill was reminded of how,

"You knew how and when to cry and when to stop when your needs were met. You didn't even have to think about when you were hungry; you just knew. And, when food arrived, you knew how to suckle and swallow, and how that naturally progressed to when you would take in small bits of food, coordinating your lips and tongue and swallowing the food automatically. Later still, you learned to coordinate the muscles of your fingers and hands and arms, knowing just how to bring them up to your mouth under your command with Cheerios or other favorite foods that were so enjoyable to eat . . . all by yourself. How proud you may have been as you continued acquiring new

skills, one building on the earlier one, until you were able to not only eat what you were served but became able to prepare the food that you ate, and you were able to do that all without really having to work to remember how. Most importantly, it is interesting to remember how good it felt to eat and drink at a pace that was just right for you, free of anyone else's demands, and fully comfortable with the deep-felt feeling that you could take just as much time as you wished. Just taking things in at your pace and under your command."

Over the next few minutes, Bill's head nods, body posture, and general muscle tone conveyed increased responsiveness to the evoked memories. The swallowing reflex that occurred specifically when *unconscious memories consciously recognized* of initially learning how to eat and swallow at the *appropriate developmental time* (i.e., even though he didn't actually remember learning to eat and swallow he absolutely accepted that he must have learned how) were suggested further reinforced the impression of his increasing absorption in the hypnotic process.

The conscious acceptance that he did once know how to swallow and digest without difficulties reinforced a yes-set that further readied him to undo the learned habit and reestablish or redo the previously learned natural habits of eating, swallowing, and digesting. The core themes of the session—(a) that you already know what to do; (b) that the learning was interrupted by life experience; and that (c) now it was finally time to reaccess the memories of how to swallow comfortably without regurgitation, which have just been waiting for the right time to be retrieved—were repeatedly reinforced during the session.

He smiled at various points as we worked. At one point, while still in trance, he stated, "Do you mean if I just take my time, I can be okay?" This spontaneous comment was responded to at several levels, each reflecting a different aspect of his statement. The first part of his comment, "I just take my time," was responded to with the suggestion that, *"knowing that you can—and should—take all the time you need, that there is no need to rush, that you are not under fire, and that you can really relax and enjoy your eating."* This suggestion spoke to those aspects of Bill's personality that were still used to "taking orders." Hearing that he "could and should" take all the time he needed was accepted as a directive. The second message expressed his need for reassurance that the desired change was possible. In a strong and direct voice, I suggested, *"It is time to be okay . . . again . . . just like before. Yes. You can be okay, again."*

At one month follow-up, Bill reported that the frequency of the regurgitation had significantly lessened. He was taking more time to eat, chewing more fully, and swallowing only when he was good and ready. In effect, he'd developed a habit of *mindful eating*, which is described as being so useful for a variety of conditions, from compulsive overeating to positive habit change in individuals with a range of disordered eating habits. No follow-up with Bill beyond the second session occurred.

SUMMARY AND NEXT STEPS

Having a basic understanding of the oral cavity and how it operates when someone exhibits dysphagia is certainly worthwhile. However, as in most of clinical practice, it is best to remember to apply the message attributed to William Osler. He said, "The good physician treats the disease; the great physician treats the *patient* who has the disease." There is no substitute for taking a careful history that affords the clinician the opportunity to absorb the historical details of the patient's concerns (i.e., the "disease"). But, it will be in the cadences of their speech, the metaphors that arise automatically through their words, and the emotional and physiological responses spontaneously, but unconsciously, exhibited through which you will learn their clinical autobiographical narrative (i.e., the "person" with the disease). Transforming this into an individualized clinical intervention is thereby made easier and likely infinitely more clinically effective.

In working with clients presenting with dysphagia, the core elements presented here are easily summarized. Swallowing is a neuromuscular habit well-learned long ago. The memory trace of that learning still exists. Hypnosis can be used to reaccess it and enable the client to rehearse it repeatedly, in and out of trance, so that it initially becomes conscious and then once again submerges into the automatic unconscious where it resides along with the many other automatic physiological habits upon which our daily functioning relies.

If indicated, hypnosis can be utilized to address anxiety-based aspects of swallowing. For many, anticipation of the swallowing difficulty will tighten relevant muscles and can constrict breathing, increasing the odds of experiencing the dysphagia. Many approaches for evoking relaxation of mind and body are available. Matching the approach to the person is the key. The law of successive approximations is relevant to successful treatment of dysphagia. Just as we learned to chew and swallow a bite of steak only long after learning to swallow milk from the breast, restoring normal swallowing in individuals with dysphagia requires gradual mastery of basic steps involved in coordinating breathing, chewing, and swallowing. Deconstruction of those neuromuscular steps in ways specific to the client's presentation and history can increase the odds of achieving therapeutic success.

Finally, especially when first learning to practice clinical hypnosis, there tends to be an overreliance on scripts and prepackaged protocols. They have their place, but rarely in the office setting where the key involves the dynamic and evolving interaction *between* the clinician and the client. The ideas in this chapter are merely offered as a therapeutic guide. The true measure of their benefit is in how they enable the reader to tailor them to meet the specific and particular needs of each client. After all, Francis Bacon once said, "Some books are to be tasted, others to be swallowed, and some few to be chewed and digested."

REFERENCES

Arvedson, J. C. (2006). Swallowing and feeding in infants and young children. *GI Motility online*. doi:10.1038/gimo17

Dane, J. R. (1996). Hypnosis for pain and neuromuscular rehabilitation with multiple sclerosis: Case summary, literature review, and analysis of outcomes. *International Journal of Clinical and Experimental Hypnosis*, 44(3), 208–231.

de Benedittis, G. (1996). Hypnosis and spasmodic torticollis–report of four cases: A brief communication. *International Journal of Clinical and Experimental Hypnosis*, 44(4), 292–306. doi:10.1080/00207149608416094

Dysphagia Fact Sheet. (n.d.). Retrieved from https://bismarck.sanfordhealth.org/vitalstim/DysphagiaFactSheet.pdf

Elinoff, V. (1991). Remission of dysphagia in a 9-year-old treated in a family practice office setting. *American Journal of Clinical Hypnosis, 35*(3), 205–208.

Elkins, G. (1984). Hypnosis in the treatment of myofibrositis and anxiety: A case report. *American Journal of Clinical Hypnosis, 27*(1), 26–30.

Galmiche, J. P., Clouse, R. E., Bálint, A., Cook, I. J., Kahrilas, P. J., Paterson, W. G., & Smout, A. J. (2006). Functional esophageal disorders. *Gastroenterology, 130*(5), 1459–1465.

Kearney, D., & Chang, J. B. (2008). Complementary and alternative medicine in IBS for adults: Mind-body medicine. *Nature Clinical Practice Gastroenterology and Hepatology, 5*, 624–636.

Klinger, R., & Strang, P. (1987). Psychiatric aspects of swallowing disorders: An increasing role for psychological and behavioral interventions. *Psychosomatics, 28*(11), 572–576.

Kopel, K., & Quinn, M. (1996). Hypnotherapy treatment for dysphagia. *International Journal of Clinical and Experimental Hypnosis, 44*(2), 101–105.

Lagrone, R. (2011). Hypnobehavioral therapy to reduce gag and emesis with a 10-year-old pill swallower. *American Journal of Clinical Hypnosis, 36*(2), 132–136.

Lindfors, P., Unge, P., Arvidsson, P., Nyhlin, H., Björnsson, E., Abrahamsson, H., & Simrén, M. (2012). Effects of gut-directed hypnotherapy on IBS in different clinical settings: Results from two randomized, clinical trials. *American Journal of Gastroenterology, 107*(2), 276–285.

Magonet, A. P. (1961). Hypnosis in dysphagia. *International Journal of Clinical and Experimental Hypnosis, 9*(4), 291–295. doi:10.1080/00207146108409682

Mathisen, B., Worrall, L., Masel, J., Wall, C., & Shepherd, R. W. (1999). Feeding problems in infants with gastro-esophageal reflux disease: A controlled study. *Journal of Pediatrics and Child Health, 35*(2), 163–169.

Nash, M. (2009). Clinical research on the utility of hypnosis in the prevention, diagnosis, and treatment of medical and psychiatric disorders. *International Journal of Clinical and Experimental Hypnosis, 57*(4), 443–450.

Palsson, O. (2002). Hypnosis treatment for severe irritable bowel syndrome: Investigation of mechanisms and effect on symptoms. *Digestive Diseases and Sciences, 47*(11), 2605–2614.

Salkind, N. (2004). *An introduction to theories of human development.* Thousand Oaks, CA: Sage.

Spankus, W., & Freeman, L. (1962). Hypnosis in cerebral palsy. *International Journal of Clinical and Experimental Hypnosis, 10*(3), 135–139.

Sugarman, L. I., Garrison, B. L., & Williford, K. L. (2013). Symptoms as solutions: Hypnosis and biofeedback for autonomic self-regulation in autism spectrum disorders. *American Journal of Clinical Hypnosis, 56*(2), 152–173. doi:10.1080/00029157.2013.768197

Thompson, K. (2004). The oral cavity: The emotional learning center of the body–the dentist is a therapist too! In K. Olness (Ed.), *The art of therapeutic communication: The collected works of Kay F. Thompson* (p. 331). Williston, VT: Crown House Publishing.

Wilbur, K. (1996). *Up from Eden: A transpersonal view of human evolution.* Wheaton, IL: Theosophical Publishing House.

Wilkins, T., Gillies, R., Thomas, A., & Wagner, P. (2007). The prevalence of dysphagia in primary care patients: A HamesNet research network study. *American Board of Family Medicine, 20*(2), 144–150.

Enuresis

Jeffrey E. Lazarus

Enuresis refers to having urinary accidents. The main focus of this chapter is on how to treat patients with nocturnal enuresis (NE), commonly referred to as *bed-wetting*.

Nocturnal enuresis refers to urinary accidents that occur during the night only, while patients are asleep. Daytime incontinence refers to leakage of urine during the day.

Primary nocturnal enuresis (PNE) means that the patient has never been dry every night for 6 months in a row, or longer. Secondary nocturnal enuresis (SNE) refers to patients who have had a stretch during which they have been dry for at least 6 months straight. SNE is often, but not always, associated with other comorbid psychiatric conditions, or an upsetting life event (Hjälmås et al., 2004).

Medical hypnosis can be effective for patients with NE and no evidence of lower urinary tract symptoms and no history of bladder dysfunction. Patients with both NE and daytime incontinence need to be evaluated by a pediatric urologist before considering hypnosis as a treatment.

The prevalence of NE decreases with age. About 15% of 5-year-olds, 5% of 10-year-olds, and 1% of patients 15 years of age and older are affected (Glazener & Evans, 2004; Glazener, Evans, & Peto, 2004).

The *ICD-10, Diagnostic and Statistical Manual of Mental Disorders* (5th ed., *DSM-5*) and the International Children's Continence Society identify age 5 years as the cutoff point for pathological NE. In general, the author feels that this is too young. The older patients are, the more motivated they are to become dry at night. Therefore, the author usually does not treat patients until they are at least 8 years old.

RESEARCH

The most common treatments for NE include medication and the enuresis alarm.

There are two main classes of medication used to treat NE. Desmopressin is the drug most commonly used. It allows the kidneys to produce more concentrated urine so that the bladder fills up more slowly during the night. Occasionally desmopressin can cause hyponatremic seizures (seizures due to water loading).

The other medications used to treat NE are the antidepressants imipramine and mianserin. These have fallen out of favor due to potential side effects that are rare, but serious. Infrequently, imipramine can cause cardiac arrhythmias. This last statement leads to the question posed by Laurence Sugarman, "Why would you take a potentially life-threatening medication and use it to treat a non–life-threatening medical condition?" (personal communication, 2000).

When medication has been used to treat NE, the placebo effect has ranged from 37% (Rombis, Triantafyllidis, Balaxis, Kalaitzis, & Touloupidis, 2005; Hjälmås, Hanson, Hellström, Kruse, & Sillén, 1998) to 59% (Smellie, McGrigor, Meadow, Rose, & Douglas, 1996).

The enuresis alarm is an electronic device that utilizes a pad that detects moisture and is placed in the patient's undergarments at bedtime. When moisture is detected, a signal is sent to the alarm so that it wakes the patient with a loud noise and/ or a vibration.

According to the Cochrane reviews, significant parental involvement is required for both the medication and the alarm. The medication provides 1 to 2 more dry nights per week, on average, but this improvement does not last once the medication is stopped. The alarm can take up to 4 months to work (when it is successful) and is effective in two-thirds of patients. However, after discontinuing the alarm, half of those children start having urinary accidents again (Austin et al., 2014; Glazener & Evans, 2009; Glazener, Evans, & Peto, 2009; National Institute for Health and Care Excellence, 2010).

Most reported studies utilizing hypnosis for enuresis have been retrospective case series. Olness (1975) and Stanton (1979) reported two separate retrospective series of patients with NE. About three-quarters of the patients in each group were dry within the first month, and this persisted for 6 to 28 months in Olness's study and 1 year in Stanton's series.

The largest retrospective series of patients with NE was reported by Kohen, Olness, Colwell, and Heimel (1984). Most of these patients had already tried an enuresis alarm or medication prior to learning self-hypnosis (SH). Of the 257 children treated, 113 became completely dry (dry 30 nights in a row and one year later without relapse) and 80 of them had significant improvement. This meant that 75% had a positive long-term response. Two of Kohen's most important findings were that more failures occurred in (a) families where the parents were too involved and (b) children who were not motivated.

Gottsegen (2003) reported four patients who were each completely cured after only one session involving learning about the brain–bladder biofeedback mechanism. Only one of these patients experienced formal trancework.

Banerjee, Srivastav, and Palan's (1993) prospective study compared imipramine with SH, with 25 patients aged 5 to 16 years in each group. After three months, 76% of the imipramine group and 72% of the SH group had improved. The medication was then discontinued and the SH group was encouraged to continue doing SH. Six months later, 24% of the imipramine group and 68% of the SH group were still doing well.

TECHNIQUE AND TRANSCRIPT

Prior to using hypnosis to treat a patient with NE, it is imperative that the patient be evaluated by

his or her primary care clinician or a specialist. The workup is usually pretty simple, requiring only the history, physical examination, and a urinalysis to rule out diabetes mellitus, diabetes insipidus, and urinary tract infection.

The most common cause of nocturnal enuresis is constipation. Other medical conditions that can contribute to this problem include encopresis (of course, this is typically related to constipation); sleep apnea; spina bifida; diabetes mellitus; diabetes insipidus; urinary tract infection; urethral; genital; or midline skin abnormalities; and seizures.

Steve Hodges's book, *It's No Accident* (Hodges & Scholsberg, 2012), is a wonderful resource for both lab people and professionals. In his book, Dr. Hodges outlines very practical solutions for patients with constipation.

Medical hypnosis treats only a symptom. If the patient has other psychological/psychiatric problems, such as generalized anxiety disorder, that are getting in the way of his or her life more than the NE is, then those must be addressed first. When those are addressed, the NE may resolve spontaneously.

When I receive a referral for a patient with NE, I speak with the parent(s) over the phone to determine:

1. If the child has any medical or psychological issues that might be contributing to the problem, such as constipation, depression, generalized anxiety, and so on
2. If the child is motivated
3. That the child has been evaluated by his or her clinician, including having obtained a urinalysis.

Frequently, particularly with younger children, the NE bothers the parents, but not the children. If this is the case, then the parents are advised to be patient and wait until the child is ready.

Once it is determined that the family is ready, it is recommended to meet with the parents alone *in person* before meeting with the child so that they are in agreement with the approach that will be used. At this initial parent visit, they talk about EVERYTHING, including school, sports, hobbies, friends, family, sleep, and screen time. At the end, the approach outlined in this chapter is explained. Parents are requested to give an update with an e-mail or voice mail on the day before each patient visit. This way, the parents do not have to be brought in during the patient visit, further reinforcing the child's independence.

A letter similar to the example shown subsequently can be sent to the patient:

Dear John/Jane:

I'm looking forward to meeting with you to help you keep the bed dry at night.

Attached are the imagery/discomfort and enuresis questionnaires that are borrowed, with the permission of the authors, from a pediatric textbook (Kohen & Olness, 1996). You will notice that some of the questions on the imagery/discomfort questionnaire don't apply to you so just ignore those. You will also notice that it allows you to be creative, so enjoy it!

Please be sure to bring the completed questionnaires for our initial visit. We will be meeting on: [List planned visits.]

Again, John/Jane, I look forward to helping you help yourself.

First patient visit: The history is obtained and rapport is developed. In obtaining the history, it is important to use the same words for urine and bowel movement that the child uses. Many children and adolescents use the terms that their family used when they were younger. For example, in the United States, instead of "urine," people often say "pee," or "pee-pee," or "tinkle." And, instead of "bowel movement," they may say "poop," or "poo," or something else.

Motivation is determined. Some children are not yet ready to be dry at night because they are afraid that if they are dry, they will have to go to other peoples' homes for a sleepover. Others are simply not bothered by sleeping in pull-ups. If the child is not motivated, then it is best to wait until he or she is ready. You can reassure the child, in a nonjudgmental way, that if he or she changes his or her mind, it would be a pleasure to work together.

At some point during the visit, the patient is guided through a brief visualization experience. This is typically introduced after discussing the patient's favorite sports or hobbies. You may use a simple guided imagery experience, or, if you have the time, you may do an SH session with the specific focus on being dry every night (see subsequent hypnosis transcript in the second visit).

The patient is taught in detail about the brain–bladder biofeedback mechanism using the following diagram from Kohen and Olness's book (2011).

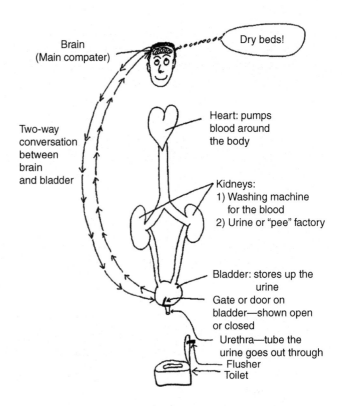

At the end of the first visit, homework is assigned to help him or her think about the problem in different ways than he or she is used to thinking about it.

The homework includes the following:

1. Keep a calendar of DRY NIGHTS ONLY.
   a. For example, if someone is dry twice in one week, the clinician can say, "Gee, I see you wet the bed five times last week. Why was that?" Or, the clinician can say, "Gee, I see you were dry twice last week! That's fantastic! How did you do that?"

   This is discussed with the patient, of course, so that he or she understands why we are looking for positive reinforcement.
2. Learn and draw the brain–bladder biofeedback picture.
3. Do the visualization (guided imagery) exercise at least three times a day.
4. Everytime you urinate, START-STOP-AND HOLD IT . . . THEN START-STOP-AND HOLD IT . . . THEN START-STOP-AND HOLD IT. . . .
   a. We are all taught to empty our bladders completely. And, when we start-stop-and hold it, we are reinforcing the connection between our brains and bladders. Plus, we are making the bladder's sphincter muscle even stronger. I then ask patients, " . . . so

that when it is stronger during the day, what will happen during the night?" Invariably, they respond with a positive reply.

5. What is good about being dry?
   a. Even though we have discussed this during the visit, I believe that it is helpful for the patient to write down the reasons to reinforce them and to make a commitment to the process.
6. What is good about not being dry?
   a. See 5a
7. No more pull-ups or diapers.
   a. These give a mixed message. They tell the patient that it is all right to have a urinary accident with no consequences.
8. If you have a urinary accident during the night, you are responsible for changing the sheets, putting the sheets and bed clothing in the washing machine and dryer, and making the bed. This is not done to punish you, rather, it is simply your responsibility.
   a. For example, if a 10-month-old spills milk on the floor, who should clean it up?
   b. Answer: The parent.
   c. But if a 10-year-old spills milk on the floor, who should clean it up?
   d. Answer: I think it should be the 10-year-old.
9. Draw a picture of your bedroom and bathroom and count how many steps there are from your bed to the toilet.
10. Draw a picture of you being dry in the future.

    a. Perhaps enjoying a sleepover, or being at a sleep-away camp, or sleeping in your new bed.

At the end of the visit, the parents and the child can be met with together to review suggestions for the family to follow to maximize the chances of success in this process. The main thing is that the parents are to stay out of the process. For example, they are not to ask to see the child's dry night calendar, or ask if he or she is doing the exercises that he or she learned in the office, and so on.

Dan Kohen's study (Kohen et al., 1984) illustrated an inverse relationship between parental involvement and the child's success. There may be a few reasons for this:

1. It infantilizes the patient by giving the message, "You can't do this without our help."

2. It is one more thing for the parents to nag the child to do. If the child is motivated, he or she will do it!
3. It may give the child the message that he or she is "not good enough." Some parents may inadvertently give the message that they are being judgmental about their child, and that they are disappointed *in the child* because he or she is not yet dry at night.

We discuss that if the patient has not done the homework, or has forgotten to bring it, that we will take the time in the office at the next visit to do this. This is not meant to threaten or punish the patient. It is to let the patient know that homework is part of the process. For younger children, I ask them if they would like their parent to remind them to bring the homework (not to help them *do* the homework!), as it would be a shame to have the child do the work and then waste time in the office doing it again. For older children, this is not suggested. I tell the parents, alone, that the best thing they can do is to give the unwritten, unspoken message that their child can do this. They are not to act as cheerleaders. They are simply to provide an attitude that shows that they believe in their child.

Second patient visit: This visit always begins with an open-ended question, such as, "What's been happening since our last visit?" This allows the patient to decide what to discuss first. Some kids like to discuss what they have been learning about in school, or a recent sporting event, or dance recital. Others prefer to immediately review their homework.

Once you and the patient are ready to have a hypnosis session, you should ask the patient what his or her goal is for this particular session. As Michael Yapko (2012) says, "Every hypnosis session should have a goal. If you are not able to articulate the goal in 25 words or less, then you probably should not be having the session." The goal needs to be specific, and, in this case, it should be pretty easy: "to be dry at night," or "to have dry beds every night."

After the homework is reviewed, trancework is done with specific focus on being dry at night.

Induction: As the patient has already been practicing SH, which was taught briefly at the first visit, this should already be a little easier to do. The patient is invited to go to his or her special place, and the goal is stated. For older children, above age 12 years, an audio recording is made for them to take home.

The yes-set is introduced, going from general to specific (Yapko, 2012). After asking each question, wait for the patient to answer, "Yes," or nod his or her head. In this particular case, the object is to set up the unconscious expectation for the urine to go into the toilet. Here is an example.

"Wouldn't you agree that where some things go is not important?"

[Pause and wait for yes/head nod]

"And wouldn't you agree that where some things go is moderately important?"

"And wouldn't you agree that where some things go is extremely important?"

Then, when you and the patient are ready, the following is an example of a hypnosis session transcript:

"And, I invite you to picture yourself going through your night-time routine, getting ready for bed tonight. You can picture yourself emptying your bladder [urinating, 'peeing,' going 'pee-pee,' or using the term that the patient uses for urinating], *then washing your hands, brushing your teeth, and walking those 14 steps and climbing into that nice, DRY, comfortable, DRY, cozy, DRY, wonderful, DRY bed . . . and as you drift off to sleep, your brain and bladder start talking with each other, just as they have been doing all day long:*

Brain: How was your day?

Bladder: I had a great day! John/Jane has been exercising me by starting-stopping-and holding it every time we urinate. As you know, it used to take only 10 seconds, and now we are up to 45 seconds each time! And, I'm clearly getting stronger!

And, Brain, how was YOUR day?

Brain: I had a great day, too! We went to school and it was very interesting today. We ate lunch with a couple friends, and after school, we played soccer and that was a lot of fun!

So, as you drift off to sleep, your brain and bladder continue to talk with each other. After a little while, the brain may ask the bladder, 'How are we doing?' . . . or, 'Are you full of urine? Do we need to get up and go to the bathroom?' And, the bladder may reply, 'We're doing fine. I'll let you know.' And, a little while later, the brain checks in on the bladder again, and the bladder may reply, 'You know, Brain, I'm feeling really strong tonight. In fact, I think we'll be able to go the entire night without having to wake up and go to the bathroom.' And the brain replies, 'Okay. Keep me posted.' And, they check in with each other a few more times, and before you know it, you wake up DRY . . . having spent the entire night without having to go to the bathroom! How will that feel? [Pause.] *That's right. Now take a few moments and enjoy that feeling. And then you can picture yourself putting a 'D,' or a smiley face, or a star, on your DRY NIGHT CALENDAR. And, again, how will that feel?* [Pause.] *Now take a few moments and enjoy that feeling.*

And, I'm wondering if you can picture being dry TWO NIGHTS IN A ROW . . . and, how will life be different when that happens? [Here the clinician uses the exact words that the patient used in the homework from the first visit.] *No more worrying about being dry at night . . . no more feeling like a baby . . . no more smelly sheets . . . no more having to change the bed and wash the sheets . . . being able to go to sleepovers confidently . . . being able to get that new bed . . . knowing that you are now able to attend sleep-over parties and sleep-away camp confidently, without fear of embarrassment from having had an accident. And, how will that feel? . . .* [Pause.] *That's right . . . now take a few moments and allow yourself to enjoy that feeling. . . ."*

Then, after you have spent all the time you want in this vein, do the same exercise, starting at the beginning of their nighttime routine . . . repeating the same words, word for word, only this time, during the night, encourage the patient to have the bladder tell the brain,

"Bladder: Brain?

Brain: Yes, Bladder?

Bladder: Brain, I think we need to wake up now. I'm getting pretty full and don't think we should wait till tomorrow morning.

Brain: Well done, Bladder! I'm so glad that you were able to recognize this and to wake us up! Okay, Bladder, squeeze that muscle . . . you know the one, the one that you've been exercising during the day every time you urinate, and the one that prevents us from having an accident during school, or while we're outside at recess, or while we're playing soccer.

And, now, the brain says to the body: 'All right, Body, let's get up and get out of bed now . . . left foot, right foot . . . let's walk those 14 steps to the toilet, [for boys, lift up the seat,] urinate, [for boys put the seat back down,] wash your hands, and walk those 14 steps back to that nice, DRY, comfortable, DRY, cozy, DRY, wonderful, DRY bed . . . and, as you drift off back to sleep, the brain and bladder will continue to talk with each other . . . only this time, the bladder reassures the brain each time that it is not necessary to wake up and that it is fine to wait until morning . . . and, before you know it, you wake up . . . DRY . . . in that nice bed! And, how will that feel? And, now picture putting that 'D,' or sticker, or smiley face, onto that DRY NIGHT CALENDAR . . . and how will that feel? And, now, take a few moments and enjoy that feeling . . . that's right. . . .

And, now. . . picture yourself in the future . . . with dry beds, every night . . . how will life be different? [Pause. . . .]"

Here the clinician will use the earlier script.

You might also suggest that the bladder has a door, or a gate, and that when the child goes to sleep, he or she can simply lock that door or gate "tight, tight, tight, through the night, night, night!" And repeat that: "tight, tight, tight, through the night, night, night!"

The use of metaphors can be very powerful, particularly while patients are in the state of hypnosis. A metaphoric story can be used at the end of the hypnosis session to reiterate the concept of the urine going into the toilet. Here are a few examples of metaphors.

I had one boy who spent his summers at his grandparents' farm and enjoyed milking the cows. Of course, this was used as a metaphor:

"When you're milking a cow, of course, the milk goes in the pail. And, when you are first learning to milk a cow, some of the milk may squirt onto the floor of the barn. And, with practice, you get better at it until all the milk, every drop, goes into the pail where it belongs."

Another example includes using a story about a father and daughter at the father's worksite.

"Lee's father was in construction and operated a crane. Occasionally he would allow Lee to sit with him while he worked. Lee was always fascinated by this. She enjoyed climbing to the top of the crane with her father and seeing him use the shovel to dig up dirt to make a hole for a new building. Then he would maneuver the crane so that the shovel was directly over a dump truck, and he would drop the dirt into the truck. The truck would then drive away and deposit the dirt to an area that needed it, usually another hole in the ground. Lee decided that when she grew up, she wanted to run a crane, too, just like her father did.

So, when she was older, she studied and trained and became a crane operator. At first, it was difficult, and she ended up spilling a lot of dirt on the way from the hole to emptying it into the dump truck. Then, with practice, she became better and better at it, and before long, she was able to move the dirt without spilling any of it except into the dump truck, where it belonged. She was quite proud of herself for this, and her parents and boss were proud, too. She learned that the more she practiced, the better she got at it. And, the more she practiced, the easier it became. And, the more she practiced, the faster she got at it."

Other metaphors might include telling the patient something similar to the following:" *. . . and, just as the object in soccer is to get the ball into the goal, and the aim in basketball is to get the ball to go through the hoop and into the net . . . the goal* *with urine is to put it all in the toilet* (Lazarus, 2009).

At the end of the second visit, the homework includes the following:

1. Continue the calendar of DRY NIGHTS ONLY.
2. Continue to start, stop, and hold it. . . .
3. Do the visualization exercise at least three times each day.
    a. At the end, each time, remember to imagine yourself in the future:
        i. How will life be different?
        ii. How will that feel?
        iii. Now take a few moments and enjoy that feeling. . . .
4. Bonus: Draw another picture of you doing something in the future because you now have dry beds.

Third patient visit: Again, begin with an open-ended question, such as, "So what's been happening since our last visit?"

Then, review the homework. Celebrate the successes and praise the patient for dry nights. If there have not yet been dry nights, it is appropriate to empathize about this with the patient.

To ensure the patient is practicing the SH exercise effectively, have the patient do the SH exercise in the office. It is recommended to give the patient 2 to 4 minutes to do this. Afterwards, revise, refine, and have the patient practice the technique again, with you, in the office. The analogy the author tells his patients is that this is like learning to hit a tennis serve. First you meet with the tennis coach/instructor, and he or she works with you on your serve. Then, you go home and practice. Then you return and the coach may help you adjust what you are doing, offering you some suggestions, and then you go home and practice again. We are like coaches. We teach patients some skills and they, in turn, have to go home and practice. And, you can tell your patients, "just like hitting a tennis serve, the more you practice this technique, the better you get at it. And the more you practice, the easier it gets. And the more you practice, the faster you get at it."

The homework at the end of the third visit includes:

1. Continue to keep the calendar of DRY NIGHTS ONLY.
2. Continue the start, stop, and hold it exercise.

3. Continue to do the SH exercise at least three times a day.
4. Return in one to two weeks.

Fourth patient visit: Typically there is significant improvement after three visits. If this is not the case, it is important to carefully review if the patient and family have been following all of their instructions. If everything is being done properly, then the patient is encouraged to continue to do what he or she is doing. If there is no improvement, this needs to be explored.

CASE EXAMPLES

A 10-year-old boy who had never been dry. He was sent the introductory letter and we met for his first visit. He returned 1 week later having been dry 5 out of the previous 7 nights. He was taught SH and never returned for a third visit because he had fixed his problem.

A 13-year-old boy who had never been dry. He received his introductory material and came in for his first visit 2 weeks later. It turned out that he had been dry every night since the letter arrived! I tell all of my patients this story and then ask them, "How do you explain that?"

A 13-year-old girl who had never been dry. I met with her parents for an extended visit, then met with the girl three times. She still was not dry. I met alone with the parents again. They were not doing everything perfectly, and neither was the girl. Yet, I felt that there still should have been some improvement.

We scheduled a fourth visit for the girl. Before that visit, I met with her mother alone. The girl had still not had one dry night. I asked the mother, "What am I missing? What am I not asking? What are you not telling me?" She replied, "We were embarrassed to tell you that for the last 2 years our daughter has been seeing a psychologist because of depression. And for the past 2 months she's been suicidal. Do you think that could have anything to do with it?" It was then clear that her mood disorder was getting in the way of her life more than the NE was, and she needed a change in her mental health therapy.

A 19-year-old female college student. She was referred by her pediatric urologist 1 month prior to going to college. The day before her second visit, her mother called asking for a note so that she could have a private room at college. When the young woman came in, this was mentioned, and she said, "No. Absolutely not! I want to be like every other college freshman and have a roommate. Besides, I've been dry every night since we met!"

An 8-year-old girl with NE . . . a humbling case. At age 3 years, she required urologic surgery which was felt to be curative. At age 8 years, she was referred for NE by her pediatric urologist. After two visits, she became dry.

She went away to an overnight camp for 1 week during which time she relapsed. Her parents thought this was due to laziness on her part, as did the author.

A couple days later, her nanny noticed that the girl's urine smelled funny and it turned out that she had developed a urinary tract infection while away at camp! She was treated with antibiotics and became dry again within 2 days. This was a very humbling experience for me. The lesson here is that if something changes or a relapse occurs, it is important to consider all possible reasons, psychological and physical.

CONCLUSION

Medical hypnosis has been used successfully to treat NE even after the enuresis alarm and/or medication have failed. The high placebo effect for medication (Hjälmås et al., 1998; Rombis et al., 2005) to 59% (Smellie et al., 1996) speaks of how powerful the mind is and perhaps makes SH even more attractive not only to patients, but also to clinicians.

There are important factors to consider prior to starting treatment, with motivation of the patient being the most important. For this treatment to work, parent motivation is irrelevant. It is the motivation of the *patient* that will determine the patient's likelihood for success. Parent involvement is discouraged and can be counterproductive when treating a patient with this approach. It is also important to remember that hypnosis is only part of the treatment plan. The education piece where patients are taught about the brain and bio-feedback system is crucial in their understanding of the control they can have over this issue. The

homework assignments are designed to encourage patients to start thinking about their problem in different ways. When these components are combined in a treatment program, patients have a greater chance for success in gaining control over their NE.

Again, it is important to remember that hypnosis is only part of the treatment plan. For a more complete approach, like the one described in this chapter, visit KeepingtheBedDry.com. Keeping the Bed Dry® is a comprehensive home video program that utilizes medical hypnosis to help children and adolescents gain control over their NE (Lazarus, 2013). Keeping the Bed Dry has been praised by patients, parents, and clinicians.

REFERENCES

Austin, P. F., Bauer, S. B., Bower, W., Chase, J., Franco, I., Hoebeke, P., . . . Nevéus, T. (2014). The standardization of terminology of lower urinary tract function in children and adolescents: Update report from the standardization committee of the International Children's Continence Society. *Journal of Urology, 191*(6), 1863–1865.

Banerjee, S., Srivastav, A., & Palan, B. M. (1993). Hypnosis and self-hypnosis in the management of nocturnal enuresis: A comparative study with imipramine therapy. *American Journal of Clinical Hypnosis, 36*(2), 113–119.

Glazener, C. M. A., & Evans, J. H. C. (2004). Simple behavioural and physical interventions for nocturnal enuresis in children. *Cochrane Database Systematic Review, 2.* doi:10.1002/14651858.CD003637.pub2

Glazener, C. M. A., & Evans, J. H. C. (2009). *Desmopressin for nocturnal enuresis in children.* Chincester: Wiley.

Glazener, C. M. A., Evans, J. H. C., & Peto, R. E. (2004). Complex behavioural and educational interventions for nocturnal enuresis in children. *Cochrane Database Systematic Review, 1.* doi:10.1002/14651858. CD004668

Glazener, C. M. A., Evans, J. H. C., & Peto, R. E. (2009). *Alarm interventions for nocturnal enuresis in children.* Chincester: Wiley.

Gottsegen, D. N. (2003). Curing bedwetting on the spot: A review of one-session cures. *Clinical Pediatrics, 42*(3), 273–275. doi:10.1177/000992280304200312

Hjälmås, K., Arnold, T., Bower, W., Caione, P., Chiozza, L. M., von Gontard, A., . . . Yeung, C. K. (2004). Nocturnal enuresis: An international evidence based management strategy. *Journal of Urology, 171*(6), 2545–2561.

Hjälmås, K., Hanson, E., Hellström, A. L., Kruse, S., & Sillén, U. (1998). Long-term treatment with desmopressin in children with primary monosymptomatic nocturnal enuresis: An open multicentre study. Swedish Enuresis Trial (SWEET) Group. *British Journal of Urology, 82*(5), 704–709.

Hodges, S. J., & Scholsberg, S. (2012). *It's no accident: Breakthrough solutions to your child's wetting, constipation, UTIs, and other potty problems.* Guilford, CT: Globe Pequot Press.

Kohen, D., & Olness, K. (1996). *Hypnosis and hypnotherapy with children.* New York, NY: Routledge.

Kohen, D., & Olness, K. (2011). *Hypnosis and hypnotherapy with children.* New York, NY: Routledge.

Kohen, D. P., Olness, K. N., Colwell, S. O., & Heimel, A. (1984). The use of relaxation-mental imagery (self-hypnosis) in the management of 505 pediatric behavioral encounters. *Journal of Developmental and Behavioral Pediatrics, 5*(1), 21–25.

Lazarus, J. (2009). L'enuresi pediatrica: La diagnosi e il trattamento con l'uso dell'autoipnosi. In M. Fasciana (Ed.), *L'ipnosi con I bambini e gli adolescenti: Tecniche psicoterapeutiche in eta evolutiva. (Pediatric enuresis: The diagnosis and treatment using self-hypnosis. In Hypnosis in children and adolescents: Psychotherapeutic techniques for different stages of development).* Milano, Italy: FrancoAngeli.

Lazarus, J. E. (2013). *Keeping the bed dry* [Video series]. Retrieved from www.keepingthebeddry.com

National Institute for Health and Care Excellence. (2010). *Nocturnal enuresis: The management of bedwetting in children and young people.* NICE clinical guideline 111.

Olness, K. (1975). The use of self-hypnosis in the treatment of childhood nocturnal enuresis. A report on forty patients. *Clinical Pediatrics, 14*(3), 273–278.

Rombis, V., Triantafyllidis, A., Balaxis, E., Kalaitzis, C., & Touloupidis, S. (2005). Nocturnal enuresis in children. A four-year experience in outpatient clinics of pediatric urology. *Folia Microbiologica, 47*(2), 24–28.

Smellie, J. M., McGrigor, V. S., Meadow, S. R., Rose, S. J., & Douglas, M. F. (1996). Nocturnal enuresis: A placebo controlled trial of two antidepressant drugs. *Archives of Disease in Childhood, 75*(1), 62–66.

Stanton, H. E. (1979). Short-term treatment of enuresis. *American Journal of Clinical Hypnosis, 22*(2), 103–107.

Yapko, M. D. (2012). *Trancework: An introduction to the practice of clinical hypnosis.* New York, NY: Routledge.

Hypnosis and Fibromyalgia

Giuseppe De Benedittis

According to the American College of Rheumatology (ACR), fibromyalgia syndrome (FMS) is a complex, debilitating, functional pain syndrome characterized by the presence of continual, severe, widespread musculoskeletal pain for three months or longer, and tenderness in specific points of the body (Wolfe et al., 1990). In addition to pain, patients with FMS report fatigue; nonrestorative sleep; psychopathological concomitants (such as anxiety and depression); cognitive dysfunction in attention, concentration, and memory; and other symptoms, such as irritable bowel syndrome and morning stiffness with significant negative consequences for patients' quality of life and daily functioning (De Benedittis, 2012; Lami, Martínez, & Sánchez, 2013; Yunus, 2000). In the latest diagnostic criteria review, Wolfe et al. (2010) emphasized the clinical approach and proposed pain, sleep disturbance, cognitive dysfunction, and physical symptoms as the most important diagnostic variables.

The location of the nine paired tender points that comprise the 1990 American College of Rheumatology (Wolfe et al., 1990) criteria for FSM are shown in Figure 25.1.

EPIDEMIOLOGY

In Europe, FMS affects 2.9% to 4.7% of the general population, mostly middle-aged women, generating considerable economic, social, and personal costs (Lami et al., 2013).

What is the incidence of FMS? A dramatic increase in the incidence of patients with FMS referred to a pain clinic, such as our Pain Clinic of the University of Milan, has been reported in the last decade, with frequency more than doubled in the last five years (De Benedittis & Malafronte, 2014). Female prevalence is striking (in a recent study of female patients in our clinic it was found that 85% out of 167 consecutive patients met diagnostic criteria for fibromyalgia; De Benedittis & Malafronte, 2014).

PATHOPHYSIOLOGY

Pathogenesis of FMS is still poorly understood. Despite widespread somatic symptoms and signs, including pain and multiple trigger points, the evidence of peripheral dysfunction (e.g., muskuloskeletal) is lacking. On the other hand, an increasing body of evidence supports the notion of a complex, central dysfunctional pain syndrome with hyperalgesia likely due to central hyperexcitability and loss of descending inhibition, as structural brain changes and neurocognitive impairment suggest (De Benedittis, 2012, 2014).

Neuroimaging studies. Recent neuroimaging studies have shown accelerated brain gray matter loss (in terms of density; the associative network or *connectoma*) in patients with FMS as compared with healthy controls, suggesting a premature aging of the brain. Regions showing significantly less gray matter density included the left parahippocampal gyrus (PHG), the left and right mid/posterior cingulate gyrus (CG), the left insular cortex (IC), and the medial frontal cortex (MFC). On the whole, FMS patients showed gray matter loss 3.3 times more than in controls and loose brain gray matter 9.5 times more than in normal aging (Kuchinad et al., 2007)!

Another study (Robinson, Craggs, Price, Perlstein, & Staud, 2011) has shown pain-related brain areas associated with decreased gray matter densities in patients with FMS compared with normal controls. These areas include the left rostral and mid–anterior cingulate cortex (ACC), as well as left mid-insula.

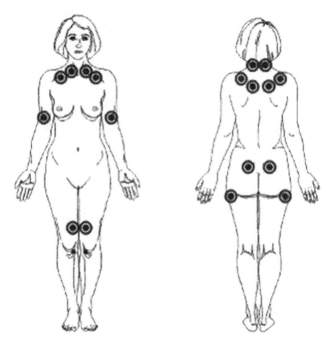

FIGURE 25.1 The location of the nine paired tender points that comprise the 1990 American College of Rheumatology criteria for fibromyalgia syndrome (FMS). From Wolfe et al. (1990).

A possible explanation for the decreased gray matter density in these disorders might include differential mechanisms, not mutually exclusive, such as: (a) chronic nociceptive input; (b) effect of chronic psychosocial stressors; (c) cytochemic excitotoxicity, that is, atrophy secondary to excitotoxicity and/or exposure to inflammation-related agents, such as cytokines; (d) maladaptive allocation of attentional resources in anticipating/amplifying the nociceptive input ("overuse atrophy"); and (e) predisposing central sensitization factors (De Benedittis, 2012).

Cognitive Impairment in Patients With FMS

Functionally speaking, patients with FMS perform no differently from healthy adults 20 years older than their chronological age on most cognitive tasks (Park, Glass, Minear, & Crofford, 2001). In a recent study (Inglese, Zago, Delli Pozzi, & De Benedittis, 2012), the cognitive functioning of patients with chronic pain was investigated. Within this group, patients suffering from FMS and nonspecific chronic low back pain (NS-CLBP) were comparatively evaluated with standardized neuropsychological tests, focusing on three key cognitive domains: attention, memory, and frontal executive functions.

Results of the study showed that more than one third of chronic pain patients complained of cognitive impairment. Memory disorders were considerably prevalent (70%) in patients with FMS, associated with attention control disorders (30%), while frontal executive function disorders were prevalent (50%) in patients with NS-CLBP, associated with attention control disorders (40%) and memory disorders (30%). Cognitive impairment was independent of such variables as age, pain duration, and pain intensity. Our preliminary results of neuropsychological evaluation were positively related with neuroimaging studies. Patients suffering from discrete pain syndromes showed different cognitive impairments possibly related to specific morphological and functional changes of the Pain Matrix. A selective neuropsychological battery has proved to be a useful tool to differentially evaluate cognitive dysfunctions in chronic pain populations.

Now, we face a crucial question: which causes which? Is the cognitive dysfunction the consequence or the cause of accelerated loss of gray substance, or is there a circular relationship between these two variables? Or are they moderated by a third variable? We still do not know as further studies are needed in order to elucidate causative relationships.

FMS and Abuse

Adverse life events such as emotional, physical, and sexual abuse in childhood and adulthood have been discussed as potential etiologic factors in FMS since the seminal study by Hudson and Pope (1995).

The trauma hypothesis of FMS assumes a link between these types of abuse and potential pathophysiologic mechanisms of FMS, such as perturbed neuroprocessing of grievous stimuli or hypereactivity of the hypo-thalamo-pituitary-adrenal (HPA) gland axis.

Abuse is the improper usage or treatment of an entity, often to unfairly or improperly gain benefit. Abuse can come in many forms, such as physical or verbal maltreatment; injury; sexual assault, violation, rape, or unjust practices; wrongful practice or custom; offense; crime; or verbal aggression.

Clinical phenomenology of abuse or victimization include (a) passive and (b) active abuse. The most common form of passive abuse is neglect (both physical and emotional), in which the perpetrator is responsible for providing care to a person (victim) who is unable to care for oneself, but fails to provide adequate care to meet the victim's needs, thereby resulting in the victim's demise. Active abuse includes physical, emotional, and sexual abuse. Physical abuse is abuse involving contact intended to cause feelings of intimidation, pain, injury, or other physical suffering or bodily harm. Psychological or emotional abuse, also referred to as mental abuse, is a form of abuse characterized by a person subjecting or exposing another to behavior that is psychologically harmful. Such abuse is often associated with situations of power imbalance, such as abusive relationships, bullying, child abuse, and mobbing in the workplace. Sexual abuse is the forcing of undesired sexual behavior by one person on another, when that force falls short of being a sexual assault. When the victim is younger than the age of consent, it is referred to as child sexual abuse. Rape, also referred to as sexual assault, is an assault by a person involving sexual intercourse with or without sexual penetration of another person without that person's consent.

What is the relevance of abuse in patients with FMS? Starting with Taylor's study (1995) on 40 patients compared with a healthy control group, no prevalent difference could be found between the two groups. At variance, Walker et al. (1997), comparing 36 patients with FMS with an equivalent number of patients with rheumatoid arthritis (RA), found significantly more physical, sexual, and emotional abuse in patients with FMS than in the control group. In 2009, Paras et al. published the first meta-analysis on 23 randomized controlled trial (RCT) and 4,640 patients, showing definitely a prevalence of sexual abuse in patients with FMS. This observation was confirmed by the recent, comprehensive meta-analytical study by Häuser, Kosseva, Üceyler, Klose, and Sommer (2011) on 18 RCT and 13,095 patients, with a striking prevalence of physical and sexual abuse in patients with FMS.

FMS and Posttraumatic Stress Disorder

Posttraumatic stress disorder (PTSD) is definitely a trauma and stress-related disorder, according to the *Diagnostic and Statistical Manual of Mental Disorders* (5th ed., *DSM-5*; American Psychiatric Association, 2013).

The main diagnostic criteria include (a) exposure to real or threatened death, injury, or sexual violence; (b) avoidance of behaviors of physical or temporal reminders of the traumatic experience(s); (c) negative alterations in cognition and mood associated with the traumatic event(s); (d) increased arousal and reactivity; (e) duration of symptoms for at least one month; and (f) the disturbance is not due to the effects of a substance or another medical condition.

A number of neuroimaging studies (Lanius, Bluhm, Lanius, & Pain, 2006) suggest that brain areas most commonly activated in PTSD patients are the medial prefrontal and ventromedial cortex, as well as the amygdala. These areas partially overlap with brain areas activated in patients with FMS, suggesting some common pathways.

A recent study by Häuser et al. (2013) evaluated the incidence of PTSD in a population of 395 consecutive patients with FMS as 45.3% as compared with 3% only in the healthy controls. In more than two-thirds of the cases, adverse events antedated the onset of FMS; in less than one-third of the cases, these events followed the onset of FMS, with adverse events occurring in the same year of FMS in 4% of the cases.

FMS, Abuse, and PTSD

What is the relationship among FMS, abuse, and PTSD? In order to try to solve the FMS conundrum, our working hypothesis was to test whether adverse childhood events (ACE) acted as early stressors for delayed, somatized PTSD, such as antecedents or precursors of FMS.

An RCT was set up by comparing patients with FMS with patients with NS-CLBP (38 patients, respectively), matched for age, sex, pain duration, and severity (De Benedittis, 2014).

Results of this study showed that patients with FMS reported a significantly higher percentage of multiple ACE on the ACE scale (Felitti et al., 1998) as compared with the NS-CLBP group. As far as the type of abuse, patients with FMS had a significantly higher percentage of physical, sexual, and emotional abuse, and, though at a lesser extent, neglect. Concomitantly, patients with FMS scored significantly higher than NS-CLBP in the posttraumatic severity (PTS) symptom scale (Foa, Cashman, Jaycox, & Perry, 1997).

The conclusions of our study suggest that childhood/adolescence abuse might induce a PTSD with

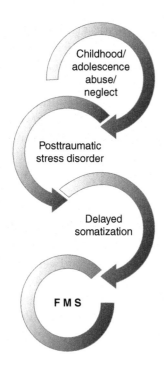

FIGURE 25.2 Childhood/adolescence abuse might induce a PTSD with delayed somatization (at least in a significant proportion of patients), eventually leading to FMS.

FMS, fibromyalgia syndrome; PTSD, posttraumatic stress disorder.

delayed somatization (at least in a significant proportion of patients), eventually leading to FMS (Figure 25.2). Is this *really* the missing link? As of yet, we do not know, as further longitudinal studies are needed to solve this intriguing puzzle.

TREATMENT

Owing to the complex pathophysiological mechanisms involved in the genesis and maintenance of FMS, and considering a psychobiological model in order to fully understand the pain experience, current treatments involve multidisciplinary approaches. Evidence-based treatment guidelines mostly recommend multimodal approaches that include pharmacological treatment, physical exercise, and psychological treatments, specifically cognitive behavioral treatment (CBT), though there is currently a controversy about the effectiveness and positive results of psychological treatments in FMS, as well as their long-term maintenance, possibly due to heterogeneity of the studies and potential methodological biases (Glombiewski et al., 2010).

Systematic reviews have reached different conclusions. Sim and Adams (2002) compared different kinds of nonpharmacological treatments for patients with FMS and concluded that there was not enough evidence to highlight any intervention over the others. Glombiewski et al. (2010) analyzed 23 studies and found that psychotherapy significantly reduced pain intensity and depressive symptoms, and that interventions based on relaxation/biofeedback were especially effective for sleep disturbance. At the same time, Bernardy, Füber, Klose, and Häuser (2011) conducted a review of CBT in FMS and did not identify any significant effects after treatment on pain intensity, fatigue, and subjective sleep disturbance.

In a context of public health systems, it is crucial to evaluate the cost–benefit of treatment. Therefore, there is a need for more controlled studies of treatment effectiveness that meet the standard methodological requirements. More research is needed to identify moderating and mediating variables that lead to a suitable match between the psychological characteristics of patients and treatment (Lami et al., 2013).

THE ROLE OF HYPNOSIS IN FMS

What is the role of hypnosis and hypnotherapy in patients with FMS?

We know very well that management of FMS may be challenging, as it seems to be refractory to most treatments. Hypnosis used alone, as well as in combination with other treatments, has been shown to be effective in the control of chronic pain of various origin (Elkins, Jensen, & Patterson, 2011). A few case studies and controlled trials of patients with FMS support the potential efficacy of hypnosis for this condition (Bernardy et al., 2011).

Table 25.1 shows RCT and meta-analysis evaluating the efficacy of hypnosis and hypnotherapy in FMS. Starting with the seminal study by Haanen et al. (1991) of 40 patients, comparing hypnosis and physical therapy (with a follow-up ranging between 12 and 24 weeks), the meta analysis found a better pain relief in the hypnotic group. In 2007, Castel, Pérez, Sala, Padrol, and Rull could not detect any difference in pain relief

TABLE 25.1

RCT AND META-ANALYSIS EVALUATING THE EFFICACY OF HYPNOSIS AND HYPNOTHERAPY IN FMS					
Authors	**Year**	**No.**	**Study**	**Follow-Up**	**Results**
Haanen et al.	1991	40	RCT (hypnosis vs. physical therapy)	12 to 24 weeks	↓ Better pain relief with h.
Castel et al.	2007	47	Hypnosis vs. relaxation	n.a.	Hypnosis ≠ relaxation
Martínez-Valero et al.	2008	6	Hypnosis vs. CBT vs. drugs	n.a.	Hypnosis/CBT better than drugs
Thieme and Gracely	2009	201	Psychological treatments—meta-analysis (5 hypnosis RCT)	n.a.	Mild effect of hypnosis
Bernardy et al.	2011	256	Meta-analysis (6 hypnosis RCT)	8 weeks (average)	Large effect on pain relief, medium on sleep, HrQoL unchanged
Picard et al.	2013	59	RCT (hypnosis vs. waiting list as control)	24 weeks	Hypnosis better than controls
De Benedittis	2014	24	RCT (hypnosis + ST vs ST alone)	24 weeks	Hypnosis + ST better than ST alone in the long run

FMS, fibromyalgia syndrome; RCT, randomized controlled trials; ST, standard therapy.

between hypnosis and relaxation. In a small RCT, Martínez-Valero et al. (2008) reported that hypnosis and CBT did better than drugs, with no significant difference in-between. In 2009, Thieme and Gracely published a meta-analysis on the efficacy of psychological treatments (including five RCT with hypnotherapy) showing mild effects of hypnosis. A meta-analysis by Bernardy et al. (2011) reviewed 6 RCT including 256 FMS cases with a follow-up of 8 weeks (average), showing a large effect on pain relief and a medium effect on sleep, whereas quality of life (QoL) remained unchanged.

A recent RCT (Picard et al., 2013) contrasted the effects of five nonstandardized sessions of hypnosis over two months in 59 women with FMS who were randomly assigned to treatment ($n = 30$) or a waiting list control group ($n = 29$). Patients in the treated group were encouraged to practice self-hypnosis. The fibromyalgia impact questionnaire (FIQ), medical outcomes study (MOS)sleep scale, multidimensional fatigue inventory (MFI), cognitive strategy questionnaire (CSQ), and patient global impression of change (PGIC) were administered at baseline, three months (M3), and six months (M6) after inclusion. Compared to the control, the hypnosis group reported better improvement on PGIC ($p = .001$ at M3, $p = .01$ at M6) and a significant improvement in sleep and CSQ dramatization subscale (both at M6).

A more recent RCT (De Benedittis, 2012, 2014) included 24 consecutive patients with a diagnosis of FMS. Owing to ethical reasons, a placebo-controlled study was not feasible. Patients were randomly assigned to hypnotherapy plus standard pharmacological treatment ($n = 12$) (H group) or purely standard pharmacological treatment as controls ($n = 12$) (C group). Follow-up evaluations were at M3 and M6. Our primary outcome was pain relief, as measured by means of a visual analog scale (VAS) and numerical rating scale (NRS). Secondary outcomes included health-related quality of life (HRQoL), energy (or fatigue reduction), and sleep. Mean pain relief was 61% in the H group and 53% in the C group, respectively. The difference was not statistically significant. Long-term (M6) mean pain relief for H and C patients was 70% and 25%, respectively ($p = .001$). Moreover, hypnosis proved to be significantly superior to standard treatment as far as QoL, energy, and restorative sleep were concerned in the long run. Patients' satisfaction after treatment was significantly higher in the H group (75%) as opposed to the C group (37%).

In conclusion: The study showed that hypnotherapy plus standard medical treatment produced greater pain relief and improvement in HRQoL than standard medical treatment alone in the long run, but not in the short run, thus suggesting that pain reduction can be maintained and even improved across time. The patient's satisfaction was significantly greater in the hypnotic group than in controls. Continued home practice coupled with periodic "booster" sessions possibly accounted for maintenance of gains. Safety of hypnotic treatment was excellent, with no adverse events related to hypnosis/self-hypnosis being reported.

Hypnosis may be a useful adjunct tool to manage chronic pain and dysfunctional symptoms in patients with FMS. A far greater population of patients and further research are still needed to establish the efficacy of hypnotherapy in FMS.

Hypnotic Procedures

One weekly hypnotic session was administered to the patients for the first three months, with two monthly sessions for the next three months. Hypnosis was synergized with self-hypnosis on a twice-a-day basis.

As far as hypnotic procedures were concerned, following standard trance induction by eye fixation, deepening of hypnosis was achieved with suggestions for multisensory imagery and progressive relaxation. Subsequently, indirect (Ericksonian) suggestions were given as target suggestions for cognitive modulation of pain in an indivualized form.

These included (a) dissociation ("pain does not belong to you"); (b) imagining to swim in a magic swimming pool; (c) respiratory pacing (slow breathing, shown to be effective in reducing pain); (d) age progression (being projected in a pain-free future); and (e) partial posthypnotic amnesia for the pain experience.

Some other, rather innovative hypnotherapeutic methods were used in selected cases. Algovisual synesthesia (De Benedittis, 2001) has been successfully applied to patients with FMS: the rationale is to cognitively modulate pain by multisensory cross talk. In one case, the patient with FMS was asked, during trance, to associate her pain experience with a color. The starting color was a pink. Subsequently, the patient was asked to associate another color with the experience of well-being. In this case, the ending color was a white, marble color. In the following hypnotic session, suggestions were given to trance-form the starting pink-rose color into the ending white-marble color, thereby resulting in significant pain relief without even mentioning the term *pain*. In another case, the patient was asked to trance-form the starting deep-blue color, associated with pain, into the ending sky-blue color, associated with the sense of well-being, thereby resulting in significant pain relief.

Finally, in two selected cases of highly hypnotizable subjects with a clear history of abuse and PTSD, hypnoanalytical treatment was successfully established. Unconscious trauma and conflicts were unveiled by age regression and worked through. This eventually led to (almost complete) symptom resolution.

CASE EXAMPLE

A 48-year-old woman complained of long-lasting severe, widespread musculoskeletal pain, associated with other debilitating symptoms (e.g., fatigue, morning stiffness, depression, insomnia, and self-perceived very poor quality of life). History of sexual abuse in her adolescence was reported and PTSD symptoms were present. Diagnosis of FMS was made on clinical grounds, with the patient being refractory to previous medical and physical treatments. Management included hypnosis, combined with self-hypnosis on a twice-a-day basis, plus standard medical treatment (amitryptiline 75 mg/day) for a duration of six months. Indirect (Ericksonian) suggestions were given for cognitive modulation of pain in an individualized form. These included (a) dissociation; (b) imagining swimming in a magic swimming pool; (c) respiratory pacing; (d) age progression; and (e) partial posthypnotic amnesia for the pain experience.

Substantial pain relief (50%) was obtained within the first three months of treatment. Outcome results were maintained and even improved (pain relief: 68%) after six months, concomitant with an improvement of the quality of life.

TRANSCRIPT: RAPID INDUCTION FIBROMYALGIA RELIEF (RIFR)

"I'd like to talk with you for a moment to see if you'd like to feel more comfortable and relaxed than you might expect. OK, then . . . the best way to begin feeling more comfortable is to just begin by sitting as comfortably as you can right now . . . go ahead and adjust yourself to the most comfortable position you like . . . that's fine. Now, I'd like you to notice how much more comfortable you can feel by just taking one very big, satisfying deep breath. That's fine. You may already notice how good that feels . . . how warm your neck and shoulders can feel. . . . Now, I'd like you to take four more very deep, very comfortable breaths . . . and, as you exhale, notice . . . just notice how comfortable your shoulders can become . . . and notice how comfortable your eyes can feel when they close . . . and when they close, just let them stay closed . . . that's right, just notice that . . . and notice, too, how, when you exhale slowly and deeply, you can just feel that relaxation is beginning to sink in. . . .

I want you to concentrate on your breathing . . . breathing in pure relaxation and exhaling all the tension in the body . . . feel all of the tension leaving the chest as you exhale . . . feel yourself relaxing even deeper with each and every breath . . . and your breathing is so regular . . . so easy and effortless and you are relaxing more and more . . . and your entire body is completely and totally relaxing as you drift even deeper down with each and every breath . . . and you feel a warm, wonderful sense of relaxation and going even deeper down. . . .

Good, that's fine . . . now, as you continue breathing gently, comfortably and deeply, all I'd like you to do is to picture in your mind . . . just imagine a beautiful and safe staircase, any kind you like . . . with 10 steps, and you at the top . . . Now, in a moment, I'm going to begin to count, out loud, from ten to one, and as I count each number I'd like you to take a step down that staircase . . . see yourself stepping down, feel yourself stepping down, one step for each number I count . . . and all you need to do is notice, just notice, how much more comfortable and relaxed you can feel at each step, as you

go down the staircase . . . one step for each number that I count . . . the smaller the number, the farther down the staircase . . . the farther down the staircase, the more comfortable you can feel . . . all right, you can begin to get ready . . . now, I'm going to begin. . . . NINE, one step down the staircase . . . EIGHT, two steps down the staircase . . . that's fine . . . SEVEN . . . three steps down the staircase . . . and maybe you already notice how much more relaxed you can feel . . . I wonder if there are places in your body that feel more relaxed than others . . . perhaps your shoulders feel more relaxed than your neck . . . perhaps your legs feel more relaxed than your arms . . . I don't know, and it really doesn't matter . . . all that matters is that you feel comfortable . . . that's all. . . . SIX . . . four steps down the staircase, perhaps already feeling places in your body beginning to relax . . . I wonder if the deep relaxing, heaviness in your forehead, is already beginning to spread and flow . . . down, across your eyes, down across your face, into your mouth and jaw . . . down through your neck. Deep, restful, heavy . . . FIVE . . . five steps down the staircase . . . half of the way down, and already beginning, perhaps, to really enjoy your relaxation and comfort . . . FOUR . . . six steps down the staircase . . . perhaps beginning to notice that the sounds which were distracting become less so . . . that all the sounds you can hear become a part of your experience of comfort and relaxation . . . anything you can notice becomes a part of your experience of comfort and relaxation . . . THREE . . . seven steps down the staircase . . . that's fine . . . perhaps noticing the heavy, restful, relaxing feeling spreading down into your shoulders, into your arms . . . I wonder if you notice one arm feeling heavier than the other . . . perhaps your left arm feels a bit heavier than your right . . . perhaps your right arm feels heavier than your left . . . I don't know, perhaps they both feel equally, comfortably heavy. . . . It really doesn't matter . . . just let yourself become more and more aware of that comfortable heaviness . . . or is it a feeling of lightness? . . . I really don't know, and it really doesn't matter . . . TWO . . . eight steps down the staircase . . . and ONE . . . nine steps down the staircase, breathing comfortably, slowly, and deeply . . . noticing that heaviness is really beginning to sink in, as you continue to notice the pleasant, restful, comfortable relaxation just spread through your whole body . . . and now, TEN steps down the staircase, wondering perhaps what might be happening, perhaps *wondering if anything at all is happening . . . and yet, knowing that it really doesn't matter, feeling so pleasantly restful, just continuing to notice this growing, spreading, comfortable relaxation. . . .*

And while you continue to relax, you'll be surprised to find yourself in the middle of a beautiful, secret, enchanted garden. It is the beginning of summer. The air is warm and balmy. The garden stretches for miles and miles. You are walking down a path under a shadowy bower of white, sweet-smelling jasmines. And while enjoying your walk, you might notice at either side of the bower wonderful flower beds with blossoms . . . and you may wonder how Nature may have blended such extraordinary variety of flowers in an endless harmony of colors and perfumes. At your right-hand side, your attention might be captured by a flower bed with so many blossom roses with different, seductive shades of colors: a fleshy pink, a brilliant yellow, an intriguing orange, a very vivid red color. And while you are marveling at this symphony of colors, shades, and tones, mysterious scents filled with joy will spread through the sweet air, blending with a full explosion of colors. It seems as if any color has its own scent, and any perfume its own color. Now, you've come across the long, shadowy bower and just in the middle of this secret garden, there is a delightful swimming pool. I wonder whether you'll like to walk along the edge of the swimming pool, enjoying the peaceful calm of clear, pure waters. You may even wish to take a swim, letting your body float in the waters, drifting way down now . . . deeper and deeper relaxed. Imagine floating on the water surface, allowing the fresh, magic liquid to penetrate your skin, into your muscles, throughout your body, soothing your pain. From now on I want you to have a positive image of your body. Whenever you look at yourself or think of your body image you will do it in a positive manner. Looking at your body in a positive manner will help you feel good about yourself and to continue to progress toward the body image that you really want. You no longer need to think painful thoughts or to feel painful experiences in your body. Your body is your temple. It is your sacred private property. You own it and you want the best for it. So from now on I want you to think only positive thoughts

and have positive feelings toward your body. You are becoming happy, confident, energetic, and progressing toward making yourself the best you that you can be. Feel good about yourself, having a good self image . . . and continuing to move onward . . . you are in full control.

And now I want you to make a wonderful, cosmic journey. One minute of actual time will seem like 10 minutes to you. Time will go by very, very slowly. It will seem an eternity. You are lying in a large, round bed in a huge, circular, black room. It's midnight. You are looking up at the ceiling, which is a glass dome, a clear, transparent bubble. Suddenly you notice that the room is beginnning to turn, going round and round and the room is spinning. You are hurled off the bed. You shoot upward and outward into the space, faster than the speed of light. Flashes of light pass you by as you go traveling through the deep space. It's a wonderful trip. Now you are beginning to fall through the space, back to earth, but in a near future time, full of positive expectations, energy and almost pain free. You are continuing to drift and float into a timeless space. And you are really enjoying this incredible experience of well-being, full of energy. I wonder if you'll notice that you'll feel surprised that your experience here today is so much more pleasant and comfortable than you might have expected . . . I wonder if you'll notice that surprise . . . that there are no other feelings. . . . I wonder if you'll be pleased to notice that today . . . or any other day . . . you'll be reminded of how very comfortable you are feeling right now . . . even more comfortable than you feel even now . . . comfortable, relaxed . . . nothing to bother, nothing to disturb . . . I don't know exactly how it will seem . . . I only know, as perhaps you also know . . . that your experience will seem surprisingly more pleasant, more comfortable, more restful than you might expect . . . with nothing to bother, nothing to disturb . . . whatever you are able to notice . . . everything can be a part of your experience of comfort, restfulness and relaxation . . . nothing really matters but your experience of comfort and relaxation . . . absolutely deep comfort and relaxation . . . that's fine. . . . And now, as you continue to enjoy your comfortable relaxation, I'd like you to notice how very nice it feels to be this way. . . to really enjoy your own experience, the feelings your whole body can give you . . . and in a moment, but not yet . . . not until you're ready . . . but in a moment, I'm going to count from one to ten . . . and as you know, I'd like you to feel yourself going back up the steps . . . one step for each number . . . you'll have all the time you need . . . after all, time is relative . . . feel yourself slowly and comfortably going back up the steps, one step for each number I count . . . when I reach eight, your eyes will be almost ready to open . . . when I reach nine, they will be opened . . . and, when I reach ten, you'll be alert, awake, refreshed . . . perhaps as though you'd had a nice nap . . . alert, refreshed, comfortable . . . and even though you'll still be very comfortable and relaxed, you'll be alert and feeling very well . . . perhaps surprised, but feeling very well . . . perhaps ready to be surprised . . . no hurry, you'll have all the time you need, as you begin to go back up these restful steps . . . . ONE . . . TWO . . . THREE . . . that's right, feel yourself going back up the steps . . . ready to be surprised . . . FOUR . . . FIVE. . . halfway back up the stairs . . . SIX . . . a quarter of the way back up, more and more alert . . . no rush, plenty of time . . . feel yourself becoming more and more alert . . . SEVEN . . . that's right . . . EIGHT . . . NINE . . . TEN . . . that's right . . . wide awake, alert, relaxed, refreshed . . . that's fine. How do you feel? Relaxed? Comfortable?"

CONCLUSION

FMS is a complex, debilitating, functional pain syndrome characterized by chronic, severe, widespread musculoskeletal pain associated with fatigue, nonrestorative sleep, psychopathological concomitants (such as anxiety and depression), cognitive dysfunction, and overall poor quality of life. Management of FMS may be challenging, as it seems to be refractory to most treatments. However, recent evidence supports the notion that hypnosis, combined with a daily practice of self-hypnosis, may be an effective adjunct tool, in addition to standard medical treatment for pain control and improved quality of life. Long-term treatment is often needed for positive therapeutic outcome with pain relief being maintained and even improved across time.

REFERENCES

American Psychiatric Association. (2013). *DSM-5 Diagnostic and statistical manual of mental disorders.* Arlington, VA: American Psychiatric Press.

Bernardy, K., Füber, N., Klose, P., & Häuser, W. (2011). Efficacy of hypnosis/guided imagery in fibromyalgia syndrome: A systematic review and a meta-analysis of controlled trials. *BMC Musculoskeletal Disorders, 12*(1), 133. doi:10.1186/1471-2474-12-133

Castel, A., Pérez, M., Sala, J., Padrol, A., & Rull, M. (2007). Effect of hypnotic suggestion on fibromyalgic pain: Comparison between hypnosis and relaxation. *European Journal of Pain, 11*(4), 463–468.

De Benedittis, G. (2001). The revolving doors of pain: Hypnotic synaesthesia for modulation of the pain experience. In C. Loriedo & B. Peter (Eds.), *The new hypnosis. The utilization of personal resources* (pp. 33–48). Münich: MEG-Stiftung.

De Benedittis, G. (2012). *Hypnotherapy for fibromyalgia: A long-term controlled study.* Presented at the 14th World Congress on Pain, Milan, Italy.

De Benedittis, G. (2014). *Fibromyalgia and post-traumatic stress disorder: The missing link?* Presented at the 15th World Congress on Pain, Buenos Aires, Argentina.

De Benedittis, G., & Malafronte, M. L. (2014). *Coping with fibromyalgia: What we have learned from hypnosis, a review of the literature and new, innovative hypnotic approaches to widespread, refractory pain.* Presented at the 15th World Congress on Pain, Buenos Aires, Argentina.

Elkins, G., Jensen, M. P., & Patterson, D. R. (2011). Hypnotherapy for the management of chronic pain. *International Journal of Clinical Experimental Hypnosis, 55,* 275–287.

Felitti, V. J., Anda, R. F., Nordenberg, D., Williamson, D. F., Spitz, A. M., Edwards, V., . . . Marks, J. S. (1998). Relationship of childhood abuse and household dysfunction to many of the leading causes of death in adults: The adverse childhood experiences (ACE) study. *American Journal of Preventive Medicine, 14*(4), 245–258.

Foa, E. B., Cashman, L., Jaycox, L., & Perry, K. (1997). The validation of a self-report measure of posttraumatic stress disorder: The posttraumatic diagnostic scale. *Psychological Assessment, 9*(4), 445–451.

Glombiewski, J. A., Sawyer, A. T., Gutermann, J., Koenig, K., Rief, W., & Hofmann, S. G. (2010). Psychological treatments for fibromyalgia: A meta-analysis. *Pain, 151*(2), 280–295.

Haanen, H. C., Hoenderdos, H. T., van Romunde, L. K., Hop, W. C., Mallee, C., Terwiel, J. P., & Hekster, G. B. (1991). Controlled trial of hypnotherapy in the treatment of refractory fibromyalgia. *Journal of Rheumatology, 18*(1), 72–75.

Häuser, W., Galek, A., Erbslöh-Möller, B., Köllner, V., Kühn-Becker, H., Langhorst, J., . . . Glaesmer, H. (2013). Posttraumatic stress disorder in fibromyalgia syndrome: Prevalence, temporal relationship between posttraumatic stress and fibromyalgia symptoms, and impact on clinical outcome. *Pain, 154*(8), 1216–1223.

Häuser, W., Kosseva, M., Üceyler, N., Klose, P., & Sommer, C. (2011). Emotional, physical, and sexual abuse in fibromyalgia syndrome: A systematic review with meta-analysis. *Arthritis Care & Research, 63*(6), 808–820.

Hudson, J. I., & Pope, H. G. (1995). Does childhood sexual abuse cause fibromyalgia? *Arthritis and Rheumatism, 38*(2), 161–163.

Inglese, S., Zago, S., Delli Pozzi, A., & De Benedittis, G. (2012). *Cognitive impairment in patients with fibromyalgia syndrome and non-specific chronic low back pain: A comparative study.* Presented at the 12th World Congress on Pain, Milano, Italy.

Kuchinad, A., Schweinhardt, P., Seminowicz, D. A., Wood, P. B., Chizh, B. A., & Bushnell, M. C. (2007). Accelerated brain graymatter loss in fibromyalgia patients: Premature aging of the brain? *The Journal of Neuroscience: The Official Journal of the Society for Neuroscience, 27*(15), 4004–4007.

Lami, M. J., Martínez, M. P., & Sánchez, A. I. (2013). Systematic review of psychological treatments in fibromyalgia. *Current Pain and Headache Reports, 17*(7), 345

Lanius, R. A., Bluhm, R., Lanius, U., & Pain, C. (2006). A review of neuroimaging studies in PTSD: Heterogeneity of response to symptom provocation. *Journal Psychiatric Research, 40,* 709–729.

Martínez-Valero, C., Castel, A., Capafons, A., Sala, J., Espejo, B., & Cardeña, E. (2008). Hypnotic treatment synergizes the psychological treatment of fibromyalgia: A pilot study. *American Journal of Clinical Hypnosis, 50*(4), 311–321.

Paras, M. L., Murad, M. H., Chen, L. P., Goranson, E. N., Sattler, A. L., Colbenson, K. M., . . . Zirakzadeh, A. (2009). Sexual abuse and lifetime diagnosis of somatic disorders: A systematic review and meta-analysis. *Journal of the American Medical Association, 302*(5), 550–561.

Park, D. C., Glass, J. M., Minear, M., & Crofford, L. J. (2001). Cognitive function in fibromyalgia patients. *Arthritis and Rheumatism, 44*(9), 2125–2133.

Picard, P., Jusseaume, C., Boutet, M., Dualé, C., Mulliez, A., & Aublet-Cuvellier, B. (2013). Hypnosis for management of fibromyalgia. *International Journal of Clinical and Experimental Hypnosis, 61*(1), 111–123.

Robinson, M. E., Craggs, J. G., Price, D. D., Perlstein, W. R., & Staud, R. (2011). Gray matter volumes of pain-related brain areas are decreased in fibromyalgia syndrome. *Journal of Pain, 4,* 436–443.

Sim, J., & Adams, N. (2002). Systematic review of randomized controlled trials of nonpharmacological interventions for fibromyalgia. *Clinical Journal of Pain, 18,* 324–336.

Taylor, S. J. (1995). Evaluations of children who have disclosed sexual abuse via facilitated communication. *Archives of Pediatrics & Adolescent Medicine, 149*(11), 1287–1288.

Thieme, K., & Gracely, R. H. (2009). Are psychological treatments effective for fibromyalgia pain? *Current Rheumatology Reports, 11*(6), 443–450.

Walker, E. A., Keegan, D., Gardner, G., Sullivan, M., Bernstein, D., & Katon, W. J. (1997). Psychosocial factors in fibromyalgia compared with rheumatoid arthritis: Sexual, physical, and emotional abuse and neglect. *Psychosomatic Medicine, 59*(6), 572–577.

Wolfe, F., Clauw, D. J., Fitzcharles, M. A., Goldenberg, D. L., Katz, R. S., Mease, P., . . . Yunus, M. B. (2010). The American College of Rheumatology preliminary diagnostic criteria for fibromyalgia and measurement of symptom severity. *Arthritis Care & Research, 62*(5), 600–610.

Wolfe, F., Smithe, H. A., Yunus, M. B., Bennett, R. M., Bombardier, C., Goldenberg, D. L., . . . Sheon, R. P. (1990). The American College of Rheumatology 1990 criteria for the classification of fibromyalgia: Report of the multicentre criteria committee. *Arthritis and Rheumatology, 33,* 160–172.

Yunus, M. B. (2000). Central sensitivity syndromes: A unified concept for fibromyalgia and other similar maladies. *Journal of Industrial Rheumetology, 8,* 27–33.

Headaches—Adults

Giuseppe De Benedittis

Probably the most common pain complaint in medical practice today is a headache. It accounts for one of the most burdensome and costly medical issues in the world. Its management still remains one of great concern, despite treatment with analgesics and psychophysiological modalities (De Benedittis & Villani, 1991).

Chronic headaches are broadly classified as "primary" or "secondary" headaches. Chronic primary headaches (CPH) are generally benign, recurrent headaches not caused by underlying disease or structural problems, such as migraine or tension-type headache (TTH). Ninety percent of all headaches are primary headaches (De Benedittis & Villani, 1991). CPH can cause substantial levels of disability and impose a significant health burden not only to patients and their families, but also to society as a whole owing to its high prevalence in the general population.

Secondary headaches are caused by an underlying disease, like a tumor, cerebral hemorrhage, or infection. Consequently, they may be dangerous symptoms of a serious life-threatening disease.

EPIDEMIOLOGY

Overall, the current global prevalence of headache is 47%, migraine is 10%, and TTH is 38% (Jensen & Stovner, 2008). As expected, the lifetime prevalences are higher: 66% for headache, 14% for migraine, and 46% for TTH (Jensen & Stovner, 2008).

The male:female ratio for migraine among adults varies from 1:2 to 1:3. In prepubertal children, there is generally no sex difference. The male:female ratio for TTH is 4:5, indicating that, unlike for migraine, women are only slightly more affected than men (Jensen & Stovner, 2008). Adults aged 20 to 50 years are the most likely sufferers, but children and adolescents are affected, too.

The Role of Stressful Events

Although CPH are acknowledged as multifactorial (De Benedittis, 1998), psychological stress has been assumed to play a significant role in the predisposition to and/or exacerbation of headache, particularly of the two most common syndromes: migraine and TTH. Emotional dynamics may play an important role in the precipitation/aggravation of many CPH attacks. Prolonged stress or tension, "let-down" after intense emotional events, internalized anger, inner conflicts, and a wide variety of other emotional factors exert an undisputed influence in provoking headache attacks. Major stressful life events may be associated with the onset of CPH, possibly serving as illness precursors or headache antecedents. In terms of event content, exits or losses are prominent in being perceived as stressful (De Benedittis, Lorenzetti, & Pieri, 1990).

Seen this way, CPH fit well into the category of psychosomatic or psychophysiological disorders, those in which pathophysiological mechanisms and, at times, structural processes are influenced by psychological determinants (De Benedittis, 1998).

CLASSIFICATION

CPH include a wide range of headaches, but the most common types are migraine and TTH; they account for the vast majority of CPH. Other, less common headaches include mixed headache (i.e., combined TTH with migraineous attacks), cluster headache, posttraumatic headache, and psychogenic headache.

Migraine

Migraine can be divided into two major subtypes: (a) migraine without aura (MwoA) and (b) migraine with aura (MwA).

Migraine is believed to be due to a mixture of environmental and genetic factors. About two-thirds of cases run in the family. The risk of migraine usually decreases during pregnancy, at variance with TTH (Olesen, Goadsby, Ramdan, Tfelt-Hansen, & Welch, 2006).

A significant number of patients (mainly women) with a history of migraine experience frequent and excessive use of ergotamine, triptans, or nonnarcotic analgesics, which perpetuate and worsen headaches rather than relieving them [the so-called "medication overuse headache" (MOH); De Benedittis & Villani (1991)].

Signs and Symptoms

MwoA is a chronic neurological disorder characterized by recurrent moderate-to-severe headaches often in association with a number of autonomic nervous system symptoms. It accounts for 90% of all migraine attacks. According to the International Headache Society (IHS) diagnostic criteria (Headache Classification Committee of the International Headache Society, 2013), typically the headache affects one half of the head, is pulsating in nature, and lasts from 4 to 72 hours. Associated symptoms may include nausea, vomiting, photophobia, and sonophobia (sensitivity to light, sound, or smell.) The pain is generally made worse by physical activity.

MwA is characterized by an aura, a transient visual, sensory, language, or motor disturbance, which signals that the headache will soon occur. Aura usually develops gradually over 5 to 20 minutes and lasts for less than 60 minutes. Occasionally an aura can occur with little or no headache following it [aura without migraine or migraine equivalent; De Benedittis & Villani (1991)].

Pathophysiology

Migraines are believed to be a neurovascular disorder, with evidence supporting its mechanisms starting within the brain and then spreading to the blood vessels (Olesen et al., 2006). High levels of the neurotransmitter serotonin, also known as 5-hydroxytryptamine, are believed to be involved (Olesen et al., 2006).

Aura. Cortical-spreading depression, or *spreading depression* is bursts of neuronal activity followed by a period of inactivity, which is seen in those with migraines with an aura (Olesen et al., 2006). After the burst of activity, the blood flow to the cerebral cortex in the area affected is decreased for two to six hours. It is believed that when depolarization travels down the underside of the brain, nerves that sense pain in the head and neck are triggered (Olesen et al., 2006).

Pain. The exact mechanism of the headache that occurs during migraine is unknown, but the role of vasodilatation of the extracranial arteries associated, in particular, concomitant with activation of the trigeminovascular system, is believed to be significantly associated with the algic phase of migraine attack (Shevel, 2011).

Tension-Type Headache

TTH is the most common type of primary headache (Olesen et al., 2006). It may be categorized as one of two major subtypes: chronic or episodic. The chronic subtype is a serious disease causing greatly decreased quality of life and high disability.

Symptoms and Signs

TTH presents with daily or very frequent episodes of headache lasting minutes to days. The pain is typically bilateral, pressing, or "bandlike" in quality and of mild to moderate intensity, and it does not worsen with routine physical activity. There may be mild nausea, photophobia, or phonophobia. The only really useful distinguishing feature is tenderness on manual palpation, and not evidenced from surface electromyography (EMG) or pressure algometry (Headache Classification Committee of the International Headache Society, 2013).

Pathophysiology

The exact mechanisms of TTH are not known. For decades, dispute has prevailed concerning the importance of a muscle contraction mechanism, but conclusive studies are still lacking. Involuntary tightening in muscles, whether mentally or physically induced, is certainly important, but may be inadequate to produce the headache (De Benedittis & Villani, 1991).

Peripheral pain mechanisms are most likely to play a role in episodic TTH, whereas central pain mechanisms play a more important role in chronic

TTH. Moreover, a dysfunction in pain inhibitory systems may also play a role in the pathophysiology of this syndrome (Headache Classification Committee of the International Headache Society, 2013).

Psychogenic Headache

There are other headaches that do not appear to possess a peripheral, or central physiological, or structural basis, according to our current knowledge. Although the term *psychogenic headache* is imprecise and shamefully misused (De Benedittis, 1998, 2008), it will be used here to describe that headache condition apparently unassociated with known pathophysiological pain-producing mechanisms, and for which there is reasonable evidence or strong presumption that the symptom is linked to psychological factors or conflicts [*Diagnostic and Statistical Manual of Mental Disorders (DSM-5)*; American Psychiatric Association (2013)]. *Conversion headache* is perhaps the most frequently described psychogenic headache (De Benedittis, 1998, 2008). Pain may represent a psychic device to exteriorize a painful conflict (Engel, 1959).

HYPNOTIC TREATMENT FOR HEADACHE: REVIEW OF THE LITERATURE

There is a considerable body of literature on the use of hypnosis in the treatment of CPH [see review in Hammond (2007)]. Interest in hypnosis for pain management has increased with recent evidence that hypnosis can reduce pain (and costs) associated with medical procedures (Lang & Rosen, 2002), and there are now an adequate number of controlled studies of hypnosis to draw meaningful conclusions from the literature regarding chronic pain (Barber & Bejenke, 1996; De Benedittis, 2009, 2012; Elkins, Jensen, & Patterson, 2011; Flammer & Aladdin, 2007; Hammond, 2007; Jensen & Patterson, 2014; Montgomery, DuHamel, & Redd, 2000).

Most approaches are directed primarily toward modifying the symptoms of migraine or TTH, but they do not attend directly to cognitive-emotional mediating variables. Yet, in a significant number of cases [approximately 30%, according to Brown and Fromm (1986)], symptom removal by using hypnosis

may fail to permanently relieve headache. The reason palliative hypnotherapy can be unsuccessful is that important determinants of psychological or psychophysiological disorders might be of unconscious origin (De Benedittis, 1998). As a consequence, in a truly comprehensive approach to the subject of headache, it is important to be open to considering repressed psychic conflicts and their corresponding emotions that produce the painful perceptions.

Chronic Primary Headache

Spanos et al. (1993) randomly assigned a sample of 136 patients with chronic headache to either one or four sessions of imagery-based hypnotic treatment, one or four sessions of a placebo treatment ("subliminal reconditioning"), or to a no-treatment control group. The follow-up was at 8 weeks. Of the total sample, 15% were classified as having migraines, 54% as suffering with TTH, and 32% as having mixed tension/migraine headaches. Control patients reported no significant changes in headache activity, whereas hypnotic and placebo subjects reported significant ($p < .05$) but equivalent changes. Medication usage in treated subjects decreased significantly ($p < .001$).

In a randomized, controlled study, ter Kuile et al. (1994) evaluated autogenic training in comparison to cognitive self-hypnosis training and a waiting-list control condition in treating patients with chronic headache. Treatment consisted of seven individual manualized treatment sessions once weekly, with three reinforcement sessions at 2, 4, and 6 months, with encouragement to use a 15-minute tape twice daily. Cognitive self-hypnosis training included relaxation, imaginative inattention, pain displacement and transformation, and hypnotic analgesia. At the conclusion of treatment, there was a significant ($p < .004$) reduction in headache index scores (i.e., headache month frequency) for both treatment groups compared with the waiting-list controls, and no significant differences were observed between the two conditions. At 35-week follow-up, the improvements were maintained, with no significant differences between the treatment groups.

Migraine

Andreychuk and Skriver (1975) randomly assigned 33 subjects with migraine to one of three experimental treatment groups: self-hypnosis training, biofeedback training for hand warming combined with listening to autogenic training tapes, or electro-encephalogram (EEG)-biofeedback alpha-training. All three treatment groups experienced a significant reduction in migraines from pretreatment levels, reaching significance at the .025 level for alpha training and self-hypnosis training groups and .01 level for the hand-temperature training group. High hypnotizable subjects demonstrated significant ($p < .05$) reduction in migraine rates compared with low hypnotizable subjects.

In a controlled study, Anderson, Basker, and Dalton (1975) compared outcomes in 47 patients who were randomly assigned to receive either medication treatment ($n = 24$) with prochlorperazine and ergotamine, or to hypnotherapy ($n = 23$). Hypnotic treatment, which consisted of induction, deepening, suggestive therapy, and ego-strengthening, included six sessions at intervals of 10 to 14 days. Patients were also told to visualize the arteries in the neck and head as being swollen and throbbing and to then imagine them becoming smaller and more comfortable. Moreover, daily self-hypnosis was included to avert migraine attacks. Follow up was done for one year. The results found that the number of migraines per month and of "blinding attacks" were significantly less ($p < .0005$ and $p < .005$, respectively) in the hypnosis group. At one-year follow-up, the number of hypnosis patients who had experienced complete remission of migraines during the previous three months was 43.5%, compared with 12.5% of the patients in the medication treatment condition ($p < .039$).

Emmerson and Trexler (1999) utilized group hypnosis with relaxation and manipulation of the cerebrovascular tone (imagery of a cool helmet with freezer coils behind the protective cover) to evaluate the effectiveness of hypnosis in reducing migraine duration, frequency, severity, and need for medication. Posttreatment duration of migraine was found to be significantly shorter ($p < .0005$), frequency of migraines was significantly lower ($p < .0001$), and medication usage was reduced by almost 50% ($p < .0005$).

Tension-Type Headache

The effectiveness of four sessions of hypnosis and self-hypnosis training in comparison with a waiting-list control group in the treatment of chronic TTH was evaluated by Melis, Rooimans, Spierings, and Hoogduin (1991) in a single-blind study. The one-hour hypnosis sessions utilized eye fixation and relaxation inductions, followed by imagery modification in which the patient visualized an image of the headache gradually changing. Suggestions were also given to transform the pain into sensations that were easier to tolerate, and for transferring the pain from the head to a less disabling part of the body. Each patient received a self-hypnosis tape. Patients were randomly assigned to a hypnosis ($n = 11$) or a waiting-list control condition ($n = 15$). At four-week follow-up, the hypnosis group was found to be experiencing significant reductions ($p < .05$) in number of headache days, hours, and intensity of headaches compared with the waiting-list control group. They also showed a significant reduction in anxiety ($p < .01$).

A Dutch group published a series of studies on TTH. Van Dyck, Zitman, Linssen, Corry, and Spinhoven (1991) investigated the relative efficacy of autogenic training versus self-hypnosis training utilizing future-oriented hypnotic imagery in the treatment of TTH. Fifty-five patients were randomly assigned to the two therapy conditions (28 to autogenic training and 27 to hypnosis). The two procedures were found to be equally effective in reducing headache pain, usage of pain medication, depression, and state anxiety. Hypnotizability was positively correlated with ratings of pain reduction.

Zitman, Van Dyck, Spinhoven, Linssen, and Corry (1992) compared an abbreviated form of autogenic training to a hypnosis group that used a technique of future-oriented hypnotic imagery (imagining the self in the future, pain-free), and to a third condition that used the future-oriented hypnotic imagery but without presenting it as being hypnosis. Ninety-six patients were enrolled for this study. All three interventions emphasized muscular and mental relaxation, and treatment lasted eight weeks. The three treatments were equally effective in reducing headaches at posttreatment, but, after a six-month follow-up period, the future-oriented hypnotic imagery that had been explicitly presented as hypnosis was found to be superior to autogenic training.

Spinhoven, Linssen, Van Dyck, and Zitman (1992) compared manualized treatment (physical therapy) with various self-hypnotic techniques or autogenic training in 56 patients with chronic tension headache. Patients served as their own controls. There were no differences between treatment groups at conclusion of treatment or at six-month follow-up. Patients in both conditions significantly ($p < .05$) reduced their headaches and psychological distress ($p < .05$) compared with the waiting-list period. Improvements were maintained at follow-up.

Ezra, Gotkine, Goldman, Adahan, and Ben-Hur (2012) enrolled 97 patients with TTH to compare hypnotic relaxation (HR) and amitryptiline (AMT). Fifty-three (57.6%) patients chose HR, while 39 (42.4%) chose pharmacological therapy with AMT. Seventy-four percent of the patients in the HR group and 58% of patients in the AMT group had a 50% reduction in the frequency of headaches ($p = .16$). Long-term adherence to treatment with HR exceeded that of AMT.

Juvenile Headache

A prospective, randomized, double-blind, placebo-controlled study with classic juvenile migraine (MwA) was conducted by Olness, MacDonald, and Uden (1987), comparing placebo, propranolol, and self-hypnosis. Children (aged 6–12) were included in a 12-week treatment period for each treatment. They were asked to practice self-hypnosis twice daily for 10 minutes, including several techniques being offered for self-regulation of pain from which the patient could choose things to incorporate into his or her self-hypnosis practice. At the end of one year, hypnosis proved superior to both placebo and propranolol in reducing the number of migraine attacks.

Kohen and Zajac (2007) studied the effect of self-hypnosis in a prospective, open study of 178 juvenile patients suffering from recurrent headache. The study included four training sessions focused on progressive relaxation and pleasant imagery (favorite place). Results showed a significant reduction in frequency, intensity, and duration. No adverse effects were reported.

In a subsequent study (Kohen, 2010), in 52 out of the previous 178 patients, years after treatment, 85% reported continued relief with self-hypnosis, 44% reported decreased headache frequency, 31% noted decreased severity, and 56% reported that self-hypnosis reduced headache intensity.

CONCLUSION

On clinical evidence base, the use of hypnosis with CPH qualifies as a well-established treatment that is both efficacious and specific (Hammond, 2007). The efficacy of hypnosis with headaches has been demonstrated to be statistically superior or equivalent in comparison with commonly used medication treatments, in a double-blinded placebo controlled study, in comparison with established biofeedback treatments, and in research performed by many different investigators. The consensus of the outcome studies is that hypnotically facilitated relaxation and imagery (or imagery modification) techniques, combined with encouraging the daily practice of self-hypnosis, are usually effective without requiring more complex or multifaceted hypnotic techniques. "Explicit hypnosis" seems more effective than "implicit hypnosis," while the effect of hypnotizability on the therapeutic outcome remains a controversial issue because of inconclusive findings (De Benedittis, 2009).

Not only has hypnosis been shown to be efficacious with CPH, but it is also a treatment that is relatively brief and cost effective. At the same time, it has been found to be virtually free of the side effects, risks of adverse reactions, and the ongoing expense associated with the widely used medication treatments. Hypnosis should be recognized by the scientific, health care, and medical insurance communities as being an efficient evidence-based practice (Hammond, 2007).

CLINICAL APPLICABILITY AND HYPNOTIC STRATEGIES FOR CPH

Clinical Applicability

Although hypnosis can be used in most CPH, the following subtypes are more likely to be treated successfully by hypnotic treatment: (a) TTH; (b) MwoA and MwA; (c) mixed headache (TTH + migraine headache); and (d) psychogenic headache (i.e., conversion headache).

Hypnotic Strategies

Basically, the hypnotic approach to headaches can be (a) symptomatic treatment aimed at relieving frequency and intensity of headache attacks, without removing the cause of headache, and (b) causative treatment aimed at removal of the primary cause of the headache (e.g., unconscious conflicts) with subsequent permanent cure of the disease.

Most hypnotic treatments are symptomatic. Indirect (Ericksonian) approaches appear to be more effective than direct approaches, though no clear superiority has been shown in evidence-based studies (De Benedittis, 2009).

Causative approach can be used in select cases, whenever unconscious conflicts seem somehow related to the origin of the headache. In these cases, hypnoanalysis is definitely the tool of choice (De Benedittis, 1998). Hypnoanalytical approach with age regression might help in uncovering and working through unconscious conflicts. Highly hypnotizable subjects are more likely to benefit from this curative approach, as deep hypnosis facilitates age regression.

Therapeutic Goals in Symptomatic Approach to Headaches

Symptomatic approach to headaches includes (a) treatment of the acute attack; (b) prevention of the acute attack (abort attack); and (c) prophylactic treatment.

Hypnosis can be used as a stand-alone treatment or with self-hypnosis, which enhances synergistically the efficacy of hypnosis. In most cases, however, a multimodal approach is the treatment of choice. This includes hypnosis, self-hypnosis, and prophylactic pharmacotherapy, if needed. The multimodal approach optimizes the therapeutic outcome of patients with headache (Figure 26.1).

There are contraindications and some precautions are needed:

1. Diagnosis is mandatory!
2. Paroxysmal pain (e.g., cluster headache, trigeminal neuralgia) is not suitable for hypnotic treatment
3. Inadequate motivations
4. Unrealistic expectations
5. Secondary gains (e.g., pending litigation)

CASE EXAMPLE

A 36-year-old woman presented with severe, daily headache since the age of 5. Diagnosis of MwoA was originally made. Headache frequency and intensity worsened with age, refractory to most treatments (drugs, acupuncture, homeopathy). In addition, triptan abuse was reported. At referral to our pain clinic, an overall diagnosis of disabling MOH was made.

The patient's treatment plan included:

1. In-patient triptan withdrawal program (detoxification + prednisone 60–75 mg/day for 7–10 days, then tapered slowly)
2. Multimodal approach: combined hypnosis + prophylactic treatment [i.e., tricyclic antidepressants (TCA), trifluoperazine]

Combined hypnosis + self-hypnosis + prophylactic treatment (e.g., tca, tricyclic antidepressants such as amitryptiline, beta-blockers such as propranolol).

One weekly hypnotic session (treatment duration depending on clinical patterns).

Self-hypnosis twice/day (20 minutes).

Rescue self-hypnotic session if needed (at onset of headache attack) with sleep posthypnotic suggestion to facilitate headache resolution.

Bedtime or early bird self-hypnosis (to prevent let-down or week-end headache).

Primary goals:

In the short run, hypnosis + self-hypnosis act synergistically with prophylactic drugs.

In the long run, developing and enhancing hypnotic skills and headache self-control, while progressively tapering off drugs.

FIGURE 26.1 Multimodal protocol for headache control.

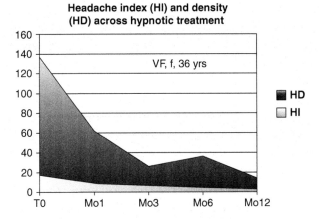

FIGURE 26.2 Headache index (HI): headache monthly frequency. Headache density (HD): headache monthly frequency per intensity (VAS).

3. One weekly hypnotic session (for 3 months, then bimonthly reinforcement for the duration of a year)
4. Self-hypnosis twice a day

Outcome results are shown in Figure 26.2.

HYPNOTIC TECHNIQUES

As headaches represent the most common chronic pain, direct and, particularly, indirect (Ericksonian) techniques for chronic pain apply also for CPH (De Benedittis, 2009). In addition, some special techniques can be used for discrete headaches, such as migraine and TTH. Some techniques are disease specific (such as hypnothermobiofeedback for migraine), whereas some others can be used effectively in both conditions.
Special Techniques for Discrete Headaches

1. Progressive relaxation (see transcript; for both TTH and migraine).
2. Pain dislocation (for both TTH and migraine): the painful sensations in the diseased part of the head can be displaced to another, smaller or economically less important, part of the body (e.g., to the extremities, which are more tolerable and less life-threatening than in other sites of the body).
3. Future-oriented imagery (for both TTH and migraine): this type of fantasy and hallucination can be used to transport the person away from the present in which he or she is experiencing pain. The patient may, for example, be guided by age progression to a time in the future where pain and illness will have been left behind; this is useful in order to mobilize and direct expectations and resources toward the therapeutic goal.
4. Time distortion (for both TTH and migraine): time distortion can be utilized to transform the perception of long hours of suffering to that of a few short minutes. Each attack—because of suggested amnesia for the pain experience—comes as a complete surprise and triggers a profound trance of 10 to 20 seconds' duration. Deep trance can be utilized to suggest even partial or total amnesia for all past headache attacks and the patient emerging from the trance would have neither awareness of having been in hypnosis nor recollection of suffered pain.
5. Headache flooding (for both TTH and migraine): first, headache can be deliberately increased by posthypnotic suggestion. If this is done, volitionally it can eventually be decreased.
6. Posthypnotic suggestion of trance induction at migraine attack, time distortion, and postattack amnesia (mainly for migraine): the patient is instructed to go into a deep trance at migraine onset in order to significantly reduce the impact (intensity and duration of the attack); time distortion and posthypnotic amnesia can be associated to decrease the perceived duration of the attack and its poisonous memory.
7. Hypnothermobiofeedback (see transcript) (for migraine).

Rationale

This technique is a (virtual) adaptation of the biofeedback paradigm in hypnotic setting. Biofeedback may be defined as the technique of using electronic equipment to reveal to human beings some of their internal physiological events, normal and abnormal, in the form of visual and auditory signals in order to teach them to manipulate these otherwise involuntary or unfelt events by manipulating the displayed signals. The individual undergoing biofeedback training is thus enabled to see or hear (or both) fluctuations of physiological activity that are ordinarily below the threshold of conscious awareness.

The biofeedback paradigm, currently interpreted as a form of cognitive learning in which higher mental processes are brought into play in the self-regulation of physiological activity, has been applied in the learned control of such functions as muscle tension, skin temperature, skin conductance, heart rate, and blood pressure.

The modality of biofeedback most commonly used for migraine therapy is thermobiofeedback, a reflection of the changes in the skin temperature associated with the constriction or dilation of peripheral blood vessels. Teaching patients to increase the difference between finger and forehead temperature could be effective in aborting or preventing a migraine attack. Because the pain in migrainous headaches is associated with the cranial blood vessels' vasodilation phase of the attack, it was theorized that this thermobiofeedback treatment aborted the migraine attack by shunting blood flow away from the affected vessels. The real mechanism of this treatment is still far from being clear. Interestingly, it has been reported that headache improvement in biofeedback training correlates with the hypnotizability of the patient (De Benedittis, 2009).

In conclusion, the rationale for hypnothermobiofeedback is to induce cerebrovascular vasoconstriction by suggesting peripheral vasodilation (i.e., hand warming).

TRANSCRIPTS FOR HEADACHES

TTH: Hypnotic Progressive Relaxation, Amnesia, and Pain Displacement Technique

"Now take two deep, deep breaths and close your eyes. Take another two very deep breaths and start feeling relaxed. Now allow your whole body to relax . . . allow all your muscles to go limp . . . and now let's focus on particular muscle groups . . . to relax even more. . . . Let's start with your arms. . . . Imagine that all the muscles and tendons in your arms are relaxing . . . and as your arms relax, being aware of those sensations that let you know that your arms feel more relaxed . . . perhaps a sense of warmth, or of heaviness, perhaps an interesting tingling sensation, whatever sensation that lets you know that your arms are becoming more and more relaxed . . . limp, heavy, warm, and comfortable. And now allow that relaxation to spread . . . up, up into your legs . . . down to your

feet. Your whole legs becoming more and more relaxed, relaxed and heavy. All the tension draining away, as your legs feel heavier, and heavier, almost as if they were made of lead. So comfortable, so relaxed. And now . . . allow your awareness to move now to the muscles of your abdomen, your breast, and your back. Imagine that all the muscles and tendons are relaxing . . . and as these muscles relax, being aware of any sensation that lets you know that your muscles feel more relaxed . . . whatever sensation that lets you know that your muscles are becoming more and more relaxed . . . limp, heavy, warm, and comfortable.

And as you continue, as you allow both of your legs and both of your arms to feel more and more relaxed . . . as well as the muscles of your abdomen, breast, and back, you can be aware that the relaxation continues to spread . . . to your shoulders. All the muscles in your shoulders letting go, relaxing, feeling the support of the (chair/bed), sinking into the (chair/bed), letting all the tension drain out of your shoulders. . . . Feeling so relaxed, so heavy, and more and more at ease . . . and the relaxation continues to spread . . . to your neck. All the muscles and tendons of your neck letting go, one by one. Just allowing your head to rest back, the feelings letting you know that your neck is relaxing, more and more, as you feel more and more comfortable, more and more at ease. Your whole body becoming relaxed, very, very relaxed, relaxed . . . heavy, calm and peaceful. . . .

As you know, there are periods of time that you feel less headache, and times that you feel more headache. Headache can come . . . and headache can go. Now here is something very interesting . . . listen carefully . . . after any period of time that you might have experienced more headache, on average, you will be surprised, sometimes very surprised . . . to look back and notice that you do not seem to be able to remember very well, if at all, any periods of greater discomfort. You may have the sense that something has happened during that period of time, but you will not recall that you felt any pain during that period. With time you will start to realize that your memories are becoming increasingly pleasant. Wouldn't it be interesting to find that the more and more you focus on, and recall, periods of increased comfort, your memories of the most important periods of your life consist of periods of hope, comfort, and pleasant confidence? . . .

Right now, and for some time, you have been experiencing discomfort in your head. We both know that this has not been something that you have been very happy with, and that you would like to change. I wonder if you have ever thought about the experience of having that discomfort in a different part of your body. You may not have, because it doesn't make much sense, does it? Why should you feel uncomfortable in your right arm when the discomfort has been in your head? Or why should you feel uncomfortable in your left hand . . . when it was once in your head? If you really think about it, however, the experience of pain is never consistent or stable. It never really remains in the same place . . . for the same amount of time . . . at the same intensity. It is always changing . . . sometimes slowly, sometimes surprisingly fast. And perhaps what you will notice now, right now . . . is that any discomfort you used to experience in your head is starting to change . . . change even more than it usually does. This time it is moving up your arm, or into your shoulder. It may be that it is moving all the way into your left hand, or even somewhere else. Somewhere where it really does not bother you half as much . . . a quarter as much. It is important to realize that the discomfort never stays in one place, and as you find it moving easily into your arm or your leg or your stomach, you find that it bothers you less. As you can move your pain, you can also control how much it bothers you. And now enjoy this moment of calm and long-lasting relaxation. . . . When you are ready, I'll awaken you from hypnosis by counting down from ten to one."

Migraine: Hypnothermobiofeedback

"Now take two deep, deep breaths and close your eyes. Take another two very deep breaths and start feeling relaxed.

You are walking along a beautiful beach and a turquoise sea, in the heart of summer. It's late afternoon, but still very, very hot.

You are barefoot. Feel the hot, dry sand beneath your feet. Walk closer to the waterline. Feel the wet, cold seawater rolling on the sand.

Hear the bearing of the waves, the rhythmic back and forth, to and from, of the water against the sand. Hear the loud, high cries of the seagulls circling overhead.

You continue walking and eventually you come to the end of this wonderful beach.

You may now sit down and focus your attention on the index finger of your right hand. Imagine the warm rays of the sun focused just upon your finger, that becomes warmer and warmer.

And as you feel it warmer than your body, the vessels of your brain stop swelling. And as they become more constricted, you'll start to feel a pleasant relief of your headache.

(As soon as this happens, please let me know by raising a finger of your hand.)

Now enjoy this moment of calm and long-lasting relaxation and when you are ready, I'll awaken you from hypnosis by counting down from ten to one. Are you ready?"

PSYCHOGENIC HEADACHE

The basic mechanism of psychogenic headache appears to be the somatic expression of a psychiatric conflict (De Benedittis, 1998, 2008).

When such conflicts appear to be present, psychoanalysis could be the treatment of choice. Unfortunately, it is time consuming and extremely expensive. The psychoanalytical process, however, may be considerably facilitated and shortened by using hypnotic procedures (Brown & Fromm, 1986; De Benedittis, 1998; Watkins, 1992; Wolberg, 1948).

The main advantages of hypnoanalysis, as compared with psychoanalysis, are how (De Benedittis, 1998): (a) it facilitates the rapid uncovering of the repressed material; (b) it fosters an easier evocation of Freudian free associations; (c) it leads itself admirably to the development and the analysis of a transference relationship; (d) it may facilitate the dissolution of transference resistances; (e) it allows induction and manipulations of dreams (spontaneous nocturnal and hypnotic analogues); and (f) the hypnotic language is congruent with the symptomatic language of the patient.

A major drawback of the procedure is that it can be used only in select cases, as deep hypnosis is generally required.

The following case example is a further contribution to this important, although neglected, area (De Benedittis, 1998).

CASE EXAMPLE

Case History

A 31-year-old married woman, a school teacher, presented herself at our pain center with a history of persistent, disabling headache which has been going on since the age of 16. Pain involved the occipital region and the neck bilaterally. The patient described her pain as "squeezing" and "biting" in nature. Headache was constant, with superimposed accessional migrainous-like throbbing pain. Occasional paroxysms were associated with accompanying symptoms, such as nausea and vomiting, photophobia and sonophobia, and heightened sensory awareness. Emotional stress, anxiety, repressed anger as well as "let-down" after intense emotional events were the most significant precipitants of headache attacks. Medical treatment history included ergotamine, nonsteroidal anti-inflammatory drugs (NSAIDs), and beta-blockers without any beneficial effect.

Neurological examination and neuroradiological investigations were both negative, whereas physical examination showed tenderness and tightness of muscles in the occipital region, shoulders, neck, and temporomandibular joint.

Psychometric and psychopathological evaluation showed highly significant neurotic patterns associated with a considerable degree of introversion. Somatization reaction, reactive depression, denial of emotional problems, and high levels of free-floating anxiety were present.

The overall diagnostic impression was the following:

1. Mixed headache (combined MwoA and TTH)
2. Conversion reaction with depressive neurosis

Relevant History

The patient was a young woman, who, on her first visit, stated that if it were not for the headache she would be entirely problem-free. It soon became evident that this was not the case. Although the patient complained of an almost complete amnesia for significant events of her infancy and childhood, she could describe herself as unhappy during that period, as she was entirely devoid of any love or affection from her parents.

She suffered from competition and rivalry with her siblings (particularly her older brother) for the attention, affection, and esteem of her parents. She felt somehow rejected by her parents for giving preference to her brother and later on to her younger sister; however, she never actively expressed any anger or resentment toward them. The patient rationalized parents' attitudes as a consequence of her insufferable and bizarre behavior.

She described herself as a difficult child to take care of, nasty and disobedient, repeatedly devising situations to provoke or exasperate her parents.

The patient could recall only two significant episodes of her early childhood, both somehow related with physical pain involving her face and head. Once her mother hit her with a belt buckle on the face, which was stained with blood. She could not remember the reason for being hit, but argued: "At that time I was a naughty girl!" At the age of 5, she would compulsively slip into her parents' bedroom almost every night, waiting silently for a long time by her father's bedside, without apparent reason. Whenever her father realized her presence there, he got angry with her and repeatedly struck her on the face and the head. At the age of 11, she was expelled from school because of disciplinary problems.

The headaches began at the age of 16 when her father was reduced to bankruptcy and the family was forced to move from Milan to a small, isolated province town. She felt angry and humiliated, holding her father responsible for all that but unable to overtly express those feelings.

The patient was married when she was 23. A few months later, she became pregnant. Despite a refusal attitude toward motherhood, she accepted to carry the child to term. Shortly after her daughter's birth, she had frequent quarrels with her mother-in-law. On one occasion, she recalled to have been violently slapped on the face and head by her. "I was so angry that I could kill her," she confessed, "but I just went out slamming the door." A severe exacerbation of her headache occurred as a result of this traumatic event.

Disappointed by the husband's attitude, who pleaded his mother's cause, she rushed headlong into her teaching profession, without much satisfaction. She became meticulous, perfectionistic, and a workaholic. Despite the efforts, she eventually realized that she had failed to make successful life adjustments as she was a "ne'er do well" person.

Two years before examination, she engaged in an extramarital relationship, but soon after she gave it up out of guilt. Also, on this occasion, the headaches became more severe and intolerable.

Hypnoanalysis

A short induction training period preceded the beginning of the therapy. Hypnosis was induced and the patient turned out to be an excellent subject, reaching the somnambulistic state with a spontaneous, self-protective, posthypnotic amnesia.

Following a brief training period, the analytical phase was instituted. Free associations and age regression techniques were used in order to explore and uncover repressed memories and/or traumatic events. The patient was induced into an extremely deep trance and slowly disoriented to time and place. She was then reoriented to earlier and earlier periods by appropriate, direct suggestions. Each time regression spontaneously occurred to the age of 5, presumably because this was a significant period to her. During the first attempts, the patient was encouraged to recall happy episodes that occurred during that period, such as Christmas Eve, her birthday, and so forth. Following successful recall of those neutral episodes, a cautious open-ended exploration of the traumatic aspects of memory was carried out.

In deep hypnosis, the patient experienced a true age regression (revivification), actually returning to the previous epoch with a reliving of the same traumatic experience that seemed to exist originally. She revivified being raped by a 16-year-old boy, who was working at that time in her grandfather's farm, and whom she adored as a father substitute. Following a forced orogenital intercourse, the boy sneered at her saying, "Well, that's what

your mother and father like best!" She ran away from the boy, horrified and disgusted, harboring death wishes toward him.

Once the repressed, traumatic material had been divulged during hypnosis, the patient was slowly prepared to face the exhumed material at nonhypnotic levels. Even though the patient could consciously master the repressed material, her symptoms did not subside, but shifted their patterns instead. Headaches became nocturnal in onset, although less severe, and more somatizations appeared while the patient became more anxious and depressed. Despite this, the relationships with her daughter and her husband unexpectedly began to improve. It was apparent that some inner conflicts were still uncovered.

These further resistances were worked through, requiring quite a long period of time. Eventually, the patient revivified the crucial episode which occurred a few months after having been raped. One night, she awoke from sleep and compulsively walked softly to her parents' bedroom. She needed to know the "truth" about what that boy had told her concerning her parents. She hid behind the door, which was ajar. It was mere chance that she witnessed sexual intercourse between her parents (the "primal scene"). Thereafter, she heard her father tell her mother that he did not love his daughter (i.e., the patient) and would rather have another daughter. From then onward, the little girl slipped every night into her parents' bedroom, as she believed it was the only chance she had for asserting her presence and her right to be loved by them. At the same time, by interposing herself between her father and mother, she attempted to prevent the birth of a new, undesired sister. She was also prepared to pay dearly for that. Whenever they realized her presence, her father got angry and would strike her on the face and the head. Despite the efforts, all her plans failed and a few months later a new sister was born. She eventually desisted in trying to regain the affection of her parents and repressed the intolerable and painful feeling of rejection into her unconscious mind.

A careful flow of the material into awareness was allowed after the termination of hypnosis, and the patient experienced a great deal of emotional relief as a result of this discovery. She realized that she had been suffering all her life due to feeling rejected by her father, and that her rebellious behavior might have been an unconscious reaction to that. In the following sessions, the patient could elaborate at a conscious level the ambivalent relationship with her father, entangled death wishes toward him blended with feelings of guilt. She recognized the fact that her headaches had constituted for her a smoke screen behind which she hid her feelings of death wishes, rejection, and self-devaluation. She could also recall, however, the unique chance she had of eventually reconciling with her father when he was dying of cancer many years later.

During the last sessions the patient became symptom-free. Headache and multiple somatizations had completely disappeared. A 12-year follow-up confirmed that the patient had been permanently cured.

Discussion

As shown in this case report, hypnoanalysis may be an excellent diagnostic tool and treatment method for CPH. The psychoanalytical paradigm provides an appropriate frame of reference for elucidating the patient's psychodynamics. According to (Engel, 1959), pain may represent a psychic device to exteriorize a painful conflict. Suffice to point out, from the case report, the strong tendency of this patient to reexperience painful physical symptoms, which tended to be overdetermined. Beginning early in her life, the head and face were intimately linked with significant conflict situations that became repressed (she was repeatedly struck, on different occasions, by her mother, father, and mother-in-law). When current frustrating circumstances (i.e., father's bankruptcy or quarrels with her mother-in-law) mobilized the old repressed impulses, the associated symptoms appeared instead, having their origin either in symptoms that the patient may have actually experienced at the time of the original conflict, or in symbolic meaning.

In conclusion, hypnoanalysis has proved to be a unique psychodynamic investigation tool and the treatment of choice for CPH in select cases.

CONCLUSION

The efficacy of hypnosis with headaches (e.g., migraine and TTH) has been demonstrated to be superior or equivalent in comparison with commonly used medication treatments and established psychophysiological treatments (i.e., biofeedback, autogenic training) in RCT studies. Self-hypnosis, on a regular basis, might enhance synergistically the efficacy of the hypnotic treatment. "Explicit-hypnosis," without requiring more complex or sophisticated hypnotic techniques, seems more effective than "implicit-hypnosis," while the effect of hypnotizability on the therapeutic outcome remains a controversial issue. Not only has hypnosis been shown to be efficacious with headaches but it is also a treatment that is relatively brief and cost effective. It is also virtually free of side effects, risks of adverse reactions, and ongoing expense associated with medication treatments. Hypnosis should be recognized by the scientific and health care communities as being an effective, reliable evidence-based practice for headache management.

REFERENCES

American Psychiatric Association. (2013). *DSM-5 Diagnostic and statistical manual of mental disorders.* Arlington, VA: American Psychiatric Press.

Anderson, J. A., Basker, M. A., & Dalton, R. (1975). Migraine and hypnotherapy. *International Journal of Clinical and Experimental Hypnosis, 23*(1), 48–58.

Andreychuk, T., & Skriver, C. (1975). Hypnosis and biofeedback in the treatment of migraine headache. *International Journal of Clinical and Experimental Hypnosis, 23*(3), 172–183.

Barber, J., & Bejenke, C. J. (1996). *Hypnosis and suggestion in the treatment of pain: A clinical guide.* New York, NY: W. W. Norton.

Brown, D. P., & Fromm, E. (1986). *Hypnotherapy and hypno-analysis.* Hillsdale, NJ: Lawrence Erlbaum Associates.

De Benedittis, G. (1998). The poisoned gift: The use of hypnosis in the treatment of severe chronic headache (a long term follow-up case report). *American Journal of Clinical Hypnosis, 41*(2), 118–129. doi:10.1080/00029 157.1998.10404198

De Benedittis, G. (2008). *Is it all in your mind? Psychogenic pain revisited.* Presented at the Satellite Symposium, 11th World Congress of Pain, Milano, Italy.

De Benedittis, G. (2009). *Hypnosis and headache: Efficacy, clinical strategies and advanced hypnotic techniques.* Presented at the 18th International Congress of Hypnosis, Rome, Italy.

De Benedittis, G. (2012). The hypnotic brain: Linking neuroscience to psychotherapy. *Contemporary Hypnosis and Integrative Therapy*, 29(1), 103–115.

De Benedittis, G., Lorenzetti, A., & Pieri, A. (1990). The role of stressful life events in the onset of chronic primary headache. *Pain*, 40(1), 65–75.

De Benedittis, G., & Villani, R. (1991). Chronic primary headache. In F. Moody, W. Montorsi, & M. Montorsi (Eds.), *Advances in surgery* (pp. 423–430). New York, NY: Raven Press.

Elkins, G., Jensen, M. P., & Patterson, D. R. (2011). Hypnotherapy for the management of chronic pain. *International Journal of Clinical and Experimental Hypnosis*, 55, 275–287.

Emmerson, G. H., & Trexler, G. (1999). A hypnotic intervention for migraine control. *Australian Journal of Clinical and Experimental Hypnosis*, 27, 54–61.

Engel, G. L. (1959). 'Psychogenic' pain and the pain prone patient. *American Journal of Medicine*, 26(6), 899–918. doi:10.1016/0002-9343(59)90212-8

Ezra, Y., Gotkine, M., Goldman, S., Adahan, H. M., & Ben-Hur, T. (2012). Hypnotic relaxation vs amitriptyline for tension-type headache: Let the patient choose. *Headache*, 52(5), 785–791.

Flammer, E., & Alladin, A. (2007). The efficacy of hypnotherapy in the treatment of psychosomatic disorders: Meta-analytical evidence. *International Journal of Clinical and Experimental Hypnosis*, 55(3), 251–274.

Hammond, D. C. (2007). Review of the efficacy of clinical hypnosis with headaches and migraines. *International Journal of Clinical and Experimental Hypnosis*, 55(2), 207–219.

Headache Classification Committee of the International Headache Society (IHS). (2013). The international classification of headache disorders. *Cephalalgia: An International Journal of Headache*, 33(9), 629–808.

Jensen, M. P., & Patterson, D. R. (2014). Hypnotic approaches for chronic pain management: Clinical implications of recent research findings. *American Journal of Psychology*, 69(2), 167–177.

Jensen, R., & Stovner, L. J. (2008). Epidemiology and comorbidity of headache. *The Lancet Neurology*, 7(4), 354–361.

Kohen, D. P. (2010). Long-term follow-up of self-hypnosis training for recurrent headaches: What the children say. *International Journal of Clinical Experimental and Hypnosis*, 58(4), 417–432.

Kohen, D. P., & Zajac, R. (2007). Self-hypnosis training for headaches in children and adolescents. *Journal of Pediatrics*, 150(6), 635–639.

Lang, E. V., & Rosen, M. P. (2002). Cost analysis of adjunct hypnosis with sedation during outpatient interventional radiologic procedures. *Radiology*, 222(2), 375–382.

Melis, P. M., Rooimans, W., Spierings, E. L., & Hoogduin, C. A. (1991). Treatment of chronic tension-type headache with hypnotherapy: A single-blind controlled study. *Headache*, 31(10), 686–689.

Montgomery, G. H., DuHamel, K. N., & Redd, W. H. (2000). A meta-analysis of hypnotically induced analgesia: How effective is hypnosis? *International Journal of Clinical and Experimental Hypnosis*, 48(2), 138–153.

Olesen, J., Goadsby, P. J., Ramdan, N. M., Tfelt-Hansen, P., & Welch, K. M. (2006). *The headaches*. Philadelphia, PA: Lippincott Williams and Wilkins.

Olness, K., MacDonald, J. T., & Uden, D. L. (1987). Comparison of self-hypnosis and propranolol in the treatment of juvenile classic migraine. *Pediatrics*, 79(4), 593–597.

Shevel, E. (2011). The extracranial vascular theory of migraine—A great story confirmed by the facts. *Headache*, 51(3), 409–417.

Spanos, N. P., Liddy, S. J., Scott, H., Garrard, C., Sine, J., Tirabasso, A., & Hayward, A. (1993). Hypnotic suggestion and placebo for the treatment of chronic headache in a university volunteer sample. *Cognitive Therapy and Research*, 17, 191–205.

Spinhoven, P., Linssen, A. C., Van Dyck, R., & Zitman, F. G. (1992). Autogenic training and self-hypnosis in the control of tension headaches. *General Hospital Psychiatry*, 14(6), 408–415.

ter Kuile, M. M., Spinhoven, P., Linssen, A. C., Zitman, F. G., Van Dyck, R., & Rooijmans, H. G. (1994). Autogenic training and cognitive self-hypnosis for the treatment of recurrent headaches in three different subject groups. *Pain*, 58(3), 331–340.

Van Dyck, R., Zitman, F. G., Linssen, A. C., & Spinhoven, P. (1991). Autogenic training and future oriented hypnotic imagery in the treatment of tension headache: Outcome and process. *International Journal of Clinical and Experimental Hypnosis*, 39(1), 6–23.

Watkins, J. G. (1992). *Hypnoanalytic techniques*. New York, NY: Irvington.

Wolberg, L. R. (1948). *Medical hypnosis*. London, UK: Grune and Stratton.

Zitman, F. G., Van Dyck, R., Spinhoven, P., Linssen, G., & Corry, A. (1992). Hypnosis and autogenic training in the treatment of tension headaches: A two-phase constructive study design with follow-up. *Journal of Psychosomatic Research*, 36(3), 219–228.

Headaches—Children

Daniel P. Kohen

Before a discussion of what I do, how I do it, and how much children and teenagers with headaches have taught me, it's important to remember what we know about headaches in children.

It is well known that chronic, recurrent headaches (HA) are common in children and youth, so much so that they are the cause of considerable discomfort and distress, as well as functional disability. As many as 10% of children aged 5 to 15 years may experience recurrent HA, and some report that 17% of children in the United States have frequent or severe HA (Abu-Arefeh & Russell, 1994; Blume, Brockman, & Breuner, 2012). Adolescents have an even higher prevalence, as high as 28%; compared with 13% of adults, almost 20% of children experience migraine HA (Headache Classification Committee of the International Headache Society, 2013; Split & Neuman, 1999).

While medications have often been used initially to treat recurrent HA, they may not be successful, and sometimes can have unpleasant side effects. Although prescription analgesics may help relieve periodic HA, they also may not; some medications to abort HA can contribute to rebound HA if used excessively (Fisher, 2005). Triptan medications and beta-blocking agents are often prescribed not only for adults, but also for children and adolescents. Unfortunately, however, they are much less effective in children and may cause more side effects than benefits (Lewis et al., 2004).

Research by Olness, MacDonald, and Uden (1987) noted that self-hypnosis (SH) and biofeedback were superior to propranolol, a commonly prescribed beta-blocker which, in this study, was no more effective than placebo. Training in SH has been shown to be an effective therapeutic approach for self-management of HAs in children and adolescents (Eccleston, Yorke, Morley, Williams, & Mastroyannopoulou, 2003; Kohen & Olness, 2011; Kohen & Zajac, 2007; Kröner-Herwig,

Mohn, & Pothmann, 1998; Larsson & Carlsson, 1996; Masek, 1999; McGrath, 1999). The review by Holden, Deichmann, and Levy (1999) found good evidence for the efficacy of both SH and relaxation in reducing pain. However, few reports have investigated outcomes in large groups of children and adolescents who have had training in and used SH for HA problems.

SH has many advantages over pharmacotherapy as a therapeutic strategy for HA. In addition to cost savings (of not purchasing either prescription or over-the-counter medications), training in SH enjoys the advantage of having no adverse effects as compared with medications.

We examined the clinical effects of SH in a large group of children and adolescents with migraine and other chronic HA, as well as its therapeutic effects over time. We demonstrated that most patients experienced substantial improvement in their HA, decreasing their frequency, their duration, the intensity of their HAs, or combinations thereof (Kohen & Zajac, 2007). Kohen and Zajac (2007) also noted that "as a form of active coping and self-regulation, SH also reflects an internally derived and self-reinforcing treatment compared with treatments (e.g., medications) that come from outside of the individual."

We are all reminded that any therapist (physician, psychologist, nurse, social worker, etc.) considering helping a child/teen with HAs with storytelling/hypnosis or other counseling/psychotherapies must assure that either the therapist or a colleague has first also conducted a thorough medical and family/social history along with a thorough physical examination, including neurological evaluation. A recent study (Pavone et al., 2012) reported on the frequency of comorbidities in primary HAs in children. In a well-controlled study, 280 children with primary HA were consecutively enrolled. They and their families were carefully interviewed about the association of their HAs with different conditions. A comparable group of 280 children without HAs and matched for age, sex, race, and socioeconomic status functioned as a control group. While no significant association was found between HAs and other medical conditions, overall behavioral disorders were more common in children with HAs than in controls. Most importantly, HAs were significantly associated with anxiety and depression ($p < .001$), but not with any other psychiatric conditions [including attention deficit hyperactivity disorder (ADHD), tic disorders, obsessive-compulsive disorder (OCD), or learning disorders]. This is an important caveat. As with all conditions for which we may effectively utilize hypnosis, we must be sure that the child has had a thorough diagnostic evaluation, and that we—or appropriate colleagues—are providing treatment as needed for other conditions that may be comorbid.

VALUE OF STORYTELLING

This section highlights and focuses specifically on the value of stories integral to the hypnotherapeutic experience in teaching young people self-management of HAs.

The value of storytelling for children has been well known for centuries by their best therapists, that is, their parents, grandparents, and community elders! Through fairy tales, family stories of older generations, and newly created stories, children have been calmed and soothed, sung and "storied" to sleep, and trance-ported away from their discomfort and worries. We have long known that in this sense, parents, grandparents, and *their* grandparents were the first "hypnotherapists" as they listened and loved unconditionally, and knew both nonverbally (snuggles, hugs, rocking) and verbally how to provide needed comfort through stories.

In our modern era, therapeutic storytelling has had substantial resurgence and attention with the work of Mills and Crowley in *Therapeutic Metaphors for Children and the Child Within* (1986), Doris Brett's wonderful work in *Annie Stories* (1986) and *More Annie Stories* (1992), Leora Kuttner's *Favorite Stories* (1988), Beata Jencks' inspirational story of *Twinkle* for thousands of preschool children with asthma (Kohen

& Wynne, 1997), and Linda Thomson's *Harry the Hypno-Potamus* (2005, 2009), to name just a few. Gary Elkins' book for children, *My Doctor Does Hypnosis* (1997), uses storytelling and cartoon figures (drawn by a teenager) to capture the attention of children, and to demystify and "demythify" potential misconceptions about hypnosis before moving into utilization of hypnosis and hypnotic stories for individualized therapy.

Milton Erickson, perhaps the ultimate modern master storyteller (after the writers of the Bible, of course!), told stories to most of his patients, young and old alike, recognizing the implicit value of not only the story but also the process of "the telling" in engaging the child patient/client, thereby facilitating their narrowed focus, and preparing them(selves) for whatever now easier shifts in attention, intention without detention, pretention, or tension, but, instead, with surprise and pretending (Erickson, 1964; Zeig, 1994). Erickson even told stories from his own family TO his own children in the interest of motivating, offering metaphorical and indirect suggestions that surely if a sibling could accomplish comfort, so could the child who was injured and suffering (Erickson, 1958).

Value of OWN Stories

The utilization of imagery of a child's OWN favorite activities/stories positively drives rapport, transference, confidence, and competence in the patient and therapist alike. Awareness of this allowed and encouraged the evolution of this approach.

■ "I Knew This Kid Once . . ." Approach

Perhaps most influential on my work with young people has been Erickson's "My friend John" technique/approach/story, also borrowed, embraced, and modeled regularly in her teaching by my first hypnosis teacher, Kay F. Thompson, of blessed memory (Erickson, 1964; Kane & Olness, 2004).

Described subsequently in detail, my adaptation of this approach/strategy occurs most often "intuitively" during the course of an interview, and often (though not always) during my first encounter with a child with HA (or any other problem!). To the outside, casual observer, and perhaps to the parent and even (perhaps intentionally so?!) to the child, this may seem like a kind of "tangent," or "by the way . . .," or "toss-off" remark during the course of history taking. As such, it is intended (designed) to capture attention by being a surprise, bypassing of critical judgment or analysis, and instead, to be FUN! This can be understood as being much the same way someone may spontaneously use humor and say, for example, "You know, what you just said reminds me of a joke: Did you hear about . . . ?" Such "interruptions" or "disruptions of the [expected] mindset" have the characteristic hypnotic ingredient of intention without any formal "ceremony" of "hypnotic induction." They (temporarily) disrupt the child's focus and mindset (e.g., on how frequent and how bad their HAs are, or have been), and instead bring the focus onto the "story" or the "joke." Without consciously developing it this way, my "way" of doing this has evolved into rather abruptly saying something like, "You know, I knew a kid once who had . . ." and off I go into a story . . . or two . . . or three. Always depending upon the personal history and circumstances of an individual case, this story might be told in a way analogous to Erickson's original introduction of this by telling the current child patient something like: *In fact, they were sitting on that very same couch, just over there, you could imagine or pretend they are there now if you like"* (Erickson, 1964). Further variable *ingredients* of such a story are described in detail in the examples that follow.

Often, suggestions to children for imagery during their self-hypnotic trance are best fashioned around their favorite activities or favorite imagined [future or hoped-for] experiences (Kohen, 2010; Kohen & Olness, 2011; Kohen & Zajac, 2007). It is evident, therefore, that to get to and learn this information, the essential and critical value of the clinician's rapport with the child may not be overstated.

It is similarly evident that in the context of that rapport, the clinician can and MUST learn what the child LOVES to do, what the child does BEST, what the child's favorite right-now activities are, and what the child's hoped/dreamed-for experiences are for their future. Toward this, methodically and openly take notes while the child tells me about his or her favorite things. I am clear to ask permission, "I hope it's okay if I write these things down/take notes? I don't want to forget what you tell me." (The "meta" message to the child is, of course, "I like you, I care about you, I want to get to know you better, SO THAT I can help you to

help yourself.") I've never had a child say, "No, don't take notes!" I have cultivated the ability to make notes without losing much eye contact with the child. This has its most obvious value in having complete, thorough records to which one can refer repeatedly as necessary, and which obviates the problem of the clinician "forgetting" what was discussed. Much more importantly, however, one should refer to these (or remember them!) when DOING hypnosis and offering suggestions for imagination.

In the formulation of hypnotic suggestions, these stories/ideas/favorite activities can and should be "given back to the child" as part of the MENU from which to "internally select" a focus for his or her own hypnotic imagery and "own stories" experience(s). One might even tell the child something like this:

"I really appreciate knowing what you enjoy, BECAUSE that helps me to help you. NOW that you have settled into a nice [FIRST] hypnotic experience with your [e.g., slower, even breathing, muscle relaxation, and inside calm feeling], I don't know what you will imagine, but you will know— you can just notice what comes into your mind OR you can allow/let your inside mind CHOOSE—I don't know if it will be [and here one can note three or four things the child has mentioned and described as favorite activities . . .], for example, riding your bike with your sister, playing soccer on your team, snuggling with your teddy bear, or helping grandmother bake cookies, or, maybe something else, like a vacation you've always wanted to have, and you CAN HAVE NOW in your imagination BECAUSE you're the BOSS of your IMAGINATION. . . ."

In this way children are *telling themselves their own stories* and can add how to USE those stories as a context in which to offer the variety of HA-resolving/preventing suggestions.

Setting the tone/encouraging own stories can occur through the use of "You know, I knew this kid once" as integrated and interwoven with the process of history taking and rapport building as described earlier.

As a seeming tangent during history taking, for example, "You know, I knew a kid once . . ." as well as in my storytelling in and out of trance, I always make the FIRST STORY about a child who was:

"a little different than you. . . . First of all, this child I was thinking of was a girl, not a boy [or a boy, not a girl] *and she* [or he] *was 'only' a year or two YOUNGER than you* [the patient in your office]."

As such, the first story is of a child of the opposite sex who is younger than the patient. The INTENTION here—never discussed, but simply and indirectly IMPLIED—is that the patient's indirect and internal expected conclusion will be something like "surely if an 8-year-old GIRL can do this, I as a 9-year-old BOY can most certainly do it as well, and probably even better, easier, and PROBABLY faster." I continue by offering a story of how that child got rid of his or her tummy aches. Then, I commonly and matter-of-factly would add "then there was this *other kid*—perhaps same sex as my patient, perhaps younger or same age . . .," and so on.

INGREDIENTS OF EFFECTIVE SH TRAINING

Nothing is more important than effective therapist–client (doctor–patient) rapport; and no therapy—hypnotic storytelling or otherwise—should expect or presume to proceed until there is a positive, mutual respect and rapport between the client and clinician. This may take several or more visits in some patients. This may mean that formal hypnosis per se may not be at all appropriate in a first visit, while conversational hypnosis, positive expectations, and thoughtful storytelling as ways of "being hypnotic" may be entirely appropriate both in generating rapport and being therapeutic.

In thinking about this, I realized that it was perhaps best said by (my teacher) Kay Thompson (1994), "In looking for commonalities in what takes place, I find a consistency in my acknowledgment and appreciation of individual differences. I cannot utilize others' pre-determined approaches like frozen entrees, or even canned recipes, although I may start with the same cookbook. Nor must I rely on theories in those cookbooks. I *must work with the ingredients on hand,* [emphasis added] and I must have a taste for what is simmering with this one patient, different from

any other I have seen, demanding a new adaptation of any recipe."

To be sure, each of our professional disciplines (psychology, medicine, social work, nursing, etc.) and each of us as individual clinicians has our own personal style and methodology to obtain a clear and comprehensive history, including of course the circumstances of the evolution of the problem, the attendant "triggers" to the symptoms, and the presence or absence of related and unrelated other signs and symptoms. The challenge is to allow and create that "history taking" in the context of rapport building so that it becomes in and of itself THERAPEUTIC, through the interspersal of hypnotic language, indirect, so-called "waking suggestions," and anticipatory preparation for the further therapeutic HISTORY. Specifically, I believe it is essential to help the patient find a way, or for the clinician to SUGGEST a way, to MEASURE the symptoms (of the HAs) *so that* he or she can REALLY KNOW when he or she is improving as measured by the patient. While I typically use the idea of 0 to 12 because of the convention of our American 12-inch ruler, one can easily utilize 0 to 10 (and use centimeters!). I believe it is very important to "set up" and characterize this "scale" in a mutually acceptable and believable fashion. Thus, consider the following example.

At the initial visit, and in the context of obtaining the history, methods for measuring and monitoring HAs—and also language for the hypnosis that has not yet been introduced!—are suggested, agreed upon, and utilized, both in initial discussion and in self-monitoring before any discussion of hypnosis.

For purposes of (a) driving our rapport and (b) letting the patient know that I value his or her opinion and it is IMPORTANT, indeed ESSENTIAL, in this new clinical relationship, I always ask the child to "PLEASE help me understand these HAs that USED to bother you." Handing the child the 12-inch wooden ruler from my desk, I ask "WHAT could it measure?" or I might immediately move into "Let's say that we (or you) could MEASURE HAs and let's say that 12 was the worst most imaginable, crying, vomiting HA anyone could ever have; and let's say that the other end is zero, is NO HA whatsoever. Okay?" I would continue inquiring about the patient's history with the questions framed

TABLE 27.1

HEADACHE HISTORY "BY THE NUMBERS"
• What was the average HA rating 6 months ago? Three months ago? Last month? Last week?
• What was the worst ever? (They sometimes will know the precise day, circumstances)
• What number is it when you first NOTICE it?
• How slow/fast does it increase? So, does it go gradually and slowly up higher, or does it ZOOM UP—BANG! and it's *suddenly* an 8 when a moment ago it was a 2, or 3, or 4? • What makes the average one of, for example, 6 go up to 8 or 9 or more? This of course is a question about "triggers."
• How high does the USUAL HA go?
• How high does it have to go to make you cry?
• What does it have to be to not want to eat?
• What does it have to be to get nauseated?
• What does it have to be to cause you to throw up/vomit?
• How high does it have to be to stop you from doing regular things?
• (SHIFTING without warning) What does it have to go DOWN to so that you can be your "regular self"? (It is my experience that children *know* these answers, rarely hesitate, and most do NOT need it to go down to 0 to feel better and be active.)
• How far **down** does it have to go to not be **bothered** by it? (nb: reframe from hurt to "bother")
• How **low** does it have to go to be able to play? To eat? To do homework?
• Right now what **helps** it to go down? NOTE: This presumes and reinforces a positive expectation that they [already] know how to lower it!
• [When you have a HA] Do you prefer light or dark? Quiet or sound? (Music?)

in that context (Table 27.1): children ALWAYS have the answer immediately, often much to the amazement of their parents.

And, so it is that *getting* the history in this way is, in effect, the child learning that he or she *helps himself or herself* by *telling me the child's own story.* My role as the "coach" in soliciting this story is to ask the right kinds of reframing questions that allow *the story to begin to change* in the way the child understands it and wants it to change.

Thus, while taking the history about HAs, I would like to know when they occur—morning, day, evening—if it awakens the child from sleep (HAs that are very precise = "RIGHT HERE doctor!" pointing to a spot, and/or that awaken people from sleep are usually *very* significant medically and should be referred to the child's primary physician or for emergency evaluation as soon as possible). Seeking to understand the child's *motivation for change*, I always want to

know how it interferes with daily life . . . and *how life will be different* WHEN (not 'IF') *the HA is gone.* (Of course, this is indeed a so-called "waking hypnotic suggestion.")

I generally do very little, if any, mention of, or formal talking about, hypnosis at a first visit. This is not to ignore the patient, but rather to convey the most important principles of rapport and history taking which must precede any therapeutic intervention. Of course if the patient or family bring up "hypnosis or hypnotizing," we discuss their ideas, beliefs, and any misconceptions in the moment and as needed.

In conveying this in advance, I may very well say the same kinds of things to the child long before we ever formally DO hypnosis, by beginning to talk with the child about what I am going to do and what THE CHILD can DO *WHEN* we do the hypnosis "in a few minutes" or "at your next visit." Whether we call this informal or indirect or conversational hypnosis, or not hypnosis at all, it is, to be sure, future programming/future projection and positive expectations for what will follow.

INTRODUCING HYPNOSIS

Talking about hypnosis should follow the development of rapport and evolution of the history; it should precede any "doing" of hypnosis (other than the hypnotic language that has become integral to our everyday language of positive expectancy, such as "You'll probably be surprised how easy and fun this turns out to be, that's what most kids notice after they learn and get into it").

How we decide to discuss what hypnosis is, and what it is not, and what myths we have to dispel, will depend entirely upon how it is that the family came to us in the first place. Thus, did the patient/family go looking for someone who does hypnosis because they already have a favorable outlook based on knowing clinicians who do hypnosis? **OR** is their expectation based upon another family member's positive experience? **OR** is it based upon being referred by someone they trust and hold in high regard? **OR**, by contrast, are they seeking "magic" as perhaps they have seen hypnosis portrayed in a movie, or cartoons, or on a stage show?

While we all must do this in our own way, I do so in a *natural part of our initial visit* by asking directly, "How come you came over to see me?" in order to learn the history. Once details about the HAs are clear, if I have not heard any mention of hypnosis, I will typically ask, "What was I supposed to do? What did you HEAR about coming HERE?" Sometimes even if they have been referred FOR hypnosis, the child or the parent(s) may not mention the "H" word, reflecting perhaps their anxiety or uncertainty about the word *hypnosis*, the process, what will follow, and so on. When hypnosis is eventually mentioned and "on the table," I typically ask *them* what that IS, that is, what *they* think, or have heard, thought, or believed. That leads quite naturally to a discussion about what is true and known and what is not. Young people typically make a gesture of a "swinging pocket watch" to which I respond, "Really? *Then* what happens?" And they typically say something like their eyes then go all "swirly" from watching that, and they close them, and then they do whatever the

"hypnotist" tells them to do, and then when the hypnotist snaps his fingers they "wake up," and they do not remember anything and they do whatever he told them to do when they were hypnotized. I usually look at them with incredulity and ask, "Do you **BELIEVE** that?" and, most often, they say "Nahhh" but also of course they *did* believe it, at least partially. I then give an explanation—varying with and depending on my perception of how much they seem to need to learn:

First, they cannot "wake up" because they were not asleep. Hypnosis is NOT sleep. And I repeat that: "Hypnosis is NOT sleep; in fact, people in hypnosis are MORE alert, more aware, and MORE in control than people not in hypnosis. Hypnosis is a SPECIAL state of mind that we ALL have been in before, it is the same (or similar to) the feeling we have when we are daydreaming, YOU know how THAT feels, right?" And they (children and parents) always agree. OR (for a younger child) it feels like you do when you PRETEND SOMETHING FUN, YOU know how pretending feels just like you were doing that thing, only you are pretending, only it feels like you are not, and that you are REALLY doing it, because you ARE really doing it, INSIDE your pretend. Pretty cool, hey? OR (for an older child), it is like when you zone out or imagine about something that you would *rather* be doing, like that concert you went to, or hanging out with your friends, or playing video games, or whatever. In this way, the tone is beginning to be set for paying attention to imagination and stories.

"Would you like to see a VIDEO about hypnosis?" I typically then show a couple of very brief (less than 5 minutes each) video clips of children/teens both talking about hypnosis FOR HEADACHES and doing it (Kohen, 1991; Sugarman, 1997). BOTH videos talk very matter-of-factly about "I imagine about this, and then . . . and then . . . and then . . . ," one being about imagining playing golf *because the child in the video loves to play golf,* and the other being about imagining being in the "safest place I can be, somewhere with a drawing table in the middle of nowhere, I'm all alone." The child goes on to say, "I draw a number scale (to measure headaches) at the top of the page and whatever my headache is on, I then just erase that and it goes away."

As also described in the following examples, the level of positive, matter-of-fact belief in the voices of these children in the videos is quite extraordinary, and undoubtedly reflects their self-confidence and reinforces their practice, their application of SH, and their success in using stories in modulating, eliminating, and preventing HAs. THEIR stories, then, continue to set the tone that stories can and will be helpful. Discussion after the video should give the child/parent an opportunity to respond to "What did you think?" Often the reply is brief like "Pretty cool," or "I don't know." When it is not clear how much the child was paying attention or may have absorbed, I ask, "So, let's say when you get home tonight your dad wonders about this appointment 'cause he was not able to come, what would you tell him?" and most kids will say, "Well, this one boy was meditating (that word is NOT mentioned in the video but children often use it to describe what they saw) and he meditated about golf and his headache went away!"

INTERVENTION—THE STORIES

Hearing the therapist tell them—before and again during trance—that they *can imagine themselves anywhere they want* empowers children from the beginning that their *own stories* of *their own favorite activities* are the keys to at least beginning to use their imagination (= self-hypnosis) to their benefit, and to improving and resolving their HA problems. As they learn more—as illustrated subsequently—they will learn how they can benefit from *other* children's *stories* along with their own.

Experiencing Stories

For me this discussion is most commonly not held until the second visit, and occasionally later. The decision about when should be mutual, and if the child is not in a readiness to proceed, I wait. I might say, "Let me know when you think it will be the right time for you to be ready to learn SH to get rid of those HAs that *used to bother you*. . . ." When we begin, I often describe many, if not all, of the details of what the hypnosis will entail before "officially" or "formally" doing anything. This is intended to provide education, comfort, and demystification to take this out of the realm of "peculiar" or "magical."

"When we do this in a little while, I'll sit here and you can sit there [anchoring, assuring comfort], *then I'll show you a cool way* [it's not just A way, it's a COOL way] *to begin the hypnosis . . . you're going to really like this . . .* [positive expectation] *then I'll talk about imagination which you already know you're good at doing, and then I might say it might be a good idea to close your eyes, because you know when your eyes are closed then other things around you don't bother or distract you, and besides, it is often easier to see things quite clearly when your eyes are closed* ['Seeing' here = understanding].

Then I'll probably talk about paying attention to breathing and to the way your muscles relax and stuff like that; and you don't have to do any work at all, just listen, like you are now [the word 'JUST' here implies 'it's easy!']. *Along the way I'll probably tell you some stories of how other kids solved their headache or stomachache or other problems, you know? Of course before you finish you will learn* [note the embedded suggestion in this not-yet-official-formal hypnotic language] *how to DO this self-hypnosis for yourself when* [not 'if'] *you practice at home. OKAY?* [Though this is a question, I have never had any child or parent say no].

Once they agree, I make the transition with a simple 'Ready to learn?' or 'Okay, do you think we should let your mom and dad learn at the same time, or should we ask them to wait in the waiting room because this is YOURS to learn?' The parent who has learned, been listening, and is well oriented, typically will get up and leave and I'll tell him or her 'we'll be about 20 minutes'].

Some parents ask "Well, is it okay if I stay and learn too, then I can help them better at home?" In this case I usually agree and make a note to myself that it will be all the more important to emphasize to this parent and child later that the "practice" of SH at home is *not* for the parent's involvement, reminders, or coaching. Rather, that it IS a contract between the child and clinician/therapist (= coach), and if the child comes to the parent with questions, the parent should direct them to call or e-mail the coach/therapist. Most parents understand this but some, even those who understand, have more trouble than others "letting go" and that could interfere both with the process and success of practicing. I am very clear to inform parents that this is not the same as school homework or practicing piano. We do NOT have a goal that the child will hear at home, "Now, you get in your bedroom RIGHT NOW and PRACTICE THAT SELF-HYPNOSIS, NOW GO!!!" Indeed, the moment the child gets the idea from this kind of directive that the parent (at least thinks he or she is) in charge of the SH practice, all is potentially lost in rebuilding the child's ego-strength and empowerment to take charge of and eliminate the problem.

The exception to this is that younger children, for example, 5- or 6-year-olds, or younger, may well need, appreciate, and want parental help with practice, much as they would enjoy a bedtime story. Stories about children with HAs or other discomfort can be effectively utilized (Kohen & Olness, 2011; Kohen & Wynne, 1997; Kuttner, 1988; Thomson, 2005, 2009).

Once it is established whether or not the parents will join in the learning, I ask them to sit in a different place (e.g., not on the same couch as the child), encourage them to "go along with learning how to go into hypnosis," and ask them to remember and understand that I will be talking primarily to their child and not to them, so they can enjoy their hypnosis.

I then proceed to talk with the child, sometimes doing perhaps a more formalized hypnotic procedure in much the same way I had just described. In effect, however, this is really the second hypnotic induction as the forgoing "prehypnosis conversation" was really the first hypnotic experience and was "priming the pump."

Induction can and should be whatever the clinician is most comfortable with (Kohen & Olness, 2011; Kohen & Zajac 2007). Invariably, critical elements of the "beginning" are *"imagination of doing something you really love to do."*

Intensification (Deepening)

Irrespective of how the patient moves into a trance, once he or she has developed the beginnings of

a trance everything that follows is, and should be, understood as potentially and intentionally enhancing/intensifying/deepening the trance experience. Any or all of the following are examples of how to do that.

■ Favorite Place Imagination

"As your eyes close and you begin to notice feeling comfortable and a bit 'different,' let your mind wander to imagine that you're not even here, but instead that you're somewhere where you really enjoy where you are, where nothing bothers or disturbs you, and where you are really happy. I [therapist] *do not know what you will imagine, but you WILL KNOW because it's YOUR imagination . . . PERHAPS* [= they get to choose] *it will be* [and here the clinician can offer two, or three, or four options which he or she knows the child enjoys as gleaned from the history taking/rapport building portions of the child's initial visit(s)] *. . . in your grandmother's kitchen making cookies, OR maybe you'll be riding your bicycle with your friends or by yourself* [CHOICE!], *OR maybe you'll be in your bedroom listening to your iPod and your favorite music, OR maybe you'll be hanging out with your friends, OR maybe you'll be on vacation with your family. I don't know BUT YOU'LL KNOW BECAUSE you're learning to be the boss of your imagination and the boss of your body.* [Note the intentional incorporation of elements of the child's own stories into suggestions.]"

■ Multisensory Imagery

"As you're imagining something just right for you, maybe you'll do that by just [= it's easy!] *feeling like you're there, or maybe you'll do it by picturing it on a movie screen and there you are on the screen in a video! Notice everything about it . . . what you see there, what you hear there, what you are doing (moving, running, dancing, laying down), what the smells and tastes are—maybe you'll imagine having a snack or your favorite meal, and you can notice that as though you were really having it now, because you ARE REALLY having it in your MIND, and I know you won't mind using your mind this way! WHEN you can notice yourself at least part way in your mind, somewhere else, just let your head nod, and then I'll know* [response is usually very fast]. [This is important as one of

many ways to ratify the trance and for the child to know that you know and CARE that he or she is "with" you. Note: One can be more specific when the patient has shared WHERE he or she is imagining a place, in which case sensory suggestions can be specifically integrated to reflect that favorite place imagery.]"

Trance Ratification and Ego-Strengthening

"I'll bet that you have noticed some wonderful things that have changed and happened since you started, maybe without knowing that you notice them until now . . . but you are doing this self-hypnosis exactly right! Probably you noticed that your face muscles got all relaxed and droopy kind of all by themselves even though I didn't say anything about muscles relaxing [sometimes they will smile and nod even without a request for a response]. *This is because when the mind is relaxing doing self-hypnosis this way, the body listens and muscles relax. And, you can even notice that you can spread that relaxing feeling dooowwwwwwwnnnn your body at the right speed for you . . . so, after your face muscles relax, you can let that relaxed, cozy feeling of soft muscles move down into your neck, and then as you breathe* <u>out</u>, *you can let it* [= that feeling] *move into your shoulders and then down your arms around the bend at the elbows, and down into your hands, and wrists, and finger-tips . . . right! In fact, your fingers might get a little of that tingly, buzzy feeling this time or another time when you practice. And, it's natural for that relaxing feeling to move down your body at the right speed for you, when you're ready, past your chest, down into your belly, and all the way past your hips and thighs, down into your ankles, your feet, and your toes, until all the tension, or tightness, or stress that you want to get rid of can just go out of your body through the bottom of your feet and into the ground/floor. And as a therapist I pace a deep breath out with the patient's exhalation 'Ahhhhhhhh, that's right'".*

Therapeutic Suggestions

Utilization or storytelling continues *when* the patient is ready (as it already began in the pre-hypnosis conversational suggestions and as part

of favorite place imagery), and the therapist can either assume, or guess, or ask. Asking is best! For example, during or after progressive relaxation, one can say, "When you have all the relaxation you need/want for this practice time AND you're READY to use this great feeling that you have given yourself to help get rid of those [note the hypnotic dissociation suggestion, not "your" headaches, but "those" headaches] HEADACHES that USED TO bother you [more embedded suggestions, i.e., "used to" means past tense, implication is that they are now not bothering any more; and "bother" is a softer discomfort than "hurt"), THEN let me know [or, "let your head nod," not "nod your head" which is a conscious act, but "let your head nod" is a request for an unconscious = ideomotor response).

Stories

Using their OWN STORIES and creating the story within it, the child is invited to:

"Just imagine [baking cookies, swinging on swings, walking in the woods, playing video games, etc.], *or something else you really like."* Then, *"While you are doing that* [OR, while you are watching yourself on a video doing that = dissociation] *somewhere there you will see that 0 to 12 headache scale—I don't know where you'll see it, but you'll know. It might be in your pocket on a piece of paper, or in the sky writing in the clouds, or on a picnic table over there, or floating on a lake. I don't know what color it is or what it is made out of, but you'll know, and when you see it, just let your head nod. . . . Great! Now, notice what color the scale/ruler is and what color the numbers are. And now, just have a pretend or imaginary headache and see what number the scale is on. Maybe you'll be able to tell because that number is bigger or a different color or has a light around it or an arrow pointing to it, and let your head nod when you notice it. You could tell me about it now or later. I don't know how in your story you'll notice how that* [girl, boy, Susie, Michael, whatever] *begins to lower it to feel better. Maybe they'll notice a dial on the side of the ruler and just turn it down?* [note, use of "just" implies that it is EASY!] *OR, maybe it's a video game and every time you get to the next level of success it goes down another number or two, OR, maybe you're imagining playing basketball and*

every basket lowers it one or two or more numbers on your scale. OR, maybe some other way . . . I don't know how it will happen in your story, but you'll find out, and you can tell me about it NOW or you can wait until another time. Please give me a signal when the headache has gone down to as low as you want it to go down right now."

■ Stories of Other Kids

Commonly, in order to reinforce personal control and power, I continue to offer *menu options* after offering the earlier-described guidance for using children's own favorite activities as stories for themselves. This comes in the form of the "my friend John" (Erickson, 1964), as discussed earlier, and the "I knew this kid once . . ." techniques.

"You know, I meant to tell you earlier, but I knew this kid once who had a problem a little different than yours . . . [if the patient is a girl, I speak first of a boy who is younger]. He was 9 [she is 10 or 11] and had a problem with stomachaches; and what he decided to do because he loved to go to big buildings was whenever he had a stomachache, he'd pretend he was in an elevator with his mom or dad—and if he had like a 10 or 11 stomachache, he'd just imagine that he was in an elevator at the 11th floor . . . and then he'd watch himself reach over and push the button for 10, and the light would go off at 11 and on at 10 [pacing], and then he'd push 9 and the light would go off at 10 and . . . on at 9 . . . and then he'd push 8 and the light would . . . go . . . off . . . at 9 . . . and on at 8. And then he'd push like 4 or 5 and it would skip a few floors and the light came on at 5 and then pretty soon all the way to 0, and he'd get off the elevator and his stomachache was gone, it was now at ZERO!

One time I told that story to a little boy who was only 6 years old and he had headache problems even more often than yours, but he was afraid of elevators, so when I started to tell him that story, he got kind of upset, and then all of a sudden he got this smile on his face and got really relaxed, and he told me, 'left the elevator and went to the water park and there's this slide and it's 12 at the top and then it twists and turns and ends

up at 0 in the water. . . . So when I was day-dreaming about it, I went zooming down from 12-11-10-9-8-7-6-5-4-3-2-1 and SPLASHED! into the cool water at ZERO! And my headache was gone!'

And, then there was this 17-year-old girl who had terrible migraines. Her very favorite thing to do was to ride horses, and she was lucky enough to have her own horse. So she rides her real horse whenever she can arrange it and have time, AND she could ride her horse in her imagination whenever she wanted. SHE taught ME a lot, and one day after she had learned self-hypnosis, she was having hardly any migraines at all. I asked her 'How did you DO THAT?' She told me that she told herself this story: 'I picture myself riding my horse, and it feels like I am, and there I am riding on the beach near the ocean . . . and there on the sand is my 0 to 12 headache scale ruler in big numbers. And I think to myself if I have a headache then I just ride right over to the scale where that number is, like 8 or 7 or 11 or 5 or whatever, and as the horse walks slowly his hooves erase the next lower number, my headache number goes down too, and pretty soon the headache is GONE!'"

Varying forms of these "I knew a kid once . . ." stories are told. Other methods for pain control (of HAs) might be easily integrated into stories, including, for example, teaching changing of sensation with hypnoanalgesia, and transferring a remembered sensation and experience of local anesthesia to the site of the HA; another option is, within the story, giving the HA a shape and a color and then changing it to the shape and color of comfort, "throwing away discomfort" (the "jettison technique"). While there is a multitude of hypnotic suggestions for pain (HA) control/modulation, these are beyond the scope and focus of this discussion; however, they can be reviewed elsewhere (see Kohen & Olness [2011]; Sugarman & Wester [2014]).

Recently, a completed research project allowed us to learn the power of children's own stories in helping to eliminate HA AND in maintaining freedom from HA. Many such stories were related in response to an open-ended question in a survey of patients whom we had previously seen for HA problems, who learned hypnosis, and with whom we had no contact for as many as 10 to 12 years.

The patients were asked simply, "Is there anything else you would like to tell us about your self-hypnosis experience?" The responses were astounding (Kohen & Olness, 2011).

A 16-year-old young man wrote, "I *imagine* myself walking thru the woods. I do my self-hypnosis wherever I am *when I need to do* it. I listen to the air currents in the room, and I imagine that I'm chasing Magic (my uncle's dog) through the woods. When I catch the dog I know my headache is gone. I also use self-hypnosis when I'm really nervous. It helps me calm down so I can concentrate on whatever I need and am doing. Sometimes I use it when I am angry. It helps me calm down" (Kohen & Olness, 2011).

A 24-year-old woman who learned SH when she was 13 years old wrote: "I lay down in a dark room and close my eyes and *picture myself* standing on a beach in the sun. As I begin to walk down the beach, there are *numbers written in the sand* beginning with whatever number my headache is currently at. I use my feet to erase the numbers. When I reach zero, I sit or lay down on the beach and *focus* on what a pain-free head feels like. Usually I fall asleep at this point. I *use my scene* now whenever I feel overwhelmed . . . even if it's not headache related. . . I simply begin my numbers at the point of stress rather than my pain scale, and I've also felt an aura coming on and used them to *calm myself down into relaxation before a full aura starts*" (Kohen & Olness, 2011).

A 25-year-old woman wrote: "I begin by sitting on my bed with some relaxing music playing softly. My eyes closed and I begin to visualize a staircase. The staircase leads to a hot tub, and after relaxing my hot tub leads me to a meadow and at the end is a pond with a seat. While at the pond, I concentrate on relieving any pain I might have and completely relax. I use it on a daily basis to unwind after work, or just a long day. I have also used it for sleep. I had a very complicated pregnancy and quite a bit of pain, and imagery helped me to control the pain" (Kohen & Olness, 2011). "I lie down on my bed and *pretend* I am at my cabin fishing . . ." from a 13-year-old boy.

As we were making a video recording of our visit, I asked my patient, a 16-year-old young woman, to please tell the (prospective) viewer(s) of the video, "What you do in your hypnosis and how?" She replied: "I imagine my most favorite and relaxing place, which is our cabin in a small country town . . . and I just imagine what I do in the summer [a lot], which is lay on the grass near the lake and read and I like to write . . . and I like to take a walk on a little road and [notice the] leaves falling, and the wind blowing . . . and it gives me a chance to relax and get some peace from a stressful day at school. . . . When I am at the cabin in the summer my headache is usually better than when I'm in school." Then, in response to the question "What do you DO in your hypnosis to program yourself to get rid of headaches?," she said, "In my hypnosis I picture my discomfort, maybe in the sky or on a thermometer and I notice where it [the HA] is when I start and then as I relax I notice it from time to time, and notice it goes down and then tell myself to keep it at that level when I finish my hypnosis . . . I was actually astonished at how well it works!!"

I have since then often told her story as "I knew this teenager once who had such bad headaches that they were *every single day* . . . at least until she started keeping track of them, AND as she learned self-hypnosis she kept track of her self-rating of how she is *dealing with headaches* . . . and as time went on her numbers for headache went down, and so did the *dealing with it numbers* [lower dealing with it = dealing with it easier and easier, better and better the lower the number] and when I asked her to tell me about what her imagination was DOING, she told me that story." Another adolescent male with a long history of chronic daily headache created his own "story" through poetry (Kohen, 2011; Kohen & Olness, 2011).

After the first time learning SH (and practicing at home), it is essential to debrief children regarding what they have DONE at home, have them tell you *what they did, how* they did it, and what *stories* they told themselves while reacting/imagining something fun, exciting, or relaxing (or all three!). I write this down and ask for details, embellishment, and then permission to "give this right back" to them when we practice hypnosis a few moments later.

CONCLUSION

As the children and youth who are our patients—and their parents—have taught us, stories "work"! As we are invited into the lives of young people and their families as helpers and storytellers, we can help them create their own stories, and use various combinations of stories told and developed, and stories heard, and make them an integral part of their SH as they create comfort and healing for themselves.

REFERENCES

Abu-Arefeh, I., & Russell, G. (1994). Prevalence of headache and migraine in schoolchildren. *BMJ (Clinical Research Ed.)*, 309(6957), 765–769.

Blume, H. K., Brockman, L. N., & Breuner, C. C. (2012). Biofeedback therapy for pediatric headache; factors associated with response. *Headache*, 52(9), 1377–1386.

Brett, D. (1986). *Annie stories*. Victoria, Australia: McPhee Gribble Publishers Pty Ltd Fitzroy.

Brett, D. (1992). *More Annie stories–therapeutic storytelling techniques*. New York, NY: Magination Press–Brunner-Mazel.

Eccleston, C., Yorke, L., Morley, S., Williams, A. C., & Mastroyannopoulou, K. (2003). Psychological therapies for the management of chronic and recurrent pain in children and adolescents. *Cochrane Database Systematic Review*, 1, 1–46.

Elkins, G. (1997). *My doctor does hypnosis*. Chicago, IL: American Society of Clinical Hypnosis Press.

Erickson, M. H. (1958). Pediatric hypnotherapy. *American Journal of Clinical Hypnosis*, 1(1), 25–29.

Erickson, M. H. (1964). The "surprise" and "my-friend-John" techniques of hypnosis: Minimal cues and natural field experimentation. *American Journal of Clinical Hypnosis*, 6, 293–307.

Fisher, P. (2005). Help for headaches: A strategy for your busy practice. *Contemporary Pediatrics*, 22, 34–41.

Headache Classification Committee of the International Headache Society (IHS). (2013). The International Classification of Headache Disorders, 3rd edition (beta version). *Cephalalgia*, 33(9), 629–808.

Holden, E., Deichmann, M. M., & Levy, J. D. (1999). Empirically supported treatments in pediatric psychology: Recurrent pediatric headache. *Journal of Pediatric Psychology*, 24(2), 91–109.

Kane, S., & Olness, K. (Eds.). (2004). *The art of therapeutic communication: The collected works of Kay F. Thompson*. Wales: Crown House Publishing.

Kohen, D. P. (1991). *Children and hypnosis dimension*. Minneapolis, MN: WCCO Television.

Kohen, D. P. (2010). Long term follow-up of self-hypnosis training for recurrent headaches: What the children say. *International Journal of Clinical and Experimental Hypnosis*, 58(4), 417–432.

Kohen, D. P. (2011). Chronic daily headache: Helping adolescents help themselves with self-hypnosis. *The American Journal of Clinical Hypnosis*, 54(1), 32–46.

Kohen, D. P., & Olness, K. (2011). *Hypnosis and hypnotherapy with children*. New York, NY: Routledge, Taylor & Francis.

Kohen, D. P., & Wynne, E. (1997). Applying hypnosis in a preschool family asthma education program: Uses of storytelling, imagery and relaxation. *American Journal of Clinical Hypnosis*, 39(3), 169–181.

Kohen, D. P., & Zajac, R. (2007). Self-hypnosis training for headaches in children and adolescents. *Journal of Pediatrics*, 150(6), 635–639.

Kröner-Herwig, B., Mohn, U., & Pothmann, R. (1998). Comparison of biofeedback and relaxation in the treatment of pediatric headache and the influence of parent involvement on outcome. *Applied Psychophysiology and Biofeedback*, 23(3), 143–157.

Kuttner, L. (1988). Favorite stories: A hypnotic pain reduction technique for children in acute pain. *American Journal of Clinical Hypnosis*, 30(4), 289–295.

Larsson, B., & Carlsson, J. (1996). School-based, nurse-administered relaxation training for children with chronic tension-type headache. *Journal of Pediatric Psychology*, 21(5), 603–614.

Lewis, D., Ashwal, S., Hershey, A., Hirtz, D., Yonker, M., & Silberstein, S. (2004). Practice parameter: Pharmacological treatment of migraine headache in children and adolescents. *Neurology*, 63(12), 2215–2224.

Masek, B. J. (1999). Commentary: The pediatric migraine connection. *Journal of Pediatric Psychology*, 24(2), 110.

McGrath, P. J. (1999). Commentary: Recurrent headaches: Making what works available to those who need it. *Journal of Pediatric Psychology*, 24(2), 111–112.

Mills, J., & Crowley, R. J. (1986). *Therapeutic metaphors for children and the child within*. New York, NY: Brunner/Mazel.

Olness, K., MacDonald, J. T., & Uden, D. L. (1987). Comparison of self-hypnosis and propranolol in the treatment of juvenile classic migraine. *Pediatrics*, 79(4), 593–597.

Pavone, P., Rizzo, R., Conti, I., Verrotti, A., Mistretta, A., Falsaperla, R., . . . Pavone, L. (2012). Primary headaches in children: Clinical findings on the association with other conditions. *International Journal of Immunopathology and Pharmacology*, 25(4), 1083–1091.

Split, W., & Neuman, W. (1999). Epidemiology of migraine among students from randomly selected secondary schools in Lodz. *Headache*, 39(7), 494–501.

Sugarman, L. I. (Producer). (1997). *Imaginative medicine: Hypnosis in pediatric practice*. Retrieved from lisdsp@rit.edu

Sugarman, L. I., & Wester, W. C. (2014). *Therapeutic hypnosis with children and adolescents*. Bancyfelin, Carmarthen, Wales, UK: Crown House Publishing.

Thompson, K. F. (1994). Whose story is this anyway? A history of his-story. In J. Zeig (Ed.), *Ericksonian methods: The essence of the story* (pp. 136–144). New York, NY: Brunner-Mazel.

Thomson, L. (2005). *Harry the Hypno-potamus: Metaphorical tales for pediatric problems.* Bancyfelin, Carmarthen, UK: Crown House Publishing.

Thomson, L. (2009). *Harry the Hypno-potamus–Volume II: More metaphorical tales for pediatric problems.* Bancyfelin, Carmarthen, UK: Crown House Publishing.

Zeig, J. K. (1994). *Ericksonian methods: The essence of the story (Proceedings of the Fifth International Congress on Ericksonian Approaches to Hypnosis and Psychotherapy).* New York, NY: Brunner/Mazel.

The Treatment of Hypertension With Hypnosis

Edit Jakubovits and Zoltán Kekecs

Close to 1 billion people live with hypertension worldwide, which is rated as one of the biggest causes of premature death by the World Health Organization (WHO, 2014). The direct medical costs associated with hypertension, in the United States alone, are estimated to reach $100 billion annually (Hodgson & Cai, 2001); thus, there is an evident need for new, innovative, and cost-effective approaches to the prevention and treatment of hypertension. Although pharmacological treatments of hypertension exist, uses of medical therapies are limited by side effects and low patient compliance. As concluded by several reviews of the topic, nonpharmacological therapies usually produce more lasting effects than drug therapies alone, and can have "spill-over" benefits as well, like increased quality of life (Hedayati, Elsayed, & Reilly, 2011; Rosen, Brondolo, & Kostis, 1993). The most popular nonpharmacological techniques for managing hypertension are (a) introducing a healthy diet, (b) weight loss, (c) exercise (Beck, Martin, Casey, & Braith, 2014; Hagberg, Park, & Brown, 2000; Vander José das Neves, Redondo, Soci, Melo, & de Oliveira, 2014), (d) decreased alcohol intake, and (e) psychological interventions for stress and anxiety reduction (Jonas, Franks, & Ingram, 1997; Markovitz, Matthews, Kannel, Cobb, & D'Agostino, 1993).

Hypnotherapy is a good candidate for directly delivering or supporting such nonpharmacological interventions. Several studies have shown that hypnotherapy can directly reduce chronically high blood pressure (BP; Deabler, Fidel, Dillenkoffer, & Elder, 1973; Friedman & Taub, 1977, 1978; Gay, 2007; Raskin, Raps, Luskin, Carlson, & Cristal, 1999; Tosi, Rudy, Lewis, & Murphy, 1992). These studies used a protocol in which the suggestions were mostly focused on deep relaxation. The script also contains posthypnotic suggestions to increase motivation for healing, to cooperate with the physician, and to comply with lifestyle change. Furthermore, the script offers tools to cope with everyday stressors. The hypnosis regimen utilized both therapist-delivered and self-hypnosis techniques. With an average of seven therapist-delivered sessions and instructions for daily home practice using self-hypnosis, these interventions yielded an average of 9 mmHg and 7 mmHg decrease in systolic and diastolic BP, respectively. Importantly, this decrease in blood pressure was found to be retained even after one year of follow-up, which emphasizes the success of an empowering approach (self-hypnosis training). However, self-hypnosis in itself does not seem to be enough to treat hypertension, as demonstrated by the study of Case, Fogel, and Pollack (1980); thus, therapist-delivered sessions also seem to be necessary. Most of these studies did not select for high hypnotizable participants. Therefore, the significant treatment effects suggest that some degree of success can be expected regardless of hypnotizability. Randomization and group allocation are usually not sufficiently detailed in these studies, and in most cases there was no attempt to blind the participants, the therapist, or the researchers regarding group allocation. These methodological shortcomings somewhat weaken the strength of the evidence.

Hypnosis can also be used to target the risk factors of hypertension, such as obesity, anxiety, and stress. Several studies show that hypnosis can be effective to assist weight loss. For a review on the topic in the context of diabetes, see Xu and Cardeña (2007), although there is no consensus on the size of the added benefit of hypnosis to cognitive behavioral therapy (CBT), and there is not enough research to judge the efficacy of hypnosis as a standalone therapy for obesity either (Shaw, O'Rourke, Del Mar, & Kenardy, 2005). Hypnotherapy has also been confirmed to reduce anxiety and stress, in some cases even more effectively than CBT (Golden, 2012; Schoenberger, 2000). During their recent review of the topic, Cardeña, Svensson, and Hejdström (2013) concluded that hypnosis interventions in general, and especially those using imagery, reduced the experience and physiological effects of everyday stressors, such as work stress, exam-related stress, or stress associated with medical procedures. Another important risk factor of developing and maintaining hypertension is excessive alcohol consumption. Accordingly, there have been some attempts in the literature to examine the effectiveness of hypnotherapy for alcohol cessation; however, based on the evidence accumulated so far we cannot claim that including hypnotherapy in the treatment of alcohol abuse would have significant added benefits (Crocker, 2004; Pekala et al., 2004; Wadden & Penrod, 1981; Young, 1996).

THERAPEUTIC SUGGESTIONS

The main goal of hypnotherapy is to improve the physical condition of the client, not to simply decrease his or her blood pressure. This is achieved by (a) reducing stress and anxiety, (b) self-strengthening (to continue medical therapy and to persevere the lifestyle changes), (c) exploring the psychological background of the illness, and (d) improving cooperation with the physician. Hypertension is not painful and is usually unnoticed by the person suffering from it; while lifestyle and dietary changes for the management of hypertension require considerable effort, patients are often noncompliant. Thus, the importance of improving compliance and cooperation cannot be overstated. The hypnotherapist also has to work closely with the physician during the therapy.

COMPOSITION OF THE HYPNOTHERAPY

The content of the suggestions needs to be personalized, integrating the following points:

1. The patient's own notions about his or her bodily functions and medications.
2. The social psychobiological model of hypnosis (Bányai, 1998): "Social"—suggestions involving family, friends, work relationships, and the cooperation of the cells or organs of the body; "psycho"—suggestions facilitating the mobilization of mental resources; "biological"—suggestions concerning the physical body, emphasizing the communication involving the body.
3. Medical knowledge about the illness: If the patient understands the condition and the treatment, he or she will be more likely to actively participate in the therapy. The hypnotherapist is also able to use more appropriate suggestions with accurate medical knowledge.

As emphasized earlier, exercise is one of the most accepted therapeutic techniques in the treatment of hypertension. Thus, instead of a regular relaxational technique, our example here uses active alert hypnosis as an induction method (Bányai & Hilgard, 1976; Bányai, Zseni, & Túry, 1993; Bíró, 2012; Zseni, 1988). Another advantage of an active alert approach is that psychological and physiological stress and tension—often displayed in hypertension cases—can be rechanneled into physical activity. The equipment used for the induction can be a stationary bicycle, or treadmill. (The following script is designed for a stationary bicycle.)

EXAMPLE OF A 10-SESSION THERAPEUTIC PLAN

Session 1: Introducing hypnosis, revitalization, finding positive emotions and personal pace, recalling the joy of physical activity (motivation, relationship building, self-strengthening, mobilizing resources). *Sessions 2–3:* Enhancing the healing of the blood vessels with metaphors of the river and renovating a house. *Sessions 4–5:* Tour inside the body, direct suggestions. *Sessions 6–7:* Understanding the "message" of the body and the illness, dissolving psychological blockades, utilizing inner resources, metaphors, and results achieved so far. *Session 8:* Facilitating independence and cooperation with the physician. *Sessions 9–10:* Self-hypnosis training.

The active alert hypnosis is 10 to 20 minutes long, which is shorter than a classic relaxational session; however, there is more discussion needed at the end of each session because this approach results in more associations. The voice of the therapist is strong, active, and lively. It adapts to the changes in the pace of movement. The therapist should ask for feedback frequently (feedback can be a simple head nod), and should also give feedback of the client's condition. The setup of the equipment at the start of the session contains suggestions in its own right. The therapist needs to be aware of this and utilize this stage as well.

EXAMPLE FOR A HYPNOSIS SCRIPT

The following material was used for the development of the hypnosis script and metaphors: Ewin (2011a, 2011b), Hammond (1990), Kekecs and Varga (2013), Varga (2004, 2011a, 2011b), and Varga and Diószeghy (2001). Pauses (marked as "...") are usually shorter than in a relaxation induction.

"Preparation: We will set the equipment now, with which you will take a magical journey, so that your body can find its own healthy rhythm. Is the height of the seat alright? Please set the resistance so that movement is not too hard, nor too easy. You can adjust it any time on the go. Overexertion is not a goal here. The goal is to have a steady, rhythmical motion in your body. You can achieve this with a steady, slow movement as well.

Induction: Please start pedaling ... very good! Your eyes can remain open if you would like, but maybe closing them will help you even more to pay attention to internal sensations. The important thing is to feel yourself secure and comfortable. The only things that matter are the ones I point out to you and the things that are happening inside. The hypnosis now helps you to rediscover the joy of movement, the flexibility of the body, the flexibility of the blood vessels, and the red blood cells ... it helps you to find your own pace, in your own way, in your own tempo.

I would like to ask you to concentrate your attention on the sensations in your legs, even more so than you would normally do. While you pedal and focus your attention on these sensations in your legs, this concentrated attention synchronizes the

neurons with each other and your legs more and more, this way helping you to reach the hypnotic state. [The pace of the voice should match that of the movement.] *As you focus your attention intensely onto the sensations in your legs, so are you able to enter into a deeper and deeper hypnosis. Thus, it is easier and easier to pedal. Very good! Great!*

Notice what kind of sensations the pedals produce as you push one of them down, and you feel its hardness, while the other one comes up and becomes light. Notice what it feels like that on one side your ankle and knee extend out, while on the other side they bend and rise. They extend and bend, rhythmically, in synchrony. Your ankle and knee bends on one side, and extends on the other, one after the other, rhythmically ... in synchrony ... in deeper and deeper hypnosis. ... Notice what it feels like as the muscles in the shin and thigh contract and relax. Pay close attention, how one leg moves after the other, how one contracts while the other relaxes. The left and the right. One of them in front, the other in the back. One is up, the other is down. The left and the right. Automatically ... in synchrony ... deeper and deeper in hypnosis. ... Great! [The pace of the voice should match the movement.]

As you pedal, you get closer and closer to yourself, to your deeper feelings. As you feel your muscles and joints stretching and bending more and more, rhythmically, in synchrony, so you perceive your feelings about movement and about your health more and more. For some, this goes easily and they enjoy the tempo, while for others it is harder or they feel tired. Whichever way it might be, the nervous system gets more and more tuned with the legs, and you drift into a deeper and deeper hypnosis, closer and closer to noticing your own feelings. As your nervous system gets more and more synchronized with your legs, so do other cells of the body get more in synchrony. More and more cells join in to help the movement and to fight tiredness! Notice how other muscles support the movement. How do the hips, the back and the neck move. Notice how your head helps so that you can better concentrate! Pay attention on how your shoulders and arms move, how they help you find your own rhythm and movement. And there are those arms and hands! Notice how hard and secure their grip is on the handles. How do the handles feel? They support the movement, they support the hypnosis! The muscles are getting more and more synchronized . . . just like a dance, just like your favorite physical activity [Here the therapist can use the favorite physical activity of the client from a previous interview]. . . . *As you listen to the rhythmic movement, you go into a deeper and deeper hypnosis, and you feel it more and more that you can keep up the pace and to achieve your goal. You can do it!*

How are you? How do you feel? [Wait for response, give encouragement and reinforcement using the answer.] *Notice how the heart, the blood vessels, and the lungs work together. The heart and the lungs support the functioning of the muscles more and more, they get aligned with the rhythm. Notice how you can breathe better so that oxygen can travel everywhere in your body where it is needed. The fresh air blows away fatigue. It refreshes your whole body! Your muscles, your nervous system, your whole body is refreshed! This way you are able to discover your own rhythm. The flexibility in your lungs, the heart, the blood vessels. Notice how the more and more flexible lungs, blood vessels, and heart muscles are helping. More flexible, more easy, more resolute. Maybe you already feel that warmth, that tingling sensation in your legs, as the blood flow gets livelier and livelier. More and more fresh blood flows there, to carry oxygen and nutrition, and to wash away the tiredness. The breathing and the heartbeat gets stronger as well, just as much as needed. Not only your muscles, but also your whole body and mind get refreshed through this blood flow. You can concentrate better and better to reach your goals. You are more and more able to focus, to pedal persistently, to reach your goals. With every movement you get into an even deeper and deeper hypnosis, and your movement gets more and more synchronized, automatic. You enjoy it more and more, and you get more and more refreshed by it. How are you? It is enough to just nod if you are alright.*

As the body gets more and more refreshed, the movement suddenly gets over a point from which it gets easier and easier, and more and more free! Automatic! You start to feel the runner's high! Very good! Your legs are no longer driving pedals, they drive a power generator. With every pedaling, stronger and stronger, more and more free.

In deeper and deeper hypnosis your legs already move on their own, with joy, freely. [If the movement does not get faster at all, or if it slows down, the therapist should inquire about how the client feels, what is happening, where is the client in his imagery right now.]

With every movement it gets easier and easier! Because you can do it! Because you know: one leg after the other, one leg up, the other one down! One of the muscles contracts, the other one relaxes, in synchrony, rhythmically, in the front and in the back, up and down, and with every movement it gets easier and easier! It is like our lives, as we move on from the difficulties. Let's go! One leg after the other, one leg up, the other one down! And you are able to keep yourself on track toward the goal. [The pace of the voice should match the movement.] *Where are you? What is happening?* [Wait for answer. Encourage and reinforce the answer.] *Is that right? Very good! Let's go forward!*

You already feel the joy of movement and that of synchronized functioning more and more! The other muscles are helping, the circulation, the brain, and the whole body, so that you can rediscover the joy of movement, the flexibility of the body, the flexibility of blood vessels and red blood cells. You find your own rhythm, in your own way, in your own pace, together with the others, in synchrony. With greater and greater enjoyment, rhythmically, in your own tempo, for your own pleasure. Nothing else matters now but the joy of movement, your own rhythm, your own pace! More flexible, more automatic! You are able to find those movements in your everyday life that give your body and your blood vessels more and more pleasure and flexibility. Your body helps you, you should also help your body! Your cells will be grateful! You feel that great synchrony and cooperation more and more! Your muscles on the outside and on the inside contract and relax, contract and relax rhythmically and flexibly. [This type of induction can bring forth sexual experiences or experiences from the time of birth.] *Fresh, oxygen-rich blood is flowing, full of nutrition, just enjoy, because you can do it! In deeper and deeper hypnosis the refreshed blood washes away obstructions from deeper and deeper!. . . It washes away obstructions from deeper and deeper! From now on with every breath difficulties and obstructions are washed away, and the blood flows more and more freely in the flexible blood vessels! From here on with every breath, as long as it is needed. This freshness stays with you after hypnosis as well, you will be surprised how pleasant you will feel. Your whole body will be filled with the flow, the freshness, the joy of movement, the feeling of being able. Very good! Where are you? What is happening?* [Wait for answer.] *Very good!*

Posthypnotic suggestions: From now on with every breath, difficulties and obstructions are washed away, and the blood flows more and more freely in the flexible blood vessels! From here on with every breath, as long as it is needed. This freshness stays with you after hypnosis as well, you will be surprised how pleasant you will feel. Your whole body will be filled with the flow, the freshness, the joy of movement, the feeling of being able. You will also be able to handle every stressful event in your day-to-day life easier and easier, more and more flexible. Is that right? Very good!

Therapeutic phase: [Here the therapist can integrate the appropriate therapeutic suggestions according to the progress of the therapy. Some examples are listed, using the metaphors of a river, renovating a house, and changing pipelines. After every question, we can utilize the answers of the client. Developing some of the experiences can take a whole session; there is no need to fit all the experiences into the same session.]

Example 1—organ-tour: As you start to discover your wonderful blood vessels, in which your blood flows like a river, notice what this river is like. What are the shores of this river like? How do the blood vessels look like from the inside? Are they smooth, or are there interesting things on the walls of the blood vessels? What are those like?

You feel it more and more that you are capable to clean anything that you find that does not belong there. In what way do you start to do this? Some people scrub it with great force with a scrub, or hit and pound the sediment with a hammer. Some people fight and push between the obstructions until they feel that the way is clear and they are free to go forward. [This might even mobilize experiences from the time of birth.] *Some people just brush this injury lovingly and let the light of love dissolve the problem . . . . Some people simply release a dissolvent, or omega-3 oil in their bloodstream, which smoothes and cleans the inner surface of the blood vessels with their magical powers.*

What is your solution? Notice what, or who helps in this. Pay attention to the sounds . . . the bodily feelings . . . the colors . . . and the lights! Notice how the walls of the blood vessels get cleaned because of your exercise . . . how the blood flows more and more freely, and brings the joy of well done work into your whole body. . . .

[The therapist should elaborate on whichever solution the client chooses. For example, if the client chooses exertion of force, we can encourage him or her like this:] *That's right, yes, let's do this, you can do it! Bring it on! The cheerleaders are all cheering for you on the sides! The fans are all roaring . . . your team is going to win!!! Feel the pleasant feeling of victory! Notice how good this feels! Do you want to clean even more areas, or was it enough for today and you want to rest? However might it be, I want you to know that your cells are doing their jobs, making it sure that the cleaning of the blood vessels is continuous. How do you help your cells? With healthy diet? Exercise? Self-knowledge? Relaxation techniques? Or you can do more than one of these? The fact that you are here already shows that you have already made your decision that you want to get better . . . this is the most important. . . . Pay attention and feel that your cells accept these presents of yours gratefully! How do you feel this? What is your own experience? Do you see the happier and happier and livelier and livelier cells in the heart, in the walls of the blood vessels, as they contract or relax joyfully? Or are you simply filled with a pleasant and restful feeling? Or is it simply pleasant to think about this and listen to the words of encouragement? However it might be, I want you to know that your whole body appreciates that it has your undivided attention now . . . I am curious when and how you will notice the changes first. Right at the end of this hour? Tomorrow? Or a month from now? I am looking forward to your experiences.*

Example 2—metaphors for dissolving a blockade: Now I would like you to imagine a special, strong, and beautiful river, which gives you strength. It is possible that you already know this river, or that you only saw it on a picture, or that you just met it now for the first time. . . . What is this river like? Would you like to take a walk on its banks? Or to take a swim in it? . . . Just observe and experience. . . . What is the shore like? What is the water like? What are the colors, lights, and sounds? What does the water and the place smell like? How does it feel to touch the water?

As you experience this more and more, I am curious whether you have already thought about people utilizing the safe and strong power of rivers: for example, we irrigate plants. What is your favorite plant, that will get more and more beautiful and healthy as this magical river feeds it with its power. . . . It is so delightful. . . . So delicious. . . .

Or do the rivers drive a power plant? What is your power plant like? Is it old fashioned with turning wheels like a watermill? Or is it a modern system with all the turbines? What is your own power plant like? Maybe it will need a little refurbishing. How do you do that? Do you do it on your own or do you bring others to help? You can do anything! In the magical world of hypnosis you are completely free. . . . How does this refurbishing go? Sometimes it is sweaty and hard work, but you can do it! How wonderful it is that you progress forward and the power plant gets more and more beautiful and clean. What does your own newly refurbished power plant use the power for? What kinds of things does it build, feed, clean . . . or what do you do with this clean power? Just notice how joyfully your environment receives this power. . . .

A beautiful and strong river can also carry ships. . . . They can be cargo ships or passenger ships, small or large, or even a small flatboat or rowboat. . . . What does your own look like? What does it carry and where it is headed? I would like you to follow it and I want you to know that if you find any obstacle in your way, you can deal with it. You are able to solve it. . . . What is this obstacle like? And what is your solution? Notice how joyful it is to solve these problems, and to sail onward toward your goal, which might even be the ocean . . . where the horizon opens up. . . .

Rivers sometimes overflow . . . or something might obstruct their flow. . . . As you travel with your own river toward the ocean, what does your river show you, what kinds of problems do you find? What do you experience? Would you like to observe what that is? Would you like to clear this area? Notice the obstacles. Sometimes it is sludge, or branches, other times it is alluvium that obstructs the flow.

The goal is that the strong river will travel to the ocean in its safe riverbed, while giving you useful experiences, even if sometimes this is hard. You are more and more capable to direct the flow of this power, freely. The river is cleaner and cleaner. The river flows with more and more joy. The goal is for the strong river to reach the ocean in its safe riverbed, while giving you useful experiences. . . . What is this union with the ocean like?

Example 3—renovating a house: The walls of the heart, the blood vessels, and the red blood cells carrying the oxygen are more and more flexible, and they can incorporate the materials they get from nutrition more and more. . . . For example, these special omega-3 oils . . . notice how they smooth and oil the wall of the heart, the walls of the blood vessels, the red blood cells, as if you would paint using this golden oil with a soft paintbrush . . . . As the brush dips into the oil and then gently brushes the walls of the blood vessels. . . . With every brushstroke the heart, the blood vessels, and the red blood cells get cleaner and more and more flexible. As if the cells would be just swimming in this magical substance. They stretch with joy and they contract flexibly, one cell after the other . . . they are soaked with the wonderful substance . . . the layers between the cells are also clearer and cleaner, and the cells are enjoying themselves more and more . . . amongst them the flexible muscle cells, the elastic fibers, and the endothelial cells are all happier and happier, as the brush covers them with the healing substance. . . . Brilliant! Very good!

As the walls of the blood vessels get cleaner and stronger, maybe you will notice that here and there are still some flaws on the surface and the inside. Like when you renovate your house and the window frames still need to be repaired, or when you have to scrape the old rendering. It is possible that the pipes in the wall need to be changed. The walls might have to be opened to get to these pipes. You might already hear the sound of the hammering as the wall comes apart, fractions of it flying all around, and you can already sense the bad smell of the old pipes. . . . And the hands of the repairmen work skillfully, as they swiftly change the pipes, they put the new ones in, they pad them with insulation, and the wall is rebuilt quickly. But this is a fine new pipe now, a fine new wall.

You can smell the good odors of the new materials . . . maybe it is still a bit wet if you touch it . . . and maybe you can already hear as they turn the faucet on, and the water rushes out freely . . . the beautiful, clear water is flowing . . . the invigorating fresh water flows freely in the whole house in new, clean pipes . . .

As the water pipes are done, they can work more easily in the rooms and the other parts of the house. . . . Just observe how your brush works with the magical substance in the rooms, and how does the whole house revive. There are places where it is not that simple, and where you have to apply force, to scrape the old rendering or the tapestry . . . just apply that force, and notice that fantastic feeling when it gets cleaner and cleaner and that you are doing this! As you feel that it is hard, bring it on, you can do it, there is more and more area that is complete! Very good! Painting can come after that. As you take the brush out of the bucket, maybe it spills out a bit, but that's alright, you are already painting, vigorously repairing the wall . . . very good, and you can apply the final layer of paint, or the tapestry, whichever you like. Come on, what does it feel like? You are more and more confident and free, in your own way, in your own pace . . . in your own colors!

As you step back, you can see what it looks like. If you perceive any flaws, just repair it now, you have time, with every breath of air the blood vessels are getting more and more clean and flexible, as long as it is needed. . . . That's right! How is it now? When you feel that you are satisfied, please take a step back and enjoy your creation, enjoy the experience. . . it is as you always wanted it to be. . . . The newly renovated house, the rooms, the hallways, the water pipes, the faucets are clean and bright. There is a nice smell in the air, the smell of cleanliness. If you would touch the walls, you would feel how the fresh paint makes your fingers smooth and wet. . . . What are the colors and lights like? The residents also feel really nice. Notice as the new blood cells play hide and seek as little children, and that they can now squeeze through even the tightest spots, they are so flexible and lively.

Dehypnosis: [If the client gets tired earlier, we compliment him or her for holding out for this long and that he or she accepted his or her feelings. These feelings are really important and we can work with them.] *I would like you to take another walk around your whole body! Notice where the body feels the absolute best right now. Just let this feeling fill you up. . . . With every session the switch between states of consciousness gets easier and easier, more and more flexible. Now I would like you to take what was the most important in today's practice, and compress it into one memory: this could be a picture, a sound, a feeling, an odor, a word, a thought. Place this in your body to a place that calls out for this experience the most. If there is no such place now, then to a place which comes into your mind first. After hypnosis it will feel good to repeatedly recall this empowering experience, which recalls the joy of movement, flexibility, the joy of being able, which fills you now in your own way.*

After you have found and recorded this important experience, you can start to return from hypnosis. I would like to ask you to pay attention to the bicycle once again, to the sensation the pedals generate on your feet, the sensation of the seat under you, and the handle in your grip. The movement of the equipment starts to slow down, but the joy of movement and capability continue to flow, to help to find healthy experiences in the day-to-day life, in cooperation with the doctors, in your own way. Return to your normal state of consciousness, full of strength, rested, full of experiences. The movement of the bicycle is slowing down, and stopping. . . . You are here in the office again. Return here, while retaining and utilizing all of the things that were important to you from this practice. Return from hypnosis to the here and now, into the office, on the way toward healing, change, and development. The hypnosis is over. Please sit back in the chair, and tell me about your experiences from the point you started pedaling. . . ."

Experiences from clients: "First I was tired. And suddenly it changed as if I was not pedaling on a bicycle anymore, but like I was walking against the wind. After that, my bodily sensations were gone, and a beautiful rose developed in me from the bottom up. It opened up, it was gorgeous. I recorded this in my memory." "Suddenly I became a big bird, which flies upward furiously, but I was struck by lightning. I was paralyzed and I started to fall down. This was really painful, but somehow I regained strength and I felt myself so powerful. I was flying again, freely. I felt that I can do anything. I became one with everything."

Contraindications: Health conditions that prevent physical activity, for example, angina pectoris, can be contraindications. It is vital to contact the physician of every client and inquire about the level of physical activity allowed. For patients who cannot do physical activity, active alert hypnosis can still be used, but the exercise is only performed in mental imagery. Active alert hypnosis is also contraindicated in cases with excessive mental activity and disorientation.

Side effects: BP might be monitored during or after sessions. Physical activity must not be excessive. It can be increased gradually, but has to be started slower and easier at the first sessions. Hypnosis can be reached even with a slow, but rhythmic pace. The client's resistance to the therapy can manifest as injuries in the day-to-day life, which prevent them from riding the bicycle. The background of such injuries has to be explored. Decreasing BP can cause fatigue in some cases.

REFERENCES

Bányai, É. I. (1998). The interactive nature of hypnosis: Research evidence for a social-psychobiological model. *Contemporary Hypnosis, 15*(1), 52–63.

Bányai, É. I., & Hilgard, E. R. (1976). A comparison of active-alert hypnotic induction with traditional relaxation induction. *Journal of Abnormal Psychology, 85*(2), 218–224.

Bányai, É. I., Zseni, A., & Túry, F. (1993). Active-alert hypnosis in psychotherapy. In J. Rhue, S. Lynn, & J. Kirsch (Eds.), *Handbook of clinical hypnosis* (pp. 271–290). Washington DC: American Psychological Association.

Beck, D., Martin, J., Casey, D., & Braith, R. (2014). Exercise training improves endothelial function in resistance arteries of young prehypertensives. *Journal of Human Hypertension, 28*, 303–309.

Bíró, G. (2012). A relaxációs és az aktív-éber hipnózis szerepe a sport coaching terén [The role of relaxation and active alert hypnosis in sport coaching]. In K. Varga & A. Gősi-Greguss (Eds.), *Tudatállapotok, hipnózis, egymásra hangolódás [States of consciousness, hypnosis, tuning to each other]* (pp. 391–413). Budapest: L'Harmattan Kiadó.

Cardeña, E., Svensson, C., & Hejdström, F. (2013). Hypnotic tape intervention ameliorates stress: A randomized, control study. *International Journal of Clinical and Experimental Hypnosis, 61*(2), 125–145.

Case, D. B., Fogel, D. H., & Pollack, A. A. (1980). Intrahypnotic and long-term effects of self-hypnosis on blood pressure in mild hypertension. *International Journal of Clinical and Experimental Hypnosis, 28*(1), 27–38.

Crocker, S. M. (2004). *Hypnosis as an adjunct in the treatment of alcohol relapse* (Doctoral dissertation). Washington State University, Pullman, WA.

Deabler, H. L., Fidel, E., Dillenkoffer, R. L., & Elder, S. T. (1973). The use of relaxation and hypnosis in lowering high blood pressure. *American Journal of Clinical Hypnosis, 16*(2), 75–83.

Ewin, D. M. (2011a). *101 things I wish I'd known when I started using hypnosis*. Wales: Crown House Publishing Ltd.

Ewin, D. M. (2011b). The laws of hypnotic suggestion. In K. Varga (Ed.), *Beyond the words* (pp. 75–83). New York, NY: Nova Science Publishers.

Friedman, H., & Taub, H. A. (1977). The use of hypnosis and biofeedback procedures for essential hypertension. *International Journal of Clinical and Experimental Hypnosis, 25*(4), 335–347.

Friedman, H., & Taub, H. A. (1978). A six-month follow-up of the use of hypnosis and biofeedback procedures in essential hypertension. *American Journal of Clinical Hypnosis, 20*(3), 184–188.

Gay, M. C. (2007). Effectiveness of hypnosis in reducing mild essential hypertension: A one-year follow-up. *International Journal of Clinical and Experimental Hypnosis, 55*(1), 67–83.

Golden, W. L. (2012). Cognitive hypnotherapy for anxiety disorders. *American Journal of Clinical Hypnosis, 54*(4), 263–274.

Hagberg, J. M., Park, J.-J., & Brown, M. D. (2000). The role of exercise training in the treatment of hypertension. *Sports Medicine, 30*(3), 193–206.

Hammond, D. C. (1990). *Hypnotic suggestions and metaphors*. New York, NY: W. W. Norton.

Hedayati, S. S., Elsayed, E. F., & Reilly, R. F. (2011). Non-pharmacological aspects of blood pressure management: What are the data & quest. *Kidney International, 79*(10), 1061–1070.

Hodgson, T. A., & Cai, L. (2001). Medical care expenditures for hypertension, its complications, and its comorbidities. *Medical Care, 39*(6), 599–615.

Jonas, B. S., Franks, P., & Ingram, D. D. (1997). Are symptoms of anxiety and depression risk factors for hypertension? Longitudinal evidence from the National Health and Nutrition Examination Survey I Epidemiologic Follow-up Study. *Archives of Family Medicine, 6*(1), 43.

Kekecs, Z., & Varga, K. (2013). Positive suggestion techniques in somatic medicine: A review of the empirical studies. *Interventional Medicine and Applied Science, 5*(3), 101–111.

Markovitz, J. H., Matthews, K. A., Kannel, W. B., Cobb, J. L., & D'Agostino, R. B. (1993). Psychological predictors of hypertension in the Framingham study: Is there tension in hypertension? *Journal of the American Medical Association, 270*(20), 2439–2443.

Pekala, R. J., Maurer, R., Kumar, V., Elliott, N. C., Masten, E., Moon, E., & Salinger, M. (2004). Self-hypnosis relapse prevention training with chronic drug/alcohol users: Effects on self-esteem, affect, and relapse. *American Journal of Clinical Hypnosis, 46*(4), 281–297.

Raskin, R., Raps, C., Luskin, F., Carlson, R., & Cristal, R. (1999). Pilot study of the effect of self-hypnosis on the medical management of essential hypertension. *Stress and Health, 15*(4), 243–247.

Rosen, R. C., Brondolo, E., & Kostis, J. B. (1993). Nonpharmacological treatment of essential hypertension: Research and clinical applications. In R. Gatchel & E. Blanchard (Eds.), *Psychophysiological disorders: Research and clinical applications* (pp. 63–110). Washington, DC: American Psychological Association.

Schoenberger, N. E. (2000). Research on hypnosis as an adjunct to cognitive-behavioral psychotherapy. *International Journal of Clinical and Experimental Hypnosis, 48*(2), 154–169.

Shaw, K., O'Rourke, P., Del Mar, C., & Kenardy, J. (2005). Psychological interventions for overweight or obesity. *Cochrane Database Systematic Review, 2*(2).

Tosi, D. J., Rudy, D. R., Lewis, J., & Murphy, M. A. (1992). The psychobiological effects of cognitive experiential therapy, hypnosis, cognitive restructuring, and attention placebo control in the treatment of essential hypertension. *Psychotherapy: Theory, Research, Practice, Training, 29*(2), 274–284.

Vander José das Neves, T. F., Redondo, F. R., Soci, U. P., Melo, S. F., & de Oliveira, E. M. (2014). Exercise training in hypertension: Role of microRNAs. *World Journal of Cardiology, 6*(8), 713–727.

Varga, K. (2004). The possible explanation of metaphors in re-interpreting negative life events: Our experiences with the critically ill. *Hypnos, 31*(4), 201–207.

Varga, K. (Ed.). (2011a). *Beyond the words: Communication and suggestion in medical practice.* New York, NY: Nova Science Publishers.

Varga, K. (2011b). Suggestions–Step by step. In K. Varga (Ed.), *Beyond the words: Communication and suggestion in medical practice* (pp. 413–421). New York, NY: Nova Science Publishers.

Varga, K., & Diószeghy, C. (2001). *Hűtésbefizetés, avagy szuggesztiók alkalmazása az orvosi gyakorlatban* [*Application of suggestions in medical practice*]. Budapest: Pólya kiadó.

Wadden, T. A., & Penrod, J. H. (1981). Hypnosis in the treatment of alcoholism: A review and appraisal. *American Journal of Clinical Hypnosis, 24*(1), 41–47.

World Health Organization. (2014). *Hypertension.* Retrieved from http://www.world-heart-federation .org/cardiovascular-health/cardiovascular-disease-risk-factors/hypertension

Xu, Y., & Cardeña, E. (2007). Hypnosis as an adjunct therapy in the management of diabetes. *International Journal of Clinical and Experimental Hypnosis, 56*(1), 63–72.

Young, G. K. (1996). *Hypnosis as an adjunctive modality in the relapse prevention component of an alcoholism treatment program* (Doctoral dissertation). Pacific Graduate School of Psychology, Palo Alto, CA.

Zseni, A. (1988). Terápiás tapasztalatok egy új hipnózis indukciós eljárással. Az aktív-éber dinamikus hipnózis módszer [*Therapeutic experiences with a new hypnosis induction method. The active alert dynamic hypnosis technique*]. *Psychiatria Hungarica, 3*(4), 311–320.

Irritable Bowel Syndrome

Olafur S. Palsson

Irritable bowel syndrome (IBS) is one of the most common ailments of the gastrointestinal tract, characterized by recurrent or constant abdominal pain and associated episodes of diarrhea and/or constipation. It has been estimated to be present in 11.2% of adults worldwide, based on a meta-analysis of 81 studies in numerous countries (Lovell & Ford, 2012). The disorder is more common in women than men (14.0% vs. 8.9% on average in the same meta-analysis). It declines in prevalence across the adult age range, especially after age 50. IBS is a chronic disorder by definition, and most people have it continually for many years after it first presents itself. However, epidemiological studies show that between one-third and half of individuals who qualify for IBS diagnosis at a baseline time point no longer have the disorder a decade later (Ford, Forman, Bailey, Axon, & Moayyedi, 2008; Halder et al., 2007; Olafsdottir, Gudjonsson, Jonsdottir, Bjornsson, & Thjodleifsson, 2012).

IBS represents a substantial burden both on health care systems and on individual sufferers. Even though the symptoms of the majority of people with the disorder are sufficiently mild for them not to seek any medical care, IBS is nonetheless the reason for 25% to 50% of all visits to gastroenterologists and 10% to 15% of all primary care visits (Choung & Locke, 2011). Estimated direct annual health care costs attributable to IBS are $742 to $7,547 per patient in the United States, £90 to £316 in the United Kingdom, and $259 in Canada (Canavan, West, & Card, 2014). IBS has been found to impact quality of life more on average than serious organic disorders like diabetes mellitus and dialysis-dependent end-stage renal disease (Gralnek, Hays, Kilbourne, Naliboff, & Mayer, 2000), and has been estimated to reduce overall work productivity of people who have the disorder by 20% (Dean et al., 2005).

Abdominal pain is the cardinal symptom of IBS and the fulcrum of the diagnosis. To meet the Rome III diagnostic criteria for IBS (Rome Foundation, 2006), which is the most widely recognized standard for diagnosis, patients must have abdominal discomfort or pain at least three days a month and also experience two of the three following associated characteristics: (a) relief of the pain with defecation, (b) change in stool frequency associated with the start of pain episodes, and (c) change in stool consistency with start of pain episodes. This symptom picture must have been present for at least six months for an individual to qualify for diagnosis.

Subsets of patients with IBS exhibit different and relatively stable patterns of stool consistency abnormality, and are classified accordingly into subtypes. Some patients predominantly suffer from hard or lumpy stools (IBS-C subtype), others mostly have a problem with mushy or watery stools (IBS-D subtype), and still others characteristically experience a mixture of the two (IBS-M subtype). However, most patients with IBS (79%) of all subtypes fluctuate in their stool consistency between mushy or watery stools and hard or lumpy stools (Palsson, Baggish, Turner, & Whitehead, 2012). It should also be noted that the majority of bowel movements of patients of all subtypes are of normal stool consistency (i.e., they are neither diarrhea nor constipation).

Some individuals with IBS only experience the bowel symptoms a few days a month, but for most of them the symptoms are more frequent. We found in a recent study that tracked the symptoms of a large group of patients with IBS in online diaries over months that, on average, the patients had bowel symptom episodes on about two of every three days (Palsson, Baggish, & Whitehead, 2014).

IBS is defined as a functional gastrointestinal disorder, which is a classification it shares with more than 20 other health problems, and which sets it apart from organic disorders of the gut. The term refers to the fact that the functioning of the bowels (pain sensitivity and intestinal motility) is disturbed in this disorder, whereas no structural problems, lesions, or clear biochemical abnormalities can be detected. This means that IBS is not a dangerous disorder even though it often causes much suffering and trouble for patients; it does not cause damage to the body and it does not turn into a more serious disease like cancer or colitis (Chey et al., 2010). The absence of organic abnormalities also means that no specific tests exist that are diagnostic for IBS, and physicians can generally make the diagnosis with confidence based on the symptom pattern and history without any test results. However, IBS symptoms overlap with, and can be confused with, those of a number of organic bowel diseases that are more harmful, including ulcerative colitis, Crohn's disease, bowel cancer, or celiac disease. Tests such as colonoscopy, fecal occult blood test, screening test for celiac disease, blood and stool tests to detect infection, and breath test for small bacterial overgrowth do have a limited role in IBS diagnostic work-up on a case-by-case basis for ruling out alternative explanations for the bowel symptoms. Such tests are especially applicable when certain red-flag symptoms are present, such as age of onset over 50, weight loss, self-reported bloody stools, fever, or nocturnal awakening due to abdominal pain (Camilleri, Heading, & Thompson, 2002).

The etiology of IBS has been intensively investigated over several decades, and is now understood to be multifactorial and heterogeneous, meaning that different constellations of contributing factors may underlie symptoms in different individuals. Hypersensitivity of the intestines to pain stimuli, smooth muscle hyperreactivity of the bowel wall, and dysfunctions in the brain's regulation of intestinal functions and processing of sensations from the intestines are all thought to be key causal factors (Drossman, Camilleri, Mayer, & Whitehead, 2002). Additionally, elevated life stress, psychological distress, and dysfunctional coping (especially catastrophizing) are known to exacerbate IBS symptoms (Drossman, 1999). Immune activation of the bowels may also play some role in the onset and maintenance of symptoms; in a subset of individuals, the symptoms of the disorder first begin after acute bacterial or viral gastroenteritis (Thabane & Marshall, 2009), and several studies have reported that patients with IBS show evidence of subclinical inflammation of the intestinal mucosa (Ford & Talley, 2011). Food sensitivities are moreover unusually prevalent in patients with IBS, and some patients benefit substantially from changes in diet, suggesting that adverse food reactions play a role in driving the bowel symptoms for many individuals (Hayes, Fraher, & Quigley, 2014). Finally, altered balance of populations of different intestinal bacteria in IBS have gained considerable attention in the past few years, but it is not yet clear whether those abnormalities contribute significantly to IBS symptoms (Collins, 2014). As can be seen from this summary, the causal picture of IBS is highly complex, and there is no easy way at the present time to know what combination of factors causes this health problem for a given individual—a fact that frustrates both clinicians and patients and poses major difficulties for treatment.

Because of its etiological complexity and multisymptom nature, IBS has proved challenging to treat effectively. A study by our team found that only 49% of patients with IBS in a large health maintenance organization reported that their bowel symptoms were at least somewhat better when surveyed six months after seeing a doctor for those symptoms (Whitehead et al., 2004). Few medications are available that have been tested and approved for IBS treatment specifically; each of them is suited only for limited subsets of patients, and all show relatively modest success in impacting the overall symptom picture. The most common medical approaches to treat the disorder, at least in the United States, are advice on dietary changes and stress reduction (both of which actually have relatively limited empirical support as effective IBS interventions), as well as medications that are not specifically intended for IBS but are used off-label to treat individual bothersome presenting symptoms like diarrhea or constipation (Whitehead et al., 2004).

The fact that a large proportion of IBS sufferers gains little or no relief from their symptoms from usual medical care approaches highlights a great need for adjunctive therapies that can help improve clinical outcomes, especially for the numerous patients who continue to have severe and life-impairing symptoms in spite of the best that standard medical care has to offer. To date, psychological treatments have been the most researched options for such supplemental interventions for treatment-refractory patients with IBS. In numerous published trials over the past three decades, psychological interventions, and especially cognitive behavioral therapy and hypnosis, have consistently shown themselves to be efficacious in improving IBS symptoms (Palsson & Whitehead, 2013). This extensive body of empirical work has gained psychological interventions the status of recommended therapy options for certain IBS cases by the two main membership organizations in gastroenterology in the United States: The technical review on IBS by the American Gastroenterological Association recommends psychological treatment for moderate and severe patients, those with inadequate response to standard medical care, and patients in whom psychosocial factors clearly exacerbate symptoms (Drossman et al., 2002). The current evidence-based position statement of the American College of Gastroenterology gives psychological treatment a "strong recommendation" rating for improving global IBS morbidity (Brandt et al., 2008).

Although it may seem odd at first thought to utilize psychological approaches to treat a bowel disorder, there are two key reasons that make psychological intervention a very logical option. One is the fact that elevated psychological distress is strikingly common in IBS and it amplifies the bowel symptoms. In tertiary care settings, 40% to 90% of patients have affective disorders, such as major depression and generalized anxiety (Whitehead, Palsson, & Jones, 2002). Diagnosable affective disorders are somewhat less common in patients with general clinical IBS, but are still two to three times as frequent as in other medical patients (Whitehead et al., 2007). Patients suffering from anxiety or depression, who often also have associated trauma history or maladaptive cognitive coping styles, tend to have more severe gastrointestinal symptoms (Drossman, 1999; Levy et al., 2006; van Oudenhove et al., 2011). Mental stress has furthermore been shown in the laboratory to lower visceral pain thresholds and amplify the motility and neuroendocrine responses in the colon and small bowel of patients with IBS in a way that is not seen in control subjects (Posserud et al., 2004; Whitehead, 1996). Although it remains

unclear to what extent psychological factors play a causal role in the onset of IBS in general, evidence in postinfectious IBS has furthermore clearly indicated that if individuals have elevated psychological distress when they get bacterial or viral gastroenteritis (such as due to food poisoning or contaminated drinking water), they are significantly more likely to develop persistent bowel symptoms that turn into IBS (Dai & Jiang, 2012).

The second reason why psychological treatment is a logical option for improving bowel symptoms is that it is now recognized that the brain plays a very active role in modulating visceral perception and gastrointestinal tract functioning, via the brain–gut axis, which is a busy two-way communication highway between the central nervous system and the enteric nervous system of the gut (Mayer & Tillisch, 2011). The brain continually filters incoming neural signals from the gut to control the threshold of awareness and the intensity of sensory experience from the bowels. The brain also modulates smooth muscle activity and the amount of fluid secretion in the intestines via the hypothalamopituitary-adrenal (HPA) axis. Both these aspects of the brain's regulating influence via the brain–gut axis (that is, the filtering of gut signals and modulation of gut functions) are affected by emotional states and life stress load (Mayer & Tillisch, 2011; Van Oudenhove, Demyttenaere, Tack, & Aziz, 2004). This recent understanding of the continual and important regulating role that the brain plays in gut perception and gut functioning makes it reasonable to treat intestinal pain and dysfunctions by addressing the brain by means of a verbal intervention. The results of trials of hypnosis treatment for IBS (and cognitive behavioral therapy as well) confirm that this is not only possible but that it can be done with a high rate of success.

RESEARCH ON HYPNOSIS TREATMENT FOR IBS

Twenty-two published studies have tested the therapeutic effects of clinical hypnosis on IBS symptoms (not including single-case reports, follow-up papers, or studies primarily on the mechanism of effect). Almost universally (the single exception being one of the studies reported in a paper by Lindfors and colleagues in 2012; Lindfors et al., 2012), these studies have reported significant improvement in bowel symptoms after hypnosis treatment. Affective symptoms, quality of life, and nongastrointestinal body symptoms have also generally been found to improve significantly as well in these studies if those parameters were measured. Importantly, this empirical literature on IBS hypnosis treatment includes 10 randomized controlled trials (summarized in Table 29.1), which are the types of studies that have the research design usually considered necessary for formally determining efficacy of treatment. A systematic review and meta-analysis of those randomized controlled trials was published in 2014 (Schaefert, Klose, Moser, & Häuser, 2014). It included eight of these studies, all of which exclusively tested hypnosis intervention on IBS patients who had failed to benefit from typical medical care for IBS. Analysis of the pooled samples across those eight studies confirmed that

hypnosis was highly efficacious, and the investigators found that hypnosis treatment produced long-term adequate symptom relief for 54% of these treatment-refractory patients.

The research shows that improvement of IBS by hypnosis treatment can generally be expected to last a long time. Three of the randomized controlled trials have included extended follow-up, and they reported therapeutic gains in treatment responders to be well maintained at 10 months (Palsson et al., 2002), 15 months (Moser et al., 2013), and 18 months (Whorwell, Prior, & Colgan, 1987) after treatment. Additionally, one of these investigative teams published a large case series of 204 consecutive patients with IBS whose symptoms were reassessed annually for years after hypnotherapy, and they found that 81% of patients maintained their treatment gains fully for up to five years (Gonsalkorale, Miller, Afzal, & Whorwell, 2003).

In summary, the outcome trials published to date collectively demonstrate that hypnosis treatment is

TABLE 29.1

PUBLISHED RANDOMIZED CONTROLLED TRIALS ON HYPNOSIS TREATMENT FOR IRRITABLE BOWEL SYNDROME				
	Subjects per Group	What Improved	Nature of Control Group	Between-Groups Results
Whorwell, Prior, and Faragher (1984)	15 H, 15 C	G, E	Supportive therapy + placebo pills	Hypnosis superior
Galovski and Blanchard (1998)	5 H, 6 C	G, E	Waiting list	Hypnosis superior
Forbes, MacAuley, and Chiotakakou-Faliakou (2000)	25 H, 27 C	G, E	Audiotapes	Hypnosis superior
Palsson, Turner, Johnson, Burnett, and Whitehead (2002) (Study II)	15 H, 9 C	G, E, P	Waiting list	Hypnosis superior
Roberts et al. (2006)	40 H, 41 C	G	Usual medical care	Hypnosis superior
Vlieger, Menko-Frankenhuis, Wolfkamp, Tromp, and Benninga (2007)	27 H, 25 C	G	Medical care + supportive therapy	Hypnosis superior
Lindfors et al. (2012) (Study 1)	45 H, 45 C	G	Supportive therapy	Hypnosis superior
Lindfors et al. (2012) (Study 2)	25 H, 23 C	E	Waiting list	Hypnosis = control group
Moser et al. (2013)	46 H, 44 C	G, E, Q	Supportive therapy	Hypnosis superior
Dobbin, Dobbin, Ross, Graham, and Ford (2013)	30 H, 31 C	G, E, P	Biofeedback	Hypnosis = control group

C, control group; E, emotional symptoms; G, gastrointestinal symptoms; H, hypnosis group; P, nongastrointestinal physical symptoms. Q, quality of life.

a powerful intervention for substantially improving gastrointestinal symptoms in the long term for individuals with IBS who have not improved from standard medical care. A shortcoming of this literature, however, is that most of the published studies provide little or no details about the tested hypnosis intervention and therefore cannot be replicated by others who want to use the same method for their patients. The exceptions to this are two empirical protocols that have been tested and found efficacious in multiple studies to date and have been described in sufficient detail to make their specific techniques useful for clinicians. One is the Manchester Method, originally developed by Peter Whorwell in Manchester, England, who headed the first randomized clinical trial of hypnosis for IBS (Whorwell et al., 1984). The Manchester approach generally consists of 12 weekly hypnosis sessions following a common outline of suggestion types and metaphors, while also individualizing or tailoring treatment to some degree to the idiosyncratic presentation of different patients. The other protocol is the North Carolina Protocol, a fully scripted seven-session treatment course (authored by this chapter's author) that is suited to be delivered verbatim. Both of these protocols represent accessible frameworks for clinicians wishing to deliver evidence-based therapy with dependable success. Papers describing each of these approaches in great detail, including sample session scripts, can be found in the January 2006 issue of the *International Journal of Clinical and Experimental Hypnosis* (Gonsalkorale, 2006; Palsson, 2006). Although there are significant differences between the two protocols (such as explicit emphasis on the patient's control over the bowels in the Manchester Method, which is entirely absent in the North Carolina Protocol), they also have many similarities, including utilization of similar types of therapeutic suggestions and employing a three-month therapy course. Clinical trials using these two approaches have generally shown high and largely comparable efficacy (Gonsalkorale, Houghton, & Whorwell, 2002; Palsson et al., 2002): success rates of 70% or better, reduction of abdominal pain by about half on average, and substantial impact on other bowel symptoms as well, and significant reduction in psychological symptoms and somatization (i.e., the amount of nongastrointestinal physical symptoms).

CRAFTING A SUCCESSFUL HYPNOSIS TREATMENT FOR IBS

Even though hypnosis treatment approaches for IBS have varied greatly among the published studies and in clinical practice, a common key to reliable success is that the treatment is firmly gut directed. This means that the principal focus of the intervention should be to influence and improve the actual bowel symptoms, rather than making affective or behavioral changes as the main therapy targets (unless those changes directly serve to improve the physical symptoms). To keep this therapy focus clear, it is helpful to think of the IBS problem in terms of three intervention aims: (a) reduction or elimination of abdominal pain; (b) normalization of bowel functioning—that is, reduction in diarrhea and/or constipation and restoration of normal intestinal muscle activity, and (c) reduction of disturbance of the bowels from psychological influences or stress. This trio of aims is applicable to any patient with IBS, and is best addressed in multiple ways with suggestions and metaphors in every session of the treatment course.

A variety of hypnotic and posthypnotic suggestions are useful to achieve these aims. In the fully scripted North Carolina Protocol, five types of suggestions in particular are utilized extensively across the seven-session treatment course, and this can be a useful framework for reference in crafting suggestions. These are suggestions for (a) lessening attention to bowel symptoms; (b) altering perceptual experience of the symptoms—that is, reducing intensity and frequency, and changing the symptom qualitatively into something more pleasant; (c) increasing overall sense of health and comfort; (d) disconnecting or protecting the intestines from disturbance from internal or external stimuli; and (e) restoring healthy rhythm and functioning of the bowels. Examples of all these five types of suggestions can be found in the following sample script.

Metaphors for therapeutic change should be used along with suggestions in the treatment course. These are best implemented as vivid and detailed visualizations that symbolically represent desired therapeutic effects. For example, a secluded garden with high walls hiding it from the outside world, a log cabin, or a cave can be used to convey protection of the intestines from discomfort and outside disturbance. Being far out in the country, up in the mountains or on an island, miles away from everything that usually causes stress and challenges in normal life, can be used to instill a sense of disconnect or distance from stressors and social pressures. A river metaphor to represent the bowels is very useful for normalization of bowel functioning (it is a standard technique in the Manchester Method). It can be utilized in different ways, for example, to associate vividly with the intestines the powerful sense of imperturbability of a mighty river, which always flows by at a steady rate regardless of what goes on around it; or to equip the patient with magical imagined power to mentally slow the flow of the river to treat diarrhea or speed it up to treat constipation. An amusement park water slide is one of my favorite metaphors to use for treating constipation. It is a fun way to metaphorically convey a sense of easy and trouble-free movement of digestive contents through the gut and effortless elimination. For pain reduction, an imagined strong protective coating applied to the inside of the intestinal wall can be used, for example, or imagery of a pain sensitivity rheostat that the patient visualizes connected to the bowel wall and dials down and leaves on a lower setting.

For added impact, the therapeutic suggestions should be explicitly tied to the metaphors used, for example:

"More and more, your intestines will feel comfortable and protected from any disturbance regardless of what goes on around you, just like you feel completely protected from the winter storms outside as you enjoy relaxing, perfectly at ease, inside this comfortable log cabin."

To achieve the greatest treatment impact, it is desirable to use several types of suggestions in each session (preferably some or each of the five types previously listed), and to use several different metaphors across the treatment course. It is also preferable to use the therapeutic suggestions and metaphors only when the patient is likely to be in the most receptive mental state in the hypnosis session, to avoid interference from critical-analytic thinking. This means that the suggestions and metaphors should not follow right after hypnotic

induction, but rather after extensive deepening and guided progressive whole-body relaxation to create a low-arousal physiological state, and preferably also after some kind of dissociation from the here-and-now (such as by transporting the patient mentally to a vividly experienced imagined new environment).

Therapeutic triggers are very helpful additions to suggestions and metaphors as intervention elements for some patients, especially those who experience sudden and intense symptoms such as bowel cramps and pain that interfere with daily activities. These triggers are behaviors imbued with therapeutic power by means of suggestions and originally practiced in the hypnosis sessions. They can then be implemented in everyday life to deal with symptoms when needed. A good example of this is the soothing hand on the belly technique (which plays an integral part in the Manchester Method). The author has provided a variant of this technique in the following sample script.

In order to give the hypnosis treatment a fair chance to achieve its full effect on IBS symptoms, it is important to provide adequate length of treatment. A shorter course than six or seven sessions is not advisable, as it may compromise the therapeutic response for some patients. Even if the patients exhibit impressive reduction in symptoms in the first few sessions, a full therapy course should nonetheless be completed, for this is likely to lead to even more profound and more sustained improvement. Experience has shown that improvement in bowel symptoms from hypnosis intervention is often gradual and takes months, and it is therefore also important to not concentrate all the treatment sessions in a short period. This is why both the North Carolina Protocol and the Manchester Method use a three-month treatment course, and this should generally be emulated whenever possible. It is noteworthy that the clinical trials in the empirical literature on hypnosis for IBS that used the fewest intervention sessions and shortest treatment courses show weak symptom impact (Dobbin et al., 2013) and lack of persistence of the therapeutic effects (Roberts et al., 2006) that compares unfavorably with most of the other trials. Finally, home practice with audio-recorded hypnosis sessions is an important part of successful treatment protocols for IBS, and should contain some of the same suggestions as used in the office sessions. Generally the author suggests that patients both in clinical practice and in research studies use these recordings five times a week throughout the treatment course.

CASE EXAMPLE

A 38-year-old woman presented in the author's behavioral medicine clinic with a 20-year history of IBS-type bowel symptoms. In the intake session it was confirmed that she met the Rome criteria for IBS and had been diagnosed with IBS by primary care doctors multiple times over the years, and more recently by her gastroenterologist. She had completed a colonoscopy and anorectal motility testing within the past few months without any abnormal findings. She described suffering daily from abdominal pain that at times impaired her concentration and productivity at work, and interfered markedly with her ability to enjoy social activities, causing "a big drag on her life overall." Additionally, she reported great difficulty passing stool, spending a lot of time daily in the bathroom trying to do so, with her attempts culminating either in painful and difficult defecation or in failure to pass stool. She described experiencing a great deal of anxiety and frustration before and during defecation. The patient reported using laxatives on and off with limited benefit. Her IBS severity scale score (Francis, Morris, & Whorwell, 1997) at intake was 325, which is classified as severe IBS. A two-week baseline bowel symptom diary prior to treatment showed abdominal pain every day and four to five bowel movements a week, with 77% of stools rated hard. The seven-session treatment course mostly followed the North Carolina Protocol (Palsson, 2006) verbatim. However, it was augmented by a water slide metaphor in three of the sessions to reinforce a sense of easy passage of stool, and supplemental suggestions about letting go spontaneously and relaxing on the toilet. A customized audio-recorded session for home hypnosis practice was created for her, centering on the "soothing hand on the belly technique" to ease abdominal pain, and suggestions for easy defecation and normalization of bowel motility. By the third treatment visit, the patient reported having occasional days without any abdominal pain or discomfort for the first time in years. She had also started using the soothing hand technique at her desk at work without her audio recording, and said she found it very helpful when she was having bouts of intense abdominal pain. At the end of the three-month treatment course, the patient's bowel diaries showed abdominal pain present only once a week or less, and much milder than before. Stool frequency was unchanged from pretreatment diaries, but only 18% of stools were rated hard. The IBS severity score was 120, which classified her as having mild IBS. A follow-up visit 3.5 months after the end of the treatment course included a booster hypnosis session involving the water slide imagery for easy stool passage and further reinforcement of the soothing hand technique. The patient reported that the great majority of her bowel movements were still of normal consistency, and estimated that she had experienced abdominal pain one to two days a week since the end of treatment. She moreover stated that bowel symptoms no longer interfered with her social or work life. Finally, an e-mail exchange with the patient a year after treatment termination revealed even further improvement: she was now entirely pain-free, experienced only occasional hard stools, and had no problems with passing stool.

SAMPLE SCRIPT

This intervention module is administered by the therapist after a hypnotic induction, deepening, and extensive guided physical relaxation.

"I would like to ask you now, while you let your body continue to relax, to focus your whole attention on your right hand. Think about your right hand now, as it lies there resting, and notice every sensation in it. Notice what it feels like. Picture your hand in your mind as clearly as you can. Picture your right hand . . . see it in your mind even though your eyes are closed, see it clearly as it lies there resting. And I would like to ask you to imagine that this hand is becoming warmer and warmer. Imagine this happening . . . and notice whether you can feel it happening. Let the warmth . . . the healthy warm feeling that comes from relaxing your body flow out into your hand and allow that warmth to collect in your hand. Imagine this warm feeling flowing down your arm and into your hand from your

body, making your hand warmer. Your hand is becoming warmer and warmer. Imagine wave after wave of this wonderful warmth flowing down your arm and into your hand, each time you breathe out . . . like breathing out is pumping warmth into your right hand. Just experience this as vividly as you can, using your imagination and concentration. Breathing out, breath after breath, as you breathe slowly and freely . . . makes your right hand gradually warmer. Warmer each time you exhale. Whatever you can feel or cannot feel is fine . . . just use your imagination to the best of your ability . . . but you can probably feel this happening more and more clearly now . . . feel your hand becoming noticeably warmer . . . as the comfortable warmth flows into your hand and builds up in your hand . . . making your hand distinctly warmer than it was before. And perhaps you can imagine that this warmth in your hand has a healing effect . . . that it has a healing power. Maybe you can even imagine that the hand is beginning to glow from this warmth—imagine it glowing with healing power. And I would like to ask you now to lift your warm right hand and place it on top of your stomach—low on your stomach, over your intestines. Put your hand on your stomach now, with your palm lying flat against your stomach . . . and just let it rest there. Hand on the stomach . . . with the palm flat on the stomach . . . [Note: If the patient is not moving the hand to the stomach, then say *"I am going to take your hand now in a moment and assist you in placing your hand right on the stomach."* Then, after a pause, pick up the patient's right hand gently and place it on the patient's lower stomach, and continue]. *That's right. Rest your hand on your belly like that, and notice if you can feel this soothing healing warmth flow deep inside you . . . feel it flowing from the hand and into your belly . . . you probably can feel it clearly now if you concentrate. Feel it now, and imagine this healing warmth going all the way deep down into your intestines . . . picture it in your mind and feel it as clearly as you can. Perhaps you can picture this flow of healing warmth in your mind like warm light or glow flowing from your hand deep inside you . . . filling you with soothing comfort inside . . . making you more and more comfortable inside . . . so wonderfully comfortable inside. . . . Imagine this soothing warmth*

spreading all the way down through your intestines, and also up into your stomach.

As you let your hand continue to rest on your belly, allowing the wonderful warmth from your hand to continue to flow inside you and fill you inside, this is causing a healthy and powerful change in the functioning of your intestines . . . a healthy change that will remain with you long after you wake up from this state in a little while. It is like this feeling of warmth and comfort is nourishing the intestines and restoring their natural health . . . making them feel naturally healthy and comfortable . . . naturally healthy and comfortable. . . . In the coming days and weeks, this feeling of natural health will remain with you and will grow stronger. You may be surprised to notice that things that you might have expected to bother you inside, like perhaps certain kinds of food or things going on in your life, just don't seem to be able to interrupt this natural healthy feeling inside you anymore. More and more, from day to day and week to week, your intestines keep their natural comfortable rhythmic functioning regardless of what is going on in your life.

More and more it will feel like your intestines are protected from all discomfort . . . like nothing can disturb them. This powerful healing effect of the warmth that is filling you inside is restoring your natural health inside, making your intestines so comfortable that you won't even notice many of the sensations that were uncomfortable before. . . . In situations where you might have experienced bowel discomfort or pain before, you will most likely be surprised to realize that you only feel pleasant, warm, soothing sensations. . . . And even if you feel discomfort inside, you will most likely notice that it is surprisingly weak, much milder than before, as your sensitivity to bowel pain and discomfort steadily fades away and disappears. More and more, you can trust your intestines to keep functioning with a natural, healthy, and comfortable rhythm, free from pain or discomfort, without you having to think about what is going on inside your body at all. This will allow you to enjoy your everyday life more without being disturbed or bothered. You might therefore notice in the coming days and weeks that you are paying less and less attention to your intestines, without even thinking about it . . . paying less and less attention to what is happening inside you from day to day . . . focusing your attention instead more on the enjoyable and interesting things in your life. . . ." [Followed by suggestions for normalization of sensations in the right hand, and gradual realerting guided by counting.]

CONCLUSION

IBS is a complex functional gastrointestinal disorder defined by abdominal pain and associated diarrhea and/or constipation, which has proven challenging to treat effectively by conventional medical care approaches. It has been demonstrated to be responsive to hypnosis treatment in more than 20 studies, including 10 randomized controlled trials. Results from the controlled trials collectively indicated that 54% of patients who were unresponsive to medical care gain long-term relief from hypnosis treatment. As a health problem afflicting 1 in every 10 adults, IBS represents a very substantial and rewarding practice opportunity for clinicians offering hypnosis services. For best treatment success, the hypnosis approach needs to be gut focused and consist of no less than six or seven sessions over a three-month period with audio-recorded home-treatment hypnosis sessions used between office sessions. The principal aims of the intervention should be: (a) reduction or elimination of abdominal pain; (b) normalization of bowel functioning (reduction in diarrhea and/or constipation); and (c) elimination of disturbance of the bowels from psychological influences or stress. These treatment aims can be achieved through a combination of targeted metaphors and hypnotic and posthypnotic suggestions.

REFERENCES

Brandt, L. J., Chey, W. D., Foxx-Orenstein, A. E., Quigley, E. M., Schiller, L. R., Schoenfeld, P. S., . . . Moayyedi, P. (2008). An evidence-based position statement on the management of irritable bowel syndrome. *American Journal of Gastroenterology, 104*(1), S1–S35. doi:10.1038/ajg.2008.122

Camilleri, M., Heading, R. C., & Thompson, W. G. (2002). Clinical perspectives, mechanisms, diagnosis and management of irritable bowel syndrome. *Alimentary Pharmacology & Therapeutics, 16*(8), 1407–1430.

Canavan, C., West, J., & Card, T. (2014). Review article: The economic impact of the irritable bowel syndrome. *Alimentary Pharmacology & Therapeutics, 40*(9), 1023–1034. doi:10.1111/apt.12938

Chey, W. D., Nojkov, B., Rubenstein, J. H., Dobhan, R. R., Greenson, J. K., & Cash, B. D. (2010). The yield of colonoscopy in patients with non-constipated irritable bowel syndrome: Results from a prospective, controlled US trial. *American Journal of Gastroenterology, 105*(4), 859–865. doi:10.1038/ajg.2010.55

Choung, R. S., & Locke, G. R. (2011). Epidemiology of IBS. *Gastroenterology Clinics of North America, 40*(1), 1–10. doi:10.1016/j.gtc.2010.12.006

Collins, S. M. (2014). A role for the gut microbiota in IBS. *Nature Reviews. Gastroenterology & Hepatology, 11*(8), 497–505. doi:10.1038/nrgastro.2014.40

Dai, C., & Jiang, M. (2012). The incidence and risk factors of post-infectious irritable bowel syndrome: A meta-analysis. *Hepato-Gastroenterology, 59*(113), 67–72. doi:10.5754/hge10796

Dean, B. B., Aguilar, D., Barghout, V., Kahler, K. H., Frech, F., Groves, D., & Ofman, J. J. (2005). Impairment in work productivity and health-related quality of life in patients with IBS. *American Journal of Managed Care, 11*(1), 17–26.

Dobbin, A., Dobbin, J., Ross, S. C., Graham, C., & Ford, M. J. (2013). Randomized controlled trial of brief intervention with biofeedback and hypnotherapy in patients with refractory irritable bowel syndrome. *Journal of the Royal College of Physicians of Edinburgh, 43*(1), 15–23. doi:10.4997/JRCPE.2013.104

Drossman, D. A. (1999). Do psychosocial factors define symptom severity and patient status in irritable bowel syndrome? *American Journal of Medicine, 107*(5), 41–50. doi:10.1016/S0002-9343(99)00081-9

Drossman, D. A., Camilleri, M., Mayer, E. A., & Whitehead, W. E. (2002). AGA technical review on irritable bowel syndrome. *Gastroenterology, 123*(6), 2108–2131. doi:10.1053/gast.2002.37095

Forbes, A., MacAuley, S., & Chiotakakou-Faliakou, E. (2000). Hypnotherapy and therapeutic audiotape: Effective in previously unsuccessfully treated irritable bowel syndrome? *International Journal of Colorectal Disease, 15*(5–6), 328–334. doi:10.1007/s003840000248

Ford, A. C., & Talley, N. J. (2011). Mucosal inflammation as a potential etiological factor in irritable bowel syndrome: A systematic review. *Journal of Gastroenterology, 46*(4), 421–431. doi:10.1007/s00535-011-0379-9

Ford, A. C., Forman, D., Bailey, A. G., Axon, A. T., & Moayyedi, P. (2008). Irritable bowel syndrome: A 10-year natural history of symptoms and factors that influence consultation behavior. *American Journal of Gastroenterology, 103*(5), 1229–1239. doi:10.1111/j.1572-0241.2007.01740.x

Francis, C. Y., Morris, J., & Whorwell, P. J. (1997). The irritable bowel severity scoring system: A simple method of monitoring irritable bowel syndrome and its progress. *Alimentary Pharmacology & Therapeutics, 11*(2), 395–402. doi:10.1046/j.1365-2036.1997.142318000.x

Galovski, T. E., & Blanchard, E. B. (1998). The treatment of irritable bowel syndrome with hypnotherapy. *Applied Psychophysiology and Biofeedback, 23*(4), 219–232.

Gonsalkorale, W. M. (2006). Gut-directed hypnotherapy: The Manchester approach for treatment of irritable bowel syndrome. *International Journal of Clinical and Experimental Hypnosis, 54*(1), 27–50. doi:10.1080/00207140500323030

Gonsalkorale, W. M., Houghton, L. A., & Whorwell, P. J. (2002). Hypnotherapy in irritable bowel syndrome: A large-scale audit of a clinical service with examination of factors influencing responsiveness. *American Journal of Gastroenterology, 97*(4), 954–961. doi:10.1111/j.1572-0241.2002.05615.x

Gonsalkorale, W. M., Miller, V., Afzal, A., & Whorwell, P. J. (2003). Long term benefits of hypnotherapy for irritable bowel syndrome. *Gut, 52*(11), 1623–1629.

Gralnek, I. M., Hays, R. D., Kilbourne, A., Naliboff, B., & Mayer, E. A. (2000). The impact of irritable bowel syndrome on health-related quality of life. *Gastroenterology, 119*(3), 654–660.

Halder, S. L., Locke, G. R., Schleck, C. D., Zinsmeister, A. R., Melton, L. J., & Talley, N. J. (2007). Natural history of functional gastrointestinal disorders: A 12-year longitudinal population-based study. *Gastroenterology, 133*(3), 799–807. doi:10.1053/j.gastro.2007.06.010

Hayes, P. A., Fraher, M. H., & Quigley, E. M. (2014). Irritable bowel syndrome: The role of food in pathogenesis and management. *Gastroenterology and Hepatology (NY), 10*(3), 164–174.

Levy, R. L., Olden, K. W., Naliboff, B. D., Bradley, L. A., Francisconi, C., Drossman, D. A., & Creed, F. (2006). Psychosocial aspects of the functional gastrointestinal disorders. *Gastroenterology, 130*(5), 1447–1458. doi:10.1053/j.gastro.2005.11.057

Lindfors, P., Unge, P., Arvidsson, P., Nyhlin, H., Björnsson, E., Abrahamsson, H., & Simrén, M. (2012). Effects of gut-directed hypnotherapy on IBS in different clinical settings-results from two randomized, controlled trials. *American Journal of Gastroenterology, 107*(2), 276–285. doi:10.1038/ajg.2011.340

Lovell, R. M., & Ford, A. C. (2012). Global prevalence of and risk factors for irritable bowel syndrome: A meta-analysis. *Clinical Gastroenterology and Hepatology: The Official Clinical Practice Journal of the American Gastroenterological Association, 10*(7), 712–721. doi:10.1016/j.cgh.2012.02.029

Mayer, E. A., & Tillisch, K. (2011). The brain-gut axis in abdominal pain syndromes. *Annual Review of Medicine, 62*, 381–396. doi:10.1146/annurev-med-012309-103958

Moser, G., Trägner, S., Gajowniczek, E. E., Mikulits, A., Michalski, M., Kazemi-Shirazi, L., . . . Miehsler, W. (2013). Long-term success of GUT-directed group hypnosis for patients with refractory irritable bowel syndrome: A randomized controlled trial. *American Journal of Gastroenterology, 108*(4), 602–609. doi:10.1038/ajg.2013.19

Olafsdottir, L. B., Gudjonsson, H., Jonsdottir, H. H., Bjornsson, E., & Thjodleifsson, B. (2012). Natural history of functional gastrointestinal disorders: Comparison of two longitudinal population-based studies. *Digestive and Liver Disease, 44*(3), 211–217. doi:10.1016/j.dld.2011.10.009

Palsson, O. S. (2006). Standardized hypnosis treatment for irritable bowel syndrome: The North Carolina protocol. *International Journal of Clinical and Experimental Hypnosis, 54*(1), 51–64. doi:10.1080/00207140500322933

Palsson, O. S., & Whitehead, W. E. (2013). Psychological treatments in functional gastrointestinal disorders: A primer for the gastroenterologist. *Clinical Gastroenterology and Hepatology, 11*(3), 208–216. doi:10.1016/j.cgh.2012.10.031

Palsson, O. S., Baggish, J. S., Turner, M. J., & Whitehead, W. E. (2012). IBS patients show frequent fluctuations between loose/watery and hard/lumpy stools: Implications for treatment. *American Journal of Gastroenterology, 107*(2), 286–295. doi:10.1038/ajg.2011.358

Palsson, O. S., Baggish, J., & Whitehead, W. E. (2014). Episodic nature of symptoms in irritable bowel syndrome. *American Journal of Gastroenterology, 109*(9), 1450–1460. doi:10.1038/ajg.2014.181

Palsson, O. S., Turner, M. J., Johnson, D. A., Burnett, C. K., & Whitehead, W. E. (2002). Hypnosis treatment for severe irritable bowel syndrome: Investigation of mechanism and effects on symptoms. *Digestive Diseases and Sciences, 47*(11), 2605–2614.

Posserud, I., Agerforz, P., Ekman, R., Björnsson, E. S., Abrahamsson, H., & Simrén, M. (2004). Altered visceral perceptual and neuroendocrine response in patients with irritable bowel syndrome during mental stress. *Gut, 53*(8), 1102–1108. doi:10.1136/gut.2003.017962

Roberts, L., Wilson, S., Singh, S., Roalfe, A., & Greenfield, S. (2006). Gut-directed hypnotherapy for irritable bowel syndrome: Piloting a primary care-based randomised controlled trial. *British Journal of General Practice: The Journal of the Royal College of General Practitioners, 56*(523), 115–121.

Rome Foundation. (2006). Guidelines—Rome III diagnostic criteria for functional gastrointestinal disorders. *Journal of Gastrointestinal and Liver Diseases, 15*(3), 307–312.

Schaefert, R., Klose, P., Moser, G., & Häuser, W. (2014). Efficacy, tolerability, and safety of hypnosis in adult irritable bowel syndrome: Systematic review and meta-analysis. *Psychosomatic Medicine, 76*(5), 389–398. doi:10.1097/PSY.0000000000000039

Thabane, M., & Marshall, J. K. (2009). Post-infectious irritable bowel syndrome. *World Journal of Gastroenterology, 15*(29), 3591–3596.

van Oudenhove, L., Demyttenaere, K., Tack, J., & Aziz, Q. (2004). Central nervous system involvement in functional gastrointestinal disorders. *Best Practice & Research. Clinical Gastroenterology, 18*(4), 663–680. doi:10.1016/j.bpg.2004.04.010

van Oudenhove, L., Vandenberghe, J., Vos, R., Holvoet, L., Demyttenaere, K., & Tack, J. (2011). Risk factors for impaired health-related quality of life in functional dyspepsia. *Alimentary Pharmacology & Therapeutics, 33*(2), 261–274. doi:10.1111/j.1365-2036.2010.04510.x

Vlieger, A. M., Menko-Frankenhuis, C., Wolfkamp, S. C., Tromp, E., & Benninga, M. A. (2007). Hypnotherapy for children with functional abdominal pain or irritable bowel syndrome: A randomized controlled trial. *Gastroenterology, 133*(5), 1430–1436. doi:10.1053/j.gastro.2007.08.072

Whitehead, W. E. (1996). Psychosocial aspects of functional gastrointestinal disorders. *Gastroenterology Clinics of North America, 25*(1), 21–34.

Whitehead, W. E., Levy, R. L., von Korff, M., Feld, A. D., Palsson, O. S., Turner, M., & Drossman, D. A. (2004). The usual medical care for irritable bowel syndrome. *Alimentary Pharmacology & Therapeutics, 20*(11–12), 1305–1315. doi:10.1111/j.1365-2036.2004.02256.x

Whitehead, W. E., Palsson, O., & Jones, K. R. (2002). Systematic review of the comorbidity of irritable bowel syndrome with other disorders: What are the causes and implications. *Gastroenterology, 122*(4), 1140–1156.

Whitehead, W. E., Palsson, O. S., Levy, R. R., Feld, A. D., Turner, M., & von Korff, M. (2007). Comorbidity in irritable bowel syndrome. *American Journal of Gastroenterology, 102*(12), 2767–2776. doi:10.1111/j.1572-0241.2007.01540.x

Whorwell, P. J., Prior, A., & Colgan, S. M. (1987). Hypnotherapy in severe irritable bowel syndrome: Further experience. *Gut, 28*(4), 423–425.

Whorwell, P. J., Prior, A., & Faragher, E. B. (1984). Controlled trial of hypnotherapy in the treatment of severe refractory irritable-bowel syndrome. *The Lancet, 2*(8414), 1232–1234.

Labor and Delivery

Anette Werner

Childbirth is one of the most intense and demanding events that a woman is likely to experience, and both physical and psychological resources must be mobilized to cope with the labor process (Larkin, Begley, & Devane, 2009). Meaningful and adequate support must be given to the woman undergoing labor and delivery because the costs for society and the individual of a negative childbirth experience may be substantial. Negative and traumatic birth experiences have been associated with an increased risk of both short-term and long-term consequences, including bonding problems between mother and child (Taylor, Atkins, Kumar, Adams, & Glover, 2005; van Bussel, Spitz, & Demyttenaere, 2010), childbirth-related posttraumatic stress and postpartum depression (Creedy, Shochet, & Horsfall, 2000; Leeds & Hargreaves, 2008; Olde, van der Hart, Kleber, & Van, 2006; Soderquist, Wijma, & Wijma, 2002), poor health (Schytt & Waldenstrom, 2007), preferences for delivery by cesarean birth in future pregnancies (Pang, Leung, Lau, & Hang Chung, 2008; Waldenstrom, Hildingsson, & Ryding, 2006), and refraining from having more children (Gottvall & Waldenstrom, 2002).

A woman's childbirth experience is affected by many factors, and some of the most profound seem to be labor pain, loss of control, coping skills, support from the caregivers, anxiety and fear, and expectations for the upcoming birth (Hodnett, 2002; Larsson, Saltvedt, Edman, Wiklund, & Andolf, 2011; Waldenstrom, Borg, Olsson, Skold, & Wall, 1996; Waldenstrom, Hildingsson, Rubertsson, & Radestad, 2004). For example, an optimistic and positive attitude is associated with a positive birthing experience and negative expectations with a negative birthing experience (Green, Coupland, & Kitzinger, 1990; Hodnett, 2002; Slade, MacPherson, Hume, & Maresh, 1993; Waldenstrom, 1999; Waldenstrom et al.,

1996). Fear of and worries about the upcoming childbirth are relatively well-established risk factors for having a negative experience (Alehagen, Wijma, Lundberg, & Wijma, 2005; Lang, Sorrell, Rodgers, & Lebeck, 2006; Saisto & Halmesmaki, 2003; Waldenstrom, 1999).

Medical interventions, for example, emergency operative delivery and augmentation of labor, as well as prolonged labor, also affect the childbirth experience negatively (Mackey, 1995; Waldenstrom, 1999; Waldenstrom et al., 1996). However, a woman's subjective childbirth experience may be the most important factor determining her mental health in the postpartum period (Garthus-Niegel, Von, Vollrath, & Eberhard-Gran, 2013).

The pain experience during labor is complex and consists of an interaction among multiple physiological and psychological factors. The complexity of the pain experience during childbirth is illustrated by studies showing that removal of the pain does not necessarily result in a more satisfying childbirth, and that the intensity of the pain during labor is not necessarily related to the woman's satisfaction with the childbirth. Labor pain differs from other types of pain by being purposeful. If the woman can distract herself from or redefine the pain into a larger motivational context, it can be experienced as positive and as a necessity in order to give birth to the child (Lowe, 2002). For some women, labor pain can actually lead to feelings of fulfillment and achievement (Hodnett, 2002; Salmon, Miller, & Drew, 1990; Waldenstrom, Bergman, & Vasell, 1996).

The woman's confidence in her ability to cope with labor and delivery is strongly associated with a decreased perception of pain and a decreased use of analgesia during childbirth (Crowe & von Baeyer, 1989; Lowe, 1996; Manning & Wright, 1983; Wuitchik, Hesson, & Bakal, 1990).

Therefore, a woman's subjective experience of pain may be intensified if her personal control of the labor and birth is diminished; therefore, it is important to support a woman's ability to cope with the birthing process.

EVIDENCE FOR THE EFFECT OF HYPNOSIS ON CHILDBIRTH

Hypnotizability

The ability to experience hypnosis increases in pregnancy (Alexander, Turnbull, & Cyna, 2009; Tiba, 1990). Tiba (1990) showed that the degree of hypnotizability increased from the second to the third trimester of pregnancy. A recent study tested hypnotizability in the third trimester and subsequently between 14 and 28 months postpartum. The results also suggested that pregnant women are more susceptible to the effects of hypnosis during late pregnancy (Alexander et al., 2009).

Antenatal Hypnosis Training

Various studies show the beneficial effects of training pregnant women in hypnosis and self-hypnosis when preparing for childbirth (Brann & Guzvica, 1987; Cyna, Andrew, & McAuliffe, 2006a; Davidson, 1962; Freeman, Macaulay, Eve, Chamberlain, & Bhat, 1986; Guse, Wissing, & Hartman, 2006; Guthrie, Taylor, & Defriend, 1984; Harmon, Hynan, & Tyre, 1990; Jenkins & Pritchard, 1993; Letts, Baker, Ruderman, & Kennedy, 1993; Maris, 1995; Martin, Schauble, Rai, & Curry, 2001; Mehl-Madrona, 2004; VandeVusse et al., 2007; Werner, Uldbjerg, Zachariae, Wu, & Nohr, 2013). However, many studies also fail to show an effect of hypnosis (Cyna et al., 2006a; Fisher, Esplin, Stoddard, & Silver, 2009; Freeman et al., 1986; Madden, Middleton, Cyna, Matthewson, & Jones, 2012; Martin et al., 2001; Werner, Uldbjerg, Zachariae, & Nohr, 2013; Werner, Uldbjerg, Zachariae, Rosen, & Nohr, 2012). A Cochrane Review from 2012 outlined these results and did not find an effect of hypnosis on use of pharmacological pain relief, spontaneous vaginal birth, coping with labor, satisfaction with the childbirth experience, admissions to the neonatal intensive care unit, and breastfeeding at discharge from the hospital. There was some

evidence of benefit in the women in the hypnosis group compared with the control group with regard to pain intensity and length of labor and maternal hospital stay, but these findings were based on single studies with small numbers of women. Pain intensity was found to be lower in women in the hypnosis group than in those in the control group in one trial of 60 women. The same study found that the average length of labor was significantly shorter in women in the hypnosis group. Another study found that a smaller proportion of women in the hypnosis group stayed in the hospital for more than two days after the birth compared with women in the control group. The authors of the review concluded that further research is needed before recommendations can be made regarding the clinical usefulness of hypnosis for pain management (Madden et al., 2012).

However, in most of the trials included in the review, the hypnotic method and the control conditions were not well described (Fisher et al., 2009; Freeman et al., 1986; Harmon et al., 1990; Martin et al., 2001; Mehl-Madrona, 2004; Rock, Shipley, & Campbell, 1969). Moreover, the birth settings were not contemporary (Freeman et al., 1986; Harmon et al., 1990; Rock et al., 1969), and that complicates the generalizability of the studies.

The most recent trial included in the review was the HATCh trial from Australia. It was a large trial, and the hypnotic method was well described. It compared three groups: one given a brief course in self-hypnosis late in pregnancy supplemented with audio recordings late in pregnancy, another that received only the audio recordings, and a third group that was given usual care. According to a Cochrane Review, no differences across the three groups were found with regard to analgesic use and experienced pain (Cyna et al., 2006b; Madden et al., 2012).

A large, randomized controlled trial from Denmark using a similar intervention, a brief course in self-hypnosis to ease childbirth, was reported in 2012 and it was not included in the Cochrane Review. The trial found no effect on the use of epidural analgesia during birth and self-reported labor pain in a group that was given a brief course in relaxation and awareness techniques compared with a group given usual care. Furthermore, no effect was seen on the duration of birth and other maternal and neonatal outcomes at birth, lactation success, caring for the child, well-being, and postpartum depression (Werner et al., 2012; Werner et al., 2013a).

However, the hypnosis intervention had a positive impact on the childbirth experience, and women who had high hypnotic susceptibility seemed to benefit the most. Fewer women in the hypnosis group preferred a cesarean section in future pregnancies because of the fear of childbirth and negative birth experiences (Werner et al., 2012; Werner et al., 2013b).

In England, a similar trial has taken place, but no results have been reported yet. It will be very exciting to see the results of this trial in the near future (Downe, 2013).

We now need further studies that deal with and focus on the start of intense interventions early in pregnancy.

Hypnosis During Labor and Childbirth

Only one trial has evaluated hypnosis provided by a hypnotherapist during labor and childbirth. The results showed a lesser use of analgesics, less self-rated pain, and more observed comfort in the hypnosis group compared with the control group (Rock et al., 1969). However, the trial was performed in 1969 and is therefore not contemporary.

It seems that by working consciously with structured behavior and hypnosis during surgery, good results may be achieved. In these situations, the patients' level of anxiety and stress is high. This is knowledge that may presumably be transferred to the childbirth situation, which may also be characterized by anxiety and stress. Hopefully, future studies will also focus on hypnosis interventions that take place during labor and delivery.

CASE EXAMPLES

Hypnosis can be used to help prepare women for childbirth during both pregnancy and labor. In the Danish study that showed that hypnosis was able to facilitate a positive birth experience, the participants took part in a short, group course on hypnosis (antenatal hypnosis training) that consisted of three one-hour lessons with supplementary CDs (Werner et al., 2013b). The content of the course is described in Appendix A. Later, the participants had the opportunity to comment on whether the

course had helped them during childbirth, and if so, how. Following are the comments from six different women (Werner, 2013).

"Hypnosis helped me manage breathing, gave me the ability to focus on the situation, and I experienced that the labor pains were soon over. And I also had the feeling that my body would be able to manage . . . I felt ready to give birth."

"I was very pleased with the techniques I learned. I was in a trance-like state during childbirth. I could focus on strengths and on the positive."

"I got really good help from the techniques I learned during hypnosis. From the beginning of labor until I had given birth I used the calm given by hypnosis between my contractions. I'm sure that this helped make childbirth less traumatic and overwhelming. I'm so happy I took part in the course."

"The hypnosis itself helped me relax at home. During childbirth the use of the techniques helped me cope with the pain, but I was only able to concentrate for short periods of time."

"I used hypnosis during all the time I was at home. It gave me a preliminary calm and joy at the thought of the coming childbirth. And the hypnosis itself meant that we could be at home for almost ten hours before we went to the hospital."

"I used what I had learned. I became especially aware of how much I used it when we talked about the childbirth afterward. It helped me focus and concentrate on the childbirth, making it a fantastic experience!"

MEDICAL APPLICATIONS

The following section contains a selection of suggestions that would be advantageous to include in a booklet to be used as part of the preparation for childbirth. It would also be possible to use the suggestions during childbirth itself and thus be a guide for a woman in labor. In both situations, it is important to obtain an adequate history, establish good contact with the women, and make use of utilization of individual preferences of the patient.

Progressive Relaxation

There are many good reasons to include progressive relaxation in the deepening process. The relaxation itself can give a sensation of control and relief of pain. The same is true for deep and regular breathing.

"And you can feel how nice it is to relax, in your whole face, and in the muscles around the eyes and eyebrows that just get heavier and heavier. The mouth might open a bit when you release the tension in the jaw muscles. Likewise, the muscles in the back of the head become softer, and the process of relaxation spreads down over the neck, so that the neck becomes long and soft and relaxed, and the same relaxation flows further down to your shoulders, so that they drop and the muscles are at rest—and it's as if the pleasant feeling spreads throughout the whole body . . . more and more every time you exhale.

You can let the gentle feeling of relaxation and heaviness move down through the arms—the upper arms softly relaxed, elbows with space and freedom, the lower arms loose, wrists at ease, your hands soft and gentle, fingers relaxed. And it's possible to let this pleasant feeling spread throughout your whole body. From the shoulders down over the shoulder blades, all the way down along the spine and over the thighs and buttocks while the chest rises and falls with each breath, in and out, and out. Just feel that your whole body is resting safe and secure. And it is possible to relax with a feeling of release of tension down through the chest, peace of mind, the diaphragm, the belly with the uterus, and the uterus with the baby, and let the feeling of heaviness spread to the legs, thigh muscles soft and heavy, and knees, and further down to the calf muscles and the whole lower leg and ankles, and feel the weight and heaviness, and the feet heavy and light, warm, and all the way out into the toes, a sense of complete relaxation. A feeling that your whole body is resting safe and secure. Deeper and deeper each time you exhale . . . rest, relaxation, peace. . . ."

Information About Childbirth and Labor

In some of the scientific studies on hypnosis and obstetrics, HypnoReflexology™ techniques have been used with advantage. Through informative instruction given in preparation for childbirth, an expectant feeling of the normal progression of

pregnancy and childbirth is gained that can lead to a conditioned reflex/response that embodies a sense of control and pleasure. The idea is to minimize anxiety by achieving a feeling of control (Schauble, Werner, Rai, & Martin, 1998; Werner, Schauble, & Knudson, 1982).

There is focus on the structure of the uterine muscle and what to expect with regard to labor pains, which are the result of the contraction of this muscle. The muscular contractions that cause labor pains are compared with other muscular contractions, ones you do many times daily and which do not cause pain or unpleasantness:

"The term muscular contraction should be very familiar to you because you've had them all your life. Every time you move a part of your body, it takes one or more muscular contractions to accomplish it. Every time you breathe, it takes many muscular contractions. Now remember, muscles have been contracting for you since the moment of your birth. You have hardly paid any attention to them at all. Why? Because they're completely natural. So, you know instinctively muscles have been contracting for you all your life, while you've been completely comfortable. And remember . . . the whole mechanism of the first stage of your labor is a series of muscular contractions . . . of the muscles in the walls of the uterus." (Schauble et al., 1998, p. 277)

Ego-Strengthening

It is a fundamental requirement that the woman is supported in her belief that she can get through labor and delivery and manifest the strengths needed. Thus, a large part of the preparations for childbirth deal with increasing the woman's self-confidence, self-esteem, and personal effectiveness.

Here are some possibilities for linking ego-strengthening with information on childbirth.

"Great and small changes take place in the body during pregnancy. The body adjusts itself to the child and the pregnancy, and many of the changes are related to assuring an easy and safe birth of your child. During childbirth, uterine contractions come and go. Most birthing women concentrate on the long rests between contractions. All these long, wonderful rests fill them with a surplus of energy

and strength—much more than they actually need to safely and effortlessly give birth to their baby.

You can trust your body—you can deliver your child safely and in comfort. You have the ability to let go and relax. If you want to, you can use this ability in any and all situations. You are in control. But you don't need to remember it or think about it—just maintain control by letting things take their course. The ability to relax will be there if you need it."

Managing Labor Pains

Clinical experience suggests that a large part of the management of labor pains deals with helping the birthing woman to keep focused. Attention should be diverted from contractions to pauses, from tension to relaxation, from the unknown to the known. The women must be helped to reframe labor pains from something unpleasant to something helpful. In addition, focus should be placed on the women's strength, composure, peace of mind, and the result of the effort being the little child.

■ Anchoring (Using the Psychological Process)

"It is an advantage to secure an anchor to something. This can be done in many different ways. One way is to anchor to the physiological process like the labor contractions themselves.

Every contraction may remind you about how easy it is to relax and feel comfortable . . . just being confident that the body knows what to do . . . how to deliver your baby easily and safely.

The more powerful the contractions become, the easier it becomes to feel comfortable . . . while you breathe, easily and deeply . . . in and out, and out, just breathing easily. . . ."

■ Time Distortion

Through the phenomenon of time distortion, it is possible to lengthen or shorten our subjective experience of time. This can be applied to the birthing process so each pause between labor contractions is experienced as longer than it actually is and each contraction as being shorter. "Every contraction is

followed by a rest . . . a long, comfortable rest. The more powerful the contractions get, the shorter and more distant you may experience them . . . and the more powerful the contractions get, the longer the rest periods in between may seem. Just let this happen . . . there is no need to think about why and how. . . ."

■ Amnesia

A good strategy is to forget the labor contractions that have passed and not think about those that are coming, but just concentrate and enjoy the pauses between contractions.

"When the contraction abates and disappears, you will forget everything about it. It will demand so much energy that it is much easier just to forget . . . just forgetting everything about the contraction when it is gone. It is much easier to just forget everything about the last contraction and focus on the long and pleasant rest."

■ Peace and Quiet

"When you exhale, the experience of tranquility will increase and peace and quiet will spread throughout the body from the inside to the outside, from the outside to the inside, all the way out to each little finger and toe, and fill you with a spirit of quietness and peace."

■ Metaphors

Metaphors are very useful for the highly susceptible pregnant woman. Here is an example of how positive emotional conditioning on childbirth, amnesia, and purposeful contractions can be worked. In addition, contractions can be reframed from something painful to a useful positive force.

"If your safe place is a beach, there might be a wave that you could look at. A wave that begins as a weakly colored line in the sea and that builds up just like a contraction. The color changes and foam appears on the top, and you can see it break in a powerful crash, casting water upon the beach with such great energy that you can *almost taste and feel the salty spray, and then the water recedes just like a contraction abates. Maybe you'll see how the water rushes further and further back into the sea, and you know that you will never see that wave again—that you will never feel that contraction again, you can forget about it—it has brought you closer to the moment, the high tide, and the safe and comfortable appearance of your baby.*

You know that all waves are different, and you can accept that your contractions develop in just the right tempo for you and your child. When the wave is over and the contraction has passed, you can forget all about it, and you know that you have come closer to the point when you will see your baby for the first time."

■ Safe Place

A strategy could be to separate yourself from the contraction and move to your own safe place.

"When you have the first sign that the uterus is beginning to contract, you can breathe in and feel the strength, breathe out and feel the heaviness. You might think of a wonderful experience you have had—a long time ago—or one you have had recently, or maybe just imagine that you are in a place you'd like to be. Maybe you imagine yourself to be somewhere outside in nature, or at home on the couch, or in a lovely garden. It doesn't make any difference where you decide to travel to in your thoughts—just that it is a place that is comfortable, safe, and secure. It's all right just to be safe and relaxed and comfortable.

And you can concentrate on your own safe place—be there with all your senses. Feel the comfortable temperature. Imagine it for yourself—the color and shapes of the place, the patterns of light and shade. . . . Maybe there are some sounds in your own special place. Deep and high notes, close or so far away that you have to concentrate to hear them—or it's the sound of almost complete silence that fills you. If you take a deep breath, nice aromas may pass through your nostrils and permeate your whole body. Maybe there's a delicious taste. Just notice how it feels to be there where you are in your own special place. Maybe there are other people

present in your place. You can take along all those you want. Or maybe you just want to be alone . . . complete peace, quiet, and security. Just let good, nice, pleasant, and wonderful things happen . . . precisely the way you want it to be in your safe place. Maybe you'll do things you like to do, or do things you did a long time ago, or things you would like to do.

Have you noticed that the more time you spend here, the more a feeling of pleasure and contentment becomes a part of you—a feeling of pleasure and security fills you, from the inside to the outside and from the outside to the inside, and you relax more and more now, and become aware of where your own inner peace and security lives.

When you are here in your safe place, you may be so obsessed by the place that you forget everything else . . . so completely preoccupied by your special place that you forget everything else. It is almost as if the contractions distance themselves from you while you are so involved with what is happening in your own safe place."

■ Immunization to Unhelpful Noises During Labor

Women in labor are in a dissociated mental trance-like state and therefore very open to suggestions. To protect the women from negative words and comments from midwives, doctors, relatives, and others, immunization can be worked on.

"You can be happy that we all have a natural ability to focus our attention on certain things and keep other things out of our consciousness. This is the way it will be during delivery. You will be able to focus on the sensory impressions from your surroundings, noises, words, and comments that are important to you and that you can use. You will be able to shut out all the other words, comments, and impressions—you register them without thinking more about them, let them glide more and more into the background, maybe almost as if they were a foreign language or background noise, so that you are conscious of only useful words and comments that support and help you. Completely relaxed and at ease while you are only aware of things that are useful to you and your child."

■ Analgesia

There are many hypnoanalgesic methods to ease pain during labor and delivery. The following script deals with dissociation and analgesia of the lower body and has been inspired by Cyna and McCarthy (Cyna et al., 2006a; McCarthy, 2001). As always, it is important to take a good history so that previous negative experiences with analgesia are not reactivated.

The woman is first guided to her "safe place" and from there to "the spa."

". . . You can see that it is a spa, a very special spa—maybe you'd like to look more closely at it. From the spa you can look over to your own safe place. You can even see yourself at a distance, see how you rest comfortably in your safe place, see how you appear smaller because of the distance—and here, in your spa place you can make sure that you are comfortable. The temperature is surely just right, and there are some pleasant smells. Is the light dimmed? Does music fill the air? Is there a tray with refreshing drinks? You can make your spa and its surroundings to be just what you want them to be. Maybe you can see the water and see the color. Maybe you can feel how you are filled with peace and comfort here in your spa place. Here is everything you need right now.

Did you notice that there were some bottles beside the spa? They are filled with a fluid, and there seems to be bubbles in the fluid, just like in a bubble bath. The fluid in the bottles has a very beautiful clear color. . . . Actually, it is a very special fluid; it's a local anesthetic. There are enormous amounts of local anesthetic fluid in the bottles, all you'll ever need. So take one of the bottles and pour the clear local anesthetic into the spa. See how the color of the water changes, maybe there are bubbles when the local anesthetic saturates the fluid. In a moment, you'll go into the water, into the water the local anesthetic is mixed with. So you go down the steps into the tub so that your feet are covered by the water. The water has a very pleasant temperature and small bubbles swirl around your feet. Note how the local anesthetic begins to seep through the skin and into your feet and ankles. The local anesthetic seeps in even further, into the muscles and nerves. Maybe you can sense how the feet and ankles begin to feel differently.

Maybe it reminds you of some other time when you were given an anesthetic and you experienced a tingly sensation, maybe the feet feel heavy—there is certainly a numb feeling in them now. As the local anesthetic seeps deeper and deeper into the ankles and feet and as the feeling in them changes, they become more and more numb, you realize that is a very helpful feeling. It makes you feel safer and more comfortable. Maybe you like to go a step further down into the spa so that the water reaches your knees. When you stand with the water up over the knees, you feel the water's pleasant temperature, how it swirls around with small bubbles that tingle refreshingly against the skin. The local anesthetic seeps through the skin of the knees and downward, seeps through skin, flesh, muscles, nerves—further and further in. You can feel a new sensation in the knees and the lower part of the legs. It pricks, tingles, and maybe there's a cold sensation. You look at it with wonder because you know that the sensation is very helpful, usable, for you. The more you concentrate on the tingling, numbing sensation, the more it expands—and the safer you feel.

When you feel that you are numb from the knees down, you can go further into the water. Maybe a step deeper, or maybe you sit down so that the water covers you from the waist down. You can lean against the wall of the tub. Maybe you are floating in a swim ring. Whatever you do, your body is covered by the wonderful tepid water from the waist down: the belly, hips, thighs, legs, and feet—the rest of your body is above the water. The bubbles swirl around and the water comfortably supports your back and loins. The refreshing bubbles softly prick the skin, and you feel how the fluid slowly and surely seeps into the genital area, thighs, buttocks, lower body—into the womb, pelvis, tailbone. . . . You feel a different sensation from the waist down. You relax, float, pleasantly supported by the water. You feel safe and comfortable because you know it's good for you. You know that you can recreate this different, pleasant numb feeling any time you want. It gives you a good and safe feeling to know that you can recreate the different, pleasant numb feeling. Every time you want to create this helpful feeling of being numbed, you can step into your local anesthetic spa—and each time you want to be numbed and step into the local anesthetic spa, you'll be able to create the sensation even better, more clearly, and it will be even more helpful for you.

If at any time a problem arises in that part of your body where you have created this helpful sensation of numbness, you will have the symptoms that are necessary to diagnose the problem. When you get the symptom, you can return to the helpful, tingling sensation of being anesthetized. Each time you step into the local anesthetic spa remember to step out of it again at some point—you will always be able to go back. . . . Right now you can give yourself the right to float comfortably in the warm water in your very own spa—float at ease and relax more and more. If you are still in your spa, now it's time to get out of it again. You can take all the feelings with you, even though you have gotten out of your spa. See how you get up, you are now standing with water to your knees, and later the water covers only your ankles and feet—and you are out of the water. Maybe you're in your own special place—walk up the steps back to your own body—all the way back and feel your body. . . ."

CONCLUSION

Childbirth is one of the most intense and demanding events that a woman is likely to experience, and both physical and psychological resources must be mobilized to cope with the labor process. Meaningful and adequate support must be given to the woman undergoing labor and delivery. The pregnant woman is highly susceptible to suggestion, which indicates that hypnosis could be a strategy to cope with labor and delivery. Hypnosis can have a positive impact on the childbirth experience; we need further studies on hypnosis and childbirth.

Hypnosis can be provided as antenatal training and during labor and delivery as self-hypnosis or as guided hypnosis. Attention should be paid to ego-strengthening, reframing the labor and childbirth process, and helping the pregnant and laboring woman to keep a positive focus. Basic hypnotic strategies such as progressive relaxation and securing a safe place can be very useful.

Suggestions for analgesia of the lower body can be used for pain management.

REFERENCES

Alehagen, S., Wijma, B., Lundberg, U., & Wijma, K. (2005). Fear, pain and stress hormones during childbirth. *Journal of Psychosomatic Obstetrics and Gynecology, 26,* 153–165.

Alexander, B., Turnbull, D., & Cyna, A. (2009). The effect of pregnancy on hypnotizability. *American Journal of Clinical Hypnosis, 52,* 13–22.

Brann, L. R., & Guzvica, S. A. (1987). Comparison of hypnosis with conventional relaxation for antenatal and intrapartum use: A feasibility study in general practice. *Journal of the Royal College of General Practitioners, 37*(303), 437–440.

Creedy, D. K., Shochet, I. M., & Horsfall, J. (2000). Childbirth and the development of acute trauma symptoms: Incidence and contributing factors. *Birth, 27,* 104–111.

Crowe, K., & von Baeyer, C. (1989). Predictors of a positive childbirth experience. *Birth (Berkeley, Calif.), 16*(2), 59–63.

Cyna, A. M., Andrew, M. I., & McAuliffe, G. L. (2006a). Antenatal self-hypnosis for labour and childbirth: A pilot study. *Anesthetic Intensive Care, 34,* 464–469.

Cyna, A. M., Andrew, M. I., Robinson, J. S., Crowther, C. A., Baghurst, P., Turnbull, D., . . . Whittle, C. (2006b). Hypnosis Antenatal Training for Childbirth (HATCh): A randomized controlled trial. *BMC Pregnancy and Childbirth, 6*(1), 5. doi:10.1186/1471-2393-6-5

Davidson, J. A. (1962). An assessment of the value of hypnosis in pregnancy and labour. *British Medical Journal, 2,* 951–953.

Downe, S. (2013). *Self-hypnosis for intrapartum pain management (SHIP) trial* [Electronic version]. Retrieved from http://www.controlled-trials.com/ISRCTN27575146

Fisher, B., Esplin, S., Stoddard, G., & Silver, R. (2009). 125: Randomized controlled trial of hypnobirthing versus standard childbirth classes: Patient satisfaction and attitudes towards labor. *American Journal of Obstetrics and Gynecology, 201*(6), S61–S62.

Freeman, R. M., Macaulay, A. J., Eve, L., Chamberlain, G. V., & Bhat, A. V. (1986). Randomized trial of self-hypnosis for analgesia in labour. *British Medical Journal, 292,* 657–658.

Garthus-Niegel, S., Von, S. T., Vollrath, M. E., & Eberhard-Gran, M. (2013). The impact of subjective birth experiences on post-traumatic stress symptoms: A longitudinal study. *Archives of Women's Mental Health, 16,* 1–10.

Gottvall, K., & Waldenstrom, U. (2002). Does a traumatic birth experience have an impact on future reproduction? *BJOG: An International Journal of Obstetrics and Gynaecology, 109*(3), 254–260. doi:10.1111/j.1471-0528.2002.01200.x

Green, J. M., Coupland, V. A., & Kitzinger, J. V. (1990). Expectations, experiences, and psychological outcomes of childbirth: A prospective study of 825 women. *Birth, 17,* 15–24.

Guse, T., Wissing, M., & Hartman, W. (2006). The effect of a prenatal hypnotherapeutic program on postnatal maternal psychological well-being. *Journal of Reproductive and Infant Psychology, 24,* 163–177.

Guthrie, K., Taylor, J. D., & Defriend, D. (1984). Maternal hypnosis induced by husbands. *Journal of Obstetrics and Gynecology, 5*(2), 93–95.

Harmon, T. M., Hynan, M. T., & Tyre, T. E. (1990). Improved obstetric outcomes using hypnotic analgesia and skill mastery combined with childbirth education. *Journal of Consulting and Clinical Psychology, 58,* 525–530.

Hodnett, E. D. (2002). Pain and women's satisfaction with the experience of childbirth: A systematic review. *American Journal of Obstetrics and Gynecology, 186,* S160–S172.

Jenkins, M. W., & Pritchard, M. H. (1993). Hypnosis: Practical applications and theoretical considerations in normal labour. *BJOG: An International Journal of Obstetrics and Gynaecology, 100*(3), 221–226. doi:10.1111/j.1471-0528.1993.tb15234.x

Lang, A. J., Sorrell, J. T., Rodgers, C. S., & Lebeck, M. M. (2006). Anxiety sensitivity as a predictor of labor pain. *European Journal of Pain, 10,* 263–270.

Larkin, P., Begley, C. M., & Devane, D. (2009). Women's experiences of labour and birth: An evolutionary concept analysis. *Midwifery, 25,* e49–e59.

Larsson, C., Saltvedt, S., Edman, G., Wiklund, I., & Andolf, E. (2011). Factors independently related to a negative birth experience in first-time mothers. *Sexual Reproductive Healthcare, 2,* 83–89.

Leeds, L., & Hargreaves, I. (2008). The psychological consequences of childbirth. *Journal of Reproductive and Infant Psychology, 26,* 108–122.

Letts, P. J., Baker, P. R., Ruderman, J., & Kennedy, K. (1993). The use of hypnosis in labor and delivery: A preliminary study. *Journal of Women's Health, 2,* 335–341.

Lowe, N. K. (1996). The pain and discomfort of labor and birth. *Journal of Obstetrics and Gynecology, 25,* 82–92.

Lowe, N. K. (2002). The nature of labor pain. *American Journal of Obstetrics and Gynecology, 186,* S16–S24.

Mackey, M. C. (1995). Women's evaluation of their childbirth performance. *Maternal and Child Health Journal, 23,* 57–72.

Madden, K., Middleton, P., Cyna, A. M., Matthewson, M., & Jones, L. (2012). Hypnosis for pain management during labour and childbirth. *Cochrane Database Systematic Review, 11.* doi:10.1002/14651858.CD009356.pub2

Mairs, D. A. (1995). Hypnosis and pain in childbirth. *Contemporary Hypnosis, 12,* 111–118.

Manning, M. M., & Wright, T. L. (1983). Self-efficacy expectancies, outcome expectancies, and the persistence of pain control in childbirth. *Journal of Personal and Social Psychology, 45,* 421–431.

Martin, A. A., Schauble, P. G., Rai, S. H., & Curry, R. W. (2001). The effects of hypnosis on the labor processes and birth outcomes of pregnant adolescents. *Journal of Family Practice, 50,* 441–443.

McCarthy, P. (2001). *The use of hypnosis in surgery and anesthesiology.* Springfield, IL: Charles C. Thomas Publisher.

Mehl-Madrona, L. E. (2004). Hypnosis to facilitate uncomplicated birth. *American Journal of Clinical Hypnosis, 46,* 299–312.

Olde, E., van der Hart, O., Kleber, R., & Van, S. M. (2006). Posttraumatic stress following childbirth: A review. *Clinical Psychological Review, 26,* 1–16.

Pang, M. W., Leung, T. N., Lau, T. K., & Hang Chung, T. K. (2008). Impact of first childbirth on changes in women's preference for mode of delivery: Follow-up of a longitudinal observational study. *Birth, 35,* 121–128.

Rock, N. L., Shipley, T. E., & Campbell, C. (1969). Hypnosis with untrained, nonvolunteer patients in labor. *International Journal of Clinical and Experimental Hypnosis, 17,* 25–36.

Saisto, T., & Halmesmaki, E. (2003). Fear of childbirth: A neglected dilemma. *Acta Obstetrica et Gynecologica Scandinavia, 82,* 201–208.

Salmon, P., Miller, R., & Drew, N. C. (1990). Women's anticipation and experience of childbirth: The independence of fulfillment, unpleasantness and pain. *British Journal of Medicine and Psychology, 63*(3), 255–259.

Schauble, P. G., Werner, W. E., Rai, S. H., & Martin, A. (1998). Childbirth preparation through hypnosis: The hypnoreflexogenous protocol. *American Journal of Clinical Hypnosis, 40,* 273–283.

Schytt, E., & Waldenström, U. (2007). Risk factors for poor self-rated health in women at 2 months and 1 year after childbirth. *Journal of Women's Health (2002), 16*(3), 390–405. doi:10.1089/jwh.2006.0030

Slade, P., MacPherson, S. A., Hume, A., & Maresh, M. (1993). Expectations, experiences and satisfaction with labour. *British Journal of Clinical Psychology, 32*(4), 469–483.

Soderquist, J., Wijma, K., & Wijma, B. (2002). Traumatic stress after childbirth: The role of obstetric variables. *Journal of Psychosomatic Obstetrics and Gynecology, 23,* 31–39.

Taylor, A., Atkins, R., Kumar, R., Adams, D., & Glover, V. (2005). A new mother-to-infant bonding scale: Links with early maternal mood. *Archives of Women's Mental Health, 8,* 45–51.

Tiba, J. (1990). Clinical, research and organizational aspects of preparation for childbirth and the psychological diminution of pain during labour and delivery. *British Journal of Experimental & Clinical Hypnosis, 7,* 61–64.

van Bussel, J. C., Spitz, B., & Demyttenaere, K. (2010). Three self-report questionnaires of the early mother-to-infant bond: Reliability and validity of the Dutch version of the MPAS, PBQ and MIBS. *Archives of Women's Mental Health, 13,* 373–384.

VandeVusse, L., Irland, J., Healthcare, W. F., Berner, M. A., Fuller, S., & Adams, D. (2007). Hypnosis for childbirth: A retrospective comparative analysis of outcomes in one obstetrician's practice. *American Journal of Clinical Hypnosis, 50,* 109–119.

Waldenstrom, U. (1999). Experience of labor and birth in 1111 women. *Journal of Psychosomatic Research, 47,* 471–482.

Waldenstrom, U., Bergman, V., & Vasell, G. (1996). The complexity of labor pain: Experiences of 278 women. *Journal of Psychosomatic Obstetrics and Gynecology, 17,* 215–228.

Waldenstrom, U., Borg, I. M., Olsson, B., Skold, M., & Wall, S. (1996). The childbirth experience: A study of 295 new mothers. *Birth, 23,* 144–153.

Waldenstrom, U., Hildingsson, I., & Ryding, E. L. (2006). Antenatal fear of childbirth and its association with subsequent caesarean section and experience of childbirth. *British Journal of Obstetrics and Gynecology, 113,* 638–646.

Waldenstrom, U., Hildingsson, I., Rubertsson, C., & Radestad, I. (2004). A negative birth experience: Prevalence and risk factors in a national sample. *Birth, 31,* 17–27.

Werner, A. (2013). *Antenatal hypnosis training—the effect on pain experience, duration of birth and other birth outcomes* (Unpublished doctoral dissertation). Health Aarhus University, Aarhus, Denmark.

Werner, A., Uldbjerg, N., Zachariae, R., & Nohr, E. A. (2013). Effect of self-hypnosis on duration of labor and maternal and neonatal outcomes: A randomized controlled trial. *Acta Obstetrica er Gynecologica Scandinavia, 92,* 816–823.

Werner, A., Uldbjerg, N., Zachariae, R., Rosen, G., & Nohr, E. A. (2012). Self-hypnosis for coping with labour pain: A randomized controlled trial. *British Journal of Obstetrics and Gynecology: An International Journal of Obstetrics & Gynecology, 120*(3), 346–353.

Werner, A., Uldbjerg, N., Zachariae, R., Wu, C. S., & Nohr, E. A. (2013). Antenatal hypnosis training and childbirth experience: A randomized controlled trial. *Birth, 40,* 272–280.

Werner, W. E., Schauble, P. G., & Knudson, M. S. (1982). An argument for the revival of hypnosis in obstetrics. *American Journal of Clinical Hypnosis, 24,* 149–171.

Wuitchik, M., Hesson, K., & Bakal, D. A. (1990). Perinatal predictors of pain and distress during labor. *Birth, 17,* 186–191.

Appendix A: Training Program

Content	Hypnosis and Self-Hypnosis
Duration of training	First session: 1 hour Second session: 1 hour Third session: 1 hour
Group size	3 to 12 participants

First session	**Introduction to hypnosis and self-hypnosis**
	• Introduction to the course.
	• A basic introduction to hypnosis and self-hypnosis.
	• Focus on the participant's expectations, fears, and worries toward the upcoming birth through dialogue. A possibility to process negative expectations through informal hypnosis is given.
	• Guided hypnosis that includes parts of script from audio compact disc 1 (CD1).
	• CDs[1] for hypnosis training handed over. The participants are instructed to listen to CD1 every day during the next week.
	
	CD features:
	  • Induction by progressive muscle relaxation and guided imagery to an autobiographical safe and comfortable place according to the women's preference with integration of perceptions of all the senses.
	  • Suggestions and imagery for:
	    • Ego-strengthening
	    • Confidence during labor
	    • Control of labor
	    • Deep and easy breathing
	    • Positive emotional condition
	    • Child's well-being
	    • Basic information about first stage of labor
	    • Letting go of worries
	    • Immunization for unhelpful communication and noises during labor

Second session	**Adding hypnosis to labor**
	• Follow-up on "homework" and questions.
	• Knowledge about the mechanisms of labor and breathing.
	• Effort on self-hypnosis. Suggestions for coping with labor by inducing a feeling of control, strength, and belief in own ability to manage labor. Further on focus on breathing to improve relaxation, time distortion to experience labor as shorter and rest periods as longer, amnesia to forget contractions. Fractionation technique[2] is used to exercise labor (McCarthy, 2001).
	• Guided hypnosis consisting of parts of script from CD2.
	• The participants are instructed to listen to CD2 every day during the next week.
	
	CD features:
	  • Induction by progressive muscle relaxation and guided imagery to an autobiographical safe and comfortable place according to the women's preference with integration of perceptions of all the senses.
	  • Suggestions and imagery for:
	    • Fractionation
	    • Ego-strengthening
	    • Confidence during labor
	    • Control of labor
	    • Deep and easy breathing
	    • Positive emotional condition
	    • First and second stage of labor
	    • Reminder to let worries go
	    • Amnesia
	    • Time distortion
	    • Immunization to unhelpful communication and noises during labor

Content	Hypnosis and Self-Hypnosis
Third session	**Pain management techniques and coping strategy for labor** • Follow-up on "homework" and questions. • Suggestions for third stage of labor, breastfeeding, and recovery in the postpartum period. • Pain management techniques: focus on dissociation and lower body anesthesia by using "spa" ("filled with local anesthesia") imagery (McCarthy, 2001). • Guided hypnosis consisting of parts of script from CD3. • Coping strategy for labor: Self-hypnosis. Basically dissociation techniques. A CD (20 min) was developed to support the participants if needed during labor. • The participants are instructed to listen to CD3 every day until birth. If needed, CD3 can be replaced by CD1 or CD2. CD features: • Induction by progressive muscle relaxation and guided imagery to an autobiographical safe and comfortable place according to the women's preference with integration of perceptions of all the senses. • Suggestions and imagery for: • Fractionation • Ego-strengthening • Confidence during labor • Control of labor • Deep and easy breathing • Positive emotional condition • Whole labor process • Reminder to let worries go • Amnesia • Time distortion • Immunization to unhelpful communication and noises during labor • Analgesia of lower body • Breastfeeding • Recovery in the postpartum period

[1]The author may be contacted for additional information on the recorded scripts and CDs used in this program. Anette Werner: awerner@health.sdu.dk.

[2]Moving between state of alertness and relaxation.

Loin Pain Hematuria

Lauren Koep Crawshaw

Loin pain hematuria is a medical condition that can cause the following symptoms: recurrent or persistent unilateral or bilateral flank pain, loin tenderness, microscopic or macroscopic amounts of blood in the urine, low-grade fever, painful urination, and abnormal amounts of protein in the urine. These symptoms can be severe and often result in excessive use of pain medications and significant interference with activities of daily living. Additionally, psychological symptoms, such as depression and anxiety, have been associated with the condition (Coffman, 2009).

Loin pain hematuria originates in the kidneys but is often difficult to identify using standard diagnostic tests. The majority of patients diagnosed with loin pain hematuria have been female and Caucasian (Dube, Hamilton, Ratner, Nasr, & Radhakrishnan, 2006), though prevalence is not known. Treatments for loin pain hematuria have included analgesia with nonsteroidal anti-inflammatory drugs (NSAIDs) and opioids, prolonged courses of antibiotics, antiplatelet therapy with aspirin or sulfinpyrazone, anticoagulation with warfarin, renal autotransplantation, intra-ureteric capsaicin treatment, nephrectomy, and renal denervation. However, outcomes from these treatments are not consistently successful for even short-term pain relief, and most are unsuccessful at providing long-term pain relief. Additionally, surgical interventions for loin pain hematuria are often dangerous and high-opiate doses are associated with multiple negative side effects.

RESEARCH

Though it is known that loin pain hematuria is a form of kidney disease, the exact etiology of loin pain hematuria is poorly understood. As a result, the research on treatment options for patients diagnosed

with loin pain hematuria is limited. This is problematic due to the need to address the physical and psychological symptoms, which are often severe and can be debilitating. Previous studies have found hypnotherapy to be effective for pain (Dufresne et al., 2010; Eitner, Bittner, Wichmann, Nickenig, & Sokol, 2010; Elkins, Jensen, & Patterson, 2007; Kohen, 2010; Mackey, 2010; Nash & Tasso, 2010; Patterson & Jensen, 2003; Patterson, Jensen, Wiechman, & Sharar, 2010; Tan, Fukui, Jensen, Thornby, & Waldman, 2010) as well as for symptoms of anxiety and depression associated with medical conditions (Barabasz & Watkins, 2005; Elkins et al., 2008). To the author's knowledge, only one case study (Elkins, Koep, & Kendrick, 2012) has been published examining hypnotherapy for the treatment of the physical and psychological symptoms associated with loin pain hematuria.

CASE EXAMPLE

The case study focuses on a single, 17-year-old Caucasian female patient. She presented for treatment with uncontrolled, excruciating, constant pain in her right flank associated with loin pain hematuria. She reported severe pain, inability to achieve sufficient pain control, and frustration associated with interference in her quality of life, despite multiple attempts at seeking medical intervention for her symptoms.

The onset of her symptoms occurred in May 2009 when she first noticed spots of blood in her urine followed by the sudden onset of severe, bilateral flank pain. Initial diagnostic work confirmed hematuria, and subsequent treatment involved a course of antibiotics. However, she continued to experience pain and an increase in the blood volume in her urine. On seeking treatment again, she was given another course of antibiotics and a recommendation to take up to eight ibuprofen every four hours. Even while following these recommendations, the patient's pain worsened, leading to withdrawal from school and initiation of a home-bound educational program. She sought emergency room care nine times over the course of two months due to uncontrolled pain. Her treatment in the emergency room primarily consisted of narcotic medications. The patient's constant need for pain relief resulted in tolerance to the narcotics and consequent larger doses and stronger medications.

Throughout this struggle, the patient's physical discomfort was exacerbated by her inability to find relief from her symptoms. She also experienced mistrust from her medical providers, as her hematuria was inconsistent and did not necessarily correspond with her pain level. When lack of adequate pain control led her to present to the emergency room for the tenth time, NSAIDs were discontinued and blood was drawn for laboratory analysis. When her lab values displayed elevated creatinine levels, indicating kidney failure, she was admitted to the hospital. While inpatient, the patient was examined by a nephrologist, who confirmed that her kidneys were the source of her symptoms and advised her to avoid NSAIDs. She attempted to tolerate her pain for several weeks without any medications. However, as before, uncontrolled pain restricted almost all of the patient's waking activities and again stimulated frequent emergency room visits. It was postulated during some of these visits that the patient was medication seeking, but she reported a significant aversion to the effects of narcotic medications, stating that they left her somnolent and irritable.

When the patient returned to her nephrologist for follow-up, she was diagnosed with loin pain hematuria and referred to a pain clinic for management of this condition. Her treatment through the pain clinic consisted of up to eight 10 mg doses of Norco and three 30 mg doses of morphine daily. While under the effects of these medications, she spent up to 22 hours asleep each day while still suffering from residual pain and nausea, a side effect of the medications. In response to her continued symptom experience, the patient underwent right renal denervation in September 2009, as recommended by her nephrologist. After recovering from an abscess caused by the initial denervation, she then underwent left renal denervation in November 2009. Left renal denervation resulted in lessening of the patient's pain, but pain persisted on her right side even after the surgical intervention. She therefore continued treatment in the pain management clinic and utilized high doses of over-the-counter acetaminophen and sleep medication.

The patient returned for nephrology follow-up with unremitting pain. At that visit, she was educated that her next option would be another surgery, autotransplantation. The risks of this surgery included a future possibility that she may be unable to carry a pregnancy to full term. Out of concerns about this potential adverse effect, the patient was then referred for hypnosis for symptom management.

TECHNIQUE

The patient was seen for an initial consultation and assessment. She was then treated with eight one-hour hypnotherapy sessions over five months. Each session was initiated with a standard hypnotic induction following the transcript outlined by Elkins and Handel (2001). Because pain reduction was a primary goal of treatment, suggestions were made for her experience of pain to become *"less and less severe, every day."* It was suggested that during hypnosis, she would feel greater comfort and *"no pain, the deeper the relaxation the greater the comfort"* and for her to experience *"greater control over any pain that remains."* Additional suggestions for pain management included suggestions that she would be able to *"become so deeply relaxed that any feeling of discomfort would fade to the background."* She was able to achieve feelings of relaxation and to respond to imagery to deepen relaxation by visualizing *"walking down a staircase,"* and at the bottom of the stairs seeing *"a beautiful lake and feeling calm, relaxed, and very comfortable."* Additionally, each hypnotherapy session included suggestions that the functioning of her immune system would improve, and the symptoms of her loin pain hematuria would lessen. Examples of such suggestions include *"allowing comfort and healing to become more and more complete"* with each practice of hypnosis, and *"your immune system will improve and your kidneys and body will return to normal functioning."* Each session of hypnosis also involved suggestions for comfort, calmness, and a sense of well-being. Additionally, the patient was provided with suggestions to *"be able to sleep well and to feel calm most of the time."*

To address her overall symptom experience and provide empowerment, it was suggested that she *"imagine a time in the future when she is no longer bothered by loin pain or symptoms."* Finally, in order to reduce the interference with the patient's activities of daily living, the clinician suggested that she would *"be able to return to school as symptoms of pain and anxiety become less and less"* and that she would *"feel a sense of confidence and well-being and feelings of control over her body."*

In addition to these face-to-face hypnosis sessions, the patient was provided with recordings of the hypnosis sessions and encouraged to listen to the recordings daily. She was taught to practice self-hypnosis as a tool to achieve comfort and independent control over her pain experience.

CONCLUSION

Baseline, endpoint, and follow-up measures were administered to examine the effectiveness of the hypnotic intervention. Measures included the General Health Questionnaire, Hospital Anxiety and Depression Scale (HADS), McGill Pain Questionnaire, Pain Discomfort Scale, and visual analog measures of pain, academic interference, and social interference. Upon the patient's endpoint session and at 12-month follow-up, her self-report and responses on these measures demonstrated substantial reduction in depression, pain, and anxiety.

Her score on the General Health Questionnaire (GHQ28) improved by 84.7% from baseline to endpoint and by 98.3% at 12-month follow-up. This indicates a clinically significant reduction in symptoms. Her score on the Anxiety subscale of the HADS improved by 35.0% from baseline to end of treatment, and by 100.0% by her follow-up session. Similarly, her score on the Depression subscale of the HADS demonstrated a 73% reduction in symptoms from baseline to end of treatment, and a 100% reduction in symptoms by 12-month follow-up. These changes from endpoint to 12-month follow-up suggest that difficulties with mood and anxiety continued to improve after treatment was concluded because the patient continued to practice self-hypnosis. Additionally, her total score on the McGill Pain Questionnaire improved by 73.7% from baseline to endpoint and by 100.0% at follow-up. Further,

her score on the Pain Discomfort Scale improved by 64.7% from baseline to endpoint, and by 100.0% at follow-up. Improvement on this instrument indicates lessening of pain intensity and negative affect associated with pain. The patient's scores on several visual analog measures also demonstrated marked improvement. On a visual analog scale of pain level, her score improved by 80.5% from baseline to endpoint, and by 97.5% by her follow-up session. On a visual analogue scale of academic interference, her score improved by 100.0% from baseline to endpoint and remained in complete remission at follow-up. Finally, on a visual analogue scale of social interference, her score improved by 83.9% from baseline to end of treatment and by 100.0% at 12-month follow-up. The patient reported almost complete amelioration of her pain at 12-month follow-up and she was therefore able to return to full academic, social, and extracurricular functioning outside the home.

The results reported in this case study indicate that hypnotherapy may be useful in addressing the physiological discomfort, emotional distress, and lifestyle interference associated with loin pain hematuria. Additionally, hypnosis provides a medically benign and conservative alternative to surgical interventions and narcotic medications. The qualitative data gathered from this case study demonstrate that one particularly helpful aspect of hypnosis is that it restores an individual's sense of control, which is especially valuable for patients struggling to cope with chronic medical problems. Hypnosis helped this patient to manage her symptoms of loin pain hematuria, achieve lasting pain relief, return to an appropriate level of functioning, and improve her quality of life. These findings are similar to treatment outcomes of other kinds of pain conditions using hypnosis (Dufresne et al., 2010; Eitner et al., 2010; Kohen, 2010; Mackey, 2010; Nash & Tasso, 2010; Patterson et al., 2010; Tan et al., 2010).

REFERENCES

Barabasz, A., & Watkins, J. (2005). *Hypnotherapeutic techniques*. New York, NY: Brunner-Routledge.

Coffman, K. L. (2009). Loin pain hematuria syndrome: A psychiatric and surgical conundrum. *Current Opinion in Organ Transplantation, 14*(2), 186–190.

Dube, G. K., Hamilton, S. E., Ratner, L. E., Nasr, S. H., & Radhakrishnan, J. (2006). Loin pain hematuria syndrome. *Kidney International, 70*(12), 2152–2155.

Dufresne, A., Rainville, P., Dodin, S., Barré, P., Masse, B., Verreault, R., & Marc, I. (2010). Hypnotizability and opinions about hypnosis in a clinical trial for the hypnotic control of pain and anxiety during pregnancy termination. *International Journal of Clinical and Experimental Hypnosis, 58*(1), 82–101.

Eitner, S., Bittner, C., Wichmann, M., Nickenig, H. J., & Sokol, B. (2010). Comparison of conventional therapies for dentin hypersensitivity versus medical hypnosis. *International Journal of Clinical and Experimental Hypnosis, 58*(4), 457–475.

Elkins, G. R., & Handel, D. L. (2001). Clinical hypnosis: An essential in the tool kit for family practice. *Behavioral Medicine in Family Practice: Clinics in Family Practice, 3*(1), 113–126.

Elkins, G. R., Jensen, M. P., & Patterson, D. R. (2007). Hypnotherapy for the management of chronic pain. *International Journal of Clinical and Experimental Hypnosis, 55*(3), 275–287.

Elkins, G. R., Koep, L. L., & Kendrick, C. E. (2012). Hypnotherapy intervention for loin pain hematuria: A case study. *International Journal of Clinical and Experimental Hypnosis, 60*(1), 111–120.

Elkins, G. R., Marcus, J., Stearns, V., Perfect, M., Rajab, M. H., Ruud, C., . . . Keith, T. (2008). Randomized trial of a hypnosis intervention for treatment of hot flashes among breast cancer survivors. *Journal of Clinical Oncology:*

Official Journal of the American Society of Clinical Oncology, 26(31), 5022–5026.

Kohen, D. P. (2010). Long-term follow-up of self-hypnosis training for recurrent headaches: What children say. *International Journal of Clinical and Experimental Hypnosis, 58*(4), 417–432.

Mackey, E. F. (2010). Effects of hypnosis as an adjunct to intravenous sedation for third molar extraction: A randomized, blind, controlled study. *International Journal of Clinical and Experimental Hypnosis, 58*(1), 21–38.

Nash, M. R., & Tasso, A. (2010). The effectiveness of hypnosis in reducing pain and suffering among women with metastatic breast cancer and among women with temporomandibular disorder. *International Journal of Clinical and Experimental Hypnosis, 58*(4), 497–504.

Patterson, D. R., & Jensen, M. P. (2003). Hypnosis and clinical pain. *Psychological Bulletin, 129*(4), 495–521.

Patterson, D. R., Jensen, M. P., Wiechman, S. A., & Sharar, S. R. (2010). Virtual reality hypnosis for pain associated with recovery from physical trauma. *International Journal of Clinical and Experimental Hypnosis, 58*(3), 288–300.

Tan, G., Fukui, T., Jensen, M. P., Thornby, J., & Waldman, K. L. (2010). Hypnosis treatment for chronic low back pain. *International Journal of Clinical and Experimental Hypnosis, 58*(1), 53–68.

Menopause—Hot Flashes

Gary Elkins and Yesenia Mosca

Hot flashes are the most prevalent symptom associated with menopause and are characterized by sudden warmth, primarily in the face and chest, sweating, chills, anxiety, and irritability (Elkins, Kendrick, & Koep, 2014; Freedman, 2001; Kendrick et al., 2015). Hot flashes can disrupt sleep and result in discomfort and distress, which can negatively affect quality of life (Kendrick et al., 2015; Sideras & Loprinzi, 2010). The onset of hot flashes coincides with a decrease in estrogen levels that occurs during the menopausal transition; therefore, hormone replacement therapy has been the most commonly used treatment for hot flashes (Freedman, 2001).

It is estimated that the prevalence of hot flashes among menopausal women in the general population ranges from 30% to 80% (Sideras & Loprinzi, 2010). In the United States, it is estimated to occur in 68% to 82% of women (Lobo, 2007). The number of menopausal women who experience hot flashes is expected to exceed 23 million in the following years, with a significant portion experiencing severe hot flashes (Ziv-Gal & Flaws, 2010).

Menopause, the cessation of the menstrual cycle, typically occurs between the ages of 45 and 55 when the release of estrogen and progesterone declines dramatically. The transition from premenopausal to postmenopausal is around four years and begins with changes in the normal menstrual cycle, culminating in amenorrhea (Blake, 2006; Nelson, 2008; Pearce, Thøgersen-Ntoumani, Duda, & McKenna, 2014). Hot flashes are most commonly observed in postmenopausal women and can persist for years (Ziv-Gal & Flaws, 2010). The severity of hot flashes varies greatly from a small change in temperature, to sudden sensations of extreme heat that can impact daily activities (Kronenberg, 1990). Women who have induced menopause due to a surgical procedure for the treatment of a disease tend to experience more severe and longer lasting hot flashes (Bruce & Rymer, 2009).

Increasing the levels of estrogen that are present after the menopausal transition has been the main focus for alleviating symptoms. The most widely used treatment for hot flashes is hormone replacement therapy, which has shown to be very effective at reducing hot flashes (Ziv-Gal & Flaws, 2010). Hormone replacement therapy involves administering estrogen, or a combination of estrogen and progesterone, to supplement the decreasing levels of these hormones (Nelson, 2008). With hormone replacement therapy, a reduction of 75% to 95% in the frequency of hot flashes is typical. The severity of each episode is also reduced (Grady, 2006; Nelson, 2008).

Hormone therapy has been linked to an increase in the risk of developing breast cancer, cardiovascular disease, as well as increasing the risk of having a stroke (Elkins, Johnson, Fisher, Sliwinski, & Keith, 2013; Grady, 2006). For this reason, it should not be used in women who have a history of or are considered high risk for developing any of these problems (Grady, 2006).

The treatment of some cancers, including breast cancer, relies on hormonal deprivation therapies that can result in menopausal-like symptoms, the most common one being hot flashes (Vilar-González, Pérez-Rozos, & Cabanillas-Farpón, 2011). For these women, hormone replacement therapy is not an option for treating their hot flashes, and alternative treatments should be considered (Bordeleau, Pritchard, Goodwin, & Loprinzi, 2007). Nonhormonal treatments have been studied and found to reduce the frequency of hot flashes, although they are not as effective as traditional hormone replacement therapy. Selective serotonin reuptake inhibitors (SSRIs) have been shown to have up to 50% or higher success in the reduction of the frequency of hot flashes (Imai,

Matsunami, Takagi, & Ichigo, 2013; Morrow, Mattair, & Hortobagyi, 2011). Antidepressants can also have unwanted side effects, and when taken in conjunction with other medications that cancer patients use, could lead to more problems (Nachtigall, 2010).

Other preliminary studies showed hypnosis combined with cognitive behavioral therapy to be an effective alternative to pharmacological therapies (Cramer et al., 2015), but a more recent study compare clinical hypnosis and structured-attention control group (Elkins et al., 2013).

RESEARCH

Elkins et al. (2013) conducted a study in which the effects of clinical hypnosis could be measured against a control group. Frequency of hot flashes was measured both subjectively and physiologically, using daily diaries and a skin conductance monitoring system. A hot flash score (product of frequency by severity) was also recorded for each participant. As expected, the hypnosis group showed a reduction in subjective hot flash mean frequency of 63.87% compared with 9.24% reduction in the control group. Hot flashes continued to decrease in frequency when measured again at the week 12 follow-up, with a mean reduction of 74.16%. The control group had a mean reduction of 17.13% at week 12. A similar trend was found for the physiologically measured frequency where the mean reduction for the hypnosis group was 40.92% compared with the control group, which showed an increase in frequency of 7%. Both groups showed reduction in the frequency of hot flashes at the 12-week follow-up. Hot flash scores also decreased on average by 71.36% for the hypnosis group compared with 8.32% in the control group. This study demonstrated that hypnosis could significantly reduce the amount as well as the severity of hot flashes in postmenopausal women.

Additionally, Elkins et al. (2013) conducted a study and found that guided self-hypnosis also resulted in fewer hot flashes. This is more evidence that hypnosis can be used effectively and could eventually be administered in settings that may not have enough trained professional hypnotherapists to deliver the intervention to the large

population of postmenopausal women who suffer with hot flashes.

While we now have a growing number of studies that continue to show hypnosis as a good alternative to traditional treatments, the mechanisms by which hypnosis reduces hot flashes is still unknown (Cramer et al., 2015; Elkins et al., 2013). One theory that has been tested regards the idea that hypnosis reduces hot flashes by reducing stress (Kendrick et al., 2015). Changes in salivary cortisol concentrations were used to measure changes in stress. There was a significant reduction in cortisol when the saliva sample was collected in the morning, but upon further analysis, changes in salivary cortisol concentration were not found to mediate the effect hypnosis had on the reduction of hot flashes (Kendrick et al., 2015). Future research is needed to understand how hypnosis, whether administered by a trained hypnotherapist or through guided self-hypnosis, causes the changes in the frequency of hot flashes. As Elkins, Kendrick, and Koep (2014) show, hypnosis may benefit not only postmenopausal women or breast cancer survivors, but also men with a history of prostate cancer.

CASE EXAMPLE

The effective use of hypnotic relaxation therapy for reduction of hot flashes is described in detail in the publication, *Relief From Hot Flashes: The Natural, Drug-Free Program to Reduce Hot Flashes, Improve Sleep, and Ease Stress* (Elkins, 2014). This program provides the hot flash daily diaries for recording hot flashes, session-by-session guidance, and audio recordings for practice of hypnotic relaxation with suggestions and mental imagery for reduction of hot flashes.

In the following case study, adapted from *Relief From Hot Flashes: The Natural, Drug-Free Program to Reduce Hot Flashes, Improve Sleep, and Ease Stress* (Elkins, 2014), the patient was a 57-year-old woman who was experiencing moderate to severe hot flashes during the menopause transition. She was married and employed as a teacher. She reported having about nine hot flashes per day (counting night sweats). As a result of hot flashes, she experienced frequent sweating and flushing, and night sweats were interfering with her sleep. She reported anxiety due to the frequent hot flashes as well. She was asked to identify any triggers for hot flashes and she noted that she was most prone to have hot flashes in a warm room or during times of stress. However, most of the time she was not aware of any specific triggers. She was referred by her family physician and she was interested in hypnotic relaxation therapy as an alternative to hormone or drug therapies. She kept a hot flash daily diary for one week before starting her practice of hypnotic relaxation. She completed hypnotic inductions with suggestions for "coolness" and mental imagery for reduction of hot flashes. In addition, she was instructed in daily practice of hypnotic relaxation using audio recordings at home. She was seen for five weekly sessions and by the end of treatment had reduced her hot flashes by approximately 77%. She had a preference for mental imagery, such as walking down a mountain path with a cool breeze and snow around her. The following is an example of the transcript used.

TRANSCRIPT

"Hypnotic induction begins with a focus of attention, suggestions for relaxation, deepening suggestions, and mental imagery for coolness. Following the initial induction, suggestions are given for goal-directed mental imagery as follows. . . .

Now, in a moment, I am going to ask you to notice some images in your mind . . . you can hear my voice with one part of your mind and with another part of your mind going to a pleasant, peaceful place where you notice and experience everything that is there, every sound, every sight, every sensation of coolness . . . images and scenes that allow you to experience even more comfort and control . . . now allow yourself to see a door in front of you . . . a special door that will lead you to experience more comfort . . . soon going through that door and going to a place where you find the comfort that you need . . . learning to use hypnosis to remain more comfortable and relaxed. Everyday . . . and here finding a coolness and comfort. Now walking to that door and perhaps going through the door to a place where it is cool

and so comfortable . . . as you walk through that door finding that you are in the mountains . . . it is cool here; in fact, there is snow all around . . . the air is very cool and it is pleasant to notice the white snow on the trees and on the ground . . . you might want to take a deep breath of the crisp, cool air . . . and feeling cool waves of comfort flowing over you and through you . . . and feel more refreshed . . . it is the kind of day when the cool and the cold snow feels very good . . . this is a very beautiful place and perhaps you can see a lake in the distance . . . there is a path before you and you might enjoy walking down that mountain path. With every step you take feeling the cool air, the fresh cool feeling of feeling the air on your face, your forehead, and a gentle breeze across your ears.

It is just so pleasant there and just notice the coolness while standing at the top of this snow-covered mountain . . . cool waves of comfort flowing over you and through you . . . and while you are there it is possible that your mind could drift to other times when you have felt such a coolness and comfort. Perhaps the coolness of standing in front of an air conditioner . . . feeling the cold air . . . or the coolness one could experience when opening a refrigerator, or a cool drink of ice water when one is really thirsty and feeling the cool feeling of the water that is clear and clean and so refreshing. . . .

Now it is possible to enter an even deeper state of hypnosis . . . deeper and deeper relaxed . . . now letting all the tension go and as you do beginning to enter an even deeper level of hypnosis . . . now as this occurs you may notice a change in sensations . . . this may be a floating sensation . . . a drifting sensation and perhaps just less aware of your body . . . just floating in space. Your body floating in a feeling of comfort and your mind, just so aware of being in that pleasant place where you find coolness and a sense of well-being . . . just noticing a detached feeling . . . floating within feelings of coolness and comfort . . . drifting and floating . . . more and more . . . as your body floats, find even more comfort. Now as this occurs, finding that it is so natural that your mind blocks from conscious awareness any excessive discomfort and it is possible that you can feel more detached from your body . . . feeling the coolness . . . as you become more relaxed.

... and as you become more comfortable ... you will find a sense of being more in control ... and as this occurs you will find that more and more, you are able to sleep very well, your feelings of well-being will improve, and your quality of life will improve. You will not be bothered by any excessive anxiety, and any hot flashes will become less and less frequent and less severe. As time passes you simply will be less bothered by hot flashes ... more calm and relaxed and comfortable ... every day.

... Now, see yourself in the future in a way and a place where you experience that coolness and calm feelings. See how well you are able to feel and you will feel calm and comfortable and very relaxed, no matter if times become stressful or difficult. You will be able to remain calm and relaxed, both now and in the future.

... In a few moments return to conscious alertness. Return to conscious alertness in your own time and your own pace, in a way that just feels about right for you today. Feeling very good, normal, with good and normal sensations in every way as you return to full conscious alertness.

... Return to conscious alertness as I count from the numbers four to one, or perhaps you will want to just drift a little deeper relaxed and return to conscious alertness when it is just right for you.

4 ... 3 ... 2 ... 1."

CONCLUSION

The studies completed so far have shown that hypnosis can be used to successfully treat hot flashes. The mechanisms that drive the changes, however, are still unknown. Future research into how these changes occur is the logical next step. This could include combining new knowledge about the hormonal changes that occur during menopause.

Hypnotic relaxation therapy can be adapted to effectively treat hot flashes—both the frequency and severity of the hot flashes. It can therefore be used to treat women who are seeking an alternative option to hormone replacement therapy and with breast cancer survivors. A pilot study has

indicated that guidance with a therapist with audio recordings of hypnotic relaxation inductions may be helpful to some women. The use of hypnotic relaxation therapy for reduction of hot flashes is described in detail in *Relief From Hot Flashes: The Natural, Drug-Free Program to Reduce Hot Flashes, Improve Sleep, and Ease Stress* (Elkins, 2014), along with audio recordings that may be of use to clinicians who treat patients, postmenopausal women, or breast cancer survivors who are experiencing hot flashes and associated symptoms. When administering hypnosis, it is best to individualize the session by determining what the patient associates with feelings of coolness and calmness to facilitate participation of the hypnotic intervention (Elkins et al., 2010). Increasing the awareness that hypnotic relaxation therapy can be used to help women with hot flashes can be an important step in bringing hypnosis to hospitals and clinics.

REFERENCES

Blake, J. (2006). Menopause: Evidence-based practice. *Best Practice & Research Clinical Obstetrics & Gynaecology, 20*(6), 799–839. doi:10.1016/j.bpobgyn.2006.07.001

Bordeleau, L., Pritchard, K., Goodwin, P., & Loprinzi, C. (2007). Therapeutic options for the management of hot flashes in breast cancer survivors: An evidence-based review. *Clinical Therapeutics, 29*(2), 230–241. doi:10.1016/j.clinthera.2007.02.006

Bruce, D., & Rymer, J. (2009). Symptoms of the menopause. *Best Practice & Research. Clinical Obstetrics & Gynaecology, 23*(1), 25–32. doi:10.1016/j.bpobgyn.2008.10.002

Cramer, H., Lauche, R., Paul, A., Langhorst, J., Kümmel, S., & Dobos, G. J. (2015). Hypnosis in breast cancer care: A systematic review of randomized controlled trials. *Integrative Cancer Therapies, 14*(1), 5–15. doi:10.1177/1534735414550035

Elkins, G. R. (2014). *Relief from hot flashes: The natural, drug-free program to reduce hot flashes, improve sleep, and ease stress.* New York, NY: Demos Health Publishing.

Elkins, G. R., Fisher, W. I., Johnson, A. K., Carpenter, J. S., & Keith, T. Z. (2013). Clinical hypnosis in the treatment of postmenopausal hot flashes: A randomized controlled trial. *Menopause: The Journal of the North American Menopause Society, 20*(3), 291–298.

Elkins, G. R., Johnson, A., Fisher, W., Sliwinski, J., & Keith, T. (2013). A pilot investigation of guided self-hypnosis in the treatment of hot flashes among postmenopausal women. *International Journal of Clinical and Experimental Hypnosis, 61*(3), 342–350. doi:10.1080/00207144.2013.784112

Elkins, G. R., Kendrick, C., & Koep, L. (2014). Hypnotic relaxation therapy for treatment of hot flashes following prostate cancer surgery: A case study. *International Journal of Clinical and Experimental Hypnosis, 62*(3), 251–259. doi:10.1080/00207144.2014.901051

Elkins, G., Marcus, J., Bunn, J., Perfect, M., Palamara, L., Stearns, V., & Dove, J. (2010). Preferences for hypnotic imagery for hot-flash reduction: A brief communication. *International Journal of Clinical and Experimental Hypnosis, 58*(3), 345–349. doi:10.1080/00207141003761239

Freedman, R. R. (2001). Physiology of hot flashes. *American Journal of Human Biology: The Official Journal of the Human Biology Council, 13*(4), 453–464. doi:10.1002/ajhb.1077

Grady, D. (2006). Management of menopausal symptoms. *New England Journal of Medicine, 355*(22), 2338–2347. doi:10.1056/NEJMcp054015

Imai, A., Matsunami, K., Takagi, H., & Ichigo, S. (2013). New generation nonhormonal management for hot flashes. *Gynecological Endocrinology: The Official Journal of the International Society of Gynecological Endocrinology, 29*(1), 63–66. doi:10.3109/09513590.2012.705380

Kendrick, C., Johnson, A. K., Sliwinski, J., Patterson, V., Fisher, W. I., Elkins, G. R., & Carpenter, J. S. (2015). Hypnotic relaxation therapy for reduction of hot flashes in postmenopausal women: Examination of cortisol as a potential mediator. *International Journal of Clinical and Experimental Hypnosis, 63*(1), 76–91. doi:10.1080/00207144.2014.931169

Kronenberg, F. (1990). Hot flashes: Epidemiology and physiology. *Annals of the New York Academy of Sciences, 592*(1), 52–86.

Lobo, R. A. (2007). *Treatment of the postmenopausal woman: Basic and clinical aspects.* San Diego, CA: Academic Press.

Morrow, P. K., Mattair, D. N., & Hortobagyi, G. N. (2011). Hot flashes: A review of pathophysiology and treatment modalities. *The Oncologist, 16*(11), 1658–1664. doi:10.1634/theoncologist.2011-0174

Nachtigall, L. E. (2010). Nonhormonal treatment of hot flashes—a viable alternative? *Nature Reviews. Endocrinology, 6*(2), 66.

Nelson, H. D. (2008). Menopause. *The Lancet, 371*(9614), 760–770. doi:10.1016/S0140-6736(08)60346-3

Pearce, G., Thøgersen-Ntoumani, C., Duda, J. L., & Mckenna, J. (2014). Changing bodies: Experiences of women who have undergone a surgically induced menopause. *Qualitative Health Research, 24*(6). doi:10.1177/1049732314529664

Sideras, K., & Loprinzi, C. L. (2010). Nonhormonal management of hot flashes for women on risk reduction therapy. *Journal of the National Comprehensive Cancer Network, 8*(10), 1171–1179.

Vilar-González, S., Pérez-Rozos, A., & Cabanillas-Farpón, R. (2011). Mechanism of hot flashes. *Clinical & Translational Oncology: Official Publication of the Federation of Spanish Oncology Societies and of the National Cancer Institute of Mexico, 13*(3), 143–147. doi:10.1007/s12094-011-0633-x

Ziv-Gal, A., & Flaws, J. A. (2010). Factors that may influence the experience of hot flashes by healthy middle-aged women. *Journal of Women's Health (2002), 19*(10), 1905–1914. doi:10.1089/jwh.2009.1852

Morgellons Disease

Ashley Gartner

Morgellons disease is a mysterious, poorly understood condition characterized by nonhealing skin lesions, fibrous growths protruding from the skin, and subcutaneous stinging sensations. These dermatological symptoms are frequently accompanied by mood fluctuations, sleep disturbance, fatigue, joint pain, and hair and weight loss. Additionally, some individuals with these symptoms also report cognitive decline, often described as "brain fog" (Savely, Leitao, & Stricker, 2006). Because the biological and physiological bases of these symptoms are poorly understood, the condition is somewhat controversial. Some physicians view symptoms associated with Morgellons disease as stemming from delusions or hypochondriasis, rather than from an actual medical condition. Although the Centers for Disease Control and Prevention (CDC) briefly recognized Morgellons disease, they later recanted, and there is currently no widely accepted method of diagnosing this condition.

The Morgellons Research Foundation (www.morgellons.org) claims to have registered over 12,000 families who profess to have been affected by these symptoms. In 2006, the CDC began funding an epidemiological investigation in order to rule out an environmental toxin or new strain of infection as the source of these symptoms (Paquette, 2007). That investigation revealed no clear infectious cause or environmental link (Pearson et al., 2012). A subsequent study found that filament formation associated with Morgellons disease may be related to abnormal keratin and collagen expression, and that spirochetal infection may be a factor in Morgellons disease symptoms (Middelveen et al., 2013).

RESEARCH: HYPNOSIS FOR MORGELLONS DISEASE

To date, little research has been conducted regarding hypnosis as a possible treatment for Morgellons disease. However, a case study involving a woman reporting symptoms of Morgellons disease found significant reduction in physical and mood symptoms following treatment with hypnosis. In the aforementioned case study, based upon self-report of symptom severity, the patient reported a 75% decrease in anxiety from pretreatment to posttreatment. Additionally, the patient reported a significant decrease in skin infections and lesions, feelings of being "bitten," skin pain, joint pain, fatigue, and "brain fog." The reduction in symptoms was maintained at a follow-up appointment conducted three months after the final hypnosis session. Furthermore, the patient reported additional reduction in brain fog, fatigue, joint pain, and skin pain between her final hypnotherapy session and her follow-up appointment, which is likely related to continued practice of self-hypnosis (Gartner, Dolan, Stanford, & Elkins, 2011).

In addition, previous studies have found hypnotherapy to be effective for patients suffering from various dermatological conditions, including eczema, atopic dermatitis (Stewart & Thomas, 1995), alopecia, rosacea, hyperhidrosis, verruca (Ewin, 1992; Noll, 1994; Spanos, Williams, & Gwynn, 1990), lichen planus, and urticaria (Fried & Hussain, 2008). Thus, hypnosis may be beneficial for the treatment of the physical and psychological symptoms associated with Morgellons disease.

CASE EXAMPLE

Ms. J. is a divorced, 42-year-old woman who complained of skin lesions and fibrous growths protruding from her skin, which she believed to be related to Morgellons disease. Ms. J. reported significant sharp pain, as well as burning, stinging, and itching sensations. She likened her discomfort to "being sandblasted" or "stabbed constantly." Ms. J. also reported frequent sadness as well as anxiety and worry that her symptoms would become increasingly debilitating. Further, she reported impaired memory and attention span.

Prior to presenting for hypnosis treatment, Ms. J. had been treated with mood stabilizers and antidepressant medications. She had discontinued use of those medications due to her perception that they had not benefitted her or resulted in any reduction in symptoms. Ms. J. presented in a somewhat defensive manner, frequently stating that she was not "making up" her symptoms. Like many individuals who present with such symptoms, she described frustration with previous treatment providers who had labeled her delusional and a hypochondriac. Physically, Ms. J. had numerous observable spots of discoloration on her skin. She was thin, and appeared frail and older than her actual age.

Through clinical interview, psychosis and hypochondriasis were ruled out. Prior to beginning the hypnosis treatment, Ms. J. completed a self-report questionnaire, rating the severity of her primary symptoms on a scale of 0 (not a problem) to 10 (severe problem). In addition, she rated her overall stress level, sleep quality, and mood, to assess the impact of her symptoms on her functioning and quality of life. The Stanford Hypnotic Susceptibility Scale—Form C was administered to assess Ms. J.'s susceptibility to hypnosis (Weitzenhoffer & Hilgard, 1962). She then participated in six sessions of hypnosis, occurring once per week for 1 hour. At each session, she completed the self-report questionnaire to track changes in her symptoms. Three months following her final hypnosis session, Ms. J. attended a follow-up session, where she again rated her symptoms. She was instructed to continue practicing self-hypnosis following her final in-person hypnosis session.

TRANSCRIPT

The following is an example of a transcript that may be used or adapted for use with patients reporting symptoms of Morgellons disease:

"As I count from the numbers 1 to 10, feeling more and more relaxed. 1—feeling the wave of relaxation starting at the top of your head. 2—feeling the wave of relaxation in your face. 3—feeling the relaxation now in your neck and shoulders. 4—the wave of relaxation moving down through your arms and fingers. 5—feeling the wave of relaxation in your upper back and lower back. 6—that wave of relaxation now in your chest. 7—the wave of relaxation moving down through your legs and feet. 8—release all the tension from every muscle in your body. 9—more and more relaxed. 10—completely relaxed, completely comfortable.

Finding that you are so relaxed, so comfortable, that you are no longer in this room. Instead, you are in the mountains. You can feel the crisp, cool mountain air gently blowing across your face and through your hair. Noticing that you are approaching a path as you walk toward the mountain. Perhaps you might like to walk along that mountain path. With each step, feeling more and more relaxed. Feeling more and more comfortable. Nothing else is as important now as how beautiful and enjoyable it is to be walking along this mountain path. Feeling completely relaxed; completely comfortable. Finding that any skin discomfort is so slight, so minimal, that you can just push it to the back of your mind. It doesn't even bother you. And as you continue along this mountain path, feeling more and more relaxed, more and more comfortable. Noticing that any skin irritation or discomfort becomes less and less severe. You are less and less bothered by your skin as time passes. As you continue along the mountain path, hearing the gentle rustling of the mountain air as it gently blows through the trees and across the lake. Feeling a sense of well-being. You are not bothered by any excessive sadness or anxiety. Feeling more and more at peace every day, no matter if times becomes stressful or difficult. Imagining a time in the future when you are no longer bothered by any skin irritation or discomfort. Imagining how well you are able to feel. Allowing the comfort and relaxation to become more and more complete."

In addition to the weekly hypnosis sessions with the clinician, the clinician may wish to provide the patient with a recording or transcript of a hypnosis session. This allows patients to practice self-hypnosis between sessions or after completing the hypnosis treatment.

CONCLUSION

Currently, there are no established treatments for Morgellons disease. Its physiological and biological bases are not completely known. It is possible that such patients may have symptoms related to somatization as well as a disease process. Thus, clinicians may wish to ensure a complete diagnostic evaluation is completed. Hypnotherapy is a promising treatment for symptoms associated with Morgellons disease. While research on hypnosis for treating Morgellons disease is limited, hypnosis has been reported to reduce comorbid symptoms of depression and anxiety, as well as to improve sleep and reduce stress, and may provide some relief for patients with symptoms of Morgellons disease.

REFERENCES

Ewin, D. M. (1992). Hypnotherapy for warts (verruca vulgaris): 41 consecutive cases with 33 cures. *American Journal of Clinical Hypnosis, 35*(1). 1–10. doi:10.1080 /00029157.1992.10402977

Fried, R. G., & Hussain, S. H. (2008). Nonpharmacologic management of common skin and psychocutaneous disorders. *Dermatologic Therapy, 21*(1), 60–68. doi:10.1111/j.1529-8019.2008.00171.x

Gartner, A. M., Dolan, S. L., Stanford, M. S., & Elkins, G. R. (2011). Hypnosis in the treatment of Morgellons disease: A case study. *International Journal of Clinical and Experimental Hypnosis, 59*(2), 242–249. doi:10.1 080/00207144.2011.546263

Middelveen, M. J., Burugu, D., Poruri, A., Burke, J., Mayne, P. J., Sapi, E., . . . Stricker, R. B. (2013). *Association of spirochetal infection with Morgellons disease*. Retrieved from http://www. ncbi.nlm.nih.gov/pubmed/24715950; doi:10.12688/ f1000research.2-25.v1

Noll, R. B. (1994). Hypnotherapy for warts in children and adolescents. *Journal of Developmental & Behavioral Pediatrics, 15*(3), 170–173. doi:10.1097/00004703-199406000-00003

Paquette, M. (2007). Morgellons: Disease or delusions? *Perspectives in Psychiatric Care, 43*(2), 67–68. doi:10.1111/j.1744-6163.2007.00113.x

Pearson, M. L., Selby, J. V., Katz, K. A., Cantrell, V., Braden, C. R., Parise, M. E., . . . Eberhard, M. L. (2012). Clinical, epidemiologic, histopathologic and molecular features of an unexplained dermopathy. *PLoS One, 7*(1), e29908. doi:10.1371/journal. pone.0029908

Savely, V. R., Leitao, M. M., & Stricker, R. B. (2006). The mystery of Morgellons disease: Infection or delusion? *American Journal of Clinical Dermatology, 7*(1), 1–5.

Spanos, N. P., Williams, V., & Gwynn, M. I. (1990). Effects of hypnotic, placebo, and salicylic acid treatments on wart regression. *Psychosomatic Medicine, 52*(1), 109–114.

Stewart, A. C., & Thomas, S. E. (1995). Hypnotherapy as a treatment for atopic dermatitis in adults and children. *British Journal of Dermatology, 132*(5), 778–783.

Weitzenhoffer, A. M., & Hilgard, E. R. (1962). *Stanford Hypnotic Susceptibility Scale, Form C*. Palo Alto, CA: Consulting Psychologists Press.

Nail Biting

Daniel P. Kohen

Nail biting (fancy name onychophagia) is a common oral habit in children, adolescents, and young adults, and less so in older adults (Ghanizadeh & Shekoohi, 2011; Leung & Robson, 1990).

Nail biting is commonly understood to be the most common habit in the general population, being present overall in 10% of the (adult) population (Infante, 1976; Malone & Massler, 1952; Pennington, 1945) and more prevalent in children and youth. Indeed, the presence in 10% of the population begs the question as to whether or not it should be considered "abnormal" or part of the range of normal habit behaviors. This philosophical or nomenclature question is not addressed in this discussion.

EVIDENCE

Some estimate that as many as one third of children aged 7 to 10 years and 45% of adolescents experience nail biting (Leung & Robson, 1990). A recent study from Iran (Ghanizadeh & Shekoohi, 2011) reported that 24.4% of boys and 20% of girls noted nail biting in a survey of 743 primary school children. Hegde and Xavier (2009) noted that nearly 20% of school children between 4 and 15 years had adverse oral habits of which nail biting was the most prevalent.

Like many habit behaviors, the vast majority of people who bite their nails do not seek assistance/treatment for this problem; even with children in whom it is more common, only a small percentage are brought for "help" by their parent or other caregiver. Professionals who are asked to help in management/elimination of these habit problems often include pediatricians, family physicians, internists, dentists, or therapists of various kinds including psychologists, social workers, or marital and family therapists. Sometimes, children/teens are brought for consultation because they personally desire assistance in eliminating the habit; more often, their parents seek consultation/assistance because they have developed adverse consequences, such as frequent bleeding of nails/cuticles and/or infection (paronychia), and/or because other family members find the habit to be "annoying" or "disturbing" to observe, and/or because they recognize the habit as a symptom/consequence of stress or anxiety and the habit is a "ticket" of admission to treatment of a more important underlying condition, such as anxiety and/or adjustment problems or challenges.

The role of anxiety and stress has been well documented for decades (Leung & Robson, 1990; Moritz, Treszl, & Rufer, 2011), and most authors (Leung & Robson, 1990; Moritz, Treszl, & Rufer, 2011) consistently recommend that therapeutic approaches should be directed not only to the habitual response behavior of nail biting, but also concurrently to the precipitating cause(s) of stress.

A variety of approaches—behavioral, pharmacological, and combinations thereof—have been utilized to treat nail biting with varying degrees of success. Most recently, the nutraceutical N-acetyl cysteine (NAC) has been touted to be potentially effective for habit problems such as nail biting and trichotillomania, in theory at least in part because of antioxidant properties that may impact on mood and mediate the impulsivity associated with the target habit behavior. A report by Berk et al. (2009) describes the potential promising role of this agent. Leonard et al. (1991) reported on a double blind comparison of clomipramine and desipramine in the pharmacological approach to severe nail biting. A specific pharmacological agent with a predictable and high degree of success in eliminating nail biting has yet to be identified.

Of the behavioral approaches described, aversive taste treatment has been described repeatedly (Allen, 1996; Friman, Barone, & Christophersen,

1986) but has always seemed to this author to be inappropriate and not ethically acceptable, particularly as regards the treatment of children and youth with this problem. Various other behavioral treatments have focused upon habit reversal therapy (Azrin & Nunn, 1973; Miltenberger, Fuqua, & Woods, 1998) and related behavior modification (Moritz, Treszl, & Rufer, 2011) with varying degrees of success. We have long thought that the training and process of habit reversal has elements which are similar, if not identical, to hypnotic/hypnotherapeutic approaches, but as time and space do not permit a theoretical investigation of this, we leave further distinctions and similarities to the discretion of the discerning reader.

Most authors also agree that treatment should include behavior modification strategies, ongoing follow-up and reinforcement, and appropriate care of the nails; and that reminders by others (parents, friends, spouses) should, whenever possible, be avoided (Kohen, 1996; Kohen & Olness, 2011), or only used with the prior agreement and consent of the child (or spouse) who agrees and prefers reminders regarding the behavioral modification.

One might legitimately ask what is the "So what?" about this behavior before launching into a treatment program. Identifying the "So what?" comes from the elements of good rapport and a comprehensive history that defines the patient's reasons for seeking help, and what the patient hopes, believes, and seeks to be different in his or her life *when* (not "if") the nail biting is no longer happening. Answers to these questions usually help the thoughtful clinician to answer the accompanying "Now what?" question, and to design an approach that will be a "good fit" with the presenting client/patient.

Hypnosis per se for nail biting and/or related habit problems has been described in clinical reports, but in no comprehensive study that we were able to identify. A study of hypnobehavioral treatment involving multiple baseline analyes was reported by Bornstein et al. (1980), and de Luca and Holborn (1984) compared relaxation training and competing response training toward the elimination of hair pulling and nail biting. In 1991, 1996, and 2011, we published detailed case reports and descriptions of the application of hypnosis to habit problems (Kohen, 1991), to trichotillomania (Kohen, 1996), and more generally (Kohen & Olness, 2011). Clinical experience teaches that hypnosis—and, more precisely, training in

self-hypnosis—when used appropriately by experienced clinicians, is a safe, easy, and very effective treatment to eliminate the habit of nail biting. An example follows.

CASE EXAMPLE

K. was 16 when referred by his pediatrician for help with "test anxiety" and his nail biting habit disorder.

The first portion of the patient's initial 75-minute visit focused on rapport development and learning details of the problem of test anxiety, which was K.'s focus. In fact, he did not even mention the fingernail biting at all. Beyond coming to know him and his likes and dislikes, strengths, and concerns, I clarified with K. my orientation to focus on feelings, to think carefully about what we say and how we say it.

I asked K. by way of continuing the present illness history, "What have you done so far to help yourself with this problem?" He said, "At least I study a lot and I know I've gone over the material so that when I go into a test I'm very confident." Having set the tone for focus on language, I asked him, "Is that confident with a C or a small 'c'?" and he said clearly "Capital 'C,' VERY confident." I asked K. how his body acts when he gets "nervous," which is his word of choice rather than "anxiety," "worry," or some other word. His first response was to say, "I don't know," but I didn't accept that response and asked him to just think about it. Shortly thereafter he said "My hands shake" and he reluctantly showed me a fine tremor of his hands when I asked him to "Please show me." He said that it continues until the end of the test even though he may be getting easy questions and doing fine, and that he considered the shaking a lot when I offered him a choice of "a little, in between, or a lot." I asked him specifically if there was any change in his heartbeat, his breathing, or any other part of his body, and he said there was not. I asked him explicitly, "What do you do to stop the shaking?" In reply, he said "I can't, I try." This led me to talking about language and most specifically I told him:

How we speak is how we think.
How we think is how we feel.
How we feel is how we act.

And then I explained, "Therefore, if we want to change an action or behavior, it doesn't work to say 'Don't do that' and it doesn't work to tell somebody to feel differently, like 'Don't worry!' because they are *already* worried!" I asked him and his mom to "please do an experiment" and invited them to close their eyes and then said, "Whatever you do, don't think of a pink elephant." They opened their eyes and Mom laughed and said she thought of a pink elephant and K. also said he thought of a pink elephant, even though I had explicitly said "Don't." We then did a different experiment, asking K. to tell me the color of three successive things that I pointed to, each of which was white, and then asked him, "What do cows drink?" Predictably, he answered promptly, "Milk," which he then corrected by saying, "No, the correct answer is water." They both laughed and I spoke for a few moments about conditioning responses and how conditioned all humans are and how easy it is to fall into a habitual response even without thinking about it. I purposely did NOT speak of the natural connection of this habituated response to his habituated response of hands shaking or feeling test anxiety that starts and then seems to continue throughout the remainder of the test even when there is no further stimulus of a negative question or not knowing an answer.

At the end of the visit I told K. and his mother that I was 100% certain that I could be of help to him helping himself with this problem. Almost in a "Columbo-like fashion" with her "hand on the doorknob," Mom brought up the observation that "he's a nail biter, besides his anxiety he [also] has a problem for a long time of biting his fingernails." In the few minutes left, an examination showed that no fingernails were chewed down, no cuticles were torn or bleeding, and there were no scabs, or jagged nails. I told him and his mother that as someone who bites his nails *sometimes,* he is part of 10% of the U.S. population (universalizing the problem). Clarifying that people are *not* their problem, I suggested he is a person who has a nail biting problem *sometimes* and is <u>not</u> a "nail biter." [I explained that I don't believe in "ic" or "er" words as people are not their problem or their disorder and therefore I am "against" use of words like nail bit*er*, bedwett*er*, leukem*ic*, epilept*ic*, and diabet*ic*.]

At the second visit when I asked what he had thought about our first visit, he said, "Well, I guess that it's in my head. . . that's what I kind of realized," referring to his anticipation of his anxiety-causing tremor/shaking of his hands.

I told him a story of an 18-year-old tall young man with a tall mother who had been referred to me for help with thumb sucking. I told K. how I had asked the patient (whom I called Bob in the story) to "show me in slow motion please HOW you suck your thumb." The purpose of the story-telling was both to model a not very distant metaphorical story, a self-hypnotic way of managing the problem and solving it, as well as to offer hope in the process. K. was rightfully shocked and annoyed to hear the rest of the story, that is, of how Bob's mother forcefully knocked the thumb out of 18-year-old Bob's mouth before the thumb could make it all the way to the mouth.

Seeming to change the subject, I asked K. to do an *experiment.* I gave him a pen and a pad of paper and asked him to sign his name. Curiously, he said "I do not have a signature" and he proceeded to print his name! I proceeded with the "experiment" and after he had printed his name I asked him to close his eyes and print his name again. Though one could tell the difference upon looking at them (even though the two printed "signatures" were pretty close), I thought it was quite good and would have in any case still asked him "HOW did you DO that?" Unwittingly providing the ideas and solutions to his problem, he surprised me with his answer: "Muscle memory." He said he was familiar with muscle memory from coaching by a guitar teacher and from being successful in his sport of trap-shooting. He agreed that he had good muscle memory.

Shifting again, I began talking about the nail biting habit disorder that he says he does "when I have nothing else to do" and was able to relate this to the thumb sucking described previously as something "that seems to be automatic."

Having demonstrated to him the slow-motion technique with Bob's thumb sucking, I asked him to do the following "experiment":

"Please show me *in slow motion* exactly how you used to usually bite your nails."

He began to move his hand quickly to his mouth. I stopped him.

"Oh, sorry, much too fast, *please do it in slow motion so I can really see and understand. . . .*"

He began to do it a bit more slowly but I stopped him again (pattern interruption continues).

"That's much better, now about *twice as slow* (= a funny way of speaking but clearly understood by the unconscious mind)."

He began to move very slowly.

When his hand was about three-quarters of the way from lap to mouth, I abruptly said,

"Okay, STOP, leave your hand right there [= levitated, cataleptic] *. . . great . . . let your eyes close* [not "Close your eyes"]. *Great. NOW, in your mind's imagination picture a STOP SIGN as though you were looking at one out the window, or you were walking and came to one at a corner. . . .* [He smiled, and nodded.]

Let the STOP SIGN grow until it fills the screen in your mind . . . notice what color and shape it is, what color the letters are . . . I am going to touch your right (other) hand now. . . . [I took his right hand and placed it on top of his left hand and gently pushed the left hand down back onto his lap, saying] *These hands have known each other all their lives and know how to help each other create a new pattern of behavior to replace the old pattern that is of no value anyway."*

I asked him to then do the same thing AGAIN, and he let his left hand "float" slowly up toward his mouth, on his own, then STOPPED it, closed his eyes, and his right hand went over to the left and gently pushed it back to his lap.

I commented simply "Great! Now do the opposite" and he knew implicitly to let the opposite (= right) hand float up, stop, and have the left hand reach over to help the right go back down to the lap, without either hand ever getting to the mouth to chew/bite the fingernails.

I congratulated him on the effectiveness of this and suggested to him quite directly that changing any habit or pattern requires practice and "everyone knows that the more you do it the better you get."

I suggested, therefore, that it might be very helpful to him to practice doing this for two minutes before going to bed every night, for a minute or two before starting his day in the morning, and to be surprised how quickly the pattern changes and the problem starts to disappear.

Relying upon his own history and knowledge of muscle memory, I also noted how much "new memory" there NOW was of the hands knowing how to help each other.

There was never any discussion of "hypnosis."

At the third visit I asked K. what he had thought about and done following the previous (and first

private) visit a month earlier. He told me that he thought at first that it was odd but that after a while he thought that it made sense and he said that he had practiced it about four to five times since we last met (about once a week). I purposely did not talk at all about or ask to see his fingernails, or whether he had noticed any difference, or if anybody else had commented about it.

At the end of the visit I offered the "waking suggestion" that it might be appropriate for him to practice his hands helping hands experience a bit more often, noting that "changing patterns requires creating new patterns and it's probably worth five minutes of your time before going to sleep, you know, to train the muscle memory." I briefly told him as a truism that "obviously the ultimate goal is to train those hands to know automatically to STOP at the first urge to lift toward the mouth rather than having to each time have the hand come all the way up almost to the mouth and have the other hand reach over and move it down to the lap." He nodded.

At the fourth visit a month later, K. proudly showed me his nails were good and remained "unbitten." He was delighted when I asked permission to take a photo of his fingernails. I told him in waking hypnotic suggestion that *"of course once you have undone a prior pattern* [nail-biting] *and replaced it with a new pattern* [of keeping fingers away from his mouth], *it's very easy for the new pattern to just continue without thinking about it."* At follow-up months later, K. proudly displayed his continuing pattern of healthy fingernails.

CONCLUSION

As illustrated in the case example, essential to the success of a hypnotic approach to nail biting is, as with all patients, first and foremost, the development of a positive rapport. The client/patient must come to believe early in their therapeutic relationship that the clinician is experienced and confident that he or she can be of substantial help in alleviating and eliminating this problem. As rapport is developed in the context of learning and understanding the history of the nail biting habit, the clinician must discern any readily identifiable precipitating causes or triggers for the emergence of the habit, as well as any comorbid features that may require concurrent and/or separate therapeutic work. In this patient, K. identified "test anxiety" as *his* primary concern, whereas his mother was equally concerned about his nail biting. K. chose to work on the test anxiety first and did so quickly and easily by identifying the mind–body connection, that is, his success in managing anxiety and body responses in other situations, such as playing trumpet or guitar, and as a competitive trap-shooter. He was able to almost simultaneously then utilize this awareness and success to apply it to changing and then eliminating his fingernail biting habit pattern.

As we and others have described (Kohen, 1991, 1996; Kohen & Olness, 2011), this "hands helping hands" is one variation of perhaps limitless ways of helping patients find and decide to repeatedly rehearse a new and preferred pattern to replace the undesired pattern of biting their fingernails.

REFERENCES

Allen, K. W. (1996). Chronic nailbiting: A controlled comparison of competing response and mild aversion treatments. *Behavior Response Therapy*, 34(3), 269–272.

Azrin, N. H., & Nunn, R. G. (1973). Habit reversal: A method of eliminating nervous habits and tics. *Behavior Research and Therapy*, 11, 619–628.

Berk, M., Jeavons, S., Dean, O. M., Dodd, S., Moss, K., Gama, C. S., & Malhi, G. S. (2009). Nail-biting stuff? The effect of N-acetyl cysteine on nail-biting. *CNS Spectrums*, 14(7), 357–360.

Bornstein, P. H., Rychtarik, R. G., Mcfall, M. E., Winegardner, J., Winnett, R. L., & Paris, D. A. (1980). Hypnobehavioral treatment of chronic nailbiting: A multiple baseline analysis. *International Journal of Clinical and Experimental Hypnosis*, 28(3), 208–217.

de Luca, R. V., & Holborn, S. W. (1984). A comparison of relaxation training and competing response training to eliminate hair pulling and nail biting. *Journal of Behavioral Therapy and Experimental Psychiatry*, 15(1), 67–70.

Friman, P. C., Barone, V. J., & Christophersen, E. R. (1986). Aversive taste treatment of finger and thumb sucking. *Pediatrics*, 78(1), 174–176.

Ghanizadeh, A., & Shekoohi, H. (2011). Prevalence of nail biting and its association with mental health in a community sample of children. *BMC Research Notes*, 11(4), 116.

Hegde, A., & Xavier, A. (2009). Childhood habits: Ignorance is not bliss–A prevalence study. *International Journal of Clinical Pediatric Dentistry*, 2(1), 26–29. doi:10.5005/jp-journals-10005-1037

Infante, P. F. (1976). An epidemiologic study of finger habits in preschool children, as related to malocclusion, socioeconomic status, race, sex, and size of community. *ASDC Journal of Dentistry*, 43, 33–38.

Kohen, D. P. (1991). Applications of relaxation and mental imagery (self-hypnosis) for habit problems. *Pediatric Annals*, 20(3), 136–144.

Kohen, D. P. (1996). Management of trichotillomania with relaxation/mental imagery (self-hypnosis): Experience with five children. *Journal of Developmental and Behavioral Pediatrics*, 15(5), 328–334.

Kohen, D. P., & Olness, K. (2011). *Hypnosis and hypnotherapy with children*. New York, NY: Routledge–Taylor and Francis Group.

Leonard, H. L., Lenane, M. C., Swedo, S. E., Rettew, D. C., & Rapoport, J. L. (1991). A double-blind comparison of clomipramine and desipramine treatment of severe onychophagia (nail biting). *Archives of General Psychiatry*, 48(9), 821–827.

Leung, A. K., & Robson, L. M. (1990). Nailbiting. *Clinical Pediatrics*, 12(12), 690–692.

Malone, A. J., & Massler, M. (1952). Index of nailbiting in children. *Journal of Abnormal and Social Psychology*, 47, 193–202.

Miltenberger, R. G., Fuqua, R. W., & Woods, D. W. (1998). Applying behavior analysis to clinical problems: Review and analysis of habit reversal. *Journal of Applied Behavior Analysis*, 31(3), 447–469. doi:10.1901/jaba.1998.31-447

Moritz, S., Treszl, A., & Rufer, M. (2011). A randomized controlled trial of a novel self-help technique for impulse control disorders: A study on nail-biting. *Behavior Modification*, 35(5), 468–485. doi:10.1177/0145445511409395

Pennington, L. A. (1945). The incidence of nail-biting among adults. *American Journal of Psychiatry*, 102(2), 241–244.

Peterson, A. L., Campise, R. L., & Azrin, N. H. (1994). Behavioral and pharmacological treatments for tic and habit disorders: A review. *Journal of Developmental and Behavioral Pediatrics*, 15(6), 430–441.

Reaney, J. B. (1984). *Hypnosis in the treatment of habit disorders*. In W. Wester, & A. Smith (Eds.), *Clinical hypnosis: A multidisciplinary approach* (pp. 305–324). Philadelphia, PA: Lippincott Williams & Wilkins.

Tanaka, O. M., Viral, R. W., Tanaka, G. Y., Guerrero, A. P., & Camargo, E. S. (2008). Nailbiting, or onychophagia: A special habit. *American Journal of Orthodontic Dentofacial Orthopedics*, 134(2), 305–308.

Zawoyski, A. M., Bosch, A., Vollmer, T. R., & Walker, S. F. (2014). Evaluating the effects of matched and unmatched stimuli on nail biting in typically developing children. *Behavioral Modification*, 38(3), 428–447.

Nausea Associated With Chemotherapy

Alexander A. Levitan

Major advances have been made in preventing chemotherapy-induced nausea and vomiting (CINV) in patients receiving chemotherapy. Nevertheless, it does occur in those patients receiving highly emetogenic therapy, such as cisplatin and dacarbazine. Certain factors predispose patients to CINV. These include age under 50 years and the female gender (Acupuncture, 2014; Roscoe, Morrow, Aapro, Molassiotis, & Olver, 2011). A variety of highly effective antinausea medications are currently available and customarily employed. In addition, hypnosis and similar complementary therapies have also been shown to be of significant benefit in this regard.

Acute nausea and vomiting (N&V) can develop within a few hours of receiving chemotherapy. Delayed N&V may occur more than 24 hours after chemotherapy. Breakthrough vomiting may also occur despite use of antinausea medication. Anticipatory N&V occurs as a consequence of learned conditioning from previous chemotherapy experiences (Acupuncture, 2014; Akechi et al., 2010; Dupuis et al., 2014; Kamen et al., 2014).

Certain chemotherapy drugs, such as cisplatin and dacarbazine, given without antinausea medications, have a 90% chance of causing N&V. Other chemotherapy drugs, such as vinblastine, have less than a 10% incidence of N&V even without the concomitant use of antinausea medications (Hesketh et al., 1997; Hurley, Trezona, & Pexzalska, 2005).

Highly effective antinausea medications, such as ondansetron, olanzapine, and granisetron, called 5HT3 antagonists, and aprepitant, called substance P antagonists, often completely prevent CINV. They act upon the brain centers that respond to chemotherapy agents introduced into the body (Aapro, Jordan, & Feyer, 2013; Molassiotis, Brearley, & Stamataki, 2011; Mustian et al., 2011; Richardson et al., 2007). The specific mechanism by which chemotherapeutic drugs cause N&V relates to the effect of both serotonin and dopamine on receptors located in the chemoreceptor trigger zone of the postrema of the medulla oblongata. This area of the brain is outside of the blood–brain barrier and thus is immediately responsive to chemical changes in the blood and may have benefited our ancestors by causing immediate vomiting after the ingestion of toxic substances. Other mechanisms associated with nausea in conjunction with chemotherapy include psychological factors as well as activation of substance P and neurokin-1 receptors, which are present throughout the central and peripheral nervous systems. It is common to use a combination of drugs which block both acute and delayed CINV by acting at different stages of the biological responses.

Hypnosis, acupuncture, and mindfulness-based therapy have all been shown to be of significant benefit to patients undergoing chemotherapy, whether or not antinausea medication is simultaneously employed (Acupuncture, 2014; Ezzo et al., 2006; Jacknow, Tschann, Link, & Boyce, 1994; Néron & Stephenson, 2007; Zainal, Booth, & Huppert, 2013). The expectation of the patient prior to receiving therapy is of major importance in the eventual outcome of all oncologic therapy, and, in particular, the side effects caused by the therapy. The initial psychological impact begins as early as the first discussion of obtaining consultation from an oncologist. If the topic is raised in a positive and enthusiastic fashion, the patient's expectations are likely to be much more favorable than if a neutral or even negative phraseology is used. A typical positive suggestion might be: "I'm going to refer you to a specialist colleague of mine who has had great success in treating and assisting in the cure of many patients with your type of cancer." This is as opposed to a referral preceded by a comment such as: "I don't think there's much we can do, but perhaps, to be sure, you should see a local oncologist."

In a similar fashion, even something as trivial as calling for an appointment can have a great impact on the patient, depending upon the response received. If the receptionist scheduling the appointment confirms that the doctor has had good success with many other patients having an identical problem, this will be of benefit to the patient even before he or she presents at the oncologist's office for consultation. It is also useful to arrange the patient's appointment such that he or she is bracketed by other patients with the same condition and who have had successful outcomes, because patients frequently discuss their illnesses while sitting in the waiting room.

Misconceptions in regard to chemotherapy should also be discussed and dispelled. Some patients believe that if they do not experience N&V with their chemotherapy, it is not being effective. The truth of the matter is that, with modern antinausea medications used skillfully in combination, most patients rarely experience vomiting and few even experience nausea.

Teaching patients to control their bodies in various fashions is extremely useful. This can begin with teaching the patient glove anesthesia for use with blood drawing and intravenous medication administration. Many patients find that after having mastered this skill, it is easy for them to extrapolate to the control of other body sensations, such as nausea. In this fashion, the locus of control is returned to the patient and he or she need not be at the mercy of bewildering circumstances.

It is important that the patient be kept informed about all aspects of the treatment, including the scientific basis for the selected regimen. Many patients fear the unknown but can effectively deal with circumstances once they have the knowledge to do so. In this regard, it is critical to be absolutely honest in dealing with patients with cancer and for all members of the therapeutic team to present accurate information to the patient. It is also important to acknowledge uncertainty, should it exist, in an honest and straightforward manner. It is often hard to tell a patient "I don't know," when indeed the information is unavailable. But this is always the best course of action.

It is helpful to anticipate problems before they occur and provide suggestions for their prevention. Among these are hypnotic suggestions to counter negative suggestions and remarks, to maintain normal appetite and bowel function, and to prevent anticipatory emesis. The latter phenomenon occurs in patients who have not had adequate control of N&V in association with previous chemotherapy administration or medical procedures (Roscoe et al., 2011). These patients describe the onset of nausea in anticipation of visiting the oncologist or the chemotherapy suite. This can be effectively prevented with hypnotherapy, particularly when posthypnotic suggestions of amnesia are given for all previous chemotherapy experiences.

As a consequence, the patient need have no memory of previous negative experiences of chemotherapy and thus would have none in the future. Similarly, suggestions can be given to neutralize the impact of any negative or ambiguous statements the patient might overhear and not understand negating the possibility of an adverse psychological impact.

It is beneficial for the clinicians to share their accumulated experience with the patient in the form of suggestions for avoiding or reducing complications of chemotherapy. Among these are the use of such things as mouthwashes and saliva replacements for sore throat and gum irritation following chemotherapy. Other suggestions include cooling caps, gloves, and foot covers to reduce hair loss, hand–foot syndrome, and nail damage from certain chemotherapeutic agents. In this regard, it is necessary for all personnel caring for the patient to understand the therapeutic program being proposed and any potential side effects that might occur. All of the previous suggestions will augment confidence in the therapeutic team and make suggestions relative to N&V even more effective.

RESEARCH

Many case studies and clinical examples have been written reporting the benefits of hypnosis in reducing nausea associated with chemotherapy. However, there have been a limited number of well-controlled clinical trials. Hurley et al. reported on 25 women receiving moderately emetogenic chemotherapy with self-hypnosis experiencing significantly less nausea than controls at a p level of .042 (Hurley et al., 2005). Zeltzer et al. reported on 20 children who were able to use fewer antinausea medications after being taught hypnosis at a p level of .04 to .02 (Zeltzer, LeBaron, & Zeltzer, 1984).

A recent review of research evidence covering the use of hypnosis for CINV also supports the benefits of this intervention (Richardson et al., 2007). Several recent papers confirm the use of hypnosis for the prevention and treatment of anticipatory N&V due to chemotherapy (Figueroa-Moseley et al., 2007; Kamen et al., 2014; Marchioro et al., 2000; Roscoe et al., 2011). Research also suggests that hypnosis can reduce pain and anxiety as well as nausea among breast cancer patients. This was demonstrated in an exceptionally well-conducted randomized clinical trial by Montgomery et al. who reported on 200 patients undergoing excisional breast biopsy or lumpectomy and found less need for anesthesia, less anxiety, and less nausea in patients using hypnosis versus a control group with a 95% confidence interval (Montgomery et al., 2007). Taken together, the existing research has consistently confirmed the benefit of hypnotherapy in management of cancer-related nausea. Studies have shown hypnosis for nausea to have few risks and that it can be provided to patients in as few as one or two individual sessions while in other cases more sessions of hypnotherapy may be required.

CASE EXAMPLE

R.G. is a 46-year-old female who recently began to experience hot flashes suggestive of menopause and who noted a left breast mass while showering. She consulted her family physician who confirmed a left upper outer quadrant nodule and arranged for a mammogram with needle biopsy if indicated. The patient underwent fine-needle biopsy which was positive for invasive ductal carcinoma. She then had sentinel lymph node mapping with resection of one positive node. She subsequently underwent a left mastectomy and was found to be estrogen-receptor positive, progesterone-receptor negative, and HER2 negative. The tumor was 1 mm in the greatest dimension, and thus she was determined to be a stage IIA, T1, M1, M0. She was started on a regimen of doxorubicin and cyclophosphamide intravenously every 14 days for four cycles, after which she was to receive paclitaxel intravenously every 14 days for an additional four cycles. Before the chemotherapy, the patient was given antinausea medications consisting of ondansetron, dexamethasone, and aprepitant. The latter two agents were continued orally from the second through the fourth day following her chemotherapy. She was also given a supply of prochlorperazine in both suppository and oral forms to be used should she have any breakthrough nausea or vomiting.

The patient presented for hypnotherapy because of anxiety concerning the treatment and its eventual outcome, as well as the onset of nausea when she contemplated the next cycle of chemotherapy, or when she was preparing to go to the doctor's office for her treatment. She was able to control some but not all of her symptoms with the medications she had been given for breakthrough nausea. She was also upset about the possibility of losing her hair and concerned that her husband would not be able to accept her in her present condition, despite the fact that he had been totally supportive during all phases of her evaluation and treatment.

Hypnotherapy techniques focusing on the patient's constellation of problems are illustrated in the following transcript.

TRANSCRIPT: HYPNOSIS FOR CANCER-RELATED NAUSEA

"Now that you're totally relaxed and perfectly comfortable, I invite you to go forward in time to the day before your next chemotherapy is due. See yourself taking a moment at least once an hour to allow your forefinger and thumb of one hand to come together like a magic switch allowing a sudden rush of comfort, peace and relaxation to flow down over your body, concentrating in exactly the location where it is most needed, almost like stepping under a magic waterfall, feeling that serenity washing down over your body, washing away all the tension, all the stress, all the worry; not only washing the outside of your body but cleansing every inner part of your body as well. Feel that fresh, clean feeling as you step out from under that

waterfall. Know that each time you practice relaxing it will be as if you were instantly transported to the same lovely place.

You may even find it interesting to note that on occasion, your finger and thumb will come together automatically, almost like a magic thermostat that detects your need for relaxation and comfort. See yourself pleasantly surprised at how good you feel. See your family members noticing the benefit you have achieved and admiring your accomplishment. Notice the way your husband looks at you. See the admiration, love, and respect in his eyes. He doesn't care about your missing breast. He cares about you and how important you are to him and the family. See yourself resting comfortably the night before your appointment. See yourself enjoying supper as well as a good night's rest, and breakfast the next morning. See yourself driving comfortably to the infusion center, knowing that all will go well today. See yourself forgetting to remember, or remembering to forget, any negative experiences from the past. In this way each treatment will be the first experience and you need have no memories or concerns about prior treatments. In a similar fashion, anything that is said to, or overheard by, you that is less than helpful will be as if it is spoken in a foreign language that you simply don't understand. If anything, it will make it easier and more comfortable for you to succeed.

See the chemotherapy nurse pleasantly surprised at how confident and comfortable you appear. See her asking you to turn off the pain switch to the hand or arm you've chosen. See her inserting the IV comfortably and easily. See her injecting the medication to prevent nausea and notice it flowing through your body precisely to where it is most needed and effective. See the color changing in that area from a pink to a tranquil blue. See the chemotherapy being administered easily and comfortably. See it, too, flowing exactly where it is needed and not bothering any other part of your body. See it seeking out and destroying any remaining cancer cells, no matter where they may be located. See them shrinking and disappearing. See the normal tissue replacing them completely. See yourself being disconnected from the IV and looking forward to comfortably going home and enjoying your next meal. See yourself pleasantly

surprised to discover that the time has passed so rapidly that the treatment is over almost before it begins. See yourself leaving the memory of each treatment completely behind each time as you drive home, almost like writing on a child's magic slate and lifting up the covering sheet, erasing everything that was written there. In a similar way, should you ever have any hint of queasiness you can allow your finger and thumb to come together and be instantly transported away to your favorite place of peace and comfort and contentment. Any negative feelings will disappear like the writing on the magic tablet, or like pressing the delete button on a magic keyboard. You may enjoy letting them be replaced by a special taste in your mouth, such as fresh mint or a flavor of your preference.

Perhaps you've had the experience of sitting in a sunlit room watching little particles of dust dancing in the sunlight as is streams in a nearby window. Those little particles are like the negative thoughts and feelings we all share. Notice what happens when a cloud drifts across the sun, blocking the rays and causing all those little particles to instantly disappear.

Perhaps you'd like to think about a lovely beach at sunset with a brilliant orange red sun slowly descending into a turquoise ocean. See the sun slowly disappearing on the horizon, taking its reflection with it. Notice the beautiful tranquility that results just after sunset when the water is completely still and glass-like, and sound seems to travel a great distance. Know that that feeling is available on an instant's notice any time you have need for it.

Remember the taste of your favorite ice cream or fruit. Taste it now and enjoy the rich, delightful flavor. Notice the pleasant anticipatory hunger as you look forward to your next bite. Take an emotional snapshot of that feeling; then, feel free to take it out and reexperience the sensation any time you need it. Feel free to take all negative feelings and put them in a sturdy container and close the lid securely. Take the container and place it high on the back of a shelf in a place you need never visit. Perhaps you'd prefer to leave it on the curb for the trash hauler to pick up and dispose.

You might enjoy thinking about the little person inside each of us who looks after our well-being. See that little person in a control room containing various switches and dials that are being adjusted to keep all parts of our body functioning optimally. See that little person knowing each time you practice relaxation; you are showing your concern and care for that person's well-being. See that little person reciprocating by keeping everything going smoothly. Similarly, see that little person taking a bucket of paint and a ladder and climbing down into your body to paint over and heal any area that needs care and attention. See the paint changing the color of the area from red to blue; feel the peace and contentment as the paint is being applied exactly where it is needed. It's nice to know that you're in charge and that you are in control.

Your mind can and should control your body. You can choose to find the switch that controls sensations in various parts of your body. Notice that each switch has a light over it, indicating whether it is off or on. If ever you should have a sensation that you don't wish to have, find the switch that controls that feeling and turn it off and allow the light over the switch to go out. Feel free to turn off all the unnecessary feelings and replace them with comfort and peace. Feel free to make my words those you most want and need to hear. Feel free to feel refreshed as if you've had a lovely long nap; feel every part of your body vibrant and alive, feel good in every possible way, and when you're ready to . . . come back."

CONCLUSION

Hypnosis is a well-established and highly valuable resource for patients undergoing chemotherapy. It diminishes unpleasant side effects and augments a sense of self-worth. The very fact that the therapist wants to help the patient indicates that the patient has value and is deemed worthy of receiving assistance.

Hypnosis prevents anticipatory nausea and reduces the need for antinausea medications and their side effects. Even when nausea and vomiting do occur, it reduces the physical and emotional effect of the experience. Patients have stated that when they did have vomiting, "it did not feel as if I was being turned inside out," as had been the case in the past.

It is often wise to block negative experiences before they occur. For this reason, suggestions of amnesia for previous chemotherapy experiences are given so that, never having had chemotherapy, the patient cannot have a negative anticipation of the next cycle. Similarly, learned aversions to certain foods caused by ingesting them following chemotherapy with resultant N&V can also be avoided or negated. Patients can also be prevented from being influenced by less-than-helpful comments expressed in their presence.

The treatment of cancer is a complicated enterprise deeply affecting the physical and mental status of the recipient. It is important that each member of the support team be fully informed about all aspects of the therapeutic undertaking so that the patient will have confidence in the team effort. If the mental health provider is unfamiliar with some aspects of the treatment, it is imperative that he or she contact appropriate members of the oncology team, such as the oncology nurse or physician, to be certain that they understand the planned course of action, and its potential side effects.

Physical and emotional contact via touch and sharing of the therapist's life experiences can reduce the patient's perception of being an unworthy or a damaged person. It is helpful to have family pictures on the therapist's desk to share with the patient. It is also useful to ask favors of patients in order to give them a sense of self-worth. A request for a recipe, a flower from the patient's garden, or a taste of a cookie baked by the patient all establish that the patient is of value to the therapist and worthy of the oncology team efforts.

Lastly, remember that one out of three of us will have cancer during our lifetime. Treat your patients as you would like to be treated—you might eventually be one yourself.

REFERENCES

Aapro, M., Jordan, K., & Feyer, P. (2013). Antiemetic prophylaxis of chemotherapy-induced nausea and vomiting: Prevention of nausea and vomiting in cancer patients. *Springer Healthcare*, 37–43. doi:10.1007/978-1-907673-58-0_6

Acupuncture (PDQ®)—National Cancer Institute. (2014). Retrieved from http://www.cancer.gov/cancertopics/pdq/cam/acupuncture/healthprofessional

Akechi, T., Okuyama, T., Endo, C., Sagawa, R., Uchida, M., Nakaguchi, T., . . . Furukawa, T. A. (2010). Anticipatory nausea among ambulatory cancer patients undergoing chemotherapy: Prevalence, associated factors, and impact on quality of life. *Cancer Science*, *101*(12), 2596–2600.

Dupuis, L. L., Robinson, P. D., Boodhan, S., Holdsworth, M., Portwine, C., Gibson, P., . . . Sung, L. (2014). Guideline for the prevention and treatment of anticipatory nausea and vomiting due to chemotherapy in pediatric cancer patients. *Pediatric Blood & Cancer*, *61*(8), 1506–1512.

Ezzo, J. M., Richardson, M. A., Vickers, A., Allen, C., Dibble, S. L., Issell, B. F., . . . Zhang, G. (2006). Acupuncture-point stimulation for chemotherapy-induced nausea or vomiting. *Cochrane Database of Systematic Reviews*, *2*(2). doi:10.1002/14651858.CD002285.pub2

Figueroa-Moseley, C., Jean-Pierre, P., Roscoe, J. A., Ryan, J. L., Kohli, S., Palesh, O. G., . . . Morrow, G. R. (2007). Behavioral interventions in treating anticipatory nausea and vomiting. *Journal of the National Comprehensive Cancer Network*, *5*(1), 44–50.

Hesketh, P. J., Kris, M. G., Grunberg, S. M., Beck, T., Hainsworth, J. D., Harker, G., . . . Lindley, C. M. (1997). Proposal for classifying the acute emetogenicity of cancer chemotherapy. *Journal of Clinical Oncology: Official Journal of the American Society of Clinical Oncology*, *15*(1), 103–109.

Hurley, R., Trezona, E., & Pexzalska, C. (2005). A randomized trial of self-hypnosis to contol nausea in women receiving moderately emetogenic chemotherapy. *Journal of Clinical Oncology: Official Journal of the American Society of Clinical Oncology*, *23*, 81–82.

Jacknow, D. S., Tschann, J. M., Link, M. P., & Boyce, W. T. (1994). Hypnosis in the prevention of chemotherapy-related nausea and vomiting in children: A prospective study. *Journal of Developmental and Behavioral Pediatrics*, *15*(4), 258–264.

Kamen, C., Tejani, M. A., Chandwani, K., Janelsins, M., Peoples, A. R., Roscoe, J. A., & Morrow, G. R. (2014). Anticipatory nausea and vomiting due to chemotherapy. *European Journal of Pharmacology*, *722*, 172–179. doi:10.1016/j.ejphar.2013.09.071

Marchioro, G., Azzarello, G., Viviani, F., Barbato, F., Pavanetto, M., Rosetti, F., . . . Vinante, O. (2000). Hypnosis in the treatment of anticipatory nausea and vomiting in patients receiving cancer chemotherapy. *Oncology*, *59*(2), 100–104. doi:10.1159/000012144

Molassiotis, A., Brearley, S. G., & Stamataki, Z. (2011). Use of antiemetics in the management of chemotherapy-related nausea and vomiting in current UK practice. *Supportive Care in Cancer: Official Journal of the Multinational Association of Supportive Care in Cancer*, *19*(7), 949–956. doi:10.1007/s00520-010-0909-7

Montgomery, G. H., Bovbjerg, D. H., Schnur, J. B., David, D., Goldfarb, A., Weltz, C. R., . . . Silverstein, J. H. (2007). A randomized clinical trial of a brief hypnosis intervention to control side effects in breast surgery patients. *Journal of the National Cancer Institute*, *99*(17), 1304–1312. doi:10.1093/jnci/djm106

Mustian, K. M., Devine, K., Ryan, J. L., Janelsins, M. C., Sprod, L. K., Peppone, L. J., . . . Morrow, G. R. (2011). Treatment of nausea and vomiting during chemotherapy. *US Oncology & Hematology*, *7*(2), 91–97.

Néron, S., & Stephenson, R. (2007). Effectiveness of hypnotherapy with cancer patients' trajectory: Emesis, acute pain, and analgesia and anxiolysis in procedures. *International Journal of Clinical and Experimental Hypnosis*, *55*(3), 336–354. doi:10.1080/00207140701338647

Richardson, J., Smith, J. E., Mccall, G., Richardson, A., Pilkington, K., & Kirsch, I. (2007). Hypnosis for nausea and vomiting in cancer chemotherapy: A systematic review of the research evidence. *European Journal of Cancer Care*, *16*(5), 402–412. doi:10.1111/j.1365-2354.2006.00736.x

Roscoe, J. A., Morrow, G. R., Aapro, M. S., Molassiotis, A., & Olver, I. (2011). Anticipatory nausea and vomiting. *Supportive Care in Cancer: Official Journal of the Multinational Association of Supportive Care in Cancer*, *19*(10), 1533–1538. doi:10.1007/s00520-010-0980-0

Zainal, N. Z., Booth, S., & Huppert, F. A. (2013). The efficacy of mindfulness-based stress reduction on mental health of breast cancer patients: A meta-analysis. *Psycho-Oncology*, *22*(7), 1457–1465. doi:10.1002/pon.3171

Zeltzer, L., LeBaron, S., & Zeltzer, P. M. (1984). The effectiveness of behavioral intervention for reduction of nausea and vomiting in children and adolescents receiving chemotherapy. *Journal of Clinical Oncology: Official Journal of the American Society of Clinical Oncology*, *2*(6), 683–690.

Pain Control—Acute and Procedural

Elvira Lang

Many classic hypnotic interventions can be guided leisurely in the privacy of the office. However, management of acute and procedural pain unfolds in view of others, under pressure of time, and is increasingly subject to patient evaluation with potential considerable financial consequences for the practice in which it is provided. Furthermore, patients in a medical setting may not only NOT expect the offer of hypnotic techniques, but also show skepticism and resistance that need to be quickly addressed. This chapter thus focuses on this unique setting.

In managing acute and procedural pain over the past 20 years, my team and I had the opportunity to test various approaches in rigorous clinical and research trials. Spurred on by suggestions (demands) of the funding agencies and journal editors, we came to adopt very structured approaches, worked with scripts, and standardized the training of those guiding patients in self-hypnotic relaxation. I also came to realize that there is no need (and no time) for classic hypnotherapy, extensive patient preparation, or even any preparation before entering the procedure suite, operating room, or dental suite. Everything has to happen fast and without disruption of the procedure workflow. While this may seem a challenge, the situation also offers the immense advantage that the patient is already in a state of trance by just being there. Thus, all that needs to be done is to find the "right" words. Establishing rapport and the considerate choice of verbiage comprises 80% to 90% of what is needed to help the patient toward a better experience; only 10% to 20% represent a more formal type of induction. After two decades of clinical and educational research, we were able to distill effective and teachable skills using a Comfort Talk® approach that any medical professional can become quite efficient in.

DYNAMICS AND CLINICAL MANAGEMENT OF THE ACUTE PAIN EXPERIENCE

Time plays an essential role in the experience of acute pain. During medical procedures, pain increases linearly over time under standard care conditions (Lang et al., 2000; Lang et al., 2006; Lang et al., 2008; Figure 36.1). This increase is relatively independent of the severity of stimuli applied, regardless of any sedatives and anesthetics given, as long as the patient is conscious (Lang, Tan, Amihai, & Jensen, 2014). An analysis of procedure data obtained during vascular and renal procedures even shows pain to correlate positively with the amount of drugs given (Figure 36.2)—leaving open the chicken/egg question of whether more pain resulted in more drug deliveries or whether greater reliance on drugs brought out a greater focus on pain. While these data were obtained with patients largely determining how many drugs they received in a patient-controlled analgesia model, the usage of drugs becomes even more complicated in the standard setting where nursing or other staff determine the amounts of sedatives and narcotics given. In a prior study, we found that drivers of staff-administered medication were initially fearful that the patient might be anxious, then that the patient displayed anxiety, then fear of pain, and only lastly overt pain

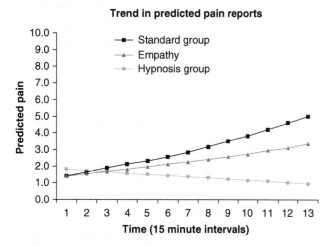

Trend in predicted pain reports

FIGURE 36.1 Increase in pain over time under standard care conditions. When patients are assisted by a provider displaying empathic attention (rapport skills, avoidance of negative suggestions, and matching of verbal and nonverbal preferences), the increase is less steep. When the self-hypnotic script is read at the onset of the case by a person who also displays empathic attention, there is no increase in pain perception over time. Analysis of data from Lang et al. (2000). Pain ratings on a scale of 0 = no pain at all to 10 = worst pain possible.

Source: Lang et al. (2014).

(Lang, Chen, Fick, & Berbaum, 1998). The problem with this type of prophylactic drug application is that much of the medication is given when not needed, resulting in respiratory depression. When the drugs are needed, the ability to give them may already have been maxed out.

Any hypnosis coach who accompanies a patient to a procedure or performs the procedure himself or herself has to expect a certain resistance to non-pharmaceutical approaches from personnel whose own approach is intimately linked to their perception of caring. On the other hand, one can see how decreasing the expression of anxiety in itself can already open the path to less unnecessary drugging of patients and leave options for more effective and safer medication schemes. The goal is not the entire elimination of drugs—and one should avoid feeling guilty for "having failed" when the patient requests medication. To take pressure off the patients of wanting to please the coach in settings where IV drugs are available, an attention bell can be provided that the patient can ring and receive medication; no questions asked as long as blood pressure and breathing are in a safe range.

The pain experience in general depends on a combination of type and severity of the stimulus, what it is interpreted to be, and its meaning to the individual. The relative independence of the increase in pain over time in the procedure suite suggests that stimulus severity is not the critical component of the equation but rather the way stimuli are interpreted in themselves and successively. In the context of ambiguity, the subconscious interprets stimuli in the most negative sense so that even innocuous stimuli may be interpreted as painful (Ewin & Eimer, 2006). Once one stimulus has been experienced as painful, all subsequent stimuli tend to also be interpreted as painful, regardless of whether they are or are not (Bayer, Coverdale, Chiang, & Bangs, 1998). The mind then continues on the upward trajectory of pain perception unless a reframing happens early on. The very good news is that even in very lengthy—hours-long—procedures, reframing at the onset in as short as one to three minutes suffices to interrupt these unhelpful dynamics (see also Figure 36.1). In our experience, reading from an appropriate self-hypnotic relaxation script by trained personnel at the onset of surgeries on awake patients reliably provides such reframing.

HYPNOTIC INTERVENTIONS FOR ACUTE PROCEDURAL PAIN

There is ample evidence over a wide range of procedures including dressing changes, dentistry, endoscopies, percutaneous invasive procedures, and open surgeries that hypnotic interventions work well for management of procedural pain (Elkins et al., 2006; Everett, Patterson, Burns, Montgomery, & Heimbach, 1993; Faymonville et al., 1995; Flory, Salazar, & Lang, 2007; Fredericks, 1978; Ginandes, Brooks, Sando, Jones, & Aker, 2003; Lang et al., 2006, 2008; Liossi & Hatira, 2003; Lucas, 1965; Macones, Tuuli, Houser, Nicholas, & Kurnit, 2008; Marc, Rainville, & Dodin, 2008; Meurisse et al., 1999; Montgomery et al., 2007; Montgomery, David, Winkel, Silverstein, & Bovbjerg, 2002; Richardson, Smith, McCall, & Pilkington, 2006; Roberts, 2006; Ruiz & Fernandez, 1960; Spiegel, 2007; Weinstein & Au, 1991; Wright & Drummond, 2000).

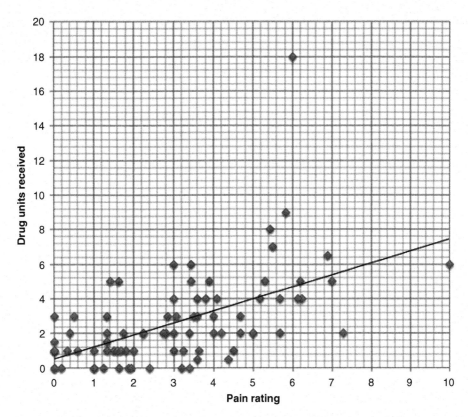

FIGURE 36.2 Amount of drugs received in relation to average pain ratings on a scale of 0 = no pain at all and 10 = worst pain possible. Midazolam and fentanyl given in combination with 1 drug unit corresponding to either 1 mg midazolam or 50 mcg fentanyl. Data from the standard care group of a vascular and renal intervention trial.

Source: Lang et al. (2000).

Based on a meta-analysis on hypnosis for surgery, Montgomery and colleagues concluded that on average 89% of patients benefited from adjunctive hypnosis compared with standard care (Montgomery et al., 2002). Positive effects of hypnosis were observed with regard to pain perception, amount of pain medication given, physiological indicators, complications, treatment time, recovery, and emotional well-being. Lang et al. and Montgomery et al. also documented significant cost savings (Lang & Rosen, 2002; Montgomery et al., 2007). Hypnotic techniques in the literature varied widely in terms of approach and time invested. Because of the intimate familiarity with the techniques validated in our own clinical trials, the following focuses on what worked best in our experience.

Because procedural pain increases linearly over time, it stands to reason that overall patient comfort improves when either the increase in pain is less steep and/or the procedure can be completed faster. Guidance in self-hypnotic relaxation can achieve both: a significant flattening of the pain-trend curve over time (Lang et al., 2014; Figure 36.1) as well as reduction in procedure time (Butler, Symons, Henderson, Shortliffe, & Spiegel, 2005; Lang et al., 2000; Montgomery et al., 2007). An explanation for the latter may lie in the effect of a relaxed patient on the treatment team. Behavior tends to be contagious (Neumann & Strack, 2000). Relaxing just one person in the operating room (in this case the patient) can mirror to the team to let go of their own stress, focus better on the task at hand, and thus complete faster—and with fewer complications.

When we first investigated the effects of hypnotic techniques, we used a model that would be applicable in regular clinical practice and not require extra patient preparation. As such, it was essential that the patient coach could quickly establish rapport, explain the concept of the ensuing intervention, and get started in a reproducible and teachable fashion. More extensive guidance can be found in print and online form (Lang, 2014a; Lang & Laser, 2009).

GETTING READY

Stepping into an often stress-laden procedure room as hypnosis coach takes guts. Staff will be busily going about their work and will not stop. A display of confidence is a must as in any other situation requiring team integration and cooperation of all involved (Moss Kanter, 2004). For anyone engaging in direct operating room work it is thus helpful to have privately anchored oneself in a prior self-hypnosis to a scenario of confidence with a self-signal that can be used to summon self-confidence whenever needed immediately [for examples see Chapter 1 (Lang & Laser, 2009) or Lang (2014)].

The hypnosis coach should always remember the following two key points—particularly when the patient does not enter a deep trance right away or appear in full bliss: (a) All one can (and should) do is help patients help themselves—the patient has to be willing to go on the journey with you. Although most patients are very motivated to be helped during a procedure, rejection of the hypnosis offer can in itself be a very powerful boost in a setting where the patient has few other options of exerting control. *Thus, refusal of the offer is not a failure, and research shows that even that improves outcomes.* (b) The clinical trials have shown that guidance in self-hypnotic relaxation significantly reduces pain and anxiety. This does not mean that every patient has zero pain and zero anxiety. It means that the patients will have less pain and less anxiety than they would have had without the intervention, typically in ways that they find acceptable and with the management of which they are more satisfied (Lang & Berbaum, 1997; Lang et al., 2013). Keeping that conviction in mind will be particularly helpful when a patient still expresses discomfort, and an unrealistic expectation of zero pain and zero anxiety would be counterproductive. Keeping one's confidence up is key—as it will eventually rub off on everyone present.

Establishing rapid rapport is essential and best achieved by initial matching of the patient's emotional state, leading to a more resourceful demeanor (Lang, 2012). Attention and matching of verbal and nonverbal preferences further helps [for more detail see Lang & Laser (2009)].

HYPNOSIS BY SCRIPT

There was debate as to whether a free-hand completely customized approach is more helpful in the procedure suite or whether a script can be successful. Our research in clinical trials alleviated these concerns, particularly once several safeguards and options were included. Reading a script removes concerns of "hocus-pocus" or mind control from the equation—reading is a familiar activity to most and not typically associated with nefarious intentions of the reader. The script has been used on thousands of patients, refined over the years, and rigorously tested in clinical trials and is now available in app form (Lang, 2014b). As noted, every word and sentence is important to avoid redundancy and to make the effort short—a few minutes at most. Then it suffices to just be quiet or say an occasional "hmm" or "that's right" unless the patient wishes to interact in conversation about his or her experience, or when announcement of pending stimuli may be integrated in terms of the patient's chosen imagery.

Note the important specifics included in the script: immunization against noise and unhelpful suggestions is essential. Having the patients use all the sounds and noises in the room to structure their own experience wins half the battle and that alone may produce a trance as opposed to the patients feeling bothered by clunking equipment or phones ringing. Suggesting to disregard unhelpful suggestions is also critical—they will occur and could otherwise derail a successful session. Health care professionals love to give negative suggestions that increase pain and anxiety (Lang et al., 2005), and on occasion the coach may inadvertently slip in some imagery that is not helpful for the patient and could otherwise result in an adverse reaction (e.g., suggesting a walk in a meadow for a patient who has pollen allergies).

The 1-2-3 eyeroll induction is used as it proved the simplest to apply in an area prone to interruptions. Should a patient return to his or her natural state of awareness because of interest in the case or because of being interrupted, the eyeroll is easy to reapply. In conjunction with a 3-2-1 reorientation, the combination gives patients an extra layer of control to reenter and leave the state of concentration whenever they may need to do so later on.

The patient is anchored early on in a place where he or she feels safe so that in case of an abreaction in response to ongoings in the operating room or sudden emergence of traumatic memories, one always has a safe haven to return to.

Once the patient is in a trance, often no specific pain management becomes necessary short of the prophylactic admonition to focus on heat or cold or a delicious sense of tingling (the same wording is also used, for example, when local anesthetic is applied rather than "a prick and a burn" or other negative suggestions that worsen the experience). The script also contains options for more advanced pain and anxiety management if necessary.

SCRIPT

"We want you to help us to help you to learn a concentration exercise to help you get through the procedure more comfortably. It can be a way to help your body be more comfortable through the procedure and also deal with any discomfort that may come up during the procedure. It is just a form of concentration, like getting so caught up in a movie or a good book that you forget you are watching a movie or reading a book.

Now you may be interested to learn how you can use your imagination to enter a state of focused attention and physical relaxation. If you hear sounds or noises in the room, just use these to deepen your experience. And use only the suggestions that are helpful for you. There are a lot of ways to relax, but here is one simple way:

On one, you can do one thing—look up.

On two, two things—slowly close your eyes and take a deep breath.

On three, three things—breathe out, relax your eyes, and let your body float.

Good. Just imagine your whole body floating, floating right through the table, with each breath deeper and easier. Right now imagine that you are floating somewhere safe and comfortable, in a bath, a lake, a hot tub, or just floating in space, with each breath deeper and easier. Just notice how with each breath you let a little more tension out of your body as you let your whole body float, safe and comfortable; each breath deeper and easier. Good, now with your eyes closed and remaining in this state of concentration, please describe for me how your body is feeling right now. Where do you imagine yourself being? What is it like? Can you smell the air? Can you see what is around you? Good. Now this is your safe and pleasant place to be and you can use it in a sense to play a trick on the doctors (or this whole procedure). Your body has to be here, but you don't. So just spend your time being somewhere you would rather be.

Now, if there is some discomfort, and there may be some with the procedure as they prepare you and insert the line, or as you feel the dye entering your body, there is no point in fighting it. You can admit it, but then transform that sensation. If you feel some discomfort, you might find it helpful to make that part of your body to feel warmer, as if you were in a bath. Or cooler—if that is more comfortable—as if you had ice or snow on that part of your body. This warmth and coolness becomes a protective filter between you and the pain.

If you have any discomfort right now, imagine that you are applying a hot pack or that you are putting snow or ice on it and see what it feels like. Develop the sense of warm or cool or delicious tingling numbness to filter the hurt out of the pain.

With each breath, breathe deeper and easier, your body is floating, filter the hurt out of the pain.

Now, again with your eyes closed and remaining in the state of concentration, describe what you are feeling right now."

(Option 1) If the patient is at his or her safe and comfortable place—reinforce it. Say:

"What is it like now? What do you see around you? What are you doing?"

(Option 2) If the patient is in pain—address it. Say:

"The pain is there but see if you can add coolness or more warmth or make it lighter or make it heavier."

(Option 1) If the patient is no longer in pain, say:

"Good. Continue to focus on those sensations."

(Option 2) If the patient is still in pain, say:

"Focus on sensations in another part of your body. Now rub your fingertips together and notice all of the delicate sensations in your fingertips and see how much you can observe about what it feels like to rub your thumb and forefingers together. How do you feel now?"

(Option 1) If the patient is not in pain, say:

"Good. Continue to focus on these sensations."

(Option 2) If the patient is still in pain, say:

"Now imagine yourself being at _____ [patient's safe place] where you said you felt relaxed and comfortable. What is it like now? What is the temperature? What do you see around you?"

(Option 3) If the patient states that he or she is worried—address it. Say:

"Okay, your main job right now is to help your body feel comfortable so we will talk about what is worrying you. But first, no matter what we discuss, concentrate on your body floating. So let's get the floating back into your body. Imagine that you are in this favorite spot and when you are ready let me know by nodding your head; and then we will talk about what is worrying you. But remember, no matter what we discuss, concentrate on your body floating and feel safe and comfortable. So what is worrying you? [Discuss.]

How do you feel now?"

(Option 1) If the patient is no longer worried, say:

"Good. Now continue to concentrate on your body floating, and feel safe and comfortable in your favorite place."

(Option 2) If the patient is still worried, say:

"Okay, picture in your mind a screen like a movie screen, TV screen, or a piece of clear blue sky. First you might see a pleasant scene on it. Now picture a large piece of blue screen divided in half. All right. Now on the left half, picture what you are worrying about on the screen. Now on the right half of the screen, picture what you will do about it, or what you would recommend someone else do about it. Keep your body floating. And if you are worrying about the outcome, it is okay to admit it to yourself, but your body does not have to get uptight about it. You may, but your body does not have to.

Good. You know that whatever happens there is always something you can do. But for now just concentrate on keeping your body floating and feeling safe and comfortable."

From time to time throughout the procedure, say:

"If you feel any sense of discomfort, you are welcome to let me know about it. You may use the filter to filter the hurt out of the pain, but by all means let me know and I will do what I can to help you with it as well. Whatever you do, just keep your body floating and concentrate on being in the place where you feel safe and comfortable."

When the procedure is finished, say:

"Okay, the procedure is completed now. We are going to formally leave this state of concentration by counting backward from three to one. On three, get ready; on two, with your eyes closed, roll up your eyes; and on one, let your eyes open and take a deep breath and let it out. That will be the end of the formal exercise, but when you come out of it, you will still have the feeling of comfort that you felt during the exercise. Ready . . . three, two, one."

If the patient opens the eyes, say:

"Take a deep breath, and feel refreshed and proud about having helped yourself through this procedure."

If the patient has not followed, say:

"Three—get ready. Two—with your eyes closed, roll up your eyes. One—let your eyes open and take a deep breath, and feel refreshed and proud about having helped yourself through this procedure."

CONCLUSION

Guiding patients through medical procedures and acute pain situations is one of the more rewarding experiences in medicine. Backed by scientific evidence, it can be done with the confidence that patients are better off and with improved outcomes than if it had not been offered.

REFERENCES

Bayer, T. L., Coverdale, J. H., Chiang, E., & Bangs, M. (1998). The role of prior pain experience and expectancy in psychologically and physically induced pain. *Pain, 74*(2–3), 327–331.

Butler, L. D., Symons, B. K., Henderson, S. L., Shortliffe, L. D., & Spiegel, D. (2005). Hypnosis reduces distress and duration of an invasive medical procedure for children. *Pediatrics, 115*, 77–85.

Elkins, G., White, J., Patel, P., Marcus, J., Perfect, M. M., & Montgomery, G. H. (2006). Hypnosis to manage anxiety and pain associated with colonoscopy for colorectal cancer screening: Case studies and possible benefits. *International Journal of Clinical and Experimental Hypnosis, 54*(4), 416–431.

Everett, J. J., Patterson, D. R., Burns, G. L., Montgomery, B., & Heimbach, D. (1993). Adjunctive interventions for burn pain control: Comparison of hypnosis and ativan: The 1993 clinical research award. *Journal of Burn Care & Rehabilitation, 14*(6), 676–683.

Ewin, D. M., & Eimer, B. N. (2006). *Ideomotor signals for rapid hypnoanalysis*. Springfield, IL: Charles C. Thomas Publishers.

Faymonville, M. E., Fissette, J., Mambourg, P. H., Roediger, L., Joris, J., & Lamy, M. (1995). Hypnosis as adjunct therapy in conscious sedation for plastic surgery. *Regional Anesthesia, 20*(2), 145–151.

Flory, N., Salazar, G. M., & Lang, E. V. (2007). Hypnosis for acute distress management during medical procedures. *International Journal of Clinical and Experimental Hypnosis, 55*(3), 303–317.

Fredericks, L. E. (1978). Teaching of hypnosis in the overall approach to the surgical patient. *American Journal of Clinical Hypnosis, 22*, 175–183.

Ginandes, C., Brooks, P., Sando, W., Jones, C., & Aker, J. (2003). Can medical hypnosis accelerate post-surgical wound healing? Results of a clinical trial. *American Journal of Clinical Hypnosis, 45*(4), 333–351.

Lang, E. V. (2012). A better patient experience through better communication. *Journal of Radiology and Nursing, 31*(4), 114–119.

Lang, E. V. (2014a). *Comfort Talk® Online Training Module*. Retrieved from http://www.hypnalgesics.com/pages/pr.OnlineTraining.html

Lang, E. V. (2014b). *My comfort talk app*. Retrieved from https://itunes.apple.com/us/app/comfort-talk/id823174763?mt=8

Lang, E. V., Benotsch, E. G., Fick, L. J., Lutgendorf, S., Berbaum, M. L., Berbaum, K. S., . . . Spiegel, D. (2000). Adjunctive non-pharmacologic analgesia for invasive medical procedures: A randomized trial. *The Lancet, 355*(9214), 1486–1490.

Lang, E. V., & Berbaum, K. S. (1997). Educating interventional radiology personnel in nonpharmacologic analgesia: Effect on patients' pain perception. *Academic Radiology, 4*(11), 753–757. doi.org/10.1016/s1076-6332(97)80079-7.

Lang, E. V., Berbaum, K. S., Faintuch, S., Hatsiopoulou, O., Halsey, N., Li, X., . . . Baum, J. (2006). Adjunctive self-hypnotic relaxation for outpatient medical procedures: A prospective randomized trial with women undergoing large core breast biopsy. *Pain, 126*(1–3), 155–164.

Lang, E. V., Berbaum, K. S., Pauker, S. G., Faintuch, S., Salazar, G. M., Lutgendorf, S., . . . Spiegel, D. (2008). Beneficial effects of hypnosis and adverse effects of empathic attention during percutaneous tumor treatment: When being nice does not suffice. *Journal of Vascular and Interventional Radiology, 19*(6), 897–905.

Lang, E. V., Chen, F., Fick, L. J., & Berbaum, K. S. (1998). Determinants of intravenous conscious sedation for arteriography. *Journal of Vascular and Interventional Radiology, 9*(3), 407–412.

Lang, E. V., Hatsiopoulou, O., Koch, T., Berbaum, K., Lutgendorf, S., Kettenmann, E., . . . Kaptchuk, T. J. (2005). Can words hurt? Patient-provider interactions during invasive procedures. *Pain, 114*(1–2), 303–309.

Lang, E. V., & Laser, E. (2009). *Patient sedation without medication. Rapid rapport and quick hypnotic techniques. A resource guide for doctors, nurses, and technologists*. Raleigh, NC: Lulu.

Lang, E. V., & Rosen, M. P. (2002). Cost analysis of adjunct hypnosis for sedation during outpatient interventional procedures. *Radiology, 222*(2), 375–382.

Lang, E. V., Tan, G., Amihai, I., & Jensen, M. P. (2014). Analyzing acute procedural pain in clinical trials. *Pain, 155*(7), 1365–1373.

Lang, E. V., Yuh, W. T., Ajam, A., Kelly, R., Macadam, L., Potts, R., & Mayr, N. A. (2013). Understanding patient satisfaction ratings for radiology services. *American Journal of Roentgenology, 201*(6), 1190–1196.

Liossi, C., & Hatira, P. (2003). Clinical hypnosis in the alleviation of procedure-related pain in pediatric oncology patients. *International Journal of Clinical and Experimental Hypnosis, 51*(1), 4–28.

Lucas, O. N. (1965). Dental extractions in the hemophiliacs: Control of emotional factors by hypnosis. *American Journal of Clinical Hypnosis, 7,* 301–307.

Macones, G. A., Tuuli, M., Houser, M., Nicholas, S., & Kurnit, K. (2008). Hypnotic analgesia during first-trimester termination: Marc. *American Journal of Obstetrics and Gynecology, 199*(5), 579–580.

Marc, I., Rainville, P., & Dodin, S. (2008). Hypnotic induction and therapeutic suggestions in first-trimester pregnancy termination. *International Journal of Clinical and Experimental Hypnosis, 56*(2), 214–228.

Meurisse, M., Defechereux, T., Hamoir, E., Maweja, S., Marchettini, P., Gollogly, L., . . . Faymonville, M. E. (1999). Hypnosis with conscious sedation instead of general anaesthesia? Applications in cervical endocrine surgery. *Acta Chirurgica Belgica, 99*(4), 151–158.

Montgomery, G. H., Bovbjerg, D. H., Schnur, J. B., David, D., Goldfarb, A., Weltz, C. R., & Silverstein, J. H. (2007). A randomized clinical trial of a brief hypnosis intervention to control side effects in breast surgery patients. *Journal of the National Cancer Institute, 99*(17), 1304–1312.

Montgomery, G. H., David, D., Winkel, G., Silverstein, J. H., & Bovbjerg, D. H. (2002). The effectiveness of adjunctive hypnosis with surgical patients: A meta-analysis. *Anesthesia and Analgesia, 94*(6), 1639–1645.

Moss Kanter, R. (2004). *How winning streaks & losing streaks begin and end.* New York, NY: Crown Business.

Neumann, R., & Strack, F. (2000). "Mood contagion": The automatic transfer of mood between persons. *Journal of Personality and Social Psychology, 79*(2), 211–233.

Richardson, J., Smith, J. E., McCall, G., & Pilkington, K. (2006). Hypnosis for procedure-related pain and distress in pediatric cancer patients: A systematic review of effectiveness and methodology related to hypnosis interventions. *Journal of Pain Symptom Management, 31*(1), 70–84.

Roberts, K. (2006). Hypnosis in dentistry. *Dentistry Update, 33*(5), 312–314.

Ruiz, O. R., & Fernandez, A. (1960). Hypnosis as an anesthetic in ophthalmology. *American Journal of Opthalmology, 50*(1), 163.

Spiegel, D. (2007). The mind prepared: Hypnosis in surgery. *Journal of the National Cancer Institute, 99*(17), 1280–1281.

Weinstein, E. J., & Au, P. K. (1991). Use of hypnosis before and during angioplasty. *American Journal of Clinical Hypnosis, 34,* 29–37.

Wright, B. R., & Drummond, P. D. (2000). Rapid induction analgesia for the alleviation of procedural pain during burn care. *Burns, 26*(3), 275–282.

Pain Management—
Chronic Pain

Mark Jensen

Chronic pain is common and contributes to significant emotional suffering and physical disability worldwide (IOM, 2011; Leadley, Armstrong, Lee, Allen, & Kleijnen, 2012; Tsang et al., 2008). For example, individuals with chronic pain endorse substantially more symptoms of depression and anxiety than those without chronic pain (Asmundson & Katz, 2009; Fishbain, Cutler, Rosomoff, & Rosomoff, 1997). People with chronic pain also report higher levels of disability than those without chronic pain (Aronoff, Feldman, & Campion, 2000), and pain interferes significantly with important quality-of-life domains, including sleep quality (Smith & Haythornthwaite, 2004), social relationships (Forgeron et al., 2010; Haythornthwaite & Benrud-Larson, 2000), and work functioning (Leadley et al., 2012; Patel et al., 2012). For too many people, pain and its effects can become the single most important focus of their lives, interfering with their ability to participate in pleasurable activities and to achieve their most valued goals.

Chronic pain is, by its very nature, refractory to available treatments. This refractory nature of chronic pain is due, in part, to a tendency among many to view the problem from a narrow biomedical perspective—to search for a medical treatment or treatments that will relieve suffering. By far, the most common treatments of chronic pain are analgesic medications, including opioid drugs. Unfortunately, while opioid medications may reduce (many patients say, "take the edge off"— that is, not eliminate) the severity of chronic pain in the short run, the pain relief associated with chronic opioid use is now known to be minimal (Stein, Reinecke, & Sorgatz, 2010). There is no such thing as a "pain killer." Moreover, increasing evidence indicates that chronic opioid use can cause a number of harms, including overdose deaths, diversion,

tolerance, and various toxicities and negative side effects, such as decrements in cognitive functioning, respiratory dysfunction, fractures, myocardial infarction, and sexual dysfunction, among many others (Baldacchino, Balfour, Passetti, Humphris, & Matthews, 2012; Chou et al., 2015; Holliday, Hayes, & Dunlop, 2013; Papaleontiou et al., 2010; Teichtahl & Wang, 2007). As a result, many experts now view chronic opioid use as inappropriate for the treatment of many, if not all, chronic pain conditions (Painter & Crofford, 2013).

Chronic pain is not primarily a biomedical problem, and is therefore not easily resolved with a single simple biomedical treatment. Rather, we now understand that chronic pain is a biopsychosocial problem that requires the consideration of, and treatments that address, the many biological, psychological, and social factors that can contribute to its severity and impact (Makris, Abrams, Gurland, & Reid, 2014; Novy, Nelson, Francis, & Turk, 1995; Salama-Hanna & Chen, 2013). Treatments or treatment programs that focus on *only* one component are not likely to have profound beneficial effects on the majority of individuals with chronic pain. Instead, clinicians and health care providers need to take into account the entire person in the context of his or her environment and develop a treatment program that will address each factor that is contributing to that person's pain and suffering.

Among the many treatments that address psychological factors,[1] those that incorporate hypnosis may be the most effective (Montgomery, DuHamel, & Redd, 2000; Patterson, 2010). The purpose of this chapter is to provide an introduction to the use of hypnosis for the treatment of chronic pain for the clinician who is interested in incorporating hypnotic approaches into his or her clinical practice. The first section provides a basic overview of a contemporary biopsychosocial model of pain—a model that should be clearly understood by health care professionals who work with individuals with chronic pain. The next section describes a detailed and specific protocol for training patients in the use of self-hypnosis for chronic pain management. This protocol has been shown in clinical trials to be effective in reducing pain severity and improving physical functioning in individuals with chronic pain (Jensen, 2011; Jensen, Barber, Romano, Hanley, et al., 2009; Jensen, Barber, Romano, Molton, et al., 2009; Jensen et al., 2011). However, it is important to remember that the presentation of a very specific protocol (with examples of scripts for hypnotic inductions and suggestions) in this chapter is not meant to imply that this protocol should be followed precisely as described for every patient. Rather, the details are provided so that clinicians can use them as a starting point, with the idea that the most effective hypnotic treatment will occur with the use of induction strategies and suggestions that are tailored to the specific needs of each client or patient.

THE BIOPSYCHOSOCIAL MODEL OF CHRONIC PAIN

As mentioned previously, many patients, and even some current health care providers, view chronic pain primarily from a narrow biomedical perspective. It was not long ago, and perhaps as recently as the late 1960s, that most pain experts viewed chronic pain from this model. In this simplistic view, pain is thought to be directly related to the amount of tissue damage or injury; more tissue damage should result in more pain, and more pain should be indicative of more tissue damage. Clinicians who hold this view and who then evaluate patients reporting significant pain in the absence of clear signs of tissue damage might think that the patient is malingering or has significant psychopathology that is being expressed using the language of pain and suffering. They might communicate to the patient indirectly, or even directly, that the patient is imagining or exaggerating the pain. Clinicians viewing chronic pain from this perspective are also at risk to make harmful suggestions without being aware of just how harmful these suggestions

are, such as telling the patient that "nothing can be done" or that the patient "must learn to live with" the pain. These suggestions imply that the patient and clinician are helpless and that suffering will continue, both of which are patently untrue if the patient learns strategies for better managing pain and its impact.

Patients who view their chronic pain from a simple biomedical perspective often go "doctor shopping" until they find a physician who is willing to provide them with biomedical treatments. Because health care providers are both trained to provide and paid for providing health care, it is often easy for patients to find health care providers willing to prescribe biomedical treatments or perform invasive procedures. Patients who receive only biomedical treatments may end up receiving escalating doses of opioids or sedatives, even as their daily pain intensity and suffering increase over time. Worse, some patients with a biomedical focus might seek out and receive repeated invasive medical interventions (surgeries, spinal blocks) that have not been shown to be superior to nonsurgical treatment in terms of effects on pain, but which are associated with significant risks and tissue damage that themselves can contribute to the overall pain problem (Reddi & Curran, 2014; Wang, Wanyan, Tian, & Hu, 2014).

A profound turning point in our understanding of chronic pain occurred with the publication of the gate control theory of pain in the 1960s (Melzack & Wall, 1965). This model provided an easily understandable neurophysiological explanation for how patients who are neither exaggerating nor have significant psychopathology can experience severe pain in the absence of identifiable tissue damage, and how this pain can persist for many years long after tissue healing occurs. According to the gate control theory, the signals from the periphery associated with physical damage or the potential for physical damage—signals referred to as *nociception*—are modulated at the level of the spinal cord. This signal modulation can be influenced by both "ascending" (toward the brain from the periphery) activity from peripheral nerves and "descending" (down to the spinal column from the brain) activity from the brain.

Ascending influences on pain intensity can occur with the activation of nerve fibers by massage or by movement, because the activation of these nerve fibers releases neurotransmitters in the spinal cord that inhibit the influence of nociceptive signals. A good example of this process is when you injure your hand by hitting it against an object, and then rub your hand to reduce the intensity of the pain. The neurons that transmit nociceptive signals to the spinal cord can also be influenced by activation of neurons on the brain that transmit descending signals. An example of a descending influence would be the effects of fear about possible injury, which can cause the system to be more aware—sometimes acutely aware—of sensations from the periphery, even in the absence of physical damage. This process is not the same as "malingering" or even "exaggerating" pain. It is, in fact, a biological process that has significant survival benefits. A system that is more sensitive to pain in the presence of real danger is more likely to survive in the long run, even when that system causes more pain. The problem, of course, is that in the context of chronic pain, the pain signal has lost its beneficial effects and only results in more pain and suffering. The gate control theory provided an important new model for how pain can be influenced by both biological and psychological factors. It inspired a profound increase in pain research (Cervero, 2013) and increased acceptance for the development of more complex biopsychosocial models of pain (Novy et al., 1995).

Biopsychosocial models recognize that biological components and mechanisms can play a significant role in the perception of pain. Importantly, they also incorporate the findings from research performed over the last few decades demonstrating that psychological and social factors also have important influences on pain intensity, psychological distress, and the effects of pain on day-to-day life. From a clinical perspective, a biopsychosocial model emphasizes that all three factors—biological, psychological, and social—should be considered when evaluating pain and developing effective treatment plans. What many clinicians who treat patients with chronic pain do not yet understand is that hypnosis can play a positive role in many, if not most, of these treatment plans.

The biological factors that contribute to pain can vary significantly between patients and specific chronic pain conditions. They include, but by no means are limited to, the amount of ongoing inflammation in the areas associated with pain (more inflammation usually contributes to higher levels of pain), the relative strength and mobility of the muscles and tendons in the areas associated with pain (in general, muscles and tendons that are stronger and better stretched hurt less), the amount and nature of any ongoing nerve damage (patients with nerves that are being compressed, that have been damaged, or that are deteriorating owing to neuromuscular conditions tend to report more pain), or even the amount and nature of immune cell activity in the spinal cord (recent evidence suggests that immune cell activity in the spinal cord can increase pain sensitivity; Wieseler-Frank, Maier, & Watkins, 2005).

Just as patients with chronic pain should not be treated by only biomedical treatments without consideration of psychological and social factors, these individuals should also not be treated using *only* hypnosis or *only* any psychological intervention, without a thorough evaluation and consideration of biomedical factors by a trained pain physician. Appropriate biomedical treatments might include medication management (often discontinuing or decreasing medications thought to be harmful in the long run, such as opioids and sedatives, but sometimes also initiating or increasing selected medications with evidence supporting their long-term efficacy for specific conditions), graded reactivation or exercise, and, for some pain problems, appropriate medical procedures.

Psychological factors that impact pain and its effects on function in persons with chronic pain include such variables as beliefs and attributions about the pain (including its specific meaning to the patient), coping strategies used to manage pain, the presence of significant depressive or anxiety symptoms, and psychosocial history (Jensen, 2011; Novy et al., 1995). The three most important social factors that have been identified in empirical research as playing a role in pain severity and its impact are: (a) the level of social support available to the patient, (b) how the important people in the patient's life respond to the patient when he or she communicates pain (via "pain behaviors," such as groaning, limping, etc.), and (c) the patient's work (or lack of work) environment (Jensen, 2011).

The primary clinical implication of contemporary biopsychosocial models of pain is the understanding that pain treatment should begin with a thorough evaluation of the biological, psychological, and social factors that may be contributing to an individual patient's pain and suffering. This evaluation should then inform the development of the treatment plan. The goals of treatment, and the patient's readiness to participate in treatment, will have a profound impact on whether hypnosis should even be offered, and, if offered, on the specific suggestions that should be used during hypnosis. It is beyond the scope of this chapter to describe in detail the medical and psychosocial evaluation of a patient with chronic pain. Such descriptions are available elsewhere [e.g., for discussions of medical evaluations, see Loeser (2001); for discussions of psychosocial evaluations, see Jensen (2011) and Turner & Romano (2001)]. The critical point here is that such evaluations are necessary. To the extent that these evaluations indicate that a trial of training a patient in the use of self-hypnosis for managing chronic pain and its negative effects is indicated—and they often will, given the overall efficacy of hypnosis in light of the lack of negative side effects (Jensen et al., 2006)—clinicians might consider providing one or more of the hypnotic treatments described in the remainder of this chapter.

SELF-HYPNOSIS TRAINING FOR CHRONIC PAIN

The treatment protocol described in this section for helping a patient learn self-hypnosis for chronic pain is based on the findings from a long-standing and ongoing research program on the development and evaluation of hypnotic treatments for chronic pain (Jensen & Barbar, 2000; Jensen et al., 2008, 2015; Jensen, Barber, Romano, Hanley, et al., 2009; Jensen, Barber, Romano, Molton, et al., 2009; Jensen et al., 2005, 2011). Before the specific protocol is presented, it would be useful to discuss some of the findings from the research that has used the protocol, and the clinical implications of these findings. These findings include that (a) the treatment outcome is variable, and only partially associated with, or explained by, trait hypnotizability; (b) the treatment appears to have two important effects—a significant reduction in chronic daily pain intensity that maintains for many months (or longer) posttreatment and an increase in the use of the skill of self-hypnosis, a skill that allows many patients to experience periods of increased comfort on a regular basis; and (c) the "side effects" of the hypnosis treatment are overwhelmingly positive.

Treatment Outcome Is Variable

Not everyone benefits in the same way after learning self-hypnosis skills. If the *only* treatment outcome of interest to the patient is a reduction in daily pain intensity, substantial numbers of patients with chronic pain who learn self-hypnosis skills will be disappointed. What constitutes a "meaningful" reduction in pain of course varies from person to person. However, there is a consistent finding that, on average, a reduction of about 30% in average pain intensity is meaningful for most patients (Dworkin et al., 2008; Farrar, Young, LaMoreaux, Werth, & Poole, 2001). So, while many patients may say that they hope for a complete elimination of pain with treatment, those who report reductions from pretreatment levels of 9 or 10 to a 6, or from pretreatment levels of 6 or 7 to a 4 on a 0 to 10 scale of pain intensity report that they obtained substantial and meaningful pain reductions.

These reports are consistent with findings regarding the impact of pain intensity on functioning; pain intensity levels in the "mild" range of 1 to 4 are reported as noticeable but often manageable by patients (Alschuler, Jensen, & Ehde, 2012; Jensen, Smith, Ehde, & Robinson, 2001; Serlin, Mendoza, Nakamura, Edwards, & Cleeland, 1995). Pain levels in the "moderate" range of 5 to 6 are reported as having fairly substantial negative impact on a patient's quality of life. Many patients who report pain intensities at this level seek treatment. For patients with average pain intensity levels in the "severe" range of 7 or greater on a 0 to 10 scale, pain often becomes a central factor in their lives, associated with ongoing efforts to find strategies to reduce the pain. Thus, a 30% reduction in pain associated with treatment means that patients experience a reduction from one primary category of pain intensity to another—severe to moderate, or moderate to mild. Moreover, because most individuals seek treatment for pain only when it has become moderate or severe—that is, they often begin treatment with their average or "worst" pain as a "6" or higher on a 0 to 10 scale—a reasonable treatment goal to consider is to help patients learn to reduce their pain intensity to the "mild" range (i.e., 1–4 on the 0–10 scale).

How many patients with chronic pain achieve a meaningful pain reduction in daily pain with hypnosis treatment? In our studies, the rate has varied as a function of the patient population.

Among individuals with chronic pain associated with spinal cord injury—a population whose pain is particularly refractory to all available treatments—the treatment response rate ranges from 22% to 27% (Jensen, Barber, Romano, Hanley, et al., 2009; Jensen et al., 2005). We have also found that the response rates of individuals with multiple sclerosis and chronic pain are higher—the 33% to 47% range (Jensen, Barber, Romano, Molton, et al., 2009; Jensen et al., 2005). People with chronic pain associated with amputation have even higher response rates—60% (Jensen et al., 2005). Importantly, although the amount of improvement in pain intensity that patients experience with hypnosis treatment can vary, the evidence indicates that those individuals who are able to achieve meaningful decreases in daily pain with hypnosis treatment are able to maintain those benefits for at least a year following treatment (Jensen et al., 2008). In short, while many individuals with chronic pain have a good chance of obtaining significant and meaningful pain reductions with hypnosis treatment, for most if not all chronic pain conditions, there will be individuals who do not respond to this treatment with clinically meaningful reductions in daily pain. Nonetheless, hypnosis treatment often provides other significant benefits for these individuals, as noted in the following section.

Self-Hypnosis Training Has Two Primary Beneficial Effects on Pain Intensity

Given our findings that not all people who receive hypnosis treatment for chronic pain report clinically meaningful pain reductions with treatment, we were somewhat surprised to learn in follow-up interviews that only 3% of individuals reported "no benefit" to hypnosis treatment (Jensen et al., 2006). Moreover, the vast majority of patients who receive self-hypnosis training—80% to 85%—continue to practice self-hypnosis following treatment (Jensen, Barber, Romano, Hanley, et al., 2009; Jensen, Barber, Romano, Molton, et al., 2009). This raised a question: Why would so many individuals continue to practice self-hypnosis despite no reports of meaningful reductions in ongoing *daily* pain intensity?

To investigate this, we asked study participants about the effects of self-hypnosis practice. In short, they reported that when they practiced self-hypnosis, they experienced an *immediate* reduction in pain that often lasted for hours (but not necessarily all day) following practice (Jensen, Barber, Romano, Hanley, et al., 2009; Jensen, Barber, Romano, Molton, et al., 2009). In short, although some (but not all) individuals experience substantial reductions in daily pain with hypnosis treatment, the great majority—upwards of 80% to 85%—learn and use self-hypnosis as a coping response to experience immediate but short-term reductions in pain.

Thus, self-hypnosis training for chronic pain management appears to have *two* effects on pain intensity. First, hypnotic treatment can have a substantial effect on the way that some patients' brains process sensory information on a daily basis; effects that result in substantial and clinically meaningful reductions in chronic pain that is long-lasting, and may require little additional effort on the part of the patient. This effect by no means happens to everyone—and even happens to a minority of individuals with some highly refractory pain conditions—but it occurs in the majority of patients with some pain conditions, such as individuals with amputation-related chronic pain. Second, training in self-hypnosis teaches patients a specific skill that they can use whenever they choose to experience an immediate reduction in pain intensity that can last for several hours—much like they might use a medication (but one with few negative side effects, as discussed in the next section) to experience short-term pain reductions. This short-term beneficial effect on pain intensity is consistent with evidence showing that the immediate effects of hypnosis on *current pain* can be very large. For example, we have found that 87% of individuals with chronic pain (Jensen, Barber, Romano, Molton, et al., 2009) report clinically meaningful (30% or more) *immediate* reductions in pain intensity with hypnosis.

Self-Hypnosis Has Many More Benefits Than Just Pain Reduction

During and after hypnosis treatment, many of the participants in our studies—including many of those who did not report clinically meaningful reductions in daily chronic pain intensity—spontaneously reported a very high degree of satisfaction with treatment. To understand what might have contributed to this very high level of satisfaction, we asked the study participants about both benefits and negative side effects of hypnosis treatment (Jensen et al., 2006). We were pleasantly surprised at the results.

First, the ratio of positive to negative benefits (32:3) was extremely high. Moreover, the three "negative" effects about the treatment were in fact not that negative. One was that the treatment ". . . didn't work," another was that the treatment was less effective than was hoped, and the third was that the treatment benefits did not last as long as the person hoped it would. Interestingly, and despite the fact that the focus of the hypnotic suggestions in the study was pain reduction, only nine of the treatment benefits identified were pain related. The three most common pain-related benefits were pain reduction, an increased sense of control over pain, and a sense of having a new option or tool for pain management.

To our surprise, the majority of the benefits identified were not pain related. The most common of these included general positive comments about how much they enjoyed the treatment and an increased sense of overall relaxation and positive affect. Other benefits included a feeling of increased energy, increased self-awareness, improved sleep, and lowered blood pressure.

Moreover, 2 of the 30 participants interviewed attributed major positive shifts in their overall life perspective to the treatment. One said that the treatment had ". . . a profound implication in every aspect of my life—I got to do things like get a job." The other said that the treatment ". . . gave me a whole different perspective on my life and how I was approaching it." It is notable that these positive shifts occurred even though the treatments were focused only on pain management and the suggestions were not tailored to the patients; they were script driven.

Imagine if you will a drug that (a) produces substantial and clinically meaningful decreases in chronic daily pain for 22% to 60% (depending on the population) of patients with chronic pain—decreases that maintain for at least a year after treatment, (b) continues to be used by 80% to 85% of individuals who are prescribed the drug, and (c) has overwhelmingly positive "side effects" including an improvement in mood, energy, and sleep quality, among many others. This drug would be a billion dollar blockbuster for whatever company developed and patented it. It would also likely be a first-line treatment for individuals with chronic

pain. Training in self-hypnosis is such a treatment. Perhaps the time has come to offer it to more individuals.

Clinical Implications of the Effects of Self-Hypnosis Training

The findings from our clinical trials regarding (a) variability in treatment outcome, (b) the effects that hypnosis has on overall daily chronic pain intensity and immediate but short-term pain relief, and (c) the overwhelmingly positive additional benefits described earlier have important clinical implications. First, these findings emphasize the importance of helping patients have realistic but positive outcome expectancies about the treatment. This is important, given evidence supporting the positive effects of outcome expectancies on outcome with hypnosis treatment (Jensen et al., 2015). Thus, and especially for patients who indicate that meaningful pain reduction is a primary treatment goal, it is important to plant the seeds for positive expectancies about other additional outcomes. This can be accomplished by saying something along the lines of the following at some point during the initial evaluation:

> You may be interested to learn what you can expect with this treatment. If what you are looking for is the complete elimination of all of your pain, I can tell you that this does not happen with everyone. Only a few patients I have treated finished treatment with no pain, although *it has happened*. If what you want is to experience a *substantial* and meaningful reduction in your usual daily pain intensity, then this outcome is more likely. Importantly, almost everyone is able to learn how to use self-hypnosis to achieve substantial reductions in pain when they practice, and this relief often lasts for several hours. Perhaps more importantly, virtually everyone finds some *additional* benefits with this treatment. Many report they are more relaxed and feel improvements in their overall mood. Or they report health benefits, such as reduced blood pressure and improved sleep. Because everyone is different, I cannot say right now which of *these or other benefits* you will be able to achieve with treatment . . . want to find out?

A second clinical implication of our findings is that it is important to target the suggestions provided during treatment to both of the beneficial effects on pain intensity with posthypnotic suggestions (i.e., include suggestions for both (a) permanent changes in how the brain processes sensory information so the patient feels comfortable throughout the day, every day, and (b) an ability to use self-hypnosis whenever the patient chooses to achieve immediate comfort that lasts for hours or even days). The protocol presented later in this chapter presents the specific wording used to achieve these two effects.

Finally, in the clinical setting, it is useful to include inductions and suggestions that are tailored to the patient's specific goals and needs. Patients who feel or experience more "stress" than they like and wish to feel more relaxed could be provided with suggestions for feeling relaxed, when appropriate, throughout the day. Patients with sleep problems (and this is the majority of patients with chronic pain) can be provided with suggestions for improved sleep (Jensen, 2011). A patient who reports any benefits that surprise them (and perhaps the clinician) can be provided with additional suggestions to enhance and utilize these benefits.

Treatment Protocol

The protocol presented in this section is based on the protocols used in our clinical trials, which have demonstrated efficacy for benefiting individuals with chronic pain (Jensen, Barber, Romano, Hanley, et al., 2009; Jensen, Barber, Romano, Molton, et al., 2009; Jensen et al., 2011). Given the scope of this chapter, many details regarding the protocol must be left out, and more information is available from a published therapist manual (Jensen, 2011). However, the description provided here provides the clinician with the basics needed to get started.

When we began our research program in this area almost 20 years ago, we provided 10 sessions of hypnosis treatment. Each session began with time to check in with the patient, review the treatment goals for the session, provide the hypnosis portion of the session (usually, about 20 to 30 minutes), and finish with time to debrief the patient and discuss goals for the week (Jensen, Barber, Romano, Hanley, et al., 2009; Jensen, Barber, Romano, Molton, et al., 2009; Jensen et al., 2005). We noticed, however, that many of the treatment benefits emerged following just two to four sessions. Therefore, we are now evaluating four-session protocols in our clinical trials (Jensen

et al., 2011), including two studies that are currently underway. Indeed, in a recent study, we found that while patients with chronic pain who received eight sessions of hypnosis treatment reported slightly greater improvements in outcomes than those who received just two sessions, the differences we noted were not statistically significant (Tan et al., 2015). Currently, when treatment will involve only or primarily hypnosis to focus on a very specific treatment goal (e.g., pain management), in my clinical practice I suggest that we plan on four sessions of treatment to begin with. Patients or clients presenting with more complex issues or who have multiple treatment goals, of course, often require more than just four treatment sessions. For the majority of patients, and as long as they practice self-hypnosis regularly between sessions (see following paragraph), four sessions is often enough. For others, once the first four sessions are completed, we may agree that an additional four to six sessions would be helpful to build on and consolidate treatment gains.

Because the model of hypnosis treatment presented here is a model of self-hypnosis training—that is, hypnosis as something that patients learn to do and use for themselves, rather than something that is done *to* patients—between-session practice is critical. Thus, an audio recording is made of each hypnosis session and provided to the patient in his or her preferred form (e.g., as a CD or audio file). The patients are asked to listen to the entire recording or practice on their own for about the same amount of time without the recording (if they have a great deal of hypnotic skill when treatment begins) at least once each day. They are also asked to practice self-hypnosis for very brief periods multiple times throughout the day, every day. They can begin each of the two to five minute practice sessions with the cue ("Take a deep breath. . .") and then focus on positive suggestions that address their primary goals. After treatment, some patients say that they are able to use self-hypnosis without listening to audio recordings of the sessions, while others report that they respond better if they continue to use the audio recordings. I tell them to choose whichever method works best, although I do continue to encourage regular practice, "as often as you find helpful," once treatment ends.

The rest of this chapter presents a summary of the typical protocol (including scripts) used in a single hypnosis session. It is divided into subsections that discuss and present the five primary components of a hypnosis session: the induction, therapeutic suggestions, posthypnotic suggestions, reorienting, and session debriefing. It bears emphasizing again that the protocol described here should be considered as at most a starting point or as "ideas to be considered," and should not be administered (or read to) patients exactly as written without consideration of the patient's specific aptitudes, needs, and treatment goals. At the same time, it may be useful to keep in mind that the wording presented here has been used and edited by a number of very skilled clinicians over many years of protocol development and refinement,[2] so it would be worth considering using at least some of the text, as appropriate.

Inductions

We use three primary inductions in our clinical trials: a relaxation induction, followed by a countdown deepening strategy, which then moves into favorite place imagery. We start with a relaxation induction for a number of reasons. First, almost everyone has had at least some experience at some point in their lives with feeling relaxed. Thus, this is an experience that resonates with many individuals; it is relatively "easy" for many individuals to feel relaxed, at least when they are invited to do so by a clinician. Second, the experience of relaxation is inconsistent with the experience of pain. Thus, even in the presence of severe pain, suggestions for experiencing relaxation can disrupt a patterned response, which then disrupts the experience of pain. As a result, many patients report experiencing some pain relief and greater control over pain during the induction itself, even before any suggestions related to pain relief are given. This can help to create and build positive outcome expectancies very early in the session. Finally, teaching patients to be able to experience relaxation (which is almost always—but not always—experienced as pleasant) even while experiencing pain starts to help patients learn that the presence of pain does not necessarily have be associated with negative affect. This is a critical truth that can be associated with significant improvements once it is clearly understood by a patient.

Although rare, some patients find the experience of relaxation uncomfortable. For some, this is psychological discomfort associated with a sense of "losing control." Others describe a physical

sensation of "falling" when they feel relaxed, which can be distressing. Still, others have reported an increase in spasms and/or pain with relaxation suggestions—perhaps due to a decrease in activity in areas of the brain that are needed and being used for sensory and/or spasm suppression. To help decrease the chances that the patient would feel like he or she is "falling" with relaxation suggestions, and to encourage a mindset associated with feeling "supported" by the clinician, the following script contains wording that refers to experiencing the "strong support" of the chair. However, in the rare case that a patient finds suggestions for relaxation uncomfortable, simply use other inductions, including perhaps the deepening induction included here, or a favorite place induction. The most important thing, of course, is that the patient be able to focus his or her mind increasingly on the clinical suggestions provided following the induction.

In the absence of a history of trauma, following the relaxation induction and a simple countdown deepening procedure, the clinician can invite the patient to experience dissociation (see following script) to deepen the experience, and to provide an introduction to the skill of dissociation from physical sensations. If the patient is a trauma survivor, he or she may have used dissociation to cope, making it necessary to be particularly careful with the use of dissociation suggestions. Again, a thorough evaluation of the biological, psychological, and social factors is essential before treatment.

Alternatively, the clinician can move right into inviting the patient to experience himself or herself in a favorite place—a favorite beach, a favorite room, anywhere that the patient finds enjoyable. Prior to the induction, it is a good idea to tell the patient that the session will include an invitation for him or her to experience being in a place where he or she feels comfortable and at ease—a "favorite place." The patient can be told that this can be a real place that he or she has actually been to, or that the place can be imaginary; however, some experienced clinicians believe that the number of times the patient has been in the place is associated with the overall degree of "presence" he or she will experience because the memories of that place may be more readily available. For this reason, use of an actual place that the patient has been to (e.g., a recent vacation) may be preferred. The patient should also be told that this need not always be the same place. In fact, changing details about the place every so often may keep the place "fresh" and make it even more interesting and engaging.

The important thing is for participants to select a place that they can very clearly imagine in detail. It is often useful to elicit from them as many of the details about the place as they would like to share (e.g., sandy beach, mountain meadow, meadow filled with flowers, mountain top, living room; ideal temperature; color of any water and the sky; plants or other objects around them) as a way to give them concrete memories or experiences to enhance the experience during the induction. However, it is also important to be very permissive during the induction ("I do not know exactly where you will choose to go today, perhaps it is a beach . . . or a mountain top . . . or a favorite room . . ."), which will allow the audio recording to be useful to them when and if they choose to use different locations as their favorite place.

Just before the induction, we always begin by inviting the patient to engage in a prehypnosis cue; specifically to "*. . . take a deep, refreshing breath and hold it. . . . Hold it for a moment. . . . And let it go. . . .*" This suggestion is given to provide the participant with a cue he or she can use for experiencing self-hypnosis outside of the sessions without the recording. The specific wording that we are currently using in our clinical trials for the induction component of treatment is as follows:

"*Okay . . . just settle back. . . .*
If eyes open, say, *and close your eyes.*
If eyes closed say, *and let the eyes stay closed.*

Now . . . I'm going to talk to you for a while . . . all you have to do is listen to what I'm saying and allow yourself to have as pleasant an experience as you know how. Go ahead and adjust yourself to the most comfortable position you can.

Observe subject. Wait until adjusting is completed before continuing.

That's fine. And remember, you can feel free to make any adjustments, at any time, to help yourself be comfortable, and this need not interrupt your concentration or ability to maintain a deep state of comfortable relaxation.

Now . . . I'd like you to notice that you can increase your comfort, right now. . . . Take a deep, satisfying breath and hold it just for a moment. That's right . . . hold it for a moment . . . and let it go. Let yourself notice how good that feels."

Relaxation Induction
"*And now . . . allow the whole body to relax . . . allow all of your muscles to go limp . . .* [wait about three seconds] *and then allow special muscle groups to relax even more . . . starting with the hands. . . . Imagine that all the muscles and tendons in the hands are relaxing . . . and as the hands relax, being aware of any sensations that let you know that the hands feel more relaxed . . . perhaps a sense of warmth, or of heaviness, perhaps some other interesting and comfortable sensation, whatever sensation that lets you know that the hands are becoming more and more relaxed . . . limp, heavy, warm, and comfortable. And now allow that relaxation to spread . . . up, up into the wrists . . . the forearms, the elbows, and upper arms. The arms becoming more and more relaxed, relaxed and heavy. All the tension draining away, as the arms feel heavier, and heavier, almost as if they were made of lead. Or perhaps they might be feeling lighter and lighter. Or even both at the same time. I don't know exactly what sensations of relaxation and comfort you are noticing, and it really doesn't matter, as long as you experience greater comfort . . . greater relaxation.*

And as this process continues, as you continue to allow both arms to feel more and more relaxed, you can be aware that the relaxation continues to spread . . . into the shoulders. All the muscles in the shoulders letting go, relaxing, feeling the support of the chair/bed, perhaps sinking into the chair/bed, while also feeling so very supported and safe, letting all the tension drain out of the shoulders. . . . Feeling so relaxed, heavy, and . . . . More and more relaxed. . . .

And the relaxation continues to spread . . . into the neck. All the muscles and tendons of the neck letting go, one by one. Just allowing the head to rest, being aware of the sensations that let you know that the neck is relaxing, more and more, as you feel more comfortable, more and more at ease. The whole body becoming relaxed, very, very relaxed . . . heavy, calm, and peaceful . . . allowing the feelings of comfortable relaxation to spread up around the ears . . . the scalp . . . letting all the tension drain away, the muscles around the eyes letting go, relaxing, as do the muscles in the face . . . the jaw . . . limp, relaxed, comfortable, and at peace . . . as relaxed as you have ever been . . . it feels so good to take a vacation from stress . . . and the relaxation continues, down the back . . . into the chest . . . the stomach. . . .

And then down into the legs . . . the legs feeling limp, so very heavy . . . comfortable . . . all the tension draining out. . . . Feeling the support of the chair/ bed, as the legs feel heavier, and heavier . . . and so comfortable. All the tension draining out of the legs, to be replaced by comfort . . . a heavy, pleasant comfortable and deep relaxation.

The whole body relaxing. . . . And when it feels like you are as relaxed as you can be, you can allow yourself to relax even more, becoming even more relaxed . . . more comfortable, without a care in the world. . . . The whole body relaxed, and comfortable . . . so relaxed, in fact, that you might even lose awareness of sensations from some parts of the body, almost as if parts of the body were disappearing as they become more comfortable . . . and you might experience yourself as a point of consciousness, without any body at all, just floating comfortably and safely in space. You are in space, and know that you are in space.

Yet while there, you can also imagine that you are somewhere else. You can imagine that you are, with me, in an elevator. . . . This is a special elevator that takes us down to levels of deeper and deeper comfort and well-being . . . even deeper than you are right now. . . ."

[You can change the way of going down if the participant does not like elevators, or to motivate the participant by using a variety of scenes.]

Deepening

"*In a moment, I'm going to count from 1 to 10. As I count each number, I'd like you to imagine that we are descending, one level for each number I count. . . . And notice . . . just notice that, as we descend to each level, you can feel more and more*

absorbed by feelings of comfort and well-being. While you descend, continue to take nice deep, satisfying breaths. When we reach 10, the deepest level, you can really enjoy a deep sense of comfort and well-being.

Let's begin now.

One. One level down into deeper comfort. That's right. You might already notice interesting and comfortable sensations and feelings, maybe a deep sense of relaxation.

Two. Two levels down. That's right . . . deeper into yourself.

Three. Three levels down. . . . Perhaps noticing, every sensation you can feel . . . and these can also become more and more a part of your experience of comfort and well-being. . . .

Four. Four levels down. . . . And I wonder if you are beginning to enjoy the freedom of this experience. Right now, there is nothing you have to do. This is an opportunity . . . just for you . . . to feel deeply absorbed in comfort and well-being.

Five. Half way down. . . . Becoming more and more absorbed in this moment . . . no need to focus on the past, or the future . . . just focusing on your breath in this moment . . . and all the ways to enjoy this time for comfort and well-being. . . .

Six. Six levels down. . . . Really noticing pleasant feelings and sensations. Feelings that seem to wash through the body . . . across your forehead . . . around your eyes and face . . . into your mouth and jaw, down through your neck . . . and into your shoulders . . . and on and on . . . down through the body. . . .

Seven. Seven levels down. . . . Even as you imagine that the body feels heavier and heavier, you also know that you are actually just floating in space, and can enjoy a feeling of weightlessness . . . as if your mind is just floating . . . effortlessly, and so comfortably . . . drifting and floating. . . .

Eight. Eight levels down. Hearing the sound of my voice, without even trying to listen. Understanding my words without any particular effort. Allowing yourself to be more and more absorbed by comfort and well-being. . . . As if nothing else matters . . . just your comfort and well-being. Nine. . . . Nine levels down. . . . Almost to the very bottom of this elevator to comfort. And now. . . .

Ten. The tenth level of relaxation. Comfort . . . well-being . . . perhaps curious about just how deeply comfortable, how deeply at ease you can feel. During this time, you can continue to let yourself rest more and more deeply, as deeply as you know how.

And the elevator doors open, and as we leave the elevator, you can imagine that you are in a peaceful, beautiful, and safe place. Picture this place in as much detail as possible . . . so that it feels as if you are really there, right now. Take a moment, right now, to use all your senses to take in every detail you can about this peaceful place, this place of comfort, relaxation, and well-being."

Favorite Place Imagery

Now invite the participant to continue to experience the place using all of his or her senses for about five minutes. Keep in mind that the patient will be listening to a recording of this session, so do not provide so much detail that might ultimately be inconsistent with a new place he or she imagines months or even years from now. Rather, invite the patient to create the place and experience it in great detail; to touch objects, and experience how they feel. Invite the patient to experience the colors. Add any sensations that the patient has described previously as present as being a part of the place. Encourage the patient to experience positive emotional experiences (calmness, a sense of confidence and connectedness to nature). Suggest that the individual see, hear, and smell all the possible details of this place, wherever he or she is as he or she approaches it and moves through it. Pause long enough to let the patient create these experiences for himself or herself.

After three to four minutes, and if the participant previously indicated that sitting, laying, or floating in a body of water in the peaceful place would be of some benefit, you can describe a body of water. Be sure to follow the individual's preferences for the nature of the body of water, ideal temperature, and so on. Ask the participant to imagine that the warm/cool/other healing

water is soothing any areas of the body that are uncomfortable. Suggestions will vary depending on individual preferences.

If the subject previously indicated that entering the body of water would not be of any particular benefit or might be scary or uncomfortable, *do not* mention it here. Rather, talk with him or her about being able to imagine a "healing energy that is just the right color and just the right temperature" that surrounds and protects him or her.

For example,

". . . and as you step into your favorite, comfortable place . . . you can notice a sense of relief . . . a sense of deep physical and emotional comfort . . . it is like a vacation from stress . . . you can really let go, knowing that you are so very safe . . . with nothing to bother you, and nothing to disturb you. . . .

This is your time . . . a time to charge your batteries . . . you step onto the sand, and can feel its warmth on your feet . . . actually feel that warm sand . . . the texture . . . and as you look around . . . everything is so beautiful. Looking into the sky, you can see that it is incredibly blue . . . as blue a sky as you have ever seen . . . and if there are clouds, they are just floating there . . . so easily . . . white and fluffy . . . they look as relaxed as you feel. . . .

There is nothing, nothing at all, that you have to do here. No one you have to please, no one to take care of. . . .

And you can smell the salt in the air . . . and hear the waves . . . [timed with the patient's breathing] back and forth, back and forth, the sound of the waves, so relaxing. . . .

Perhaps there are plants. And you can focus on the leaves. They are so green, perhaps waving a little in the breeze, feeling the breeze against the skin. The temperature is just right . . . just right for feeling so relaxed, focused, able to hear my voice, without really having to listen at all. . . .

And in front of you, you can see a tub of water. It is as if it were built just for you. You know that it fits you just right . . . and you know that the healing water in this tub can make you feel even better . . . even more relaxed, comfortable, and strong.

You might decide to allow yourself to move to the tub, to sit back, feeling the support of a built-in chair, supporting your head above the water. And the water just feels so good. It, too, is just the right temperature. The perfect amount of warmth or coolness. You can actually feel the water all around your body, breathing so naturally and easily with your head supported.

Maybe noticing how the healing liquid seems to soak into areas of the body that could benefit from feeling better, stronger, and more energized. Of course, you know that this state of focused awareness is so healthy for you. It strengthens your immune system, it relaxes you and gives you more energy, it allows the mind to relax, and yet feel more focused at the same time.

You might enjoy just letting yourself go, and allow your mind and body to heal, as you experience a timeless feeling of relaxation."

■ Clinical Suggestions

Following the induction, the clinician then makes the suggestions that are consistent with the patient's needs and treatment goals. A number of examples of suggestions, pulled from the treatment manuals of some of our currently ongoing clinical trials, are presented here. Additional ideas for suggestions that could be useful to patients with chronic pain are presented in various books and text books (Hammond, 1990; Patterson, 2010), including the book that is also based on our clinical research program (Jensen, 2011). When working with an individual with chronic pain, goals related to all of these issues should be considered and included as a part of treatment, when appropriate.

Because many of the issues listed earlier that are a part of chronic pain (sleep difficulties, inactivity, etc.) are addressed elsewhere, the clinical suggestions that follow focus on those that are most closely associated with managing chronic pain, in particular. They include suggestions for (a) a decreased awareness of uncomfortable suggestions, (b) an increased awareness of comfort and comfortable sensations, (c) a decrease in pain

unpleasantness (i.e., distinguishing the affective and sensory aspects of pain), and (d) acceptance of all sensations, including pain.

Decreased Awareness of Uncomfortable Sensations
"*As we continue, you can let yourself stay in this peaceful place, or you can drift somewhere else, as you wish, but you can remain very relaxed, and it will become easier and easier to hear my voice and understand my words . . . and to respond to suggestions that are appropriate for your comfort and well-being.*

Now take another nice deep breath. [Wait until the patient does so.]

[Continue with:] *. . . and hold it, hold it for a moment . . . now let it all the way out, and as you do so, just let yourself sink even deeper, into a profound level of relaxation. As your mind relaxes, it becomes easier and easier to hear my voice, no matter what else is going through your mind. If there are any thoughts or images that you would rather not focus on, just allow them to drift on by, like leaves floating down a stream. . . . It is becoming easier and easier to respond to suggestions for your comfort and well-being. . . .*

With every breath you take, breathing comfort in and breathing discomfort out, you can wonder how you can be feeling more and more comfortable, right here and now. You may be pleased, of course, but you may also be surprised that it's so much easier now to simply focus on relaxation and comfort, to be increasingly aware of your comfort. . . . So much easier to enjoy the relaxing, peaceful comfort of each breath. So simple, so natural, to attend to your breathing.

And at the same time, you can notice, almost as a side effect, that any uncomfortable feelings are drifting farther and farther away. You might even imagine these feelings as an image . . . perhaps as leaves on a stream . . . or as a fire burning on a piece of wood, or even as some other image floating on a log or piece of wood . . . you can actually see them. I don't know what color they are, or what the image is . . . but you do. . . . You can see details, watching the image change. Perhaps floating slowly, drifting down the stream . . . or if it is a fire, watching the fire burning out. Either way, the image is getting smaller and smaller. Disappearing. . . .

And now, maybe you can take whatever image you have of the uncomfortable sensations, and imagine, in your mind's eye, lowering this into a strong insulated box with a secure lid. Into the box it goes. And you can see yourself shutting the lid and securing it. . . . Muffling the sensations . . . and then putting this box into a second very secure box, and shutting the lid. The sensations are in there, but muffled. . . . And putting this second box into yet another box. . . . And shutting the lid. Securing it. Nothing can get out. And then, and you can use your creativity here, imagine sending the box far far away. . . . Maybe deep into space . . . maybe across the ocean . . . but really imagine it going away . . . picturing it. Far far away. . . . So much easier to ignore now. . . .

And with those sensations so far away, it is even easier to feel the comfort of every breath. So easy to let yourself daydream about a peaceful place, to imagine a happy time in your life or a happy time you'd like to have. Letting yourself feel free, right now, to just let your mind wander. . . .

You can trust that your unconscious mind will notice any feelings that you need to pay attention to. If your health requires that you notice any uncomfortable feelings, you will do so. It's so nice, though, that any old, chronic discomforts can fade away . . . it feels so good to be in such control of your health . . . your well-being . . . you are in charge. . . .

Such a pleasure to be here, with nothing to bother you and nothing to disturb you. With every breath you take, breathing comfort in and tension or discomfort out, just notice how naturally you feel more and more comfort. And any feelings of discomfort seem to have lessened and maybe even disappeared altogether. Like some memory long forgotten. Or something you have stored away but no longer in your awareness. Letting each breath you take. . . contribute to your comfort and well-being."

Increased Awareness of Comfort and Comfortable Sensations

"Now take another nice deep breath. [Wait until the patient does so.]

[Continue with:] *. . . and hold it, hold it for a moment . . . now let it all the way out, and as you*

do so, just let yourself sink even deeper, into a profound level of relaxation. As your mind relaxes, it becomes easier and easier to hear my voice, no matter what else is going through your mind. If there are any thoughts or images that you would rather not focus on, just allow them to drift on by, like leaves floating down a stream. . . . It is becoming easier and easier to respond to suggestions for your comfort and well-being. . . .

One way that many people manage to feel more comfortable is to create for themselves an increased ability to notice comfortable sensations that can overwhelm other sensations. Like being in a bath that is just the right temperature seems to drain away and overwhelm any feelings of discomfort or tension. This is why, of course, many people enjoy soaking in a tub of water. Your mind can do this, by noticing feelings that are comfortable and pleasant; feelings that grow and grow. You may already have been noticing some different, more pleasant sensations during our time so far, or you may begin to notice these more pleasant sensations now . . . sensations that can slowly and easily fill your awareness.

Because the mind is so powerful . . . it can magnify and enhance feelings that are interesting and pleasant. I do not know what those feelings might be for you today. You might not even know what they are until they happen. As we continue, you can enjoy discovering that comfortable feelings just seem somehow to change, that comfortable feelings can spread and grow, as you become even more aware of them. With every breath you take, you can notice how feelings of relaxation and comfort seem to become more and more clear, more and more strong . . . as if they are spreading farther and farther throughout your body . . . taking up more and more space in your awareness. . . . If there are any sensations that suggest a change in your health, you'll be able to notice them and take care of yourself as needed.

You have noted some feelings that are often pleasant for you in the past. Maybe these are some of the feelings you are noticing. Or maybe some other interesting, calming, good feelings. But wouldn't it be interesting if they were the feelings that were just right for you, right now, right here? Notice that as you notice these feelings, notice, really notice, all of the pleasant sensations that your body is giving you. . . . As these sensations are noticed, as they build, you probably feel more and more calm, peaceful . . . more and more relaxed.

. . . You are training your nervous system so that it is possible to be more aware of pleasant sensations and helpful feelings, so aware of pleasant sensations and feelings, in fact, that it is hard to notice any other type of feelings. Noticing, just noticing, how your mind focuses more and more on these feelings of calmness, comfort, and relaxation.

If floating or being partially submerged in water was discussed as something that could be pleasant, you can describe how a sense of being in healing water can contribute to the patient's comfort. Suggestions will vary based on the patient's preferences, and may involve soaking a painful body part, drifting and floating on top of the water, and so on. Focus on whatever sensations the subject finds pleasant.

In fact, your nerves are sending all kinds of interesting feelings to your brain all the time, and your brain can learn to filter out some sensations, and become increasingly absorbed in new, more comfortable feelings. As you pay attention to this, you can start to notice interesting feelings that are comfortable and pleasant, in any areas that you want to feel more comfortable. And now you can relax further and allow these other feelings to grow, to expand, to take up more and more of your attention, so that your mind is less and less able to be aware of any other feelings. I wonder if you might be curious about just how absorbed you can become in noticing these comfortable and pleasant feelings . . . or whatever other pleasant feelings you notice. How good this feels. And your ability to do this is growing, and becoming more and more automatic all the time. Not only that, but the more you notice these good feelings, the better you feel emotionally . . . calmer and calmer . . . more and more hopeful and confident. . . . You can just . . . feel good. . . ."

Decreased Pain Unpleasantness and Pain Acceptance

"Now take another nice deep breath. [Wait until the patient does so.]

[Continue with:] *. . . and hold it, hold it for a moment . . . now let it all the way out, and as you do so, just let yourself sink even deeper, into a profound level of relaxation. As your mind relaxes, it becomes easier and easier to hear my voice, no matter what else is going through your mind. If there are any thoughts or images that you would rather not focus on, just allow them to drift on by, like leaves floating down a stream. . . . It is becoming easier and easier to respond to suggestions for your comfort and well-being. . . .*

As you sink deeper into comfort, you can be aware of just how well you can feel, with nothing to bother you, and nothing to disturb you. It is possible for you, right now, to notice that even though the body provides input into the mind, it is the mind that creates sensations out of that input. And these sensations are always changing . . . they wax and wane, like all natural processes. But this is not what is most important right now, what is important is this: that you are able to simply accept any sensations the mind creates, just as they are. They come, they go. But you do not have to do anything about them. You can experience the sensations almost as if they were happening to someone else, or a different version of you . . . from a distance . . . and just notice them with an emotional detachment . . . perhaps a curiosity about how they might change . . . but knowing that whatever sensations there are . . . they do not have to bother you. . . . Imagine them as leaves floating down a stream . . . arriving, passing by, and continuing down the stream. Sometimes more leaves, sometimes fewer. . . . Sometimes none at all. . . . Being somewhat interested, but also interestingly detached.

Isn't it interesting how the sensations that we experience, and our emotional reaction to them, are different things? The sensations are one thing. Our emotional reaction is another. We can experience small sensations and have large emotions about them, or experience large sensations, and be detached; hardly any emotion at all. It is possible to have a calm, warm, comfortable acceptance of our sensations; they simply are what they are. And notice how calming and reassuring this realization is . . . it can feel physically relaxing . . . a kind of letting go . . . not have to worry or bother anymore about these sensations, whatever they are . . . freeing you up to think about the things in your life that are most important. . . .

Many people are surprised to find that it becomes easier and easier to relax the more they practice these skills. To feel relaxed and calm, emotionally, no matter what is happening physically. I wonder if you will be surprised to find that you can experience this, too. It might help to remember that you have the ability to take good care of your health as you need to. If there's any change in your feelings or sensations, your mind can notice this, and you will be able to take care of yourself as needed. But this can be done from a detached, calm, relaxing perspective. No matter what type of sensations you have, you really don't need to feel bothered by them. . . . As you focus on this, notice that you may have started to feel more and more calm, less and less bothered by anything in particular, without having to do anything at all . . . it just happens.

Because with any of the old feelings, you know that you don't need to do anything at all about them. Just . . . accept . . . calmly accept them. It's just so satisfying to notice that, for some reason, all the sensations you can feel, all the feelings you can notice, can become more and more a part of your experience of comfort and well-being, with nothing to bother you and nothing to disturb you. . . . Your comfort can grow . . . it is possible for you to feel better now . . . and in the future. . . . Although you can notice feelings . . . from a distance . . . there are no feelings that bother you or disturb you right now. . . ."

Age Progression to Increase Adaptive Coping, Hope, and Positive Affect

"Now take another nice deep breath. [Wait until the patient does so.]

[Continue with:] . . . and hold it, hold it for a moment . . . now let it all the way out, and as you do so, just let yourself sink even deeper, into a profound level of relaxation. As your mind relaxes, it becomes easier and easier to hear my voice, no matter what else is going through your mind. If there are any thoughts or images that you would rather not focus on, just allow them to drift on by, like leaves floating down a stream. . . . It is becoming easier and easier to respond to suggestions for your comfort and well-being. . . .

And now, you can open up a new channel of concentration . . . whereby you focus on taking a special trip into the future. . . . Experience yourself in a special imaginary time machine . . . you can now push the button that takes you into the future when you are managing even better than you are now. I do not know when that will be . . . it might be a month from now . . . a year . . . two . . . or even five years from now . . . it might be different every time you practice this exercise . . . but you are moving forward in your time machine, and stopping at some period of time when you are doing well. You have successfully learned the cognitive and hypnosis skills you are practicing right now. Your mind is able to note your thoughts and evaluate them quickly, easily, and automatically, and adjust them for you as needed so you can feel more comfortable, physically and emotionally . . . you are able, whenever you wish, to enter a state of total relaxation . . . and to calmly evaluate your symptoms . . . so that they do not bother you at all . . . you can see yourself feeling so good, actually see yourself . . . so relaxed . . . able to manage any symptoms comfortably and easily . . . any symptoms really do not bother you . . . the part of you that is YOU is able to focus on and enjoy the things that really matter.

You are no longer surprised at your abilities to manage your thoughts and symptoms . . . your skills in this area are now second nature . . . when you were first learning to add numbers together as a child, 1 and 1 = 2, 2 and 2 = 4, you might have had to use your fingers, you really had to concentrate and focus . . . and you may not even remember when you first learned to walk . . . but when you did, you had to focus your attention on each step . . . you needed help . . . to hold on to people and to furniture . . . but with time and continued practice . . . walking became second nature . . . so automatic that you never really had to even think about it anymore . . . and in your mind's eye, as you see yourself sometime in the future . . . your ability to manage your symptoms . . . and even more importantly your positive reaction to your sensations . . . or even lack of reaction to your sensations—whichever is more helpful—is automatic. . . . You see yourself as confident . . . you can actually see yourself smiling . . . feeling so good. . . .

And now . . . in this time in the future . . . you move into the body . . . and can feel, actually feel, what it is like to feel so good . . . so confident . . . before you saw yourself smiling . . . now you can feel yourself smiling . . . so relaxed . . . and in control . . . you are feeling even better than you imagined you might . . . you have the abilities and the skills to manage . . . your thoughts . . . and your sensations. . . .

And taking a deep breath . . . go ahead. . . . A deep breath . . . and hold it . . . that's right . . . hold it for a moment, and let go . . . and as you exhale, you can really experience an enhanced tranquility . . . and now get ready to travel back from the future in your imaginary time machine. As you come back, bring with you all of these positive experiences of joy, comfort, delight, accomplishments . . . and SKILLS. Bring them back as your special gifts from the future, and let them stay with you consciously and subconsciously, guiding you on your own journey of healing . . . and now your time machine has arrived to the present, and you can see yourself moving out of the time machine carrying with you these special gifts you have brought with you. . . ."

Posthypnotic Suggestions

In this protocol, the goals of the posthypnotic suggestions are to teach the participant how to use the hypnotic skills on his or her own, and to make any beneficial changes permanent, consistent with our findings that hypnosis can have two categories of benefits, discussed earlier in this chapter. The general idea is to suggest that (a) the experience of analgesia, relaxation, and comfort will stay with the patient and linger beyond the session, lasting for ". . . hours, days, weeks, and years . . ."; (b) the more the patient practices, by listening to a recording of the session and also by using the cue to enter a hypnotic state and reexperience the comfort of hypnosis without the recording, the more effective and long-lasting the suggestions will be; and (c) the participant will be able to enter this relaxed and absorbed state using a specific cue more easily with time and practice, and can do so any time he or she wishes to experience comfort. The posthypnotic suggestions are also designed to increase the patient's confidence in using these skills and a sense of control over pain and its impact.

"Now we have reached the time to extend any comfort and relaxation you have gained in this session into the rest of your day, and your daily life. Begin by taking a deep, comfortable, relaxing breath and hold it . . . hold it for a moment . . . and then let it all the way out. That's right. [Attend to the subject's breathing and coordinate your speaking emphasis with the subject's breath.] *Really feel the sensations of each breath. Notice that breathing in feels different than breathing out. Now, I'd like you to imagine that you are breathing comfort in each time you breathe in . . . actual comfort, each time you breathe in . . . and imagine you are breathing tension or discomfort out each time you breath out.* [Continue, repeating with the subject's breathing, two times.] **As you do so, maybe you already notice a feeling of comfort washing over you, like warm water in a bath.**

Any time you want to feel more comfortable, just rest back and take a very deep, very satisfying breath, and hold it . . . and then, as you let it all the way out . . . let your eyelids close and focus on your breathing. Breathe comfort in, and tension out with each breath you take. Really focus your mind on each breath. Let each breath contribute to your comfort. With each breath you take, you can feel yourself filling your awareness with comfort. Then you can let your mind go to your peaceful place if you like, or anywhere else it wishes to go, or just become more and more absorbed by your breath . . . and your comfort. . . .

All the time you are learning new ways of helping yourself to feel more comfortable . . . and these skills are becoming more automatic and effortless each time you practice. You have the ability to feel more comfortable and peaceful, any time you want. And the more you practice these skills, the easier it will be to keep the comfort with you. This comfort is yours . . . to keep with you, wherever you are, whatever you are doing. You may even find that later today, or tomorrow, or . . . I don't know when . . . you may suddenly notice that you are keeping the comfort with you for longer and longer . . . perhaps longer than you would have expected.

I don't know exactly how you will choose to practice. You may have a longer practice each day, and a number of shorter times, maybe even for a minute or less. But the more you practice, the more your mind will be able to use these skills, automatically, throughout the day, so that you can find comfort and relaxation when you need it. When you are finished practicing and are ready to end the experience, you'll find that your eyes open, and your mind is clear and alert, ready to go on with the day . . . yet no matter how clear and alert your mind is, this inner comfort, this inner sense of ease, can remain with you and grow. And because this is your experience, you can have it whenever you need to."

Reorienting

The goal of reorienting is to bring a patient out of hypnosis, while also maximizing the chances that he or she will bring any benefits of the sessions, including any feelings of calmness and relaxation, into his or her day.

"Now . . . imagine we're back in the elevator. As I count from 10 back to 1 . . . I want you to come back up the elevator with me, one level for each number that I count . . . and when I reach the number 'one' you will still have your eyes closed but they will be about to open. What will happen is that your mind will allow you to open your eyes only when you are fully alert, but still relaxed and at ease. The feelings of comfort, relaxation, and calmness you have been feeling, these feelings will stay for longer and longer.

Let's begin now. Ten, nine, eight . . . more alert with each number. . . . Seven, six . . . feeling more refreshed with each level of the elevator. . . . Five, four . . . noticing more and more how your mind starts to be more alert, your attention more expanded, and your body more and more active. . . . Three . . . more alert but calm at the same time. . . . Two, almost there. . . . One, your eyes are still closed but they are ready to open when you know that you are ready to feel safe, awake, and more and more alert. . . . You will notice how it becomes a signal from your mind that you are ready to come out by your eyes starting to open. And when they open, you will continue to feel more and more awake and more and more alert. Whenever you are ready, you notice that your eyes seem to be open if they have not opened yet. As you start reorienting yourself, you start feeling alert and active but at ease and comfortable. [Wait for the patient to be ready to open his or her eyes and elaborate more if the patient does not seem to be more alert yet.] *Eyes open, feeling alert, oriented,*

and active. Fully, fully alert and active, and at the same time at ease . . . ready to go on with your day, with all your activities. . . ."

■ Debriefing

The goals of the session debriefing include (a) ensuring that the patient is actually alert and not just sitting, compliantly with his or her eyes open, and (b) understanding how the patient responded to the induction and the suggestions, in order to inform what changes, if any, should be made in these for the next session. If, after conversing with the patient, it appears that he or she is not yet completely alert, you might give him or her some time to reorient on his or her own. Or, if needed, you might provide additional suggestions for being alert.

Then discuss with the patient how he or she is feeling right now and his or her experience during the hypnosis session. Modifications in the hypnosis suggestions may be made based on the information obtained from this discussion (e.g., if a participant states that a suggestion was not helpful, or did not like it, that suggestion should be dropped or reworded; if the participant describes a specific suggestion or image that was particularly helpful, that suggestion or image might be emphasized in the next session). Also, of course, this is a good time to address any questions or concerns about the hypnosis session or hypnosis in general, as appropriate.

At some point, explain to the patient how he or she might practice self-hypnosis before the next session. In our trials, we say:

You can practice hypnosis with the recording we made in the session and you can also practice on your own.

When you are practicing self-hypnosis you will enter into a state of focused attention (also referred to as "hypnotic trance" by some people), and let your mind play with the ideas in order to experience more comfort. Several times during the day, but at least three times every day, take two to five minutes (or more if you wish) and go through the steps to enter a state of hypnosis, starting with taking a deep breath and holding it . . . and letting it go. Allow the body to relax, imagine going down the elevator, and go to your special place. Give yourself suggestions for comfort, relaxation in general, or for any other sensation that is helpful for you to cope with pain. Stay there for as long as you like.

CONCLUSION

In this chapter, I emphasized the importance of viewing chronic pain from a biopsychosocial perspective and ensuring that each patient has had a thorough medical and psychological evaluation (and is receiving appropriate medical and psychological care) prior to beginning treatment. Hypnosis and hypnotic interventions can, and often should, be a part of chronic pain treatment. But few, if any, patients should be offered or provided only hypnosis. The chapter also contained a detailed protocol of inductions and some suggestions that are derived from a number of clinical trials and that therefore have evidence supporting their efficacy. More details of the protocol are available for those who are interested (Jensen, 2011). The protocol presented here, when considered in light of the other chapters in this text, provides a good start for someone interested to see if he or she wishes to incorporate hypnosis and hypnotic procedures into his or her practice.

Hypnosis—defined here very simply as an induction that encourages focused awareness followed by suggestions to experience greater control and comfort—has demonstrated efficacy for reductions in pain intensity and increases in a large range of positive outcomes with very few negative side effects. Self-hypnosis training is empowering, and gives patients greater control over pain and its negative effects on their lives. Given this outcome profile, the evidence indicates that hypnosis should be offered to more individuals than it currently is.

ENDNOTES

1. Psychological treatments with evidence supporting their efficacy include cognitive behavioral therapy, operant treatment, biofeedback, graded exposure therapy, group therapy, and family therapy, as well as some relatively new approaches such as acceptance-based therapy (McCracken & Vowles, 2014) and Motivational Interviewing (Jensen, 2002).
2. Clinicians who have contributed ideas to the protocol over the years, in alphabetical order, include Drs. Joseph Barber, Tiara Dillworth, Dawn Ehde, Marisol Hanley, Adam Hirsh, M. Elena Mendoza, Ivan Molton, Travis Osborne, David Patterson, Katherine Raichle, Joan Romano, Brenda Stoelb, and Gabriel Tan.
3. Based largely on the work of Moshe Torem (Torem, 1992, 2006). See also Chapters 16 and 56 of this volume.

REFERENCES

Alschuler, K. N., Jensen, M. P., & Ehde, D. M. (2012). Defining mild, moderate, and severe pain in persons with multiple sclerosis. *Pain Medicine, 13*(10), 1358–1365.

Aronoff, G. M., Feldman, J. B., & Campion, T. S. (2000). Management of chronic pain and control of long-term disability. *Occupational Medicine, 15*(4), 755–770.

Asmundson, G. J., & Katz, J. (2009). Understanding the co-occurrence of anxiety disorders and chronic pain: State-of-the-art. *Depression and Anxiety, 26*(10), 888–901.

Baldacchino, A., Balfour, D. J., Passetti, F., Humphris, G., & Matthews, K. (2012). Neuropsychological consequences of chronic opioid use: A quantitative review and meta-analysis. *Neuroscience and Biobehavioral Reviews, 36*(9), 2056–2068.

Cervero, F. (2013). Pain research: What have we learned and where are we going? *British Journal of Anaesthesia, 111*(1), 6–8.

Chou, R., Turner, J. A., Devine, E. B., Hansen, R. N., Sullivan, S. D., Blazina, I., . . . Deyo, R. A. (2015). The effectiveness and risks of long-term opioid therapy for chronic pain: A systematic review for a National Institutes of Health Pathways to Prevention Workshop. *Annals of Internal Medicine, 162*(4), 276–286.

Dworkin, R. H., Turk, D. C., Wyrwich, K. W., Beaton, D., Cleeland, C. S., Farrar, J. T., . . . Zavisic, S. (2008). Interpreting the clinical importance of treatment outcomes in chronic pain clinical trials: IMMPACT recommendations. *Journal of Pain: Official Journal of the American Pain Society, 9*(2), 105–121.

Farrar, J. T., Young, J. P., LaMoreaux, L., Werth, J. L., & Poole, R. M. (2001). Clinical importance of changes in chronic pain intensity measured on an 11-point numerical pain rating scale. *Pain, 94*(2), 149–158.

Fishbain, D. A., Cutler, R., Rosomoff, H. L., & Rosomoff, R. S. (1997). Chronic pain-associated depression: Antecedent or consequence of chronic pain? A review. *Clinical Journal of Pain*, 13(2), 116–137.

Forgeron, P. A., King, S., Stinson, J. N., Mcgrath, P. J., Macdonald, A. J., & Chambers, C. T. (2010). Social functioning and peer relationships in children and adolescents with chronic pain: A systematic review. *Pain Research & Management: The Journal of the Canadian Pain Society*, 15(1), 27–41.

Hammond, D. C. (1990). *Handbook of hypnotic suggestions and metaphors*. New York, NY: W. W. Norton.

Haythornthwaite, J. A., & Benrud-Larson, L. M. (2000). Psychological aspects of neuropathic pain. *Clinical Journal of Pain*, 16(Suppl 2), S101–105.

Holliday, S., Hayes, C., & Dunlop, A. (2013). Opioid use in chronic non-cancer pain—part 1: Known knowns and known unknowns. *Australian Family Physician*, 42(3), 98–102.

IOM. (2011). *Relieving pain in America: A blueprint for transforming prevention, care, education, and research*. Washington, DC: The National Academics Press.

Jensen, M. P. (2002). Enhancing motivation to change in pain treatment. In D. Turk & R. Gatchel (Eds.), *Psychological approaches to pain management: A practitioner's handbook* (pp. 71–93). New York, NY: Guilford Press.

Jensen, M. P. (2011). *Hypnosis for chronic pain management: Therapist guide*. Oxford, UK: Oxford University Press.

Jensen, M. P., Adachi, T., Tomé-Pires, C., Lee, J., Osman, Z. J., & Miró, J. (2015). Mechanisms of hypnosis: Towards the development of a biopsychosocial model. *International Journal of Clinical and Experimental Hypnosis*, 63(1), 34–75.

Jensen, M. P., & Barbar, J. (2000). Hypnotic analgesia of spinal cord injury pain. *Australian Journal of Clinical and Experimental Hypnosis*, 28(2), 150–168.

Jensen, M. P., Barber, J., Hanley, M. A., Engel, J. M., Romano, J. M., Cardenas, D. D., . . . Patterson, D. R. (2008). Long-term outcome of hypnotic analgesia treatment for chronic pain in persons with disabilities. *International Journal of Clinical and Experimental Hypnosis*, 56(2), 156–169.

Jensen, M. P., Barber, J., Romano, J. M., Hanley, M. A., Raichle, K. A., Molton, I. R., . . . Patterson, D. R. (2009). Effects of self-hypnosis training and EMG biofeedback relaxation training on chronic pain in persons with spinal-cord injury. *International Journal of Clinical and Experimental Hypnosis*, 57(3), 239–268.

Jensen, M. P., Barber, J., Romano, J. M., Molton, I. R., Raichle, K. A., Osborne, T. L., . . . Patterson, D. R. (2009). A comparison of self-hypnosis versus progressive muscle relaxation in patients with multiple sclerosis and chronic pain. *International Journal of Clinical and Experimental Hypnosis*, 57(2), 198–221.

Jensen, M. P., Ehde, D. M., Gertz, K. J., Stoelb, B. L., Dillworth, T. M., Hirsh, A. T., . . . Kraft, G. H. (2011). Effects of self-hypnosis training and cognitive restructuring on daily pain intensity and catastrophizing in individuals with multiple sclerosis and chronic pain. *International Journal of Clinical and Experimental Hypnosis*, 59(1), 45–63.

Jensen, M. P., Hanley, M. A., Engel, J. M., Romano, J. M., Barber, J., Cardenas, D. D., . . . Patterson, D. R. (2005). Hypnotic analgesia for chronic pain in persons with disabilities: A case series. *International Journal of Clinical and Experimental Hypnosis*, 53(2), 198–228.

Jensen, M. P., McArthur, K. D., Barber, J., Hanley, M. A., Engel, J. M., Romano, J. M., . . . Patterson, D. R. (2006). Satisfaction with, and the beneficial side effects of, hypnotic analgesia. *International Journal of Clinical and Experimental Hypnosis*, 54(4), 432–447.

Jensen, M. P., Smith, D. G., Ehde, D. M., & Robinsin, L. R. (2001). Pain site and the effects of amputation pain: Further clarification of the meaning of mild, moderate, and severe pain. *Pain*, 91(3), 317–322.

Leadley, R. M., Armstrong, N., Lee, Y. C., Allen, A., & Kleijnen, J. (2012). Chronic diseases in the European Union: The prevalence and health cost implications of chronic pain. *Journal of Pain & Palliative Care Pharmacotherapy*, 26(4), 310–325.

Loeser, J. D. (2001). Medical evaluation of the patient with pain. In J. Loeser, S. Bulter, C. Chapman, & D. Turk (Eds.), *Bonica's management of pain* (pp. 267–278). Philadelphia, PA: Lippincott Williams & Wilkins.

Makris, U. E., Abrams, R. C., Gurland, B., & Reid, M. C. (2014). Management of persistent pain in the older patient: A clinical review. *Journal of the American Medical Association*, 312(8), 825–836.

McCracken, L. M., & Vowles, K. E. (2014). Acceptance and commitment therapy and mindfulness for chronic pain: Model, process, and progress. *American Psychologist*, 69(2), 178–187.

Melzack, R., & Wall, P. D. (1965). Pain mechanisms: A new theory. *Science*, 150(3699), 971–979.

Montgomery, G. H., DuHamel, K. N., & Redd, W. H. (2000). A meta-analysis of hypnotically induced analgesia: How effective is hypnosis? *International Journal of Clinical and Experimental Hypnosis*, 48(2), 138–153.

Novy, D. M., Nelson, D. V., Francis, D. J., & Turk, D. C. (1995). Perspectives of chronic pain: An evaluative comparison of restrictive and comprehensive models. *Psychological Bulletin*, 118(2), 238–247.

Painter, J. T., & Crofford, L. J. (2013). Chronic opioid use in fibromyalgia syndrome: A clinical review. *Journal of Clinical Rheumatology: Practical Reports on Rheumatic & Musculoskeletal Diseases*, 19(2), 72–77.

Papaleontiou, M., Henderson, C. R., Turner, B. J., Moore, A. A., Olkhovskaya, Y., Amanfo, L., & Reid,

M. C. (2010). Outcomes associated with opioid use in the treatment of chronic noncancer pain in older adults: A systematic review and meta-analysis. *Journal of the American Geriatrics Society, 58*(7), 1353–1369.

Patel, A. S., Farquharson, R., Carroll, D., Moore, A., Phillips, C. J., Taylor, R. S., & Barden, J. (2012). The impact and burden of chronic pain in the workplace: A qualitative systematic review. *Pain Practice: The Official Journal of World Institute of Pain, 12*(7), 578–589.

Patterson, D. R. (2010). *Clinical hypnosis for pain control.* Washington, DC: American Psychological Association.

Reddi, D., & Curran, N. (2014). Chronic pain after surgery: Pathophysiology, risk factors and prevention. *Postgraduate Medical Journal, 90*(1062), 222–227.

Salama-Hanna, J., & Chen, G. (2013). Patients with chronic pain. *Medical Clinics of North America, 97*(6), 1201–1215.

Serlin, R. C., Mendoza, T. R., Nakamura, Y., Edwards, K. R., & Cleeland, C. S. (1995). When is cancer pain mild, moderate or severe? Grading pain severity by its interference with function. *Pain, 61*(2), 277–284.

Smith, M. T., & Haythornthwaite, J. A. (2004). How do sleep disturbance and chronic pain inter-relate? Insights from the longitudinal and cognitive-behavioral clinical trials literature. *Sleep Medicine Reviews, 8*(2), 119–132.

Stein, C., Reinecke, H., & Sorgatz, H. (2010). Opioid use in chronic noncancer pain: Guidelines revisited. *Current Opinion in Anaesthesiology, 23*(5), 598–601.

Tan, G., Rintala, D. H., Jensen, M. P., Fukui, T., Smith, D., & Williams, W. (2015). A randomized controlled trial of hypnosis compared with biofeedback for adults with chronic low back pain. *European Journal of Pain, 19*(2), 271–280.

Teichtahl, H., & Wang, D. (2007). Sleep-disordered breathing with chronic opioid use. *Expert Opinion on Drug Safety, 6*(6), 641–649.

Torem, M. S. (1992). "Back from the future": A powerful age-progression technique. *American Journal of Clinical Hypnosis, 35*(2), 81–88.

Torem, M. (2006). Treating depression: A remedy from the future. In M. Yapko (Ed.), *Hypnosis and treating depression: Applications in clnical practice* (pp. 97–119). New York, NY: Routledge.

Tsang, A., Von Korff, M., Lee, S., Alonso, J., Karam, E., Angermeyer, M. C., . . . Watanabe, M. (2008). Common chronic pain conditions in developed and developing countries: Gender and age differences and comorbidity with depression-anxiety disorders. *Journal of Pain: Official Journal of the American Pain Society, 9*(10), 883–891.

Turner, J. A., & Romano, J. M. (2001). Psychological and psychosocial evaluation. In J. Loeser, S. Butler, C. Chapman, & D. Turk (Eds.), *Bonica's management of pain* (pp. 329–341). Philadelphia, PA: Lippincott Williams & Wilkins.

Wang, X., Wanyan, P., Tian, J. H., & Hu, L. (2015). Meta-analysis of randomized trials comparing fusion surgery to non-surgical treatment for discogenic chronic low back pain. *Journal of Back and Musculoskeletal Rehabilitation.* 28(4):621-627. doi: 10.3233/BMR-140571

Wieseler-Frank, J., Maier, S. F., & Watkins, L. R. (2005). Central proinflammatory cytokines and pain enhancement. *Neuro-Signals, 14*(4), 166–174.

Palliative Care

Daniel Handel

CHAPTER 38

Patients facing advanced medical illness often experience significant symptoms such as pain, anxiety, insomnia, nausea, or cachexia. Integrated treatment strategies that combine traditional pharmacological treatments with mind–body approaches are increasingly being utilized to improve outcomes. Patients must also work through the denial and anger that commonly accompany new diagnoses. Families often struggle to support the patient through physical and psychological symptoms of advancing illness. Demand for complementary approaches has dramatically increased, and professional training in these therapies has become more generally available (Eisenberg, 1997; Eisenberg et al., 1993).

This chapter discusses the clinical applications and the evidence for efficacy of hypnosis in palliative care, and proposes the incorporation of hypnotic suggestion as an adjunctive strategy to manage pain, nausea, and anxiety in patients with advanced illness. As hypnosis has received growing acceptance by physicians, nurses, and other health care practitioners, it has received past recognition by the American Medical Association (AMA) and British Medical Association. Studies by the National Institutes of Health (NIH) Panels of specific modalities that include mind–body techniques, such as hypnosis, include chronic pain and insomnia (NIH, 1996), chronic pain (Deyo et al., 2014a, 2014b), end-of-life care (Crawley, Marshall, Lo, & Koenig, 2002), and cancer symptom management (Patrick et al., 2004).

Hypnosis can produce independent beneficial changes in palliative care patients, augment other therapeutic palliative care modalities, and be reinforced by team members through therapeutic language to activate previous hypnotic suggestions.

EVIDENCE FOR PALLIATIVE CARE HYPNOTIC APPLICATIONS AND EXAMPLES

Hypnosis differs from nonhypnotic states of awareness in several critical ways. Its narrowed and intensified focus of attention combined with its relaxation and decreased reality orientation fosters a suspension of critical judgment, which facilitates potentially powerful alterations in sensate and cognitive experiences.

Whether the state of consciousness characterized by hypnosis or the relationship between patient and therapist drives outcomes in hypnosis remains controversial. With regard to hypnotic analgesia, the social and expectancy theories assert that pain control is achieved through a cooperative therapeutic relationship between patient and practitioner that enhances responsiveness built upon expectancy (Spanos, 1986, 1989). More recent research posits a neurophysiological explanation involving central nervous system inhibition, or the "gating" of signals associated with specific aspects of pain perception (Melzack, 1993). Melzack's neuromatrix model is also consistent with hypnotic theory, which states that hypnotic suggestion can *directly* activate pain control in the patient through top-down control mechanisms (Chaves, 1989; Hilgard, 1973, 1975; Kirsch, 1990; Rainville, Bao, & Chrétien, 2005). Despite competing theories, it is generally agreed that hypnotic suggestion can mediate major changes in both perception and belief by selectively modifying sensory or the emotional (suffering) aspects of pain. Both mechanisms result in downregulation of painful stimuli in a top-down fashion.

Pain and palliative care patients are good candidates for hypnotic training for several reasons. First, hypnotic outcomes are better in motivated patients, and many patients with chronic or intractable pain are highly motivated to gain some sense of control. This sense of need fosters an openness to learning new methods for pain control. A common complaint of cancer and palliative care patients is that daily life feels controlled by pain and its treatment. Hypnotic training can create an "inner space" for these individuals, away from burdensome existential tension and physical symptoms. As successful training requires significant involvement and work by the patient, enhanced motivation improves outcomes. Second, hypnosis often is accompanied by a state of relaxation, which is independently helpful in managing pain. Third, self-hypnosis is easily learned, immediately helpful, and can be utilized in many situations without elaborate preparation. As such, hypnosis can act as a routinely employed adjunctive therapy. For example, hypnosis can aid patients in "memorizing" the therapeutic effects of other traditional and nontraditional therapies and interventions (Handel, 2001; Lang et al., 2006), reinforcing positive effects. These results are similar to the "conditioned response" that independently triggers therapeutic results (Ader, 1981).

In addition to reducing pain, hypnosis helps reduce levels of anxiety and stress. Anxiety can predate and potentiate pain perception, particularly in chronic or progressive medical conditions. Because hypnotic training is easily taught, it should be considered for interested patients with problematic anxiety or when stress is linked to exacerbations of pain. Early mastery of self-hypnosis can reduce anxiety and consequently lessen the suffering associated with pain. This enhances self-confidence and mastery. By offering the following suggestions during routine home hospice care for a patient with painful cancerous bone metastases, one can begin training a relaxation response and begin to link suggestions for muscular relaxation, mental ease and relaxation, and then dissociation to past pleasant times, experiences, and feelings.

"Just allow each of your muscles to go deeply relaxed . . . as your bath cares begin . . . at the hands of your aide . . . as if those muscles that had previously been noted to feel so tight . . . are feeling increasingly smooth, soft, and relaxed . . . more and more comfortable with each breath . . . and as your breathing becomes more deeply relaxed, your muscles notice how they feel more smoothly comfortable, effectively relaxed . . . that's right.

And as you notice those beginnings of comfortable relaxation, your mind might notice itself wandering . . . back to a more pleasant time . . . as your body relaxes more completely . . . and you will find this relaxation guiding you to peaceful and calm feelings . . . that fill you with just-right feelings . . . as your cares are provided . . . and each visit's cares remind you of rightfully loving, caring feelings . . . right back to other comfortable times . . . to others' loving feelings for you . . . feeling just right for longer, and feeling confident longer."

The hospice patient, for example, who learns to respond to this suggestion can find during simple hospice routine care delivered by an aide a stimulus for profound mental and emotional relaxation and an opportunity for an enhanced sense of well-being, loving kindness, and peace. What is more, trained health care paraprofessionals can effectively and respectfully enhance such helpful suggestions during these interactions. Patients can similarly be cued to automatically enter hypnotic states during preprocedure routines, promoting a sense of relaxation, self-control, and distance from bothersome sensation (Faymonville et al., 1997; Lang et al., 2006).

It is interesting to note that patients often act upon verbal and nonverbal suggestions with or without the help of hypnosis. The induction of hypnosis, however, is known to enhance patients' responsiveness to suggestion, helping them to respond more readily either to their own or to someone else's suggestions (Handel, 2001; Hilgard, 1973). Hospice and palliative care practitioners can employ informal hypnotic suggestions in daily practice, because patients in ill health or in dependent situations often exhibit behavior that more readily responds to suggestion. The use of positive "healing language" and avoidance of negative suggestions promotes positive attitudes and beliefs by patients and families in such circumstances (Elkins & Handel, 2001). Hypnotic training can be incorporated into medical visits and reinforced by health care professionals during potentially pain-producing hospice procedures, such as repositioning, bathing, enemas, toileting, or other activities. Palliative and hospice care patients often report difficulties with the quality and amount of sleep due to pain, other symptoms, or to emotional distress and worry. Important hypnotic suggestions can easily and quickly be incorporated into medical settings.

"As you take a few deep breaths and listen to my voice, you'll begin to notice a growing sense of loose relaxation . . . a spreading wave of deep relaxation . . . notice where that begins . . . and how it feels as it settles into that part which had been a bother to you . . . settling possibly into your mid and lower back . . . and as that feeling spreads down . . . deep into your muscles . . . you'll feel more deeply relaxed and comfortable. You might be surprised tonight at how easily this feeling returns . . . on its own bringing smooth relaxed comfort . . . as you prepare for bed . . . each part of you in the mirror . . . relaxing . . . easily and smoothly relaxing . . . as you notice your image in the mirror . . . preparing parts of you for rest . . . noticing each movement in that mirror . . . and how more relaxed that image becomes with each movement . . . and as that images relaxes, notice relaxation spreading . . . calming thoughts . . . calming feelings . . . feeling more and more ready for a deeply restorative sleep . . . and later you will drift smoothly asleep, soundly asleep, and return easily to sleep . . . after taking care of any necessary business . . . should you awaken before the end of your sleep."

Applying hypnotic techniques to help manage cancer pain has been reported repeatedly over the last four decades. The benefits of hypnotic training to cancer pain management has been reported over several decades and repeated in diverse populations (Butler, 1954, 1955; Lea, Ware, & Monroe, 1960). Cangello's studies demonstrate statistically significant and sometimes dramatic reductions in pain, with varying depths of trance, proposing a relationship between depth of trance and reductions in pain levels and analgesic use (Cangello, 1960, 1961). Controlled studies utilizing hypnosis and cognitive behavioral strategies for pain and nausea demonstrate significant benefit from both techniques (Faymonville et al., 1995; Faymonville et al., 1997; Syrjala, Cummings, & Donaldson, 1992). Hypnotic training has proven beneficial for pain and nausea associated with advanced illness, as preparation for painful procedures, and as a coping strategy for anxiety-producing events.

Studies on hypnotically induced analgesia demonstrate a moderate-to-large strength of effect for hypnotic pain management techniques (Miller, Barabasz, & Barabasz, 1990; Miller & Bowers, 1993; Montgomery et al., 2007). These results suggest broader application of these techniques for clinical pain, but are limited by imperfect methodological rigor.

Patients experiencing progressive illnesses often report isolation, depression, loss of hope, and existential suffering. A study of self-hypnosis and group support demonstrates less suffering, improved function, reduced pain complaints, and a startling increase in survival in women with metastatic breast cancer. Even as larger subsequent multicenter studies have not reliably replicated a survival benefit for self-hypnosis and group support model in advanced illness, these studies have consistently demonstrated reduced symptom burden and lessened existential and spiritual suffering. With newer research technology, we are also unravelling the underlying actual mechanisms that underlie these findings.

Neuropsychological PET and fMRI studies vividly mechanistically demonstrate the specific pathways and brain areas responsible for hypnotic pain reduction. Elegant study designs demonstrate the physiological mechanisms whereby talented subjects make specific and discreet changes through central nervous system (CNS) networks for pain processing in response to specific hypnotic suggestions (Rainville et al., 1999; Rainville, Bao, & Chretien, 2005). Hypnosis seems to uniquely enable changes in attentional processes in response to pain (resulting in "bother" by pain), and separately to trigger downregulation in the actual cortical sensate registration of pain. Many relaxation and cognitive techniques teach patients how to distance or distract from the painful experience through the pain transmission circuit involving the spinal cord–thalamic–anterior cingulate (ACC)–frontal cortex pathway. This pathway plays a role in the subjective psychological responses to pain stimuli, gated through the ACC, and modulated by the limbic system's activation of the autonomic system. This descending inhibitory system, reaching down from the frontal cortex through the periaqueductal gray region, modulates pain signal processing at the level of the spinal cord. This results in either augmentation or inhibition of pain transmission, respectively, during states of arousal or during hypnotic relaxation. Specific hypnotic suggestion is documented to separately and specifically modulate the processing of the painful sensate intensity at the primary and secondary sensory cortex. This involves the spinal cord–thalamic–periaqueductal gray–somatosensory cortex pathway (Hofbauer et al., 2001). These recent neurophysiological findings suggest specific physiological mechanisms responsible for selectively disattending or alternately downregulating sensate processing of painful stimuli—each in response to specific hypnotic suggestions and each through unique mechanistic pathways.

Commonly employed hypnotic techniques include hypnotic distraction from pain, suggestions for hypnotic analgesia, displacement, substitution, anesthesia, and the use of amnesia for past pain. Patients can be offered suggestions to decrease or "turn off" pain:

". . . that burning, electric-like pain that you had noticed in that arm will become less and less noticed . . . until it begins to feel as if the controlling center of that nerve has been turned down . . . or off . . . and the pain will settle away from your awareness . . . leaving that arm cool and numbingly comfortable."

To substitute a less bothersome sensation:

". . . you may notice that as that headache becomes less and less noticeable, a small buzzing sensation may gently grow and persist in your little finger . . . not so much as to be really bothersome . . . more as a background buzzer reminder . . . just a reminder of how successful your relaxation has become . . . as that headache fades gently into the background . . . less noticed . . . less of a bother . . . that you really do not notice nearly so much anymore."

Or not to recall pain at a later time:

". . . and as you settle more comfortably into this relaxed state you can begin noticing now how well you can learn to forget parts that do not add significantly to the whole . . . parts of pain that can be remembered to forget . . . specifically to not recall . . . at specific times . . . all that your subconscious chooses to forget . . . like the comfortable feelings of floating in the trough behind a gently rolling ocean wave, where you can neither see in front nor behind . . . when in the trough of the wave you can enjoy the heavenly vistas above . . . the stars . . . the sun . . . passing clouds . . . blue skies . . . and you will comfortably learn to forget those past pain events . . . beyond this present trough . . . and rest comfortably in this present moment . . . comfortable and confident that you are coping better . . . feeling better . . . more confident and capable in managing comfort."

In addition to helping patients cope with pain, hypnosis can alleviate the distressing sensation of nausea that so commonly occurs as the result of advancing illness; medications, including chemotherapy; or surgical procedures (Carey & Burish, 1987; Cotanch, Hockenberry, & Herman, 1985). In some cases, nausea can be an even more debilitating symptom than pain. Nausea can also become a conditioned response causing emesis in response to specific sensations, such as ward aromas or the sight of medications.

Several studies have evaluated efficacy of hypnotic interventions in the management of cancer treatment–related nausea and vomiting in both children and adults (Handel, 2001; Jelicic, Bonke, & Millar, 1993; Kekecs, Nagy, & Varga, 2014; Montgomery et al., 2007; Syrjala, Cummings, & Donaldson, 1992). Jacknow's innovative research on the benefits of hypnotic suggestion on chemotherapy-associated nausea in pediatric cancer patients, all with access to supplemental antiemetic medication, measured nausea and vomiting, antiemetic medication during two chemotherapy cycles, and anticipatory nausea and vomiting at two and four months after diagnosis (Jacknow et al., 1994). Patients practicing hypnosis used significantly less antiemetic medication and reported less anticipatory nausea than the medication-only group. This effect was most pronounced early in the treatment course. Realistically, hypnosis is an effective adjunctive treatment and may assist patients to experience less anxiety, fewer anticipatory problems, and more pronounced positive responses to antiemetic medications.

When cure no longer is possible, self-hypnosis becomes a self-management strategy for symptom control and can aid one in preparation for death. Hypnosis can create an opportunity for patients to transcend physical and emotional pain and positively transform experience (Giese-Davis et al., 2011; Handel, 1998; NIH, 2004; Olness, 1981; Patrick et al., 2004; Spiegel et al., 2007). Capable individuals seem determined to separate their identity and their wellness from their disease; this cognitive reframe can positively affect their families as well.

CONCLUSION

Patients with progressive illness face many challenges including physical symptoms; existential challenges brought through isolation, infirmity, reduced activity, and challenged self-identity; and spiritual questions brought through death's inevitability and proximity. There is growing evidence that hypnotic training should be introduced early and reinforced throughout the care of patients with life-threatening illness. Individual studies demonstrate efficacy in managing individual symptoms such as pain, nausea, hot flashes, anxiety, and insomnia. Hypnosis training can both benefit symptoms and improve the patient's sense of mastery and self-efficacy. Through therapeutic relationship and multi-level communication, hypnotic suggestion can also enhance acceptance and peacefulness, as well as promote personal growth at the end of life.

REFERENCES

Ader, R. (1981). *Psychoneuroimmunology*. New York, NY: Academic Press.

Butler, B. (1954). The use of hypnosis in the cancer patient. *Cancer*, 7(1), 1–14.

Butler, B. (1955). The use of hypnosis in the cancer patient. *British Journal of Medical Hypnosis*, 6, 2–12.

Cangello, V. W. (1960). The use of hypnotic suggestion for pain relief in malignant disease. *International Journal of Clinical Medical Hypnosis*, 9, 17–22.

Cangello, V. W. (1961). Hypnosis for the patient with cancer. *American Journal of Clinical Hypnosis*, 4, 215–226.

Carey, M. P., & Burish, T. G. (1987). Providing relaxation training to cancer chemotherapy patients: A comparison of three delivery techniques. *Journal of Consulting and Clinical Psychology*, 55(5), 732–737.

Chaves, J. F. (1989). Hypnotic control of clinical pain. In N. P. Spanos & J. F. Chaves (Eds.), *Hypnosis: The cognitive-behavioral perspective* (pp. 242–272). Buffalo, NY: Prometheus.

Cotanch, P., Hockenberry, M., & Herman, S. (1985). Self-hypnosis as anti-emetic therapy in children receiving chemotherapy. *Oncology Nursing Forum*, 12(4), 41–46.

Crawley, L. M., Marshall, P. A., Lo, B., & Koenig, B. A. (2002). Strategies for culturally effective end-of-life care. *Annual Journal of Internal Medicine*, 7(136), 673–679.

Deyo, R. A., Dworkin, S. F., Amtmann, D., Andersson, G., Borenstein, D., Carragee, E., . . . Vernon, S. W. (2014a). National Institutes of Health State-of-the-Science Conference Statement: Symptom management in cancer: Pain, depression, and fatigue. *Journal of the National Cancer Institute*, 32, 9–16.

Deyo, R. A., Dworkin, S. F., Amtmann, D., Andersson, G., Borenstein, D., Carragee, E., . . . Weiner, D. K. (2014b). Focus article: Report of the NIH task force on research standards for chronic low back pain. *European Spine Journal: Official Publication of the European Spine Society, the European Spinal Deformity Society, and the European Section of the Cervical Spine Research Society*, 23(10), 2028–2045. doi:10.1007/s00586-014-3540-3

Eisenberg, D. (1997). Advising patients who seek alternative medical therapies. *Annals of Internal Medicine*, 127–140.

Eisenberg, D. M., Kessler, R. C., Foster, C., Norlock, F. E., Calkins, D. R., & Delbanco, T. L. (1993). Unconventional medicine in the United States. *New England Journal of Medicine*, 328(4), 246–252. doi:10.1056/NEJM199301283280406

Elkins, G. E., & Handel, D. L. (2001). Clinical hypnosis: An essential in the tool kit for family practice. *Clinics in Family Practice*, 3(1), 113–126.

Faymonville, M. E., Fissette, J., Mambourg, P. H., Roediger, L., Joris, J., & Lamy, M. (1995). Hypnosis as adjunct therapy in conscious sedation for plastic surgery. *Regional Anesthesia*, 20(2), 145–151.

Faymonville, M. E., Mambourg, P. H., Joris, J., Vrijens, B., Fissette, J., Albert, A., & Lamy, M. (1997). Psychological approaches during conscious sedation. Hypnosis versus stress reducing strategies: A prospective randomized study. *Pain*, 73(3), 361–367.

Giese-Davis, J., Collie, K., Rancourt, K. M., Neri, E., Kraemer, H. C., & Spiegel, D. (2011). Decrease in depression symptoms is associated with longer survival in patients with metastatic breast cancer: A secondary analysis. *Journal of Clinical Oncology: Official Journal of the American Society of Clinical Oncology*, 29(4), 413–420. doi:10.1200/JCO.2010.28.4455

Handel, D. L. (1998). Hypnotherapy and dying: Joshua's journey. In W. Matthews & J. Edgette (Eds.), *Current thinking and research in brief therapy: Solutions, strategies, narratives* (pp. 119–136). Philadelphia, PA: Taylor & Francis.

Handel, D. L. (2001). Complementary therapies for cancer patients: What works, what doesn't, and how to know the difference. *Texas Medicine*, 97(2), 68–73.

Hilgard, E. R. (1973). A neodissociation interpretation of pain reduction in hypnosis. *Psychological Review*, *80*(5), 396–411.

Hilgard, E. R. (1975). Alleviation of pain by hypnosis. *Pain*, *1*(3), 213–231.

Hockenberry, M. J., & Cotanch, P. H. (1985). Hypnosis as adjuvant antiemetic therapy in childhood cancer. *Nursing Clinics of North America*, *20*(1), 105–107.

Hofbauer, R. K., Rainville, P., Duncan, G. H., & Bushnell, M. C. (2001). Cortical representation of the sensory dimension of pain. *Journal of Neurophysiology*, *86*(1), 402–411.

Jacknow, D. S., Tschann, J. M., Link, M. P., & Boyce, W. T. (1994). Hypnosis in the prevention of chemotherapy-related nausea and vomiting in children: A prospective study. *Journal of Developmental and Behavioral Pediatrics*, *15*(4), 258–264.

Jelicic, M., Bonke, B., & Millar, K. (1993). Effect of different therapeutic suggestions presented during anaesthesia on post-operative course. *European Journal of Anesthesiology*, *10*, 343–347.

Kekecs, Z., Nagy, T., & Varga, K. (2014). The effectiveness of suggestive techniques in reducing postoperative side effects: A meta-analysis of randomized controlled trials. *Anesthesia and Analgesia*, *119*(6), 1407–1419. doi:10.1213/ANE.0000000000000466

Kirsch, I. (1990). *Changing expectations: A key to effective psychotherapy*. Pacific Grove, CA: Brooks/Cole.

Lang, E. V., Berbaum, K. S., Faintuch, S., Hatsiopoulou, O., Halsey, N., Li, X., . . . Baum, J. (2006). Adjunctive self-hypnotic relaxation for outpatient medical procedures: A prospective randomized trial with women undergoing large core breast biopsy. *Pain*, *126*(1–3), 155–164. doi:10.1016/j.pain.2006.06.035

Lea, P., Ware, P., & Monroe, R. (1960). The hypnotic control of intractable pain. *American Journal of Clinical Hypnosis*, *3*, 3–8.

Melzack, R. (1993). Pain: Past, present and future. *Canadian Journal of Experimental Psychology = Revue Canadienne De Psychologie ExpéRimentale*, *47*(4), 615–629.

Miller, M. E., & Bowers, K. S. (1993). Hypnotic analgesia: Dissociated experience or dissociated control? *Journal of Abnormal Psychology*, *102*(1), 29–38.

Miller, M. F., Barabasz, A. F., & Barabasz, M. (1990). Effects of active alert and relaxation hypnotic inductions on cold pressor pain. *Journal of Abnormal Psychology*, *100*, 223–226.

Montgomery, G. H., Bovbjerg, D. H., Schnur, J. B., David, D., Goldfarb, A., Weltz, C. R., . . . Silverstein, J. H. (2007). A randomized clinical trial of a brief hypnosis intervention to control side effects in breast surgery patients. *Journal of the National Cancer Institute*, *99*(17), 1304–1312. doi:10.1093/jnci/djm106

NIH Technology Assessment Panel on Integration of Behavioral and Relaxation Approaches Into the Treatment of Chronic Pain and Insomnia. (1996). Integration of behavioral and relaxation approaches into the treatment of chronic pain and insomnia. *Journal of the American Medical Association*, *276*(4), 313–318.

NIH State-of-the-Science Conference Statement on improving end-of-life care. (2004). *NIH Consensus and State Scientific Statements*, *21*, 1–26.

Olness, K. (1981). Imagery (self-hypnosis) as adjunct therapy in childhood cancer: Clinical experience with 25 patients. *American Journal of Pediatric Hematology and Oncology*, *3*, 313–321.

Patrick, D. L., Ferketich, S. L., Frame, P. S., Harris, J. J., Hendricks, C. B., Levin, B., Vernon, S. W., & National Institutes of Health State-of-the-Science Panel. (2004). National Institutes of Health State-of-the-Science Conference Statement: Symptom management in cancer: Pain, depression, and fatigue. *Journal of the National Cancer Institute. Monographs*, *32*(32), 9–16. doi:10.1093/jncimonographs/djg014

Rainville, P., Bao, Q. V., & Chrétien, P. (2005). Pain-related emotions modulate experimental pain perception and autonomic responses. *Pain*, *118*(3), 306–318. doi:10.1016/j.pain.2005.08.022

Rainville, P., Carrier, B., Hofbauer, R. K., Bushnell, M. C., & Duncan, G. H. (1999). Dissociation of sensory and affective dimensions of pain using hypnotic modulation. *Pain*, *82*, 59–71.

Spanos, N. P. (1986). Hypnotic behavior: A social psychological interpretation of amnesia, analgesia, and "trance logic." *Behavioral and Brain Sciences*, *9*, 449–467.

Spanos, N. P. (1989). Experimental research on hypnotic analgesia. In N. P. Spanos & J. F. Chaves (Eds.), *Hypnosis: The cognitive-behavioral perspective* (pp. 206–240). Buffalo, NY: Prometheus.

Spiegel, D., Butler, L. D., Giese-Davis, J., Koopman, C., Miller, E., Dimiceli, S., . . . Kraemer, H. C. (2007). Effects of supportive-expressive group therapy on survival of patients with metastatic breast cancer: A randomized prospective trial. *Cancer*, *110*(5), 1130–1138. doi:10.1002/cncr.22890

Syrjala, K. L., Cummings, C., & Donaldson, G. W. (1992). Hypnosis or cognitive behavioral training for the reduction of pain and nausea during cancer treatment: A controlled clinical trial. *Pain*, *48*(2), 137–146.

Parkinson's Disease

Jim Sliwinski and Gary Elkins

Parkinson's disease is a severe neurological disorder that results in the progressive diminishment of the physical and mental health of those affected. The disease attacks neurons located in the basal ganglia and substantia nigra of the brain (Fearnley & Lees, 1991). This results in a gradual diminishment of one's ability to produce and process dopamine (Kimble, 1988; Schuepbach et al., 2013). Damage to these brain structures, along with the subsequent decrease in dopamine availability, leads to the hallmark symptoms of the disease, which include rest tremor, rigidity, and slowed or difficult movement, also known as bradykinesia. Another common symptom, involuntary muscle movement, or dyskinesia, is brought about by the long-term usage of levodopa, which is the most commonly prescribed treatment for the disorder (Hellmann, Melamed, Steinmetz, & Djaldetti, 2010).

Apart from these motor complications, Parkinson's disease is associated with a number of severe psychological concerns as well. In fact, over 60% of patients with Parkinson's disease either report or display neuropsychiatric symptoms (Aarsland et al., 1999). Common symptoms include anxiety, depression, sleep disturbance, and impulsiveness. Thus far, research has been unable to determine the extent to which these symptoms occur in response to the physical limitations of the disease, or whether they are more directly brought on by changes occurring within the brain (Medd, 1999; Truong, Bhidayasiri, & Wolters, 2008). However, evidence suggests that psychological symptoms may actually precede motor complications in some patients (Truong et al., 2008). Furthermore, successful treatment of psychological concerns has been associated with improvement in rest tremor severity (Wain, Amen, & Jabbari, 1990).

Estimates suggest that 7 to 10 million people are currently living with Parkinson's disease worldwide (Parkinson's Disease Foundation, 2014). Men are 1.5 times more likely than women to be diagnosed, and only 4% of patients will contract the disease before age 50. Roughly 60,000 Americans are diagnosed with Parkinson's disease each year.

RESEARCH

Although no large-scale studies examining the benefits of hypnosis for treating Parkinson's disease have been published, case studies suggest that hypnotherapy can be used to treat a variety of parkinsonian symptoms. In an early study (Stambaugh, 1977), a male patient, whose motor symptoms were successfully treated with levodopa, received six sessions of hypnosis over a two-week period. Treatment was focused on alleviating the patient's severe depression while also improving sleep. Hypnotic suggestions were given for glove analgesia, deep relaxation, and the isolation of ruminating thoughts.

Following treatment, the patient reported that he was able to sleep through the night, after having previously experienced an average of six awakenings per night (Stambaugh, 1977). He also reported the absence of pain after his fourth session, as well as a significant improvement in his appetite. At one year follow-up, the patient was gainfully employed and reported an absence of depressive symptomatology.

In a more recent study (Wain et al., 1990), a 76-year-old man suffering from bradykinesia as well as severe resting tremor on his left side, which had been made worse through years of treatment with levodopa, received two sessions of hypnosis. He was also taught self-hypnosis, which he reported practicing for approximately 12 minutes each day. Suggestions were given for deep relaxation and time distortion.

Results indicated that rest tremor ceased in the patient's left foot and hand during hypnosis (Wain et al., 1990). This most commonly occurred following suggestions for deep relaxation. Tremors returned whenever the patient was asked to speak and also when hypnosis sessions were ended. However, despite these limitations, the patient reported improvements in the intensity of his resting tremor and stiffness that lasted for several hours following treatment. These improvements were maintained at six-month follow-up.

In the most recent case study to have been conducted (Elkins, Sliwinski, Bowers, & Encarnacion, 2013), three sessions of hypnotherapy proved effective for significantly improving the anxiety, depression, sleep, libido, pain, stiffness, rest tremor, and quality of life of a 51-year-old male patient. This study is illustrated in the following case example.

CASE EXAMPLE

John was a 51-year-old school teacher and coach who had been diagnosed with Parkinson's disease 21 months ago. John's chief symptom of complaint was resting tremor in his left hand and foot that persisted despite treatment with carbidopa, levodopa, and ropinirole. John was referred to our lab for hypnotherapy by his neurologist after it had become clear that his symptoms could not be successfully managed through medication alone.

During John's initial visit to our lab, he reported that, along with his resting tremor, he also experienced significant pain and stiffness on his left side, and that these symptoms were particularly troublesome during the early hours of the day. He also reported taking medication for anxiety that had resulted from his diagnosis and reported that this was a severe detriment to his sleep. John reported that he was excited to begin hypnosis treatment and that he had no existing bias either for or against hypnotherapy or alternative medicine in general. However, he was slightly worried about the possibility that any new treatment might exacerbate his condition. John's goals entering therapy were improved sleep and slowing the progression of his symptoms. Prescreening indicated that John was moderately hypnotizable.

During John's first hypnotic session, steps were taken to clear up any misconceptions he might have had about hypnotherapy. He then received a standard hypnotic induction (Elkins & Handel, 2001), which was followed by suggestions for increased relaxation, diminishment of resting tremor, and greater control over dopamine release. Sessions 2 and 3 proceeded in the same manner; however, relaxation imagery had been personalized to include a relaxing lake scene from John's childhood. John also received an audio recording of his first hypnotic session and was instructed to listen to the recording at least once a day.

Following three weeks of treatment, John experienced a 94% reduction in the severity of his resting tremor. He also experienced an 89% reduction in pain, and a 97% reduction in stiffness. Nonmotor symptoms were also improved. Despite discontinuing his anxiety medication during the course of the study, John experienced a 75% improvement in his anxiety level following treatment. He also reported significant improvements in his levels of depression, sleep disturbance, libido, and quality of life. Many of these symptoms showed continued improvement at an eight-week follow-up visit. During this follow-up visit, John indicated that his symptoms had improved to a level that he had not thought possible prior to receiving hypnosis.

TRANSCRIPT: HYPNOSIS FOR PARKINSON'S DISEASE

The following transcript includes many of the same elements that were used during our case study with John, and can easily be adapted to suit a variety of patients.

"If you are comfortable, I would like you to focus your attention on a spot on the ceiling. You may close your eyes if you like, but try to imagine yourself at the top of a staircase that will lead you to a comfortable room. As you begin to descend the staircase, you may notice that you are becoming more and more relaxed. Hypnosis is a state of deep relaxation, and as you descend the first few steps, notice that you are drifting deeper into a relaxed and calm hypnotic state. Now, descending the next few steps, you feel yourself becoming

more and more relaxed with every breath. And as you are now, so deeply relaxed, you will be able to respond to each hypnotic suggestion without effort. There is a powerful relationship between the mind and body, and as you descend the next few stairs, drifting deeper and deeper into relaxation, you will notice that your tremors begin to decrease . . . your dopamine levels begin to increase . . . and your stiffness begins to subside. Now, nearing the bottom of the staircase, completely relaxed, you notice a door that will lead you to a comfortable room. When you are ready, descend the last few steps of the staircase and open the door to enter the room. Perhaps this room contains a cozy chair next to a fire. If you like, have a seat in the chair, and notice that there is a large window in the room that looks out over a beautiful landscape. And as you gaze at the landscape, still completely relaxed, continue to notice your levels of dopamine increasing . . . your tremors subsiding . . . and the pain and stiffness leaving your body. You can revisit this scene whenever you like . . . whenever you feel the need for further relaxation and comfort. Now, notice that even after you leave this room you will continue to have comfort and relief from your pain and stiffness . . . your rest tremors will continue to be significantly diminished . . . and your dopamine levels will be under your control."

CONCLUSION

Parkinson's disease is a progressive neurological disorder that can severely diminish the quality of life of the patient. Clinicians who wish to utilize hypnosis to help treat their patients with Parkinson's disease should familiarize themselves with the myriad of symptoms that accompany the disease. While some patients may seek relief from the physical manifestations of the disorder, others may be more discomforted by psychological symptoms, such as hallucinations, anxiety, and depression. Still others may find autonomic system irregularities, such as incontinence, hyperhidrosis, and sexual dysfunction, the most difficult symptoms to manage. A thorough history screening will allow clinicians to adapt their hypnotic suggestions to best suit the needs of their patients.

Although the research on hypnosis for Parkinson's disease is limited, results, thus far, have been promising. While additional investigation is needed to determine whether certain demographic factors, such as age, ethnicity, and gender, influence treatment efficacy, hypnosis has proven effective at treating many of the symptoms of Parkinson's disease and may offer hope to patients who have not responded favorably to treatment as usual.

REFERENCES

Aarsland, D., Larsen, J. P., Lim, N. G., Janvin, C., Karlsen, K., Tandberg, E., & Cummings, J. L. (1999). Range of neuropsychiatric disturbances in patients with Parkinson's disease. *Journal of Neurology, Neurosurgery & Psychiatry, 67*(4), 492–496. doi:10.1136/jnnp.67.4.492

Elkins, G., & Handel, D. (2001). Clinical hypnosis: An essential in the tool kit for family practice. *Clinics in Family Practice, 3*(1), 113–126. doi:10.1016/S1522-5720(05)70070-2

Elkins, G., Sliwinski, J., Bowers, J., & Encarnacion, E. (2013). Feasibility of clinical hypnosis for the treatment of Parkinson's disease: A case study. *International Journal of Clinical and Experimental Hypnosis, 61*(2), 172–182. doi:10.1080/00207144.2013.753829

Fearnley, J. M., & Lees, A. J. (1991). Ageing and Parkinson's disease: Substantia nigra regional selectivity. *Brain: A Journal of Neurology, 114 (Pt 5)*, 2283–2301.

Hellmann, M. A., Melamed, E., Steinmetz, A. P., & Djaldetti, R. (2010). Unilateral lower limb rest tremor is not necessarily a presenting symptom of Parkinson's disease. *Movement Disorders: Official Journal of the Movement Disorder Society, 25*(7), 924–927. doi:10.1002/mds.23030

Kimble, D. P. (1988). *Biological psychology*. New York, NY: Holt, Rinehart & Winston.

Medd, D. Y. (1999). Hypnosis with selected movement disorders. *Contemporary Hypnosis, 16*(2), 81–86. doi:10.1002/ch.155

Parkinson's Disease Foundation. (2014). *Statistics on Parkinson's*. Retrieved from http://www.pdf.org/en/parkinson_statistics

Schuepbach, W. M., Rau, J., Knudsen, K., Volkmann, J., Krack, P., Timmermann, L., Deuschl, G., EARLYSTIM Study Group. (2013). Neurostimulation for Parkinson's disease with early motor complications. *New England Journal of Medicine, 368*(7), 610–622. doi:10.1056/NEJMoa1205158

Stambaugh, E. E. (1977). Hypnotic treatment of depression in a parkinsonian patient: A case study. *American Journal of Clinical Hypnosis, 19*(3), 185–186. doi:10.1080/00029157.1977.10403869

Truong, D. D., Bhidayasiri, R., & Wolters, E. (2008). Management of non-motor symptoms in advanced Parkinson disease. *Journal of the Neurological Sciences*, 266(1-2), 216–288. doi:10.1016/j .jns.2007.08.015

Wain, H. J., Amen, D., & Jabbari, B. (1990). The effects of hypnosis on a parkinsonian tremor: Case report with polygraph/EEG recordings. *American Journal of Clinical Hypnosis*, 33(2), 94–98. doi:10.1080/0002915 7.1990.10402910

Pediatrics

Karen Olness

When Benjamin Franklin chaired a commission to assess the validity of Mesmer's claims, children were among the subjects of the commission's experiments. Franklin's commission concluded that the success of Mesmer's work related to application of imagination, rather than magnetic rods and/or mesmeric passes (Tinterow, 1970). Because most children have imagination skills superior to those of adults, it makes sense that they have the potential to do well with hypnosis.

Subsequently, James Braid, the English surgeon who first used the word *hypnotism,* did surgery with hypnosis as the sole anesthesia. Some of his patients were children. Auguste Liebeault and Hippolyte Bernheim worked with children in France and found that children were able to pay attention and understand instructions for hypnosis (Tinterow, 1970). Hypnosis was first mentioned in a U.S. publication (*Science*) in 1891 in a paper titled "Suggestion in infancy" (Baldwin, 1891). Franz Baumann, a pediatrician in California, began using hypnosis with children in the 1950s after attending workshops with Milton Erickson. He reported many successes in working with children who had enuresis, encopresis, or asthma (Baumann & Hinman, 1974). Following Dr. Baumann's lead, child health professionals began to teach hypnosis to children for habit problems, pain, performance anxiety, and other anxieties associated with chronic illness. London published the children's hypnotic susceptibility scales (London, 1963), and Morgan and Hilgard published the Stanford Hypnotic Clinical Scale for Children (Morgan & Hilgard, 1979). The first hypnosis workshop on children and hypnosis took place in Philadelphia in 1976.

Since then, there has been substantial research documenting not only the therapeutic efficacy of hypnosis with children but also achievement of psychophysiological controls by children who use hypnosis.

CHILD DEVELOPMENT AND HYPNOSIS WITH CHILDREN

Most children learn hypnosis easily. They often engage in games involving their imaginations that lead to spontaneous hypnotic states. The child professional who teaches hypnosis to children must consider the child's developmental stage. A hypnotic training approach that is accepted easily by a 4-year-old is unlikely to be enjoyed by a 9-year-old and vice versa. If a child is intellectually disabled, the hypnotic training approach should relate to his cognitive, not his chronological, age.

HYPNOSIS AS PRIMARY OR ADJUNCT THERAPY IN PEDIATRICS

Children may benefit from learning hypnosis as either primary or adjunct therapy for a variety of problems including:

- Sleep problems: difficulty falling asleep, nightmares, or night wakings
- Performance anxiety, including anxiety about sports, music, speaking in front of a group, or examinations
- Habit problems such as thumb sucking, coughing, nail biting, hair pulling
- Enuresis
- Warts
- Chronic conditions, including migraines, asthma, hemophilia, diabetes

- Tics, including Tourette's
- Conditioned fears or anxiety
- Pain associated with procedures
- Chronic pain, including abdominal pain, rheumatoid arthritis, cancer
- Dysfluencies
- Conditioned physiological responses, such as perspiration, hives, blushing, and tremors
- (Kohen & Kaiser, 2014; Kohen & Olness, 2011; Sugarman & Wester, 2014)

RESEARCH RELATED TO CHILDREN AND HYPNOSIS

There is substantial clinical and laboratory research to validate the use of hypnosis in pediatrics. However, the variability in preferences, learning styles, and developmental stages among children complicate the design of research protocols that study hypnosis with children. To accommodate reviewers, protocols are often written to describe identical hypnotic inductions, often recorded, to be used at prescribed times. Measured independent variables are unlikely to include the child's preferred mental imagery, whether or not the child focuses on his or her own preferred imagery instead of following taped instructions, or whether the child has subtle learning impairments.

Several controlled laboratory studies have demonstrated an association between practicing self-hypnosis and changes in humoral or cellular immunity in children (Hall, Minnes, Tosi, & Olness, 1992; Hewson-Bower and Drummond, 1996, 2001; Olness, Culbert, & Uden, 1989; Olness, Theoharides, Hall, Schmidt, & Rozniecki, 1999). There are several controlled studies documenting the ability of children to change autonomic responses while practicing hypnosis (Bothe, Grignon, & Olness, 2014; Dikel & Olness, 1981; Lee & Olness, 1996).

Controlled clinical studies have documented the efficacy of hypnosis in treating juvenile migraines, functional abdominal pain, warts, and procedure-related pain in children (Felt et al., 1998; Olness, MacDonald, & Uden, 1987; Tome-Pires & Miro, 2012; Vlieger, Menko-Frankenhuis, Wolfkamp, Tromp, & Benninga, 2007).

EVALUATION OF THE PEDIATRIC PROBLEM

Depending on the presenting problem and whether the child is to be seen in a hospital or an outpatient setting, much information can be obtained before seeing the child. Useful previsit questionnaires include screens for anxiety, depression, or attention; questionnaires specific for enuresis or headaches or pain; and also those which provide more general information about the child.

It is important that all patients, including children, have careful and thorough diagnostic assessments before making decisions about treatment. Does the child need diagnostics, such as laboratory or radiological tests? If a child is referred specifically to learn hypnosis, the child health professional must be certain that prior diagnostic assessments have been sufficient. For example, enuresis may be caused by constipation, diabetes, hyperthyroidism, diastematomyelia, or urinary tract infections. Headaches may be caused by brain tumors, allergies, carbon monoxide exposure, or sinus infections.

Cyclic vomiting may be caused by a biochemical deficiency such as oxalotranscarbamylose deficiency. It is essential that the child health professional be certain that the problem will not be more effectively treated with another approach that may require medications or a surgical procedure.

If it is appropriate to teach a child hypnosis, then it is important that the child's health professional assess the child's cognitive ability and preferred learning style. This can be done by asking parents and/or teachers about school performance, study habits, and knowledge of any learning disabilities.

The child health professional should ascertain how interested the child is in reducing or eliminating the problem. Are parents more concerned than the child? And if the child wishes to address the problem, what does he or she or the family members know about hypnosis? Are there misconceptions? Do they understand that practice at home is important to success?

It is often helpful to make drawings for school-age children that relate to the problem, such as enuresis or pain, and then to ask the child to do his or her own drawing. The child may do that drawing in the office or at home and then bring it along at the next visit. Discussion about the drawing may clarify the problem for the child and also provide the child health professional with important information about the child.

SELECTING A HYPNOTIC APPROACH FOR CHILDREN

The child health professional must take the time to learn about the child before making decisions about a hypnotic approach. This can be facilitated with the questionnaires completed before the appointment and discussion with the child. What are the child's interests, strengths, and weaknesses? What are his or her fears? Have there been past traumatic experiences related to family events or medical procedures? Does the child have visual imagery or auditory imagery? Can the child imagine tastes and smells or kinesthetic experiences such as the feeling of water in a pool or shower or bath?

The choice of a hypnotic induction for a child must take into account his or her age and developmental stage. Preschoolers generally are not comfortable closing their eyes during a hypnotic induction. They are also very concrete and respond best to concrete suggestions. They may prefer to hug a favorite stuffed animal while they are doing hypnosis. Children ages 6 to 11 years old usually like approaches that relate to their favorite places or activities. It is especially important to assure adolescents that they are in control of their hypnotic experience and to offer them choices.

The child health professional may elect not to teach hypnosis during the first visit but rather to use the first visit for thorough evaluation and establishing rapport with the child. After hypnosis is taught for the first time, it is important to ask the child what was helpful or enjoyable and what might be changed. Give the child the option to change his or her imagery. Then ask the child to repeat the practice according to his or her preferences. After the child does self-hypnosis, there should be some discussion about a reminder system for practice. What reminder system appeals to the child?

If the child is learning self-hypnosis to control a habit or to reduce performance anxiety, it is important to include suggestions about a future without the problem. Ideally, this should be tied to a pleasant anticipated event in the child's future, an event that the child chooses to imagine.

At a subsequent visit, the child health professional can offer to record a training session and to give a copy of the recording to the child. It is important to emphasize that the recording is to be used as "training wheels on a bike," only as long as is needed, after which the child can do the self-hypnosis practice without such assistance. Another option for the child is that he or she make the recording; this reinforces the child's control.

PARENT INVOLVEMENT

Whether or not parents should observe the teaching of hypnosis or be involved in practice at home depends on the problem and the needs of the child. Because it is important to emphasize the child's mastery and control, it is preferable for habit and performance problems to teach the child without parents' presence and to encourage the child to explain what he or she is doing to the parents. An alternative is to video record the training and to show the video to the parents. In general, it is better that the child and parents agree on a reminder system that does not involve the parents. In situations where the child is chronically ill or very young, it may be preferable to involve parents in coaching (Kuttner, 1986, 1998) and also to teach parents how to use self-hypnosis for themselves.

FACTORS IMPACTING EFFICACY OF HYPNOTHERAPY WITH CHILDREN

The milieu is important. The attitude of parents or other family members, members of a health care team, or cultural norms will impact outcomes, either encouraging or discouraging a child. The child's developmental stage, interest, fatigue level, and cognitive ability affect the child's capacity to learn and practice self-hypnosis. The context of the symptom or problem is also important. For example, a child who has warts that are causing no discomfort and are covered with clothing may have little interest in eliminating them.

WHEN NOT TO TEACH HYPNOSIS TO CHILDREN

One should not proceed if there is a more appropriate treatment for the problem or if further diagnostics are needed. One should not proceed if the child is fearful or disinterested. It may be possible to establish rapport to overcome fear or disinterest but this must be done before any attempt to teach hypnosis. If two parents or guardians disagree about hypnosis, it is unwise to proceed. If a child has mental health problems such as depression or posttraumatic stress disorder (PTSD), it is essential that the person teaching hypnosis be a qualified child psychologist or psychiatrist, or that he or she work closely with a qualified child psychologist or psychiatrist who is also seeing the child. Depending on where they are developmentally, children and adolescents have limited decision-making capacity. Special consideration must be given to ethical issues when any type of treatment is under consideration for a child (Etzrodt, 2013).

USE HYPNOSIS TO FACILITATE THE CHILD'S SENSE OF MASTERY

1. Emphasize that the child is in control.
2. Offer to be the teacher or coach.
3. Offer choices or options.
4. Explain that the child can use hypnosis when he or she chooses.
5. In general, we ask that parents not remind children to practice.

CASE EXAMPLE

Note: This case report represents one child. The child's name has been changed for reasons of privacy. Each child is different and it is not appropriate to use identical approaches or words for other children. The child health professional must think about the characteristics of each child patient and individualize the approach accordingly (Kaiser, 2011).

Jason, a 9-year-old boy, was referred by his family physician because he had developed test anxiety in school. When the boy arrived in the office with his mother, the child health professional had already reviewed questionnaires completed by the boy and his mother a week earlier. These included the children's behavior checklist (CBCL) and a general questionnaire about his health, sleep, peers, strengths, preferred activities, and preferred mental imagery. Copies of school reports from the past year were also reviewed. The CBCL did not flag any concerns. The general questionnaire provided information that Jason was in the fourth grade and doing well. He enjoyed school except for tests and often had play dates with friends from school. He was taking guitar lessons and sometimes practiced without reminding. He was on a soccer team and soccer was his favorite sport. He had an older brother and a younger sister. His parents were married and one set of grandparents lived nearby. Jason enjoyed spending time with his grandparents. He usually slept 10 hours a night. School reports indicated that he had done very well through third grade and that his grades in academic subjects declined after the first period of fourth grade. This led to the referral. The first two visits were scheduled during the holiday break.

The child health professional greeted Jason and his mother and invited them into her office. She thanked the mother for sending the questionnaires and school reports. She told Jason she was impressed that he played the guitar and would practice without reminders. Jason smiled and said that sometimes he was reminded. The child health professional asked him about music he was playing and about his guitar teacher. Jason said that he was learning some classical guitar pieces and that he looked forward to his weekly lessons. His mother nodded in agreement. The child health professional then asked about basketball and Jason said he was on a team that had practice in the fall and winter. He said that his dad was one of the basketball coaches and that basketball was his favorite sport. Sometimes he and his dad and grandfather attended high school or college basketball games and Jason looked forward to those times.

The child health professional asked Jason why he came in to see her today. Jason hesitated and then said, "Because I can't take tests in school."

She asked if Jason could tell her when he began worrying about tests. Jason said this started in November when he got two wrong in a spelling test. Another boy in his class saw his graded test and said he was "really dumb" to not know how to spell those words. After this, Jason said, he felt "shaky" before every exam, especially spelling and math tests. He said he couldn't finish exams because he was "so nervous." His mother said that he didn't show signs of anxiety when he was playing a basketball game or playing his guitar at a recital. She also said she had talked to school officials about the child who had criticized Jason.

The child health professional told Jason that many children and adults have the same problem of being nervous before tests, and that she knew several children who overcame the problem by learning self-hypnosis. The health professional said, "I learned from the questionnaire that you have a good imagination and that you can imagine pictures in your head and also you can imagine the sound of your favorite music. I'm glad to know that because that makes it easy to learn self-hypnosis."

She said that she could be his coach or teacher if he would like to learn self-hypnosis. "I can teach you what to do but I am not going home with you. So it would be up to you to do the practice at home. Is that agreeable to you?" Jason nodded vigorously.

"Good, then I will ask your mother to wait in the waiting room while I teach you. You can then explain to your mother how you do this practice and the two of you can talk about how you will remind yourself to practice while you are on the way home today."

After his mother left the room, the child health professional said, "Please make yourself comfortable in the chair and, while you listen, you can keep your eyes open or shut. Some children find it easier if they close their eyes." (Jason then closed his eyes.)

"That's good. We talked about your good imagination and about your favorite sport, basketball. Just go ahead and imagine you are shooting free throws and making every one. When you have made ten free throws in your imagination, let me know by nodding or by lifting one of your fingers."

After two minutes, Jason nodded.

"Great, and now imagine playing one of your favorite guitar pieces, playing it very well and enjoy hearing the sound of your music. Take all the time you need."

After a pause, the child health professional said, *"When you have played that guitar music and you are feeling very comfortable, please let me know."*

After a minute, Jason nodded.

"You did that well. Now, as you are comfortable, imagine you are at home wherever you do your homework and you ask your mother or dad to do a practice spelling test with you. And you write the words so easily and correctly and, when the practice test is done, you see that all the words are correct. Enjoy that good feeling of being in control of the spelling words. Take all the time you need to enjoy that feeling and then, slowly, comfortably, and easily, you can open your eyes and we can talk about what you did for yourself."

After two minutes Jason opened his eyes and smiled.

The child health professional said, "Were you comfortable?" Jason nodded.

"What did you like best?" Jason said, "Shooting baskets."

"Well, that's fine. You can shoot even more baskets if you like. How many words were on the spelling test?"

Jason said, "Eight. And I got them all right."

"Good. You have done well. Do you have any questions?"

Jason shook his head, "No."

"Now, to help you remember this practice, it would be good for you to do the self-hypnosis by yourself. I will be quiet and you go ahead, shoot baskets, play the guitar, and take a spelling test at home. Just make yourself comfortable in the chair and go ahead. I will wait for you."

Jason closed his eyes again. After five minutes he opened them.

"How was that for you?"

Jason said, "Good."

"So you can explain your practice to your mom and I recommend you practice this twice a day until the next time I see you, because the more you practice, the better you get. If you have any questions before you come back to see me, you can leave a message with my office and I will call you back."

Follow-Up: Second Visit

Jason returned a week later. He said that he had practiced his self-hypnosis once or twice each day. The child health professional asked if there was anything that he would like to change. Jason said that he was shooting 20 baskets instead of 10 and that he was playing a different song on his guitar.

"That's fine. You are in control of your self-hypnosis. Today you can repeat your self-hypnosis and add two more parts. You just go ahead and do your self-hypnosis the way you have been doing at home and let me know after you finish the spelling test with your parents. You can nod your head or lift a finger to let me know when you are ready for me to tell you about the next parts."

Jason did his self-hypnosis and nodded his head after about six minutes.

"That's good. Now, staying very comfortable, imagine yourself taking a spelling test in school and enjoying writing the answers because you are comfortable and in control. Just let me know when you have finished the test."

Jason nodded again after two minutes.

"You've done well. Now take time to imagine something you are looking forward to doing by yourself or with a friend or with someone in your family. Please let me know when you are imagining doing something special."

After Jason nodded she said,

"And it's nice to know that you can enjoy that special time and, at the same time, enjoy knowing that you no longer have worries about taking tests. Enjoy that special time and enjoy being in control, a little while longer, as long as you wish and then slowly, comfortably, and easily open your eyes and enjoy the rest of today."

When Jason opened his eyes he smiled.

"How was that?"

Jason said, "It was good, I went to a Final Four basketball game."

"Wow, I bet that was exciting!" Jason smiled and said "Yes!"

"Do you have any questions?'

Jason answered, "Should I do this practice at home now?"

"Yes, if possible, practice twice a day at home. If you wish, when you are in school and about to have a test, you can imagine making 20 free throws first."

"Great idea," said Jason.

Follow-Up: Third Visit

Jason returned two weeks later. He had done well in two exams in school. He was practicing once a day at home and said that he made imaginary free throws before the exams in school.

In a phone follow-up a month later, his mother said he had no further test anxiety and that his grades had improved.

CONCLUSION

Children learn hypnosis easily. They can apply hypnosis as either primary or adjunct therapy for both acute and chronic problems.

It is essential to do a careful assessment of each child, including the history of the problem and the child's personality and interests before teaching hypnosis. It is important to consider the child's age and developmental stage in making decisions about communicating with the child and selecting a hypnotic approach.

It is essential that the coach or teacher emphasize that the child is in control and can use his or her self-hypnosis when and where he or she wishes.

REFERENCES

Baldwin, J. M. (1891). Suggestion in infancy. *Science*, *17*(421), 113–117. doi:10.1126/science.ns-17.421.113

Baumann, F. W., & Hinman, F. (1974). Treatment of incontinent boys with non-obstructive disease. *Urology*, *111*, 114–116.

Bothe, D. A., Grignon, J. B., & Olness, K. N. (2014). The effects of a stress management intervention in elementary school children. *Journal of Developmental and Behavioral Pediatrics*, *35*(1), 62–67. doi:10.1097/DBP.0000000000000016

Dikel, W., & Olness, K. (1981). Self hypnosis, biofeedback and voluntary peripheral temperature control in children. *Pediatrics*, *66*, 335–340.

Etzrodt, C. M. (2013). Ethical considerations of therapeutic hypnosis and children. *American Journal of Clinical Hypnosis*, *55*(4), 370–377. doi:10.1080/00029157.2012.746933

Felt, B. T., Hall, H., Olness, K., Schmidt, W., Kohen, D., Berman, B. D., . . . Young, M. H. (1998). Wart regression in children: Comparison of relaxation–imagery to topical treatment and equal time interventions. *American Journal of Clinical Hypnosis, 41*(2), 130–137. doi:10.1080/00029157.1998.10404199

Hall, H. R., Minnes, L., Tosi, M., & Olness, K. (1992). Voluntary modulation of neutrophil adhesiveness using a cyberphysiologic strategy. *International Journal of Neuroscience, 63*(3-4), 287–297.

Hewson-Bower, B., & Drummond, P. D. (1996). Secretory immunoglobulin A increases during relaxation in children with and without recurrent upper respiratory tract infections. *Journal of Developmental and Behavioral Pediatrics, 17*(5), 311–316.

Hewson-Bower, B., & Drummond, P. D. (2001). Psychological treatment of recurrent symptoms of colds and flu in children. *Journal of Psychosomatic Research, 51*(1), 369–377.

Kaiser, P. (2011). Childhood anxiety, worry, and fear: Individualizing hypnosis goals and suggestions for self-regulation. *American Journal of Clinical Hypnosis, 54*(1), 16–31. doi:10.1080/00029157.2011.575965

Kohen, D. P., & Olness, K. (2011). *Hypnosis and hypnotherapy with children.* New York, NY: Routledge.

Kohen, D., & Kaiser, P. (2014). Review: Clinical hypnosis with children and adolescents: What? Why? How? Origins, applications and efficacy. *Children, 1*(2), 74–98. doi:10.3390/children1020074

Kuttner, L. (1986). *No fears, no tears.* [DVD].

Kuttner, L. (1998). *No fears, no tears 13 years later.* [DVD].

Lee, L. H., & Olness, K. N. (1996). Effects of self-induced mental imagery on autonomic reactivity in children. *Journal of Developmental and Behavioral Pediatrics: JDBP, 17*(5), 323–327.

London, P. (1963). *Children's hypnotic susceptibility scale.* Palo Alto, CA: Consulting Psychologists Press.

Morgan, A. H., & Hilgard, E. R. (1979). The Sanford hypnotic clinical scale for children. *American Journal of Clinical Hypnosis, 21,* 148–169.

Olness, K., Culbert, T., & Uden, D. (1989). Self regulation of salivary immunoglobulin A by children. *Pediatrics, 83*(1), 66–71.

Olness, K., Macdonald, J. T., & Uden, D. L. (1987). A prospective study comparing self hypnosis, propranolol and placebo in management of juvenile migraine. *Pediatrics, 79*(4), 593–597.

Olness, K., Theoharides, T. C., Hall, H., Schmidt, W., & Rozniecki, I. (1999). Mast cell activation in child migraine patients before and after training in self regulations. *Headache, 41,* 130–138.

Sugarman, L. I., & Wester, W. C. (2014). *Therapeutic hypnosis with children and adolescents.* Bethel, CT: Crown House.

Tinterow, M. M. (1970). *Foundations of hypnosis from Mesmer to Freud.* Springfield, IL: Charles C. Thomas.

Tomé-Pires, C., & Miró, J. (2012). Hypnosis for the management of chronic and cancer procedure-related pain in children. *International Journal of Clinical and Experimental Hypnosis, 60*(4), 432–457. doi:10.1080/00207144.2012.701092

Vlieger, A. M., Menko-Frankenhuis, C., Wolfkamp, S. C., Tromp, E., & Benninga, M. A. (2007). Hypnotherapy for children with functional abdominal pain or irritable bowel syndrome: A randomized controlled trial. *Gastroenterology, 133*(5), 1430–1436. doi:10.1053/j.gastro.2007.08.072

Pre-Surgery

Linda Thomson

Around the world, millions of minor and major surgical procedures are performed every year. Surgery is a traumatic injury that stimulates the stress response that delays wound healing and surgical recovery. Hypnosis has the potential to mitigate the stress response. The use of hypnosis for surgical patients can be very effective in enhancing their coping skills, managing stress and anxiety, reducing pain, and increasing their sense of self-mastery, thus having an enormous positive impact on both their surgical course and their recovery.

Until the 1800s, surgery was often an option of last resort as patients preferred a certain death over the pain of surgery. Alcohol and herbal extracts were used for thousands of years in an attempt to achieve sedation and anesthesia. In the 1800s, mesmerism began to be used as the sole anesthetic for both minor and major surgeries. Esdaile (1850) and Elliotson (1843) in England published reports outlining the success of their work using these techniques to increase the surgical patient's comfort and reduce both morbidity and mortality. Their work, which in essence was hypnoanesthesia, was minimized when ether was discovered in 1846 and chloroform in 1847. Certainly, the safety and efficacy of anesthetic agents have increased dramatically over the past 170 years. However, chemical anesthesia is not without its risks and side effects and does nothing to empower the patient.

Today, surgical patients are asked to sign an informed consent document that itemizes everything that could possibly go wrong, leaving patients to anticipate pain, complications, and even fear for their lives. They are stripped of their control and their clothing, are immobilized on a gurney and taken to a cold room far removed from family or friends, and filled with masked strangers and scary equipment. For surgical procedures, a huge spotlight shines down and for interventional radiological procedures, the room is plunged into darkness. The iatrogenic ingredients for anxiety and the nocebo effect are all there. Negative health consequences may result when patients avoid diagnostic or surgical procedures due to acute procedural anxiety.

Surgical procedures on adults older than 65 years account for a disproportionately large percentage of operations performed each year. Pharmacodynamic sensitivity to chemical agents affecting the central nervous system increases with age (Rivera & Antognini, 2009). It is recognized, although not fully understood, that older patients have a higher incidence of postoperative delirium and cognitive deficits following general anesthesia (Silverstein, Timberger, Reich, & Uysal, 2007). The duration of the drug effect from intravenous and volatile anesthetics is frequently prolonged in adults older than 40. The postoperative cognitive decline has been found to be especially prevalent in cardiac surgery patients as well as patients with diabetes and hypertension. It is postulated that because anesthesia affects so many diverse brain processes and areas that it may have unforeseen consequences, which may be linked to neurodegeneration (Faymonville, Meurisse, & Fissett, 1999). In a recent large cohort study of nearly 25,000 patients older than 50, there was a nearly twofold increase in dementia in the anesthesia/surgery group as compared with controls (Chen et al., 2013). Anesthesia may promote inflammation of the neural tissue, beta-amyloid plaques, and neurofibrillary tangles implicated as a precursor of dementia. The hypotensive and respiratory depressant effects of sedatives and narcotic agents are exaggerated in older adults in addition to increasing the risk of poor perfusion, postoperative apnea, and respiratory failure (McLean & Le Couteur, 2004). It is apparent that there are significant potential benefits to decreasing the dosage of anesthetics, anxiolytics, sedatives, and narcotics in surgical patients. Research has shown that hypnosis can be effective in potentiating the efficacy of anesthetics and analgesics so that lower dosages can be used (Peebles-Kleiger, 2000). Hypnosis for surgery preparation can also facilitate postoperative healing and help maintain the stability of vital signs. When necessary, hypnosis can also be used as the sole anesthetic for surgery in patients with above average hypnotizability (Barabasz & Watkins, 2005).

RESEARCH

Hypnosis can be effectively used in children to decrease the distress of parental separation and the induction of anesthesia. The drugs used to sedate children can have unwanted harmful effects such as airway obstruction and behavior changes (Yip, Middleton, Cyna, & Carlyle, 2009). A simple surgical procedure can be a traumatic experience for a child with long-lasting psychological effects. When midazolam and hypnosis were compared for preoperative anxiety in children, it was found that hypnosis was equally effective and without any risks or adverse effects. Hypnosis was superior in reducing anxiety during the induction of anesthesia (Calipel, Lucas-Polomeni, Wodey, & Ecoffey, 2005). Butler, Symons, Henderson, Shortliffe, and Spiegel (2005) evaluated the effectiveness of hypnotic relaxation for children during voiding cystourethrography (VCUG). The research showed significant improvement in comfort, especially during the catheterization, and the length of the procedure was reduced by 20 minutes.

In a randomized controlled study, children experienced significantly less pain, state anxiety, and had shorter hospital stays when preoperative hypnotic guided imagery was used (Lambert, 1996). Adolescents who received self-hypnosis training before undergoing a Nuss procedure for pectus excavatum had statistically significant improved pain control as compared with the nonhypnosis group. The results of this study suggest that hypnosis provides an effective opioid-sparing adjunctive therapy for the management of moderate to severe pediatric postoperative pain (Manworren et al., 2014). An earlier study using perioperative hypnosis for the Nuss surgical procedure showed reduced length of hospitalization in children (Lobe, 2006).

Glaser et al. (1999) showed that there are stress-related changes in proinflammatory cytokines in wounds that can delay healing. A study by Ginandes, Brooks, Sando, Jones, and Aker (2003) looked at the effect of hypnosis on wound healing following reduction mammoplasty. The hypnosis group had statistically significant improved functional recovery, less postoperative pain, and a greater degree of healing than those in the control and supportive attention groups.

Many studies have shown the positive effects of hypnotic intervention therapy on surgical patients with reduced postoperative nausea and vomiting, decreased anxiety during the procedure, less pain, fewer postoperative side effects, decreased use of analgesics and anxiolytics, and quicker recovery time (Blankfield, 1991; Cupal & Brewer, 2001; de Klerk, du Plessis, Steyn, & Botha, 2004; Eitner et al., 2006; Enqvist, Björklund, Engman, & Jakobsson, 1997; Faymonville et al., 1995, 1997, 1999; Fredericks, 2001; Ginandes et al., 2003; Lang et al., 2000, 2006, 2008; Saadat et al., 2006; Schnur et al., 2008; Tusek, Church, & Fazio, 1997; Van Wijk, Buchanan, & Coulson, 2009; Wain, 2004; Williams, Hind, Sweeney, & Fisher, 1994).

Montgomery, David, Winkel, Silverstein, and Bovbjerg (2002) performed a meta-analysis of the controlled studies that looked at the effectiveness of hypnosis with surgical patients. They found that surgical patients in the hypnosis groups had better outcomes than 89% of the patients in control groups. Their analysis showed that there was no difference between live intervention and taped hypnosis. They also determined that it was not just the highly hypnotizable that could benefit from this intervention. Kessler and Dane (1996) found that a patient's overall recovery from surgery is only partially related to his physical state and significantly related to psychological factors that can be favorably impacted with hypnosis.

Following Lang et al.'s study (2000) using hypnosis for invasive vascular and renal procedures, which showed reduced pain and decreased anxiety despite the use of less analgesia, fewer anxiolytics, and greater hemodynamic stability, she and her colleagues did a cost analysis using adjunctive hypnosis with sedation during interventional radiological procedures (Lang & Rosen, 2002). They determined that a cost savings of $338 per case was achieved when adjunctive hypnosis was used. In large part, due to the improved hemodynamic stability when hypnosis was used, room time could be reduced. Even if room time was increased by 58.2 minutes, it would still be cost-effective.

CASE EXAMPLE

In large part due to a catastrophic skiing accident, I have had more than two dozen surgeries. For only the past four did I know about ad utilize hypnosis as an adjunct to or in place of anesthesia. Following my first ASCH Basic workshop in clinical hypnosis, I asked an anesthesiologist who was part of my experiential skill practice group if he would create a hypnosis recording for me to be used as an adjunct to anesthesia for an upcoming abdominal surgery. I began listening to the recording three days before surgery. I took it to the hospital and listened to it in the pre-op area. Starting an intravenous infusion in my small, deep, and rolling veins is always a challenge. After failed attempts at starting an IV in my arms, hands, and feet, the anesthesiologist decided to try the external jugular vein in my neck. I remember the doctor saying, "This one is really going to hurt," to which the nurse responded, "I don't think she can feel anything. I think she has numbed her entire body." I was comfortably listening to my hypnosis CD during the multiple unsuccessful attempts to start an IV. Following the total hysterectomy, I was up walking in the halls two and a half hours later and required no pain medication.

Several years later, I required rotator cuff surgery on my shoulder and created a hypnosis recording for myself. I was comfortably relaxed in the preoperative area listening to my hypnosis recording when the anesthesiologist arrived and asked if I wanted something for anxiety. From my totally relaxed hypnotic haze, I responded, "You have got to be kidding! Do I look like I need anything for anxiety?" Following the surgery, the orthopedic surgeon came into the recovery area and announced to my husband and myself that they had found more damage in my shoulder than expected and that when the scalene block wore off, I "could anticipate being in a tremendous amount of pain." Fortunately, two of the suggestions I had given to myself on the hypnosis recording were that the sensations I would feel after surgery would be those of healing and mending and need not bother me and that if anyone said anything to me that was less than helpful, it would be as if they were speaking in a foreign language that I did not understand. I never heard the surgeon telling me that I would be in a tremendous amount of pain; my husband told

me what he had said 3 days later. I never needed any pain medication. It wasn't that I didn't feel any pain, it just didn't bother me. I preferred the mild discomfort to the dopey, groggy feeling that results from narcotics.

I subsequently needed knee surgery. As I was discussing the options for anesthesia, the same orthopedist remarked, "You could have a general anesthetic, a spinal, or we could do it under local and you could do your hypnosis stuff." I chose the local and to do my "hypnosis stuff." When I arrived in the operating room, they had Frank Sinatra's "I Did It My Way" playing. I was able to leave the hospital 30 minutes after he finished the surgery and required no pain medication. Two years later, I tore my meniscus in the other knee and again needed arthroscopic surgery. Once again, "I Did It My Way."

From my own personal experience and those of the patients that I have prepared hypnotically for surgery, hypnosis has been an incredibly effective adjunct to anesthesia and hastened healing and surgical recovery.

TRANSCRIPT: HYPNOSIS FOR SURGERY

Before beginning hypnosis, it is important to obtain a careful history from the patient while establishing rapport. The clinician should obtain information concerning the what, where, who, and when of the procedure, along with the why. Why is the patient having the surgery and how will his or her life be better when the surgery has been successfully completed are important questions to ask and utilize in trance. It is helpful for the clinician to know the expected postoperative course and the patient's wishes, worries, and fears. Has the patient had previous hospitalizations, surgeries, and prior experience with hypnosis? Depending on the patient's personal spiritual beliefs, the patient may request scripture, prayer, or a meaningful poem to be included in the hypnosis session. It may also be comforting for the individual to have specific background music during the session. It is most helpful when the hypnosis is recorded. Depending on the availability of the necessary equipment and the technological capabilities of both the patient and the clinician, the session can be recorded directly on the patient's device, an audio file can be e-mailed to the patient, or a CD can be burned of the session and given to the patient for use both preoperatively and intraoperatively.

Utilizing a rapid induction followed by a lengthier deepening or intensification gives the patient a tool to use to quickly return to a trance when interrupted or disturbed. Variations of the eye roll or Easy as 1-2-3 rapid inductions can be effectively used.

"It's as easy as One. . . . Two. . . . Three. On One you do one thing: Look up, up, up. On Two you do two things: Take a deep breath in and hold it. On Three you do three things: Slowly, slowly allow your eyes and eyelids to drift down together into a comfortable space, exhale, and just float . . . float.

There is no drug that can compete with hypnosis for empowering the patient. You have incredible inner strength. Strength you may never have known you have, and I am going to help you tap into that strength so that you can go through your surgery in comfort and safety, surrounded by the love and healing wishes (or prayers) of your family and friends. Feel their love and good wishes surrounding you now. While you are enjoying your special place of peacefulness, comfortable and relaxed, I will prepare you for surgery. Dr. _____ will perform what is necessary to your _____ skillfully, carefully. The doctors and nurses will take good care of you."

This can be followed by diaphragmatic breathing, progressive muscle relaxation, and, most importantly, the creation of a safe place of comfort that the patient can return to whenever he or she wants or needs to. It is helpful to suggest a technique to the patient to get rid of unwanted worries or fears.

"If there are any thoughts or concerns that are getting in the way of your comfort and relaxation, perhaps you would like to put them on a cloud and notice how the cloud floats off, taking those worries farther and farther away . . . smaller and smaller . . . further and further."

For a patient who has requested inclusion of a higher power, the following may be included:

"Feel yourself lying in the palm of God's hand, safe and secure, feel His presence in this room. Feel the comfort of His strength and power, the warmth of His love. Know that He is here guiding the hands of your doctor and nurses. Feel His healing light shining down around you."

A patient in the preoperative area who is listening to a hypnosis recording or practicing self-hypnosis can anticipate multiple interruptions. The patient may be asked questions, required to sign forms, meet the anesthesiologist, or have an IV started or the operative area washed or shaved. Through fractionation these interruptions can be utilized to deepen the patient's trance.

"You will be interested to note that as you are asked to answer questions or are asked to do anything, that it does not disrupt your level of comfort. If questioned directly, you can respond easily. In fact, anytime during your journey that you open your eyes or are asked to move from one place to another, you will notice when you close your eyes again, you will feel yourself going even more deeply relaxed. From the time you arrive at the hospital until you are in the recovery room, pay attention only to the voice that is speaking directly to you. All other sounds will seem pleasantly far away, a lolling, soothing sound like background music, that drowsy, dreamy, sleepy feeling will increase with each sound, making you go deeper and deeper relaxed. And if anyone says anything to you that is less than helpful, it will be as if he or she is speaking in a foreign language that you do not understand. It will be interesting to note that your inner mind will translate that foreign language to the words that are most helpful to you—words of comfort and words of health and healing.

The doctors and nurses will be with you all the time, watching over you, making sure you are comfortable and safe. You will feel a gentle clip on your finger and the hug of a blood pressure cuff around your arm, making you feel very safe and secure. You may notice all the high-tech equipment around you, all there to help your surgery go well. You may be surprised to discover how safe it makes you feel.

You will be pleased to remain in this deep state of relaxation. You may hear sounds or noise that you may choose to ignore or you may wish to incorporate as part of your very pleasant daydream. These sounds do not need to bother or disturb you. How pleasant it is to know you do not have to respond to anything unless it is directed especially at you. You may remain deeply relaxed in your special place of comfort, comfortable from head to toe. Let your unconscious mind record this feeling and when they are ready to take you for the procedure, use your journey to the operating room, your journey of healing, to take you even deeper relaxed."

Operating rooms are kept cool intentionally, so it is helpful to offer suggestions about warmth.

"From your special place of comfort, bring with you the warmth to make you as comfortable and relaxed as you need to be. You may experience the warmth as absorbing warm rays of energy and healing."

Hemodynamic stability can be enhanced with the following suggestions: *"As your _____ [operative area] is being washed with the antiseptic solution, your inner mind will constrict the blood vessels to that area, diverting blood to all other organs. Your inner mind will regulate your blood flow, blood pressure, and blood glucose to the level that is perfect for you. It will protect you; your blood pressure will stay at the level that is right for you. Sending just the right amount of blood to your brain, your heart, your kidneys, and all your other organs, filling you with nutrients and oxygen. Your body knows how to fill every cell of your body with just the right amount of nutrients and supply glucose and oxygen to your tissues, not too much, not too little, just the right amount.*

When you are ready to receive the wonderful anesthesia, take a deep breath of comfort, a breath of tranquility from your special place of comfort where nothing needs to bother or disturb you. Your body will make the operative area relaxed and comfortable through-out the procedure and afterwards until you are completely healed.

Creating positive expectancy is especially reassuring. Your surgery will go well, successful as planned. When you are as comfortable and nicely relaxed as you are now, your surgical team will be able to do what needs to be done to your _____ to correct the problem (remove the cancer, replace the knee, etc.)."

Your procedure will soon be complete and the healing can begin immediately. Continue to let your team of doctors and nurses take good care of you, knowing also that you can do anything you need to do to increase your comfort."

Specific suggestions are helpful to enhance postoperative pain control, encourage lung expansion, promote earlier return of bodily functions, and decrease nausea and vomiting.

"When your procedure is complete, you will awaken as if from a pleasant, peaceful, natural sleep. You will feel relaxed and pleased to feel so good, so happy to be free of _____ and the concern, worry, and aggravation that surrounded it. Happy and confident that this procedure was so successful. The sensations you feel will be those of healing and mending and need not bother you. Your body is setting everything right, so you need not mind the healing sensations. As you begin to awaken, breathe in a very deep breath of comfort and peacefulness. Allow that wonderful air to fill your lungs and your body with healing. You can now recover quickly, completely, and comfortably. Note with pleasure how soon all your bodily functions will return to normal. How easily and fully you regain control of your bladder and bowel functions. You will swallow to clear your throat. This will be a signal to your digestive system—one way going straight down bringing nourishment and healing to your body. One way, only going down, comfortably easily. You will look forward to the good food and find it so satisfying to drink fluids again, your stomach welcoming the nourishment."

Additional personalized suggestions may be given depending on the particular surgery (orthopedic, cardiac, GI, GU/Gyn, cancer, spinal, etc.).

Reframing postoperative pain can have significant positive effects. *"As your body heals, you will experience different physical sensations. I am not sure what they will be—perhaps a slight discomfort, or pulling, pressure, or warmth as your body mends and the healing process continues. As your body heals, changes do occur and you can cooperate with the work of your body by remaining as calm as you are now, feeling the gentle rhythm of your breathing. The more relaxed you are, the less tension you have, the less discomfort that you have, and the more comfort you will have.*

You are on a journey of healing. The wind has changed direction. It is at your back now. Feel its gentleness. encouraging you forward to the place you want to be—physically, emotionally well, healthy, and strong. Nothing needs to disturb you now, nothing needs to bother you. Everything is being taken care of. All you need to concentrate on is getting better, completely healed. No demands are being placed on you, no expectations. There is no one to please, no one to satisfy. The only thing for you to do right now is to feel and experience the gentle rhythm of your body, feeling a sense of comfortable stillness. At any time during your recovery, you can go right back to this place of comfort and relaxation for your own benefit. You can daydream as fully as you would like without any need to pay attention to all the goings on of the hospital.

You may choose to remember to forget or forget to remember as much or as little of this experience as you want or need to, but remember to remember that you were able to give yourself an amazing amount of comfort.

As my voice leaves you now, you will remember my voice in your place of comfort and healing surrounded by the love and good wishes (prayers) of your family and friends. Feel the strength and healing power of their love and care surrounding you.

Whenever you are ready to come back from this very pleasant daydream, knowing you can return again to your place of comfort and relaxation at any time, simply count to 3 and realert feeling good, feeling healthy, comfortable, and very calm. Taking all the time you need, allowing yourself to retain that feeling of comfort and sense of well-being."

CONCLUSION

By helping the surgical patient achieve a relaxed, confident, and comfortable state of mind, hypnosis can have a profound impact on the patient's surgical experience. Research has shown that by using pre-operative hypnotic intervention therapy, the patient will be in the best psychological condition for optimal experience, outcome, and healing. The hypnotically prepared patient can expect to experience less preoperative anxiety, fewer operative complications, less postoperative discomfort, and faster healing. Hypnosis accesses the most powerful pharmacy in the world located within the individual. Hypnosis empowers the surgical patient to take charge of his or her recovery, increase his or her comfort, and hasten healing more powerfully than any pharmaceutical and without any negative side effects.

REFERENCES

Barabasz, A., & Watkins, J. G. (2005). *Hypnotherapeutic techniques.* New York, NY: Brunner Routledge.

Blankfield, R. P. (1991). Suggestion, relaxation, and hypnosis as adjuncts in the care of surgery patients: A review of the literature. *American Journal of Clinical Hypnosis, 33*(3), 172–186.

Butler, L. D., Symons, B. K., Henderson, S. L., Shortliffe, L. D., & Spiegel, D. (2005). Hypnosis reduces distress and duration of an invasive medical procedure for children. *Pediatrics, 115*(1), 77–85.

Calipel, S., Lucas-Polomeni, M. M., Wodey, E., & Ecoffey, C. (2005). Premedication in children: Hypnosis versus midazolam. *Paediatric Anaesthesia, 15*(4), 275–281.

Chen, P. L., Yang, C. W., Tseng, Y. K., Sun, W. Z., Wang, J. L., Wang, S. J., . . . Jong-Ling, F. (2013). Risk of dementia after anaesthesia and surgery. *British Journal of Psychiatry 204*(3), 188–193.

Cupal, D., & Brewer, B. (2001). Effects of relaxation and guided imagery on knee strength, reinjury anxiety, and pain following anterior cruciate ligament reconstruction. *Rehabilitation Psychology, 46*(1), 28–43.

de Klerk, J. E., du Plessis, W. F., Steyn, H. S., & Botha, M. (2004). Hypnotherapeutic ego-strengthening with male South Africa coronary artery bypass patients. *American Journal of Clinical Hypnosis, 47*(2), 79–92.

Eitner, S., Wichmann, M., Schultze-Mosgau, S., Schlegel, A., Leher, A., Heckmann, J., . . . Holst, S . (2006). Neurophysiologic and long-term effects of clinical hypnosis in oral and maxillofacial treatment: A comparative interdisciplinary clinical study. *International Journal of Clinical and Experimental Hypnosis, 54*(4), 457–479.

Elliotson, J. (1843). *Numerous cases of surgical operations without pain in the mesmeric state.* Philadelphia, PA: Lea and Blanchard.

Enqvist, B., Björklund, C., Engman, M., & Jakobsson, J. (1997). Preoperative hypnosis reduces postoperative vomiting after surgery of the breasts. A prospective, randomized and blinded study. *Acta Anaesthesiologica Scandinavica, 41*(8), 1028–1032.

Esdaile, J. (1850). On the operation for the removal of scrotal tumors. *London Medical Gazette, 11*, 449–454.

Faymonville, M. E., Fissette, J., Mambourg, P. H., Roediger, L., Joris, J., & Lamy, M. (1995). Hypnosis as adjunct therapy in conscious sedation for plastic surgery. *Regional Anesthesia, 20*(2), 145–151.

Faymonville, M. E., Mambourg, P. H., Joris, J., Vrijens, B., Fissette, J., Albert, A., & Lamy, M. (1997). Psychological approaches during conscious sedation. Hypnosis versus stress reducing strategies: A prospective randomized study. *Pain, 73*(3), 361–367.

Faymonville, M. E., Meurisse, M., & Fissette, J. (1999). Hypnosedation: A valuable alternative to traditional anaesthetic techniques. *Acta Chirurgica Belgica, 99*(4), 141–146.

Fredericks, L. E. (2001). *The use of hypnosis in surgery and anesthesiology: Psychological preparation of the surgical patient*. Springfield, IL: Charles C. Thomas Publisher.

Ginandes, C., Brooks, P., Sando, W., Jones, C., & Aker, J. (2003). Can medical hypnosis accelerate post-surgical wound healing? Results of a clinical trial. *American Journal of Clinical Hypnosis, 45*(4), 333–351.

Glaser, R., Kiecolt-Glaser, J. K., Marucha, P. T., MacCallum, R. C., Laskowski, B. F., & Malarkey, W. B. (1999). Stress related changes in proinflammatory cytokine production in wounds. *Archives of General Psychiatry, 56*(5), 450–456.

Kessler, R., & Dane, J. R. (1996). Psychological and hypnotic preparation for anesthesia and surgery: An individual difference perspective. *International Journal of Clinical and Experimental Hypnosis, 44*(3), 189–207.

Lambert, S. A. (1996). The effects of hypnosis/guided imagery on the postoperative course of children. *Journal of Developmental and Behavioral Pediatrics, 17*(5), 307–310.

Lang, E. V., & Rosen, M. P. (2002). Cost analysis of adjunct hypnosis for sedation during outpatient interventional procedures. *Radiology, 222*(2), 375–382.

Lang, E. V., Benotsch, E. G., Fick, L. J., Lutgendorf, S., Berbaum, M. L., Berbaum, K. S., . . . Spiegel, D. (2000). Adjunctive nonpharmacologic analgesia for invasive medical procedures: A randomized trial. *The Lancet, 355*(9214), 1486–1490.

Lang, E. V., Berbaum, K. S., Faintuch, S., Hatsiopoulou, O., Halsey, N., Li, X., . . . Baum, J. (2006). Adjunctive self-hypnotic relaxation for outpatient medical procedures: A prospective randomized trial nonpharmacologic analgesia adjuncts. *Pain, 126*(1–3), 155–164.

Lang, E. V., Berbaum, K. S., Pauker, S. G., Faintuch, S., Salazar, G. M., Lutgendorf, S., . . . Spiegel, D. (2008). Beneficial effects of hypnosis and adverse effects of empathic attention during percutaneous tumor treatment: When being nice does not suffice. *Journal of Vascular and Interventional Radiology, 19*(6), 897–905.

Lobe, T. E. (2006). Perioperative hypnosis reduces hospitalization in patients undergoing the Nuss procedures for pectus excavatum. *Journal of Laparoendoscopic & Advanced Surgical Techniques: Part A, 16*(6), 639–642.

Manworren, R., Girard, E., Verissimo, A. M., Riccardino, S., Ruscher, K. A., Weiss, R., & Hight, D. (2014). Effectiveness of hypnosis for post-operative pain management of minimally invasive thorascopic approach to repair pectus excavatum: Retrospective analysis. Poster presentation, American Pain Society.

McLean, A. J., & Le Couteur, D. G. (2004). Aging biology and geriatric clinical pharmacology. *Pharmacology Review, 56* (2), 163–184.

Montgomery, G. H., David, D., Winkel, G., Silverstein, J. H., & Bovbjerg, D. H. (2002). The effectiveness of adjunctive hypnosis with surgical patients: A meta-analysis. *Anesthesia and Analgesia, 94*(6), 1639–1645.

Peebles-Kleiger, M. J. (2000). The use of hypnosis in emergency medicine. *Emergency Medicine Clinics of North America, 18*(2), 327–338.

Rivera, R., & Antognini, J. F. (2009). Perioperative drug therapy in elderly patients. *Anesthesiology, 110*, 1176-1181.

Saadat, H., Drummond-Lewis, J., Maranets, I., Kaplan, D., Saadat, A., Wang, S. M., & Kain, Z. N. (2006). Hypnosis reduces preoperative anxiety in adults. *Anesthesia and Analgesia, 102*(5), 1394–1396.

Schnur, J. B., Bovbjerg, D. H., David, D., Tatrow, K., Goldfarb, A. B., Silverstein, J. H., . . . Montgomery, G. H. (2008). Hypnosis decreases presurgical distress in excisional breast biopsy patients. *Anesthesia and Analgesia, 106*(2), 440–444.

Silverstein, J. H., Timberger, M., Reich, D. L., & Uysal, S. (2007). Central nervous system dysfunction after noncardiac surgery and anesthesia in the elderly. *Anesthesiology, 106*(3), 622-628.

Tusek, D., Church, J. M., & Fazio, V. W. (1997). Guided imagery as a coping strategy for perioperative patients. *AORN Journal, 66*(4), 644–649.

Van Wijk, A., Buchanan, H., & Coulson, N. (2009). Psychological interventions for reducing postoperative morbidity in dental surgery in adults. *Cochrane Database of Systematic Reviews, 2.*

Wain, H. J. (2004). Reflections on hypnotizability and its impact on successful surgical hypnosis: A sole anesthetic for septoplasty. *American Journal of Clinical Hypnosis, 46*(4), 321–331.

Williams, A. R., Hind, M., Sweeney, B. P., & Fisher, R. (1994). The incidence and severity of postoperative nausea and vomiting in patients exposed to positive intra-operative suggestions. *Anesthesia, 49*(4), 340–342.

Yip, P., Middleton, P., Cyna, A. M., & Carlyle, A. V. (2009). Non-pharmacological interventions for assisting the induction of anaesthesia in children. *Cochrane Database of Systematic Reviews, 3*(3). doi: 10.1002/14651858.CD006447.pub2

Prostate Cancer

Cassie Kendrick

Prostate cancer is the second most common malignancy among men: Approximately one in six men are expected to be diagnosed with prostate cancer in their lifetime (American Cancer Society, 2013). Depending upon treatment needs, hormone therapy is often utilized to reduce overall androgen levels or the chances of androgens reaching cancer cells. The goal of antiandrogen hormone therapy, which can be chemical or surgical in nature, is to shrink or slow the growth of prostate cancer cells.

Cancer of any type is often accompanied by uncomfortable physical symptoms and symptoms of psychological distress, such as feelings of anxiety, sadness, irritability, and nervousness (Portenoy et al., 1994). In addition to the distress associated with any cancer diagnosis, a diagnosis of prostate cancer often produces a unique and significant set of distressing physical and emotional challenges related to urinary, erectile, and bowel dysfunctions. In addition, prostate cancer is associated with a higher level of psychological distress than is typical among the general population, and the unique stressors associated with prostate cancer can have a deleterious effect upon marital relationships (Manne et al., 2010).

Psychological distress is not only associated with the symptoms of the cancer itself, but also with its treatment. Hot flashes, which can be a clinically significant problem for those who undergo either chemical castration (androgen deprivation via gonadotropin-releasing hormone analogues or oral antiandrogens) or surgical castration (bilateral orchiectomy; Adelson, Loprinzi, & Hershman, 2005; Quella et al., 1999), have been reported to be among the most distressing of all the symptoms associated with prostate cancer treatments (Spetz, Zetterlund, Varenhorst, & Hammar, 2003). Further, difficult experiences with hot flashes have been shown to be a significant predictor of cancer-related distress (Ulloa, Salup, Patterson, & Jacobsen, 2009), and some prostate cancer patients have discontinued androgen deprivation treatment due to hot flashes (Frisk, 2010).

In addition, men who are forced to discontinue androgen replacement therapy that they had been subjected to for low testosterone and hot flashes associated with androgen deficiency (Spetz et al., 2007) prior to a prostate cancer diagnosis can experience a resurgence of hot flashes. Though not as well known, hot flashes experienced by men who undergo hormone therapy for prostate cancer can be of greater frequency, severity, and duration than those that accompany the female menopausal transition (Adelson, Loprinzi, & Hershman, 2005), and they can persist for as many as 8 years following the initial onset of symptoms (Engstrom, 2008; Spetz, Zetterlund, Varenhorst, & Hammar, 2003). Moreover, hot flashes are a significant problem for as many as 80% of patients undergoing prostate cancer treatments (Clark, Wray, & Ashton, 2001; Engstrom, 2008); up to 50% of those patients experience hot flashes that are severe enough to require treatment (Suzuki, Kobayashi, & Tokue, 2003).

Physiologically, hot flashes are experienced as "a sudden sensation of heat over the face, neck and chest" (Spetz, Hammar, Lindberg, Spångberg, & Varenhorst, 2001, p. 517) or "a subjective sensation of heat that is associated with objective signs of cutaneous vasodilation and a subsequent drop in core body temperature" (Boekhout, Beijnen, & Schellens, 2006, p. 642). These events, which are also referred to as vasomotor events or hot flashes, vary in duration, but can last up to several minutes and are associated with a number of challenging symptoms, including excess daytime sweating and night sweats (Finck, Barton, Loprinzi, Quella, & Sloan, 1998; Kronenberg, 1994; Sievert, Obermeyer, & Price, 2006), heart palpitations, anxiety, irritability, and distress (Finck et al., 1998; Kronenberg, 1994).

Currently, several pharmaceutical treatment options are available to treat hot flashes associated with prostate cancer treatments. These include selective serotonin reuptake inhibitors (e.g., Loprinzi, Barton, Carpenter, et al., 2004), serotonin-norepinephrine reuptake inhibitors (e.g., Evans et al., 2005), gabapentin (Moraska et al., 2010), and progesterones and estrogens (Spetz, Zetterlund, Verenhorst, & Hammar, 2003). The effects of some mind–body therapies, such as acupuncture, have also been examined (Adelson, Loprinzi, & Hershman, 2005). However, research has yet to establish firm conclusions regarding the efficacy of current treatments, and the safety of such treatments is not yet fully established.

EVIDENCE

Although research into the effects of hypnosis for the treatment of hot flashes in breast cancer survivors (Elkins, Marcus, Stearns, & Rajab, 2007; Elkins et al., 2008) and postmenopausal women (e.g., Elkins, Fisher, Johnson, Carpenter, & Keith, 2013) has been growing in recent years, research examining hypnosis for the treatment of hot flashes in prostate cancer survivors is extremely limited. To the author's knowledge, only one case study (Elkins, Kendrick, & Koep, 2014) has been published examining the effect of hypnosis upon hot flashes among prostate cancer survivors.

CASE EXAMPLE

Mr. W was a 69-year-old married African American with uncontrolled hot flashes. He had a history of androgen deficiency and was treated with testosterone replacement therapy prior to discovering he had prostate cancer in October 2010. Following his diagnosis, he subsequently discontinued his hormone therapy, and approximately 8 weeks after his prostatectomy his hot flashes reemerged, resulting in an increasing number of distressing hot flashes that he was unable to control. Mr. W was seen for 7 weekly individual sessions of hypnotic relaxation therapy with the primary aims of therapy being

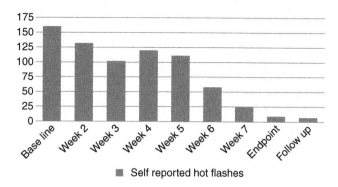

FIGURE 42.1 Daily subjective/perceived hot flash frequency.

(a) reducing hot flash frequency; (b) reducing hot flash severity; and (c) improving sleep quality. He was also provided with a CD for at home practice and was encouraged to practice daily. In addition, beginning in session 2, imagery was individualized to Mr. W's personal preference, and once Mr. W had completed session 3, he was instructed in self-hypnosis without the use of an audio recording.

Outcome measures included self-reported (Hot Flash Symptoms Diary) hot flash frequency and severity, physiologically measured hot flashes (Biolog™ Ambulatory Skin Conductance Monitor), and sleep quality (Pittsburgh Sleep Quality Index). Mr. W completed all measures at baseline, endpoint, and at 12-week follow-up. At endpoint, Mr. W's self-reported hot flashes had decreased by 94% (see Figure 42.1), physiologically measured hot flashes decreased by 100% (see Figure 42.2), and sleep quality improved by 87.5% in comparison to baseline. These improvements remained at 12-week follow-up, with self-reported hot flashes still decreased by 95%, physiologically measured hot flashes decreased 95%, and sleep quality improved 37.5% over baseline.

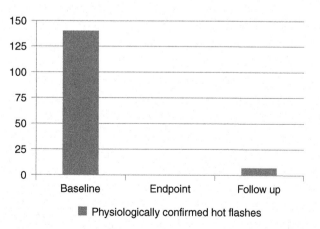

FIGURE 42.2 Ambulatory monitored physiological hot flash frequency.

TECHNIQUE

The intervention utilized with Mr. W followed what had been followed with postmenopausal women and breast cancer survivors and has been previously described elsewhere (Elkins, 2013; Elkins, Fisher, Johnson, Carpenter, & Keith, 2013; Elkins et al., 2008). Additional details of this intervention can be found in an Chapter 32 of this book.

As a part of the standard hypnotic relaxation induction for hot flashes, the therapist provided suggestions that Mr. W would experience feelings of comfort and coolness; that he would feel a *"cool, cold breeze coming in from the lake"* and that he would *"feel the cold air on [his] face."* Suggestions were also provided for dissociation from hot flashes, *"and it is possible that you can feel more detached from your body . . . waves of coolness and comfort flowing over you and through you."* Posthypnotic suggestions were also given for self-hypnosis and for increased feelings of control: *"and as you become more comfortable . . . so you will find a sense of being more in control."*

Although Mr. W primarily received a standardized induction aimed at reducing hot flashes, it was important that the therapist include individualized imagery as a part of treatment. Thus, beginning in session 2, sessions were modified to include imagery reported by the patient following therapist-administered sessions or at-home practice. Mr. W. reported that, during hypnosis, he imagined being at a favorite fishing spot early in the morning. He imagined himself sitting on a bucket between two trees on a long shore of grass at his favorite fishing spot and watching the water early in the morning. These images were incorporated into the therapist-delivered hypnotherapy sessions.

"And now, seeing before you a path . . . a path leading down to your favorite spot at the lake. It is still dark out, in the cool, early morning hours. Just feeling the coolness, the stillness, the calm peaceful feeling of this special place and time in the morning. As you walk down that path, notice the peaceful stillness, the calmness, the coolness of the morning surrounding you. The air is very cool there, and with every step you take going down the path, sinking deeper and deeper into this coolness, this calmness . . . sinking deep down into this relaxing, hypnotic state. . . .

And notice now, as you walk down the path, there is a special place you can sit, a special place you can relax . . . a long shore of grass where you can sit and relax and look out across the water. You know this place well. It is a place of comfort, of peace, of relaxation. And as you rest there, feeling the cool, crisp morning air, you can look out across the water, the stillness reflected by the image of the moon and stars on the water. It is just so pleasant there. . . . And as you relax, just gazing out at the moonlit lake, you can take a deep breath of that cool, crisp morning air, just noticing the coolness, the pleasantness of this peaceful place."

CONCLUSION

Hot flashes are a major source of physical discomfort and psychological distress among a majority of men undergoing hormone therapy as a part of prostate cancer treatment, and safe, effective treatments are needed. Though evidence is currently limited and additional research is needed, evidence from at least one case study suggests that hypnotherapy may hold promise as an effective, safe intervention for the treatment of hot flashes in prostate cancer patients and survivors.

In applying hypnosis for hot flashes for prostate cancer patients and survivors, clinicians should be mindful of individual patient needs and incorporation of individualized imagery relevant to the patient. Further, it is important to normalize the experience of hot flashes among this patient population, lest beliefs about hot flashes in men impede progress. In addition, monitoring treatment compliance (via a hypnosis practice diary) and progress (through a hot-flash daily diary) is important and will help the clinician pinpoint potential downfalls of treatment success.

REFERENCES

Adelson, K., Loprinzi, C., & Hershman, D. (2005). Treatment of hot flushes in breast and prostate cancer. *Expert Opinion on Pharmacotherapy*, 6, 1095–1106.

American Cancer Society. (2013). *Cancer facts and figures, 2013.* Retrieved from http://www.cancer.org/acs/groups/content/@epidemiologysurveilance/documents/document/acspc-036845.pdf

Boekhout, A. H., Beijnen, J. H., & Schellens, J. H. (2006). Symptoms and treatment in cancer therapy-induced early menopause. *The Oncologist, 11,* 641–654.

Clark, J. A., Wray, N. P., & Ashton, C. M. (2001). Living with treatment decisions: Regrets and quality of life among men treated for metastatic prostate cancer. *Journal of Clinical Oncology, 19,* 72–80.

Elkins, G. (2013). *Hypnotic relaxation therapy: Principles and applications.* New York, NY: Springer Publishing Company.

Elkins, G. R., Kendrick, C., & Koep, L. (2014). Hypnotic relaxation therapy for treatment of hot flashes following prostate cancer surgery: A case study. *International Journal of Clinical and Experimental Hypnosis, 62,* 251–259.

Elkins, G., Fisher, W., Johnson, A., Carpenter, J., & Keith, T. (2013). Clinical hypnosis in the treatment of postmenopausal hot flashes: A randomized controlled trial. *Menopause, 20,* 291–298.

Elkins, G., Marcus, J., Stearns, V., & Hasan Rajab, M. (2007). Pilot evaluation of hypnosis for the treatment of hot flashes in breast cancer survivors. *Psycho-Oncology, 16,* 487–492.

Elkins, G., Marcus, J., Stearns, V., Perfect, M., Rajab, M. H., Ruud, C., . . . Keith, T. (2008). Randomized trial of a hypnosis intervention for treatment of hot flashes among breast cancer survivors. *Journal of Clinical Oncology, 26,* 5022–5026.

Engstrom, C. A. (2008). Hot flashes in prostate cancer: State of the science. *American Journal of Men's Health, 2,* 122–132.

Evans, M. L., Pritts, E., Vittinghoff, E., McClish, K., Morgan, K. S., & Jaffe, R. B. (2005). Management of postmenopausal hot flushes with venlafaxine hydrochloride: A randomized controlled trial. *Obstetrics & Gynecology, 105,* 161–166.

Finck, G., Barton, D. L., Loprinzi, C. L., Quella, S. K., & Sloan, J. A. (1998). Definitions of hot flashes in breast cancer survivors. *Journal of Pain and Symptom Management, 16,* 327–333.

Frisk, J. (2010). Managing hot flushes in men after prostate cancer—A systematic review. *Maturitas, 65,* 15–22.

Kronenberg, F. (1994). Hot flashes: Phenomenology, quality of life, and search for treatment options. *Experimental Gerontology, 29,* 319–336.

Loprinzi, C. L., Barton, D. L., Carpenter, L. A., Sloan, J. A., Novotny, P. J., & Christensen, B. J. (2004). Pilot evaluation of paroxetine for treating hot flashes in men. *Mayo Clinic Proceedings, 79,* 1247–1251.

Manne, S., Badr, H., Zaider, T., Nelson, C., & Kissane, D. (2010). Cancer-related communication, relationship intimacy, and psychological distress among couples coping with localized prostate cancer. *Journal of Cancer Survivorship, 4,* 74–85.

Moraska, A. R., Atherton, P. J., Szydlo, D. W., Barton, D. L., Stella, P. J., Rowland, K. M., . . . Loprinzi, C. L. (2010). Gabapentin for the management of hot flashes in prostate cancer survivors: A longitudinal continuation study—NCCTG trial. *Journal of Supportive Oncology, 8,* 128–132.

Portenoy, R. K., Thaler, H. T., Kornblith, A. B., McCarthy Lepore, J., Friedlander-Klar, H., Coyle, N., . . . Scher, H. (1994). Symptom prevalence, characteristics and distress in a cancer population. *Quality of Life Research, 3,* 183–189.

Quella, S. K., Loprinzi, C. L., Sloan, J., Novotny, P., Perez, E. A., Burch, P. A., . . . Pisansky, T. M. (1999). Pilot evaluation of venlafaxine for the treatment of hot flushes in men undergoing androgen ablation therapy for prostate cancer. *Journal of Urology, 162,* 98–102.

Sievert, L. L., Obermeyer, C. M., & Price, K. (2006). Determinants of hot flashes and night sweats. *Annals of Human Biology, 33,* 4–16.

Spetz, A. C., Hammar, M., Lindberg, B., Spångberg, A., & Varenhorst, E. (2001). Prospective evaluation of hot flashes during treatment with parenteral estrogen or complete androgenablation for metastatic carcinoma of the prostate. *Journal of Urology, 166,* 517–520.

Spetz, A. C., Zetterlund, E. L., Varenhorst, E., & Hammar, M. (2003). Incidence and management of hot flashes in prostate cancer. *Journal of Supportive Oncology, 1,* 263–272.

Spetz, A.-C. E., Palmefors, L., Skobe, R. S. P., Strömstedt, M. T., Fredriksson, M. G., Theodorsson, E., & Hammar, M. L. (2007). Testosterone correlated to symptoms of partial androgen deficiency in aging men (PADAM) in an elderly Swedish population. *Menopause, 14,* 999–1005.

Suzuki, K., Kobayashi, M., & Tokue, A. (2003). Clinical evaluation of hot flushes developing during endocrine therapy for prostate carcinoma. *Nippon Hinyokika Gakkai Zasshi, 94,* 614–620.

Ulloa, E. W., Salup, R., Patterson, S. G., & Jacobsen, P. B. (2009). Relationship between hot flashes and distress in men receiving androgen deprivation therapy for prostate cancer. *Psycho-Oncology, 18,* 598–605.

Raynaud's Syndrome

Aimee Johnson

Raynaud's syndrome is a disorder of the peripheral circulation distinguished by episodic vasospasm in the fingers and toes (Anderson & Couch, 1983). Serious complications such as scleroderma can result, as well as tissue damage and the loss of fingers (Gilliland & Mannik, 1983; Jones, Raynor, & Medsger, 1987). Raynaud's disease was first characterized in 1888 as a reduction of peripheral blood flow in response to exposure to cold temperature and emotional stress (Raynaud, 1888).

Estimates of its prevalence range from 4.3% in women to 2.7% in men (Weinrich, Maricq, Keil, McGregor, & Diat, 1990). According to estimates from general practitioners in the United Kingdom, prevalence of Raynaud's ranges from 19% of women to 11% of men (Silman, Holligan, Brennan, & Maddison, 1990). Raynaud's syndrome is estimated to be five times more common in women than men (Marcus, Weiner, Suzuki, & Kawn, 1991; Spittell, 1972; Taub, 1977). Wise, Malamet and Wigley (1987) estimate that 5% to 15% of the population in the United States suffers from this disorder. More recent data suggests that 2.2% of women and 1.6% of men suffer from Raynaud's syndrome (Suter, Murabito, Felson, & Fraenkel, 2005).

Raynaud's symptomology is commonly divided into primary Raynaud's disease and secondary Raynaud's phenomenon. Primary Raynaud's disease is an idiopathic type of paroxysm digital vasospasm (Sedlacek & Taub, 1996). This denotes the primary form of the disorder in which the symptoms cannot be explained by an identifiable disease such as scleroderma, or other collagen vascular disease (Freedman, 1993). The diagnosis of primary Raynaud's disease is made according to the following criteria: (a) bilateral attacks in the extremities without evidence or organic arterial disease; (b) trophic changes limited to the skin (no gangrene); (c) no evidence of any other disease; and (d) symptoms present for at least 2 years (Allen & Brown, 1932). Approximately 30% to 60% of people seeking treatment for Raynaud's symptoms have primary Raynaud's disease (Shepard, 2008).

Symptoms will often begin when a person is in his or her teens or twenties (Sedlacek & Taub, 1996). Symptoms may be mild, but in some cases of Raynaud's phenomenon, they may progress to ulcerations that are difficult to heal, and in rare cases amputation (Adee, 1993; Sedlacek, 1979). Raynaud's phenomenon typically has more severe symptoms and results from an underlying organic disease (Adee, 1993). For example, secondary Raynaud's phenomenon is related to connective tissue disease, arterial occlusive disease, and drugs (e.g., ergot derivatives, beta-blockers, nitroglycerine, chemotherapy agents) (LeRoy & Medsger, 1992). Additionally, it may also be brought on by repetitive trauma and is seen in a higher proportion of carpal tunnel syndrome patients (Pal, Keenan, Misra, Moussa, & Morris, 1996).

Symptoms of Raynaud's phenomenon typically display a triphasic discoloration (Desai & Headley, 2006; Levien, 2010). The discoloration begins as a whiteness of the affected area. If left untreated for a period of time, the white discoloration can turn into a blue discoloration. The third phase of the triphasic cycle is redness, as blood returns to the affected area. Other symptoms of Raynaud's include numbness and a drop in skin temperature (Herrick, 2005). Onset is typically due to exposure to cold, but may be brought on by emotional stress or tobacco use (Ko & Berbrayer, 2002).

Some cases of primary Raynaud's disease may progress into Raynaud's phenomenon after a period of time, suggesting an initial organic basis was undetected, or minimally expressed (Sedlacek & Taub, 1996). Some authors suggest the use of the term *Raynaud's syndrome* for all Raynaud's symptoms (Surwit & Jordan, 1987). However, it is recommended when diagnosing Raynaud's disease or Raynaud's phenomena to reserve Raynaud's syndrome for cases for which there is difficulty making an exact diagnosis (Marcus et al., 1991).

The usual treatment of primary Raynaud's syndrome involves keeping warm, smoking cessation, medications (long-lasting calcium-channel-blocking drugs, prostacyclin analogues), and behavioral therapies (hypnosis, behavior modification, and biofeedback) (Black et al., 1998; Gjrøup, Hartling, Kelback, & Nielsen, 1986; Jacobson, Hackett, Surman, & Sliverberg, 1973; Keefe, Surwit, & Pilon, 1980). The side effects of the common prescribed medications consist of lowered blood pressure, dizziness, and headaches (Garcia-Carrasco et al., 2008). Such side effects occur due to the inherent inability to target the drug to only the affected area (Freedman, 1987). Another recent method for treating symptoms of Raynaud's disease is the wearing of special gloves. The gloves are ceramic-impregnated gloves, and are shown to significantly improve symptoms of Raynaud's disease (Ko & Berbrayer, 2002). However, effectiveness is largely dependent upon the patient wearing the gloves for several hours per day, which may be intrusive upon a patient's daily lifestyle. Several studies have shown hypnosis as well as biofeedback to be effective for treatment of Raynaud's syndrome.

RESEARCH

Hypnosis administered by a professional hypnotherapist has shown to increase blood flow and hand temperature, which are the two main symptoms of Raynaud's syndrome (Bregman & McAllister, 1981). An early case study of Raynaud's disease utilized a combination of hypnosis and operant conditioning (Jacobson, Hackett, Surman, & Sliverberg, 1973). The patient, diagnosed with primary Raynaud's, discontinued pharmacological treatment due to side effects of depression. The combined treatment of hypnosis and operant conditioning resulted in an increase of 4.3°C in digital skin temperature. Furthermore, this increase was maintained at the 7-month follow-up. Jacobson, Sliverberg, and Manschreck (1978) treated eight cases of Raynaud's disease with a combination of temperature biofeedback, relaxation, and

psychotherapy. Study results demonstrated that approximately half the participants reported subjective improvement, which was maintained at the follow-up. Conn and Mott (1984) reported success in treating a case of Raynaud's disease with hypnosis alone. The results showed the patient's digital blood volume had increased four times over baseline.

Biofeedback is one of the most researched alternative therapies for Raynaud's disorder (Middaugh et al., 2001). Biofeedback treatment of Raynaud's focuses on controlling skin temperature. Initially, Taub and Emurian (1976) demonstrated that skin temperature could be self-regulated in healthy participants. This was followed by successful clinical accounts utilizing biofeedback to improve Raynaud's symptomology (Freedman, 1993; Freeedman, Ianni, & Wenig, 1983; Freedman, Lynn, Ianni, & Hale, 1981; Keefe, Surwit, & Pilon, 1980; Sedlacek, 1979, 1989; Taub & Stroebel, 1978). Furthermore, case studies demonstrate that Raynaud's patients report fewer symptoms after treatment with biofeedback alone, or in combination with relaxation procedures (Blanchard & Haynes, 1975; Surwit, 1973).

Freedman's research demonstrates the effectiveness of thermal biofeedback using participants with primary Raynaud's disease (Freedman, Ianni, & Wenig, 1983). In a controlled study, 32 primary Raynaud's disease participants were randomized into three conditions and each received two pretreatment sessions followed by 10 biweekly training sessions. Finger temperature was collected using automated ambulatory skin temperature monitoring. Results showed a 32.6% reduction in vasospastic attacks using autogenic therapy, a 66.8% reduction utilizing thermal biofeedback, and a 92.5% reduction using thermal biofeedback plus cold stress training. There is much evidence to support that biofeedback provides significant increases in finger temperature and blood flow, whereas autogenic training, frontalis EMG biofeedback, or simple instructions to increase finger temperature do not (Freedman, 1993; Freedman et al., 1981, 1983; Sedlacek & Taub, 1996).

Multiple comparison studies have been conducted to determine the efficacy of hypnosis compared with biofeedback for the treatment of Raynaud's symptoms. For example, an early study compared the efficacy of hypnotic suggestion and biofeedback in improving Raynaud's symptoms

(Barabasz & McGeorge, 1978). Participants (*n* = 78) were assigned to one of four conditions to receive either audio biofeedback, "sham" biofeedback, relaxation instructions, or hypnosis with specific suggestions to increase hand warmth. Participants were not screened for hypnotic susceptibility. The hypnosis condition showed significant increase in hand temperature from the end of the baseline period compared with a temperature reading taken after the hypnotic treatment. This study suggests hypnotic suggestion for increased blood flow to the hands was more effective than biofeedback (Barabasz & McGeorge, 1978). In addition, another study comparing biofeedback to hypnotic suggestion showed hypnotic suggestions separate from biofeedback training can allow participants to successfully control their hand temperature (Keefe, 1978). While some studies have compared the effectiveness of hypnosis and biofeedback, other studies have compared the effects of combined treatments. Hypnosis in conjunction with biofeedback has shown successful results in raising skin temperature and may be used as a treatment in Raynaud's disease (Shenefelt, 2002). In sum, it is encouraging that the literature indicates that 80% to 89% of persons with Raynaud's disease may obtain substantial relief through the use of hypnosis, mental imagery, and biofeedback treatments (Sedlacek & Taub, 1996). In many cases, it appears that biofeedback procedures may not have any advantage over hypnosis and mental imagery relaxation-training methods (Surwit, 1982).

Hypnosis has been effective at improving symptoms of Raynaud's syndrome; since biofeedback therapy utilizes many relaxation-imagery suggestions similar to those used in hypnosis, the question arises as to what is the role of suggestion in biofeedback (Barabasz & Wright, 1975; Gaarder, 1977). Barabasz and McGeorge (1978) questioned the need for the extensive development and sale of biofeedback equipment, suggesting that hypnosis may be the most important factor in thermal biofeedback. The evidence remains inconclusive. Some investigators have found a greater degree of temperature control with hypnosis and biofeedback used together than with either used alone (Roberts, Kewman, & MacDonald, 1973) while others have not. Given the study results, it is likely that the control of skin temperature is a complex process in which patients' individual preferences for mental imagery and relaxation may be an important consideration for hypnosis and/or biofeedback.

CASE EXAMPLE

The case study is centered on a 22-year-old single female. The patient was a college athlete and played basketball for her university. The patient was diagnosed with primary Raynaud's disease when she was 16 years old. Her condition became worse at age 19 with her fingers turning white in response to variable weather conditions. The patient's primary complaint is chronic cold fingers and feelings of numbness; all previous attempts at relieving these symptoms had failed. She noticed that stress exacerbated her condition, and her fingers would turn white and become numb. The patient did not want to take medication for her condition. Her coping strategy involved running her fingers over hot water. She was referred by her family physician and was interested in hypnosis for the treatment of Raynaud's disease.

The patient tabulated the daily temperature ratings. This individual was seen for five weekly sessions of hypnosis for Raynaud's syndrome. The sessions averaged approximately 45 minutes in length. In each session, the patient was told to visualize lying on a sandy beach on a hot summer day and experience warmth in her hands and feet from the hot sun. Additionally, she was instructed to practice hypnosis using an audio-recording containing visual imagery of a hot summer beach day.

At her first session, a case history was taken, and the hypnosis treatment was discussed. At the end of the session, some information was given relative to the hypnosis procedures.

The second session was held a week later. The patient was very interested in receiving help for her condition. The patient enjoyed being on the beach during the summer, so this imagery was used to produce body warmth while under hypnosis. She was instructed to picture herself lying on the beach during a hot summer day and to visualize a bright sun warming her body, hands, and feet. Also, she was given imagery of the warm sand running through her fingers and toes, which slowly warmed each of her fingers and toes. The patient needed a 45-minute session in order to achieve some warmth in her hands, fingers, feet, and toes. Toward the end of the session, she was instructed to listen to an audio-recording containing imagery of the hot summer beach day.

During the third session, the patient indicated she practiced her visualization of the beach for seven days, through which she was able to achieve warmth in her hands. The session consisted of the same induction techniques and hypnotic instructions that were used as the second session. During this session, the patient was more relaxed, and the session yielded better success than the second session. She obtained warmth in her hands, fingers, and feet. At the end of the session, she was instructed in self-hypnosis. The patient was provided with a worksheet to aid in self-hypnosis and individualization of imagery throughout the week.

From the fourth through the fifth session, the same procedures and instructions were used as in sessions 2 and 3. However, she experienced greater success. In this session, she indicated that she was able to feel moderate warmth in her hands, fingers, feet, and toes when practicing self-hypnosis. During the session, she experienced warmth in all extremities, which lasted for several days. The fifth hypnosis session was also successful in producing positive symptoms of warmth for five days. Additionally, the fifth session was used as a summary and discussion of progress and changes in treatment. The patient reported that she continued her self-hypnosis sessions, which have been very helpful. The cold features returned for short intervals of time and were less intense than she experienced before treatment. Follow-up a month later revealed an 80% improvement in her Raynaud's symptoms.

TRANSCRIPT: HYPNOSIS FOR RAYNAUD'S SYNDROME

"To begin your practice of hypnotic relaxation therapy, keep your eyelids open for a moment . . . and pick a point on the wall or ceiling. . . . Focus your attention on that point. . . . As you concentrate, begin to feel more relaxed. Now, concentrate on that point, so intensely that other things begin to fade into the background. . . . Just let them fade into the background. . . . Beginning the process of deep hypnotic relaxation now, by just taking a deep breath of air, holding it for a moment, and as you breathe out, letting all the tension go.

Good. As this occurs, allow your eyelids to close. As the eyelids close, notice more of a relaxed feeling. Allow the eyelids to close, and allow them to feel heavy as they close. To begin the process of deepening this hypnotic relaxation, please now take another deep breath of air, hold it for a moment, and as you release the air and breathe out, just letting all tension go, drifting into a very deep state of relaxation. In fact, each time you breathe out, thinking the word 'relax,' silently to yourself. As you think this word, relax. The mind and the body work together to achieve a deep state of comfort and relaxation. . . . With each breath of air, let go of all tension, drift deeply relaxed. Every muscle, every fiber of your body, becoming so deeply relaxed. . . .

Deeper relaxed. Your neck can go limp, your jaw can go slack, as all the tension drifts away. Becoming so deeply relaxed that you can notice more and more feelings associated with warmth and calmness. Memories of warmth and calmness can begin to come to you as your mind can drift and remember a time when you felt so warm and calm. Within your own experience, go back within your memories to a time when you felt very warm, feeling calm, relaxed, and secure. Your own personal mental imagery of a time when you can remember calmness in such a place and time, and you may notice sounds, remembering sounds like the sound of wind, or the sound of an ocean as the waves come in on the shore. Let that wave of relaxation spread across your arms and shoulders, arms become so deeply relaxed that they become limp and heavy, as all the tension drifts away, draining out through your arms and hands and out your fingertips.

And finding now as you can hear my voice with a part of your mind, with another part of your mind, going to that pleasant, peaceful place, where you find even more relaxation and comfort. You may find that you notice a beautiful beach where you can watch the waves come in on the sandy beach. You may notice the warm sand running through your fingers as you listen to the ocean waves. You feel warm, safe, and secure.

Metaphor for hand warming: The mental image of a beautiful sandy beach may come to you . . . you are lying on a beach . . . you dig your fingers into the warm sand . . . deeper and deeper . . . your right hand feels pleasantly warm . . . your fingers feel warmer . . . the warmth spreads from your hands down to your fingertips . . . your whole right hand is pleasantly warm . . . warmer . . . warmer . . . so you will feel the sand warming your left hand . . . good . . . digging your left hand into the sand . . . deeper . . . deeper . . . feeling the warmth of the hot sun spreading over both your hands . . . so relaxed . . . so you can effortlessly . . . naturally . . . feel . . . warmth spreading throughout your fingers and toes . . . warmth . . . good. . . .

Individualization of suggestions: I'm just going to be silent for a moment, as you are there, becoming completely absorbed in these feelings of warmth and a deeper state of hypnotic relaxation. And as you enter an even deeper level of relaxation, your own, personal images can come to you . . . images that take you deeper and deeper. . . . You may at times notice a floating feeling or even more heaviness. You may notice that your breathing becomes more comfortable and at ease; certainly as you enter a deeper level of hypnotic relaxation, blood pressure decreases and muscle tension becomes less. And just experience being in your own personal, individual place, where there is warmth and calmness.

Posthypnotic suggestion: Now, just going a little deeper into this state of hypnotic relaxation, and allow each suggestion to occur, each positive suggestion, to achieve whatever needs to be achieved, for you to find you are able to experience warmth spreading throughout your hands and fingers, and become deeply relaxed, drifting into your own personal place, your own mental imagery, your own experience of relaxation and calmness. I'm just going to remain silent for a moment as you drift to such a personal place, and then I will give you suggestions to return to conscious alertness."

CONCLUSION

In review of the literature, it appears that hypnosis and biofeedback offer promise for the treatment for Raynaud's symptomology. Future research studies, with the goal of developing a standardized treatment protocol for Raynaud's symptomology,

should emphasize: replication with large randomized controlled studies, improved physiological measurement, and specific guidelines for controlling confounding variables.

In utilizing hypnotherapy, it is necessary for clinicians to have an understanding of the diagnosis of Raynaud's symptomology. It is important to differentiate between primary Raynaud's disease, in which symptoms cannot be explained by an identifiable disease, and Raynaud's phenomenon, which typically has more severe symptoms and occurs due to an underlying organic disease. The patient must have a clear diagnosis from a physician.

Once the practitioner is certain about the patient's diagnosis, the practitioner should develop a behavioral assessment and a treatment plan (Freedman, Lynn, Ianni, & Hale, 1981). The treatment plan should include (a) tracking the number of vascular attacks (e.g., self-report diary), (b) temperature training, (c) homework involving finger temperature training with home monitoring, and (d) a goal of warming the fingers 3° to 9°F (1.7° to 2.2°C). Patients should be instructed to stop or restrict substances with peripheral vasoconstrictive effects, such as tobacco and caffeine, as well as stimulants. Drugs such as pseudoephedrine, ephedrine, or any other vasoconstrictive should be reviewed by the physicians and practitioner for possible reduction (Sedlacek & Taub, 1996). Also, by reviewing the relevant findings from the research literature with patients, practitioners can assist them to make informed decisions about available treatment options and alternatives and to decide if the inclusion of hypnosis is appropriate for the patient.

REFERENCES

Abramson, D. (1974). *Vascular disorders of the extremities.* New York, NY: Harper & Row.

Adee, A. C. (1993). Managing Raynaud's phenomenon: A practical application. *American Family Physicians, 47,* 823–829.

Allen, E. V., & Brown, G. W. (1932). Raynaud's disease: A critical review of minimal requisite for diagnosis. *American Journal of Medical Science, 183,* 187–200.

Anderson, R. J., & Couch, N. P. (1983). Pain in the extremities. In R. G. Petersdorf, R. D. Adams, E. B. Braunwald, K. J. Isselbacher, J. B. Martin, & J. D. Wilson (Eds.), *Harrison principles of internal medicine* (10 ed., pp. 45–49). New York, NY: McGraw-Hill.

Barabasz, A. F., & McGeorge, C. M. (1978). Biofeedback, mediated biofeedback and hypnosis in peripheral vasodilation training. *American Journal of Clinical Hypnosis, 21*(1), 28–37. doi:10.1080/00029157.1978.10403954

Barabasz, A. F., & Wright, G. W. (1975). Treatment of collagen vascular disease by hypnotic imagery. *Hypnosis Quarterly, 19,* 1–15.

Black, C. M., Halkier-Sørensen, L., Belch, J. J., Ullman, S., Madhok, R., Smit, A. J., . . . Watson, H. R. (1998). Oral ilioprost in Raynauds phenomenon secondary to systemic sclerosis: A multicenter, placebo-controlled, dose-comparison study. *British Journal of Rheumatology, 37*(9), 952–960.

Blanchard, E., & Haynes, M. (1975). Biofeedback treatment of a case of Raynaud's disease. *Journal of Behavior Therapy & Experimental Psychiatry, 6,* 230–234.

Bregman, N. J., & McAllister, H. A. (1981). Effects of suggestion on increasing or decreasing skin temperature control. *International Journal of Neuroscience, 14*(3-4), 205–210.

Conn, L., & Mott, T. (1984). Plethysmographic demonstration of rapid vasodilation by direct suggestion: A case of Raynaud's disease treated by hypnosis. *American Journal of Clinical Hypnosis, 26*(3), 166–170. doi:10.1080/00029157.1984.10404158

Desai, T., & Headley, R. (2006). Raynaud's phenomenon. *ACS Surgery: Principles and Practice, 24,* 1–4.

Freedman, R. R. (1993). Raynaud's disease and phenomenon. In R. J. Gatchel & E. B. Blanchard (Eds.), *Psychophysiological disorders* (pp. 245–267). Washington, DC: American Psychological Association.

Freedman, R. R., Ianni, P., & Wenig, P. (1983). Behavioral treatment of Raynaud's disease. *Journal of Consulting and Clinical Psychology, 151,* 539–549.

Freedman, R. R., Lynn, S. J., Ianni, P., & Hale, P. A. (1981). Biofeedback treatment of Raynaud's disease and phenomenon. *Biofeedback and Self-Regulation, 6*(3), 355–364.

Freedman, R. (1987). Long-term effectiveness of behavioral treatments for Raynauds disease. *Behavioral Therapy, 18,* 387–399.

Gaarder, K. R. (1977). *Clinical biofeedback: A procedural manual.* Baltimore, MD: Lippincott Williams & Wilkins.

Garcia-Carrasco, M., Jimenez-Hernandez, M., Escarcega, R. O. P., Pardo-Santos, R., Levy, R., Maldoanado, C. G., & Cervera, R. (2008). Treatment of Raynaud's phenomenon. *Autoimmunity Review, 8,* 62–68.

Gilliland, B. C., & Mannik, M. (1983). Progressive systemic sclerosis. In R. G. Petersdorf, R. D. Adams, E. B. Braunwald, K. J. Isselbacher, J. B. Martin, & J. D. Wilson (Eds.), *Harrison principles of internal medicine* (pp. 2002–2005). New York, NY: McGraw-Hill.

Gjørup, T., Hartling, O. J., Kelbaek, H., & Nielsen, S. L. (1986). Controlled double blind trial of nisoldipine in the treatment of idiopathic Raynaud's phenomenon. *European Journal of Clinical Pharmacology, 31*(4), 387–389.

Herrick, A. L. (2005). Pathogenesis of Raynaud's phenomenon. *Rheumatology, 5,* 587–596.

Jacobson, A. M., Silverberg, E., Hackett, T., & Manschreck, T. (1978). Treatment of Raynaud's disease: Evaluation of a behavioral approach. *Psychiatric Clinics (Basel), 11*(3), 125–131.

Jacobson, A. M., Hackett, T. P., Surman, O. S., & Silverberg, E. L. (1973). Raynaud phenomenon: Treatment with hypnotic and operant technique. *JAMA, 225*(7), 739–740.

Jones, N. F., Raynor, S. C., & Medsger, T. A. (1987). Microsurgical revascularisation of the hand in scleroderma. *British Journal of Plastic Surgery, 40*(3), 264–269.

Keefe, F. (1978). Biofeedback vs. instructional control of skin temperature. *Journal of Behavioral Medicine, 1*(1), 383-390.

Keefe, F. J., Surwit, R. S., & Pilon, R. N. (1980). Biofeedback, autogenic training and progressive relaxation in the treatment of Raynaud's disease. *Journal of Applied Behavior Analysis, 13*(1), 3–11. doi:10.1901/jaba.1980.13-3

Ko, G. D., & Berbrayer, D. (2002). Effect of ceramic impregnated "thermaflow" gloves on patients with Raynaud's syndrome: Randomized, placebo-controlled study. *Alternative Medicine Review, 3,* 328–335.

Leroy, E. C., & Medsger, T. A. (1992). Raynaud's phenomenon: A proposal for classification. *Clinical and Experimental Rheumatology, 10*(5), 485–488.

Levien, T. L. (2010). Advances in treatment of Raynaud's phenomenon. *Vascular Health and Risk Management, 6,* 167–177.

Marcus, S., Weiner, S. R., Suzuki, S. M., & Kwan, L. (1991). Raynaud's syndrome. *Postgraduate Medicine, 89*(4), 171–187.

Middaugh, S. J., Haythornthwaite, J., Thompson, B., Hill, R., Brown, K., Freedman, R., & Smith, E. (2001). The Raynaud's Treatment Study: Biofeedback protocols and acquisition of temperature biofeedback skills. *Applied Psychophysiological Biofeedback, 26*(4), 251–278.

Pal, B., Keenan, J., Misra, H. N., Moussa, K., & Morris, J. (1996). Raynaud's phenomenon in idiopathic carpal tunnel syndrome. *Scandinavian Journal of Rheumatology, 25*(3), 143–145.

Raynaud, M. (1888). *New research on the nature and treatment of local asphyxia of the extremities.* London, UK: New Sydenham Society.

Roberts, A. H., Kewman, D. G., & MacDonald, H. (1973). Voluntary control of skin temperature: Unilateral changes using hypnosis and feedback. *Journal of Abnormal Psychology, 82*(1), 163–168.

Sedlacek, K. (1979). Biofeedback for Raynaud's disease. *Psychosomatics*, 20(8), 535–541. doi:10.1016/S0033-3182(79)70776-6

Sedlacek, K. (1989). Biofeedback treatment of primary Raynaud's disease. In J. V. Basmajian (Ed.), *Biofeedback: Principle and practice for clinicians* (pp. 317–321). Baltimore, MD: Lippincott William & Wilkins.

Sedlacek, K., & Taub, E. (1996). Biofeedback treatment of Raynaud's disease. *Professional Psychology: Research and Practice*, 27, 548–553.

Shenefelt, P. (2002). Complementary psychotherapy in dermatology: Hypnosis and biofeedback. *Dermatology*, 20, 595–601.

Shepard, R. F. (2008). Upper extremity and arterial disease: Raynaud's syndrome, occlusive arterial disease, and thoracic outlet syndrome. In T. W. Rooke, T. M. Sullivan, & M. R. Jafee (Eds.), *Vascular and endovascular* (pp. 26–43). Oxford, UK: Society for Vascular Medicine and Biology.

Silman, A., Holligan, S., Brennan, P., & Maddison, P. (1990). Prevalence of symptoms of Raynaud's phenomena in general practice. *BMJ (Clinical Research Ed.)*, 301(6752), 590–592.

Spittell, J. A. (1972). Raynaud's phenomenon and allied vasospastic conditions. In J. F. Fairbairn, J. L. Juergens, & J. A. Spittell, Jr. (Eds.), *Peripheral vascular disease* (pp. 387–419). Philadelphia, PA: Saunders.

Surwit, R. S., & Jordan, J. S. (1987). Behavioral tratment of Raynaud's syndrome. In J. P. Hatch, J. G. Fisher, & J. D. Rough (Eds.), *Biofeedback*. New York, NY: Plenum Press.

Surwit, R. S. (1973). Biofeedback: A possible treatment for Raynaud's disease. *Seminars in Psychiatry*, 5(4), 483–490.

Surwit, R. S. (1982). Behavioral treatment of Raynaud's syndrome in peripheral vascular disease. *Journal of Consulting and Clinical Psychology*, 50(6), 922–932.

Suter, L. G., Murabito, J. M., Felson, D. T., & Fraenkel, L. (2005). The incidence and natural history of Raynaud's phenomena in the community. *Arthritis and Rheumatism*, 52(4), 1259–1263. doi:10.1002/art.20988

Taub, E. (1977). Self-regulation of human tissue temperature. In G. Schwartz & J. Beatty (Eds.), *Biofeedback: Theory and practice* (pp. 265–300). New York, NY: Academic Press.

Taub, E., & Emurian, C. S. (1976). Feedback-aided self-regulation of skin temperature with simple feedback locus. *Biofeedback and Self-Regulation*, 1(2), 147–168.

Taub, E., & Stroebel, C. F. (1978). Biofeedback in the treatment of vasoconstrictive syndromes. *Biofeedback and Self-Regulation*, 3(4), 363–373.

Weinrich, M. C., Maricq, H. R., Keil, J. E., McGregor, A. R., & Diat, F. (1990). Prevalence of Raynaud's phenomenon in the adult population of South Carolina. *Journal of Clinical Epidemiology*, 43(12), 1343–1349.

Wise, R. A., Malamet, R., & Wigley, F. M. (1987). Acute effects of nifedipine on digital blood flow in human subjects with Raynaud's phenomenon: A double blind placebo controlled trail. *Journal of Rheumatology*, 14(2), 278–283.

Rehabilitation: Amelioration of Suffering and Adjustment

Philip R. Appel

This chapter deals with the subject of hypnosis in rehabilitation, as it pertains to the amelioration of suffering from untoward medical events that alter a person's physical, intellectual, or emotional capacities. The genesis of suffering from a lasting medical event includes the wounding of self and the narcissistic injury or threat that incurred. In this chapter, we will look at one particular approach to restoring a sense of self that is not identified necessarily with the self as a physical being alone or as an agent or narrator of one's life. When medical illness or injury creates a lasting disability, then the facets of the self are confronted as the remembered sense of self may be in conflict with the experienced sense of self (Appel, 2003a). Livneh and Antonak (2005) point out that one's self-concept and self-identity are often linked to body image; for individuals with visible disabilities, it is the successful transformation of body image and self-perception that mitigate the erosion of self-esteem. Consistent with this approach, Murugami (2009) concluded that a person with a disability has the capability of constructing a sense of self not rooted in impairment but independent of it and seeing the disability as just one characteristic of self rather than a reflection of the entire self.

Suffering from injury or disability is increased when the cognitive self cannot create a meaningful narrative that integrates the loss of function and ability. Suffering may be difficult to overcome when the patient tries to cope by grasping onto the former sense of self that was, and/or having an aversion to the present experience of self. Gallagher (2000) points out that the narrative self relies on the repetition of the story about self (which relies on intactness of the brain where memory is stored) and when the narrative must change because of loss of function and disability, then there is a diminishment in the experience of self.

LOSS, TRAUMA, AND SUFFERING

Chapman and Gavrin (1999, p. 2223) state that "suffering is the perception of serious threat or damage to the self, and it emerges when a discrepancy develops between what one expected of one's self and what one does or is." For Cassell (1991), suffering is the consequence of perceived impending destruction of the person or of some essential part of the person. Wilke (1981) stated that we define suffering as perceived damage to the integrity of the self, which is a psychological construct that represents a subjective sense of identity. Higgins (1987) also addresses the notion of suffering as a threat to or damage to the integrity of the self and further points out that it arises from the discrepancy between what one expects of oneself and what one is capable of doing.

Scheiman and Turner (1988) point out that when there is disability, it affects the sense of mastery, which is all about being able to live one's life as one chooses as opposed to fate. Another finding that was consistently supported in the literature was the issue of an increased awareness of one's vulnerability, and particularly of one's mortality following a traumatic episode. Soeken and Carson (1987) pointed out that the onset of an illness or disability may be the first opportunity of one's life to confront and contemplate the finite nature of life. "One's personal belief in the effectiveness of one's self as agent is self-efficacy. This belief has an important role in adjustment to painful disease conditions" (Keefe, Lefebvre,

Maxiner, Salley, & Caldwell, 1997). Marks, Allegrante, and Lorig (2005) discuss the importance of promoting and increasing self-efficacy in managing the consequences of illness or injury that creates disability. For without the individual's personal confidence in beliefs about his or her capacity to undertake behavior or behaviors that may lead to desired outcomes such as improved health or adaptation to disability, not only may such behaviors not be undertaken, but the sense of self is diminished. Yet at the same time, Squier (2004, p. 29) points out that the Western concept of "triumphing over mind, body or soul" with sufficient determination is an illusion and an unwinnable battle. Striving and overcoming is directly related to self agency and is a part of the American character of rugged individualism and pulling yourself up by your bootstraps. Our culture does not advocate acceptance as it equates it with surrender; therefore, acceptance can become identified with being a loser. Margaretha-Strandmark (2004, p. 135) stated that "the essence of ill health is powerlessness, which is made by a self-image of worthlessness, a sense of being imprisoned in one's life situation, and emotional suffering. The individual views her/himself as worthless, based on societal norms, attitudes and human models. Incapability and a sense of worthlessness cause the individual to distrust her/him self and others. She/he is imprisoned in her/his own life situation due to limited choices and ability." To alleviate suffering in part, steps must be undertaken to help the individual disidentify from his/her narrative, beliefs, sensations, and emotions in a way that would allow the individual to identify with the experiencer as opposed to the experience.

USE OF HYPNOSIS IN REHABILITATION

I have written extensively about the use of hypnosis in working with rehabilitation patients (Appel, 1990, 1992a, 1992b, 1999, 2003a, 2003b) and portraying how hypnotically mediated interventions have been used to assist with rehabilitation goal attainment, adjustment to disability, and treatment of coexisting premorbid conditions impacting rehabilitation. As hypnosis can be used to promote a greater awareness of the ongoing flow of experience by giving suggestions to attend to additional aspects of experience (e.g., sensations, imaginings, thoughts, emotions, intuitions, or impulses) that the patient usually attends to in his or her everyday discrete pattern of conscious awareness, it can be used easily for reframing an experience or disidentifying from an experience or letting the focal point of attention recede into the background of awareness. The goals in alleviation of suffering from the discordant experience of self arising from an inability to be in the world the way one wishes involves transcendence . . . transcendence of beliefs, pain, and inabilities. From another standpoint, hypnotically mediated interventions facilitate change and accelerate learning (Wright, 1960); and in this case, hypnosis is being used to bring about change in awareness and sense of self. The use of relaxation strategies helps as well as hypnotically mediated interventions for pain control or performance enhancement as they promote awareness of the "agent self." The major challenge is helping to facilitate adjustment to disability, dealing with the permanent changes in the neurological self, within the body, as well as the cognitive self, from whence the narrative arises.

RESEARCH

While research specific to hypnosis and mindfulness is limited, Grossman, Niemann, Schmidt, & Walach (2004, p. 35) performed a meta-analysis of mindfulness-based stress reduction and showed the efficacy of such interventions in increasing awareness "to provide more veridical perception, reduce negative affect and improve vitality and coping". Several authors (Alladin, 2014; Holroyd, 2003; Otani, 2003; Semmens-Wheeler & Dienes, 2012; Yapko, 2011) have written about the relationship of hypnosis and mindfulness and their integration, as mindfulness techniques are especially effective for reduction of patient identification of self with injury or illness. The Italian psychiatrist Roberto Assagioli (1971), a contemporary of Freud and Jung, promoted extensively the concept of "disidentification," stating that anything we identify with will control and dominate us, and everything from which we disidentify we can influence. Assagioli's unabridged "disidentification" exercise will be presented in the case example that follows. Thus, when an individual with impaired motoric, sensory, or cognitive abilities identifies with the impairments as self, suffering arises as all that is usually seen as self is the disability. It is to these ends that helping an individual learn to tolerate dysphoric experiences needs to be addressed to avoid negative self-reflections, because the attributions made about the self when the experienced disability is perceived as identical with self often lead to suffering. One way of changing the conditioned pattern of awareness, the individual's everyday discrete state of consciousness (Tart, 1972) through which the world of objects and self as object is experienced, is through the use of a choiceless awareness mindfulness meditation exercise that incorporates hypnotic language, expectancy, and suggestion. Further, Squier (2004, p. 34) writes about meditation as a "survival aide" for the person with a disability as it helps one disidentify from experience and acquired notions of self.

CASE EXAMPLE

A 62-year-old married, college-educated female who broke her jaw (in three different places) as the result of a bicycle accident was referred for hypnotherapy to assist in rehabilitation. She had suffered multiple injuries that affected her sense of self and pain that she was experiencing. She had broken nine teeth, lacerated her liver, and broke her hand. The original operation on the jaw involved three titanium plates and screws. She later underwent surgery to remove one of the plates. Two years later, she underwent an anterior cervical disc fusion to repair damage to the spine that was also sustained in the fall. She reported that the pain was always on the top of her consciousness and that eating, speaking, and making facial expressions was a strain. Even her sense of taste had been compromised. She reported that she had developed biomechanical issues in her jaw and her jaw was now much smaller.

She reported that she had been rushing to catch up to her partner who was ahead of her and had not been paying attention to her and how far behind she was. As she was rushing to catch up, she had to stop suddenly to avoid hitting another bicyclist. Stopping so quickly threw her over the bike and onto the ground, which is how she sustained her injuries. She remembered telling herself, "I was going to die there and he was on his phone, not paying attention to me." She reported having occasional intrusive images of her broken teeth on the ground and has vivid memories of the accident every few months. She reported that she has become a negative person. She reported that she became hopeless when she realized that she would never look better, that she now looked aged and disfigured in her face. She always wore a scarf to cover up her neck. While engaged in an ego-state intervention with the part of her that felt ugly and old, as soon as she saw that ego-state, the pain in her jaw increased, revealing the emotional component of her pain. There was no prior history of mental health contacts or psychological problems. She has been married for 37 years, had two children, and had worked for much of her life outside of the home.

The patient was initially taught Gunther's (1968) relaxation protocol coupled with autogenics and safe-place imagery (permissive instructions to imagine being in a safe, peaceful place, which could be a seashore, forest, mountains, or desert; and to notice all that is within that landscape or seascape, the objects, the colors, and so on, and to feel the warmth of the sun, and to feel a gentle breeze on one side of the face with a fragrance on the wind that could be smelled), to which she responded well, and Oyle's (1975) protocol for pain reduction. Oyle's protocol (Appel & Bleiberg, 2005) is a light hypnotic "imagery based intervention in which the patient is given the suggestion to convert the kinesthetic qualities of the pain into an image (visual or an auditory based on preferred sensory modality)." Patients are then given a suggestion to create a second image of health and healing, followed with a suggestion to observe the interaction of both their images in a way that is better for them. Alternatively for individuals who have difficulty coming up with a three-dimensional form, they can be asked to see the color of the intensity of their pain and then the color of health and healing and then given the suggestion to see the color of health and healing dilute the color of their pain until all they can see is the color of health and healing. I usually give the metaphor of pouring milk into coffee, and assuming an infinite supply of milk, the coffee eventually becomes coffee-flavored milk; with more milk, the coffee cannot be tasted, smelt, or seen. She responded to the color variation. Given her feelings of resentment and anger toward her partner for the accident, I engaged her in ego-state therapy to target the part of the self that was resentful and negative. By acknowledging the feelings and offering thanks and an apology for all that, that part of the psyche had to endure a noticeable lessening of tension in her chest and a peaceful mood ensued. By targeting the angry blaming part of the patient's self against the partner, she was better able to be in relation to her partner, from whom she needed support, as well as shift from her fear of lack of control to caring for self now. She was next taught the choiceless awareness mindfulness meditation described previously, which diminished her awareness of the pain as well as the negative internal dialogue. The therapist talked to her to understand the consequence of expanded versus concentrated awareness, particularly when that which is concentrated upon is pain. Again, ego-state therapy was engaged with the part of her that felt unattractive. She immediately felt an increase in pain as she visualized that part of herself as an old hag. The hypnotist engaged with that part and offered loving kindness and acceptance. She pointed out that the part of her that looked like a hag felt unloved and unaccepted by her, and that was painful. In addition, it was her projection onto this part of her psyche that made her look like an old hag. As she gained insight into her inner dynamics and changed her thoughts and communication, she felt more relief. In another session, she talked about being mournful about all that had happened. To trace the origins of that feeling, she was in the "corridor of time" (Edelstein, 1988) uncovering technique and she became aware of loss related to her daughter going off to college. She was able to see that there were several issues related to her sense of mourning and it was not all about the accident. There were also generational issues present as she was a "child of the Holocaust"; although both parents survived Nazi concentration camps, she remembered a fear that had been with her since childhood that her father would die that is. She had been a caretaker of her parents even when young until they died, and had also been a caretaker of her own children. While that ego-state mourned the loss of that role, it was now given the assignment to care for self and experience self in an individuated way that also deserved attention and could exist without being in relation to others as a caretaker.

TRANSCRIPTS: HYPNOSIS IN THE AMELIORATION OF SUFFERING AND ADJUSTMENT TO REHABILITATION

I teach all of my patients this adaptation of a choiceless awareness mindfulness exercise as it rapidly expands awareness and promotes neutral observation of experiences. The following is a transcript of the exercise I use.

"Go ahead and close your eyes right now, and allow yourself to become aware of what it's like to have your eyes covered by your eyelids. The whole time that you are experiencing what it's like to have your eyes covered by your eyelids you can also become aware of your breath, you can become aware of the flow of air in your nostrils, and the temperature of your exhalations compared with your inhalations. The whole time that you are observing your breath and what it is like to have your eyes covered by your eyelids, you can experience the movement in your body. You can feel the rise and fall of your chest as you breathe, the movement of your diaphragm, the beating of your heart, your pulse throughout the body, and any random movement you may be making in your limb, torso, neck, or head. The whole time you are in the chair experiencing the movement in the body and the breath and what it's like to have your eyes covered by your eyelids, you can become aware of all your sensations. You can feel the weight of your body in the chair, the texture of the cloth of your clothing against your skin, your ring on your finger, your watch on your wrist, your glasses on the bridge of your nose, as well as any sensation within your limb, torso, neck, or head. The whole time that you are experiencing all the different sensations, and the movement, of the body, and the breath and what it is like to have your eyes covered by your eyelids, you can also experience all the sounds around you that you can hear. You can notice the sound of the air conditioner, the sounds of traffic coming in through the window, sounds filtering in from outside the office within the hospital, my voice, and you can notice how still and quiet you are compared to all that you. The whole time that you are listening to all the sounds and experiencing the sensations and the movement and the breath and what it's like to have your eyes covered by your eyelids, you can

also become aware of the contents of your mind, you can be aware of any thoughts, memories, images, fantasies, or impulses that may be present in your awareness. And you can begin to observe how every moment your experience changes and how you do not have to respond or react to any part of your experience in any particular way. You can observe your experiences without becoming them. And so you begin to realize that the experiencer is not the experience; that the thinker is not the thought, that the feeler is not the feeling, that the sensor is not the sensation. You are he or she who is aware of all of this and does not have to be identified with any one experience, nor do you have to respond to any experience. In a moment I'm going to ask you to envision hearing and thinking and feeling and sensing and breathing and moving. When you open your eyes, see without looking at any one thing in particular. See all that there is to see at the same time that you are aware of the entirety of your experience, allowing yourself to be aware of all that is happening with all your senses."

I find that using the previous intervention helps teach the patient about impermanence and change and facilitates being open to what is arising without resistance and without aversion, which fuels suffering. It helps the patient to find refuge in the moment, in the now, away from memories of loss or fears of future happenings. Squier (2004, p. 36) points out that the practice of meditation can be used as a medical treatment to shift "from the narrow focus on illness, pain, and loss of control to a broader project of integrating the vicissitudes inevitable in life within an experience of health and well-being." Neff (2003, p. 89) wrote that "when individuals are not being mindful of their painful thoughts and feelings, they are not accepting their experience for what it is, and this non-acceptance may manifest as the refusal to bring it into conscious awareness (Hayes, Wilson, Gifford, Follette, & Strosahl, 1996), or else as intense emotional resistance to the pain, so that one is caught up and swept away by one's aversive reaction." I have found that this intervention readily teaches through an expansion of awareness of all that can be experienced that the previous focal point of dysphoria that has been resisted drops away.

Disidentification

I also use Assagioli's (1971) exercise in disidentification (original given in the following text) to further help the patient identify with a self that is beyond narrative, to identify with the narrator who has yet to tell a story; to identify with a self that is the center of awareness, a center of consciousness, and not identified with the contents of consciousness. In other words, identifying with the experiencer, not the experience, not thoughts, not emotions, not sensations, not impulses, but he or she who is aware of all this.

When engaged in the disidentification exercise, I give suggestions for relaxation using Gunther's approach (1968) unless the experience of being weighted has negative associations and then instruct the patient *"to hear my words as their words to him/her self and to then experience deeply what I am suggesting to them."* I then begin. . . .

"I have a body but I am not my body. My body may find itself in different conditions of health or sickness, it may be rested or tired, but that has nothing to do with myself, my real self. I value my body as my precious instrument of experience and of action in the outer world, but it is only an instrument. I treat it well, I seek to keep it in good health, but it is not myself.

'I have a body, but I am not my body.'

Focus your attention on the central thought here: 'I have a body but I am not my body.'

Attempt, as much as you can, to realize this as an experienced fact in your consciousness."

I have emotions, but I am not my emotions. My emotions are diversified, changing, and sometimes contradictory. They may swing from love to hatred, from calm to anger, from joy to sorrow, and yet my essence—my true nature—does not change. 'I' remain. Though a wave of anger may temporarily submerge me, I know that it will pass in time; therefore, I am not this anger. Since I can observe and understand my emotions, and then gradually learn to direct, utilize, and integrate them harmoniously, it is clear that they are not myself.

I have emotions, but I am not my emotions.

Focus your attention on the central thought here: 'I have emotions but I am not my emotions.'

Attempt, as much as you can, to realize this as an experienced fact in your consciousness.

I have desires but I am not my desires. Desires are aroused by drives, physical and emotional, and by other influences. They are often changeable and contradictory, with alternations of attraction and repulsion; therefore, they are not myself.

I have desires, but I am not my desires.

Focus your attention on the central thought here: 'I have desires but I am not my desires.'

Attempt, as much as you can, to realize this as an experienced fact in your consciousness.

I have a mind but I am not my mind. My mind is a valuable tool of discovery and expression, but it is not the essence of my being. Its contents are constantly changing as it embraces new ideas, knowledge, and experience. Sometimes it refuses to obey me. Therefore, it cannot be me, myself. It is an organ of knowledge in regard to both the outer and the inner worlds, but it is not myself.

I have a mind, but I am not my mind.

Focus your attention on the central thought here: 'I have a mind but I am not my mind.'

Attempt, as much as you can, to realize this as an experienced fact in your consciousness.

I engage in various activities and play many roles in life. I must play these roles and I willingly play them as well as possible, be it the role of son or father, wife or husband, teacher or student, artist or executive. But I am more than the son, the father, the artist. These are roles, specific but partial roles, which I, myself, am playing, agree to play, can watch and observe myself playing.

Therefore, I am not any of them. I am self-identified, and I am not only the actor, but the director of the acting.

Focus your attention on the central thought here: 'I have many roles in life but I am not my roles.'

Attempt, as much as you can, to realize this as an experienced fact in your consciousness."

Next comes the phase of identification.

"What am I then? What remains after having disidentified from my body, my sensations, my feelings, my desires, my mind, and my actions? It is the essence of myself—a center of pure self-consciousness. It is the permanent factor in the ever-varying flow of my personal life. It is that which gives me a sense of being, of permanence, of inner balance. I affirm my identity with this center and realize its permanency and its energy. [Pause] I recognize and affirm myself as a center of pure self-awareness and of creative, dynamic energy. I realize that from this center of true identity I can learn to observe, direct, and harmonize all the psychological processes and the physical body. I choose to achieve a constant awareness of this fact in the midst of my everyday life, and to use it to help me and give increasing meaning and direction to my life.

Focus your attention on the central realization: I am a center of pure self-consciousness and of will. Attempt, as much as you can, to realize this as an experienced fact in your awareness."

I have found the previous intervention lets the patient liberate himself or herself from existing notions of what is self to center on a new sense of self that is not disabled. As whatever experience is unfolding, no matter how that experience may be tempered by damage to sensory or cognitive abilities, it is what it is and the experiencer can observe that which is arising in the moment. Obviously patients who have sustained profound traumatic brain injuries or stroke and who have limited attention and concentration may not benefit. However, I did write (Appel & Bleiberg, 2000) about a patient who sustained a mild to moderate brain injury in an industrial accident who with continued practice was able to enter into hypnotic meditative states for several hours.

As regards a new awareness of the self, Fitzgerald (1997) and Frazee (1999) discussed the notion of reclaiming the self, and redefining the self to incorporate the disability, but not being defined by it.

Ego States

Helen Watkins, in her 1993 article on an "overview of ego-state therapy," points out that many clinicians have theorized about the "segmentation" of personality and that others have used it in their clinical practice successfully to bring about therapeutic outcomes. She (1993, p. 233) states that "an ego state may be defined as an organized system of behavior and experience whose elements are bound together by some common principle." She goes on to say (1993, p. 236) that "Ego-state therapy is the utilization of family and group-therapy techniques for the resolution of conflicts between the different ego states that constitute a 'family of self' within a single individual. It is a kind of internal negotiation that may employ any of the directive, behavioral, abreactive, or analytic techniques of treatment, usually under hypnosis." Frederick (2005) pointed out that "in the normal personality, ego states relate almost seamlessly. Their relationships with one another are harmonious. The normal personality does have the capacity, however (via different ego states within it assuming the executive position), for a great deal of variation. A single individual may think, act, feel and behave quite differently from one time to another as a function of which personality part has the most energy." Alladin (2013) talks about the efficacy of healing the wounded self when confronted with loss using ego-state therapy.

McNeal and Fredick (1993) point out how easy it is to use ego-strengthening with ego-states and to facilitate a "conflict-free ego state." Hageman and Frederick (2013) have discussed the phenomenological-based research that points to the effectiveness of ego-state therapy. McNeal and Frederick (1993), Rossman (1987), Schwartz (1995), Torem and Gainer (1995), Comstock (1991), and Watkins and Watkins (1997) have discussed the use of a conflict free ego-state to facilitate change. Ginandes (2006, p. 121), in a discussion of types of ego-states associated with medical illness, talks about a "healing guide" that "seems to embody the patient's deep wellspring of inner knowledge about how to restore health in the complex ecosystem of the body . . . and on the spiritual level, may appear as an ego state that can provide hope,

inspiration, and wisdom about moving in the direction of recovery."

Ego-state therapy can be used to target "the narrative self" or any aspect of the psyche that is suffering from the medical condition and disability arising from such. It allows for uncovering the deep structure of experience that can facilitate the attributions and beliefs that are being utilized as part of the narrative that is being resisted against for its painful narcissistic reflection of a self that is now broken or less than in some manner. Once the ego-state that is struggling with what has happened is identified, then a variety of interventions can be employed to provide ego-strengthening (including disidentification), reframe the situation, and provide unconditional positive regard and compassion for self through intervening with that part of the psyche, that ego-state that is suffering.

Ego States, Loving Kindness, and Compassion

Using ego-state therapy makes it easier to offer compassion toward self. I suggest that using a naturalistic induction style to listen for a significant statement related to the inability to tolerate present medical circumstance and resulting disability is a place to begin. I ask the patient to repeat the target statement silently to self three times and to notice how that thought feels when experienced. I then ask the patient to locate the epicenter of that feeling in the body. Holding that feeling state in mind, the patient is then asked to see the part of self that is thinking that thought and feeling this way. Once the suffering ego-state is seen, the patient is asked to convey respect and empathy for all that part has endured and to apologize for leaving that part to deal all alone with the disability. I often reframe the declarative statements made by the suffering ego-state as a question that is being asked of self and have the patient address it. For example, as in the previous case the statement "*I am an old Hag!*" is reframed as "*I am an old Hag?*" I give the suggestion to address the needs of different aspects of the psyche and to not take every utterance literally, as well as to identify the goal and to separate out the behavior to meet that goal.

Neff, Kirkpatrick, and Rude (2007) described how studies have shown that self-compassion promotes adaptive psychological functioning and helps protect against self-evaluative anxiety when confronted with personal weaknesses. Neff (2003, p. 85) stated that "self-compassion entails three main components: (a) self-kindness—being kind and understanding toward oneself in instances of pain or failure rather than being harshly self-critical, (b) common humanity—perceiving one's experiences as part of the larger human experience rather than seeing them as separating and isolating, and (c) mindfulness—holding painful thoughts and feelings in balanced awareness rather than over-identifying with them." Neff (2003, p.87) goes on to say that self-compassion involves being touched by and open to one's own suffering, not avoiding or disconnecting from it, generating the desire to alleviate one's suffering and to heal oneself with kindness.

CONCLUSION

Kenneth Bowers (1983) once described hypnosis as "semantic input for somatic output" and the power of words to create experience. Hypnotically mediated psychotherapeutic interventions are a powerful means to bring about changes every day in a discrete state of consciousness. As stated previously, suffering arises from resistance, from aversion to what is happening. When an individual acquires a disability and the narrating self identifies with the disability as opposed to experiencing disability, then there is suffering as the self is no longer experienced as whole and perhaps "broken." The ego-states, the subpersonalities that evolved through the developmental years into adulthood, all respond to the existential challenge differently given their function and degree of knowledge and insight. The teaching of self-regulation skills not only in the sensory, cognitive, and affective realms but in awareness training can mitigate the experience of suffering. The acquisition of skills addresses the needs of the agent self, and the awareness training meets the needs of the narrative self to create a more accommodating narrative. The transforming power of empathy and compassion directed toward self brings about a rapprochement within and does much to ameliorate the narcissistic wound that arose in the face of disability.

REFERENCES

Alladin, A. (2013). Healing the wounded self: Combining hypnotherapy with ego state therapy. *American Journal of Clinical Hypnosis, 56*(1), 3–22.

Alladin, A. (2014). Mindfulness-based hypnosis: Blending science, beliefs, and wisdoms to catalyze healing. *American Journal of Clinical Hypnosis, 56*(3), 285–302.

Appel, P. R. (1990). Clinical applications of hypnosis in the physical medicine and rehabilitation setting: Three case reports. *American Journal of Clinical Hypnosis, 33*(2), 85–93.

Appel, P. R. (1992a). Performance enhancement in physical medicine and rehabilitation. *American Journal of Clinical Hypnosis, 35*(1), 11–19.

Appel, P. R. (1992b). The use of clinical hypnosis in physical medicine and rehabilitation. *Psychiatric Medicine, 10*(1), 133–148.

Appel, P. R. (1999). Hypnosis and suggestion in physical medicine and rehabilitation. In W. Matthews & J. Edgette (Eds.), *Current thinking and research in brief therapy: Solutions, strategies, narratives.* New York, NY: Brunner Mazel.

Appel, P. R. (2003a). Clinical hypnosis. In E. Leskowitz (Ed.), *Complementary and alternative medicine in rehabilitation* (pp. 97–108). St. Louis, MO: Harcourt Health Sciences.

Appel, P. R. (2003b). Clinical hypnosis. In S. Wainapel & A. Fast (Eds.), *Alternative medicine and rehabilitation: A guide for practitioners.* New York, NY: Demos.

Appel, P. R., & Bleiberg, J. (2000). Evaluation and treatment of anxiety in neuromuscular rehabilitation. In D. I. Mostofsky & D. H. Barlow (Eds.), *The management of stress and anxiety in medical disorders.* Needham Heights, MA: Simon & Schuster.

Appel, P. R., & Bleiberg, J. (2005). Pain reduction is related to hypnotizability but not to relaxation or to reduction in suffering: A preliminary investigation. *American Journal of Clinical Hypnosis, 48*(2–3), 153–161.

Assagioli, R. (1971). *Psychosynthesis: A collection of basic writings.* New York, NY: Viking Press.

Bowers, K. S. (1983). *Hypnosis for the seriously curious.* New York, NY: Norton.

Cassell, E. J. (1991). *The nature of suffering and the goals of medicine.* New York, NY: Oxford University Press.

Chapman, C. R., & Gavrin, J. (1999). Suffering: The contributions of persistent pain. *The Lancet, 353,* 2223–2237.

Comstock, C. (1991). The inner self-helper and concepts of inner guidance: Historical antecedents, its role within dissociation, and clinical utilization. *Dissociation, 4,* 165–177.

Edelstein, G. (1988, March). *Comments during a meeting at the Annual Scientific Meeting of the American Society of Clinical Hypnosis*. Chicago, IL.

Fitzgerald, J. (1997). Reclaiming the whole: Self, spirit, and society. *Disability & Rehabilitation, 19*(10), 407–413.

Frazee, C. (1999). Balance and movement. In M. A. McColl & J. E. Bickenbach (Eds.), *Introduction to disability and handicap* (pp. 59–71). London, UK: WB Saunders.

Frederick, C. (2005). Selected topics in ego state therapy. *International Journal of Clinical and Experimental Hypnosis, 53*(4), 339–429.

Gallagher, S. (2000). Philosophical conceptions of the self: Implications for cognitive science. *Trends in Cognitive Sciences, 4*(1), 14–21.

Ginandes, C. (2006). Six players on the inner stage: Using ego state therapy with the medically ill. *International Journal of Clinical and Experimental Hypnosis, 54*(2), 113–129.

Grossman, P., Niemann, L., Schmidt, S., & Walach, H. (2004). Mindfulness-based stress reduction and health benefits: A meta-analysis. *Journal of Psychosomatic Research, 57*(1), 35–43.

Gunther, B. (1968). *Sense relaxation: Below your mind*. New York, NY: Collier.

Hageman, J. H., & Frederick, C. (2013). Phenomenological and evidence based research in ego state therapy: Recognized and unrecognized successes and future directions. *American Journal of Clinical Hypnosis, 56*(1), 66–85.

Hayes, S., Wilson, K., Gifford, E., Follette, V., & Strosahl, K. (1996). Experiential avoidance and behavioral disorders: A functional dimensional approach to diagnosis and treatment. *Journal of Consulting and Clinical Psychology, 64*(6), 1152–1168.

Higgins, E. T. (1987). Self-discrepancy: A theory relating self and affect. *Psychological Review, 94*(3), 319

Holroyd, J. (2003). The science of meditation and the state of hypnosis. *American Journal of Clinical Hypnosis, 46*(2), 109–128.

Keefe, F. J., Lefebvre, J. C., Maxiner, W., Salley, A. N., & Caldwell, D. S. (1997). Self-efficacy for arthritis pain: Relationship to perception of thermal laboratory pain stimuli. *Arthritis Care Research, 10*(3), 177–184.

Livneh, H., & Antonak, R. F. (2005). Psychosocial adaptation to chronic illness and disability: A primer for counselors. *Journal of Counseling & Development, 83*(1), 12–20.

Margaretha Strandmark, K. (2004). Ill health is powerlessness: A phenomenological study about worthlessness, limitations and suffering. *Scandinavian Journal of Caring Sciences, 18*(2), 135–144.

Marks, R., Allegrante, J. P., & Lorig, K. (2005). A review and synthesis of research evidence for self-efficacy-enhancing interventions for reducing chronic disability: Implications for health education practice. *Health Promotion Practice, 6*(2), 148–156.

McNeal, S., & Frederick, C. (1993). Inner strength and other techniques for ego strengthening. *American Journal of Clinical Hypnosis, 35*(3), 170–178.

Murugami, M. W. (2009). Disability and identity. *Disability Studies Quarterly, 29*. Retrieved from http://dsq-sds.org/article/view/979/1173

Neff, K. (2003). Self-compassion: An alternative conceptualization of a healthy attitude toward oneself. *Self and Identity, 2*(2), 85–101.

Neff, K. D., Kirkpatrick, K. L., & Rude, S. S. (2007). Self-compassion and adaptive psychological functioning. *Journal of Research in Personality, 41*(1), 139–154.

Otani, A. (2003). Eastern meditative techniques and hypnosis: A new synthesis. *American Journal of Clinical Hypnosis, 46*(2), 97–108.

Oyle, I. (1975). *The healing mind: You can cure yourself without drugs*. Berkeley, CA: Celestial Arts.

Rossman, M. L. (1987). *Healing yourself: A step-by-step program for better health through imagery*. New York, NY: Walker and Company.

Scheiman, S., & Turner, A. (1988). Age, disability, and the sense of mastery. *Journal of Health and Social Behavior, 29*(2), 169–186.

Schwartz, R. C. (1995). *Internal family systems therapy*. New York, NY: Guilford Press.

Semmens-Wheeler, R., & Dienes, Z. (2012). The contrasting role of higher order awareness in hypnosis and meditation. *Journal of Mind–Body Regulation, 2*(1), 43–57.

Soeken, K. L., & Carson, V. J. (1987). Responding to the spiritual needs of the chronically ill. *The Nursing Clinics of North America, 22*(3), 603–611.

Squier, S. (2004). Meditation, disability, and identity. *Literature and Medicine, 1*, 29–45.

Tart, C. T. (1972). *Altered states of consciousness*. Upland, CA: Hawking Books.

Torem, M. S., & Gainer, M. J. (1995). The center core: Imagery for experiencing the unifying self. *Hypnosis, 22*, 125–131.

Watkins, H. H. (1993). Ego-state therapy: An overview. *American Journal of Clinical Hypnosis, 35*(4), 232–240.

Watkins, J. G., & Watkins, H. H. (1997). *Ego states: Theory and therapy*. New York, NY: W. W. Norton.

Wilke, J. T. (1981). Personal identity in the light of brain physiology and cognitive psychology. *Journal of Medical Philosophy, 6*, 323–333.

Wright, M. E. (1960). Hypnosis and rehabilitation. *Rehabilitation Literature, 21*, 2–12.

Yapko, M. D. (2011). *Mindfulness and hypnosis: The power of suggestion to transform experience*. New York, NY: W. W. Norton.

Skin Disorders

Philip D. Shenefelt

For skin disorders, hypnosis may help decrease pain and pruritus (itching) in the skin, allow exploration of and intervention in psychosomatic aspects of skin diseases, and lead to the resolution of some skin diseases, including verruca vulgaris (viral warts). Suggestion without formal trance induction may be effective in some cases. Sulzberger and Wolf (1934) reported on the use of suggestion to treat verrucae. For example, hypnosis may be utilized to regulate blood flow to the skin and other autonomic functions such as sweating that are not usually under conscious control. The relaxation response that occurs with hypnosis also affects the neurohormonal systems that regulate many body functions including those of the skin. Studies on the influence of hypnosis on immediate immune responses have shown the ability of hypnotized volunteers to significantly decrease the flare reaction to the skin histamine prick test. Similarly, in one study, the effect of hypnotic suggestion on delayed cellular immune responses showed a significant effect on the size of erythema (redness) and on palpable induration but no significant effect in other studies (Shenefelt, 2000).

Also, hypnotic relaxation can be quite useful during skin surgeries to reduce anxiety. Supportive (ego-strengthening) therapy while in a hypnotic state includes positive suggestions of self-worth and effectiveness. Posthypnotic suggestion is often included, and further strengthening of the effect can be obtained by making a recording that the patient can repeatedly use for self-hypnosis later. The strengthened ego is better able to repress or confront discordant elements that inhibit healing.

Direct suggestion while in the hypnotic state is a frequently used method of decreasing discomfort from pain, pruritus, burning sensations, anxiety, and insomnia. Again, posthypnotic suggestion and repeated use of a recording for self-hypnosis can help reinforce the effectiveness of direct suggestion. Direct suggestion may produce a sufficiently deep anesthesia in highly hypnotizable individuals for cutaneous surgery. Direct suggestion can also be used to reduce repetitive acts of skin scratching or picking, nail biting or manipulating, and hair pulling or twisting. Unwanted psychophysiological responses such as hyperhidrosis (excessive sweating), blushing, and some types of urticaria (hives) can also be controlled by direct suggestion. Some skin lesions such as verrucae (warts) can even be induced to resolve by using direct suggestion.

In addition, hypnosis is a tool that can be used to reveal and overcome psychological and behavioral roadblocks to healing. Therapies that can be enhanced by hypnosis include supportive (ego-strengthening) therapy, direct suggestion, symptom substitution, and psychosomatic hypnoanalysis. These uses of hypnosis in the treatment of skin disorders are illustrated in this chapter.

HYPNOTIC RELAXATION DURING DERMATOLOGIC SURGERY

A variety of skin procedures can produce pain or anxiety in patients. Procedures that are somewhat painful but usually do not require a local anesthetic include moderate-depth chemical peels, cryodestruction of skin lesions, curettage of molluscum, excision of skin tags, extrusion of comedones, incision and expression of milia, laser treatment of vascular lesions, strong microdermabrasion, and sclerotherapy. Procedures that require a local anesthetic include electrodesiccation and curettage, incision and drainage of an abscess, laser ablation of skin lesions, liposuction, punch biopsy, shave biopsy, surgical excision, and surgical repair. Procedures that may require conscious sedation include deep chemical peels, dermabrasion, laser resurfacing, and extensive liposuction. All of these procedures may be augmented by hypnotic relaxation and/or hypnotic analgesia.

RESEARCH

Faymonville et al. (1997) randomly assigned 60 patients undergoing skin plastic surgery with conscious sedation either to a control group with stress-reducing strategies or to a hypnosis group (Faymonville et al., 1997). Intraoperative and postoperative anxiety and pain were significantly lower, and significantly smaller amounts of medication were required for conscious sedation in the hypnosis group. Light and medium trance states are sufficient for most purposes, but a deep trance state is required for hypnotic anesthesia for surgery. Montgomery, Weltz, Seltz, and Bovbjerg (2002) studied 20 women randomized to standard care versus preoperative hypnosis for excisional breast biopsy (Montgomery et al., 2002). They found brief (10-min) hypnosis to be effective in reducing postsurgery pain and distress both before surgery and after surgery. Defechereux et al. (1999) reported a prospective randomized study of thyroid and parathyroid procedures performed under hypnosis, local anesthesia, and minimal conscious sedation in patients compared with similar surgery performed under conventional anesthesia in 20 patients. Defechereux et al. (1999) found that patients in the hypnoanesthesia group had significantly fewer instances of inflammatory response, hemodynamic dysregulation, postoperative pain, postoperative fatigue, and convalescence time. Bleeding, operative times, and surgical comfort were similar in both groups.

Lang et al. (2000) conducted a prospective randomized trial of adjunctive hypnotic relaxation and analgesia for invasive radiological procedures in three groups: percutaneous vascular radiological intraoperative standard intravenous conscious sedation care; structured attention; and intravenous conscious sedation that included self-hypnotic relaxation (Lang et al., 2000). Pain increased linearly with time in the standard group and in the structured attention group, but it remained flat in the hypnosis group. Anxiety decreased over time in all three groups but more so in the hypnosis group. Drug use was significantly higher in the standard group, intermediate in the structured

attention group, and lowest in the self-hypnosis group. Hemodynamic stability was significantly higher in the hypnosis group than in the other two groups. Procedure times were significantly shorter in the hypnosis group than in the standard group. Individual imagery was quite varied (Fick et al., 1999).

Permitting the patient to choose his or her own self-guided imagery seems to allow most individuals to reach a state of relaxation during skin procedures. The author used the technique from the invasive radiological studies modified for dermatology with good success in dermatological surgery (Shenefelt, 2003). Eye-roll induction was most commonly used by the author; this method works quickly for most patients. The author also conducted a prospective randomized control trial of hypnotic relaxation for skin procedures. Pain was not an issue because local anesthesia is quite effective for skin procedures. Anxiety was significantly decreased in the live induction hypnosis group compared with the control group (Shenefelt, 2013). The recorded induction hypnosis group was similar to the control group without much anxiety reduction.

CASE EXAMPLE

A needle-phobic 51-year-old female became more and more agitated during a skin surgery procedure to remove a melanoma from her upper arm. She asked that the procedure be terminated before completion. When offered hypnotic relaxation, she readily accepted. She had had no prior experience with hypnosis or meditation. She shifted into a trance within a minute and remained so until realerted after the end of the skin surgery procedure. This case is an example of dissociation and self-distraction in a trance by the patient imagining being where he or she would rather be.

TRANSCRIPT

"Now what I will do is show you how you can use your imagination to enter a state of focused attention and physical relaxation. If you hear sounds or noises in the room, just use them to deepen your experience. Here is a simple way to relax:

First, do one thing: Look up as far as you can, that's right, look way up toward the top of your head. Keep looking up.

Second, now do two things: Let your eyes close slowly and take a deep breath. That's right.

Third, now do three things: Breathe out, relax your eyes, and let your body float . . . float . . . float.

That's right, continue to imagine your body floating, floating through the table, each breath deeper and easier. Imagine yourself floating in a safe place where you are comfortable and feel protected, in a bath, or a lake, or a hot tub, or just floating in space, each breath deeper and easier. Notice how with each breath you let a little more tension out of your body as you continue to let your body float, safe and comfortable, each breath deeper and easier. That's right . . . now with your eyes closed and remaining in this state of concentration, describe for me how your body is feeling right now. Where do you imagine yourself being? What is it like? Can you smell the air? Can you see what is around you? Can you hear the pleasant sounds or silence? Can you feel the comfort? Good, now you can continue to be in this safe and comfortable place. Your body has to be here but you don't, so just spend your time being somewhere you would rather be. That's right, continue to float, each breath deeper and easier.

That's right, continue to float, each breath deeper and easier. Continue to enjoy being where you would rather be. Now if there is some discomfort, imagine that part to be cooler, if that's more comfortable, as if you had cool water or ice or snow on that part of your body. That's right, and continue to float.

That's right, continue to float. Now that the procedure is over, you may gradually come back to alert consciousness. As you realert yourself, you will continue to feel comfortable and relaxed, and that comfort will stay with you for the rest of the day. You may now, when you are ready, open your eyes and feel alert. That's right. How do you feel?" (Adapted from Spiegel & Spiegel, 2004)

Results: The patient was very grateful to have the procedure finished and had been relaxed and comfortable throughout the rest of the procedure.

HYPNOTHERAPY FOR SPECIFIC SKIN DISORDERS

Much of the older literature about the effectiveness of hypnosis on specific skin disorders is based on one or a few uncontrolled cases. In recent years, randomized controlled trials have produced more reliable information but are not available yet for most of the skin disease categories. The list of dermatological conditions in the following text is not all-inclusive, but it does include most of the skin disorders for which hypnosis is reasonably helpful in reducing symptoms or in improving aspects of the condition. They are arranged on the basis of the strength of scientific evidence for the effectiveness of hypnosis, starting with the strongest evidence (Shenefelt, 2000). Those dermatological conditions supported by only one or a few case reports are listed in alphabetical order toward the end of this section, followed by a case example for acne excoriée.

RESEARCH

Verruca Vulgaris

The early report by Sulzberger and Wolf (1934) on the efficacy of suggestion in treating warts has since been confirmed numerous times. Numerous reports attest to the efficacy of hypnosis in treating warts (Noll, 1994; Sinclair-Gieben & Chalmers, 1959). In a well-conducted randomized control study by Spanos, Williams, and Gwynn (1990) that serves as a typical example, 53% of the experimental group had improvement of their warts 3 months after the first of five hypnotherapy sessions, while none of the control group had improvement. If the warts fail to improve or resolve with direct suggestion, psychosomatic hypnoanalysis may be of benefit. Ewin (1992) reported 41 cases of warts where direct suggestion had failed, and in 33 of those cases, resolution occurred following psychosomatic hypnoanalysis.

Psoriasis

Stress is often a factor in the onset, exacerbation, and prolongation of psoriasis. Hypnosis and suggestion have been shown to have a positive effect on psoriasis. Tausk and Whitmore (1999) performed a small randomized double-blind control trial by using hypnosis as adjunctive therapy in psoriasis, with significant improvement in individuals who were highly hypnotizable. Hypnosis can be useful as an adjunct therapy for resistant psoriasis, especially if an emotional factor is significant in the triggering of the psoriasis.

Atopic Dermatitis

Stewart and Thomas (1995) treated 18 adults with extensive atopic dermatitis whose conditions had been resistant to conventional treatment with hypnotherapy. In a nonrandomized control study, they used relaxation, stress management, direct suggestion for nonscratching behavior and for skin comfort and coolness, ego strengthening, posthypnotic suggestions, and instruction in self-hypnosis. The results were statistically significant for reduction in itching, scratching, sleep disturbance, and tension. The use of topical corticosteroids decreased from the original amount by 40% at 4 weeks, 50% at 8 weeks, and 60% at 16 weeks.

Alopecia Areata

Gupta, Gupta, and Watteel (1997) found a strong correlation between high stress reactivity and depression in patients with alopecia areata. Willemsen, Vanderlinden, Deconinck, and Roseeuw (2006) used hypnotherapy for 21 patients, nine with alopecia universalis and 12 with extensive alopecia areata. After hypnotherapy, all patients had significantly lower anxiety and depression. Complete scalp hair regrowth occurred in nine patients, including four with alopecia universalis and two with ophiasis. Over 75% scalp hair regrowth occurred in another three patients. Five patients had a significant relapse of alopecia. Hypnosis is appropriate as a stress reducer and sometimes is successful as a primary treatment method for alopecia areata.

Urticaria

Two cases of urticaria responding to hypnotic suggestion were reported in a study (Shenefelt, 2000). The study included an 11-year-old boy whose urticarial reaction to chocolate could be blocked by hypnotic suggestion so that hives appeared on only one side of his face in response to that hypnotic suggestion. A case series study of hypnosis with relaxation therapy on 15 patients with chronic urticaria for an average duration of 7.8 years showed that within 14 months, six patients' conditions had cleared and those of eight had improved, with decreased medication requirements reported by 80% of the patients. One patient's condition did not improve.

Ciguatera Toxicity

A case of mysterious intense burning pain of the feet that kept the man awake at night was diagnosed through psychosomatic hypnoanalysis as resulting from ciguatera toxicity and its resultant persistent neuropathic pain. Suggestions in trance for coolness and comfort greatly reduced the discomfort and permitted the man to sleep through the night again (Laser & Shenefelt, 2012).

Congenital Ichthyosiform Erythroderma

Several cases of remarkable clearing of congenital ichthyosiform erythroderma of Brocq have been reported following direct suggestion for clearing under hypnosis. For example, Kidd (1966) reported improvement in a 34-year-old father and his 4-year-old son. Hypnosis, in addition to the use of emollients, may potentially be useful.

Dyshidrotic Dermatitis

Reduction in the severity of dyshidrotic dermatitis has been reported with the use of hypnosis as a treatment. Griesemer's (1978) data indicate a significant psychosomatic component for dyshidrosis; therefore, hypnosis may be useful as a therapy.

Erythema Nodosum

Resolution of erythema nodosum of 9-year duration occurred in a 44-year-old woman after hypnoanalysis (Shenefelt, 2007). Five of the seven key C.O.M.P.A.S.S. factors (conflict, organ language, motivation, past experience, active identification, self-punishment, suggestion or imprint) were positive in this case.

Erythromelalgia

One case report exists of successful treatment of erythromelalgia in an 18-year-old woman using hypnosis alone followed by self-hypnosis (Shenefelt, 2000). Permanent resolution occurred.

Furuncles

Jabush (1969) described a 33-year-old man with recurrent multiple furuncles since age 17 years, which contained *Staphylococcus aureus*. The furuncles were unresponsive to multiple treatment modalities. The patient had a negative self-image. Hypnosis and self-hypnosis with imagined sensations of warmth, cold, tingling, and heaviness resulted in dramatic improvement over 5 weeks, with full resolution of the recurrent furuncles. He also substantially improved from a mental standpoint. The hypnosis was hypothesized to have helped in some way to normalize the immune response to the bacteria. Conventional antibiotic therapy is the first line of treatment for furuncles; however, in unusually resistant cases with significant psychosomatic overlay, hypnosis may help to end the recurrent cycles of infection.

Glossodynia

When oral pain has a psychogenic component, hypnosis may be effective as a primary treatment. Even with organic disease, hypnosis may temporarily relieve pain (Golan, 1997).

Herpes Simplex

Lessening of discomfort from herpes simplex eruptions is similar to that for postherpetic neuralgia. Reduction in the frequency of recurrences of herpes simplex following hypnosis has also been reported. In cases with an apparent emotional trigger factor, hypnotic suggestion may be useful as a therapy for reducing the frequency of recurrence.

Hyperhidrosis

Hypnosis and autogenic training may be useful as adjunctive therapies for hyperhidrosis (Shenefelt, 2000).

Ichthyosis Vulgaris

A 33-year-old man with chronic ichthyosis vulgaris that was better in the summer and worse in the winter began hypnotic suggestion therapy in the summer and was able to maintain the summer improvement throughout the fall, winter, and spring. Hypnosis may be useful as an adjunct therapy for ichthyosis (Shenefelt, 2000).

Lichen Planus

Both the pruritus and the lesions may be reduced in selected cases by using hypnosis as a therapy for lichen planus (Scott, 1960).

Nummular Dermatitis

Reduction of pruritus and resolution of lesions have been reported with the use of hypnotic suggestion as complementary therapy for nummular dermatitis (Scott, 1960).

Postherpetic Neuralgia

The pain of acute herpes zoster and, in some cases, postherpetic neuralgia can be reduced by hypnosis. The author had a 71-year-old male patient who had lived with excruciating pain from postherpetic neuralgia for 6 years with minimal relief from many different medical procedures and medications. He found the pain very debilitating. As a result, he retired early from practicing trial law due to the pain and was limited to playing one or two holes of golf and then having to stop. After being taught self-hypnosis, he felt like he got control of his life back and his attitude changed much for the better. Although he described only temporary reductions in pain, he found the pain much more bearable, and he was able to complete nine holes of golf without stopping.

Pruritus

The intensity of pruritus may be modified and improved by hypnosis. For example, a man with chronic myelogenous leukemia had intractable pruritus, which improved with hypnotic suggestion (Shenefelt, 2000).

Rosacea

Improvement of rosacea, especially the vascular blush component, has been reported in selected cases of resistant rosacea where hypnosis has been added as a therapy (Shenefelt, 2000).

Trichotillomania

Several cases of successful adjunctive treatment of trichotillomania with hypnosis have been reported (Barabasz, 1987).

Vitiligo

Hautmann and Panconesi (1997) detailed the psychoneuroendocrinimmunologic aspects and mechanisms of vitiligo. Occasional cases of vitiligo have improved by using hypnotic suggestion as a therapy.

Acne Excoriée

Hollander (1959) reported success in controlling the picking aspects of acne excoriée in two cases by using posthypnotic suggestion. While in a hypnotic state, the patient was instructed to remember the word *scar* whenever she wanted to pick her face and to refrain from picking by saying "scar." The excoriations (scratch marks) resolved but not the underlying acne. The author has also used this technique successfully (Shenefelt, 2004).

CASE EXAMPLE

A 32-year-old pregnant female had mild-to-moderate papular acne with multiple excoriations. She said that she had been picking at her acne for 15 years and wanted to stop. Appropriate treatment for the acne during pregnancy was instituted and she was instructed to stop scratching at her acne. The acne improved gradually over several weeks, but she continued to pick at her acne. After some discussion, she consented to medical hypnosis. She had previous experience with hypnosis for a prior pain issue. This case is an example of direct suggestion.

TRANSCRIPT

"First, do one thing: Look up as far as you can, that's right, look way up toward the top of your head. Keep looking up.

Second, now do two things: Let your eyes close slowly and take a deep breath. That's right.

Third, now do three things: Breathe out, relax your eyes, and let your body float . . . float . . . float.

That's right, continue to imagine your body floating, floating through the chair, each breath deeper and easier. Imagine that you are walking down toward a safe and comfortable place, walking 1, 2, 3, 4, 5, 6, 7, 8, 9 toward that place, and arriving 10 at that safe place. Enjoy the sights, sounds, fragrance, feel, and other sensations of that special place. You can return here whenever you wish. As you become aware of your face, become aware that you are beautiful with slight imperfections just as nature is beautiful with slight imperfections, and that adds to your natural beauty. Perfection is the enemy of good and perfection is less beautiful than natural is. You will visualize a scar and think of the word scar *every time you reach your hand toward your face to pick your skin. You will continue to feel calm and tranquil throughout the rest of the day. Each day you will use self-hypnosis to relax and to reinforce that you will think of 'scar' every time you reach toward your face. Continue for a few more moments to enjoy your special safe place. Now begin to walk up toward ordinary awareness, 10, 9, 8, 7, 6, 5, 4, 3, 2, and 1 becoming fully alert and awake. Do you feel like you are fully back?"*

The patient was seen in clinic 6 days later, and her facial excoriations had already healed. She reported that she had stopped picking at her face on the day of the initial hypnosis and had used self-hypnosis for reinforcement. She still had mild papular acne on the face with slow improvement of the acne over time. When seen 2 weeks later, she had continued to refrain from picking, and this lasted for 8 months until she got very busy with her new baby and did not maintain the self-hypnosis. She then occasionally lapsed into a little picking but could stop it with further self-hypnosis. She was continuing to do well at a follow-up in 2 years.

PSYCHOSOMATIC HYPNOANALYSIS WITH IDEOMOTOR SIGNALING FOR SKIN DISORDERS

Psychosomatic hypnoanalysis with ideomotor signaling may benefit patients with chronic psychosomatic skin disorders who are nonresponsive to other simpler approaches. The author coined the term *psychosomatic hypnoanalysis* to indicate that the primary method of analysis uses the somatic bridge technique followed by exploration using LeCron's (1961, 1964) list of the seven most common factors causing emotional difficulties and illnesses. Those factors are conflicts, motivation, the effect of suggestion, organ language, identification, self-punishment, and the effect of past experiences. Ewin and Eimer (2006) have provided a user-friendly method of detecting and neutralizing the emotional impact of sensitizing or precipitating events. They use ideomotor signaling to obtain recollection of significant memories that may be preverbal or nonverbal. Results may occur more rapidly than with standard psychoanalysis. The author has discussed the successful use of psychosomatic hypnoanalysis in dermatology (Shenefelt, 2007). The author slightly modified Ewin's mnemonic for LeCron's seven key factors to C.O.M.P.A.S.S. as conflict, organ language, motivation, past experiences, active identification, self-punishment, and suggestion (Shenefelt, 2010). This technique can be used for screening for psychosomatic factors related to skin disorder triggering or exacerbation. It is possible to rule out a likely psychosomatic component if the focused history and C.O.M.P.A.S.S. ideomotor questioning for all seven factors is negative. When one or two factors are positive, a psychosomatic component likely exists and appropriate reframing may be sufficient, but with more factors positive, more intensive psychotherapy would be appropriate. If sufficient improvement still does not occur, exploration on the spiritual level may be indicated (Shenefelt & Shenefelt, 2014). For example, several cases of neurodermatitis (psychogenic excoriations) have reportedly resolved by using hypnosis as a therapy (Lehman, 1978). The neurodermatitis remained resolved for up to 4 years of follow-up. Iglesias (2005) reported three cases of neurodermatitis that failed to respond to direct suggestion under hypnosis but that responded to hypnoanalysis with ideomotor signaling followed by reframing. The author had a similar case that failed to respond to direct suggestion but that responded following psychosomatic hypnoanalysis (Shenefelt, 2010, 2011).

CASE EXAMPLE

A 32-year-old female complained of sores on her nose and glabellum (forehead between the eyebrows). Cognitive behavioral instructions to become aware of the urge to pick, keep her elbows straight, and clench her fists until the urge had passed failed to stop the picking. She was given direct suggestions in hypnosis to think and visualize "scar" as her hand approached her face. She was told that natural imperfections are more beautiful than artificial perfection. When she was seen 2 weeks later, her glabellar excoriation was almost healed and her nasal excoriation was still crusted but not picked open. She still had the urge to pick, so further focused history questions were asked followed by hypnoanalysis using the C.O.M.P.A.S.S format.

For conflict, she regressed to about 3 to 4 years of age and remembered being scared about her "bad" part as her parents were arguing with each other about her behavior. For organ language, she regressed to about 10 to 15 years of age and remembered her mother telling her, "Don't cut off your nose to spite your face." With respect to motivation, she said that at age 10 to 15 years, the picking felt good. As a past experience at age 10 to 15 years, her mother taught her to squeeze blackheads out of her nose, which her father opposed and chastised her mother for teaching her. With respect to active identification at age 10 to 15 years, her mother repeatedly told her that her mother thought her own nose was ugly and that the patient had a cute button nose. As to self-punishment at age 10 to 15 years, the patient felt guilty about undisclosed behaviors and self-punished with picking. She was not aware of any suggestion. The author offered her reframing suggestions for each of the six positive elements of the C.O.M.P.A.S.S. and suggested that she discuss them with her therapist. On a subsequent visit, her glabellar forehead and nose areas had no fresh scratch marks and continued to heal and she reported no urge to pick.

TRANSCRIPT

"First, do one thing: Look up as far as you can, that's right, look way up toward the top of your head. Keep looking up.

Second, now do two things: Let your eyes close slowly and take a deep breath. That's right.

Third, now do three things: Breathe out, relax your eyes, and let your body float . . . float . . . float.

That's right, continue to imagine your body floating, floating through the chair, each breath deeper and easier. Imagine that you are walking down toward a safe and comfortable place, walking 1, 2, 3, 4, 5, 6, 7, 8, 9 toward that place, and arriving 10 at that safe place. Enjoy the sights, sounds, fragrance, feel, and other sensations of that special place. You can return here whenever you wish."

[C.O.M.P.A.S.S. Points Ideomotor Hypnoanalysis Questioning]

[Establish ideomotor finger signals for "Yes," "No," and "I Don't Want to Answer."]

1. CONFLICT

A conflict occurs when you feel that you want to do one thing but that you ought to do the opposite. Do you have a conflict that relates to your skin disorder? If YES, ask Would it be alright for you to know at a conscious level what it is? And is it alright for you to tell me what it is?

[REFRAME by having patient make a decision, choosing between want and ought.]

2. ORGAN LANGUAGE

Have you or someone else mentioned your skin or skin appendages in a negative way, such as 'My skin problem is a real pain', or 'I have been itching to do that?' If YES, ask Would it be alright for you to know at a conscious level the specific phrase that has been affecting you? And is it alright for you to tell me what it is?

[REFRAME by rewording the phrase omitting mention of or allusion to the skin.]

3. MOTIVATION (Secondary Gain)

Do you sense that you are motivated to have this symptom, that it somehow serves a useful or protective purpose for you? If YES, ask What good could come from having this skin problem; how is it helpful or protective for you?

[REFRAME by finding a better and healthier way to cope with the problem or change the way that the problem is perceived.]

4. PAST EXPERIENCE

Do you feel that this skin problem started with a significant experience in your past? If YES, ask Did it happen before age 20? 15? 10? 5? Let your mind go back to the very beginning. When you are there, your Yes finger will rise. Every time you encounter something emotionally important to you, your No finger will rise. When you are finished, your thumb will rise. Is it alright to bring it up to a conscious level and tell me what happened?

[REFRAME by having the patient view it from an adult perspective and see it in a different way.]

5. ACTIVE IDENTIFICATION

Did someone whom you are or were emotionally close to have the same or a similar skin problem? If YES, ask Is it alright to know who it is?

REFRAME by separating the identities. Everyone is unique and you are not bound by the other's problems.

6. SELF-PUNISHMENT

Do you sense that this symptom/skin problem is a form of self-punishment? If YES, ask Would it be alright to know what you feel you shouldn't have done?

[REFRAME by finding a remedy for the offense or by having the patient forgive himself/herself.]

7. SUGGESTION OR IMPRINT

Do you sense that you are being affected by a suggestion that was introduced to you at a highly emotional time? If YES, ask Was it given by some authoritative person? If NO, ask Was it an idea that you gave yourself?

[REFRAME the suggestion by identifying and removing it.]

You may now gradually come back to alert consciousness. As you realert yourself, you will continue to feel comfortable and relaxed, and that comfort will stay with you for the rest of the day. You may now, when you are ready, open your eyes and feel alert. That's right. How do you feel?" (Adapted from Ewin & Eimer 2006; Shenefelt, 2012)

CONCLUSION

Hypnosis may be used to increase healthy behaviors, to decrease situational stress, to reduce needle phobias, to control harmful habits such as scratching, to provide immediate and long-term analgesia, to ameliorate symptoms related to diseases such as itching or pain, to accelerate recovery from surgery, and to enhance the mind–body connection to promote healing. Hypnosis, when combined with hypnoanalysis, can be especially helpful in dealing with skin diseases that have a psychosomatic aspect. For example, Griesemer (1978), who was trained both in dermatology and in psychiatry, recorded the incidence of emotional triggering of skin disorders in his patients during 1 year of his practice. From this, he developed an index for various skin diseases, with 100 indicating an absolute psychosomatic component and 0 indicating no psychosomatic component for the skin disorder. In a resource book for patients, Grossbart and Sherman (1992) discuss mind–body interactions in skin diseases and include hypnosis as a recommended therapy for a number of skin conditions. The responsiveness of skin diseases to hypnosis has been noted for many years (Scott, 1960), and hypnosis can be a very useful tool in treating these disorders.

REFERENCES

Barabasz, M. (1987). Trichotillomania: A new treatment. *International Journal of Clinical and Experimental Hypnosis, 35*(3), 146–154. doi:10.1080/00207148708416050

Defechereux, T., Meurisse, M., Hamoir, E., Gollogly, L., Joris, J., & Faymonville, M. E. (1999). Hypnoanesthesia for endocrine cervical surgery: A statement of practice. *Journal of Alternative and Complementary Medicine, 5*(6), 509–520. doi:10.1089/acm.1999.5.509

Ewin, D. M. (1992). Hypnotherapy for warts (verruca vulgaris): 41 consecutive cases with 33 cures. *American Journal of Clinical Hypnosis, 35*(1), 1–10. doi:10.1080/00029157.1992.10402977

Ewin, D., & Eimer, B. N. M. (2006). *Ideomotor signals for rapid hypnoanalysis: A how-to manual.* Springfield, IL: Charles C. Thomas Publishers.

Faymonville, M. E., Mambourg, P. H., Joris, J., Vrijens, B., Fissette, J., Albert, A., & Lamy, M. (1997). Psychological approaches during conscious sedation. Hypnosis versus stress reducing strategies: A prospective randomized study. *Pain, 73*(3), 361–367.

Fick, L. J., Lang, E. V., Logan, H. L., Lutgendorf, S., & Benotsch, E. G. (1999). Imagery content during nonpharmacologic analgesia in the procedure suite: Where your patients would rather be. *Academic Radiology, 6*(8), 457–463.

Golan, H. P. (1997). The use of hypnosis in the treatment of psychogenic oral pain. *American Journal of Clinical Hypnosis, 40*(2), 89–96. doi:10.1080/00029157.1997.10403413

Griesemer, R. D. (1978). Emotionally triggered disease in a dermatological practice. *Psychiatric Annals, 8*(8), 49–56.

Grossbart, T. A., & Sherman, C. (1992). *Skin deep: A mind/body program for healthy skin.* Santa Fe, NM: Health Press.

Gupta, M. A., Gupta, A. K., & Watteel, G. N. (1997). Stress and alopecia areata: A psychodermatologic study. *Acta Dermatologica Et Venereologica, 77*(4), 296–298.

Hautmann, G., & Panconesi, E. (1997). Vitiligo: A psychologically influenced and influencing disease. *Clinics in Dermatology, 15*(6), 879–890.

Hollander, M. B. (1959). Excoriated acne controlled by post-hypnotic suggestion. *American Journal of Clinical Hypnosis, 1*, 122–123.

Iglesias, A. (2005). Three failures of direct suggestion in psychogenic dermatitis followed by successful intervention. *American Journal of Clinical Hypnosis, 47*(3), 191–198. doi:10.1080/00029157.2005.10401483

Jabush, M. (1969). A case of chronic recurring multiple boils treated with hypnotherapy. *Psychiatric Quarterly, 43*(3), 448–455.

Kidd, C. B. (1966). Congenital ichthyosiform erythroderma treated by hypnosis. *British Journal of Dermatology, 78*(2), 101–105.

Lang, E. V., Benotsch, E. G., Fick, L. J., Lutgendorf, S., Berbaum, M. L., Berbaum, K. S., . . . Spiegel, D. (2000). Adjunctive non-pharmacological analgesia for invasive medical procedures: A randomised trial. *The Lancet, 355*(9214), 1486–1490. doi:10.1016/S0140-6736(00)02162-0

Laser, E. D., & Shenefelt, P. D. (2012). Hypnosis to alleviate the symptoms of ciguatera toxicity: A case study. *American Journal of Clinical Hypnosis, 54*(3), 179–183. doi:10.1080/00029157.2011.613489

Lecron, L. M. (1961). *Techniques of hypnotherapy.* New York, NY: Julius Publishers.

Lecron, L. M. (1964). *Self-hypnotism: The technique and its use in daily living.* Englewood Cliffs, NJ: Prentice-Hall.

Lehman, R. E. (1978). Brief hypnotherapy of neurodermatitis: A case with four-year follow-up. *American Journal of Clinical Hypnosis, 21*(1), 48–51. doi:10.1080/00029157.1978.10403957

Montgomery, G. H., Weltz, C. R., Seltz, M., & Bovbjerg, D. H. (2002). Brief presurgery hypnosis reduces distress and pain in excisional breast biopsy patients. *International Journal of Clinical and Experimental Hypnosis, 50*(1), 17–32. doi:10.1080/00207140208410088

Noll, R. B. (1994). Hypnotherapy for warts in children and adolescents. *Journal of Developmental and Behavioral Pediatrics, 15*, 170–173.

Scott, M. J. (1960). *Hypnosis in skin and allergic diseases.* Springfield, IL: Charles C. Thomas Publishers.

Shenefelt, P. D. (2000). Hypnosis in dermatology. *Archives of Dermatology, 136*(3), 393–399.

Shenefelt, P. D. (2003). Hypnosis-facilitated relaxation using self-guided imagery during dermatologic procedures. *American Journal of Clinical Hypnosis, 45*(3), 225–232. doi:10.1080/00029157.2003.10403528

Shenefelt, P. D. (2004). Using hypnosis to facilitate resolution of psychogenic excorations in acne excoriee. *American Journal of Clinical Hypnosis, 46*(3), 239–245. doi:10.1080/00029157.2004.10403603

Shenefelt, P. D. (2007). Psychocutaneous hypnoanalysis: Detection and deactivation of emotional and mental root factors in psychosomatic skin disorders. *American Journal of Clinical Hypnosis, 50*(2), 131–136. doi:10.1080/00029157.2007.10401610

Shenefelt, P. D. (2010). Hypnoanalysis for dermatologic disorders. *Journal of Alternative Medicine Research, 2*(4), 439–445.

Shenefelt, P. D. (2011). Ideomotor signaling: From divining spiritual messages to discerning subconscious answers during hypnosis and hypnoanalysis, a historical perspective. *American Journal of Clinical Hypnosis, 53*(3), 157–167. doi:10.1080/00029157.2011.10401754

Shenefelt, P. D. (2012). Hypnoanalysis for skin disorders. In L. V. Berhardt (Ed.), *Advances in medicine and biology* (pp. 163–175). Hauppauge, NY: Nova Science Publishers.

Shenefelt, P. D. (2013). Anxiety reduction using hypnotic induction and self-guided imagery for relaxation during dermatologic procedures. *International Journal of Clinical and Experimental Hypnosis, 61*(3), 305–318. doi:10.1080/00207144.2013.784096

Shenefelt, P. D., & Shenefelt, D. A. (2014). Spiritual and religious aspects of skin and skin disorders. *Psychology Research and Behavior Management, 7*, 201–212. doi:10.2147/PRBM.S65578

Sinclair-Gieben, A. H., & Chalmers, D. (1959). Evaluation of treatment of warts by hypnosis. *The Lancet, 2*, 480–482.

Spanos, N. P., Williams, V., & Gwynn, M. I. (1990). Effects of hypnotic, placebo, and salicylic acid treatments on wart regression. *Psychosomatic Medicine, 52*(1), 109–114.

Spiegel, H., & Spiegel, D. (2004). *Trance and treatment: Clinical uses of hypnosis.* Arlington, VA: American Psychiatric Association.

Stewart, A. C., & Thomas, S. E. (1995). Hypnotherapy as a treatment for atopic dermatitis in adults and children. *British Journal of Dermatology, 132*(5), 778–783.

Sulzberger, M. B., & Wolf, J. (1934). The treatment of warts by suggestion. *Medical Record, 140*, 552–556.

Tausk, F., & Whitmore, S. E. (1999). A pilot study of hypnosis in the treatment of patients with psoriasis. *Psychotherapy and Psychosomatics, 68*(4), 221–225. doi:12336

Willemsen, R., Vanderlinden, J., Deconinck, A., & Roseeuw, D. (2006). Hypnotherapeutic management of alopecia areata. *Journal of the American Academy of Dermatology, 55*(2), 233–237. doi:10.1016/jaad.2005.09.025

Spasmodic Torticollis

Giuseppe De Benedittis

Dystonia is a neurological movement disorder, in which sustained muscle contractions cause twisting and repetitive movements or abnormal postures (Donaldson, Marsden, Schneider, & Bhatia, 2012; Evatt, Freeman, & Factor, 2011). The movements may resemble a tremor. Dystonia is often initiated or worsened by voluntary movements, and symptoms may "overflow" into adjacent muscles (Balint & Bhatia, 2014).

Primary dystonia is suspected when the dystonia is the only sign and there is no identifiable cause or structural abnormality in the central nervous system.

Secondary dystonia refers to dystonia brought on by some identified cause, such as birth-related or other physical trauma, infection, poisoning (e.g., lead poisoning), or reaction to pharmaceutical drugs, particularly neuroleptics (Balint & Bhatia, 2014).

CLASSIFICATION

There are multiple types of dystonia (Donaldson, Marsden, Schneider, & Bhatia, 2012): (a) generalized, (b) focal, and (c) segmental.

The most frequent form of focal dystonia is referred to as spasmodic torticollis. However, since it is not always spasmodic and it does not always consist of torticollis, this term is most confusing. The term *idiopathic cervical dystonia* (ICD) as a generic descriptor of dystonic movements or postures involving the neck seems a more appropriate designation for this condition (Donaldson, Marsden, Schneider, & Bhatia, 2012; Evatt, Freeman, & Factor, 2011).

EPIDEMIOLOGY

Worldwide, it has been reported that the incidence rate of spasmodic torticollis is at least 1.2 per 100,000 persons per year (Claypool, Duane, Ilstrup, & Melton, 1995), and a prevalence rate of 57 per 1 million (the Epidemiological Study of Dystonia in Europe [ESDE], 2000). There is a higher prevalence of spasmodic torticollis in females; females are 1.5 times more likely to develop spasmodic torticollis than males. The prevalence rate of spasmodic torticollis also increases with age; most patients show symptoms from age 50 to 69. The average onset age of spasmodic torticollis is 41 (Jankovic, Tsui, & Bergeron, 2007).

SIGNS AND SYMPTOMS

Spasmodic torticollis is a painful, chronic neurological movement disorder causing the neck to involuntarily turn to the left, right, upward, and/or downward (Chan, Brin, & Fahn, 1991; Donaldson, Marsden, Schneider, & Bhatia, 2012; Evatt, Freeman, & Factor, 2011). Most patients have constant head deviation at rest to the left (i.e., chin to the left; De Benedittis, 1996). Both agonist and antagonist muscles contract simultaneously during dystonic movement. Initial symptoms of spasmodic torticollis are usually mild. Then the head may turn, pull or tilt in jerky movements, or sustain a prolonged position involuntarily. Over time, the involuntary spasm of the neck muscles will increase in frequency and strength until it reaches a plateau. Symptoms can also worsen while the patient is walking or during periods of increased stress. Other symptoms include muscle hypertrophy, neck pain, dysarthria, and tremor (Donaldson, Marsden, Schneider, & Bhatia, 2012; Evatt, Freeman, & Factor, 2011). Studies have shown that over 75% of patients report neck pain, and 33% to 40% experience tremor of the head (Jankovic, Tsui, & Bergeron, 2007).

The muscles most frequently involved are the sternocleidomastoid (SCM) and the trapezius, but the excessive activity is not confined to these muscles and may "overflow" into adjacent muscles.

A variety of factors are found to influence ICD. As in other dyskinesias, emotional stress is the most common aggravating factor. Patients are made worse by emotional stress, exertion, and/or fatigue. Corrective maneuvers, gestures, or other sensory tricks (*geste antagonistique* of the French writers or counterpressure) are frequent. Maneuvers most commonly used involve minimal support to the back of the neck or lightly touching the chin with the hand. Symptoms usually improve by sleep and lying down and are made progressively worse when the patient sits up, is standing, or walking (Balint & Bhatia, 2014; Donaldson, Marsden, Schneider, & Bhatia, 2012).

PATHOPHYSIOLOGY

The Controversial Nature of Spasmodic Torticollis

The term *torticollis* was used by the psychiatrists and neurologists of earlier periods for very different pathological conditions. Torticollis represents one of the most confusing problems as to its underlying anatomical substrate and physiological mechanisms, as to the site and type of pathological changes, and as regards the bizarre symptoms that are often refractory to treatment.

The remarkable influence on torticollis of emotional factors and sensory stimuli is of more than historical importance. However, until a few decades ago, the question whether the condition was of "psychogenic" or "organic" origin remained undecided. It is only in recent years that the disease has been regarded as an organic, extrapyramidal disorder, with psychogenic factors contributing only secondarily to the development of torticollis in many instances (*see* reviews of earlier studies in De Benedittis, 1996, 2004; Evatt, Freeman, & Factor, 2011; Podivinsky, 1969).

Today, most neurologists do not consider ICD as a psychogenic disorder but as a focal dystonia, in agreement with the view of Marsden and associates (Donaldson, Marsden, Schneider, & Bhatia, 2012; Marsden & Quinn, 1990). Physiological and pathological data derived from studies of the anatomical relationships of the basal ganglia served as a basis for the recent concept of torticollis as an organic disorder of the brain. However, neuropathological and neurochemical studies have shed little light on the pathophysiology of ICD.

On the other hand, psychoanalytic studies reemphasize the role of psychodynamics and personality patterns in ICD patients (*see* review in Rentrop, 1987). In a study of 81 patients (23 of whom were treated psychoanalytically), Mitscherlich (1979) postulates torticollis as a psychosomatic disease understood in terms of a presentative symbolic event and as a compensation for the loss of cognitive ability to symbolize in the field of language. The pathological internal object relations, ego regression to the pregenital level in the form of the omnipotence of motion, and the inability for developing an own self were the prominent features observed in these patients, confirmed in a study by Taylor (1993). More recently, a study by Scheidt et al. (1998) showed that the General Symptom Index of the Symptom Checklist 90-Revised in 27% of the patients ranged above the double standard deviation of the normal controls, indicating a clinically significant psychopathology.

Actually, more questions are raised concerning the pathogenesis of ICD than are being answered in spite of the acquisition of new information on neurophysiological and psychophysiological mechanisms.

Genetic and Neurophysiological Mechanisms of Spasmodic Torticollis

The pathophysiology of spasmodic torticollis is still poorly understood. In many cases, it may involve some genetic predisposition toward the disorder combined with environmental conditions. Furthermore, psychological factors may modulate significantly the disorder.

The role of genetic factors has been investigated and studies have shown that the DYT7 locus on chromosome 18p in a German family and the DYT13 locus on chromosome 1p36 in an Italian family are associated with spasmodic torticollis

(Waddy, Fletcher, Harding, & Marsden, 1991). The inher-itance for both loci is autosomal dominant with reduced pen-etrance. Although these loci have been found, the extent of influence the loci has on spasmodic torticollis is still not clear.

Although there is no identifiable cause or structural abnormality, it is suspected to be caused by a pathology of the central nervous system, likely originating in those parts of the brain concerned with motor function, such as the basal ganglia, and the gamma-aminobutyric acid (GABA)–producing Purkinje neurons. Functional MRI (fMRI) and PET studies have shown abnormalities of the basal ganglia and hyperactivation of the cortical areas (Vacherot et al., 2007). Studies have suggested that there is a functional imbalance in the striatal control of the globus pallidus, specifically the substantia nigra pars reticulata. The studies hypothesize the hyperactivation of the cortical areas is due to reduced pallidal inhibition of the thalamus, leading to overactivity of the medial and prefrontal cortical areas and underactivity of the primary motor cortex during movement (Uc & Rodnitzky, 2003). It has also been suggested that the functional imbalance is due to an imbalance of neurotransmitters such as dopamine, acetylcholine, and GABA. These neurotransmitters are secreted from the basal ganglia and travel to muscle groups in the neck. An increase in neurotransmitters may cause spasms to occur in the neck, resulting in spasmodic torticollis (de Carvalho Aguiar & Ozelius, 2002).

Malfunction of the sodium-potassium (Na+ -K+) pump in the basal ganglia may be a factor in some dystonias. The Na+ -K+ pump has been shown to control and set the intrinsic activity mode of cerebellar Purkinje neurons. The dystonia aspect is thought to be attributable to malfunctioning Na+ -K+ pumps in the cerebellum (that act to corrupt its input to the basal ganglia), possibly in Purkinje neurons (Forrest, Wall, Press, & Feng, 2012).

DIAGNOSIS

Diagnosis of spasmodic torticollis is made mainly upon physical grounds, due to lack of specific clinical criteria. The most commonly used scale to rate the severity of spasmodic torticollis is the Toronto Western Spasmodic Torticollis Rating Scale (TWSTRS; Albanese et al., 2013). There are three scales in the TWSTRS: torticollis severity scale, disability scale, and pain scale. These scales are used to represent the severity, the pain, and the general lifestyle of spasmodic torticollis.

TREATMENT

Dystonia and particularly ICD are neuromuscular disorders that are extremely resistant to most therapies (physical, medical, and surgical); unless the etiological investigation reveals a specific theapeutic intervention, therapy is symptomatic. It includes supportive therapy and counseling, physical therapy, pharmacotherapy (e.g., trihexyphenidyl, tetrabenazine, levodopa and dopamine agonists), intrathecal infusion of baclofen, neurosurgical procedures (e.g., thalamotomy, pallidotomy, and pallidal deep brain stimulation; see reviews in (Balash & Gilady, 2004; Velickovic, Benabou, & Brin, 2001; Vidailhet, Jutras, Grabli, & Roze, 2013). Botulinum toxin (A and B) injections have been the standard of care in the symptomatic management of this condition since their approval for this indication in the early 2000s (Albanese et al., 2011; Comella, Buchman, Tanner, Brown-Toms, & Goetz, 1992; Figgitt & Noble, 2002; Jankovic & Brin, 1991; Marsh, Monroe, Brin, & Gallagher, 2014; Velickovic, Benabou, & Brin, 2001). When injected into skeletal muscle, botulinum toxins act to disrupt neurotransmitter release at the neuromuscular junction, inducing a transient weakening of the muscle. Because of the temporary nature of the effect of botulinum toxins, they need to be readministered regularly to maintain clinical improvement (Marsh, Monroe, Brin, & Gallagher, 2014).

Recent EBM reviews on the efficacy of botulinum toxin in the treatment of cervical dystonia have established an obvious benefit (Albanese et al., 2011; Balash & Gilady, 2004), but the treatment is symptomatic only; the mean duration of effect is 93 to 95 days (13.2–13.5 weeks). This suggests that, in general, patients with ICD treated with botulinum toxin A should require ~4 treatments per year (Marsh, Monroe, Brin, & Gallagher, 2014). Significant side effects are not infrequent, and the outcome is often equivocal

(Colosimo, Tiple, & Berardelli, 2012; Comella, Tanner, De Foor-Hill, & Smith, 1992; Holds, Fogg, & Anderson, 1990).

Torticollis is also one of the most difficult problems to treat with hypnosis (Crasilneck & Hall, 1985). Anecdotal reports of successful treatment of ICD with hypnosis have been published (Avampato, 1975; De Benedittis, 1996, 2004; Friedman, 1965; Kampman & Ihalainen, 1974; Kirkner, 1956; Kraines, 1943; Kröger, 1977; LeHew, 1971; Medd, 2006a, 2006b; Schneiderman, Leu, & Glazeski, 1987; Schneiderman, Leu, & Glazeski, 1987; Trenerry & Jackson, 1983). Electromyography (EMG)-biofeedback also has reportedly proved beneficial in treating this refractory disorder (Jahanshahi, Sartory, & Marsden, 1991; Korein & Brudny, 1976).

The author reported four cases of ICD successfully treated with hypnosis, two of them in combination with EMG-Biofeedback (De Benedittis, 1996).

All patients had constant head deviation at rest to the left (i.e., chin to the left) and some degree of rotational torticollis. One patient had severe neck pain and stiffness. Two patients were unemployed because of ICD-related disability. There was multiple muscle group involvement (i.e., trapezius, splenius, scalenus, and platysma), although the SCM was most frequently affected.

A history of major stressful life events (mostly in terms of exits or losses), associated with a cognitive–emotional appraisal of their negative impact on life patterns, appeared to herald the onset of torticollis in all cases, possibly serving as illness antecedents or precursors (De Benedittis, 1996). Two patients reported nocturnal panic attacks within a few months prior to the onset of torticollis. The other two patients developed torticollis shortly after significant loss events (i.e., mother's death and family member's serious illness).

Patients with idiopathic disease had no evidence by history, examination, or laboratory studies of any identifiable cause for the dystonic symptoms. No prior history of neurological illness or exposure to drugs known to cause acquired dystonia (e.g., dopamine receptor blocking agents) was reported. Neurological examination and diagnostic studies (such as MRI and EMG) were normal in all cases.

Psychometric assessment revealed abnormal personality patterns in all cases. All subjects complained of a marked state of anxiety and two of them were found to have previously suffered from depressive tendencies requiring treatment. Most of them also mentioned difficulty in controlling their emotions, impulsiveness, irritability, and aggressive tendencies. Using the paradigm of "organ language," the torticollis seems to be a symbolic expression of trying to "turn away" the subject from a relevant problem, with the head frequently turning toward the left, which could be understood in terms of symbolic averting of anxious–aggressive impulses. Denial, suppressed aggressiveness, somatization, and avoidance learning represent some other defense mechanisms observed in these patients. Obsessive-compulsive patterns were most common in our group of patients, providing additional support for the theory of a link between basal ganglia-related involuntary movement disorders and psychiatric disorders, namely, obsessive-compulsive disorders (Bihari, Hill, & Murphy, 1992). Furthermore, three out of four patients reported that at least one family member suffered from psychotic disorders. Finally, a risk of psychotic breakdown was present in two cases.

All four patients reported significant improvement with hypnosis alone or combined with EMG-Biofeedback treatment. Excellent results were obtained in three out of four cases, whereas a good result was reported in the remaining case. Significant changes in activities in daily living included return to work, improvement of social and marital life, return of ability to drive a car, and so forth. A significant improvement in mood and emotional control, with concomitant reduction of anxiety levels, was also noted.

All subjects were followed from 1 year up to 10 years (mean: 4.5 years; median: 2.3 years). All cases maintained improvement, with no significant relapse being reported.

HYPNOTIC TECHNIQUES

Subjects are gradually introduced to hypnosis through the use of relaxation techniques, leading into induction and deepening procedures. This relaxation increases control of their symptoms. As they progress over a few sessions, "postural hypnosis" (i.e., hypnosis in standing position; De Benedittis, 1996) is employed in order

FIGURE 46.1 Postural hypnosis (i.e., hypnosis in standing position) is employed in order to counteract and minimize muscle spasms due to postural reflexes. Suggestions are given to displace somatized and unbound anxiety from the neck muscles to the clenched fist of the dominant arm.

to counteract and minimize muscle spasms due to postural reflexes (Figure 46.1). Since hypnoanalytic treatment with insight might be difficult and pose more risks because of possible psychotic breakdown in some of our patients, a covert hypnobehavioral approach is adopted. Hierarchical hypnodesensitization is introduced, depicting most aspects of stressful situations frequently associated with worsening of the symptoms, while the patient is relaxed and in hypnosis. Patients are instructed to place themselves in the scenes that they are observing. This permits the hypnotized individual to better cope with and to overcome some of the potential sources of failures often associated with desensitization by reciprocal inhibition (Wolpe, 1958). Suggestions are given to displace somatized and unbound anxiety from the neck muscles to the clenched fist of the dominant arm.

Sensory-imagery conditioning is also used, with the subject being instructed to imagine pleasant events to be associated with a normal alignment of his or her head and neck. Posthypnotic suggestions are given that he or she could, if he or she wishes, increase the intensity of the torsion. It is further explained that whenever one could increase the severity of a symptom, one could deliberately decrease it! When appropriate, "silent abreaction" is also elicited to discharge feelings associated with unpleasant events.

Hypnosis facilitates differential muscle retraining (i.e., decreasing the tone of the spasmodic SCM muscle and increasing the tone of the antagonist, contralateral muscle) and helps patients regain their former behavioral patterns through several sessions ("forgotten assets"). These patterns, strongly imprinted in every life situation, had been completely erased by the neuromuscular disorder. They are restored and positively extended.

The ego defenses, permanently breached in certain areas, are rebuilt in a projective manner by ego-boosting suggestions. Throughout the hypnotherapeutic treatment, attention is given to inchoate patient's emotions from a regressive, sensorimotor level of experience to a more mature representational level, where they could be valued for their signal function and modulated through emotional sensory imaging and communication with others.

Twice-weekly hypnotic sessions are usually needed. Patients are encouraged to practice self-hypnosis twice a day for 20 minutes as a supporting device.

Duration of the treatment is of crucial importance. The hypnotherapeutic process is usually gradual and slow, taking several months to induce and stabilize significant changes as well as to reverse the anatomo-functional imbalance of the neck muscles. Duration of treatment ranges from 6 to 12 months.

CASE EXAMPLES

Case #1

The patient was a 44-year-old man, who had a 7-year history of torticollis to the left. His father died when he was 35 years old. He tried to get through with this terrible loss by rushing headlong into his job, but during a period of severe work-related stress, the patient developed panic attacks, characterized by sudden heart palpitations and fear of death, particularly at night. The patient was reassured by his cardiologist about the psychological nature of his symptoms, but a few months later, spasmodic torticollis to the left began. The onset was associated with pain in the neck and head, concomitant with oscillatory movements. The involuntary movements became more intense with emotional stimuli, exertion, fatigue, and when in an upright position. The patient had to stop driving a car and often had difficulty in sleeping at night, although lying down was the most comfortable position. He used postural cues while sitting (usually supporting his chin or the back of his neck with his right hand), which aided him in maintaining head position. A variety of medical and psychiatric treatment regimens (including a hypnotic trial) proved totally ineffective. After 12 months of combined hypnotic and EMG-Biofeedback treatment, the patient achieved control of head and neck position; pain disappeared, sleep was undisturbed, and he could now drive a car again. Daily home self-hypnosis was prescribed during the treatment period. He maintained good results during the 10-year follow-up after initial treatment, although his two sons had developed borderline personality disorders, which required psychiatric treatment. He is still continuing to practice self-hypnosis on a regular basis for relaxation.

Case #2

This 43-year-old man had a 4-month history of rotational torticollis and laterocollis to the left. The patient's symptoms began a few months after his mother's death, following surgery for suspected pancreatic cancer. He harbored feelings of guilt for his mother's death, which he just could not accept, and felt that his life was over. Soon after, his neck started turning to the left, as if he unconsciously wished to turn his head away from the unbearable reality of his loss. Because of the disabling severity of his torticollis, he had to give up his job; this worsened his reactive depression. A variety of medical and psychiatric treatments proved ineffective. After 11 months of hypnotic treatment (hypnosis + self-hypnosis), he regained full control of his head and neck

position. Alleviation of his anxiety and feelings of guilt, together with the sensory-imagery conditioning and with hypnotic manipulation of the symptom, eventually resulted in dissolution of the torticollis and in a better adaptation to life situations and demands. He has been symptom-free since then (follow-up: 4.6 years) except for occasional bending of the head during times of emotional upset or fatigue. Reinforcement sessions were not needed and self-hypnosis was tapered off a few months after the end of the treatment.

TRANSCRIPT

Postural Hypnosis for ICD (Spasmodic Torticollis)

"While you're comfortably standing against the wall, I would like you to pay attention to the strong tension in all the muscles of your body, particularly those of your neck. And now you might want to release all that unsufferable tension. Relax, letting all the tension go . . . focusing on these muscles as they just relax completely, noticing what it feels like as the muscles become more and more relaxed . . . focusing all your attention on the pleasant feelings associated with relaxation flowing into the muscles of your face and of your neck . . . spreading into your shoulders and upper arms . . . enjoy the feelings in the muscles as they loosen up, smooth out, unwind, and relax more and more deeply . . . pay attention only to the sensations of relaxation as the relaxation process takes place.

Imagine yourself in the place and during the activity and situations where more often you experience your discomfort. Observe yourself in that place, in those situations . . . picture yourself doing those things, feeling completely comfortable, relaxed, and in full control.

Now close your hand and make a tight fist and let all the tension in your neck or those painful feelings flow into that hand . . . and as the tension and those strong feelings flow into the hand, the fist will become tighter and tighter. . . . And now you can open your fist, slowly and safely, and let as much of the tension [or feelings] *as you want to get rid of flow away into the air . . . and as the tension streams away from you, you will go deeper and deeper into trance.*

As you drift along, you feel yourself relaxed, deeper and deeper relaxed—way down—so that more and more you know that your body is getting under your complete control. You have the ability to control your neck muscles, stop your tension, and relax. . . . Your mind might wonder how easy and comfortable you could be pulling your chin to the right and to the left, forward and backward . . . or just keeping it in a straight position . . . that's okay. . . . When you find this happening, just relax . . . and each time you practice, you get better and better, more and more relaxed and able to control your muscles and posture.

CONCLUSION

Dystonia and, particularly, focal ICD (the so-called spasmodic torticollis) are rather common neuromuscular disorders, whose etiology remain uncertain. Whether ICD is a neurological disorder involving the basal ganglia, a psychogenic condition, or a combination of both is still controversial. It is likely to be a psychophysiological spectrum, whose pathophysiological and psychopathological determinants are strictly cross-linked.

ICD is extremely resistant to most therapies (physical, medical, and surgical). A wide variety of psychiatric and psychophysiological treatments have been proposed to alleviate ICD, including hypnosis. Hypnosis, alone or combined with EMG-Biofeedback, may be a useful therapeutic tool in the treatment of ICD. A hypnobehavioral model, focused upon postural hypnosis (i.e., hypnosis in standing position), is the treatment of choice to counteract and minimize muscle spasms due to postural reflexes. Hypnotic strategies include hierarchical desensitization, sensory-imaging conditioning, and ego-boosting suggestions, combined with hypnosis-facilitated differential muscle retraining.

Although the hypnotherapeutic process is usually gradual and slow, taking several months to induce and stabilize significant changes, immediate and long-term results are encouraging, with marked reduction of the torticollis and the hypertrophy of the neck muscles as well as a reduced interference in normal patterns of daily living.

REFERENCES

Albanese, A., Asmus, F., Bhatia, K. P., Elia, A. E., Elibol, B., Filippini, G., . . . Valls-Solé, J. (2011). EFNS guidelines on diagnosis and treatment of primary dystonias. *European Journal of Neurology, 18*(1), 5–18.

Albanese, A., Sorbo, F. D., Comella, C., Jinnah, H. A., Mink, J. W., Post, B., . . . Schrag, A. (2013). Dystonia rating scales: Critique and recommendations. *Movement Disorders: Official Journal of the Movement Disorder Society, 28*(7), 874–883.

Avampato, J. J. (1975). Hypnosis: A cure for torticollis. *American Journal of Clinical Hypnosis, 18*(1), 60–62.

Balash, Y., & Gilady, N. (2004). Efficacy of pharmacological treatment of dystonia: Evidence-based review including meta-analysis of the effect of botulinum toxin and other cure options. *European Journal of Neurology, 11*(6), 361–370.

Balint, B., & Bhatia, K. P. (2014). Dystonia: An update on phenomenology, classification, pathogenesis and treatment. *Current Opinion in Neurology, 27*(4), 468–476.

Bihari, K., Hill, J. L., & Murphy, D. L. (1992). Obsessive-compulsive characteristics in patients with idiopathic spasmodic torticollis. *Psychiatric Research, 42*, 267–272.

Chan, J., Brin, M. F., & Fahn, S. (1991). Idiopathic cervical dystonia: Clinical characteristics. *Movement Disorders: Official Journal of the Movement Disorder Society, 6*(2), 119–126.

Claypool, D. W., Duane, D. D., Ilstrup, D. M., & Melton, L. J. (1995). "Epidemiology and outcome of cervical dystonia (spasmodic torticollis) in Rochester, Minnesota." *Movement Disorders: Official Journal of the Movement Disorder Society, 10*(5), 608–614. doi.org/10.1002/mds.870100513.

Colosimo, C., Tiple, D., & Berardelli, A. (2012). Efficacy and safety of long-term botulinum toxin treatment in craniocervical dystonia: A systematic review. *Neurotoxin Research, 22*(4), 265–273.

Comella, C. L., Buchman, A. S., Tanner, C. M., Brown-Toms, N., & Goetz, C. G. (1992). Botulinum toxin injection for spasodic torticollis: Increased magnitude of benefit with electromyographic assistance. *Neurology, 42*, 878–882.

Comella, C. L., Tanner, C. M., De Foor-Hill, L., & Smith, C. (1992). Dysphagia after botulinum injections for spasmodic torticollis: Clinical and radiological findings. *Neurology, 42*, 1307–1310.

Crasilneck, H. B., & Hall, J. A. (1985). *Clinical hypnosis. Principles and applications.* New York, NY: Grune & Stratton.

De Beneditts, G. (1996). Hypnosis and spasmodic torticollis—report of four cases. *International Journal of Clinical and Experimental Hypnosis, 44*(4), 292–306.

De Benedittis, G. (2004). Postural hypnosis and EMG-Biofeedback in idiopathic cervical dystonia. *Hypnosis, 31*(3), 136–145.

de Carvalho Aguiar, P. M., & Ozelius, L. J. (2002). Classification and genetics of dystonia. *Lancet Neurology, 1*(5), 316–325.

Donaldson, I., Marsden, C. D., Schneider, S. A., & Bhatia, K. P. (2012). *Marsden's book of movement disorders.* Oxford, UK: Oxford University Press.

Epidemiological Study of Dystonia in Europe (ESDE) Collaborative Group. (2000). A prevalence study of primary dystonia in eight European countries. *Journal of Neurology, 247*(10), 787–792.

Evatt, M. L., Freeman, A., & Factor, S. (2011). Adult onset dystonia. In W. J. Weiner & E. Tolosa (Eds.), *Handbook of hyperkinetic movement disorders* (pp. 481–512). Amsterdam: Elsevier.

Figgitt, D. P., & Noble, S. (2002). Botulinum toxin B. Review of its therapeutic potential in the management of cervical dystonia. *Drugs, 62*(4), 705–722.

Forrest, M. D., Wall, M. J., Press, D. A., & Feng, J. (2012). The sodium-potassium pump controls the intrinsic firing of the cerebellar Purkinje neuron. *PloS One, 7*(12), e51169. doi:10.1371/journal.pone.0051169

Friedman, H. (1965). Brief clinical report: Hypnosis in the treatment of a case of torticollis. *American Journal of Clinical Hypnosis, 8*(2), 139–140.

Holds, J. B., Fogg, S. G., & Anderson, R. L. (1990). Botulinum A toxin injection. Failures in clinical practice and a biomechanical system for the study of toxin-induced paralysis. *Opthalmic Plastic Reconstructive Surgery, 6,* 252–259.

Jahanshahi, M., Sartory, G., & Marsden, C. D. (1991). EMG biofeedback treatment of torticollis: A controlled outcome study. *Biofeedback and Self-Regulation, 16*(4), 413–448.

Jankovic, J., & Brin, M. F. (1991). Drug therapy: Therapeutic uses of botulinum toxin. *New England Journal of Medicine, 324*(17), 1186–1194.

Jankovic, J., Tsui, J., & Bergeron, C. (2007). Prevalence of cervical dystonia and spasmodic torticollis in the United States general population. *Parkinsonism & Related Disorders, 13*(7), 411–416

Kampman, R., & Ihalainen, O. (1974). A changing dream in the hypnoanalytic treatment of spastic torticollis patient. *American Journal of Clinical Hypnosis, 16*(3), 206–209.

Kirkner, F. J. (1956). *Hypnosis and its therapeutic applications.* New York, NY: McGraw-Hill.

Korein, J., & Brudny, J. (1976). Integrated EMG feedback in the management of spasmodic torticollis and focal dystonia: A prospective study of 80 patients. *Research Publications—Association for Research in Nervous and Mental Disease, 55,* 385–426.

Kraines, S. H. (1943). *The therapy of the neuroses and psychoses.* Philadelphia, PA: Lea & Febiger.

Kröger, W. S. (1977). *Clinical and experimental hypnosis in medicine. Dentistry and psychology.* Philadelphia, PA: Lippincott Williams & Wilkins.

LeHew, J. L. (1971). Use of hypnosis in the treatment of long standing spastic torticollis. *American Journal of Clinical Hypnosis, 14*(2), 124–126.

Marsden, C. D., & Quinn, N. P. (1990). Dystonias. *BMJ (Clinical Research Ed.), 300*(6718), 139–144.

Marsh, W. A., Monroe., D. M., Brin, M. F., & Gallagher, C. J. (2014). Systematic review and meta-analysis of the duration of clinical effect of onabotulinum toxin A in cervical dystonia. *BMC Neurology, 14*:91. doi: 10.1186/1471-2377-14-91

Medd, D. Y. (2006a). Dystonia and hypnosis. *Contemporary Hypnosis, 14*(2), 121–125.

Medd, D. Y. (2006b). Hypnosis with selected movement disorders. *Contemporary Hypnosis, 16*(2), 81–86.

Mitscherlich, M. (1979). The theory and therapy of hyperkineses (torticollis). *Psychotherapy and Psychosomatics, 32*(1-4), 306–312.

Podivinsky, F. (1969). Torticollis. In P. J. Vinken & G. W. Bruyn (Eds.), *Diseases of the basal ganglia. Handbook of clinical neurology* (pp. 563–567). Amsterdam: North Holland Publishing Company.

Rentrop, E. (1987). Zur Geschichte der Psychotherapie des Torticollis. Eine historische Ubersicht. *Zeitschrift für Psychosomatische Medizin und Psychoanalyse, 33*(3), 266–275.

Scheidt, C. E., Rayki, O., Nickel, T., Heinen, F., Wissel, J., Poewe, W., . . . Deuschl, G. (1998). Psychosomatic aspects of idiopathic spasmodic torticollis. Results of a multicenter study. *Psychotherapy and Psychosomatic Medicine and Psychology, 48*(1), 1–12. doi.org/10.1155/1996/292504.

Schneiderman, M. J., Leu, R. H., & Glazeski, R. C. (1987). Use of hypnosis in spasmodic torticollis: A case report. *American Journal of Clinical Hypnosis, 29*(4), 260–263.

Taylor, G. J. (1993). Clinical application of a dysregulation model of illness and disease: A case of spasmodic torticollis. *International Journal of Psycho-analysis, 74*(Pt 3), 581–595.

Trenerry, M. R., & Jackson, T. L. (1983). Hysterical dystonia successfully treated with post-hypnotic suggestions. *American Journal of Clinical Hypnosis, 26*(1), 42–44.

Uc, E. Y., & Rodnitzky, R. L. (2003). Childhood dystonia. *Seminars in Pediatric Neurology, 10*(1), 52–61.

Vacherot, F., Vaugoyeau, M., Mallau, S., Soulayrol, S., Assaiante, C., & Azulay, J. P. (2007). Postural control and sensory integration in cervical dystonia. *Clinical Neurophysiology: Official Journal of the International Federation of Clinical Neurophysiology, 118*(5), 1019–1027.

Velickovic, M., Benabou, R., & Brin, M. F. (2001). Cervical dystonia pathophysiology and treatment options. *Drugs, 61*(13), 1921–1943.

Vidailhet, M., Jutras, M. F., Grabli, D., & Roze, E. (2013). Deep brain stimulation for dystonia. *Journal of Neurology, Neurosurgery, and Psychiatry, 84*(9), 1029–1042. doi.org/10.1136/jnnp-2011-301714.

Waddy, H. M., Fletcher, N. A., Harding, A. E., & Marsden, C. D. (1991). A genetic study of idiopathic focal dystonias. *Annual Journal of Neurology, 29*(3), 320–324. doi.org/10.1002/ana.410290315.

Wolpe, J. (1958). *Psychotherapy by reciprocal inhibition.* Stanford, CA: Stanford University Press.

Vocal Cord Dysfunction

Ran D. Anbar and Benedicto A. Fernandes

Vocal cord dysfunction (VCD) or paradoxical vocal-fold motion (PVFM) is a disorder characterized by abnormal adduction (moving together) of the vocal cords upon inspiration. In contrast, vocal cords normally abduct (move apart) during inspiration. Patients tend to experience symptoms such as throat tightness, persistent cough, inspiratory difficulty, and often times stridor (Kenn & Balkissoon, 2011).

The mechanisms that cause the paradoxical movement noted in VCD are incompletely understood and may be multifactorial (Kenn & Hess, 2008). VCD most commonly is triggered by psychological stressors but sometimes is associated with physical issues such as asthma, chronic rhinosinusitis with postnasal drainage, gastroesophageal reflux, and organic brain pathology (Bahrainwala & Simon, 2001; Greenberger & Grammer, 2010; Greenlee, Donovan, Hasan, & Menezes, 2002). A common psychological trigger of VCD is self-imposed stress by elite athletes engaged in athletic competitions. Less commonly associated psychological stressors include sexual abuse, academic difficulties, and conflicts with family members or peers (Freedman, Rosenberg, & Schmaling, 1991). Anbar (2014) documented that patients who were diagnosed with VCD accounted for 17% of 1,666 children (up to 21 years old) referred to a pediatric pulmonary center over a 15-year period, who reported symptoms suggestive of psychological difficulties associated with their respiratory symptoms.

Definitive diagnosis of VCD requires direct visualization of the adducted cords during inhalation via laryngoscopy. However, it may be difficult to visualize the abnormality, given its intermittent nature. Thus, the diagnosis often is made based on its characteristic clinical presentation. In one report, a patient with suspected VCD agreed to induce an episode by following a suggestion given during hypnosis (Anbar & Hehir, 2000). In this way the diagnosis was confirmed, and the patient also learned that with hypnosis, he could control his VCD.

Prompt recognition and treatment is important as ineffective interventions are costly and may be associated with significant morbidity. However, one of the difficulties in making the diagnosis on clinical grounds is related to the frequent comorbidity of VCD and asthma. For example, over half of patients with VCD also had concurrent asthma in one report (Newman, Mason, & Schmaling, 1995). In some patients, asthma appears to trigger VCD episodes, which could be the result of either the physical or psychological factors related to an asthma exacerbation. Thus, patients with VCD often are mischaracterized as having asthma only (Kenn & Hess, 2008). In other cases, VCD alone has been confused with asthma when its associated inspiratory stridor (resulting from an upper airway obstruction) was confused with expiratory wheeze (as a result of lower airway obstruction that is characteristic of asthma; see Chapter 15). As a result, patients with VCD often have been treated with beta-agonist bronchodilators and/or corticosteroids that are appropriate for asthma but ineffective for VCD. Sometimes, patients have required multiple hospitalizations and have even undergone intubation and tracheostomy placement because of recurrent episodes of undiagnosed VCD (Bahrainwala & Simon, 2001; Ibrahim, Gheriani, Almohamed, & Raza, 2007).

Reported treatments for VCD include

1. Behavioral interventions such as speech therapy and breathing techniques (Sullivan, Heywood, & Beukelman, 2001). Warnes and Allen (2005) reported that weekly speech therapy for 10 weeks along with biofeedback alleviated the symptoms of VCD. Thurston and Fiedorowicz

(2009) documented that a 1-year course of psychotherapy along with speech therapy can help patients with their VCD symptoms. In contrast, Bahrainwala and Simon (2001) reported that even one session of speech therapy can be sufficient to teach the breathing exercises necessary to alleviate and even resolve the symptoms of VCD, although some patients required extra sessions for reinforcement.

2. Psychological interventions such as application of relaxation techniques, cognitive behavioral therapy (Richards-Mauzé & Banez, 2014), biofeedback (Warnes & Allen, 2005), and one to three sessions of hypnosis (Anbar, 2002; Caraon & O'Toole, 1991).

3. Physical interventions for treatment of underlying organic triggers of VCD such as asthma, allergies, or gastroseophageal reflux, use of inhaled ipratropium in order to prevent VCD induced by exercise (Doshi & Weinberger, 2006), intralaryngeal injection of botulinum toxin (Maillard et al., 2000), and use of a mixture of helium and oxygen to resolve acute episodes of VCD (Reisner & Borish, 1995).

RESEARCH

No studies have yet compared the efficacy of the various therapies for VCD. It is our opinion that unless an underlying organic trigger requires medical therapy, physical interventions for VCD should be used only if behavioral or psychological interventions are ineffective, given the cost and potential morbidity associated with physical interventions. Further, significant underlying psychological stressors may need to be addressed before VCD symptoms can resolve with the use of behavioral interventions or psychological techniques that do not focus on dealing with the stressors directly (such as relaxation techniques or biofeedback).

Published reports regarding the use of hypnosis for VCD have been limited to case reports and case series. As part of a case series involving pediatric patients who were treated with hypnosis for respiratory issues, Anbar (2002) reported 33 patients with VCD who were offered hypnosis, out of whom 29 accepted. After a single hypnosis session, 20 patients experienced either resolution or improvement of their symptoms, two patients did not improve, and seven were lost to follow-up.

Anbar and Geisler (2005) conducted a retrospective study of pediatric patients who were offered hypnotherapy for a range of respiratory diagnoses including VCD. Hypnosis was taught in one or two 15- to 45-minute sessions. Out of the 81 patients who received instruction in self-hypnosis for their respiratory symptoms, 75% returned for a follow-up assessment and 95% of these patients reported improvement and/or resolution of their symptoms.

Anbar and Hummell (2005) reported a case series of 22 patients with VCD who were taught hypnosis. Of these, 14 patients experienced either resolution or improvement of their symptoms, one patient did not improve, and seven were lost to follow-up. Caraon and O'Toole (1991) reported a case where an adolescent developed VCD related to psychosocial stressors in school. His symptoms resolved after two sessions of hypnotherapy.

CASE EXAMPLE

The patient was a 15-year-old who presented with a 2-year history of developing shortness of breath during cross-country meets. Initially, she was diagnosed by her primary care provider as having exercise-induced asthma, for which she was treated with albuterol prior to exercise without associated improvement in her symptoms.

Because of her ongoing complaint of shortness of breath, she was referred to an allergist, who documented by skin scratch testing that she was allergic to grass and prescribed the use of an oral antihistamine, which was not associated with an improvement in her symptom. The allergist proposed initiation of allergy immunotherapy (involving monthly injections), but the patient and her family did not want to commit to such an intervention.

The patient then was referred for evaluation by an otolaryngologist who documented by laryngoscopy that her tonsils and adenoids were enlarged but no other upper airway abnormality was present. She underwent a tonsillectomy and adenoidectomy that helped resolve her mild snoring but did not change the nature of her shortness of breath.

Finally, the patient was referred to a pediatric pulmonologist who elicited the history that her shortness of breath was associated with inspiratory stridor, and difficulty with inhalation, which are symptoms characteristic of VCD. The pulmonologist taught the patient how to use hypnosis in order to calm herself (with instruction similar to that used in the Chapter 15 case example), and also how to utilize a gesture (i.e., a relaxation sign, as described in Chapter 20) that would trigger her relaxation response and that she could employ prior to running or should she develop shortness of breath while running.

A month later, the patient reported that she no longer developed shortness of breath with exercise. She commented that once she realized she could control her shortness of breath, she no longer feared it and therefore no longer developed VCD as a result of anxiety about it. She said she only ended up employing her relaxation sign before running on two occasions, and thereafter was symptom-free.

TECHNIQUES: HYPNOSIS FOR VOCAL CORD DYSFUNCTION

It is important to recognize that all symptoms, including VCD, are triggered by an underlying abnormality. Treatment directed at a symptom can provide short-term relief, but long-term improvement or resolution of a symptom depends on the amelioration or spontaneous improvement of its underlying trigger.

In the case of VCD that is caused by self-imposed pressure to succeed, such as occurs commonly with high-achieving athletes, instruction in the use of self-hypnosis to achieve a relaxed state has been shown often to lead to resolution of the symptom. In addition, some patients benefit from using imagery specific to resolution of the abnormal tightening of the vocal cords similar to how imagery specific to airway constriction can be helpful in the hypnotic management of asthma.

When a psychological trigger of VCD is related to issues that are not relieved by relaxation alone, therapy should be directed at dealing with the underlying issue. For example, an athlete whose VCD is triggered by the desire to stop competing may need to learn how to verbalize his or her feelings and desires (Anbar & Linden, 2010). Some patients develop VCD as a way of resolving a significant psychological conflict; thus, their symptom

represents a conversion disorder. For example, one girl was reported to have developed VCD in association with being abused sexually by her stepfather. With hypnosis, she was able to express her worries about disclosing uncomfortable information to her mother and that the VCD was of help to her by preventing her from talking (Anbar, 2004).

Hypnosis can be used in a number of ways to help identify and/or address psychological issues that may be underlying the development or persistence of VCD. Being in a hypnotically induced relaxed state can allow patients to better verbalize feelings that usually are anxiety provoking and thus more difficult to express during therapy.

Metaphors can be used as a way of allowing the patient to indirectly explore and deal with stressors without necessarily bringing them to conscious awareness. For example, in the case of a patient who developed VCD related to a feeling that he could not compete adequately with his peers, a discussion regarding how a seed can grow into a powerful oak tree gave sufficient ego strengthening that he was able to feel better about his likelihood of success. This was associated with resolution of his symptoms.

Psychological stressors that can trigger VCD in children include

1. A past event that has ended and is unlikely to recur (e.g., a child who was bullied in a former school)
2. A past event that is likely to recur (e.g., the bully is still around)
3. An ongoing event over which the patient has some control (e.g., the school has encouraged students to report bullying)
4. An ongoing event over which the patient has no control (e.g., the school refuses to take adequate action against a bully)
5. Anticipation of a future event over which the patient has some control (a child worries bullying will recur at a new school)
6. Anticipation of a future event over which the patient has no control (a child worries that the principal at a new school will be unsympathetic, should bullying recur)

Hypnotic techniques should be varied in order to better address the patient's needs in each of the aforementioned circumstances.

1. If a past event is unlikely to recur, the nature and outcome of the event can be processed with various hypnotic techniques or counseling, which sometimes requires referral to a mental health care provider. Thereafter, hypnotic techniques that can help patients let go of the memory of the event include: *"Place the event into a helium balloon. Let the balloon go, and notice how the event can seem to have less and less impact on you the farther away the balloon travels. Until it is gone." "You might choose to bury the event in a treasure chest, with a lock. You could throw away the key, or keep it around so that you can reopen the chest if you like."*

2. If a past event is likely to recur, it can be suggested that with new coping skills the patient has learned as a result of using hypnosis, he or she will be much more capable of dealing with the same type of event in the future. Sometimes, it is beneficial for the patient to rehearse how he or she will react to the event differently than in the past. *"You now have the ability to remain calm even in the face of a stressful situation, through use of your relaxation sign." "Notice how much more confident you feel in thinking about how you can cope with such an event." "Perhaps you would care to get rid of the event memory by erasing it or blowing it up?"*

3. If the event is ongoing and is partially in the patient's control, the patient should be encouraged to consider how to best address the situation in order to reduce stress resulting from the event. Hypnotic suggestions that can help patients cope better in this situation include, *"You can help yourself deal better with the event by rehearsing how you can remain calm while working toward improving the situation." "Imagine how good you will feel once the nature of the event changes as a result of your proactive actions."*

4. If the event is ongoing but is not in the patient's control, the patient can be coached how to deal better with such a situation. A thought that has been helpful for patients to consider is a quote that commonly has been attributed to Reinhold Neibuhr: *"God grant me the serenity to accept the things I cannot change, the courage to change the things I can, and the wisdom to know the difference." "You will become stronger by dealing confidently with a difficult situation. Embracing the difficulty will help you deal with it better."*

5. To help deal with anxiety about future events that can be controlled, the patient can be encouraged about his or her ability to cope through changing his or her thinking pattern, and mental rehearsal regarding how he or she might deal with such an event when and if it occurs. Patients can benefit by considering a suggestion such as, *"The difference between a good and a bad day can often be found in a person's attitude."*

6. Patients can be coached how to let go of anxiety regarding future events over which they have no prospect of control. *"While you may not have control about the nature of the event, you do have control regarding how you react." "Focus on the present rather than an uncertain future. In this way you can remain calmer."*

CONCLUSION

VCD is a relatively common condition that often is misdiagnosed as asthma. Use of hypnosis in order to achieve relaxation often is associated with rapid resolution. In some cases, patients require guidance regarding how to address the underlying psychological trigger of their VCD in order to achieve resolution of the symptom. As hypnosis typically works for VCD in one to three sessions without associated side effects and can preclude some more expensive medical evaluations and therapies with their associated morbidity, it should be considered a first-line therapy for this condition.

REFERENCES

Anbar, R. D. (2002). Hypnosis in pediatric: Applications at a pediatric pulmonary center. *BMC Pediatrics*, 2(11). doi:10.1186/1471-2431-2-11

Anbar, R. D. (2004). Stressors associated with dyspnea in childhood: Patients' insights and a case report. *American Journal of Clinical Hypnosis*, 47(2), 93–101. doi:10.1080/00029157.2004.10403628

Anbar, R. D. (2014). Addressing psychological issues affecting children with pulmonary disease. *American Journal of Respiratory and Critical Care Medicine*, A4039.

Anbar, R. D., & Geisler, S. C. (2005). Identification of children who may benefit from self-hypnosis at a pediatric pulmonary center. *BMC Pediatrics*, 5(1), 6.

Anbar, R. D., & Hehir, D. A. (2000). Hypnosis as a diagnostic modality for vocal cord dysfunction. *Pediatrics, 106*(6). doi:E81.10.1542/peds.106.6.e81

Anbar, R. D., & Hummell, K. E. (2005). Teamwork approach to clinical hypnosis at a pediatric pulmonary center. *American Journal of Clinical Hypnosis, 48*(1), 45–49.

Anbar, R. D., & Linden, J. H. (2010). Understanding dissociation and insight in the treatment of shortness of breath with hypnosis: A case study. *American Journal of Clinical Hypnosis, 52*(4), 263–273.

Bahrainwala, A. H., & Simon, M. R. (2001). Wheezing and vocal cord dysfunction mimicking asthma. *Current Opinion in Pulmonary Medicine, 7*(1), 8–13.

Caraon, P., & O'Toole, C. (1991). Vocal cord dysfunction presenting as asthma. *Irish Medical Journal, 84*(3), 98–99.

Doshi, D. R., & Weinberger, M. M. (2006). Long-term outcome of vocal cord dysfunction. *Annals of Allergy, Asthma & Immunology, 96*(6), 794–799.

Freedman, M. R., Rosenberg, S. J., & Schmaling, K. B. (1991). Childhood sexual abuse in patients with paradoxical vocal cord dysfunction. *Journal of Nervous and Mental Disease, 179*(5), 295–298.

Greenberger, P. A., & Grammer, L. C. (2010). Pulmonary disorders, including vocal cord dysfunction. *Journal of Allergy and Clinical Immunology, 125*(Suppl 2), S248–S254. doi:10.1016/j.jaci.2009.09.020

Greenlee, J. D., Donovan, K. A., Hasan, D. M., & Menezes, A. H. (2002). Chiari I malformation in the very young child: The spectrum of presentations and experience in 31 children under age 6 years. *Pediatrics, 110*(6), 1212–1219.

Ibrahim, W. H., Gheriani, H. A., Almohamed, A. A., & Raza, T. (2007). Paradoxical vocal cord motion disorder: Past, present and future. *Postgraduate Medical Journal, 83*(977), 164–172. doi:10.1136/pgmj.2006.052522

Kenn, K., & Balkissoon, R. (2011). Vocal cord dysfunction: What do we know? *European Respiratory Journal, 37*(1), 194–200. doi:10.1183/09031936.00192809

Kenn, K., & Hess, M. M. (2008). Vocal cord dysfunction: An important differential diagnosis of bronchial asthma. *Deutsches Ärzteblatt International, 105*(41), 699–704. doi:10.3238/arztebl.2008.0699

Maillard, I., Schweizer, V., Broccard, A., Duscher, A., Liaudet, L., & Schaller, M. D. (2000). Use of botulinum toxin type A to avoid tracheal intubation or tracheostomy in severe paradoxical vocal cord movement. *Chest, 118*(3), 874–877.

Newman, K. B., Mason, U. G., & Schmaling, K. B. (1995). Clinical features of vocal cord dysfunction. *American Journal of Respiratory and Critical Care Medicine, 152*(4), 1382–1386.

Reisner, C., & Borish, L. (1995). Heliox therapy for acute vocal cord dysfunction. *Chest, 108*(5), 1477.

Richards-Mauzé, M. M., & Banez, G. A. (2014). Vocal cord dysfunction: Evaluation of a four session cognitive-behavioral intervention. *Clinical Practice in Pediatric Psychology, 2*(1), 27–38. doi:10.1037/cpp0000044

Sullivan, M. D., Heywood, B. M., & Beukelman, D. R. (2001). A treatment for vocal cord dysfunction in female athletes: An outcome study. *Laryngoscope, 111*(10), 1751–1755.

Thurston, N. L., & Fiedorowicz, J. G. (2009). Improvement of paradoxical vocal cord dysfunction with integrated psychiatric care. *Psychosomatics, 50*(3), 282–284. doi:10.1176/appi.psy.50.3.282

Warnes, E., & Allen, K. D. (2005). Biofeedback treatment of paradoxical vocal fold motion and respiratory distress in an adolescent girl. *Journal of Applied Behavior Analysis, 38*(4), 529–532.

Warts

Yimin Yu and Juliette Bowers

48

CHAPTER

Warts are skin lesions caused by the human papillomavirus (HPV). Most warts are considered benign, but their effects differ based on the dozens of forms of HPV as well as other environmental and individual differences. Warts vary in their physical appearance and their location on the body but can be frequently found on the hands, feet, or genital areas. The shape, size, clustering, and depth of a wart may affect the degree of impact on the patient, which can range from superficial unsightliness to physical pain, and therefore inform treatment (Sterling, Handfield-Jones, & Hudson, 2001). In terms of treatment, there is no single treatment that is 100% effective. Treatment methods can vary from spontaneous remission to cryotherapy to hypnosis, depending on the cause of the wart and its effect on the patient (Dall'Oglio, D'Amico, Nasca, & Micali, 2012; Sterling, Handfield-Jones, & Hudson, 2001).

Nongenital warts are primarily found in children and young adults, with estimates suggesting that 3% to 20% of the population of children and adolescents will suffer from cutaneous warts and that about 360,000 people in the United States are diagnosed with genital warts a year (CDC Fact Sheet, 2014; Kikenny & Marks, 1996; Sterling, Handfield-Jones, & Hudson, 2001). In children, genital warts may require assessment of sexual abuse in the home environment. When studied beyond young adulthood, nongenital warts tend to be more prevalent in adults who work with raw meat and fish (Kikenny & Marks, 1996). In people who have immunocompetence, warts can remit naturally, but others may require additional treatment to resolve. Treatment of warts ranges from home-based, alternative remedies such as heat treatment and hypnosis to medical approaches such as cryotherapy and salicylic acid.

Research on the treatment of warts tends to review stages of treatment as appropriate on a case-by-case basis because no one treatment is 100% effective (Springer International Publishing, 2012). Stages include first-line, second-line, and third-line treatments that should be evaluated based on the history of the individual presenting the problem. Salicylic acid is considered to be a first-line therapy treatment due to its general effectiveness and relative ease of administration (Dall'Oglio et al., 2012). Salicylic acid is a destructive treatment method that attacks the virus and attempts to stimulate the immune system. Salicylic acid is effective in approximately 67% of the population (Sterling, Handfield-Jones, & Hudson, 2001). This includes salicylic acid to treat a variety of warts including flat warts, plantar warts, and periungual warts (Sterling, Handfield-Jones, & Hudson, 2001; Dall'Oglio et al., 2012). When compared with other destructive treatments such as cryotherapy, salicylic acid is generally considered more cost-effective, especially when administered at home (Keogh-Brown et al., 2007). One of the problems with salicylic acid treatment is that it may be uncomfortable for use in genital warts, which limits its applicability.

One of the primary second-line treatments is cryotherapy, another destructive treatment that includes using an agent, such as liquid nitrogen, to freeze the tissue and force an immune response from the body. Cryotherapy is considered a more aggressive treatment than salicylic acid (Dall'Oglio et al., 2012) and is less cost-effective as a treatment (Keogh-Brown et al., 2007). Research is mixed on the effectiveness of cryotherapy, which may be due to the variety of techniques that are used in the process of cryotherapy as well as the difference in each wart. Techniques can range based on the administration time, the number of times that it is administered, and the method of administration (Dall'Oglio et al., 2012).

Third-line treatments for warts, according to Dall'Oglio et al. (2012), are for resistant and recurrent warts. Treatments in this category include topical treatments (Dall'Oglio et al., 2012) or laser removal (Sterling, Handfield-Jones, & Hudson, 2001), potentially in conjunction with other third-line treatments such as home remedies including duct tape and other folk remedies. Focht, Spicer, and Fairchok (2002) compared treatment of warts with duct tape versus cryotherapy and found that duct tape eliminated more warts than cryotherapy in their sample. Interestingly, in both groups, most warts were eliminated in the first month of treatment. Hypnosis in the treatment of warts is an area of research with inconsistent evidence (Felt et al., 1998; Keogh-Brown et al., 2007; Sterling, Handfield-Jones, & Hudson, 2001; Shenefelt, 2000, 2003). Despite the inconsistency in support of hypnosis as a treatment for warts, hypnosis remains as an alternative and noninvasive treatment for warts that may be inaccessible by other means or those that have been unresponsive to other treatments.

RESEARCH

Clinicians have used hypnosis in the treatment of warts for approximately 50 years, but there has been inconsistent evidence of its efficacy, likely due to a lack of research focus on the area and the increase in the availability and feasibility of other medical treatments such as cryotherapy, salicylic acid, and other topical treatments. Overall, the literature suggests that use of hypnosis for the regression of warts may infer longer term benefits as compared with those treated topically, with longer clearance rates at 6- to 12-week follow-ups as compared with both placebo and no-treatment controls (Barabasz, Higley, Christensen, & Barabasz, 2009; Lankton, 2007; Spanos, Williams, & Gwynn, 1990). While there has been no proposed mechanism for the regression of warts as a result of hypnosis, reasonable hypotheses have been put forth stating that hypnosis may be more effective for warts that are psychosomatic in nature and likely a result of increased stress response in the body (Barber, 1961; Shenefelt, 2000). In these cases, hypnosis can improve healthful behaviors, diminish situational stress and alleviate phobias, and be

helpful as a complementary therapy in addition to medical treatment or a stand-alone alternative therapy for warts (Shenefelt, 2000, 2003).

One of the earliest randomized controlled studies by Spanos et al. (1990) compared the efficacy of four different conditions: hypnotic suggestion, topical salicylic acid, topical placebo, and no-treatment control. Each participant was randomly assigned to one of the conditions and each condition had an equal number of subjects. The hypnotic treatment group was orally administered a 10-minute hypnotic induction that included suggestions for wart regression, informing the participants that the skin around their warts was "beginning to tingle and grow warm" before shrinking and dissolving away (Spanos et al., 1990). The participants were asked to practice this wart regression imagery once per day for 6 weeks. Results indicated a significant difference in warts lost in the hypnotic treatment group as compared with the other three conditions. Spanos et al. (1990) also looked at hypnotizability using the Carleton University Responsiveness to Suggestion Scale (CURSS), which did not yield significant differences in hypnotizability among the participants. This study showed robust results in support of using hypnotic therapy as a treatment for the regression of warts over and above topical salicylic acid and topical placebo and suggests that there may be psychosomatic underpinnings in the cause for wart appearance and maintenance.

More recently, Barabasz et al. (2009) conducted a study comparing the effects of medical-only therapies with hypnosis-only therapies in treating HPV infection in a rural and urban population of adult women. There were 12 women in the rural sample and 14 in the urban sample, and all participants self-selected the therapy they wished to participate in after exposure to information and brochures about HPV. Participants in the hypnosis treatment received biweekly sessions in the urban sample and weekly sessions in the rural sample for 12 weeks and instructions for self-hypnosis. During the hypnosis treatment, the hypnotherapists gave suggestions for vasodilation of the infected areas and increased immunity. Results indicated that both hypnosis and medical procedures resulted in statistically significant reductions in areas and number of lesions, which suggested equal efficacy between the two treatments. However, at the 12-week follow-up, five hypnosis therapy participants showed complete clearance compared with only one in the medical group. While the results show support for hypnosis as a potential alternative to medical treatment of HPV warts, the small sample size of the study and lack of randomized selection process in methodology detract from the robust nature of the results. Another study by Felt et al. (1998) compared relaxation mental imagery to standard topical treatment and equal time control interventions in children ranging from 6 to 12 years of age. The study included four visits over 8 weeks and a phone follow-up at 6 to 18 months after study entry. While results showed no statistical group differences after the first 8 weeks, follow-up results showed a trend for more relaxation imagery and standard topical treatment participants to report complete wart resolution. These results suggest that hypnosis may play a role in the maintenance of wart regression and resolution and may be a complementary treatment in addition to a topical treatment.

There have also been case studies of using hypnosis in the treatment of wart regression in children and adults (Lankton, 2007). In the study by Kellis, the patient was an 11-year-old boy who had warts on his feet and hands. The treatment was preceded by psychoeducation for both the boy and his mother about hypnosis and warts and a thorough review regarding the boy's favorite TV show, which was incorporated into his individualized hypnosis treatment. The study included one hypnosis session, one follow-up phone call 1 week later, and another phone call follow-up in 6 weeks. The patient reported during the follow-up phone call that he experienced complete regression of all of his warts with no negative side effects. His mother confirmed these results at the 6-week follow-up. These results are similar to those reported in the Spanos et al. study (1990); however, it is difficult to discern the causes of the client's success and the role that aspects of hypnosis played in the necessary parts in the client's wart regression. Another case study looked at wart regression in a 16-year-old female who had exhausted all medical treatments for warts on her hands and legs that were negatively affecting her social functioning, self-image, and self-confidence. The hypnosis treatment began approximately 7 months after the last medical treatment, thus minimizing as much as possible the effect of residual medical treatments. The hypnosis treatment included initial psychoeducation about hypnosis and the potential benefits of this modality of treatment and about the physiology of the immune system. The therapist included suggestions for increased immune function in specific immune cells including T cells,

white corpuscles, and antibodies. The client attended five sessions, with 30 days in between her first and second session and a week in between all following sessions. By session 5, the client noted regression of all warts. It is difficult to discern from one case study the causative variables that may have been instrumental in the success of this hypnotic treatment as compared with the other unsuccessful treatments. The authors speculated on an increase in overall immune system function powered by expectancy, increased relaxation, and a placebo effect caused by the suggestions. As with all case studies, the sample size detracts from the generalizability of these results to the population. However, the results are consistent with those from bigger trials in support of hypnosis as a possible alternative route for the treatment of warts.

CASE EXAMPLE

A 25-year-old female entered treatment for warts on her feet and hands. The client reported that she first began having warts in her early teenage years and was told by doctors that her symptoms would likely reduce after high school. Her warts spread so that she also had genital warts that were not only embarrassing for her but also painful. The client felt embarrassed by her warts and had tried cryotherapy, salicylic acid, and many home remedies such as nail polish and duct tape, as well as patience. Despite this, the client's warts had persisted. Her doctor recommended her to a hypnotherapist who specialized in dermatological treatments. The hypnotherapist conducted several sessions of hypnotherapy with the client that included suggestions for reduced blood flow to the wart and feelings of coolness such as a cold mountain lake or snowy forest. After a series of sessions, the client began to notice improvements and was able to terminate the sessions and continue to use self-hypnosis techniques to reduce her warts.

TRANSCRIPT

The following transcript is a sample that may be used over the course of treatment for wart removal on the feet or other parts of the body. The session may begin with a rhypnotic elaxation induction or other induction as well as including suggestions for deepening before suggestions are included.

"And now, as you continue to relax into your chair, it might be nice to imagine yourself in a peaceful place. Perhaps a beach or a forest . . . perhaps on a mountain or near a lake. Imagine this lake in your mind, it is a calming place, a place where you feel relaxed. The day is comfortably warm and you can enjoy the sunshine and peaceful feelings. And maybe, as you sit watching this serene lake, you begin to feel warm . . . and staring at the cool lake water, you may decide to stick your feet in the lake . . . imagine sticking your feet in the cool lake water. Touching the cool water, you feel calm and at ease. The warts on your feet feel cool, no discomfort. And the coolness penetrates these warts, shutting off the blood flow to these warts, making your feet feel healthier every moment that they are in the water. And perhaps, while your feet are in this cooling, healing water, you could place water on other areas of your body with warts, allowing the cooling water to penetrate these warts as well, cooling each wart so much that the blood supply to these warts stops, not allowing them to remain on your body any longer. And your body and mind will know when the water has stopped as much blood flow as it can today, and when it is ready, you may choose to step out of the water, again absorbing the serene atmosphere that this lake has provided and the healing water that the lake has produced, feeling content and relaxed.

And your body may continue to reduce blood flow to the warts over time, ridding yourself of the warts at a gradual but steady pace. Pain and discomfort will diminish even before visible signs of the warts diminishing begin."

CONCLUSION

Warts are formations found on the skin, mainly hands, feet, and genital areas, which are caused by HPV. Cutaneous warts are commonly found in children and young adults and can remit naturally over the course of a few months in those with immunocompetence. At times, warts can be painful and may spread in a localized area of the body, leading to a decrease in various domains of functioning such as self-image and self-confidence. The severity of the symptoms and the depth of impact for the patient should inform the appropriate treatment for the warts. While there is no known treatment for warts that is 100% effective, there are various accepted treatments such as using salicylic acid or cryotherapy, which attack the warts, or home remedies, such as duct tape and hypnosis, which reduce oxygen to the wart. These treatments range in cost-effectiveness and efficacy depending on the type and location of the wart. Studies have shown that hypnosis can be a viable alternative or complementary treatment for warts in addition to medical means or as a stand-alone treatment, particularly for warts that may be resistant to medical treatment or are located in areas that are not conducive to destructive treatments.

CLINICAL SUMMARY

- Like many of the treatments for warts, there is inconsistent research in the literature on the treatment of warts using hypnosis, with a few randomized controlled trials and some case studies. The results indicate that hypnosis may be viable as an adjunct therapy in addition to medical treatment or as a stand-alone treatment, depending on the patient, cause of the warts, and the location and physical properties of the warts.
- Use individualized imagery as much as possible for the client and regularly ask for feedback on the client's experience of the session and imagery. For example, suggestions for coolness may be very helpful for some clients and not necessary for others.
- Suggestions for increased immune function may be effective in wart regression treatment.
- Secondary emotional symptoms may also be present with clients, such as depression or anxiety based on the social consequences of warts. These may need additional treatment from a qualified provider.
- Genital or anal warts may also be a sign of possible sexual assault and should be followed up by a qualified provider.

REFERENCES

Barabasz, A., Higley, L., Christensen, C., & Barabasz, M. (2009). Efficacy of hypnosis in the treatment of human papillomavirus (HPV) in women: Rural and urban samples. *International Journal of Clinical and Experimental Hypnosis, 58*(1), 102–121. doi:10.1080/00207140903310899

Barber, T. X. (1961). Physiological effects of hypnosis. *Psychological Bulletin, 58*(5), 390.

Boy, Y. O. (2011). The treatment of warts with a little help. *Australian Journal, 39*(2), 181–188.

Dall'Oglio, F., D'Amico, V., Nasca, M. R., & Micali, G. (2012). Treatment of cutaneous warts: An evidence-based review. *American Journal of Clinical Dermatology, 13*(2), 73–96.

Felt, B. T., Hall, H., Olness, K., Schmidt, W., Kohen, D., Berman, B. D., & Young, M. H. (1998). Wart regression in children: Comparison of relaxation-imagery to topical treatment and equal time interventions. *American Journal of Clinical Hypnosis, 41*(2), 130–137. doi:10.1080/00029157.1998.10404199

Focht, D. R. III, Spicer, C., & Fairchok, M. P. (2002). The efficacy of duct tape vs cryotherapy in the treatment of verruca vulgaris (the common wart). *Archives of Pediatric and Adolescent Medicine, 156*, 971–974.

Keogh-Brown, M. R., Fordham, R. J., Thomas, K. S., Bachmann, M. O., Holland, A. J., Avery, S. J., &

Harvey, I. (2007). To freeze or not to freeze: A cost-effectiveness analysis of wart treatment. *British Journal of Dermatology, 156*, 687–692.

Kikenny, M., & Marks, R. (1996). The descriptive epidemiology of warts in the community. *Australasian Journal of Dermatology, 37*(2), 80–86.

Lankton, S. (2007). Psychotherapeutic intervention for numerous and large viral warts with adjunctive hypnosis: A case study. *American Journal of Clinical Hypnosis, 49*(3), 211–218. doi:10.1080/00029157.2007.10401583

Shenefelt, P. D. (2000). Hypnosis in dermatology. *Archives of Dermatology, 136*(3), 393–399.

Shenefelt, P. D. (2003). Biofeedback, cognitive-behavioral methods, and hypnosis in dermatology: Is it all in your mind? *Dermatologic Therapy, 16*(2), 114–122.

Spanos, N. P., Stenstrom, R. J., & Johnston, J. C. (1988). Hypnosis, placebo, and suggestion in the treatment of warts. *Psychosomatic Medicine, 50*(3), 245–260.

Spanos, N. P., Williams, V., & Gwynn, M. I. (1990). Effects of hypnotic, placebo, and salicylic acid treatments on wart regression. *Psychosomatic Medicine, 52*(1), 109–114.

Springer International Publishing. (2012). Treat cutaneous warts on a case-by-case basis, taking into account patient factors and the available clinical evidence. *Drugs and Therapy Perspectives, 28*(8), 15–19.

Sterling, J. C., Handfield-Jones, S., & Hudson, P. M. (2001). Guidelines for the management of cutaneous warts. *British Journal of Dermatology, 144*, 4–11.

Psychological Applications

Addictions and Relapse Prevention

Ronald J. Pekala

Substance abuse disorders are a major health issue facing many countries around the world. In the United States, the lifetime and 12-month prevalence rates of alcohol abuse were 17.8% and 4.7%, respectively; for alcohol dependence, they were 12.5% and 3.8%, respectively (Hasin, Stinson, Ogburn, & Grant, 2007). Whereas alcohol abuse typically results in harm to one's heath, interpersonal relationships, and one's ability to work, alcohol dependence subsumes not only abuse but also physical dependence: tolerance (the increased need for more alcohol to feel the same effect) and withdrawal (symptoms when the effects of alcohol wear off, such as anxiety, trembling, sweating, nausea, insomnia, irritability, etc.). Over a decade ago, it was estimated that more than 85,000 deaths a year were directly attributed to alcohol use in the United States at an annual economic cost of at least $185 billion (Harwood, 2000).

Concerning illicit drug use, the lifetime and 12-month prevalence rates for such drug abuse in the United States were 7.7% and 1.4%, respectively; for drug dependence, they were 2.6% and 0.6%, respectively (Compton, Thomas, Stinson, & Grant, 2007). Rates for drug abuse and dependence were usually greater for men than women; those of lower socioeconomic status; and those individuals who were never married or were widowed, separated, or divorced. It is of interest that "most individuals with drug use disorders have never been treated, and treatment disparities exist among those at high risk, despite substantial disability and comorbidity" (Compton et al., 2007, p. 566).

When the various drugs of abuse and alcohol were cluster analyzed across chronic drug/alcohol abusers (Pekala et al., 2000), six clusters/groups were found to emerge. These were the use of (in terms of the largest to smallest number of participants per cluster group) cocaine and alcohol; alcohol, cocaine, and marijuana; alcohol only; heroin, cocaine, and marijuana; polysubstance abuse; and a second alcohol, marijuana, and cocaine use group. This research suggests that with a chronic substance abuse population, usually a mixture of drugs and alcohol is abused.

The most severe substance abuse among the six groups, the polysubstance abusers, "reported experiencing the highest levels of child abuse across all five (abuse) subscales: physical/verbal abuse, sexual abuse, inappropriate punishment, parental dysfunctioning, and neglect" (Pekala et al., 2000, p. 38). Hence, childhood abuse appears to be a factor in the more severe forms of drug and alcohol abuse. Since dissociation, as measured by the Dissociative Experiences Scale (Carlson & Putnam, 1992, 1993), appears to be significantly correlated with child abuse (Pekala et al., 2000), the use of hypnosis with such dissociative types may be helpful.

RELEVANT LITERATURE

The literature on using hypnosis with individuals suffering from drug and alcohol use disorders has been largely anecdotal. Over 30 years ago, Erickson (1976) reported that he had limited success in using hypnosis with alcoholics, believing that hypnosis encouraged an unhealthy negative transference and dependence on the therapist. Hartman (1972) reviewed the use of hypnosis in the treatment of drug addiction through the early 1970s. Reviewing individual and group case studies and one controlled study, Hartman (1972, p. 37) concluded that the "use of hypnosis in the treatment of drug addiction shows a great deal of promise," indicating consistent success rates of between "60% and 70%" for programs employing hypnosis. Hypnotic interventions included "traumatizing the drug addict against any use of a needle"; "autohypnosis for withstanding the disagreeable subjective sensations of withdrawal"; using hypnosis to revivify a "good trip" (so the person learns to get high naturally on hypnosis, instead of an illegal substance); and extensive hypnoanalysis to "uncover very significant neurosis" (Hartman, 1972, p. 36).

Katz in 1980 suggested that hypnosis had not been well integrated into behavioral therapy and could be better utilized in the addictions field. He stressed interfacing hypnosis with the gains that had been made in behavior therapy as applied to self-control approaches and using hypnosis as a cognitive self-control skill model: "Newer types of hypnotic inductions which attempt to 'train rather than trance' through education of subjects in the most important principles responsible for successful hypnotic response" (Katz, 1980, p. 44) were advocated. He believed that by teaching clients how cognitions affect behaviors, control over behavior could be enhanced via cognitive, and possibly hypnotic, techniques.

In 1981, Wadden and Penrod published a review of studies on the hypnotic treatment of alcoholism since 1964. They concluded that although positive results were reported in individual and group case studies, these results should be viewed with caution due to the methodological shortcomings of the research. In reviewing two experimental studies using hypnosis, they noted that the use of a hypnotic induction did not add leverage to conventional therapies for alcoholism. When hypnotic therapies were successful in the treatment of problem drinking, their efficacy was probably attributable to nonhypnotic factors rather than to the use of hypnosis per se. They concluded, however, that final conclusions concerning the efficacy of hypnosis with alcoholism could not be reached until the contribution of hypnotic susceptibility to treatment outcome was determined.

In a comprehensive *Psychological Bulletin* review of the clinical use of hypnosis, Wadden and Anderton (1982) concluded that the experimental use of hypnosis for alcoholism has lagged behind the hypnotic experimental research for obesity or cigarette smoking. In a national survey of state hospitals, hypnotherapy was only used in 3% of

those hospitals for alcoholism. They concluded that "a hypnotic induction does not appear to add leverage to a standard treatment for alcoholism" (Wadden & Anderton, 1982, p. 227).

Stoil (1989) observed that hypnosis has been applied to treating alcoholics for over a century and hypnosis has been accepted by the American Medical Association (AMA) as a medically valid tool. However, systematic experimental evaluation of the use of hypnosis with alcoholism

has been hampered by the unique role of hypnosis as a cultural artifact, by problems in defining and verifying hypnotic interventions, by individual and situational variation in hypnotizability, and by difficulty in separating hypnosis from the therapies to which it is applied. (Stoil, 1989, p. 31)

He suggested that the experimental situation makes it difficult to appropriately assess and control for the integration of hypnotic routines into various treatments and implied that clinicians are likely to continue to use hypnosis in the treatment of alcoholics, basing their claims for "its effectiveness on intuition, especially since no study has demonstrated that hypnotherapy is contraindicated for patients requesting its use" (Stoil, 1989, p. 31).

Orman (1991) used hypnotherapy as a reframing technique with an individual addicted to cocaine and alcohol. He used age regression, age progression, reframing, ideodynamic finger responses, and symbolic task suggestions along with more direct suggestions. Drug and alcohol abstinence was maintained at 6- and 12-month follow-up for this client. Page and Handley (1993) reported on an unusual case of cocaine addiction in which an individual successfully treated herself, using a commercial hypnosis weight loss tape in which she mentally substituted "weight control" for the word "coke." There was no external therapeutic support for this person, and the client also remained in an environment in which drugs were readily available. The client remained drug-free for 9 years. The client credited her success to the practice of the self-hypnosis tape on a twice-a-day basis for 2 years.

Miller (1991) suggested that hypnosis "has not been developed to its fullest potential in treatment programs for addictive and compulsive behaviors" (p. 2) and that it is underutilized in the addictions field. He felt that hypnosis could enable the patient to develop greater self-control and self-discipline. Observing that "suggestion" is a "very powerful healing tool in the mind/body healing process" Miller (1991, p. 7) suggested that hypnosis could be helpful to the alcoholic in enhancing rapport, changing belief systems, controlling physiological responses, and helping with personality reintegration. He concluded that suggestive therapy and hypnosis could provide an opportunity to help a person disrupt usual patterns of behavior, break free of those usual patterns, and begin to make changes to promote new growth and development.

MODELS OF ADDICTION AND POSSIBLE HYPNOTIC INTERVENTIONS

Hypnosis has been found effective in altering cognitive and affective states (Brown & Fromm, 1986; Hammond, 1990; Nash & Barnier, 2008). Since negative affective states lead to relapse (Deffenbacher, 1995; Kassinove, 1995; Marlatt & Gordon, 1985; Reilly, Clark, Shopshire, Lewis, & Sorensen, 1994), using hypnosis as a treatment modality to reduce and control anxiety, anger, and other negative affects may be helpful in reducing potential triggers to relapse. Given a counterconditioning model (Sarafino, 2001), if individuals can learn to not only reduce negative affect but also substitute positive affective states when in high-stress situations, they may develop the skills necessary to prevent the vicious cycle back to drug and alcohol abuse.

McPeake, Kennedy, and Gordon (1991) theorized that attaining altered states of consciousness is a basic human motive, a motive that is destructively pursued by substance-dependent individuals. Failing "to address patient's needs for alternative methods of achieving altered states of consciousness" (McPeake, Kennedy, & Gordon, 1991, p. 75) may be part of the reason for relapse. Hence, integrating hypnosis into substance abuse treatment as a way of achieving a more "healthy" or "productive" altered state of consciousness may facilitate relapse prevention.

Prochaska, DiClemente, and Norcross (1992, 1994) developed a "stage" model for better understanding addictions. Their "stages of change" model links particular processes of change with the five major stages of change: precontemplation, contemplation, preparation, action, and maintenance. Cognitive processes appear more important in the earlier stages of precontemplation and contemplation, while behavioral change processes are more effective during the action and maintenance stages (Prochaska et al., 1992). Prochaska et al. (1994) suggest that when individuals are in the action phase of change, these individuals should concentrate on the change processes of counterconditioning, stimulus control, and contingency management. These are the processes for which Prochaska et al. (1994) found support in reference to 12 problematic behaviors including nicotine and cocaine addiction. Hence, hypnotic suggestions may be useful in modifying cognitive and behavioral processes to help with substance abuse cessation and relapse prevention.

Witkiewitz and Marlatt (2004) developed a dynamic model of relapse in which tonic processes interact with phasic responses, in the context of high-risk situations, leading to possible relapse back into substance abuse. Staying abstinent or, conversely, relapsing is a function of intrapersonal determinants (self-efficacy, outcome expectancies, cravings, motivation, coping skills, emotional states) and interpersonal determinants (positive social support, negative peer pressure). Using hypnosis to modify any of these determinants may be helpful with augmenting abstinence and preventing relapse.

A RANDOMIZED, CONTROLLED STUDY OF HYPNOSIS FOR RELAPSE PREVENTION

Pekala et al. (2004) completed a randomized controlled study comparing hypnosis with relaxation/stress management, a transtheoretical approach to the addictions (Prochaska et al., 1994), and a control group, looking at relapse prevention within a chronic substance abuse population. Two hundred and sixty-one participants suffering from chronic drug and alcohol abuse were matriculated into a study on relapse prevention. The average age of the participants was 47 years. Each participant had an average alcohol use of 24 years, five years of heroin use, nine years of cocaine use, and 11 years of marijuana use. For the hypnosis intervention, individuals were asked to play one of these four self-hypnosis protocols (relapse prevention, self-esteem enhancement, negative affect reduction/control, serenity enhancement) on a once-a-day basis for several months. The individuals were contacted after discharge at about seven-week follow-up.

Multivariate analysis of variance (MANOVA)/ analysis of variance (ANOVA) "interaction analyses for the hypnosis intervention suggest(ed) that with severely addicted individuals practicing a self-hypnosis audiotape at least 4 times a week post-discharge was associated with increased self-esteem and serenity, and decreased anger/ impulsivity" (Pekala et al., 2004, p. 292), in comparison to individuals who played the audiotapes less often or the control group. (No such effects were found for the relaxation/stress management or the transtheoretical interventions.) Of those individuals in the hypnosis group who remained abstinent after discharge, 15% of the relative variance, as assessed by regression analyses, was due to practice of the self-hypnosis audio tapes. Twenty-two percent of the relative variance of those who practiced the self-hypnosis audio tapes was predicted from the Phenomenology of Consciousness Inventory: Hypnotic Assessment Procedure (PCI-HAP) hypnoidal state score, an estimator of Weitzenhoffer's (2002) conception of "trance" (Pekala & Maurer, 2013), suggesting that practice of the audio self-hypnosis audiotapes was related to hypnotic responsivity. (The PCI-HAP [Phenomenology of Consciousness Inventory: Hypnotic Assessment Procedure; Pekala, 1995a, 1995b] was used to measure hypnotic responsivity.)

SERENITY ENHANCEMENT

Pekala, Kumar, Maurer, Elliott-Carter, and Moon (2009) looked at the relationships between self-esteem, serenity, and anger/impulsivity within a chronic substance abuse population. Their research suggested that besides targeting negative feelings such as anger and anxiety, that is, teaching strategies to reduce and control such negative feelings, therapists should also focus on enhancing positive feelings, such as those of serenity, and fostering a

sense of connection with a meaningful universe or "higher power." Roberts and Cunningham (1990) reported that serenity encompasses more than just inner peace and tranquility; it also includes unconditional self-acceptance, an equanimous present-centeredness, and a spiritual or meaningful perspective of one's world and one's self.

The positive and existential effects (May, Angel, & Ellenberger, 1958) associated with establishing feelings of inner serenity within a more meaningful universe may allow individuals dependent on alcohol/other drugs to begin to understand and try to transcend their struggle with illicit substances. This is why Bill Wilson, when under treatment of severe alcoholism, was able to cofound Alcoholics Anonymous (AA) only after he had his transcendental or spiritual experience:

> Suddenly, the room lit up with a great white light. I was caught up into an ecstasy which there are not words to describe. It seemed to me, in the mind's eye, that I was on a mountain and that a wind not of air but of spirit was blowing. And then it burst upon me that I was a free man. Slowly the ecstasy subsided. I lay on the bed, but now for a time I was in another world, a new world of consciousness. All about me and through me there was a wonderful feeling of Presence, and I thought to myself, "So this is the God of the preachers!" A great peace stole over me. (May, Angel, & Ellenberger, 1958, p. 63)

Allowing the person dependent on alcohol/other drugs to actively participate in feelings of inner serenity, possibly through self-hypnosis, meditation, and other types of spiritual practices, may allow this individual to access a healthy substitution of existential (Marcel, 1950) or spiritual (Evans, 1993) meaningfulness, a meaningfulness that he or she was previously trying to find through "spirits" and other types of destructive, mind-altering pharmacological substances. As mentioned previously, McPeake, Kennedy, and Gordon (1991) theorized that attaining altered states of consciousness is a basic human motive, a motive that is destructively pursued by individuals dependent on alcohol/other drugs. Hence, failing "to address patient's needs for alternative methods of achieving altered states of consciousness" (McPeake, Kennedy, & Gordon, 1991, p. 75) may be a reason for relapse.

The following transcript was one of the four hypnosis protocols that were used as hypnotic interventions with the substance abuse population reported in the preceding text (Pekala et al., 2004). The other three hypnotic interventions were self-esteem enhancement, anxiety and anger (negative affect) management/reduction, and relapse prevention. The particular transcript in the following text focused on serenity enhancement. (As mentioned, individuals who played the self-hypnosis audiotapes at least four times a week had increased self-esteem and decreased anger/impulsivity in comparison to individuals who played the self-hypnosis audiotapes less often.)

Prior to the transcript listed in the following text, participants experienced a "body scan" relaxation protocol (progressive relaxation but without the tensing), and a "mind-calm" deepening routine: "counting from 10 to 1, while your mind becomes more and more calm and more and more empty." Space limitations precluded including the full (deepening) transcript here.

". . . You are now deeply relaxed. Your mind is very, very calm and very much at ease. Just continue to relax and experience the deep hypnotic state that you are now in. In that state it is much easier for your conscious, subconscious, and unconscious to work together as one to help you become more the person you would like to be. It is much easier to give you suggestions, for you to give yourself suggestions, to become more the person you would like to be.

A very good way to help you let go of urges related to the use of drugs and alcohol is to enter into a serene and peaceful state of mind. When your mind is serene, tranquil, and peaceful, you are able to make better judgments, solve everyday problems more effectively, and remain free of the desire to use drugs and alcohol.

I am going to show you how to enter this serene and tranquil state of mind, a serene state of mind that you can use to lead a better, happier, and more productive life, one that is free of drug and alcohol use. I am going to show you a way to cultivate a serene and a peaceful state of mind that will help you become a happier, more productive, and a more serene person.

By practicing this self-hypnosis serenity technique, you will be able to attain a calm, peaceful, and serene state of mind. This inner serenity that will allow you to feel more at home and at peace with yourself. Such serenity can help you enjoy the little ordinary things of life with a sense of thankfulness and a sense of wonder. By experiencing this inner joy and serenity, you will be better able to enjoy the little things of life, appreciating the beauty and joy of existence, by living each day fully and deeply in the present. By enjoying deeply this inner serenity, you will feel a peace and contentment, an inner sense of bliss and joy as you begin to live fully and deeply in the present, becoming absorbed and enchanted with the pure mystery of life.

You can begin to use your breathing to begin to access this inner serenity. All you need to do is inhale and slowly exhale, and as you slowly exhale, feel yourself moving deeper and deeper into a joyful state of inner peace, inner tranquility, inner serenity. As you inhale and especially as you slowly exhale, allow yourself to let go of urges and conflicts and move deeper and deeper into this serene state of mind. You can use this inner state of inner peace and inner tranquility to cultivate a state opposite to the state of wanting to use drugs or alcohol, for you can begin to experience and enjoy the beauty, the zest, and excitement of living the mystery of life with an openness to all that it has to offer.

By focusing on your breathing, you can let go of the tension and worry and move deeper and deeper into feelings of serenity and inner joy. As you exhale, let your exhalation be about twice as long as your inhalation and allow yourself to move deeper and deeper, deeper and deeper into this state of inner peace and serenity, a state of mind where you feel very safe, secure, and very at ease. This is a state of mind within your heart and your soul that you can go to whenever you start to feel anxious or insecure or have cravings. As you enter this serene state of mind, you find that your feelings of anxiety, insecurity, and any cravings simply fade and vanish away. In their place, feel an increased desire to become a better and more productive person, a desire to help the world become a better place to live, and a need to do service toward others.

For the next minute I'm going to stop talking, and I want you to use your breathing, and as you exhale, allow yourself to move deeper and deeper, and deeper into that state of inner peace, inner tranquility, inner serenity, where there is hope, where there is inner harmony and inner contentment. A state of total peace and total contentment. So for the next minute, continue to relax to your breathing and allow yourself to move deeper and deeper into the serene state of mind. After a minute I will start talking again, and will then give you a variety of other suggestions and affirmations. [Pause one minute.]

That's fine. And as I continue to talk, allow yourself to continue to be bathed in these feelings of inner peace, inner serenity, and inner tranquility.

Many people have suggested that one of the best ways to deal with urges is to develop a spiritual perspective, a spiritual approach to the universe. By spiritual I do not necessarily mean religious, or partaking of one particular religious creed or code of conduct. Rather I mean an openness to the goodness, the bounty of the universe. Feel connected within that universe, feel a meaningful connection with that universe, where you have a necessary and important role to play. And in the deep hypnotic state that you are now in, I want you to begin to feel a connectedness with the universe. No longer feeling lost or alone, no longer feeling apathetic or empty, but realizing you have an important part to play in the bigger scheme of things. Helping yourself to be a better person, helping the world to become a better place to be.

Feel connected with the universe. Allow yourself to feel more comfortable with who you are. Feel more connected with those around you with an increased sense of trust in the wisdom of the universe. Allow yourself to live within that wisdom. Let go of the past and the future, and live within the present, taking one day at a time, living deeply and fully in the present.

Taking one day at a time, but remaining firmly focused on your sobriety. Firmly focused on your conviction to remain abstinent. Let go of the past and its mistakes. Let go of the fears of the future. Live fully and deeply in the present. Living in the

present does not necessarily mean being attached to the present. Addiction to drugs and alcohol usually means excessive attachment to these substances and other addictions that may come our way.

You want to be able to live within the present without being attached to the present. Being in the world, but not of the world, as the saying goes. Allow yourself to begin to let go of desires and negative emotions, of desires for drugs, alcohol, and other addictions. Allow yourself to develop an even-minded position or perspective on the world. A perspective on the world where you won't become attached to drugs, to alcohol, or to other things like sex or ego.

And as you continue to practice this exercise as best you can on your own, you'll become better and better at becoming aware of urges when they begin to arise and being able to let go of those urges, becoming detached from those urges, and moving instead into the serenity and peace within. You'll become better and better at being able to let go of those urges, becoming detached from those urges, and moving instead into the serenity and peace within. Knowing that the wisdom of the universe is there to help you, to support you.

But the universe helps those who help themselves. So you realize the importance of actively pursuing all reasonable avenues available for effective problem solving. You will find yourself becoming better at developing strategies to deal with the problems in living as they arise. You will be more proactive instead of reactive in dealing with the problems that confront you in day-to-day living. And you will willingly and actively pursue all reasonable avenues to deal with problems as they arise.

In your everyday life, some situations may be quite difficult to change. Even in those difficult situations, you will find that you will be able to maintain a sense of serenity and do what needs to be done to stay away from alcohol and drugs. You will be able to accept situations, which you cannot change. You will not return to your old ways of getting away from difficult situations by using alcohol or drugs. And in those situations that are very difficult to change, you will allow yourself the flexibility to make the internal changes that are needed to cope more effectively and more easily without returning to past drug and alcohol use.

As you develop an increased self-acceptance, you will realize that sometimes we can feel too self-important, too puffed up with our own goals and desires that we forget to give to others and forget the needs of others. It is the belief of many spiritual paths that it is only in giving to others that we can receive what we need from the universe. So you will become increasingly aware of the part, of the meaning you have within your universe, and do what needs to be done, not only to make your life more meaningful and healthier but also to give to others as a way to be a part of the larger scheme of things, to make a contribution to a larger cause.

With an increase in self-acceptance, you will also find that you will become increasingly accepting of others to establish more meaningful relationships. And not only will you give to others but you will also find yourself becoming more forgiving of others. Many times we harbor resentments, we harbor ill feelings because of the ways we have been treated or because of what has been done to us. As you increase your feelings of inner serenity, you will find it easier and easier for you to let go of those past resentments and you will be able to forgive others and yourself. This sense of inner serenity and spirituality will allow you to live fully in the present . . . letting go of past resentments . . . trusting in the wisdom of the universe . . . and the wonderful spiritual and healing energy that you have begun to feel and experience.

At this point I'd like you to become more aware, more deeply aware than ever before, of a spiritual energy, a feeling of spiritual upliftment or a spiritual essence within you. Now that I call your attention to it, I want you to become increasingly aware of this spiritual essence or energy within you. Allow this spiritual energy to give you the commitment, the willpower, and the strength you need to deal more appropriately, more effectively with problems as they arise. Feel energized and supported in your desire and goal to remain drug- and alcohol-free. Feel your whole body, your mind and spirit being permeated with this benevolent spiritual healing energy so you can go forward with hope and optimism for a better life.

Some people may feel this spiritual energy bubbling up from within; bubbling up from within the area of your heart, or your stomach, or your diaphragm. Or, you may feel it coming from without as if a divine, heavenly light from above is pouring down upon you. Or, you may feel this spiritual healing energy not only bubbling up from within but also shining down from above. Allow yourself to feel the beneficence, the spiritual healing energy of the universe enveloping you in feelings of hope, and joy, and care.

For the next minute or so, I'm going to stop talking and I want you to feel that benevolent healing spiritual energy becoming a part of who you are. Allow yourself to feel stronger, allow yourself to feel that inner joy, that inner spiritual energy permeating your body, your mind, your soul and spirit. Allow yourself to become more and more committed than ever before to this spiritual path without drugs and alcohol. Committed to becoming the healthiest, the most fully functioning person you can envision yourself to be.

In a few moments I'm going to stop talking and I want you to feel this spiritual, healing energy bubbling up from within and shining down upon you from above. Feel this spiritual, healing energy uplifting your soul, your spirit, your mind, and your body, helping you to become stronger, more harmonious, more in tune with the spiritual aspects of yourself that need to be developed. So for the next minute or so, just enjoy that spiritual healing energy permeating your entire being. Allow your mind and spirit to be bathed and healed in this golden light of spiritual, healing energy. See and visualize yourself within this golden spiritual energy and feel it healing you. I will stop talking for the next minute or so. After about a minute I will start talking again.

[Pause one minute.]

That's fine. Continue to feel that soothing, spiritual energy permeating your entire being. In a few moments I'm going to count from 1 to 7, and as I do, you'll wake up, you'll come out of the state you are now in and be in your normal, waking state. Yet that spiritual healing energy will continue to stay with you. Just continue to remain relaxed and at ease, relaxed and calm. I'm going to count *aloud from 1 to 7 and as I do, I would like you to count along silently with me. With each number that I say aloud, with each number that you say silently to yourself, you will become more and more alert, more and more awake, more and more aware. At 7, your eyes will begin to open, and you will wake up feeling alert, refreshed, relaxed, and at ease. No longer hypnotized, but in your normal, waking state of consciousness. And that spiritual healing energy will continue to remain with you in the hours and days ahead.*

Here we go. 1 . . . 2 . . . 3. Becoming more and more alert, more and more awake. 4 . . . 5. More and more awake, more and more alert, more and more aware. 6 . . . 7. Eyes beginning to open. Awake, alert, relaxed, and at ease. Eyes opened. Revitalized with a renewed sense of feeling of a strong spiritual connection that will keep you serene in the most difficult of situations in your daily life."

CONCLUSION AND FUTURE DIRECTIONS

Despite the checkered history of hypnosis within the addictions field, the aforementioned review suggests that hypnosis may be useful as an adjunctive strategy for helping individuals with drug and alcohol addiction issues and also for relapse prevention. Integrating hypnosis with suggestions for increasing self-esteem and serenity, and decreasing anger/impulsivity, variables that prior research (Connors, Toscova, & Tonigan, 1999; Hill & Durm, 1997; Reilly et al., 1994) have shown to be associated with abstinence, may be a means to help individuals deal better with their drug and alcohol problems, and also assist with relapse prevention.

Self-hypnosis training may allow the drug and alcohol user to access altered states of consciousness in a nonpharmacological, nondestructive manner, while augmenting self-esteem, serenity, and positive behavioral processes such as counterconditioning, stimulus control, and contingency management (Prochaska et al., 1992). Probably more so than relaxation and meditation, self-hypnosis training can be used for not only letting go of negative effect but also fostering positive affective strategies by targeting those specific areas that may need to be better developed. Via the use of

such hypnotic suggestions and associated hypnotic interventions, the drug and alcohol user may then begin to substitute more positive and healthy cognitive/behavior patterns for the previous self-destructive ones.

DISCLAIMER

The content of this chapter does not represent the views of the Department of Veterans Affairs or those of the United States Government.

REFERENCES

Brown, D. P., & Fromm, E. (1986). *Hypnotherapy and hypnoanalysis*. Hillsdale, NJ: Lawrence Erlbaum.

Carlson, E. B., & Putnam, F. W. (1992). *Manual for the dissociative experiences scale*. Beloit, WI: Beloit College.

Carlson, E. B., & Putnam, F. W. (1993). An update on the dissociative experiences scale. *Dissociation*, 6, 16–27.

Compton, W. M., Thomas, Y. F., Stinson, F. S., & Grant, B. F. (2007). Prevalence, correlates, disability, and comorbidity of *DSM-IV* drug abuse and dependence in the United States: Results from the national epidemiological survey on alcohol and related conditions. *Archives of General Psychiatry*, 64(5), 566–576. doi:10.1001/archpsyc.64.5.566

Connors, G. J., Toscova, R. T., & Tonigan, J. S. (1999). Serenity. In W. R. Miller (Ed.), *Integrating spirituality into treatment* (pp. 235–250). Washington, DC: American Psychological Association.

Deffenbacher, J. L. (1995). Ideal treatment package for adults with anger disorders. In H. Kassinove (Ed.), *Anger disorders: Definition, diagnosis, and treatment* (pp. 151–172). Washington, DC: Taylor & Francis.

Erickson, M. H. (1976). The interspersal technique for symptom correction and pain control. *American Journal of Clinical Hypnosis*, 8, 198–200.

Evans, D. (1993). *Spirituality and human nature*. Albany, NY: State University of New York Press.

Hammond, D. C. (1990). *Handbook of hypnotic suggestions and metaphors*. New York, NY: W. W. Norton.

Harwood, H. (2000). *Updating estimates of the economic costs of alcohol abuse in the United States: Estimates, update methods, and data*. Rockville, MD: National Institute on Alcohol Abuse and Alcoholism.

Hartman, B. J. (1972). The use of hypnosis in the treatment of drug addiction. *Journal of the National Medical Association*, 64(1), 35–38.

Hasin, D. S., Stinson, F. S., Ogburn, E., & Grant, B. F. (2007). Prevalence, correlates, disability, and comorbidity of *DSM-IV* alcohol abuse and dependence in the United States: Results from the National Epidemiological Survey on alcohol and related conditions. *Archives of General Psychiatry, 64*(7), 830–842. doi:10.1001/archpsyc.64.7.830

Hill, T. D., & Durm, M. W. (1997). Temporal association of substance abuse and self-esteem. *Psychological Reports, 80*(3 Pt 1). 1058 doi:10.2466/pr0.1997.80.3.1058

Kassinove, H. (1995). *Anger disorders: Definition, diagnosis, and treatment.* Washington, DC: Taylor & Francis.

Katz, N. W. (1980). Hypnosis and the addictions: A critical review. *Addictive Behaviors, 5*(1), 41–47.

Marcel, G. (1950). *The mystery of being.* South Bend, ID: Gateway Editions.

Marlatt, G. A., & Gordon, J. R. (1985). *Relapse prevention: Maintenance strategies in the treatment of addictive behaviors.* New York, NY: Guilford Press.

May, R., Angel, E., & Ellenberger, H. F. (1958). *Existence: A new dimension in psychiatry and psychology.* New York, NY: Simon and Schuster.

McPeake, J. D., Kennedy, B. P., & Gordon, S. M. (1991). Altered states of consciousness therapy: A missing component in alcohol and drug rehabilitation treatment. *Journal of Substance Abuse Treatment, 8*(1–2), 75–82.

Miller, W. A. (1991). Using hypnotherapy in communicating with the recovering addicted patient. *Alcoholism Treatment Quarterly, 8,* 1–18.

Nash, M. R., & Barnier, A. J. (2008). *The Oxford handbook of hypnosis: Theory, research, and practice.* Oxford, UK: Oxford University Press.

Orman, D. J. (1991). Reframing of an addiction via hypnotherapy: A case presentation. *American Journal of Clinical Hypnosis, 33*(4), 263–271. doi:10.1080/00029157.1991.10402944

Page, R. A., & Handley, G. W. (1993). The use of hypnosis in cocaine addiction. *American Journal of Clinical Hypnosis, 36*(2), 120–123. doi:10.1080/00029157.1993.10403054

Pekala, R. J. (1995a). A short, unobtrusive hypnotic-assessment procedure for assessing hypnotizability level: I. Development and research. *American Journal of Clinical Hypnosis, 37,* 271–283.

Pekala, R. J. (1995b). A short unobtrusive hypnotic induction for assessing hypnotizability level: II. Clinical case reports. *American Journal of Clinical Hypnosis, 37,* 284–293.

Pekala, R. J., Ainslie, G., Elliott, N. C., Mullen, K. J., Salinger, M. M., Masten, E., & Kumar, V. K. (2000). Assessing substance abuse: An automated self-report inventory. *Federal Practitioner, 17,* 27–39.

Pekala, R. J., Kumar, V. K., Ainslie, A., Elliott, N. C., Mullen, K. J., Salinger, M. M., & Mullen, P. (2000). The child abuse and trauma scale: Reliability, validity, and subtypes in a substance abuse population. *Indian Journal of Clinical Psychology, 27,* 262–272.

Pekala, R. J., Kumar, V. K., Maurer, R., Elliott-Carter, N. C., & Moon, E. (2009). Self-esteem and its relationship to serenity and anger/impulsivity in an alcohol/other drug dependent population: Implications for treatment. *Alcoholism Treatment Quarterly, 27,* 94–112.

Pekala, R. J., & Maurer, R. M. (2013). A cross-validation of two differing measures of hypnotic depth. *International Journal of Clinical and Experimental Hypnosis, 61*(1), 81–110. doi:10.1080/00207144.2013.729439

Pekala, R. J., Maurer, R., Kumar, V. K., Elliott, N. C., Masten, E., Moon, E., & Salinger, M. (2004). Self-hypnosis relapse prevention training with chronic drug/alcohol users: Effects of self-esteem, affect, and relapse. *American Journal of Clinical Hypnosis, 46*(4), 281–297. doi:10.1080/00029157.2004.10403613

Prochaska, J. O., DiClemente, C., & Norcross, J. C. (1992). In search of how people change. *American Psychologist, 47*(9), 1102–1114. doi.org/10.1037/0003-066x.47.9.1102.

Prochaska, J. O., Diclemente, C. C., & Norcross, J. C. (1994). *Changing for good.* New York, NY: Avon.

Reilly, P. M., Clark, H. W., Shopshire, M. S., Lewis, E. W., & Sorensen, D. J. (1994). Anger management and temper control: Critical components of posttraumatic stress disorder and substance abuse treatment. *Journal of Psychoactive Drugs, 26*(4), 401–407. doi:10.1080/02791072.1994.10472460

Roberts, K., & Cunningham, G. (1990). Serenity: Concept analysis and measurement. *Educational Gerontology, 16,* 577–589.

Sarafino, E. P. (2001). *Behavior modification: Understanding principles of behavior change.* Mountain View, CA: Mayfield Publishing.

Stoil, M. J. (1989). Problems in the evaluation of hypnosis in the treatment of alcoholism. *Journal of Substance Abuse Treatment, 6*(1), 31–35. doi.org/10.1016/0740-5472(89)90017-2.

Wadden, T. A., & Anderton, C. H. (1982). The clinical use of hypnosis. *Psychological Bulletin, 91*(2), 215–243.

Wadden, T. A., & Penrod, J. H. (1981). Hypnosis in the treatment of alcoholism: A review and appraisal. *American Journal of Clinical Hypnosis, 24*(1), 41–47. doi:10.1080/00029157.1981.10403282

Weitzenhoffer, A. M. (2002). Scales, scales, and more scales. *American Journal of Clinical Hypnosis, 44*(3-4), 209–220. doi:10.1080/00029157.2002.10403481

Witkiewitz, K., & Marlatt, G. A. (2004). Relapse prevention for alcohol and drug problems: That was Zen, this is Tao. *American Psychologist, 59*(4), 224–235. doi:10.1037/0003-066X.59.4.224

Affect Regulation

Carolyn Daitch

Patients who present with affect dysregulation suffer from a variety of clinical and subclinical impediments to their daily functioning. Affect dysregulation is an affective style that can be conceptualized as having four main components. One is a distorted and unnecessarily intense qualitative appraisal of routine stimuli and interpersonal contact. Thus, the intensity of the emotional reaction does not correspond to that indicated by the environmental trigger. The second is an accompanying psychophysiological hyperarousal. Psychophysiological markers can range from elevated heart rate and rapid breathing to the bradycardic rhythms of the freeze response that also result from autonomic nervous system arousal. The third component consists of emotional, cognitive, and/or behavioral manifestations of affect dysregulation. These frequently include the internal experience of being flooded or overwhelmed with emotion and feeling out of control. Cognitively, a person may suffer from extreme anticipatory anxiety or rumination. Behaviorally, avoidance responses, angry outbursts, crying episodes, and other manifestations of intense emotion are often exhibited. Fourth, these intense surges of emotional over-reactivity are not easily quelled. Once triggered, individuals with affect dysregulation take longer to return to a normal equilibrated state.

In addition to the internal suffering affect dysregulation causes, as this reactivity is externalized, it can precipitate relationship conflicts. Those close to the dysregulated individual may feel at the mercy of the person's labile mood and overreactions. Common interpersonal stressors such as criticism, misunderstanding, lack of consideration from the other, and fear of abandonment can be problematic in any relationship. But for those with affect dysregulation, such relational triggers can lead to a destructive escalation of interpersonal conflict.

Unchecked it blocks the healing of the inevitable ruptures particularly in intimate relationships. Not only can inability to manage affect interfere with romantic/marital relationships, it can also be problematic in other relationships with family and friends. On the work front, dysregulation can lead to conflict with colleagues and employers and can lead to termination.

Clinically, affect dysregulation is a component of diagnoses such as attention deficit hyperactivity disorder, obsessive compulsive disorder, posttraumatic stress disorder, and bipolar disorder, as well as many of the personality disorders (Daitch, 2007). In addition, affect dysregulation contributes to many subclinical problems such as marital and family problems that bring clients into psychotherapy. Whether clinical or subclinical, the strong surges of emotion that typify the experience of affect dysregulation arise rapidly, persist with overpowering force, and are not easily quelled by logic-based thoughts. This presents a challenge for the treatment of affect regulation. While cognitive interventions alone can address the distorted attributions that typify overreactivity, they are often insufficient to address the psychophysiological arousal.

BENEFITS OF INCORPORATING HYPNOSIS INTO TREATMENT

Incorporating hypnosis into the treatment of affect dysregulation provides a powerful and effective means to address this psychophysiological arousal. Hypnotic interventions can address the psychophysiological overload that typifies affect dysregulation by providing patients with quick, explicit techniques to help them manage their emotions. . . . The relaxation response alone, usually elicited in a hypnotic state, can diminish the physiological arousal and emotional flooding that together often lead to escalation of internal and external conflict. Hypnosis is an ideal intervention to help clients stabilize emotions (Horevitz, 1996).

Contributions by those such as Hammond (1990) and Fromm and Nash (1992) have established the effectiveness of hypnosis as an adjunct to many therapeutic treatments. The integration of hypnosis with cognitive behavioral therapy (CBT) has been demonstrated to produce more effective treatment outcomes across a variety of clinical disorders than do CBT interventions alone (Alladin & Alibhai, 2007; Kirsch, Montgomery, & Sapirstein, 1995; Schoenberger, 2000).

Hypnosis can help clients modulate emotional reactivity in the following ways (adapted from Daitch, 2007):

- Elicit a relaxation response
- Engage self-soothing
- Change cognitions
- Develop a dual perspective by working with ego states
- Rehearse desired responses
- Develop impulse control

The application of clinical hypnosis in the treatment of affect dysregulation is demonstrated in the case study that follows.

CASE EXAMPLE

Sarah, age 45, was referred to me by another therapist who was seeing her and her husband for marriage and family counseling. The other therapist felt that Sarah's volatility was impeding treatment progress. While Sarah's behaviors did not indicate any specific clinical disorder, her affect dysregulation in response to daily life stressors was causing significant disruption in her marriage and challenging her ability to parent well. Both Sarah and her husband, Terry, maintained full-time jobs while raising their two sons, ages 7 and 11. Terry worked from home as a consultant and was there at home when their sons returned from school. Conversely, Sarah's mechanical engineering job necessitated long hours as well as a long daily commute.

Sarah's Background

Sarah is the second born with five siblings. She is the eldest girl. She described her father as often remote and cold, and only intermittently gave her attention. He worked long hours to support the family and often fell asleep in front of the television after dinner. However, Sarah reported that he would welcome Sarah whenever she went to his workroom in the basement and watched him tinker with household projects. Sarah reported that these times alone with her father, away from the chaos of the family, were special to her.

Sarah was the classic parentified child, who, at an early age, had responsibilities taking care of the younger siblings along with housekeeping and preparing meals for the family. Although she would get sporadic recognition from her mother for her work, Sarah described her mother as very critical and demanding. Sarah's mother would yell at her if the children were not well behaved. One of her younger brothers was hard to control and she felt it was her task to keep him in line, an objective that she often failed to meet.

When stressed, Sarah's mother would yell at all the children, berating them with a laundry list of how they disappointed her. Sarah recalled her mother stating on a number of occasions that she wished she had pursued her career as a dancer and not had "all these kids." Sarah's mother demanded that the house be in "company-perfect condition" at all times. When asked if she had any fond memories of her mother, Sarah said she enjoyed getting her mother's attention and praise Sarah helped with the cleaning.

In view of her relationship with her mother, it was not surprising that Sarah was extraordinarily sensitive to perceived criticism. If she felt that her husband or her children were critical or judgmental, she sometimes reacted with rage or tears. At times when Sarah's emotionality was too much to bear, her husband Terry would withdraw. This withdrawal triggered the disconnection she had experienced with her father.

Sarah admitted that her anger was out of control and that the contempt she expressed toward her husband and children was not only hurtful to them but to herself as well. "I am turning into my mother," she would exclaim as she recognized that her own behavior with her children often mirrored her mother's emotional style. She knew that her angry verbal outbursts were probably destructive to her family, just as her mother's were.

She described her husband as a terrible housekeeper. She was particularly vulnerable to emotional overwhelming whenever she arrived home exhausted to find the house in a mess.

As she recounted in the first session: "Terry's working from home is great because it means he can be free to get the kids from school and supervise homework, but he never cleans up after himself—and he's teaching that to the kids. On my drive home, I dread seeing the dishes in the sink, piles of paper on the kitchen table, and the kids' afternoon snack and crumbs all over the family room. It's like going home to a disaster zone each day."

The general state of the house combined with her fatigue would often result in significant affect dysregulation. Sarah reported frequently slamming her briefcase on the counter, banging the pots and pans while fixing dinner, and responding sharply to her children's requests. "I hate myself for it, but I find myself yelling at them, berating them for being lazy and inconsiderate. I know it's reasonable for me to simply ask that everyone pick up after themselves. But I can't seem to do it without flying off the handle and yelling at everyone—even though I know that only makes things worse."

Goals of Treatment

- Modulate emotions with self-soothing
- Increase access to mature parts of self
- Change cognitions
- Develop a dual perspective by working with ego states
- Contain verbally damaging remarks
- Rehearse desired nonreactive behaviors
- Manage fatigue and blood sugar
- Link desired nonreactive behaviors with inevitably occurring triggers
- Establish and maintain the habit of taking time each day to practice emotional regulation techniques

Assessment/Psychoeducation (Session 1)

When I asked Sarah what her hope for therapy was, without hesitation she said that she wanted to break the cycle of the out-of-control parent. In our first session, after assessing her, I provided psychoeducation on affect dysregulation. In this process,

we addressed the shame that Sarah was experiencing. I validated her desire for a clean and serene home environment. Further, I stated how normal it was to be at the end of one's rope when one was hungry and tired after a long day.

Because Sarah was so damaged by judgment in childhood, addressing the shame component was essential and needed to be part of the treatment plan. The repetitive message in her childhood was that she was fundamentally flawed. In adult life, she generalized that message to her primary relationships, viewing herself as an inadequate wife and parent.

I outlined the treatment plan that we would be following. We would not begin to implement the affect-regulation interventions until the second session. However, I taught her one self-soothing technique to begin using immediately: four square breathing, an easy breathing technique for relieving stress and regulating the autonomic nervous system. For this intervention, Sarah also learned to visualize drawing a four-sided box. I directed her as follows:

"As you breathe in to the count of four, imagine drawing the first side of the box, with the line beginning at the bottom of your visual field and progressing vertically upwards. Then, as you hold your breath to the count of four, imagine the line progressing horizontally from left to right, making the top of the box. Next, while you exhale to the count of four, imagine the line progressing downward to form the right side of the box. Finally, as you hold to the count of four, complete the square by drawing the base line horizontally from left to right."

REHEARSAL AND TRANSFER

As part of the introduction to any treatment protocol, I inform clients about the importance of rehearsal of the interventions learned in the sessions. Namely, commitment to rehearsal, or practice, both during and after the clinical hour is essential to transfer the therapeutic learning. I seed the idea that therapy is not a passive process by which new skills are absorbed by simply being present. In this vein, I asked for and received

Sarah's verbal commitment to engage in at-home practice sessions throughout the course of therapy, and explained that at the close of each session she would have new tools to practice at home that week.

I concluded the first and all subsequent sessions with a 5-minute hypnotic rehearsal of the techniques learned in the session. In a trance state, I direct clients to see themselves using the tools that they learned in session outside the office in any scenarios in which they might be triggered. Accordingly, Sarah engaged in a brief hypnotic rehearsal of practicing four square breathing and visualized using the breathing technique in the garage, still in her car, before she entered the house at the end of her workday.

The Time-Out (Sessions 2 and 3)

The first step in establishing affect regulation was teaching Sarah to take immediate, interruptive breaks to cut short the beginning of an overreaction. I encouraged her to get into the habit of taking "time-outs" as soon as she noticed she was upset. These provided Sarah with quiet moments to calm inner turmoil, gain perspective, and plan appropriate dialogue with her husband and children.

■ Initiating Time-Outs (Session 2)

I began by teaching Sarah to quickly catch the warning signs—physiological, emotional, and/or cognitive—that indicated an impending overreaction and the need for a time-out. For Sarah, warning signs included irritation and frustration, accompanied by cognitions such as "I can't believe him. No matter how many times I tell Terry about keeping the house in order, he agrees to but never does." She also agreed to take a time-out every evening before entering the house after work. Sarah informed Terry and her children that she would remain in the car for about five minutes before greeting them in order to "gear down from her day."

Following a hypnotic induction, I gave Sarah the following intervention:

"Time-outs are not just for kids. Even a grown-up like yourself needs to take an immediate break when you first recognize that you are about to lose control and might react in a way that does not represent your best self. We all have reactions when we are upset or when we're triggered . . . and start to react excessively. We might notice tension in our body or tears in our eyes. We might notice our heart beating quickly, or tension in our stomachs. Or feeling that we're angry or about to burst into tears. And we also say words to ourselves. . . . These words and phrases, like 'I can't handle this,' or 'I dread going into a dirty house,' can be used as warning signs . . . they can warn you that you need to take a time-out. And you can acknowledge these indicators without judgment, but with a gentle, compassionate recognition."

■ Self-Soothing in Time-Outs (Session 2)

Next, I taught Sarah a variety of hypnotherapeutic self-soothing techniques to calm the body and mind and, in the process, to create a sense of inner safety and comfort (see Daitch, 2007, for more detailed accounts of these and other self-quieting interventions). These include the eye roll, tight fist, and other breathing techniques.

While initially developed by Spiegel and Spiegel (1978) to assess a patient's hypnotizability, the eye roll technique also allows individuals to quickly focus attention and reach a hypnotic state. I have also found it to be an effective tool to halt affect dysregulation. It is the first of the quick calming techniques I teach for the time-out. Engaging in the eye roll, Sarah directed her gaze toward her eyebrows (eyes open) as if she were trying to stare at her forehead. She held them there, took a deep breath in, and held it while continuing to hold the eyes upward. She then exhaled through her mouth, lowered her eyes, and closed her eyelids.

I taught Sarah the tight fist technique so she could quickly release muscular tension and irritability. This tool facilitates a physical release that comes from tensing and then relaxing the hand, while visualizing transforming the tension into a colored liquid that she could release out of her body.

Attending to the breath by modulating one's breathing rate is a simple but highly effective way to calm the nervous system. I direct clients to use either four square breathing (as previously explained) or any of a number of other breathing techniques I teach them (see Daitch, 2011). Because Sarah responded well to four square breathing, she used it as her second quick calming technique in her time-outs.

I used the scripts for these techniques in succession. Following a hypnotic induction, I gave Sarah the following suggestions:

Eye Roll

"*Would you be willing to learn a very quick and effective tool that could help you to interrupt your reactions? [Wait for client to nod or say "Yes."] Now I'd like you to look upward toward your forehead. Now take a deep breath in through your nose . . . hold the breath while holding your upward gaze. Good. And now just continue holding your eyes upward while slowly fluttering your eyelids closed. And exhale, and relax your eyes. That's right . . . and just go inside and you can wonder how soon you can begin to feel just a bit calmer, perhaps by releasing any unnecessary tension in your body. . . .*"

Tight Fist

"*. . . So begin to scan your body for tension, and if you notice any, imagine that all your worry, fear, and muscular tension is going into one of your hands. Or you may also note some uncomfortable feelings that are present for you, anger, worry, agitation. . . . And place those feelings into your hand as well. Now make a fist with that hand, squeeze it tightly, feel the tension, magnify it, and tighten that fist even more. Tighter . . . as tightly as you can. Now imagine that tension becoming a liquid of any color you choose; imagine your fist absorbing all the distress.*

Now gradually release your fist and imagine the colored liquid flowing to the floor and to the ground, to be absorbed deep into the soil . . . where it will be cleansed and released in the earth far away from you . . . far away from you. . . ."

Four Square Breathing

"*You have already learned that doing a simple breathing technique was a very effective way to calm yourself. So once again, you can use the four square breathing technique to deepen the relaxed state that*

you have already begun to experience. Remember, all you have to do is to breathe in to the count of 4, hold to the count of 4, exhale to the count of 4, and hold to the count of 4. Repeat this cycle 4 times, before you add the visual component you learned in our first session, drawing a box with each cycle. Please continue with this process until you hear my voice again. [Wait for 2 minutes.]

And now that you are more relaxed, you can make a few self-statements that will support your best efforts to regulate your emotions, perhaps saying, 'I can handle it' or 'I release judgment and replace it with love for myself and for my family.' Trust that whatever supportive words come up for you, from your own intuition, are just the right words you need to hear."

I selected these techniques early in treatment not only for their effectiveness but also for the ease with which they can be remembered. This builds in the client a sense of self-agency that elicits a state of equilibrium with the therapist or on her own.

■ Parts of Self in Time-Outs (Session 3)

Having learned to balance her nervous system with the self-soothing techniques, Sarah was ready to learn to access internal resources that could help her manage her emotions more effectively. The parts of self interventions draw from ego-state therapy, which asserts that a family of selves exists within each individual (Watkins, 1993). Typically, these parts of self represent varying developmental levels within the person (Daitch, 2007). In this model, the vulnerable or wounded parts of self can be both nurtured and strengthened (McNeal, 2003). Additionally, the clinician can use ego-state interventions to "selectively amplify or diminish parts of [the client's] experience in order to achieve a higher purpose" (Hammond, 1990, p. 322). The client can then access overlooked internal resources and increase ego strength and maturity (Frederick, 2005; Philips & Frederick, 1995).

The objective of using the parts of self technique was to help Sarah pause and access a mature, wise, and compassionate part. Once accessed, she could use this part to influence her perspective and modulate her reactions. In a state of equilibrium, she could determine whether it was reasonable to react, and if so, how she could best express her feelings to her family.

I taught her the parts of self intervention with the following hypnotherapeutic script. After hypnotic induction, I gave the following suggestions (adapted, with permission, from Daitch, 2007):

"When you stop to think of it, we are all made up of contrasting parts including those parts of us that are young, mature, self-absorbed, empathic, possessive, giving, superficial, and substantive. You might think of many other parts of you that come to mind now. These parts reflect our life experiences . . . losses . . . successes . . . disappointments . . . injuries to our self-esteem . . . relationships with our parents.

And we've been talking about your difficulty containing your resentments toward your husband and the children . . . a kind of reactivity that has been painful for you and for them . . . for some time . . . you and I both already know that it is more effective . . . in relationships . . . to interact from a more developed part of yourself . . . when the goal is for love and reconnection each day . . . and maintaining a wiser perspective . . . indeed the wiser perspective . . . that showing your deep love for them preempts your transient annoyance with their behaviors. It is understandable that when you are tired, stressed, and hungry you revert to the less mature part of yourselves . . . so that it is easy to be critical . . . judgmental . . . which contributes to losing sight of your long-term goal . . . that true connections require . . . empathy . . . compassion . . . generosity . . . and the flexibility to view the world from another's eyes . . . and you have these skills. It is a matter of tapping them . . . tapping your inner resources. It certainly makes sense that when you are experiencing a conflict with your family you can access a mature, strong part of yourself that can not only comfort the younger, less developed parts of yourself but can interact with Terry and the boys in a compassionate . . . understanding . . . empathic way . . . this part of you is always present, even if you temporarily overlook it. So take a minute now to get in touch with that awareness of the more mature part of yourself. . . . Perhaps it would be helpful to remember a situation that you responded to with equanimity and balance . . . when that part of you took center stage. So take a minute to get

in touch with that part now, and let a finger come up when you can feel that part of you coming into your awareness. [Pause.]

Now wait for words to come from the wisest, most evolved, strongest, or even most spiritual part of your being. Maybe images rather than words will come to mind, but really feel your strength, maturity, and compassion . . . look into the eyes of a younger, more vulnerable part of yourself . . . touch [his or her] *hand and reassure* [him or her] *that* [he or she] *is ok and that you . . . the adult part of yourself . . . will handle whatever needs to be handled. Now hold onto this part of self for a moment or two, really feeling how good it feels to be in control. . . . And you can look forward to accessing your wise part of self in your time-outs, moving into just the right state of mind to prepare for those inevitable triggers that we all experience in our lives."*

At the close of this session, Sarah expressed appreciation for the progress she had made in a short time. It is, however, the continued and repetitive application of the tools that would propel her into permanent changes in her reactive style. After an initial honeymoon of enthusiasm about treatment and adherence to time-out sessions, it is common for clients to slip up on practice. Sarah was no exception.

Dealing With Resistance (Session 4)

At the start of session 4, Sarah reported difficulty consistently initiating the time-out interventions when arriving home from work. Despite clients' desire for change at the beginning of therapy and even throughout treatment, it can be difficult to transfer successfully the therapeutic learning from the therapy office to daily life, especially in the face of affect dysregulation. Indeed, research has validated the difficulty of making enduring therapeutic changes (Jacobson & Addis, 1993). Because Sarah reported similar problems, I spent the session teaching her interventions that specifically address resistance.

Following a hypnotic induction, I provided Sarah the intervention that follows:

"It is human nature to fall back on our habituated responses. It's as if we slip mindlessly into well-traveled roads. For you, the well-worn road

is made of strong surges of irritability and judgment when you are disappointed. You and I have already spoken about the fact that it takes practice . . . and lots of practice . . . to create new default responses to old triggers that previously have led to anger . . . irritability . . . and other responses that you don't like.

Now of course, many people experience some resistance to starting or maintaining a new habit. On some days. the resistance might be mild . . . while on other days, it is strong, and may need some firmness and guidance from the part of you that is more disciplined . . . that part of you that is like your inner parent . . . that you can utilize to do what you know is in your best interest . . . even when you're not particularly motivated.

Now I'd like you to imagine taking regular time-outs at the times you have scheduled . . . and whenever you're triggered. And you may be delighted to discover that a gentle, loving pressure may be needed at first, but in time, the habit of taking regular time-outs becomes woven into your daily life. And we've already established that when you push the garage door open . . . upon returning home from work at night . . . that's a perfectly good time for you to quickly access equilibrium by using your eye roll, tight fist, four square breathing, and accessing the most mature parts of yourself. And that would be a perfectly good time for you to support yourself with statements that come to you . . . like 'I am in control of my reactions,' or 'showing love to my family is my most important value.'

And now, make a promise to yourself that you will adhere to your practice . . . contacting that wise, mature part of yourself . . . letting this promise to yourself come from a place of integrity . . . fuelled by your desire to stop the overwhelm and to treat yourself and your family in a loving and respectful way."

Making a promise to herself to practice while in a hypnotic state increased the likelihood that Sarah would follow through on her intention to take time-outs consistently. Because Sarah had shared that integrity was an important value to her, I utilized her words in the hypnotic suggestion to motivate her consistent practice.

Consolidation, Mindfulness, and Termination (Sessions 5 to 7)

In the final three sessions, we reviewed the time-out techniques and elicited Sarah's triggers so she could practice intervening to calm herself. In addition, I taught Sarah mindfulness practices. In recent years, the therapy field has recognized the effectiveness of integrating mindfulness and hypnosis in treatment (Alladin, 2014; Lynn, Das, Hallquist, & Williams, 2006; Yapko, 2011).

I taught Sarah to use mindfulness to observe her thoughts and feelings, name them, and then accept them without judgment. She appreciated learning to have an attitude of detached curiosity about and openness to her immediate experience. After a hypnotic induction, I gave Sarah the following suggestions (adapted, with permission, from Daitch, 2007):

"Sarah, when you practice mindfulness, you start replacing knee-jerk thoughts of 'this is good' or 'this is bad/horrible/not okay' with an attitude of detached observation. You take a step back to simply observe your experience. With mindfulness, you are changing the lens through which you view your emotions. And you and I both know that emotions come and go . . . transient like a change in the weather . . . inevitably shifting . . . never constant. And because they are always changing . . . it might make some sense to learn a way of becoming less controlled by them . . . less attached to them . . . experiencing the inevitable ebb and flow of emotions . . . without being engulfed by them. So, in this moment, would you be open to learning a style of peaceful, nonjudgmental detachment . . . that will allow you to respond differently . . . that will train you to experience emotions with less intensity? You can learn a simple intervention called mindfulness in which you'll learn to stand back and watch your feelings.

And . . . now . . . I would like you to remember a recent time when you were experiencing a feeling that was uncomfortable to you . . . anger, frustration, overwhelm. Just nod your head when you can bring it up again . . . Good . . . and now I want you to amplify the feeling . . . let the feelings become more intense . . . just let those feelings come up . . . remember where you were . . . how you were triggered, what you were feeling and thinking . . . and see if you can re-elicit them. It is perfectly OK to let those feelings come up now in here . . . because they're going to go away in a few moments . . . and I'm right here with you . . . and so take all the time you need to remember a time when you were triggered . . . and when you reacted too strongly. . . . Bring up the details. . . . Let yourself experience that time again . . . right now. . . . [Look for nonverbal cues.] Good . . . you're doing very well . . . and, I want you to step back . . . and. simply observe the feeling . . . without judgment . . . without self-criticism or self-contempt for feeling this way . . . with acceptance . . . releasing judgment . . . like a detached observer . . . like a scientist observing an interesting phenomenon . . . just becoming aware and observant . . . kind of like watching clouds floating by . . . or people passing you on the street . . . coming and going . . . being a kind of silent witness to your feelings, your ongoing experience . . . observing what is . . . without reactivity or self-condemnation."

At this point, Sarah, the referring therapist, and I reviewed her progress in containing her emotionality and agreed that we had met our treatment goals. We decided to terminate regular sessions. I assured her that she could return to therapy with me if she was having difficulty and needed a tune up.

Case Outcome

I saw Sarah weekly for four sessions and then bi-monthly for three sessions. In our last session, she reported that for the previous six weeks, she was consistently spending five minutes in her car after work using the tools I had taught her before entering her house and re-engaging with her family. She acknowledged that the session that focused on reinforcing consistent practice helped her to stay committed to the time-outs with self-hypnosis. The benefit of the short self-soothing time-out sessions was that she not only became able to move quickly into a state of equilibrium, but she also was successful in accessing a compassionate, mature side of herself. The patient said that because of eliciting compassion, she found it easier to join her family with a loving and tolerant attitude.

Sarah also listened to the audio recordings I made for her before she went to work each day. She also took three two-minute breaks during the

workday to manage stress with the four square breathing. In our last session, she told me that she depended on her daily practice of self-soothing to enable her to put limits on her verbal and nonverbal overreactions. As a result, her relationship with her husband had improved greatly and she rarely experienced the disconnect with him that had previously caused her so much distress. She was relieved that her increasing ability to handle her emotions and shift gears was creating positive and satisfying changes in the family environment.

CONCLUSION

This case report illustrates how hypnosis can be utilized in the treatment of affect dysregulation. Although affect dysregulation is a component of many psychological disorders, difficulty managing emotions and containing overreactive responses are also evident in clients who are not diagnosed with a specific disorder and can be classified as subclinical. Like Sarah, these individuals' inability to contain their emotional reactions often results in relationship problems. Interactions with their closest family members can cause emotional flooding. This often occurs because childhood wounds are most likely to be triggered by those close to us. Sarah, who had been shamed as a child, experienced her emotional dysregulation as ego dystonic, which worsened her already low self-esteem. Sensitivity to the patient's shame at the start of the therapy was vital to the success of the treatment.

Hypnosis calms the nervous system, which is essential for achieving affect regulation. The combination of interventions in this case included in-session hypnosis and several quick, self-hypnotic interventions to enable the patient to regain equilibrium when she was emotionally overwhelmed. Further, hypnosis conditions new and desirable response patterns that the individual can activate in the future as needed. Hypnosis also can help clients access parts of themselves (i.e., ego states) that they can use to manage their vulnerability and the emotional reactivity that follows. This was illustrated in Sarah's case by eliciting a mature, wise, compassionate part who could guide her reactions in a reasonable way.

Regardless of the presenting problem, unchecked and overwhelming emotionality shows up in the treatment room routinely. When clients' uncontained fear, anger, or anxiety hijack therapy, attention to and treatment of the affect dysregulation become paramount. Hypnosis can potentiate any treatment modalities used to address this common and significant clinical issue.

REFERENCES

Alladin, A., (2014). Mindfulness–based hypnosis: Blending science, beliefs, and wisdoms to catalyze healing. *American Journal of Clinical Hypnosis, 56*(3), 285–302.

Alladin, A., & Alibhai, A. (2007). Cognitive hypnotherapy for depression: An empirical investigation. *International Journal of Clinical and Experimental Hypnosis, 55*(2), 147–166.

Daitch, C. (2007). *Affect regulation toolbox: Practical and effective hypnotic interventions for the over-reactive client.* New York, NY: W. W. Norton.

Daitch, C. (2011). *Anxiety disorders: The go-to guide for clients and therapists.* New York, NY: W. W. Norton.

Frederick, C. (2005). Selected topics in ego state therapy. *International Journal of Clinical and Experimental Hypnosis, 53*(4), 339–429.

Fromm, E., & Nash, M. R. (Eds.). (1992). *Contemporary hypnosis research.* New York, NY: Guilford Press.

Hammond, D. (1990). *Handbook of hypnotic suggestions and metaphors.* New York, NY: W. W. Norton.

Horevitz, R. (1996). The treatment of a case of dissociative identity disorder. In S. J. Lynn, L. Kirsch, & J. W. Rhue (Eds.), *Casebook of clinical hypnosis* (pp. 193–222). Washington, DC: American Psychological Association.

Jacobson, N. S., & Addis, M. E. (1993). Research on couple therapy: What do we know? Where are we going? *Journal of Consulting and Clinical Psychology, 61*(1), 85–93.

Kirsch, I., Montgomery, G., & Sapirstein, G. (1995). Hypnosis as an adjunct to cognitive-behavioral psychotherapy: A meta-analysis. *Journal of Consulting & Clinical Psychology, 63,* 214–220.

Lynn, S. J., Das, L. S., Hallquist, M. N., & Williams, J. C. (2006). Mindfulness, acceptance and hypnosis: Cognitive and clinical perspectives. *International Journal of Clinical and Experimental Hypnosis, 54*(2), 143–166.

McNeal, S. (2003). A character in search of character: Narcissistic personality disorder and ego state therapy. *American Journal of Clinical Hypnosis, 45*(3), 233–243.

Philips, M., & Frederick, C. (1995). *Healing the divided self: Clinical and Ericksonian hypnotherapy for posttraumatic and dissociative conditions.* New York, NY: W. W. Norton.

Schoenberger, N. E. (2000). Research on hypnosis as an adjunct to cognitive–behavioral psychotherapy. *International Journal of Clinical and Experimental Hypnosis, 48,* 154–169.

Spiegel, H., & Spiegel, D. (1978). *Trance and treatment: Clinical uses of hypnosis.* New York, NY: Basic Books.

Watkins, H. (1993). Ego-state therapy: An overview. *American Journal of Clinical Hypnosis, 35*(4), 232–240.

Yapko, M. (2011). *Mindfulness and hypnosis: The power of suggestion to transform experience.* New York, NY: W. W. Norton.

Anger Management

E. Thomas Dowd

Anger is a curious phenomenon and an ambiguous psychological state. While it is generally viewed as a negative emotion to be addressed in psychological therapy, it is likewise often seen as a positive emotion. The term *righteous anger* expresses the latter feeling; many people think they have a right to be angry, are justified in being angry, even that their anger is someone else's fault (e.g., "I wouldn't get angry if other people treated me better"), or something others should just learn to handle. Angry individuals are often powerful externalizers, seeing events and other people as responsible for their difficulties. The result is that few clients ever come to treatment for an anger problem; usually it is a side aspect of another issue or because someone else (e.g., a spouse, an employer, the courts) has referred them for therapy for that issue. As a result, perhaps, the *Diagnostic and Statistical Manual of Mental Disorder, 4th edition (DSM-IV)* contains no anger diagnosis, the closest approximation being intermittent explosive disorder (IED; 312.34). In the *International Classification of Diseases (ICD)-9* anger issues are embedded within aggressive behaviors and disorders of conduct. Only in the 2014 ICD-10 does an anger diagnosis actually appear as "irritability and anger" disorder. Thus, until recently, anger and aggression were largely conflated. Emotion theorists for many years have identified anger as a primary emotion exhibited by all humans (Tafrate, Kassinove, & Dundin, 2002).

As Kassinove and Tafrate (2011) note, anger has its origins deep in our evolutionary past, as an outgrowth of the "flight–fight" response. Bodily and neurochemical changes, including adrenalin, oxytocin, and vasopressin, that occurred with and fueled anger supported aggressive behaviors toward outsiders ("the others" who were often dangerous) that enabled individuals and tribal groups to protect and enhance their resources. Anger tends to be seen as, and often is, empowering (DiGiuseppe, 2011; Kassinove & Tafrate, 2011), at least in the short run. It can often coerce and direct other people's behavior, establish social dominance, and aid in acquiring additional resources. But in the long run, an excessive level of anger can lead to health problems, poorer relationships, and diminished occupational functioning.

Resentment and irritability are closely related to anger (Dowd, 2006); indeed, they can be seen as low-grade forms of anger that occasionally flare into genuine anger. Aggression, however, is a distinct, though related and overlapping, concept and refers to a more behavioral expression of anger. Anger tends to be more verbally expressed. Kassinove and Sukhodolsky (1995) state that anger does not cause aggression, although anger makes aggression much easier to express and more likely to occur. Although they sometimes occur together, we can have either one without the other. According to Tafrate, Kassinove, and Dundin (2002), although the incidence of aggressive behavior is quite low in nonclinical and low-trait angry individuals, it rises significantly in high-trait angry individuals. In addition, behind anger, there is often a profound sense of hurt or humiliation so that anger can be seen as a mask or cover for hurt (Deffenbacher, 2011).

Deffenbacher (2011) has identified a number of themes behind anger, often revolving around a perceived or actual lack of ability to cope with a situation and feeling overwhelmed. These themes include powerlessness, control by others, being taken advantage of, rigid demands for fairness, assumptions that vulnerability and weakness are catastrophic, low frustration tolerance, and a narcissistic feeling that one should not have to put up with this (whatever "this" is). Kassinove and Tafrate (1998) report that anger has been linked to anxiety and low self-esteem as well as to the rational emotive behavior therapy (REBT) concept of "demandingness" (e.g., others *should/must* do this or that or treat me better!).

In addition, there are several types of anger. Chronic anger is exhibited by people who always seem to be angry, resentful, and have a constant defensive approach to life. They are always ready to fight—mostly verbal, sometimes physical. Explosive or volatile anger is intermittent in nature and is shown by those who periodically go into rages. When in that state they may become violent, for which they are often remorseful afterward. Avoidant anger is exhibited by those who are afraid to express any form of anger, instead suppressing it and often not even recognizing it. The result is increased tension, often of a somatic nature. Passive-aggressive anger is demonstrated in indirect ways, such as by sarcasm, contempt, ignoring people, deliberately arriving late, or sabotaging. This can be especially difficult to identify and treat because the individual or others may not recognize or accept it as anger. Anger expression toward intimates and others can be considered to be a form of emotional abuse, depending on the frequency and severity.

RESEARCH

Psychological therapy has been shown to be effective in treating anger problems (Glancy & Saini, 2005; Saini, 2009). Glancy and Saini reported that diverse approaches may be effective in reducing anger and aggression, although cognitive-behavioral approaches have more supporting research evidence. In addition, cognitive-behaviorally oriented treatments have been able to be completed in and show results by about eight sessions. Stapleton, Taylor, and Amundson (2006) found prolonged exposure, eye movement desensitization, and relaxation training to be effective—and equally effective—in reducing both trait anger and guilt and trauma-related anger and guilt.

There are few research studies specifically on the use of hypnosis in treating anger. However, anger reduction may occur when hypnosis is targeted toward reduction of anxiety and stress. For example, Sapp (1992) reported a clinical trial in which relaxation therapy was combined with hypnosis in

treatment of anxiety and stress in 16 adults. Levels of anxiety were improved and state anger and trait anger as measured by the State-Trait Anger Expression Inventory (STAEI; Spielberger, 1988) were significantly reduced. Relaxation therapy combined with hypnosis also significantly increased participants' levels of self-esteem. Follow-up data demonstrated that the reductions in anxiety and anger were maintained even after treatment sessions ended.

An alternative Buddhist description of anger treatment has recently been presented by Horn (2014). She describes a four-step process. The first step is to recognize the many forms that anger can take—from irritation to resentment to rage. The second step is to nonjudgmentally accept this anger in yourself. The third step is to investigate the nature of your anger by recognizing when it is arising, where it is located in the body, the themes of the anger, and so on, all the while maintaining a nonjudgmental attitude toward it. The fourth step is not to identify with your anger, maintaining a detached attitude toward it as you recognize that the anger may be part of you, an aspect of you, but not you.

Also, Leifer (1999) described a Buddhist conceptualization and treatment of anger that sees anger as a form of suffering because it causes pain to self and others. The fact that everyone suffers is the First Noble Truth of Buddhism. Leifer states that the causes of suffering are the three poisons of passion, aggression, and ignorance. Treatment involves three steps: taking responsibility for one's anger (not easy for externalizers), becoming aware that anger is the result of our frustrated desires and aversions, and making a decision and commitment not to act out anger but to become aware of it and reflect on it. He suggests asking two questions: "What did I want that I wasn't getting?" and "What was I getting that I didn't want?"

The clinical use of hypnosis in combination with a cognitive-behavioral conceptualization and mindfulness have been reported (Dowd, 2006). A combination of cognitive-behavioral therapy and a Buddhist conceptualization of anger in treating anger may involve the hypnotic routines around themes of perceived lack of respect from others as well as early maladaptive schemas of entitlement/grandiosity and insufficient self-control/self-discipline (Young, Klosko, & Weishaar, 2003). The combined intervention includes development of changes in cognition, emotional regulation, and often new interpersonal skills for expression of feelings.

CASE EXAMPLE

"George" (not his real name) came to see me very reluctantly. He had been referred by his wife, who said she could no longer tolerate his explosive outbursts of anger. My usual strategy in cases where a client is referred by a family member is to see both the referring party and the client privately before beginning treatment. In this case, I met with his wife first.

She reported that George had never been physically aggressive but she feared he might be in the future because his angry outbursts were increasing both in frequency and intensity. In addition, his verbal anger was becoming very wearing and upsetting to the whole family, in particular because it was unpredictable and no one knew what might "set him off." All the family members felt they were constantly "walking on eggshells" and were increasingly avoiding all interactions with him. However, that by itself could arouse his anger because he perceived (correctly) that his family was avoiding him and he felt slighted and disregarded. George's angry rages had become so great that his wife was considering leaving him with their two children (seven and five).

George admitted that he was easily angered but tended to attribute it to others (in particular, his family) ignoring his wishes and desires and doing whatever they wanted. He reported having little influence in family activities and directions in life. His wife made all the major decisions for him and for the family and often informed him about upcoming family activities (in particular, involving her family of origin) after she had made plans. He did not think he could refuse to go or there would be "hell to pay." His attempts to express his dislike of being disregarded were either ignored or denigrated and opposed. George said that he sometimes felt angry at work, too, but was afraid to express it for fear of losing his job. He therefore "stuffed it" (his term) and seethed inwardly with resentment.

I conducted an assessment of George's family of origin. He said that his father was a volatile person

as were his uncles and aunts on that side of the family. His mother was rather timid and engaged in numerous attempts to placate his father. Family members on his mother's side were not particularly volatile although several of them lived in other parts of the country and he rarely had contact with them so he did not know them well. George did admit that he liked his mother more than his father but did admire his father who was quite successful occupationally. He reported that he had attempted to please his father as a child, mostly without success he felt. But he had at least followed his father in one regard: by becoming himself very successful occupationally, although in a different field. It was not clear; however, if this had actually pleased his father, and he reported feeling very frustrated by his inability to seemingly make his father proud of him.

Although George tended to externalize the responsibility for his anger, he did recognize that it caused him difficulties in his family. After some discussion, he could see that it might potentially cause him problems at work if he dared to show it. He could also see that his anger and volatility in both areas of his life were not really getting him what he wanted, which we identified as respect. He could see that he was, to some extent, following family-of-origin behaviors in his own. Accordingly, I pointed out that what he was doing was not helping and was even hurting him in the achievement of his goal of being treated with respect. I asked him if he was willing to try something else and he reluctantly agreed.

TRANSCRIPTS

Therapy with George lasted 10 sessions, including the two intakes (with his wife and himself). Most sessions involved a combination of discussion and hypnosis. The following somewhat abbreviated hypnotic routine occurred early in our work together.

"And now, I'd like you to become comfortable— comfortable in your own skin—as you begin to relax and turn your attention inward; inward and downward; becoming aware of the tension points in your body—and as you become aware, allowing them to relax and become more comfortable.

That's right! Becoming more comfortable and more relaxed as you turn your attention inward and downward—downward and inward. And as you continue to find comfort and peace, you can listen to my words in new ways—hearing the meaning behind the words—beginning to find new associations and meanings in ways you never expected to and never thought of—beginning to learn new things, not quite sure what yet. Finding increasing comfort in your mind and in your body—not doing, not forcing but simply allowing it to happen—in its own way and at its own pace. Feeling comfortable with the process—beginning to understand that good things can happen in their own way and at their own speed. Beginning to feel the tremendous power of letting go—letting go of powerful emotionality—beginning to realize that sometimes we can sabotage our own best interests by trying to move too quickly, can't we?—expecting others to do the same—creating problems and blocks where we really don't want or need them. And you might begin to discover that you don't really need to demand respect and admiration from others—you can let respect and admiration come to you by allowing it to do so—beginning to feel comfortable and confident that it will. Beginning to realize that you can and should set limits with others but in a comfortable and confident way. Beginning to understand what that means. Comfortable and confident—confident and comfortable. And you can discover this if you allow it—and you can begin the process of allowing yourself to discover it. It's all new and exciting, isn't it? And you can allow yourself to be increasingly excited about learning and discovering new things—and the more you discover the more you can learn; the more you learn the more you can discover and the more you learn and discover the more excited you can become about the whole process. Beginning to feel better about yourself and the tremendous power in letting go, allowing things to happen in their own way, at their own speed. Now let your mind lay flat as it begins to incorporate these new ideas—new learnings—in new and different ways—learning, growing and developing. . . ."

During a subsequent session, I created a hypnotic routine to address the early maladaptive schemas described earlier. Here is a somewhat abbreviated transcript.

"In the past you learned many things, didn't you? And as you continued to grow and develop, you continued to add to those learnings, didn't you? As you became an adult, perhaps you thought you had learned everything you needed to learn, didn't you? Many people do and perhaps you did too. It's normal and natural, isn't it? Perhaps you think that way now. You may have learned, or thought you did, that some people can't be trusted sometimes. Many people do. Perhaps you began to wonder if you could ever trust anyone; some people do. Perhaps you wondered, 'will those big people who are so important to me ever really like me; ever really approve of me?' So you tried harder—and harder—and it didn't work—and perhaps you didn't trust them to be there for you when and how you needed them. It's easy to constantly look for approval, isn't it?—and perhaps you did so. Over and over—until it became a habit—and you know of course how difficult it is to break a habit. Perhaps you felt eventually that they owed you approval—and it's natural to feel that way, isn't it? Many people do and children are owed many things by those who are important to them; love, caring, affection, respect. We all want—we all need—these things, don't we? So it's natural to feel this way and perhaps you do, too. But because things are natural and normal doesn't always mean the ways of looking for them are always good—are always useful. There are better and worse ways of getting what you need—what you want—aren't there? And as you continue to learn, grow, and develop you can begin to separate the good from the bad—finding new ways to get what you need—what you want—legitimately."

After using these routines and discussing their impact, George reported that his anger and its verbal expression had begun to diminish, which his wife confirmed. However, he was still left with his feelings of resentment (a low-grade form of anger) over being left out of family decision making and his wishes being denigrated, disregarded, and ignored. One alternative would have been marital therapy with George and his wife to address these issues and his feelings about them. That might have been advantageous in letting his wife know that the family problems were not completely of George's making. Instead I chose what I thought might be a shorter and less onerous way of addressing them. Marital therapy would have meant enlisting the assistance of another therapist because I had a previous therapeutic relationship with George and it would likely have taken much longer. We discussed his feeling of lack of respect from his family and his perceived helplessness in doing anything about it. George was a conflict-avoider and consequently I used the following hypnotic routine to address his resentment.

"You have some resentment . . . about being disrespected by some important others in your life. They don't seem to care, you feel, what you think about things—that are important to you. You don't know what to do about it, don't you, so the resentment and feelings of helplessness just fester and fester and you stuff them. These feelings are normal—natural. No one likes to feel disrespected—to be ignored, do they? What can you do about it? You don't know, do you? And perhaps it seems the only thing you can do—what you do—is to get angry, hoping they will pay attention to you and to your needs and desires. But it doesn't work—it hasn't worked—and all you know to do is more of the same—which doesn't work any better the second—or third—or fourth time either. So the frustration leads to more anger, which leads to no success and in fact can make things worse, in a sort of a vicious circle of helplessness, anger, frustration, and more anger. And perhaps you can feel your anger rising right now as I talk to you about it—if so, just notice the anger, reflect upon it, and slowly allow it to diminish, becoming less and less. That's right—you can just allow it to slowly dissolve—becoming less and less without doing anything about it—just allowing it to diminish. Not doing—just allowing it to happen. Now let those thoughts roll around in your mind, slowly allowing them to sink in. . . . [Pause]. Perhaps if you think about it, you may already have discovered the tremendous power of doing nothing, or allowing your negative emotions to gradually fade away—becoming less and less, not by doing but allowing. It can be really quite powerful, isn't it—in a way perhaps you never thought. . . . [Pause]. Now turn your attention to your wife's refusal to consider your desires in making family plans. You can't really force her to consider your desires, can you? And that's what is so frustrating—leading to anger. You feel blocked, helpless, and angry in that order. What can you do? Let me suggest something different. You can't force
her to consider your wishes—but she can't force you to accept her wishes either, can she? She can only make you do what she wants if you give her the power—and so far you have. But you can say, 'No,' even though she might be irritated and even angry if you do. You can stand it because it will eventually go away. And wouldn't it be interesting—even fun—for her to be angry instead of you! You can take the power back if you say 'No' and then she might be the one to feel blocked, helpless, and angry. Kind of a reversal, isn't it? Remember, you have the power if you choose to exercise it— and if you feel powerful and act powerful you don't have to get angry because there is nothing to get angry about. Think of that; nothing to get angry about! Let that thought roll around in your mind—the tremendous power in saying 'No'— knowing 'No' can stick if you want it to, if you want to feel the power—feel the power. . . . And the more you let this idea penetrate your unconscious mind, the more at peace you can feel—calm and at peace . . . peaceful and calm."

In this final transcript, the client's feelings of powerlessness and helplessness were addressed, as well as his desires to be heard and acknowledged by his family. It may be strange to think of an angry person as feeling helpless because anger is often thought to reflect power, but in many instances, it may reflect attempts to feel more powerful when one doesn't. This is more apparent if one thinks of anger as arising from frustrated desires and blocked actions. I instead suggested to the client that although he could not force his wife to do what he wanted, neither could she force him to do what she wanted unless he allowed it. In a potentially amusing routine, I suggested that his saying "No" might in turn trigger angry responses on her part, leading perhaps to a role reversal and more empathy from her toward his anger. It has been long noted in intimate relationships that behavioral changes by one partner unbalance the system and can lead to unanticipated changes by others in the system. I also included suggestions for reducing anger by letting go, by allowing it to diminish.

After the 10 sessions for which we had contracted, George reported his anger was much reduced. He was able on a few occasions to disagree with his wife about events that she had planned without consulting him. Once he refused to go, leaving him with a new feeling of power. Although his wife was irritated by that, she did accept it somewhat gracefully. George and I discussed appropriate ways of handling his resentment and I suggested he have a proactive discussion with his wife when neither was angry and tell her of his resentment at being excluded. I instructed him on the use of self-calming techniques should the discussion become heated. I suggested marital therapy to resolve these issues if they persisted. George and I agreed to terminate with the understanding he could return if his anger resurfaced.

CONCLUSION

This case example nicely illustrates the central themes in anger management by hypnosis: letting go of frustrated desires, allowing things to happen instead of trying to force them, and finding alternative ways of obtaining what one wants and reducing what one doesn't want. Providing clients with self-calming techniques and often assertion training is crucial. It also illustrates the manner in which I use hypnosis in psychological therapy; cognitive-behavioral or otherwise. That is, hypnotic routines are interspersed within discussions of the client's psychological difficulties and subsequent discussions of the effects and reactions to the routines. These reactions can often be quite powerful and may require extensive discussion, sometimes requiring attention during the next session as well. Likewise, the initial discussions allow me to understand the major themes in the client's life, to formulate a case conceptualization, and from that to develop the hypnotic routines to address the themes. I would estimate that approximately one-third of the total client session activity might be devoted to hypnosis on the average. As therapy winds down, the percentage may be less.

REFERENCES

Deffenbacher, J. L. (2011). Cognitive-behavioral conceptualization and treatment of anger. *Cognitive and Behavioral Practice, 18*(2), 212–221.

DiGiuseppe, R. (2011). A comprehensive treatment program for a case of disturbed anger. *Cognitive and Behavioral Practice, 18*, 222–234.

Dowd, E. T. (2006). Cognitive hypnotherapy and the management of anger. In R. A. Chapman (Ed.), *clinical use of hypnosis in cognitive behavior therapy* (pp. 189–211). New York, NY: Springer Publishing Company.

Glancy, G., & Saini, M. (2005). An evidence-based review of psychological treatments of anger and aggression. *Brief Treatment and Crisis Intervention, 5*, 229–248.

Horn, E. (2014). How RAIN cools the flames of anger. *Shambhala Sum, 23*, 52.

Kassinove, H., & Sukhodolsky, D. G. (1995). Basic science and practice issues. In H. Kassinove (Ed.), *Anger disorders: Definition, diagnosis and treatment* (pp. 1–26). Washington, DC: Taylor & Francis.

Kassinove, H., & Tafrate, R. C. (1998). Anger control in men: Barb exposure with rational, irrational, and irrelevant self-statements. *Journal of Cognitive Psychotherapy: An International Quarterly, 12*, 187–211.

Kassinove, H., & Tafrate, R. C. (2011). Application of a flexible, clinically-driven approach for anger reduction in the case of Mr. P. *Cognitive and Behavioral Practice, 18*, 222–234.

Leifer, R. (1999). Buddhist conceptualization and treatment of anger. *Journal of Clinical Psychology, 55*(3), 339–351.

Saini, M. (2009). A meta-analysis of the psychological treatment of anger: Developing guidelines for evidence-based practice. *Journal of the American Academy of Psychiatry and the Law, 37*(4), 473–488.

Sapp, M. (1992). Relaxation and hypnosis in reducing anxiety and stress. *Journal of Clinical Hypnotherapy and Hypnosis, 13*(2), 39–55.

Spielberger, C. (1988). *Professional manual for the state-trait anger expression inventory.* Odessa, FL: Psychological Assessment Resources.

Stapleton, J. A., Taylor, S., & Asmundson, G. J. (2006). Effects of three PTSD treatments on anger and guilt: Exposure therapy, eye movement desensitization and reprocessing, and relaxation training. *Journal of Traumatic Stress, 19*(1), 19–28. doi:10.1002/jts.20095

Tafrate, R. C., Kassinove, H., & Dundin, L. (2002). Anger episodes in high- and low-trait community adults. *Journal of Clinical Psychology, 58*(12), 1573–1598. doi:10.1002/jclp.10076

Young, J. E., Klosko, J. S., & Weishaar, M. (2003). *Schema Therapy: A Practitioner's Guide.* New York, NY, Guilford Publications

Anxieties in Adults

Burkhard Peter

Anxiety disorders are the most common form of mental illness, with a prevalence rate of 18% in the United States and 15% in Europe (GBE, 2004; Kessler, Berglund, et al., 2005). In Germany, almost 40% of psychotherapy patients are diagnosed with an anxiety disorder (GBE, 2004). Some studies have estimated the "economic burden" of anxiety disorders to be worth more than € 74.40 billion per year in Europe (Gustavsson et al., 2011).

The classification of this mental disorder includes the following:

- Generalized anxiety disorder is characterized by a persistent and ongoing fear and worry without a specific cause or antecedent. Its lifetime prevalence is close to 30%.
- A specific phobia is a fear of an object or situation that is not proportional to its actual potential danger, such as a fear of a harmless animal or specific location (e.g., airplane). Its prevalence is 5% to 12% of the population.
- Social phobia or social anxiety disorder is characterized by an exaggerated fear of becoming humiliated or embarrassed by others. This affects 11% to 16% of the population.
- Agoraphobia is the fear of being unable to escape from a public place or situation, especially if one expects having a panic attack by being there. Approximately 2% to 11% of the population are believed to have it.
- Panic disorder is defined as a fear or discomfort that abruptly arises and peaks in less than 10 minutes but can last for several hours, in most cases without apparent cause. Its prevalence is about 3%.

With the exception of social phobias, women are twice more likely than men to be affected by an anxiety disorder. Single, divorced, and widowed people are more likely to develop this kind of disorder as well as those with a low education and/or income (Kessler, et al., 2005; Kessler, Chiu, Demler, Merikangas, & Walters, 2005; Lépine, 2002). A high level of comorbidity with depression (up to 60%) has been observed, and many patients also suffer from other Axis I disorders (Hofmeijer-Sevink et al., 2012).

Symptoms can be described on different levels. Anxious or phobic patients feel psychophysiological symptoms, such as sweating, palpitations, tachycardia, hypertension, and muscle spasms, which, in some cases, lead to fatigue or exhaustion. In terms of cognition, they have unrealistic and dysfunctional thoughts about the phobic objects. A significant problem is that most of these patients behaviorally avoid objects and situations of which they are anxious or phobic. This might be the only reason why exposure-based therapies are so effective. This, however, can become a problem in hypnotherapeutic approaches with some anxiety patients: They choose hypnosis because they hope that they can continue their avoidance behavior. There are many case examples of Erickson abstaining from hypnosis, confronting his patients directly with their phobias, and also utilizing other people at hand—like his spouse—to deter them from avoiding or escaping. In some cases, a "systemic view" might also be necessary when patients seem to use other people to serve their anxious purposes. A complex systemic problem arises within partnerships or families, for example, when a patient with a social phobia cannot leave the home alone or cannot meet other people.

EVIDENCE

Unlike cognitive behavioral psychotherapy, for which exposure is the empirically validated treatment of choice, there is, to date, insufficient scientific evidence for the effectiveness of hypnosis/hypnotherapy for anxiety disorders. Revenstorf (2006) described seven older scientific studies, five of which were conducted with nonclinical populations (i.e., students) and two were flawed in their design. Flammer (2006) conducted a more thorough meta-analysis of 18 randomized controlled clinical trials ($N = 732$) covering phobias, generalized anxiety disorders, and unspecified anxiety disorders. For pre and post comparisons, a moderate effect size ($d = .72$) was found, and a large effect ($d = 1.02$) was found when compared with a waiting control group. Hypnosis is particularly effective for phobias ($d = 1.23$) and in the treatment of children/adolescents ($d = 1.35$). For patients treated with hypnosis, 74% experienced symptom improvement in contrast to 26% of patients in a waiting control condition. Hypnotherapy also proved to be superior to attention-placebo ($d = .66$). A direct comparison with behavior therapy, however, showed no significant difference. Unfortunately, 10 out of the 18 studies examined in the meta-analysis were conducted with children, adolescents, and students with examination anxieties. The proven effectiveness of hypnosis, therefore, cannot be applied to patients of a general psychotherapeutic practice. That is, its practical efficiency has not yet been demonstrated.

There are some significant problems with behaviorally based exposure therapies. One is the acceptance of and adherence to the exposure, which, in most cases, must be continued at home. Choy, Fyer, and Lipsitz (2007), for example, showed that in vivo exposure has the highest dropout rate. Park et al. (2001) found that the degree of adherence to self-exposure at home predicted the stability of the improvement after two years. Another problem with exposure arises when there is nothing to expose. Such is the case for many panic disorder patients, who cannot identify any cues in the outside world over which they panic. These situations call for a treatment approach other than behavioral exposure. The following case is an example for this latter problem.

CASE EXAMPLE: PANIC ATTACKS AFTER AN "OPERATION ACCIDENT"

A 29-year-old housewife and mother of two young children came to therapy because of panic attacks. She had no explanation for her symptoms, which plagued her for several years and had occurred more frequently in recent times. She could not identify any situation or reason for which the symptoms would occur. Being at the subway or public spaces were typical situations, but even then she did not know with certainty whether or when it actually did happen. Why she had panic attacks even at home when, after her day's housework, she sat comfortably in her living room or on the terrace, she could never understand.

After two sessions of rather fruitless general exploration, as we could not find any meaningful contingent stimuli preceding her panic attacks, I made a new attempt with hypnosis. While being in trance following a careful induction, she suddenly remembered having these symptoms ever since she had a sinus surgery about 3 years earlier. Still, she could not initially specify any further contingencies, but rather thought of an uncle to whom the following had happened: After a relatively harmless operation in the hospital, he had found a small scar in the skin from a stitch above his heart. A kind of vision had occurred to him, in which he dreamt, either during surgery or shortly thereafter, seeing himself from a position above lying on the operating table while doctors worked hectically around him. Upon questioning where the scar on his chest came from, a doctor told him that there had been an incident during the operation, that his heart stopped and that he had to be resuscitated.

As my female patient told this story, she still could not find any connections between herself and the panic attacks. She was easily hypnotizable and could develop an arm levitation without tactile support (Peter, Piesbergen, Lucic, Staudacher, & Hagl, 2013). I took advantage of ideomotor signaling (Ewin & Eimer, 2006; Peter, 2009a) for another attempt to explore her symptoms on a subconscious level. I asked her "unconscious" whether there was a link between the sinus surgery and the subsequent panic attacks. The "Yes-hand" went up, and so I suggested that her unconscious mind would provide more detail should the Yes-hand rise further. This happened, and after some time, the patient reported, in a spontaneous age regression, being in a hospital room alone the night before a surgery while experiencing a terrible, inexplicable fear. I intervened immediately and asked her to carefully detach her mind from her body and to move so far away that she could look at this fearful woman lying in her bed from a distant position, being very quiet, thinking about her, and talking to me about her. With her being in this position as an observer, who was by now so far away that she was outside the room in the hallway, we then began to discuss the following:

It was now a very irrational situation: The woman was lying in her bed terrified of that next-day surgery because she feared that the same thing would happen to her as it did to her uncle. Thus she, the observer, now had to go to her, soothe her, and explain to her that the probability of such an incident was so small that she could easily forget about it and fall asleep. I asked her whether she would be able to do so, and upon her agreeing we both went back into the room. She sat beside the woman, took her hand, and said, partly supported by me, that what had happened to her uncle was extremely unlikely, and that it was therefore completely improbable something like that could also happen to her. Therefore, she could be quite sure that she will be safe, and so on.

As it turned out, I was wrong with these assumptions. In the next age regression during the following session, she relived how she responded paradoxically to the sedatives the next morning. Instead of being relaxed and detached, she was brought into the operating room with panic anxieties but also with flaccid muscles. She went again into an observer position and, with my support, we explained to the poor woman that this was a totally unusual and unfortunate situation. She had obviously responded unexpectedly to the anesthetic, which had no proper explanation, since it happens so rarely. Unfortunately, she was still affected by this awkward incident. However, she was told she could remain relaxed because this was "only a physical" reaction, artificially provoked by the drug. It felt like fear because of the physical signs. Further, she should detach from her body in a way and go far enough away that she could feel her mind calming down. Then she would understand everything correctly and become very relaxed again.

Finally, during several therapy meetings, the "trauma" was gradually "reconstructed," and an explanation was found for the previously seemingly unexplainable (i.e., "irrational") panic symptoms: She woke up during surgery and became conscious. She was fortunate not to feel pain, but had a very unpleasant feeling of not being able to move or breathe autonomously yet felt the tube in her throat. She saw nothing and heard only vague voices without understanding anything. Before she panicked, I intervened and explained to her that this really was an unfortunate and absurd coincidence, because this happens so extremely seldom. Unfortunately, there was again no proper explanation for this incident.

I then told her:

"Concentrate and listen very carefully to my words, and follow all my instructions precisely, because you know well that this woman on the operating table could otherwise develop a panic disorder. Ask her to let her body fall deeply asleep and become very calm so that she can leave her body completely now with her mind and join with you. Make sure that you together are so far detached from it that you can float high enough in order to look down and see her body lying on the operating table. Notice the doctors around it doing their job with no one realizing that she woke up, because all of them are so engrossed in their work that they cannot see anything else. Only you yourself or her mind, respectively, know that she is awake and probably will develop fear if we do not intervene and do the right things. Therefore, go back now and move closer to the woman on the operating table, talk to her, and soothe her. The best thing would be to take her hand at her bedside like the night before, and talk with the woman on the operating table in a very tender and quiet manner. Tell her that everything is in order, that she feels no pain, just an unneeded feeling, and that everything would be over right soon. While you caress the hand of this woman, instruct her that she still should be a bit patient. The doctors will do their job perfectly. If it takes too long, she should reflect on things about which she normally never had time to think, that you and I are with her. . . ."

I suggested that if the woman on the operating table feels that her hand is being touched, it would go up all by itself, for then she knows that everything is in order, that she can wait, be quiet, learn new things, and wait quietly until it's all over. The left hand of my real female patient went up slightly and she remained visibly calm. She confirmed after the trance session that it was hard but very satisfying work.

In subsequent hypnotic sessions, we went through this scene several times to deepen and anchor the result. Before and after each session, and not just during the trance itself, I frequently provided some physiological and psychological information and explanations. In these briefings and debriefings, I repeatedly emphasized that we had to be aware of the possibility that this reconstructed scene could be the historic truth, but we really cannot be sure unless she consulted her medical records. It could also be possible, I pointed out, that only parts were historically true and others were imagined to fill memory gaps in order for the story to make sense. She readily agreed to and accepted my concerns but made no effort to get her medical records. In the course of the following weeks, her panic attacks became less frequent and eventually disappeared completely. After 17 sessions, they were gone, and did not return even after a year, as the catamnesis revealed.

TECHNIQUES

Joseph Wolpe (1996), at the Second European Congress of Ericksonian Hypnosis and Psychotherapy in Munich, made a "formal acknowledgement of the role that hypnosis played in the development of systematic desensitization" (p. 137). He described in detail how he experimented first with narco-analysis using the barbiturate Pentothal, then with hypnosis, and finally with Jacobson's progressive muscle relaxation. He concluded that "for most cases it was not really necessary to use hypnosis. One could simply say, 'imagine so and so', without a formal hypnotic trance. Nevertheless, there are occasional cases in which it is a definite advantage to use hypnotic induction as a background for the systematic desensitization procedure" (p. 139). In his book *Psychotherapy by Reciprocal Inhibition,* Wolpe (1958) presented the standard technique of the early behavior therapy. This approach of successive approximations to the phobic stimulus was, though, preceded 10 years earlier by Lewis Wolberg (1948), who, in the chapter "Hypnosis in Desensitization" of his book *Medical Hypnosis,* gave a similar account for the use of hypnosis in the treatment of anxiety disorders. Today, there are many case examples of using hypnosis in systematic desensitization, one of the most recent from Iglesias and Iglesias (2013). "Flooding," as an alternative

to systematic desensitization, has become increasingly popular in behavior therapy since the late 1970s and developed ultimately into the contemporary exposure-based therapies with which relaxation and hypnosis techniques have been dispensed.

As already mentioned, the standard procedures of systematic desensitization and exposure therapies are not applicable to all anxiety disorders. I still recall very well a rather peculiar incident, which occurred at the end of my study of psychology, when the entire clinical department experimented with the then newly discovered technique of "flooding": A female patient with a phobia of spiders had to hold a bird spider in her palm long enough that she habituated to the look and tingling feelings of it until she felt relief from her symptoms. Very soon she exclaimed: "What a nice bird!" She was subsequently deemed as not being treatable. Behavior therapists could not handle this kind of a dissociative hallucination by exposure therapies, and they still cannot do it today.

Alladin (2014) recently discussed reasons why behavior therapeutic techniques are not applicable to some anxiety patients. He presented the concept of the "wounded self," based on Wolfe (2005), as the basis for understanding and treating anxiety disorders: Not all anxieties are traceable to unfortunate conditioning processes. Certain portions of them are meaningful to patients on an unconscious level as they represent special "relationships between certain life experiences and intense fear" (Wolfe, 2005, p. 369) that the person encountered in her or his past.

Similar reflections have been presented in many case studies by Paul Janouch (1990, 1997, 2003, 2008) and were later detailed in the form of a special hypnotherapeutic strategy (Janouch, 2001, 2009) that takes into account unconscious processes of the patient that can be revealed and utilized by hypnosis. This strategy basically entails seven steps, which are presented here:

Step 1: Orientation

"Pace" his/her specific features like sensorial orientation, nervousness, tensions, and so on. The patient's attention becomes focused and gradually oriented toward the induction of a hypnotic trance, including hand or arm levitation (Peter, Schiebler, Piesbergen, & Hagl, 2012).

Step 2: Get the Patient in Contact With the "Symptom"

Patients do not like their anxiety symptoms; some are even embarrassed by them. Instead of explaining the possible meaning and function of the symptoms directly to the patient, which certainly is a helpful strategy for some, it may be more useful to make the patient immediately familiar with his or her symptoms. One way is to let the patient remember the most recent instance when he or she experienced it, albeit in an attenuated or dissociated manner:

"As you sit here comfortably and quietly, you can imagine the last time you felt these symptoms. You can be aware of the physical or physiological signs of it . . . where and how you can feel it in your body in an intriguing and attentive manner. Now you can separate it from yourself and, as your hand goes up more and more, you can manage this distance in a way that is more and more comfortable to you. You can get in contact with this part of you that holds this strong energy unconsciously hidden in this symptom. Ask it to cooperate with your conscious mind by letting your hand going up further. [Upon an appropriate ideomotoric reaction] *Now you probably can see your anxiety in the form of an image with which you can start to talk, converse, and ask questions. . . ."*

Contact and communication are core features for the differentiation between psychopathological symptoms (to which contact and communication are lost) and phenomena of "normal" human agency, including hypnotic phenomena (Peter, 2009b), when contact and communication are in order and adaptive. As such, it might be useful to spend some time in this phase in order to bring the patient in experiential contact with his or her symptoms. The "representative technique" (Bongartz & Bongartz, 2009), which is useful with psychosomatic (Meiss, 2009) and pain patients (Peter, 2010), can be applied to anxious patients as well. The patient is asked to imagine actively (or better, to let his or her unconscious construct) a figure such as an animal or other object from nature that best symbolizes his or her fear. Hence, an active communication between the patient and this symbolic figure can be launched.

Step 3: Make a Contract With the "Symptom"

Before proceeding with the next step of uncovering meaning, content, or function of the symptom (i.e., to query the symptom-figure about these issues), a sort of a contract is recommended. Instead of the patient futilely fighting against the symptom, he or she is invited to make an honest agreement with it in order to learn and to use the inherent information and resources: "Commit yourself to stopping the fight against the symptom. Accept that it has/had a special meaning that is not yet comprehensible to you, and that you are eager to learn this meaning in the course of your therapy. In return, your symptom can respond that it will calm down, and it will indicate this by lifting up the other hand."

If this does not work properly because, for instance, the symptom or its representative is too terrifying, one should go back to step 2 and deepen his or her detachment by special dissociation techniques. One method is the projection screen technique, in which the patient sits comfortably in a chair watching a video scene of a person like her or him being struck by fear symptoms. This dissociation can be duplicated and amplified if he or she is looking at a person who sits comfortably in a chair watching a video scene or some other visual means, as illustrated by Reckert (2009).

Step 4: Exploration of the Symptom's Meaning

The core of this kind of hypnotherapeutic treatment of anxieties starts with a request:

"As soon as your unconscious mind is ready and willing to uncover the source of your anxieties, which you can feel or see in the figure of the symptom-figure, your hand/arm will rise. This might not always work the first time, so it might be necessary several times to ask the client to be patient. The possible protective intentions of the unconscious should be emphasized and any "resistance" should be respected in this phase of treatment. Once an ideomotor reaction appears (e.g., the hand lifts up), the dissociation needs to be deepened: *Take your time now to experience the willingness of your unconscious mind to uncover whatever is relevant to your symptoms. But take your time first to find*

out the right distance from which you can easily look at and understand what your symptom/your symptom-figure tells you. . . ."

Usually the patient feels very confident if an uncovered meaning is inherently consistent. If not, it is necessary to go on with further explorations.

Step 5: Solutions

In some cases, possible solutions follow resulting from uncovered materials, for which some simple reframing may suffice. In other cases, patients need more help by the therapist in order to, for instance, equalize confusions if a currently ambivalent situation is masked by old anxious feelings, of which the origin is not conscious at the moment. Yet, in other cases, there may not have been a proper solution possible in the situation when the anxiety first manifested, so life simply continued and the traumatic event fell into oblivion. Cues of the present trigger the old anxious experience as long as there is no meaningful solution for the original context. This has to be created collaboratively by the therapist, the patient, and the unconscious knowledge of the latter. Old business needs to be settled and old wounds have to be healed. Feelings of guilt and shame can also play a role in some anxiety disorders if they fit with similar feelings from the past. These are usually forgotten or repressed and operate now as a kind of permanent trigger for remorse and physiological excitement. The therapist should help the patient address directly his or her conscience in order to find ways of remission. Because these feelings are the most difficult and problematic for people, the state of a hypnotic trance in addition to ideomotor techniques are most appropriate to deal with them.

Step 6: "Ecological Validation"

If a solution has been found or sufficiently created, each part or "ego state" (Frederick, 2007) of the patient needs to be asked whether it can accept it. A simple and good test involves the patient establishing the state of solution imaginatively and physiologically and associating himself or herself with the formerly anxious situation. That is, he or she enters imaginatively into it in order to experience the newly developed reactions of staying calm and relaxed.

Step 7: Posthypnotic Suggestion and Amnesia

In order to continue all the processes that have been started to solve the problems and soothe the patient, appropriate posthypnotic suggestions at the end of each session are needed:

"Your unconscious/your conscience will continue to work on these matters so long as a good and durable solution is found. It will find the right time to do this, even at night and in your dreams, or during the day when your conscious mind is not fully absorbed by other business. And your conscious mind can forget it as it is important that you know that your anxious reactions are now over and you can confront yourself easily with what you feared in the past."

CONCLUSION

Though behaviorally based exposure therapies are currently the empirically validated treatments of choice for anxiety disorders, hypnotherapeutic approaches are also useful. They are necessary at least when exposure fails because unconscious processes still trigger the symptoms. In these cases, a thorough and detailed hypnotherapeutic strategy (à la Paul Janouch) can be appied in order to find a meaningful and satisfying solution for the patient. At least moderate hypnotizability and some capability for imaginative involvement are prerequisites for this approach. Otherwise, behaviorally based techniques are recommended. This is also true if the patient searches for hypnosis as an inherent part of his or her habit to constantly avoid exposure. Further research to validate this hypnotherapeutic approach, however, is needed.

REFERENCES

Alladin, A. (2014). The wounded self: New approach to understanding and treating anxiety disorders.

American Journal of Clinical Hypnosis, 56(4), 368–388. doi:10.1080/00029157.2014.880045

Bongartz, B., & Bongartz, W. (2009). Stellvertretertechnik. In D. Revenstorf & B. Peter (Eds.), *Hypnose in psychotherapie, psychosomatik und medizin. Ein manual für die praxis* (pp. 268–276). Heidelberg: Springer Publishing Company.

Choy, Y., Fyer, A. J., & Lipsitz, J. D. (2007). Treatment of specific phobia in adults. *Clinical Psychology Review, 27*(3), 266–286. doi:10.1016/j. cpr.2006.10.002

Ewin, D. M., & Eimer, B. N. (2006). *Ideomotor signals for rapid hypnoanalysis. A how-to-do manual.* Springfield, IL: Charles C. Thomas Publishers.

Flammer, E. (2006). Die wirksamkeit von hypnotherapie bei angststörungen. *Hypnose-ZHH, 1*(2), 173–198.

Frederick, C. (2007). Ausgewählte themen zur ego state therapie. *Hypnose-ZHH, 2*(2), 5–100.

GBE. (2004). Angststörungen. Gesundheitsberichterstattung des Bundes: Themenheft. Retrieved from http://www.gbe-bund.de

Gustavsson, A., Svensson, M., Jacobi, F., Allgulander, C., Alonso, J., Beghi, E., . . . Olesen, J. (2011). Cost of disorders of the brain in Europe 2010. *European Neuropsychopharmacology: The Journal of the European College of Neuropsychopharmacology, 21*(10), 718–779. doi:10.1016/j.euroneuro .2011.08.008

Hofmeijer-Sevink, M. K., Batelaan, N. M., van Megen, H. J., Penninx, B. W., Cath, D. C., van den Hout, M. A., & van Balkom, A. J. (2012). Clinical relevance of comorbidity in anxiety disorders: A report from the Netherlands Study of Depression and Anxiety (NESDA). *Journal of Affective Disorders, 137*(1-3), 106–112. doi:10.1016/j.jad.2011.12.008

Iglesias, A., Iglesias, A., & Iglesias, A. (2013). I-95 phobia treated with hypnotic systematic desensitization: A case report. *American Journal of Clinical Hypnosis, 56*(2), 143–151.

Janouch, P. (1990). Angstbehandlung mit hypnose. *Hypnose Und Kognition, 7*(2), 7–15.

Janouch, P. (1997). Hypnotherapie bei angststörungen. *Hypnose Und Kognition, 14*(2), 55–60.

Janouch, P. (2001). Angststörungen. In D. Revenstorf & B. Peter (Eds.), *Hypnose in psychotherapie, psychosomatik und medizin. Ein manual für die praxis* (pp. 421–433). Heidelberg: Springer Publishing Company.

Janouch, P. (2003). Anmerkungen zum prinzip der unwillkürlichkeit in der hypnose am beispiel der angsttherapie. *Hypnose Und Kognition, 20*(2), 121–126.

Janouch, P. (2008). Zur kombination von hypnotherapeutischen und verhaltenstherapeutischen techniken bei angststörungen. *Ein Fallbericht. Hypnose-ZHH, 3*(2), 111–116.

Janouch, P. (2009). Angststörungen. In D. Revenstorf & B. Peter (Eds.), *Hypnose in psychotherapie, psychosomatik und medizin. Ein manual für die praxis* (pp. 439–449). Heidelberg: Springer Publishing Company.

Kessler, R. C., Berglund, P., Demler, O., Jin, R., Merikangas, K. R., & Walters, E. E. (2005). Lifetime prevalence and age-of-onset distributions of *DSM-IV* disorders in the National Comorbidity Survey Replication. *Archives of General Psychiatry, 62*(6), 593–602. doi:10.1001/archpsyc.62.6.593

Kessler, R. C., Chiu, W. T., Demler, O., Merikangas, K. R., & Walters, E. E. (2005). Prevalence, severity, and comorbidity of 12-month *DSM-IV* disorders in the National Comorbidity Survey Replication. *Archives of General Psychiatry, 62*(6), 617–627. doi:10.1001/ archpsyc.62.6.617

Lépine, J. P. (2002). The epidemiology of anxiety disorders: Prevalence and societal cost. *Journal of Clinical Psychiatry, 63*(14), 4–8.

Meiss, O. (2009). Psychosomatische störungen. In D. Revenstorf & B. Peter (Eds.), *Hypnose in psychotherapie, psychosomatik und medizin. Ein manual für die praxis* (pp. 547–557). Heidelberg: Springer Publishing Company.

Park, J. M., Mataix-Cols, D., Marks, I. M., Ngamthipwatthana, T., Marks, M., Araya, R., & Al-Kubaisy, T. (2001). Two-year follow up after a randomised controlled trial of self- and clinicial-accompanied exposure for phobia/panic disorders. *British Journal of Psychiatry: The Journal of Mental Science, 178*, 543–548.

Peter, B. (2009a). Ideomotorische hypnoserituale. In D. Revenstorf & B. Peter (Eds.), *Hypnose in psychotherapie, psychosomatik und medizin. Ein manual für die praxis* (pp. 169–180). Heidelberg: Springer Publishing Company.

Peter, B. (2009b). Is it useful to induce a hypnotic trance? A hypnotherapist's view on recent neuroimaging results. *Contemporary Hypnosis, 26*(3), 132–145.

Peter, B. (2010). Konstruktion von symptomgestalt und symptomträger. Zwei hypnotherapeutische strategien bei chronischen schmerzpatienten. *Hypnose-ZHH, 5*(2), 163–178.

Peter, B., Piesbergen, C., Lucic, T., Staudacher, M., & Hagl, M. (2013). The role of tactile support in arm levitation. *American Journal of Clinical Hypnosis, 56*(2), 115–142.

Peter, B., Schiebler, P., Piesbergen, C., & Hagl, M. (2012). Elektromyographic investigation of hypnotic arm levitation: Differences between voluntary arm elevation and involuntary arm levitation. *International Journal of Clinical and Experimental Hypnosis, 60*(1), 88–110. doi:10.1080/00207144.20 11.622213

Reckert, H. W. (2009). Spezifische phobien. In D. Revenstorf & B. Peter (Eds.), *Hypnose in psychotherapie, psychosomatik und medizin. Ein manual für die praxis* (pp. 460–465). Heidelberg: Springer Publishing Company.

Revenstorf, D. (2006). Expertise zur beurteilung der wissenschaftlichen evidenz des psychotherapieverfahrens hypnotherapie entsprechend den kriterien des wissenschaftlichen beirats psychotherapie. *Hypnose-ZHH, 1*(2), 7–164.

Wolberg, L. R. (1948). *Medical hypnosis: The practice of hypnotherapy*. New York, NY: Grune & Stratton.

Wolfe, B. E. (2005). *Understanding and treating anxiety disorders: An integrative approach to healing the wounded self*. Washington, DC: American Psychological Association.

Wolpe, J. (1958). *Psychotherapy by reciprocal inhibition*. Stanford, CA: Stanford University Press.

Wolpe, J. (1996). Hypnosis and the evolution of behavior therapy. In B. Peter, B. Trenkle, F. C. Kinzel, C. Duffner, & A. Iost-Peter (Eds.), *Munich lectures on hypnosis and psychotherapy* (pp. 137–139). München: M.E.G.-Stiftung.

Anxiety in Children and Teens

Pamela Kaiser

Anxiety in childhood ranges from transient, normative fears at different developmental phases (e.g., fear of strangers at age 9 to 10 months and again around 20 months of age; fear of the dark or monsters at age 4 and 5, etc.), to what I've termed "normal nervous" episodes related to specific events and situations (e.g., exams, school plays, sports, starting a new school), to an intense, persistent, developmentally inappropriate chronic state of "excessive anxiety and related behavioral disturbances" that causes significant distress or impairs functioning (such as academic, peer relationships, or family life) that meets criteria for a clinical diagnosis (*Diagnostic and Statistical Manual of Mental Disorders*, fifth edition [*DSM-5*], American Psychiatric Association, 2013).

In order to discern these differences in children's presentations, clinicians must have a solid background in normal development and behavior as well as in developmental psychopathology (i.e., a theoretical and research perspective explaining potential pathways leading to the emergence of childhood mental health disorders). Research in this field shows that clinicians also need to take into account the combination of factors known to foster, fuel, and maintain clinical anxiety in children, including genetics, neurobiology, temperament, anxiety sensitivity, information processing bias, coping style, attachment and early control experiences, exposure to feared and common conditioned stimuli, parenting style, parental psychopathology, and self-regulation (Bell & Deater-Deckard, 2007; Vasey & Dodds, 2001).

Decades of research indicate that young children's "persistent fear and chronic anxiety can have lifelong consequences by disrupting the developing architecture of the brain" (National Scientific Council on the Developing Child 2010, p. 3). . . . and "can disrupt the typical development of self-regulation as well as learning, memory, and social behavior" (p. 7). Thus, the importance of incorporating hypnosis as an adjunct to a treatment plan for self-regulation and other goals to ameliorate childhood anxiety cannot be understated.

RESEARCH

Unfortunately, there is a paucity of hypnosis research on childhood anxiety. Comparable to the negligible focus on anxiety disorders in the adult hypnosis research literature (Hammond, 2010), very few hypnosis studies focus specifically on childhood anxiety disorders, for example, separation anxiety disorder, phobias, social anxiety disorder, and so on.

In fact, there are only a handful of original articles and chapters about the use of hypnosis to treat children with anxiety disorders. For example, Kaiser (2011) offers a developmental psychopathology perspective to guide the assessment and treatment planning (including individualized discrimination and self-regulation hypnosis goals and strategies) for clinically significant anxiety, worry, and fear. A companion article on childhood anxiety disorders addresses the design of individualized hypnosis sessions that build discrimination and self-regulation skills to reduce psychophysiological reactivity (Kaiser, 2014). Other internationally recognized pediatric hypnosis experts, Kohen and Olness (2011), Kuttner (2009), and Wester and William (2013), have written about hypnosis for pediatric anxiety disorders.

The largest and strongest body of research supportive of hypnosis for pediatric anxiety is found in some studies on pediatric pain related to medical procedures. Building on seminal findings from the formative leaders in this area (Kuttner, Bowman, & Teasdale, 1989; Zeltzer & LeBaron, 1982), other researchers continue to find therapeutic value in hypnosis for children anxiously experiencing painful medical procedures (e.g., Butler, Symons, Henderson, Shortliffe, & Spiegel, 2005; Liossi & Hatira, 1999, 2003; Liossi, White, & Hatira, 2006, 2009; Smith, Barabasz, & Barabasz, 1996). A 2008 Cochrane Review of randomized controlled trials of psychological interventions for needle-related procedural pain and "distress," with some studies specifically measuring anxiety, concluded that hypnosis was effective (Uman, Chambers, McGrath, & Kisely, 2008). A 2010 "integrative review" of pediatric CAM approaches for procedural pain, anxiety, and stress concluded that self-hypnosis was effective for anticipatory anxiety (Landier & Tse, 2010).

The successful use of hypnosis for pediatric primary care presentations, including anxiety, was documented in a large case series (505) conducted by Kohen and Olness and colleagues (1984), globally recognized as the foremost leaders in the field of pediatric hypnosis.

A small body of research, primarily case series, that focuses on nonclinical populations of children and/or teens experiencing "normal nervous" emotions or state anxiety, such as test anxiety (Johnson, Larson, Conn, Estes, & Ghibellini, 2009; Spies, 1979; Stanton, 1994), academic stress (Nair & Meera, 2014), and sports performance anxiety (Bagherpour, Hashim, Saha, & Ghosh, 2012; Hashim & Hanafi, 2011), report the value of relaxation therapies (including guided imagery about a "special fun place" with repetitive instructions to "relax and calm yourself").

Unfortunately, far too many clinicians limit their intervention to employing relaxation therapy "scripts" that only focus on calming and relaxing the psychophysiological symptoms of situational anxiety and fear. Such general, one-size-fits-all visualization recipes, which erroneously assume that these are the key issues, are the converse of a carefully designed, individualized hypnosis approach. It is this author's opinion that recipes are woefully insufficient because they fail to (a) target any underlying specific thinking, perceptual, feeling, and behavioral patterns that generate and maintain the anxiety, stress, and/or fear; (b) address and utilize the patient's unique resources; or (c) devise a personalized treatment plan. Because of the boundless individual differences in the presentation of

anxious and stressed children and teens, the use of scripts is not recommended.

CASE EXAMPLES

I contend that clinicians need to take a more comprehensive approach by designing customized hypnosis sessions, guided by the specific goals that address the distinctive profile and underdeveloped resources of each child or teen.

This view is drawn from extensive study with Michael Yapko, a leading expert with prolific contributions (e.g., 1988, 2001, 2012, 2015) to the hypnosis field. Yapko's hypnosis framework emphasizes the personalization of hypnosis sessions. Drawing from various fields of psychology and psychotherapy, he identified several style patterns that potentially influence the person's issue, problem, or symptom (Yapko, 1988). Examples include (but are not limited to) expectations (positive/negative), perceptual style (magnify/diminish), rigidity/flexibility, and degree of mastery over experience (internal/external locus of control). Children and teens with any kind of anxiety disorder have their own unique profile of these and other characteristics contributing to their presentation, which add complexity and challenge as well as the need for customized treatment planning. These individual differences in their style pattern have important implications when determining specific and concrete goals and therapeutic suggestions for hypnosis sessions.

Many clinically anxious youth have more than one diagnosis, so a comprehensive evaluation is essential to determine if there are additional anxiety disorders, as well as comorbid depression. Also, the older the anxious child becomes, the more likely he or she also will experience clinical depression. For these reasons, clinicians need to be familiar with the *DSM-5* descriptions of major depressive disorders as well as different domains of anxiety, including diagnoses related to generalized anxiety (i.e., excessive and persistent worry and anxiety about several domains plus physical symptoms), panic, agoraphobia, trauma and stressors, social situations, performance in front of others, selective mutism (i.e., failure to speak in certain social situations [e.g., school] despite speaking in other situations), specific phobias (e.g., medical procedures/equipment, animals/insects), separation from parents, and substance/medications.

Children and youth typically show clinical anxiety and fear in novel and unfamiliar situations, for example, the therapist's office. These emotional states create a natural trance that you can utilize upon introduction in the reception room and throughout each session. Speak calmly and somewhat slower than usual, conveying warmth and kindness, without much eye contact and without touching, for example, handshake. Provide structure by informing her or him what to expect. "I am glad to have you visit for a while (calling attention to the temporary situation). I have some collections (giraffe, spinning tops, sand timers, marbles) and some other neat things to show you in my room (not "office": too clinical). Do you have any collections? (bridging to a common interest of school-age children). Then I want to . . . *listen very carefully* . . . to what you say about why you've come to see me. You can decide where you want to sit; I have several different types of chairs. Your parent is going to sit here (determine ahead of time if the parent will do an errand, or go home nearby, and when to return). When we're done at (give the time) then it will be time for the *two of you to leave together*" (this emphasizes that the parent will remember to take the child home).

Various studies show that anxiety disorders are the most frequent mental disorders in children and adolescents, and are the earliest of all forms of psychopathology (Beesdo, Knappe, & Pine, 2009). Yet anxious youth suffer from the stigma of their developmentally inappropriate symptoms, are often embarrassed about their diminished self-regulation, and may be criticized by family and/or friends for being oversensitive or a cry-baby, wimp, sissy, or other derogatory terms. As children get older, some may blatantly minimize or even deny anxiety, fear, or worry; interestingly, they tend to be more forthcoming when asked about stress.

Listen carefully for the term students use to convey their anxiety, for example, *freaked out, stressed out, afraid, scared, nervous,* and so on. Use their term when discussing their problems and during hypnosis.

To maximize truthfulness about presence, range, and intensity of symptoms when asking about additional sources of stress, anxiety, or fear, you can normalize the question. Be hypnotic as you

say, "Everyone has some things that make them feel stressed or bothered. Let's make a (written) list of the things that bother you." (Bother is a very neutral term.) After obtaining this list, then ask about any other worries or things that make the patient feel (use the child's term here). Next, draw and explain the 0 to 10 scale to rate his or her level of distress (anxiety, worry, bother, stress, whatever the child calls it), and then ask the patient to rate each item on his or her list.

Children and teens with anxiety disorders share some common patterns in their thinking and response. They share core difficulties in accurately appraising specific situations, experiences, and other stimuli (e.g., elevators, bugs, etc.). A working paper on persistent fear and anxiety in young children written by The National Scientific Council on the Developing Child (2010) at Harvard concluded that "children who have had chronic and intense fearful experiences often lose the capacity to differentiate between threat and safety" (p. 5). Such discrimination errors are fraught with a pattern of overestimating the probability of risk, threat, or danger.

Case A

A 10-year-old presented with a 2 months history of school refusal due to strong fears and worry about being in a new academic setting that differed significantly from the former school. After getting lost in the halls for 20 minutes during recess in the first week, this student concluded, "I'm not safe there" because the very large student body and building layout meant easily getting lost again; therefore, the teachers were unable to adequately monitor the students' safety. This child overgeneralized from a single episode to an assumption, which would recur often.

Beyond this extreme school anxiety, the assessment revealed an underlying chronic separation anxiety. Both were fueled and maintained by an underlying pattern of errors in discrimination: overestimating the probability of risk, threat, or danger to his mother and himself when they were apart. This became the primary focus of his treatment plan that included designing hypnotic suggestions to enhance accurate appraisal of conventional separation experiences.

A second typical and similarly critical discernment error of anxious youth is an underestimation of their capacities and internal resources to cope, manage, and successfully handle certain situations, experiences, or stimuli (Lazarus, 2013). The case A student adamantly contended an inability to manage all day in this unfamiliar school setting, intensified by difficulty remembering the school layout and lack of courage to initiate introductions with classmates.

A third common discrimination error of most anxious youth is misinterpreting their exaggerated psychophysiological (mind–body) reactivity and its related anxiety and/or fear. These bodily sensations of racing heart and respiration rates, stomach "butterflies" or "knot," trembling, and/ or other possible rising panic reactions are typically misread as confirming signs of imminent danger. Such disturbing sensations reinforce and escalate their fear and anxiety, as well as trigger sleep-related problems (SRP) (especially insomnia, nightmares, and reluctance/refusal to sleep alone). Research shows that 88% of anxious youth (ages 6–17) experienced at least one SRP, and more than half experienced three or more (Alfano, Ginsburg, & Kingery, 2007).

In case A, the child demanded that the mother stay in his room until he was asleep. Both insomnia and nightmares resulted in significant difficulty and resistance to getting going each morning. Once up, the child would protest vociferously, screaming and crying hysterically as well as visibly shaking on the way to school and then vomiting upon getting out of the car. The principal and mother agreed that the student was too overwhelmed to attend a full day, eventually leading to nonattendance every day. The longer this child escaped and avoided (classic "safety" behaviors) school, the more it locked in his fear and anxiety.

Resolving sleep disturbances is frequently my initial treatment goal with anxious youth, given sleep deprivation's profound and pervasive negative impact on all areas of functioning. Creating a hypnosis tape focused on relaxation and respite from stress is one option, especially if the child is slow to acquire self-hypnosis skills, lacks imagination, or cannot shift attention from fears or worries.

Enhancing self-regulation, that is, shifting one's attention in order to control and modulate one's psychophysiological reactivity (panic sensations), emotions (anxiety, fear), thoughts (worries), and behavior (escape, avoid, demand reassurance) leads to various, individualized goals for treating anxious youth with hypnosis, cognitive behavioral therapy (CBT), and other mind–body approaches (Cyr, Culbert, & Kaiser, 2003; Kaiser, 2011; Kohen & Kaiser, 2014).

Because this Case A child was also visibly anxious during his initial sessions with me, I wondered aloud how his body reacted when he was scared. He did not have much insight into his mind–body connection; however, he was able to identify specific panic symptoms when I listed these while drawing a picture of a scared boy. I capitalized on his natural trance state and used conversational hypnosis, leaning on specific words and hypnotic "phrasing" to create implied directives: *So you just identified the first two signals that tell you when you're afraid. You used to* [indirect suggestion that this pattern was in the past] *interpret these as danger or threat in a situation because you were being tricked by your imagination! Listen very carefully now* [as I leaned forward, lowered my voice, and steadily looked directly into his eyes]: *Actually, these are two very important signals that say . . . it is time now to . . . use your new tricks and strategies to . . . help yourself have control . . . to calm down. You're going to . . . learn these powerful skills . . . starting now.*

I do concur with Kajander and Peper (1998) that teaching diaphragmatic breathing is an extremely useful technique to address the psychophysiological reactivity of children and teens experiencing clinically significant anxiety, stress, or fear. Kajander and Peper cogently explain that "belly breathing in through the nose stimulates the vagus nerve endings resulting in lowering of the sympathetic response and inhibiting the fight/flight response" (p. 16). By careful observations of Case A, I noted his raised shoulders with shallow, rapid breathing and his speech had a breathy quality, with comments coming in short bursts, rather than fluid sentences. Learning diaphragmatic breathing led to notable positive changes for this child, as he applied this handy technique for self-soothing, lowering anxiety, and smoother verbal communication.

If you wish to read an excellent and detailed explanation of diaphragmatic breathing and how to teach the proper technique to children, refer to Kajander and Peper (1998).

Once the child consistently demonstrates the correct technique, and is fully absorbed with focused attention on "belly breathing," the clinician can further intensify/deepen this spontaneous trance with layers of suggestions that focus on cognitive, emotional, and physiological self-regulation and adaptive coping:

"That's right. . . . As you . . . breathe in cool . . . calm . . . control . . . comfort . . . capable . . . confidence . . . competence. The 7 C's. This breathing turns on the Calming . . . Control . . . Center (CCC). Excellent. . . . Blow out the worries . . . scared feelings . . . stress . . . and anything you don't need any longer. You can . . . remember to do this . . . whenever you just start to get those signals [name them] [posthypnotic suggestion]. After all, you take your lungs with you wherever you go!"

Use the pacing technique to match these suggestions to the child's inspirations and expirations.

TRANSCRIPT: INDIVIDUALIZED HYPNOTIC SESSION

The following case transcript offers another illustration of how to incorporate a student's unique style patterns underlying her anxiety into individualized hypnosis goals and suggestions for cognitive, emotional, and physiological self-regulation and adaptive coping.

Case B

Case B was a 14-year-old very bright, articulate student athlete who presented with a phobia of vomiting. She was captain of a debate team as well as a superior soccer player. An assessment revealed a history of vomiting prior to these two activities as well as her underlying style pattern of negative expectations about upcoming situations/events, intolerance of ambiguity/uncertainty (which is inherent in such activities), and a strong need for control during these experiences. Thus, the initial hypnosis goals were to build internal control and positive expectations despite external uncontrollability, and to accept life's ambiguities, that is, being certain about upcoming uncertainty. To solely focus on the vomiting phobia would have missed the driving forces for such a fear, and likely led to an unsuccessful outcome.

Since expectancy has critical implications for the success of therapy, the clinician needs to build positive expectations from the beginning of contact. Following the assessment and development of a comfortable rapport in her first session, I used a response (aka yes) set technique to lay the groundwork for this therapeutic goal. I methodically commented: "People tend to look for what they expect. Many people make a point of expecting that things will go really well for themselves. (Pause.) Some students oppose that view and expect that things will not work out well. (Pause.) You can examine the evidence and decide . . . to anticipate that things will work out in your current life . . . so things can go much smoother."

Because we already discussed the many ways that people experience spontaneous trance states, including her highly focused naturalistic trance states during soccer games and debate meets, I used a conversational induction, as I encouraged her to

"Go ahead and just begin in any way you like . . . getting yourself more comfortable in your chair . . . as you begin to shift your focus toward your inside mind . . . comfortably . . . easily . . . resting into yourself. Allowing yourself to shift your attention . . . now . . . to becoming more internally absorbed. . . . That's right (as she closed her eyes and settled into a more comfortable position) . . . you've done this before . . . in your own way . . . you can do it again . . . and you . . . do it again."

The following segment of a longer hypnosis session also demonstrates how to utilize a child's interest (debate team) by weaving in words related to that activity. I typically take a few minutes before starting the hypnosis to generate these words (sometimes getting help from the Internet) while the student completes a questionnaire or creates some projective drawings. For example, some words in the debate field include: give a speech, make a point, defend, extend the case, rebuttal, hold the floor, "point of information," propose, motion, oppose, dispute, deliberate, examine the facts, conclusion, argue, contend, reason, maintain, consult with a coach, and flowsheet.

"I'd like to hold the floor for a bit. Expectations are an internal experience about an external experience. Many people claim that experiences

can become adventures. A reasonable case can be made that one expands his or her perspect ive on adventures near . . . and farther away. No one would dispute that there are likely to be a few detours along the way . . . despite having researched the case. One can expect, having done this before so many times, as you so well know, you can adjust . . . and extend . . . your prior perspective. So you can put into motion . . . new expectations."

I created a theme about ambiguity and anticipation of new positive possibilities: "I guess people can debate about how novel an experience is going to be. Rather than arguing the case back and forth, you can choose . . . to embrace these uncertain experiences and look forward to new possibilities . . . positive . . . for your own personal growth."

"Isn't it curious that the one thing about life that we can be certain of . . . is uncertainty? When we examine the facts . . . we don't really know 100% that all of our friends will be at school on any particular day . . . or that all the teachers will be teaching every day. . . . It's entirely reasonable that we can't be absolutely certain that the weather will be pleasant . . . or that you will have a great time when hanging out with some class friends . . . no one would contend that you can be completely sure that you will enjoy a new dish on the restaurant menu . . . and one could extend the case to say it's unclear that you will fall asleep easily every night . . . or that you will like your favorite singer's newest song. . . . In a way, we can propose that all upcoming situations are ambiguous . . . and no one could disprove that it's impossible to definitely know or anticipate what is going to happen . . . like, whether all your teammates will be giving 100% effort . . . or what the outcome of a contest will be.

In conclusion, rather than worry and defend against such ambiguity, I motion that it can be so much more pleasant to . . . create a shift in your mindset . . . deliberately . . . away from worry and . . . and move toward curiosity and anticipation of what's ahead. [Pause.] I expect that . . . YOU have the guts . . . gumption . . . and mental gifts . . . to keep your focus on positive possibilities and expectations."

CONCLUSION

In sum, chronic childhood anxiety, the earliest and most frequent mental disorder among youth, has a potentially lifelong negative impact on self-regulation, learning, memory, and social behavior. Despite the dearth and variable quality of research, hypnosis offers a valuable adjunct to psychological interventions (especially cognitive behavioral therapy) in the treatment of childhood anxiety, presenting as anxiety disorders, anticipatory and medical procedural anxiety, primary care presentations, or "normal nervous" (state anxiety) responses to developmentally based situational stressors.

Rather than superficial "scripts" for relaxation, clinicians are urged to design individualized hypnosis sessions utilizing the child's interests and presenting profile of underdeveloped internal resources (Anbar, 2003). Determining the child's pattern of underlying factors that fuel and maintain anxiety leads to specific hypnosis goals, such as more accurate discrimination skills, self-regulation, positive expectancy, tolerance of ambiguity, and other more adaptive patterns.

REFERENCES

Alfano, C. A., Ginsburg, G. S., & Kingery, J. N. (2007). Sleep-related problems among children and adolescents with anxiety disorders. *American Academy for Child Adolescent Psychiatry*, 46(2), 224–232.

American Psychiatric Association. (2013). *Diagnostic and statistical manual of mental disorders* (5th ed.). Washington, DC: American Psychiatric Association Publishing.

Anbar, R. D. (2003). Self-hypnosis for anxiety associated with severe asthma: A case report. *BMC Pediatrics*, 3(7). doi:10.1186/1471-2431-3-7

Bagherpour, T., Hashim, H. A., Saha, S., & Ghosh, A. K. (2012). *Effects of progressive muscle relaxation and internal imagery on competitive state anxiety inventory 2R among Taekwondo athletes*. International Conference on Education and Management Innovation.

Beesdo, K., Knappe, S., & Pine, D. S. (2009). Anxiety and anxiety disorders in children and adolescents: Developmental issues and implications for *DSM-V*. *Psychiatric Clinic of North America*, 32(3), 483–524.

Bell, M. A., & Deater-Deckard, K. (2007). Biological systems and the development of self-regulation: Integrating behavior, genetics, and psychophysiology.

Journal of Developmental and Behavioral Pediatrics, 28(5), 409–420. doi:10.1097/DBP.0b013e3181131fc7

Boyce, W. T., & Jemerin, J. (1990). Psychobiological differences in childhood stress response. Patterns of illness and susceptibility. Journal of Developmental and Behavioral Pediatrics, 11(2), 86–94.

Boyce, W. T., Chesney, M., Alkon, A., Tschann, J. M., Adams, S., Chesterman, B., . . . Wara, D. (1995). Psychobiologic reactivity to stress and childhood respiratory illnesses: Results of two prospective studies. Psychosomatic Medicine, 57(5), 411–422.

Boyce, W. T., Chesney, M., Kaiser, P., Alkon, A., Eisenhardt, M., Chesterman, E., & Tschann, J. (1991). Development of protocol for measuring cardiovascular response to stress in preschool children. Pediatric Research.

Burns, D. (1999). The feeling good handbook. New York City, NY: Penguin Putnam.

Butler, L. D., Symons, B. K., Henderson, S. L., Shortliffe, L. D., & Spiegel, D. (2005). Hypnosis reduces distress and duration of an invasive medical procedure for children. Pediatrics, 115, 77–85.

Cyr, L. R., Culbert, T., & Kaiser, P. (2003). Helping children with stress and anxiety: An integrative medicine approach, special issue: Pediatric integrative medicine. Biofeedback, 31, 12–33.

Hammond, C. (2010). Hypnosis in the treatment of anxiety- and stress-related disorders. Expert Review of Neuroscience, 10, 263–273.

Hashim, H. A., & Hanafi, H. (2011). The effects of progressive muscle relaxation and autogenic relaxation on young soccer players' mood states. Asian Journal of Sports Medicine, 2(2), 99–105.

Johnson, C. M., Larson, H. A., Conn, S. R., Estes, L. A., & Ghibellini, A. B. (2009). The impact of relaxation techniques on third grade students' self-perceived levels of test anxiety. Paper based on a program presented at the American Counseling Association Annual Conference and Exposition, Charlotte, NC.

Kaiser, P. (2011). Childhood anxiety, worry, and fear: Individualizing hypnosis goals and suggestions for self-regulation. American Journal of Clinical Hypnosis, 54(1), 16–31. doi:10.1080/00029157.2011.575965

Kaiser, P. (2014). Childhood anxiety and psychophysiological reactivity: Hypnosis to build discrimination and self-regulation skills. American Journal of Clinical Hypnosis, 56(4), 343–367. doi:10.1080/00029157.2014.884487

Kajander, R., & Peper, E. (1998). Teaching diaphragmatic breathing to children. Biofeedback, 26(3), 14–17.

Kohen, D. Pl., Olness, K. N., Colwell, S. O., & Heimel, A. (1984). The use of relaxation-mental imagery (self-hypnosis) in the management of 505 pediatric behavioral encounters. Journal of Behavioral Pediatrics, 5(1), 21–25.

Kohen, D. P., & Kaiser, P. (2014). Review article: Clinical hypnosis with children and adolescents–What? Why?

How?: Origins, applications, and efficacy. Children, 1, 74–98.

Kohen, D. P., & Olness, K. N. (2011). Hypnosis and hypnotherapy with children. Florence, KY: Routledge Publications.

Kuttner, L. (2009). Treating pain, anxiety and sleep disorders with children and adolescents. In D. C. Brown (Ed.), Advances in the use of hypnosis in medicine, dentistry, pain prevention and management (pp. 177–194). Bethel, CT: Crown House Publishers.

Kuttner, L., Bowman, M., & Teasdale, M. (1989). Psychological treatment of distress, pain, and anxiety for young children with cancer. Journal of Developmental & Behavioral Pediatrics, 9, 374–381.

Landier, W., & Tse, A. M. (2010). Use of complementary and alternative medical intervention for the management of procedure-related pain, anxiety, and distress in pediatric oncology: An integrative review. Journal of Pediatric Nursing, 25(6), 566–579. doi:10.1016/j.pedn.2010.01.009

Lazarus, R. S. (2013). Fifty years of the research and theory of R. S. Lazarus: An analysis of historical and perennial issues. Florence, KY: Psychology Press.

Liossi, C., & Hatira, P. (1999). Clinical hypnosis versus cognitive behavioral training for pain management with pediatric cancer patients undergoing bone marrow aspirations. International Journal of Clinical and Experimental Hypnosis, 47(2), 104–116. doi:10.1080/00207149908410025

Liossi, C., & Hatira, P. (2003). Clinical hypnosis in the alleviation of procedure-related pain in pediatric oncology patients. International Journal of Clinical and Experimental Hypnosis, 51(1), 4–28. doi:10.1076/iceh.51.1.4.14064

Liossi, C., White, P., & Hatira, P. (2006). Randomized clinical trial of local anesthetic versus a combination of local anesthetic with self-hypnosis in the management of pediatric procedure-related pain. Health Psychology: Official Journal of the Division of Health Psychology, American Psychological Association, 25(3), 307–315. doi:10.1037/0278-6133.25.3.307

Liossi, C., White, P., & Hatira, P. (2009). A randomized clinical trial of a brief hypnosis intervention to control venipuncture-related pain of paediatric cancer patients. Pain, 142(3), 255–263. doi:10.1016/j.pain.2009.01.017

Nair, P. P., & Meera, K. P. (2014). Effectiveness of progressive muscle relaxation in reducing academic stress of secondary schools students of Kerala. IOSR Journal of Humanities and Social Science, 19(8), 29–32.

National Scientific Council on the Developing Child. (2010). Persistent fear and anxiety can affect young children's learning and development: Working paper no. 9. Retrieved from http://www.developingchild.net

Smith, J. T., Barabasz, A., & Barabasz, M. (1996). Comparison of hypnosis and distraction in severely ill children undergoing painful medical procedures. Journal of Counseling Psychology, 43, 187–195.

Spies, G. (1979). Desensitization of test anxiety: Hypnosis compared with biofeedback. *American Journal of Clinical Hypnosis, 22*(2), 108–111. doi:10.1080/00029157.1979.10403207

Stanton, H. E. (1994). Self-hypnosis: One path to reduced test anxiety. *Contemporary Hypnosis, 11*, 14–18.

Uman, L. S., Chambers, C. T., McGrath, P. J., & Kisely, S. (2008). A systematic review of randomized controlled trials examining psychological interventions for needle-related procedural pain and distress in children and adolescents: An abbreviated Cochrane Review. *Journal of Pediatric Psychology, 33*(8), 842–854. doi:10.1093/jpepsy/jsn031

Vasey, M., & Dodds, M. (2001). Information-processing factors in childhood anxiety: A review and developmental perspective. In M. Vasey & M. Dodds (Eds.), *The developmental psychopathology of anxiety* (pp. 253–277). New York, NY: Oxford University Press.

Yapko, M. (1988). *When living hurts: Directives for treating depression.* Bristol, PA: Taylor & Francis.

Yapko, M. (2001). *Treating depression with hypnosis: Integrating cognitive-behavioral and strategic approaches.* Philadelphia, PA: Brunner-Routledge.

Yapko, M. (2012). *Trancework.* New York, NY: Routledge.

Yapko, M. (2015). *Essentials of hypnosis.* New York, NY: Routledge.

Zeltzer, L., & LeBaron, S. (1982). Hypnosis and non-hypnotic techniques for reduction of pain and anxiety during painful procedures in children and adolescents with cancer. *Journal of Pediatrics, 101*(6), 1032–1035.

Bereavement

Alex Iglesias and Adam Iglesias

The loss of a loved one is a ubiquitous and devastating experience. While in many cases, the bereaved is able to reach a resolution of the loss without the presence of disabling and/or prolonged characteristics, there are many instances when such loss engenders prolonged and/or debilitating grief. This chapter will review the burgeoning body of information on prolonged grief disorder (PGD), a construct that has been heretofore titled complicated grief, traumatic grief, and pathological grief with subcategories including interrupted, delayed, and absence of grief (Averill, 1968). The literature on the treatment of PGD with hypnosis also will be reviewed and a case example of hypnosis-aided behavioral treatment in a case of spousal bereavement will be presented. Included is the treatment protocol with a transcript of hypnotic suggestions, which was employed.

UNCOMPLICATED BEREAVEMENT REACTIONS

Healthy adjustment to bereavement has been described by several theoretical models (Bonanno & Kaltman, 1999; Neimeyer, 1998, 2005; Shuchter & Zisook, 1993; Stroebe & Schut, 1999; Stroebe, Schut, & Stroebe, 2005a, 2005b). These models share several features including (a) focus on resilience and adaptation, (b) premise that adaptation requires strategies in a multitude of situations, (c) the importance of developing and operationalizing coping strategies, and (d) the role that the sociocultural context plays in the adaptation process.

One model relevant to hypnotherapy for bereavement is the model of adaptation developed by Bonanno and Kaltman (1999). This theoretical model places significant importance on behavioral coping strategies, which act as emotion regulation strategies as well. It lends credence to the therapeutic value of mastering behavioral tasks considered

by the bereaved as too difficult or even impossible to achieve. Moreover, this model considers the acquisition of new behavioral skills, in graduated successive approximations, the key toward a sense of mastery and independence in the bereaved. This premise was supported by Bauer and Bonanno (2001), who found that bereaved individuals who felt self-efficacious were less likely over time to experience intense grief. Chentsova, Dutton and Zisook (2005) also supported this theoretical premise and emphasized that when conducting assessments of the functioning of widows and widowers it becomes imperative to define coping more comprehensively and to take the acquisition of new skills and improved physical, social, and occupational functioning into account. Caserta, Lund, and Obray (2004) also supported this theoretical position and posited that offering bereavement counseling services that focus on behavioral strategies, self-care behavioral methods, daily living skills, and assuming tasks that were the province of the deceased is a beneficial direction to promote the personal mastery among the bereaved.

Pursuant to this orientation, Lieberman (1978) and Ramsey (1978) developed therapeutic programs for the bereaved that focused on the behavioral therapy methods of systematic desensitization and flooding. Their aim was for the bereaved to focus their attention and confront activities associated with their loss that they were avoiding. Theoretically, this approach allows the bereaved to be exposed to the seemingly intolerable stimuli, at a gradual pace, and to achieve successive approximations of the desired goal at a rate that is tolerable to the individual. The behavior therapy orientation maintains that changed behaviors lead to a shift in feelings and thoughts (Barbato & Irwin, 1992). Controlled exposure to bereavement cues was based on the Kavanagh (1990) principle that bereaved individuals need to confront grief by deliberate exposure to bereavement cues. This principle indicates that only by deliberate exposure to bereavement cues can the bereaved develop skills for confronting and coping with the distressing signals.

PROLONGED GRIEF DISORDER

The essence of PGD is the magnification of bereavement traits rather than the diminution of the same over time. Precursors of the disorder include a history of prior trauma or loss, a history of mood and anxiety disorders, insecure attachment style, a violent cause of death, and lack of social support subsequent to the loss (Jordan & Litz, 2014). The *Diagnostic and Statistical Manual of Mental Disorders, fifth edition* (*DSM-5;* American Psychiatric Association, 2013) includes nomenclature, which references prolonged grief-related problems. These include other specified trauma and stressor-related disorder, and persistent complex bereavement disorder (PCBD). PGD is a condition that has been found to be a disorder distinct from bereavement depression and anxiety (Prigerson et al., 1996).

RESEARCH ON HYPNOSIS FOR THE TREATMENT OF GRIEF REACTIONS

The literature on hypnosis for bereavement is scarce. Perhaps the most ambitious effort of treating inordinate grief with hypnosis was provided by Gravitz (2001). A single-session hypnosis-based, imagery strategy was designed to focus and address the patient's tormenting images of her mother as she agonized during her final days. These recurrent intrusive images were hypnotically replaced with images of her loved one during happy and healthy times. It was concluded that creating hypnotically reconstructed memories is a viable approach for treating inordinate grief. Gravitz (2001) also contributed a thorough review of the hypnosis literature for bereavement. This review referenced an 1813 report wherein the hypnotic techniques of uncovering and revivification were employed to assist a young woman to cope with grief. Additional contributions to the hypnosis literature on the applications of hypnosis for the treatment

of complicated grief included the work of Fromm and Eisin (1982), wherein the authors treated a female patient with self-hypnosis to work through feelings of loss following the death of her husband. Furthermore, there were documented case reports by Turco (1981) as well as Savage (1993) in which complicated grief reactions in female patients were successfully treated with hypnosis. In addition, Gravitz (1994) reported on several cases of traumatic grief in which hypnotic strategies were employed first to bring to conscious memory the previously repressed memories of traumatic incidents. These memories were subsequently restructured, including the memory of the original event as well as the psychological meaning to the patient.

In pediatric populations, Iglesias and Iglesias (2005) developed an approach to reduce obsessive focusing on morbid and horrific details of the accidental death of a parent. The gruesome nature of the parental death complicated the children's grief reaction, interrupted their grief, and led to a PTSD reaction. The authors designed the hypnotic trauma narrative, an instrument designed to provide therapeutic elements by means of two age-progression methods. The first is a telescope metaphor/strategy created in order to allow the child to view images of the catastrophic loss through a distant vantage point (i.e., child looks through the wide end of a telescope) and facilitate the narrowing, constricting, and blurring of horrific and painful details. Second, the hypnotic trauma narrative also provides a more unstructured indirect age progression technique aimed to allow the child to orient to future possibilities (Phillips & Frederick, 1992).

CASE EXAMPLE

The patient, a 72-year-old Caucasian male who was 13 months postspousal bereavement, was referred by a local hospice. He had received 10 bereavement support group sessions with minimal results. The focus of the support group was emotion-based, which resulted in iatrogenic effects for this patient (e.g., exacerbated his sense of despair). He was deeply grieved and met the criteria for PGD. He exhibited behaviors that contributed to perpetuate the bereavement reaction. He was also not engaging in behaviors conducive

TABLE 54.1

SELF-DEFEATING BEHAVIORS AND RESOLUTION OF GRIEF EXAMPLES	
Self-Defeating Behaviors (SDB)	**Facilitators of the Resolution of Grief (FRG)**
Refuses invitations from friends	Accept invitations
Discontinues attendance to health club	Resumes attendance to health club
Eats meals on a tray/does not use dining table	Uses dining table
Stays in night clothes during the day	Out of night clothes in the morning
Does not return phone calls	Returns phone calls
Does not answer the phone	Answers the phone
Cancels grocery shopping trips	Makes grocery shopping trips
Ignores mail received Ignores personal hygiene	Attends to mail received Pays close attention to hygiene
Obsessive reminiscing of final moments	Reminiscing a host of memories
Maintains a museum-like environment Exclusive display of pictures of the deceased	Maintains a lived-in environment Displays an assortment of pictures
Ambulates aimlessly around house	Maintains an agenda and avoids aimlessness
Sleeps for large segments of the day	Avoids sleeping during the day
Overeating or undernourishment	Adheres to proper diet

to reconnect socially. The recalcitrance of his grief picture and the debilitating impact that an emotion-based treatment modality exacted on the patient were criteria used to select a behavioral treatment approach.

Technique

The treatment consisted of a hypnotically aided behavioral orientation that, rather than focus on the grief itself, addressed specific behaviors that were hindering the resolution of grief (Sobel, 1981). The focus

on behaviors as the unit of attention is consonant with the orientation of behavioral therapy (Gray & Litz, 2005). In behavior therapy, the therapist adopts a problem-solving focus and assists patients to operationalize the presenting problems, set goals, and learn new skills to replace self-defeating behaviors (Barbato & Irwin, 1992). Theoretically, this approach is based on the notion that behavior is learned and through a systematic training program, the patient can be helped to replace self-defeating behaviors with more health-promoting behaviors (Corey, 1986).

First Phase

The initial meetings involved the task of developing two lists of behaviors targeted for attention. First, the patient was instructed to identify specific behaviors associated with the present circumstance that were self-defeating (i.e., self-defeating behaviors) These behaviors were acknowledged by the patient as necessary to be reduced and even eliminated in order to resolve the grief. Stated differently, as the self-defeating behaviors diminished, resolution of the grief would be facilitated. The goal became to extinguish those self-defeating behaviors that were interfering with the resolution of grief. Second, the patient was instructed to identify behaviors that needed to be established and increased in frequency. These behaviors were designated as facilitators of the resolution of grief; establishing them and increasing their frequency became a pivotal goal. These items in essence became the antidotes to the self-defeating behaviors (SDB) shown in Table 54.1.

Second Phase

A protocol consisting of items from the facilitators of the resolution of grief (FRG) list was prepared. After inducing hypnosis using an eye fixation induction (Hammond, 1990) and relaxation (Elkins, 2014), the items from this list were presented and repeated to the patient in hypnosis. Ideomotor signaling was employed to allow for patient responses (Hammond, 1998). The following protocol was employed in the case in question.

TRANSCRIPT

"Now that you are in a comfortable hypnotic state you will be provided suggestions of behaviors we

have deemed need to be enhanced and their frequency increased. Understand that the increased frequency of these behaviors will by definition bring about a normalization of your emotions. I will ask you to visualize yourself engaging in these behaviors. See yourself performing each of the items as if you were watching a movie. The movie is played out with a minimum of feeling. This will make the process bland and maybe boring. It is expected that images that are accepted during hypnotic treatment will become accepted to be incorporated into daily use. You will keep your eyes closed to be able to see yourself clearly engaging in the behaviors that I will suggest. The activities in question may be carried out without much desire or pleasure. The important factor is that you see yourself carrying them out. Now begin by seeing yourself engaging in [item from the facilitators of the resolution of grief (FRG) list]. *Even if you do not feel like engaging in the behaviors, you can perform or carry out the same in your mind. Remember, these suggestions are medically necessary and were designed by your doctor expressly for you and with your circumstances in mind. Those tasks performed in hypnosis will be able to be carried out in daily life."*

The patient was instructed to incorporate into his agenda and carry out those items successfully rehearsed in hypnosis.

The patient was seen for six visits of individual attention on a biweekly basis. The patient was able to perform in vivo the tasks rehearsed in hypnosis. Deceased levels of emotional reactivity from the PGD reaction were recognized as an indirect result of the reconnecting and restoration efforts. The patient was able to diminish the morbid and self-defeating elements of his reaction to the loss. He was seen for follow up two months after treatment concluded. He had retained the reconnecting and restoration activities that were targeted in therapy. He was also observed to be devoid of the morbidity and melancholic elements present before treatment started.

CONCLUSION

Millions of people are bereaved every year and a proportion of them go on to develop PGD. If left untreated or improperly treated, the consequences

can be significant from a point of view of functional impairment, reduced quality of life, and increased mortality and morbidity (Jordan & Litz, 2014). Hypnotherapy is a valuable approach to treat bereavement. A hypnotic-mediated approach is presented here that emphasizes reconnecting and restoration aspects. Clinicians using this approach are encouraged to:

1. identify specific behaviors that are self-defeating in regard to resolving grief;
2. identify facilitators for the resolution of grief;
3. utilize hypnotic inductions with relaxation suggestions and control;
4. employ ideomotor signaling to confirm responses;
5. present positive suggestions to decrease self-defeating behavior and to facilitate grief resolution; and
6. consider biweekly sessions with in vivo rehearsal of grief resolution in hypnosis.

Hypnotic-mediated approaches that emphasize reconnecting and restoration aspects of PGD treatment should be considered as an invaluable part of therapy in cases (Jordan & Litz, 2014; Schut & Strobe, 2005; Stroebe & Shut, 1999) of prolonged grief.

REFERENCES

American Psychiatric Association. (2013). *Diagnostic and statistical manual of mental disorders*. Arlington, VA: American Psychiatric Association.

Averill, J. (1968). Grief: Its nature and significance. *Psychological Bulletin, 6*, 721–748.

Barbato, A., & Irwin, H. (1992). Major therapeutic systems and the bereaved client. *Australian Psychologist, 27*, 22–27.

Bauer, J., & Bonanno, G. (2001). I can, I do, I am: The narrative differentiation of self-efficacy and other self-evaluations while adapting to bereavement. *Journal of Research in Personality, 35*, 424–448.

Bonanno, G. A., & Kaltman, S. (1999). Toward an integrative perspective on bereavement. *Psychological Bulletin, 125*(6), 760–776.

Caserta, M., Lund, D., & Obray, S. (2004). Promoting self care and daily living skills among older widows and widowers: Evidence from the Pathfinders Demonstration Project. *Omega. Journal of Death and Dying, 49*, 217–236.

Chentsova Dutton, Y., & Zisook, S. (2005). Adaptation to bereavement. *Death Studies*, 29(10), 877–903.

Corey, G. (1986). *Theory and practice of counseling and psychotherapy*. Monterrey, CA: Brooks/Cole.

Elkins, G. (2014). *Hypnotic relaxation therapy: Principles and appplications*. New York, NY: Springer Publishing Company.

Fromm, E., & Eisen, M. (1982). Self-hypnosis as a therapeutic in the mourning process. *American Journal of Clinical Hypnosis*, 23, 3–14.

Gravitz, M. A. (1994). Memory reconstruction by hypnosis as a therapeutic technique. *Psychotherapy: Theory, Research, Practice, Training*, 31(4), 687–691.

Gravitz, M. A. (2001). Perceptual reconstruction in the case of inordinate grief. *American Journal of Clinical Hypnosis*, 44(1), 51–55.

Gray, M. J., & Litz, B. T. (2005). Behavioral interventions for recent trauma: Empirically informed guidelines. *Behavior Modification*, 29(1), 189–215.

Hammond, C. (1990). *Handbook of hypnotic suggestions and metaphors*. New York, NY: W. W. Norton.

Hammond, C. (1998). Ideomotor signaling: A rapid method for unconscious exploration. In D. C. Hammond (Ed.), *Hypnotic induction and suggestion* (pp. 113–121). Chicago, IL: American Society of Clinical Hypnosis.

Iglesias, A., & Iglesias, A. (2005). Hypnotic treatment of PTSD in children who have complicated bereavement. *American Journal of Clinical Hypnosis*, 48(3), 177–183.

Jordan, A., & Litz, B. (2014). Prolonged grief disorder: Diagnostic, assessment and treatment considerations. *Professional Psychology: Research and Practice*, 45(43), 180–187.

Kavanagh, D. (1990). Towards a cognitive-behavioural intervention for adult grief reactions. *British Journal of Psychiatry*, 257, 373–383.

Lieberman, S. (1978). Nineteen cases of morbid grief. *British Journal of Psychiatry: The Journal of Mental Science*, 132, 159–163.

Neimeyer, R. (1998). *The lessons of loss: A guide to coping*. New York, NY: McGraw Hill.

Neimeyer, R. (2005). Widowhood, grief and the quest for meaning: A narrative perspective on resilience. In D. Carr, R. Nesee, & C. Wortman (Eds.), *Late life widowhood in the United States*. New York, NY: Springer Publishing Company.

Phillips, M., & Frederick, C. (1992). The use of hypnotic age-progressions as prognostic, ego-strengthening, an integrating technique. *American Journal of Clinical Hypnosis*, 35(2), 99–108.

Prigerson, H. G., Bierhals, A. J., Kasl, S. V., Reynolds, C. F., Shear, M. K., Newsom, J. T., & Jacobs, S. (1996). Complicated grief as a disorder distinct from bereavement depression and anxiety: A replication study. *American Journal of Psychiatry*, 153(11), 1484–1486.

Ramsey, R. (1978). Bereavement: A behavioral treatment of pathological grief. In P. Sojoden, S. Bates, & W. Dockens (Eds.), *Trends in behavior therapy*. New York, NY: Academic Press.

Savage, G. (1993). The use of hypnosis in the treatment of complicated bereavement. *Contemporary Hypnosis*, 10, 99–104.

Schut, H., & Strobe, M. (2005). Interventions to enhance adaptation to bereavement. *Journal of Palliative Medicine*, 8, 140–147.

Shuchter, S., & Zisook, S. (1993). The course of normal grief. In M. Stroebe, W. Stroebe, & R. Hansson (Eds.), *Handbook of bereavement* (pp. 175–195). Cambridge, UK: Cambridge University Press.

Sobel, H. (1981). *Behavior change in terminal care: A humanistic approach*. Cambridge, MA: Ballinger.

Stroebe, M., & Schut, H. (1999). The dual process model of coping with bereavement: Rationale and description. *Death Studies*, 23(3), 197–224.

Stroebe, M., Schut, H., & Stroebe, W. (2005a). Attachment in coping with bereavement: A theoretical integration. *Review of General Psychology*, 9, 48–66.

Stroebe, W., Schut, H., & Stroebe, M. S. (2005b). Grief work, disclosure and counseling: Do they help the bereaved? *Clinical Psychology Review*, 25(4), 395–414.

Turco, R. (1981). The treatment of unresolved grief following loss of an infant. *American Journal of Obstetrics and Gynecology*, 141(5), 503–507.

Conversion Disorder

Camillo Loriedo and Flavio G. Di Leone

55

CHAPTER

Conversion disorder (CD) or functional neurological disorder (FND), as defined in *Diagnostic and Statistical Manual of Mental Disorders*, fifth edition (*DSM-5*; American Psychiatric Association [APA], 2013), is a neuropsychiatric condition characterized by neurological signs and symptoms that are not due to a medical condition. It is included in the somatic symptom disorder category, but differs from other somatic disorders because it affects voluntary branches of the nervous system (motor function and senses). *DSM-5* recognizes eight phenotypes: (a) weakness or paralysis, (b) abnormal movements (e.g., tremor dystonia, myoclonus, gait disorder), (c) swallowing symptoms, (d) speech symptoms, (e) attacks or seizures, (f) anesthesia and sensory loss, (g) sensory disorders (e.g., visual impairment; olfactory or hearing disturbances), and (h) mixed symptoms.

In *DSM-5*, the CD category has been completely revised. And, unlike *DSM-IV-TR*, in *DSM-5*, Criterion B ("the positive identification of psychological features") and Criterion C ("the condition should not be deliberately feigned") have both been dropped to encourage clinicians to pay attention to discriminating clinical features; in other words, to the appearance of CD, rather than restricting it to exclude other diagnoses (Stone, 2010).

Despite these efforts, the diagnosis remains controversial (Rickards & Silver, 2014). Recent findings have shown that after identifying functional signs of CD, neurologists are uncomfortable to play the psychiatrist role (Espay et al., 2009; Kanaan, 2009). Furthermore, conversion disorder and psychosomatic disorders are, in general, commonly neglected by psychiatrists (Bass, Peveler, & House, 2001; Dimsdale, Sharma, & Sharp, 2011). Because there is not a universally agreed upon conceptual framework, clinicians are not confident with the current taxonomy, and this leads to underestimation and misdiagnoses of these symptoms (Mayou,

2014). This is not a trivial issue, since a suitable diagnostic explanation is important in securing a successful start to treatment (Stone et al., 2009; Thomas, Vuong, & Jankovic, 2006), and sometimes it is enough to produce a patient's improvement (Mayor et al., 2012; Oto, Espie, & Duncan, 2010). The recommendation is: (a) tailor the explanation of the diagnosis offered to each patient, avoiding general references to "stress" or that the patient needs to "figure out" his or her own situation. (b) With communication, be inoffensive, transparent, logical, and clear, and do not share personal uncertainty or doubt with the patient. (c) Use the word *functional* to describe the nature of the symptoms, since it helps to introduce the psychological issue of the problem, and avoids any reference to the "physiological vs. psychological" dichotomy. (d) Point out that the patient's symptoms are legitimate neurological symptoms, although not due to a degenerative or structural brain disease. Therefore, the patient can improve and even fully recover. If necessary, demonstrate to the patient and his or her family the patient's diagnostic clinical signs or show neuroimaging or other laboratory studies. (e) Provide a rationale for the available treatments, focusing on the importance of the collaboration of professionals from different fields, for example, psychiatrist, psychologist, neurologist, or physiotherapist (Demartini, Batla, et al., 2014; Kanaan, Armstrong, & Wessely, 2011a, 2011b; Reuber, 2005; Ricciardi & Edwards, 2014; Stone, Carson, & Sharpe, 2005). Clinicians should always remember that patients with functional neurological symptoms need to be aware of their condition in order to seek treatment and follow the prescribed regimen.

The epidemiology of conversion disorder is diagnostically controversial, and reliable data are unavailable. However, an incidence between 4 and 12 of 100,000 per year is estimated, and a prevalence of 50/100,000 (Akagi & House, 2001), notwithstanding differences in diagnostic methodology, settings, and culture. About one out of every three patients referred to neurological clinics presents with an unexplained neurological symptom, and one out of 10 is affected by a CD symptom (Carson et al., 2003; Stone, Carson, & Duncan, 2010). It has become evident that conversion disorder is one of the most common conditions a neurologist will encounter (Carson et al., 2012).

From a recent systematic review of the literature, the CD prognosis and long-term outcome appear unfavorable. It has been shown that for the majority of patients with consistent disability and low social and professional fuctioning, symptoms will persist or worsen. However, some studies report a spontaneous and full recovery in one out of every five patients (Gelauff, Stone, Edwards, & Carson, 2013). Although misdiagnosis is rare (Stone et al., 2009), diagnostic delay is common and is the primary prognostic factor in causing chronicity, strengthening the secondary gain, and facilitating a disabled lifestyle (Green, Payne, & Barnitt, 2004). Also, socioeconomic factors contribute to the outcome, while gender, age, and even comorbid emotional disorders do not (Sharpe et al., 2010).

The psychopathology of CD varies, which reflects its multifactorial nature. Researchers, however, emphasize the role of dissociation as the etiological and maintaining factor (Bell, Oakley, Halligan, & Deeley, 2011), so much so that some authors call for a diagnostic revision (Brown, Cardeña, Nijenhuis, Sar, & van der Hart, 2007). Cognitive neuroscience studies suggest that since hypnotic, dissociative, and conversion phenomena seem to share common brain circuits, they can be considered different expressions of the same underlying mechanism (van der Kruijs et al., 2014; Vuilleumier, 2014).

Nevertheless, clear and meaningful continuity of dissociative phenomena and processes with conversion disorder have been found only in patients with psychogenic nonepileptic seizures (PNES), who show a heightened dissociative tendency (Cohen, Testa, Pritchard, Zhu, & Hopp, 2014; Reuber, House, Pukrop, Bauer, & Elger, 2003). The role of alexithymia, a mental state denoting the inability to identify emotions at a cognitive level, as well as traumatic experiences and childhood abuse/neglect have been widely reconsidered (Demartini,

Petrochilos, et al., 2014). Otherwise, difficulties with emotional regulation—the ability to adjust the intensity of a range of emotions when experiencing an emotional situation—has been demonstrated, especially in patients with PNES (Wiseman & Reuber, 2015). This and other evidence supports the hypothesis that conversion disorder could arise in a relational context, characterized by reciprocated emotional incoherence regarding ambiguous and conflicting feelings toward significant others (Güney, Sattel, Cardone, & Merla, 2015). This "interpersonal psychosomatic process" appears to involve embodied mentalization, aberrant or vigilant somatic reactivity, and attachment strategies (Hustvedt, 2014; Luyten, van Houdenhove, Lemma, Target, & Fonagy, 2012; Waller & Scheidt, 2006). We have observed that this peculiar relational context is commonly reported by all "hysterical" patients and it is grounded in what we have called a "narrative relationship." According to this model, in CD families, communication is focused on "secrets," or information considered crucial; it doesn't matter if it's true or false. This dramatized narrative, considered to be of great interest to others, becomes the facade that hides both the real individual and relational identity, and overshadows any other subject, to the point that the boundaries between fiction and reality become lost. In general, hysterical subjects offer an abundance of elaborate communication, but the content of their communication is limited and not informative. In conversion disorder, the center of communication is more specifically unresolved interpersonal conflicts regarding the emotional distance between the patient and significant others; these unresolved conflicts tend to be converted into symptomatic behaviors (Loriedo, Di Leone, & Bilardi, 2010; Loriedo, Di Leone, & Zullo, 2012). Patients with PNES may try to reduce their emotional awareness and preserve their interpersonal context, excluding some psychological elements (perceived or sanctioned as menacing for the system) by disengaging the cognitive-behavioral component from the emotional-perceptive component of interactive experience (Di Leone, 2015).

Psychotherapy is considered the primary treatment for CD, even though there is no agreement on the most effective strategy, mainly because there is little structured evidence available (Koelen et al., 2014; Stone, 2014). Different factors are involved in this limited number of studies—the clinical and etiological heterogeneity of the category, difficulty in engaging this type of patient in psychiatric and psychological trials, and an overall scarcity of researchers interested in, and experienced with, CD (Rosebush & Mazurek, 2011).

In general, cognitive behavioral therapy is acknowledged as the most common therapeutic modality for somatic symptom disorder, and there is evidence to support that it is also helpful for conversion disorder, especially PNES. Furthermore, mindfulness (Balset & Hill, 2011), therapeutic sedation (Stone, 2014), abreaction (Poole, Wuerz, & Agrawal, 2010), psychoeducation, paradoxical intervention (Ataoglu, Ozcetin , Icmeli, & Ozbulut, 2003), EMDR (van Rood & de Roos, 2009), and psychodynamic psychotherapy (Kompoliti, Wilson, Stebbins, Bernard, & Hinsen, 2014) have all shown to be somewhat valid as treatment for CD.

Pharmacotherapy is known to alleviate functional symptoms; however, it remains unclear whether the benefit for CD is a general effect on some comorbid dimensions, or a more specific effect on somatic symptoms (Somashekar, Jainer, & Wuntakal, 2013). Dramatic but controversial results have been obtained with transcranial magnetic stimulation (TMS) and there are other studies in progress (Pollak, Nicholson, Edwards, & David, 2014). Many authors emphasize the role of a placebo as effective for treating CD and encourage the use of suggestion as a therapeutic tool (Shamy, 2010).

Hypnosis is also arguably another form of effective treatment for CD, supported by two randomized controlled clinical trials carried out by Moene and coworkers. In a 10-year workstudy, the authors developed a dedicated outcome measuring scale—the Video Rating Scale for Motor Conversion Symptoms (VRSMCS)—and a hypnotic treatment protocol (Moene, 1991; Moene et al., 2001). Its effectiveness was compared with no treatment and multidisciplinary treatment (Moene, Hoogduin, & van Dyck, 1998; Moene, Spinhoven, Hoogduin, & van Dyck, 2002, 2003). The hypnotic protocol encompassed one-hour sessions once a week for 8–10 weeks, focused on self-hypnosis training for improving long-term outcomes. The authors propose two forms of hypnotic strategies: "symptom alleviation," aimed at the direct and indirect influencing symptoms by operant and cue conditioning, and "emotional expression/insight-oriented approach," involving age regression and other abreaction techniques, with the goal of recognizing and expressing dissociated emotions and memories, perceived as the causative or precipitating factors of the symptoms. In these studies, CD patients improved, compared with the baseline condition and the waiting list controls, but hypnosis was found to be no more effective than an inpatient, multidisciplinary treatment. Despite these contradictory results and a methodological problem pointed out by further systematic revisions, these studies should be considered a fundamental contribution to the reliability and consistency of hypnotic treatment for this disorder (Martelew, Pulman, & Marson, 2014; Ruddy & House, 2005).

Along with the controlled clinical trials, a number of descriptive reports illustrate the successful use of hypnosis in treating ptosis in adolescents (Al-Sharbati et al., 2001), catatonia (Jensen, 1984), dystonia and contractures (Hoogduin, Akkermans, Oudshoorn, & Reinders, 1993), hysterical aphonia and dysphonia (Giancalone, 1981; Neelman & Mann, 1993), blindness (Horsley, 1982; Patterson, 1980; Wilkins & Field, 1968), hearing loss (Attias et al., 1993; Veniar & Salton, 1983), pseudo-seizures (Caldwell & Stewart, 1981), urinary dysfunction (Freeman & Baxby, 1982), and other disorders (Bloom, 2001).

Despite the fact that these studies differ considerably in adopted theoretical perspective, approach, measurement, and outcome, they also recognize these common principles: (a) According to an early technical study (Moskowitz, 1964), hypnotic trance can effectively influence conversion symptoms, and although remission seems to be independent by the adopted hypnotic techniques, ideomotor suggestions can frequently lead to a complete symptom suppression. (b) CD patients show a high hypnotic susceptibility, but this is rather equivocal for PNES, and outcome predictability remains uncertain (Barabasz & Perez, 2007). (c) Effectiveness is usually evident within 12 weeks of treatment, supporting the choice of a short-term hypnotic intervention. (d) Symptom-oriented intervention is commonly reported as effective, but self-awareness and insight, as well as expression of emotions, are recommended for resistant patients with a long history of illness. (e) Tailoring appears to enhance efficacy, reduce dropout, and ensure a stable remission, but affects reliability and consistency of hypnotic treatment (Aybek, Hubschmid, Mossinger, Berney, & Vingerhoets, 2013).

As a fallout of these studies, hypnosis should ultimately be considered an effective form of therapy for CD. This is certainly an important conclusion, and not so different from the conclusions Pierre Janet, Paul Briquet, and Henry Lagrande Du Salle reached in the 19th century (Brussole et al., 2013).

EVIDENCE

Conversion disorder represents one of the most interesting bridges between the mind and body. Today, we witness a renewed interest in this particular form of functional disorder, mainly due to the integration of cognitive models with neurobiological evidence. Neuroimaging studies now offer the opportunity to explore neural correlates of psychogenic symptoms; however, even today, despite evidence and insight into the neural-system dysfunction of those with CD, we are still lacking a proven and accepted model.

The central inhibition theory, originally postulated by Cojan, Waber, Carruzzo, and Vuilleumier (2009), stressed that the lower activity of the somatosensory cortex in patients with motor CD is the result of enhanced activity of a wide network, including part of the frontal cortex and the limbic system. According to these findings, CD could be considered a direct interference of the cognitive brain on motor execution (de Lange, Roelofs, & Toni, 2007). Another study demonstrated a low connectivity in functional weakness between sensorimotor areas and premotor cortex, reflecting a disturbance in the generation of motor intention (de Lange, Toni, & Roelofs, 2010). Moreover, when CD patients were given an affective task, their limbic system presented impairment in habituation to fearful as well as joyful stimuli, and enhanced connectivity with the supplementary motor area, demonstrated by self-initiated actions and in nonconscious motor inhibition (Voon et al., 2010). Impaired motor generation or conceptualization, and cognitive and self-monitoring processes have also been suggested as symptomatic of CD patients (Burgmer et al., 2006; de Lange, Roelofs, & Toni, 2008; Roelofs et al., 2001; Spence, Crimlisk, Cope, Ron, & Grasby, 2000). In summary, we can assume that the limbic motor interaction provides a neural basis for the motor function disturbance by abnormal affective processes, which is a neurofunctional model of the embodiment of psychological issues. Notably, the neural network implied in generating conversion symptoms seems to be identical to the one found in hypnotic paralysis (Halligan, Athwal, Oakley, & Frackowiak, 2000; Oakley, 1999; Ward, Oakley, Frackowiak, & Halligan, 2003), and to perform the same function (Burgmer et al., 2013; Cojan, Waber, Schwartz, Rossier, Forster, & Vuilleumier, 2009). The hypothesis of a shared mechanism has generated new consideration of hypnosis for understanding CD (Deeley et al., 2013).

INTERVENTION MODEL

About 35 years ago, the senior author of this paper empirically discovered that the chances of success in treating conversion disorder with hypnosis increased when the treatment was brief. This rule doesn't seem to be applicable to other disorders treated by hypnosis, and mostly has to do with the attitude shared by CD patients. These subjects often try to manipulate the patient–therapist relationship in ways that can make long-term therapy difficult for both patient and therapist. A limited and well-defined form of therapy offers a more honest and reliable working alliance—something in which CD patients are particularly sensitive.

General Principles of the Ultrabrief Hypnotic Therapy

The model is based on an ultrabrief hypnotic therapy that includes no more than three hypnotic sessions, with an agreement that in the case that one or two sessions were sufficient for problem resolution, the remaining one(s) could be used for any other problem that might arise in the future.

The ultrabrief approach is founded on the following principles:

1. *A contract defining a limited, but clear and honest, therapeutic relationship.*
   If the subject meets the criteria to be admitted to the treatment process, then he or she is presented with a clearly written therapeutic contract. The contract text specifies that no more than three hypnotic sessions will be offered, but that there

is an allowance for a prolonged relationship if all the hypnotic sessions are not immediately used by the subject. If therapy appears to be effective, additional (nonhypnotic) sessions will be offered. The contract contains a detailed presentation of the therapeutic protocol and both therapist and subject should clearly indicate that they will consistently respect the terms of the contract.

2. *Acceptance by both participants of a limited, but meaningful, relationship.*

This type of proposed therapeutic relationship requires an honest and intense personal involvement on the part of the therapist, in that he will always respect the terms of the contract and refuse to be manipulated by the patient, who might attempt to extend the therapeutic relationship through the use of symptoms or seductive behaviors. This ensures a well-balanced relationship, with the correct emotional distance between therapist and subject, which is often difficult to achieve with CD patients.

3. *Acceptance of failure risk.*

Acceptance of the risk of failure plays an important role in the therapeutic process, since CD patients seem to specialize in trying to defeat therapists who are only trying to help the patient succeed. Offering no more than three hypnotic sessions makes failure possible; this should be accepted by the therapist in a serene attitude beginning with the first session. This prevents the tendency of CD subjects to use symptom worsening as a way to seek longer therapy, or even a seemingly endless therapeutic relationship. When a subject complains about an absence of response to therapy, or uses symptom worsening to try to gain more sessions, the therapist should be prepared to stop the treatment immediately, and only agree to continue (but never beyond the third hypnotic session) if the subject displays a strengthened motivation to be cured within the ultra-brief hypnotic treatment. If the subject does not display such motivation, treatment cessation appears to be the best option. However, control interviews should be maintained, and the unused hypnotic session(s) can be saved and resumed if the subject shows improvement, or if other favorable conditions should occur. A therapist's composed and peaceful acceptance of failure, and even an open declaration of possible failure on the part of the therapist, is not only a fundamental part of the treatment, but can activate a stronger motivation in the patient and therefore becomes important for a positive treatment outcome.

4. *Search for a basic conflict, and incorporate the conflict into the therapeutic strategy.*

One or more initial (nonhypnotic) interviews are required, because the basic conflict that is converted in somatic disorders should be uncovered by the hypnotherapist. In our experience, finding a basic conflict that is converted in the symptom is mandatory for an effective therapy. For both a definition and the typology of conflicts, we adopt Kurt Lewin's (1935) classic interpersonal approach-avoidance conflict classification. Once the basic approach-avoidance conflict has been found, hypnotic therapy will then consist of helping the subject to resolve it in a way that will produce change in the conversion symptom generated by the same conflict.

On the contrary, failing to identify the conflict or ignoring it will not allow the development of the proper therapeutic protocol; in this case, the ultrabrief model has proven to be useless or to produce relapses. Similar negative effects tend to occur when the therapeutic intervention is aimed to bring in only the symptom's change without affecting the underlying basic conflict.

5. *Search for minimal cues.*

Psychotherapists and particularly hypnotherapists should carefully consider William James's opinion: "I'm done with great things and big plans, great institutions and big success. I am for those tiny, invisible, loving, human forces that work from individual to individual, creeping through the crannies of the world like so many rootlets, or like the capillary oozing of water, which, if given time, will rend the hardest monuments of pride" (p. 90). Minimal cues (Erickson, 1964) are little, seemingly unimportant details that may have profound meaning and implication for each individual and can, if utilized for therapeutic purposes, produce enormous and often unexpected changes in a person's life. CD subjects are sensitive to the therapist's observation and utilization of minimal cues. These subjects live in a world of exhibition and appearance, and when someone pays attention to their profound but less accessible needs, they finally feel appreciated for what they are, and not for the seductive facade they tend to create.

6. *Utilization.*

According to Milton Erickson (1959), utilization is "... no more than a simple reversal of the usual procedure of inducing hypnosis. Ordinarily, trance induction is based upon securing from the patients some form of initial acceptance and cooperation with the operator. In Techniques of Utilization the usual procedure is reversed to an initial acceptance of the patients' presenting behaviors and a ready cooperation by the operator, however seemingly adverse the presenting behaviors may appear to be in the clinical situation" (p. 4).

The observation of Erickson that utilization techniques are particularly useful when treating "patients who are unwilling to accept any suggested behavior until their own resistant or contradictory or opposing behaviors have first been met by the operator" (p. 3) seems to indicate that the utilization approach is specifically helpful in dealing with the conflicting nature of CD subjects.

We have found that to obtain a higher level of therapeutic efficacy, four aspects should be utilized to produce therapeutic change: (a) subject's history and narrative, (b) subject's symptom, (c) basic conflict, and (d) minimal cues.

These four aspects and the principles of utilization, as well as the setting's limitations, all contribute in building a restricted but solid therapeutic alliance that is not too involving, but also not cold or distant. We consider this aspect of the therapy as crucial since it appears that CD patients have endless conflict between interpersonal approach and interpersonal avoidance, and are continually searching for the "right," most comfortable emotional distance.

CASE EXAMPLE

Doris is a 48-year-old self-made financial manager who dedicates herself entirely to work. She carries an enormous sense of duty, as well as a sense of pride. She is an only child, and her parents provided her with a strict education, which consisted of more reprisals and punishment than affection and warmth.

About 6 months before our first interview, Doris suddenly developed paralysis and a loss of sensitivity on the left side of her body. She had repeated neurological examinations and testing; however, the doctors could not find any physical explanation for the problem. Subsequently, due to her disability, she lost much of her autonomy and is now confined to a wheelchair. Doris is married and has two children, and all of her family members complain because, despite her limiting conditions, Doris never asks for help, although she frequently needs assistance.

The conflict between her need for help and her refusal to ask for it (no matter what the circumstances) seems to play a crucial role in her conversion disorder. This delicate balance between the need for help, but refusal to ask for it, had been compromised a few days before the symptoms occurred. After a serious kidney infection, she was informed by the doctors that dialysis was no longer an option, but a necessity, and treatment would need to be started within the coming months.

This news made Doris desperate, and a few days later she developed the paralysis. This severe bodily condition allowed her to "ask" for help without ever actually using the word *help*. Doris's condition was investigated by many specialists, and she was eventually hospitalized in a neurology unit for a month before being referred to the senior author for hypnotherapy.

TRANSCRIPT

Hypnotherapist [H]: *You never ask for help; it's like living alone.*

Doris [D]: Yes, it's like living alone. There have been moments going to bed in which I hoped not to open my eyes anymore.

[The subject completely ignores the word *help*, but responds by emphasizing the consequences of not using it, with an indirect allusion to suicidal ideation.]

H: *Okay, now close your eyes and go to bed like in those moments you don't have to do anything—don't even talk until I tell you to do so. Don't move, don't do anything. It's a difficult concept for you to understand; just don't do anything. The* *more you succeed at doing nothing, the more skillful you become.*

[The hypnotherapist's harsh tone is purposeful—tailored to the necessity of the subject to be commanded, instead of helped. And the essential content, presented in the form of orders, is aimed to transform the subject's ideas of death in an unusual induction technique.]

H: *Rest deeply. Now, you have the possibility of entering in deep contact with yourself without making the effort to encounter anyone else. You now have the chance to meet yourself as if you have an appointment that you postponed for many years, like a very busy person who had to attend many work meetings; like a businessperson who has settled many contracts, even very important ones, and who has achieved extraordinary results. But, one day, she realizes she missed the most important appointment: She didn't dedicate enough time for rest and getting in contact with herself. Finally, she decides to give an appointment to herself.*

["Now, exactly in this moment, I have an appointment with myself and I won't see anybody else."

And inside her mind, like in a cartoon, an idea develops: "Can I dedicate some time to myself every day? Maybe just a couple of minutes for myself, instead of meeting some so-called important people, who, as a matter of fact, are not that important."

Here the hypnotherapist works to transform the subject's sense of duty to the others into a sense of duty toward herself. This is a step in the direction of introducing the idea of accepting others' help.]

H: And, another question to ask yourself: "Rather than working so much to help everyone, am I able to sit still and ask others for help? Not because I have to stay still, but because I want to stay still. Not because I can't make it, but because I don't want to make it."

[Staying still and acceptance of others' help doesn't mean being paralyzed.]

H: *Now, look at the ceiling where there is an inscription. And, to see it, you have to throw your head back and gaze upward, and there it's written: "I have the right to ask for help." Then, look down and read what's written on the floor: "I have*

the duty to ask for help." You can easily walk on it without erasing the inscription. Now, you can read the words aloud on the ceiling and on the floor. You can talk.

D: I have the right to ask. I have the duty to ask.

H: *You didn't read well, there is one word missing.*

D: No.
[This is an extraordinary example of the subject's induced positive hallucination, containing in and of itself a spontaneous negative hallucination.]

H: *The right phrases are: "I have the right to ask for help" and "I have the duty to ask for help." Don't try to ignore the help, otherwise I won't help you.*

D: I have the right to ask for **help**. I have the duty to ask for **help**.
[The hypnotherapist's firm and irrefutable order is used to remove the subject's negative hallucination. The word *help* has now been pronounced by the subject for the first time, giving the hypnotherapist the opportunity to use it to induce therapeutic change, utilizing both symptom and conflict resolution.]

H: *Now, I will ask you to collaborate with your movements. But before we get to this point, I would like you to loosen all the muscles, and to release all the contractions that impede your movements and make them less effective and agile, to the point of having the most complete freedom in your movements.*

While your muscles relax, you can notice they respond promptly, and always better and better. At every movement, you will notice that you are acquiring agility and sensibility, and the reason is: There are no more choked words in your bone joints. Finally, those words will no longer hinder the ease and comfort of your movements, since from now on, all of them, all your requests for help, will come out of your mouth instead of going into your bone joints and blocking them.

[Here is an example of the process of binding the symptom and conflict together to form pseudo-logic, which is nevertheless a convincing explanation. If the explanation works, the more the subject will be able to use the repressed word, and the more sensibility and movement will be perfectly restored.]

H: *Now, your movements will become more free, and I ask you to let me know if you can lift your left leg perfectly and as easily as you once could. You can try now. Is it perfect, or is there something missing?*

[The subject moves her left leg slowly but easily, raising it up about five centimeters. The left hand that is resting on the leg is also passively moved.]

D: I still lack of sensitivity under my foot. The leg is okay, but I don't feel anything under my foot.

H: *You don't have any feelings under your foot, but the leg is okay. Is the perfection of your leg complete?*

D: Yes.

H: *Okay, it seems perfect. And are all the other body movements perfect as well?*

D: The palm of my left hand is asleep.

H: *As far as the movements are concerned?*

D: The movements are all okay, only the palm.

H: *So the sole and the palm of the left side . . . the rest is okay. Since all the movements are now okay, but there is still the problem of the sensitivity, are you also willing to ask for help for this?*

D: Yes.

[In an attempt to restore sensitivity, the subject is moving her left hand back and forth in a way that suggests to the hypnotherapist that she is caressing a pet. It is a correct intuition, but the pet is not a pet.]

H: *Is there a particular animal that you like?*

D: An animal?

H: *Yes.*

D: The horse!

H: *Can you imagine caressing a horse named Help?*

D: I don't know.

H: *You don't know if you can imagine it?*

D: I don't know if I can caress a horse named **Help**.

H: *Can you imagine a horse to caress?*

D: Yes.

[The subject smiles and her facial expression suggests that she is recognizing the pleasure of this contact.]

H: *With your left hand, can you feel the pleasure of the contact with the horse?*

D: Yes, it's beautiful.

H: *It's beautiful. And can you feel the contact with the horse's coat?*

D: Yes.

H: *Is sensitivity coming back?*

D: Yes.

H: *And who should be praised for this?*

D: I don't know.

H: *It's the help you received. There still is a foot to fix. It's not good to caress a horse with one's foot.*

D: Then it would be like kicking him.

H: *But you can put a foot in the stirrup.*

D: Yes.

H: *If I was that horse and you wouldn't accept my name, I wouldn't accept your foot in my stirrup either. I would not let you caress me, and would rather go away; he's been too kind letting you caress him.*

D: So it's my fault?

H: *It's your fault, unless you call him by his name.*

[The subject is attempting a depressive, self-blaming maneuver, but the therapist immediately blocks this path, finding the most appropriate punishment to suppress the idea that it is the subject's fault.]

D: But such a beautiful horse cannot be called **Help.**

H: *Why?*

D: Because people ask for **help** only when they suffer.

H: *True, if asking for help was only a right, but it's a duty, too; the best gift you can offer someone who's close to you is to accept being helped. So you only saw the wrong side of the horse; the other side, which is the duty's half, is much more beautiful. You have the duty to ask for help, not only the right. Waive your right if you want, but you cannot renounce your duty.*

D: But I try to do my duties the best I can.

H: *You are not doing so well. You want to change a horse's name—a name that he's had for years, maybe ages.*

D: I'll try to call him **Help.**

[A sense of duty is the strongest motivation for this subject. If asking for help is defined as a duty, the subject can no longer refuse to accept the others' help.]

H: *Try.*

D: The horse is next to me. I call him **Help** and I tell him to **help** me to mount him.

H: *Does it work?*

[Similar to all other forms of somatic disorder, with CD, patients need to undergo not only an intellectual and emotional change; they need to have and recognize a new subjective body experience, in which the symptom is gone and the conflict is solved. In this instance, the subjective experience is horse riding, and the first spontaneous request for help is: "I tell him to **help** me to mount him."]

D: Yes, but my foot hurts a little bit.

H: *Well, it was numb. . . .*

D: Yes, the horse is very beautiful.

H: *The horse is beautiful, even if he has this name?*

D: Yes.

H: *Are you becoming fond of the name?*

D: Yes, one should also become fond of the name.

[At this point, the subject seems to have accepted and experienced the idea that asking for help is necessary (since it is a duty), but her first sensation is pain. Then, she appears to see the other side of the horse ("the horse is very beautiful"), and even becomes fond of his name. In order to complete the work, the last part is to emphasize that asking for and receiving help is pleasurable, so that it can be considered more than a necessary but painful experience. Rather, it can be considered an enjoyable part of the everyday life we share with others.]

H: *A good thing in life is the experience of helping each other. If one only helps himself, it's like having sex alone, eating alone, going to the movies alone. Now I want you to relax again without talking, since I'm sure you are very tired because of the many experiences you have had. Changes always produce strain and a bit of pain; luckily, it's not so unbearable and most often so brief that it leaves no scar. At this point, let your body feel at peace with itself, as well as with the others, from whom you've accepted help. I would like you to take some deep breaths, and then you can reorient yourself perfectly. Pain?*

D: A bit.

H: *Do you take it as good or bad news?*

D: Good.

H: *Pain is not always a problem, especially if it's so short.*

D: Yes, it's okay.

H: *Is your hand awake? It has been pleasant riding the horse... short, but effective.*

D: Horse riding? I like horses very much. . . .

H: *You like horses very much?*

D: Very much!

[The way in which the subject shows profound surprise: "Horse riding? I like horses very much. . ." seems to indicate a meaningful amnesia of the entire experience with the horse.]

[At the end of the session, Doris stands up and moves her entire body, as if to check that all parts are working, and then returns to the neurology unit, carrying the wheelchair she came in with about one hour earlier].

■ The Next Day

The hypnotherapist went to visit Doris in the neurology unit. She smiled and was friendly, but she did not say hello. Instead, she immediately addressed the hypnotherapist, saying: "As you know doctor, I have to undergo dialysis." And then, still smiling but with tears in her eyes, she added in an imperative tone: "And you have to help me!"

■ One Month Later

D: No, I don't need hypnosis today. I would like to leave it for when I begin dialysis.

H: *Are you sure you will have to begin it?* D: Yes.

H: *Changes are occurring, but maybe you can elaborate on them alone.*

D: Yes.

H: *Maybe sometime you could tell us about them.*

D: Yes.

H: *Will you do it all by yourself?*

D: No, no. In my family too, I'm beginning to take more care of myself, even if I have to argue a bit.

H: *And if you need something?*

D: I ask for it.

H: *Do you want to show me how you walk now? Come toward me. Now go toward your husband. . . .*

■ One Year Later

Doris asked for and was granted a second session for the pain she was experiencing due to the shunt that was inserted, in order to postpone the dialysis.

■ About Three Years Later

The dialysis had begun and Doris asked for just a "control session," because she felt strong enough to deal with the new situation, but wanted to save the third hypnotic session for other occasions in which she might need help.

CONCLUSION

Conversion disorders are neuropsychiatric conditions characterized by neurological signs and symptoms not due to a medical condition and are part of the somatic symptom disorder category. They include weakness or paralysis, abnormal movements, swallowing symptoms, speech symptoms, attacks or seizures, anesthesia and sensory loss, sensory disorders, and mixed symptoms. CD is not a rare disorder; however, its prevalence is often underestimated by clinicians, which often leads to a delay in diagnosis that negatively impacts the prognosis. Although hypnosis appears to be a valid treatment for CD, very few controlled studies have been performed in this field. Recently, there has been a growing interest in applying hypnosis to CD both for clinical reasons and for exploring brain functioning with neuroimaging methods.

In our experience, hypnotherapy can be considered an elective model of treatment, based particularly on the peculiar therapeutic relationship these disorders require. This creates a limited but meaningful relationship, where attention is paid to minimal cues more than to the dramatic and seductive behavior these patients usually exhibit. The ultrabrief treatment of three hypnotic sessions, and several nonhypnotic control sessions, is centered on the basic conflict resolution and on the use of minimal cues to change the symptom's body experience.

To illustrate the hypnotherapeutic approach to the CD, a clinical example with commentary is reported.

REFERENCES

Akagi, H., & House, A. (2001). The epidemiology of hysterical conversion. In P. Halligan, C. Bass, & J. Marshall (Eds.), *Contemporary approaches to the study of hysteria: Clinical and theoretical perspectives.* Oxford, UK: Oxford University Press.

Al–Sharbati, M. M., Viernes, N., Al-Hussaini, A., Zaidan, Z. A., Chand, P., & Al-Adawi, S. (2001). A case of bilateral ptosis with unsteady gait: Suggestibility and culture in conversion disorder. *International Journal of Psychiatry and Medicine*, 31(2), 225–232.

American Psychiatric Association. (2013). *Diagnostic and statistical manual of mental disorders, DSM–5*. Washington, DC: American Psychiatric Publishing.

Ataoglu, A., Ozcetin, A., Icmeli, C., & Ozbulut, O. (2003). Paradoxical therapy in conversion reaction. *Journal of Korean Medical Science*, 18(4), 581. doi:10.3346/jkms.2003.18.4.581

Attias, J., Shemesh, Z., Sohmer, H., Gold, S., Shoham, C., & Faraggi, D. (1993). Comparison between self-hypnosis, masking and attentiveness for alleviation of chronic tinnitus. *International Journal of Audiology*, 32(3), 205–212.

Aybek, S., Hubschmid, M., Mossinger, C., Berney, A., & Vingerhoets, F. (2013). Early intervention for conversion disorder: Neurologists and psychiatrists working together. *Acta Neuropsychiatrica*, 25(1), 52–56. doi:10.1111/j.1601-5215.2012.00668.x

Barabasz, A., & Perez, N. (2007). Salient findings: Hypnotizability as core construct and the clinical utility of hypnosis. *International Journal of Clinical and Experimental Hypnosis*, 55(3), 372–379. doi:10.1080/00207140701339793

Baslet, G., & Hill, J. (2011). Case report: Brief mindfulness-based psychotherapeutic intervention during inpatient hospitalization in a patient with conversion and dissociation. *Clinical Case Studies*, 10(2), 95–102.

Bass, C., Peveler, R., & House, A. (2001). Somatoform disorders: Severe psychiatric illness neglected by psychiatrists. *British Journal of Psychiatry: The Journal of Mental Science*, 179, 11–14.

Bell, V., Oakley, D. A., Halligan, P. W., & Deeley, Q. (2011). Dissociation in hysteria and hypnosis: Evidence from cognitive neuroscience. *Journal of Neurology, Neurosurgery & Psychiatry*, 82(3), 332–339.

Bloom, P. B. (2001). Treating adolescent conversion disorders: Are hypnotic techniques reusable? *International Journal of Clinical and Experimental Hypnosis*, 49(3), 243–256. doi:10.1080/00207140108410074

Broussolle, E., Gobert, F., Danaila, T., Thobois, S., Walusinski, O., & Bogousslavsky, J. (2013). History of physical and "moral" treatment of hysteria. *Frontiers of Neurology and Neuroscience*, 35, 181–197.

Brown, R. J., Cardeña, E., Nijenhuis, E., Sar, V., & van der Hart, O. (2007). Should conversion disorders be reclassified as a dissociative disorders in *DSM–V*? *Psychosomatics*, 48(5), 369–378. doi:10.1176/appi .psy.48.5.369

Burgmer, M., Konrad, C., Jansen, A., Kugel, H., Sommer, J., Heindel, W., . . . Knecht, S. (2006). Abnormal brain activation during movement observation in patients with conversion paralysis. *NeuroImage*, 29(4), 1336–1343. doi:10.1016/j.neuroimage.2005.08.033

Burgmer, M., Kugel, H., Pfleiderer, B., Ewert, A., Lenzen, T., Pioch, R., . . . Konrad, C. (2013). The mirror neuron system under hypnosis: Brain substrates of voluntary and involuntary motor activation in hypnotic paralysis. *Cortex; a Journal Devoted to the Study of the Nervous System and Behavior*, 49(2), 437–445. doi:10.1016/j.cortex.2012.05.023

Caldwell, T. A., & Stewart, R. S. (1981). Hysterical seizures and hypnotherapy. *American Journal of Clinical Hypnosis*, 23(4), 294–298. doi:10.1080/00029 157.1981.10404040

Carson, A. J., Best, S., Postma, K., Stone, J., Warlow, C., & Sharpe, M. (2003). The outcome of neurology outpatients with medically unexplained symptoms: A prospective cohort study. *Journal of Neurology, Neurosurgery & Psychiatry*, 74(7), 897–900.

Carson, A. J., Brown, R., David, A. S., Duncan, R., Edwards, M. J., Goldstein, L. H., & Voon, V. (2012). Functional (conversion) neurological symptoms: Research since the millennium. *Journal of Neurology, Neurosurgery & Psychiatry*, 83(8), 842–850.

Cohen, M. L., Testa, S. M., Pritchard, J. M., Zhu, J., & Hopp, J. L. (2014). Overlap between dissociation and other psychological characteristics in patients with psychogenic non–epileptic seizures. *Epilepsy & Behavior: E&B*, 34, 47–49. doi:10.1016/j.yebeh.2014.03.001

Cojan, Y., Waber, L., Carruzzo, A., & Vuilleumier, P. (2009). Motor inhibition in hysterical conversion paralysis. *Neuroimage*, 47(3), 1026–1037.

Cojan, Y., Waber, L., Schwartz, S., Rossier, L., Forster, A., & Vuilleumier, P. (2009). The brain under self–control: Modulation of inhibitory and monitoring cortical networks during hypnotic paralysis. *Neuron*, 62(6), 862–875.

de Lange, F. P., Roelofs, K., & Toni, I. (2007). Increased self-monitoring during imagined movements in conversion paralysis. *Neuropsychologia*, 45(9), 2051–2058. doi:10.1016/j.neuropsychologia.2007.02.002

de Lange, F. P., Roelofs, K., & Toni, I. (2008). Motor imagery: A window into the mechanisms and alterations of the motor system. *Cortex; a Journal Devoted to the Study of the Nervous System and Behavior*, 44(5), 494–506. doi:10.1016/j. cortex.2007.09.002

de Lange, F. P., Toni, I., & Roelofs, K. (2010). Altered connectivity between prefrontal and sensorimotor cortex in conversion paralysis. *Neuropsychologia*, 48(6), 1782–1788. doi:10.1016/j. neuropsychologia.2010.02.029

Deeley, Q., Oakley, D. A., Toone, B., Bell, V., Walsh, E., Marquand, A. F., . . . Halligan, P. W. (2013). The functional anatomy of suggested limb paralysis. *Cortex; a Journal Devoted to the Study of the Nervous System and Behavior*, 49(2), 411–422. doi:10.1016/j. cortex.2012.09.016

Demartini, B., Batla, A., Petrochilos, P., Fisher, L., Edwards, M. J., & Joyce, E. (2014). Multidisciplinary treatment for functional neurological symptoms: A prospective study. *Journal of Neurology, 261*(12), 2370–2377.

Demartini, B., Petrochilos, P., Ricciardi, L., Price, G., Edwards, M. J., & Joyce, E. (2014). The role of alexithymia in the development of functional motor symptoms (conversion disorder). *Journal of Neurology, Neurosurgery & Psychiatry.*

Di Leone, F. (2015). Preliminary consideration for a evidence–based hypnotherapy for psychogenic non-epileptic seizures. *Ipnosi–Rivista Italiana Di Ipnosi Clinica E Sperimentale, 1*, 37–50.

Dimsdale, J., Sharma, N., & Sharpe, M. (2011). What do physicians think of somatoform disorders? *Psychosomatics, 52*(2), 154–159. doi:10.1016/j.psym.2010.12.011

Erickson, M. H. (1964). Initial experiments investigating the nature of hypnosis. *American Journal of Clinical Hypnosis, 7*(2), 152–162.

Erickson, M. H. (1959). Further clinical techniques of hypnosis: Utilization techniques. *American Journal of Clinical Hypnosis, 2*, 3–21.

Espay, A. J., Goldenhar, L. M., Voon, V., Schrag, A., Burton, N., & Lang, A. E. (2009). Opinions and clinical practices related to diagnosing and managing patients with psychogenic movement disorders: An international survey of movement disorder society members. *Movement Disorders: Official Journal of the Movement Disorder Society, 24*(9), 1366–1374. doi:10.1002/mds.22618

Foong, J., Lucas, P. A., & Ron, M. A. (1997). Interrogative suggestibility in patients with conversion disorders. *Journal of Psychosomatic Research, 43*(3), 317–321.

Freeman, R. M., & Baxby, K. (1982). Hypnotherapy for incontinence caused by the unstable detrusor. *British Medical Journal, 284*(6332), 1831–1834.

Frenzel, S., Schlesewsky, M., & Bornkessel-Schlesewsky, I. (2015). Assessing embodied interpersonal emotion regulation in somatic symptom disorders: A case study. *Frontiers in Psychology, 6*, 1–12. doi:10.3389/fpsyg.2015.00001

Gelauff, J., Stone, J., Edwards, M., & Carson, A. (2013). The prognosis of functional (psychogenic) motor symptoms: A systematic review. *Journal of Neurology, Neurosurgery & Psychiatry.*

Giacalone, A. V. (1981). Hysterical dysphonia: Hypnotic treatment of a ten–year-old female. *American Journal of Clinical Hypnosis, 23*(4), 289–293. doi:10.1080/00029157.1981.10404039

Green, A., Payne, S., & Barnitt, R. (2004). Illness representations among people with non–epileptic seizures attending a neuropsychiatry clinic: A qualitative study based on the self-regulation model. *Seizure, 13*(5), 331–339. doi:10.1016/j.seizure.2003.09.001

Halligan, P. W., Athwal, B. S., Oakley, D. A., & Frackowiak, R. S. (2000). Imaging hypnotic paralysis: Implications for conversion hysteria. *The Lancet, 355*(9208), 986–987.

Hoogduin, K., Akkermans, M., Oudshoorn, D., & Reinders, M. (1993). Hypnotherapy and contractures of the hand. *American Journal of Clinical Hypnosis, 36*(2), 106–112. doi:10.1080/00029157.1993.10403052

Horsley, I. A. (1982). Hypnosis and self-hypnosis in the treatment of psychogenic dysphonia: A case report. *American Journal of Clinical Hypnosis, 24*(4), 277–283. doi:10.1080/00029157.1982.10403316

Hustvedt, S. (2014). I wept for four years and when I stopped I was blind. *Neurophysiology Clinics, 44*(4), 305–313.

Jensen, P. S. (1984). Case report of conversion catatonia: Indication for hypnosis. *American Journal of Psychotherapy, 38*(4), 566–570.

Kanaan, R. A., Armstrong, D., & Wessely, S. C. (2011b). Neurologists' understanding and management of conversion disorder. *Journal of Neurology, Neurosurgery & Psychiatry, 82*(9), 961–966.

Kanaan, R. A., Armstrong, D., & Wessely, S. (2011a). Limits to truth–telling: Neurologists' communication in conversion disorder. *Patient Education and Counseling, 77*(2), 296–301.

Koelen, J. A., Houtveen, J. H., Abbass, A., Luyten, P., Eurelings-Bontekoe, E. H., van Broeckhuysen-Kloth, S. A., . . . Geenen, R. (2014). Effectiveness of psychotherapy for severe somatoform disorder: Meta-analysis. *British Journal of Psychiatry: The Journal of Mental Science, 204*(1), 12–19. doi:10.1192/bjp.bp.112.121830

Kompoliti, K., Wilson, B., Stebbins, G., Bernard, B., & Hinson, V. (2014). Immediate vs. delayed treatment of psychogenic movement disorders with short term psychodynamic psychotherapy: Randomized clinical trial. *Parkinsonism & Related Disorders, 20*(1), 60–63. doi:10.1016/j.parkreldis.2013.09.018

Lewin, K. (1935). *A dynamic theory of personality.* New York, NY: McGraw–Hill.

Loriedo, C., Di Leone, F. G., & Bilardi, G. (2010). Hypnotherapy for conversion disorder. *Idee in Psicoterapia, 3*(1), 88–102.

Luyten, P., van Houdenhove, B., Lemma, A., Target, M., & Fonagy, P. (2012). A mentalization-based approach to the understanding and treatment of functional somatic disorder: A contemporary psychodynamic approach. *Journal of Psychotherapy and Integrated Therapy, 23*, 250–262.

Martlew, J., Pulman, J., & Marson, A. G. (2014). Psychological and behavioral treatments for adults with non–epileptic attack disorder. *Cochrane Database Systematic Review, 11*(2).

Mayor, R., Brown, R. J., Cock, H., House, A., Howlett, S., Singhal, S., . . . Reuber, M. (2012). Short-term outcome of psychogenic non-epileptic seizures after communication of the diagnosis. *Epilepsy & Behavior: E&B, 25*(4), 676–681. doi:10.1016/j.yebeh.2012.09.033

Mayou, R. (2014). Is the *DSM–5* chapter on somatic symptom disorder any better than *DSM-IV* somatoform disorder? *British Journal of Psychiatry: The Journal of Mental Science, 204*(6), 418–419. doi:10.1192/bjp.bp.113.134833

Moene, F. C., & Hoogduin, K. A. (1999). The creative use of unexpected responses in the hypnotherapy of patients with conversion disorders. *International Journal of Clinical and Experimental Hypnosis, 47*(3), 209–226. doi:10.1080/00207149908410033

Moene, F. C. (1991). *Therapist treatment protocol.* Dordrecht: Albert Schweitzerplaas Psychiatric Center.

Moene, F. C., Hoogduin, K. A., & van Dyck, R. (1998). The inpatient treatment of patients suffering from (motor) conversion symptoms: A description of eight cases. *International Journal of Clinical and Experimental Hypnosis, 46*(2), 171–190. doi:10.1080/00207149808409998

Moene, F. C., Sandyck, P., Spinhoven, P., Hoogduin, C. A. L., van Dijk, F., & Redert, J. F. M. (2001). Assessment of conversion disorder, motor type development, reliability and validity of the VRMC, a video rating scale for motor conversion symptoms. *Psychological Assessments.*

Moene, F. C., Spinhoven, P., Hoogduin, K. A., & van Dyck, R. (2003). Randomized controlled clinical trial of a hypnosis-based treatment for patients with conversion disorder, motor type. *International Journal of Clinical and Experimental Hypnosis, 51*(1), 29–50. doi:10.1076/iceh.51.1.29.14067

Moene, F. C., Spinhoven, P., Hoogduin, K. A., & van Dyck, R. (2002). A randomized controlled clinical trial on the additional effect of hypnosis in a comprehensive treatment program for in–patients with conversion disorder of the motor type. *Psychology and Psychosomatic Disorders, 71*(2), 66–76.

Moskowitz, A. E. (1964). A clinical and experimental approach to the evaluation and treatment of a conversion reaction with hypnosis. *International Journal of Clinical and Experimental Hypnosis, 12*(4), 218–227. doi:10.1080/00207146408409108

Neeleman, J., & Mann, A. H. (1993). Treatment of hysterical aphonia with hypnosis and prokaletic therapy. *British Journal of Psychiatry: The Journal of Mental Science, 163,* 816–809.

Oakley, D. A. (1999). Hypnosis and conversion hysteria: A unifying model. *Cognitive Neuropsychiatry, 4*(3), 243–265. doi:10.1080/135468099395954

Oto, M., Espie, C. A., & Duncan, R. (2010). An exploratory randomized controlled trial of immediate versus delayed withdrawal of antiepileptic drugs in patients with psychogenic non–epileptic attacks (PNEAs). *Epilepsia, 51*(10), 1994–1999. doi:10.1111/j.1528-1167.2010.02696.x

Patterson, R. B. (1980). Hypnotherapy of hysterical monocular blindness: A case report. *American Journal of Clinical Hypnosis, 23*(2), 119. doi:10.1080/0002915 7.1980.10403250

Perez, D. L., Barsky, A. J., Daffner, K., & Silbersweig, D. A. (2012). Motor and somatosensory conversion disorder: A functional unawareness syndrome? *Journal of Neuropsychiatry and Clinical Neurosciences, 24*(2), 141–151. doi:10.1176/appi.neuropsych.11050110

Pollak, T. A., Nicholson, T. R., Edwards, M. J., & David, A. S. (2014). A systematic review of transcranial magnetic stimulation in the treatment of functional (conversion) neurological symptoms. *Journal of Neurology, Neurosurgery & Psychiatry, 85*(2), 191–197.

Poole, N. A., Wuerz, A., & Agrawal, N. (2010). Abreaction for conversion disorder: Systematic review with meta–analysis. *British Journal of Psychiatry: The Journal of Mental Science, 197*(2), 91–95. doi:10.1192/bjp.bp.109.066894

Reuber, M. (2005). Psychogenic nonepileptic seizures: diagnosis, aetiology, treatment and prognosis. *Schweizer Archiv für Neurologie und Psychiatrie, 156*(2), 47–57.

Reuber, M., House, A. O., Pukrop, R., Bauer, J., & Elger, C. E. (2003). Somatization, dissociation and general psychopathology in patients with psychogenic non–epileptic seizures. *Epilepsy Research, 57*(2–3), 159–167. doi:10.1016/j.eplepsyres.2003.11.004

Ricciardi, L., & Edwards, M. J. (2014). Treatment of functional (psychogenic) movement disorders. *Neurotherapeutics: The Journal of the American Society for Experimental NeuroTherapeutics, 11*(1), 201–207. doi:10.1007/s13311-013-0246-x

Rickards, H., & Silver, J. (2014). Don't know what they are, but treatable? Therapies for conversion disorders. *Journal of Neurology, Neurosurgery & Psychiatry, 85*(8), 830–831.

Roelofs, K., Näring, G. W., Keijsers, G. P., Hoogduin, C. A., van Galen, G. P., & Maris, E. (2001). Motor imagery in conversion paralysis. *Cognitive Neuropsychiatry, 6*(1), 21–40.

Rosebush, P., & Mzzurek, M. (2011). Treatment of conversion disorder in the 21st century: Have we moved beyond the couch? *Current Treatment Options in Neurology, 13*(3), 255–256.

Ruddy, R., & House, A. (2005). Psychosocial interventions for conversion disorder. *Cochrane Database Systematic Review, 4,* CD005331.

Shamy, M. C. (2010). The treatment of psychogenic movement disorders with suggestion is ethically justified. *Movement Disorders: Official Journal of the Movement Disorder Society, 25*(3), 260–264. doi:10.1002/mds.22911

Sharpe, M., Stone, J., Hibberd, C., Polla Warlow, C., Duncan, R., Coleman, R., & Carson, A. (2010). Neurology out–patients with symptoms unexplained by disease: Illness beliefs and financial benefits predict 1-year outcome. *Psychological Medicine, 40*(4), 689–698.

Somashekar, B., Jainer, A., & Wuntakal, B. (2013). Psychopharmacotherapy of somatic symptoms disorders. *International Review of Psychiatry, 25*(1), 107–115. doi:10.3109/09540261.2012.729758

Spence, S. A., Crimlisk, H. L., Cope, H., Ron, M. A., & Grasby, P. M. (2000). Discrete neurophysiological correlates in prefrontal cortex during hysterical and feigned disorder of movement. *The Lancet, 355*(9211), 1243–1244.

Stone, J. (2014). Psychotherapy for severe somatoform disorder: Problems with missing studies. *The British Journal of Psychiatry, 204*(3), 243–244.

Stone, J., Carson, A., & Duncan, R. (2010). Who is referred to neurology clinics? The diagnoses made in 3781 new patients. *Clinical Neurology and Neurosurgery, 112*, 747–751.

Stone, J., Carson, A., & Sharpe, A. (2005). Functional symptoms in neurology: Management. *Journal of Neurology, Neurosurgery, and Psychiatry, 76*(1), 13–21.

Stone, J., Carson, A., Duncan, R., Coleman, R., Roberts, R., Warlow, C., . . . Sharpe, M. (2009). Symptoms 'unexplained by organic disease' in 1144 new neurology out–patients: How often does the diagnosis change at follow-up? *Brain: A Journal of Neurology, 132*(Pt. 10), 2878–2888. doi:10.1093/brain/awp220

Thomas, M., Vuong, K. D., & Jankovic, J. (2006). Long-term prognosis of patients with psychogenic movement disorders. *Parkinsonism & Related Disorders, 12*(6), 382–387. doi:10.1016/j.parkreldis.2006.03.005

Uliaszek, A. A., Prensky, E., & Baslet, G. (2012). Emotion regulation profiles in psychogenic non–epileptic seizures. *Epilepsy & Behavior, 23*(3), 364–369. doi:10.1016/j.yebeh.2012.01.009

van der Kruijs, S. J. M., Bodde, N. M. G., Vaessen, M. J., Lazeron, R. H. C., Vonck, K., Boon, P., . . . Jansen, J. F. A (2012). Functional connectivity of dissociation in patients with psychogenic non-epileptic seizures. *Journal of Neurology, Neurosurgery & Psychiatry, 83*(3), 239–247. doi:10.1136/jnnp-2011-300776

van der Kruijs, S. J., Jagannathan, S. R., Bodde, N. M., Besseling, R. M., Lazeron, R. H., Vonck, K. E., . . .

Jansen, J. F (2014). Resting–state networks and dissociation in psychogenic non-epileptic seizures. *Journal of Psychiatric Research, 54*, 126–133. doi:10.1016/j.jpsychires.2014.03.010

van Dyck, R., & Hoogduin, K. (1989). Hypnosis and conversion disorders. *American Journal of Psychotherapy, 43*(4), 480–493.

van Rood, Y. R., & de Roos, C. (2009). EMDR in the treatment of medically unexplained symptoms: A systematic review. *Journal of EMDR Practice and Research, 3*(4), 248–263.

Veniar, F. A., & Salston, R. S. (1983). An approach to the treatment of pseudohypacusis in children. *American Journal of Diseases of Children (1960), 137*(1), 34–36. doi.org/10.1001/archpedi.1983.02140270030011.

Voon, V., Brezing, C., Gallea, C., Ameli, R., Roelofs, K., Lafrance, W. C., & Hallett, M. (2010). Emotional stimuli and motor conversion disorder. *Brain: A Journal of Neurology, 133*(Pt. 5), 1526–1536. doi:10.1093/brain/awq054

Vuilleumier, P., Armony, J. L., Driver, J., & Dolan, R. J. (2001). Effects of attention and emotion on face processing in the human brain: An event-related fMRI study. *Neuron, 30*(3), 829–841.

Vuilleumier, P. (2014). Brain circuits implicated in psychogenic paralysis in conversion disorders and hypnosis. *Neurophysiologie Clinique/Clinical Neurophysiology, 44*(4), 323–337. doi.org/10.1016/j.neucli.2014.01.003.

Waller, E., & Scheidt, C. E. (2006). Somatoform disorders as disorders of affect regulation: A development perspective. *International Review of Psychiatry, 18*(1), 13–24. doi:10.1080/09540260500466774

Ward, N. S., Oakley, D. A., Frackowiak, R. S., & Halligan, P. W. (2003). Differential brain activations during intentionally simulated and subjectively experienced paralysis. *Cognitive Neuropsychiatry, 8*(4), 295–312. doi:10.1080/13546800344000200

Wilkins, L. G., & Field, P. B. (1968). Helpless under attack: Hypnotic abreaction in hysterical loss of vision. *American Journal of Clinical Hypnosis, 10*(4), 271–275.

Wiseman, H., & Reuber, M. (2015). New insights into psychogenic non–epileptic seizure. *Seizure, 29*, 69–80. doi:10.1016/j.seizure.2015.03.008

Depression

Moshe S. Torem

Depression has been manifested in many medical and psychiatric conditions, and is one of the most common presenting symptoms. In fact, the World Health Organization (WHO) describes depression as the leading cause of disability in the world and the fourth leading contributor to the global burden of disease (WHO, 2009). In 2012, 350 million people were affected by depression worldwide. The World Mental Health Survey, conducted in 17 countries, revealed that on average about 1 in 20 people reported having an episode of depression in the previous year. Depressive disorders often start at a young age; they reduce people's functioning and often are recurring. For these reasons, depression is the leading cause of disability worldwidpe in terms of total years lost due to disability. The demand for curbing depression and other mental health conditions is on the rise globally. A recent World Health Assembly called on the WHO and its member states to take action to help reduce the occurrence of depression worldwide (WHO, 2012).

However, clinicians often disagree on the meaning of depression. In using the term *depression*, we sometimes mean sadness, such as that observed in a state of normal grief and mourning, and in other instances, we refer to a psychopathological condition associated with self-derogatory and self-deprecatory thoughts, feelings of guilt, and suicidal ideations. In a previous publication (Torem, 1983), I indicated the need for a distinction between depression as illness, and depression as simply a mood state of sadness. In this chapter, I plan to clarify the types of depression in which hypnosis can be useful and to explain the technique of using hypnosis as an explorative and therapeutic tool in the treatment of depression.

TYPES OF DEPRESSION AND UNDERLYING CAUSES

The *Diagnostic and Statistical Manual of Mental Disorders*, fifth edition (*DSM-5*; America Psychiatric Association [APA], 2013) classifies the various psychiatric disorders using a phenomenological approach based on behavioral observations and natural history of the illness. Little attention, however, is devoted to the underlying dynamics of psychiatric illness. Research studies in the past 20 years have consistently shown that certain types of depression have a strong biological, perhaps even genetic, etiological component. Major affective disorders were identified to be of the unipolar and bipolar type. The patients with this condition cycle in and out of depression or mania, regardless of what happens in their environment. They recover from a depressed state regardless of whether they had psychotherapy or other treatments, provided there is no suicide. These people usually respond well to mood stabilizers and antidepressant medication, which may not only shorten the cycle but even decrease the intensity of symptoms, frequency of relapses, and sometimes totally prevent the cycles of depression. If the patient has an underlying stable and healthy personality, the positive results of biological treatments can be very dramatic. However, if the patient has an affective disorder superimposed on a borderline personality structure or any other type of character disorder, the biological treatments will result in less dramatic responses, since the remaining psychopathology will still be manifested due to the patient's underlying character or order disorder

There is, however, another group of depressions in which the symptoms are not as much a manifestation of genetics. In these patients, the condition of depression may be manifested in the form of a variety of symptoms and behaviors stemming from underlying intrapsychic and interpersonal maladaptive patterns of behaviors and cognitions (Torem, 1987; Yapko, 1986, 1994, 1999).

THE SYMPTOM COMPLEX OF DEPRESSION: VARIABILITY IN MANIFESTATION

The symptoms of depression may manifest in the form of depressed mood, excessive sadness, crying spells, or aches and pains in various parts of the body. Headaches, abdominal pain, chest pains, and backaches are the most common pain symptoms. G. Engel (1959) referred to this group of patients, especially when they take on a chronic pattern, as "pain-prone patients." Depression may also be manifested by a sleep disorder, insomnia or hypersomnia, poor appetite, binge-eating episodes associated with excessive weight gain, or reduced intake of food and liquids associated with weight loss, self-neglect in physical appearance and personal hygiene, difficulties in making decisions concerning activities of daily living, and the inability to experience joy (anhedonia).

The patient's thoughts are dominated by excessive pessimism, gloom and doom, negativism, low regard for self, and ideas of being undeserving of love, respect, or success. Moreover, self-derogatory and self-deprecatory thoughts are not uncommon.

In some people, the depressed mood is not that conspicuous and instead the clinical picture is dominated by aches, pains, and other physical symptoms. This condition has been referred to as "masked depression" or "depressive equivalents"; that is, the patient has a depressive illness but it is manifested mostly by other symptoms (Lopez-Ibor, 1973; Pinchot & Hassan, 1973). Another way in which depressive psychopathology may manifest itself is in the patient's lifestyle and interpersonal relationships. These patients may not be able to tolerate success, and subconsciously may be motivated to sabotage any success in their careers or personal lives. They have been referred to in the literature as having a masochistic character (Berliner, 1958; Torem, 1979) and their behavior may also be manifested by their repeated associations in close relationships in which they are being exploited or even abused. They appear unhappy and miserable, and their actions continue to perpetuate that pattern.

THE PSYCHODYNAMICS OF DEPRESSION PATTERNS

In exploring the psychodynamics of depression patterns, the clinician will find hypnosis to be a very valuable tool, and its skillful use may facilitate a rapid uncovering of the major underlying conflicts and set the road to resolution and recovery. The following is a detailed list of such underlying psychodynamics.

An Unconscious Sense of Guilt

Self-inflicted pain and suffering serve as a way to expiate for the guilt feelings. Thus, the pain, although unpleasant, becomes the lesser of two evils. The patient's attempts to atone for his guilt may be manifested in repeated patterns of psychogenic pain, as described eloquently by G. Engel (1959) in his classic paper "Psychogenic Pain and the Pain-Prone Patient."

The following case vignette illustrates this dynamic. A 42-year-old man was admitted to the hospital complaining of chest pain and shortness of breath.

After a thorough examination, it became clear that he had no organic disease. An intensive interview revealed a man with a long history of pain and suffering associated with accidents, injuries, and repeated operations. He had felt miserable all his life, and even when the occasion called for it he could not experience happiness or joy. A further interview, using the hypnoanalytic technique of affect bridge, revealed an interesting story of the patient having lost a twin brother at the age of 5 due to an accident in which the brother was struck in the head by a heavy swing as the two were playing. This accident had a major impact on the patient's life, and he survived living with an intense subconscious sense of guilt, which was partially alleviated through self-inflicted suffering, unhappiness, and depression.

Masochism

The patient engages in a behavior that is characterized by the repetition of misery and suffering associated with interpersonal relationships.

B. Berliner, who devoted many years to the study of the phenomena of masochism, had described this condition in a number of his writings (1947a, 1947b, 1958). In his article from 1966, titled "Psychodynamics of the Depressive Character," Berliner (former president and training analyst of the San Francisco Psychoanalytic Institute) states: "The depressive character is immensely frequent, at least in western civilization." He later stated that the depressive personality is what makes masochism possible and that masochism is a symptom, not a nosological entity. Masochistic suffering is seen as a bid for affection from a parent figure who hates, rejects, and depreciates. This is not a "lust for pain."

Reenactment of Childhood Trauma

Every depressive character has its roots in a very unhappy childhood filled with traumatic experiences. This mechanism forces the patient to reenact the original childhood trauma by living in misery, sorrow, pain, and sadness, subconsciously inflicted on himself or herself without the conscious awareness of it. Consciously, the patient complains and begs for help. However, if this mechanism is not identified and uncovered (hypnosis is a very useful tool to uncover it), the patient will be locked into a vicious cycle of suffering, misery, and pain, and may even show a "negative therapeutic reaction" in the face of some symptom relief and act out in self-destructive behavior (Sandler, Holder, & Dare, 1970; Torem, 1979).

Identification With the Aggressor

In this mechanism, which was first described by Anna Freud (1946), the patient subconsciously identifies with the introjected, hateful, rejecting, and abusing parent. The trauma lives on, through self-inflicted sadness and suffering. The patient in a way turns against himself, not his own aggression, but the hate and abuse of an incorporated love-object that may have become a part of the patient's self.

Persecuting Hidden Ego States

Here, again, the patient had suffered repeated traumata in childhood, but the hateful, abusing parent was not only introjected, but later split off from conscious awareness through the mechanism of dissociation. Dissociation was followed by amnesia to the traumatic events of the past. Through hypnosis, much time can be saved in uncovering these hateful ego states that are responsible for the patient's self-derogatory and self-deprecatory thoughts.

Unresolved Grief and Anniversary Reactions

The patient's depression represents an underlying, unresolved grief or a form of pathological, prolonged, incomplete mourning reaction. When this is set off by a specific date, such as the patient reaching the age of the lost love-object at the time of death, or the patient's child reaching the age of the patient when the loss occurred, or the arrival of the calendar date of the loss, there may follow a set of depressed feelings, accompanied by low self-esteem, insomnia, aches and pains, difficulties with concentration, a sense of worthlessness, and sometimes suicidal thoughts. This phenomenon has been described by many authors (Engel, 1975; Pollock, 1970), and hypnosis can be helpful for a rather quick identification of the underlying dynamics. The following case is illustrative of such a mechanism.

A 39-year-old Caucasian, a married woman and mother of three children, was admitted to the hospital due to severe depression, insomnia, and suicidal thoughts. She had a poor appetite and had been neglecting her personal hygiene. The clinical interview elicited her wishes to die so that she could be in peace. A more detailed interview, under hypnosis, revealed that the patient had an older sister to whom she had been very close, who had died at the age of 39 in a car accident. The patient had never fully completed the process of mourning her sister's sudden death, and she reported having no memory of the funeral or the viewing. When the patient turned 39, the age of her sister at the time of her death, she became increasingly sad and depressed. The depression culminated with strong suicidal ideations on the date of the tenth anniversary of her sister's death. The use of hypnosis not only helped to uncover these dynamics, but also allowed the patient to begin the long overdue task of mourning to finally resolve the loss in a healthy way.

Maladaptive Cognitions and Behavioral Patterns

In the past 20 years, a new trend has emerged in the understanding and treatment of depression. This new trend has gradually shifted away from the exploration of a history of a past trauma or unresolved memories of childhood abuse and instead has focused on the patterns of maladaptive cognitions and behaviors that are associated with depression. In fact, Yapko (1992, 2010a) points out that depression was commonly but incorrectly understood to be caused by anger turned inward, unsettled subconscious guilt feelings, unresolved grief, childhood abuse or trauma, or some other hypothetical psychodynamic conflict. So, "despite recent evidence that none of these are true about depression, many people's outdated concept of depression has not been revised" (Yapko, 2010a). This caused, according to Yapko and others, many clinicians to predominantly use treatments of antidepressant medication and psychotherapeutic focus on the wrong issues (Wang, Berglund, & Kessler, 2000).

So, in treatment, the emphasis has gradually shifted from unresolved intrapsychic conflicts and the exploration of past traumas and childhood abuse to identifying the patterns of dysfunctional thoughts and behaviors and using cognitive behavior therapy (CBT) to correct such cognitive distortions. D. Burns (1980) described the following list of 10 cognitive distortions that are commonly found in people with depression:

All or nothing thinking
Mental filter
Jumping to conclusions
Emotional reasoning
Labeling and mislabeling
Overgeneralization
Disqualifying the positive
Magnification or minimization
Should statements
Personalization

This was also elaborated by Ellis (1977), Beck (1972, 1975, 2008; Beck & Haigh, 2014; Beck, Rush, Shaw, & Emery, 1979), and Meichenbaum (1977), who wrote prolifically on the method of CBT. In this form of therapy, patients learn to identify their cognitive distortions, name them, understand them, and develop a rational response to dissolve them and then realize how their feelings of anxiety and depression

improve and sometimes totally disappear. The focus was on the "here and now," in terms of the patient's own thinking and maladaptive behavioral patterns. Later, hypnosis has incorporated the principles of CBT and produced a more powerful and rapid intervention that allowed for an alleviation of depressive symptoms and behaviors in a shorter period of time (Alladin, 1992b, 1994, 2006, 2012, 2013; Yapko, 1986, 1992, 1993, 1994, 1995, 1997, 1999, 2001a, 2001b, 2001c, 2007). Yapko (2010a) stated that, "The emphasis [is] on empowering depressed individuals to acquire specific skills that not only reduce depression's severity and frequency but may even have preventive value." This was also supported by Beck (1976), Dozois and Dobson (2004), and Seligman (2002).

HYPNOSIS AS AN EXPLORATIVE TOOL IN THE TREATMENT OF DEPRESSION

Hypnosis can be a very useful tool in facilitating the exploration of the various underlying dynamics responsible for a patient's depression. The following is a list of the various techniques in which hypnosis can be used as an explorative tool.

The Affect Bridge

In 1971, J. G. Watkins described a technique whereby a patient, under hypnosis, is moved experientially from the present to a past incident over an affect common to the two events. In fact, it is a technique used to explore the roots of past events that are responsible for the patient's depression. In the clinical setting, the hypnotherapist guides the patient into hypnosis and instructs the patient to focus on a feeling that typifies his depressed state. This feeling is then enhanced and intensified. When it reaches its peak strength, the therapist leads the patient back in time to the origin of this feeling. Thus, the patient is "bridged" from the present to the past, to the event responsible for the patient's original emotions of depression and hopelessness. It is not uncommon for dramatic abreactions to accompany this technique, and therapists using it must be trained in handling abreactions. The uncovering of the original trauma allows the therapist to set the stage for the next phase, in which hypnosis is used as a tool to facilitate therapeutic change and promote recovery from depression.

Movie/TV Screen Imaging

The patient is guided into a hypnotic trance and is instructed to imagine a movie or television screen. He is then instructed to imagine himself watching a movie of his life, going through various events and situations that may have originated in hopelessness, helplessness, and the present-day depression. This method has the advantage of keeping the patient dissociated from the emotions and feelings associated with the original trauma. He can focus on a simple, logical reporting of the facts in a detached manner, thus avoiding the intense, sometimes premature, abreactions which may lead to the patient leaving therapy before resolution is accomplished.

The Crystal Ball Technique

In 1964, Wolberg described the use of a crystal ball with a patient who was first led into hypnosis with his eyes closed, and, while in a trance, was given the suggestion to let his eyes open. The patient was then instructed to gaze into the crystal ball and identify significant events from the past, which were related to the depression in the present. M. Erickson (1954) described a variant of this technique in which the crystal ball could be imagined or hallucinated by the patient who remained with his eyes closed.

Age Regression

The patient is led, under hypnosis, to a younger age at which he reexperiences, and, in a way, relives the original trauma that led to the depression of the present. Age regression can be accomplished with greater ease in patients who are highly hypnotizable. A variety of techniques have been used such as counting backwards from the present age to a previous age in which the depression or feelings of helplessness/hopelessness first started. Once this is accomplished, the patient is further instructed to continue the age regression to a previous time in which these depressive feelings and symptoms had not existed. The patient is then instructed to move forward so that the memory of the forgotten event can be shared and explored in greater detail; thus, the patient is ready for therapy.

Ideomotor Signaling

This technique is one of the major therapeutic options used in analytical hypnotherapy. The patient is guided into hypnosis. Then the signals for "yes," and "no," "I don't know," and "I don't want to answer" are established and agreed upon. The questions used in the interview must be constructed in a special close-ended way to avoid confusion and allow for one of the previous choices to be signaled as an answer. The best signals are finger-lifting signals, all on one hand. Although this variation was first recommended by Cheek and LeCrone in 1968, ideomotor phenomena are not new and were described before by Erickson (1954) and LeCron (1954). The whole idea of communicating with the subconscious mind though ideomotor signaling is still controversial regarding its reliability and validity, but it is the most widely used uncovering technique.

Indirect Methods of Uncovering

These methods offer an alternative mode of hypnotic exploration, which is especially useful when the direct methods have not worked.

■ Automatic Writing

The patient is guided into hypnosis and later, with his eyes open, is trained to communicate important unconscious information. Naturally, a writing note pad and pen must be at hand. Some patients respond very well when a suggestion is given that the writing hand will be dissociated and is no longer under the patient's conscious control or awareness. Thus, the questions directed at the unconscious mind will be answered in writing by the dissociated hand.

■ The Personal Diary Technique

The patient is taught self-hypnosis and, after some practice, is given the suggestion to write in the personal diary an answer to a question that is posed. The suggestion is made that the answer may come later, even during sleep or in a dream. The patient is to keep the personal diary at hand and to sign his name at the end of each entry. The patient brings the personal diary to each session and the writings are looked at and examined. Some patients make it a habit to write daily and reflect upon the events of the day, their thoughts and feelings, future plans, and internal conflicts. Not infrequently, hidden, subconscious ego states emerge to report about traumatic events from the past or internal conflicts of the present. Clues to such emerging ego states include a change in handwriting, a change in the style and vocabulary, and a change in the patient's signature at the end of the diary entry.

■ Dream Induction

Wolberg (1964) recommended giving the patient a suggestion that he will have a significant dream that night, which will have an answer and sometimes the solution to the problem. The patient will report this dream in the following session. Naturally, the therapist must be skilled in dream interpretation. Some patients can be trained to produce the dream right there in hypnosis and come out of hypnosis to report the dream relevant to the problem the patient is facing.

■ The Unconscious Body Image

This technique was described by Freytag (1961), who postulated that the hallucinated, unconscious body image is the picture that the individual forms of himself in his unconscious mind. Freytag reported that she asked the patient, under hypnosis, to hallucinate a full-length mirror and see his reflection in it. After he described it, he was told that this was just a reflection of his body as it existed in space. The patient was then told that each person has another picture of himself in his unconscious mind, which symbolically expresses significant emotional problems and conflicts. The patient was told to wait for the appearance of this unconscious body image and to describe in detail what he saw. According to Freytag, this technique is not only useful for exploration and uncovering, but also in doing hypnoanalytic therapy by suggesting changes in the unconscious body image that will affect the true mirror image of the patient.

HYPNOSIS AS A THERAPEUTIC TOOL IN DEPRESSION

In using hypnotherapy for the patient with depression, the clinician must carefully avoid a direct symptom removal approach, especially before the explorative phase has been completed and the underlying dynamics are fully understood. Such avoidance will lessen the risk of suicide attempts or other self-destructive acts that are motivated by a powerful need for self-punishment and suffering. However, general ego-strengthening techniques, focusing on calmness, relaxation, and inner peace, are safe when they are associated with permissive suggestions in which the patient is allowed to keep his sadness if he still needs it or if it serves an important function. The use of hypnosis in patients with depression is best done by therapists who are well-trained in psychodynamics and in the care of suicidal patients. Hypnosis should always be used with caution and only after the doctor–patient relationship has been well established with a stable working and therapeutic alliance.

Therapeutic Abreaction

Abreaction as a therapeutic tool was first discovered by Freud and Breuer (1955) in their studies of hysterical patients. They explained that the effectiveness of abreaction was due to a discharge of what they called "strangulated affects" attached to the suppressed mental acts. "Language," these authors said, "serves as a substitute for action." Today, we see abreaction as a process in which pent-up emotions, previously unconscious to the patient, are discharged through verbal and nonverbal expressions. Abreactions may occur spontaneously with the use of hypnosis and are most effective in the crisis intervention of patients with posttraumatic disorders. The sooner the abreaction, the more likely it is to avoid the development of a chronic posttraumatic stress disorder associated with depressive symptoms. Many depressed patients have a variety of underlying dynamics associated with traumatic events from the past. In these patients, it is not uncommon to observe spontaneous abreactions during the hypnotic explorative phase. The therapist's handling of the patient's abreaction is very important in making this a therapeutic experience rather than just reliving the traumatic event.

The therapist must be supportive and continuously provide the patient with a grounding in the present reality so that the patient is not lost in an uncontrolled regression. The following is an illustrative case example.

A. S. was a 28-year-old married woman who suffered from depression, insomnia, phobias, and low self-esteem. After two initial diagnostic interviews, the patient was instructed in the use of hypnosis, and she agreed to cooperate in further exploration of her symptoms under hypnosis. During the first hypnotic session, she spontaneously regressed to the age of 8 and abreacted emotionally to an experience in which she was raped by her uncle. She was shaking in fear, and while crying profusely she described in a quivering voice the helplessness and hopelessness she felt and her fear and humiliation. The therapist, listening in a supportive way, asked gently that the patient continue describing the events that took place using such statements as: "And then what happened?" or "Go on. I am listening," or "You are safe here. It is O.K. to cry." The facilitating statements encouraged the patient to continue describing the entire event in detail.

She was told that when she came out of hypnosis she would remember only what she needed to remember and was ready to safely handle in order to accept consciously the disturbing event. If she was not ready, she did not have to remember. When the patient came out of hypnosis, she was fully alert and remembered all the details of her abreaction. She apologized for her intense crying, but reported feeling a great relief, as if "a heavy weight has been lifted off my chest." She spontaneously started to talk about how she now understood the reason for feeling dirty and unclean around the Easter holiday, which was when the rape occurred. Therapy continued with working through the guilt and other feelings regarding the rape.

Working Through

This concept was first developed by Freud (1958), who pointed out that in psychotherapy one cannot expect an immediate cure following an abreaction. The patient often shows resistance to giving up old notions and assimilating new insight. Therefore, the material that the patient becomes consciously aware of has to be examined and reexamined repeatedly, each time from a different slant, allowing the patient time to assimilate and incorporate the new insight, thus letting go of distortions and misconceptions regarding past traumatic events. In the case of the woman who was raped by her uncle, she felt considerable guilt about the event, and the guilt contributed to her depression. In the working through process, the patient gradually accepted the notion that this happened not because she was a bad girl but because her uncle was drunk; she was simply a helpless, innocent victim. This new insight allowed her to let go of the guilt and accept what happened as an unfortunate event for which she had no responsibility.

Ego-Strengthening Suggestions

Hartland (1965, 1971) stated that only a few patients will let go of their symptoms before they feel strong enough to do without them. He pointed out that the effectiveness of symptom removal is enhanced by intensive psychotherapy in which hypnosis plays a facilitating role. Hartland's "ego-strengthening" techniques are comprised of positive suggestions of self-worth and personal effectiveness. According to Alladin (2008, 2012), ego-strengthening suggestions promote greater confidence, self-esteem, and self-efficacy. The utilization of hypnosis in this context augments the desired outcome in using therapeutic ego-strengthening suggestions as supported by Hammond (1990) and Frederick and McNeal (1999). The foundation for this approach is also based on the experimental evidence in the work of Bandura (1977), who showed that self-efficacy, the expectation and confidence of being able to cope successfully with various life situations, is one of the key elements in the effective treatment of many psychological disorders. Alladin (2012) points out that in the treatment of people with depression, it is important to craft the ego-strengthening suggestions in such a way that they appear credible and logical to the specific individual receiving the treatment. For example, rather than stating "Every day in every way, you are getting better and better," it is advisable to suggest, "As a result of this treatment and as a result of you listening to your self-hypnosis tape/CD every day, you will begin to feel better." According to Alladin, this set of suggestions sounds more logical to the depressed patient and improvement becomes contingent on continuing with the therapy and listening to the self-hypnosis tape/CD on a daily basis. The following is an example of "ego-strengthening" under hypnosis as used in a depressed patient.

Mrs. R.D. was a 28-year-old married woman, who had been referred for the evaluation and treatment of chronic depression. In the initial interview, it became evident that she suffered from a chronic state of depression, which involved poor self-esteem dating back to her childhood. The emphasis, in the first few interviews, was on establishing good rapport with the patient by meeting the patient on her level and attending to her immediate needs. This method inaugurated a good working and therapeutic alliance with the patient. She complained of much tension and a sense of restlessness. She was asked if she wanted to learn self-hypnosis to help reduce her tension and create a sense of internal calmness. She agreed and turned out to be a good subject for learning self-hypnosis. After mastering the technique of self-hypnosis, she was guided into hypnosis and the following ego-strengthening suggestions were made:

"As you are sitting here in this chair, you may allow yourself to be calm and experience a state of internal harmony, whereby your subconscious mind continues to pay attention to my voice and accepts whatever is needed so that you can go on with your life in a healthy, mature way. Whatever it was that happened in the past belongs to the past, and you can simply let go of it, even if you don't fully remember or understand all that actually happened. Living goes on in the present. Every day, you become physically stronger and more alert, more wide awake, more energetic, and more helpful. Yes, you deserve to live your life with hope and optimism. You have suffered enough. Every day, your nerves become stronger and more stable, your mood more pleasant and hopeful. You will become interested in what you do and in whatever goes on around you, and as this happens, your mind becomes more calm, serene, and peaceful, more clear and composed, more tranquil, more in harmony with your body. Your thinking will be clearer, and your concentration easier. You will accept yourself with grace and ease, viewing yourself in a positive light, developing greater confidence in your talents and gifts, and greater confidence in your abilities, with faith in your future. Now, all these things may not happen that quickly. They may take some time, but only as much time as you need for all of this to take place. Therefore, they can happen as rapidly as you want, and it is O.K. if you don't want them

to happen that fast. Now, you may want to take a moment to reflect privately on what your life will be like with all these positive changes occurring, and then, whenever you are ready, simply count back from three to one. When you get to one, your eyes will open and you will be fully alert and awake, calm and relaxed. Even though you may not remember everything, your subconscious mind will continue to retain all those positive suggestions. It will continue to guide you to a full recovery. Ready, three . . . two . . . and one. Eyes open, fully alert and awake. That's right."

In reviewing the wording of the ego-strengthening and therapeutic suggestion technique, the reader should remember the following points:

- All suggestions are phrased in the affirmative, emphasizing the positive.
- The patient is told of her own internal strengths, that the cure and healing will continue even after the session.
- Self-hypnosis is taught to avoid dependency.
- The patient is given the choice regarding the speed of her recovery.
- The patient is encouraged to reflect on the future consequences of her recovery and to get ready by using guided imagery.

There are many variations to this technique, and each therapist needs to find the techniques that are tailored to the patient's needs, incorporating the five points mentioned in the previous list.

Posthypnotic Suggestions

Alladin (2012) points out that depressed patients are predisposed to automatically ruminate with negative self-suggestions, especially when faced with stressful life situations (e.g., "I will not be able to cope"). This tendency can be viewed as a form of negative self-hypnosis (NSH) or negative posthypnotic suggestion (PHS) that inadvertently maintains and reinforces the depressive state. One way of breaking this automatic pattern of thinking is to utilize the power of posthypnotic suggestions. This is given to the patient on a regular basis at the end of each hypnosis session. Alladin gives an example countering the negative self-hypnotic suggestion (NHS) with the following statement: "While you are in an upsetting situation, you will become more aware of how to deal with it rather than focusing on your depressed feelings." Yapko (2003) considers posthypnotic suggestions as a necessary ingredient of the therapeutic process for generating motivation and fostering changes in the future. Clark and Jackson (1983) regard posthypnotic suggestions as a form of higher-order conditioning; they provided evidence that PHS enhances the effect of in vivo exposure. Kirsch and Low (2013) report on the indispensable value in understanding and utilizing the power of suggestion in the treatment of depression. They point out that the therapeutic response to antidepressant medication is based to a large extent on a placebo response. Moreover, CBT and other nonpharmacological therapies all share success based on the successful outcome of positive suggestions and expectancy. This is compatible with the published work of Raz and Wolfson (2010) and my own previous publication on the cardinal importance and relevance of suggestion to all therapeutic encounters (Torem, 2010).

Reframing and Relabeling

Watzlawick, Weakland, and Fisch (1974), defined "reframing" as changing the individual's conceptual viewpoint in relation to the situation in which it is being experienced and placing it in another frame where the "fact" still fits, but the meaning is entirely changed. In other words, the meaning attributed to the situation is entirely changed.

"Relabeling" refers simply to changing the label attached to the person's problem or symptom, without necessarily changing the frame of reference or conceptual model.

In the case of depression, the symptoms of guilt, self-accusation, and depression are relabeled to responsibility, reliability, courage, and willingness to explore, through self-examination, strong feelings and thoughts. Depression is viewed as a process of self-examination, internal review, and a willingness to reevaluate a situation and consider new options. The following case illustrates the use of hypnosis to facilitate change, through reframing and relabeling, in a patient with depression.

D.J. was a 32-year-old man who was seen for the evaluation and treatment of depression. After an extensive set of interviews in which an organic basis for his depression was ruled out, it was recommended that he be seen for brief psychotherapy

for six sessions. The patient's symptoms included low self-esteem and a set of derogatory thoughts in which he was criticized for agreeing to work for his father and allowing himself to be dominated by him. The patient revealed that he was planning to leave his father's business and look for a new job, but this father's illness complicated the situation and he could not leave him. Thus, he felt that he had no backbone. The patient's father was diagnosed as suffering from an advanced stage of cancer and was given less than one year to live. Further investigation, under hypnosis, revealed that the patient had a competitive father who needed to be admired, respected, and looked up to by others in order to maintain his own self-worth.

The patient was then given a new definition of his symptoms using the techniques of reframing and relabeling. This was first done under hypnosis, and was later reinforced with discussion when the patient was out of the hypnotic trance. While under hypnosis, the patient was told that he should continue to behave in a submissive way toward his father and continue to act helpless since this behavior gave his father a chance to show how strong and wise he was, allowing him to instruct his son on how to run the business. Moreover, the patient was told that he was a good and loving son to his father, and that by acting in a helpless way he was, in fact, showing his great and deep love for his father, who had a limited time to live. In the discussion following the hypnotic session, the patient said he never thought of it that way, and that maybe his subconscious found a mysterious way to communicate his love for his father.

These techniques of reframing and relabeling were reinforced by telling the patient that he showed a great deal of courage in wanting to search for the truth. The patient's depressed mood and self-criticism were thus reframed into a positive mode regarding his relationship with his father. The patient's symptoms disappeared within two weeks, and in a follow-up visit, seven months later, he reported that on his father's death he resolved the loss by mourning his loss in a healthy way, without any signs of guilt.

Redirecting

This technique can be especially effective for dealing with feelings of guilt and remorse. The patient is told, under hypnosis, that he made a mistake and that all humans make mistakes at times. Remorse shows a high degree of humanness, and it is a true element of courage to reflect internally in order to move forward. The technique here follows the concept mentioned by Arthur Koestler in his book *Act of Creation*. He referred to psychotherapy as an artificially induced regeneration, relying on the basic process of *reculer pour mieux sauter* to take a step backward in order to make a better leap forward. In hypnosis, the patient is told that his subconscious mind will find new ways to guide him into good deeds to expiate for his mistake. The following case illustrates the use of this technique.

A.K. was a 35-year-old man who was involved in a car accident in which he lost control of his car, ran into another car, and caused an accident in which two people were killed. Later, it was learned that he had been drinking too much at a party earlier that evening. The patient was very depressed and suffered from insomnia, feelings of guilt and remorse, and he could not forgive himself, although more than three years had passed and he had not touched a drop of alcohol in that time. During an interview, under hypnosis, an ego state of this patient emerged spontaneously and called itself "The Superego of A.K." The ego state reported that the patient, A.K., will get some emotional peace only if he joins Alcoholics Anonymous and then becomes active in the movement of Citizens Against Drunk Driving. This ego state further communicated that A.K. is to be instructed to share his experience with young, teenage drivers so that his mistake will serve as a lesson for others. When he emerged from hypnosis, the patient had only a vague memory of what was discussed. He was then instructed to join in the previously mentioned activities. Follow-up with this patient a year later revealed that he was very actively involved in activities to prevent drunk driving. Further, he was energetic and had no symptoms of depression.

Ego-State Therapy

This form of therapy involves the utilization of family and group treatment techniques for the resolution of conflicts between different ego states, which constitute a "family of self" within a single individual. According to J. and H. Watkins (1979–1980, 1981), who have written prolifically on this subject (Watkins, 1971, 1981, 1993), an ego state is defined as an organized system of behaviors and experiences, whose elements are bound together by some common principle, but are more or less permeable. In some patients with depression, the underlying dynamics may involve the persecution and expression of hostility from a hidden ego state that represents the introject of a hostile, unloving parent or authority figure. When such underlying dynamics are uncovered by the use of hypnosis, ego-state therapy is a very useful technique in alleviating the patient's depression (Alladin, 1992a; Alladin, 2014; Christensen et al., 2013; Frederick, 2005, 2014; Frederick & McNeal, 2013; Gainer & Torem, 1993; Phillips & Frederick, 2010; Torem, 1993). Each ego state involved in the patient's depression is individually activated through the use of hypnosis, followed by a thorough study of each ego state to determine its origin, its needs, its objectives, and its significance in affecting the patient's mood and thinking. The therapist becomes a diplomat, who negotiates with the persecuting ego state to change its behavior while keeping its original aim.

For example, W.D. was a 33-year-old married woman, who was evaluated for depression associated with insomnia, inability to experience pleasure, poor appetite, and crying spells. She reported thoughts of being a bad mother to her newborn baby and was afraid she might hurt her baby. A further hypnoanalytic interview revealed that this woman had suffered great neglect and physical abuse from her own mother. She later made a vow to herself not to be like her mother when she has her own children. The hypnoanalytic technique identified an ego state that represented the introjected image of the patient's mother. This ego state attempted to influence the patient's behavior toward her baby by making her do to the baby what had been done to her. These impulses were experienced as bad thoughts and impulses in the patient's adult ego state, resulting in symptoms of anxiety and depression. In treatment, using ego-state therapy, the persecuting ego state was activated. The therapist found that it felt unloved and unappreciated by the patient. The therapist negotiated an agreement between this ego state and the patient, whereby this ego state would keep its influence on the patient, but instead of instilling thoughts of neglecting the baby it would influence the patient to pay more attention to her looks, makeup, body shape, and clothes. The patient's adult ego state, in turn, agreed to recognize the hidden child ego state and include it as part of the patient's makeup.

Hypnosis-Facilitated Cognitive Therapy

Yapko, who has been very prolific in communicating his model of understanding and treating depression in combination with hypnosis (Yapko, 1986, 1988, 1992, 1993, 1994, 1995, 1996, 1997, 1999, 2001a, 2001b, 2001c, 2002, 2003, 2006, 2007, 2008, 2009, 2010a, 2010b, 2013), points out that hypnosis and depression have the following elements in common:

- Depression and hypnosis increase in their intensity based on the quality and direction of one's focus.
- Both depression and hypnosis involve certain social processes and are affected and changed by the person's relationship with other people.
- Both depression and hypnosis are by and large a product of expectancy, regardless of whether the expectation is positive or whether it is negative.
- Both depression and hypnosis involve a "believed-in imagination," which means that one's experience is based on the recognition that people get deeply absorbed in highly subjective ideas, beliefs, and perceptions that regulate the quality of their lives. Such beliefs, ideas, and perceptions can be altered in therapeutic ways during the experience of hypnosis (Yapko, 2010a).

Yapko further eloquently details the application and value of using hypnosis in the treatment of depression, stating that:

- Hypnosis helps people build and utilize a positive attention focus.
- Hypnosis facilitates the acquisition of new behavioral skills.
- Hypnosis encourages people to see themselves as more resourceful and resilient, thereby enhancing a more positive self-image.
- Hypnosis helps in the easier and more efficient transfer of useful information from one context to another.
- Hypnosis establishes helpful subjective associations more automatically and intensively.

- Hypnosis provides opportunities for therapeutic learning of new skills and insights on an experiential and multidimensional level.
- Hypnosis defines people as being actively in charge of managing their internal world, thereby fostering greater emotional self-regulation.
- Hypnosis helps people sharpen key perceptual distinctions to counter overgeneralized thinking.
- Hypnosis allows people to experience a more comfortable distance from overwhelming feelings in order to face them, re-examine them cognitively, and resolve them.
- Hypnosis encourages people to rehearse new responses and actively incorporate new possibilities in a deliberate behavioral sequence designed to achieve a successful outcome.
- Hypnosis helps people to identify and develop underutilized personal resources, and
- Hypnosis helps people detach and separate themselves from a sense of victimhood.

Yapko points out the fact that CBT alone, even when facilitated with hypnotic therapeutic experiences, may not be enough to produce the best possible treatment outcome. Jacobson and his colleagues (1996) were searching for the most effective ingredients involved in the use of CBT for depression. After a sophisticated analysis, they concluded that what makes CBT most effective was not the specific cognitive changes in thinking but rather the activation of purposeful and new goal-directed behaviors designed to bring about a transformative change in the patient's ways of dealing with daily life predicaments and challenges. In fact, Jacobson and his colleagues showed that the cognitive component of the treatment added little to the overall treatment of depression. Subsequent research has confirmed that therapeutic change is much greater in therapies that employ homework skill building exercises (Burns & Spangler, 2000; Detweiler-Bedell & Whisman, 2005). This has led to the evolution of the third generation of behavior therapy, which has been named behavioral activation therapy (BA).

Behavioral Activation Therapy

Yapko (2010b) explains that the term *behavioral activation* (Lewinsohn & Graf, 1973, Lewinsohn, 1974) was used to emphasize the importance of getting the depressed person to actually *take action* rather than merely passively acquire information or contemplate feelings, circumstances, and new thoughts. According to Yapko (2010b), since the important fundamental research of Jacobson and his colleagues (1996), behavioral activation strategies have evolved as an intervention to promote experiential learning, skill building, and proactive new behaviors, which have then evolved into a model of psychotherapy called "behavioral activation therapy," also known as BA. The general goal of behavioral activation therapy is to increase the patient's frequency of positively reinforced experiences. Depressed patients are taught strategies for successfully carrying out goal-oriented behaviors. BA is also known as a third generation behavior therapy. The principles of behavioral activation therapy have been detailed by Jacobson, Martell, and Dimidjian (2001). According to Yapko (2010b), one recent study by Dimidjian et al. (2006) has shown behavioral activation therapy to be as efficacious as antidepressant medications and to have a slight edge over simple cognitive therapy. Yapko (2010b) emphasizes the importance of structured experiential learning exercises and the use of behavioral activation strategies enhanced by hypnosis. Yapko emphasizes that none of the effective therapeutic components focus on analyzing the past or exploring unconscious guilt or intrapsychic conflicts; instead, the focus is on developing new skills and using them to take positive actions to change one's way of coping with the stresses of daily life. Yapko points out that the patient is defined as an active participant in the treatment process. This is compatible with my own previous publications on participatory pharmacotherapy (Blackwell & Torem, 1980; Torem, 2006a, 2006b, 2008, 2009, 2011, 2013).

Future-Focused Therapy and Age Progression

In previous publications (Torem, 1987, 1992a, 1992b, 2006b, 2008, 2009, 2011, 2013), I pointed out the importance of a future focus in the treatment of patients suffering from depression. One of the common symptoms in patients with depression is the feeling of hopelessness and futurelessness. The use of age progression interventions enhanced by hypnosis combined with ego-strengthening and posthypnotic suggestions provides the patient with

a future projected therapeutic experience focused on healing, recovery, and the best possible therapeutic outcome. This is experienced by the patient in all five senses, internalized on a conscious and subconscious level, and then the patient is brought "back from the future" to the present time with the therapeutic experiences having been internalized and introjected into the patient's subconscious mind. Even if the patient does not have a clear memory of what he or she experienced, the results can be very positive. Following such a therapeutic future-focused intervention, the patient is instructed to write an essay about his or her experience and bring it back to the following session. In this following session, the patient is asked to read out loud from his or her essay about the patient's future-focused experience. Typically I found that patients who use the past tense in describing their future-focused experience are those who have fully internalized and introjected the images and experiences and this serves as a positive prognosis for their recovery from depression. The following is a case example of such a future-focused therapy enhanced by hypnosis.

Aaron (not his real name) was a 42-year-old married man and the father of three children ages 12, 10, and 8. He was diagnosed with severe depression associated with suicidal thoughts. He had a history of previous treatments that included a combination of antidepressants with some supportive psychotherapy. In the process of the evaluation, it was found that his depression was characterized by feelings of hopelessness with a sense of futurelessness. He specifically felt discouraged due to the fact that several trials of antidepressant medications in various combinations had not worked for him, in part due to intolerable side effects and in part due to the lack of a therapeutic response. In the process of establishing rapport with this patient, I found that a previous therapist told him that he would never recover from his depression unless he fully remembered all the details of his childhood abuse growing up in a dysfunctional family.

When Aaron consulted me for psychotherapy, he was focused on his past, assuming this focus would eventually help him resolve his feelings about the childhood abuse he suffered. However, on the contrary, the more he focused on all of the unpleasant memories of his dysfunctional childhood, the more depressed and hopeless he was feeling in his present day-to-day living. At times, he was afraid that he might act upon his suicidal thoughts and end up killing himself by an impulsive act of momentary desperation and anger. Thus, orienting Aaron to a positive future with new coping skills was an essential part of his treatment. He learned to use the structured guided imagery I taught him, which focused his attention on a beach scene using all five senses to induce a state of calmness. That self-soothing strategy also helped him to reach an improvement in the quality and length of natural sleep at night. He was pleased with these results because it gave him a new sense of mastery. He regained some trust in his inner resourcefulness when he learned that he could calm himself and could also use his new imagery skills independently to resolve his insomnia problem.

Aaron's relationship with his wife was described as generally good. However, he repeatedly stated that he felt "she got a bad deal," explaining that he frequently felt undeserving of her kindness and loving nature. He repeatedly kept asking her, "Why do you love me? You could have done so much better with another man." Her direct statements of "I love you and I don't want anyone else—you are the best man for me" provided reassurance that was only short-lived at best.

He stated that he loved his children but would sometimes get abrupt with them.

When he would later apologize for his short temper, he would add that perhaps they should have another father. His firstborn daughter would frequently say, "You are the best dad for me; I don't want another father." These reassurances were, predictably, also short-lived in effect. In the process of discussing a plan for his recovery, Aaron responded very favorably to a dialogue focused on the future. This dialogue began with the following series of suggestions:

"Aaron, let us suppose that you and I work together and somehow you recover from this depression. And let us suppose that when your daughter Erin [age 12] is a senior in high school, you have fully recovered from your depression, and you have reached a new level of healthy functioning in day-to-day living, not only at home but also at work. . . . You found a way to separate yourself from the memories of your childhood and liberate yourself from the past to live your own life in greater freedom from the past . . . knowing that you have a right to experience your own happiness with your wife and children as a mature adult, husband, and father. You experience

a sense of mastery over any dysfunctional thoughts or feelings. You know how to handle these feelings, you recognize that anger is a feeling, and you know how to identify its meaning . . . and how to be assertive in expressing your needs appropriately without losing your temper. . . . This has improved your sense of self-worth and self-respect. . . ."

As we talked about it, his face communicated a focused attentiveness and there was a new twinkle in his eyes I had not seen previously. I asked if he was interested in taking a trip into the future when his daughter Erin is 18 years old on the day of her graduation from high school. He agreed to do so. I asked him to describe in some more detail what such a day would be like, and then we followed with the "Back from the Future" intervention. This time, the intervention was presented with structured suggestions coupled with ego-strengthening. Additional suggestions, such as "Experience the comfort of Erin hugging you and telling you, 'Dad, I love you. Thank you for being there for me all these years.'" He was instructed to see the sparkle of joy in her eyes as she was dressed in cap and gown holding the diploma in her hand. This was then followed by the family getting together for a meal. He was instructed to experience the meal with all of the five senses and with a focus on the color and shape of the food, its smell and taste, and to experience the chewing and swallowing of the food. As these suggestions were given to him, I carefully observed the front of his neck and noticed that he was swallowing several times (this is a literal sign of swallowing one's saliva in response to a particular suggestion and may symbolically indicate an act of internalizing the suggestions). He was then instructed to internalize the feelings of joy, comfort, and pride in the accomplishment of his daughter and, in addition, the overall experience of being there with his family. He was then instructed to bring these gifts back with him from the future and to let them guide him consciously and subconsciously on a daily basis as he continues to change and transform his reality internally and externally to match this man of the future. As he was guided out of this hypnotic state, he was asked to write an essay about the experience and bring it back with him to the following session.

In the following session, Aaron reported that his energy was coming back and that he and his wife began walking together every evening after dinner. He said that for the first time in a long time, when his wife was holding his hand, he did not withdraw from her. He said he felt comfortable holding her hand and felt the love and care from her warm touch. At that point, the moving thought occurred to him how fortunate he was to have her as his wife and partner.

Years later, I received a letter from Aaron following the graduation of his daughter from high school, updating me on all of his accomplishments at home and at work. He reminded me of the visualizations and imagery we did and how those images had become reality for him. He thanked me for caring for him and promised to stay in touch in the future. In Aaron's case, the shift from a past orientation of an unchangeable history to a future orientation featuring some of the best experiences life can offer was vital to his recovery from depression.

CONCLUSION

This chapter discussed the utilization of hypnosis as a tool to uncover the various dynamics involved in a patient's depression. Moreover, it also demonstrated the efficacy of hypnosis as a facilitating tool in the psychotherapy of depression by enhancing such techniques as abreaction, working through, therapeutic suggestion, ego-strengthening, reframing and relabeling, redirecting, ego-state therapy, behavioral activation therapy with structured clinical experiential learning of new skills and behaviors, and the utilization of age progression in a future-focused therapeutic strategy. The need to rule out organic, biological elements in depression before hypnotic techniques are employed was emphasized.

REFERENCES

Alladin, A. (1992a). Depression as a dissociative state. *Hypnos: Swedish Journal of Hypnosis in Psychotherapy and Psychosomatic Medicine, 19*, 243–253.

Alladin, A. (1992b). Hypnosis with depression. *American Journal of Preventive Psychiatry and Neurology, 3*, 13–18.

Alladin, A. (1994). Cognitive hypnotherapy with depression. *Journal of Cognitive Psychotherapy, 8*, 275–288.

Alladin, A. (2006). Cognitive hypnotherapy for treating depression. In R. Chapman (Ed.), *The clinical use of hypnosis with cognitive behavior therapy: A practitioner's casebook* (pp. 139–187). New York, NY: Springer Publishing Company.

Alladin, A. (2008). *Cognitive hypnotherapy: An integrated approach to the treatment of emotional disorders.* Chichester, UK: John Wiley & Sons.

Alladin, A. (2012). Cognitive hypnotherapy for major depressive disorder. *American Journal of Clinical Hypnosis, 54*(4), 275–293. doi:10.1080/00029157.20 12.654527

Alladin, A. (2013). The power of belief and expectancy in understanding and management of depression. *American Journal of Clinical Hypnosis, 55*(3), 249–271. doi:10.1080/00029157.2012.740607

Alladin, A. (2014). Healing the wounded self: Combining hypnotherapy with ego state therapy. *American Journal of Clinical Hypnosis, 56*, 3–22.

Alladin, A., & Alibhai, A. (2007). Cognitive hypnotherapy for depression. *International Journal of Clinical and Experimental Hypnosis, 55*(2), 147–166. doi:10.1080/00207140601177897

Alladin, A., & Heap, M. (1991). Hypnosis and depression. In M. Heap & W. Dryden (Eds.), *Hypnotherapy: A handbook* (pp. 49–67). London, UK: Open University Press.

American Psychiatric Association. (2013). *Diagnostic and statistical manual.* Arlington, VA: American Psychiatric Association.

Bandura, A. (1977). Self-efficacy: toward a unifying theory of behavioral change. *Psychological review, 84*(2), 191.

Beck, A. T. (1972). *Depression: Causes and treatment.* Philadelphia, PA: University of Pennsylvania Press.

Beck, A. T. (1975). *Cognitive therapy and the emotional disorders.* Madison, CT: International Universities Press.

Beck, A. T. (2008). The evolution of the cognitive model of depression and its neurobiological correlates. *American Journal of Psychology, 165*, 969–977.

Beck, A. T., & Haigh, E. A. (2014). Advances in cognitive theory and therapy. *Annual Review of Clinical Psychology, 10*, 1–24. doi:10.1146/annurev-clinpsy-032813-153734

Beck, A. T., Rush, A. J., Shaw, B. F., & Emery, G. (1979). *Cognitive therapy of depression.* New York, NY: Guilford Press.

Beck, A. T. (1976). *Cognitive therapy and the emotional disorders.* New York, NY: New American Library.

Berliner, B. (1947a). The concept of masochism. *Psychoanalytical Review, 29*, 386–400.

Berliner, B. (1947b). On some psychodynamics of masochism. *Psychoanalytics Quarterly, 16*, 459–471.

Berliner, B. (1958). The role of object relations in moral masochism. *Psychoanalytics. Quarterly, 27*, 38–56.

Berliner, B. (1966). Psychodynamics of the depressive character. *Psychoannual Forum, 1*, 243–251.

Blackwell, B., & Torem, M. (1980). The biosocial model of depression. In F. J. Ayd (Ed.), *Clinical depressions: Diagnostic and therapeutic challenges* (pp. 103–113). New York, NY: Ayd Medical Communications. Waiverly Press.

Burns, D. D., & Spangler, D. L. (2000). Does psychotherapy homework lead to improvements in depression in cognitive-behavioral therapy or does improvement lead to increased homework compliance? *Journal of Consulting and Clinical Psychology, 68*(1), 46–56.

Burns, D. D. (1980). *Feeling good*. New York, NY: William Morrow.

Burrows, G., & Broughton, S. (2001). Hypnosis and depression. In G. Burrows, R. Stanley, & P. Bloom (Eds.), *International handbook of clinical hypnosis* (pp. 129–142). New York, NY: Wiley.

Cheek, D. B., & LeCron, L. M. (1968). *Clinical hypnotherapy*. New York, NY: Grune and Stratton.

Christensen, C., Barabasz, A., & Barabasz, M. (2013). Efficacy of abreactive ego state therapy for PTSD: Trauma resolution, depression, and anxiety. *International Journal of Clinical and Experimental Hypnosis, 61*(1), 20–37. doi:10.1080/00207144.2013.729386

Clarke, J. C., & Jackson, J. A. (1983). *Hypnosis and behavior therapy: The treatment of anxiety and phobias*. New York, NY: Springer Publishing Company.

Clarkin, J. F., Pilkonis, P. A., & Magruder, K. M. (1996). Psychotherapy of depression. *Archives of General Psychiatry, 53*(8), 717–723.

Coe, W. (1993). Expectations and hypnotherapy. In J. Rhue, S. Lynn, & I. Kirsch (Eds.), *Handbook of clinical hypnosis* (pp. 73–93). Washington, DC: American Psychological Association.

Detweiler-Bedell, J., & Whisman, M. (2005). A lesson in assigning homework: Therapist, client, and task characteristics in cognitive therapy for depression. *Professional Psychology: Research & Practice, 36*, 219–223.

Dimidjian, S., Hollon, S. D., Dobson, K. S., Schmaling, K. B., Kohlenberg, R. J., Addis, M. E., . . . Jacobson, N. S. (2006). Randomized trial of behavioral activation, cognitive therapy, and antidepressant medication in the acute treatment of adults with major depression. *Journal of Consulting and Clinical Psychology, 74*(4), 658–670. doi:10.1037/0022-006X.74.4.658

Dirmaier, J., Steinmann, M., & Krattenmacher, T. (2012). Non-pharmacological treatment of depressive disorders: A review of evidence-based treatment options. *Review of Recent Clinical Trials, 7*, 141–149.

Dozois, D., & Dobson, K. (Eds.). (2004). *The prevention of anxiety and depression: Theory, research and practice*. Washington, DC: American Psychological Association. doi:10.1037/10722-000

Ellis, A. (1977). *The basic clinical theory of rational-emotive therapy*. New York, NY: Springer Publishing Company.

Engel, G. L. (1959). Psychogenic pain and the pain-prone patient. *American Journal of Medicine, 26*(6), 899–918.

Engel, G. L. (1975). The death of a twin: Mourning and anniversary reactions. Fragments of ten years of self-analysis. *International Journal of Psycho-Analysis, 56*(1), 23–40.

Erickson, M. (1954). Pseudo-orientation in time as a hypnotherapeutic procedure. *International Journal of Clinical and Experimental Hypnosis, 2*, 261–283.

Erickson, M. (1954). Special techniques of brief hypnotherapy. *Journal of Clinical and Experimental Hypnosis, 2*, 109–129.

Frederick, C., & McNeal, S. (1999). *Inner strengths*. Mahwah, NJ: Lawrence Erlbaum Associates, Publishers.

Frederick, C. (2014). The center core in ego state therapy and other hypnotically facilitated psychotherapies. *American Journal of Clinical Hypnosis, 56*, 39–53.

Frederick, C., & McNeal, S. A. (2013). *Inner strengths: Contemporary psychotherapy and hypnosis for ego-strengthening*. New York, NY: Routledge.

Frederick, C., & Phillips, M. (1992). The use of age progression as interventions with acute psychosomatic conditions. *American Journal of Clinical Hypnosis, 35*(2), 89–98. doi:10.1080/00029157.1992.10402991

Freud, S. (1958). Formulations on the two principles of mental functioning. In *The Standard Edition of the Complete Psychological Works of Sigmund Freud, Volume XII (1911-1913): The Case of Schreber, Papers on Technique and Other Works* (pp. 213–226).

Freud, A. (1946). *The ego and the mechanism of defense*. New York, NY: International Universities Press.

Freud, S., & Breuer, J. (1955). *Studies of hysteria. the collected writings of S. Freud* (standard ed.). London, UK: Hogarth Press.

Freytag, F. K. (1961). *Hypnosis and the unconscious body image*. New York, NY: Julian Press.

Gainer, M. J., & Torem, M. S. (1993). Ego-state therapy for self-injurious behavior. *American Journal of Clinical Hypnosis, 35*(4), 257–266. doi:10.1080/00029157.1993.10403017

Hammond, D. C. (Ed.). (1990). *Age-progression. Handbook of hypnotic suggestions and metaphors* (pp. 515–516). New York, NY: W. W. Norton.

Hartland, J. (1965). The value of ego-strengthening procedures prior to direct symptom removal under hypnosis. *American Journal of Clinical Hypnosis, 8*(2), 89–93. doi:10.1080/00029157.1965.10402470

Hartland, J. (1971). Further observations of the use of ego-strengthening techniques. *American Journal of Clinical Hypnosis, 14*(1). doi:10.1080/00029157.1971.10402136

Jacobson, N. S., Dobson, K. S., Truax, P. A., Addis, M. E., Koerner, K., Gollan, J. K., . . . Prince, S. E. (1996). A component analysis of cognitive-behavioral treatment for depression. *Journal of Consulting and Clinical Psychology, 64*(2), 295–304.

Jacobson, N. S., Martell, C., & Dimidjian, S. (2001). Behavioral activation treatment for depression: Returning to contextual roots. *Clinical Psychology: Science and Practice, 8,* 255–270.

Kirsch, I., & Low, C. B. (2013). Suggestions in the treatment of depression. *American Journal of Clinical Hypnosis, 55*(3), 221–229. doi:10.1080/00029157.2012.738613

Lecron, L. M. (1954). A hypnotic technique for uncovering unconscious material. *Journal of Clinical and Experimental Hypnosis, 1,* 76–79.

Lewinsohn, P. M., & Graf, M. (1973). Pleasant activities and depression. *Journal of Consulting and Clinical Psychology, 41*(2), 261–268.

Lewinsohn, P. (1974). A behavioral approach to depression. In R. Friedman & M. Katz (Eds.), *The psychology of depression: Contemporary theory and research* (pp. 157–178). Oxford, UK: John Wiley & Sons.

Lopez-Ibor, J. J. (1973). Depressive equivalents. In P. Kielholz (Ed.), *Masked depression.* Bern, Switzerland: Hans Huber Publishers.

Ma, S. H., & Teasdale, J. D. (2004). Mindfulness-based cognitive therapy for depression: Replication and exploration of differential relapse prevention effects. *Journal of Consulting and Clinical Psychology, 72*(1), 31–40. doi:10.1037/0022-006X.72.1.31

Meichenbaum, D. (1977). *Cognitive-behavior modification: An integrative approach.* New York, NY: Springer Publishing Company.

Phillips, M., & Frederick, C. (2010). Empowering the self through ego-state therapy. Retrieved from http://www.reversingchronicpain.com/prof.html.

Pichot, P., & Hassan, J. (1973). Masked depression and depressive equivalents: Problems of definition and diagnosis. In P. Kielholz (Ed.), *Masked depression.* Bern, Switzerland: Hans Huber Publishers.

Piet, J., & Hougaard, E. (2011). The effect of mindfulness-based cognitive therapy for prevention of relapse in recurrent major depressive disorder: A systematic review and meta-analysis. *Clinical Psychology Review, 31*(6), 1032–1040. doi:10.1016/j.cpr.2011.05.002

Pollock, G. H. (1970). Anniversary reactions, trauma, and mourning. *Psychoanalytical Quarterly, 39,* 347–371.

Raz, A., & Wolfson, J. B. (2010). From dynamic lesions to brain imaging of behavioral sessions: Alloying the gold of psychoanalysis with the copper of suggestion. *Neuropsychoanalysis, 12,* 5–21.

Sandler, J., Holder, A., & Dare, C. (1970). Basic psychoanalytic concepts: The negative therapeutic reaction. *British Journal of Psychiatry: The Journal of Mental Science, 117*(539), 413–435.

Seligman, M. (2002). *Authentic happiness: Using the new positive psychology to realize your potential for lasting fulfillment.* New York, NY: Free Press.

Soucy, C. I., & Provencher, M. D. (2013). Behavioural activation for depression: Efficacy, effectiveness and dissemination. *Journal of Affective Disorders, 145,* 292–299.

Torem, M. S. (1993). Therapeutic writing as a form of ego-state therapy. *American Journal of Clinical Hypnosis, 35*(4), 267–276. doi:10.1080/00029157.1993.10403018

Torem, M. S. (2013). Participatory pharmacotherapy: Ten strategies for enhancing adherence. *Current Psychiatry, 12,* 21–25.

Torem, M. (1979). Pseudomasochism: A clinical report. *Hillside Journal of Clinical Psychology, 1,* 161–192.

Torem, M. (1983). Depression as illness and mood: The implications for diagnosis and treatment. *Ohio State Medical Journal, 79,* 792–795.

Torem, M. (1987). Hypnosis in the treatment of depression. In W. Wester (Ed.), *Clinical hypnosis: A case management approach* (pp. 288–301). Cincinnati, OH: Behavioral Science Center.

Torem, M. (1990). Ego strengthening. In D. C. Hammond (Ed.), *Handbook of hypnotic suggestions and metaphors* (pp. 110–112). New York, NY: W.W. Norton.

Torem, M. (2006a). Postpartum depression. In M. Dambro (Ed.), *Griffith's 5-minute clinical consult* (pp. 888–889). Philadelphia, PA: Lippincott Williams & Wilkins.

Torem, M. (2006b). Treating depression: A remedy from the future. In M. Yapko (Ed.), *Hypnosis and treating depression: Applications in clinical practice* (pp. 97–119). New York, NY: Routledge.

Torem, M. (2008). Words to the wise: 4 secrets of successful pharmacotherapy. *Current Psychiatry, 7,* 19–24.

Torem, M. (2009). Words to the wise: 4 secrets of successful pharmacotherapy. *OBG Management, 21,* 39–47.

Torem, M. (2010). The central role of suggestion in all clinical encounters including psychoanalysis. *Neuropsychoanalysis, 12,* 43–46.

Torem, M. (2011). Beyond lithium: Using psychotherapy to reduce suicide risk in bipolar disorder. *Current Psychiatry, 10,* 39–45.

Wang, P. S., Berglund, P., & Kessler, R. C. (2000). Recent care of common mental disorders in the United States. *Journal of general internal medicine, 15*(5), 284–292.

Watkins, H. H. (1993). Ego-state therapy: An overview. *American Journal of Clinical Hypnosis, 35*(4), 232–240. doi:10.1080/00029157.1993.10403014

Watkins, J. G. (1971). The affect bridge: A hypnoanalytic technique. *International Journal of Clinical and Experimental Hypnosis, 19*(1), 21–27. doi:10.1080/00207147108407148

Watkins, J. G. (1981). Ego-state therapy. In R. J. Corsini (Ed.), *Handbook of innovative psychotherapies.* New York, NY: John Wiley and Sons.

Watkins, J. G., & Watkins, H. H. (1979–1980). Ego states and hidden observers. *Journal of Altered States and Consciousness, 5,* 3–18.

Watzlawick, P., Weakland, J., & Fisch, R. (1974). *Change: Principles of problem formation and problem resolution.* New York, NY: W. W. Norton.

World Health Organization. (2009). *World health organization: Programmes and projects/mentalhealth/ disorders management/depression.definition/en/.* Retrieved from http://www.who.int/mental_health

World Health Organization. (2012). *Depression: A global public health con*cern. Retrieved from http://www.who .int/mental_health/management/depression/who_ paper_depression_wfmh_2012.pdf?ua=1

Yapko, M. (1999). *Hand-me-down blues: How to stop depression from spreading in families.* New York, NY: St. Martins Griffin.

Yapko, M. (2003). *Trancework: An introduction to the practice of clinical hypnosis* (3rd ed.). New York, NY: Brunner/Routledge.

Yapko, M. (2007). The case of Carol: Empowering decision-making through metaphor and hypnosis. In G. W. Burns(Ed.). *Healing with stories: Your casebook collection for using therapeutic metaphors* (pp. 213–226). Hoboken, NJ: Wiley.

Yapko, M. D. (2013). Treating depression with antidepressants: Drug-placebo efficacy debates limit broader considerations. *American Journal of Clinical Hypnosis, 55*(3), 272–290. doi:10.1080/00029157.20 12.707156

Yapko, M. (1986). Depression: Diagnostic frameworks and therapeutic strategies. In M. Yapko (Ed.), *Hypnotic and strategic interventions: Principles & practice* (pp. 241–242). New York, NY: Irvington.

Yapko, M. (1988). *When living hurts: Directives for treating depression.* New York, NY: Brunner/Mazel.

Yapko, M. (1992). *Hypnosis and the treatment of depressions: Strategies for change.* New York, NY: Brunner/Mazel.

Yapko, M. (1993). Hypnosis and depression. In J. Rhue, S. Lynn, & I. Kirsch (Eds.), *Handbook of clinical hypnosis* (pp. 339–355). Washington, DC: American Psychological Association.

Yapko, M. (1994). *When living hurts: Directives for treating depression.* New York, NY: Brunner/Mazel.

Yapko, M. (1995). *Essentials of hypnosis.* New York, NY: Brunner/Mazel.

Yapko, M. (1996). A brief therapy approach to the use of hypnosis in treating depression. In S. Lynn, I. Krisch, & J. Rhue (Eds.), *Casebook of clinical hypnosis* (pp. 75–98). Washington, DC: American Psychological Association.

Yapko, M. (1997). *Breaking the patterns of depression.* New York, NY: Random House/Doubleday.

Yapko, M. (2001a). Hypnosis in treating symptoms and risk factors of major depression. *American Journal of Clinical Hypnosis, 44,* 97–108.

Yapko, M. (2001b). Hypnotic intervention for ambiguity as a depressive risk factor. *American Journal of Clinical Hypnosis, 44,* 109–117.

Yapko, M. (2001c). *Treating depression with hypnosis: Integrating cognitive-behavioral and strategic approaches.* New York, NY: Brunner/Routledge.

Yapko, M. (2002). The power of vision as an antidepressant: Rethinking the focus of therapy. In J. Zeig (Ed.), *Brief therapy: Lasting impressions* (pp. 63–78). Phoenix, AZ: The Milton H. Erickson Foundation Press.

Yapko, M. (2006). *Hypnosis and treating depression: Application in clinical practice.* New York, NY: Routledge.

Yapko, M. (2008). Hypnotic approaches to treating depression. In M. Nash & A. Barnier (Eds.), *The Oxford handbook of hypnosis: Theory, research and practice* (pp. 549–567). Oxford, UK: Oxford University Press.

Yapko, M. (2009). *Depression is contagious: How the most common mood disorder is spreading around the world and how to stop it.* New York, NY: Free Press.

Yapko, M. (2010a). Hypnosis in the treatment of depression: An overdue approach for encouraging skillful mood management. *International Journal of Clinical and Experimental Hypnosis, 58,* 137–146.

Yapko, M. (2010b). Hypnotically catalyzing experiential learning across treatments for depression: Actions can speak louder than moods. *International Journal of Clinical and Experimental Hypnosis, 58,* 186–201 doi: 10.1080/00029157.2012.707156

Zeig, J. (Ed.). (1997). Cognitive therapy: Reflections. *The evolution of psychotherapy: The third conference* (pp. 55–64). New York, NY: Bruner/Mazel.

Eating Disorders

Moshe S. Torem

Eating disorders continue to be a challenging predicament for families and clinicians engaged in the long-term care of patients diagnosed with these conditions. The incidence of anorexia nervosa in females is 8 to 19 per 100,000 per year and 2 per 100,000 in males. The prevalence of anorexia nervosa is 0.9% in females and 0.3% in males (Farooq & Siddiqui, 2015a). Bulimia nervosa shows different statistics. The incidence of bulimia nervosa for females is 28.8 per 100,000 per year and for males is 0.8 per 100,000 per year. The prevalence of bulimia nervosa is 1% to 3% in females ages 16 to 35 and 0.5% in young males (Farooq & Siddiqui, 2015b).

A review of the literature on eating disorders, including anorexia nervosa and bulimia, reveals a remarkable scarcity on the utilization of hypnosis as a therapeutic tool (Doyle, 1996; Marcus & Wildes, 2014; Walsh, 1997; Yager, 1994). However, the effectiveness of hypnotic interventions, in patients with eating disorders, has been recorded in a significant amount of the literature since the time of Pierre Janet (1907, 1919).

Numerous publications have pointed out the usefulness of hypnosis in the treatment of patients with eating disorders (Vanderlinden, Vandereeycken, & Claes, 2007). Vanderlinden and Vandereycken (1988, 1990) provide a comprehensive and excellent review of the literature on the use of hypnosis with eating disorders. Janet (1907, 1919) described how, by using hypnotic techniques, he was able to change the patients' dissociative, fixed ideas about eating and their body image, and to promote a general mental synthesis. Janet also used cognitive restructuring techniques that were successfully augmented by hypnosis. The hypothesis that many patients with eating disorders may suffer from dissociative episodes has been supported by the research of Pettinati, Horne and Staats (1982, 1985), as well as by Council (1986) and Torem (1986a, 1990).

These studies found that patients with bulimia were significantly more hypnotizable than patients with anorexia nervosa. Griffith (1989) reported the successful use of a hypnobehavioral model in the treatment of bulimia nervosa, and Gross (1984) reported the successful use of hypnosis in the treatment of patients with anorexia nervosa, thus indicating that patients with the diagnosis of anorexia nervosa should not automatically be ruled out as candidates for hypnotherapy.

This chapter will describe specific issues involved in the effective assessment of the patient with an eating disorder before the decision to utilize hypnosis is implemented. What follows is a description of a variety of hypnotherapeutic techniques and their utilization in the treatment of patients with eating disorders.

RESEARCH

The comprehensive and in-depth assessment of patients with an eating disorder is of great value for understanding the underlying dynamics of the condition, the patient's character, and the crafting of an effective treatment plan. The clinical literature identifies a variety of psychodynamics attributed to the psychopathology of eating disorders such as:

- A fear of growing up and reaching full sexual maturation (Bruch, 1973, 1974; Gross, 1984).
- Obsessive perfectionism and distorted body image (Bruch, 1973, 1974, 1978).
- Family enmeshment and struggle for autonomy (Minuchin, Rosman, & Baker, 1978).
- A fear of pregnancy, a fear of acting out hostile impulses as well as a need for self-punishment (Evans, 1982).

- An unresolved past trauma (Damlouji & Ferguson, 1985; Goodwin, 1988; Goodwin & Attias, 1993; McFarlane, McFarlane, & Gilchrist, 1988; Torem & Curdue, 1988; Vanderlinden & Vandereycken, 1993).
- A dissociative mechanism (Chandarana & Malla, 1989; Council, 1986; Grave, Oliosi, Todisco, & Vanderlinden, 1997; Pettinati, Horne, & Staats, 1982, 1985; Pettinati, Kogan, & Margolis, 1989; Sanders, 1986; Schwartz, Barrett, & Saba, 1985; Torem, 1986a, 1986b, 1989b; Vanderlinden, Spinhoven, Vandereycken, & van Dyck, 1995; Vanderlinden, Vandereycken, Van Dyck, & Vertommen, 1993).
- Underlying splitting and confused identity (Goodwin & Attias, 1993; Gutwill, 1994; Kluft, 1991; Ross, 1989; Torem, 1984, 1989a, 1990, 1993a; Torem, 1993b; Torem & Curdue, 1988).

In listening to the patient I specifically explore the possibility of ambivalence and internal conflicts regarding the eating disorder symptoms and behaviors, looking for any clues that the behaviors are ego-dystonic. In previous publications (Torem, 1989b, 1991), I have delineated examples of clues to an underlying dissociative mechanism in the patient's description of the symptoms:

1. "I sometimes do not know why I do it . . . I am so confused. . . . It is not like me."
2. "Whenever food is put in front of me, I become frightened, like a little kid. I know I need to eat but it is like an inner voice doesn't let me touch the food."
3. "A part of me wants to binge and another part of me hates it and is disgusted."
4. "Sometimes I feel like Dr. Jekyll and Mr. Hyde and it is not just about eating . . . I don't know myself anymore."
5. "Look at this body . . . isn't it a shame? . . . she used to be a fine attractive girl and then this awful thing happened . . . she is afraid of men, all men . . . she hides behind the fat."
6. "When I get into a binge . . . it feels so strange . . . as if I am in a daze . . . I don't know what comes over me . . . and then I feel so guilty and I want to throw up."
7. "Doctor, you may not believe me, but at times I don't even remember bingeing . . . my husband tells me that I do . . . but I can hardly remember doing it."
8. "I look at my body and I know the scale says I have lost more than 25 pounds but yet my body feels so fat . . . I know it doesn't make sense . . . it is as if I hear this voice in my head telling me I am too fat."
9. "You know doctor, at times I am so confused . . . sometimes I feel fat and sometimes I feel skinny . . . sometimes I want to eat and other times I'm afraid . . . I don't know what gets into me . . . I am so confused."
10. "Doctor, my mother says I am weird . . . she thinks that I am possessed by the Devil . . . that is her way of explaining my anger at myself for eating too much . . . and then wanting to throw up."

An additional method for identifying a possible underlying dissociation in patients with eating disorders is the administration of a scale to detect dissociation. The Dissociation Experiences Scale (DES; Bernstein & Putnam, 1986) is easy to administer and has been tested for its validity and reliability in large populations (Carlson et al., 1993; Putnam et al., 1996). The Perceptual Alteration Scale (PAS; Sanders, 1986) is also of use, since it has a special focus on eating disorder symptoms. In a recent study (Torem, Egtvedt, & Curdue, 1995), a high correlation between the eye roll sign (ERS) and the dissociation scores measured by the PAS indicated a likely correlation between these two assessments of dissociation. Since the capacity to dissociate is correlated with the capacity for hypnosis, the clinician may, therefore, learn in advance whether a certain patient may benefit from the use of hypnotic techniques without having to use a more lengthy assessment of hypnotizability. To complement the previously noted scales, Spiegel's Hypnotic Induction Profile (HIP) (Spiegel, 1972, 1974) may be useful; it is particularly suited to the clinical setting since it takes about 5 to 7 min to administer.

Many patients with eating disorders feel helpless, hopeless, and ashamed of having to seek psychological help. I use the principle of "meeting the patient where the patient is at," allowing patients to talk about any subject they wish to discuss, and letting them choose the priority of their concerns, even if at first it seems only remotely related to the eating disorder. I listen to metaphors in the patient's language, being aware that people communicate simultaneously on two levels: manifest and latent. For example, an 18-year-old adolescent girl communicates in the first session her story about the fact that the house she is living in is crumbling and needs to be renovated and remodeled, and that she is determined to find the resources to accomplish this goal. This patient is talking on a manifest level about her own house, which in reality may need to be renovated and remodeled; however, on a latent level, she may be referring to her own body that needs to be repaired and restored to health. In fact, this girl had lost many teeth due to repeated self-induced vomiting, and in addition had an electrolyte imbalance, abnormal liver functions, and esophageal bleeding, requiring immediate medical and dental care. The clinician's recognition that the patient communicates about her body in a metaphorical way makes the therapist an ally with the patient's subconscious mind, and creates an ideal setting for the effective use of hypnosis to facilitate the needed therapeutic change.

Therapeutic Intervention Training

When evaluating a new patient, I listen to the patient's communication regarding dysphoric feelings of helplessness, anxiety, hopelessness, inner tension, insomnia, fear, and restlessness. I introduce the idea of using hypnosis by making it relevant to the patient's presenting symptoms, saying to the patient something like this, "Would you like to learn how to use an exercise to reduce your anxiety and promote a sense of calmness?" Most patients respond affirmatively. I then proceed by teaching the patient a self-hypnosis exercise, loaded with suggestions and images of calmness and comfort, asking the patient to select a place associated in his or her mind with such feelings. Some patients select a mountain trail, others an inland lake or a state park, and many select an ocean beach.

Most patients respond positively to this exercise, which can be tailored to the patient's choice of place. At its completion, patients have an experience of success in replacing their feelings of anxiety and restlessness with new feelings of calmness and comfort. This success helps patients to become allies and believers in the healing powers of self-hypnotic imagery and conveys to them a sense of new hope. To enhance the experience of success,

suggestions and images for ego-strengthening are added (Torem, 1992a, 1992b).

Ego-Strengthening

Ego-strengthening suggestions are an important part of most hypnotherapy interventions. The technique was named by Hartland (1965, 1971), and further elaborated by Stanton (1975, 1979, 1989) and Frederick and McNeal (2013). In this intervention, the patient follows a set of general hypnotic suggestions to promote healing, strength, a sense of well-being, competence, and mastery. The following verbatim example may be used in patients with eating disorders:

"As you are sitting here in this chair in a state of self-hypnosis, and you allow yourself to experience such calmness and comfort, a state of inner harmony, you may allow yourself to accept, if you wish, whatever is necessary to promote your progress of healing and well-being, so you can go on with your life in a healthy, more mature and adaptive way. You learn to be free, live in the present as an effective, healthy human being. Every day, in every way, you are getting better and better. You become physically stronger, more alert, more wide awake, more energetic, more resourceful, trustworthy, and trusting in your own wisdom and intelligence. Yes, you deserve to live your life with respect and dignity. Yes, you deserve to experience hope, comfort and optimism. Every day in every way, your nerves become stronger and your mood more stable and pleasant. You become more interested in what you do, and what goes on around you . . . and as this happens, your mind becomes calm, serene and peaceful . . . your thoughts are clear and well composed. You experience a sense of internal tranquility in total harmony with your body, and as your body responds to your mind, it too becomes more calm and comfortable. Your concentration becomes focused and easy. You accept yourself with grace and with ease as a bona fide member of human society; you learn to see yourself in a positive light, developing greater confidence in your talents and skills, developing greater confidence with faith in a positive future. Now, all these may not happen quickly or rapidly. They may take some time, but only as much time as you really need for them all to take place . . . they can happen as rapidly and as quickly as you need for them to happen and as rapidly as your subconscious mind wants

them to happen. It is OK if you don't want them to happen too fast, only as fast as you need. Now, you may take a moment to reflect privately what your life is like with all these wonderful changes taking place. Then whenever you are ready, simply count back from three to one. At the count of three you get ready in your own mind to shift your focus to the regular state of consciousness, and go ahead and do it now. At the count of two with your eyelids closed, you look up with your eyes, and at the count of one let your eyelids open and you let your eyes come back to focus. Your subconscious mind continues to retain all these images and feelings for healing and recovery. Now, you become fully alert, awake and oriented to your surroundings, able to function safely and adaptively as you interact with your surrounding environment."

This is followed by a dialogue with the patient on practicing self-hypnosis to induce calmness and relaxation, opening one's mind to accept positive autosuggestions and imagery such as: "every day in every way I am getting better and better." The patient is instructed to practice this on a daily basis and report results in the next appointment or by a phone call.

Cognitive Reframing and Restructuring

Cognitive restructuring is described in detail by H. and D. Spiegel in their book, *Trance and Treatment* (1978, 2008), and also by cognitive-behavioral therapists such as Meichenbaum (1977) and Kroger and Fezler (1976). In essence, the patient is taught a new way of looking at an old problem and finding new, creative solutions in situations where the patient was cognitively "chasing his own tail," and feeling stuck with no way out. The patient with an eating disorder is first guided into a state of self-hypnosis, in which the patient is highly receptive to new ideas and suggestions. Under hypnosis, patients are asked to respond if they are willing to fully cooperate in this process of therapy, with the aid of ideomotor signaling.

CASE EXAMPLE

Jane was a 16-year-old Caucasian single daughter, living with her parents and attending high school. She suffered from bulimia nervosa with a pathological low weight and a BMI of 15. She engaged in behaviors of bingeing and purging using self-induced vomiting on a daily basis. She felt depressed and developed difficulties in her ability to concentrate on her academic work in school. She also complained of insomnia and constant fatigue with poor memory. Even though she was brought for treatment by her mother, she indicated a wish to get help in order to control the symptoms of bingeing and purging. She expressed guilt and shame regarding these behaviors and for some time kept them as a secret, trying to hide them even from her own parents. At the start of treatment, she was first taught self-hypnosis and imagery (choosing the ocean beach as her favorite place) to induce a state of calmness, activating the relaxation response state as described by Benson (1975, 1996). She did well in the office and then practiced at home with good results. In follow-up sessions, we used ideomotor signaling to explore her willingness to proceed with more interventions in helping her control the bingeing and purging symptoms. She responded with an affirmative ideomotor signal, and then we continued as follows:

"As you are sitting in this chair, in this special state of extra-receptivity and self-hypnosis, you realize that your subconscious mind has now become your ally, and together you are making the commitment to develop a new relationship between yourself and your body. In this new relationship you, in fact, vow to respect and protect your body for the rest of your life. You are learning to develop a new view of your body that is totally dependent on you to be taken care of. In fact, your body is like a precious plant through which you can experience life itself, and to the extent that you want to live your life to the fullest, you owe your body this respect and protection. You also become aware that if not for you, for your body, binge eating and purging are, in fact, a poison [(for bulimic patients). For anorexic patients, modify this statement to say]: For your body, if not for you, self-starvation is, in fact, a poison. You realize that you cannot live without your body. Your body is this precious plant through which you experience life itself, so you need your body to live, and to the extent that you want to live your life to the fullest, you owe your body this respect and protection. Do you agree? [waiting for an ideomotor signal of confirmation].

Now, these are the three principles which reaffirm your commitment to respect and protect your body for the rest of your life. This new commitment is going to be locked in from now on, and forever with the thought to binge, to purge, or to self-starve. When any thoughts for bingeing, purging, or self-starvation arise, they will be locked in with the new commitment to respect and protect your body. Since you and your subconscious have committed to support, strengthen, and empower this commitment to respect and protect your body, the destructive thoughts for bingeing, purging, or self-starvation are going to become weaker and weaker until they dissipate away. Are you willing to reaffirm this new commitment and your vow to respect and protect your body for the rest of your life? [Wait for the affirmative response through ideomotor signaling, or in words. If the answer is yes, proceed in the following way]: *Now, repeat after me the following statements, reaffirming your commitment as a whole person on a conscious and subconscious level: (a) for my body, if not for me, bingeing, purging, or self-starvation are, in fact, a poison* [patient verbally repeats statement]; *(b) I need my body to live* [patient verbally repeats statement]; *(c) To the extent that I want to live my life to the fullest, I owe my body this respect and protection* [patient verbally repeats statement]. *Now that you have reaffirmed your commitment and vow to respect and protect your body for the rest of your life, I suggest you do this exercise daily once every two hours. . . .*

In fact, you are going to regain a sense of mastery and control in your life as it relates to activities on your job, your plans for the future, the learning of new things, and in your relationships with other people. Now, I would like you to take a moment or so to visualize yourself as fully healed and recovered in the future. Notice the sense of joy and accomplishment as you look at your life and your healthy body. You continue your self-hypnotic exercises, which you are going to do safely and comfortably on a regular basis. . . ."

This hypnotic session is followed by a discussion with the patient whereby the patient learns to avoid self-entrapment, using the principle of "don't think about a purple elephant." The patient is asked to engage in a thought exercise whereby she is asked not to think about a purple elephant. Most patients smile and report immediately that they picture a nice, big, purple elephant. The patient is then told:

"You see, free people don't like to be told don't. Your subconscious mind does not incorporate the word 'don't,' and only hears, 'think about a purple elephant,' and then complies appropriately. The same thing happens when you say to yourself, 'don't binge,' or 'don't purge.' You are, in fact, giving your subconscious mind the suggestion to binge and to purge, and thus entrapping yourself in doing exactly what you're wishing to avoid. In this new approach, any time you experience the thought to binge, purge, or use self-starvation this is your signal to engage in a state of self-hypnosis, and reaffirm your commitment and your vow to respect and protect your body for the rest of your life. So, now you focus on your vow to respect and protect your body for the rest of your life, and on your future reality of yourself living as a healthy, recovered individual."

In a patient with anorexia nervosa, an additional method of cognitive reframing is set up whereby we talk about "gaining strength" instead of "gaining weight." The patient is instructed that each strength unit is equal to one pound of body weight. Since most patients with anorexia nervosa who are extremely emaciated get into treatment feeling tired and physically weak, these presenting symptoms are capitalized on by asking these patients, under hypnosis, whether they would be willing to regain their strength. Most patients respond positively to such a suggestion, and this method uses the principle of "meet the patient where the patient is at." Including the patient's concerns allows for the co-creation of a treatment plan that is accepted by the patient. The patient with anorexia nervosa, who suffers from a low body weight, tiredness, and physical weakness, engages more readily, and is more cooperative in activities focused on supplying her body with healthy nutrition in wholesome meals so she can regain her strength.

In this method, the patient is guided into a state of self-hypnotic relaxation and calmness induced in a nature scene of the patient's choice. This is followed by the use of symbolic guided imagery intended to introduce a variety of natural images communicating changes of maturation, differentiation, integration, growth, self-mastery, control, and freedom of choice (Baker & Nash, 1987). I like to use natural images of transformation such as the metamorphoses of a caterpillar through a cocoon into a mature, well-differentiated butterfly. The butterfly is well differentiated sexually and can fly freely from flower to flower and choose its own mate, while the caterpillar is asexual, cannot fly (is immature) and is limited with its choices of food and resources. This has a special value for the immature adolescent patient who struggles with conflicts around gender identity and physical maturation into an adult. Another useful image is "the red balloon technique" (Walch, 1976), which was adapted by Hammond (1987) as an effective adjunct in helping patients alleviate dysfunctional guilt. I also use images for gaining a sense of control and mastery by asking the patient to visualize herself driving a car, holding the steering wheel in both hands, turning to the right or left whenever she wishes to do so, changing the speed of her travel in the car, moving forward, or reversing, and using the brakes and other control instruments in the car, based on her need and travel plans. All these are suggested in association with a sense of pleasure and self-mastery.

Another image is one of the patient remodeling and redecorating her room, the room being analogous to the patient's body. First, one imagines living in an old room where the patient feels dissatisfied, then imagery is used in which the patient visualizes the remodeling and redecorating of her room to meet her needs. Emphasis is placed on the patient's choice of colors, materials, furniture, drapes, pictures, and so on. Another effective image is that of the patient adopting a puppy or kitten, perhaps a sick one from the animal shelter of the local community. Then, instruct the patient to visualize the kitten or puppy nursed into full health through the patient's commitment and dedication. The sick pet is naturally a metaphor of the patient's unhealthy body, to which he or she makes a commitment to heal and nurse back to full physical health.

"Back From the Future" Technique

In this method, hypnotic age progression techniques are utilized as described by Yapko (1984, 1986), Erickson (1980), Frederick and Phillips (1992), and Torem (1992a, 1992b, 1992c, 2006).

Here, a discussion is held with a patient about a desired future image the patient would be interested in as representing her full recovery and reaching an ideal stage regarding personal goals, as well as body image and a state of healthy living. This is particularly important with a developing adolescent patient who is in the process of change and is generally struggling with the question of "Who shall I become?" The patient is guided into a state of self-hypnosis and suggestions are structured as with the following example:

"Everyone who is committed to a process of healing and recovery has an image of the future. If you wish, you may take this very special trip in a time machine, a trip in time, into the future. Ready . . . enter into your special time machine and experience yourself moving forward in time . . . turning into the age of 17 [assuming the patient is 16 years old] moving forward into 18, 19, 20, 21, 22, 23, that's right, and now age 25. . . . By this time, you have graduated from college and you are working in a job of your choice, gainfully employed, living in your own apartment, enjoying your state of independence. You may wish to experience yourself strolling in a department store, trying on new clothes. Find yourself sitting at the counter consulting a cosmetic sales person regarding the special colors of lipstick and other make-up items that fit your skin tone and color. As you try these on, you look in the mirror and you see with joy how much you like your face, and the rest of your body, and yourself, and your blooming femininity representing the young woman in you. As this goes on, you may continue to experience yourself, on a date with a young man who truly communicates uncritical acceptance of you and loves you with respect and dignity, and, if you wish, you may experience the special joy of having a date and wondering about your natural and healthy attraction to the young man that you love too, wondering about the special compatibility and chemistry that exists between the two of you, trusting the center core of your subconscious mind that has guided you and led you to this point. On the job, you continue to excel and do what you like best, feeling a sense of self-accomplishment and self-actualization . . . going to work every day with a special feeling of looking forward to the day, being assertive, appropriately so, expressing your feelings and your emotions

verbally, clearly, representing your own point of view and at the same time, being flexible, adaptively so, to consider the opinions of other people, as well. Now, with a sense of wisdom, inner joy, intelligence, and special deep knowledge I'd like you to travel in the time machine back to the year when you turned age 16 . . . and bring with you back from the future, into the present, all these feelings of confidence and competence, the sense of self-actualization, the joys, the sense of contentment, the sense of maturity that you already have experienced at the age of 25, bringing these experiences with you back from the future into the present, and let your subconscious mind guide you and use the special feelings, . . . the joys, and the wisdom to guide you in the present in moving you forward, on your journey of healing and recovery. That's right, now, you don't have to consciously remember anything that's been discussed and experienced here by you. In fact, even if you don't remember anything at all, your subconscious will continue to do all the work every minute of the hour, every hour of the day, every day of the week, every week of the month, and every month of the year, every year for the rest of your life. However, if you wish to remember, you may remember whatever you need to remember to continue and guide you in this special journey of healing and recovery, that's right, very good, that's right."

The patient is now encouraged to return to the alert state. This is followed by a discussion with the patient on what the patient remembered of the exercise of the future-oriented hypnotic imagery. In this modification, which I have called "Back From the Future" (Torem, 1992a), the patient brings back from her trip to the future all the experiences that have already been realized in the patient's hypnotic future-oriented imagery. The patient is then given the assignment of writing in her personal journal the details of this experience of her trip to the future, and is requested to bring her completed assignment to the following session. At that time, I ask the patient to read to me her assignment and I listen carefully to the tense the patient uses in describing her trip into the future. I have found that patients who describe their trip into the future using the past tense throughout their writing assignment usually respond well to this technique, and I use it as a positive, prognostic indicator.

Many times, this has proven to be a turning point in the patient's therapy.

Metaphorical Prescriptions

As part of the whole treatment program, patients are given concrete assignments reinforced with hypnotic suggestions for improved therapeutic outcome. These assignments, which they are asked to complete, are designed so that the patient will metaphorically and concretely experience a feeling of success, as well as a sense of gaining mastery, control, and exercising new choices and options. Examples of such metaphorical prescriptions are the following:

- Chart a journey, on a map from point A to point B. Drive your car in confidence and safety from point A to point B. Choose two different routes; one with the expressway and the other with a country road.
- Redecorate your own room, or remodel the house you live in.
- Change the sheets and pillow cases on your bed, where you sleep at night.
- Buy yourself a new dress or blouse and wear it.
- Get new glasses (frames) or new contact lenses.
- Adopt a pet (kitten or puppy) and take good care of it, watch it grow to maturity.
- Build a puzzle showing the picture of a whole person.
- Plant a vegetable garden, or one tomato plant. Watch it grow and develop, and take responsibility for nurturing it. Pick the tomatoes only when ready.
- Bottle-feed a small human baby, hold it, and let it cling to you.

Age Regression; Abreactions and Catharsis

This specific technique has been found useful with patients in whom the underlying dynamic for the eating disorder is related to past trauma. This can be done by using hypnosis as a diagnostic tool with the aid of such techniques as the affect bridge (Channon, 1981; Watkins, 1978) and other methods of hypnoanalytic exploration in conjunction with ideomotor signaling (Barnett, 1981; Brown & Fromm, 1986; Cheek & Le Cron, 1968; Ewin & Eimer, 2006). Once this has been identified, the patient can be guided with the use of age regression to the original trauma to which the eating disorder is being related. Many patients then have a chance to fully abreact emotions attached to the original trauma, and the emotional catharsis in the abreaction itself already produces some relief. At times, a significant improvement (although not a full cure) of the eating disorder symptoms is apparent. This has been described in previous publications on the special subgroup of patients with eating disorders in whom the eating disorder symptoms may be a manifestation of an underlying posttraumatic stress disorder (Torem & Curdue, 1988). To make this specific technique work, additional methods should be attached such as cognitive restructuring, as well as other methods that use hypnotic suggestion for personal growth, healing, recovery, letting go of the past, and being liberated from the traumatic memories (Watkins, 1980).

Ego-State Therapy

Ego-state therapy has become a frequent focus in the hypnosis literature (Alladin, 2014; Beahrs, 1982; Edelstein, 1982; Frederick, 2005, 2014; Newey, 1986; Watkins, 1984, 1993; Watkins & Watkins, 1981a, 1981b). Ego-state therapy is defined by Watkins and Watkins (1981b) as the "utilization of family and group treatment techniques for the resolution of conflicts between the different ego states that constitute a family of self within a single individual." This method is aimed at conflict resolution and may employ any of the directive, behavioral, psychoanalytic, supportive, existential, and even relaxation and biofeedback techniques of therapy. This method of therapy concerns a notion of how much the individual's behavior is the result of dissociated ego states in a state of conflict. According to Helen and John Watkins (1981a, 1981b), the experience with ego-state therapy shows that activating, studying, and communicating with various ego states decreases the patient's tendency to dissociate. The patient who used to dissociate and experienced these changes as "mood swings," "confusion states," or "lost time" develops an awareness of her condition. Confusion is then replaced by greater clarity, understanding, new hope, and a sense of self-mastery. The goal of ego-state therapy is not total fusion of all ego states into one fully "fused" ego, but rather an increased permeability of ego-state boundaries, and an improved internal harmony

resulting in better cooperation and congruence among the various ego states. Some ego states may be maladaptive; however, the strategy is not to eliminate any ego state, even if it is responsible for maladaptive behavior. Instead, the strategy is to change the maladaptive behavior, and to help the ego state become more adaptive in its behaviors. In previous publications (Torem, 1987, 1989b), I have described in great detail the use of this method for the treatment of patients with eating disorders. This specific method is especially effective with patients in whom the underlying dynamic for the eating disorder is related to dissociated ego states, and who are in a state of conflict. This method also has been found useful in patients with eating disorders who had an underlying dissociative identity disorder (Torem, 1990, 1993b).

CONCLUSION

Any treatment modality stands to be tested based on its outcome, and the outcome of treatment must be compared to the natural history of the illness. There are insufficient data regarding the natural history of eating disorders. This needs to be compared with a variety of treatment modalities, and when treatment interventions produce better outcomes compared with the natural history of the illness, such a treatment modality may be considered as effective. The following are criteria, which may be used to measure the effectiveness of a specific treatment intervention:

- Symptom relief: Patients who come for treatment suffer from a variety of symptoms that can be measured and recorded with the psychiatric interview, the Mental Status Examination, and a variety of scales such as the Eating Disorders Inventory (EDI) (Garner, Olmsted, & Polivy, 1983), the Zung Scale for rating anxiety (Zung, 1971), and the Zung Scale for rating depression (Zung, 1965). There should be an easing of these symptoms in terms of intensity, frequency, and an improvement in the patient's ability to function adaptively with the activities of daily living.
- Behavioral change: I expect to see improvement in the patient's ability to form healthy, interpersonal relationships, his or her social skills,

his or her ability to hold a job, to be gainfully employed (for adults), and perform academically (for students).

- Improvement in self-esteem: I expect to see a change in the patient's sense and stability of a positive self-image, which can be reflected in the sentence completion test, the psychiatric interview, and specific projective testing such as the Thematic Apperception Test (TAT).
- Body image: The patient's body image should move from a distortion to a realistic assessment and perception of the patient's body image as described by Barabasz (2007) and Walsh (2008). This can be evaluated by the use of the Mental Status Examination (MSE), as well as the Eating Disorders Inventory (EDI) and the Draw a Person Test (DAP).

Some of these assessments may also be done with the aid of hypnoanalytic exploratory techniques such as ideomotor signaling. All of the assessments can be supplemented by data collected from close family members, who know the patient prior to the treatment, during the treatment, and after the treatment intervention has been completed; this will help assess how the patient has changed.

REFERENCES

Alladin, A. (2014). Healing the wounded self: Combining hypnotherapy with ego state therapy. *American Journal of Clinical Hypnosis, 56*, 3–22.

Baker, E. L., & Nash, M. R. (1987). Applications of hypnosis in the treatment of anorexia nervosa. *American Journal of Clinical Hypnosis, 29*(3), 185–193. doi:10.1080/00029157.1987.10734350

Barabasz, M. (2007). Efficacy of hypnotherapy in the treatment of eating disorders. *International Journal of Clinical and Experimental Hypnosis, 55*(3), 318–335. doi:10.1080/00207140701338688

Barnett, E. (1981). *Analytical hypnotherapy: Principles and practice.* Kingston, Ontario: Junica.

Beahrs, J. (1982). *Unity and multiplicity: Multilevel consciousness of self in hypnosis: Psychiatric disorders and mental health.* New York, NY: Brunner Mazel.

Benson, H. (1975). *The relaxation response.* New York, NY: Harper Collins Publishers.

Benson, H. (1996). *Timeless healing: The power and biology of belief.* New York, NY: Simon & Schuster.

Bernstein, E. M., & Putnam, F. W. (1986). Development, reliability and validity of a dissociation scale. *Journal of Nervous and Mental Disease, 174*(12), 727–735.

Brown, D. P., & Fromm, E. (1986). *Hypnotherapy and hypnoanalysis.* Hillsdale, NJ: Lawrence Erlbaum.

Bruch, H. (1973). *Eating disorders: Obesity, anorexia nervosa and the person within.* New York, NY: Basic Books.

Bruch, H. (1974). Eating disturbances in adolescence. In S. Arieti (Ed.), *American handbook of psychiatry* (pp. 275–286). New York, NY: Basic Books.

Bruch, H. (1978). *The golden cage: The anima of anorexia nervosa.* Cambridge, MA: Harvard University Press.

Carlson, E. B., Putnam, F. W., Ross, C. A., Torem, M., Coons, P., Dill, D. L., . . . Braun, B. G. (1993). Validity of the Dissociative Experiences Scale in screening for multiple personality disorder: A multicenter study. *American Journal of Psychiatry, 150*(7), 1030–1036. doi:10.1176/ajp.150.7.1030

Chandarana, P., & Malla, A. (1989). Bulimia and dissociative states: A case report. *Canadian Journal of Psychiatry. Revue Canadienne De Psychiatrie, 34*(2), 137–139.

Channon, L. D. (1981). Modification of the affect-bridge technique in weight control. *Australian Journal of Clinical Experimental Hypnosis, 9*(1), 42–43.

Cheek, D. P., & Le Cron, L. M. (1968). *Clinical hypnotherapy.* New York, NY: Grune & Stratton.

Council, J. R. (1986). Exploring the interface of personality and health: Anorexia nervosa, bulimia and hypnotic susceptibility. *Behavior and Medical Abstracts, 7*, 165–168.

Damlouji, N. F., & Ferguson, J. M. (1985). Three cases of post-traumatic anorexia nervosa. *American Journal of Psychiatry, 142*(3), 362–363. doi:10.1176/ajp.142.3.362

Doyle, M. M. (1996). Practical management of eating disorders. *Proceedings of the Nutrition Society, 54*, 711–719.

Edelstien, M. G. (1982). Ego-state therapy in the management of resistance. *American Journal of Clinical Hypnosis, 25*(1), 15–20. doi:10.1080/00029157.1982.10404060

Erickson, M. (1980). The case of Barbie: An Ericksonian approach to the treatment of anorexia nervosa. In J. Zeig (Ed.), *A teaching seminar with Milton H. Erickson.* New York, NY: Brunner Mazel.

Evans, J. (1982). *Adolescent and preadolescent psychiatry.* New York, NY: Academic Press.

Ewin, D. M., & Eimer, B. N. (2006). *Ideomotor signals for rapid hypnoanalysis: A how-to manual.* St. Louis, MO: Charles C. Thomas Publisher.

Farooq, U., & Siddiqui N. H. (2015b). Bulimia nervosa. In F. Domino (Ed.), *The 5-minute clinical consult standard* (pp. 182–183). New York, NY: Wolters Kluwer.

Farooq, U., & Siddiqui, N. H. (2015a). Anorexia nervosa. In F. Domino (Ed.), *The 5-minute clinical consult standard* (pp. 76–77). New York, NY: Wolters Kluwer.

Frederick, C. (2005). Selected topics in ego-state therapy. *International Journal of Clinical and Experimental Hypnosis, 53*(4), 339–429. doi:10.1080/00207140591007518

Frederick, C. (2014). The center core in ego state therapy and other hypnotically facilitated psychotherapies. *American Journal of Clinical Hypnosis, 56*, 39–53.

Frederick, C., & McNeal, S. A. (2013). *Inner strength: Contemporary and hypnosis for ego-strengthening.* New York, NY: Routledge.

Frederick, C., & Phillips, M. (1992). The use of hypnotic age progressions as interventions with acute psychosomatic conditions. *American Journal of Clinical Hypnosis, 35*(2), 89–98. doi:10.1080/0002915 7.1992.10402991

Garner, D. M., Olmsted, M. P., & Polivy, J. (1983). *Eating disorder inventory.* Odessa, FL: Psychological Assessment.

Goodwin, J. M., & Attias, R. (1993). Eating disorders in survivors of multimodal childhood abuse. In R. Kluft & C. Fine (Eds.), *Clinical perspectives on multiple personality disorder* (pp. 327–341). Odessa, FL: American Psychiatric Press.

Goodwin, J. (1988). Eating disorders as a response to multimodel child abuse. Paper Presented at the Fifth International Conference on Multiple Personality and Dissociative States, Chicago, IL.

Grave, R. D., Oliosi, M., Todisco, P., & Vanderlinden, J. (1997). Self-reported traumatic experiences and dissociative symptoms in obese women with and without binge-eating disorder. *Eating Disorders, 5*(2), 105–109.

Griffith, R. A. (1989). Hypnobehavioral treatment for bulimia nervosa: Preliminary findings. *Australian Journal Clinical Experimental Hypnosis, 17*, 79–87.

Gross, M. (1984). Hypnosis in the therapy of anorexia nervosa. *American Journal of Clinical Hypnosis, 26*(3), 175–181. doi:10.1080/00029157.1984.10404160

Gutwill, S. (1994). Eating problems in patients with multiple personality disorder. In C. Bloom, A. Gilter, S. Gutwill, L. Kogel, & L. Zaphiroponlos (Eds.), *Eating problems* (pp. 227–272). New York, NY: Basic Books.

Hammond, C. (1987). The red balloon technique. *Newsletter of the American Society of Clinical Hypnosis, 28*(2), 3.

Hartland, J. (1965). The value of ego-strengthening procedures prior to direct symptom removal under hypnosis. *The American Journal of Clinical Hypnosis, 8*(2), 89–93. doi:10.1080/00029157.1965.10402470

Hartland, J. (1971). Further observations on the use of ego-strengthening techniques. *American Journal of Clinical Hypnosis, 14*(1), 1–8. doi:10.1080/00029157. 1971.10402136

Janet, P. (1907). *The major symptoms of hysteria.* London, UK: Macmillan.

Janet, P. (1919). *Les medications psychologiques.* Paris, France: Felix Alcan.

Kluft, R. P. (1991). Clinical presentations of multiple personality disorder. *Psychiatric Clinics of North America, 14*(3), 605–630.

Kroger, W., & Fezler, W. (1976). *Hypnosis and behavior modification: Imagery conditioning.* Philadelphia, PA: Lippincott Williams & Wilkins.

Marcus, M. D., & Wildes, J. E. (2014). Evidence-based psychological treatments for eating disorders. In G. Gabbard (Ed.), *Gabbard's treatments of psychiatric disorders, DSM-5 edition* (pp. 539–548). Washington, DC: American Psychiatric Association.

McFarlane, A. C., McFarlane, C. M., & Gilchrist, P. N. N. (1988). Post-traumatic bulimia and anorexia nervosa. *International Journal of Eating Disorders, 7*, 705–708.

Meichenbaum, D. (1977). *Cognitive behavior modification.* New York, NY: Plenum Press.

Minuchin, S., Rosman, B., & Baker, L. (1978). *Psychosomatic families: Anorexia nervosa in context.* Cambridge, MA: Harvard University Press.

Newey, A. B. (1986). Ego-state therapy with depression. In B. Zilbergeld, M. Edelstein, & D. Araoz (Eds.), *Hypnosis: Questions and answers* (pp. 197–203). New York, NY: Norton.

Pettinati, H. M., Horne, R. L., & Staats, J. M. (1985). Hypnotizability in patients with anorexia nervosa and bulimia. *Archives of General Psychiatry, 42*(10), 1014–1016.

Pettinati, H. M., Horne, R. J., & Staats, J. M. (1982). Hypnotizability of anorexia and bulimia patients. *International Journal of Clinical and Experimental Hypnosis, 30*, 332.

Pettinati, H. M., Kogan, L. G., & Margolis, C. (1989). Hypnosis, hypnotizability, and the bulimic patient. In L. Hornyak & E. Baker (Eds.), *Experiential therapies for eating disorders.* New York, NY: Guilford Press.

Putnam, F. W., Bernstein-Carlson, E., Ross, C. A., Anderson, G., Clark, P., & Torem, M. S. (1996). Patterns of dissociation in clinical and nonclinical samples. *Journal of Nervous and Mental Disorders, 184*(11), 673–679.

Ross, C. A. (1989). *Multiple personality disorder.* New York, NY: Wiley.

Sanders, S. (1986). The perceptual alteration scale: A scale measuring dissociation. *American Journal of Clinical Hypnosis, 29*(2), 95–102. doi:10.1080/00029157.198 6.10402691

Schwartz, R. C., Barrett, M. J., & Saba, G. (1985). Family therapy in bulimia. In D. Garner & P. Garfnkel (Eds.), *Handbook of psychotherapy for anorexia nervosa and bulimia.* New York, NY: Guilford Press.

Spiegel, H. (1972). An eye-roll test for hypnotizability. *American Journal of Clinical Hypnosis, 15*(1), 25–28. doi:10.1080/00029157.1972.10402206

Spiegel, H. (1974). *Manual for the hypnotic induction profile: Eye-roll levitation method.* New York, NY: Soni Medica.

Spiegel, H., & Spiegel, D. (1978). *Trance and treatment: Clinical uses of hypnosis.* New York, NY: Basic Books.

Spiegel, H., & Spiegel, D. (2008). *Trance and treatment: Clinical uses of hypnosis.* Washington, DC: American Psychiatric Publishing.

Stanton, H. E. (1989). Ego-enhancement: A five-step approach. *American Journal of Clinical Hypnosis, 31*(3), 192–198. doi:10.1080/00029157.1989.10402888

Stanton, H. (1975). Ego-enhancement through positive suggestion. *Australian Journal of Clinical and Experimental Hypnosis, 3,* 32–35.

Stanton, H. (1979). Increasing internal control through hypnotic ego-enhancement. *Australian Journal of Clinical and Experimental Hypnosis, 7,* 219–223.

Torem, M. S. (1991). Eating disorders. In W. Wester & D. O'Grady (Eds.), *Clinical hypnosis with children* (pp. 230–257). New York, NY: Brunner-Mazel.

Torem, M. S. (1984, September). Anorexia nervosa and multiple dissociated ego states. Presented at the 1st International Conference on Multiple Personality and Dissociate States, Chicago, IL.

Torem, M. S. (1986a). Dissociative states presenting as an eating disorder. *American Journal of Clinical Hypnosis, 29,* 137–142.

Torem, M. S. (1986b). Psycho-dynamic ego-state therapy for eating disorders. *New Directions for Mental Health Services, 31,* 99–107.

Torem, M. S. (1987). Ego-state therapy for eating disorders. *American Journal of Clinical Hypnosis, 30*(2), 94–103. doi:10.1080/00029157.1987.10404169

Torem, M. S. (1989a). Eating disorders in MPD patients. Paper presented at the Annual Meeting of the American Society of Clinical Hypnosis, Nashville, TN.

Torem, M. S. (1989b). Ego-state hypnotherapy for dissociative eating disorders. *Hypnos, 16,* 52–63.

Torem, M. S. (1990). Covert multiple personality underlying eating disorders. *American Journal of Psychotherapy, 44*(3), 357–368.

Torem, M. S. (1992a). Back from the future: A powerful age progression technique. *American Journal of Clinical Hypnosis, 35,* 81–88.

Torem, M. S. (1992b). The use of hypnosis with eating disorders. *Psychiatric Medicine, 10,* 105–118.

Torem, M. S. (1992c). Therapeutic imagery enhanced by hypnosis. *Psychiatric Medicine, 10,* 1–12.

Torem, M. S. (1993a). Eating disorders in patients with multiple personality disorder. In R. Kluft & C. Fine (Eds.), *Clinical perspectives on multiple personality disorder* (pp. 343–353). Washington, DC: American Psychiatric Press.

Torem, M. S. (1993b). Therapeutic writing as a form of ego-state therapy. *American Journal of Clinical Hypnosis, 35*(4), 267–276. doi:10.1080/00029157.1993.10403018

Torem, M. S. (2006). Treating depression: A remedy from the future. In M. Yapko (Ed.), *Hypnosis and treating depression: Applications in clinical practice* (pp. 97–119). New York, NY: Routledge.

Torem, M. S., & Curdue, K. (1988). PTSD presenting as an eating disorder. *Stress Medicine, 4,* 139–142.

Torem, M. S., Egtvedt, B. D., & Curdue, K. J. (1995). The eye roll sign and the PAS dissociation scale. *American Journal of Clinical Hypnosis, 38*(2), 122–125. doi:10.1080/00029157.1995.10403190

Vanderlinden, J., Vandereycken, W., & Claes, L. (2007). Trauma, dissociation, and impulse dyscontrol: Lessons from the eating disorder field. In E. Vermetten, M. Dorahy & D. Spiegel (Eds.), *Traumatic Dissociation: Neurobiology and Treatment* (pp. 317–333). Arlington, VA: American Psychiatric Publishing.

Vanderlinden, J., & Vandereycken, W. (1988). The use of hypnotherapy in the treatment of eating disorders. *International Journal of Eating Disorders, 7,* 673–679.

Vanderlinden, J., & Vandereycken, W. (1990). The use of hypnosis in the treatment of bulimia nervosa. *International Journal of Clinical and Experimental Hypnosis, 38*(2), 101–111. doi:10.1080/00207149008414505

Vanderlinden, J., & Vandereycken, W. (1993). Is sexual abuse a risk factor for developing an eating disorder? *Eating Disorders, 1*(4), 282–286.

Vanderlinden, J., Spinhoven, P., Vandereycken, W., & van Dyck, R. (1995). Dissociative and hypnotic experiences in eating disorder patients: An exploratory study. *American Journal of Clinical Hypnosis, 38*(2), 97–108. doi:10.1080/00029157.1995.10403188

Vanderlinden, J., Vandereycken, W., van Dyck, R., & Vertommen, H. (1993). Dissociative experiences and trauma in eating disorders. *International Journal of Eating Disorders, 13*(2), 187–193.

Walch, S. L. (1976). The red balloon technique of hypnotherapy: A clinical note. *International Journal of Clinical and Experimental Hypnosis, 24*(1), 10–12. doi:10.1080/00207147608405592

Walsh, B. J. (2008). Hypnotic alteration of body image in the eating disordered. *American Journal of Clinical Hypnosis, 50*(4), 301–310. doi:10.1080/00029157.2008.10404297

Walsh, B. T. (1997). Eating disorders. In A. Tasman, J. Kay, & J. Lieberman (Eds.), *Psychiatry* (pp. 1202–1216). Philadelphia, PA: W. B. Saunders.

Watkins, J. G., & Watkins, H. H. (1981a). Ego-state therapy, In R. Corsini (Ed.), *Handbook of innovative psychotherapies* (pp. 252–270). New York, NY: Wiley.

Watkins, J. G., & Watkins, H. H. (1981b). Ego-state therapy. In L. Abt (Ed.), *The newer therapies: A sourcebook* (pp. 136–155). New York, NY: Van Nostrand Reinhold.

Watkins, H. H. (1978). Ego-state therapy. In J. Watkins (Ed.), *The therapeutic self* (pp. 360–398). New York, NY: Human Sciences Press.

Watkins, H. H. (1980). The silent abreaction. *International Journal of Clinical and Experimental Hypnosis, 28*(2), 101–113. doi:10.1080/00207148008409833

Watkins, H. H. (1984). Ego-state therapy. In R. Corsini (Ed.), *Encyclopedia of psychology* (pp. 420–421). New York, NY: Wiley.

Watkins, H. H. (1993). Ego-state therapy: An overview. *American Journal of Clinical Hypnosis, 35*(4), 232–240. doi:10.1080/00029157.1993.10403014

Yager, J. (1994). Eating disorders. In A. Stoudemire (Ed.), *Clinical psychiatry for medical students* (pp. 355–371). Philadelphia, PA: Lippincott Williams & Wilkins.

Yapko, M. D. (1984). *Trancework: An introduction to clinical hypnosis.* New York, NY: Irvington Press.

Yapko, M. D. (1986). Hypnotic and strategic interventions in the treatment of anorexia nervosa. *American Journal of Clinical Hypnosis, 28*(4), 224–232. doi:10.1080/00029157.1986.10402658

Zung, W. W. (1965). A self-rating depression scale. *Archives of General Psychiatry, 12,* 63–70.

Zung, W. W. K. (1971). A rating instrument for anxiety disorders. *Psychosomatic, 12,* 371–379.

Ego-Strengthening

Donald Moss and Eric Willmarth

In 1965, John Hartland proposed that before practitioners undertake direct symptom removal through hypnosis, it was advantageous to engage in a preliminary process of ego-strengthening. Hartland's approach to ego-strengthening was direct and authoritarian. Hartland introduced ego-strengthening initially as an adjunctive technique that could enhance the patient's confidence and enable him or her to become more self-reliant. He also aimed to strengthen general coping abilities, and reduce any worry or anxiety. Hartland reported that he used a series of steps including his eight-minute ego-strengthening induction to begin each hypnosis session, and further that a general practitioner, who does not take on the most challenging cases, might use the combination of ego-strengthening and direct suggestion to resolve difficulties for most patients.

EMIL COUÉ AND HARTLAND'S INTERVENTIONS

Hartland's approach resembled the work of Emil Coué's suggestive approach (Coué, 1922). Coué lived from 1857 to 1926 in France, and developed the self-suggestive affirmation approach, in which subjects learned to recite positive suggestions repeatedly, such as "Everyday in every way. I am getting better and better." Like Coué, Hartland utilized standardized instructions and direct suggestion. Hartland (1965; Hartland, 1971) described the following step-wise protocol that he used to begin most hypnotic sessions.

1. Hartland invited the patient to lie back comfortably in the chair, relax, and begin to breathe quietly. He then suggested that the patient would go to sleep.

2. He then commenced a more detailed relaxation moving from the feet and ankles upward through the body to the neck, shoulders, and arms. At each bodily region, he suggested physical relaxation and increased deepening.
3. Next he engaged in counting and more emphasis on breathing.
4. At this point, he utilized his eight-minute sequence of ego-strengthening, involving a ritualized series of suggestions for personal strengthening, fitness, clarity of thinking, well-being, feelings of safety and security, relaxation, independence, happiness, and contentment. (See Box 58.1 for the detailed text of Hartland's 1965 script.)

SUPPORT FOR EGO-STRENGTHENING APPROACH

An Australian, R. D. Calnan (1977), applied Hartland's approach in a psychiatric community mental health center, and reported that the patients uniformly reported feeling more relaxed, less depressed, and more confident. They described their experience in words derived from the Hartland script, yet did not recognize the origins of their improvements.

Shortly thereafter, another Australian, Harry Stanton (1977), conducted a controlled study comparing the effectiveness of the Hartland script to a series of positive suggestions derived from Albert Ellis's rational emotive therapy. He found that the patients in both groups reported coping more effectively with emotional problems, even though the suggestions had not specifically addressed their emotional symptoms.

In a second study, Stanton (1979) used a script combining positive suggestions derived from

---

BOX 58.1 EGO-STRENGTHENING SCRIPT

"Every day . . . you will become physically stronger and fitter. You will become more alert . . . more wide awake . . . more energetic. You will become much less easily tired . . . much less easily fatigued . . . much less easily depressed . . . much less easily discouraged.

Every day . . . you will become so deeply interested in whatever you are doing . . . so deeply interested in whatever is going on . . . that your mind will become much less preoccupied with yourself . . . and you will become much less conscious of yourself . . . and your own feelings.

Every day . . . your nerves will become stronger and steadier. . . . Your mind will become clearer . . . more composed . . . more placid . . . more tranquil. You will become much less easily worried . . . much less easily agitated . . . much less fearful and apprehensive . . . much less easily upset.

You will be able to think more clearly . . . you will be able to concentrate more easily. . . . . Your memory will improve . . . and you will be able to see things in their true perspective . . . without magnifying them, without allowing them to get out of proportion.

Every day . . . you will become emotionally much calmer . . . much more settled . . . much less easily disturbed . . . much less easily disturbed.

Every day . . . you will feel a greater feeling of personal safety . . . and security . . . than you have felt for a long, long time.

Every day . . . you will become . . . and you will remain . . . more and more completely relaxed . . . and less tense. Each day . . . both mentally and physically . . . even when you are no longer with me.

And, as you become . . . and, as you remain . . . more relaxed . . . and less tense each day. . . . So, you will develop much more confidence in yourself. Much more confidence in your ability to do . . . not only what you have to do each day . . . but, much more confidence in your ability to do whatever you ought to be able to do . . . without fear of failure . . . without fear of consequences . . . without unnecessary anxiety . . . without uneasiness.

Because of this . . . every day . . . you will feel more and more independent . . . more able to "stick up for yourself" . . . to stand upon your own feet . . . to "hold your own" . . . no matter how difficult or trying things may be. And, because all these things will begin to happen . . . exactly as I tell you they will happen, you will begin to feel much happier . . . much more contented . . . much more cheerful . . . much more optimistic . . . much less easily discouraged, much less easily depressed."

Source: George Hartland (1965), p. 91; Reprinted with permission of the *American Journal of Clinical Hypnosis.*

Hartland, Albert Ellis, and Emil Coué, emphasizing increased calmness, relaxation, and self-confidence. The participants in the study showed increased "internal locus of control" on the Rotter Internal-External scale.

OUTSIDE DEVELOPMENTS: THE EMERGENCE OF IMAGERY, THE ERICKSONIAN REVOLUTION, AND THE PERSON-CENTERED APPROACH OF CARL ROGERS

Three critical developments somewhat outside the arena of classical hypnosis opened the doors for new pathways for ego-strengthening: the emergence of guided imagery as a powerful tool, the Ericksonian revolution, and the person-centered approach of Carl Rogers.

Imagery as therapy. The increasing attention to imagery in therapeutic work introduced an effective tool for healing and transformation (Achterberg et al., 2005; Sheikh, 1983), and this tool offered greater power for ego enhancement as well. Imagery is inherent in human communication, and was present in hypnotic practice from the beginning. The power of "magnetism" as an image, the magnetized *baquet,* and the mesmeric passes were all powerful images influencing the patient's hypnotic experiences. In the 20th century, however, imagery has received increasing attention in its own right as a therapeutic tool.

One of the leaders in applying imagery for healing is Martin Rossman (2000). Rossman acknowledged the ancient origins of imagery-based healing, in the shamanic healing of indigenous healers and in the spiritual healing of the great spiritual traditions, East and West. Rossman also credited the Swiss psychoanalyst Carl Jung, who utilized a technique called "active imagination," and the Italian psychiatrist Roberto Assagioli, for bringing the power of imagery into medicine and psychiatry.

Carl Jung is known for his exploration of myths, symbols, and dreams in psychotherapy. Active imagination is an approach he developed between 1913 and 1916, in which he invited the patient's unconscious self to actualize a variety of conflicts and issues in visualization, artistic expression, and writing, often in the form of archetypal imagery (Jung, 1997). Archetypal imagery involves images and symbols from the collective unconscious, as discovered in mythology, dreams, and fairy tales.

Robert Assagioli founded the school of psychosynthesis, beginning with his doctoral dissertation in 1909, with his work reaching the American audience largely in the 1960s and 1970s (Assagioli, 1965, 1973). Psychosynthesis presented a comprehensive understanding of the psyche and a process of psychotherapy. Assagioli used imagery and meditation to give form to creative and adaptive forces within the psyche.

Martin Rossman formulated many practical techniques and scripts for guided-imagery work, as a tool for professionals to facilitate healing and personal transformation, and as a tool for the average human being to engage in self-healing. Many of his strategies are in some sense ego-strengthening. They often begin with dissolving tensions, and culminate with discovering healing resources within one's own body-mind.

Jeanne Achterberg was another leader in bringing the powers of imagery into medicine. She collaborated in the early work of Carl Simonton on the mental imagery cancer patients developed about their illnesses (Achterberg, 1978a). Achterberg found prognostic significance when patients imagined their immune systems overpowering cancer cells, rather than imagining the victory of cancer over the body. She developed an assessment tool for rating the imagery (Achterberg & Lawlis, 1984). She guided patients to develop targeted imagery of the immune system successfully vanquishing their disease, and reported many patients mobilized unexpected resilience and recovery. Simonton shifted his emphasis over time from the specific imagery of the patient to an emphasis on hope and confidence in living with cancer, and his work is continued today by the Simonton Cancer Center.

Achterberg's work later broadened to emphasize the healing power of human consciousness, the power of mind to impact physiology and healing, and the power of distant healing intentions to affect the brain and body across many miles; she continued to highlight the central role of imagery in most mind–body interventions (Achterberg, 1985; Achterberg et al., 2005).

The Ericksonian revolution. Milton Erickson abandoned the use of stereotyped rituals in which each patient would be guided through one of a handful of classical inductions favored by a specific therapist. Erickson tuned into the patient's own words, images, and mannerisms, and created conversations, drawing the contents and form of any hypnotic intervention from the patient's own inner and outer experiencing. The new guiding principle became "utilization" (Erickson, 1959; Zeig, 2014). The therapist guided by Erickson learned to view the patient's every utterance and action as a gift, to be utilized as steps for induction and suggestion. Further, the concept of hypnosis as somnolent trance went out the window, and a session of Ericksonian hypnotherapy came to resemble a conversation with life lessons and the seeds of transformation woven subtly into a conversational thread.

For ego-strengthening, the Ericksonian therapist may reconnect the patient with his or her most positive past experiences and utilize the affective tone and hopefulness of those biographical episodes as resources and strengths for approaching current challenges. The fuel for ego-strengthening came from the patient's own latent strengths and adaptive capacity, not from a verbatim script.

Prior to Erickson, hypnosis was considered to take place only with a formal induction; in the absence of an explicit step-by-step induction, there was only psychotherapy and not hypnotherapy. In the Ericksonian approach, there need not be a formal induction. There is thus no clear boundary between Ericksonian hypnosis and Ericksonian psychotherapy. Every time the Ericksonian psychotherapist enters a dialogue with a patient, there is an opportunity to use Ericksonian principles and techniques. When we apply Ericksonian perspectives to ego-strengthening, we discover a rich continuum of interventions from ego-strengthening hypnosis to ego-strengthening psychotherapy.

Person-centered therapy. Carl Ransom Rogers dedicated considerable energy to defining the necessary and sufficient conditions for positive personal transformation in psychotherapy. He concluded that when these conditions are met, the person's own inner strengths are mobilized, and the person spontaneously moves toward self-actualization.

The conditions identified by Rogers are: (a) two persons are in emotional contact with one another;

(b) one of them, here called the client, displays anxiety, distress, or "incongruence"; (c) the other, called the therapist, experiences and displays genuineness and congruence in the relationship; (d) the therapist expresses and displays "unconditional positive regard" for the client; (e) the therapist acquires an empathic understanding for the client's internal perspective and communicates this empathy to the client; and (f) the client perceives, at least to a minimal degree, the genuineness, positive regard, and empathy of the therapist (Moss, 1999; Rogers, 1957, 1961).

In the course of Rogers' career, he pursued a further exploration of how therapists and change agents outside of the therapeutic context could create these necessary and sufficient conditions and mobilize the inherent forces for positive transformation within the person. Working with Virginia Satir, he promoted the application of person-centered life-affirming principles to reconciling divided communities.

For the present context, the authors propose that Rogers' necessary and sufficient conditions serve well the therapeutic process of ego-strengthening. When a hypnotherapist establishes sustained emotional contact with a client, establishes empathy, displays personal genuineness or congruence, and communicates unconditional positive regard (affirmation), the inner resources of that client are mobilized, and the client moves spontaneously toward experiencing greater inner strengths. Hypnotic strategies, especially utilization of what is emerging, can deepen and extend that process. Hypnotic suggestion of images of trust, safety, and tranquility, when in balance with what is currently emerging for the client, are effective tools creating the optimal conditions desired by Rogers.

LATER DEVELOPMENTS IN EGO-STRENGTHENING HYPNOSIS

Gail Gardner and the sense of mastery. G. Gail Gardner (1976) explored the use of hypnosis to elicit client involvement in a mastery experience. She concluded that eliciting a sense of mastery can help hypnotic induction in clients perceiving hypnosis as a dangerous loss of control. Immersing such patients directly in a mastery experience, through imagery of mastery, facilitates induction. She reported that eliciting a sense of mastery can facilitate patients solving deep-seated problems. She also emphasized that eliciting a sense of mastery can conserve and protect gains made in hypnosis. Like Hartland, she observed that ego-strengthening, in this case eliciting a sense of mastery, facilitated patients' success in more symptomatically targeted hypnotic interventions.

Harry Stanton returns with flexible scripts and imagery. In 1989, Stanton proposed a five-step approach for ego-enhancing, his name for the process of ego-strengthening. Like Hartland's original work, Stanton's approach followed a step-wise protocol, but the protocol now relied heavily on mental imagery and integrated the patient's own ideas for images. Stanton's approach included five steps: (a) physical relaxation induced by a focus on the breath; (b) mental calmness induced by imagining the mind as a pond, the surface of which is completely still, with the subject watching individual thoughts drifting through the field of vision above the pond, and then returning attention to the stillness of the pond; (c) disposing of rubbish—the subject "dumps" mental obstacles such as fears and worries, and physical obstacles such as cigarettes and excess weight; (d) removing a barrier representing everything negative in the subject's life; and (e) enjoyment of a special place where subjects feel content, tranquil, and still. (See Box 58.2 for Stanton's five-step script.) The subjects "turn off the outside world," and discover a special place, where subjects can see themselves succeeding (p. 193). Sometimes the therapist suggests specific images or the subject may initiate his or her own special place and imagery.

Stanton encouraged practitioners to customize the script for "patient specific ego enhancement" (1989, p. 194). He suggested rich images, for example, to encourage the subjects to drop stones into the pond, representing anything they desire, such as mental calmness, physical relaxation, confidence, and happiness. But he encouraged practitioners to modify the nature of the stones to suit the subject, and to welcome the subjects to generate their own variations.

Other advances. Several authors refined the ego-strengthening approach, sometimes under the guise of raising self-esteem. T. X. Barber (1984, 1990) developed ego-strengthening suggestions, with the aim of raising client self-esteem. He began by affirming actual positive attributes visible in the client, and weaving these affirmations into his hypnotic suggestions. He developed a script to counteract parental criticism central to low esteem. Finally, he sent the client home from sessions with audio recordings of hypnotic suggestions, suggesting that a true and positive self, with much positive well-being, is now emerging. Helen Watkins (1990) published a procedure for raising the client's self-esteem. Her approach engaged the client's "loving, healing self." Newey (1986) proposed a somewhat different therapeutic strategy. Rather than strengthening general self-esteem, Newey suggested that therapists discover and work with the strong part of a client.

D. Corydon Hammond and more scripts. Hammond, in his famous "red book" (Hammond, 1990), presented an entire section, approximately 50 pages, of ego-strengthening scripts. Hammond related the ego-strengthening approach to the work in social cognitive psychology of Albert Bandura on self-efficacy, "the expectation and confidence of being able to cope successfully with various situations" (Hammond, 1990, p. 109). Bandura has pointed out how deficits in the patient's sense of self-efficacy often impede therapeutic change. When a health professional successfully installs a credible hope, a sense that not only can others face and solve this problem, but that the patient himself or herself can solve the problem, suddenly change is possible.

Hammond then introduces short articles and scripts by a host of hypnosis practitioners, including Moshe Torem, Theodore Barber, John Hartland, Harry Stanton, Helen Watkins, Alcid Pelletier, Hammond himself, and many others (pp. 110–153). The scripts are as diverse as their authors, reflecting the rich presence of imagery, approaches including age progression, suggestions for well-being, acceptance of change, self-nurturance, and metaphors such as the "ugly duckling" and the growth of a tree.

Moshe Torem proposed a central role of ego-strengthening in all medical settings, and for all patients. He pointed out the analogy between ego-strengthening and nutrition: "In my opinion, ego strengthening is a technique that is indicated for all patients who come to us looking for an alleviation of their suffering regardless of what their symptoms are. It is like saying that healthy and good nutrition is helpful to all patients regardless of what their diagnosis or illness is" (Torem, 1990, p. 110).

MAGGIE PHILLIPS, CLAIR FREDERICK, SHIRLEY MCNEAL, AND INNER STRENGTH

Several contemporary authors have evolved a well-developed approach to ego-strengthening drawing on ego-state psychotherapy, hypnosis, and extensive imagery exercises (Frederick & McNeal, 1999; McNeal & Frederick, 1993; Phillips, 2001; and Phillips & Frederick, 1992). Their approach provides some scripted interventions, but also draws heavily on the three developments highlighted previously making effective use of imagery, applying the Ericksonian principle of utilization heavily, and creating the conditions for mobilization of inner resources. In 1993, McNeal and Frederick cited two aspects of Erickson's approach critical to ego-strengthening. They cited Erickson and Rossi's (1976) notion that the human unconscious contains all the resources needed for resolving conflicts. In their perspective, ego-strengthening work in hypnosis evokes the client's unconscious resources, and exemplifies Erickson's utilization principle.

Age progression for ego-strengthening

Phillips and Frederick (1992) recalled Milton Erickson's interest in time distortion and age progression in hypnosis. Erickson (1954) used images of gazing into a crystal ball to enable clients to see themselves at the end of a series of powerful therapeutic gains. Phillips and Frederick highlighted that when a client is able to see a future where current problems are resolved, this client is also glimpsing a transformed version of self, where the ego has been enhanced or strengthened, with a deepened sense of mastery and confidence.

Phillips and Frederick described a continuum of age progression interventions, from Hartland's structured direct suggestion of enhanced hope and confidence, to a mid-ground where the therapist guides an age progression but leaves openness for the client's imagination and initiatives, to an extreme of unstructured and indirect guidance for age progression. They cited Erickson and Rossi (1989), who concluded that age progression involves "an active process of changing

---

BOX 58.2 EGO-STRENGTHENING

The technique embraces the following steps:

1. Physical relaxation induced by concentration upon the breath, following it as it flows in and out, letting go of tension, tightness, and discomfort with each breath out. Patients are encouraged to develop a detached attitude, as if they are watching someone else breathing.

The simple following-of-the-breath physical relaxation technique permits patients to "let go" of specific problems, unwanted thoughts, and physical discomforts, which have been discussed before the induction is commenced. Thus, it serves as both the first step in trance induction and the commencement of therapy.

2. Mental calmness encouraged through imagining the mind as a pond, the surface of which is completely still, like a mirror. Thoughts are watched in a detached way, being allowed to drift through above the water, attention then being brought back to further contemplation of the water's stillness.

Patients may be encouraged to imagine the area above the water as their conscious minds and that below as their unconscious minds. Accordingly, they have the power to "drop into" the pond of their mind anything they desire. This may be formulated in terms of a trance-deepening suggestion with the patient imagining a beautiful stone representing, say, mental calmness sinking down and down, deeper and deeper, until it comes to rest at the bottom of the pond. It is then suggested that the patient's mind locks around this calmness, a calmness which is to become a permanent part of his or her life.

The same procedure may be followed with other stones, each one representing a specific suggestion relevant to the particular patient, and each one assisting the deepening of the trance as the stone sinks "down and down, deeper and deeper."

As a normal practice, mental calmness, physical relaxation, confidence, and happiness comprise the "stones," but these may be replaced with others such as concentration, mental control, and healing where it seems appropriate. The "pond," then, provides a basic framework within which considerable flexibility is possible.

3. Disposing of "rubbish" as subjects imagine themselves "dumping" mental obstacles, such as fears, doubts, worries, and guilts, down a chute from which nothing can return. Physical obstacles, such as cigarettes and excess weight, may also be disposed of in this way.

Patients are also allowed flexibility in the corridor, rubbish chute, and barrier metaphors, which may be used to meet individual needs. Smokers may wish to discard their cigarettes, alcoholics their alcohol, and the obese may care to strip away their unwanted weight.

4. Removal of a barrier representing everything that is negative in the lives of subjects. Embodied in this barrier are self-destructive thoughts, forces of failure and defeat, mental obstacles, and self-imposed limitations, everything that is preventing subjects from enjoying their lives as they would like. This barrier is destroyed through use of the imagination.

5. Enjoyment of a special place where subjects feel content, tranquil, and still. In this place, they "turn off" the outside world. Once patients find their special place, it is suggested that they think of themselves as they want to be, imagining themselves behaving the way they want to behave, and "seeing" themselves achieving the success they wish to achieve. Sometimes particular images to meet the expressed needs of patients will be suggested; on other occasions, they may generate their own material.

The "special place" visualization is a common aspect of many hypnotherapeutic treatments. One particularly useful pattern is to have patients imagining themselves going through a door, which they can shut behind them to exclude the rest of the world. Suggestions may then be made that, in this place, they will be able to get into contact with the unconscious part of their minds, which will then solve any problems they might have. One aspect of such solutions will be that things that have worried or upset them in the past will simply drop out of their lives as if they never existed. Because these things have now become so unimportant, the patients will probably forget they were ever disturbed in this way.

Source: Harry E. Stanton (1989); Reprinted with permission of the *American Journal of Clinical Hypnosis.*

---

one's mental dynamics rather than the passive expression of a simple hope or fantasy" (p. 241).

Meeting inner strength. McNeal and Frederick (1993) introduced a key procedure for ego-strengthening–guiding the client to encounter his/her inner strength. The process typically begins with a hypnotic induction and a deepening process. The client is instructed to use ideomotor signaling to communicate arrival at certain points in the script. Then a rough script is followed, allowing maximal flexibility to enlist the client's own images and experiencing to modify the experience. The script directs the client to take a journey to the center of his or her being, to a still place, to encounter his or her inner strength. The client is instructed that this mythical figure

BOX 58.3 SCRIPT FOR MEETING INNER STRENGTH

"I would like to invite you to take a journey within yourself to a place that feels like the very center of your being, that place where it's very quiet . . . and peaceful . . . and still. And when you're in that place . . . it's possible for you to have a sense of finding a part of yourself . . . a part that I will refer to as your Inner Strength.

This is a part of yourself that has always been there since the moment of birth . . . even though at times it may have been difficult for you to feel . . . and it is with you now. It's that part of yourself that has allowed you to survive . . . and to overcome many, many obstacles in the past. Just as it helps you now to overcome obstacles wherever you face them. Maybe you'd like to take a few moments of time to get in touch with that part of yourself . . . and you can notice what images . . . or feelings . . . what thoughts . . . what bodily sensations are associated with being in touch with your Inner Strength. And when those images or thoughts or feelings or bodily sensations or however it is coming to you are clear to you in your inner mind, and when you have a sense that the experience is completed for you . . . then your "yes" finger can raise. In the future, when you wish to get in touch with Inner Strength . . . you will find that you can do so by calling forth these images, thoughts, feelings, bodily sensations, and that by so doing you will be in touch with Inner Strength again.

And when you're in touch with this part of yourself, you will be able to feel more confident . . . confident with the knowledge that you have, within yourself, all the resources you really need to take steps in the direction that you wish to go . . . to be able to set goals and to be able to achieve them . . . and to have the experience that dreams can come true.

When you're in touch with this part of yourself, it's possible to feel more calm, more optimistic, to look forward to the future. [At this point particular goals, which the patient has shared with the therapist, may be stated.]

And in the next days and weeks to come, you may find yourself becoming calmer and more optimistic about your life . . . and you will find that any time during the day it will be possible for you to get in touch with your own Inner Strength by simply closing your eyes for a moment, bringing your hand to your forehead, evoking the image of your Inner Strength, and reminding yourself that you have within you . . . all the resources that you really need. The more you can use these methods to be in touch with your Inner Strength, the more you will be able to trust your inner self, your intuition, your feelings, and will be able to use them as your guide."

Source: McNeal and Frederick (1993); Reprinted with permission of the *American Journal of Clinical Hypnosis.*

of inner strength is a component within self that has been present from birth, which has allowed the client to survive, and has overcome many obstacles (1993, p. 172). (See Box 58.3 for the complete script of McNeal and Frederick's "inner strength" exercise).

Age regression, age progression, and ego-strengthening. McNeal and Frederick (1993) also utilized age regression to discover some nurturing figure, even in the most abusive and traumatic childhoods, someone who has done something special for the child and lent support. The client is also guided to recollect and experience how the presence of such persons in an otherwise painful life is a foundation for a growing present-day sense of confidence and strength. They also introduced scripts for age progression, to a time when all of the client's current difficult problems have been resolved.

Ego-strengthening and EMDR. Maggie Phillips (2001) published an imaginative article suggesting strategies for combining hypnotic principles and ego-strengthening with eye movement desensitization and reprocessing (EMDR). EMDR was initially introduced by Francine Shapiro (1995) to address posttraumatic stress and correlated anxieties. EMDR consists of a technique in which the therapist uses hand movement to guide the client's eyes to move back and forth laterally while recalling painful events and emotions. EMDR is now widely used to desensitize the client to the painful reexperiencing of past traumas. EMDR is also applied more widely now to include many nontrauma-based anxiety disorders, grief, physical symptoms, and dissociative disorders (Shapiro, 1995). The process of EMDR is sometimes challenging, and it is not unusual for clients to feel overwhelmed and discontinue their EMDR sessions.

Phillips advocated combining ego-strengthening and other hypnotic strategies to help the client to build new ego-related strengths while processing traumatic memories. She proposed using safe place imagery to provide the client with a strategy for inner safety and comfort. Whenever the client feels overwhelmed, he or she can retreat to the safe place, and strengthen feelings of inner well-being. She suggested building a "positive template" strategy, similar to hypnotic age progression, directly into the EMDR process. The client is invited to picture future progress in his or her coping, while the therapist conducts lateral eye movements. Phillips provided a number of other strategies which lend themselves to combination with EMDR.

A synthesis: Ego-strengthening in hypnosis and psychotherapy. Frederick and McNeal (1999) published a book on the inner strengths approach, detailing a variety of strategies and models for pursuing ego-strengthening. John and Helen Watkins wrote a foreword to the book, and proposed that ego-strengthening is fundamental to the process of transforming human beings. The approach outlined by Frederick and McNeal is useful for empowering personal transformation in hypnosis and general psychotherapy. Ericksonian change principles do not require a trance or a specific induction, and carry over easily in any counseling or psychotherapy process.

Further, although Frederick and McNeal utilized an ego-state therapy framework, their approach to ego-strengthening can be combined with a variety of therapeutic models, from psychoanalysis, to Jungian analysis, to self-psychology. Initial and continuing attention to strengthening the client's sense of mastery, confidence, and hope tends to enhance the effectiveness of any therapeutic intervention.

The Frederick and McNeal book covers a wide range of ego-strengthening techniques and strategies, far beyond the scope of this chapter. They suggested strategies for self-soothing and development of self, the cultivation of inner resources of love, ideodynamic healing, managing performance anxiety, and addressing a variety of clinical syndromes.

NEURAL CORRELATES OF EGO-STRENGTHENING

With the birth of modern neuro-imaging, it has become possible to assess whether hypnotic interventions have a consistent measurable impact on brain processes. The new emerging field of neurophenomenology has become possible: a systematic effort to correlate the individual's phenomenological experiencing with neural processes (Gordon, 2013; Rainville & Price, 2003; Varela, 1996). It stands to reason that if ego-strengthening is a powerful intervention that consistently reduces depression, enhances subjective well-being, and catalyzes better coping,

there should be measurable changes in the brain, paralleling these psycho-emotional changes. Yet, the exploration of neural processes during ego-strengthening is in its infancy.

One study by Stevens et al. (2004) used measurement of EEG activity in the midfrontal area, which is regarded as critical in executive processing. The subjects in the study were 60 college students: all completed the Tellegen Absorption Scale, the Creative Imagination Scale, and the Stanford Form C. EEG was recorded at Fz and Oz (midpoints of the frontal and occipital areas), at baseline, and during hypnotic induction, arm levitation, progressive relaxation, and a phase of "visual imagery/ego-enhancing suggestions." The authors developed a series of specific hypotheses about the directions in which theta, beta, and alpha frequency cortical activity would change during each phase of the hypnotic process, and hypotheses about how the level of hypnotizability would impact power in each frequency range. They formed hypotheses about gamma frequency activity (36–44 Hz) as well, as gamma has been found to be elevated in some meditation states, and also to be elevated in highly hypnotizable subjects. For some reason, perhaps the level of technology available for this team, they did not analyze gamma separately from the broad beta range of cortical activity within which it falls.

Stevens et al. reported many specific findings, and their report is readily available. For the present purposes, the following findings are relevant. The highly hypnotizables and very highs showed significantly greater EEG power across all phases of the baseline and hypnotic intervention in theta and beta ranges, and in some phases in alpha and delta. The high hypnotizables also lost power in both beta and theta from baseline to eye roll and increased power steadily during arm levitation, progressive relaxation, and the ego-strengthening suggestions. The authors acknowledged that this study is a preliminary investigation, but it established, first, that the activity of ego-strengthening may produce a greater activation of theta and beta power than other hypnotic techniques used, and second, that hypnotizability also interacts with the type of intervention to produce cortical differences.

Future research should examine the entire cortex and not just select regions, utilize more sophisticated quantitative analysis of EEG to isolate the role of specific waveforms such as gamma, and draw on additional neuro-imaging such as the functional MRI to map functional systems in the brain and their activation during ego-strengthening interventions. The sequence of the various hypnotic interventions was not varied in this study, so there is no control for the order in which a specific intervention occurred—that is an order effect. Future studies should have a control by varying the sequence of interventions.

CASE EXAMPLE

Howard was a 47-year-old male, who was referred to a pain clinic psychologist because of difficulties with chronic pain and depression. He provided a history of growing up on his grandfather's farm along with his parents and a grandmother who died when he was 6 years old. At 17, Howard left the farm to study agricultural economics at Michigan State University, but returned home at 19 when his grandfather died, agreeing to work the farm with his father. He described a sharp contrast between his grandfather and father, the former being "a total optimist who made you believe that you could do anything" and the latter "a pessimist who knew that nothing you did would ever work out."

After several years, his father decided that it would cost too much to repair the harvesting equipment and entered into an agreement with a corporation that would conduct the harvest while paying a reduced price for the crop. Just at harvest time, the corporation filed for bankruptcy and Howard's father, without working equipment, lost most of his crop. He decided that the farm was hopeless and took a job in a factory where he later arranged a job for Howard. A year prior to being seen at the pain clinic, Howard was involved in a car accident that killed his parents and left him with a shattered left wrist, knee, and foot. When Howard was not able to return to his job after six months, he was informed that he no longer had a job to return to.

Howard responded well to the use of hypnosis for pain management; however, his depression, which was partially grief-related due to the loss of his parents, undermined his ability to decide what he should do with his life. With his wife's job, his wage replacement from his auto insurance, and his parent's life insurance policies, he was not in financial distress, but he was paralyzed with self-doubt about his ability to do anything productive again.

Ego-strengthening. A breakthrough came during a hypnosis session when Howard was introduced to the Council of Advisors exercise (Hammond, 1992). Following the instructions to visit the council, he was given the vague suggestion that "someone will appear who will provide you with what you need." Howard described going into an empty room with only a table and chairs, and was surprised to find that his father was the first to appear at the table at the beginning to tell him that "nothing matters, nothing you do will work." Howard's grandfather appeared "in a rage and made my father vanish." The grandfather then proceeded to reassure him that, as always, he could do anything and that everything would work out in time. The grandfather's final words: "Be me, not your father, you'll be happier."

Howard came out of the trance laughing, and when questioned he offered, "I guess I really am more than I have become!" Over the next several sessions, Howard used the Council of Advisors to reconnect with former teachers and professors who had thought highly of him in his teen years. He was able to recognize the beginnings of his depression when he not only left college but then spent years working with his father, absorbing "the negative energy that followed him everywhere" with no protection from anyone else.

As his depression lifted, Howard was able to become more engaged with the physical therapists working with him. Their praise of his effort and acknowledgment of his functional gains further boosted the ego-strengthening process. Finally, Howard was introduced to the concept of the central healing response (Willmarth, 2010), which suggests that both consciously and unconsciously the body has a natural drive toward health that would continue at its own pace.

A follow-up three months after the conclusion of treatment found that Howard, who still lived on his grandfather's original farm, had decided to convert the property to a fully organic farm. He reported only moderate improvement in his pain levels but noted a belief that he was still getting better. "My inner grandfather says that I can do this," he reported. "And I believe him!"

CONCLUSION

Ego-strengthening represents both an autonomous treatment approach and a strategy that can supplement other treatments. Since Hartland first introduced the ego-strengthening model in 1965, many patients with mental health and medical disorders have shown significant improvement in their overall well-being, and in some cases reduction in their presenting symptoms as well. Today's tool box for ego-strengthening is much expanded. We still have access to a wide range of verbatim scripts for ego-strengthening suggestions, but we also have the newer approaches using guided imagery, the inner strengths model, the process of age progression, and the mobilization of helpful ego states. At this time, in a world of damaged egos/selves, entire communities with traumatic psychological injury, and individuals battling addictive behavior, ego-strengthening psychotherapy and ego-strengthening hypnosis provide an approach applicable in most cli4nical practices.

REFERENCES

Achterberg, J., & Lawlis, G. F. (1984). *Imagery and Disease*. Champaign, Ill: Institute for Personality and Ability Testing.

Achterberg, J. (1978a). *Imagery and disease: Image-ca, image-sp, image-db, A diagnostic tool for behavioral medicine*. Champagne, IL: Institute for Personality and Ability Testing.

Achterberg, J. (1978b). *Imagery of cancer*. Champagne, IL: Institute for Personality and Ability Testing.

Achterberg, J. (1985). *Imagery in healing: Shamanism and modern medicine*. Boston, MA: Shambhala.

Achterberg, J., Cooke, K., Richards, T., Standish, L. J., Kozak, L., & Lake, J. (2005). Evidence for correlations between distant intentionality and brain function in recipients: A functional magnetic resonance imaging analysis. *Journal of Alternative and Complementary Medicine, 11*(6), 965–971. doi:10.1089/acm.2005.11.965

Assagioli, R. (1965). *Psychosynthesis: A manual of principles and techniques*. New York, NY: Hobbs, Dorman.

Assagioli, R. (1973). *The act of will*. New York, NY: Viking.

Barber, T. X. (1984). Hypnosis, deep relaxation, and active relaxation: Data, theory, and practical applications. In R. L. Woolfolk, & P. M. Lehrer (Eds.), *Principles and practice of stress management* (1st ed., pp. 164–166). New York, NY: Guilford Press.

Barber, T. X. (1990). Suggestions for raising self-esteem. In D. C. Hammond (Ed.), *Handbook of hypnotic suggestions and metaphors* (pp. 118–119). New York, NY: W. W. Norton.

Calnan, R. D. (1977). Hypnotherapeutic ego-strengthening. *Australian Journal of Clinical Hypnosis, 5*, 105–118.

Coué, E. (1922). *Self-mastery through conscious auto-suggestion (trans., A. S. van orden)*. New York, NY: Malkan Publishing.

Erickson, M. H. (1954). Pseudo-orientation in time as a hypnotherapeutic procedure. *Journal of Clinical and Experimental Hypnosis, 2*, 261–283. doi.org/10.1080/00207145408410117.

Erickson, M. H. (1959). Further clinical techniques of hypnosis-utilization techniques. *American Journal of Clinical Hypnosis, 2*, 3–21.

Erickson, M. H., & Rossi, E. L. (1976). Two level communication and the micro-dynamics of trance and suggestion. *American Journal of Clinical Hypnosis, 18*(3), 153–171. doi:10.1080/00029157.1976.10403794

Erickson, M. H., & Rossi, E. L. (1989). *The February man: Evolving consciousness and identity in hypnotherapy*. New York, NY: Brunner/Mazel.

Frederick, C., & McNeal, S. (1999). *Inner strengths: Contemporary psychotherapy and hypnosis for ego-strengthening*. Mahwah, NJ: Lawrence Erlbaum.

Gardner, G. G. (1976). Hypnosis and mastery: Clinical contributions and directions for research. *International Journal of Clinical and Experimental Hypnosis, 24*(3), 202–214. doi:10.1080/00207147608416202

Gordon, S. (Ed.). (2013). *Neurophenomenology and its applications to psychology*. New York, NY: Springer Publishing Company.

Hammond, D. C. (1992). *Manual for self-hypnosis*. Bloomingdale, IL: American Society for Clinical Hypnosis.

Hammond, D. C. (Ed.). (1990). *Handbook of hypnotic suggestions and metaphors*. New York, NY: W. W. Norton.

Hartland, J. (1971). Further observations on the use of ego-strengthening techniques. *American Journal of Clinical Hypnosis, 14*(1), 1–8. doi:10.1080/00029157.1971.10402136

Hartland, J. (1965). The value of "ego strengthening" procedures prior to direct symptom removal under hypnosis. *American Journal of Clinical Hypnosis, 8*(2), 89–93. doi:10.1080/00029157.1965.10402470

Jung, C. (1997). J. Chodorow (Ed.), *Jung on active imagination*. New York, NY: Routledge.

McNeal, S., & Frederick, C. (1993). Inner strength and other techniques for ego strengthening. *American*

Journal of Clinical Hypnosis, 35(3), 170–178. doi:10.1
080/00029157.1993.10403001

Moss, D. (1999). Carl Rogers, the client-centered
approach, and experiential therapy. In D. Moss (Ed.),
*Humanistic and transpersonal psychology: A historical
and biographical sourcebook* (pp. 41–48). Westport,
CT: Greenwood.

Newey, A. B. (1986). Ego state therapy with depression.
In B. Zilbergeld, M. G. Edelstein, & D. L. Aroaz
(Eds.), *Hypnosis: Questions and answers* (pp. 197–
203). New York, NY: W. W. Norton.

Phillips, M. (2001). Potential contributions of hypnosis
to ego-strengthening procedures in EMDR. *American
Journal of Clinical Hypnosis, 43,* 247-262.

Phillips, M., & Frederick, C. (1992). The use of hypnotic
age progressions as prognostic, ego-strengthening, and
integrating techniques. *American Journal of Clinical
Hypnosis, 35,* 99-108.

Rainville, P., & Price, D. D. (2003). Hypnosis
phenomenology and the neurobiology of consciousness.
*International Journal of Clinical and Experimental
Hypnosis, 51,* 105-129.

Rogers, C. R. (1957). The necessary and sufficient
conditions of therapeutic personality change. *Journal
of Consulting Psychology, 21*(2), 95–103.

Rogers, C. R. (1961). *On becoming a person.* Boston,
MA: Houghton Mifflin.

Rossman, M. L. (2000). *Guided imagery for self-healing.*
Novato, CA: New World Library.

Shapiro, F. (1995). *Eye movement desensitization
and reprocessing: Basic principles, protocols, and
procedures.* New York, NY: Guilford Press.

Sheikh, A. (Ed.). (1983). *Imagery: Current theory,
research and application* (pp. 391–435). New York,
NY: Wiley.

Stanton, H. E. (1977). The use of suggestions derived
from rational-emotive therapy. *International Journal
of Clinical and Experimental Hypnosis, 25*(1), 18–26.
doi:10.1080/00207147708415959

Stanton, H. E. (1979). Ego-enhancement through positive
suggestion. *Australian Journal of Clinical Hypnosis, 3,*
32–36.

Stanton, H. E. (1989). Ego-enhancement: A five step
approach. *American Journal of Clinical Hypnosis,
31*(3), 192–198. doi:10.1080/00029157.1989.1040
2888

Stevens, L., Brady, B., Goon, A., Adams, D.,
Rebarchik, J., Gacula, L., . . . Verduga, S. (2004).
Electrophysiologic alterations during hypnosis for ego-
strengthening: A preliminary investigation. *American
Journal of Clinical Hypnosis, 46,* 323–344.

Torem, M. (1990). Ego-strengthening. In D. C.
Hammond (Ed.), *Handbook of hypnotic suggestions
and metaphors* (pp. 110–112). New York, NY: W. W.
Norton.

Varela, F. (1996). Neurophenomenology: A
methodological remedy for the hard problem. *Journal
of Consciousness Studies, 3,* 330–349.

Watkins, H. H. (1990). Suggestions for raising self-
esteem. In D. C. Hammond (Ed.), *Handbook of
hypnotic suggestions and metaphors* (pp. 127–130).
New York, NY: W. W. Norton.

Willmarth, E. (2010, August). Hypnotic enhancement
of the central healing response: The power of "mere
imagination." Presidential Address for Division
30, Annual Meeting of the American Psychological
Association: San Diego, CA.

Zeig, J. K. (2014). *The induction of hypnosis: An
Ericksonian elicitation approach.* Phoenix, AZ: The
Milton H. Erickson Foundation Press.

Fear of Flying

Sharon Spiegel

There was a time in the distant past when flying was a luxury experience of being pampered, fed, and then arriving at your destination relaxed and on schedule. Air travel is now more accessible to the general public, but for the average passenger, it can also be a stressful experience of long lines, extra charges, delays, cancellations, lengthy airport screening procedures, and concerns about contagious diseases. However, for those who suffer from a fear of flying, the mere anticipation of flying can be so anxiety provoking that they avoid air travel, fly only when absolutely necessary, or fly when they have to but with high levels of anxiety (Ekeberg, Seeberg, & Ellertsen, 1989; Oakes & Bor, 2010a).

Aviophobia is one of the most common specific phobias of the situational subtype and is characterized by marked fear or anxiety about a specific object or situation that has been present for at least six months and causes clinically significant distress or impairment in social, occupational, or other important areas of functioning (American Psychiatric Association, 2013).

There is considerable variability in the prevalence statistics depending on whether people are asked if they are afraid to fly or assessed using clinical diagnostic criteria (Oakes & Bor, 2010a). Some older surveys estimate that 10% to 40% of adults in industrialized nations or 25 million Americans are afraid to fly (Dean & Whitaker, 1982; Oakes & Bor, 2010a; Van Gerwen & Diekstra, 2000; Van Gerwen, Spinhoven, Diekstra, & Van Dyck, 1997). In contrast, a significantly lower rate of 2.5% of adults meet the *Diagnostic and Statistical Manual of Mental Disorders, fifth edition (DSM-5)* diagnostic criteria (Stinson, et al., 2007). From a clinical standpoint, however, many fearful flyers who may not reach the diagnostic threshold still experience sufficient distress to warrant treatment (Dean & Whitaker, 1982;

Mühlberger, Hermann, Wiedemann, Ellgring, & Pauli, 2001; Oakes & Bor, 2010a).

Fear of flying is also a significant economic problem for the airline industry due to lost revenue from potential passengers who forego air travel. It is likely that the number of people who worry about flying has increased since the terrorist attacks of September 11, 2001, as many individuals believe that air travel increases the risk of terrorist attacks or spread of contagious diseases (Van Gerwen, Diekstra, Arondeus, & Wolfger, 2004). In one study conducted by the Boeing Corporation to determine the commercial impact of fear of flying, 17% of American respondents admitted being afraid to fly and flew only one third as often as those who were not afraid (Oakes & Bor, 2010a). An economic analysis performed in 2004 to assess the impact of the terrorist attacks revealed a 10% to 30% reduction in air travel (Ito & Lee, 2004). Although many people are content using other forms of transportation, for growing numbers of people, an inability to have "full global mobility" has serious professional, personal, and economic costs (Laker, 2012).

Fearful flyers are a diagnostically diverse group, including those with a single phobia, multiple phobias, or another primary diagnosis such as agoraphobia, generalized anxiety disorder, or panic disorder with agoraphobia. Fear of flying can also co-occur with a number of other Axis I and Axis II disorders (APA, 2013; Oakes & Bor, 2010a; McNally & Loura, 1992; Wilhelm & Roth, 1997). In view of the heterogeneity of this patient population and the possibility that other issues may complicate treatment, it is important to do a thorough assessment and to tailor the treatment program to the specific needs of the patient. A review of published research favors an individualized approach over standardized protocols (Oakes & Bor, 2010b).

A good assessment begins with questions about the underlying anxiety, as patients differ with respect to the feared catastrophic consequences of flying (Howard, Murphy, & Clarke, 1983; Oakes & Bor, 2010a; Oakes & Bor, 2010b; Van Gerwen, Spinhoven, Diekstra,& Van Dyck, 1997). In a small study of 34 patients, half of whom had a primary diagnosis of flight phobia and the other half with a primary diagnosis of agoraphobia, the agoraphobic patients were afraid of having a panic attack in flight whereas those without agoraphobia were afraid of the plane crashing (McMcNally & Louro, 1992). In my clinical practice, the majority of patients have a mixed presentation, worrying about the possibility of air disasters but far more overwhelmingly about the fear of a panic attack during the flight. I always inquire: "How would you feel about flying if you knew that your experience would be comfortable and anxiety-free?" It is not surprising that people who believe that they have a serious risk of dying in an airplane crash are far less likely to avail themselves of treatment. I'm reminded that many years ago a colleague told me she had never been in a plane because of her fear of flying. When I suggested that therapy could be very helpful, she responded by saying she was not interested because if she got over her anxiety and flew, it would be more likely she would die in a plane crash. For those people whose fear is driven by the fear of disastrous plane accidents, psychoeducation on the safety of air travel should be the first step in treatment so as to alter the perception of risk.

As treatment progresses, I find it particularly helpful to inquire about the patient's reactions to the various components of therapy. For some people, learning to reduce physiological reactivity through deep relaxation makes them less fearful of being restricted in an airplane for several hours, whereas for others, the cognitive restructuring that helps patients view flying through a different lens appears to play the primary role in creating change. This information can be used to continue to refine the focus of the treatment. In other words, I start with a treatment plan as a roadmap, but am willing to take whatever detours will most likely help us arrive at the destination of successful flight.

Finally, there is the question of what constitutes a good outcome. Empirical measures of efficacy include reduced anxiety before or during flight, increased flying behavior, or both. Although research requires standardized outcome measures,

in clinical work, it is preferable to adopt a more pragmatic approach to accommodate the patient's needs, preferences, and life circumstances. For someone whose work entails air travel, an optimal outcome would be defined as the ability to fly whenever necessary with reduced anxiety before or during the flights. However, a flying phobia is different from other phobias in that avoidance of flying after treatment can often be accounted for by a number of other practical considerations such as time, financial considerations, and opportunity (Oakes & Bor, 2010b). It is important to know at the outset whether the individual is hoping to fly frequently, only when necessary, or simply to be able to fly comfortably if the opportunity presents itself. Although therapists may be ambitious in their desire to help achieve complete freedom from the phobia, it is preferable to collaborate with the patient to determine if it is appropriate to set more limited but realistic treatment goals.

There are two special situations that challenge the therapist's flexibility and creativity but have not been addressed adequately in the literature. The first of these is the case where the fear of flying persists despite the fact that the patient has previously been in therapy for this problem. Often patients seek other types of approaches in hopes of having greater success. In these instances, treatment should capitalize on the skills that have already been built while offering additional elements that will increase the likelihood of better results. Hirsch (2012) describes one such treatment-resistant patient for whom he structured an array of components including hypnosis, virtual reality therapy, behavior therapy, and cognitive behavior therapy, all leading to a successful outcome when he accompanied the patient on a scheduled flight.

The second challenge is the patient, who during the course of psychotherapy for other issues needs to fly and asks for help with fear of flying. Many clinicians who either are reluctant to shift the focus of therapy or do not have the necessary skills to work with phobias will automatically refer those requests for adjunctive phobia treatment. It is my practice to explore the meaning and timing of the request, and then seriously consider a temporary shift in focus in cases where I believe that will best serve the patient's interests. In more complex cases, it is actually advantageous to have established a trusting relationship as well as understanding of the underlying issues that may contribute to the phobia. For example, one of my long-term therapy patients had great difficulty in getting in touch with her anger. When she needed to fly for her job, we temporarily shifted our focus to treating the phobia. Based on our ongoing work, it became clear that her panic about flying symbolized a fear that she would feel trapped, lose control, and do something crazy like lash out physically or scream expletives during the flight. Therapy enabled her to be more comfortable experiencing negative feelings and also realize that awareness of the feelings she had did not mean she had to act on them. In this case, imaginary exposure included fantasies of being overwhelmed by anger. The phobia treatment not only enabled her to fly but also enhanced the ongoing therapy that we were able to resume.

RESEARCH

The empirically validated treatment of choice for all phobias is exposure therapy that promotes experiencing rather than avoiding the fearful situations and sensations (Alpers, 2010; Antony & Barlow, 2002; Hood & Antony, 2012; Wolitzky-Taylor, Horowitz, Powers, & Telch, 2008). The type of techniques that have been used include relaxation training, breathing techniques, distraction techniques, cognitive restructuring, thought stopping, and systematic desensitization paired with either in vivo or imaginal exposure therapy (Choy, Fyer, & Lipsitz, 2007; da Costa, Sardinha, & Nardi, 2008; Gerardi, Cukor, Difede, Rizzo, & Rothbaum, 2010; Kim, et al., 2008; Krijn et al., 2007; Oakes & Bor, 2010b). Current approaches also favor a shift in emphasis from eliminating the fear to mindful acceptance of the experience (Carbonell, 2003; Eifert & Forsyth, 2005).

Numerous multimodal fear of flying group programs are sponsored by the airlines, but these are based in Europe (Oakes & Bor, 2010a; Van Gerwen, Diekstra, Arondeus, & Wolfger, 2004). Probably the most prominent of these is the multicomponent, empirically based program offered by the VALK Foundation, a collaboration between the University of Leiden in Holland, KLM Royal Dutch Airlines, and Amsterdam Airport Schiphol (Van Gerwen, Spinhoven, Diekstra, & Van Dyck, 2002). Treatment includes individual assessment

and preparation, group cognitive behavior therapy, hands-on orientation to the equipment sessions in a flight simulator, a "graduation" flight, and three-month follow-up and relapse prevention. Having easy access to a preplanned, convenient, and inexpensive airplane excursion is an extremely advantageous component as it prevents the all too common problem of patients who complete treatment successfully but procrastinate in scheduling a flight.

Frequently patients who are afraid to fly inquire about using hypnosis and there are several published case reports on the topic (Deyoub & Epstein, 1977; Diment, 1981; Hirsch, 2012; Spiegel & Spiegel, 1978). Furthermore, an interest in this approach is not a recent phenomenon, as more than 35 years ago Spiegel and Spiegel (1978) noted it was the most common phobia encountered in their clinical practice. Hypnosis has firmly established itself as a valuable adjunct in the treatment of all phobias, although there has been a dearth of empirical research on using it for aviophobia for more than 30 years (Hirsch, 2012; Spiegel, Frischholz, Maruffi, & Spiegel, 1981). Meta-analyses have demonstrated that combining hypnosis with cognitive behavioral therapy (CBT) for anxiety disorders enhances the effectiveness of treatment (Kirsch, Montgomery, & Sapirstein, 1995). Hypnosis has also been shown to be a useful complement to both cognitive behavioral and psychodynamic treatments for hypnotizable patients (Crawford & Barabasz, 1993; Humphreys, 1986; Spiegel, Frischholz, Maruffi, & Spiegel, 1981). Some ways in which it has been used to enhance phobia treatment includes promoting a deeper experience of relaxation, facilitating imaginal exposure, intensifying positive transference, utilizing direct and indirect suggestion, creating opportunities for mental rehearsal, ego-strengthening, and cognitive reframing (Hammond, 1990). In addition, when patients do not respond to standard cognitive behavioral techniques, hypnotic age regression, and unconscious exploration are valuable tools for identifying the source of the phobia or the patient's resistance to treatment.

Fortunately, many patients have a good response to a combination of reassurance, psychoeducation, and in vivo or imaginal graded exposure offered in brief individual or group protocols. However, countless numbers of sufferers avoid getting help, drop out of treatment prematurely, or have suboptimal responses to therapy and remain reluctant to fly. In a recent review on the treatment of specific phobia, I proposed four major recommendations for utilizing hypnosis in innovative ways to address these issues and improve outcomes (Spiegel, 2014). This chapter will discuss how these principles can be applied to aviophobia.

A variety of suggestions should be given for comfort, mastery, and ego-strengthening. Unfortunately, this hypnotic imaginal exposure is much less effective in the case of patients who are unable to visualize the fearful situation and the accompanying intense negative affect. Some of these patients may be low in the hypnotic talent of visualization, whereas others can imagine the scene but have difficulty recreating the anxiety. Furthermore, irrespective of level of hypnotizability, someone who has never flown doesn't have the memories of previous experiences to draw upon for imaginal exposure. Fortunately, there are other ways to augment exposure in the session by means of computer technology that simulates various aspects of the flight.

The most technologically elaborate method available to prepare for flight is virtual reality (VR)—a sophisticated computer-generated technology that allows the patient to wear a head-mounted display with small TV monitors and stereo headphones to simulate a multidimensional experience of being in the airplane. Virtual reality exposure has become the most researched method for treating fear of flying and has been shown to be highly effective (Botella, Osma, Garcia-Palacios, Quero, & Banos, 2004; Choy, Fyer, & Lipsitz, 2007: Côté & Bouchard, 2008; Maltby, Kirsch, Mayers, & Allen, 2002; Mühlberger, Hermann, Wiedmann, Ellgring, & Pauli, 2001; Powers & Emmelkamp, 2008; Rothbaum & Hodges, 1999; Rothbaum, Hodges, Smith, Lee, & Price, 2000; Rothbaum, et al 2006; Roy, 2003). Recently, a successful case was reported in the literature using both virtual reality and hypnosis in a treatment-resistant patient (Hirsch, 2012). Although the results of VR training are promising, some patients describe the animations as less compelling because they have a simulated unrealistic quality. More importantly, the equipment is extremely expensive and may not be a viable option for most clinicians.

In contrast, the Internet opens the door for the average person to sample a multitude of new and otherwise inaccessible experiences. One of the main sources of such images is the video-sharing website YouTube. Google reported that the YouTube upload rate increased dramatically to 4 billion YouTube views per day (Marks, 2012). There are a variety of ways in which these video clips can be used for exposure in the session and for homework between sessions. In a recent publication, I described a new technique I developed to combine YouTube images and hypnosis as a "low tech" inexpensive alternative to virtual reality (Spiegel, 2012). This procedure involves hypnotizing the person and then using the deepening technique of fractionation (Hammond, Haskins-Bartsch, McGhee, & Grant, 1987) to re-alert with instructions to remain in an "eyes open" trance state to watch the video as the clinician offers hypnotic suggestions. I initially developed this method to help those phobic patients who have difficulty eliciting high levels of anxiety in trance with imaginal exposure. However, because of the limited number of in vivo graded exposure opportunities available for flying, I now incorporate computer imagery for all aviophobic patients. This can be done in a variety of ways, either using the fractionation method or simply by watching YouTube videos in the waking state to elicit anxious feelings and images that can later be recalled in trance. Originally I selected the video clips before meeting with the patient, but now I have discovered that it is preferable to browse through them with the patient in session to find videos that are particularly evocative for the patient. I also record pictures or brief video footage with my iPhone whenever I fly to capture elements of the flight that may be useful for this purpose.

Another common anxiety stimulus for phobic individuals is the sense of alteration in bodily sensations. This is particularly problematic for the fearful flyer since flying at high altitudes causes a variety of shifting somatic sensations due to hypoxia, acceleration, mechanical vibrations, and the effects of changes in altitude on the vestibular system (Jaffee, 2005; Silverman & Gendreau, 2009). Research shows that some patients are higher in anxiety sensitivity, which is defined as the tendency to interpret changes in bodily sensations as signals of threat (Reiss, 1991). For those individuals, the somatic sensations that result from normal fluctuations in the plane contribute to increased flight anxiety (Vanden Bogaerde & De Raedt, 2008). Anxiety sensitivity has been found to moderate the relationship between somatic sensations and fear of flying (Vanden Bogaerde & De Raedt, 2011). For individuals high in anxiety sensitivity, it is essential to address these sensations directly and explain how the brain may be registering anxiety when there is none present. It is also worthwhile to talk with patients about experiences they have had in safe situations where similar shifts in bodily sensations did not trigger anxiety. For example, many people are able to enjoy amusement park rides even though they are associated with somatic and perceptual changes. Similarly, individuals who are hypersensitive to turbulence in flight don't even notice changing sensations when driving over bumpy roads. Patients are encouraged to seek out similar experiences where they can practice cognitive reframing as well as interoceptive exposure.

The advent of functional magnetic resonance imagery (fMRI) has led to dramatic advances in the study of cognitive neuroscience. We can now explain to our patients that there are complex neural circuits in multiple levels of the brain that are involved in the experience of fear. The structure that has been labeled the "heart and soul of the fear system" is the subcortical amygdala—a structure in the limbic system that rapidly registers signals of imminent danger. The amygdala is part of the fast neural network that responds rapidly in a reflexive mode, whereas the cortex is part of the slower system that interprets and makes sense of the experience. The phobic stimulus triggers the amygdala response so rapidly that "we are already scared when we initially perceive what is frightening us" (Cozolino, 2010, p. 242). In other words, the cortex is inadequate in managing the competing brain signals by controlling these threat-based cues from the "top down" (Bishop, 2007; Larson et al., 2006).

The phobic patient can be taught that the slower but smarter cortex needs a chance to realistically assess and override the error message given by the rapidly firing amygdala. This message is most effective when presented and discussed in the waking state and then subsequently reinforced in a more experiential manner with hypnotic suggestions to allow the "smart" part of the brain to be in charge in phobic situations. A sample script for these suggestions titled "The Cortex Knows Best" can be found in Spiegel (2014), demonstrating how suggestions for neuroplasticity were used in a case of bridge phobia. These suggestions can readily be modified and applied when working with patients who are afraid to fly. Suggestions are given for both: (a) allowing the smart part of the brain to catch up and override the inaccurate amygdala response and (b) experiencing and facilitating the changes in the way the brain is now functioning.

CASE EXAMPLE

Katherine is an intelligent, vivacious 50-year-old attorney and mother of two daughters who requested hypnosis to help her overcome the fear of flying. She denied having any other phobias, but admitted to being a chronic worrier in connection with her family's health and well-being. Approximately 10 years ago, Katherine sought psychotherapy to work on both family of origin issues and conflict with her husband. Katherine and her husband have a loving marriage, but she had been frustrated by his inability to be more emotionally demonstrative. She also felt resentment that he did not share equitably in household tasks and family responsibilities. She found therapy to be extremely helpful in reducing her anxiety and increasing her confidence in expressing her feelings.

When Katherine was single, she enjoyed domestic travel and also flew with her husband to France on their honeymoon. However, this changed when her children were born and she was obsessed with how traumatized they would be if something happened to her. This increased sense of vulnerability became connected with anxiety about flying. When their youngest daughter was 5 years old, Katherine needed to fly to Florida to visit her mother who had suffered a sudden heart attack. It was a very emotionally unsettling time as Katherine was both afraid her mother would die and worried about leaving her family behind. The flight to Florida was uneventful but during the return flight there was bad weather and a great deal of turbulence. At that time, Katherine experienced her first panic attack, and was convinced she was going to die and never see her family again. She was deeply shaken and relieved when she landed and vowed not to fly again.

When her youngest daughter went to college, Katherine started rethinking her self-imposed travel restrictions. When the family began discussing the possibility of a trip to Europe, both daughters started trying to encourage her. These events were the catalyst for her deciding to pursue treatment.

During the initial assessment, I inquired as to the precise nature of her fears. Although she had been very concerned about terrorist attacks since 9/11, she realized that was not the source of her fear of flying. Katherine's primary anxiety was focused on her fear of having a severe panic attack in the event of turbulence. There was a very strong somatic component to her experience of anxiety including dry mouth and racing heart. She was afraid that if there was persistent turbulence during the flight, her heart might beat so rapidly that it would trigger a heart attack. Although she knew about distraction and breathing techniques, she did not feel confident that she could manage her anxiety on a long flight.

Based on the assessment, my treatment plan included the following components: self-hypnosis and building self-soothing skills, psychoeducation about anxiety and flight, ego-strengthening, imaginal exposure both with hypnosis and YouTube footage, cognitive reframing, mindfulness training, and utilization of neuroscience metaphors to modulate amygdala reactivity.

We met for a total of eight sessions. Katherine was very motivated and said that she found the self-soothing training to be the most important skill in our work. She enjoyed the experience of self-hypnosis, but preferred to practice with hypnosis recordings that were made in the sessions. One of the hypnosis sessions included a hypnotic rehearsal of the experience on the day of the flight using her newly learned skills. I introduced the concept of selective perception to prepare her for the experience. During that session, I brought in examples of figure-ground drawings to illustrate how we only see a portion of what is in the picture. That theme was extended to seeing how she could shift from her habitual way of noticing anxiety-producing triggers to noticing the ordinariness of the experience. We also used future time projection in which she imagined herself sitting in her comfortable living room looking through photo albums of the wonderful vacations abroad she had taken with her family.

After the sixth session, she was comfortable enough to purchase tickets for a family trip to London. She got a prescription for a benzodiazepine from her physician, which she said felt like an insurance policy. After the vacation, she came in for a follow-up session where she reported that the flight was successful and that she never even considered taking the medicine. There were a couple of turbulent events during the flight, during which time she had some anxiety, but was able to manage it well. She focused on noticing how unaffected the flight attendants and other passengers appeared to be. Katherine was actually glad that there was some turbulence because it enabled her to see that she could manage it successfully. After her trip, she sent me an e-mail to tell me how relieved she was to have flown successfully and been able to enjoy this vacation. Although she still felt some anxiety when she thought about flying again, Katherine proudly said that she wouldn't let it stop her from future air travel.

TRANSCRIPT: HYPNOSIS FOR FEAR OF FLYING

This transcript illustrates how hypnotic suggestion can be used in support of the specific elements that will be beneficial to the patient. In this case, the goal was to help build self-soothing skills, reframe a "revved up" feeling as excitement rather than anxiety, modify reactivity to somatic sensations, manage turbulence, and increase a sense of confidence and mastery. Although these may be generic themes, the particular metaphors and images used were derived from salient details in the ongoing therapeutic dialogue. Of particular note in this case is the patient's well-developed capacity to soothe her children and a history of enjoying a number of activities that involve altered somatic sensations such as drinking wine and riding roller coasters.

"Just begin by breathing in comfort . . . exhaling tension . . . in and out. . . . Just allow yourself to filter out any extraneous noise . . . because so much is about selective perception . . . what you are focused on. . . . Just feel a wave of peace flowing over you . . . just feel ease and comfort in every breath . . . and letting yourself focus on some of the good things . . . like the excitement about the trip ahead. . . . You know so many sensations that we have of excitement and anxiety can feel similar . . . of having your heart beat quickly . . . breathing more shallowly . . . can be a sign of anxiety . . . but can also be a sign of being pumped and

excited . . . as you look forward to this trip . . . as you think, feel, and imagine how wonderful it will be . . . to be building these amazing memories with your children . . . seeing things together . . . seeing through their eyes so many of the things that will be very special.

Remembering that your body feels the sensations and your mind makes sense of them. . . . If all of a sudden your he ad felt a little weird that could make you anxious . . . but if your head felt a little weird after you enjoyed a glass or two of wine, you'd say 'Yes, that wine is giving me a little buzz' . . . and experience it in a positive way . . . enjoying the pleasure that comes from a shift in your experience. So you know that there is that part of your brain that registers fear . . . and you've learned today that it's called the amygdala . . . but then there's the smart part of your brain . . . the part of your brain that knows best . . . the cortex . . . and it's driven by reality and wisdom and knowledge . . . that can over-rule the knee-jerk reaction of the amygdala. So as you sit here you feel a wave of peace flowing over you . . . knowing it's your time . . . the world can stand still . . . be aware of your breath . . . of the sensations in your body if you feel warm or cool . . . the mindful experience of just being in the present moment . . . perhaps feeling that time is slowing down just a bit . . . feeling that wave of peace flowing over you . . . from the top of your head . . . down to your toes . . . a wave of calm and ease . . . enjoying the stillness . . . and accepting if your mind . . . your thoughts speed up or slow down . . . or stay just as they are . . . easy comfortable calm. . . calm and quiet . . . enjoying your ability to shift to this calm feeling . . . at will . . . whenever you so choose.

One of the skills and strengths we've talked about today is your ability to use your wisdom to weather different kinds of bumps . . . the ups and downs in the lives of your children when they were younger . . . and you've talked about how over the years you've seen your kids get really upset . . . when one of your sons was scared of the dark . . . or would wake up at night after having bad dreams . . . and you could be so calming and reassuring . . . with a hug . . . and your comforting voice . . . and tell him that you know it feels so real . . . but it's just a dream . . . and with

your very reassuring manner you could soothe him back to sleep . . . so easily . . . so naturally . . . or the time your other son was terrified of thunderstorms . . . you used words to show the difference between safe and not safe . . . your children looked to you as the voice of wisdom . . . and you were always able to sense their fear . . . and their sense of panic . . . perhaps you are beginning to form a picture of that in your mind right now . . . can you picture yourself talking to one of your children . . . [nods yes] . . . good . . . and you can notice that it is your words and your manner . . . that you were able to explain that the the difference between feeling something is scary and checking if it really is dangerous . . . helping them know the difference . . . because there may be times when the feelings of alarm do signal that you do something different . . . like knowing it is dangerous to be out in the open or under a tree during a lightning storm . . . you always had that talent to guide them in terms of the difference between dangerous and safe . . . with your calm manner . . . and your years of wisdom and experience . . . your children knew to trust you . . . when you said 'Don't worry' . . . you'll be good . . . you'll be just fine . . . and with those words . . . you were helping them override the reaction of the amygdala . . . even though you may not have known that was exactly what you were doing . . . you could reassure your kids who felt panicky . . . and you help them to modify those feelings and turn them into something else . . . and you watched how they began to learn that some things that initially felt scary no longer began to feel natural . . . thanks to you . . . you knew how to soothe them.

That soothing part can help you as well . . . when your inner alarm is going off but you know it is safe . . . when you are flying and you notice a shift . . . you feel scared even though your wise self tells you that you are safe . . . your body is feeling the sensations but your mind is making sense of them . . . so that wise soothing part can tell you that even though it feels bumpy . . . you're going to be just fine . . . it's bumpy but safe. And you can also allow somebody who is very wise to guide you . . . pilots with years of experience . . . and it's more than the individual pilots . . . even the FAA . . . all the information that you have read on their website . . .

explaining that turbulence is nothing more than an aggravating nuisance . . . it may feel scary but it's normal . . . the pilot knows it is completely normal . . . and the wise part of your mind knows that as well.

So imagine yourself now on that plane . . . you already know which section you're sitting in so you can see that now. . . . And let me know you have that image by saying so or by nodding your head. [I've got it] . . . Good . . . Feel the plane take off . . . and shift your way of thinking from 'Please let there not be any turbulence' . . . to the idea that turbulence is a nuisance but normal . . . just like every time you're in a car . . . you're driving along some bumpy road . . . or even go over a pothole . . . but we don't think about that so much . . . and the pilots will tell you that even in very powerful turbulence the plane remains strong . . . and upright . . . it will be annoying . . . but the plane continues on its path. So rather than fighting and praying that there are no bumps . . . welcome them . . . because every time a bump comes . . . every time there is turbulence . . . every time you say 'bring it on . . . I can take it' . . . it takes away the power of that turbulence to push that button in your amygdala . . . as you get your wise mind to say, 'That is a false alarm . . . bumpy but safe' . . . three little words to remember. So that turbulence is like that bully you are afraid of . . . running from and hiding . . . but when you stand up to the turbulence . . . and say 'OK . . . this may feel weird . . . but my smart brain is telling me that I'm safe . . . the pilots are telling me that I'm safe . . . it's annoying . . . but this is a safe flight and I'm fine.' So imagine allowing that smart part of your brain to talk to your amygdala . . . and say I know you're scared but I'm the boss . . . and I know best . . . just like you know when you talk to your clients that they need reassurance . . . and I'll bet that what has happened when people are with you for a long time . . . is that they probably learn to trust what you say . . . because you stayed with them through the bumps . . . and they have learned that they are okay. . . .

So experience that flight . . . doing the things that you enjoy doing . . . talking or reading or watching a movie . . . and on these big planes it's kind of like sitting in a big living room . . . and

most of the time it's really smooth . . . most of the time you can walk around without even having the sensation of being in a plane . . . but when you hear the flight attendant or the captain get on the air and say 'We are about to hit a little turbulence . . . please go back to your seat and fasten your seat belts' . . . you might even close your eyes and remember some of the fun times you have had in amusement parks on the roller coaster . . . remembering how you didn't fight the sensations but actually welcomed them . . . letting yourself enjoy the ups and downs . . . feeling the thrill . . . because if you know it is safe . . . your mind will change the meaning of the sensations . . . to something different and actually enjoyable . . . and before long the bully will be gone . . . he won't need to bother you anymore . . . bumpy but safe . . . and this thought can be a thought that comes to you often . . . so that on that day when you fly . . . you'll know that you're going to be just fine . . . bumpy but safe . . . perfectly safe . . . and you might even be surprised to see . . . that you will enjoy the flight . . . you will enjoy that down time . . . nothing to do but read or talk or watch a movie . . . or do whatever it is that you most enjoy . . . and before long the plane lands . . . and you can feel so good about what you have just done . . . as you get ready for this wonderful adventure . . . and the sense of strength . . . and focus . . . to know that you are free to travel . . . anytime you want . . . enjoying the experience . . . and the sense of adventure . . . that you now can continue to build. . . .

But for now it's time to return . . . as the scene begins to fade . . . and you get ready to come back to your ordinary state of being . . . and you know how to do that . . . easily and comfortably . . . as you follow the numbers back from 5 to 4 . . . as you take a deep energizing breath . . . from 4 to 3 . . . as you move hands and fingers, feet and toes . . . from 3 to 2 as you start to move around a bit . . . and from 2 to 1 as your eyes open and you come all the way back."

CONCLUSION

Aviophobia is a specific situational phobia for which people frequently seek therapy. Fearful flyers are a diagnostically diverse group, including those who (a) are fearful but whose symptoms don't fully meet the *DSM-5* criteria for aviophobia, (b) meet the criteria for aviophobia, (c) have a primary diagnosis of agoraphobia, (d) have multiple phobias, and (e) are diagnosed with additional Axis I and Axis II disorders. As a result, it is not surprising that when it comes to treatment, one size does not fit all. Although experts agree that exposure therapy is the "gold standard" for specific phobia, many individuals fail to make rapid progress or achieve only partial success with standard treatments. Clinicians need to personalize therapy to increase retention and improve outcomes. Hypnosis can be used in a variety of ways to amplify techniques and target the specific elements that keep the phobia active. Whenever possible, clinicians should individualize suggestions and metaphors to reflect the unique interests, issues, and themes of the patient.

Fearful flyers now have the promise of not only affective and behavioral changes that result from therapy but also the functional and structural brain changes that accompany the creation of new neural networks (Cozolino, 2010; Kandel, 1998). This concept of neuroplasticity can be translated into simplified terms that also lead to a more hopeful outlook for phobia sufferers. In clinical practice, I utilize hypnotic imagery and metaphors to facilitate this process as patients imagine neural networks recalibrating from phobic to non-phobic patterns.

REFERENCES

Alpers, G. W. (2010). Avoiding treatment failures in specific phobias. In M. Otto, & S. Hoffman (Eds.), *Avoiding treatment failures in the anxiety disorders. Series in anxiety and related disorders* (pp. 209–227). New York, NY: Springer Publishing Company.

American Psychiatric Association. (2013). *Diagnostic and statistical manual of mental disorders*. Arlington, VA: American Psychiatric Publishing.

Antony, M. M., & Barlow, D. H. (2002). Specific phobia. In D. Barlow & D. Barlow (Eds.), *The nature and treatment of anxiety and panic* (pp. 380–217). New York, NY: Guilford Press.

Bakal, P. A. (1981). Hypnotherapy for flight phobia. *American Journal of Clinical Hypnosis, 23*(4), 248–251. doi:10.1080/00029157.1981.10404029

Bishop, S. J. (2007). Neurocognitive mechanisms of anxiety: An integrative account. *Trends in Neurocognitive Science, 11*, 307–316.

Botella, C., Osma, J., Garcia Palacios, A., Quero, S., & Baños, R. M. (2004). Treatment of flying phobia using virtual reality: Data from a 1-year follow-up using a multiple baseline design. *Clinical Psychology & Psychotherapy, 11*, 311–323.

Carbonell, D. (2003). Fly the fearful skies: Acceptance based methods of overcoming fear of flying. Presentation at ADAA 29th Annual Conference.

Choy, Y., Fyer, A. J., & Lipsitz, J. D. (2007). Treatment of specific phobia in adults. *Clinical Psychology Review, 27*(3), 266–286. doi:10.1016/j.cpr.2006.10.002

Cozolino, L. (2010). *The neuroscience of psychotherapy* (2nd ed.). New York, NY: W. W. Norton.

Crawford, H. J., & Barabasz, A. F. (1993). Phobias and intense fears: Facilitating their treatment with hypnosis. In J. W. Rhue, S. J. Lynn, & I. Kirsch (Eds.), *Handbook of clinical hypnosis* (pp. 311–338). Washington, DC: American Psychological Association.

Côté, S., & Bouchard, S. (2008). Virtual reality exposure for phobias: A critical review. *Journal of CyberTherapy & Rehabilitation, 1*, 75–91.

da Costa, R. T., Sardinha, A., & Nardi, A. E. (2008). Reality exposure in the treatment of fear of flying. *Aviation, Space, and Environmental Medicine, 79*(9), 899–903.

Dean, R. D., & Whitaker, K. M. (1982). Fear of flying: Impact on the US air travel industry. *Journal of Travel Research, 27*, 7–17.

Deyoub, P. L., & Epstein, S. J. (1977). Short-term hypnotherapy for the treatment of flight phobia: A case report. *American Journal of Clinical Hypnosis, 19*(4), 251–254. doi:10.1080/00029157.1977.10403885

Diment, A. D. (1981). Fear of flying: Case study of a phobia. *Australian Journal of Clinical & Experimental Hypnosis, 9*, 5–8.

Eifert, G. H., & Forsyth, J. P. (2005). *Acceptance and commitment therapy for anxiety disorders: A practitioner's treatment guide to using mindfulness, acceptance, and values-based behavior change*. Oakland, CA: New Harbinger Publications.

Ekeberg, O., Seeberg, I., & Ellertsen, B. B. (1989). The prevalence of flight anxiety in Norway. *Nordic Journal of Psychiatry, 43*, 443–448.

Gerardi, M., Cukor, J., Difede, J., Rizzo, A., & Rothbaum, B. O. (2010). Virtual reality therapy for post traumatic stress disorder and other anxiety disorders. *Current Psychiatry Reports, 12*(4), 298–305. doi:10.1007/s11920-010-0128-4

Hammond, D. C. (Ed.). (1990). *Anxiety and phobic disorders in handbook of hypnotic suggestions and metaphors* (pp. 153–155). New York, NY: W.W. Norton.

Hammond, D. C., Haskins-Bartsch, C., McGhee, M., & Grant, C. W. (1987). The use of fractionation in self-hypnosis. *American Journal of Clinical Hypnosis, 30*(2), 119–124. doi:10.1080/00029157.1987.10404171

Hirsch, J. A. (2012). Virtual reality exposure therapy and hypnosis for flying phobia in a treatment-resistant patient: A case report. *American Journal of Clinical Hypnosis, 55*(2), 168–173. doi:10.1080/00029157.2011.639587

Hood, H. K., & Antony, M. M. (2012). Evidence-based assessment and treatment of specific phobias in adults. In *Intensive one-session treatment of specific phobias* (pp. 317–333). New York, NY: Springer Publishing Company

Howard, W. A., Murphy, S. M., & Clarke, J. C. (1983). The nature and treatment of fear of flying: A controlled investigation. *Behavior Therapy, 14*(4), 557–567.

Humphreys, A. (1986). Review of the literature on the adjunctive use of hypnosis in behavior therapy: 1970–1980. *British Journal of Clinical and Experimental Hypnosis, 3*, 95–101.

Ito, H., & Lee, D. (2004). Assessing the impact of September 11 terrorist attacks on U.S. airline demand. Retrieved from http://www.brown.edu/Departments/Economics/Papers/2003/2003-16_paper.pdf

Jaffee, M. S. (2005). The neurology of aviation, underwater, and space environments. *Neurologic Clinics, 23*(2), 541–552. doi:10.1016/j.ncl.2004.12.009

Kandel, E. R. (1998). A new intellectual framework for psychiatry. *American Journal of Psychiatry, 155*(4), 457–469. doi:10.1176/ajp.155.4.457

Kim, S., Palin, F., Anderson, P., Edwards, S., Lindner, G., & Rothbaum, B. O. (2008). Use of skills learned in CBT for fear of flying: Managing flying anxiety after September 11th. *Journal of Anxiety Disorders, 22*(2), 301–309. doi:10.1016/j.janxdis.2007.02.006

Kirsch, I., Montgomery, G. H., & Sapirstein, G. (1995). Hypnosis as an adjunct to cognitive behavioral psychotherapy: A meta-analysis. *Journal of Consulting and Clinical Psychology, 63*(2), 214–220.

Krijn, M., Emmelkamp, P. M., Olafsson, R. P., Bouwman, M., Van Gerwen, L. J., Spinhoven, P., . . . van der Mast, C. A. (2007). Fear of flying treatment methods: Virtual reality exposure vs. cognitive behavioral therapy. *Aviation, Space, and Environmental Medicine, 78*(2), 121–128.

Laker, M. (2012). Specific phobia: flight. *Activitas Nervosa Superior, 54*(3/4), 108.

Larson, C. L., Schaefer, H. S., Siegle, G. J., Jackson, C. A., Anderle, M. J., & Davidson, R. J. (2006). Fear is fast in phobic individuals: Amygdala activation in response to fear relevant stimuli. *Biological Psychiatry, 60*(4), 410–417. doi:10.1016/j.biopsych.2006.03.079

Maltby, N., Kirsch, I., Mayers, M., & Allen, G. J. (2002). Virtual reality exposure therapy for the treatment of fear of flying: A controlled investigation. *Journal of Consulting and Clinical Psychology, 5*, 1112–1118.

Marks, R. (2012). *Introduction to Shannon sampling and interpolation theory*. New York, NY: Springer Science & Business Media.

McNally, R. J., & Loura, C. E. (1992). Fear of flying in agoraphobia and simple phobia: distinguishing features. *Journal of Anxiety Disorders, 6*, 319–324.

Milosevic, I., & Radomsky, A. S. (2008). Safety behaviour does not necessarily interfere with exposure therapy. *Behaviour Research and Therapy, 46*(10), 1111–1118. doi:10.1016/j.brat.2008.05.011

Mühlberger, A., Hermann, M. J., Wiedemann, G. C., Ellgring, H., & Pauli, P. (2001). Repeated exposure of flight phobics to flights in virtual reality. *Behaviour Research and Therapy, 39*(9), 1033–1050.

Oakes, M., & Bor, R. (2010a). The psychology of fear of flying (part I): A critical evaluation of current perspectives on the nature, prevalence and etiology of fear of flying. *Travel Medicine and Infectious Disease, 8*, 327–338.

Oakes, M., & Bor, R. (2010b). The psychology of fear of flying (part II): A critical evaluation of current perspectives on approaches to treatment. *Travel Medicine and Infectious Disease, 8*, 339–363.

Powers, M. B., & Emmelkamp, P. M. (2008). Virtual reality exposure therapy for anxiety disorders: A meta-analysis. *Journal of Anxiety Disorders, 22*(3), 561–569. doi:10.1016/j.janxdis.2007.04.006

Reiss, S. (1991). Expectancy model of fear, anxiety, and panic. *Clinical Psychology Review, 11*(2), 141–153.

Rothbaum, B. O., & Hodges, L. F. (1999). The use of virtual reality exposure in the treatment of anxiety disorders. *Behavior Modification, 23*(4), 507–552.

Rothbaum, B. O., Anderson, P., Zimand, E., Hodges, L., Lang, D., & Wilson, J. (2006). Virtual reality exposure therapy and standard (in vivo) exposure therapy in the treatment of fear of flying. *Behavior Therapy, 37*(1), 80–90. doi:10.1016/j.beth.2005.04.004

Rothbaum, B. O., Hodges, L., Smith, S., Lee, J. H., & Price, L. (2000). A controlled study of virtual reality exposure therapy for the fear of flying. *Journal of Consulting and Clinical Psychology, 68*(6), 1020–1026.

Roy, S. (2003). State of the art of virtual reality therapy (VRT) in phobic disorders. *PsychoNology Journal, 1*, 176–183.

Silverman, D., & Gendreau, M. (2009). Medical issues associated with commercial flights. *The Lancet, 373*, 2067–2077.

Spiegel, H., & Spiegel, D. (1978). *Trance and treatment: Clinical uses of hypnosis*. New York, NY: Basic Books.

Spiegel, D., Frischholz, E. J., Maruffi, B., & Spiegel, H. (1981). Hypnotic responsivity and the treatment of flying phobia. *American Journal of Clinical Hypnosis, 23*(4), 239–247. doi:10.1080/00029157.1981.10404028

Spiegel, S. B. (2012). The use of online resources in the treatment of three cases of simple phobia. *American Journal of Clinical Hypnosis*, *55*(2), 174–183. doi:10.1080/00029157.2012.677962

Spiegel, S. B. (2014). Current issues in the treatment of specific phobia: Recommendations for innovative applications of hypnosis. *American Journal of Clinical Hypnosis*, *56*(4), 389–404. doi:10.1080/00029157.2013.801009

Stinson, F. S., Dawson, D. A., Patricia Chou, S., Smith, S., Goldstein, R. B., June Ruan, W., & Grant, B. F. (2007). The epidemiology of *DSM-IV* specific phobia in the USA: Results from the National Epidemiologic Survey on Alcohol and Related Conditions. *Psychological Medicine*, *37*(7), 1047–1060. doi:10.1017/S0033291707000086

Van Gerwen, L. J., & Diekstra, R. F. (2000). Fear of flying treatment programs for passengers: an international review. *Aviation, space, and environmental medicine*, *71*, 430–437.

van Gerwen, L. J., Spinhoven, P., Diekstra, R. F. W., & van Dyck, R. (2002). Multicomponentstandardized treatment programs for fear of flying: description and effectiveness. *Cognitive and Behavioral Practice*, *9*(2), 138–149.

Van Gerwen, L. J., Spinhoven, P., Diekstra, R. F., & Van Dyck, R. (1997). People who seek help for fear of flying: Typology of flying phobics. *Behavior Therapy*, *28*, 237–251.

vanden Bogaerde, A., & De Raedt, R. (2008). Cognitive vulnerability in fear of flying: The role of anxiety sensitivity. *Depression and Anxiety*, *25*(9), 768–773. doi:10.1002/da.20359

Van Gerwen, L. J., Diekstra, R. F., Arondeus, J. M., & Wolfger, R. (2004). Fear of flying treatment programs for passengers: An international update. *Travel Medicine and Infectious Disease*, *2*(1), 27–35. doi:10.1016/j.tmaid.2004.01.002

Wilhelm, F. H., & Roth, W. T. (1997). Acute and delayed effects of alprazolam on flight phobics during the exposure. *Behavior Research and Therapy*, *35*, 831–841.

Wolitzky-Taylor, K. B., Horowitz, J. D., Powers, M. B., & Telch, M. J. (2008). Psychological approaches in the treatment of specific phobias: A meta-analysis. *Clinical Psychology Review*, *28*(6), 1021–1037. doi:10.1016/j.cpr.2008.02.007

Flow and Peak Experiences

Juliette Bowers

Flow was conceptualized by Csikszentmihalyi (1975) as a result of research in the area of happiness and creativity. Flow is a state of absorption and concentration in the current moment. It involves intrinsic motivation and joy in the task at hand as well as a sense of balance in one's ability to accomplish the task. These features make it an optimum state of functioning that can benefit many people.

Flow consists of nine different components. Of these nine components, three areas emerge: prerequisites, experiential components, and autotelic experience. Prerequisites for flow include: (a) a challenge–skill balance, (b) clear goals, and (c) unambiguous feedback. These prerequisites set the stage for reduced anxiety and reduced boredom, finding a place in between balance and understanding. Experiential components make up the next components with: (d) loss of self-consciousness, (e) action-awareness merging, (f) transformation of time, (g) sense of control, and (h) concentration in the task at hand. These components describe the experience of what flow is like once it is achieved. The final component, (i) autotelic experience, describes a sense of intrinsic joy and motivation in an activity (Nakamura & Csikszentmihalyi, 2002).

Csikszentmihalyi (1990) proposes that flow is linked with perceived quality of life. Flow has been studied with a number of populations from different ages to different interests. Studies with an older adult population suggest that people with higher cognitive resources will be more likely to experience flow on cognitive tasks. On the other end of this spectrum, adults with fewer cognitive resources experience higher levels of flow on less cognitive tasks. This indicates that people gain from an activity that is matched to their strengths and reiterates the importance of challenge–skill balance. The authors suggest that stimulating cognition early in life will encourage people to enjoy cognitive tasks

more, which can be nurtured through the life span and then further utilized in older adulthood (Payne, Jackson, Noh, & Stine-Morrow, 2011). Another area of the life span in which flow has been studied is with college students and studying behaviors. Cermakova, Moneta, and Spada (2010) studied attentional control with flow as a mediator for attentional control and approach to studying. The researchers suggest that flow can have an influence in the learning process by creating environments that are conducive to a flow state (Cermakova et al., 2010).

A current increase in research on video game performance and flow suggests a wide use for the construct of flow. While a great amount research has studied people who have higher arousal when performing their tasks, flow can still be found in tasks that require less arousal. Research with flow and video game use complements the perceived ability and perceived demand of flow by reporting a correlation between hours of experience and frequency of flow. There is also an emphasis on the importance of intrinsic motivation (Seger & Potts, 2012). Flow has also been studied in relation with piano players, discussing the ability for performance tasks to involve high attention and positive valence, indicating a high likelihood of a flow state (de Manzano, Theorell, Harmat, & Ullén, 2010). Other areas in which flow has shown a correlation with positive performance are chess playing, writing, and various performing arts (Csikszentmihalyi & Csikszentmihalyi, 1992).

Flow can be measured using the Dispositional Flow Scale (Jackson & Eklund, 2002) and the Flow State Scale (Jackson & Eklund, 2002). The scales look at the frequency in which a person enters a flow state, both in a domain overall and from a state perspective. The scales measure the construct of flow as well as measuring each of the components of flow. Measuring flow proneness allows clinicians and researchers to understand the client's ability to enter a flow state in a specific task. Different tasks may encourage more flow proneness for a given individual. This could be based on the prerequisites and the person's perceptions or an ability to have the experiential components present. Hypnosis can help to improve a person's ability to enter a flow state by inducing a hypnotic state and giving suggestions for components of flow (Elkins, 2014). These suggestions can be to enhance perception of an experience, or to create an expectancy to have these experiences in the future. It can also be useful to use hypnosis as a mechanism to pair a trigger with the experience of flow (Pates, Oliver, & Maynard, 2001).

RESEARCH

Athletics has a strong focus on peak performance and flow. Athletes from swimmers, cyclists, golfers, basketball players, and tennis players have been researched in regards to flow (Bernier, Thienot, Codron, & Fournier, 2009; Koehn, Morris, & Watt, 2013; Lindsay, Maynard, & Thomas, 2005; Pates, Maynard, & Westbury, 2001; Pates, Oliver, & Maynard, 2001). Athletes are also one of the few populations where research has been shown to work with hypnosis inducing the flow. Research performed to study the use of hypnosis to trigger flow states in sport performance have been conducted with golfers, cyclists, and basketball players (Lindsay et al., 2005; Pates, Maynard, & Westbury, 2001; Pates, Oliver, & Maynard, 2001). Studies using this strategy report using a stage approach to the intervention. The first stage includes a progressive muscle relaxation script followed by the second stage, which is the hypnotic induction. The third stage involves a regression to a previous flow state experience, and best competitive performance, using as many sensory cues as the participants can recall. At this time, a natural trigger, such as a golf club handle, is paired with the performance. Following this, the participant will be given suggestions for alertness, followed by training to judge the control over the paired trigger. Results from these studies have shown the utility of using hypnosis to enhance peak performance

(Lindsay et al., 2005; Pates, 2013; Pates & Cowen, 2013; Pates, Cummings, & Maynard, 2002; Pates, Oliver, & Maynard, 2001).

CASE EXAMPLE

A 28-year-old male presented with concerns about his ability to be productive in his workplace. The man cited primary concerns as boredom, feeling unchallenged, feelings of unhappiness, and a desire to be more effective at work. None of these complaints reached a clinical level of significance and a recent evaluation at work revealed that the client was working at or above his expected level. When asked about his current expectations for himself, the client stated that in college, he was able to spend long hours studying when time seemed to slow down. He described a state of confidence in his ability to perform his tasks and an enjoyment executing these tasks. The client reported that he would feel more productive at work if he could have these feelings at work. Following the intake session, four to five sessions of hypnosis were conducted to help increase his drive to produce and improve optimum performance. Sessions included a relaxation-based hypnotic induction with suggestions for increased motivation, challenge–skill balance, and a sense of control.

The following is a sample of a script that may be included over a multisession treatment such as for the previous client.

TRANSCRIPT

When determining the suggestions for a particular client, it is important to note the client's strengths and weaknesses. Does the client appear to not meet the prerequisites for flow and therefore is not experiencing it? Does the client understand what it is like to be in a state that involves the experiential components? Does the client need the intrinsic motivation and joy in the task to enter a flow state? By asking these questions, suggestions can be created that will guide the peak performance experience for the client. The following transcripts were created with the concept of four to five therapy sessions that could each focus on a different skill. The appropriate skill for each session will depend on the client.

"As you continue to relax and settle into the chair, I want you to notice the relaxing of your mind. Notice how simple it is in this relaxed state to be present with your mind and your body. What you are doing and what you are thinking are simply one together . . . when you allow your brain to relax and to trust your body and your body to relax and trust your brain, your instincts take over. Instincts such as your breath as you inhale and exhale. Your body can do this with more complex tasks such as walking and talking, driving and listening to the radio. When your brain relaxes and trusts your body and your body relaxes and trusts your brain, your body is capable of functioning highly in the moment. As you sit relaxed, notice again how your action and awareness are merged and neither is fighting for control. . . .

And, perhaps you could begin to focus on your breathing . . . focus on the way that the air feels as it passes through your nose . . . the pressure of the air, the timing of the air . . . notice the way that your chest moves up and down . . . up and down. As you become aware of your breathing, I would like you to pick a part of your body and to focus on that part. Notice the sensations that occur at that one spot, whether it is warm or cool, whether anything is touching that spot. And notice how well you can focus on that one spot. When you feel comfortable with the sensations that are there, I would like you to expand your focus, noticing more and more of your whole body . . . the feelings of the chair on your body, the feelings that your breathing has on your body. And notice your ability to focus on your whole body, how easy it is . . . focusing on your body is much like concentrating at [insert relevant task] *by taking your time, by recognizing this . . . you can believe in your ability to concentrate just as well at work as you have at focusing on your body. And knowing this gives you a sense of confidence in that ability.*

Now . . . as you continue to go even deeper into this hypnotic state, you may be able to recognize how confidence is like driving a car for a long time. I would like you to imagine that you are driving a car . . . this car is one that you are very

comfortable with and have been driving for a long time . . . you know the brakes and the acceleration, and you especially know the steering in this car. You feel very comfortable driving along in this car, turning and steering, feeling in control of the vehicle. Perhaps you can imagine how life might be like driving this car . . . turning, accelerating, and decelerating at will . . . feeling in control of each situation because you know the vehicle well and feel comfortable with it. As you imagine this sense of control in your car, you feel a sense of control wash over you so that you may believe in your ability to maintain this control.

And now, I would like you to think of [specific task]. *As you think about this task, continue to relax, and perhaps notice how the task makes you feel. Does it make you feel nervous? . . . Notice whether or not you feel prepared to complete this task. It might feel nice at this time, to let those thoughts drift through your mind without care. Perhaps you could begin to imagine them as clouds drifting by on your mind. These thoughts are going to drift away. The clouds may begin as dark and dreary, drifting along with your concerns . . . as they drift along, you may notice that the clouds begin to become lighter, more white, more fluffy, and as you notice the changes in the clouds, notice that your thoughts and feelings have changed, too. You may have thoughts such as 'I am capable of this task' or perhaps 'I feel prepared for what is to come' . . . these thoughts continue to float by, making you feel lighter and more relaxed. When asked about* [specific task] *you can have these same light feelings. You feel these doubts drift away. Though the task is challenging, you feel capable of performing it well.*

Now, I want you to imagine yourself performing [specific task] *. . . as you imagine yourself performing this task, begin to notice the feelings of productivity that can occur while performing this task, notice the work you get done and the ease at which you accomplish it, perhaps a feeling of success may begin to grow inside of you. Notice the steady pace at which you are able to work. And as you notice this productivity, begin to notice the time, notice that time seems to slow when you are productive. More and more work is completed and yet, time does not seem to be flying by. You feel capable when you notice how much work you* *have accomplished in so little time, it is as if your sense of time has changed and you no longer feel a tie between the amount of work you accomplish and the time that has been spent.*

Continue to think about [the task] *that you are working on . . . what do you enjoy about this task? Think about the parts of this task that bring you joy . . . perhaps the feeling of accomplishment as you complete a part of the task or perhaps the success you feel at being able to manage the task on your own. Let yourself sit with these feelings and absorb the joy you have in your performance. As you sit with these feelings, you may feel an increased motivation to perform the task; just allow this to happen, and as you perform these tasks at* [work] *you will notice an increased motivation there as well."*

CONCLUSION

Flow is an experience that occurs when a person is performing at his or her most effective in regards to mental energy. People who have entered a flow state are intrinsically motivated and enjoy the experience. This peak experience involves a state of absorption where one experiences a balance between his expected challenge in the task and his ability level. There are currently nine identified components of flow: challenge–skill balance, clear goals, unambiguous feedback, action-awareness merging, concentration on the task at hand, sense of control, loss of self-consciousness, transformation of time, and the autotelic experience (Csikszentmihalyi, 2000).

Entering a flow state can be of benefit to people in many fields and many stages of life. Research suggests that older adults can benefit from flow (Payne et al., 2011) as well as many students (Cermakova et al., 2010) and performers from pianists (de Manzano et al., 2010), to golfers (Pates, Oliver, & Maynard, 2001), to video-gamers (Seger & Potts, 2012). Currently, hypnosis has been used to help create triggers for flow in athletes so that they may be able to pair previous flow states and recall them using the trigger (Lindsay et al., 2005; Pates, 2013; Pates & Cowen, 2013; Pates et al., 2002; Pates, Maynard, & Westbury, 2001). Using

hypnosis can be a productive way to help patients enter a flow state and experience peak performance in many areas of their lives, improving motivation and enjoyment.

CLINICAL SUMMARY

- Hypnosis sessions should be structured around the individual experience of clients. Ask clients about possible previous experiences with flow and tailor sessions around their needs.
- With so many components of flow, it is important to determine suggestions around the client's strengths and weaknesses so as not to overwhelm the client with suggestions.
- Psychological barriers such as depression or anxiety should be addressed before attempting to create a peak experience.

REFERENCES

Bernier, M., Thienot, E., Codron, R., & Fournier, J. (2009). Mindfulness and acceptance approaches in sport performance. *Journal of Clinical Sports Psychology*, *4*, 320–333.

Cermakova, L., Moneta, G. B., & Spada, M. M. (2010). Dispositional flow as a mediator of the relationships between attentional control and approaches to studying during academic examination preparation. *Educational Psychology: An International Journal of Experimental Educational Psychology*, *30*(5), 495–511.

Csikszentmihalyi, M. (1975). *Beyond boredom and anxiety: The experience of play in work and games.* San Francisco, CA: Jossey-Bass.

Csikszentmihalyi, M. (1990). *Flow: The psychology of optimal experience.* New York, NY: Harper Perrennial.

Csikszentmihalyi, M. (2000). The contribution of flow to positive psychology. In M. E. Seligman & J. Gillham (Eds.), *The science of optimism and hope.* Philadelphia, PA: Templeton Foundation Press.

Csikszentmihalyi, M., & Csikszentmihalyi, I. (1992). *Optimal experience: Psychological studies of flow in consciousness.* Cambridge, UK: Cambridge University Press.

de Manzano, O., Theorell, T., Harmat, L., & Ullén, F. (2010). The psychophysiology of flow during piano playing. *Emotion*, *10*(3), 301–311. doi:10.1037/a0018432

Jackson, S. A., & Eklund, R. C. (2002). Assessing flow in physical activity: The Flow State Scale-2 and Dispositional Flow Scale-2. *Journal of Sport and Exercise Psychology, 24,* 133–150.

Koehn, S., Morris, T., & Watt, A. P. (2013). Correlates of dispositional and state flow in tennis competition. *Journal of Applied Sport Psychology, 25*(3), 354–369.

Lindsay, P., Maynard, I., & Thomas, O. (2005). Effects of hypnosis on flow states and cycling performance. *The Sport Psychologist, 19,* 164–177.

Nakamura, J., & Csikszentmihalyi, M. (2002). The concept of flow. In C. R. Snyder & S. J. Lopez (Eds.), *Handbook of positive psychology* (pp. 89–105). Oxford, England: Oxford University Press.

Pates, J. (2013). The effects of hypnosis on an elite senior European tour golfer. *International Journal of Clinical and Experimental Hypnosis, 61*(2), 193–204. doi:10.1080/00207144.2013.753831

Pates, J., & Cowen, A. (2013). The effect of a hypnosis intervention on performance and flow state of an elite golfer: A single subject design. *International Journal of Golf Science, 2,* 43–53.

Pates, J., Cummings, A., & Maynard, I. (2002). The effects of hypnosis on flow states and three-point shooting performance in basketball players. *The Sport Psychologist, 16,* 1–15.

Pates, J., Maynard, I., & Westbury, T. (2001). An investigation into the effects of hypnosis on basketball performance. *Journal of Applied Sport Psychology, 13*(1), 84–102.

Pates, J., Oliver, R., & Maynard, I. (2001). The effects of hypnosis on flow states and golf-putting performance. *Journal of Applied Sport Psychology, 13,* 341–354.

Payne, B. R., Jackson, J. J., Noh, S. R., & Stine-Morrow, E. A. (2011). In the zone: Flow state and cognition in older adults. *Psychology and Aging, 26*(3), 738–743. doi:10.1037/a0022359

Seger, J., & Potts, R. (2012). Personality correlates of psychological flow states in videogame play. *Current Psychology, 31,* 103–121.

Forensic Interviewing and Hypnosis

Graham F. Wagstaff and Jacqueline M. Wheatcroft

The idea that hypnosis might be useful as a forensic interviewing tool gained prominence in the late 1970s and early 1980s when a number of books and articles were published describing the benefits of hypnosis in this context (see, for example, Haward, 1988; Hibbard & Worring, 1981; Reiser, 1980). However, hypnosis has now largely been superseded in this role by the cognitive interview, which has been adopted by a variety of police forces around the world.

EXPERIMENTAL LABORATORY STUDIES OF HYPNOSIS AND MEMORY

If one examines the relevant scientific literature, it is not difficult to see why hypnosis has now lost favor as a forensic interviewing tool. With a few exceptions, there now seems to be a fairly overwhelming body of experimental evidence to indicate that hypnotic procedures do not improve the accuracy of memory to a level above that achievable in motivated nonhypnotic conditions (for reviews, see Erdelyi, 1994; Kebbell & Wagstaff, 1998; McConkey & Sheehan, 1996; Smith, 1983; Steblay & Bothwell, 1994; Wagstaff, 1981, 1983, 1984, 1999a, 1999b). For example, in his seminal overview of the relevant literature, Erdelyi (1994) found that, in some cases, hypnosis did result in increases in recall of correct information, but when such instances occurred, the overall accuracy as determined by the proportion of correct to incorrect responses was not improved. In fact, memory accuracy sometimes deteriorated (i.e., there was a disproportionate increase in errors or confabulations [see e.g., Dinges et al., 1992; Dywan & Bowers, 1983]). Research has also found that hypnotic procedures may encourage witnesses to incorporate more misleading information

into their reports, and to be more confident in their reports generally, including reports of incorrect information, resulting in a "false confidence" effect (McConkey & Sheehan, 1996; Scoboria, Mazzoni, Kirsch, & Milling, 2002; Wagstaff, 1989, 2010; Webert, 2003). Indeed, as a result of expert evidence on this subject, most states in the United States have now enacted a per se exclusion rule, and banned victims and witnesses who have been interviewed with "hypnosis" from giving evidence in court (Webert, 2003). In the UK also, the Home Office has produced guidelines discouraging the use of hypnosis as a police interviewing tool (see Wagstaff, 1988).

The most generally accepted explanation for the hypnotic false-memory effect is that, because of popular expectancies associated with hypnosis (i.e., the view that hypnosis has a magical power to restore lost memories), and pressure brought to bear by the investigating hypnotist to remember more information, "hypnotized" witnesses sometimes adopt a more lax criterion for report (i.e., they become less cautious when reporting). As a result, they tend to report details as correct that they would normally reject on the basis of uncertainty. In support of this explanation, a variety of experimental research has shown that hypnotic confabulations or "pseudo-memories" can be reduced to nonhypnotic levels if subjects are given instructions that lead or invite them to adopt a more cautious criterion for reporting (Wagstaff, 1999a, 1999b; Wagstaff, Cole, Wheatcroft, Anderton, & Madden, 2008; Wagstaff, Wheatcroft, & Jones, 2011).

ANECDOTAL EVIDENCE

However, notwithstanding these considerations, hypnotic investigative interviewing continued to have, and still has, some proponents (McConkey & Sheehan, 1996; Vingoe, 1995). For example, in the UK, when the Home Office first produced guidelines on the use of investigative hypnosis in the late 1980s, the Association of Chief Police Officers alluded to a number of real-life anecdotal cases in which hypnosis had apparently been useful, and suggested that hypnosis might still be applicable in some serious cases where leads are few. Hence, although urging caution, the UK Crown Prosecution Service still explicitly states, "The police will sometimes arrange for a witness to be hypnotized in the hope that he or she will recall further details under hypnosis" (CPS, 2014). Also, in the U.S. Attorneys' Criminal Resource Manual (2014), it states that, "In certain limited cases, the use of forensic hypnosis can be an aid in the investigative process."

But why should real-life "case studies" of the effects of hypnotic interviewing appear to be more impressive than the experimental research findings? One answer may lie in the fact that the procedures adopted by hypnoinvestigators in the field are often very different from those used in routine police interviews, and may produce better results. For example, when interviewing witnesses in real life, hypnoinvestigators tend to adopt a sympathetic nonauthoritarian attitude and attempt to establish trust and rapport with interviewees; these may be particularly important factors if the witness is anxious or traumatized, making it easier for the witness to "open up" and disclose sensitive or disturbing information. Also, unlike in standard police interviews, hypnoinvestigators often employ techniques to provide memory retrieval cues, such as role-playing, picture drawing, recalling in different orders, and context reinstatement. Context reinstatement, or "revivication," which involves encouraging interviewees to report freely everything they can, including thoughts and feelings, has long been established as an effective retrieval aid in its own right (Malpass & Devine, 1981; Wagstaff, 1982). Indeed, there is considerable overlap with some of these features of hypnotic interviewing and the cognitive interview, which, as previously noted, has generally displaced hypnosis as the preferred mode of memory facilitation in police investigations. For example, the cognitive interview uses techniques such as rapport building, "report everything" instructions, focused attention, and context reinstatement (Fisher &

Geiselman, 1992; Fisher, Geiselman, & Amador, 1989; Fisher, Geiselman, Raymond, Jurkevich, & Warhaftig, 1987). Indeed, studies that have directly compared cognitive interview techniques with hypnosis indicate that performance on them is similar (Geiselman, Fisher, Mackinnon, & Holland, 1985; Kebbell & Wagstaff, 1997); however, unlike hypnosis, the majority of the evidence suggests that, in adults, the cognitive interview does not unduly affect accuracy rates, susceptibility to leading questions, or disrupt confidence accuracy relationships (Bekerian & Dennett, 1993; Geiselman, 1996; Geiselman, Fisher, Mackinnon, & Holland, 1986; Kebbell & Wagstaff, 1999; Memon & Bull, 1991; Memon, Holley, Milne, Kohnken, & Bull, 1994; Memon & Kohnken, 1992).

Nevertheless, cognitive interviewing is time-consuming in practice, not only in terms of time spent interviewing the witness, but in training the police interviewers; moreover, because of their complexity, officers often do not adhere to the specified procedures or end up avoiding it altogether (Dando, Wilcock, & Milne, 2009; Kebbell & Wagstaff, 1999; Kebbell, Milne, & Wagstaff, 1999, 2001; Wheatcroft, Wagstaff, & Russell, 2013). This has led researchers in this area to look for alternatives to the cognitive interview that are just as effective and accurate, but take less time to administer and do not involve extensive training to use. One such approach adopted by the present authors has involved the development of some ideas suggested by the first author in the early 1980s (see, for example, Wagstaff, 1982); labelled the Liverpool Interview Protocol (LIP), it was derived directly from studies of hypnotic forensic interviewing.

HYPNOTIC INTERVIEWING REVISITED: THE LIVERPOOL INTERVIEW PROTOCOL

The approach adopted by the present authors is based on the assumption that many of the procedures traditionally employed by "hypnoinvestigators" might potentially be effective tools for facilitating accurate witness memory, if divorced from the contextual label of "hypnosis" (which can create unrealistic expectancies and associated errors). The present authors, therefore, decided to revisit hypnotic interviewing to see if there are any additional techniques used in hypnotic interviewing procedures that could potentially be used by themselves, or as part of a brief but effective investigative memory facilitation technique, but divorced from the context of hypnosis. In addition to the aspects of rapport building, report everything, and context reinstatement (revivication), already found in the cognitive interview, two other features of traditional hypnotic interviewing stood out as possibly useful in forensic situations: the relaxation instructions that frequently feature in hypnotic inductions, and eyeclosure, which is another common feature in many hypnosis procedures. The result was the Liverpool Interview Protocol (LIP), which has been developed in conjunction with practicing police officers who have piloted and provided feedback on the procedures.

The LIP is presented in a generic protocol format that is easy for interviewing officers to learn and apply (i.e., all officers have to do is read the information out to the witness). It consists of the following components: (a) a very brief introduction; (b) an optional eye-closure instruction; (c) a brief focused breathing exercise; (d) a brief context reinstatement instruction, and (e) a free-recall and report everything instruction. Notably, although these are features associated with traditional hypnotic interviewing, all of these components are based on psychological principles that are known to effectively enhance witness memory. For example, as previously noted, context reinstatement and report everything have been shown to be the most effective mnemonic techniques in the cognitive interview, and work well by themselves (Davis, McMahon, & Greenwood, 2005; Hammond, Wagstaff, & Cole, 2006; Milne & Bull, 2002; Wagstaff, Cole, Wheatcroft, Marshall, & Barsby, 2007; Wagstaff, Wheatcroft, Caddick, Kirby, & Lamont, 2011). The main scientific principle underlying the effectiveness of context reinstatement and report everything instructions is that they help the witness generate a variety of general memory associations that may "trigger" more critical memories. Research is continuing on the exact mechanisms involved in the memory enhancement effects of focused breathing, but these may include reducing distractions, optimizing brain processing conditions, and making the witness (and even the interviewer) feel more relaxed and open (Wagstaff, Brunas-Wagstaff, Cole, & Wheatcroft, 2004; Wagstaff, Brunas-Wagstaff, Cole, Knapton, et al., 2004; Wagstaff & Wheatcroft, 2012). Eyeclosure, too, may help the witness to optimize attention and reduce distractions (Perfect et al., 2008; Vredeveldt, Hitch, & Baddeley, 2011; Wagstaff, Brunas-Wagstaff, Cole, & Wheatcroft, 2004).

A variety of controlled scientific studies have shown that the focused breathing and eye-closure instructions used in the LIP, both individually and in combination, can improve memory for different kinds of information, including speech, visual material (including memory for episodes encountered some years previously), and person identification. Effects are greatest, however, when the two techniques are combined. The further combination of focused breathing with context reinstatement instructions used in the LIP has also been shown to be particularly effective in enhancing memory (i.e., again the effects of the techniques are additive). Moreover, the LIP techniques have been shown to be effective with adults, irrespective of age, and children as young as 6 years old (Hammond et al., 2006; Wagstaff, Brunas-Wagstaff, Cole, & Wheatcroft, 2004; Wagstaff, Brunas-Wagstaff, Cole, Knapton, et al., 2004; Wagstaff et al., 2007; Wagstaff & Wheatcroft, 2012).

Significantly, although the LIP components, both individually and in combination, have been shown to reliably improve memory, the overwhelming empirical evidence indicates that they do not have any negative effects with regard to incorrect responses. So, for example, they do not increase false-positive responses or confabulations (saying things were present which were not), or inflate confidence in incorrect responses. Indeed, some components of the LIP have been shown to decrease errors of this kind, including a reduction in the effects of misleading information (Wagstaff, Brunas-Wagstaff, Cole, & Wheatcroft, 2004; Wagstaff, Brunas-Wagstaff, Cole, Knapton, et al., 2004; Wagstaff et al., 2007; Wagstaff, Wheatcroft, Burt, et al., 2011; Wagstaff, Wheatcroft, Caddick, et al., 2011).

CASE EXAMPLES

More recent studies have also shown that the LIP in its entirety can systematically improve memory for a variety of professional witness groups, such as police-authorized firearms officers and senior fire service officers, involved in realistic, highly demanding, training simulations. Moreover, surveys of its use in the field by police officers in the UK and Canada have shown that, so far, it has been favorably received by police officers who have been trained in its use, and by witnesses who have been interviewed with it (Wagstaff & Wheatcroft, 2012). Indeed, a majority of officers report being surprised by how simple and effective the protocol is in increasing recall of accurate, detailed information.

For example, in one case report, the officer states, "Yesterday, I interviewed a 67-year-old witness to a distraction burglary using this procedure and the result was very positive. This witness saw a male inside the targeted premises at the relevant time and so her evidence was vital. Unbelievably, from her account (using the LIP) I received the following description:"

'White skinned male, about 24 years of age. I would say he was a bit taller than me say about 5'6. He was medium in build, his shoulders a bit broader than mine and he had what I would call a tubby face. By that I mean he had plump cheeks and I remember his nose looked puffed up as though it had been broken—like a boxer's nose. The man also had bushy eyebrows and a pale complexion. He was also clean shaven but possibly had some kind of stubble, like the early stages of a moustache above his top lip. His hair was either black or brown in colour and was in a short cropped style, like a crew cut and about ¾ in length. He didn't have any sideboards and his hairline was in what I would call a teapot cut. This man was wearing either a cream or beige coloured sweatshirt, which had a roll-neck and what looked like a shiny badge on the right breast. I could not see what the man was wearing below his sweatshirt because that was below the window and out of my view. I saw this man for maybe a total of 3 to 4 seconds whilst I was at the top of the staircase and my best view of him was when he was stood right in the window. The distance between my window and Joyce's window is roughly 30 feet and positioned at about the same height. I remember the weather was fine but it had been drizzling earlier in the day so the ground was wet and it was just going dark. I could see clearly anyway because of the lighting in the street. The only thing in the way of me and this man was the windows where we were stood at. I did not recognise this man, I have never seen him before and I have not seen him since. I think he looked older than he probably was, maybe because of his nose and his bushy eyebrows. You would think that someone with nicely cropped hair would have their eyebrows trimmed as well. I would recognise this person again."

The officer adds, "Initially, the witness could only say that the male had a chubby face, so to get all of this was fantastic to say the least."

Other comments made by police interviewers in case reports include the observations that, when using the LIP, the interviewee speaks slower and more thoughtfully, which makes interviewing him or her easier; it also visibly relaxes the interviewer (in addition to the interviewee), and the interviewer automatically adopts a softer, less authoritarian tone, which is less intimidating to the witness. As one officer said: "The main advantage for me is that this technique takes away having to think of how to get the interviewee into the right frame of mind so I can concentrate on what I actually want, which is the best evidence from my witness." For example, in another case involving a teenage boy, the interviewing officer noted that in his first interview, without the LIP, the boy was "nervous and stilted" and his "responses were limited." However, after the LIP, he "stopped fidgeting, spoke slowly and concentrated far more," and the interviewers stated that they got "a lot more out of the second interview."

A SAMPLE PROTOCOL

Although there are a number of LIP variations for different types of information and witness characteristics (e.g., auditory memory, and very traumatized witnesses and victims), the following is a basic LIP protocol for use in forensic investigations.

1. The Introduction

"Before asking you any questions, we going to give you two procedures to help you relax and remember things that you have seen and heard. The first is a very brief breathing exercise, with or without your eyes closed. The second is a short set of instructions to help you think generally about what happened. They only take a few minutes. Although it may seem a little unusual to start an interview in this way, some people find these procedures helpful. Do you have any questions?" [Answer questions; show interviewee transcript of procedures if requested.]

2. The Eye-Closure Instruction

"*Many people find the procedures work best if they close their eyes while thinking about things that have happened. How do you feel about closing your eyes during these procedures and when answering questions?* [If the interviewee responds positively say], *OK I will ask you to keep your eyes closed during the procedures and the questions that follow, but remember, if at any time you feel uncomfortable and you would like to open your eyes, please do so. Do you understand this?* [Use the eye-closure option, which is in brackets in the following instructions. If the interviewee seems reticent, tell him/her]: *OK you do not need to close your eyes* [use the non-eye-closure option; i.e., ignore the instructions in brackets].

After you have received these procedures, you will be asked some questions about the incident/s in question, but please do not start to speak about these events until after I have described the procedures. I will tell you when I want you to answer some questions. Do you understand?"

3. Administer the Focused Breathing Exercise

"*OK, let's start with the relaxation procedure.* [Read slowly and in a relaxed manner.]

[Please close your eyes.] *This is a very simple focused breathing exercise designed to help you relax and concentrate. So sit comfortably; keep your spine straight; keep your back straight and focus your attention now on your breathing. As you breathe in and out in a natural manner, focus on your breathing; breathing in and out in a natural manner. Take a few deep conscious breaths but don't strain. Just focus on your breathing, breathing in and out in a natural manner. Let the flow of your breath settle into its own natural rhythm; keep focused and aware during the whole process but concentrate on your breathing, breathing in and out in a natural manner. Allow your attention to focus on the changing rhythms of your breathing; and if your attention begins to wander, gently but firmly bring it back to your breathing. Now keep focusing on your breathing as you listen to the following instructions.*

Throughout the following instructions continue focusing on your breathing, breathing in and out in a natural rhythm."

4. Administer the Context Reinstatement Instruction

"*Good, I'm now going to give you a very simple procedure, designed to help you remember what happened during the incident you witnessed.* [Remember to keep your eyes closed.] *Please do not start speaking about the events until I have finished describing the procedure and tell you to do so. OK?* [If read verbatim, read slowly and in a relaxed manner.]

I would like you to try and picture the events that you saw in the incident as if they were happening right now, right before your eyes. Run through what happened; try to replay the event in your head, as if it were a video that is replaying before you, which you are watching right now. Try to picture the scene and what it looks like. Imagine you are there, look around . . . try to mentally note everything that you see. Think about what you see and what is happening before you. Think about what you were doing at the time. Notice whether you can you hear any sounds, or recognize any smells associated with the event. Try to picture what happened as if you were still there, and seeing the event for the first time. Think about everything that you can see, noting every single detail, no matter how small, irrelevant or trivial it may seem. Notice any feelings you have. Notice your reactions to what is happening. I'd like you to keep picturing and remembering what you saw, remembering the event as you answer the following questions. Think back and play it back in your head at any point when you need help remembering."

5. Administer Free Recall/ Report Everything Instruction

"*OK* [keep your eyes closed]. *I've now finished reading out the procedures and I'm going to ask you some questions. Whilst answering these questions remember to try to keep your breathing relaxed* [and your eyes closed] *and keep trying to picture the incident in your head.*

First, I'm now going to ask you to describe as many details as you can remember about the incident in question. So now, talking slowly and keeping relaxed, please tell me everything you can remember about the incident in question; tell me now about everything that you can remember, noting every detail, no matter how small or unimportant it may seem." [Remember not to interrupt the interviewee during this first free recall attempt. When the interviewee has finished you may continue with your further follow-up questions].

GENERAL CONCLUSION: A NOTE OF CAUTION

Our work on the LIP and its components suggests that when, in the 1980s, a number of advocates of the use of hypnosis as a memory enhancement procedure argued that by rejecting the use of hypnosis outright "the baby was being thrown out with the bathwater," they might have had a point. Indeed, many of the techniques developed by hypnoinvestigators can be construed as a rich source of ideas, which may be of benefit in forensic interviewing (Wagstaff, 2009). Nevertheless, it is important to emphasize that, in practice, neither interviewees nor interviewers consider the LIP to actually involve "hypnosis" (Wagstaff, Wheatcroft, Hoyle, & Duffy, 2014). This draws attention to a potentially important practical distinction between hypnosis for forensic purposes and hypnosis as used in some clinical contexts. In many clinical situations, the client's or patient's belief in the "special properties" of hypnosis could be construed as something to be positively endorsed and encouraged (see, for example, Kirsch, Montgomery, & Sapirstein, 1995). In contrast, historically, this same public belief in the transcendent properties of "hypnosis" has likely been a, if not the, main cause of its downfall as a forensic tool. In finishing, therefore, it may be worth reemphasizing that, notwithstanding results obtained with the LIP, the use of procedures to enhance recall of memories in clinical or other situations that are explicitly or implicitly labeled by the client or patient as "hypnosis" is still potentially problematic. In such instances, if memory accuracy is a critical issue, then the evidence suggests that, at the very least, interviewees

should be advised emphatically to be cautious in their reporting, and interviewers should be extremely cautious about accepting the veracity of what is said by the interviewee.

REFERENCES

Barnier, A. J., Cox, R. E., Connors, M., Langdon, R., & Coltheart, M. (2011). Are high hypnotizables especially vulnerable to false memory effects? A sociocognitive perspective. *International Journal of Clinical and Experimental Hypnosis, 59*(1), 1–17. doi:10.1080/002 07144.2011.522863

Bekerian, D. A., & Dennett, J. L. (1993). The cognitive interview technique: Reviving the issues. *Applied Cognitive Psychology, 7*, 275–297.

Crown Prosecution Service. (2014). Hypnosis CPS public consultations. Retrieved from http://www.cps.gov.uk/legal/h_to_k/hypnosis

Dando, C., Wilcock, R., & Milne, R. (2009). The cognitive interview: Novice police officers' witness/victim interviewing practices. *Psychology, Crime and Law, 15*, 679–696.

Davis, M. R., McMahon, M., & Greenwood, K. M. (2005). The efficacy of mnemonic components of the cognitive interview: Towards a shortened variant for time-critical investigations. *Applied Cognitive Psychology, 19*, 75–93.

Dinges, D. F., Whitehouse, W. G., Orne, E. C., Powell, E. W., Orne, M. T., & Erdelyi, M. H. (1992). Evaluating hypnotic memory enhancement (hypermnesia and reminiscence) using multitrial forced recall. *Journal of Experimental Psychology: Learning Memory and Cognition, 18*, 1139–1147.

Dywan, J., & Bowers, K. (1983). The use of hypnosis to enhance recall. *Science, 22*, 184–185.

Erdelyi, M. H. (1994). The empty set of hypermnesia. *International Journal of Clinical and Experimental Hypnosis, 42*(4), 379–390. doi:10.1080/00207149408409366

Fisher, R. P., Geiselman, R. E., Raymond, D. S., Jurkevich, L. M., & Warhaftig, M. L. (1987). Enhancing eyewitness memory: Refining the cognitive interview. *Journal of Police Science and Administration, 15*, 291–297.

Fisher, R. P., Geiselman, R. E., & Amador, M. (1989). Field test of the cognitive interview: Enhancing the recollection of actual victims and witnesses of crime. *Journal of Applied Psychology, 74*(5), 722–727.

Fisher, R. P., & Geiselman, R. E. (1992). *Memory enhancing techniques for investigative interviewing: The cognitive interview.* Springfield, IL: Charles C. Thomas Publishers.

Geiselman, R.E., Fisher, R. P., Mackinnon, D. P., & Holland, H. L. (1986). Enhancement of eyewitness memory with the cognitive interview. *American Journal of Psychology, 99*, 385–401.

Geiselman, R. E., Fisher, R. P., Mackinnon, D. P., & Holland, H. L. (1985). Eyewitness memory enhancement in the police interview: Cognitive retrieval mnemonics versus hypnosis. *Journal of Applied Psychology, 70*(2), 401–412.

Geiselman, R. E. (1996). On the use and efficacy of the cognitive interview. *Psycholoquy, 7*(2).

Hammond, L., Wagstaff, G. F., & Cole, J. (2006). Facilitating eyewitness memory in adults and children with context reinstatement and focused meditation. *Journal of Investigative Psychology and Offender Profiling, 3*, 117–130.

Haward, L. R. C. (1988). Hypnosis by the police. *British Journal of Experimental and Clinical Hypnosis, 5*, 33–35.

Hibbard, W. S., & Worring, R. W. (1981). *Forensic hypnosis: The practical application of hypnosis in criminal investigation*. Springfield, IL: Charles C. Thomas Publishers.

Kebbell, M. R., Milne, R., & Wagstaff, G. (1999). The cognitive interview: A survey of its forensic effectiveness. *Psychology, Crime and Law, 5*, 101–115.

Kebbell, M. R., Milne, R., & Wagstaff, G. F. (2001). The cognitive interview in forensic investigations. A review. In G. B. Traverso & L. Bagnoli (Eds.), *Psychology and law in a changing world: New trends in theory, practice and research* (pp. 185–197). Reading: Harwood.

Kebbell, M. R., & Wagstaff, G. F. (1997). An investigation into the influence of hypnosis on the confidence and accuracy of eyewitness recall. *Contemporary Hypnosis, 14*, 157–166.

Kebbell, M. R., & Wagstaff, G. F. (1998). Hypnotic interviewing: The best way to interview eyewitnesses? *Behavioral Sciences & the Law, 16*(1), 115–129.

Kebbell, M. R., & Wagstaff, G. F. (1999). The effectiveness of the cognitive interview. In D. Canter & L. Alison (Eds.), *Interviewing and deception* (pp. 23–41). Dartmouth: Ashgate.

Kirsch, I., Montgomery, G., & Sapirstein, G. (1995). Hypnosis as an adjunct to cognitive behavioral psychotherapy: A meta-analysis. *Journal of Consulting and Clinical Psychology, 63*(2), 214–220.

Malpass, R. S., & Devine, P. G. (1981). Guided memory in eyewitness identification. *Journal of Applied Psychology, 66*, 343–350.

McConkey, K. M., & Sheehan, P. W. (1996). *Hypnosis, memory, and behavior in criminal investigation*. New York, NY: Guilford Press.

Memon, A., & Bull, R. (1991). The cognitive interview: Its origins, empirical support, evaluation and practical implications. *Journal of Community and Applied Social Psychology, 1*, 291–307.

Memon, A., & Kohnken, G. (1992). Helping witnesses to remember more: The cognitive interview. *Expert Evidence, 1*, 39–48.

Memon, A., Holley, A., Milne, R., Kohnken, G., & Bull, R. (1994). Towards understanding the effects of interviewer training in evaluating the cognitive interview. *Applied Cognitive Psychology, 8*, 641–659.

Milne, R., & Bull, R. (2002). Back to basics: A componential analysis of the original cognitive interview mnemonics with three age groups. *Applied Cognitive Psychology, 16*(7), 743–753.

Wagstaff, G. F. (1989). Forensic aspects of hypnosis. In N. P. Spanos & J. F. Chaves (Eds.), *Hypnosis: The cognitive behavioral perspective* (pp. 340-357). Buffalo, NY: Prometheus.

Reiser, M. (1980). *Handbook of investigative hypnosis*. Los Angeles, CA: Lehi.

Scoboria, A., Mazzoni, G., Kirsch, I., & Milling, L. S. (2002). Immediate and persisting effects of misleading questions and hypnosis on memory reports. *Journal of Experimental Psychology Applied, 8*(1), 26–32.

Smith, M. C. (1983). Hypnotic memory enhancement of witnessess: Does it work? *Psychological Bulletin, 94*(3), 387–407.

Steblay, N. M., & Bothwell, R. K. (1994). Evidence for hypnotically refreshed testimony: The view from the laboratory. *Law and Human Behavior, 18*(6), 635.

U.S. Attorneys. (2014). Use of hypnosis—purpose. *Criminal Resource Manual, 287*. Retrieved from http://www.justice.gov/usao/eousa/foia_reading_room/usam/title9/crm00287.htm

Vingoe, F. J. (1995). Beliefs of British law and medical students compared to an expert criterion group on forensic hypnosis. *Contemporary Hypnosis, 12*, 173–187.

Vredeveldt, A., Hitch, G. J., & Baddeley, A. D. (2011). Eyeclosure helps memory by reducing cognitive load and enhancing visualisation. *Memory & Cognition, 39*(7), 1253–1263.

Wagstaff, G. F. (1999a). Hypnosis and forensic psychology. In I. Kirsch, A. Capafons, & E. Cardena-Buela (Eds.), *Clinical hypnosis and self-regulation: Cognitive-behavioral perspectives* (pp. 277–308). Washington, DC: American Psychological Association. doi:10.1037/10282-011

Wagstaff, G. F. (1999b). Hypnotically elicited testimony. In A. Heaton Armstrong, E. Shepherd, & D. Wolchover (Eds.), *Analysing witness testimony* (pp. 277–310). Aldine Place, London: Blackstone.

Wagstaff, G. F. (2010). Hypnosis and the relationship between trance, suggestion, expectancy and depth: Some semantic and conceptual issues. *American Journal of Clinical Hypnosis, 53*(1), 47–59.

Wagstaff, G. F., Wheatcroft, J. M., & Jones, A. C. (2011). Are high hypnotizables especially vulnerable to false memory effects? A sociocognitive perspective. *International Journal of Clinical and Experimental Hypnosis, 59*(3), 310–326.

Wagstaff, G. F. (1981). The use of hypnosis in police investigation. *Journal—Forensic Science Society, 21*(1), 3–7.

Wagstaff, G. F. (1982). Helping a witness remember—A project in forensic psychology. *Police Research Bulletin, 38,* 56–58.

Wagstaff, G. F. (1983). Hypnosis and the law: A critical review of some recent proposals. *The Criminal Law Review, 3,* 152–157.

Wagstaff, G. F. (1984). The enhancement of witness memory by hypnosis: A review and methodological critique of the experimental literature. *British Journal of Experimental and Clinical Hypnosis, 2,* 3–12.

Wagstaff, G. F. (1988). Comments on the 1987 home office draft circular: A response to the comments of Gibson, Haward and Orne. *British Journal of Experimental and Clinical Hypnosis, 5,* 145–149.

Wagstaff, G. F. (1989). Forensic aspects of hypnosis. In N. P. Spanos & J. F. Chaves (Eds.), *Hypnosis: The cognitive behavioral perspective* (pp. 340-357). Buffalo, NY: Prometheus.

Wagstaff, G. F., Brunas-Wagstaff, J., Cole, J., Knapton, L., Winterbottom, J., Crean, V., & Wheatcroft, J. (2004). Facilitating memory with hypnosis, focused meditation and eye closure. *International Journal of Clinical and Experimental Hypnosis, 52*(4), 434–455. doi:10.1080/00207140490889062

Wagstaff, G. F., Brunas-Wagstaff, J., Cole, J., & Wheatcroft, J. (2004). New directions in forensic hypnosis: Facilitating memory with focused meditation. *Contemporary Hypnosis, 21,* 14–27.

Wagstaff, G. F., Cole, J., Wheatcroft, J., Marshall, M., & Barsby, I. (2007). A componential approach to hypnotic memory facilitation: Focused meditation, context reinstatement and eye movements. *Contemporary Hypnosis, 24,* 97–108.

Wagstaff, G. F., Cole, J., Wheatcroft, J., Anderton, A., & Madden, H. (2008). Reducing and reversing pseudomemories with hypnosis. *Contemporary Hypnosis, 25,* 178–191.

Wagstaff, G. F. (2009). Is there a future for investigative hypnosis? *Journal of Investigative Psychology and Offender Profiling, 6,* 43–57.

Wagstaff, G. F., Wheatcroft, J. M., Burt, C. L., Pilkington, H. J., Wilkinson, K., & Hoyle, J. D. (2011). Enhancing witness memory with focused meditation and eye-closure: Assessing the effects of misinformation. *Journal of Police and Criminal Psychology, 26,* 152–161.

Wagstaff, G. F., Wheatcroft, J. M., Caddick, A. M., Kirby, L. J., & Lamont, E. (2011). Enhancing witness memory with techniques derived from hypnotic investigative interviewing: Focused meditation, eye-closure and context reinstatement. *International Journal of Clinical and Experimental Hypnosis, 59*(2), 146–164. doi:10.1080/00207144.2011.546180

Wagstaff, G. F., & Wheatcroft, J. M. (2012). Enhancing witness memory with focused breathing, eye-closure and context reinstatement: The Liverpool Interview Protocol in practice. Paper presented to the International Investigative Interviewing Research Group: 5th Annual Conference. Toronto, Canada.

Wagstaff, G. F., Wheatcroft, J. M., Hoyle, J. D., & Duffy, C. (2014). Enhancing memory with the Liverpool Interview Protocol: Is an association with hypnosis a problem? *Contemporary Hypnosis and Integrative Therapy, 30,* 134–141.

Webert, D. R. (2003). Are the courts in a trance? Approaches to the admissibility of hypnotically enhanced witness testimony in the light of empirical evidence. *American Criminal Law Review, 40,* 1301–1327.

Wheatcroft, J. M., Wagstaff, G. F., & Russell, K. (2013). Police officers' perceptions of the cognitive interview: Usefulness, confidence and witness reliability. *Police Practice and Research: An International Journal, 1,* 1–14.

Marital Communication

Carol Kershaw

Couples develop a unique interactive relationship that often demonstrates aspects of hypnotic trance (Kershaw, 2014). Their language and expressions and the projections of the worst and best of each partner onto each other often lead to intimacy or conflict. Mental states of focused attention become patterned and habitual and lead to either pleasant or painful experiences. Each individual tends to narrow the focus of the other and stimulate patterned responses in altered states of consciousness. This is the couple's hypnotic dance (Kershaw, 1992).

When couples begin to have conflict, they act as psychobiological regulators of each other's nervous systems. For those who have difficulty modulating states of arousal, interactions tend to turn on rage and fear neural circuits, and intimacy is lost. In fact, it is the perception of threat to one's ego that creates an overreaction. A negative perception by one partner of the other creates feelings of separation and of being misunderstood.

RELEVANT RESEARCH

When partners feel misunderstood or unloved, the couple system is ripe for stimulating high levels of arousal. Cortisol levels rise, and stress in the form of physiological responses, such as headaches, tightness in the chest, and foggy thinking, characterized by high amplitudes of slow brain frequencies, can be barriers to intimacy. The greater the stress in the relationship, the less connected partners feel to each other, and whatever communication skills individuals have learned remain in amnesia, unavailable to the conscious mind (Neff & Karney, 2009).

Default attachment styles activate under stress, and a regression toward defensive and reactive behaviors promote distance for protection from emotional pain. When these styles are other than secure, and partners do not develop a level of awareness and interactional strategies that lead to calm and understanding, conflict ensues to deal with insecurity and anxiety. These dynamics often lead to a negative "hypnotic dance" (Kershaw, 1992) that creates adverse trance states in partners where the focus of attention is on everything that is wrong. Hyperfocus is an element in trance. People in trance can focus on that which is painful or pleasurable, but hyperfocusing on something painful creates an adverse trance state.

Aspects of the dance include a cycle of pursuing and withdrawal that sparks dysfunctional exchanges. The pathologizing of a partner's behavior accompanied by a feeling of contempt is certain to result in resentment and negative emotions. Over a few years, changing how the couple relates becomes more difficult to alter. To deal with difficulty, Gottman (1999) found that successful couples who find their conflicts are gridlocked use dialogue to uncover unfulfilled dreams that may be at the root of dissatisfaction. Then each partner helps the other achieve life goals. Those who are happier punctuate their conflict with humor and positive comments and characterize their partner's annoying ways as stress behavior rather than deficient or malevolent. Those who remain unhappy engage in acidic interactions characterized by criticism and contempt.

Negotiating one's sense of separateness and being together are two important aspects in the dynamics of relationships. At times, couples may find themselves too close or "wedded at the hip" and need distance. At other times, couples may feel too distant; if this happens, each needs to move toward the other. In fact, there is a common dynamic of moving together and moving apart. When one partner moves away, the other needs to respect the need and not demand closeness. At the same time, when the other partner has been distant too long, an invitation to be closer is in order. How this is done is crucial in the reconnection. Those who are successful in managing this rhythm pay attention differently than those who do not. Successful marital partners focus on the whole dynamic and realize that when one partner pulls back, it often represents a need for regeneration rather than rejection.

How able a couple is to forgive and let go of hurtful interactions is crucial to the long-term relationship. The ability to ask for forgiveness and to accept it takes a level of maturity. By shifting upset states to calmer ones and creating more benign interpretations of a partner's behavior, one learns to move into more optimal states of mind.

Couples can achieve states of synchrony when they enter into deep conversation (Levenson & Gottman, 1985). They begin to entrain their heart rate and brain frequencies through shared empathic moments. In addition, shared states of relaxation and mental clarity occur. These states can be stimulated with clinical hypnosis (William & Gruzelier, 2001). When synchrony or "whole-brain" balance is achieved, stress disappears and many possibilities open for individuals and couples for enhanced relationships and goal achievement.

It is clear that couples who practice calmer alpha states have happier and more satisfied lives and relationships. Research with couples practicing alpha states in interactional synchrony by imitating each other's movements found that the mirror neuron system was stimulated and reflected in the alpha/mu frequency band (9.2–11.5 Hz) over the right centroparietal regions of two interacting partners (Dumas, Nadel, Soussignan, Martinerie, & Garnero, 2010). Mirror neurons are activated in empathy and connection.

The research on meditation demonstrates that the practice of alpha states often leads to almost magical shifts in people's lives by changing threats to challenges (Lucas, 2012). Meditation can even turn off genes that cause inflammation so that perceptions are reflected in body chemistry (Kaliman et al., 2014). An individual can learn to stay in an optimal mental state for longer periods of time with alpha training.

How a person pays attention is crucial to making positive change in couple interaction. Whether there is a narrow focus on a problem (or partner) that occurs in a fearful state, a

negative trance state, or a wider focus looking at possibilities when one is in a calm state, a positive trance state, often determines the response. This process leads to staying connected and present at the same time. When, in hypnosis, a client focuses on "space;" that is, focusing on the space between two walls or the imaginary space in the head between the ears, which Fehmi (2007) calls "open focus" training, the brain immediately balances hemisphere functioning and moves into whole-brain alpha. This is the state where both hemispheres produce alpha at the same time. Such a focus prevents a story or explanation or inner dialogue from taking place and allows the mind to travel into deeper states, a respite from chronic disappointment and worry.

A study was conducted with 554 couples who could not conceive. Over 70% of the couples conceived after direct and indirect hypnotic interventions targeting stressors and dynamic issues. This study suggests that when a couple's mental state is calmed and shared in a state of synchrony, the partners more often attain desired results.

Panksepp identified seven emotional systems that play a part in both problem development and resolution (1998). These seven circuits are anger and rage, nurture, fear, play, lust, panic, and curiosity. Couples have the capacity to trigger these circuits in their partners for pleasant or unpleasant experiences. The circuits are also related to various individual beliefs that partners maintain such as "I can't sustain a relationship" or "I will always need someone around to take care of me."

Kershaw and Wade (2012) elaborated on Panksepp's system to demonstrate how to shift between neural circuits and enhance the psychotherapeutic results. This neurological repatterning occurs by turning off fear with curiosity. Humor shifts anger, and empathy calms anger and fear. When individuals in a couple system begin to reprogram their own habitual mental patterns through changing focus and observing erratic or irrational thoughts, they learn to stay in their own target states of calm, confidence, courage, and persistence for longer periods of time. Inner trains of thought that lead to discomfort and unhappiness begin to shift into more productive mind habits.

The thoughts and mental states in which couples engage become reflected in a partner's physiology, so a mental field is shared (Sheldrake, 2010) and circuits are easily triggered. When a partner thinks about the other, the galvanic skin response shows a change even when the person has no conscious idea this is occurring (Libet, 2005; Radin, 2006). A system develops between partners and links them in social bonding. The partners affect each other's attention, emotions, behaviors, and intentions (Sheldrake, 2010).

Another aspect of the relationship has to do with the ability of partners to soothe each other and lower emotional arousal. Partners who stay in calmer states with each other access humor and playfulness and tend to build a history of fun and anticipation in being together. The ability to soothe another emerges from practiced empathy. When one partner empathizes with another's challenges, a shared understanding and lowered emotional arousal for both occurs.

Deep connection with another is a psychophysiological and spiritual experience. When both people use self-regulation of mental states and can keep reactivity to a minimum, they are happier personally and with each other. In calmer states, a closer and deeper connection is experienced as well as deeper personal awareness. Hypnosis often provides this experience and teaches a change in focus, a change in arousal, and an ability to shift perspective.

A negatively narrowed attention or overfocusing on a partner's perceived faults results in the sympathetic nervous system activating into high arousal. By taking the mind away from emergency states, better thinking is available. When couples experience hypnosis, which moves their attention away from upsetting but non-life-threatening experiences toward constructing positive interactions, their quality of attention changes; they move into a deeper relationship with more empathy, understanding, and flexibility; and they report more intimacy and a "honeymoon" effect where early feelings of being in love were shared by both people.

CASE EXAMPLE

Judith and William came to marital therapy after being married for 12 years. They complained that the connection they once had seemed quite dim.

Daily life was entirely separate and the weekends were filled with other work duties, so time spent with each other was limited. Both felt like strangers and missed their once close relationship.

When asked "How many feet each had in the relationship, one or two?" (representing their commitment), Judith and William each confessed to having two, but it was an effort. They reported wanting to rediscover the intimacy they once had before life's disappointments knocked some of their idealistic views off course.

Each person reported high levels of daily stress that was never relieved by coming home. The couple had forgotten how to soothe each other and themselves and lived in habitual anxiety and frustration. Because there was a need to remember what a calm mind and body was like and to be able to reconnect emotionally, they were asked to participate in marital hypnosis. In the following transcript, each person's needs are addressed as well as those of the couple system.

TRANSCRIPT OF TECHNIQUE

"Now I would like both of you to make some adjustments in how you are sitting, to maximize relaxation, and to close your eyes. With your feet flat on the floor, just begin to develop a deeper level of comfort. Breathe yourself into more relaxation with the awareness that your partner is sitting next to you having a similar but different experience.

You are sitting here separately and together wondering how to set feelings of upset aside and reconnect to the loving, compassionate, and passionate emotions that reside inside. The conscious mind may question this but as each of you have said, you still have "two feet" in the marriage. And two is always better than one to have a more profound experience in your life journey.

Judith, as you sit there and move into a deeper calm that can now pervade the whole body, you may become aware of a longing in you to connect with William like you did in the past. Perhaps you can remember a time when there was easiness between you, an effortless flow that was natural so that being together was natural and what you wanted to do when you came home. You might remember how you delighted in William's smile and your experience that he wanted to be with just you.

And William, perhaps you can remember a time when Judith was so engaged with you when you talked with her about something. She doted on every word and thought you were brilliant. The sense of respect and appreciation danced between you, and you experienced a vibrant love in your body and mind. So your minds may tell you what you either need to forgive or let go of to recover those warm feelings.

When you calm your mind, and you breathe more easily, a perspective shifts; you begin to remember your connection, heart to heart. It is only a habit of mind to suffer and blame the other. When you feel afraid, the mind begins to run the worst horror movies. But when you calm your nervous system, something profound occurs. You begin to remember; you begin to wonder. Can you have more fluidity in the relationship; can you expand your awareness and consciousness into greater acceptance of yourself? Can you slow the movies in the mind and focus on space in just a moment as I instruct how to accomplish that process? Can you, in fact, forgive the other, and begin to appreciate again why you are together and what you receive from each other?

So just now, allow yourself to move to a deeper place of mind down beneath any worry and know that your unconscious mind has the ability to problem-solve without your conscious activity now. Focus on the deeper comfort that you both have the ability to achieve together and separately. In fact, there is a pool of self-compassion deeper inside you. When you reach this place inside, you may want to dip your toes into it or jump completely in, and enjoy this place of inner sanctuary that regenerates and replenishes.

Take a moment and, with eyes closed, focus on the imaginary space between your eyes in your head. Now shift and focus on the imaginary space between your ears in your head. Now move your attention outside yourself and focus on the space between the walls in this room. Gently move the attention to the space above the building you are sitting in.

Move your attention to the space between earth and the moon. Now move your attention to the imaginary space in the galaxy. And now to the universe.

Can you begin to let go of the idea that there should be no tension, conflict, or trouble ever in your relationship? But that whatever comes up is merely an expression of a need in the moment that deserves a different kind of attention, a wider focus?

Remember a time in the past when you looked at each other and saw the best in your partner. What did you notice? Those qualities are still there. It is like noticing a tree growing in the yard. The tree expands its roots deep into the soil over time and grows almost imperceptibly. Noticing from time to time the amazing beauty of this gift of nature while feeling more calm and relaxed is a ritual you can develop.

We have a cat who loves to sit with us in the evening and watch television. Her tail gently flits from one person's arm to the other's, creating a bridge of connection and sweet affection. She gently lets us know she is there, nonintrusive but a gentle reminder that we are all connected, in a sweet experience that occurs almost every evening by creating the time and space for bonding.

Then, when you begin to feel upset about something, your mind can gently ask, "Why is this a problem?" There may be a legitimate complaint that needs a different behavior by the other but everything can be negotiated if you still have deep feelings and sparks for each other. And you can "respark" your relationship when you move into a deeper space of appreciation for the person you deeply love.

When you understand the vulnerabilities that your partner brings into the relationship, you can focus on the genuine pleasant aspects of your partner while you have this time together. Is it the way he or she looks at you; is it the way he or she laughs at your jokes or listens to your deepest dreams and desires?

Now as you contemplate these ideas, it is nice to be reminded, is it not? It is expansive to renew the mind, to remind your mind, that you can reconnect, set upset aside, work things out with kindness, and place your relationship once again first.

Perhaps you both can imagine your most optimal mental state. That state might be calm, courage, connected, confidence, or persistence. Allow your mind to enter this state now. Now being in your optimal mental states together, I wonder if you can begin to feel a flow between you? I don't know exactly how you might experience the flow and balance, but you can notice it now.

In a moment, allow yourselves to return to the room. As you come back, you can realize how both of you are sitting here together having had an experience together, and perhaps you would find it interesting to understand what it was like for your partner."

After the couple reorients, it is useful to have each describe his or her individual experience. It is wise for the clinician to help devise a plan of action for the couple over the next few weeks that includes creating time together for fun and sharing interesting experiences with each other. The plan can entail an assignment.

An example of homework is the following: "What if you were transported 1,000 years into the future where your minds were more mature, empathic, and understanding? What would be different about your perceptions and interactions with each other? What level of self-mastery could you demonstrate?" When the couple keeps this idea in mind and discusses the ramifications, subtle shifts in interactions begin to take place.

CONCLUSION

There are several aspects to a couple's hypnotic dance that can be addressed with clinical hypnosis. First, lowered levels of emotional arousal and shared mental states of calm can lead to more positive interactions over time. Self-regulation of potential reactivity is crucial for keeping romantic feelings alive as well as the constant practice of admiration and respect for the partner. The calming of emotional arousal usually entails mental training and an awareness that productive solutions for problems usually emerge from these calmer states of mind. Some couples find that practicing self-hypnosis together and separately can facilitate the best of their relationship over time.

There are several principles of marital communication relating to keeping levels of arousal low that can be taught to couples. First, the key to successful relationships comes from the ability to shift mental states. If people feel annoyed or upset with their partners, taking time to calm reactivity is useful, and communication from lowered states of arousal leads to better outcomes.

Second, the brain entrains to the most dominant frequency in the room, and emotional states are contagious. Couples have the capacity to turn on and off the partner's emotional neural circuits whereby they focus the partner's attention.

Third, by using several positive mental habits, couples can reinforce positive interactions. These include the use of consistent empathy in communication and the reinforcement of positive states of mind. Attention to reduced complaining is crucial in maintaining strong ties. When couples are on the same "wavelength" and producing synchronous brain states, they have the capacity to maintain loving states for longer periods of time.

Finally, the clinician needs to enter the mental state she or he wants to teach to the couple as a "target" or optimal state, in order to model that for them. This state is empathic, kind, and understanding. When another feels empathy, upset dissolves. As the clinician models this state, the couple unconsciously begins to model this state with each other.

REFERENCES

Dumas, G., Nadel, J., Soussignan, R., Martinerie, J., & Garnero, L. (2010). Inter-brain synchronization during social interaction. *PloS One*, 5(8), e12166. doi:10.1371/journal.pone.0012166

Fehmi, L. (2007). *The open-focus brain: Harnessing the power of attention to heal mind and body.* New York, NY: Shambhala Publications.

Gottman, J. (1999). *The seven principles for making marriage work: A practical guide from the country's foremost relationship expert.* New York, NY: Crown Publishers.

Kaliman, P., Alvarez-López, M. J., Cosín-Tomás, M., Rosenkranz, M. A., Lutz, A., & Davidson, R. J. (2014). Rapid changes in histone deacetylases and inflammatory gene expression in expert meditators. *Psychoneuroendocrinology, 40*(96). 96–107. doi:10.1016/j.psyneuen.2013.11.004

Kershaw, C. (1992). *The couple's hypnotic dance: Ericksonian strategies in marital therapy.* New York, NY: Brunner/Mazel.

Kershaw, C. (2014). *The couple's hypnotic dance: Ericksonian strategies in marital therapy.* Houston, TX: Awake Press.

Kershaw, C., & Wade, J. (2012). *Brain change therapy: Clinical interventions for self transformation.* New York, NY: W. W. Norton.

Levenson, R. W., & Gottman, J. M. (1985). Physiological and affective predictors of change in relationship satisfaction. *Journal of Personality and Social Psychology, 49*(1), 85–94. doi:10.1037/0022-3514.49.1.85

Libet, B. (2005). *Mind time: The temporal factor in consciousness.* Boston, MA: Harvard University Press.

Lucas, M. (2012). *Rewire your brain for love.* Carlsbad, CA: Hay House.

Neff, L. A., & Karney, B. R. (2009). Stress and reactivity to daily relationship experiences: How stress hinders adaptive processes in marriage. *Journal of Personality and Social Psychology, 97*(3), 435–450. doi:10.1037/a0015663

Panksepp, J. (1998). *Affective neuroscience: The foundations of human and animal emotions.* Boston, MA: Oxford University Press.

Radin, D. (2006). *Entangled minds: Extrasensory experiences in a quantum reality.* New York, NY: Paraview Pocket Books.

Sheldrake, R. (2010). Morphic fields and morphic resonance. *Journal of Noetic Science, 4.*

Williams, J. D., & Gruzelier, J. (2001). Differentiation of hypnosis and relaxation by analysis of narrow band theta and alpha frequencies. *International Journal of Clinical and Experimental Hypnosis, 49*(3), 185–206. doi:10.1080/00207140108410070

Mindfulness and Hypnosis

Nicholas Olendzki and Gary Elkins

Mindfulness is commonly defined as "paying attention in a particular way: on purpose, in the present moment, and nonjudgmentally" (Kabat-Zinn, 1994). It is an important element of "third-wave" cognitive behavioral therapies (CBTs) that involve addressing psychological and physiological symptoms through changing a client's relationship with his or her own experience (e.g., metacognitions, cognitive decentering). This chapter focuses on mindfulness as a psychological trait and presents a brief review of the evidence supporting the mindfulness-based and mindfulness-influenced therapies, which have emerged over the past 35 years. This review is followed by an examination of the empirical literature, which may be useful when considering the use of hypnosis to deliver a mindfulness intervention, as well as a case example and sample hypnosis transcript.

On a practical level, mindfulness may be easiest to understand in contrast to more traditional CBTs. For example, if an individual presents with generalized anxiety disorder in an outpatient clinic, common CBT interventions might include addressing anxiety-provoking thoughts through "thought stopping" in order to *avoid* the harmful thoughts or through *changing* irrational beliefs in order to ameliorate their impact. In contrast, a mindfulness-based intervention may ask a client to pay attention to what the anxiety feels like as it arises, with an attitude of acceptance and open curiosity toward the experience. Thus, rather than avoiding or *changing* anxiety-provoking thoughts, the client modifies his or her *reaction* to them. While this approach may seem counterintuitive at first, the end result is often a reduction in reactivity to negative emotions and pathogenic thoughts, thus reducing psychological distress.

Bishop et al. (2004) characterize mindfulness as having two primary components. The first characteristic component of mindfulness is

a self-regulation of attention, including sustained attention on present moment experiences and an inhibition of elaborative processing. The second major component of mindfulness is an orientation to experience characterized by curiosity, openness, and acceptance. Over the course of a mindfulness-based therapy, this shift in a client's attitude toward experiences is often supported by experiential exercises including, but not limited to, meditation, body scan, or mindful stretching. The common factor among these mindfulness exercises is that the client focuses his or her attention on the flow of experience unfolding in the present moment, with an attitude of openness, curiosity, and acceptance toward those experiences. Ideally, continued practice with this state of mind leads to mindfulness becoming a dispositional trait that occurs frequently throughout the day, and a mindful state becomes easier to evoke at will when needed.

The study of mindfulness as a beneficial psychological state coincided with the advent of Buddhism in 400 BCE, although it was not until much later that the concept received formal scientific scrutiny. Growing interest in Buddhism and Eastern philosophy in the West during the latter half of the 20th century provoked professional interest in the potential applications of mindfulness to psychotherapy practice (see, e.g., Fromm, Suzuki, & de Martino [1960] or Smith [1975]). In 1982, John Kabat-Zinn published the first secular, clinical mindfulness intervention for chronic pain (Kabat-Zinn, 1982), which is now known as mindfulness-based stress reduction (MBSR). The success of this program led to further studies validating its usefulness for other presenting problems and may have helped pave the way for other mindfulness interventions such as dialectical behavioral therapy (DBT; Linehan, 1987), acceptance and commitment therapy (ACT; Hayes, 1987; Hayes & Wilson, 1993), and mindfulness-based cognitive therapy (MBCT; Teasdale et al., 2000). Each distinct mindfulness intervention incorporates mindfulness into treatment in a slightly different way, and although there are slight theoretical distinctions between each of these interventions, they are united in their focus on modifying a client's relationship to his or her experiences. Collectively, these interventions have come to be empirically validated for use with a variety of populations and for many different conditions. Among the most promising avenues of intervention are stress and anxiety, chronic pain, borderline personality disorder, mood disorders, and adverse psychological sequelae of physical diseases such as cancer.

ANXIETY AND MOOD

Although the study of mindfulness interventions has suffered from a dearth of large randomized controlled trials (RCTs), the evidence collected to date seems to support the conclusion that mindfulness is efficacious in the treatment of anxiety disorders. This conclusion seems to hold true for heterogeneous anxiety disorders (Arch et al., 2013; Vøllestad, Sivertsen, & Nielsen, 2011), social anxiety disorder (Goldin & Gross, 2010; Koszycki, Benger, Shlik, & Bradwejn, 2007), and generalized anxiety disorder (Evans et al., 2008; Roemer & Orsillo, 2002). The majority of findings from meta-analyses indicate that mindfulness has a medium-to-large effect size (Grossman, Niemann, Schmidt, & Walach, 2004; Hofmann, Sawyer, Witt, & Oh, 2010; Piet, Würtzen, & Zachariae, 2012; Powers, Zum Vorde Sive Vording, & Emmelkamp, 2009).

When third-wave therapies are compared with more traditional treatments such as CBT for stress, anxiety disorders, and mood symptoms, the studies that have been conducted to date indicate that mindfulness-based therapies and traditional CBT are equally effective after intervention (Arch et al., 2013; Forman, Herbert, Moitra, Yeomans, & Geller, 2007), although one study comparing CBT to a third-wave therapy for anxiety and depression found that at 3-year follow-up, individuals maintained gains on depression scores slightly better in the CBT group than in the ACT group (Forman et al., 2012). Further research is needed to confirm the generalizability of this finding to other third-wave treatments and to other disorders, given that

long-term follow-up studies of third-wave therapies tend to show good maintenance of gains for anxiety and mood symptoms (Miller, Fletcher, & Kabat-Zinn, 1995; Teasdale et al., 2000) as well as for other presenting problems (Ljótsson et al., 2011; Ong, Shapiro, & Manber, 2009).

CHRONIC PAIN

The evidence for the efficacy and effectiveness of mindfulness interventions for chronic pain appears to be mixed. In one meta-analytic analysis of 22 studies of chronic pain, Veehof, Oskam, Schreurs, and Bohlmeijer (2011) found that third-wave therapies have a small but statistically significant effect size of 0.37 for reductions in pain intensity. This finding was found to be relatively homogeneous across studies of third-wave therapies for chronic pain and roughly equivalent to the more traditional approach of CBT for chronic pain. In discussing these results, the authors note that although reductions in pain intensity were present in these studies, reductions in experienced pain are not the focus of third-wave therapies; rather, the reduction of pain is secondary to changing the patient's relationship with pain such that distress is minimized and pain-related quality of life and functioning increases. Therefore, the authors recommend further research, which incorporates these measures.

Other studies have been more guarded in the prognosis for chronic pain patients treated with mindfulness. Two additional reviews of mindfulness interventions for chronic pain were conducted since the study by Veehof et al. (2011) and have each concluded that while mindfulness may be helpful in increasing acceptance of psychological distress and mood symptoms associated with pain, there is insufficient evidence to support mindfulness in comparison to attention control and waitlist control conditions (Cramer, Haller, Lauche, & Dobos, 2012; Song, Lu, Chen, Geng, & Wang, 2014). The apparent contradictions between these findings may be partially due to heterogeneity in measures of pain, heterogeneity in pain conditions included, small sample size in the studies reviewed, and using broad versus narrow criteria for the degree of rigor in reviewed studies. In short, while mindfulness may or may not have an impact on physical pain symptoms, the literature presents more consistent findings that the emotional correlates of pain are improved with mindfulness treatment.

BORDERLINE PERSONALITY DISORDER

Borderline personality disorder and the parasuicidal tendencies that often accompany the condition are notoriously difficult to successfully treat. One of the potential treatments that has emerged is DBT, which includes mindfulness skills training as an important element of treatment. Despite initial empirical support for the treatment and early adoption by many clinicians, DBT (like many mindfulness therapies) has been critiqued for the quality and size of the empirical trials evaluating its efficacy. The most comprehensive compilation of these critiques can be found in a special section of *Clinical Psychology: Science and Practice* published in 2000 (Koerner & Dimeff, 2000; Scheel, 2000; Swenson, 2000; Westen, 2000; Widiger, 2000). Since this review, there have been additional studies that address many of these concerns about the empirical basis of DBT presented in these articles, as summarized in Lynch, Trost, Salsman, and Linehan (2007).

In a meta-analysis of the effects of DBT on parasuicidal behavior in individuals with borderline personality disorder, Kliem, Kröger, and Kosfelder (2010) found that RCTs of DBT had an estimated effect size of $g = 0.60$ with regard to reducing self-injurious behavior. This estimated effect size remained relatively stable with the inclusion of nonrandomized controlled studies ($g = 0.56$); this finding coincides with the meta-analytic finding of $g = 0.62$ by Panos, Jackson, Hasan, and Panos (2013). In the past two decades, research into the effects of DBT has expanded to include the effects on comorbid conditions previously classified as Axis I disorders (Harned et al., 2008; Linehan et al., 2002; Linehan et al., 1999) and with different populations such as veterans (Koons et al., 2001) and adolescents (Goldstein et al., 2015). While DBT is still best known for its utility in treating borderline personality disorder, there have also been investigations into its use for eating disorders (Palmer et al., 2003; Safer, Telch, & Agras, 2001; Telch, Agras, & Linehan, 2000, 2001; Wisniewski & Kelly, 2003)

and other conditions (Bohus et al., 2013; Hejazi, Sobhi, & Sahrzad, 2014).

RESEARCH REGARDING THE USE OF MINDFULNESS IN HYPNOSIS

Given that there is empirical support for mindfulness and that hypnotherapy can be a useful and effective mechanism for delivering psychotherapy interventions, it seems probable that mindfulness can be delivered in a hypnotherapeutic context. Regardless, clinicians seeking to integrate mindfulness into hypnotherapy should be aware that to date, no empirical studies have been published, which test this supposition directly. This represents a significant gap in the literature, which persists despite clear overlaps between these two approaches, sound theoretical support for the benefits of integration, and recent professional interest in the intersection of these two approaches to therapy.

With regard to examining the theoretical compatibility of hypnotherapy and mindfulness, several peer-reviewed articles have compared the phenomenological and physiological correlates of mindfulness and hypnosis (Brown, Forte, Rich, & Epstein, 1982; Sabourin, Cutcomb, Crawford, & Pribram, 1990; Walrath & Hamilton, 1975). Findings indicate that although the physiological responses to mindfulness meditation and hypnosis are fairly similar to one another (Walrath & Hamilton, 1975), the phenomenological experience of the two states are distinct (Brown & Forte, 1983).

In a special issue on mindfulness and hypnosis, several authors contributed articles to the *Journal of Mind-Body Regulation* with different perspectives on the overlap between these two interventions. In one article, Lynn, Malaktaris, Maxwell, Mellinger, and van der Kloet (2012) argued that hypnosis and mindfulness inhabit a common domain involving suggestion. After comparing and contrasting mindfulness and hypnotic approaches to suggestion, the authors discuss some of the clinical implications for their conclusions. For instance, mindfulness and hypnosis could be used interchangeably according to variable client characteristics, or hypnosis could be used to enhance the effectiveness of a mindfulness intervention. The authors go on to highlight the fact that hypnosis and meditation have barely been explored from an empirical standpoint and suggest that controlled empirical trials studying the overlap of hypnosis and mindfulness are "vitally important" (Lynn et al., 2012, p. 21). In the same issue, Grant (2012) offers a cautionary commentary where he highlights some of the methodological difficulties of meaningfully comparing hypnosis to mindfulness. His arguments include the fact that meditation and even mindfulness can include a diverse array of interventions. He also points out that several benefits of mindfulness are attained only by long-term practice, whereas secular clinical interventions often focus on the effects of short-term practice. While none of his arguments is prohibitive for empirically investigating the possibility that hypnosis and mindfulness inhabit a common domain, they do emphasize the importance of clear definitions of the constructs under investigation and careful methodology when investigating those constructs.

Harrer (2009) described a complementary and synergistic relationship between mindfulness and hypnosis, where each intervention presents unique expressions of the same central constructs. Harrer presents eight constructs with analogues in hypnosis and mindfulness for the reader's consideration, such as the fact that hypnosis is often characterized by attentional "absorption," whereas mindfulness is usually described in terms of an "open awareness." Rather than viewing these two poles of attention as diametrically opposed, Harrer suggests that there is a spectrum of clinically useful experiences between the two and that using only hypnosis or mindfulness is unnecessarily restrictive. A logical consequence of Harrer's line of reasoning is that it may be possible to integrate mindfulness and hypnosis into a personalized intervention, which is superior to either intervention alone. Along similar lines, Lynn, Surya Das, Hallquist, and Williams (2006) suggest that

> hypnosis and mindfulness-based approaches can be used in tandem to create adaptive response sets and to deautomatize maladaptive response sets. . . . They also suggest that mindfulness can serve as a template for generating an array of suggestions that provides cognitive strategies to contend with problems in living and to ameliorate stress and negative affect more generally (p. 145).

More recently Lynn, Barnes, Deming, and Accardi (2010) have published a sample hypnotic mindfulness induction for use in MBCT courses and call the combination of mindfulness and hypnosis "a natural marriage with excellent prospects." Furthermore, Yapko (2011) published a book detailing the theoretical argument for the integrated use of mindfulness and hypnosis, though he does not describe a specific clinical guide for this mindfulness–hypnotherapy intervention.

Therefore, although evidence and theory are clearly converging on the possibility that mindfulness and hypnosis are compatible therapeutic modalities, which might be productively combined into a single, integrated intervention, research has not yet been conducted to confirm or deny this supposition. Despite professional interest in combining hypnosis and mindfulness approaches as well as theoretical descriptions of such an approach, there is currently no treatment for an integrated mindfulness and hypnosis intervention, nor has there been any empirical investigation into the feasibility or the clinical effects of combining these approaches.

CASE EXAMPLE

The patient "Lynn" was a 20-year-old biracial (Black and Caucasian) female who presented to an outpatient clinic with symptoms consistent with generalized anxiety disorder. She was a self-described perfectionist and said that she had been a constant worrier all of her life, but elaborated that since arriving at college her anxiety had been interfering with nighttime sleep and her ability to perform well on tests. She had consulted her primary care physician regarding her symptoms, but after a trial of anxiolytics and soporifics 1 year previous, Lynn had discontinued their use due to unwanted side effects and was now seeking an alternative to medication for her anxiety and sleep symptoms.

During the first session, baseline scores for anxiety and sleep were acquired, a case history was taken, and basic information about mindfulness and hypnosis were provided including common misconceptions about hypnosis. Lynn had never experienced hypnosis or mindfulness before but felt open to this avenue of treatment and optimistic that with the proper guidance she could reduce her anxiety and improve her sleep. She agreed to a trial of eight weekly, 1-hour sessions of hypnotherapy using mindfulness to address her primary symptoms, with the understanding that if she was showing good progress at 8 weeks, additional sessions could be added as necessary.

In Lynn's second session, she seemed eager to get started. After explaining her pattern of persistent worry and mental preparation across several domains of her life, Lynn was introduced to a hypnotic induction focused on mindful awareness of the breath. During the induction, she was instructed to pay attention to each nuance of the physical sensations of breathing. She was guided through the experience of being "present" with her breath, without controlling it, and simply accepting it as it is. During the posthypnotic inquiry, Lynn described this experience as relaxing and stated that there were things about her breath that she had never noticed before. She also noted that she looked forward to using this technique to "get rid of" or "control" her anxiety whenever it became irksome. This is a common sentiment in early stages of mindfulness therapies; while these desires are perfectly natural, they may be counterproductive to the work of later sessions and continued progress within a mindfulness framework. Lynn was encouraged to focus nonjudgmentally on her breathing frequently throughout the week, but reminded that an important aspect of treatment would be to let go of her *need* to control her anxiety, and instead maintain an attitude of nonjudgmental awareness of her stream of experiences.

The progression of the following sessions followed a similar format. The first half of each session was characterized by a didactic discussion of the stressors in Lynn's life and exploring how she might begin to approach her internal reaction to these stressors in new ways through mindfulness while becoming increasingly aware of how her previous, compulsive attempts to manage and control her worry were part of her presenting problem rather than the solution. During the first half of each session, new aspects of mindfulness were introduced and Lynn's efforts to be more mindful in her daily life were discussed. During the second half of each session, Lynn was guided through a hypnotic induction with suggestions for mindfulness, with variations appropriate to the themes explored during that session.

Lynn's progress was aided by a systematic approach to treatment: starting with awareness of the present moment and progressing through nonjudgmental awareness of bodily sensations, before transitioning to more difficult topics such as nonjudgmental awareness of thoughts and emotions. In the early stages of therapy, Lynn found it easier to become accustomed to being nonjudgmentally aware of neutral or pleasant experiences; with practice, she was gradually able to experience even stressful events with a greater degree of equanimity and markedly less *distress*. This reduction in stress *about* stress and her ability to habitually return to present moment awareness also had the effect of reducing the frequency and intensity of her worried thoughts about the future and her ability to discriminate productive worry from rumination.

Given that Lynn displayed significant improvements in anxiety and sleep at the conclusion of her eighth session, she elected to taper off of therapy with three more sessions spread over the next 3 months in order to solidify her gains and maintain the self-hypnosis and mindfulness habits that had helped her to improve. By the end of the 11th session, Lynn no longer met the criteria for generalized anxiety disorder and was consistently getting 7 to 8 hours of sleep, with only rare exceptions when studying for midterms and finals.

TRANSCRIPT: MINDFULNESS-BASED HYPNOTHERAPY

"You may begin by allowing your body to relax, discovering a sense of ease, and clearing your mind . . . you might begin this process by taking a series of three deep breaths . . . and you may find that as you relax . . . so deeply . . . your eyes may begin to get heavy . . . and you may allow your eyes to close whenever it feels most natural to you . . . now taking a deep breath, and holding it for a moment . . . hold . . . and as you exhale, allow all of your muscles to relax . . . unwinding . . . tension draining from your body . . . and when you're ready, take another deep, deep breath . . . and hold . . . and now exhaling all of your cares and worries . . . perhaps feeling lighter as your burdens pass from you . . . a sense of ease settling deeply into your being . . . and in a moment . . . your final deep, deep breath will carry you into the present moment . . . becoming deeply mindful and present even more easily than

you have in the past . . . effortlessly. Breathing in now for the third time . . . and hold . . . and as you breathe out, entering the present moment . . . leaving concerns of the past and the future behind."

Focus on Breathing and Narrowing of Attention

"Now settling more and more into the present moment . . . and as your focus on the present moment becomes more complete . . . perhaps noticing now [timed with in-breath] *both the in-breath . . .* [timed with out-breath] *and the out-breath . . . as they occur. As you breathe, you may find that your breath is made up of many stages . . . and as your focus narrows, it would be possible and even natural to become aware of each part of the process of breathing as it happens . . . more and more focused on each stage of the breath . . . perhaps becoming aware of the sensations at the very beginning of the in-breath, the middle of the in-breath, and the end . . . as your lungs are filled with air . . . and noticing the unique sensations that occur at each point in the out-breath. Each breath is unique . . . nuanced . . . if your attention were to waver, you might miss something interesting about your breath . . . something you never noticed before. And as people focus on their breath with this level of detail . . . unwavering . . . they sometimes find that there is a whole universe of interesting and ever-changing sensations. As they observe these sensations as they come and go . . . there is no desire to attend to anything else . . . and everything else except my voice fades to insignificance . . . in the background of awareness.*

Now as you focus more and more . . . on each sensation as it comes . . . it may be possible to find a point of absolute focus and stillness . . . in the present moment . . . as you allow this awareness of your breathing to carry you into a deep relaxation . . . everything else fading into the background . . . relaxed and serene. . . ."

Deepening Suggestions

". . . And this sensation can allow you to sink deeper into hypnosis . . . journeying inward . . . toward a place of complete and utter serenity . . . a place of calmness and relaxation . . . where your mind

is at ease, and nothing troubles you . . . where your thoughts are clear like a cool mountain lake . . . still, and serene . . . not burdened by the slightest care . . . this may be a familiar place . . . and you may find it pleasant to journey inward toward that place within you now . . . and as you hear my voice count from 5 to 1, with each number finding yourself settling into an even deeper level of hypnosis . . . deeper toward that place of complete mental and physical relaxation within you. . . .

5 . . . Setting your cares aside now as you embark on this inner journey . . . feeling a sense of relief . . . and as your body relaxes . . . it leads the way . . . bringing a sense of deep relief. . . .

4 . . . Deeply calm . . . number 4 and already so deeply relaxed . . . and you may begin to notice a warmth or tingling sensation in your body, as it relaxes even further. . . .

3 . . . And now a sense of profound calmness begins to blossom . . . unfolding . . . effortless, like a flower to the sun . . . and as you feel this, you might realize that mental and physical relaxation is not something that you do . . . it is a process of letting go. . . .

2 . . . Letting go of struggles and cares . . . letting go of any tension . . . letting go and simply being . . . in the present moment. . . .

1 . . . At the final step of your own inner journey . . . comfortably and deeply hypnotized . . . resting in the present moment . . . your thoughts uncluttered . . . still . . . and calm."

Suggestions for Breathing, Acceptance, and Awareness of the Present Moment

"And in this place . . . you will find that your experience of mindfulness will soon begin to deepen . . . aware of the breath . . . focusing on the sensations of breathing in . . . and breathing out . . . focusing on the nuances of the sensations . . . letting go of expectations of what this experience will be like . . . letting go of what it was like in this past moment . . . letting go of thinking about the breathing . . . just noticing what it is unfolding

now . . . *abiding in this beautiful present moment as your experiences flow past you . . . like a rock in the midst of a gentle stream . . . you will begin to feel a growing sense of peace . . . calmness . . . and as you feel these things just nodding your head yes. . . . Good, being present with your experiences . . . accepting them as they flow past you . . . sensations, sounds, thoughts, feelings . . . accepting them without judgment . . . in the simplicity of nonjudgmental awareness . . . in this present moment . . . the mind becomes relaxed, clear, and focused . . . noticing thoughts and feelings as these arise, and returning your attention to the breath if or when they pass . . .*

. . . aware of the present moment . . . accepting your experiences without trying to push them away or cling to them . . . a rock in a gentle stream . . . and in a moment . . . I will be silent to allow you to mindfully observe this experience . . . that is growing within you. When I speak to you again . . . you will remain . . . in a deep state of hypnosis and mindfulness . . . able to easily respond to each suggestion that I give. [Pause for 90 seconds.]"

Posthypnotic Suggestion

"Very good . . . and this experience of mindfulness . . . is now becoming more a part of you . . . and more and more, every day . . . you will find that . . . mindfulness has become a part of the way you perceive and experience the world . . . nonjudgmental awareness of the present moment . . . whenever your mind is not needed to plan or reflect . . . able to experience things from your five senses with equanimity and peacefulness . . . able to experience thoughts and feelings and remain grounded, steady, and calm. . . . Practice of mindfulness-based hypnotherapy on a regular basis enables you to thrive, and you will find it easy to continue to practice self-hypnosis and mindfulness on a regular basis . . . and each time you do so, you will feel more grounded . . . more steady regardless of your circumstances."

Alerting

"In a few moments, it is possible to begin returning to conscious alertness. Returning to conscious alertness in your own time and at your own

pace, in a way that just feels about right for you today. . . . Feeling very good, normal, with good sensations in every way as you return to full conscious alertness . . . soon, you will hear a tone that will signal for you to return to conscious alertness. When that tone sounds, you will begin to gently return to alertness . . . gradually opening your eyes as the sounds fade . . . and when the sound can no longer be heard, your eyes will be open. You will be fully awake and alert, in your normal state of wakefulness. Ready now? Returning to alertness with the sound of the tone. . . ."

CONCLUSION

Mindfulness involves a focus on present moment experience, with an attitude of curiosity and acceptance free from judgmental thoughts about the experiences that are arising. The state/trait of mindfulness can be a useful addition to a clinician's repertoire and eschews changing the *contents* of experience such as thoughts and feelings in favor of focusing on an individual's *reactions and attitudes* toward the contents of experience. Mindfulness is a central element of third-wave cognitive therapies such as MBSR, ACT, DBT, and MBCT, and although more large, well-controlled studies are clearly needed, there is already a substantial evidence base for the use of mindfulness in therapy for mood disorders, borderline personality, and even some evidence for chronic pain.

Despite the fact that there is a sound theoretical basis for delivering a mindfulness-based intervention in a hypnotherapeutic context, there are no current empirical trials to demonstrate the outcome of such an approach. Regardless, there has been intense interest from both the mindfulness and hypnosis communities of professionals in developing, studying, and using such an intervention. The sample case study and hypnosis script presented in this chapter may serve qualified clinicians as a template for implementing a combined mindfulness and hypnosis approach. In the event that this approach is indicated as the best option for a client, a clinician may also find that additional training in and research from the fields of hypnosis and mindfulness will be helpful in creating an integrated, theory-informed intervention.

REFERENCES

Arch, J. J., Ayers, C. R., Baker, A., Almklov, E., Dean, D. J., & Craske, M. G. (2013). Randomized clinical trial of adapted Mindfulness-Based Stress Reduction versus group cognitive behavioral therapy for heterogeneous anxiety disorders. *Behaviour Research and Therapy*, 51(4–5), 185–196. doi:10.1016/j.brat.2013.01.003

Bishop, S. R., Lau, M., Shapiro, S., Carlson, L., Anderson, N. D., Carmody, J., & Velting, D. (2004). Mindfulness: A proposed operational definition. *Clinical Psychology: Science and Practice*, 11(3), 230–241.

Bohus, M., Dyer, A. S., Priebe, K., Krüger, A., Kleindienst, N., Schmahl, C., . . . Steil, R. (2013). Dialectical Behaviour Therapy for post-traumatic stress disorder after childhood sexual abuse in patients with and without borderline personality disorder: A randomised controlled trial. *Psychotherapy and Psychosomatics*, 82(4), 221–233. doi:10.1159/000348451

Brown, D., Forte, M., Rich, P., & Epstein, G. (1982). Phenomenological differences among self hypnosis, mindfulness meditation, and imaging. *Imagination, Cognition and Personality*, 2(4), 291–309.

Cramer, H., Haller, H., Lauche, R., & Dobos, G. (2012). Mindfulness-Based Stress Reduction for low back pain. A systematic review. *BMC Complementary and Alternative Medicine*, 12(1), 162. doi:10.1186/1472-6882-12-162

Evans, S., Ferrando, S., Findler, M., Stowell, C., Smart, C., & Haglin, D. (2008). Mindfulness-Based Cognitive Therapy for generalized anxiety disorder. *Journal of Anxiety Disorders*, 22(4), 716–721. doi:10.1016/j.janxdis.2007.07.005

Forman, E. M., Herbert, J. D., Moitra, E., Yeomans, P. D., & Geller, P. A. (2007). A randomized controlled effectiveness trial of Acceptance and Commitment Therapy and cognitive therapy for anxiety and depression. *Behavior Modification*, 31(6), 772–799. doi:10.1177/0145445507302202

Forman, E. M., Shaw, J. A., Goetter, E. M., Herbert, J. D., Park, J. A., & Yuen, E. K. (2012). Long-term follow-up of a randomized controlled trial comparing Acceptance and Commitment Therapy and standard cognitive behavior therapy for anxiety and depression. *Behavior Therapy*, 43(4), 801–811. doi:10.1016/j.beth.2012.04.004

Fromm, E., Suzuki, D. T., & de Martino, R. (1960). *Zen buddhism & psychoanalysis*. New York, NY: Harper.

Goldin, P. R., & Gross, J. J. (2010). Effects of Mindfulness-Based Stress Reduction (MBSR) on emotion regulation in social anxiety disorder. *Emotion*, 10(1), 83. doi:10.1037/a0018441

Goldstein, T. R., Fersch-Podrat, R. K., Rivera, M., Axelson, D. A., Merranko, J., Yu, H., . . . Birmaher, B. (2015). Dialectical Behavior Therapy for adolescents with bipolar disorder: Results from a pilot randomized trial. *Journal of Child and Adolescent Psychopharmacology*, 25(2), 140–149. doi:10.1089/cap.2013.0145

Grant, J. A. (2012). Towards a more meaningful comparison of meditation and hypnosis. *Journal of Mind-Body Regulation*, 2(1), 71–74.

Grossman, P., Niemann, L., Schmidt, S., & Walach, H. (2004). Mindfulness-Based Stress Reduction and health benefits: A meta-analysis. *Journal of Psychosomatic Research*, 57(1), 35–43. doi:10.1016/S0022-3999(03)00573-7

Harned, M. S., Chapman, A. L., Dexter-Mazza, E. T., Murray, A., Comtois, K. A., & Linehan, M. M. (2008). Treating co-occurring Axis I disorders in recurrently suicidal women with borderline personality disorder: A 2-year randomized trial of Dialectical Behavior Therapy versus community treatment by experts. *Journal of Consulting and Clinical Psychology*, 76(6), 1068. doi:10.1037/a0014044

Harrer, M. E. (2009). Mindfulness and the mindful therapist: Possible contributions to hypnosis. *Contemporary Hypnosis*, 26(4), 234–244.

Hayes, S. C. (1987). A contextual approach to therapeutic change. In N. S. Jacobson (Ed.), *Psychotherapists in clinical practice: Cognitive and behavioral perspectives* (pp. 327–387). New York, NY: Guilford Press.

Hayes, S. C., & Wilson, K. G. (1993). Some applied implications of a contemporary behavior-analytic account of verbal events. *The Behavior Analyst/MABA*, 16(2), 283–301.

Hejazi, M., Sobhi, A., & Sahrzad, F. (2014). Effectiveness of Dialectical Behavior Therapy (DBT) in reducing depression and anxiety in women with breast cancer. *Indian Journal of Health and Wellbeing*, 5(3), 392.

Hofmann, S. G., Sawyer, A. T., Witt, A. A., & Oh, D. (2010). The effect of mindfulness-based therapy on anxiety and depression: A meta-analytic review. *Journal of Consulting and Clinical Psychology*, 78(2), 169. doi:10.1037/a0018555

Kabat-Zinn, J. (1994). *Wherever you go, there you are: Mindfulness meditation in everyday life*. New York, NY: Hyperion.

Kabat-Zinn, J. (1982). An outpatient program in behavioral medicine for chronic pain patients based on the practice of mindfulness meditation: Theoretical considerations and preliminary results. *General Hospital Psychiatry*, 4(1), 33–47.

Kliem, S., Kröger, C., & Kosfelder, J. (2010). Dialectical Behavior Therapy for borderline personality disorder: A meta-analysis using mixed-effects modeling. *Journal of Consulting and Clinical Psychology*, 78(6), 936. doi:10.1037/a0021015

Koerner, K., & Dimeff, L. A. (2000). Further data on Dialectical Behavior Therapy. *Clinical Psychology: Science and Practice*, 7(1), 104–112.

Koons, C. R., Robins, C. J., Tweed, J. L., Lynch, T. R., Gonzalez, A. M., Morse, J. Q., & Bastian, L. A. (2001). Efficacy of Dialectical Behavior Therapy in women veterans with borderline personality disorder. *Behavior Therapy, 32*(2), 371–390.

Koszycki, D., Benger, M., Shlik, J., & Bradwejn, J. (2007). Randomized trial of a meditation-based stress reduction program and cognitive behavior therapy in generalized social anxiety disorder. *Behaviour Research and Therapy, 45*(10), 2518–2526. doi:10.1016/j.brat.2007.04.011

Linehan, M. M. (1987). Dialectical Behavioral Therapy: A cognitive behavioral approach to parasuicide. *Journal of Personality Disorders, 1*(4), 328–333.

Linehan, M. M., Dimeff, L. A., Reynolds, S. K., Comtois, K. A., Welch, S. S., Heagerty, P., & Kivlahan, D. R. (2002). Dialectical Behavior Therapy versus comprehensive validation therapy plus 12-step for the treatment of opioid dependent women meeting criteria for borderline personality disorder. *Drug and Alcohol Dependence, 67*(1), 13–26.

Linehan, M. M., Schmidt, H., Dimeff, L. A., Craft, J. C., Kanter, J., & Comtois, K. A. (1999). Dialectical Behavior Therapy for patients with borderline personality disorder and drug-dependence. *American Journal on Addictions/American Academy of Psychiatrists in Alcoholism and Addictions, 8*(4), 279–292.

Ljótsson, B., Hedman, E., Lindfors, P., Hursti, T., Lindefors, N., Andersson, G., & Rück, C. (2011). Long-term follow-up of Internet-delivered exposure and mindfulness based treatment for irritable bowel syndrome. *Behaviour Research and Therapy, 49*(1), 58–61. doi:10.1016/j.brat.2010.10.006

Lynch, T. R., Trost, W. T., Salsman, N., & Linehan, M. M. (2007). Dialectical Behavior Therapy for borderline personality disorder. *Annual Review of Clinical Psychology, 3*(1), 181–205. doi:10.1146/annurev.clinpsy.2.022305.095229

Lynn, S., Surya Das, L., Hallquist, M. N., & Williams, J. C. (2006). Mindfulness, acceptance, and hypnosis: Cognitive and clinical perspectives. *International Journal of Clinical and Experimental Hypnosis, 54*(2), 143–166. doi:10.1080/00207140500528240

Lynn, S. J., Barnes, S., Deming, A., & Accardi, M. (2010). Hypnosis, rumination, and depression: Catalyzing attention and mindfulness-based treatments. *International Journal of Clinical and Experimental Hypnosis, 58*(2), 202–221.

Lynn, S. J., Malaktaris, A., Maxwell, R., Mellinger, D. I., & van der Kloet, D. (2012). Do hypnosis and mindfulness practices inhabit a common domain? Implications for research, clinical practice, and forensic science. *Journal of Mind-Body Regulation, 2*(1), 12–26.

Miller, J. J., Fletcher, K., & Kabat-Zinn, J. (1995). Three-year follow-up and clinical implications of a mindfulness meditation-based stress reduction intervention in the treatment of anxiety disorders. *General Hospital Psychiatry, 17*(3), 192–200.

Ong, J. C., Shapiro, S. L., & Manber, R. (2009). Mindfulness meditation and cognitive behavioral therapy for insomnia: A naturalistic 12-month follow-up. *Explore: The Journal of Science and Healing, 5*(1), 30–36.

Palmer, R. L., Birchall, H., Damani, S., Gatward, N., McGrain, L., & Parker, L. (2003). A Dialectical Behavior Therapy program for people with an eating disorder and borderline personality disorder—description and outcome. *The International Journal of Eating Disorders, 33*(3), 281–286. doi:10.1002/eat.10141

Panos, P. T., Jackson, J. W., Hasan, O., & Panos, A. (2013). Meta-analysis and systematic review assessing the efficacy of Dialectical Behavior Therapy (DBT). *Research on Social Work Practice, 24*(2), 213–223. doi:10.1177/1049731513503047

Piet, J., Würtzen, H., & Zachariae, R. (2012). The effect of mindfulness-based therapy on symptoms of anxiety and depression in adult cancer patients and survivors: A systematic review and meta-analysis. *Journal of Consulting and Clinical Psychology, 80*(6), 1007. doi:10.1037/a0028329

Powers, M. B., Zum Vorde Sive Vording, M. B., & Emmelkamp, P. M. (2009). Acceptance and Commitment Therapy: A meta-analytic review. *Psychotherapy and Psychosomatics, 78*(2), 73–80. doi:10.1159/000190790

Roemer, L., & Orsillo, S. M. (2002). Expanding our conceptualization of and treatment for generalized anxiety disorder: Integrating mindfulness/acceptance-based approaches with existing cognitive-behavioral models. *Clinical Psychology: Science and Practice, 9*(1), 54–68.

Sabourin, M. E., Cutcomb, S. D., Crawford, H. J., & Pribram, K. (1990). EEG correlates of hypnotic susceptibility and hypnotic trance: Spectral analysis and coherence. *International Journal of Psychophysiology, 10*(2), 125–142.

Safer, D. L., Telch, C. F., & Agras, W. S. (2001). Dialectical Behavior Therapy for bulimia nervosa. *American Journal of Psychiatry, 158*(4), 632–634. doi:10.1176/appi.ajp.158.4.632

Scheel, K. R. (2000). The empirical basis of Dialectical Behavior Therapy: Summary, critique, and implications. *Clinical Psychology: Science and Practice, 7*(1), 68–86.

Smith, J. C. (1975). Meditation as psychotherapy: A review of the literature. *Psychological Bulletin, 82*(4), 558.

Song, Y., Lu, H., Chen, H., Geng, G., & Wang, J. (2014). Mindfulness intervention in the management of chronic pain and psychological comorbidity: A meta-analysis. *International Journal of Nursing Sciences, 1*(2), 215–223.

Swenson, C. R. (2000). How can we account for DBT's widespread popularity? *Clinical Psychology: Science and Practice, 7*(1), 87–91.

Teasdale, J. D., Segal, Z. V., Williams, J. M., Ridgeway, V. A., Soulsby, J. M., & Lau, M. A. (2000). Prevention of relapse/recurrence in major depression by Mindfulness-Based Cognitive Therapy. *Journal of Consulting and Clinical Psychology, 68*(4), 615.

Telch, C. F., Agras, W. S., & Linehan, M. M. (2000). Group Dialectical Behavior Therapy for binge-eating disorder: A preliminary, uncontrolled trial. *Behavior Therapy, 31*(3), 569–582.

Telch, C. F., Agras, W. S., & Linehan, M. M. (2001). Dialectical Behavior Therapy for binge eating disorder. *Journal of Consulting and Clinical Psychology, 69*(6), 1061.

Veehof, M. M., Oskam, M. J., Schreurs, K. M., & Bohlmeijer, E. T. (2011). Acceptance-based interventions for the treatment of chronic pain: A systematic review and meta-analysis. *Pain, 152*(3), 533–542. doi:10.1016/j.pain.2010.11.002

Vøllestad, J., Sivertsen, B., & Nielsen, G. H. (2011). Mindfulness-Based Stress Reduction for patients with anxiety disorders: Evaluation in a randomized controlled trial. *Behaviour Research and Therapy, 49*(4), 281–288. doi:10.1016/j.brat.2011.01.007

Walrath, L. C., & Hamilton, D. W. (1975). Autonomic correlates of meditation and hypnosis. *American Journal of Clinical Hypnosis, 17*(3), 190–197.

Westen, D. (2000). The efficacy of Dialectical Behavior Therapy for borderline personality disorder. *Clinical Psychology: Science and Practice, 7*(1), 92–94.

Widiger, T. A. (2000). The science of Dialectical Behavior Therapy. *Clinical Psychology: Science and Practice, 7*(1), 101–103.

Wisniewski, L., & Kelly, E. (2003). The application of Dialectical Behavior Therapy to the treatment of eating disorders. *Cognitive and Behavioral Practice, 10*(2), 131–138.

Obesity and Weight Loss

Marty Sapp

Overweight and obesity rates have increased at striking rates in the United States, more than doubling in the past 30 years. Overweight and obesity are defined based on body mass index (BMI), which is calculated as weight (kg) divided by height^2 (m). A BMI range of 18.5 to 24.9 is considered healthy. Overweight is defined as a BMI of 25 to 29.9 and obese is defined as a BMI of at least 30. A BMI over 35 is considered morbidly obese. Results from the 2005–2006 National Health and Nutrition Examination Survey (NHANES) indicate that approximately 32.7% of American adults age 20 and over are overweight, 34.3% are obese, and 5.9% are extremely obese (BMI of 40 or higher; Allison & Baskin, 2009; Flegal, Carroll, Ogden, & Johnson, 2002; Hurt, Frazier, McClave, & Kaplan, 2011). This problem also extends to children and adolescents, with 8% to 13% of preschoolers and 13% to 22% of children and adolescents considered overweight, and an additional 31% at risk for becoming overweight (American Heart Association, 2005; Byom, 2009; Byom & Sapp, 2013; Centers for Disease Control and Prevention, National Center for Health Statistics, 2005–2006; Entwistle et al., 2014; Lehnert, Sonntag, Konnopka, Riedel-Heller, & König, 2012; National Institute of Health, 1998).

Obesity has been associated with type 2 diabetes, hypertension, coronary heart disease, and several other illnesses. As previously stated, there is a strong correlation between BMI and mortality (Byom, 2009). Sapp (2015) stated that type 2 diabetes is more common in adults than children and adolescents, but it is becoming more common with children and adolescents. Type 1 diabetes is insulin dependent and is an autoimmune disease; this means that the immune system attacks the body and the beta cells of the pancreas are destroyed. Essentially with type 1 diabetes, the pancreas does not produce enough insulin or little insulin, if any at all. Insulin is used to break down glucose or blood sugar, but after the beta cells of the pancreas are destroyed, sugar accumulates in the bloodstream. After the glucose levels of the blood increase, the kidneys extract glucose from the blood in an attempt to control blood sugar levels. Some of the symptoms of type 1 diabetes are increased urination, increased thirst, dehydration, increased hunger, fatigue, weight loss, and electrolyte imbalance. One major danger of type 1 diabetes is when fatty acids become metabolized and acids build up in the bloodstream. This leads to ketoacidosis and can result in coma and death (Barabasz, Olness, & Boland, 2009; Barte et al., 2010; Kihslinger & Sapp, 2006). Even though type 2 diabetes can occur with children, it is mostly associated with adults and is sometimes called adult-onset diabetes. Type 2 diabetes is insulin resistant, or the pancreas produces little or no insulin. Insulin resistance is when the body does not respond to or becomes resistant to insulin. Uncontrolled type 2 diabetes can result in the same results as type 1 diabetes, such as strokes, heart attacks, blindness, amputations, and kidney disease. Sadly, minorities such as African Americans, Latinos, Asian Americans, Native Americans, and Pacific Islanders are particularly at risk for type 2 diabetes (Sapp, 2015).

Hypnosis can treat the psychological aspects of type 2 diabetes such as stress, cognitive distortions, depression, and so on. Stress is one factor that can increase blood sugar levels; hypnosis can be used to reduce stress and the reduction in stress leads to reduced blood sugar levels. Some of the cognitive distortions that patients have about type 2 diabetes are "I do not really have this disease" "If I do not control my blood sugar levels, I will still be fine." Essentially, the treatment for type 2 diabetes involves a multimodal treatment plan of monitoring blood sugar levels, diet, exercise, and weight reduction.

Behavioral approaches are the common treatment for obesity, and behavioral principles include classical conditioning, operant conditioning, social learning theories, and cognitive behavior therapies. Typically, behavioral treatments result in a weight loss of 8% to 10%, and the fringe benefits of weight loss are improved blood pressure, lower cholesterol levels, reduced blood sugar levels, and other health benefits. The literature suggests that the goal for obesity treatment programs is a weight loss of 5% to 10% (Byom & Sapp, 2013; Stubbs & Lavin, 2013). The effects of behavioral treatment can be augmented with hypnosis (Kirsch, Montgomery, & Sapirstein, 1995). Even though there are many theories of hypnosis such as regression, dissociation, socio-phenomenological, Ericksonian hypnosis, and sociocognitive theories, the major debate has been between the special process theories and nonstate theories (Sapp, 2015). Special process theories believe that hypnosis is an altered state of consciousness and that physiologically hypnotic states are different from nonhypnotic states (Barabasz, 2012). In contrast, the nonstate theories do not question patients' reports of changes in subjective experiences during hypnosis, but they challenge the notion that these subjective experiences are the results of an altered state of consciousness that differs from normal consciousness (Byom & Sapp, 2013). Recently, data supporting the dissociated control theory of hypnosis provids additional information to explain hypnosis as dissociation and a change in brain functioning; this is an altered state of consciousness theory of hypnosis (Sapp, 2015). Sapp (2004a) reported that hypnosis had an average d effect size of 1.82, and he reported a 95% confidence interval around the population d effect size of .8025 for the lower limit and 1.0163 for the upper limit. Four hundred seventy-five studies were included in this analysis. Flammer and Bongartz (2003), in a meta-analysis of hypnosis, using 57 studies, found that hypnosis had a weighted or adjusted average effect size for d of .56. For disorders diagnosed in the *Diagnostic and Statistical Manual of Mental Disorders* (4th ed., *DSM-IV*; American Psychiatric Association, 2001), they found that hypnosis had a d effect size of .63. In addition, they performed a meta-analysis on 444 hypnosis studies and found a d effect size of 1.07. The d effect size for randomized studies was .56 and for nonrandomized studies the d effect size was 2.29. Like other studies, they found

a correlation of .44 between hypnotic susceptibility and treatment outcomes (Elkins, Fisher, & Johnson, 2012; Levitt, 1993; Sapp, 2015).

RESEARCH

A meta-analysis by Kirsch et al. (1995) analyzed 18 studies (1974 to 1993) that compared a cognitive behavioral treatment to the same treatment with the addition of hypnosis. The combined number of participants for this study was 577. The effect sizes were calculated for each hypnosis group versus the comparison group (no hypnosis), and these were referred to as d effect size. Presenting problems included pain, insomnia, hypertension, anxiety, obesity, snake phobia, self-concept and athletic performance, duodenal ulcer, and public speaking anxiety. The mean effect size across the studies was .87 standard deviations, indicating that hypnosis significantly increased the effectiveness of the cognitive behavioral treatment. The studies of obesity (eight studies) had the largest effect sizes and were omitted from the calculation of overall effect size in order to give a more conservative estimate. The most conservative estimate was an approximate .5 standard deviation, and this suggested that the average client receiving cognitive behavioral hypnotherapy benefited more than at least 70% of clients receiving cognitive behavioral treatment alone. Another study challenged this assertion, however, maintaining that including hypnosis only leads to a small effect size on average (Allison & Faith, 1996).

Allison and Faith (1996) conducted a meta-analysis on six of the obesity studies (two studies were not included due to their questionability) reported in Kirsch et al. (1995) and found an effect size of .28; this was considered to be small. Kirsch et al. (1995) reanalyzed their meta-analysis and found an effect size of .98 (weighted according to sample size), which was different from the previous two meta-analyses, but still indicated a large effect when hypnosis was combined with cognitive behavioral treatments. Sapp, Obiakor, Scholze, and Gregas (2007) addressed the conflicting findings by providing confidence intervals that provided the upper and lower limits of hypnosis in the treatment of obesity for the Allison and Faith study and the Kirsch study. They found a

95% confidence interval around the population d of (−.4662, .9549) for the Allison and Faith study, and (−.0440, 1.9449) for the Kirsch (1996) study. When a statistical test of the effect size obtained by Allison and Faith was compared to effect size found by Kirsch, a statistically significant difference was not found; the statistical power value for this analysis was .4915. These results indicated that both Allison and Kirsch (1996) were correct with their point estimates of effect, but confidence intervals showed how their results overlapped (Sapp, 2004a, 2004b, 2008). The Allison and Faith study represents the lower limit of effect and the Kirsch study represents the upper limit of effect. Sapp et al. (2007) found that the statistical power level was low for both studies and that more studies were needed. They also stated that a limitation of the current research regarding using hypnosis to treat obesity is that many of the studies only used female participants and that male subjects are needed for future studies.

Byom and Sapp (2013) investigated the effects of three group treatments for weight loss. The population was comprised of undergraduate and graduate students at a large urban university in the Midwest. The independent variable consisted of three treatment groups. One group received a standard cognitive behavioral treatment for weight loss adapted from the LEARN Program for Weight Management (Brownell, 2004). The second group received the identical cognitive behavioral treatment with the addition of hypnosis. For the hypnosis aspect, participants received hypnotic inductions and suggestions for weight loss. The third group received information about weight loss and exercise. Each group met for 8 weeks. The dependent variable was body weight recorded by a standard scale. Thirty-two women and five men participated in this study and they were randomly assigned to one of these three groups. A one-way analysis of variance (ANOVA) did not find any statistically significant differences among these three groups after treatment. A one-way ANOVA with percentage of weight loss as the dependent variable and treatment group as the independent variable found a power value of .22 or a 22% chance of the study correctly detecting a statistically significant difference. In other words, there is a 78% chance that a type II error was committed. This low power value explains why statistical significance was not found. The overall effect size was calculated by a formula suggested by Stevens (1999) and is expressed in terms of the F-statistic.

$$f = \sqrt{(k-1)F/N}$$

The overall effect size was .32 and showed the impact of the three treatments on weight loss. Cohen (1977) classified an f of .1 as a small effect size, .25 as a medium effect, and anything above .4 as a large effect size. An f of .32 would therefore be considered by Cohen to be indicative of a moderate effect size. Sapp (2015) stated that effect size must be interpreted within a substantive area and one cannot rely blindly on Cohen's broad guidelines. A d effect size of .28 was found between the LEARN Program for Weight Management and this program combined with hypnosis. A 95% confidence interval around the population d was (−.68, 1.24). When the hypnosis group combined with cognitive behavioral treatment was compared to the nutrition group, it produced a d of .85, and the 95% confidence interval around the population d was (−.34, 2.04). Finally, combining the cognitive behavioral group to the nutrition group resulted in a d of .61, and the 95% confidence interval around the population d was (−.49, 1.71). The hypnosis combined with cognitive behavioral treatment had a large effect size when compared with the nutrition group. The cognitive behavioral group had a moderate effect size when compared with the nutrition group. In summary, hypnosis in addition to a standard cognitive behavioral treatment for weight loss was found to be effective, and it had a large effect size.

CASE EXAMPLE

This case presentation concerns a 45-year-old married woman with a 15-year-old daughter. The client entered psychotherapy because of obesity and extreme anxiety. This client had a BMI of over 35 (morbidly obese). Let us refer to this client as Sara. Sara had been married to the same man for over 20 years. Throughout that period, she experienced many issues with her weight gain. She had a low evaluation of herself, and she relied, almost entirely, on her husband to direct her life. For example, because Sara feared disapproval, she feared expressing her ideas or opinions to her husband. Sara's issues with her weight were related to low levels of self-efficacy and some personality dynamics.

PREPARING CLIENTS FOR HYPNOSIS

Clinicians should be aware that if they cannot treat a disorder without hypnosis, then hypnosis should not be employed, because hypnosis is only an adjunctive procedure and not a complete therapy in and of itself. This general rule also applies to hypnosis for weight loss.

Clients should be educated about hypnosis. First, I usually point out that hypnosis is an adjunctive procedure. Second, I state that there are different types of hypnosis, such as guided imagery, cognitive behavioral, Ericksonian, and so forth. Next, I tell clients that all hypnosis is essentially self-hypnosis. Furthermore, I describe to clients how imagery and relaxation can lead to hypnosis. It is important to address clients' misconceptions about hypnosis, such as loss of consciousness, the weakening of the will, the giving away of secrets, and the inability to be dehypnotized. I stress with clients that nothing can occur through hypnosis that they do not want to happen.

Finally, I describe some everyday notions of hypnosis, such as driving and not being aware of how many miles one has driven, or becoming absorbed in a television show, movie, or book. Clinically, even though it has not been demonstrated consistently experimentally, absorption is a feature of hypnosis. In closing, I describe some uses of hypnosis such as for the treatment of trauma, anxiety, personality disorders, unipolar depression, dissociative disorders, ego strengthening, sexual disorders, nail-biting, obesity, smoking, and pain control.

Another way of preparing a client for hypnosis is through the use of Level I and II psychotherapy skills (Sapp, 2015). Level I psychotherapy skills are designed to help a client to explore his or her emotions. This phase of psychotherapy involves paraphrasing statements back to the client. For example, *"You are feeling nervous about hypnosis. You are not sure what will happen during hypnosis. You have some fears about hypnosis."* It is important to reassure clients that uncertain or apprehensive feelings toward hypnosis are natural.

And it is important to emphasize that anxiety, nervousness, apprehension, and so forth, are signs of intelligence and that you expect that hypnosis will be helpful. The hallmark of this phase of psychotherapy is to respond to clients' feelings, which can lead to clients experiencing genuineness and respect. The most important phase of Level I is responding to clients' feelings and the content that they communicate. Finally, this is also called the exploration phase of psychotherapy.

Level II, also called integrative understanding, is where clients continue to process information through the counseling process, and the counseling relationship gets stronger. The psychotherapist uses several psychotherapy skills during this phase such as summarizing content communicated by the client, challenging skills, and so forth. The highlight of this stage is the psychotherapists' ability to help clients to establish goals for hypnosis. When a client has been prepared for hypnosis, hypnotic screening tests can be used to determine the client's ability to respond to hypnosis (Sapp, 2015).

HYPNOSIS AND WEIGHT LOSS TRANSCRIPT

The patient I mentioned earlier, Sara, lost 50 pounds receiving hypnosis and counseling over a 1-year period. Normally, I process the client's reactions to the induction and make the appropriate changes for the following induction.

"Get as comfortable as you wish in that chair, or wherever you have yourself positioned. I am going to demonstrate a relaxation technique you can use to develop a very deep and pleasant hypnotic experience. Whenever you are ready to enter a relaxed state, clasp your hands together tightly in front of your body [the therapist should model this behavior].

Once you have them clasped together, begin to exert tension in that area. That's it. You will feel the force straining from both of your arms. In a little while your hands, arms, shoulders, and eyes will tire from the strain and want to relax. It will feel difficult for your fingers and hands to come apart. It will feel as if they are stuck together, but they will begin to come apart. That's it. As they do, you will correspondingly feel your eyes blinking and then eventually closing and then your hands will rest in your lap. This is very relaxing to say the least. This very pleasant feeling will travel throughout your body. It may appear that blood is streaming throughout your entire body. This can produce a warm, tingly, and relaxing effect.

Of course, I will guide you throughout this process. At times, it may feel as if my voice corresponds to the pattern of your relaxation and matches the rhythm of your breathing; that's fine. Just to help you become more relaxed, I will count down from 10 to 1. I will continue talking until it's time for you to come out of this trance feeling very, very good. Now, 10 . . . 9 . . . 8 . . . 7 . . . 6 . . . 5 . . . 4 . . . 3 . . . 2 . . . and 1. Now it is up to you at your own pace and rate. Good!

I want you to enjoy feeling comfortable. . . . Yes, that delightful feeling of relaxation spreading through the muscles of your face, neck, back, stomach, legs, and feet . . . floating downward through your shoulders . . . back . . . melting like butter. . . . If you want, you can allow yourself to melt like butter in that chair. [Adjust the wording to fit the position the client is in.] *Allow the chair to hold you, feel the peacefulness and comfort that is moving down through your stomach, thighs, legs, and toes. You are becoming more and more relaxed. If at any time you need to adjust your posture, feel free, because I would like you to enjoy feeling very comfortable. Yes . . . have you noticed how deeply relaxed you are? Now I would like to explain something to you. When you first went to school and learned to recognize numbers and letters, you didn't know it at that time that you were learning those numbers and letters for all the rest of your life. You formed a mental picture of those numbers and you formed mental visual pictures that would stay with you the rest of your life. You learned to form a mental visual picture of each letter of the alphabet without thinking about the fact that you would keep the visual image the rest of your life. In looking at that spot in your mind you have chosen, you have already formed a visual mental picture.* (Erickson & Rossi, 1979)

As I talk to you, you can keep looking mentally at that picture. As I talk to you, if you want, you can hear any sounds that you wish [mention any sounds in the environment]. *Actually, the only important thing for you is the sound of my voice and the meaning of what I have to say to you, so you do not really need to give attention to anything else unless you have a particular interest in the sounds in the room* [mention any other things in the environment].

Now, I will discuss your problem, and I will do it in this way. I will sketch it in general, and I want you to realize that I am only going to ask you to do things that you are capable of doing. There are many things we can do of which we are unaware. We can attend a lecture and because the lecturer is so interesting and stimulating, we do not even notice the passage of time. We are just interested in what the lecturer is saying.

If we attend a lecture that is dull, boring, and tiresome, one would feel the hardness of the seats. Yet, it could be the same seat in which one could sit and listen to an interesting lecturer and never feel all the discomforts and distress of not moving and the hardness of a seat. With a good lecturer, you don't even hear anything except his or her voice. Now, you are here to listen to me. You are here to do certain things. In your lifetime of experience you have felt things and you have not felt some things that you could have felt if you had paid attention to them [confusional technique; Erickson & Rossi, 1979]. *You have had much experience in forgetting things that would seem, upon ordinary thinking, to be unforgettable.*

For example, you were introduced to someone and you reply, 'I am very pleased to meet you,' but later you cannot [a change in tense in order to change the client's sense of time] *remember the person's name. You have forgotten it just as fast as you heard it. In other words, you can do any of the things that I will ask of you. You know how to move. You also know how not to move. You can lower your blood pressure, yet you don't know how you do that. You can slow down your heartbeat, but you don't know how you do that; but all of the things I ask you to do, every one of them, will be within the range of your experiences, so just listen carefully, knowing that I will ask of you only those things that I know you can do.* (Erickson & Rossi, 1979)

First of all, I want you to enjoy feeling very comfortable. In fact, you can enjoy yourself so much that you can let your unconscious mind listen to me while your conscious mind relaxes or busies itself with thoughts about things far removed from us, because many of the things that I want to assist you in accomplishing are governed by your unconscious mind. So now, continue as you are, at ease, in comfort, and at the proper time, I will give you all the directions necessary for you to take care of your problems, all of those you need to deal with.

Well, I am going to ask you to try to open your eyes as you imagine this. Yes, to try to open your eyes, but you will not be able to do so. Yes, the harder you try to open your eyes, the more they will stay closed.

So imagine and tell yourself that a bright ray of glaring, bright light is shining directly in your eyes, glaring, bright light directly in your eyes. . . . Now, try, yes, try to open them, but you will not be able to because the harder you try, the more they will want to stay closed. Try, try in the glaring light. [After about 10 seconds, say the following.] *All right, you can relax. You did fine. Now, as you relax deeply, you can allow the relaxation from the light to warmly relax your entire body. Let the light disappear. It went behind the clouds. Relax . . . you have demonstrated by the ability of your mind that you can exert control over your body. Good! You have within yourself the ability to relax . . . to imagine . . . and to utilize your own inner resources to control your physiological processes.*

As you remain deeply in a trance, open your eyes. Open your eyes, now! The intense light is gone. That's fine. Just look around the room and pick some spot to look at steadily as you continue to relax deeply with your eyes open. Look at any spot there . . . and do not touch it. Yes, just keep looking at that spot. Now there is no need to talk. No need to move. You really don't need to pay attention to me because your unconscious mind will hear me, and it will understand. You really don't need to pay attention to me.

While you have been sitting there, you've been doing the same thing that you did when you first went to school. Remember when you first learned

the task of writing the letters of the alphabet? It seemed like an impossible task . . . and how do you recognize a 'b?' How is it different from a 'd?' Numbers: Is a 6 an upside down 9, or is a 9 an upside down 6 . . . while you were mastering those problems, you were forming mental images that would stay with you for the rest of your life. Now, you did not know it then, but while you were sitting there the same thing has been happening to you now that happened to you then. Your respiration has changed. Your blood pressure has changed, and you have a mental image, a visualized image of that spot and now you may project on that spot, your favorite relaxing place, as you close your eyes, now! (Erickson & Rossi, 1979)

Now you can enjoy the comfort of going even deeper into the trance. I want you to enjoy every moment of it . . . and you can have a lot of pleasure in becoming aware of the comforts . . . within yourself. One of those is the understanding you can go back, and perhaps you might have the experience of sensing as you rest and relax . . . the incredible healing forces at work . . . restoring . . . nourishing . . . improving your memory . . . improving your health. If distracting thoughts enter your mind, do not fight them. Be aware of these thoughts.

Each time you experience hypnosis, you will have a greater awareness of the present and the unpleasant events of the past will become less important. If you like, focus your attention on your breathing and recognize how easily deep breathing alone can help to produce a nice state of relaxation. According to its own natural rhythm, let your body breathe by itself. Slowly . . . easily . . . and deeply. . . . Whatever you feel is your body's way of acknowledging the experience of relaxation, comfort, and peace of mind.

Remember your breathing . . . slowly and deeply. As you concentrate your attention on your breathing, give your body a few moments to relax deeply and fully. Feel all the tension, tightness, or discomfort draining away, down your spine, down your legs, and into the ground. With each breath, you may be surprised to feel yourself becoming more and more deeply relaxed . . . comfortable . . . and at ease. Enjoy this nice state of relaxation.

Every day . . . you will become physically stronger and fitter. You will become more alert . . . more wide awake . . . more energetic. You will become much less easily tired . . . and less easily fatigued . . . much less easily tired . . . much less easily fatigued . . . much less easily discouraged. Every day, your nerves will become stronger and steadier. You will become so deeply interested in whatever is going on . . . that your mind will become much less preoccupied with yourself.
(Adapted from Hartland, 1966)

Every day, you will become emotionally much calmer . . . much more settled . . . much less easily disturbed. Every day, you will feel a greater sense of awareness for the present and events of the past will become less and less meaningful. Every day . . . you will feel a greater feeling of personal safety and security . . . than you have felt for a long, long time. Every day . . . you will become . . . and you will remain . . . more and more completely relaxed . . . both mentally and physically.

All of these things will happen. . . . Exactly as I say they will happen. . . . You are going to feel much happier . . . much more contented . . . much more cheerful . . . much more optimistic . . . much less easily discouraged . . . much less easily depressed. As you relax and enjoy how wonderful it feels to be comfortable, peaceful, and at ease. . . . Tell yourself that you can return any time you wish . . . simply by letting go and taking a few moments to relax yourself and letting your imagination carry you there. . . . Each time you come to visit, you will find it even more beautiful, more serene, and more peaceful as new horizons are opened for you to experience. It is so easy . . . so accessible . . . so available to you, even when you are no longer with me, my voice will be with you. . . . It will be the voice of a member of your family. . . . It will be the voice of the wind . . . the rain . . . and, yes, the voice of the sun. . . . You will remember that the secret lies within you.

When using hypnosis for weight loss, the thing to concern yourself with is your diet. Weight loss occurs when your caloric consumption decreases. Your short-term weight loss goal should be between one to three pounds a week. High-bulk, low-calorie foods are the building blocks of an important diet, which, of course, must become a way of life.

Another thing you will find yourself doing is using a diet journal. That is, you will monitor your caloric intake. Also, you will remember to eat very slowly so that the hypothalamus of your brain can register fullness.

You will change your eating situation by eating at prescribed times in a certain room and following a certain ritual that will help you reduce your caloric intake. The last important factor of your weight loss program is exercise. You will need to exercise at least two to three times per week for at least 30 minutes.

As you start losing weight, you will feel better about yourself, and you will be able to elicit self-hypnosis, which will allow you to manage cravings and hunger. Remember, when you make a mistake during your weight loss plan, just recover and start over again.

Just to show you that you can achieve what you set out to, and that you are able to use hypnosis to help yourself, in a few moments, I will say the word 'now.' When I say this word, you will begin to count to yourself from 1 to 10. As the numbers increase, you will feel yourself becoming more and more alert. When you say the number 10 to yourself, you will open your eyes and come out of the trance feeling alert, refreshed, and also very comfortably relaxed . . . and whenever you go to sleep, you will really be able to enjoy the comfort of your bed. You will have a very deep and restful sleep, like one you had a long . . . long . . . time ago. When you awaken, you will feel calm and secure, rested, comfortable, and confident. Yes, confident in your ability to easily go into and come out of a trance, and to comfortably carry out this treatment, easier and easier. 'Now,' it is up to you, at your own pace and rate. Good!"

CONCLUSION

When I use hypnosis for weight loss, I find that it is useful to work along with my client's physician. Hypnotic suggestions that I use are similar to the ones for other habit disorders, such as smoking. Levitt (1993) reported the effectiveness of hypnosis in treating obesity. Bolocofsky, Coulthard-Morris, and Spinler (1984) found no significant differences in weight between participants receiving a behavioral management program and participants receiving the same program with the addition of hypnosis immediately after treatment. However, at an 8-month and 2-year follow-up, participants in the hypnosis group continued to lose weight, while participants in the behavioral management group without hypnosis did not. Thus, hypnosis had a significant effect on weight loss until follow-up. This suggests that the full benefits of hypnosis may not be realized immediately after treatment.

As previously stated, Byom and Sapp examined the specific aspects of hypnosis that may contribute to weight loss. For example, participants found suggestions to be slightly more effective than imagery, and it appears that hypnosis was most effective in increasing feelings of self-control. Results of this study may be used to design a hypnotic treatment protocol that, when combined with cognitive behavioral treatment, may assist individuals in losing more weight than with a cognitive behavioral treatment alone. Clearly, hypnosis is useful for weight reduction, but follow-up data are needed for hypnosis and weight reduction studies (Gelo et al., 2014).

REFERENCES

Allison, D. B., & Baskin, M. L. (2009). *Handbook of assessment methods for eating behaviors and weight-related problems: Measures, theory, and research*. Los Angeles, CA: Sage.

Allison, D. B., & Faith, M. S. (1996). Hypnosis as an adjunct to cognitive-behavioral psychotherapy for obesity: A meta-analytic reappraisal. *Journal of Consulting and Clinical Psychology, 64*(3), 513–516.

American Heart Association. (2005). *Heart disease and stroke statistics—2005 update*. Dallas, TX: American Heart Association.

American Psychological Association. (2001). *Publication manual of the American Psychological Association*. Washington, DC: Author.

Barabasz, A. F., Olness, K., & Boland, R. (2009). *Medical hypnosis primer: Clinical and research evidence*. Hove, UK: Routledge.

Barabasz, M. (2012). Cognitive hypnotherapy with bulimia. *American of Clinical Hypnosis, 54*(4), 353–364.

Barte, J. C. M., Ter Bogt, N. C. W., Bogers, R. P., Teixeira, P. J., Blissmer, B., Mori, T. A., & Bemelmans, W. J. E. (2010). Maintenance of weight loss after lifestyle interventions for overweight and obesity: A systematic review. *Obesity, 11*, 899–906.

Bolocofsky, D. N., Coulthard-Morris, L., & Spinler, D. (1984). Prediction of successful weight management from personality and demographic data. *Psychological Reports, 55*(3), 795–802.

Brownell, K. D. (2004). *The LEARN Program for Weight Management*. Dallas, TX: American Health Publishing Company.

Byom, T. K. (2009). *A comparison of the effectiveness of three group treatment for weight loss* (Doctoral dissertation). Retrieved from http://gradworks.umi .com/33/99/3399277.html

Byom, T., & Sapp, M. (2013). Comparison of effects of three group treatments for weight loss. *Sleep and Hypnosis, 15*(1–2), 1–10.

Centers for Disease Control and Prevention, National Center for Health Statistics. (2005–2006). *National health and nutrition examination survey data*. Hyattsville, MD: U.S. Department of Health and Human Services, Centers for Disease Control and Prevention.

Cohen, J. (1977). *Statistical power analysis for behavioral sciences*. New York, NY: Academic Press.

Elkins, G., Fisher, W., & Johnson, A. (2012). Assessment of hypnotizability in clinical research: Development, reliability, and validation of the Elkins' Hypnotizability Scale. *BMC Complementary and Alternative Medicine, 12*(1), 86.

Entwistle, P. A., Webb, R. J., Abayomi, J. C., Johnson, B., Sparkes, A. C., & Davies, I. G. (2014). Unconscious agendas in the etiology of refractory obesity and the role of hypnosis in their identification and resolution: A new paradigm for weight-management programs or a paradigm revisited. *Experimental Hypnosis, 62*(3), 330–359.

Erickson, M. H., & Rossi, E. (1979). *Hypnotherapy: An exploratory casebook*. New York, NY: Irvington.

Flammer, E., & Bongartz, W. (2003). On the efficacy of hypnosis: A meta-analytic study. *Contemporary Hypnosis, 20*(4), 179–197.

Flegal, K. M., Carroll, M. D., Ogden, C. L., & Johnson, C. L. (2002). Prevalence and trends in obesity among US adults, 1999-2000. *Journal of the American Medical Association, 288*(14), 1723–1727.

Gelo, O. C., Zips, A., Ponocny-Seliger, E., Neumann, K., Balugani, R., & Gold, C. (2014). Hypnobehavioral and hypnoenergetic therapy in the treatment of obese women: A pragmatic randomized clinical trial. *International Journal of Clinical and Experimental Hypnosis, 62*(3), 260–291.

Hartland, J. (1966). *Medical and dental hypnosis*. London, UK: Bailliere.

Hurt, R. T., Frazier, T. H., McClave, S. A., & Kaplan, L. M. (2011). Obesity epidemic: Overview, pathophysiology, and the intensive care unit conundrum. *Journal of Parenteral and Enteral Nutrition, 35*, S1–S13.

Kihslinger, D., & Sapp, M. (2006). Hypnosis and diabetes: Application for children, adolescents, and adults. *Australian Journal of Clinical Hypnotherapy and Hypnosis*, 27(1), 19–27.

Kirsch, I. (1996). Hypnotic enhancement of cognitive-behavioral weight loss treatments–Another meta-reanalysis. *Journal of Consulting and Clinical Psychology*, 64(3), 517–519.

Kirsch, I., Montgomery, G., & Sapirstein, G. (1995). Hypnosis as an adjunct to cognitive-behavioral psychotherapy: A meta-analysis. *Journal of Consulting and Clinical Psychology*, 63(2), 214–220.

Lehnert, T., Sonntag, D., Konnopka, A., Riedel-Heller, S., & König, H. H. (2012). The long-term cost effectiveness of obesity prevention interventions. Systematic literature review. *Obesity Reviews*, 13(6), 537–553.

Levitt, E. E. (1993). Hypnosis in the treatment of obesity. In J. W. Rhue, S. J. Lynn, & I. Kirsch (Eds.), *Handbook of clinical hypnosis* (pp. 533–553). Washington, DC: American Psychological Association.

National Institute of Health. (1998). Clinical guidelines on the identification, evaluation, treatment of overweight and obesity in adults: The evidence report. *NIH Publication, 8*, 4083.

Sapp, M. (2004a). *Cognitive-behavioral theories of counseling: Traditional and nontraditional approaches.* Springfield, IL: Charles C. Thomas.

Sapp, M. (2004b). Confidence intervals within hypnosis research. *Sleep and Hypnosis*, 6(4), 169–176.

Sapp, M. (2008). The effect sizes r and d in hypnosis research. *European Journal of Clinical Hypnosis*, 8(1), 41–59.

Sapp, M. (2015). *Hypnosis, dissociation, and absorption.* Springfield, IL: Charles C. Thomas.

Sapp, M., Obiakor, F., Scholze, S., & Gregas, A. (2007). Confidence intervals and hypnosis in the treatment of obesity. *Australian Journal of Clinical Hypnotherapy and Hypnosis* . 28(2), 25.

Stevens, J. P. (1999). *Intermediate statistics: A modern approach.* Mahwah, NJ: Lawrence Erlbaum.

Stubbs, R. J., & Lavin, J. H. (2013). The challenges of implementing behavior changes that lead to sustained weight management. *Nutrition Bulletin, 38*, 5–22.

Posttraumatic Stress Disorder

Ciara Christensen

The majority of individuals experience a violent situation at some point during their lives, such as robberies, assault, natural disasters, major accidents, combat, captivity, sexual abuse, torture, or being first responders (Levine, 2010; van der Kolk, 2014; Vermetten & Christensen, 2010). Distressing cues can precipitate a cascade of anxiety and fear-related symptomatology, with all the sights, sounds, and odors reminiscent of the original traumatic event (Scurfield & Platoni, 2013). Estimates of the prevalence of posttraumatic stress disorder (PTSD) in the United States alone is approximately 3.5% of adults, with the estimated lifetime risk for PTSD being 8.7% (American Psychiatric Association, 2014). However, the risk of onset and severity of PTSD differs across cultural groups as a result of variation in the type of traumatic exposure (e.g., genocide). Thus, the clinical expression of symptoms or symptom clusters of PTSD may vary culturally as well (*Diagnostic and Statistical Manual of Mental Disorders*, 5th ed. [*DSM-5*]; American Psychiatric Association [APA], 2013, p. 278). Data suggest that PTSD is more prevalent among females than males. This appears to be attributable to a greater likelihood of exposure to traumatic events such as rape and other forms of interpersonal violence (van der Kolk, 2014; *DSM-5*; APA, 2013, p. 278). For example, more accurate reporting has revealed that 12 million women in the United States alone have been victims of rape. Tragically, more than half of all rapes occur in girls below the age of 15 (van der Kolk, 2014). The aftermath of such unexpected, beyond-normal experiences can leave human lives in ruins.

reactions to a situational cue may be experienced. They may have little understanding as to why that response is being experienced, and it can leave them unable to respond effectively (Barabasz, Barabasz, Christensen, French, & Watkins, 2013; Barabasz, Barabasz, & Watkins, 2011, 2012; Christensen, Barabasz, & Barabasz, 2013; Emmerson, 2003; Frankel, 1994; Vermetten & Christensen, 2010). Given such reactions, trauma can be understood as a basic rupture, and individuals may feel any number of emotions including a sense of futility, detachment, or withdrawal. Such a feeling or loss of connection does not necessarily occur rapidly; rather, it may be a gradual process. Although slight and possibly unbeknownst to the individuals, their feelings are the by-product of an instinctive response, which enables them to endure the tremendous distress of (a) traumatic event(s). The person enters a dissociative "survival mode" when the slightest threat cue is perceived. This can render him or her stuck in a highly aroused mode. Physiologically, this response is intended for an immediate defensive action, not a longer term adaptation (Curran, 2010; Levine, 2010; Levine & Kline, 2006). For us as humans, being stuck in survival mode means that as long as the mind is defending itself against invisible assaults, our closest bonds are threatened, along with our ability to imagine, plan, play, learn, and pay attention to the needs of others (van der Kolk, 2014). This highlights the complex interplay between external factors inherent in the trauma itself and the biological, psychological, and social factors related to PTSD (Conner & Butterfield, 2003).

OVERVIEW OF PTSD

For individuals exposed to traumatic event(s), at any time, a variety of emotionally charged

DIAGNOSTIC CATEGORIES

Development of PTSD, Acute Stress Disorder (ASD), or combat stress injury (Figley & Nash,

2007) can occur after exposure to or witnessing traumatic event(s), after learning trauma occurred to someone close, or repeated extreme exposure to aversive aspects of traumatic events (i.e., first responders).

Symptoms typically are divided into four categories:

1. *Re-experiencing* the event, including symptoms of intrusion such as involuntary memories or dreams; dissociative reactions or flashbacks; and intense psychological distress at exposure to internal or external cues that symbolize or reassemble an aspect of the trauma.
2. *Avoidance responses,* including efforts to avoid distressing memories, thoughts, or feelings associated with the event, and/or efforts to avoid external reminders (people, places, activities, etc.) that evoke distressing memories.
3. *Negative alterations in cognition/mood,* including feelings such as persistent and distorted sense of blame of self or others, estrangement from others or markedly diminished interest in activities, or an inability to remember key aspects of the event.
4. *Alterations in arousal/reactivity,* including marked irritability, recklessness or self-destructive behavior, hypervigilance, problems with concentration, exaggerated startle response, and/or sleep disturbance (*DSM-5*; APA 2013, p. 272).

Criteria for ASD includes development of symptoms that begin immediately after the trauma and persist for at least 3 days and up to a month (*DSM-5*; American Psychiatric Association, 2013, p. 281). In order to meet the diagnostic threshold for PTSD, however, symptoms must lead to functional impairment and persist beyond 3 months after exposure (*DSM* 4th ed. [*DSM-IV*]; APA, 2000; *DSM-5*; APA, 2013).

It is not uncommon for patients to meet criteria for other psychiatric disorders as well. Comorbidities such as depression, substance abuse, and anxiety disorders are frequently seen in clinical settings (Kessler, Sonnega, Bromet, Hughes, & Nelson, 1995). Guilt, shame, self-blame, and/or feeling ashamed are commonly associated emotions of PTSD (Watkins, 1942, 1949, 1951). In the most acute expression, the constellation of symptoms generally resembles agitated depression

(i.e., individuals display hostility toward others, experience recurrent dreams of friends dying, and/or distance themselves from others for fear of abandonment; Barabasz, Barabasz, Christensen, French, & Watkins, 2013; Barabasz, Barabasz, & Watkins, 2011, 2012; Christensen, Barabasz, & Barabasz, 2013).

Symptoms of PTSD are also highly intercorrelated with dissociation, somatization, and affect dysregulation (Bower & Sivers, 1998; Butler, Duran, Jasiukaitis, Koopman, & Spiegel, 1996; Cahill, 1997; Herman, 1997; Spiegel, 2006; Spiegel, Hunt, & Dondershine, 1988; van der Kolk, 2014; Vermetten & Christensen, 2010; Vermetten, Dorahy, & Spiegel, 2007). These symptoms are especially evident in prolonged trauma, such as with a childhood onset (i.e., incest, physical abuse, torture, or neglect), and can lead to significantly hindered personality development, including relatedness and identity. In turn, these individuals are vulnerable to repeated harm, both self-inflicted and at the hands of others (Curran, 2010; van der Kolk, 2014; Vermetten & Christensen, 2010). For clinicians, it is important to be aware of the onset of the trauma, (i.e., whether onset was early in life or later as an adult). In early-life trauma, the psychopathology is usually complex (Herman, 1997; van der Kolk, 2014; Vermetten & Christensen, 2010); thus, the clinical presentation may also include many problems other than the core symptoms of PTSD.

EVIDENCE

"Working through of traumatic stimuli or memories requires careful consideration" (Cardena, Maldonado, van der Hart & Spiegel, 2000, p. 255). Complications arise from the fact that the traumatic stimuli may not always be easy to identify and may be evoked by any number of things including exposure to a movie, an odor, or something more subtle, such as a physical gesture or voice. However, Cardena et al. (2000) noted that hypnotic techniques help to reduce such complications and that hypnosis provides a safe environment in which the memories associated with the trauma do not overwhelm patients.

Research has revealed that hypnosis is effective in the treatment of PTSD when used adjunctively with cognitive behavioral interventions (Degun-Mather, 2001; Spiegel & Vermetten, 1994). Some examples include exposure therapy using elements of cognitive therapy (Lynn & Cardena, 2007) and "cognitive behavioral" therapy (Blanchard, Hickling, Devineni, Veazey, Galovski, et al., 2003; Bryant, Moulds, Guthrie, & Nixon, 2005; Bryant et al., 2006). Research has also shown that hypnosis has been effective for those who experience dissociation (Barabasz, 2008; Frederick & McNeal, 1999; Kwan, 2009; Spiegel & Vermetten, 1994; van der Hart & Brown, 1992; Vermetten & Christensen, 2010; Watkins & Barabasz, 2008).

More recent research focused on examining the hypnotic techniques that offer greater potential for the resolution of physical and emotional responses has emerged; specifically, hypnotic interventions, which use abreactive hypnosis, such as those conducted in Ego-State Therapy (EST; Watkins & Barabasz, 2008; Watkins & Watkins, 1997) during the course of treatment. Most recent studies conducted using manualized abreactive EST (Barabasz, Barabasz, Christensen, & Watkins, 2012; Barabasz, Christensen, & Watkins, 2010; Barabasz et al., 2013; Christensen et al., 2013) treatment to target the symptoms of PTSD have been promising. For example, in the Christensen et al. (2013) study, the significant differences between those who received abreactive EST and those who received the active control treatment on measures of PTSD, depression, and anxiety revealed that participants exposed to manualized single-session abreactive EST showed significantly lower PTSD symptoms after treatment and over extended periods of time, compared with the control participants. Consistent with Christensen and colleagues, in the Barabasz et al., (2013) study, which also used single-session manualized abreactive EST, findings indicated this treatment provided rapid and thorough resolution of PTSD symptomatology immediately after treatment and follow-ups.

CASE EXAMPLE

In this example, a 42-year-old divorced woman presented for therapy. She was diagnosed with bi-polar disorder (she was not able to specify bipolar I or II) and had been taking Cymbalta (duloxetine) 60 mg, Abilify (aripiprazole) 10 mg, and Wellbutrin (bupropion) 100 mg daily for symptom management. The trauma she wanted to focus on related to being molested by her father at the age of 4. Her primary complaint was "flashbacks," which she stated occurred in the evening.

This individual was seen for one session. Two therapists met with her for 6 consecutive hours. A single session of manualized abreactive EST treatment, specifically honed to the symptoms of PTSD, was employed. During the first 45 minutes of treatment, her hypnotic ability as well as her symptoms were assessed. She presented with mild depression, Beck Depression Inventory-II (BDI-II; Beck, Steer, & Brown, 1996) score of (17) and severe anxiety, Beck Anxiety Inventory (BAI; Beck & Steer, 1993) score of (28). The Modified Scale for Suicidal Ideation (MSSI; Miller, Norman, Bishop, & Dow, 1986) score of 0 indicated she was not currently experiencing suicidal ideation and her Hypnotic Induction Profile (HIP; Spiegel, 1977) score (8) was indicative of high-range hypnotizability on the 10-point scale. Her symptoms of PTSD as measured by the Davidson Trauma Scale (DTS; 102) were quite elevated. She was also provided information about the therapy that would be used; in this case, manualized abreactive EST (Barabasz, Barabasz, Christensen, & Watkins, 2012; Barabasz, Christensen, & Watkins, 2010; Barabasz et al., 2013; Christensen et al., 2013) and hypnosis. Finally, we discussed questions/concerns about the intervention. Upon the completion of therapy, it was observed that her complexion appeared fresh and rejuvenated. She reported feeling tired and indicated that she felt "much better." Her posttreatment DTS (total score = 65) was consistent with her report, as were her posttreatment BAI and BDI-II measures, with both showing dramatic positive results of the EST treatment (BAI = 0, BDI-II = 1). At 1-month follow-up, she continued to report lower PTSD symptoms in contrast to her pretreatment and posttreatment measures as suggested by her modified DTS (total score = 28). Additionally, she maintained lower anxiety and depressive symptoms as suggested by her BDI-II score (3) and BAI (2). At 3 months follow-up, this individual continued to maintain PTSD symptom alleviation as shown by her modified DTS total score = 27, as well as relief from depression (BDI = 2) and anxiety (BAI = 2).

The following transcripts include many of the elements that were used during the manualized abreactive EST session.

Summer Scene Induction (Freedom From Distraction)

Inducing hypnosis by asking the patient to visualize a pleasant, relaxing scene is often effective in achieving greater hypnotic depth. The summer scene induction is a typical example of this approach (see also Barabasz & Watkins, 2005, p. 194):

"Just imagine that it is a warm summer afternoon and you are lying on a green, grassy slope on a hillside, miles away from where anybody or anything could disturb you. It is so peaceful, so very, very peaceful. The grass is very soft and thick. There are a few trees in the distance. The landscape is like a meadow, covered with thick, plush green grass and a few beautiful wild flowers. It is quiet and the sky overhead is a deep, rich blue with only a few soft, fluffy clouds floating in it. The sun is beaming down, and you feel so peaceful, so relaxed, so safe, and so comfortable that you are allowing yourself to be drowsy, more and more drowsy. It is as if the only thought you have is one, which goes round and round in your head and says, 'Deeper relax, deeper relax, deeper relax.'"

The therapist may continue to describe this scene as the patient becomes increasingly involved in the pleasurable fantasy, *(Proceed to next phase of therapy.)*

Progressive Warm, Heavy Feeling Induction (Optional Add-On to the Above)

This deepening technique can be added to this summer scene, as follows:

"There is a warm, numb feeling beginning to form in your forehead just above the eyes. Now it starts to spread over the top of your head, into your face, and all through your head. Your head feels warm and heavy. This is like a numb wave of warmness that is sweeping down through your body. It brings the most pleasant sensation of heaviness and relaxation. Now it moves down

through your neck, and your neck becomes heavy. You make it heavy. Heavy . . . heavy . . . heavy! This warm, numb, heavy feeling now goes through your shoulders and down into your arms and hands. They feel like the limbs on a tree. And now this warm, heavy feeling moves into the center of your body, down through your chest and your abdomen, and the center of your body feels so warm, comfortable, and heavy. See if you can let this feeling now drift down into your legs [Pause], *your thighs* [Pause], *the calves of your legs* [Pause], *and into your feet* [Pause]. *And they, too, can feel warm and numb and heavy."*

This pattern may be repeated several times and can easily be adapted to suit a variety of patients. Some therapists prefer to have the "warm, numb, heavy feeling or a relaxed" feeling start in the feet and move up the body. The patient's report of the way that causes him or her to respond best should guide the choice.

CONCLUSION

PTSD can severely diminish the quality of life of the patient. Clinicians who wish to utilize hypnosis to help treat patients presenting with PTSD should familiarize themselves with the symptomatology and utilize appropriate screening measures. A thorough history screening will provide clinicians with important information regarding the onset of the trauma (i.e., early in life vs. later). Utilizing this information, clinicians are better able to adapt their treatment as well as the use of hypnotic suggestions to best suit the needs of their patients.

Research on hypnosis for PTSD adjunctively with other treatments has been promising. While additional investigation is needed to determine which hypnotic techniques offer greater potential for the resolution of PTSD symptomatology, more recent studies have demonstrated support in favor of using manualized abreactive EST as a rapid psychological intervention for the treatment of PTSD providing durable symptom relief.

REFERENCES

American Psychiatric Association. (2013). *Diagnostic and statistical manual of mental disorders (DSM-5)*. Washington, DC: American Psychiatric Press.

American Psychiatric Association. (2014). Retrieved from http://www.psychiatry.org/ptsd

Barabasz, A. (2008, August 15–17). *Ego-state therapy and hypnoanalysis.* Presented at the 116th American Psychological Association Convention, Boston, Convention Center, Boston, MA.

Barabasz, A., Barabasz, M., & Watkins, J. G. (2012). Single-session manualized ego state therapy (EST) for combat stress injury, PTSD, and ASD, Part 2: The procedure. *International Journal of Clinical and Experimental Hypnosis, 60*(3), 370–381. doi:10.1080/00207144.2012.675300

Barabasz, A., Barabasz, M., Christensen, C., & Watkins, J. (2012). *Abstractive ego state therapy, manual for combat stress injury, PTSD & ASD.* Palouse, WA: Authors. Retrieved from arreed_barabasz@wsu.edu

Barabasz, A., Barabasz, M., Christensen, C., French, B., & Watkins, J. G. (2013). Efficacy of single-session abreactive ego state therapy for combat stress injury, PTSD, and ASD. *International Journal of Clinical and Experimental Hypnosis, 61*(1), 1–19. doi:10.1080/00207144.2013.729377

Barabasz, A., Barabasz, M., Christensen, C., Riegel, S., & Watkins, J. G. (2013). *Abreagierende ego state therapie ein wegeiser für kamphbding te störungen, PTBS und ASD [Manualized abreactive ego state therapy for PTSD and ASD].* Self-published manuscript. Palouse, WA: Arreed Barabasz. Retrieved from arreed_barabasz@wsu.edu

Barabasz, A., Christensen, C., & Watkins, J. G. (2010). *Ego state therapy manual: PTSD, & ASD* (research ed.). Self-published manuscript, replaced by Barabasz, A., Barabasz, M., Christensen, C., & Watkins, J. (2012).

Barabasz, A. F., Barabasz, M., & Watkins, J. G. (2011). Single-session manualized ego state therapy (EST) for combat stress injury, PTSD, and ASD, Part 1: The theory. *International Journal of Clinical and Experimental Hypnosis, 59*(4), 379–391. doi:10.1080/00207144.2011.595349

Barabasz, A., & Watkins, J. G. (2005). *The hypnotherapeutic techniques.* New York, NY: Brunner-Rutledge.

Beck, A. T. & Steer, R. A. (1993). *Beck anxiety inventory manual.* San Antonio, TX: Harcourt Brace and Company.

Beck, A. T., Steer, R. A., & Brown, G. K. (1996). *Manual for the Beck Depression Inventory-II.* San Antonio, TX: Psychological Corporation.

Blanchard, E. B., Hickling, E. J., Devineni, T., Veazey, C. H., Galovski, T. E., Mundy, E., . . . & Buckley, T. C. (2003). A controlled evaluation of cognitive behaviorial therapy for posttraumatic stress in motor vehicle accident survivors. *Behaviour research and therapy, 41*(1), 79–96.

Bower, G. H., & Sivers, H. (1998). Cognitive impact of traumatic events. *Development and Psychopathology, 10,* 625–653.

Bryant, R., Moulds, M., Guthrie, R. M., & Nixon, R. (2005). The additive benefit of hypnosis and cognitive behaviorial therapy in treating acute stress disorder. *Journal of Consulting and Clinical Psychology, 73,* 334–340.

Bryant, R., Moulds, M., Nixon, R., Mastrodomenico, J., Flemingham, K., & Hopwood, S. (2006). Hypnotherapy and cognitive behavior therapy of acute stress disorder: A 3-year follow-up. *Behavior Research and Therapy, 44,* 1331–1335.

Butler, L. D., Duran, R. E., Jasiukaitis, P., Koopman, C., & Spiegel, D. (1996). Hypnotizability and traumatic experience: A diathesis-stress model of dissociative symptomatology. *American Journal of Psychiatry, 153*(7), 42–63.

Cahill, L. (1997). The neurobiology of emotionally influenced memory: Implications for understanding traumatic memory. *Annals of the New York Academy of Sciences, 821,* 238–246.

Cardena, E., Maldonado, J., van der Hart, O., & Spiegel, D. (2000). Hypnosis. In E. B. Foa, T. M. Keane, & M. J. Friedman (Eds.), *Effective treatments for PTSD* (pp. 247–279). New York, NY: Guilford Press.

Christensen, C., Barabasz, A., & Barabasz, M. (2013). Efficacy of abreactive ego state therapy for PTSD: Trauma, resolution, depression and anxiety. *International Journal of Clinical and Experimental Hypnosis, 61,* 20–37.

Connor, K., & Butterfield, M. (2003). Posttraumatic stress disorder. *FOCUS, 1,* 247–262.

Curran, L. A. (2010). *Trauma competency: A clinician's guide.* Eau Claire, WI: PESI.

Degun Mather, M. (2001). The value of hypnosis in the treatment of chronic PTSD with dissociative fugues in a war veteran. *Contemporary Hypnosis, 18*(1), 4-13.

DSM-5 American Psychiatric Association. (2013). *Diagnostic and statistical manual of mental disorders.* Arlington, TX: American Psychiatric Publishing.

Emmerson, G. (2003). *Ego state therapy.* Wales, UK: Crown House Publishing.

Figley, C. R., & Nash, W. P. (2007). *Combat stress injury.* New York, NY: Routledge.

Frankel, F. (1994). The concept of flashbacks in historical perspective. *International Journal of Clinical and Experimental Hypnosis, 4,* 321–336.

Frederick, C., & McNeal, S. (1999). *Inner strengths: Contemporary psychotherapy and hypnosis for ego-strengthening.* Mahwah, NJ: Lawrence Erlbaum Associates.

Herman, J. L. (1997). *Trauma and recovery: The aftermath of violence from domestic abuse to political terror.* New York, NY: Basic Books.

Kessler, R. C., Sonnega, A., Bromet, E., Hughes, M., & Nelson, C. B. (1995). Posttraumatic stress disorder in the national comorbidity survey. *Archives of General Psychiatry, 52,* 1048–1060.

Kwan, P. S. K. (2009). The application of hypnosis in the treatment of a woman with complex trauma. *Australian Journal of Clinical and Experimental Hypnosis, 34*(2), 204–215.

Levine, P. A. (2010). *In an unspoken voice: How the body releases trauma and restores goodness.* Berkley, CA: North Atlantic Books.

Levine, P. A., & Kline, M. (2006). *Trauma through a child's eyes: Awakening the ordinary miracle of healing.* Berkley, CA: North Atlantic Books.

Lynn, S. J., & Cardeña, E. (2007). Hypnosis and the treatment of posttraumatic conditions: An evidence-based approach. *International Journal of Clinical and Experimental Hypnosis, 55*(2), 167-188.

Miller, I. W., Norman, W. H., Bishop, S. B., & Dow, M. G. (1986). The modified scale for suicidal ideation: Reliability and validity. *Journal of Consulting and Clinical Psychology, 54*(5), 724-725.

Scurfield, R. M.,. & Platoni, K. T. (2013). *Healing war trauma.* New York, NY: Routledge.

Spiegel, D. (2006). Recognizing traumatic dissociation. *American Journal of Psychiatry, 163,* 4.

Spiegel, D., Hunt, T.,. & Dondershine, H. (1988). Dissociation and hypnotizability in posttraumatic stress disorder. *American Journal of Psychiatry, 145,* 301–305.

Spiegel, D., & Vermetten, E. (1994). Physiological correlates of hypnosis and dissociation. In D.

Spiegel (Ed.), *Dissociation, culture, mind and body.* Washington, DC: Academic Press.

Spiegel, H. (1977). The Hypnotic Induction Profile (HIP): A review of its development. In W. E. Edmonston (Ed.), *Conceptual and investigative approaches to hypnosis and hypnotic phenomena. Annals of the New York Academy of Sciences, 296,* 129–142.

van der Hart, O., & Brown, P. (1992). Abreaction re-evaluated. *Dissociation, 5,* 127–140.

van der Kolk, B. A. (2014). *The body keeps the score: Brain, mind, and body in the healing of trauma.* New York, NY: Viking.

Vermetten, E., Dorahy, M. J., & Spiegel, D. (Eds.). (2007). *Traumatic dissociation: Neurobiology and treatment.* Washington, DC: American Psychiatric press.

Vermetten, E., & Christensen, C. (2010). Posttraumatic stress disorder (PTSD). In A. Barabasz, K. Olness, R. Boland, & S. Kahn (Eds.), *Medical hypnosis primer: Clinical and research evidence* (pp. 41–53). New York, NY & London: Routledge.

Watkins, J. G. (1949). *Hypnotherapy of war neuroses.* New York, NY: Ronald Press.

Watkins, J. G. (1951). Hypnotherapy in a military setting. *Journal of Personality, 1,* 318–315.

Watkins, J. G., & Barabasz, A. (2008). *Advanced hypnotherapy: Hypnodynamic techniques.* New York, NY & London: Routledge.

Watkins, J. G.,. & Watkins, H. H. (1997). *Ego states theory and therapy.* New York, NY: W. W. Norton.

Watkins, J. G. (1942). Offensive psychological warfare. *Journal of Consulting Psychology, 6*(3), 117–122. doi:10.1037/h0056480

Sexual Self-Image

Gary Elkins, Debra Barton, and Alisa Johnson

Sexual health is a concept comprised of numerous important variables that can impact and be impacted by overall psychological, social, and physical health. The World Health Organization (WHO), in 2002, defined *sexual health* in part as "a state of physical, emotional, mental and social well-being in relation to sexuality" (WHO, 2006). *Sexuality* was defined, in the same WHO meeting, as "a central aspect of being human throughout life encompasses sex, gender identities and roles, sexual orientation, eroticism, pleasure, intimacy and reproduction." Hence, sexual health and sexuality are important aspects for those working in physical and mental health fields to be able to assess and help their patients and clients.

There is a high prevalence of sexual dysfunction reported for the general population (Dunn, Croft, & Hackett, 1998; Lewis et al., 2004) and even higher for many cancer survivors (Basson, 2010; Falk & Dizon, 2013; Speer et al., 2005). A few longitudinal studies in women with breast or gynecological cancer provide insights into the predictors of reduced sexual health after cancer. These predictors include vaginal dryness/symptoms, negative body image, decreased feelings of sexual attractiveness, poor mental health, a history of receiving chemotherapy, and partner issues (Burwell, Case, Kaelin, & Avis, 2006; Carmack Taylor, Basen-Engquist, Shinn, & Bodurka, 2004; Ganz, Desmond, Belin, Meyerowitz, & Rowland, 1999). Psychosocial issues were prominent in these data, along with vaginal symptoms, leading to the justification of a psychosocial approach to improving sexual health in women.

Sexual self-image, often referred to as sexual self-schema, is defined by Andersen and Cyranowski (1994) as a person's cognitive representation of his or her sexual self. This concept can inform the development of a cognitive approach to addressing sexual health concerns. According to Andersen and Cyranowksi (1994, p. 1079), sexual self-schemas of individuals are "derived from past experience, manifest in current experience, influential in the processing of sexually relevant social information, and they guide sexual behavior." It is hardly surprising then that a person's sexual self-image plays a large role in sexual health and functioning.

Sexual self-image is an important psychological component of sexual well-being and health-related quality of life (Carpenter, Andersen, Fowler, & Maxwell, 2009; Reissing, Lalibert, & Davis, 2005). The experience of diagnosis and treatment for diseases such as gynecological and breast cancer can lead to sexual dysfunction, resulting in a negative sexual self-image (Carpenter et al., 2009; Hoyt & Carpenter, 2015; Quintard & Lakdja, 2008; Shell, 2008; Sheppard & Ely, 2008). Sexual self-schema has been shown to be predictive of a person's ability to recover and adjust sexually after such adverse events (Reissing et al., 2005); a positive sexual self-schema can lessen the effects of adverse events on sexuality and quality of life (Carpenter et al., 2009; Hoyt & Carpenter, 2015).

Sexual self-image is malleable and can fluctuate across the life span, often in response to psychological and physical circumstances. Women transitioning through menopause often find that their psychological and physical symptoms (mood disruption, hot flashes, vaginal dryness and atrophy, fatigue) contribute to decreased sexual functioning and lowered sexual self-image (Dennerstein, Dudley, & Burger, 2001; Gracia et al., 2004). Improving cognitive representations of sexuality can lead to improved sexual functioning among menopausal women.

Other issues that may affect sexual self-image include trauma and childhood abuse. Cognitive mechanisms are involved in the development of sexual dysfunction following childhood abuse. Among the most common problems reported following childhood sexual abuse are promiscuity, hypoactive sexual desire, female orgasmic disorder, and risky sexual behaviors (Rellini, Ing, & Meston, 2011). Negative sexual self-schemas are frequent among survivors of childhood sexual abuse (Blain, Galovski, & Peterson, 2011; Reissing, Binik, Khalifé, Cohen, & Amsel, 2003) and may be crucial components of physical sexual interference.

Sexual self-image has been shown to mediate the relationship between body satisfaction and satisfaction with life (Donaghue, 2009). Negative sexual self-image contributes to the association between avoidant sexual behavior and negative body image (La Rocque & Cioe, 2011). Donaghue (2009) found that the passionate–romantic dimension of sexual self-schema was associated with life satisfaction and positive affect, while the embarrassed–conservative dimension of sexual self-schema correlated to negative affect, and concluded that cognitive representations of the sexual self are influential components of happiness and life satisfaction.

RESEARCH

Hypnosis has long been utilized in the treatment of sexual dysfunction and ego strengthening (Hammond, 1990; Strauss, 1990). Hypnosis has been successfully used to strengthen the ego and improve negative self-schema following trauma (Poon, 2007). A case study using a multimodal therapy approach in which nine of 14 sessions included hypnosis was successful in resolving issues experienced by a 33-year-old survivor of childhood sexual abuse (Poon, 2007). The case study showed that hypnosis is an effective adjunct to psychotherapy in the treatment of trauma symptoms (including negative self-image) in an adult survivor of childhood sexual abuse.

Although clinical research is somewhat limited regarding hypnosis for sexual self-image, many case studies report favorable outcomes for the use of hypnosis to improve sexual dysfunction (Benham & Younger, 2008). A case study utilizing hypnosis was effective in treating secondary vaginismus and performance anxiety (Dolan, 2009). Through the incorporation of hypnosis into the psychotherapeutic experience, the therapist was able to quickly establish trust and rapport with the

patient. This integrative approach was successful in addressing the patient's performance anxiety, breaking the muscular spasm causing vaginismus, and helping the patient to achieve a greater level of self-awareness, leading to a deeper understanding of other underlying issues contributing to her sexual dysfunction.

Many case studies are available that show the potential favorable outcomes of using hypnosis to improve sexual self-image (Benham & Younger, 2008). Another example involved a young woman seeking therapy following the breakup of an intimate relationship (Kellis, 2010). The patient presented with symptoms of anxiety, depression, and low self-esteem. The use of hypnosis in conjunction with cognitive behavioral therapy was successful in reducing anxiety and depression, ego-strengthening, and improving self-image.

This study demonstrates the ability of hypnosis to alter faulty cognitive representations that contribute to negative sexual self-image. The authors of this chapter have been working on a hypnotic relaxation intervention to improve sexual self-schema and self-image to improve sexual health among female cancer survivors. Feasibility data are encouraging and are being used to develop a randomized phase II study, which is supported by the Breast Cancer Research Foundation. The following case study example is a composite of the benefits women reported in the feasibility work.

CASE EXAMPLE

T.W. is a 53-year-old woman who was diagnosed with breast cancer 3 years ago. She underwent adjuvant chemotherapy and is now on a medication called an aromatase inhibitor to keep estrogen levels extremely low. As a result, T.W. reports issues with body image, decreased libido, hot flashes, and sleep issues. T.W. states that she feels like a "shriveled-up prune," old beyond her years, unattractive, and unhappy with her body. She is married and grieves the loss of her sexually intimate relationship with her husband, which has been absent for 2.5 years.

T.W. underwent four sessions of hypnotic relaxation where suggestions were provided for improved body image and increased desire for sexual activity and intimacy. Additional suggestions for cooling were provided for hot flash relief and also for sound, restful sleep. T.W. was also given an audio recording of the induction, which she was asked to use at least four times during the week. Before and after each session with the research therapist, T.W. rated her anxiety and comfort with her body on a 0-to-10 scale, with 0 being "no anxiety and no body comfort" and 10 being "worst anxiety ever" and "total body comfort." Before session 1, T. W. reported her anxiety at a 7 and her body comfort at a 2. After the first session, anxiety was rated a 0 and body comfort at 8. Improvements in body comfort were demonstrated over the 4-week intervention as each presession rating improved, indicating the intervention was having lasting effects week to week.

At the end of the 4 weeks, T.W. reported markedly reduced hot flashes, vast improvements in sleep, and more energy, and she also reported having sexual fantasies and spontaneous arousal. Perhaps most important, T.W. stated that she was able, during the hypnotic inductions, to go back to a time in her childhood where she was actually excited about her body. Being able to do that helped her remember what those positive feelings were like and she was able to get to a point, with her self-hypnosis practice, to revisit those feelings so that they eventually became the norm again. The conversation then turned to how to reinitiate intimate behavior with her husband, as she felt ready.

An example of the induction content being explored in this program of research is provided in the following text.

TRANSCRIPT: HYPNOSIS FOR SEXUAL SELF-IMAGE

"To begin your practice of hypnotic relaxation therapy, focus your attention on a spot on the wall. Focus your attention on that one spot. As you concentrate, you begin to feel more relaxed. Concentrate intensely now so that other things begin to fade into the background, drifting into a deep hypnotic state.

Now take a deep breath of air, hold it, and now as you breathe out, let all of the tension go. Good. As this occurs, your eyelids close. Notice a more and more relaxed and heavy feeling. Now

take another deep breath of air, hold it, and as you release the air and breathe out, feel yourself going into a very deep state of hypnosis. Each time you breathe out, think the word 'relax' silently to yourself. The mind and the body now working together to achieve a deep state of comfort and relaxation.

With each breath, let go of all of the tension, every muscle and every fiber of your body becoming deeply relaxed. More and more noticing a feeling of 'letting go' and becoming so deeply relaxed, so deeply relaxed that you can notice a peaceful feeling, calm and secure in your thoughts and feelings. There is a connection between the mind and the body. Your neck can go limp, your jaw can go slack, as all the tension drifts away. Drifting into hypnosis, changes in sensations naturally occur.

Now see a path before you that will lead you to a beautiful flower garden. There is a picket fence with a gate. Go through the gate now and see all the beautiful flowers. As you follow the path, you will drift into a deeper state of hypnosis. The path is clean and smooth. Notice the path and each step you take takes you to many flowers of different colors. There are trees along the path and a comfortable breeze in the air. The sun is warm and it is pleasant there. And as you are there, it is possible to reflect on many things, the sense of relaxation and well-being, a feeling of acceptance and love for yourself, feeling better and better about your body and who you are as a sexual person. Within this peaceful garden, you may become more aware of and more comfortable with your own sexuality and your desire for emotional closeness and intimacy. You will be able to feel better and better about your body, feel better and better about yourself as a sexual person.

And finding now as you can hear my voice with a part of your mind, with another part of your mind go to that pleasant, peaceful place, where you notice and experience everything that is there, images and scenes of your own preference that allow you to experience even more comfort. As I now suggest that you begin to have images and experiences that allow you to experience in your own way a more positive sexual self, a more positive body image, a more positive overall mood. As these personal images come to you now [personal imagery for achievement of goals may be inserted here], *you will see a light. This light is an indication of your sexual self. As the light becomes brighter and brighter, you begin to feel better and better about your body, you feel more and more positive about experiencing sexual feelings. As the light becomes brighter and brighter, you will notice that your overall mood is brighter and brighter. You will be able to give yourself permission to be more in touch with your sexual feelings, feeling more satisfied with your body, your sexual experiences, and more comfortable with your own sexual desire and interest.*

And each time you experience hypnotic relaxation, you will find a sense of being more comfortable, an improved sense of well-being. You will be able to have positive feelings about your body, you will experience more satisfaction in your sexual experiences, positive feelings about your overall sexual self, and more emotional closeness during intimacy. You will be able to experience sexual arousal when you want to and with greater confidence. You will be pleased as these things occur both now and in the future. In a few moments, it is possible to begin returning to conscious alertness, at your own pace, in your own time."

CONCLUSION

Preliminary evidence, including clinical experience, suggests that hypnosis is a promising treatment for improving sexual self-image. Sexual self-image plays a crucial role in healthy sexual functioning. More clinical studies are needed to evaluate hypnosis as a treatment for the improvement of sexual self-image.

The use of hypnosis to improve sexual self-image should only be conducted by trained clinicians who understand the complexities and vulnerabilities of patients presenting negative sexual self-schemas and sexual dysfunction. It is important for the trained clinician to be aware of both the physical and psychological manifestations of sexual dysfunction and for proper diagnosis to be made prior to treatment, particularly the need to assess for sexual trauma and abuse. Once a diagnosis is made, it is then crucial for a treatment plan to be established that develops trust and rapport between

the clinician and the patient. Then, and only then, can hypnosis be successfully used in treating such a sensitive topic.

Treatment plans should include suggestions that are appropriate for the patient as well as suggestions for relaxation, anxiety reduction, and self-acceptance.

REFERENCES

Andersen, B. L., & Cyranowski, J. M. (1994). Women's sexual self-schema. *Journal of Personality and Social Psychology, 67*(6), 1079–1100.

Basson, R. (2010). Sexual function of women with chronic illness. *Women's Health, 6*(3), 407–429. doi:10.2217/whe.10.23

Benham, G., & Younger, J. (2008). Hypnosis and mind-body interactions. In M. Nash & A. Barnier (Eds.), *The Oxford handbook of hypnosis: Theory, research, and practice*. Oxford, UK: Oxford University Press.

Blain, L. M., Galovski, T. E., & Peterson, Z. D. (2011). Female sexual self-schema after interpersonal trauma: Relationship to psychiatric and cognitive functioning in a clinical treatment-seeking sample. *Journal of Traumatic Stress, 24*(2), 222–225. doi:10.1002/jts.20616

Burwell, S. R., Case, L. D., Kaelin, C., & Avis, N. E. (2006). Sexual problems in younger women after breast cancer surgery. *Journal of Clinical Oncology: Official Journal of the American Society of Clinical Oncology, 24*(18), 2815–2821. doi:10.1200/JCO.2005.04.2499

Carmack Taylor, C. L., Basen-Engquist, K., Shinn, E. H., & Bodurka, D. C. (2004). Predictors of sexual functioning in ovarian cancer patients. *Journal of Clinical Oncology: Official Journal of the American Society of Clinical Oncology, 22*(5), 881–889. doi:10.1200/JCO.2004.08.150

Carpenter, K. M., Andersen, B. L., Fowler, J. M., & Maxwell, G. L. (2009). Sexual self schema as a moderator of sexual and psychological outcomes for gynecologic cancer survivors. *Archives of Sexual Behavior, 38*(5), 828–841. doi:10.1007/s10508-008-9349-6

Dennerstein, L., Dudley, E., & Burger, H. (2001). Are changes in sexual functioning during menopause midlife due to aging or menopause? *Fertility and Sterility, 76*(3), 456–460.

Dolan, L. (2009). An integrative approach to the psychotherapeutic treatment of vaginismus incorporating hypnosuggestion and hypnoanalysis. *Australian Journal of Clinical and Experimental Hypnosis, 37*(1), 60–73.

Donaghue, N. (2009). Body satisfaction, sexual self-schemas and subjective well-being in women. *Body Image*, 6(1), 37–42. doi:10.1016/j.bodyim.2008.08.002

Dunn, K. M., Croft, P. R., & Hackett, G. I. (1998). Sexual problems: A study of the prevalence and need for health care in the general population. *Family Practice*, 15(6), 519–524.

Falk, S. J., & Dizon, D. S. (2013). Sexual dysfunction in women with cancer. *Fertility and Sterility*, 100(4), 916–921. doi:10.1016/j.fertnstert.2013.08.018

Ganz, P. A., Desmond, K. A., Belin, T. R., Meyerowitz, B. E., & Rowland, J. H. (1999). Predictors of sexual health in women after a breast cancer diagnosis. *Journal of Clinical Oncology: Official Journal of the American Society of Clinical Oncology*, 17(8), 2371–2380.

Gracia, C. R., Sammel, M. D., Freeman, E. W., Liu, L., Hollander, L., & Nelson, D. B. (2004). Predictors of decreased libido in women during the late reproductive years. *Menopause*, 11(2), 144–150.

Hammond, D. C. (1990). Metaphoric suggestions and word plays for facilitating lubrication. In D. C. Hammond (Ed.), *Handbook of hypnotic suggestions and metaphors* (pp. 364–365). New York, NY: W. W. Norton.

Hoyt, M. A., & Carpenter, K. M. (2015). Sexual self-schema and depressive symptoms after prostate cancer. *Psycho-Oncology*, 24(4), 395–401. doi:10.1002/pon.3601

Kellis, E. (2010). Clinical hypnosis and cognitive-behaviour therapy in the treatment of a young woman with anxiety, depression, and self-esteem issues. *Australian Journal of Clinical and Experimental Hypnosis*, 38-39(1–2), 155–165.

La Rocque, C. L., & Cioe, J. (2011). An evaluation of the relationship between body image and sexual avoidance. *Journal of Sex Research*, 48(4), 397–408. doi:10.1080/00224499.2010.499522

Lewis, R. W., Fugl-Meyer, K. S., Bosch, R., Fugl-Meyer, A. R., Laumann, E. O., Lizza, E., & Martin-Morales, A. (2004). Epidemiology/risk factors of sexual dysfunction. *Journal of Sexual Medicine*, 1(1), 35–39. doi:10.1111/j.1743-6109.2004.10106.x

Poon, M. W. (2007). The value of using hypnosis in helping an adult survivor of childhood sexual abuse. *Contemporary Hypnosis*, 24(1), 30–37.

Quintard, B., & Lakdja, F. (2008). Assessing the effect of beauty treatments on psychological distress, body image, and coping: A longitudinal study of patients undergoing surgical procedures for breast cancer. *Psycho-Oncology*, 17(10), 1032–1038. doi:10.1002/pon.1321

Reissing, E. D., Binik, Y. M., Khalifé, S., Cohen, D., & Amsel, R. (2003). Etiological correlates of vaginismus; sexual and physical abuse, sexual knowledge, sexual self-schema, and relationship adjustment. *Journal of Sex & Marital Therapy*, 29(1), 47–59. doi:10.1080/713847095

Reissing, E. D., Lalibert, G. M., & Davis, H. J. (2005). Young women's sexual adjustment: The role of sexual self-schema, sexual self-efficacy, sexual aversion, and body attitudes. *Canadian Journal of Human Sexuality*, 14(3-4), 77–85.

Rellini, A. H., Ing, A. D., & Meston, C. M. (2011). Implicit and explicit cognitive sexual processes in survivors of childhood sexual abuse. *Journal of Sexual Medicine*, 8(11), 3098–3107. doi:10.1111/j.1743-6109.2011.02356.x

Shell, J. A. (2008). Sexuality and body image concerns after treatment for breast cancer. *Oncology Nurse Edition*, 22(4), 38–42.

Sheppard, L. A., & Ely, S. (2008). Breast cancer and sexuality. *Breast Journal*, 14(2), 176–181. doi:10.1111/j.1524-4741.2007.00550.x

Speer, J. J., Hillenberg, B., Sugrue, D. P., Blacker, C., Kresge, C. L., Decker, V. B., . . . Decker, D. A. (2005). Study of sexual functioning determinants in breast cancer survivors. *Breast Journal*, 11(6), 440–447. doi:10.1111/j.1075-122X.2005.00131.x

Strauss, B. S. (1990). Suggestions and metaphors for support and ego strengthening in cancer patients. In D. C. Hammond (Ed.), *Handbook of hypnotic suggestions and metaphors* (pp. 203–204). New York, NY: W. W. Norton.

World Health Organization. (2006). *Defining sexual health: Report of a technical consultation on sexual health, 28–31, January 2002, Geneva*. Retrieved from http://www.who.int/reproductivehealth/publications/sexual_health/defining_sexual_health.pdf

Increasing Slow-Wave Sleep by Hypnotic Suggestions

Maren Cordi and Björn Rasch

We spend one third of our lives asleep. Sleep is highly important for our well-being and health, and very often we only learn to appreciate its regular companionship when sleep quality declines. In this chapter, we will first discuss the function of sleep and characterize potential causes of sleep disturbances. Thereafter, we will present new scientific data on the potential use of hypnotic suggestions to increase the amount of slow-wave sleep, a sleep stage known to benefit health, cognition, and well-being.

WHAT IS SLEEP?

Sleep is defined as "a reversible behavioral state of perceptual disengagement from and unresponsiveness to the environment" (Carskadon & Dement, 2000, p. 15). Sleep is typically measured and characterized by oscillatory brain activity using electroencephalography (EEG). Dependent on the patterns of electrical activity appearing in the EEG signal, sleep can be divided into four stages and their relative amount can be defined (Iber, Ancoli-Israel, Chessonn, & Quan, 2007; see Figure 67.1): N1 characterizes the transition from wakefulness to sleep and covers about 2% to 5% of nocturnal sleep (Gross & Mink, 2014). With an amount of 45% to 55% per night, N2 makes up the predominant sleep stage (Gross & Mink, 2014). N3, also known as slow-wave sleep (SWS), is the deepest stage, named according to the prevalent slow waves visible in the EEG signal. Its amount of 20% strongly varies with age as its prevalence decreases across the life span. The characteristic slow waves during SWS have a frequency of around 0.5 to 4.5 Hz, and activity in this frequency band is called slow-wave activity (SWA). SWA is a more precise quantitative measure of sleep depth that reflects sleep pressure (Finelli, Baumann, Borbély, & Achermann, 2000) and is associated with brain plasticity, immune function, and memory consolidation (Huber et al., 2006; Huber, Ghilardi, Massimini, & Tononi, 2004; Lange, Dimitrov, & Born, 2010). Together, N1, N2, and SWS are referred to as NonREM sleep, in contrast to the rapid eye movement (REM) sleep, which is hallmarked by large, irregular, and rapid bursts of eye movements, accompanied by a low muscle tone and which covers about 20% to 25% of sleep (Dijk, 2009). The two major sleep phases, REM and non-REM sleep, alternate across the night with a cyclic duration of roughly 90 min, with the amount of SWS gradually decreasing over the course of a night of sleep. The average sleep duration in the healthy population is roughly 7.5 hours, although sleep duration can strongly vary between individuals from 6 to 9 hours (Patel & Hu, 2008). These differences can be partly explained by genetic disposition for longer or shorter sleep without obvious health consequences (Allebrandt et al., 2010). However, a great number of individuals indeed suffer from sleep disturbances or insufficient sleep duration, representing a major challenge for modern societies.

SLEEP DISTURBANCES AND THEIR POTENTIAL CAUSES

More and more people report at least one symptom of a sleep disturbance, such as nocturnal awakenings, difficulties falling asleep, and waking up unrefreshed or too early and not being able to fall asleep again. For instance, the U.S. There has been an upward trend in the reported prevalence of sleep problems from 62% in 1999 to 75%

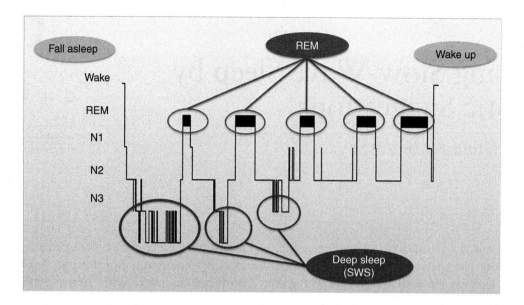

FIGURE 67.1 Hypnogram.

Note: The hypnogram displays the sleep structure across a whole night of 8 hours of sleep. The y-axis indicates sleep stage, whereas the x-axis represents time.

Wake, wakefulness; REM, rapid eye movement sleep; N1–N3, Stage N1–N3 sleep, N3 sleep is equivalent to deep sleep or slow-wave sleep (SWS).

in 2005 (http://sleepfoundation.org/sites/default/files/2005_summary_of_findings.pdf). Four of 10 respondents indicated that their poor sleep quality impacted on their wake time (e.g., feeling sleepy at least three days a week, having an increased error rate or having missed events). Sleep depth has proven to be an especially important determinant of daytime sleep propensity (Dijk, Groeger, Stanley, & Deacon, 2010), subjectively reported sleep quality (Akerstedt, Hume, Minors, & Waterhouse, 1997), and alertness (Lentz, Landis, Rothermel, & Shaver, 1999). Thus, the deepest sleep stage (i.e., SWS) is considered the most restful sleep stage (Dijk, 2009). Impaired sleep is even more common in elderly people (Foley et al., 1995). In an epidemiological study in the United States, almost 80% of over 9,000 adults older than 65 reported sleep complaints (Goldman et al., 2007), and studies show that sleep naturally becomes less deep, shorter, and more fragmented with increasing age even in healthy participants (Ohayon, Carskadon, Guilleminault, & Vitiello, 2004).

Various factors can elicit sleep disturbances. The "5 Ps" indicate the range of causes, which can be of pharmacological, physiological, psychological, physical, or psychiatric nature (see Figure 67.2) (Möller, Laux, & Deister, 2005). Due to this variety, a thorough diagnosis and investigation of the underlying mechanism is essential for choosing the adequate intervention. A hypnotherapeutic intervention might not be sufficient to treat sleep disturbances, which result from pharmacological and physical reasons, while sleep problems, which are elicited by physiological, psychological, or psychiatric reasons, might well be reduced. For these cases, certain stress-reducing hypnotherapeutic interventions exist that focus on the treatment of arousing daytime events. In this chapter, however, we present hypnotic suggestions that refer to a direct and specific manipulation of the sleep process itself.

EXPERIENCES REPORTED BY A PARTICIPANT BEFORE PARTICIPATION

"With increasing age, sleep worsens anyway. Then, however, some private issues summed up that bothered me. I had no problems falling asleep, but I woke up at night and restarted to ruminate about events of the day. Either I was unable to go back to sleep again or only hardly fell asleep. The following day I was of course tired, distressed, and depressed. I took the medicine which I was

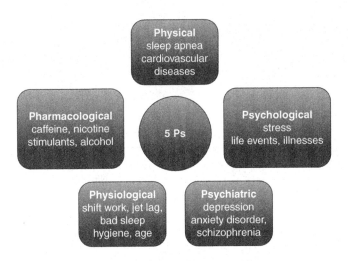

FIGURE 67.2 5 Ps of sleep problems.
Note: Schematic illustration of possible causes of sleep disorders.

prescribed only with great respect and after the first injury that happened one night when I was sedated, I refrained from it out of fear. The calming teas tasted very well, but they are of course not helpful enough."

ROLE OF SLOW-WAVE SLEEP FOR HEALTH AND COGNITION

Deep sleep (SWS) is considered the most restful sleep stage. Disruptions of SWS have a strong impact on daytime alertness and subjectively reported sleep quality; in addition, body functions, such as the immune system, were shown to particularly benefit from slow-wave sleep (Bryant, Trinder, & Curtis, 2004; Lange et al., 2010). Consequently, sleep complaints are also related to poorer self-rated mental, physical, and behavioral health (e.g., intake of medication, alcohol abuse, smoking, etc.) (Goldman et al., 2007), higher mortality (Ancoli-Israel, 2009), and several major diseases such as hypertension, cardiovascular disease, obesity, depression, anxiety, bipolar disorders, and Alzheimer's disease (Aydin et al., 2013; Gangwisch, Feskanich, Malaspina, Shen, & Forman, 2013; Ju et al., 2013; Newman, Enright, Manolio, Haponik, & Wahl, 1997; Ohayon & Vecchierini, 2005; Vorona et al., 2005). Vice versa, major illnesses like depression, heart disease, or bodily pains are often comorbid with sleep disturbances and reduced amounts of SWS (Roberts, Shema, & Kaplan, 1999). Besides

poor health and body function, consequences of reduced SWS include impaired cognitive functions as well in young adults (Curcio, Ferrara, & de Gennaro, 2006) and in the elderly (Blackwell et al., 2006). There is numerous evidence indicating that SWS, in particular, benefits memory functioning and new learning the next day (for review, see Rasch & Born, 2013; Tononi & Cirelli, 2006). Several studies have shown that reducing the amount of SWS during sleep by acoustical stimulation impairs cognitive functions and memory processes (van der Werf et al., 2009), whereas increasing the amount of SWS by electrical or auditory stimulation improves learning and memory (Marshall, Helgadóttir, Mölle, & Born, 2006; Ngo, Claussen, Born, & Mölle, 2013). Thus, SWS is a highly important target for sleep-related interventions to improve well-being, health, and cognition functions.

DISADVANTAGES OF MEDICAL TREATMENTS

Very often, sleep problems remain untreated. In a survey conducted in 1998 in Detroit, 26% of the respondents indicated that their sleep was aided by using some substance: 13% reported drinking alcohol and nearly 18% used medication, 58% thereof over-the-counter aids (Johnson, Roehrs, Roth, & Breslau, 1998). Medication to improve sleep is also commonly prescribed and also offers effective temporary help. However, most sleep-inducing substances and medications often impede the occurrence of SWS, decline in effectiveness during the long term, and are associated with adverse side effects and a high risk of addiction (Hajak & Rüther, 2006; Riemann & Perlis, 2009). Regarding the role of SWS for health, well-being, and cognition, the possibility to increase its amount by hypnotic suggestions is highly relevant. Consequently, it is highly warranted to develop efficient and risk-free tools to improve sleep. Thus, psychological and behavioral interventions should be chosen for treating insomnia (Pallesen, Nordhus, & Kvale, 1998).

USE OF HYPNOSIS TO TREAT SLEEP PROBLEMS

Among nonpharmacological treatments, hypnosis represents a promising approach to positively influence sleep and is considered free of risk (Deivanayagi, Manivannan, & Fernandez, 2007).

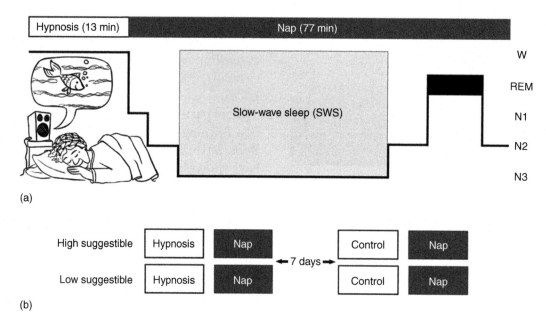

FIGURE 67.3 The session flow.

Note: Displays the session flow of our study. (a) Participants listened to the hypnotic suggestions, lying in bed over loudspeakers. They were allowed to fall asleep directly afterward and we recorded their sleep with EEG. (b) Subjects high and low in suggestibility were measured twice within two weeks. Before the nap they either listened to the hypnotic suggestions or the control text in a randomized order.

A clinical study compared the efficacy of an insomnia therapy, including hypnosis with a progressive relaxation, self-relaxation, and a no-treatment control group. All treatments reduced the number of awakenings per night and boosted feelings of being rested in the morning. Additionally, the progressive and hypnotic relaxation resulted in a reduced time to fall asleep. This demonstrated the effectiveness of the hypnotic relaxation method to achieve sleep improvements (Borkovec & Fowles, 1972). A later study confirmed the positive effect of hypnotic relaxation on sleep-onset latency (Stanton, 1989). Symptom reductions or eliminations of sleep problems after one or two sessions of hypnotherapy were maintained even after a five-year follow-up retest (Hauri, Silber, & Boeve, 2007). Stanton (1999) presented case reports about three patients suffering from diverse sleep disturbances, which could all be treated successfully and enduringly. These cases impressively underlined the effectiveness of treating sleep problems with hypnotic relaxation or imagination. However, all these studies relied on case studies or subjective reports and did not include objective analyses of the sleep EEG. It is, however, known that subjective estimations of sleep quality and objective measures need not necessarily correspond with each other (Baker,

Maloney, & Driver, 1999). Moreover, the specific effect on deep sleep could not be uncovered with these methods. Thus, sleep and its structure must be analyzed objectively with EEG to answer the question whether the reported improvements of sleep are based on an objectively measurable change and to conduct more detailed analyses concerning the characteristics of deep sleep.

THE STUDY

In our studies (Cordi, Schlarb, & Rasch, 2014; Cordi, Hirsiger, Mérillat, & Rasch, 2015), we tested whether suggestions "to sleep deeper" given during hypnosis are an effective tool to increase objective measures of sleep (SWS and SWA). For this purpose, we invited 70 healthy, German-speaking young females (aged 18–35, mean 23.27 ± 3.17 years) and 39 healthy older adults (aged 60–82, mean 67.08 ± 4.39) to take part in the experiments. In a first session, the Harvard Group Scale of Hypnotic Susceptibility (Bongartz, 1985) was conducted to divide the sample into high and low suggestible subjects. Moreover, subjects were explicitly informed about the intention of the used

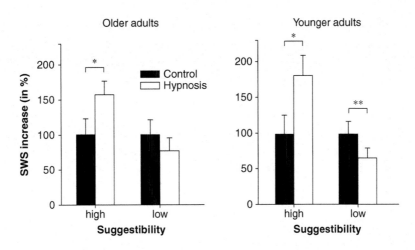

FIGURE 67.4 Effect of hypnotic suggestions on deep sleep (SWS).
Note: hypnotic suggestions increased SWS by 57% and 81% in older and young adults, respectively.

suggestions to increase their amount of SWS. After a second session, which took place in the sleep laboratory and aimed at familiarizing participants with the session flow and the laboratory, two experimental sessions followed. In both sessions, subjects were allowed to nap for 90 minutes after the attachment of the EEG, which recorded the sleep pattern. Before falling asleep, either the hypnotic suggestions or a control tape were presented via loudspeakers (the order was randomized). The hypnotic tape started with 4 minutes of induction, which was followed by the hypnotic suggestion (see the text that follows). The text was spoken with a gentle, soft, and calm voice. In contrast, the control text was a documentation of mineral deposits and was spoken with an everyday voice and speed. Subjects were allowed to fall asleep directly after the end of the tape (see Figure 67.3). To measure the effect of the hypnotic suggestions, we compared both sleep patterns within one person.

THE HYPNOTIC TEXT

"Choose a comfortable position. . . . I would like you to focus your eyes on a point . . . select any point you can rest your view on. . . . You can change your position one more time . . . and find a position so that you are comfortable . . . noises that you perceive can be familiar . . . or even strange . . . just as the electrodes on your body, which you can simply perceive and know that everything is fine . . . and this can be the starting point from which you begin . . . any tension can be collected in one place in the body . . . while the rest of your body can relax . . . sooner or later, you can see through the point . . . by having put your view far . . . it may be pleasant to close the eyelids when they are heavy . . . or to see through the things without losing sight of them . . . and while you forget . . . to notice . . . you can relax deeper and deeper . . . while soon I will count from 1 to 10 . . . you can take the time . . . and one by one take your steps . . . maybe like on the stairs. . . .

1 . . . the first step you took long ago . . . 2 . . . all things have two sides . . . 3 . . . all good things have three . . . on to . . . 4 . . . four sides by the table . . . four corners and edges . . . on an image . . . 5 . . . five fingers on one hand . . . on to . . . 6 . . . a number that you can flip on its head . . . 7 . . . seven at one blow . . . on to . . . 8 . . . two zeros one over the other . . . they give eight and take eight . . . 9 . . . is a flipped 6 . . . let it loose and play with it . . . on to 10 . . . you do the last step alone. . . .

And perhaps you have already arrived in a state that is just right for you. And I would like to invite you now on a little trip . . . and perhaps first you would like to imagine the image again . . . imagine an image of the sea . . . and you can begin to see the color of the water . . . and I do not know exactly what color the water is . . . perhaps it is more blue . . . perhaps more greenish . . . maybe the water glistens in the sun . . . reflects . . . pleasantly warm . . . so that you can simply drift . . . drift into your image you can experience . . . the sun is reflected . . . and you can let yourself drift along in this water . . .

simply drift along in this water . . . effortless, simply drifting . . . and perhaps you can see a fish, perhaps a dolphin . . . swimming there . . . quite easily . . . just as everything goes all by itself . . . floating easily . . . feeling like a fish in the water . . . in the water . . . drifting effortlessly . . . floating easily . . . while the noises get further and further away . . . only you and the sea. . . . Sensing the tranquility . . . soothing and calming . . . to know that you can simply relax now. . . . Let go . . . and enjoy this pleasant feeling . . . that everything comes by itself . . . and you feel safe and secure . . . and I do not know how everything looks . . . there in the water . . . the colorful fishes . . . bright corals . . . different plants of the sea. . . . You can perceive all this vividly and keep on drifting, keep on drifting on your way . . . and you can see the fish . . . or your dolphin in front of you . . . and it may be further down, more quiet and pleasant . . . beautiful and soothing . . . simply deeply relaxing . . . you can simply dive and enjoy the tranquility . . . completely relaxed . . . relaxing deeply . . . relaxing deeply . . . relaxing the whole body . . . all by yourself . . . and maybe you can notice that the fish finally slowly submerges . . . and while it slowly dives and it can see the things in the water, small fishes swim by . . . colorful coral fields . . . and then swimming deeper . . . even calmer . . . diving deeper and deeper. Simply like by itself. . . . In order to feel more peace. . . . And everything remains colorful . . . highly visible. . . . To feel the tranquility around . . . a pleasant calmness . . . simply to drift . . . and let go. . . . With every breath . . . drifting simply deeper into sleep . . . deeper and deeper. . . . Just letting yourself to drift . . . and while the fish swims deeper and deeper, you can notice how your arms and legs will be pleasantly heavy . . . more and more tired. Everything gets more tired and heavy . . . simply tired and heavy . . . resting. . . . Everything wants to sleep . . . and relax . . . simply to sleep deeply . . . in peace. To sleep . . . to fall deep and deeper into sleep . . . all by itself. And with every breath you can sink deeper and deeper into sleep . . . sink into the sleep . . . and feel safe . . . with each breath deeper. While all can relax . . . in deep sleep . . . the body can relax . . . and still every important thing remains where it is . . . every important thing just remembered later . . . and probably

you can remember your image . . . the image of the sea . . . and of the depth of sleep . . . and you can submerge by yourself deeper and deeper . . . submerge in sleep . . . sleeping deeply . . . sleeping deeply and relaxed . . . while everything can relax . . . every single part of your body . . . can rest . . . relaxing deeply . . . resting . . . very deep . . . to the bottom of the image . . . sinking deep . . . relaxing . . . for a long time . . . relaxing deeply . . . simply letting go . . . knowing that everything is in order. . . ."

EXPERIENCES REPORTED BY A PARTICIPANT DURING PARTICIPATION

"Until then, I had located hypnosis to the cabaret. The fact that hypnotherapy was clearly distinguished from that and the method was said to be helpful to treat diverse problems, increased my interest in the study even more. However, I did not expect to benefit personally from participation. During the hypnotic text, I was able to relax very well. I very much liked the picture of the fish; the calm, the colors, the drowning . . . just the whole atmosphere. I could very well project my thoughts in there and swim together with the fish. I did not feel the effect on sleep per se, but I had a feeling that there is something about this method that I want to follow up on."

Comparing both naps revealed that, after listening to the hypnotic suggestions "to sleep deeper," SWS in highly suggestible young females increased by 81% compared with the amount of SWS after the control nap, while no other sleep stages were influenced (see Figure 67.4). Additionally, SWA was significantly increased after the hypnotic suggestions. These results demonstrated the specific influence and effectiveness of hypnotic suggestions to sleep deeper in objectively measured parameters. Moreover, the higher the objective SWS difference, the higher subjects rated their experienced difference in sleep quality.

As mentioned, subjects were explicitly told that our hypnotic suggestions intend to result in higher amounts of SWS. To exclude effects of expectancy, a second group of young female subjects was also informed that the hypnotic suggestions will increase SWS, while the metaphor given before sleep suggested shallow and light sleep (a boat resting on the surface of the sea) instead of deep sleep. If mere expectancy was sufficient for the increase of SWS, we should have seen a similar SWS increase in this experiment. However, we observed no differences between sleep after hypnosis and the control text, indicating that mere expectancy of deepened sleep is not sufficient to elicit the effect observed in the main experiment. This conclusion was further strengthened in a third control group (for details, see Cordi, Schlarb, & Rasch, 2014).

Additionally, we tested the effects in low suggestible young females using the same texts as in the main experiment (hypnotic suggestion "to sleep deeper" and the control text). For this group, we observed an opposite result pattern: After listening to the hypnosis, low-suggestible subjects showed a reduced amount of SWS compared with the control nap. Even explicitly asking the low-suggestible participants to simulate the effects of the hypnotic suggestions was not effective in increasing SWS as observed in highly suggestible females (see Cordi et al., for details).

As SWS declines as a function of age, we replicated the study in a sample of older adults (see Cordi et al., under revision). The SWS-specific increase of 57% after listening to the hypnotic suggestions compared with the control nap confirmed that hypnotic suggestions are effective in increasing the amount of SWS in highly suggestible females (see Figure 67.4). Furthermore, on average, SWS was reached significantly earlier (after 15 minutes compared with 27 minutes after the control text). Also in the elderly, left frontal SWA increased by 5% after hypnotic suggestions compared with sleep after the control text. As SWS is known to be vital for cognition, we also tested prefrontal cognitive functioning before and after sleep. Comparing cognitive performance benefits from both naps demonstrated that cognition improved by 28% across the deepened nap while performance did not increase across the control nap. Thus, deepened sleep was significantly more beneficial for prefrontal functioning than sleep after the control text. Low-suggestible females did not show any differences in sleep after the hypnotic suggestions compared with the control text. Comparing the effects in young and older adults showed that hypnotic suggestions increase SWS and SWA robustly and independently of age. The results of both studies are highly relevant when considering the benefits of using hypnotic suggestions to influence sleep

instead of a medical treatment. Besides avoiding side effects, the effects of hypnotic suggestions on SWS were higher compared with pharmacological means (Rasch, Born, & Gais, 2006). This hints at the conclusion that the possibility to use hypnosis as a tool to positively influence sleep could be highly relevant for health and healthy aging, as advanced age is associated with an SWS decrease.

EXPERIENCES REPORTED BY A PARTICIPANT AFTER PARTICIPATION

"After participating in the study, I bought a hypnosis CD for sleep training. I used it in the evening before falling asleep and I was always looking forward to hearing it. After about two weeks, I already felt a positive effect on my sleep and appreciated it more and more. Later, I bought even more CDs, also on serenity and release, which I listened to before going to bed or when I could not fall back to sleep after the first period of deep sleep. Meanwhile, the intervals are longer, as my sleep has improved very much on its own. If I still wake up at night, I remember the pictures and the atmosphere, transferred in the CD, or I listen to it again and usually fall asleep quickly, even before it ends. Only in case of emergency, if I realize that I am in a period of increased tension, I resort to the CDs. I told already many friends, who also struggle with sleep problems about this method. I think that not only sleep training, but also serenity and release helped my sleep."

CONCLUSION

Together, sleep is a state that is important for our health, well-being, and cognition. However, its vulnerability compromises many people to experience sleep quality decline. Very often, sleep depth is reduced as a consequence of sleep disturbances or increasing age. Due to aversive side effects of pharmaceutical as well as self-prescribed sleep aids, it is vital to develop a successful tool to improve sleep and increase sleep depth. Our hypnotic suggestions showed to objectively increase the amount of SWS and SWA independent from age. This increase was associated with improved subjective sleep quality. Furthermore, its benefit for cognition could be measured in older adults. Our findings provide scientific, well-controlled data demonstrating the effectiveness of hypnotic suggestions to positively influence sleep and thereby support well-being and cognition.

LIMITATIONS

The present data lay the foundation for further studies aiming at broadening the usability of hypnotic suggestions. First, it is important to capture the suggestion's effect on a whole night of sleep. Second, longitudinal follow-ups should be set up to investigate the development of hypnotic effects in long-term applications. The ease of achieving the hypnotic state would be expected to increase with "training." Third, as we tested healthy sleepers, we cannot infer on the effectiveness of the hypnotic suggestions used in our setting for clinical sleep disturbances. Further, strictly speaking, we also have to limit our conclusions to women as we have only tested female participants. Although some studies found females to achieve higher scores in tests of suggestibility (Page & Green, 2007), we would clearly predict that suggestible men should also benefit from hypnotic suggestion to improve sleep.

PRACTICAL TIPS

To ensure standardization in our study, each subject received the same hypnotic suggestion played from an audio file. According to previously outlined case reports, individually suited metaphors would be expected to be even more effective (Stanton, 1999). Thus, in a therapeutic setting, it might be indicated to vary the exact content of the metaphor dependent on fears, experiences, or the patient's concrete sleep problem. Similarly, live hypnosis could be more efficient than a tape recording. In a therapeutic interaction, the hypnotist could for instance include tests to infer on the level of hypnotic depth before implementing the metaphor, which was not possible in our setting. Further, to enable "training," the session can be recorded and handed to the patient to regularly benefit from it. Although our results demonstrated that only highly suggestible subjects slept deeper

after the hypnotic suggestions, we would not consider it practical to make the decision whether hypnosis is implemented or not conditional on a previously conducted suggestibility test. The participant we interviewed for this chapter was actually scored as low suggestible and neither reported subjectively improved sleep nor could we measure deeper sleep during her participation. However, at least on the long run, hypnosis still improved her sleep and was an adequate and effective method for her as her final statement demonstrates:

"The information-sheet of the study told that participation inherits no personal benefit. I had one."

REFERENCES

Akerstedt, T., Hume, K., Minors, D., & Waterhouse, J. (1997). Good sleep—its timing and psychological sleep characteristics. *Journal of Sleep Research*, 6(4), 221–229.

Allebrandt, K. V., Teder-Laving, M., Akyol, M., Pichler, I., Müller-Myhsok, B., Pramstaller, P., . . . Roenneberg, T. (2010). CLOCK gene variants associate with sleep duration in two independent populations. *Biological Psychiatry*, 67(11), 1040–1047. doi:10.1016/j.biopsych.2009.12.026

Ancoli-Israel, S. (2009). Sleep and its disorders in aging populations. *Sleep medicine*, 10, S7–S11.

Aydin, A., Selvi, Y., Besiroglu, L., Boysan, M., Atli, A., Ozdemir, O., . . . Balaharoglu, R. (2013). Mood and metabolic consequences of sleep deprivation as a potential endophenotype in bipolar disorder. *Journal of Affective Disorders*, 150(2), 284–294. doi:10.1016/j.jad.2013.04.007

Baker, F. C., Maloney, S., & Driver, H. S. (1999). A comparison of subjective estimates of sleep with objective polysomnographic data in healthy men and women. *Journal of Psychosomatic Research*, 47(4), 335–341.

Blackwell, T., Yaffe, K., Ancoli-Israel, S., Schneider, J. L., Cauley, J. A., Hillier, T. A., . . . Stone, K. L. (2006). Poor sleep is associated with impaired cognitive function in older women: The study of osteoporotic fractures. *Journals of Gerontology Series A, Biological Sciences and Medical Sciences, 61*, 405–410. Retrieved from http://www.ncbi.nlm.nih.gov/pubmed/16611709

Bongartz, W. (1985). German norms for the Harvard group scale of hypnotic susceptibility, Form A. *International Journal of Clinical and Experimental Hypnosis*, 33(2), 131–139. doi:10.1080/00207148508406643

Borkovec, T. D., & Fowles, D. C. (1972). Controlled investigation of the effects of progressive and hypnotic relaxation on insomnia. *Journal of Abnormal Psychology, 82*(1), 153–158.

Bryant, P. A., Trinder, J., & Curtis, N. (2004). Sick and tired: Does sleep have a vital role in the immune system? *Nature Reviews Immunology, 4*(6), 457–467. doi:10.1038/nri1369

Carskadon, M. A., & Dement, W. C. (2000). Normal human sleep: An overview. *Principles and Practice of Sleep Medicine, 4*, 13–23.

Cordi, M. J., Hirsiger, S., Mérillat, S., & Rasch, B. (2015). Improving sleep and cognition by hypnotic suggestion in the elderly. *Neuropsychologia, 69*, 176-182.

Cordi, M. J., Schlarb, A. A., & Rasch, B. (2014). Deepening sleep by hypnotic suggestion. *Sleep, 37*(6), 1143–1152. doi:10.5665/sleep.3778

Curcio, G., Ferrara, M., & de Gennaro, L. (2006). Sleep loss, learning capacity and academic performance. *Sleep Medicine Reviews, 10*(5), 323–337. doi:10.1016/j .smrv.2005.11.001

Deivanayagi, S., Manivannan, M., & Fernandez, P. (2007). Spectral analysis of EEG signals during hypnosis. *International Journal of Systemics, Cybernetics and Informatics*, 75–80.

Dijk, D. J. (2009). Regulation and functional correlates of slow wave sleep. *Journal of Clinical Sleep Medicine: JCSM: Official Publication of the American Academy of Sleep Medicine, 5*(2), 6–15.

Dijk, D. J., Groeger, J. A., Stanley, N., & Deacon, S. (2010). Age-related reduction in daytime sleep propensity and nocturnal slow wave sleep. *Sleep, 3*(2), 211–223.

Finelli, L., Baumann, H., Borbély, A. A., & Achermann, P. (2000). Dual electroencephalogram markers of human sleep homeostasis: Correlation between theta activity in waking and slow-wave activity in sleep. *Neuroscience, 101*(3), 523–529. Retrieved from http://www.ncbi.nlm.nih.gov/pubmed/11113301

Foley, D. J., Monjan, A. A., Brown, S. L., Simonsick, E. M., Wallace, R. B., & Blazer, D. G. (1995). Sleep complaints among elderly persons: An epidemiologic study of three communities. *Sleep, 18*(6), 425–432. doi.org/10.1097/00006842-199903000-00011.

Gangwisch, J. E., Feskanich, D., Malaspina, D., Shen, S., & Forman, J. P. (2013). Sleep duration and risk for hypertension in women: Results from the nurses' health study. *American Journal of Hypertension, 26*(7), 903–911. doi:10.1093/ajh/hpt044

Goldman, S. E., Stone, K. L., Ancoli-Israel, S., Blackwell, T., Ewing, S. K., Boudreau, R., . . . Newman, A. B. (2007). Poor sleep is associated with poorer physical performance and greater functional limitations in older women. *Sleep, 30*(10), 1317–1324. Retrieved from http://www.pubmedcentral.nih.gov/articlerender.fcgi?a rtid=2266278&tool=pmcentrez&rendertype=abstract

Gross, R. A., & Mink, J. W. (2014). *Sleep medicine in neurology*. West Sussex: John Wiley & Sons.

Hajak, G., & Rüther, E. (2006). Therapie von Ein- und Durchschlafstörungen. In A. Möller (Ed.), *Therapie psychischer Erkrankungen* (pp. 1015–1055). Stuttgart: Thieme.

Hauri, P. J., Silber, M. H., & Boeve, B. F. (2007). The treatment of parasomnias with hypnosis: A 5-year follow-up study. *Journal of Clinical Sleep Medicine: JCS: Official Publication of the American Academy of Sleep Medicine, 3*(4), 369–373. Retrieved from http://www.pubmedcentral.nih.gov/articlerender.fcgi?artid=1 978312&tool=pmcentrez&rendertype=abstract

Huber, R., Ghilardi, M. F., Massimini, M., & Tononi, G. (2004). Local sleep and learning. *Nature, 430*(6995), 78–81. doi:10.1038/nature02663

Huber, R., Ghilardi, M. F., Massimini, M., Ferrarelli, F., Riedner, B. A., Peterson, M. J., & Tononi, G. (2006). Arm immobilization causes cortical plastic changes and locally decreases sleep slow wave activity. *Nature Neuroscience, 9*(9), 1169–1176. doi:10.1038/nn1758

Iber, C., Ancoli-Israel, S., Chessonn, A., & Quan, S. (2007). *The AASM manual for the scoring of sleep and associated events: Rules, terminology and technical specifications. American Academy of Sleep Medicine* (1st ed., pp. 1–70). Westchester, IL: American Academy of Sleep Medicine.

Johnson, E. O., Roehrs, T., Roth, T., & Breslau, N. (1998). Epidemiology of alcohol and medication as aids to sleep in early adulthood. *Sleep, 3*(1), 178–186.

Ju, Y. E., Mcleland, J. S., Toedebusch, C. D., Xiong, C., Fagan, A. M., Duntley, S. P., . . . Holtzman, D. M. (2013). Sleep quality and preclinical Alzheimer disease. *JAMA Neurology, 70*(5), 587–593. doi:10.1001/ jamaneurol.2013.2334

Lange, T., Dimitrov, S., & Born, J. (2010). Effects of sleep and circadian rhythm on the human immune system. *Annals of the New York Academy of Sciences, 1193*, 48–59. doi:10.1111/j.1749-6632.2009.05300.x

Lentz, M. J., Landis, C. A., Rothermel, J., & Shaver, J. L. (1999). Effects of selective slow wave sleep disruption on musculoskeletal pain and fatigue in middle aged women. *Journal of Rheumatology, 26*(7), 1586–1592. Retrieved from http://www.ncbi.nlm.nih.gov/ pubmed/10405949

Marshall, L., Helgadóttir, H., Mölle, M., & Born, J. (2006). Boosting slow oscillations during sleep potentiates memory. *Nature, 444*(7119), 610–613. doi:10.1038/nature05278

Möller, H.-J., Laux, G., & Deister, A. (2005). Schlafstörungen. In *Psychiatrie und psychotherapie* (pp. 294–305). Stuttgart: Thieme Verlag.

Newman, A. B., Enright, P. L., Manolio, T. A., Haponik, E. F., & Wahl, P. W. (1997). Sleep disturbance, psychosocial correlates, and cardiovascular disease in 5201 older adults: The Cardiovascular Health Study. *Journal of the American Geriatrics Society, 45*(1), 1–7.

Ngo, H. V., Claussen, J. C., Born, J., & Mölle, M. (2013). Induction of slow oscillations by rhythmic acoustic stimulation. *Journal of Sleep Research*, 22(1), 22–31. doi:10.1111/j.1365-2869.2012.01039.x

Ohayon, M. M., & Vecchierini, M. F. (2005). Normative sleep data, cognitive function and daily living activities in older adults in the community. *Sleep*, 28(8), 981–989.

Page, R. A., & Green, J. P. (2007). An update on age, hypnotic suggestibility, and gender: A brief report. *American Journal of Clinical Hypnosis*, 49(4), 283–287. doi:10.1080/00029157.2007.10524505

Pallesen, S., Nordhus, I. H., & Kvale, G. (1998). Nonpharmacological interventions for insomnia in older adults: A meta-analysis of treatment efficacy. *Psychotherapy*, 35(4), 472–482.

Patel, S. R., & Hu, F. B. (2008). Short sleep duration and weight gain: A systematic review. *Obesity*, 16(3), 643–653. doi:10.1038/oby.2007.118

Rasch, B. H., Born, J., & Gais, S. (2006). Combined blockade of cholinergic receptors shifts the brain from stimulus encoding to memory consolidation. *Journal of Cognitive Neuroscience*, 18(5), 793–802. doi:10.1162/jocn.2006.18.5.793

Rasch, B., & Born, J. (2013). About sleep's role in memory. *Physiological Reviews*, 93(2), 681–766. doi:10.1152/physrev.00032.2012

Riemann, D., & Perlis, M. L. (2009). The treatments of chronic insomnia: A review of benzodiazepine receptor agonists and psychological and behavioral therapies. *Sleep Medicine Reviews*, 13(3), 205–214. doi:10.1016/j.smrv.2008.06.001

Roberts, R. E., Shema, S. J., & Kaplan, G. A. (1999). Prospective data on sleep complaints and associated risk factors in an older cohort. *Psychosomatic Medicine*, 61(2), 188–196. doi.org/10.1097/00006842-199903000-00011.

Ohayon, M. M., Carskadon, M. A., Guilleminault, C., & Vitiello, M. V. (2004). Meta-analysis of quantitative sleep parameters from childhood to old age in healthy individuals: Developing normative sleep values across the human lifespan *Sleep* 27(7), 1255–1273. Retrieved from http://www.ncbi.nlm.nih.gov/pubmed/15586779.

Stanton, H. E. (1989). Hypnotic relaxation and the reduction of sleep onset insomnia. *International Journal of Psychosomatic: Official Publication of the International Psychosomatics Institute*, 36(1-4), 64–68. Retrieved from http://www.ncbi.nlm.nih.gov/pubmed/2689375

Stanton, H. E. (1999). Hypnotic relaxation and insomnia: A simple solution? *Sleep and Hypnosis*, 1, 64–67.

Tononi, G., & Cirelli, C. (2006). Sleep function and synaptic homeostasis. *Sleep Medicine Reviews*, 10(1), 49–62. doi:10.1016/j.smrv.2005.05.002

van der Werf, Y. D., Altena, E., Schoonheim, M. M., Sanz-Arigita, E. J., Vis, J. C., de Rijke, W., & van Someren, E. J. (2009). Sleep benefits subsequent hippocampal functioning. *Nature Neuroscience*, 12(2), 122–123. doi:10.1038/nn.2253

Vorona, R. D., Winn, M. P., Babineau, T. W., Eng, B. P., Feldman, H. R., & Ware, J. C. (2005). Overweight and obese patients in a primary care population report less sleep than patients with a normal body mass index. *Archives of Internal Medicine*, 165(1), 25–30. doi:10.1001/archinte.165.1.25

Smoking Cessation

Joseph P. Green and Steven Jay Lynn

The harmful effects of smoking on health are well known. From increased risk of many types of cancers, cardiovascular and pulmonary disease, stroke, and ulcerative disease, smoking is the leading cause of premature mortality and morbidity in the United States and worldwide (U.S. Department of Health and Human Services [USDHHS], 2010a). The U.S. government projects that 5.6 million of our children and adolescents will die prematurely from smoking (USDHHS, 2014). Furthermore, there is no safe level of exposure to second-hand smoke (USDHHS, 2006, 2014). Public campaigns against smoking, educational efforts, and improved treatment programs have contributed to the U.S. adult smoking rate being cut in half since 1962 (USDHHS, 2010a). Nevertheless, some 45 million American adults and adolescents continue to smoke (USDHHS, 2012), and the declining adult smoking rate appears to have stalled (USDHHS, 2010a). Still, within 10 years of quitting, the excess risk of lung cancer decreased by up to 50% (Shopland & Burns, 1993; USDHHS, 2010b). Clearly, the need for effective and widely disseminated programs that promote long-term abstinence is a public health priority (USDHSS, 2014).

RESEARCH

As a cost-effective and brief intervention, hypnosis represents a viable and promising approach for achieving smoking cessation and thereby could significantly reduce smoking-related health risks. Fortunately, there are good reasons to believe that hypnosis can play an integral role in an empirically grounded smoking cessation intervention. Qualitative reviews and meta-analytic studies consistently document the effectiveness of hypnosis in treating a variety of other psychological and medical conditions, ranging from acute and chronic pain to obesity (e.g., Lynn, Rhue, & Kirsch, 2010). Moreover, meta-analyses have found that hypnosis can enhance treatment gains of cognitive-behavioral procedures (Kirsch, Montgomery, & Sapirstein, 1995). In tandem with these developments, hypnosis has gained popularity as a smoking cessation intervention with the promise to reach a wide audience of consumers. For example, Sood, Ebbert, Sood, and Stevens (2006) reported that 27% of their sample of 1,117 patients at an outpatient tobacco treatment specialty clinic designated hypnosis as most promising in terms of future use among complementary and alternative medical techniques for smoking.

Apart from the popular appeal of hypnosis, empirical studies provide a reason for optimism regarding hypnosis as a means to achieve abstinence. Narrative reviews (Aabbot, Barnes, White, Barnes, & Ernst, 2000; Green & Lynn, 2000; Law & Tang, 1995), meta-analyses (Green, Lynn, & Montgomery, 2006, 2008; Viswesvaran & Schmidt, 1992), and individual studies provide support for the use of hypnosis in smoking cessation treatment, with quit rates typically in the range of approximately 25% to 35%. In perhaps the most promising study to date, Elkins, Marcus, Bates, Rajab, and Cook (2006) randomly assigned 20 participants to either an intensive hypnotherapy condition (eight visits over two months) or to a wait list condition. Smoking status was confirmed by carbon monoxide assessment. Thirty percent of the participants in the hypnosis condition reported continuous abstinence at both three- and six-month follow-ups, compared with no reports of abstinence in the control conditions. After six months, 40% of individuals who experienced hypnosis reported they were abstinent during the previous seven days, corroborated by carbon monoxide assessments. Still, other studies have produced mixed results and hypnosis may not be superior to alternative treatment approaches (Abbott, Stead, White, Barnes, & Ernst, 2000).

For more than two decades, beginning in 1992, we have strived to develop and refine a state of the science, brief, cost-effective cognitive-behavioral program for smoking cessation that uses self-directed hypnotic methods to achieve long-term abstinence. The initial 90-minute program was created with the support of a grant from the American Lung Association of Ohio, with the goal of integrating the content of the much more lengthy Freedom From Smoking program, with the addition of self-hypnosis exercises. In our initial evaluation of the program, 18.5% of participants reported they were abstinent after a six-month interval (Neufeld & Lynn, 1988).

Ahijevych, Yerardi, and Nedilsky (2000) later reported a roughly similar abstinence rate of 22% at 5 to 15 months post-treatment among participants who enrolled in the hypnosis program offered by the American Lung Association of Ohio. More recently, Carmody et al. (2008) tested a later developed, expanded two-session version of our program with smokers at the San Francisco Veterans Affairs Medical Center. These researchers found that 29% of the participants who were hypnotized reported abstinence over the past seven days at six-month follow-up, compared with 23% of individuals who participated in a behavioral counseling group. Self-reports were confirmed with a biochemical or proxy measure in 26% of hypnotized participants versus 18% of behavioral counseling participants. At 12 months, 24% of participants reported that they were abstinent over the past seven days, compared with 16% of individuals in the behavioral group, with biochemical or proxy confirmation of 20% of participants who were hypnotized, compared with 14% of participants in behavioral counseling.

TRANSCRIPTS AND PROGRAM DESCRIPTION: HYPNOSIS FOR SMOKING CESSATION

Over the course of Carmody et al.'s (2008) research and after their study, we continued to develop and refine our two-session program. Our revamped and restructured program ties interventions more closely to the current literature on cognitive behavioral approaches and hypnosis and incorporates mindfulness-based strategies.

In Session 1, our presentation is based on a slide show in which we (a) provide information regarding the history of the program; (b) overview the program; (c) emphasize the importance of motivation and persistence; (d) invite participants to generate reasons to stop smoking and estimate the number of times they have raised a cigarette to their mouth; (e) highlight the importance of social support, value-driven action, and self-reward for abstinence; and (f) offer strategies to minimize weight gain, manage stress, and sleep better. We also present a video clip in which a nurse provides psychoeducation regarding the health risks of smoking and the benefits of smoking cessation. After the nurse presents health risk information, she states the following:

"Strong smoking urges typically fade after a couple of days. And after about one month, sometimes sooner, most people report no strong urges to smoke.... Soon, you'll begin to breathe easier, cough less, and strengthen your immune system.... So while the risks of smoking are great, the benefits of stopping smoking are well worth facing any temporary discomfort you may experience. I am confident that this program will give you the tools to succeed, and I wish you the very best of luck."

We systematically organize the treatment into suites of strategies that focus on cognition, affect, and behavior, and encourage participants to employ many strategies to increase the likelihood of achieving abstinence (Brandon, Tiffany, Obremski, & Baker, 1990; Carmody et al., 2008). The strategies we present encompass demonstrably effective approaches including self-monitoring, stimulus control, self-reward, behavioral substitution (e.g., focused breathing, walking or stretching, squeezing a stress ball), behavioral contracting, counterconditioning, social support, cue exposure, and avoidance of high-risk situations (e.g., Brown, 2003; Burton & Tiffany, 1997; Shiffman & Balabanis, 1995). We also caution against the pitfalls of irrational thinking, cognitive distortions, and widespread erroneous beliefs (e.g., emotional reasoning, labeling, magnification, black/white thinking, weight gain inevitable) linked with the persistence of smoking. We emphasize that for the duration of the program, stopping smoking should be the highest priority.

We also incorporate techniques from motivational interviewing to facilitate reflection on the smoking habit and readiness for change (Steinberg, Ziedonis, Krejci, & Brandon, 2004). To do so, we created a video clip of an interview with a coping model who participated in the treatment. The following passage relates to her experience in response to the question, "Is there anything in particular that really helped you?"

"I was able to accept myself and not get down on myself for past failures. I know that your program teaches people to be kind to themselves, stay positive and never give up, and keep trying to make progress. I used to say that I could never stop smoking. I used to tell people, 'I'm different from everyone else. Somehow, I just need cigarettes.' Now, looking back, I realize how foolish that belief was. I never needed cigarettes. And, deep down, I knew I could stop if I psyched myself up to do so. So, when I took your program, I didn't give myself any excuses. When I felt like smoking, I did something else. When I felt an urge, I would chew gum. I remember chewing a lot of gum—and I still do [model chuckles]. After a while, I learned that the urge didn't last long. I'd have an urge and then it would go away. I think one of the phrases you used was 'surf the urge.' That image seemed to help."

Motivation and positive expectancies are likewise key to maximizing hypnotic responses (Council, 1999; Council, Kirsch, & Hafner, 1986; Milling, Reardon, & Carosella, 2006). We use empirically supported procedures—developed in our laboratories and elsewhere—to optimize suggestibility by disabusing participants of myths regarding hypnosis and boosting positive treatment expectancies (Gfeller, Lynn, & Pribble, 1987; Gorassini & Spanos, 1986, 1999) by way of education, discussion, and presentation of a video clip of a model successfully using self-hypnosis. We frame the procedures as self-hypnosis to enhance the likelihood of transfer and maintenance of gains apart from the original treatment context (Lynn & Kirsch, 2006).

The self-hypnosis script invites participants to take slow deep breaths and become absorbed in their experience, with deepening suggestions and a body scan; with suggestions to release tension through the breath, fingertips, and toes; and to

"go just as deep as you would like to go." In the self-hypnosis induction, we describe the state-like features of hypnosis in keeping with our theme of acceptance as:

". . . a state of absorption in moment-to-moment experiences and suggestions, including acceptance of whatever goes through your mind and whatever you experience in your body, a state of attunement with your intentions and values, acceptance of your experience, with each breath, more and more accepting yet aware on a deep level of your being of what you want to accomplish, what you are striving for, what you can achieve as you become a nonsmoker. Allow yourself to the extent possible to stretch yourself in your self-hypnosis and get absorbed in going just as deep as you would like to go with each breath, just as deep and comfortable and absorbed as you allow yourself to be, simply noticing and aware and accepting."

The 15-minute self-hypnosis exercise includes an embedded anchoring procedure as follows:

"Now bring your thumb and forefinger together . . . make what I call an anchor . . . anchor your intention, your willingness to let your experiences come and go, to be tolerant and accepting of yourself and others, patient and understanding, yet more and more in tune with your intentions, your intention to be a nonsmoker, to become absorbed in what you need to do to become a nonsmoker. . . ."

Although the historical focus of our approach has been on hypnosis-based strategies, we have updated our program with emerging research and clinical developments in the broader field of psychology, as we were particularly encouraged by early reports of successful use of mindfulness and acceptance-based approaches for smoking cessation (e.g., Gifford, Kohlenberg, Hayes, Antonuccio, & Piasecki, 2004; Hernández-López, Luciano, Bricker, Roales-Nieto, & Montesinos, 2009). For example, we invite participants to be aware of and to increasingly accept urges to smoke as well as other emotional and mental experiences associated with nicotine withdrawal. As the previous passages imply, the key is awareness and acceptance without acting on the urge. We suggest a number of ways to do this, including "surfing the urge" by acknowledging the impulse and waiting it out, accepting cravings as normal, and not equating an urge to smoke with negative self-evaluation or negative predictions about successfully stopping smoking. In addition to interspersing mindfulness-based strategies throughout our program, we use hypnotic suggestions to reinforce the idea that one can be mindful and accept a craving yet not act on the impulse to smoke. Participants also develop detailed, personalized plans to cope with smoking urges by substituting more healthy behavioral alternatives to smoking. These ideas are further exemplified in the following passages in the self-hypnosis exercise:

"As I have been speaking, maybe you have noticed your thoughts come and go, if you have paid attention to your thoughts at all, as you have become more and more absorbed in your experience of self-hypnosis. Now here's something you might think about should you experience an urge to smoke, simply let that urge come and go, come and go, perhaps passing with each breath . . . moving further and further away, further and further away, as you tap into your motivation, your desire, your sincere intention to become a non-smoker, and with the simple passage of time. And as you turn off that struggle switch in your mind, you discover that there's no need to struggle with the urge, to fight it so much, or do battle with it; simply accept, and here's the key—without acting on it; learn that it may come, but it WILL go, quite naturally while you live your life. You can act in terms of your values and deepest sense of what is good for you and what you need to do, and put your energy into doing something that's meaningful and life enhancing, as you surf the urge, ride it out, see its energy dissipate, just as the force of a wave on the ocean dissipates, as the once powerful wave becomes a barely perceptible ripple in the water, merging with the shore and the sand, becoming one with the vast ocean itself. And as you become aware of the energy and life within you, as your conviction to protect and preserve your deepest self and your physical body grows, and you prepare yourself to become absorbed in what is the next right thing to do, living your life in the moment is the next right thing to do."

In the days between Sessions 1 and 2, participants are instructed to listen daily to an audio recording of the first self-hypnosis session; watch an hour-long DVD of the entire educational program with a significant other who will be supportive and provide encouragement, if such a person is available; secure a co-signer to a behavioral contract to stop smoking; review reasons to stop smoking; post reminders of their goal to stop smoking in highly visible places (e.g., desk, dresser, refrigerator, car dashboard); and complete a self-monitoring form regarding the number of cigarettes smoked. Although participants are instructed to gradually reduce their consumption of cigarettes between the first and second sessions, Session 2 is designated as the official "stop smoking forever" day.

Session 2 begins with a review of the strategies presented in the first session. Participant monitoring of smoking behaviors and self-hypnosis practice serves as a springboard for a broad discussion of smoking triggers, high-risk situations and relapse prevention, alternative behaviors to smoking, urge management, and reactions to practicing self-hypnosis. In a "goal achievement ceremony," participants are invited to share a primary reason for stopping smoking, their struggles with cigarettes, and their conviction to never smoke again, as they rip up/destroy a package of cigarettes (or a supplied picture of cigarettes) in front of the audience when the program is group administered.

As described in Lynn, Green, Elinoff, Baltman, and Maxwell (2016), we use the second 25 to 30 minute self-hypnosis exercise to (a) crystallize reasons for stopping smoking; (b) enhance self-efficacy; (c) facilitate acceptance, mindfulness, and urge management, including imaginative rehearsal of resisting smoking in high-risk situations; (d) engage in imaginative scenes where one successfully resists the urge to smoke and instead chooses an alternative, more healthy behavior; (e) suggest sensory awakening of taste and smell following smoking cessation; (f) teach cue-controlled relaxation (anchoring) in stressful situations; (g) redefine image of self from a "smoker" to a "nonsmoker" and visualize the self as a nonsmoker in a variety of situations with people complimenting them for being a nonsmoker; (h) suggest mindful eating and enjoyment of eating in moderation; (i) review plans for action; (j) increase motivation to take valued action pertaining to one's health; and (k) give examples of how to deal with counterproductive and self-defeating thoughts. Our program relies on the use of imagery techniques to achieve multiple goals, as reflected in the following examples. The first passage suggests imagery for a place of security, the second uses imagery to reassess the "faulty basis" for initiating the smoking habit, and the third uses imagery to facilitate relapse prevention:

1. *"Now, let's try something a bit different. Imagine a favorite scene, a scene of a special place, your place, your spot, where you feel just right, centered, and secure. A scene that is pleasant, safe, and calm. Perhaps, it is a scene of a place that you have visited before or maybe it is one that you've only imagined. It can be any scene you wish to visit in your mind. In this space, you are comfortable, happy, and able to think clearly. You can use this mental space you have created to help any urge pass, just one more way, of many ways, you can help yourself to manage urges if they ever arise."*

2. *"Here is something interesting to think about. Most people report that the very first time that they smoked, it tasted awful and the smell was horrible. Most people have to train themselves over many years to tolerate the awful taste and the nasty smell of smoking. Now recall the very first time you ever smoked. Try to remember the very first time. Think clearly about the situation. Recall the sights and sounds, whether you are alone or with someone else. What was your motivation to smoke? Why did you start this terrible habit in the first place? Perhaps you were trying to fit in . . . to be cool . . . or maybe you wanted to be accepted by others? Was it peer pressure? Were you trying to feel like an adult? . . . to impress your friends? Were you trying to prove your independence? See if you can understand why you smoked in the first place. What need did smoking fill for you? Do this now [Pause]. Recognize that whatever your reason to start smoking . . . why you started in the first place . . . is probably no longer valid today, and you can find other ways of fulfilling the original need. Do you really need to smoke to be happy or accepted? You are, of course, older now . . . and maybe much wiser now. Is being a smoker really the person you want to be? Is smoking consistent with your goals and values? Let yourself become absorbed in the idea that you can take valued action!"*

3. *"Now think of a situation where you were once likely to smoke. What is the particular time and location; who are the people you are with? Mentally recreate your surroundings. Take in the sights, smells, and sounds of this place. What are you doing? What time of year is it? What are you wearing? Now become aware of the urge to smoke. Acknowledge the urge. Say to yourself, 'I feel the urge to smoke.' And, in your imagination, say to yourself, 'I don't have to smoke. I can choose to do something different.' Say this to yourself now, 'I don't have to smoke.' Think of yourself doing something other than smoking. Perhaps you take a drink of water, stretch your legs, and take a deep breath. Think of an action you can do instead of smoking . . . a valued action, the next right thing to do. And as you choose this course of action, notice that the urge fades away to nothing, as you live your life in each moment, intentionally."*

At the conclusion of Session 2, we provide participants with an audio copy of the second meeting self-hypnosis script and encourage practice on a daily basis for at least one week. We also instruct participants to listen to scripts from either session, over subsequent weeks, as needed.

CONCLUSION

Our multifaceted hypnosis intervention combines elements of behavior therapy, cognitive behavioral therapy, and mindfulness and acceptance-based approaches based on empirically supported principles and methodologies. Our program can be presented in an individual or group format and can be tailored to consider the individual's smoking history, personal needs, and treatment preferences. In a series of case studies (Green, 1996, 1999, 2000, 2010), we have illustrated how our program can be personalized as well as expanded to address other habit control problems, such as excessive eating. Moreover, our program can be implemented with or without nicotine replacement therapy (NRT). We have created handouts that describe the nature and pros and cons of NRT and recommend its use in conjunction with our program, consistent with evidence indicating that NRT can contribute to the success of cognitive behavioral interventions for smoking (Fiore et al., 2008; Hughes, 1995;

Tonnesen, 2009). We look forward to controlled trials of our program that compare the efficacy and effectiveness of our intervention with no treatment, alternative treatments, and experimental conditions that control for nonspecific effects of treatment.

REFERENCES

Abbot, N. C., Barnes, J., White, A. R., Barnes, J., & Ernst, E. (2000). Hypnotherapy for smoking cessation. *Cochrane Database Systematic Review, 2,* 1–8.

Ahijevych, K., Yerardi, R., & Nedilsky, N. (2000). Descriptive outcomes of the American Lung Association of Ohio hypnotherapy smoking cessation program. *International Journal of Clinical and Experimental Hypnosis, 48*(4), 374–387. doi:10.1080/00207140008410367

Brandon, T., Tiffany, S., Obremski, K., & Baker, T. (1990). Post-cessation cigarette use: The process of relapse. *Addictive Behaviors, 5*(2), 105–114.

Brown, R. A. (2003). Intensive behavioral treatment. In D. B. Abrams, R. Niaura, R. A. Brown, K. M. Emmons, M. G. Goldstein, & P. M. Monti (Eds.), *The tobacco dependence treatment handbook: A guide to best practices* (118–177). New York, NY: Guilford.

Burton, S. M., & Tiffany, S. T. (1997). The effect of alcohol consumption on craving to smoke. *Addiction, 92*(1), 15–26.

Carmody, T. P., Duncan, C., Simon, J. A., Solkowitz, S., Huggins, J., Lee, S., & Delucchi, K. (2008). Hypnosis for smoking cessatio: A randomized trial. *Nicotine & Tobacco Research: Official Journal of the Society for Research on Nicotine and Tobacco, 10*(5), 811–818. doi:10.1080/14622200802023833

Council, J. R. (1999). Hypnosis and response expectancies. In I. Kirsch (Ed.), *Expectancy, experience and behavior.* Washington, DC: American Psychological Association.

Council, J. R., Kirsch, I., & Hafner, L. P. (1986). Expectancy versus absorption in the prediction of hypnotic responding. *Journal of Personality and Social Psychology, 50*(1), 182–189.

Elkins, G., Marcus, J., Bates, J., Rajab, H. M., & Cook, T. (2006). Intensive hypnotherapy for smoking cessation: A prospective study. *International Journal of Clinical and Experimental Hypnosis, 54*(3), 303–315. doi:10.1080/00207140600689512

Fiore, M. C., Jaen, C. R., Baker, T. B., Bailey, W. C., Benowitz, N. L., & Curry, S. J. (2008). *Treating tobacco use and dependence: 2008 update. Clinical AHCPR supported guide and guidelines.* Rockville, MD: Agency for Health Care Policy and Research (US).

Gfeller, J., Lynn, S. J., & Pribble, W. (1987). Enhancing hypnotic susceptibility: Interpersonal and rapport factors. *Journal of Personality and Social Psychology, 52,* 586–595.

Gifford, E. V., Kohlenberg, B. S., Hayes, S. C., Antonuccio, D. O., & Piasecki, M. M. (2004). Acceptance-based treatment for smoking cessation. *Behavior Therapy, 35,* 689–704.

Gorassini, D. R., & Spanos, N. P. (1986). A social-cognitive skills approach to the successful modification of hypnotic susceptibility. *Journal of Personality and Social Psychology, 50*(5), 1004–1012.

Gorassini, D. R., & Spanos, N. P. (1999). The Carleton skill training program: Original version and variations. In I. Kirsch, A. Capafons, E. Cardena, & S. Amigo (Eds.), *Clinical hypnosis and self-regulation: Cognitive-behavioral perspectives* (pp. 141–177). Washington, DC: American Psychological Association.

Green, J. P. (1996). Cognitive-behavioral hypnotherapy for smoking cessation: A case study in a group setting. In S. J. Lynn, I. Kirsch, & J. W. Rhue (Eds.), *Casebook of clinical hypnosis* (pp. 223–248). Washington, DC: American Psychological Association.

Green, J. P. (1999). Hypnosis and the treatment of smoking cessation and weight loss. In I. Kirsch, A. Capafons, E. Cardena-Buelna, & S. Amigo (Eds.), *Clinical hypnosis and self-regulation: Cognitive-behavioral perspectives* (pp. 249–276). Washington, DC: American Psychological Association.

Green, J. P. (2000). Treating women who smoke: The benefits of using hypnosis. In L. M. Hornyak & J. P. Green (Eds.), *Healing from within: The use of hypnosis in women's health care* (pp. 91–117). Washington, DC: American Psychological Association.

Green, J. P. (2010). Hypnosis and smoking cessation: Research and application. In S. J. Lynn, J. W. Rhue, & I. Kirsch (Eds.), *Handbook of clinical hypnosis, II* (pp. 593–614). Washington, DC: American Psychological Association.

Green, J. P., & Lynn, S. J. (2000). Hypnosis and suggestion-based approaches to smoking cessation: An examination of the evidence. *International Journal of Clinical and Experimental Hypnosis, 48*(2), 195–224. doi:10.1080/00207140008410048

Green, J. P., Lynn, S. J., & Montgomery, G. H. (2006). A meta-analysis of gender, smoking cessation, and hypnosi: A brief communication. *International Journal of Clinical and Experimental Hypnosis, 54*(2), 224–233. doi:10.1080/00207140500528497

Green, J. P., Lynn, S. J., & Montgomery, G. H. (2008). Gender-related differences in hypnosis-based treatments for smoking: A follow-up meta-analysis. *American Journal of Clinical Hypnosis, 50*(3), 259–271. doi:10.1080/00029157.2008.10401628

Hernández-López, M., Luciano, M. C., Bricker, J. B., Roales-Nieto, J. G., & Montesinos, F. (2009). Acceptance and commitment therapy for smoking cessation: A preliminary study of its effectiveness in comparison with cognitive behavioral therapy. *Psychology of Addictive Behaviors: Journal of the Society of Psychologists in Addictive Behaviors, 23*(4), 723–730. doi:10.1037/a0017632

Hughes, J. R. (1995). Combining behavioral therapy and pharmacotherapy for smoking cessation: An update. In L. S. Onken, J. D. Blaine, & J. J. Boren (Eds.), *Integrating behavior therapies with medication in the treatment of drug dependence: NIDA research monograph* (pp. 92–109). Washington, DC: U.S. Government Printing Office.

Kirsch, I., Montgomery, G., & Sapirstein, G. (1995). Hypnosis as an adjunct to cognitive behavioral psychotherapy: A meta-analysis. *Journal of Consulting and Clinical Psychology, 63*(2), 214–220.

Law, M., & Tang, J. L. (1995). An analysis of the effectiveness of interventions intended to help people stop smoking. *Archives of Internal Medicine, 155*(18), 1933–1941.

Lynn, S. J., Green, J. P., Elinoff, V., Baltman, J., & Maxwell, R. (2016). When worlds combine: Hypnosis, mindfulness, and acceptance in psychotherapy and smoking cessation. In A. Raz & M. Lifshitz (Eds.), *Hypnosis and meditation: Toward an integrative science of conscious planes.* New York, NY: Oxford University Press.

Lynn, S. J., & Kirsch, I. (2006). *Essentials of clinical hypnosis: An evidence-based approach.* Washington, DC: American Psychological Association.

Lynn, S. J., Rhue, J. W., & Kirsch, I. (2010). *Handbook of clinical hypnosis.* Washington, DC: American Psychological Association.

Milling, L. S., Reardon, J. M., & Carosella, G. M. (2006). Mediation and moderation of psychological pain treatments: Response expectancies and hypnotic suggestibility. *Journal of Consulting and Clinical Psychology, 74*(2), 253–262. doi:10.1037/0022-006X.74.2.253

Neufeld, V., & Lynn, S. J. (1988). A single-session group self-hypnosis smoking cessation: A brief communication. *International Journal of Clinical and Experimental Hypnosis, 36*(2), 75–79. doi:10.1080/00207148808409331

Shiffman, S., & Balabanis, M. (1995). Associations between alcohol and tobacco. In J. B. Fertig & J. P. Allen (Eds.), *Alcohol and tobacco: From basic science to clinical practice.* Bethesda, MD: NIAAA.

Shopland, D. R., & Burns, D. N. (1993). Medical and public health implications of tobacco addiction. In C. T. Orleans & J. Slade (Eds.), *Nicotine addiction: Principles and management* (pp. 105–128). New York, NY: Oxford University Press.

Sood, A., Ebbert, J. O., Sood, R., & Stevens, S. R. (2006). Complementary treatments for tobacco cessation: A survey. *Nicotine & Tobacco Research: Official Journal of the Society for Research on Nicotine and Tobacco, 8*(6), 767–771. doi:10.1080/14622200601004109

Steinberg, M. L., Ziedonis, D. M., Krejci, J. A., & Brandon, T. H. (2004). A single-session motivational interviewing intervention for engaging smokers with schizophrenia in treatment for tobacco dependence. *Journal of Consulting and Clinical Psychology, 72*(4), 723–728. doi:10.1037/0022-006X.72.4.723

Tønnesen, P. (2009). Smoking cessation: How compelling is the evidence? A review. *Health Policy, 91*(Suppl. 1), S15–S25. doi:10.1016/S0168-8510(09)70004-1

U.S. Department of Health and Human Services. (2006). *The health consequences of involuntary exposure to tobacco smoke: A report of the surgeon general.* Atlanta, GA: U.S. Department of Health and Human Services, Centers for Disease Control and Prevention.

U.S. Department of Health and Human Services. (2010a). *Ending the tobacco epidemic: A tobacco control strategic action plan for the U.S. Department of Health and Human Services.* Washington, DC: Office of the Assistant Secretary for Health.

U.S. Department of Health and Human Services. (2010b). *How tobacco smoke causes disease: The biology and behavioral basis for smoking attributable disease: A report of the surgeon general.* Atlanta, GA: U.S. Department of Health and Human Services, Centers for Disease Control and Prevention, National Center for Chronic Disease Prevention and Health Promotion, Office on Smoking and Health.

U.S. Department of Health and Human Services. (2012). *Preventing tobacco use among youth and young adults: A report of the surgeon general.* Atlanta, GA: U.S. Department of Health and Human Services, Centers for Disease Control and Prevention, National Center for Chronic Disease Prevention and Health Promotion, Office on Smoking and Health.

U.S. Department of Health and Human Services. (2014). *The health consequences of smoking–50 years of progress: A report of the surgeon general, executive summary.* Atlanta, GA: U.S. Department of Health and Human Services, Centers for Disease Control and Prevention, National Center for Chronic Disease Prevention and Health Promotion, Office on Smoking and Health.

Viswesvaran, C., & Schmidt, F. L. (1992). A meta-analytic comparison of the effectiveness of smoking cessation methods. *Journal of Applied Psychology, 77*(4), 554–561.

Sports Performance

Roland A. Carlstedt

The purpose of this chapter is to present sport hypnosis as a mental training (MT) procedure that is specifically designed to facilitate the enhancement of performance during actual training and, especially, official competition. An integrative, ecological, and biomarker-based hypnosis protocol containing strong accountability components is advanced to address some of the limitations of previous research, as well as weaknesses and oversights that have marked conventional procedural and methodological approaches to sport hypnosis (Carlstedt, 2012; Morgan, 2012). Heart rate variability (HRV) monitoring is a central component of the presented protocol and is used to help determine intervention/MT efficiency (biomarker changes and behavioral responses/cues associated with hypnosis) and efficacy (effect of hypnosis/hypnosis-related biomarkers on sport-specific outcomes).

THE CARLSTEDT PROTOCOL: SPORT HYPNOSIS

Sport-specific hypnosis is a priming MT intervention that is designed to induce motor, technical, tactical, and brain–heart–mind–body responses that are associated with optimum performance. In contrast to clinical hypnosis that usually attempts to "relax" a patient, hypnotic procedures for enhancing sport performance should attempt to progressively raise levels of activation that are necessary to efficiently engage in sport-specific tasks (e.g., getting out of the blocks quickly in a 100-meter race; Carlstedt, 2004, 2012). The feeling that one attempts to generate is mental alertness, intense focus, and mind–body control even at high levels of activation and in the presence of competitive pressure. Inductions should be designed to reduce or eliminate negative intrusive thoughts that vulnerable athletes (e.g., those who are high in neuroticism) frequently experience prior to action

and especially during critical moments of competition (Carlstedt, 2004, 2012). Once mental alertness and focus have been established (using sport-specific induction analytics) as reflected in changes in differential autonomic nervous system (ANS) responses from the baseline to hypnosis condition, active–alert hypnosis can be used to further raise activation or intensity levels and prime motor–technical responses (Bányai & Hilgard, 1976). Active–alert hypnosis involves linking induction instructions, coaching prompts, and tips to sport-specific motor and technical motions and tactical sequences that are crucial to peak performance. As physical and technical/motor actions can be impacted by negative intrusive thoughts, inductions and PHSs are designed to mitigate or shut them down completely using integrative multimodal procedures starting with video–audio guided induction (Figure 69.1), programmed PHSs, prompts, and key words that are intended to trigger a cascade of sport-specific mind–body–motor responses. They are intended to reduce competitive anxiety or awareness of situational pressure, thereby facilitating technical and tactical action parameters that are associated with optimum performance.

The initial video-supported hypnotic induction can be brief and prompt oriented as opposed to lengthy and wordy, as clinical inductions can be. While longer scripts can be used for ancillary sport-relevant and supportive purposes, for example, to facilitate relaxation and recovery, in the context of on-the-playing-field performance, task/action-specific short phrases or one-word prompts or reminders that are repeatedly conveyed in conjunction with performance-supportive video are preferred and can serve as PHSs. For example, if an athlete is being trained to eliminate technical weaknesses, he or she will hear a prompt each time the specific technical action that is associated with such a technical problem is seen in a video, or imagined as part of the induction process, or

FIGURE 69.1 Video-audio supported hypnotic induction with HRV monitoring (with practitioner and self-hypnosis).

while engaged in active–alert hypnosis on the playing field. A slalom skier who constantly takes too indirect a route going into a gate might receive the prompt "direct" every time an upcoming gate is hypnotically envisioned per video priming or simulated when active–alert hypnosis is being engaged in. If successfully hypnotized, the prompt "direct" should "pop" into the skier's mind (PHS catalyst) as he or she approaches each gate, thereby facilitating motor and tactical control, leading to a more direct line of attack into the gate, which is ultimately reflected in faster times.

Prompts and short phrases are repeatedly delivered in conjunction with video-based and imagined optimum technique. The process of repeating or sequentially reproducing perfect technical motions visually/internally through external (video-role model) actions, giving way to subliminal self-repeated hypnotic-induced prompts during self- and active-alert hypnosis, and eventually during training and actual competition, is hypothesized to facilitate motor priming and subsequent action. The induction and prompt process also attempts to suppress interfering intrusive thoughts and overwriting consolidated negative technical and motor actions that must be eliminated during competition. In technically

proficient athletes, prompts and PHSs, by contrast, are primarily structured to eliminate negative intrusive thoughts during preaction phases of sports that psychologically vulnerable athletes frequently experience as a function of real and perceived pressure situations (e.g., a break point in tennis).

INDUCTION AND HYPNOTIC SUGGESTIONS: A SCRIPTED MATCH SCENARIO FOR AN ELITE TENNIS PLAYER

The following script was designed to help improve the psychological performance of a professional tennis player who was high in hypnotic susceptibility and neuroticism and low in repressive coping, scoring a "most vulnerable" in Athlete's Profile (AP; Carlstedt, 2012). The player lacked self-confidence and feared "going for his shots" when it counted the most during competition. Even though he had a good technical game, it frequently broke down under pressure. It was decided to implement video–audio guided hypnosis/self-hypnosis, leading to active–alert hypnosis that emphasized the priming of technical skills/motor action in implicit memory prior to competition. The goal was to facilitate intense subliminal focus on priming of technical and tactical action sequences that frequently occur during competitive tennis that this player had failed to master, weaknesses that surfaced especially during critical moments when mental pressure is expected to be the greatest for an athlete with such an AP. The active–alert script was created to allow for frequent repetitions of technical and tactical sequences he would have to master and involved a scenario that simulated real competition. It is important that a scripted scenario is as realistic as possible to induce a state in which an athlete believes that he or she is actually in the throes of competition that requires a level of intensity that is commensurate with the demands of a specific sport (this mind–body dynamic can be captured using biomarkers, ideally with ambulatory HRV monitoring instrumentation; e.g., POLAR RS800CX system). Realism is thought to be beneficial for reducing stress and enhancing performance during actual competition because the hypnotized athlete is expected to experience real competition no differently than the active–alert hypnosis MT preparation phase. This dynamic can be further reinforced by integrating "punishment" and "reward" components into MT in an attempt to inoculate or habituate an athlete to ongoing competitive stress during training (Carlstedt, 2012).

This hypnotic script also attempts to induce dissociation and suppression of negative intrusive thoughts from surfacing in an athlete who is high in neuroticism. As negative intrusive thoughts in this player usually centered on his technical weaknesses, the script focused on technical details and parameters associated with optimum tennis strokes or technique. Thus, although it is widely held that athletes should not think about their technique and "just do it," faulty technique must be corrected and reprogrammed, something active–alert hypnosis can facilitate independent of thinking about things too much and at the wrong time. Because, in this particular player, the way to achieve psychological improvement was through technical mastery; it was vital to correct flawed technique in order to boost his self-confidence and eventually eliminate negative intrusive thoughts associated with his technical problems. The intense repetition of prompt-based corrective technical commands and supportive active–alert hypnosis is designed to help subliminally consolidate improved motor skills in implicit memory more efficiently and prime them for action when under pressure. Faulty technique can lead to poor results and outcome, which in turn can cause a vulnerable athlete to obsess on negative intrusive thoughts such as, "Why can't I hit a winning shot when I have to?" or, "Why did I miss that backhand?" Such cognitions can be insidious and prevent even an elite athlete from performing up to peak potential consistently.

VIDEO–AUDIO GUIDED INDUCTION AND ACTIVE–ALERT HYPNOSIS SCRIPT

"Envision yourself preparing for your first round tennis match. Start by going through all of your strokes in a slow and deliberate manner, visualize the different parts of each stroke you have been working on, including the back swing, swing to contact, contact point, and follow through. Try to feel the length of your back swing, as well as your swing. After each completed stroke, get back into the ready position. Think about a tactical sequence you are going to carry out in the upcoming match, and then carry it out in a slow and

deliberate manner until you have completed all the strokes involved in this sequence. Pay attention to keeping your feet moving and going forward toward the ball. Imagine yourself attacking the ball. As you go through the stroke sequences, practice improving the weakness you were recently made aware of, remembering to stay sideways with your shoulders parallel to the sideline until you have completed the entire backhand stroke [this introductory induction is video–audio based, using "role model" footage and repetitive prompts/key words]. *As you warm up, pick up the pace progressively. Imagine that you are on the court in front of thousands of spectators, and feel yourself become eager to show what you can do. You are gaining confidence, your muscles are loosening up, your breathing is steady and indicative of someone who is in control, and you're absolutely calm and certain that you will play to the best of your ability. As you continue through the warm-up sequence, you are playing points out in your mind. When playing these points out, imagine the tactics you are going to carry out to beat your opponent. You are aware that this player will charge the net after most serves, so that you are ready to hit your best passing shots. You know that you'll have to keep your head down when hitting the ball, and if you're trying to pass him with the backhand your shoulders will remain parallel to the sideline DOWN-PARALLEL* [prompt]. *Things are going well, you are falling deeper and deeper into a state of absolute concentration. When you go out onto the court you will notice nothing but the court, the crowd will not be there, you will be totally focused on playing your best tennis. When you start to warm-up against your opponent, your motor system will feel like a finely tuned machine, the prematch routine will have worked wonders. You will feel as though you can beat anyone because you are confident that your technical skills have been optimally prepared and have the ideal game plan to beat this player. Once you are on the court you must rely on yourself, but you will continue to hear me remind you to do certain things, although I will do so only prior to action when you are returning serve or serving. Once action starts, you will react and everything for which you trained will flow in a natural and effortless manner; you can't beat yourself because you are ready. When the match starts, try to detach yourself from everything that may disturb you. Don't let anything intrude on your thoughts and interfere with your concentration. Don't pay attention to anything but what has been called to your attention. Concentrate on your positioning and balance and the feel of your racquet in your hands. Your level of concentration and confidence are increasing in preparation for action. As you anticipate the start of the match and returning serve you feel primed and ready to play. You are looking forward to the opportunity of playing in front of many tennis fans. You can feel a mild positive tension building in your feet and legs as you anticipate the first point. On each point, before your opponent's racquet starts to accelerate toward the ball, you are already in motion and preparing to return it. When returning serve you have a neutral grip, but are preparing your free hand to change to the proper grip depending on where the ball is hit. All systems are go. Continue to concentrate, time your breathing I N H A L E–EXHALE* [prompt in preaction phase; note: <u>letter separation illustrates the length of inhale (longer) vs. exhale phase (shorter) cycles</u>] *to your opponent's serving motion and just before you start your split step, take a deep breath I N H A L E and make your heart decelerate; EXHALE for a few beats, feel it happen, and your reactions will be very quick in response to the serve. When you say 'NOW'* [preaction prompt based on this sequence] *to yourself you will explode . . . EXPLODE* [prompt] *out of the ready position and react to the serve. Remember to use your free hand to get the proper grip, take a short back swing, and step toward the ball. As you swing you notice a free-flowing acceleration of the racquet, and just before you make impact with the ball your grip becomes more forceful, allowing you to transfer all of your power through the ball as you hit and follow through. Accelerate through the ball, hit it with confidence, then get back to the neutral position and prepare for the next shot. NOW! After a point ends listen to the chair umpire call out the score* [PHS/subliminal prompt]. *Whenever he does this you will know that you have a maximum of 20 to 25 seconds until the next point starts. Hearing the score* [PHS] *will help you concentrate and prepare for the next point. During this period you will prime your mind and body for the next point. You will think about an appropriate strategy that you have learned and practiced and will be getting ready during this 20- to 25-second interval. Just prior to action your*

mind will be blank, you will be totally focused on the ball and will carry out the tactic you thought about. Just as you or your opponent commences action say I N H A L E-EXHALE. . . . NOW."

COMMENTARY

This script was designed for an elite tennis player. It assumes a high level of technical competence and ability to carry out numerous tactical strategies. The player's weaknesses were addressed in the preparatory phases, the first taking place 30 minutes before the player was called out to the court. This practice session involved the induction phase of active–alert hypnosis. During this period, the player went through a so-called shadow stroke routine in which he practiced entire stroke sequences without actually hitting the ball. This phase is marked by the constant repetition of key messages that are designed to increase hypnotic depth while simultaneously priming implicit motor memory for impending action. In addition, suggestions for creating the impression that the practice session is a real match were administered. This is intended to raise levels of activation while reducing the mental stress associated with competition. It is hoped that a realistic scenario will reduce precompetition anxiety by desensitizing the player to common distractions, including crowd noise, the opponent's presence, and internal intrusive thoughts. Once the active–alert hypnosis session has been completed and a player is sufficiently activated and primed (both mentally and physically) PHSs are administered. These suggestions are intended to induce autosuggestion or self-hypnosis when the player is on the court and can no longer be coached or prompted exogenously. A well-hypnotized athlete is capable of generating his or her own active–alert script internally or it can be delivered on the playing field by a practitioner/coach.

In the earlier script, whenever the chair umpire announced the score, the player self-prompted himself to go through a mental preparation routine prior to the upcoming point. In this period, the player became aware, subliminally, of PHSs that were hypnotically embedded in the induction phase, in this case, mentally preparing to implement an appropriate tactical strategy (similar to what was rehearsed in the active–alert match simulation phase of the earlier practice session) and induce heart rate deceleration (HRD) prior to action, using cognitive strategies and breathing techniques (INHALE–EXHALE, PHS). Thereafter, another PHS, saying "NOW," functioned as a cue to ready the athlete for immediate action.

INTERVENTION EFFICIENCY AND EFFICACY ANALYTICS

Sport hypnosis procedures must always be individualized and should be considered experimental. The onus is on the practitioner to demonstrate empirically both intervention efficiency and efficacy at the intraindividual level, irrespective of claims of efficacy that are based on group studies, anecdotal accounts, or self-report. *Intervention efficiency* refers to the extent to which a conceptually procedure-relevant biomarker (e.g., HRV measures) changes from baseline to an intervention endpoint (e.g., after 15 minutes of hypnotic induction) and/or the extent to which PHS-prompted behavior or actions during competition are evident/observable. For example, if a hypnosis/active–alert hypnosis script is structured to generate a PHS-prompted action at specific times (e.g., taking a deep breath prior to each point, or saying "NOW"), the number of times such an action is observed is notated. In a tennis match with, for example, 100 points (preaction phases), if a PHS prompt action/behavior (prescribed and trained breathing cycle) is only observed 20 times, intervention efficiency (0.20 or 20%) would be considered very low. By contrast if a PHS behavior is observed 90 times, intervention efficiency would be considered very high (0.90 or 90%). Conceptually relevant HRV biomarkers, such as preaction HRD, would also be expected to occur concomitant to the PHS-exhibited action or behaviors in line with specific cardiac responses (HRD) being associated with mental preparation, giving way to preaction motor priming (criterion-referenced validation of PHS behavior with HRV biomarker; Andreassi, 2000; Carlstedt, 2001, 2012). HRD biomarker and PHS behavior/action analyses during preaction phases can help further distinguish whether a behavioral action is hypnosis induced or merely part of an athlete's preaction routine that occurs independent of hypnosis

or is a random occurrence. HRD is a distinct psychophysiological response that is discernable in HRV analyses that are obtained through continuous instrument-based monitoring (e.g., Polar RS800 CX system; Carlstedt, 2012) and offers revealing insight into MT (hypnosis) mind–body dynamics.

Intervention efficiency and efficacy are established on the basis of the following temporal intervention engagement parameters/measures: (a) when a MT (hypnosis) session started, (b) how long it lasted, (c) how many times prompts/PHS were reinforced, (d) mind–body response changes from the baseline to the intervention condition (as reflected in HRV/HRD), (e) observable PHS behaviors, and/or (f) how much of the variance in sport-specific macrolevel and microlevel outcome measures can be explained on the basis of hypnosis-related predictor measures.

The ANS reports in Figure 69.2 emanated from the tennis player in the earlier case study.

HRV was monitored for the duration of the self-hypnosis session. An ANS report was generated immediately after its completion. The report in Figure 69.2 depicts HRV data from a 10'28" video-based self-hypnosis induction session. Session length can vary due to scheduling and other factors that cannot be controlled, but should be adjusted normatively after efficiency and efficacy analyses have been performed over the course of numerous measurement occasions (40–60 to achieve acceptable statistical power; Carlstedt, 2012) to determine the session length that is most associated with positive performance outcomes. Ideally, sessions should be carried out within 30 minutes of practice or match time to minimize degradation of the achieved hypnotic state over time. HRV–ANS reports are used to determine intervention efficiency and efficacy. Relative to MT efficiency, global changes in any number of the previous HRV measures across the intervention and change-assessment condition determine initial intervention efficiency (reflective of depth of hypnosis). Because there are no group intervention efficiency norms for any MT modality, they must be established using a repeated measures design for each individual athlete. Consistent with the *individual zone of optimum functioning* (IZOF; Hanin, 2006) model, an intervention like self-hypnosis can lead to disparate ANS responses between the baseline, across the post-MT assessment conditions as a

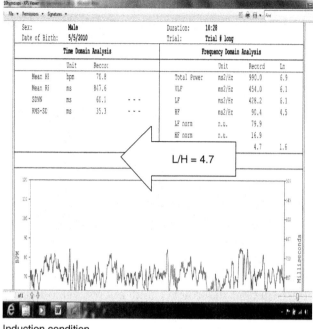

Induction condition

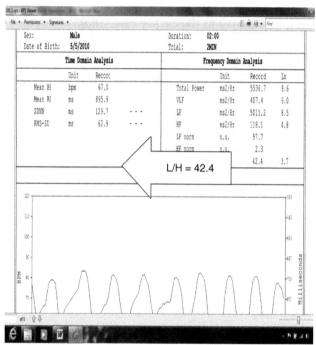

Postinduction assessment

FIGURE 69.2 Established intervention efficiency as reflected in large change in HRV, L/H frequency after induction (player's normal L:H frequency MEAN over 11 matches and training = 6.7).

function of the AP (Carlstedt, 2012), and other individual differences or factors that nevertheless, and paradoxically, can be associated with similar outcomes (e.g., the same SDNN predicting better performance in one and worse in another). Hence,

the need for individualized analyses to determine what hypnosis-mediated and/or reflective ANS/HRV measures/parameters are associated with sport-specific macrolevel or microlevel successful outcome statistical indicators (e.g., batting average during critical moment level 5 at-bats [the highest level of competitive situational pressure; Carlstedt, 2012]).

The greater the difference between the baseline or postintervention assessment and the intervention condition in most conceptually relevant ANS/HRV responses, the greater the intervention efficiency is hypothesized/expected to be (i.e., the greater the hypnotic depth). In this case, the player's post–self-hypnosis SDNN (the HRV index) more than doubled from 60 to 130 milliseconds with low frequency (LF) activity increasing more than tenfold (from 454 to over 5,000; ms^2/hz), resulting in a very high low:high frequency ratio of 42.4 immediately after the induction phase (hypothesized biomarker indicator of being hypnotized with strong hypnotic depth, increasing from 4.7 during the induction phase endpoint). Conceptually, it is expected that being hypnotized will lead to changes in ANS responding, as most interventions, especially those that have strong mental manipulative components, whether volitionally or subliminally induced (as with hypnotic procedures), will lead to differential increases or decreases in cognitively mediated ANS responses (intervention efficiency). The greater a conceptually consistent change in an ANS response across the induction phase to its conclusion, the more potent and enduring a hypnotic state is expected to be. Hypnotic response variability ([HYP]RV) is a methodological advance that allows for the statistical delineation of the hypnotic process, commencing with the induction phase and ending at the conclusion of therapy, or in the case of performance, the end of training or competition (Carlstedt, 2012). [HYP]RV can be calculated using biomarkers such as HRV, EEG, hypnosis behavioral engagement cues (HBEC), and/or macro and micro therapy or sport-specific outcome measures (Carlstedt, 2012).

Intervention-induced ANS/HRV statistically significant changes, as in this case, are expected to be enduring and predominate (= intervention efficiency). That is, baseline to postintervention ANS/HRV changes that are induced by hypnosis are expected to lead to consistent situational responses that reflect MT efficiency over the course of competition (e.g., a change in SDNN or heart rate [HR] each time the player engages in a behavior or action that is indicative of engaging in a PHS that reflects intervention/hypnotic efficiency). ANS/HRV responses that are documented immediately after a MT session (hypnosis here) establish a new MT response or intervention-mediated baseline/threshold (change from prehypnosis baseline L:H ratio of 4.7 to 42.4; see Figure 69.2) that is expected to be maintained over time as a function of the strength of differences in HRV measures between conditions (pre/during action and postcompetition) and subsequent intervention-based PHS reinforcement throughout competition. It is hypothesized that the greater the difference in ANS/HRV-specific responses between the intervention and postintervention assessment conditions, the greater the intervention efficiency and likelihood that such intervention-induced response-differences will remain stable over time (e.g., the entire duration of competition; see Figure 69.3, player intervention efficiency HRV biomarkers).

This player's intervention efficiency was relatively high, a conclusion that was reached on the basis of conceptually relevant HRV measures exhibiting strong changes from baseline (PRE) induction (HYP) to the posthypnosis condition (POST), especially heart rate (HYP vs. POST, HR, $p = .003$), SDNN (PRESD vs. POSTSD, .02), L:H ratio (LHHYP vs. POSTLH, .001), and L:H ratio (PRELH vs. POSTLH, .009), to name a few. All in all, the player exhibited statistically significant changes in five out of six conceptually most-relevant HRV biomarkers (0.83 or 83%). This data strongly suggests that the player was hypnotized and that the induction held for the entire match (about 2 hours).

INTERVENTION EFFICACY

It is important to note that intervention efficiency does not necessarily equate with or predict intervention efficacy, especially in sport performance situations. Such must be determined empirically using both variance explained/regression methodologies and macrolevel pre vs. intervention phase analytic procedures (e.g., T-test, χ^2). The

Paired samples test

		Paired differences							
					95% confidence interval of the difference				
		Mean	Std. Deviation	Std. Error Mean	Lower	Upper	t	df	Sig. (2-tailed)
Pair 1	HRHYP - PREHR	-.6667	3.9370	1.3123	-3.6929	2.3596	-.508	8	.625
Pair 2	HRHYP - POSTHR	-16.3333	11.9373	3.9791	-25.5092	-7.1575	-4.105	8	.003
Pair 3	PREHR - POSTHR	-13.1111	12.2622	4.0874	-22.5367	-3.6856	-3.208	8	.012
Pair 4	SDHYP - PRESD	-18.7778	26.4423	8.8141	-39.1031	1.5476	-2.130	8	.066
Pair 5	SDHYP - POSTSD	3.7778	28.6914	9.5638	-18.2764	25.8319	.395	8	.703
Pair 6	PRESD - POSTSD	23.6667	24.1609	8.0536	5.0949	42.2384	2.939	8	.019
Pair 7	VLHYP - PREVL	-19.4444	183.9783	61.3261	-160.8627	121.9738	-.317	8	.759
Pair 8	VLHYP - POSTVL	250.8889	164.6591	54.8864	124.3207	377.4571	4.571	8	.002
Pair 9	PREVL - POSTVL	235.6667	270.7393	90.2464	27.5580	443.7753	2.611	8	.031
Pair 10	LHYP - PRELO	-1150.89	1777.3531	592.4510	-2517.08	215.3057	-1.943	8	.088
Pair 11	LHYP - POSTL	245.7778	121.9946	40.6649	152.0044	339.5512	6.044	8	.000
Pair 12	PRELO - POSTL	923.7778	1271.9524	423.9841	-53.9314	1901.4870	2.179	8	.061
Pair 13	HHYP - PREH	-33.0000	130.6292	43.5431	-133.4105	67.4105	-.758	8	.470
Pair 14	HHYP - POSTH	-90.3333	246.5806	82.1935	-279.8720	99.2053	-1.099	8	.304
Pair 15	PREH - POSTH	-25.8889	222.8017	74.2672	-197.1495	145.3717	-.349	8	.736
Pair 16	LHHYP - PRELH	-6.1333	12.3889	4.1296	-15.6563	3.3896	-1.485	8	.176
Pair 17	LHHYP - POSTLH	3.1556	1.7444	.5815	1.8147	4.4964	5.427	8	.001
Pair 18	PRELH - POSTLH	4.7667	4.2172	1.4057	1.5250	8.0083	3.391	8	.009

FIGURE 69.3 Prehypnosis HRV versus posthypnosis induction HRV comparisons to determine intervention efficiency. HYP, HRV after induction; POST, HRV immediately after competition; PRE, pre-induction HRV measures.

self-hypnosis progression should be systematically structured, documented, and analyzed as follows: An athlete with performance psychological problems "a" and "b" and technical issue "c" that are known to manifest themselves, especially under pressure conditions, can be eradicated by "x_1" amount of precompetition video-based self-hypnosis and/or "x_2" amount of active–alert hypnosis and "x_3"amount of posthypnotic situation-specific prompt-induced mental–motor–technical corrective, performance-facilitative reinforcement pertaining to a, b, and c. To illustrate, if 15 minutes of video-guided hypnotic induction (x_1), followed by 15 minutes of active–alert hypnosis (x_2) and 5 minutes of PHS reinforcement (x_3), are associated with an enhanced level of "a" (attention threshold) and "b": (greater HRD in preaction phases of a sport), as well as reduction in "c" (technical error), then intervention efficacy has been demonstrated (i.e., if changes are statistically significant; baseline assessment vs. intervention trial x or in terms of variance in outcome measures that can be explained on the basis of hypnotic temporal parameters and/ or associated biomarker changes [e.g., change in HRV from baseline or preaction HRD and points won across numerous competitions with an A-B design]).

In this case study, player macrolevel HRV outcome measures of note included the following: LF in the hypnosis condition (across the entire match duration) was correlated with Games Lost (LF, 0.63, $p < .05$) as was prematch very low frequency HRV (VLF, 0.81, 0.005). VLF in the prematch baseline condition is reflective of relative sympathetic nervous system (SNS) predominance, a biomarker associated with high neuroticism (the player was high in N; Carlstedt, 2012; Wickramaskera, 1988). By contrast, posthypnotic induction heart rate (HR) was correlated with games won (HR, 0.70, 0.02). Interestingly, total time engaged in hypnosis (induction) was correlated with posthypnosis induction VLF activity, suggesting that hypnotic procedures may have contributed to generating and sustaining a level of activation, as reflected, subsequently (posthypnosis/active–alert hypnosis and PHS behavior during competition) in higher HR that was associated with more games won across entire matches (intervention efficiency being associated with intervention efficacy). This state and outcome may have been facilitated by prematch

active–alert hypnosis (induction phase II), helping transform what at face value could be considered a clinically negative state (excessive VLF) into performance facilitative SNS/VLF activation that can be considered adaptive/facilitative in sport action contexts (higher HR). Physical activity is known to attenuate nervousness and psychological distress associated with excessive SNS activity (e.g., prematch anxiety in this player), a self-regulation technique that appears to divert cortical resources away from the prefrontal lobes to the motor cortex, thereby reducing or eliminating frontal lobe-based negative intrusive thoughts and facilitating preaction motor priming and subsequent action (Carlstedt, 2012; Dietrich, 2003, 2006). High HR is correlated with increased SNS—a state that is associated with higher global levels of activation that are necessary for optimum physical and technical performance in many action sports. Hence, sport-specific hypnosis may have initiated and helped maintain the described cascade of mind–body responses that were associated with successful performance.

CONCLUSION

Applied intervention efficiency and efficacy analytics allow practitioners to go well beyond clinical intuition by quantifying variance explained in performance and mind–body–behavior outcome measures that can be attributed to interventional procedures (such as hypnosis). In this case spanning 9 matches, (49%) of the variance in games won could be attributed to an hypothesized, hypnosis-mediated biomarker, in this case, heart rate, preliminarily establishing the efficacy of hypnosis in this player (Intervention Efficacy Quotient of 0.49). The applied methodology also provides insight into the differential impact of hypnosis-related HRV biomarkers and negative outcome (–IO = negative intervention outcome) whereby, in this case, postinduction hypnosis and associated LF-HRV was correlated with games lost. These findings are conceptually consistent with greater SNS activation, and are expected to be performance facilitative in a sport like tennis. By contrast, a mixed para-SNS/SNS HRV measure (LF) can, as in this case, be indicative of a level of activation that is not conducive to winning games.

Individualized intervention (hypnosis) biomarker-derived measures across entire competitions allow for the future tweaking or customization of hypnosis protocols to optimize performance by enhancing performance facilitative ANS/HRV responses and reducing the impact of ANS/HRV measures that are found to be detrimental to successful outcomes. This can be done by adjusting temporal hypnosis engagement parameters (time engaged), changing the content of scripts, reinforcing PHS prompts/cues, and training athletes, in vivo and ecologically (on the playing field), to increase the frequency of PHS behaviors/actions that are associated with performance facilitative mind–body responses (HRV) and concomitant successful, sport-specific outcomes (e.g., winning a point).

REFERENCES

Andreassi, J. L. (2000). *Psychophysiology: Human behavior and physiological responding.* Hillsdale, NJ: Lawrence Erlbaum.

Bányai, E. I., & Hilgard, E. R. (1976). A comparison of active-alert hypnotic induction with traditional relaxation induction. *Journal of Abnormal Psychology,* 85(2), 218–224.

Carlstedt, R. A. (2001). Ambulatory psychophysiology and ecological validity in studies of sport performance: Issues and implications for intervention protocols in biofeedback. *Biofeedback,* 29(4), 18–22.

Carlstedt, R. A. (2004). *Critical moments during competition: A mind-body model of sport performance when it counts the most.* New York, NY: Psychology Press.

Carlstedt, R. A. (2012). *Evidence-based applied sport psychology: A practitioner's manual.* New York, NY: Springer Publishing Company.

Dietrich, A. (2003). Functional neuroanatomy of altered states of consciousness: The transient hypofrontality hypothesis. *Consciousness and Cognition,* 12(2), 231–256.

Dietrich, A. (2006). Transient hypofrontality as a mechanism for the psychological effects of exercise. *Psychiatry Research,* 145(1), 79–83. doi:10.1016/j.psychres.2005.07.033

Hanin, Y. L. (2006). Individual zones of optimal functioning (IZOF) model: Emotion-performance relationships in sport. In Y. L. Hanin (Ed.), *Emotions in sport.* Champaign, IL: Human Kinetics.

Morgan, W. P. (2012). Hypnosis in sport and exercise psychology. In J. L. van Raalte & B. W. Brewer (Eds.), *Exploring sport and exercise psychology* (pp. 151–181). Washington, DC: American Psychological Association.

Wickramasekera, I. E. (1988). *Clinical behavioral medicine.* New York, NY: Plenum. doi:10.1007/978-1-4757-9706-0

Stress Management

Robin Chapman

A Google search of the word *stress* reveals a diverse and dizzying array of articles addressing broad issues of health, work, and relationships. A recent *Time* magazine article identified Florida as the most "stressed-out" state, due to high unemployment and a higher number of people without health insurance (Frizell, 2014). Several websites promise to provide solutions aimed at reducing your stress. For example, the National Institute of Mental Health (2014) publication "Adult Stress—Frequently Asked Questions" answers questions about stress and overall health, and how to cope with stress. The World Health Organization cites stress as the second most frequent health problem, and notes that it impacts one third of the employed people in the European Union (Varvogli & Darviri, 2011).

Clinical practitioners treat countless clients for stress and related concerns. Clients often describe stress as resulting from an external event or person such as, "My boss is causing me to be stressed." Clients may also refer to internal stress that is physiological, "My stress is making my stomach hurt." Clients often use the term *stress* to refer to people, things, and events they perceive as aversive. Clinical practitioners identify the following sources of stress: environmental demands, coping with social stressors, physiological reactions, and thoughts (Davis, Eshelman, & McKay, 2008).

Stress management is an ubiquitous topic of professional seminars and journal articles, popular magazines, and media. However, there is no shared, clear definition of stress. Stress has been associated with job burnout, cardiovascular disease, cancer, substance abuse, depression, and anxiety. In an effort to better understand this widely used term, a brief summary of the historical and scientific use of this term will follow.

Ancient Stoic philosophers in Europe identified stress and the need for training to deal with the problems of life. While in the East, Buddhism focused on the first noble truth of suffering, which can be roughly translated as stress. This ancient thinking and wisdom not only identified stress, but provided the foundation for current cognitive behavioral therapy. Stress has been a difficult word to define and has changed throughout time, describing hardship, adversity, overwork, and fatigue. Physics in the 19th century defined stress scientifically as " . . . force applied to objects that could potentially result in deformation or strain" (Woolfolk, Lehrer, & Allen, 2007, p. 6).

Stress has been associated with biochemical, physiological, emotional, and behavioral changes. The early conceptualizations of stress were associated with physiological changes. Walter Cannon's (1939) fight-or-flight response is often cited as a model of the stress response. Stress is thought to occur with the constant and unneeded mobilization of the body to prepare for aggression or fleeing danger.

Hans Seyle (1956) elaborated on the fight-or-flight response, describing three stages of stress: (a) alarm stage, (b) adaptive-resistance stage, and (c) exhaustion stage. This model emphasized the concept of homeostasis, which describes the body's process of returning to the state prior to arousal. A disruption of this process may result in burnout.

A recent model of stress incorporates the concept of allostasis (Goldstein & McEwen, 2002). Allostasis is similar to homeostasis; however, it emphasizes stability through change in the functions of glucocorticoids and catecholamines. The concept of allostatic load refers to the cumulative cost, which can result in serious pathophysiology.

The aforementioned theories focus on the physiological, while other theories emerged that were based in psychology. Lazarus and Folkman (1984) developed a highly influential psychological model of stress, the appraisal theory. This view emphasized the role of cognitive mediation in stress, emphasizing the negotiation between environmental demands, constraints, and personal beliefs.

Resource models evolved later to challenge the appraisal-based theories. The conservation of resources theory attempted to clarify the nature of stress. People are thought to strive to retain, protect, and build resources in response to potential or actual loss of valued resources. Individuals rely on the objective and cultural views of the environment rather than on their personal constructs (Hobfoll, 1989, 2001).

A recent integrative model, derived from allostasis theory, highlights the role of the brain as a dynamically adapting interface between the biological self and the changing environment (Ganzel, Morris, & Wethington, 2010). This model includes the physical, social, and cultural context, the internal regulation of bodily processes, and health outcomes.

While far from comprehensive, this brief summary of the history and theories of stress provides a basic introduction to the varied physiological and psychological complexities related to models of stress. Conceptualizations of stress have been broad and imprecise. Therefore, stress may best be viewed as an umbrella concept that helps identify and categorize this multiplicity of phenomena. Stress as a nebulous concept may facilitate discussion among clinicians and researchers, leading to an increase in the treatment and investigation of these stress-related phenomena (Woolfolk, Lehrer, & Allen, 2007).

Clinical practitioners searching the new *Diagnostic and Statistical Manual of Mental Disorders*, fifth edition (*DSM-5*) will not find a specific stress disorder that describes their client's experience of stress (American Psychiatric Association, 2013). However, the impact of stress can be found in many of the depressive and anxiety diagnoses. Specific stressors such as trauma-evoking events are central to the diagnosis of acute stress disorder and posttraumatic stress disorder. The general concept of stress is also incorporated in the diagnostic category of adjustment disorders.

A recent American Psychological Association (2011) Stress in America survey found that nearly 75% of Americans who responded to an online survey said that their stress levels are so high that they feel unhealthy. To provide clarity, the American Psychological Association's definition

of stress will be used (Gerrig & Zimbardo, 2002). Stress is described as "the pattern of specific and nonspecific responses an organism makes to stimulus events that disturbs its equilibrium and taxes its ability to cope."

Clinical practitioners from diverse theoretical and psychotherapeutic approaches use hypnosis in the treatment of stress-related problems. The following presents summaries of stress management techniques and an integrated hypnosis and cognitive behavioral model for treatment of stress.

STRESS MANAGEMENT TREATMENT REVIEW

Clinical practitioners employ a wide range of stress management techniques: progressive muscle relaxation (Bernstein, Carlson, & Schmidt, 2007), meditation and mindfulness (Carrington, 2007; Kabat-Zinn, 2005), visualization (Kosslyn, 1994), biofeedback (Gevirtz, 2007; Schwartz & Andrasik, 2003), diaphragmatic breathing (Davis, Eshelman, & McKay, 2008; Varvogli & Darviri, 2011), relaxation response (Benson & Klipper, 2000), hypnotic methods, cognitive methods, and numerous other approaches (Lehrer, Woolfolk, & Sime, 2007). Many of these techniques share commonalities and may be used in an integrated hypnosis and cognitive behavioral treatment approach. The focus of this chapter is hypnotic and cognitive behavioral strategies for the treatment of stress. A comprehensive review of these techniques is beyond the scope of this chapter.

Cognitive Behavioral Therapy

Multiple forms of cognitive behavioral therapy exist today and may appear quite different from one another. These diverse forms of cognitive behavioral therapy share principles of learning theory, such as operant, classical, and social learning. Three distinct, but overlapping, waves of modern behavioral and cognitive therapies have been identified as behavioral, cognitive, and mindfulness (Hayes, 2004).

Cognitive therapy (Beck, 1979) is the most studied and widely used approach. Cognitive therapy includes assessment, case conceptualization, and cognitive and behavioral treatment techniques. This approach is time limited and is characterized by collaboration, structure, guided discovery, and Socratic questioning.

Behavioral techniques may include graded task assignments, activity scheduling, social skills training, assertiveness training, behavioral rehearsal, in vivo exposure, relaxation training, behavioral experiments, fixed role therapy, and bibliotherapy. Cognitive techniques may include daily thought records, understanding idiosyncratic meaning, guided discovery, challenging absolutes, reattribution, direct disputation, labeling of distortions, decatastrophizing, challenging dichotomous thinking, mental imagery techniques, desensitization, and considering pros and cons (Freeman, Pretzer, Fleming, & Simon, 2004).

Cognitive therapy for stress ". . . focuses on reducing the hyperactivity of the individual's controlling schemas, modifying dysfunctional cognitions, and improving the individual's ability to cope effectively" (Pretzer & Beck, 2007, p. 493).

Stress inoculation training (Meichenbaum, 1985, 2007) is a form of cognitive behavioral therapy that is multifaceted, flexible, and can be tailored to the individual. It was developed in the mid-1980s to provide stress prevention and reduction procedures for individuals with acute, sequential, and chronic stress. In medicine, vaccines often use weaker forms of the disease for inoculation against diseases. Stress inoculation training is similar as it focuses on minor stressors that foster psychological preparedness and promote resilience.

Stress inoculation training is composed of three interlocking and overlapping phases: (a) conceptual educational phase, (b) skills acquisition phase, and finally, (c) application and follow-through phase. Specific applications for stress inoculation have included medical problems, high stress occupations, and treating victims of trauma.

Hypnosis

Hypnosis, one of the oldest of psychotherapeutic techniques, can be traced to the work of Anton Mesmer during the 1770s. Research into trance states, the role of social and cognitive factors, and, most recently, neural correlates has been conducted in an effort to understand the phenomenon of hypnosis.

Many definitions of hypnosis exist today. Marc Oster (2006a) suggests that the combination of definitions is useful to understanding hypnosis. "Hypnosis can be defined as a highly focused, heightened awareness that purifies the treatment field—the mind, enabling the client or patient to be more receptive to alternative ideas and experiences. As a result of this collaborative relationship, the client or patient can experience alterations in sensation, perception, thoughts and behaviors" (p. 30).

Many modern clinical practitioners consider all hypnosis as forms of self-hypnosis. The client's hypnotic experience appears related to their level of cooperation, motivation, expectations, attitudes, and the ability to become absorbed in suggestion-related thinking and imagining (Barber, 1979). One of the most consistent and reliable ways of teaching clients self-hypnosis is progressive relaxation. Golden, Dowd, and Friedberg (1987) described hypnosis for fears, phobias, and stress-related disorders that is consistent with a cognitive behavioral therapy approach.

Today, hypnosis is used as a stress management tool for a variety of psychological and physical disorders (Karlin, 2007). Research over the last decade has suggested that an integrated approach combining hypnosis and cognitive behavioral therapy increases the efficacy of treatment (Bryant, Moulds, Guthrie, & Nixon, 2005; Kirsch, Montgomery, & Sapirstein, 1995). Several models have emerged that provide integration of hypnosis and cognitive behavioral therapy (Alladin, 2008; Chapman, 2006; Dowd, 2000; Yapko, 2006; Zarren & Eimer, 2002).

HYPNOSIS AND COGNITIVE BEHAVIORIAL THERAPY

Clinical hypnosis alone is not psychotherapy and is not sufficient for treatment and must be combined with other psychotherapies for treatment of stress. An integrated approach combining hypnosis and cognitive behavioral therapy would offer a flexible and effective treatment. Cognitive behavioral strategies have been used to effectively treat a wide range of stress-related disorders. In cognitive behavioral therapy, clinical hypnosis has been used effectively for relaxation, focusing, mobilization of imagery, heightening expectations of success, changing self-defeating thoughts, and initiating new behaviors (Oster, 2006b). Anxious clients may try unsuccessfully to relax, using breathing or progressive muscle relaxation. However, they successfully achieve relaxation during hypnosis. The client no longer has to focus on trying to relax while in the role of the hypnotized subject (Karlin, 2007). Clinical hypnosis can be thought of as a lens that sharpens the person's focus on cognitive behavioral strategies, or can be considered the glue holding these strategies together.

Assessment and case conceptualization are critical to the selection of hypnotic and cognitive behavioral strategies, and the individualized treatment interventions are guided by this process. Many approaches to case conceptualization are possible; however, these approaches share many important elements, allowing for the most effective treatment of an individual. Persons's (1989, 2008) case conceptualization model has been chosen for the following clinical case of Samantha, as this provides structure for a comprehensive approach.

RESEARCH

Evidence-based treatments for stress include progressive muscle relaxation, autogenic training, relaxation response, biofeedback, guided imagery, mindfulness-based therapy, and cognitive behavioral therapy (Varvogli & Darviri, 2011).

Hypnosis, when utilized with medical procedures and presurgical anxiety, meets the criteria for being a well-established treatment that is both effective and specific. Self-hypnosis training has been effective when used for the treatment of anxiety-related disorders such as tension headaches, migraines, and irritable bowel syndrome (Hammond, 2010).

Hypnosis, used in combination with cognitive behavioral therapy, has shown substantial enhancement of outcomes. This was demonstrated in a meta-analysis of 18 studies in which a variety of conditions were treated with cognitive behavioral therapy and then compared with cognitive behavioral therapy with the addition of hypnosis (Kirsch, Montgomery, & Sapirstein, 1995).

CASE STUDY

Stress is ubiquitous in our modern world, which presents a challenge when choosing a case that is emblematic of hypnosis and cognitive behavioral therapy treatment. This case represents the treatment of a single person, living in post-Katrina New Orleans, Louisiana, but aspects are universal to others throughout the world facing similar stressors.

New Orleans is known for its unique culture that attracts people from all over the world for its celebrations, food, and music. It also has a history of vulnerability to damage from tropical storms and hurricanes. Hurricane parties and sheltering in place were common prior to Hurricane Katrina in 2005; however, the magnitude of the approaching storm resulted in many people fleeing. When the levees were breached, 80% of the city was flooded. The widespread loss of life and devastation of property was chronicled on television and in newspapers.

Identifying Information

Samantha is a 36-year-old White female. She has a Bachelor of Fine Arts degree from a college in her home state of Mississippi. She was raised in a conservative faith that she no longer practices. The client's fiancée works as a cook and she works as a bartender at the same high-end restaurant.

Samantha came to New Orleans to work as an artist. She was originally trained in sculpture, but has recently taken up pottery. The client does not have her own pottery studio so she rents time, when she can afford the fee, at a studio. The studio provides equipment that she needs for her pottery work. While New Orleans has a thriving artist community, many artists cannot make a livable income from their work and have to take jobs in the hospitality service industry.

Samantha met her fiancée at the restaurant and they have been together for the last 10 years. They have no children. The client expressed frustration with their relationship as she desires to marry and have a family. Her fiancée cites financial problems as a barrier to marriage and children.

The couple relocated to her parents' home in central Mississippi during Hurricane Katrina. Their apartment sustained some water and wind damage but was not flooded. However, they lived in Mississippi for nine months before they could move back to New Orleans. This resulted in conflict with her parents about her choice of work, mate, and career. The restaurant opened quickly when people were allowed to reenter the city and the couple returned to work. The client reported that she cried for days when they returned as there was so much damage. Many coworkers had disappeared and some were assumed dead from the storm.

The client "hates" her current job as a bartender because "it's a dead end, I'm not doing my art." Samantha identified the following stressors: arguments with parents, work problems, inability to pursue her career, and relationship problems.

The client was seen at a community health center, which serves the uninsured and underinsured of New Orleans. Many people who work in the hospitality industry do not have health insurance. The patient arranged an appointment with primary care due to her chest and stomach pain, fearing that she had cardiac problems or an ulcer. These problems were ruled out by a medical examination. The patient's primary care provider referred her to behavioral health for assessment and treatment of stress.

Samantha reported that her stress was due to expectations of her parents, her significant other's refusal to consider marriage, financial problems, and difficulty finding time and money to do art and working in a dead-end job. Symptoms include insomnia, being short tempered with her significant other and coworkers, and stomach and chest pain.

The couple left New Orleans before Hurricane Katrina and the resulting devastation. However, she witnessed the television coverage and frequent calls from friends and coworkers who rode out the storm. Upon her return to the city, she witnessed the aftermath of the storm and devastation of the city that she had "come to love." Nine years later, she reports that she no longer thinks about the storm until the hurricane season begins in June and people turn their attention to prepare for potential storms. The effects of Hurricane Katrina can be seen today throughout the city with the FEMA markings still on many buildings, buckled sidewalks and streets, and the blighted houses pockmarking many neighborhoods.

Assessment and Diagnosis

The assessment was conducted using a multimodal approach (Lazarus & Lazarus, 1991). Seven modalities are assessed: behavior, affect, sensation, imagery, cognition, interpersonal, and drugs and biology. This is consistent with the biopsychosocial approach of many primary care clinicians and increases the likelihood of obtaining information that allows the development of effective treatment interventions.

Behavior: irritability with others
Affect: anxious
Sensation: pain in stomach and chest
Imagery: homelessness and seeing herself living under the bridge
Cognition: "I am wasting my time in a dead-end job." "I need time to do my art."
"My fiancée is going to dump me." "My biological clock is ticking." "Stress is my problem."
Interpersonal: frequent arguments with fiancée. Parents are critical and unsupportive of her lifestyle and future plans.
Drugs/Biology: slightly elevated blood pressure, prescribed lisinopril. Reports drinking one to three glasses of wine per week. Experiences insomnia several nights per week.

DSM-5 Diagnoses

The diagnosis of posttraumatic stress disorder (PTSD) requires consideration, given Samantha's experience of Hurricane Katrina. However, Samantha does not meet the criteria for this diagnosis as she does not report reexperiencing or avoidance of the trauma. This does not rule out the emotional, cognitive, and behavioral problems that may be related to the storm, such as increased anxiety, irritability, and sleep problems.

Samantha's symptoms of anxiety, irritability, somatic complaints, and relationship problems appear most consistent with an unspecified anxiety disorder. A specific disorder may arise as more assessment is completed.

Case Conceptualization

A. Client Problems
1. Anxiety, nervousness
2. Stomach and chest pain
3. Irritability with others, conflict with parents
4. Relationship problems
5. Insomnia

B. Hypothesized Underlying Mechanism(s)
The following mechanisms (cognitive, behavioral, and biological variables) are thought to cause and maintain Samantha's current problems, usually in interaction with stressful events.

The cognitive variables include maladaptive assumptions that often center on rejection, somatic concerns, and poor judgment. Samantha fears that her fiancée will leave her and she will be alone. Physical sensations in the chest or stomach signal a serious medical condition. Samantha feels that she is not accepted by her parents due to her poor judgment, as she questions her choice of careers and mate.

Her behavioral variables may best be understood from a traditional behavioral analysis perspective. This includes identification of antecedents, behaviors, and consequences.

Stressful situations such as talking to her parents lead to increased levels of anxiety, resulting in argumentative and irritable behavior. This, in turn, gives way to avoidance, which decreases her anxiety level temporality without a long-term coping strategy. These stressful conversations may also lead to a tightening of chest and stomach muscles. This unpleasant sensation and increased anxiety further increase her avoidance of discussions.

Samantha's biological variables include a possible physiological vulnerability. Many clients with anxiety can identify other family members who have experienced panic attacks or elevated anxiety. Samantha does not remember another family member with anxiety as this was not discussed in her family.

C. How Mechanism Produces the Problems

Samantha's perception of stress and experience of anxiety may be due to an upset in regulatory functions of her cognitive system. This leads to indiscriminate interpretation of environmental events and physiological sensations as dangers. Samantha is likely to have difficulty coping and managing her anxiety, leading to irritability and avoidance of others. This lack of coping strategies may also result in worry and result in vulnerability to insomnia.

D. Current Precipitants of the Problem

Samantha's arguments with her parents have increased over the last few months. Samantha continues her bartending job after her inability to find an affordable art studio space. This has increased Samantha's self-doubt and worry about the future of her career, and her relationships with her fiancée and her family.

E. Origins of the Mechanism

Samantha remembers a very controlled and restrictive childhood. She recalled not being able to play like the other children due to her parents' strict attitudes. Samantha no longer adheres to her parents' expectations and has pursued her own interests. This has resulted in feelings of anxiety, frustration, and rejection. Samantha often thinks about the things she missed as a child and young adolescent and how her life could have been different. This restrictive early life may have resulted in schemas about meeting expectations of others and pleasing others at your own expense.

F. Treatment Plan

Samantha's treatment plan included weekly clinical hypnosis and CBT for treatment of anxiety. The possible hypnosis and cognitive behavioral interventions are described in the following list:

- Provide a cognitive behavioral conceptualization of anxiety and stress.
- Introduce Samantha to the CBT approach, emphasizing collaboration, structure, problem solving, and eventual self-reliance. Also introduce her to self-hypnosis as a method to augment and strengthen the treatment effects of CBT.
- Teach Samantha relaxation skills to decrease her anxiety and aid in the teaching of self-hypnosis, and to identify negative thoughts and develop adaptive alternatives.

G. Predicted Treatment Obstacles

The origin of Samantha's maladaptive schemas most likely began during childhood and formed her personality. These schemas will be resistant to change. This is a short-term treatment, given the community health center model; therefore, only 10 to 20 sessions will be available. Samantha may require longer term treatment to address these well-learned, and closely held, schemas.

Samantha had a short course of psychotherapy upon her return from Hurricane Katrina to treat stress-related symptoms of sleeplessness and anxiety. This psychotherapy appeared to be supportive but did not offer coping skills. Samantha did not remember specifics of her treatment, or her therapist's name. She described this treatment as pleasant but not helpful, so she held out hope that hypnosis would be different.

Treatment

Samantha was provided psychoeducation about the cognitive behavioral model of stress and anxiety and the role of clinical hypnosis in augmenting and strengthening CBT. Self-hypnosis, mood monitoring, and use of daily thought record were taught in early sessions (Chapman, 2014). Samantha entered treatment with positive expectations about hypnosis.

The clinical practitioner has a vast array of options for teaching self-hypnosis, such as the relaxation method, eye fixation combined with hand heaviness, and Chiasson's method (Golden, Dowd, & Friedberg, 1987). Training in self-hypnosis can reduce anxiety for both general and specific problems (Hammond, 2010). Many practitioners consider all hypnosis self-hypnosis, as the client generates the suggested imagery and determines involvement in what is suggested, regardless of the origin of the suggestion (Green, Laurence, & Lynn, 2014). One of the most reliable and consistent methods to teach self-hypnosis is progressive muscle relaxation, which is familiar to many practitioners of cognitive and behavioral therapy. Progressive muscle relaxation was used to teach Samantha self-hypnosis.

Samantha was taught the five steps of self-hypnosis: preparation, progressive muscle relaxation, deepening relaxation, working, and termination. Progressive muscle relaxation was conducted without the tensing phase. The deepening step employed imagery of a circle of energy, while the working step used coping imagery and positive suggestion and re-alerting.

Mood monitoring is also referred to as the Subjective Units of Discomfort Scale (SUDS). This was developed by Wolpe (1973) to assess change. Samantha's level of distress was self-rated, resulting in lower scores when she felt less stressed. The common use of rating from 1 to 100 was used.

Samantha was introduced to the use of a daily thought record, which is usually comprised of three columns: situation, thoughts, and feelings. Clients are asked to note strong feelings, the situation in which the feelings occurred, and then the thoughts that accompany these feelings. A worksheet was used with the three columns for Samantha to record this information.

Session 1 focused on assessment and psychoeducation around the nature and treatment of stress. Couples' counseling was explored given the client's relationship problems; however, this was not possible given the couple's conflicting work schedules. Samantha's fiancée was not willing to change his current schedule for sessions. Individual psychotherapy was begun. Stress was presented through the lens of the fight-or-flight model (Cannon, 1939). The relaxation response was offered as rationale for treatment (Benson & Klipper, 2000). Samantha appeared comfortable with this model of stress and treatment.

Sessions 2 to 5 provided training in self-hypnosis, mood monitoring, and the use of a daily thought record. Samantha was receptive to the skill training aspect of self-hypnosis. Training in self-hypnosis can reduce anxiety related to myths and inaccurate information. Psychoeducation regarding modern clinical hypnosis was also provided.

Samantha easily developed a mood monitoring scale of 0 to 100 for relaxation. This scale described 100 as the highest level of anxiety, 50 as an everyday level of tension, and 0 as no anxiety.

The client, using the daily thought record, easily identified strong feelings and situations. However, she had great difficulty identifying accompanying thoughts and images. Samantha identified significant feelings of anxiety, which she rated when getting ready for work (situation) but could not identify her thoughts or images (thoughts).

The self-hypnosis training protocol taught in earlier sessions was used for relaxation. This included abbreviated progressive muscle relaxation with emphasis on breathing in relaxation. This was followed with a deepening exercise using the image of descending a staircase with deepening relaxation. Once Samantha reached a level of deep relaxation as evidenced by slowed breathing and smooth facial muscles, the following imagery exercise was conducted.

"Now you have reached a comfortable level of relaxation.

Breathing in relaxation and breathing out tension.

Having let all the tension flow out of your body.

Letting your muscles become smooth and relaxed.

Allow your mind to wander back to last Friday as you prepared for work.

Viewing this time without discomfort or worry, like watching someone else on TV.

Notice carefully what you are thinking or imagining while getting ready for work.

All the while comfortably relaxing.

Take your time, allowing the thought or image to emerge slowly.

Once you have this thought or image, signal with a raised finger or slight nod of your head.

Your unconscious mind will allow you to share this thought or image upon re-alerting."

The following daily thought record is completed with Samantha's thoughts identified during self-hypnosis. Samantha had great difficulty identifying these thoughts without hypnosis. Samantha explained, "I was just too tense to notice what I was thinking."

Situation	Thoughts	Feelings
Preparation for work, personal hygiene, bathing, and choosing clothes	This is useless, I'm wasting my time. How will I ever do something useful?	Feeling anxious (65–75) SUDS 100 highest level of anxiety, 50 moderate level of anxiety, and 0 as no anxiety

Self-hypnosis training, mood monitoring, and cognitive strategies such as daily thought record, guided discovery, and Socratic questioning were procedures used in the first five sessions.

Session 5 focused on self-hypnosis and coping skills using imagery. Samantha had developed skills for self-hypnosis and had continued to use daily thought records. Information from the daily thought records was used in sessions to test thoughts and develop alternatives. Samantha reported some relief with these interventions, but reported that at times she felt "overwhelmed by my parents' criticism, rejection by fiancée, and my dead end job with little time or resources left to do pottery." This cascade of negative thoughts usually began following "difficult and heated conversations" with her parents or fiancée. Samantha identifies these negative thoughts as beginning roughly around her evacuation during Katrina. Samantha

expressed that her evacuation "forced her to deal with things" that she had avoided.

While Samantha did not meet the criteria for post-traumatic stress disorder, many of her symptoms can be traced back to the effect of the hurricane. Samantha's complex and multifaceted symptom presentation resembles the impact of trauma. A cognitive behavioral intervention with hypnosis used for treatment of posttraumatic stress disorder was implemented (Oster, 2006b).

Samantha was led through the stages of hypnosis similar to the self-hypnosis that had been implemented in the earlier sessions and practiced as homework. This coping imagery follows the deepening stage.

"Imagine feeling totally at ease and relaxed.

Imagine along in your mind's eye.

A comfortably lit room with a large control panel.

Sitting down in a comfortable chair before a panel with many dials and switches.

At first, the control panel is confusing with so many controls.

But soon the purpose of this panel becomes clearer.

Imagine each dial is labeled with problems in your life.

Your parents' rejection, your fiancée's indecision, your job, questions about your future.

There are dials and switches for other problems and stressors that arise in your mind.

Resting comfortably at the control panel, feeling relaxed.

Imagine these controls and switches are labeled low, moderate, and high stress.

Allow the unconscious part of your mind to adjust these controls.

Adjusting these controls for both comfort and effectiveness."

The previous coping imagery exercise was focused on creating a sense of safety and structure when faced with multiple stressors. This exercise also helped Samantha develop coping skills to deal with her daily stress and anxiety.

Sessions 6 to 10 continued the previous strategies of self-hypnosis training, daily thought record, with disputation techniques and practice of coping imagery (control panel).

CONCLUSION

At the termination of treatment, Samantha reported that she was less stressed and had more time and energy to pursue her pottery and rated her daily stress 40 to 60 on her SUDs scale. This was a significant drop from her initial overall rating of 55 to 100. Samantha was encouraged to consider booster sessions if needed. It is important to note that many other cognitive behavioral and hypnotic interventions could be employed for treatment with additional sessions.

This case is representative of clients briefly treated in a community health center. An integrated approach using cognitive behavioral treatment and hypnosis provides an effective, structured, and time-limited approach for clients with complex stress-related problems. This integrated approach can be modified for a variety of potential stress-related problems given its reliance on individual case conceptualization and treatment planning.

REFERENCES

Alladin, A. (2008). *Cognitive hypnotherapy: An integrated approach to treatment of emotional disorders*. Chichester, UK: Wiley.

American Psychiatric Association. (2013). *Diagnostic and statistical manual of mental disorders*. Washington, DC: American Psychiatric Publishing.

American Psychological Association. (2011). Stress in America 2010. Retrieved from http://www.apa.org/news/press/releases/stress/index.aspx

Barber, T. X. (1979). Suggested hypnotic behavior: The trance paradigm versus an alternative paradigm. In E. Fromm & R. E. Shor (Eds.), *Hypnosis: Developments in research and new perspectives*. New York, NY: Adline.

Beck, A. T. (Ed.). (1979). *Cognitive therapy of depression*. New York, NY: Guilford press.

Benson, H., & Klipper, M. Z. (2000). *The relaxation response*. New York, NY: Harper Torch.

Bernstein, D. A., Carlson, C. R., & Schmidt, J. E. (2007). Progressive relaxation, abbreviated methods. In P. M. Lehrer, R. L. Woolfolk, & W. E. Sime (Eds.), *Principles and practice of stress management* (pp. 88–122). New York, NY: Guilford Press.

Bryant, R. A., Moulds, M. L., Guthrie, R. M., & Nixon, R. D. (2005). The additive benefit of hypnosis and cognitive behavioral therapy in treating acute stress disorder. *Journal of Consulting and Clinical Psychology, 73*(2), 334–340. doi:10.1037/0022-006X.73.2.334

Cannon, W. (1939). *The wisdom of the body*. New York, NY: W. W. Norton.

Carrington, P. (2007). Modern forms of mantra meditation. In P. M. Lehrer, R. L. Woolfolk, & W. E. Sime (Eds.), *Principles and practice of stress management* (pp. 363–392). New York, NY: Guilford Press.

Chapman, R. A. (2014). *Integrating clinical hypnosis and CBT: Treating depression, anxiety and fears*. New York, NY: Springer Publishing Company.

Chapman, R. (2006). *The clinical use of hypnosis in cognitive behavior therapy*. New York, NY: Springer Publishing Company.

Davis, M., Eshelman, E. R., & McKay, M. (2008). *The relaxation and stress reduction workbook* New York, NY, New Harbinger Publications.

Dowd, T. E. (2000). *Cognitive hypnotherapy*. Lanham, MD: Rowman & Littlefield.

Freeman, A., Pretzer, J., Fleming, B., & Simon, K. (2004). *Clinical applications of cognitive therapy*. New York, NY: Springer Publishing Company.

Frizell, S. (2014, June 8). This is the most stressed-out state in America. Retrieved from http://time.com/2845160/stress-state-america-study

Ganzel, B. L., Morris, P. A., & Wethington, E. (2010). Allostasis and the human brain: Integrating models of stress from the social and life sciences. *Psychological Review, 117*(1), 134–174. doi:10.1037/a0017773

Gerrig, R. J., & Zimbardo, P. G. (2002). *Psychology and life* American Psychological Association, glossary of psychological terms. Retrieved from http://www.apa.org/research/action/glossary.aspx?tab=18

Gevirtz, R. N. (2007). Psychophysiological perspectives on stress-related and anxiety disorders. In P. M. Lehrer, R. L. Woolfolk, & W. E. Sime (Eds.), *Principles and practice of stress management* (pp. 209–226). New York, NY: Guilford Press.

Golden, W. L., Dowd, E. T., & Friedberg, F. (1987). *Hypnotherapy: A modern approach*. New York, NY: Pergamon Press.

Goldstein, D. S., & McEwen, B. (2002). Allostasis, homeostats, and the nature of stress. *Stress, 5*(1), 55–58.

Green, J. P., Laurence, J. R., & Lynn, S. J. (2014). Hypnosis and psychotherapy: From Mesmer to mindfulness. *Psychology of Consciousness: Theory, Research and Practice, 1*, 199–212.

Hammond, D. C. (2010). Hypnosis in the treatment of anxiety and stress related disorders. *Expert Reviews Neurotherapeutics, 10*, 263–273.

Hayes, S. C. (2004). Acceptance and commitment therapy, relational frame therapy and third wave of behavioral and cognitive therapies. *Behavioral Therapy, 35*, 639–665.

Hobfoll, S. E. (1989). Conservation of resources: A new attempt at conceptualizing stress. *The American Psychologist, 44*(3), 513–524.

Hobfoll, S. E. (2001). The influence of culture, community, and the nested-self in the stress process: Advancing conservation of resources theory. *Applied Psychology: An International Review, 50*, 337–421.

Kabat-Zinn, J. (2005). *Full catastrophe living: Using the wisdom of your body and mind to face stress, pain, and illness* (15th anniversary ed.). New York, NY: Delta Trade Paperback/Bantam Dell.

Karlin, R. A. (2007). Hypnosis in the management of pain and stress; mechanisms, findings and procedures. In P. M. Lehrer, R. L. Woolfolk, & W. E. Sime (Eds.), *Principles and practice of stress management* (pp. 125–150). New York, NY: Guilford Press.

Kirsch, I., Montgomery, G., & Sapirstein, G. (1995). Hypnosis as an adjunct to cognitive behavioral psychotherapy: A meta-analysis. *Journal of Consulting and Clinical Psychology, 63*(2), 214–220.

Kosslyn, S. M. (1994). *Image and the brain: The resolution of the imagery debate.* Cambridge, MA: MIT Press.

Lazarus, A. A., & Lazarus, C. N. (1991). *Multimodal life history inventory.* Champaign, IL: Research Press.

Lazarus, R. S., & Folkman, S. (1984). *Stress, appraisal and coping.* New York, NY: Springer Publishing Company.

Lehrer, P. M., Woolfolk, R. L., & Sime, W. E. (2007). *Principles and practice of stress management.* New York, NY: Guilford Press.

Meichenbaum, D. (1985). *Stress inoculation training.* New York, NY: Pergamon Press.

Meichenbaum, D. (2007). Stress inoculation training: A preventive and treatment approach. In P. M. Lehrer, R. L. Woolfolk, & W. E. Sime (Eds.), *Principles and practice of stress management* (pp. 497–516). New York, NY: Guilford Press.

National Institute of Mental Health. (2014). Adult stress—frequently asked questions, how it affects our health and what you can do about it. Retrieved from http://www.nimh.nih.gov/health/publications/stress/stress_factsheet_ln.pdf

Oster, M. (2006a). Hypnosis: History, definitions, theory and applications. In R. Chapman (Ed.), *The clinical use of hypnosis in cognitive behavior therapy* (pp. 25–44). New York, NY: Springer Publishing Company.

Oster, M. (2006b). Treating treatment failures: Hypnotic treatment of posttraumatic stress disorder. In R. Chapman (Ed.), *The clinical use of hypnosis in cognitive behavior therapy* (pp. 213–242). New York, NY: Springer Publishing Company.

Persons, J. B. (1989). *Cognitive therapy in practice: A case formulation approach.* New York, NY: W. W. Norton.

Persons, J. B. (2008). *The case formulation approach to cognitive-behavior therapy.* New York, NY: Guilford Press.

Pretzer, J. L., & Beck, A. T. (2007). Cognitive approaches to stress and stress management. In P. M. Lehrer, R. L. Woolfolk, & W. E. Sime (Eds.), *Principles and practice of stress management* (pp. 465–496). New York, NY: Guilford Press.

Seyle, H. (1956). *The stress of life.* Toronto: McGraw Hill.

Varvogli, L., & Darviri, C. (2011). Stress management techniques: Evidence-based procedures that reduce stress and promote health. *Health Science Journal, 5*, 74–89.

Wolpe, J. (1973). *The practice of behavior therapy.* New York, NY: Pergamon.

Woolfolk, R. L., Lehrer, P. M., & Allen, L. A. (2007). Conceptual issues underlying stress management. In P. M. Lehrer, R. L. Woolfolk, & W. E. Sime (Eds.), *Principles and practice of stress management.* New York, NY: Guilford Press.

Yapko, M. D. (2006). *Hypnosis and treating depression: Applications in clinical practice.* New York, NY: Routledge, Taylor & Francis.

Zarren, I., & Eimer, B. N. (2002). *Brief cognitive hypnosis: Facilitating the change in dysfunctional behavior.* New York, NY: Springer Publishing Company.

Professional Issues

IV

SECTION

Ethics

Thomas F. Nagy

This chapter focuses on the ethical application of hypnosis among practitioners, teachers, and researchers. It will not address the generic informed consent matters common to all health care providers, hypnotic and nonhypnotic alike (e.g., confidentiality, fees, record keeping, emergency availability, cancellation policies, and untimely interruption to treatment, to name a few). Although practitioners belonging to professional hypnosis associations (e.g., American Society of Clinical Hypnosis [ASCH], the Society of Clinical and Experimental Hypnosis [SCEH], or the International Society of Hypnosis [ISH]), must comply with their ethics codes, or "codes of conduct," they are also ethically required to maintain membership in their primary professional discipline—medicine, psychology, social work, and so on. By so doing, members agree to abide by the ethical standards of those associations, whether they teach, do research, or provide health care services to clients and patients. The ethics codes of these associations do not specifically address hypnosis; however, they are far broader in scope and provide much more ethical guidance and education for practitioners than any hypnosis association to date.

In addressing the topic at hand, this chapter considers the variety of ethical practices of hypnosis, the nature of ethics codes in general, sanctions for ethical violations, codes of ethics from professional associations, and, finally, general ethical concepts that guide all practitioners of hypnosis. It also provides brief fictional vignettes to help in understanding the ethical issues as they apply to various areas of teaching, research, and practice. Because of the broad diversity of professionals and the range of ethical and legal rules and guidelines of those in the hypnosis community, it will not be possible to address every situation relevant to each discipline. For a specific area that is not covered, readers would be well advised to consult

any of the following: (a) the ethics code of their individual association, (b) the Ethics Committee of a hypnosis association, (c) the Ethics Committee of their primary professional association, or (d) an attorney specializing in ethical and legal issues in health care.

DIVERSITY IN ETHICAL PRACTICE OF HYPNOSIS

The early chapters of this book addressed the history, definitions, and various theories of hypnosis and how hypnotic treatment has been applied to a variety of human complaints and symptoms. Those who practice hypnosis constitute a broad range of disciplines—psychologists, psychiatrists, clinical social workers, physicians, dentists, and nurses qualified to practice independently. Similarly, there is a broad conceptual range of theories and application of hypnotic intervention with clients and patients.

It is a daunting task to develop a code of ethics for a professional association whose membership draws from so many disciplines. Within the mental health domain, there is considerable variability in how hypnosis is used. Consider those who do guided imagery, Ericksonian hypnosis, hypno-analysis, hypnosis as an adjunct to psychotherapy (i.e., to assist with depression, anxiety, anger), hypnosis for habit patterns (e.g., sleep onset, weight loss, nicotine addiction, bruxism), and hypnosis for diagnosed medical disorders (e.g., tension and migraine headaches, irritable bowel syndrome, chronic pain), to name a few. A sample of medical applications includes hypnosis for childbirth, cystic fibrosis, diabetes, Parkinson's disease, fibromyalgia, menopause, nausea associated with chemotherapy, and vaginismus. How could any ethics code address all the areas that are raised by this diverse group of practitioners? As a means of addressing the topic, I will first discuss ethics codes in general, and then those pertaining to hypnosis specifically. I will conclude the chapter by addressing eight ethical areas that are interdisciplinary in nature and have application for all health care professionals.

THE NATURE OF ETHICS CODES

Although there is much variety in the construction of ethics codes among the health care professions, they share several core concepts that were articulated 2,500 years ago by the physician Hippocrates (www.nlm.nih.gov/hmd/greek/greek_oath.html). The Hippocratic oath required physicians to reflect on their professionalism as well as the quality of the intervention about to be administered. It also required physicians to honor their teachers and mentors and to pledge to avoid harming patients (*primum non nocere*) by their actions as well as maintaining patients' privacy and confidentiality.

Most of these concepts have survived for centuries and now reappear, greatly elaborated, in current ethics codes, legal statutes, and professional standards of practice. Twenty-five hundred years of clinical practice has yielded a large database from which to derive general ethical principles and specific codes of conduct that benefit both those receiving and providing health care services. The former group (clients and patients) benefits by a reduced likelihood of suffering harm from provider incompetence, carelessness, or exploitation. The latter group (providers) benefits by staying out of trouble (avoiding litigation and complaints to state licensing boards and ethics committees of their professional association) as well as experiencing the gratification of providing competent care to those who are suffering or wish to make fundamental changes in their lives.

Many ethics codes are bipartite in nature, consisting of (a) general ethical principles, such as beneficence, nonmaleficence, or autonomy, and (b) specific rules of conduct, or "standards" such as confidentiality, record keeping, competence, and avoiding conflicts of interest. As mentioned, members of professional associations are obligated to learn their code of ethics and understand how they apply to individual clinical situations.

General ethical principles may be written in broad, lofty language, and are usually aspirational in nature (i.e., they provide a general way to think about values in making difficult decisions, but they do not require absolute compliance). They focus on concepts that create a mind-set for practitioners when confronted with ethical dilemmas. For example, what approach might a health care provider take with a new patient who had a bad experience with a prior doctor who used a very domineering approach to hypnosis, known as "father hypnosis" (Ferenczi, 1926). Considering the general principles of beneficence (i.e., providing interventions that are helpful to clients and patients) or nonmaleficence (i.e., avoiding interventions that might harm clients and patients) may assist the clinician to think about how to reduce defensiveness, enhance feelings of safety, and maximize clinical results, even though it might mean using a hypnotic approach that might diverge somewhat from his or her customary approach.

The specific rules of conduct, known as "ethical standards," "codes of conduct," "principles with annotations," or some similar term, describe the mandatory aspects of professional practice—what practitioners are required to do or prohibited from doing in the course of their professional work as clinicians, researchers, or teachers. Many of these rules are also incorporated into state or federal laws pertaining to health care providers, and some states and licensing boards incorporate entire codes of ethics into their mental health code, empowering individual ethical standards with the force of law.

Ethical standards constitute the "musts" and "must-nots" of clinical practice—such as the prohibition against entering a secondary role with a current client or patient, in addition to the primary one of psychotherapist. As an example, initiating a joint business venture or writing a book with a current psychotherapy patient might also be prohibited by this standard. All health care providers are prohibited from having sexual relations with a current client or patient, and some require a two-year waiting period of time after the treatment has terminated before a sexual relationship could begin—and even then, certain variables may need to be taken into account (i.e., the nature of the termination, mental status of the former patient, history of the patient's boundary violations, etc.; American Psychological Association, 2002). Some disciplines and some states go even further into the future, with an ethical or legal rule prohibiting sexual contact with former patients forever (American Psychiatric Association, 2003).

SANCTIONS FOR ETHICAL VIOLATIONS

As previously mentioned, ethical standards of professional associations focus upon specific professional conduct, and they are generally mandatory in nature, not discretionary (i.e., members of professional associations must comply with them unless the professional association clearly has a "voluntary" code of ethics). Failure to comply with ethical standards could result not only in harm to clients and patients, but ultimately harm to the clinician as well. Ethics committees of professional associations and state licensing boards are empowered to impose sanctions for serious ethical violations, such as reprimands, censure, or even expulsion from the professional association, for extreme transgressions such as sex with a patient. Some sanctions could require that the health care provider have additional education in ethics, seek formal consultation or supervision of his or her clinical practice for a length of time, or even have psychotherapy where there is evidence of substance abuse or psychological impairment of another sort.

One of the more unfortunate situations involves a well-meaning therapist who lacks competence, resulting in harm to a client or patient. Consider the case of Dr. Lisa Ware, who failed to properly realert a hypnosis patient before allowing her to leave her office. While still somewhat dissociated, the patient wandered out of the office building and into a busy intersection, and while crossing a street outside of a crosswalk was struck by a motorcycle. Her resulting injuries required months of physical therapy for chronic pain and also psychotherapy for depression. One year later, the patient filed an ethics complaint against Dr. Ware for failing to alert her fully before allowing her to leave her office. She also considered filing a civil suit for her medical injuries and subsequent psychological depression.

State licensing boards also have the authority to administer sanctions to those professionals who have committed major infractions, such as administering treatment that fell below the standard of care (competence), mismanagement of financial matters (e.g., failure to follow through with completing insurance forms), or other conduct that resulted in harm to a client or patient or violated a state or federal law (e.g., Medicare fraud or billing an insurance company for missed sessions or telephone session while claiming that they actually did occur in the office). In addition to the range of sanctions previously listed, these sanctions could include limiting one's practice, suspending the license of a practitioner, or even more harsh penalties (monetary fines or imprisonment) where there has been a finding of serious damage to a patient (e.g., sex with a current patient).

HYPNOSIS CODES OF ETHICS—GENERAL INTRODUCTION

Professional hypnosis associations, such as the American Society of Clinical Hypnosis, the British Society of Clinical Hypnosis, the European Society of Hypnosis, the International Society of Hypnosis, and the Society for Clinical and Experimental Hypnosis, each have ethics codes that require or prohibit certain conduct on the part of its members. There is a general consensus that members must restrict their use of hypnosis to their individual level of competence, as determined by their education, training, and legal scope of practice. For example, physicians or dentists (untrained in psychotherapy) should not attempt to offer hypnotherapy to patients who, in reality, may need psychotherapy from a trained mental health care provider. This might include those with psychotic disorders, dissociative disorders, posttraumatic stress disorder, certain personality disorders, or suicidal patients, to name a few. (This will be discussed more fully in the section on "Competence.")

There is also a general consensus among ethics codes of professional hypnosis associations that members must never use hypnosis for entertainment. For example, demonstrating hypnotic phenomena at your daughter's birthday party or some other social gathering for general amusement is clearly prohibited. Although hypnosis may have fascinated people for generations, and even health care providers may occasionally be tempted to demonstrate its powers in social settings, it should generally be restricted to clinical, research, or teaching settings.

The teaching of hypnosis has ethical constraints as well. Certainly health care providers may teach clients and patients how to use hypnosis for their own benefit, and how to self-induce hypnotic trance. However, they are generally discouraged from teaching laypeople how to induce trance in others, as this could possibly result in harm to individuals with certain mental disorders (e.g., panic attacks, undiagnosed dissociative disorders). There are exceptions to this rule, however, as dictated by good judgment of the health care provider. An example would be training parents to help their own children who have pain or must undergo invasive or uncomfortable medical interventions (Butler, Symons, Henderson, Short liffe, & Spiegel, 2005).

Health care professionals are also generally prohibited from teaching or supervising lay professionals in the use of hypnosis. The rationale here is that hypnosis is considered to be adjunctive to health care treatment—medicine, psychotherapy, and dentistry—and, as such, belongs primarily to the domain of health care per se. It is one of many tools to be used in the context of providing medical, dental, or psychological treatment. It is not considered to be an intervention to be competently used by those outside the health care field with individuals suffering psychological or medical symptoms. The reason for this is that health care providers have extensive education, training, and supervision in their specific discipline. In addition to learning how to carry out research, they also learn how to evaluate, diagnose, and treat individuals suffering a broad variety of medical and psychological disorders. They must also qualify to provide treatment to clients and patients by passing examinations administered by their state licensing board in order to become licensed. Finally, they are legally required to maintain and upgrade their skills by means of continuing education for their entire professional life.

Demonstrating or teaching hypnosis in the media also has ethical rules that limit what may be publicly presented. Those who participate in television or online presentations must not demonstrate a complete hypnotic induction; they are encouraged to mute the sound, or only show part of an induction. Although there is little in hypnosis ethics codes that specifically addresses online

activities as of this writing, as technology has advanced much more rapidly than have ethical or legal regulations, practitioners are generally urged to use caution when educating the public about the uses and application of hypnosis so as to avoid specific training in the induction of trance. Again, the rationale for this lies in the assumption that the application of hypnosis should be used within the context of medical, dental, or psychological care by those who are knowledgeable about dissociation and competently trained in the science and art of hypnosis.

Ethical guidance helps reduce the risk of harm to those requesting hypnosis when presenting with a symptom of a serious medical nature that should first be evaluated by a medical doctor, such as acute headache or abdominal pain. A patient may request hypnotic intervention of a non-medical provider (e.g., psychologist, clinical social worker) for migraines, gastrointestinal complaints, blurred vision, excessive menstrual bleeding, other localized or generalized pain, fatigue, or other symptoms. Although the practitioner might be tempted to administer hypnotic treatment, encouraged by the patient's strong faith in hypnosis, she should first consider the risk of harm to the patient (nonmaleficence) by acceding to the patient's request and failing to refer for a medical diagnostic evaluation.

GENERAL ETHICAL CONCEPTS FOR ALL HEALTH CARE PROVIDERS

The following nine sections address ethical issues pertinent to all health care providers using hypnosis. Although drawn from the ethics codes that regulate and guide the work of psychologists, psychiatrists, clinical social workers, dentists, physicians, nurses, and other health care professionals, it is necessarily general in nature, and the reader is advised to always consult the ethics code of his or her relevant discipline, as well as state laws and federal laws (e.g., Health Insurance Portability and Accountability Act [HIPAA]) that regulate their practice. The upcoming sections are: (a) Competence, (b) Assessment (c) Informed Consent, (d) Record Keeping, (e) Avoiding Harm and Exploitation, (f) Telehealth and Online Presentations, (g) Research, (h) Teaching, Training, and Supervising, and (i) Advertising and Public Statements. The following topics are not covered in this chapter as they do not address concepts unique to those who practice hypnosis, but rather apply in some form to all health care providers: confidentiality and its exceptions (e.g., mandated reporting—child and elder abuse, Tarasoff warnings), sexual harassment, treating gender and ethnically diverse patients, fees, barter, interruption and termination of services, reporting and publishing research results, and colleague relationships and collaboration.

Competence

Achieving and maintaining competence in clinical practice consists of two general areas: (a) competence in the knowledge, research, and application of hypnosis itself, and (b) competence in treating the specific disorder or symptom presented by the patient.

Competence in the knowledge, research, and application of hypnosis. Practicing within one's area of professional competence is a generally accepted ethical rule that also carries the force of law in any health care discipline. Certainly one's area of competence can change, but practitioners would then be required to undergo additional formal academic and/or clinical training in the new area of competence that could include supervised experience, a qualifying examination, and any other experience required by the state licensing board. Competence in hypnosis increasingly involves the practitioner in the concept of "evidence-based practice." In medicine and dentistry, clinical practice has long been reliant upon scientific research in diagnosis and treatment. For example, a physician must be able to competently differentially diagnose an autoimmune disorder from a bacterial or viral infection before considering how to treat the patient. And an anesthesiologist or an interventional radiologist must have adequate training in inducing and maintaining a trance with a patient prior to using hypnosis with a patient.

For those in the mental health field, evidence-based practice similarly requires practitioners to integrate science and practice when undertaking clinical work. Specifically, according to the American Psychological Association Task Force on Evidence-Based Practice, clinicians must give serious attention to the best available research, clinical expertise, and patient characteristics (e.g., gender, race, culture,

values, and preferences) when providing mental health services (American Psychological Association, 2010). This includes applying empirically supported principles of assessment, case formulation, therapeutic relationship, and intervention. In general, clinicians are increasingly being expected to rely upon current research in their work with patients—both for patient welfare and for enhancing their own clinical skills. It does not mean that every therapeutic intervention or hypnotic phrase must be literally grounded in empirical studies. However, it does require professionals to be aware of the ongoing literature in the field of hypnosis and how it informs their clinical work.

For example, emerging research is helpful in conceptualizing when it may be important to assess the hypnotic ability in the patient ("hypnotizability"), when it is unwise to use hypnosis (contraindications), how to efficiently induce a trance in various situations with various individuals (dental practice, emergency room patients, PTSD patients in psychotherapy, young children, elders with some degree of dementia, etc.), and how or if to attempt to gauge the depth of trance while carrying out hypnotic work. Empirical research also has a bearing on selecting the type of intervention for a particular situation, such as using guided imagery, hypnoanalysis, Ericksonian hypnosis, teaching self-hypnosis, or applying some other hypnotic intervention. And research also addresses vigilance about realerting the patient, hypnosis with couples and groups, integrating hypnotic work with the ongoing work of a primary psychotherapist referring the patient, the use of recordings as an adjunct for one's own patients, the use of recordings for the general public, the use of telehealth (telephone or web-based videoconferencing), and many other topics.

As an example, consider the therapist whose new patient requests hypnosis for tinnitus, a symptom never previously encountered by the therapist. Principles of "evidence-based practice" would suggest that the therapist should consult the literature in clinical hypnosis or consult colleagues to learn about whether hypnosis has proven to be a successful treatment. Failure to find support for such an intervention would not necessarily preclude its use with the new patient. However, relevant research might provide guidance to the therapist about what to "avoid" in offering an intervention as well as what to include, and it might also have implications for "informed consent"—what the therapist actually tells the patient prior to initiating treatment for tinnitus.

Competence in treating a specific symptom or disorder presented by the patient. Competence in treating a specific disorder or symptom demands that practitioners already be proficient in providing clinical care for a particular patient presenting with a particular symptom without hypnosis, before they attempt to use a hypnotic intervention. This takes into account one's legal scope of practice and prior education and training that underlies all clinical practice. Learning hypnosis does not bestow competence with a patient or symptom where it did not already exist for that patient with that symptom. For example, a dentist who takes a hypnosis workshop in the use of hypnosis for depression would likely not be qualified to begin using therapeutic hypnotic interventions on his clinically depressed dental patient, or his patient with a marital problem, even though he may feel passionate about the use of hypnosis in these situations. However, this very same dentist may well be qualified to apply hypnosis, both formal and informal, to a dentally phobic patient, given proper training.

Likewise, a psychotherapist who normally does not treat children and is untrained to do so should not offer hypnosis to children, merely because she may have taken a workshop or two on pediatric hypnosis. On the other hand, a pediatrician or child psychiatrist who chooses to obtain training in hypnotic intervention with children would be within her area of competence by using hypnosis with her familiar patient population. Also, a psychotherapist who has had little or no training in treating posttraumatic stress disorder (PTSD) or doing marital therapy would probably not be within his boundaries of competence by attempting to use hypnosis with a veteran of war returning from Afghanistan presenting with PTSD or a high-conflict couple on the verge of divorce.

In summary, hypnosis is to be used as an adjunctive technique, by a health care professional, with a particular population and diagnosis with which the provider is already competent to treat without hypnosis.

Assessment

As mentioned in the previous section, formally assessing and diagnosing a client or patient generally precedes providing treatment or hypnotic intervention. Yet there are situations where a comprehensive evaluation would not be appropriate. The physician in an emergency room or trauma center would not attempt to take the history of a patient with an urgent, painful symptom such as a burst appendix or serious burn prior to administering hypnosis for pain reduction in addition to ongoing medical treatment. However, taking a comprehensive history may well be the standard of care when providing individual psychotherapy for a patient with symptoms of chronic pelvic pain, a personality disorder, or anorexia. How do ethics codes provide guidance to practitioners of hypnosis about assessment, history taking, and psychological evaluation prior to using hypnosis with a particular client or patient? As we shall see, they generally do not.

Assessment and history taking before using hypnosis with patients may not be a normative practice for many practitioners, and many patients might prefer to "get on" with hypnosis and not "waste time (and money)" on a lengthy process of history taking. However general ethical principles such as beneficence, nonmaleficence, respect for people's rights and dignity, and others suggest that failure to learn at least some of the patient's history may prove to be harmful, even with such seemingly narrowly focused symptoms as nicotine addiction, weight loss, or insomnia.

As an example, consider a 40-year-old man whose wife recently divorced him. He wishes to stop smoking, yet he has suffered chronic depression for many years and drinks to the point of intoxication on many weekends. Some would argue that he would be a poor risk for hypnotic intervention for nicotine addiction, due to his current depressed state, recent major life transition (divorce), and alcohol dependency. The therapist who blindly complies with this patient's request may be ignoring two out of three relevant factors of evidence-based treatment. The three factors previously mentioned are: best available research, clinical expertise, and patient characteristics. There is substantial research on the temporary beneficial effects of nicotine on mood, particularly depression; it may be essential for the therapist to address the patient's mood disorder prior to initiating hypnosis for nicotine addiction. Also, this particular patient's characteristics include an ongoing history of the abuse of alcohol and a recent divorce, neither of which would necessarily be a favorable prognosticator for ending his use of such a highly addictive substance as nicotine. By agreeing to administer hypnosis to this man without first evaluating the appropriateness of it at this particular time, with his particular diagnosis, history of major loss, and history of substance abuse, the therapist may significantly be increasing the odds of failure. Such a failure may further add to the patient's loss of self-esteem, depression, and alcohol consumption. A more prudent approach might be to encourage the patient to engage in treatment for depression first (with or without antidepressants), to evaluate how alcohol dependency may complicate any progress in psychotherapy, and defer smoking cessation to a time when the patient has improved mental health. On the other hand, an argument might be made that the man's attempt to stop smoking could represent a first step in changing his life, and that hypnosis could be used to help with depression or other symptoms as well, possibly as an entrée into psychotherapy. In any case, the taking of a complete history would assist the therapist's judgment in conceptualizing the course of treatment, with or without hypnosis, even though the presenting complaint was simply nicotine addiction.

There may be specific "red flags" that a therapist would want to observe prior to beginning hypnosis with a new patient. This would vary, of course, with the presenting complaint of the patient and the theoretical orientation of the therapist. The following questions represent a partial list to consider: current health status (e.g., illness, chronic pain, history of medical interventions, current medications), current mental health status (i.e., mood disorder, thought disorder, personality disorder), presenting complaints (e.g., anticipatory anxiety, social phobia, nightmares, or some other psychological symptom), history of psychiatric hospitalization, history of child abuse (i.e., physical, sexual, or emotional abuse), major boundary or important trust betrayals (e.g., sex with a former therapist), prior use of hypnosis, and the patient's expectancies or fears about hypnosis, to name a few.

Many therapists may hold assumptions about the new patient and the appropriateness of complying with his request for hypnosis without taking a formal history or doing a formal evaluation, and in many cases, there may be little risk. However, it is often the outlier in the distribution, the "gray area," that could present a risk of harm to a patient—the individual who may "seem" appropriate for hypnosis, but has a history that would convince a competent therapist to avoid hypnosis for the present, if only he had taken the time to learn it.

Informed Consent

Securing informed consent from patients about what to expect from hypnosis may not only be wise, but may be required of many health care providers according to their ethics codes or state laws. Because there is variability in legal and ethical requirements concerning informed consent, practitioners are encouraged to be familiar with licensing board regulations and professional association's ethics codes that bear on this topic. Certainly carrying out clinical research with adults or children and offering many clinical services would require authorization, according to state law and federal law (HIPAA regulations) (Fisher, 2003). And many health care providers already are required to secure informed consent prior to offering services, in general. But is there a separate requirement to secure informed consent from a new patient when hypnosis is to be used? Two questions come to mind about securing informed consent: (a) When is it actually required that health care providers secure informed consent from patients, and (b) What constitutes adequate informed consent in different settings (e.g., psychotherapy, dentistry, medical practice)?

When to Secure Informed Consent? Informing a patient about what to expect from hypnosis varies with the type of intervention offered and the credential of the provider. A clinical social worker offering hypnosis as an adjunct to psychotherapy would likely have a more in-depth discussion about the nature of hypnosis than a dentist using hypnosis with an anxious patient facing an extraction. And the emergency room physician treating a new patient with severe and painful injuries from an industrial accident would likely use hypnosis with little or no informed consent, due to the urgency of the situation and acute pain and anxiety of the patient. Providing informed consent may largely be a question of judgment on the part of the provider, guided by principles such as beneficence, nonmaleficence, and autonomy. How the provider helps the patient, avoids harming him, and promotes self-interested decision making about his own anticipated health care are all significant factors in what the provider actually discusses, asks about, or presents in the process of providing informed consent.

Many health care providers commonly use informal hypnotic language as a standard intervention in helping children and adults cope with difficult medical procedures. And, as mentioned, there are times when informed consent may be suspended altogether. For example, a physician or nurse giving an injection to a frightened child might well use hypnotic language to reduce anxiety and promote cooperation without having a discussion about "the nature of hypnosis" beforehand. And more invasive medical procedures, such as those done by an interventional radiologist or urologist (cystoscopy, urethral dilation), may also be greatly assisted with the use of hypnotic language, with a minimum of informed consent (Anderson, 2015, personal communication; Lang & Laser, 2009).

Using hypnosis as an adjunct to psychotherapy may require a higher level of informed consent of the therapist—involving a discussion of the pragmatics of such an intervention. Honoring the principle of nonmaleficence (avoiding harm) would address such issues as the patient's unrealistic expectations of hypnosis, prior negative experiences with a hypnotherapist, or potential legal risks of employing hypnosis if the patient is involved in litigation. What to include in securing informed consent is the topic of the next section.

What Constitutes Adequate Informed Consent? How practitioners conceptualize and communicate with patients about hypnosis depends in part upon: (a) the professional discipline (e.g., physician, dentist, psychotherapist, marital therapist, forensic hypnotist), (b) what has already been presented at the outset of treatment (e.g., psychotherapy, medical or dental procedure, presurgical preparation), (c) the specific symptoms to be treated with hypnosis (e.g., essential hypertension, chronic pain, neurodermatitis, performance anxiety), (d) patient variables (e.g., presenting complaint, age, gender, culture, ethnicity, education level, beliefs/expectations about hypnosis), and (e) the psychotherapist's theoretical orientation (e.g., Ericksonian, psychoanalytic, Jungian, cognitive behavior therapy, acceptance and commitment therapy, etc.).

General factors to consider when discussing hypnosis include using simple and understandable language with the patient, encouraging the patient to voice questions or concerns about hypnosis, and informing the patient of any risk factors that might apply. The following bullet points present a broad range of options with varying degrees of relevance to practitioners in various clinical situations. In general, before carrying out hypnosis, practitioners may wish to:

- Address possible legal consequences of hypnosis. The psychotherapist should inform the patient that using hypnosis under certain circumstances could invalidate the patient's credibility in civil or criminal litigation, particularly if the hypnotic work focuses on the patient's memory surrounding the event in question. For example, consider the request for hypnotic "refreshing" of Mr. Blank's memory about the details of an accident in which he struck a bicyclist at a busy intersection, and the victim is now suing him for damages. In this situation, the court may be reluctant to accept his accounting of the accident if he had undergone hypnosis on the presumption that hypnosis could have altered his memory of the events.

- Explore and address the patient's prior use of hypnosis, questions, "magical" expectations, ambivalence, fears, or apprehensions regarding the use of hypnosis. Patients may have false ideas about hypnosis (e.g., amnesia is a necessary part of trance, only weak-minded people can be hypnotized). It is useful in general to address false ideas or prior history of being hypnotized.

- Explain the potential benefits of using hypnosis. This may include the fact that hypnosis may: accelerate psychological treatment (e.g., anticipatory anxiety, depression, low self-esteem, shame), bring relief from medical symptoms (e.g., pain, headaches, gastrointestinal disorders, skin disorders, hot flashes, etc.), help with habit patterns (e.g., smoking cigarettes, insomnia, overeating, enuresis, skin picking, hair pulling, etc.), improve sports performance (e.g., golf, tennis, etc.), and child birth, to name a few.

- Possibly provide a printed handout of hypnosis, such as that of the American Psychological Association's Division 30, or create your own handout describing how you conceptualize and use hypnosis with patients.

- Agree on the goals of hypnosis. The provider can help the patient clarify the goals of using hypnosis—generalized relaxation, symptom reduction, habit pattern control, preparation for a medical procedure, resolving past trauma, exploring secondary gain, and so on.

- Explain the risks of using hypnosis, both clinical and legal. In general, hypnosis may be considered to be a benign intervention, with a minimum of side effects when used in a health care setting. However, certain risks may still apply. A psychotherapy patient may "discover" a repressed memory of abuse that never happened, as experiences in hypnosis may seem to be more real than they actually are. A particular anxious patient who already is dissociative or reexperiencing flashbacks from the stress of past traumas may not be suitable for hypnosis at the present time when other psychological or psychopharmacological interventions may be required first.
- Avoid giving actual guarantees of outcomes. It is possible to be optimistic about hypnosis and hold strong convictions that are evidence-based, without guaranteeing outcomes (e.g., "You will lose 30 lbs. in two months," "you will definitely stop smoking in one session," etc.). There are no guarantees in life or in hypnosis.
- Address memory of hypnotically recalled events. The psychotherapist can address the plasticity of memory, both with and without hypnosis, and how recalled events are not necessarily accurate in either case. The patient should not be led to believe that events are always encoded objectively and can be accessed with hypnosis. Events in hypnosis can be seen as "experiences," "sensations," "impressions," and so on, but not necessarily as "facts." Verification of hypnotic memories, if important, may sometimes be achieved by review of old medical records (child abuse), police records, or other forms of relevant documentation.
- Describe the "nuts and bolts." Provide general information about how therapy and hypnosis will proceed, and interact, as warranted—frequency of sessions, duration, goals, involvement of self-hypnosis training, use of recordings, and so on.
- Explain that hypnosis may be understood as a psychological state but does not constitute psychotherapy by itself. The psychotherapist can clarify that hypnosis itself is not necessarily therapy, but is a dissociated state that can provide an opportunity for therapy to move forward more efficiently. It is an adjunct to psychotherapy, but it should be understood that there also will be nonhypnotic therapy sessions as well, and that

the patient's wishes and needs will be taken into account.
- Secure written informed consent from the patient before making a video recording of the hypnotic session for forensic purposes. Failure to comply with standard forensic protocol for hypnosis could further undermine the patient's credibility in litigation. For example, a forensic hypnotist might ultimately detract from the witness' or victim's credibility if he or she failed to videotape the entire procedure, failed to obtain the patient's pre-hypnotic account of the event, or applied hypnosis in a manner that might alter the patient's memory (California Evidence Code). This would likely apply if your patient were the witness of a crime, victim, or perpetrator, although relevant laws vary by state. Practitioners should have formal training in forensic hypnosis before agreeing to offer this service.
- Secure written informed consent when teaching and training others. If an instructor includes a hypnotic experience as part of a workshop, he or she must inform participants in advance and allow them to withdraw from the experience if they wish. Also, particular attention must be paid to fully realerting attendees before they are permitted to leave the workshop (Kluft, 2012a).

Record Keeping

Health care providers commonly document their clinical work with clients and patients for a variety of reasons. Recording information about a patient's history and course of treatment not only helps with continuity of care with ongoing patients, but also helps the provider to conceptualize, reflect upon, and evaluate the treatment over time. The contents of clinical records may include presenting symptoms and complaints, medical or psychological history, results of clinical tests, functional status, assessment or summary data (e.g., psychological testing, structured clinical interviews), diagnostic impressions, evaluation of risk factors of harm to self or others, medications prescribed, documentation of mandated disclosure (e.g., risk to self, child or elder abuse, threatened harm to third parties), treatment plan, progress to date, consultations with others (e.g., psychotherapists, primary care physicians, neurologists, gastroentomologists, pain clinics), e-mails, and telephone calls, to name a few.

Record keeping also helps the provider respond to any future complaints regarding the clinical care provided, as the record accurately documents specifics of diagnosis and treatment that a health care provider would not normally remember years later. In addition to identifying information, the contents of clinical records may be informed by ethical standards, professional guidelines, HIPAA, and state laws. Also, if the provider uses a computer for keeping records or e-mail or fax machine for transmitting clinical information, she must comply with HIPAA regulations (federal law) concerning securing informed consent from patients at the outset of treatment and the process of record keeping itself. Clarity on HIPAA requirements may be achieved by consulting one's professional association's ethics committee or legal resources. Encrypting and backing-up computerized records is essential (and often legally mandated), with the current pervasiveness of Internet hacking, computer and identity theft, abuse of social media, and other fraudulent online activities.

What is to be included when documenting the use of hypnosis? This may be less clear to the practitioner, particularly since practice guidelines and ethical standards rarely address this question. Certainly the context, setting, and patient variables are important factors in deciding how to document clinical hypnosis. For example, first responders will likely keep a different sort of record than the physician, pediatrician, or psychotherapist. And the level of detail in general, as well as the specifics of the hypnotic intervention in particular, will vary greatly depending upon the nature of the patient, diagnosis, type of hypnosis employed, setting, and goals. In any case, it may be useful to consider the following as a general guide for documenting hypnosis in the course of treatment:

- Rationale for using hypnosis with a particular patient
- Informed consent (e.g., what the patient was informed about hypnosis, discussion of patient's misconceptions or fears about hypnosis)
- The number of the hypnotic session (e.g, "first," "second") and whether it was recorded for the patient's use
- Symptom to be treated (e.g., migraine headaches, presurgical preparation, stopping smoking, pain management, hypnoanalysis, forensic use)
- The type of induction used and patient's response to it

- Length of the hypnotic session
- Patient's response to hypnosis (e.g., arm levitation, catalepsy, autonomic responses—weeping, respiration changes, blanching or blushing)
- Contents of the session as appropriate (e.g., topics, imagery, clinical information acquired via ideomotor questioning, automatic writing, or other means)
- Realerting (e.g., rapid or resistant realerting, lingering dissociation, spontaneous remarks)
- Posthypnotic processing if warranted (e.g., discussion or review of the hypnotic experience, depending on the following variables: setting, goals of hypnosis, theoretical orientation of practitioner, questions raised by the patient, lingering negative psychological or physical effects, didactic training in self-hypnotic use, to name a few).

In carrying out clinical work, professionals may focus more on clinical issues and be less mindful of the potential ethical risks of practice, such as future patient complaints to an ethics committee or grievances to a state licensing board. Depending upon the patient population, every practitioner should maintain sound risk-management practices concerning record-keeping, and should not hope to rely upon memory alone in defending against a patient complaint. A patient who feels harmed by her doctor may end treatment peremptorily and initiate a complaint years later, depending upon the statute of limitations imposed by professional associations. It is possible that the patient herself may have kept better records (private journal) about the treatment than the treating physician or psychotherapist did. She may feel that the therapist was incompetent in his use of hypnosis, violated boundaries (touched inappropriately or behaved seductively), implanted "memories" that were false, induced new symptoms that were more distressing than the original ones, or intervened in some other way that fell below the standard of care or was harmful to her. In defending oneself against such allegations, the practitioner will be called upon to rely upon documentation (e.g., the clinical record) in mounting a defense. Whether collaborating with an attorney in defending himself against a licensing board investigation or simply responding to questions from an ethics committee on his own, the professional will depend on the clinical record, not his own memory of what transpired so long ago. And any investigating body will likely request a copy of the clinical record as part of the investigation. The author has reviewed hundreds of psychotherapist's clinical records in the course of participating in ethics investigations over the years and can state with confidence that there is an immense variability in how clinical work is documented. Those who pay attention to this critical aspect of clinical care could still become the subject of a complaint, but they will feel more secure if they have attempted to keep adequate records of the treatment.

Also, every practitioner should consider the possibility that he or she could be drawn into litigation, even if he or she is a paragon of hypnotic competence and peerless in his or her ethical observance. We live in a litigious culture, and it is not uncommon for a health care provider to become a part of ongoing litigation simply by virtue of having offered treatment to a suffering patient. Consider the following example.

Mr. Lowe had unsuccessful back surgery for chronic pain, and experienced increased unrelenting pain, psychological depression, insomnia, and sexual dysfunction as a result. He sought hypnotic intervention from Dr. Charm, a psychologist, four months after the surgery. Little did Dr. Charm suspect that his patient would eventually initiate a lawsuit against his surgeon, Dr. Hacker, for malpractice, claiming that the surgery had made him worse. After seven months, Mr. Lowe ended his successful treatment with Dr. Charm, and sued Dr. Hacker. The surgeon's attorney subpoenaed Dr. Charm's clinical records in order to determine if Mr. Lowe had a mental disorder that would detract from his credibility or present evidence that he was in fact malingering and exaggerating his pain or other symptoms. Fortunately, Dr. Charm had kept excellent clinical records and was pleased that he did, as his participation in his patient's lawsuit was requested over two years after therapy ended with Mr. Lowe. When deposed, Dr. Charm consulted his notes and reported on his patient's diagnosis of major depressive disorder, chronic pain, primary insomnia, and erectile dysfunction. He could also reliably describe the course of psychotherapy and hypnotic intervention for each of the symptoms presented by his former patient, and several digital recordings he made of hypnosis for home use. His testimony was used by the attorney to substantiate the postsurgical psychological and physical suffering experienced by Mr. Lowe and his good faith attempt to seek help by consulting a psychologist and complying with treatment. Mr. Lowe was grateful that Dr. Charm had kept good records and could provide documentation of his diagnosis and treatment.

Although documenting clinical work may seem unnecessary and less compelling in some ways than the clinical intervention of performing hypnosis, there are sound pragmatic, clinical, ethical, and legal reasons for doing so. Practitioners of hypnosis should develop their own ways of tracking what they do in the office, for optimizing patient care, dealing with possible future litigation, and participating in their own defense should a question of competence ever be raised by a former patient.

Avoiding Harm and Exploitation

It is always important to avoid harming clients, patients, and trainees with hypnosis, but what steps are reasonable to take that would reduce the risk of harm in the everyday course of one's professional work? Certainly, securing informed consent and practicing within one's boundaries of competence are two ways of minimizing the possibility of harm to others in both clinical work and teaching settings. But sometimes harm can be unintentional by the well-meaning practitioner. Consider the following examples.

A urologist who had attended two workshops in hypnosis attempted age regression with a 33-year-old female patient presenting with chronic pelvic pain, hoping to ascertain if there was a psychological etiology of her pain. The doctor was not a psychotherapist, nor had he taken a comprehensive history prior to treatment. But he had a keen interest in psychology, and thought that catharsis from a traumatic past event would be helpful. In fact, the patient had repressed a sexual trauma at the age of 7, when her uncle had sexually assaulted her. In hypnosis, she experienced overwhelming panic while reliving the trauma in the urologist's office. Unfortunately, the urologist was not able to provide adequate intervention for her panic when recalling the assault or follow-up with psychotherapy subsequently.

A psychologist accepted a 42-year-old male alcoholic patient who was a commercial airlines pilot. He was seeking a "quick fix" with hypnosis, rather than enter rehabilitation, attend Alcoholics

Anonymous meetings, and participate in ongoing psychotherapy. The psychologist accepted him for hypnotic treatment, and although he had a strong response to hypnosis, and enjoyed the experience, he never achieved sobriety. Eventually, the airline company terminated his employment due to a near-accident. While suffering the symptoms of a hangover on an early morning flight he had a lapse in judgment, resulting in a near miss on take-off from a congested airport.

A psychologist treating a high-conflict couple decided to offer hypnosis to the wife in an individual session to help treat her impulsivity and overly angry reactions to her husband. He did not consider how treating the wife independently while simultaneously attempting couples therapy might complicate their therapy. Although he observed that the wife probably met the criteria for borderline personality disorder, and he had never treated such a patient before, he felt confident that hypnosis would be a useful tool nevertheless. Partway into the induction using the reverse-arm-levitation technique, requiring a gentle grasp of her wrist with a slight lifting motion, the patient opened her eyes and said in a strident voice, "What the hell do you think you're doing?" She then accused him of touching her improperly, without her permission, and stated that he probably was attempting to "seduce" her, just like her last therapist. She withdrew from treatment and several days later went online to blog publicly about her "awful experience" at the hands of this "incompetent and unprofessional therapist."

In each of these cases, a well-meaning professional intervened in the life of another with destructive consequences—the patient felt harmed, coerced, or exploited in some way. Whether the cause of harm was practicing outside one's area of competence (Vignette 1—the urologist), using hypnosis with little empirical basis for ameliorating the symptom (Vignette 2—alcoholic patient), or failing to ask permission about physical touch (Vignette 3—angry borderline patient), these professionals put the welfare of others at risk by their own failure to integrate ethical principles with their clinical work. Although these transgressions were unintended on the part of the provider, they resulted, in each case, with the subjective perception of harm to the patients, nevertheless

There are situations when health care providers sometimes are not so blameless, however, such as when their choices deliberately serve to gratify their own needs at the expense of clients and patients. Exploiting clients or patients is a subset of harming them, but unlike the examples presented previously these actions involve a conscious choice on the part of the provider that disregards ethical principles of beneficence and nonmaleficence. Exploitative providers show little regard for or awareness of professional boundaries, and may view clients and patients merely as objects to prey upon. A simple example of exploitation would be the hypnotherapist who has a sexual attraction to his patient and includes subtle language in the hypnotic work to promote similar sexual feelings in his patient. But some exploitative conduct may be even more nuanced. Consider the following.

A journalist whose weekly "Focus on Mental Health" show appeared on a local cable TV channel contacted Dr. Silverman, a psychiatrist, to give a presentation on her hypnotic work with transgender and transsexual clients, her new area of specialty. She also invited her to bring a patient to the TV studio in order to present "the patient's viewpoint." As Dr. Silverman was recently licensed, and wished to expand her psychiatric practice, she was actively seeking means to promote herself and viewed this as a good business opportunity. Although uncertain about the ethicality of asking a patient to participate, she did not consult with colleagues, but yielded instead to the pressure of her financial needs and the anticipation that the locally aired cable presentation might substantially increase visibility. She asked a patient to participate with her, who had only had two hypnotic sessions, having just begun treatment that month. He suffered clinical depression in addition to gender ambivalence. The patient agreed to the media interview, fearing that refusing might disappoint his new therapist and interfere with their therapeutic relationship. After the presentation, however, he felt it was a mistake to have participated, as he was asked questions by the moderator that elicited anxiety and shame—feelings that he had never addressed in therapy. For the week following the interview, his depression worsened, and he had difficulty sleeping and going to work Dr. Silverman recognized all too late that she had allowed her own entrepreneurial interests to trump several ethical principles—patient welfare, fidelity, privacy, autonomy, beneficence, and nonmaleficence—resulting in harm to her patient.

Dr. Lord was a skilled surgeon in a private cosmetic surgery clinic who recently had learned hypnosis from a training program offered by a lay-hypnotist. There was no ethical training as a part of the program, however, as the emphasis was on rapid induction and helping prepare patients for surgery. Dr. Lord was a quick study, and learned a variety of powerful induction techniques. He decided to practice his hypnotic skills on one of his nurses, inducing glove anesthesia, catalepsy, and a variety of other phenomena. He informed his nurse that this practice was "necessary" in order to increase his competence in hypnosis. He went beyond medical hypnosis, however, when he used his skills for his own entertainment, causing embarrassment to his nurse—such as giving suggestions that she could not stand up from her chair when attempting to leave his office, or having her legs "freeze" when she attempted to walk. As time went on, he even included suggestions of a sexual nature, with amnesia, for his own private gratification. He saw his behavior as perfectly acceptable, as he paid his employees well and felt entitled to their loyalty. His nurse was reluctant to openly resist his exploitative and sexually harassing conduct, as she was a single parent and needed financial security to provide for her young children. Over time, however, her mood deteriorated with increasing depression due to the ongoing exploitation, and she initiated a medical leave from work. Subsequently she began psychotherapy where she not only addressed the exploitation of her former employer but also some traumatic issues from her past—extensive childhood abuse. This abuse had contributed to a lifetime of low self-esteem, contributing to a susceptibility to easy re-victimization by authority figures.

Exploitation of clients and patients can be subtle, as in Vignette #1, or blatant, as in Vignette #2. Practitioners and teachers who exploit others may be unaware of the potential for harm. They may be aware of conflicting impulses, however. Dr. Silverman was "uncertain" about asking a current psychotherapy patient to appear in a media presentation. She may have wondered about the secondary role introduced by such an experience—that of "co-presenter"—in addition to her primary role of psychotherapist. She might have wondered about the power differential between patient and therapist, and how a patient might lack sufficient ego

strength to decline an invitation from her therapist to participate in a media presentation.

The more obvious exploitation by Dr. Lord is reminiscent of the predatory practitioners who feel entitled to take advantage of those in less powerful positions (e.g., employees, clients, patients, supervisees, students) in a variety of ways. Ultimately, some are able to acquire a keener sense of professional boundaries and respect for the autonomy of others through mandated experiences from the state licensing board—education in ethics, supervision or consultation concerning their clinical work, psychotherapy, or something else. Unfortunately, however, most "predators" are likely incapable of rehabilitation.

Telehealth and Online Presentations

Telehealth is a term describing the use of state-of-the-art technology to deliver health care interventions to clients and patients living some distance from the provider. The technology could include a telephone, cell phone, tablet, computer, or other device to enable a health care provider to diagnose and treat long distance. It should be noted that there are clinical, legal, and ethical risks that may attend such interventions, and these will be only addressed briefly here due to space limitations. For in-depth guidelines concerning telehealth, readers are referred to practice guidelines published by their own professional associations, as well as guidelines and rules published by state licensing boards. For telehealth in mental health services, the reader will benefit from consulting Maheu and her associates both online and in print (Maheu, Pulier, Wilhelm, McMenamin, & Brown-Connoly, 2005).

The use of technology offers a convenient means of delivering hypnosis remotely, but it may also present risks that could degrade the quality of care and potentially harm clients and patients. Some of the benefits include providing hypnosis to patients who have moved away, are housebound (chronically ill, disabled, etc.), live in a remote area, are on vacation, or are unable to come to the office for some other reason. However, for a variety of reasons, there may also be potential risks of using the telephone or videoconferencing in offering hypnosis. And when practitioners use telehealth for hypnosis without ever having had any training or read the research or clinical guidelines for doing so, they may put themselves at risk for making clinical errors that could impact patient welfare and safety.

The following variables may factor heavily into the clinical success of hypnosis by telehealth: the type and purpose of hypnosis, theoretical orientation of the practitioner, diagnosis of the patient, goals of the session, previous history of face-to-face contact, and the practitioner's awareness of the patient's medical history and mental health. Also, there are unique risk factors for telehealth to be addressed before offering long-distance hypnosis to clients and patients. The following list is not from any ethics code, nor is it exhaustive, but it highlights critical factors to be considered.

The use of telehealth requires a working knowledge of relevant state laws when the recipient of services resides in a state where the provider does not hold a license to practice. In general, health care providers are licensed to practice only within the state of their residence. There are exceptions for brief or short-term interventions, such as vacations or travel, but each state has different laws addressing these situations and practitioners must know them prior to offering hypnosis or treatment of any kind across state lines.

The use of telehealth requires a knowledge of HIPAA regulations, including implementation of a technology platform that will optimize privacy and stability (Cason & Brannon, 2011).

The use of telehealth may inadvertently encourage taking short-cuts in securing informed consent. Normally, in nonemergency situations, the therapist or physician may have a brief discussion with the patient concerning the nature of hypnosis, the patient's concerns and expectations, the patient's prior success or failures with hypnosis, goals of the hypnotic session, and anything else that would be relevant for the session. Also, some state laws require providing informed consent to patients and documenting the same in the clinical record.

The use of telehealth may inadvertently encourage taking short cuts in history taking and diagnosing before offering hypnosis that a therapist normally would avoid in a face-to-face session. This could result in attempting to provide relief with hypnosis to a chronic pain patient who also has a personality disorder or PTSD (unknown to the therapist). Such a patient might have a complicated response to dissociation, such as flashbacks to earlier trauma. What began as an attempt to reduce chronic pain and provide tools to the patient to use

on her own could end with a traumatic reexperiencing of abuse requiring psychotherapeutic intervention, possibly best handled in person.

Telehealth may curtail awareness of important visual cues. By relying on the telephone or a laptop screen showing only the head of the patient, a therapist cannot view body posture, tension or nervous movement in the hands or feet, changes in breathing, a tear trickling down one side of the face, changes in skin color in the face and hands, or other subtle cues that are normally used (consciously or unconsciously) by the provider. In hypnotic work involving ideomotor responses or other movements, of course, it would be critical to have appropriate visual access as needed.

Using telehealth may compromise confidentiality. Although the provider may be in a professional office, the recipient could be at home where others could sometimes eavesdrop on the session (e.g., spouse, parents, children). This may not only interfere with the patient's feelings of privacy and security, but could also result in an unintended trance of the "eavesdropper," over which the provider would have no control or even awareness. And when the recipient is at the workplace, he or she may be vulnerable to a different kind of confidentiality breach: the electronic information may travel through a server in the office, allowing the employer or others to legally access the hypnotic session, thereby compromising confidentiality.

Technical "glitches" may occur when using videoconferencing over which providers have little or no control. Calls get dropped, phone or Internet service providers randomly stop functioning—for seconds, minutes, or hours—and laptop or cell phone batteries run out, to name a few. It could be awkward or harmful for a hypnotic session to be interrupted for a half-hour due to technical difficulties while the patient is in a trance and no realerting can take place. It is wise to address these issues in advance by seeking out an information technology consultant who can provide guidance about privacy, encryption, system stability, and related matters.

The use of telehealth may require using a separate informed consent document that addresses relevant issues, such as those previously listed, and presenting a comprehensive list of possible risks for the consumer. This would constitute good preparation for the patient and safe practice for the clinician, if anything untoward were to occur.

The previous examples generally involve one provider and one known client or patient for an individual session of hypnosis or ongoing treatment. The clinical and ethical problems may be amplified exponentially for prerecorded Internet presentations available forever to millions of "unseen" adults and children who have no opportunity to follow up with the creator of the video or a local practitioner of hypnosis. Typically, hypnosis may be presented online for relaxation, sleep, pain control, weight loss, smoking cessation, memory enhancement, or other habit pattern or physical or psychological symptom. However, in these situations there may be no opportunity for disclaimers, introductions, discussions of the nature of hypnosis, or discussions of risks for those already in treatment for past traumas or dissociation, to name a few of the problems that could surface. And patient variables such as age, gender, race, ethnicity, physical and mental health history, and diagnosis all remain unknown to the creator of the hypnotic recording. For the majority of viewers there may be no ill effects, yet some may experience lingering dissociation, uncomfortable changes in mood, a return of traumatic memories, headaches, or other symptoms unanticipated and irremediable by the creator of the video.

There are few ethical proscriptions or words of guidance involving the offering of hypnosis to the general public by electronic means, as technology seems to always outstrip wisdom about its application. Members of the American Society of Clinical Hypnosis are ethically required to "take care to ensure that any demonstration of hypnosis is done in such a way as to prevent or minimize risk to unknown audience participants" (ASCH, 2003). This rule invokes the principle of nonmaleficence, avoiding harm, but it does not offer guidance about implementation, or how to determine if individuals were in fact harmed. Members of the Society for Clinical and Experimental Hypnosis are ethically required to avoid offering "their professional use of hypnosis via newspapers, radio, television or similar media" (SCEH Code of Ethics, 2003). This would seem to rule out the use of videoconferencing for hypnosis with clients and patients via computers, tablets, smartphones, or similar media. Yet there is already a vast array of hypnotic offerings and training opportunities available on the Internet

currently (nearly 11 million offerings as of this writing), many but not all created by individuals and groups who are not credentialed and licensed health care providers. Delivering hypnosis to consumers by means of telehealth is an ever-evolving and largely unexplored area by health care professionals, and much research remains to be done on the benefits and range of potential ill effects on the recipients of these presentations.

Research

Ethical and legal regulations for those carrying out research in hypnosis are similar in nature to those in biomedical ethics, which have evolved in the medical profession for many years. Historically, these include elements from such well-known documents as The Nuremburg Code (U.S. Department of Health and Human Services, 1949), The World Medical Association's Declaration of Helsinki (1964; Human & Fuss, 2001), and the Belmont Report (U.S. Department of Health and Human Services, 1979), as well as documents from NIH's Office of Research Integrity. Current guidance and requirements for those carrying out research with human participants on any topic comes from a variety of sources: (a) ethics codes from primary professional associations (American Medical Association, American Psychological Association, National Association of Social Workers, etc.), (b) The U.S. Department of Health and Human Services (http://www.hhs.gov) and HIPAA rules pertaining to the acquisition and disposition of data acquired from human subjects, (http://www.hhs.gov/ocr/privacy/hipaa/understanding/special/research/), (c) institutional review boards of hospitals, clinics, universities, professional schools, and other institutions that oversee and approve research protocols of their faculty and trainees, (d) state laws and regulations of state licensing boards concerning research, and (e) to a very slight extent, ethics codes from professional hypnosis associations (e.g., ISH, SCEH, ASCH).

General concepts of ethics in research honor the principles of autonomy, beneficence, nonmaleficence, and justice in relationships (Beauchamps & Childress, 2001). These are reflected in deliberate acts of the researcher that not only contribute to the science of hypnosis but simultaneously promote the autonomy, welfare, dignity, safety, and privacy of research participants. This is achieved by the design of the research protocol itself and also by securing informed consent from participants at the outset. Specific topics must be addressed in a printed informed consent document that describes experiences to which the participant will be exposed in easily understandable language. He or she must be able to read and ask questions about participation, and ultimately sign the document prior to participating. The following list of elements of informed consent provide a basic understanding of what must be communicated to research participants in advance of the study (Nagy, 2005). It does not constitute a comprehensive list, however, and depending upon the nature of the hypnotic question being addressed, it should be modified accordingly.

1. *Description of the research.* Describe the nature of the hypnotic research and what will be expected of participants. What is the subject of the investigation? Why is it important?
2. *Time involvement.* What are the time requirements? Is there flexibility?
3. *Compensation.* Will there be compensation of any sort (e.g., money, academic credit toward a course)?
4. *Confidentiality and privacy.* What are the threats to confidentiality? If video recording is a part of the procedure—who will view these recordings in the future (e.g., scientific audience, future trainees, the media)? If the participant's personal health information is used, how will privacy be maintained?
5. *Voluntary participation and consequences of withdrawing from the research.* Inform participants that their participation is voluntary and that they may withdraw without being penalized. Will there be any consequences for dropping out of the research (e.g., loss of financial compensation, being required to complete another academic project instead—research paper, presentation—in order to receive course credit)?
6. *Risks and benefits.* What are the foreseeable risks and benefits of participation in hypnotic research? What would affect their willingness to participate in the research? Are there any physical or psychological risks, discomfort, or potential adverse effects (e.g., sleep deprivation, unpleasant emotional or physical sensa-

tions, pain, sexual arousal)? Will medication be administered? Will participants benefit by learning self-hypnosis techniques to use for a variety of purposes?
7. *Minors.* Permission from parents or legal guardians must generally be obtained for hypnotic or any other research involving children and adolescents. In some cases, such as classroom activities and minimal-risk situations, a partial waiver of parental consent may be acceptable. Because hypnosis may hold exaggerated, magical, or even nefarious connotations for some, it might be considered wisest to *always* obtain parental permission whenever children are to be engaged in hypnotic research, even in classroom activities or minimal risk situations. Investigators should not risk even giving the appearance of diminishing the autonomy, welfare, or safety of a minor by using an intervention such as hypnosis to which some may attribute overwhelming power. In addition, investigators must comply with requirements of the institutional review board examining their protocol as well as those of the individual school or school system, which holds jurisdiction.
8. *At-risk populations.* Are there specific groups who are more likely to suffer adverse effects of participating in hypnotic research? These might include those who have disabilities, live in institutionalized settings (e.g., prisoners, in-patients, assisted living residents), are currently in psychotherapy or have a diagnosis of a mental disorder, have physical symptoms that could be exacerbated by hypnosis research on pain tolerance (e.g., chronic pain, migraine headaches, irritable bowel, essential hypertension), are elderly, are children, are from diverse cultures or religions (race/ethnicity/spirituality), or speak English as a second language. Investigators should develop exclusion criteria or take other steps to protect those potential participants who could otherwise be harmed by hypnotic research.
9. *Questions about participants' rights.* Some institutions may require investigators to supply participants with names and telephone numbers of administrators who can respond to questions or complaints about participants' rights that may have been abridged during research.

10. *Deception and debriefing.* Finally, if deception is involved, debriefing should occur as soon as feasible following the person's active participation in the research. If debriefing might compromise the naiveté of future participants, then it could legitimately occur at the end of all the data gathering, unless such a delay might increase the risk of harm to the participant.

Although not involving the specific use of hypnosis, the infamous Stanford Prison experiment could be said to include informal elements of hypnosis, and it provides examples of various ethical considerations, on hindsight, that the investigators have written and lectured about ever since. It originally was to be a two-week psychological study that had to be terminated after only six days because of strong aversive effects on participants (Haney, Banks, & Zimbardo, 1973). Zimbardo reports randomly dividing 18 mentally healthy, volunteer college students into two groups, "guards" and "prisoners," and, with little specific instructions, observing the cruel behavior that ensued while participants were confined to a makeshift "prison" (i.e., a 35-foot-long room in the basement of the Psychology Building at Stanford University).

Over the course of the experiment, some "prisoners" decompensated with extreme anxiety, hopeless feelings (being told they could not leave), and crying, while guards experienced little remorse until much later, upon reflecting on the inhumane conduct of which they were capable. On hindsight, honoring the ethical concepts of autonomy, beneficence, and nonmaleficence would likely have involved some of the following anticipatory safeguards: securing adequate informed consent, building in safeguards at each stage to protect the welfare of students participating in the research, developing clear criteria for terminating the study in advance, arranging for therapists to be on call and intervene, if needed, and considering avoiding using deception (e.g., stating that the "prisoners" could not withdraw from the prison experiment).

To his credit, Zimbardo openly addressed the issues that developed in this experiment, which seemed to form a partial basis for his later book—*The Lucifer Effect: Understanding How Good People Turn Evil* (Zimbardo, 2007). Years later, he wrote about the questions raised by a psychology colleague during the experiment and how he arrived at the decision to end the experiment prematurely, due to the increasing risk of harm to participants. Also, he acknowledged his surprise at his own subjective degree of psychological involvement in the drama of the research.

The assumption of formal roles by college males seemed to have had many of the trappings of implied hypnotic directives to become fully immersed as prisoner or guard, and temporarily suspend their normal human values, critical judgment, objectivity, free will, and natural empathy and compassion for others. The lesson for investigators here is that ethical values such as autonomy, beneficence, nonmaleficence, and respect for people's rights and dignity must always be accorded high priority in designing and executing research on hypnosis or dissociation, regardless of the prospective psychological value attributed to the research hypotheses by the investigator.

Teaching, Training, and Supervising

In addition to clinical work, many health care providers customarily assume teaching roles, such as clinical supervisors overseeing pre- and post-doctoral trainees, professors teaching a hypnosis course, workshop faculty at a professional meeting, consultants to a group of peers, and those offering online webinars to distant learners, to name a few. It may come as a surprise to consider that harm can occur in training roles also, and that ethical guidance may apply broadly in the teaching of hypnosis (as with any didactic presentation), not just in clinical work. Consider the following example involving a workshop faculty member.

A clinical social worker teaching an introductory workshop in hypnosis to 30 attendees asked a particularly highly hypnotizable trainee to volunteer three times over the course of a six-hour workshop for the purpose of demonstrating induction techniques. With each induction, the trainee had a deeper experience than the last, with slower realerting, and some lingering dissociation feelings, but she felt that she was benefitting from the calming experience by being a volunteer. The trainee had volunteered in hopes of reducing subjective feelings of anxiety, and the teacher enjoyed using her for demonstration purposes because her facility for entering a trance was exceptionally good.

Unfortunately, however, due to time pressure, the instructor paid little attention to formally realerting her for the final session, or using criteria or strategies to ensure full reorienting from hypnosis, such as the Howard Alertness Scale (Kluft, 2012b). During a coffee break in the afternoon, the trainee noticed feelings of disorientation and depersonalization growing stronger, and found that she was becoming tearful, agitated, and flooded with sadness. Not wanting to return to the workshop, or disturb the instructor, she simply left the building, walking on the sidewalk of the hotel in the vicinity. Fortunately, she accidentally encountered a fellow attendee at the conference who noticed her condition and was compassionate. He spent the next several hours helping her to emerge from her dissociated state and regain her customary level of alertness.

In this vignette, the experienced faculty member had failed to take an adequate history of the volunteer's recent history of stress or loss (her father had died several months before) and, by repeatedly inducing a trance over six hours, essentially subjected her to a fractionation technique that seemed to progressively deepen her level of dissociation with each session. It may well be customary for workshop faculty to engage trainees as volunteers without taking a history, with little or no risk of adverse effects. However, the "perfect storm" of using powerful induction techniques with a trainee who is prone to dissociation, has a mental disorder, or has a history of trauma or recent major loss may result in unplanned experiences that require more care and attention than a single instructor is prepared to manage while teaching a workshop. Kluft has addressed this issue by suggesting a number of remedies, one of which might involve including extra clinicians to be present in the room to observe and intervene with lingering dissociation among trainees who had either experienced group hypnosis or volunteered for an individual experience (Kluft, 2012a).

Another important ethical requirement in teaching and training would include securing informed consent of the trainee in advance when anticipating an individual or group supervisory session, group didactic experience, or some other educational experience—either in-person or as a distant learner—about the training experience itself. Will it include experiencing hypnosis? Will there be safeguards built in? What are the risks of participation,

if any? Are there exclusion criteria for attendees (e.g., being a current psychotherapy patient, having a prohibitive mental disorder, suffering a major life stress in the recent past?

Informed consent for formal supervisory experiences is best addressed by a letter of agreement, contract, checklist of planned experiences, or some other manner that clearly describes what the supervisee will be encountering during the course of clinical supervision. Indeed, some professional ethics codes and state laws require that professional supervisory experiences be documented ahead of time in some fashion (Thomas, 2010). Clinical consultation, however, would not necessarily require informed consent in advance, as it generally occurs between two professionals already licensed to practice independently, with clinical and legal responsibility to the patient being retained by the one seeking consultation. It may still be wise, however, for the consultee to document in the clinical record that he or she sought an external consultation in the course of rendering treatment. By respecting the mandate of securing informed consent in advance, teachers, trainers, and supervisors increase the likelihood of providing a safe and effective learning environment for students of hypnosis, while minimizing the risk of harm, confusion, embarrassment, disappointment, or resentment on the part of supervisees and students.

And finally, in compliance with ethical standards of some professional hypnosis associations, teachers and trainers should be cautions about whom they accept and whom they reject for training and membership. Decisions about refraining from teaching certain individuals by virtue of their academic credential or state licensure may at times be difficult, seem unfairly discriminatory, or place the "bar" too high. Should trainers teach induction techniques and applications of hypnosis to physical therapists, nurses trained at the bachelor's level of education, rehabilitation therapists, medical technicians, college tutors, special education teachers for students with learning disorders, or elementary school teachers? Likewise, should they teach these skills to high-school tennis coaches to help their players win matches? And finally—should they teach those in the business sector—managers of a marketing team or Silicon Valley CEOs, for that matter? Where does one draw the line?

Just because hypnotic skills could readily be taught to those outside the health care setting, should they be taught? Ethical standards declare that (a) anyone lacking professional education and clinical training in a health care discipline (ASCH Code of Ethics) or (b) anyone who is not a member of a recognized therapeutic or scientific profession (SCEH Code of Ethics) is to be considered a "layperson," and therefore should *not* be taught hypnosis (except for their own personal use, of course). Nevertheless, there are ongoing controversies within professional hypnotic associations about which groups should be admitted to membership and taught hypnotic principles and which should be excluded.

Ethics codes inform us that membership is restricted to those who maintain a license to practice at the independent, unrestricted, or unsupervised level (ASCH Code of Ethics), yet there are those who would encourage a much broader dissemination of hypnotic skills. One rationale for such broadening of the reach of hypnosis seems to be loosely based on the general ethical principle of general beneficence—the notion that many more people could be helped by learning how to use and apply hypnosis in their lives who would not ordinarily consult a psychologist or a psychiatrist—they could more readily learn from their physical therapist, tutor, or tennis pro instead. Another rationale is based on the principle of pragmatism—the notion that anyone seeking to learn hypnosis could easily find a book on self-hypnosis, search the Internet for self-training, or consult a lay hypnotist in order to acquire skills—therefore, those considered most skilled in the ethical application of clinical hypnosis (e.g., licensed health care professionals) might be better positioned to do the training instead, thereby increasing the level of teaching to potential trainees.

Whatever decisions one makes concerning the recipient of his or her hypnotic training, they should be grounded in careful thought, an evaluation of potential for psychological risks to members of the public who could be adversely affected, and a review of all ethical and legal prerequisites that may apply. Such decisions might also include consideration of the recipient's motivation for acquiring hypnotic skills, the intended setting and population where the recipient will employ hypnosis, as well as personal factors—the recipient's current mental health status, history of trauma, or other factors that might contraindicate training the individual in the use of hypnosis on others.

Advertising and Public Statements

When advertising hypnotic services in the print media, by radio or television, over the Internet, on one's professional website, or in any other manner, health care providers are held to the same standards as when advertising their nonhypnotic services. That is, they are obliged to be truthful and accurate in their statements, to avoid exaggeration or "spin," to avoid giving guarantees of services, and also to avoid deceptive or false statements about their qualifications, credentials, or training. The media is rife with examples of those advertising hypnosis who are not bound by ethics codes or the laws regulating the clinical practice of licensed health care providers, giving false hope to clients and patients.

Some practitioners use testimonials from satisfied clients who have achieved excellent results, although there may have been no long-term follow-up ascertaining whether there has been a relapse or a substitution of symptoms. However, some ethics codes prohibit soliciting testimonials if the individual is still a current psychotherapy patient (American Psychological Association Ethical Principles of Psychologists and Code of Ethics, 2002).

Even when presenting hypnosis to the public in the form of a lecture, a panel discussion, or an interview with a radio or TV journalist, health care providers are required to be accurate in how they portray hypnotic intervention and outcomes. If Dr. Allgood appears in a PBS special describing his latest hypnotic approach for weight loss, he must limit his statements to those that are supported by his actual clinical results. This might include disclaimers such as the following: individuals don't all have the same hypnotic ability; mental health status could impact the results of treatment; major ongoing life stress, transition, or loss (e.g., loss of job, deaths, divorce) could also impact the results of treatment, and so on.

Professionals may portray hypnotic intervention to future clients and patients with optimism, enthusiasm, and hope, as they might with any other psychological or medical intervention. Such a portrayal, however, whether in print, online, or presented face-to-face, need not cross the line into providing unrealistic faith in hypnosis as a panacea, guaranteeing outcomes, creating deceptive ideas about the potency of hypnosis, or perpetuating other myths or concepts about hypnosis that do not have at least some basis in the scientific literature.

CONCLUSION

The topics of this chapter have hopefully provided an introductory view of general ethical concepts that guide our work as health care providers using hypnosis. Specific areas that could be explored further are: the process of ethical decision making, what to do after becoming aware of an ethical conflict, what to do after becoming aware of a colleague's transgression, seeking consultation from senior clinicians or those who teach and specialize in ethics, seeking consultation from health care attorneys, actively remaining up-to-date on state and federal laws concerning health care in general or hypnosis in particular, and actively remaining up-to-date on clinical hypnosis (e.g., reading books and journals, reading your professional associations position papers or evolving practice standards concerning hypnosis, attending workshops, attending grand rounds if near a hospital, participating in a consultation group, seeking mentoring and individual consultation if needed).

Being aware of forensic hypnosis and current legal risk management practices for health care providers is also essential. I recommend that every clinician take at least one workshop in the area of forensics at his or her earliest convenience, in order to learn about the pragmatics of handling a subpoena, appearing for depositions, testifying in court, and minimizing risk when dealing with litigious patients. It is better to be prepared in advance (e.g., maintaining thorough records compliant with HIPAA and state law, being thorough in the initial evaluation of the patient about ongoing litigation) and knowing how to present in the adversarial situation of the legal arena—a radically different experience from the routine clinical setting of diagnosing and treating patients for which clinicians normally have little or no preparation.

Individual self-care is also a critical area for health care providers that could be further explored—how the professional senses his own impairment, at times, due to burnout, major life transitions (e.g., divorce, death of a parent or child), or some other cause, and knows to seek consultation, psychotherapy, or some other restorative experience. Indeed, it may be true that there is an ethical imperative to preserve one's own mental health as a prerequisite to maintaining clinical competence. Perhaps, after his prime directive of *primum non nocere,* Hippocrates might have added a second directive for clinicians: *mentis salute vestram servetis* ("Preserve your own mental health"), for health care providers may be subject to unique stressors from difficult patients that undermine their mental health over time or activate unresolved psychological insults from the past. For this reason, maintaining one's own mental health may be one of the most salient features of competence in the healing arts, requiring awareness of metrics for one's own impairment, yet it may be a process in which both neophyte and senior clinicians have minimal training.

It is the hope of the author that this chapter has presented professional ethics as a sensitive GPS that can help guide and direct the clinical use of hypnosis, rather than as simply a list of rules to be memorized. There are good personal and profession reasons to continue one's ethics education by various means before ethical quandaries develop, in order to reduce the likelihood of poor decision making. This is when one will feel more secure to have developed a firmer foundation in the ethics of research, teaching, and clinical work in advance, as it may well be true in matters ethical as well as in health, that *Ne unciae libram cura valet* ("an ounce of protection is worth a pound of cure").

REFERENCES

American Psychiatric Association. (2003). The principles of medical ethics with annotations especially applicable to psychiatry. *American Psychologist, 61*(4), 271–285.

American Psychological Association. (2002). Ethical principles of psychologists and code of conduct. *American psychologist, 57*(12), 1060–1073.

American Psychological Association. (2010). *Ethical principles of psychologists and code of conduct, 2010 amendments.* Retrieved from www.apa.org/ethics/code/principles.pdf

American Society of Clinical Hypnosis. (2003). *Code of conduct* . Retrieved from www.asch.net/Portals/0/PDF-content/.../revised-code-of-conduct_3-8-09.pdf.

APA Div 30. *Hypnosis: What it is and how it can make you feel better.* Retrieved from http://www.apadivisions.org/division-30/index.aspx

Beauchamps, T., & Childress, J. (2001). *Principles of biomedical ethics.* Oxford, UK: Oxford University Press.

Butler, L., Symons, B., Henderson, S., Shortliffe, L., & Spiegel, D. (2005). Hypnosis reduces distress and duration of an invasive medical procedure for children. *Pediatrics, 115,* 77–85.

California Evidence Code, Chapter 6—Credibility of Witnesses, Article 2—Attacking or Supporting Credibility, Chapter 7—Hypnosis of Witnesses §795.

Cason, J., & Brannon, J. (2011). Telehealth regulatory and legal considerations: Frequently asked questions. *International Journal of Telerehabilitation, 3*(2). doi:10.5195/ijt.2011.6077

Ferenczi, S. (1926). The problem of acceptance of unpleasant ideas: Advances in knowledge of thesense of reality. *International Journal of Psychoanalysis, 7,* 312–323.

Fisher, C. (2003). Informed consent and clinical research involving children and adolescents: Implications of the revised APA ethics code and HIPAA. *Journal of Clinical and Child and Adolesent Psychology, 33*(4), 832–839.

Haney, C., Banks, C., & Zimbardo, P. (1973). Interpersonal dynamics in a simulated prison experiment. *International Journal of Criminology and Penology, 1,* 69–97.

Human, D., & Fluss, S. S. (2001). *The World Medical Associations Declaration of Helsinki: Historical and Contemporary Perspectives.* World Medical Association.

Kluft, R. (2012a). Enhancing workshop safety: Learning from colleagues' adverse experiences. *American Journal of Clinical Hypnosis, 55*(1), 85–103.

Kluft, R. (2012b). Enhancing workshop safety: Learning from colleagues' adverse experiences. *American Journal of Clinical Hypnosis, 55* (1), 104–122.

Lang, E., & Laser, E. (2009). *Patient sedation without medication: Rapid rapport and quick hypnotic techniques.* Seattle, WA: CreateSpace Independent Publishing Platform.

Maheu, M., Pulier, M., Wilhelm, F., McMenamin, J., & Brown-Connoly, N. (2005). *The mental health professional and the new technologies: A handbook for practice today.* Mahwah, NJ: Lawrence Erlbaum Associates.

Nagy, T. (2005). *Ethics in plain English: An illustrative casebook for psychologists.* Washington, DC: American Psychological Association.

Society for Clinical and Experimental Hypnosis. (2003). *Code of Ethics.* Retreived from: http://www.sceh.us/code-of-ethics.

Thomas, J. T. (2010). *The ethics of supervision and consultation: Practical guidance for mental health professionals.* Washington, DC: American Psychological Association.

Zimbardo, P. (2007). *The Lucifer effect: Understanding how good people turn evil.* New York, NY: Random House.

Certification in Hypnosis and Specialty Boards

David Alter

We live in a time when "truthiness" has come into common usage thanks to the wit of television satirist Stephen Colbert. Truthiness is defined as the quality of being considered to be true because of what the believer wishes or feels, regardless of the facts (C.E.D., 2010). The relevance of this term to how current training in hypnosis is obtained is worth exploring. Hypnosis today continues to be contaminated by unfortunate misappropriations or misattributions of its core healing qualities based on how it has been practiced and/or understood throughout its history. Sadly, clinical hypnosis remains subject to numerous myths and misconceptions sufficient that professional training in clinical hypnosis often begins with efforts to teach what hypnosis is not before proceeding to teach what hypnosis is and what it can do in the hands of well-trained clinicians (Hammond & Elkins, 1994). How do we distinguish enduring "truths" about hypnosis from the "truthiness" that pervades what the public and even other health professionals have come to believe about what clinical hypnosis entails? A solid appreciation of professionally accredited training opportunities is an important step for any clinician seeking to incorporate clinical hypnosis into her or his therapeutic armamentarium.

There exist well-defined pathways to acquire training in clinical hypnosis through professionally accredited organizations, though what "professional accreditation means" in today's world can be another instance of what we might call "professional truthiness." The accredited organizations that this author views as legitimate maintain well-delineated criteria defining the core clinical academic and experiential foundations in clinical practice that must exist prior to seeking training in hypnosis. In short, prior to engaging in practice using clinical hypnosis, accredited professional organizations require the clinician to be licensed to practice in his or her relevant health professional discipline independent of subsequent training in clinical hypnosis. You must have the requisite foundational academic and clinical training to treat someone without hypnosis before the acquisition of hypnosis skills adds anything of value to the aspiring clinician.

This distinction constitutes a major demarcation between licensed clinicians trained in different forms of health care practice from those individuals trained through lay organizations such as the National Guild of Hypnotists. While the latter clearly defines its mission as "advancing the field of *hypnotism*" (see www.ngh.net), professionally accredited organizations incorporate clinical hypnosis as but one means of advancing the broader field of science and clinical practice, whether that be through medicine, psychology, dentistry, or other allied health care fields. Viewing clinical hypnosis as an extension of a demonstrated competency in a specific health care discipline helps avoid application of the wise adage that, "if all you've got is a hammer, then everything looks like a nail." Hypnosis as a standalone clinical skill distinct from the appropriate professional training is akin to that hammer. (A partial listing of recognized and accredited clinical hypnosis training associations is offered at the conclusion of this chapter.)

THE ROAD TO HYPNOTIC COMPETENCY

Before describing the paths by which one demonstrates increasing skills and evidence-based competence in clinical hypnosis, a step back in time is warranted to better appreciate how and why such paths exist in the first place (Goldman & Schafer, 2011). The tradition of Western-based medical practice in the United States dates to the early 17th century, when three groups of medical practitioners existed: physicians, surgeons, and apothecaries. There existed hierarchical classism that placed physicians on top and apothecaries at the bottom. Practitioners of other forms of healing were relegated to the margins of what were recognized as legitimate and valid treatment protocols. This vertical stratification by social status didn't last long in the face of America's emphasis on pragmatism and entrepreneurialism.

From the mid-1700s through the early 1800s, medical practice evolved regulations, practice standards, codes of ethical practice, and processes for certifying doctors. New Jersey led the way, creating the nation's first medical society in 1766. The need to identify a core educational, research, and practice curriculum for physicians reduced the wide variability in individual practice patterns that were promoted by proprietary medical colleges that sprang up in different states in the first generations of our nation's existence. This need for greater practice standardization led to the creation of the American Medical Association (AMA) in 1847. Finally, in 1893, Johns Hopkins School of Medicine opened and became the model for subsequent medical education by wedding together education, research, and practice in ways that other schools rapidly adopted.

Two more developments on the road to clinical competency in medicine, as practiced in the United States, are worth noting as they relate to training in clinical hypnosis. In 1910, Abraham Flexner published the "Flexner Report" (Flexner, 1910). It highlighted the appalling lack of consistent quality that still permeated medical education in this country. His report was like a lightning rod, prompting quality improvement efforts in medical education and training. The second was the influence of Sir William Osler, a brilliant Canadian physician who established the first residency program in the United States at Johns Hopkins School of Medicine. For the first time, Osler's influence brought physicians to the bedside of patients. Previously, physicians learned by reading books, and did not encounter "live" patients until they went into clinical practice. The end of diploma mills producing "degreed" but often clinically underqualified physicians soon followed.

Note the parallels to the process by which individuals can continue to acquire hypnosis skills and hang out their shingles attesting to the fact that they are "certified" hypnotists, in spite of often limited and highly variable or even irrelevant foundational academic and clinical training experience. Will the equivalent of a contemporary Flexner Report on hypnosis training emerge to rectify the quackery with which hypnosis is linked? Will the use of hypnosis by well-meaning but inadequately trained individuals seeking to ease people's suffering be redirected back toward the community of professionals who may rightly deserve to be primary disseminators of its clinical benefits by virtue of their academic and scientific training? Clearly, having admission criteria for obtaining training in clinical hypnosis that goes beyond inquiring whether an applicant has ever been convicted of a felony, which is the case with a popular lay training organization, would be prudent.

We need not wait for such developments. For clinical hypnosis to emerge from its unwarranted association with all manner of healers, entertainers, and magicians, clinicians involved in learning clinical hypnosis can incorporate lessons learned by following the path blazed by health professionals from different disciplines who created the process culminating in board certification in clinical hypnosis.

ACCREDITED CERTIFICATION TRACKS . . . AND BEYOND

Certification in Clinical Hypnosis

The American Society of Clinical Hypnosis (ASCH), established in 1957 by Milton H. Erickson, MD, remains the largest North American-based organization involved in the training of health and mental health care professionals in the use of clinical hypnosis. ASCH will be used as an illustrative model of who can pursue training in clinical hypnosis and how that training can be pursued.

A caveat is that this chapter focuses on training opportunities in North America. This training differs substantially from training standards that exist in other parts of the world. For example, to practice hypnosis in Israel, one requires possession of a license distributed by the Ministry of Health.

To qualify for such a license, the applicant must possess a license to practice medicine, dentistry, or psychology, and have a graduation certificate in hypnosis studies issued by one of the recognized Israeli universities or a private hypnosis school recognized by the Ministry of Health. Thus, the road to practicing clinical hypnosis in other parts of the world appears to traverse narrower or more restrictive roads than those traveled in the United States.

Before being eligible to obtain training in clinical hypnosis in North America, a prospective ASCH member must have obtained a master's degree or higher (e.g., MD, PhD) in the fields of medicine, dentistry, osteopathy, podiatry, psychology, nursing, marriage and family therapy, social work, or counseling that has been duly accredited by the appropriate regional accrediting body or organization. Moreover, such individuals must show that they are members, or are eligible for membership, of a professional society consistent with their degree. As should be apparent, hypnosis training is by no means the first qualifying step in determining an individual's readiness to pursue hypnosis training. The individual seeking the training must have first acquired rigorous academic and professional practice experience before eligibility for hypnosis training is even considered.

In addition to requiring an advanced degree in a relevant health field, as previously outlined, a prospective member of ASCH must also hold a valid state/provincial license for independent practice in his or her field. There are many individuals who offer hypnosis as independent practitioners, many of them trained by lay organizations that certify them as capable of independent practice. However, a major distinguishing feature of the professionally accredited practitioner trained through ASCH is that he or she is licensed to engage in his or her practice of hypnosis by the state or province in which the individual intends to practice. While many individuals may rightly claim to be "certified," the operative questions are certified by whom, and what are the qualifications for such certification?

In the event that a licensing system is not in effect in the state or province in which the mental applicant practices, the following criteria are recognized as legitimate substitutes.

• National Register of Health Service Providers in Psychology

• Certification by the Academy of Certified Social Workers or the National Board of Examiners in Clinical Social Work
• Certification by the American Nurses Association or other equivalent national certifying body
• Full membership in the American Association for Marriage and Family Therapy
• Certification by the National Board of Certified Counselors

Before individuals can seek the first level of ASCH certification, they must have been in independent practice in their respective field for a minimum of two years and be able to provide a description of the ways in which they have incorporated hypnosis into their work during the previous two years of practice. Letters of recommendation from professional colleagues (who are themselves trained by ASCH or an equivalent organization) who are familiar with the work of the individuals seeking certification from ASCH must be received. The letters attest to the applicants' professional ethics, use of clinical hypnosis, and personal character and must be submitted to ASCH for any individual who has been a member of ASCH for less than five years.

Assuming eligibility criteria for membership in a recognized and accredited organization such as ASCH have been met, there are also ongoing continuing education requirements that must be met in order to become eligible for different levels of certification in hypnosis by ASCH. The first level of certification requires the professional to have completed a minimum of 40 hours of post-degree, ASCH-approved education. Those 40 hours must include at least 20 hours of training in the fundamentals of clinical hypnosis (basic training) and a minimum of an additional 20 hours of intermediate-level training. As well, 20 hours of individualized training must be obtained in consultation with an ASCH-approved consultant. Those hours of consultation may be obtained via a one-to-one consultation or through small group-based training and consultation, although attainment of individually tailored training goals is still required. The individualized training goals are pursued by creating a learning contract with the consultant, outlining the specific learning objectives that are being pursued, the methods and resources by which the objectives will be sought, and the means by which attainment of the desired learning goals will be measured. This contract assures that the learning process is individually tailored to meet the unique interests and needs of each adult learner, which nicely mirrors the manner in which the use of hypnosis with patients or clients is individually tailored to meet each person's unique needs.

APPROVED CONSULTANT IN CLINICAL HYPNOSIS

The second level of certification offered by ASCH involves being recognized as an approved consultant in clinical hypnosis. In addition to all of the aforementioned educational and license-related requirements, an applicant for approved consultant must have completed a minimum of 100 hours of post-degree ASCH-approved training and 20 hours of one-on-one or group-based individually tailored training with an ASCH-approved consultant in clinical hypnosis. At present, efforts are underway within ASCH to refine and more firmly establish the specific skills needed to demonstrate the ability to serve as a consultant beyond involvement in educational trainings and ongoing use of hypnosis clinically. Ways of solidifying the mentor–mentee relationship model for those individuals seeking to become approved consultants are being explored.

BOARD CERTIFICATION IN CLINICAL HYPNOSIS

At present, neither the certification status nor the approved consultant status is associated with a formal and standardized assessment of an individual's breadth of knowledge of theories and practices related to hypnosis, as well as explicit demonstration of the knowledge as applied to an actual clinical situation. That designation is reserved for those individuals who elect to pursue board certification in clinical hypnosis through one of the certifying specialty boards that exist under the umbrella of the American Board of Professional Hypnosis. Certifying boards currently exist for physicians, social workers, psychologists, and dentists, while establishment of a similar board for master's level nurses is currently in development.

Becoming a diplomate in clinical hypnosis of one of the certifying boards involves a series of steps that are surprisingly humane, attainable, and ultimately personally and professionally rewarding. A curious visitor to the website for the American Board of Psychological Hypnosis, for example, will find two entries providing a description of the process involved in preparing for the board "examination." However, above and beyond the preparatory process that is detailed, the reader will find testimonials attesting to the personally and professionally transformative value the writers found through their individual pursuits of the Diploma in Clinical Hypnosis. The statements mirror the personal experience of the author.

Applications for the diploma from the relevant specialty board require that the applicant

- Have possession of an earned doctoral-level degree (e.g., MD, DDS, PhD, PsyD, DSW, EdD) from a regionally accredited university or professional school
- Have accrued at least five years of post-degree experience in the relevant field of professional practice
- Must hold membership in a national professional organization at the Member or Fellow level (e.g., AMA, APA, ADA)
- Must hold a state-level license or certification for independent practice.

And for individuals functioning in an academic, research/experimental role, the applicant must

- Document a minimum of five years of continuous engagement doing research in hypnosis
- Demonstrate significant research publications in the field of hypnosis
- Document sufficient training in clinical principles of hypnosis to work safely with hypnosis in the course of his or her research activities.

Assuming the individual has met eligibility criteria and set about preparing for the certification process, appreciating the collegial nature of the examination can make the overall process more enticing. Aside from the application fee and completion of the application form, the preparatory process entails three elements. The first is the study process itself, which covers five topic areas. The candidate is expected to: (a) demonstrate knowledge of relevant theories and conceptualizations of hypnosis; (b) become generally familiar with research relevant to hypnosis (e.g., responsiveness, phenomena, or applications of hypnosis); (c) show awareness of a range of hypnotic techniques; (d) exhibit awareness of professional issues in the field of hypnosis (e.g., ethics related to the practice of hypnosis); and (e) exhibit evidence of contributions to the field of hypnosis in the form of teaching, scholarship, or professional hypnosis society/association involvement. The study process is greatly aided by a detailed study guide relevant to each professional discipline highlighting the areas the candidate is expected to be familiar with in advance of the certification examination.

The second element involves preparation of a work sample. The work sample involves a videotaped recording of a therapeutic interaction with a client or patient obtained with his or her consent. Copies of transcripts of the recorded session, along with a description of the candidate's rationale for doing what the video depicts, are forwarded to the committee that will conduct the oral examination of the candidate. This element provides the candidate with the opportunity to demonstrate assimilation and integration of the five study areas described previously as applied to his or her work with a videotape of a client or patient. In the case of a hypnosis researcher, the candidate prepares representative samples of his or her research.

The third element of the preparation for the hypnosis diploma involves the examination itself. Unlike prior experience with examinations with which prospective candidates are all too familiar, the Hypnosis Board Examination involves an active, lively, and often vigorous discussion about the candidate's work sample in relation to the five topic areas previously outlined. The discussion lasts approximately two hours. As an example, if a candidate's work sample involved utilization of a hypnotic process reflecting ego-strengthening techniques, the candidate might be asked to describe other techniques that might have been used, and why; the rationale for use of ego-strengthening in the clinical context shown; the research support for the technique used; or the ethical considerations relevant to the use of that particular hypnotic approach given the personal history, and particular diagnostic or demographic features of the client/patient in question.

Following completion of this examination process, the committee reviews the candidate's materials and makes a determination as to whether the diploma is conferred. The candidate is informed of this decision, in writing, with detailed guidance as to areas of concern and options to retake the examination should the candidate not successfully meet the requirements for the diploma. However, upon successful passage of the examination, the candidate's pupa opens and a diplomate newly certified by their respective hypnosis board emerges.

The implicit assumption, of course, is that learning and skill building does not end with attainment of board certification. Improving hypnotic proficiency and interactive "fluency" is an ongoing and evolving endeavor. When it comes to hypnotic skill development, it is helpful to remind ourselves to apply the answer given to the harried person on the busy New York City street who stops a passerby to ask, "How do I get to Carnegie Hall?" The answer received was, "Practice, practice, practice."

A FINAL COMMENT

We began this chapter talking about "truthiness." We applied that concept to hypnosis by reviewing standards by which to discriminate between the various forms of training that invite the clinician's time, attention, and dollars. With regard to hypnosis training in particular, there are plenty of competitors offering all sorts of training that do not presuppose a professional clinical training foundation upon which the hypnosis training will build: No educational background requirements. No graduate degree from an accredited educational institution. No prerequisite for a license to engage in independent clinical practice. Such is the current larger "community" of practitioners of hypnosis who market directly to an uninformed public.

The future relevance of clinical hypnosis training to a health professional's clinical practice depends upon appreciation of what hypnosis offers the clinician, let alone the client or patient. Specifically, the unique capacity of hypnosis to enhance a clinician's efficacy and improve clinical outcomes warrants hypnosis's preservation as a fundamental and even essential skill to acquire and hone over time.

This chapter has outlined several of the steps by which that training can be obtained. If the chapter has achieved its intended goal, it will be reflected in the reader's recognition that hypnosis entails gradually building social attunement skills that facilitate the clinician's ability to support the client/ patient in his or her particular change efforts. From the author's perspective, there is nothing more important than the commitment to continuously refine those skills. After all, hypnosis isn't a stand-alone skill or collection of techniques. As Benedetti said, healing is about more than the *material medica,* for "the patient's mind, emotions and beliefs also matter and play a central part in any therapy" (Benedetti, 2009). And our charge is to immerse ourselves in ongoing efforts to learn the means by which we are able to enable to utilize those internal resources for the client's/patient's personal betterment and the betterment of his or her lives.

Listing of Nationally Recognized Professional Training Associations

American Society of Clinical Hypnosis (www.asch.net)

Society for Clinical and Experimental Hypnosis (www.sceh.us)

International Society of Hypnosis (www.ishhypnosis.org)

Society for Psychological Hypnosis (APA Division 30) (www.apa.org)

Milton H. Erickson Foundation (www.erickson-foundation.org)

REFERENCES

Benedetti, A. (2009). *Placebo effects: Understanding the mechanisms in health and disease.* Turin, Italy: Oxford University Press.

C.E.D. (2010). *Collins english dictionary—complete & unabridged* (10th ed.).UK: HarperCollins

Flexner, A. (1910). *Medical education in the United States and Canada.* Washington, DC: Science and Health Publications.

Goldman, L., & Schafer, A. (2011). Approach to medicine, the patient, and the medical profession. In Goldman (Ed.), *Cecil medicine* (24th ed.). Philadelphia, PA: Saunders Elsevier.

Hammond, D., & Elkins, G. (1994). *Standards of training in clinical hypnosis*: American Society of Clinical Hypnosis Press.

Placebo Effects and Hypnosis

Irving Kirsch

What is a hypnotic induction? Procedures that have been used to induce hypnosis include clanging gongs, flashing lights, applying pressure to subjects' heads, having them close their eyes, and asking them to keep their eyes open while focused on a stationary or moving object. Most contemporary inductions include suggestions for relaxation, but alert inductions are also effective (e.g., Capafons, 2004; Cardeña, Alarcón, Capafons, & Bayot, 1998). The only common ingredient to these historical and current inductions is the label hypnosis.

When the effect of administering a drug is found to be independent of its specific ingredients (i.e., when an inert preparation produces the same effect), that drug is deemed to be a placebo. Similarly, hypnotic inductions are expectancy manipulations, akin to placebos, because their effects on suggestibility are independent of any specific component or ingredient. In fact, it is possible to produce all of the suggestive effects of hypnosis by giving subjects placebos and telling them that the medication produces a hypnotic state (Baker & Kirsch, 1993; Glass & Barber, 1961). It is also possible to produce these effects by giving suggestions without either a hypnotic induction or the administration of a placebo pill (Braffman & Kirsch, 1999; Mazzoni et al., 2009; McGeown et al., 2012; Raz, Kirsch, Pollard, & Nitkin-Kaner, 2006).

Although hypnosis and placebo effects are similar in their dependence on suggestion and belief, they differ in the degree to which responsiveness to these suggestions acts like a stable trait (Piccione, Hilgard, & Zimbardo, 1989). Whereas the stability of hypnotic suggestibility has been well-established, placebo responsiveness seems very unstable and context dependent. Simply changing the name of the placebo can reduce very high test–retest correlations to zero (Whalley, Hyland, & Kirsch, 2008). Nevertheless, responsiveness to hypnotic

suggestion has been found to be moderately correlated with responsiveness to placebos in some circumstances (Baker & Kirsch, 1993; McGlashan, Evans, & Orne, 1969). Although the associations are modest, they are about the same magnitude as those between hypnotic suggestibility and traits like absorption and fantasy proneness (Braffman & Kirsch, 1999).

Response expectancy is correlated with both hypnosis and placebo (Braffman & Kirsch, 1999; Whalley et al., 2008) and may be the common factor uniting the two phenomena. Still, correlation does not establish causality and it is possible that expectancy is an epiphenomenon rather than a cause of responsiveness to hypnotic suggestion and placebo. More convincing evidence of causality is provided by studies in which manipulated expectancies produced changes in responsiveness (Kirsch, Wickless, & Moffitt, 1999; Wickless & Kirsch, 1989). The effect of an expectancy manipulation was so strong that 73% of the subjects scored in the high range of responsiveness (9–12) on form C of the Stanford Scale, and no subject scored in the low range (0–4). Similarly, expectancy manipulations have been found to have a profound impact on placebo-induced pain reduction (Kirsch et al., 2014; Montgomery & Kirsch, 1997; Price et al., 1999; Watson, El-Deredy, Bentley, Vogt, & Jones, 2006). Furthermore, the expectancy manipulations producing enhanced hypnotic responsiveness and enhanced placebo responsiveness are very similar. Both use surreptitiously altered environmental conditions to convince participants that they are responding successfully.

These data provide strong evidence for a causal relation between expectancy and hypnotic suggestibility, but they still leave some variance in responsiveness unexplained. It is possible that expectancy is the sole proximal determinant of hypnotizability and that the residual variance is a result of measurement error. Conversely, the unexplained variance may be due to a talent or personality characteristic, the nature of which is yet to be established. In either case, it is clear that enhancing response expectancies can be a means of enhancing outcome.

HYPNOSIS AS A NONDECEPTIVE EXPECTANCY MANIPULATION

The identification of expectancy with placebo effects, which are regarded as artifacts in pharmacological research, has led to a connotative degradation of the construct in psychotherapeutic theory. Expectancy effects are seen by most writers as somehow less real than those of other hypothesized psychological mechanisms. But in what way is expectancy any less legitimate a psychological mechanism than abreaction, conditioning, cognitive restructuring, and so on? I can think of only one way in which response expectancies are different from most other psychological variables, and that is that they seem to have a broader range of effects. Response expectancy is the only psychological variable that is pervasive enough to be controlled for routinely in medical research.

Clearly, this is not a reason for psychotherapists to avoid expectancy effects. Instead, we should want to maximize them (Fish, 1973). However, there is a legitimate barrier to the manipulation of expectancy by clinicians, and that is the fact that the use of placebos typically entails deception. Psychotherapists, in particular, are rightfully concerned about deceiving their patients in any way. Expectancy is only one of the powerful psychological factors upon which the outcome of treatment is dependent. Trust is another, and in the long run, psychotherapists will earn their patients' trust only if they (the therapists) behave in a trustworthy manner. The problem, then, is how to maximize our clients' therapeutic outcome expectancies without deception.

Hypnosis is one solution to this dilemma. It is seen by many people as a powerful procedure that may help one lose weight, stop smoking, overcome fears, block pain, recover childhood memories, and so on. There is empirical support for some of these claims (e.g., Kirsch, Montgomery, & Sapirstein, 1995; Patterson & Jensen, 2003) and refutation for

at least one of them (Lynn, Barnes, & Matthews, 2008). Like placebos, hypnosis produces therapeutic effects by changing the client's expectancies, but it does not require deception in order to be effective. Whereas placebos are presented deceptively as pharmacological treatments (but see Kaptchuk et al., 2010, for an exception), hypnosis is presented honestly as a psychological procedure. Furthermore, honestly informing clients about what has been learned through research about the nature of hypnosis may reduce resistance and increase responsiveness to hypnotic interventions.

CLINICAL IMPLICATIONS

Deciding to Use Hypnosis

Hypnosis is an adjunct to therapy, rather than a treatment in its own right. Consequently, whatever can be done in hypnosis can also be done outside of hypnosis. Conversely, anything that can be done without hypnosis can also be done in a hypnotic context. How, then, is the clinician to decide whether to use hypnosis in working with a particular client?

Assessment of hypnotic suggestibility is sometimes suggested as a precursor to its clinical use. The assumption is that because responsiveness to hypnosis is relatively stable, its use with clients who do not possess the hypothesized trait of hypnotic suggestibility amounts to nothing more than administering a placebo. For this reason, nonhypnotic treatments are sometimes recommended for clients who achieve low hynotizability scores (Bates, 1994). Yet the effectiveness of placebos in alleviating physical and psychological distress reveal the fallacy in this reasoning. The placebo effect is not something to be avoided, provided that it can be elicited without deception. Instead, we should attempt to maximize the impact of this powerful psychological mechanism.

The addition of hypnosis to treatment can yield important therapeutic effects independently of the client's hypnotic suggestibility. Schoenberger and colleagues, for example, demonstrated that a cognitive-behavioral treatment for anxiety was enhanced substantially by the addition of hypnosis (Schoenberger, Kirsch, Gearan, Montgomery, & Pastyrnak, 1997). Within the group treated in a hypnotic context, however, anxiety reduction was not related to suggestibility. Thus, omitting hypnosis for clients with low suggestibility scores could deprive them unfairly of a potentially beneficial treatment component.

Thinking of hypnosis as a powerful nondeceptive placebo suggests that we should be more concerned with clients' attitudes and expectancies than with their hypnotic abilities. Yet mildly negative initial attitudes need not preclude the use of hypnosis. Although some people have very set negative attitudes toward hypnosis and are likely to drop out of treatment if its use is insisted upon, most people who have not yet experienced hypnosis have tentative and unstable expectancies (Council, Kirsch, & Hafner, 1986) that can be changed substantially by their initial experience of hypnosis. Also, clients' attitudes toward hypnosis can be improved by the correction of mistaken preconceptions.

The best way to decide whether to use hypnosis with a particular client is to ask the client, following a factual presentation about the nature of hypnosis, its potential benefits, its limitations, and the dependence of its effects on the characteristics of the client. Because treatment outcome depends at least partially on response expectancies, clients generally are excellent judges of what will work best for them. Lest we forget, it was the client, Anna O., rather than her therapist, who invented the "talking cure." Furthermore, the therapeutic efficacy of allowing clients to choose their treatments has been verified experimentally (Devine & Fernald, 1973; Kanfer & Grimm, 1978).

Hypnosis is contraindicated for clients with strong negative attitudes toward it. Fortunately, because whatever can be done in hypnosis can also be done outside of hypnosis, all that is needed is a change in the name and explanation of what is being done. In fact, imagery-based behavior therapies such as systematic desensitization, covert sensitization, and covert modeling are typical hypnotic interventions, minus the "hypnosis" label.

Presenting a Therapeutic Rationale

Therapeutic rationales are important because they provide a foundation for therapeutic outcome expectancies. Research indicates that identical treatment procedures can have dramatically different effects depending on the clients' understanding of them (Southworth & Kirsch, 1988).

The effective clinician will present a convincing rationale and then check to ensure that it has been accepted by the client. This can be facilitated by taking the client's worldview into account when formulating the rationale. A particular treatment can be explained in different ways, and an explanation that is consistent with the client's beliefs is most likely to be accepted.

If the client rejects the rationale, a different treatment strategy might be considered. Sometimes this may entail nothing more than a change in labels. "Hypnosis" can be replaced by "relaxation" and "imagery," or vice versa. Changing the label can make a substantial difference in treatment outcome, especially when clients' preferences are taken into account (Lazarus, 1973).

Preparing Clients for Hypnosis

It has become commonplace to prepare clients for hypnosis by debunking myths and misconceptions that might engender apprehension or fear. Expectancy theory suggests going even further, by challenging the idea of hypnosis as an altered state. Because decades of research have failed to confirm the altered state hypothesis (Kirsch, 2001; Kirsch & Lynn, 1995; Mazzoni, Venneri, McGeown, & Kirsch, 2013), we are well-justified in considering it yet another myth in need of debunking.

Debunking the altered state myth can enhance the effects of hypnosis in at least two ways. First, many people without prior hypnotic experience are afraid of the idea of going into a "trance." Second, people who think of hypnosis as an altered state are less likely to experience its effects (McConkey, 1986). In contrast, honest debunking of the altered state myth allows the client to interpret relaxed involvement as evidence that the induction was successful, thereby facilitating response to suggestion. Clients can be told that "hypnosis is largely a question of your willingness to be receptive and responsive to ideas and to allow these ideas to act upon you" (Weitzenhoffer & Hilgard, 1959, p. 8).

Besides debunking myths and misconceptions, hypnosis can be facilitated by teaching clients to generate suggested responses prior to hypnotic induction. This can be done by teaching them to use fantasy creatively to produce changes in perception and experience. In some hypnotizability training programs, subjects are also told to generate behavioral responses intentionally (Gorassini

& Spanos, 1986). This, however, may encourage simple compliance without further enhancing suggestibility. The same training procedures with instructions for intentional responding deleted produce equivalent response enhancement, but with less compliance (Gearan, Schoenberger, & Kirsch, 1995). Besides increasing hypnotic responsiveness, training procedures of this sort encourage a cognitive set in which therapy is seen as something done by—rather than to—the client. This, of course, is a cognitive set that facilitates therapeutic change.

Inducing Hypnosis

It is widely believed that hypnotic phenomena can be enhanced by careful attention to the procedures used in the induction and during the administration of suggestions. Although this belief has not as yet been substantiated by research (Lynn, Neufeld, & Maré, 1993), it is instructive to examine the nature of some of these procedures. Hypnotists are taught to observe their subjects carefully and to suggest the behaviors they observe, so that the subject will interpret those behaviors as evidence that they are entering a trance. In addition, when subjects fail to respond to suggestions, attempts are made to convince them that they actually did respond. For example, when subjects show only a small response to the suggestion that their hands will move apart, the hypnotist might take their hands and move them together slowly, telling them that this is being done so that they can feel how much their hands have moved apart. Another widely used ploy is to word suggestions in ways that generate double binds, so that the subject cannot fail. These procedures are clearly designed to convince subjects that they are responding successfully, thereby enhancing their expectancies for future responding.

Assessing Responsiveness Without Lowering It

Although an assessment of responsiveness is not needed for the purpose of deciding whether to use hypnosis, it can be helpful in deciding how to use it. Highly responsive subjects may benefit from very difficult suggestions, whereas these same suggestions might lower the self-efficacy of those who find themselves unable to experience their effects. Unfortunately, the act of assessing hypnotic suggestibility could produce this same negative effect in less responsive clients. By highlighting their lack

of hypnotic ability, it might lower their expectations about the therapeutic effects that hypnosis might have for them.

Many therapists judge trance depth from signs of relaxation, such as slowed breathing and flaccid facial muscles. However, there are no data indicating that these manifestations are correlated with responsiveness to suggestion. The only way to assess suggestibility is to observe a client's responses to suggestions. Here are some procedures by which responsiveness can be estimated without running the risk of lowering initially positive expectancies.

The clinician can begin assessing suggestibility by administering one or two very easy suggestions prior to the induction. The Chevreul pendulum illusion, in which the client holds a small pendulum between the thumb and the forefinger and imagines it to be moving in a particular direction, can be used for this purpose. Most people are amazed to find the pendulum moving, seemingly by itself, in the suggested direction. The experience is impressive enough to provide striking experiential confirmation of the power of suggestion. The main purposes of administering easy prehypnotic suggestions are to enhance response expectations and to convey the notion that hypnotic responses are under the control of the client rather than the therapist. At the same time, clients who have great difficulty getting the pendulum going are likely to be relatively unresponsive to more difficult hypnotic suggestions. Hypnosis might still be used with these clients, but ideomotor and challenge suggestions should be avoided.

During the induction, further evaluation of responsiveness can be accomplished by giving simultaneous suggestions for heaviness and immobility in one arm and lightness in the other (Kirsch, Lynn, & Rhue, 1993). Signs of a lightness response (e.g., movement of the fingers in one hand) lead the therapist to convert this to a permissively worded arm levitation suggestion (e.g., "I wonder how much higher your hand can continue to lift"). In the absence of signs that the subject is successfully responding to the lightness suggestions, the therapist focuses on heaviness and immobility, without ever providing the challenge to "try" to move the arm. The client's response to this dual suggestion allows gross classification into upper or lower ranges of responsiveness, while at the same time preventing the experience of failure that might otherwise detract him or her from the therapeutic use of hypnosis.

Clients' abilities to experience some of the more difficult cognitive suggestions can be inferred from their experiences of suggested imagery during the induction. Using beach imagery, for example, clients can be asked to feel the warmth of the sun on their faces or chests, to see soft billowy clouds, to hear birds in the distance, to experience thirst and relieve it with a cool drink, and so on. Suggestions such as taste aversion, sometimes used in habit control, are more likely to be effective in clients who report clear sensory experiences during the imagined scenes. Of course, it is important that the client's experiences be probed in a manner that does not set implicit standards that might have failed. Because virtually all clients are able to imagine a pleasant scene, responses to these suggestions can always be interpreted as successful.

Enhancing Expectancies Throughout the Course of Treatment

Although patients' initial expectancies play an important role in determining the outcome of therapy, it is equally important to monitor and influence changing expectations throughout the course of therapy. This is facilitated by including therapeutic procedures that are likely to provide clients with feedback, indicating that treatment is successfully producing therapeutic changes. Exposure treatments for phobic disorders ensure that clients will experience feedback of this sort. Repeated or prolonged exposure to the phobic stimulus produces temporary habituation, which the client interprets as evidence that the treatment is working, an interpretation that converts temporary physiological habituation into lasting therapeutic change.

Expectancies vary along two independent dimensions. One is the degree of certainty that change will occur. The other is the speed and amount of change that is expected. Ensuring that positive feedback will be experienced during treatment is facilitated by certainty that improvement can occur, but also by the expectancy that it will begin with small, gradual changes. This allows small increments, such as those produced by random fluctuations, to be interpreted as signs of therapeutic success, in much the same way as a twitch of a finger is interpreted as the beginning of arm levitation. Similarly, the assignment of easy initial tasks ensures early successes, which bolster the client's confidence in treatment.

Clinicians trained in the use of hypnosis habitually monitor and intervene in ways designed to enhance clients' expectations, often without awareness that this is what they are doing. Many of the clinical innovations of Milton Erickson, for example, are aimed at accomplishing this goal. Their ingenuity indicates an intuitive mastery of art of changing expectations.

CONCLUSION

Hypnotic procedures have evolved as if their creators were aware of the importance of shaping subjects' response expectancies. Altering response expectancies is an important therapeutic task. Accordingly, hypnosis can be thought of as an analogue of psychotherapy. Familiar hypnotic strategies exemplify sound therapeutic practice, as illustrated in the following maxims, which are as useful in conducting nonhypnotic therapy as in maximizing hypnotic effects:

- Be permissive.
- Present and respect choices.
- Present choices as therapeutic double-binds, so that either choice promotes improvement.
- Prevent failure by beginning with easy tasks that the client is almost certain to accomplish.
- Proceed gradually to more and more difficult tasks.
- Define tasks so that failure is impossible.
- Evaluate performances at any level as indications of success.
- Structure expectations so that even small improvements are seen as significant beginnings.
- Be alert to random fluctuations and capitalize on those that occur in a desired direction.
- Prepare clients for setbacks by labeling them in advance as inevitable, temporary, and useful learning opportunities.

These strategies can function as hypnosis-inspired nondeceptive placebos and enhance the outcome of therapy.

REFERENCES

Baker, S. L., & Kirsch, I. (1993). Hypnotic and placebo analgesia: Order effects and the placebo label. *Contemporary Hypnosis, 10,* 117–126.

Bates, B. L. (1994). Individual differences in response to hypnosis. In J. W. Rhue, S. J. Lynn, & I. Kirsch (Eds.), *Handbook of Clinical Hypnosis* (pp. 23–54). Washington D.C: American Psychological Association.

Braffman, W., & Kirsch, I. (1999). Imaginative suggestibility and hypnotizability: An empirical analysis. *Journal of Personality and Social Psychology*, 77(3), 578–587.

Capafons, A. (2004). Clinical applications of "waking" hypnosis from a cognitive behavioural perspective: From efficacy to efficiency. *Contemporary Hypnosis*, 21(4), 187–201.

Cardeña, E., Alarcón, A., Capafons, A., & Bayot, A. (1998). Effects on suggestibility of a new method of active-alert hypnosis: Alert hand. *International Journal of Clinical and Experimental Hypnosis*, 46(3), 280–294. doi:10.1080/00207149808410008

Council, J. R., Kirsch, I., & Hafner, L. P. (1986). Expectancy versus absorption in the prediction of hypnotic responding. *Journal of Personality and Social Psychology*, 50(1), 182–189.

Devine, D. A., & Fernald, P. S. (1973). Outcome effects of receiving a preferred, randomly assigned, or nonpreferred therapy. *Journal of Consulting and Clinical Psychology*, 41(1), 104–107.

Fish, J. M. (1973). *Placebo therapy: A practical guide to social influence in psychotherapy*. San Francisco, CA: Jossey-Bass.

Gearan, P., Schoenberger, N. E., & Kirsch, I. (1995). Modifying hypnotizability: A new component analysis. *International Journal of Clinical and Experimental Hypnosis*, 43(1), 70–89. doi:10.1080/00207149508409376

Glass, L. B., & Barber, T. X. (1961). A note on hypnotic behavior, the definition of the situation, and the placebo effect. *Journal of Nervous and Mental Disease*, 132, 539–541.

Gorassini, D. R., & Spanos, N. P. (1986). A social-cognitive skills approach to the successful modification of hypnotic susceptibility. *Journal of Personality and Social Psychology*, 50(5), 1004–1012.

Kanfer, F. H., & Grimm, L. G. (1978). Freedom of choice and behavioral change. *Journal of Consulting and Clinical Psychology*, 46(5), 873–878.

Kaptchuk, T. J., Friedlander, E., Kelley, J. M., Sanchez, M. N., Kokkotou, E., Singer, J. P., . . . Lembo, A. J. (2010). Placebos without deception: A randomized controlled trial in irritable bowel syndrome. *PloS One*, 5(12), e15591. doi:10.1371/journal.pone.0015591

Kirsch, I. (2001). The altered states of hypnosis. *Social Research*, 68(3), 795–807.

Kirsch, I., Kong, J., Sadler, P., Spaeth, R., Cook, A., Kaptchuk, T. J., & Gollub, R. (2014). Expectancy and conditioning in placebo analgesia: Separate or connected processes? *Psychology of Consciousness: Theories, Research, and Practice*, 1(1), 51–59.

Kirsch, I., & Lynn, S. J. (1995). The altered state of hypnosis—changes in the theoretical landscape. *American Psychologist*, 50(10), 846–858.

Kirsch, I., Lynn, S. J., & Rhue, J. W. (1993). Introduction to clinical hypnosis. In J. W. Rhue, S. J. Lynn, & I. Kirsch (Eds.), *Handbook of clinical hypnosis* (pp. 3–22). Washington, DC: American Psychological Association.

Kirsch, I., Montgomery, G., & Sapirstein, G. (1995). Hypnosis as an adjunct to cognitive-behavioral psychotherapy: A meta-analysis. *Journal of Consulting and Clinical Psychology*, 63(2), 214–220.

Kirsch, I., Wickless, C., & Moffitt, K. H. (1999). Expectancy and suggestibility: Are the effects of environmental enhancement due to detection? *International Journal of Clinical and Experimental Hypnosis*, 47(1), 40–45. doi:10.1080/00207149908410021

Lazarus, A. A. (1973). "Hypnosis" as a facilitator in behavior therapy. *International Journal of Clinical and Experimental Hypnosis*, 21(1), 25–31. doi:10.1080/00207147308409302

Lynn, S. J., Barnes, S., & Matthews, A. (2008). Hypnosis and memory: From Bernheim to the present. In K. D. Markman, W. M. P. Klein, & J. A. Suhr (Eds.), *Handbook of imagination and mental simulation* (pp. 103–118). New York, NY: Psychology Press.

Lynn, S. J., Neufeld, V., & Maré, C. (1993). Direct versus indirect suggestions: A conceptual and methodological review. *International Journal of Clinical and Experimental Hypnosis*, 41(2), 124–152. doi:10.1080/00207149308414543

Mazzoni, G., Rotriquenz, E., Carvalho, C., Vannucci, M., Roberts, K., & Kirsch, I. (2009). Suggested visual hallucinations in and out of hypnosis. *Consciousness and Cognition*, 18(2), 494–499. doi:10.1016/j.concog.2009.02.002

Mazzoni, G., Venneri, A., McGeown, W. J., & Kirsch, I. (2013). Neuroimaging resolution of the altered state hypothesis. *Cortex; a Journal Devoted to the Study of the Nervous System and Behavior*, 49(2), 400–410. doi:10.1016/j.cortex.2.012.08.005

McConkey, K. M. (1986). Opinions about hypnosis and self-hypnosis before and after hypnotic testing. *International Journal of Clinical and Experimental Hypnosis*, 34(4), 311–319. doi:10.1080/00207148608406996

McGeown, W. J., Venneri, A., Kirsch, I., Nocetti, L., Roberts, K., Foan, L., & Mazzoni, G. (2012). Suggested visual hallucination without hypnosis enhances activity in visual areas of the brain. *Consciousness and Cognition*, 21(1), 100–116. doi:10.1016/j.concog.2011.10.015

McGlashan, T. H., Evans, F. J., & Orne, M. T. (1969). The nature of hypnotic analgesia and placebo response to experimental pain. *Psychosomatic Medicine*, 31(3), 227–246.

Montgomery, G. H., & Kirsch, I. (1997). Classical conditioning and the placebo effect. *Pain, 72*(1-2), 107–113.

Patterson, D. R., & Jensen, M. P. (2003). Hypnosis and clinical pain. *Psychological Bulletin, 129*(4), 495–521.

Piccione, C., Hilgard, E. R., & Zimbardo, P. G. (1989). On the degree of stability of measured hypnotizability over a 25-year period. *Journal of Personality and Social Psychology, 56*(2), 289–295.

Price, D. D., Milling, L. S., Kirsch, I., Duff, A., Montgomery, G. H., & Nicholls, S. S. (1999). An analysis of factors that contribute to the magnitude of placebo analgesia in an experimental paradigm. *Pain, 83*(2), 147–156.

Raz, A., Kirsch, I., Pollard, J., & Nitkin-Kaner, Y. (2006). Suggestion reduces the Stroop effect. *Psychological Science, 17*(2), 91–95. doi:10.1111/j.1467-9280.2006.01669.x

Schoenberger, N. E., Kirsch, I., Gearan, P., Montgomery, G. H., & Pastyrnak, S. L. (1997). Hypnotic enhancement of a cognitive behavioral treatment for public speaking anxiety. *Behavior Therapy, 28*(1), 127–140.

Southworth, S., & Kirsch, I. (1988). The role of expectancy in exposure-generated fear reduction in agoraphobia. *Behaviour Research and Therapy, 26*(2), 113–120.

Watson, A., El-Deredy, W., Bentley, D. E., Vogt, B. A., & Jones, A. K. (2006). Categories of placebo response in the absence of site-specific expectation of analgesia. *Pain, 126*(1-3), 115–122. doi:10.1016/j.pain.2006.06.021

Weitzenhoffer, A. M., & Hilgard, E. R. (1959). *Stanford hypnotic susceptibility scale: Forms A and B.* Palo Alto, CA: Consulting Psychologists Press.

Whalley, B., Hyland, M. E., & Kirsch, I. (2008). Consistency of the placebo effect. *Journal of Psychosomatic Research, 64*(5), 537–541. doi:10.1016/j.jpsychores.2007.11.007

Wickless, C., & Kirsch, I. (1989). Effects of verbal and experiential expectancy manipulations on hypnotic-susceptibility. *Journal of Personality and Social Psychology, 57*(5), 762–768.

Precautions to the Use of Hypnosis in Patient Care

Richard P. Kluft

Unwanted sequelae of therapeutic trance states were observed in the healing temples of ancient Greece (MacHovec, 1986). The scientific study of unwanted effects begins with Benjamin Franklin's investigation of Mesmer's animal magnetism. While serving as president of the French Royal Commission, Franklin studied seven subjects experiencing mesmeric inductions. Two developed headaches and a third suffered eye pain and tearfulness; in other words, 42.8% experienced unwanted after-effects (Shor & Orne, 1965).

Hypnosis, like other beneficial therapeutic modalities, is inevitably associated with instances of unintended, unwanted, and undesirable consequences (Gruzelier, 2000; Hilgard, 1974; Hilgard, Hilgard, & Newman, 1961; Kleinhauz & Eli, 1987; Kluft, 2012c; Lynn, Myers, & Mackillop, 2000; Meares, 1961; Mott, 1992; Orne, 1965; Shor, 1959). These range from transient and trivial discomforts to more lasting mild through severe uncomfortable forms of physical, psychophysiological, and psychological distress.

These consequences include (a) failures of realerting, resulting in persistent residual waking hypnosis or confused hybrid states with a range of persistent characteristics of the hypnotic state; (b) distress/dysphoria (including psychophysiological and/or somatoform elements; (c) intrusive memories, abreactions, or the intrusion of isolated BASK (behavior, affect, sensation, knowledge) elements (Braun, 1988); (d) behavioral abnormalities associated with persistence of suggestions or ongoing vulnerability to suggestion; (e) disinhibition of dissociative or psychotic symptoms/disorders; and (f) phenomena due to error or malfeasance facilitated by hypnosis but not expressions of hypnosis itself (derived from Gruzelier, 2000; Kluft, 2012c; MacHovec, 1986).

The field of hypnosis has developed a common wisdom, passed along in workshop settings. It holds that adverse effects are infrequent in research settings, uncommon in both clinical work and workshop trainings, and quite frequent in stage hypnosis. Furthermore, it is generally taught that when adverse effects occur, they are easily detected. However, these statements are the legends and myths of our field. Neither thorough reviews of the literature (e.g., Gruzelier, 2000; MacHovec, 1986) nor recent research (Kluft, 2012c) sustains these widely held beliefs.

Gruzelier's masterful review (2000) cites a number of studies that indicate that when subjects are queried carefully, the administration of the classic Stanford Scales in a research setting may be attended with unwanted consequences in over 30% of normal subjects. Page and Handley (1993) found that educational efforts to demystify hypnosis and prevent negative outcomes have some success in reducing posthypnotic sequelae, but are not notably successful in effecting meaningful reductions in the occurrence of other unwanted phenomena during hypnosis. Further, Kluft discovered that among 30 subjects who suffered adverse experiences in workshops, in only one instance (3%) was the subject's distress both evident to others and freely reported by that subject.

Therefore, it can be argued that when efforts are made to make detailed inquiry about unwanted effects, their incidence may prove higher than anticipated, that there is reason to believe that still others will decline to reveal their distress, and that the absence of follow-up studies leaves it open as to whether other negative sequelae may exert impacts never appreciated as such after contact with the health professional, hypnosis instructor, or researcher has terminated. These indeed were repeated findings in Kluft's studies (2012c).

Kluft also found that every adverse incident in his series was associated with a failure to achieve adequate dehypnosis. Many of his discoveries were rediscoveries. Intent upon studying adverse sequelae to the research administration of Stanford Scales, Josephine Hilgard (1974) concluded that most of the phenomena being classified as unwanted consequences of hypnosis would be more accurately understood as the unwanted persistence of hypnosis (i.e., the realerting aspects of the research instruments did not reliably accomplish their tasks). Additional relevant research will be noted in the following text. The findings of Crawford, Hilgard, and Macdonald (1982) indicate that adverse sequelae are differentially associated with the use of cognitive elements (imagery and suggestions). Many have followed Orne (1965) in observing that the use of standard imagery rather than imagery crafted for the individual patient may enhance the risk of unwanted consequences. Unfortunately, Orne's proposed solution for research purposes was to create more impersonal standard suggestions and images, the very types later discovered to be associated with so many unwanted consequences, because what is upsetting is in the mind of the subject, not in the hypotheses or models of the experimenter. Ironically, gross estimates of the incidence of the adverse sequelae of stage hypnosis, generally 15% (MacHovec, 1986) to 20% (Echterling & Emmerling, 1987), are lower than those often encountered in research settings, but these figures are not comparable, because the researchers reported a wider range of sequelae, including more minor events.

Limitations of focus and space preclude detailed discussion of the complex issue of whether a particular unwanted phenomenon associated with hypnosis should be attributed to hypnosis itself or some related or concomitant factor. Pragmatically, it is customary to consider what can be attributed to hypnosis itself, to the skill and person of the hypnotist, to the unique qualities and vulnerabilities of the subject, to the techniques that have been employed, and to the circumstances surrounding the use of hypnosis. MacHovec (1986) summarized these as the hypnosis, hypnotist, subject, and environmental risk factors. To date, the literature remains rather unconvincing that hypnosis itself is associated with deleterious consequences associated with its use. The possible interaction of the neuropsychophysiolgical aspects of hypnosis with other factors in the triggering of psychosis remains a subject of study (e.g., Gruzelier, 2000).

PRACTICING TO MINIMIZE UNWANTED EFFECTS

The most diligent efforts of the most skillful and experienced clinicians will never succeed in completely eliminating all risk of unwanted sequelae. Nonetheless, consistent with Hippocrates's injunction, "Firstly, do not harm," we must take steps to prevent as many mishaps as possible, identify mishaps when they occur, and bring them to a rapid resolution. I will offer brief remarks about what steps best prevent the six categories of problems listed previously, and then address certain issues more extensively.

1. Complications due to inadequate dehypnosis/reawakening are best prevented by achieving a rough estimate of hypnotizability prior to proceeding, benchmarking the characteristics of alertness prior to hypnosis (see the following text), and assessing whether they have been restored, using assertive dehypnosis efforts if they have not.
2. Distress and dysphoria incipient and manifest in session is best handled by a thorough prehypnotic evaluation of the patient, which may make it possible to select less upsetting approaches; and intervening at the first sign of distress to prevent whatever is beginning from gathering momentum. Routine inquiry about subjective well-being even in the absence of overt signs is essential, because most upsetting matters remain covert and are best identified while there is still enough time to address potentially emergent problems.
3. Intrusive phenomena are best prevented through prehypnotic history taking, with special attention to traumatic/abusive/rejection/neglect experiences. Alerted to the possibility that painful material may be triggered, the clinician can plan accordingly. Of course, those who either withhold or have no awareness of having had such experiences would not be detected by such efforts.

4. Persistent suggestions are best prevented by meticulous cancellation of every suggestion other than therapeutic instructions prior to realerting, vigorous dehypnosis efforts, and rechecking for persistent trance and suggestion-related responses.

5. Disinhibition is best avoided by making a prehypnotic estimate of hypnotizability, taking a meticulous history, and performing a mental status prior to proceeding.

6. Error is best reduced by circumspection, modesty in one's estimation of one's prowess, and a commitment to lifelong learning. Unethical behavior is beyond the range of general advice.

The implicit message in these observations is the importance of patience, thoroughness, and skillful time management.

PSYCHOEDUCATION AND INFORMED CONSENT

Preparing the patient for hypnosis is a basic topic in hypnosis workshops and textbooks and will not be addressed here. Further, informed consent, especially in the context of litigation in recent decades about memory and hypnosis, is too complex a topic to address in brief or in passing. It is important to appreciate that when pursued as a part of the therapeutic alliance instead of a perfunctory or anxiety-fraught matter, it can enhance the treatment relationship. Forms are never comprehensive enough to cover all contingencies, so it is useful to augment any such formality with notes consistent with Appelbaum and Gutheil's (2006) concept of informed consent as a process, and to note your discussion of and the patient's understanding and consent to any new direction the treatment begins to take, or any new techniques or other interventions that might be added to the treatment as time goes on.

KNOW AND RESPECT YOUR LIMITATIONS

Hypnosis is a facilitator and catalyst. As such, it magnifies the impact of interventions, indifferent to whether they are skilled, inept, or misguided. Martin Orne often remarked in workshops and discussion, "Don't try to treat anything with hypnosis that you don't know how to treat without hypnosis." Mastering the rudiments or even the advanced aspects of hypnosis does not automatically translate into mastery of its use for any particular purpose. Nor does knowing an appropriate technique suffice. Internet LISTSERVs abound with inquiries that take the form, "How do I use modality X to treat condition Y?" Following the thread often reveals that the person asking for advice knows modality X, but is in the dark about condition Y.

It is a breach of ethics for a practitioner to treat a condition outside the domain of his or her training, professional discipline, and licensure. Understanding a condition is essential for good practice, and may suggest interventions that a practitioner dealing with symptoms alone would never consider.

SEEK RELIABLE SOURCES OF INFORMATION

While the Internet is a wonderful resource, it often restricts colleagues' searches for information to what is readily available and free, and provides information that may not prove applicable to the unique circumstances of one's individual patient. Relevant literature and knowledgeable colleagues may be harder to find, but the effort is worth it. Key articles not available for free on the net and expert consultation may be worth acquiring rather than bypassing.

WHAT DOES IT MEAN TO KNOW YOUR PATIENT?

When I began in hypnosis, Harold Crasilneck (Crasilneck & Hall, 1989) and many of the wise senior figures in hypnosis advised against beginning the use of hypnosis before completing the evaluation of the patient. As of this writing, a different set of expectations with different economic contingencies prevail, and many practitioners now begin to use hypnosis during their first contact with a new patient. My experience in practice, consultation, and in researching workshop casualties convinces me that in any contact designed to be more than a time-limited approach to symptom relief, and sometimes in those circumstances as well, safety is best served by a full initial evaluation that includes an extensive psychological and medical history and a mental status.

Much of the work we do is safer and more effective if it is carefully individualized. Our stances and choices of language, metaphor, imagery, and technique tend to be more accurately and empathically attuned the better we know those with whom we work. The six misadventures summarized in the following list were directly related to clinicians' insufficient understanding of their patients' circumstances.

1. The use of imagery involving a river and flowing water was followed by angina pectoris. The patient did not know how to swim and panicked.
2. The patient was instructed to let her limbs feel heavy. She responded with anxiety and weeping. She was profoundly ashamed of her weight problems.
3. A patient was instructed to let her hands feel cool. Her hands became blue and ischemic. Her nonmedical therapist did not understand the physiology of her patient's Raynaud's syndrome. Her suggestions triggered its symptoms.
4. Deepening was suggested by the image of descending a staircase. The patient experienced intrusion of a previously unavailable memory of being thrown down the stairs and raped. She did not reveal her flashback, and sought treatment elsewhere. Several years later, she shared her experience with the person who had done the hypnosis.
5. A patient was instructed to relax her muscles completely. She fell over and injured herself when she attempted to stand up after her hypnotic treatment. The nonmedical therapist was unaware that the patient's antihypertensive regimen made her vulnerable to orthostatic hypotension if she rose quickly, and the additional lowering of her blood pressure caused by the relaxation instructions endangered her.
6. A therapist instructed a patient to reexperience the warmth a child might feel in the arms of a loving mother. The patient said nothing about the terror she felt. On leaving this session, she consulted another therapist immediately. Had the therapist taken a more thorough history, she would have known that the patient's mother had tried to kill her.

Adequate preparation requires more than a superficial knowledge of the patient's medical and psychological background. It remains possible that many of these situations might not have been revealed in a first interview. The woman who reacted so poorly to deepening instructions had been completely amnestic regarding the information that burst into her awareness. However, more information and attention to individualizing interventions might have prepared clinicians to avoid the other five mishaps.

CRAFTING INTERVENTIONS FOR THE INDIVIDUAL PATIENT

The more we get to know those we treat, the more we appreciate their uniqueness as individuals. This pays dividends for clinician and patient alike when it comes to crafting interventions for the individual patient. I will discuss this subject using imagery as an example, because many wise students of hypnosis (e.g., Gruzelier, 2000; Orne, 1965) have cautioned against the general clinical use of scripted imagery, yet students learn hypnosis inductions by reading scripts involving imagery protocols provided by the instructors, and spend far less time learning to develop imagery for the individual patient.

What does research show? Imagery is among the aspects of the Stanford Scales most associated with adverse sequelae (reviewed in Gruzelier, 2000). I have published instances of the problems caused by my own use of scripted imagery, and of my emergency interventions when others' favorite images proved to be traumatic to others (Kluft, 2012b, 2012c).

Sadly, calling attention to the downside of making repetitive use of one's favorite imagery is often responded to not as a circumspect observation, but as proof that the person making such remarks exemplifies the offensive ignorance of a Philistine. From the perspective of a published novelist as well as a clinician, I understand that as a writer I am permitted to exercise poetic license, rule the fictive universe I have created, and shape it to the needs of my projects. As a healer, I do not enjoy such privileges. Instead, it is my duty to subordinate my creative notions to the needs of my patients. The failure to do so injects an unnecessary degree of jeopardy into the therapeutic enterprise.

When the clinician knowingly or unknowingly privileges the clinician's concerns over those of the patient, or is unable to differentiate the two, a dignity violation is inflicted upon the patient (Hicks, 2011; Kluft, 2016b) that enables the clinician to rationalize a countertransferential stance that disrespects the patient as a person (Hirsch, 2008; Kluft, 2016b).

It is neither threatening nor difficult to review imagery or other interventions one might use with a patient; simply ask if they are acceptable or problematic, and modify accordingly. In the following example quoted from a forthcoming novel (Kluft, 2016a, pp. 143–144), an instructor is trying to help a workshop participant whose dehypnosis was incomplete. Both know the student is still in a trance. The instructor proposes to use imagery to extricate the student from his residual trance. He asks,

"Any problem with stairways or escalators or elevators?"
"I fell down the stairs once. I was stuck in an elevator for 2 hours last year."
"OK. Just imagine yourself at the foot of a very safe escalator."

This type of simple inquiry would have prevented four of the six adverse incidents described previously.

It is also useful to bear in mind that the values of which the therapist is mindful, whether personal or societal, may blind the therapist to powerful therapeutic opportunities. Several times a year I encounter a male patient who states he cannot be hypnotized. Heroic attempts by competent practitioners have failed. I usually find that the images and suggestions that have been proposed have not resonated with the patient, whose values are not "politically correct." He has found what was offered either boring, irrelevant, or sissified.

I asked one such patient what interested him, what captured his imagination. He immediately responded, "Fishing and fighters." The pilot of a cargo plane during the Korean conflict, he resented not being assigned to a fighter group. He dreamed of flying the iconic fighters of World War II. Fishing-wise, he dreamed of going offshore for "the big ones," but never had. Five minutes after

we began talking about things that interested him, he was making approach to an aircraft carrier deck he envisioned on my blank wall with his eyes wide open, gripping the imaginary stick and swaying when I warned him that a cross wind was picking up. With imagery individualized to what he loved and valued, he went from refractory to profoundly cooperative in under 10 minutes.

UNDERSTANDING YOURSELF IN YOUR RELATIONSHIP WITH YOUR PATIENT

The modern practitioner of hypnosis has many advantages over his predecessors, and one distinct disadvantage. As cognitive-behavioral models become increasingly predominant in undergraduate and professional curricula, there has been an increasing de-emphasis on approaches that study the subjective experiences of the patient and the therapist within the treatment dyad. Many professionals learning hypnosis today have had scant exposure to the importance of psychodynamics and the relational aspects of healer–patient interaction.

Often professional skill and virtuosity seem sufficient to power hypnotically facilitated treatments, and rapport suffices to sustain the therapeutic enterprise. But when things begin to veer off track, the skill set based on the use of one's self as a caring, concerned person may be insufficient to restore a constructive thrust and direction. For therapists taught to minimize the importance of transference and countertransference, there is ongoing danger that one misstep may set the stage for the next, that personal reactions to the patient and what transpires may become increasingly problematic and/or disconnected with the core of the patient's therapeutic needs, leaving the helping professional feeling deskilled and deprived of mastery.

In the literature of hypnosis, the term *unconscious* often refers to dissociated/split aspects of the mind that can easily be engaged in conversation. In most other literature, this term refers to material that is inaccessible to the conscious mind and unavailable for interpersonal dialog. Ideomotor inquiries, as useful as they are, tap into split/dissociated configuration of the mind but may not access the deeper layers of the mind.

Often when hypnotic efforts fail to prosper, or evoke problematic reactions, the problems can be accessed with ego state, ideomotor, and other approaches. But when the problematic material is less accessible, they may prove unavailing.

Clinicians are well served by familiarizing themselves with basic concepts in the study of transference and countertransference, and with their relational and traumatic manifestations, in addition to more classic concerns. Enacted rather than expressed attitudes may sabotage the treatment and directly precipitate unwanted events.

A useful skill I teach my students is to try to figure out what figures in their lives most resemble their patient, and to recall both what attitudes they had/have toward those individuals and what attitudes those figures had/have toward them. It matters less what one thinks and feels than that one uses the information this exercise provides to learn from.

PREPARING TO GO FORWARD

Over my 45 years of practicing clinical hypnosis, I have gradually adopted a number of practices designed to reduce the likelihood that my use of this modality will be associated with unwanted consequences. I offer my own approach not as a set of definitive recommendations, but as an illustration of how I have struggled with my concerns. I have already spoken about the importance of taking a detailed history and a commitment to individualizing therapeutic efforts.

I learned the Spiegel eye-roll sign (Spiegel & Spiegel, 2004) and have assessed it in virtually every patient I have evaluated ever since. This sign co-occurs with hypnotizability rather than measures hypnotizability as a construct. It offers an early clue to the role hypnotic talent may play in my patient's clinical picture.

After experimenting with a number of methods, I discovered that Billie Strauss's "Apple test" is just right for my practice (Strauss, 1991). The subject is invited to pick up, describe, heft, and smell the apple prior to taking a bite. Inquiry is made about the juice, the taste, the crunchiness, and how the crunchiness sounds. Then inquiry is made about the experience of swallowing the ingested bite. I ask my subject to take another couple of bites and describe the sensations of those as well, and then to tell me what the apple looks like half eaten. I note if any sensory modality seems to be avoided or less

responsive to suggestion. Naturally, if apples are unacceptable due to taste or symbolic implications, I can find a substitute.

With these two inquiries, I tap a biological correlate of hypnotizability, assess suggestibility in a nonthreatening manner, learn which senses I can call upon to establish and intensify imagery, and get an indication of how abruptly, vividly, and powerfully intrusive elements may make themselves known.

I track all signs of discomfort and ask about them. Sometimes this provides information that would not otherwise have been shared for one reason or another. I try to avoid allowing anything linked with avoidance or discomfort to play a role in my interventions because I want to avoid building anything linked with discomfort into my early interventions.

I combine some workshop advice from Cory Hammond (see also Hammond, 1990) with creating a list of possible indicators of problematic areas. I list my actual interventions with some key details, including suggestions, images, methods of dehypnosis, and my patient's responses. It is very easy to lose track of what I actually have done and succumb to the seductive pulls of guesswork and stereotypy. If problems occur, I want to have the information I will need to review what I have done and reassess its impact.

My problematic indicators will include anything that strikes me as "off" in any way. Here is an example of how this works. Headaches are a common form of discomfort in hypnosis. They also are a common indicator of intense conflict in general, and conflict between the pressure of material and/or affect to emerge and the pressure to keep it out of awareness. Since the unanticipated emergence of traumatic dissociated material is a well-known unwanted effect in hypnosis work, ongoing reports of headaches or pressures, however vague, warn me that unstructured explorations may confront me with challenging crises. I may well discuss my concerns with the patient and schedule a longer session to inquire further rather than find us stumbling into an emergency.

WHEN PRECAUTIONS FAIL

No preparations, however thorough, cover all eventualities. While my preventive steps have proven remarkably effective, life goes on. Events and experiences in patients' lives trigger unfortunate reactions. Others' comments about hypnosis/treatment may undermine my best efforts and persuade my patient that this modality is problematic/unacceptable.

When an unexpected negative event occurs, my first step is to consider whether anything in the conduct of our work might have contributed to it. I am particularly worried about the possibility that some empathic failure or inadvertent error of mine may have caused my patient to feel unsafe, abandoned, or retraumatized, changing the valence of a pattern of interaction that had previously been effective. Luborsky's (Luborsky & Auerbach, 1969) symptom context research has demonstrated that most symptoms emerging suddenly in therapy sessions can be traced to transference-related material in the few previous minutes. Exploring emergent symptoms usually leads to relational issues or dissociated material. Prompt apologies for inadvertent misunderstandings or heavy-handed comments or interventions has had a more productive impact than techniques of any sort.

Clinicians must bear in mind that when patients in hypnotically facilitated treatments suddenly become highly distressed, hysterical psychosis or psychosis not otherwise specified should be considered. Very often, such episodes of distress signify the emergence of traumatic material and/or declare the presence of a dissociative disorder. Prompt therapist responses often make it possible to use ideomotor signals to learn something about the threat to the patient's stability, and to obtain consent for containing the distress or dealing with it bit by bit (Kluft, 1988, 1989, 2013).

In 45 years of practice, every emergent traumatic scenario, dissociative disorder, or apparently psychotic symptom has proven manageable, rarely requiring neuroleptics. However, several skilled colleagues have reported different experiences. I do not doubt others' accounts of the emergence of classic schizophrenia in the context of hypnosis (e.g., Gruzelier, 2000). Perhaps my interest in trauma has led to my seeing a different patient population, or that changing definitions of the major psychoses may cause different clinicians to interpret the same phenomena differently. I have addressed the confusion of dissociative disorders with schizophrenia elsewhere (Kluft, 1987; see also Tutkun, Yargic, & Sar, 1996).

DEHYPNOSIS AND REALERTING: THE FRONTIER OF PREVENTING UNWANTED EVENTS

My recent research (Kluft, 2012c) demonstrated that many subjects have sufficient ego strength to contain the overt expression of their distress when they suffer adverse responses to hypnosis. Further, most hypnosis professionals are accustomed to using gradual and permissive approaches to dehypnosis and realerting, and have a high toleration for persistent signs of less than complete alertness. Their thresholds for suspecting something is amiss are unrealistically high, even if they see their subjects manifesting residual trance phenomena. All too often if a subject rubs and opens his or her eyes, stretches, and moves about a bit, it is assumed that the task of realerting has been achieved; any residua are no cause for concern, and surely will dissipate rapidly.

This is completely fallacious predicate logic (the principle of Von Domarus). It falsely equates the presence of some descriptor of something with that thing itself, a quality attributed to psychotic thinking (Arieti, 1974). If eyes are open and the person can move about, that person is "awake," out of the trance. Yet it is well known that individuals can be in a trance with their eyes wide open and while they are engaged in vigorous physical activity (e.g., Bányai & Hilgard, 1976; Wark, 2006)! Vogt's fractionation methods involve deepening by reintroducing a trance to a person who has recently come out of a trance, literally piling one trance on top of another (see Kroger & Yapko, 2008; Kluft, 2012c, 2013). Kluft (2012c) follows Hilgard (1965) in maintaining that it could be argued that most of what has been described as problematic sequelae of hypnosis might be better described as the unrecognized persistence of hypnosis, a phenomenon documented in 100% of Kluft's (2012c) series. Gruzelier (2000) has commented on the problems associated with the unrecognized persistence of hypnosis.

The types of unwanted events most commonly linked with hypnosis are all related to the persistence/noncancellation of hypnotically facilitated changes. All are well-known hypnotic phenomena, arguably evidence of persistent trance or hybrid trance/wakeness states (Gruzelier, 2000; Howard, in preparation; Kluft, 2012c).

It should be self-evident that permitting a person to leave a training, research experiment, or clinical encounter with prominent trance phenomena still activated and potentially problematic is unwise at the least, and probably deserving of considerable censure. Yet, if permissive approaches to dehypnosis are utilized, the opportunity to prevent such circumstances and the unwanted consequences associated with them may be forfeited (Kluft, 2012a, 2012b, 2012c).

The persistence of residual trance may be difficult to detect both because the index of suspicion for it may be low and its manifestations may be kept private, subtle, and covert, or simply misunderstood. However, two interventions used in conjunction show promise in identifying and interdicting the persistence of the vast majority of unwanted events associated with hypnosis: (a) the use of the Howard Alertness Scale (Howard, 2008, in preparation; scale reproduced with permission in Kluft, 2013); and (b) the replacement of permissive methods of dehypnosis with directive approaches (Kluft, 2012a, 2012b, 2012c).

The Howard Alertness Scale (HAS; Howard, 2008) bypasses the difficulties associated with defining hypnosis by benchmarking and tracking the subject's alertness. The subject is asked to attend to the vividness and clarity of his or her sensory experiences. Alertness is assessed globally prior to the use of hypnosis, and again after dehypnosis or realerting has been attempted. In Kluft's (2013) modification of Howard's method, several sensory perceptions are elicited, and estimates are made for them as well. The successfulness of dehypnosis or realerting is gauged by the degree to which the benchmarked baseline(s) is (are) restored.

The power of this approach resides in its conceptual straightforwardness and its establishing a baseline by eliciting experiences that subjects actually will endorse with a paucity of defensiveness and are able to observe over time. If the second estimates indicate that the benchmark values have not been restored, additional efforts to effect dehypnosis are indicated. The initial use of the HAS with groups is described in Kluft (2012c), and its use with individuals is illustrated in Howard (in preparation).

When further efforts at realerting are indicated, and simple repetition of the original attempt proves ineffective, it is usually helpful to transition to directive methods of dehypnosis, methods characterized by clear, crisp instructions and a solid predictable structured exodus from trance. Counting a patient out of trance in conjunction with an image suitable to the occasion, as in the earlier fictional illustration, is typical, although for those who are averse to counting numerous other metaphoric approaches are available. These interventions may require elaboration and repetition.

APPROACHES TO THE PATIENT IN A REFRACTORY TRANCE

While some individuals indeed seem to remain in a trance despite efforts to extricate them because they indeed value the experience and are gratified by the relief and escape the trance has afforded them, and others seize upon the occasion to make a statement related to their issues with autonomy, control, or defiance of authority, most remain stuck because important dynamics have become activated or adverse psychological experiences are taking place. Rarely, profound fatigue compromises the subject's ability to concentrate.

However, in most instances, after a period of time, the trance becomes somewhat less enmeshed with the forces that drove its inception, and takes on a life of its own. At that point, it often can be addressed as a problem in itself. I have described trances that behave in that manner as "rogue trances" (Kluft, 2011, 2012a). Elsewhere (Kluft, 2012a) I described 15 ways to approach the resolution of rogue or persistent trances. Three of these may stand on their own, but they are usually used in connection with, or to serve as a foundation for, the other 12 methods.

In addressing any refractory trance, it becomes important to avoid proceeding in a hurried manner. D. Corydon Hammond (personal communication, July 10, 2011) reminds us that it is an unfortunate commonplace for clinicians to spend quite a while establishing a trance and then try to terminate that trance in a comparatively rapid manner. This may result in the patient's being unable to emerge completely from trance within the time allotted. It is preferable to manage so that ample time is reserved for dehypnosis, including enough time for several approaches in case the first is unavailing.

Most efforts to remove patients from rogue trances will (1) revisit, review, and possibly repeat the induction and dehypnosis that was used;

(2) replace permissive dehypnosis with directive realerting; and (3) build upon an improved or different set of induction suggestions to induce a deeper trance, a rescue trance, in an attempt to capture the rogue trance and dehypnotize the subject from both. Such efforts are worth repeating before going on.

Another approach (4) involves the systematic emphatic undoing of all the suggestions associated with the trance and interventions associated with the establishment of the trance that went awry.

Another approach (5) utilizes future-oriented techniques in which the patient is helped to look forward to having recovered, and encouraged to look back from that vantage point and share what made that possible. Hypnoprojective techniques (6) may be used to request information that may indirectly yield information about what might be helpful in bringing about an end to the unwanted trances. (7) Age regression may be used to capture a good state of mind not locked in a trance and bring it back to the present. (8) It is common to ask a person stuck in a trance to develop imagery of what he or she most values, and use its assumed strength to engage the individual. Elsewhere I have expressed caution about this method and do not use it (Kluft, 2012a). If it fails, something deeply cherished may become devalued.

(9) Ego-state methods (Watkins & Watkins, 1997) may be used to appeal to parts of the mind with relevant hidden knowledge useful to resolve the situation. (10) Those with psychodynamic training may be able to offer an interpretation of the matters that are keeping the patient stuck in a trance. Applying superficial levels of understanding may well backfire. If a story (11) derived from understanding the individual can be created and told in a manner to encourage an adaptive emergence from trance, it may be helpful. At times it becomes possible (12) to propose that the patient take a rain check to put aside whatever is keeping the patient in the trance, and allow it to emerge in the next session or some other time of mutual agreement. Such arrangements often succeed if carried out with high hypnotizables/dissociative patients using ideomotor signals. In essence, confrontation of the problematic matter is postponed.

I have been pleasantly surprised by successes with what I will call (13) desensitization to alertness. Alertness is understood to be something that is being avoided, as if the patient were phobic of returning to an alert state. The current mental alertness is rated on a 1 to 100 scale, with 100 signifying full alertness. The patient is encouraged to rise a few percentage points toward alertness, and then to return to the level of the refractory trance state. This is repeated, and slowly the degree of alertness is increased. It has been my experience that after several returns to the refractory state, the patient either cannot resume it, or simply achieves alertness. I have never had to do a full desensitization. This approach has much in common with my fractionated abreaction technique (Kluft, 1988, 2012a, 2013).

Methods involving (14) physical touch, such as pressure on the shoulders and release of that pressure, offer a physical analog to being down, and then being able to rise. Another approach I have used involves a series of acupressure points. This is most unlikely to work well in the hands of those who are not experienced with this modality, but I have seen someone who knew nothing about acupressure build up expectations and take a shot in the dark by pressing random places and sufficiently impact the patient in some manner that she emerged from a very prolonged refractory trance. For many patients, such approaches are contraindicated. In all instances permission should be requested and granted before physical methods are applied.

Finally, (15) alternative modalities might be involved. Sometimes when things become problematic, the modality being used loses valence and credibility with the patient, a phenomenon I have described as paradigm exhaustion (Kluft, 1992). The patient simply will not respond to any form of the problematic modality. I have broken a number of refractory trances using EMDR via tactile stimuli after being granted permission to do so.

CONCLUSION

While unwanted responses to hypnosis are more common and covert than has been generally understood, the risk of their occurrence can be markedly reduced by the more thorough evaluation of the patient, the regular use of rather basic and straightforward clinical interventions, and the individualization of the techniques and imagery brought to bear in the treatment setting. Further, initially unrecognized incipient problems often can be identified and nipped in the bud by monitoring alertness with the clinician- and patient-friendly Howard Alertness Scale (HAS) and the more assertive use of directive approaches to dehypnosis.

Only a small percentage of unwanted effects prove either beyond prevention or beyond clinicians' abilities to affect their rapid remediation and resolution.

REFERENCES

Appelbaum, P., & Gutheil, T. (2006). *Clinical handbook of psychiatry and the law*. Baltimore, MD: Lippincott Williams & Wilkins.

Arieti, S. (1974). *Interpretation of schizophrenia*. New York, NY: Basic Books.

Bányai, E. I., & Hilgard, E. R. (1976). A comparison of active-alert hypnotic induction with traditional relaxation induction. *Journal of Abnormal Psychology*, 85(2), 218–224.

Braun, B. G. (1988). The BASK model of dissociation. *Dissociation*, 1(1), 4–23.

Crasilneck, H., & Hall, J. (1989). *Clinical hypnosis: Principles and applications*. New York, NY: Pearson.

Crawford, H. J., Hilgard, J. R., & Macdonald, H. (1982). Transient experiences following hypnotic testing and special termination procedures. *International Journal of Clinical and Experimental Hypnosis*, 30(2), 117–126. doi:10.1080/00207148208407377

Echterling, L. G., & Emmerling, D. A. (1987). Impact of stage hypnosis. *American Journal of Clinical Hypnosis*, 29(3), 149–154. doi:10.1080/00029157.1987.10734344

Gruzelier, J. (2000). Unwanted effects of hypnosis: A review of the evidence and its implications. *Contemporary Hypnosis*, 17(4), 163–193. doi:10.1002/ch.207

Hammond, D. C. (1990). *Handbook of hypnotic suggestions and metaphors*. New York, NY: W. W. Norton.

Hicks, D. (2011). *Dignity*. New Haven, CT: Yale University Press.

Hilgard, E. R. (1965). *Hypnotic susceptibility*. New York, NY: Harcourt, Brace and World.

Hilgard, J. R. (1974). Sequelae to hypnosis. *International Journal of Clinical and Experimental Hypnosis*, 22(4), 281–298. doi:10.1080/00207147408413008

Hilgard, J. R., Hilgard, E. R., & Newman, M. (1961). Sequelae to hypnotic induction with special reference to earlier chemical anesthesia. *Journal of Nervous and Mental Disease*, 133(6), 461–478.

Hirsch, I. (2008). *Coasting in the countertransference: Conflicts of self-interest between analyst and patient*. New York, NY: Routledge.

Howard, H. (2008). The Howard Alertness Scale. *Focus*, 50(2–3), 3–4.

Howard, H.(In preparation). *The role of an alertness scale in clinical hypnosis*.

Kleinhauz, M., & Eli, I. (1987). Potential deleterious effects of hypnosis in the clinical setting. *American Journal of Clinical Hypnosis*, 29(3), 155–159. doi:10.1080/00029157.1987.10734345

Kluft, R. P. (1987). First-rank symptoms as a diagnostic clue to multiple personality disorder. *American Journal of Psychiatry*, 144(3), 293–298. doi:10.1176/ajp.144.3.293

Kluft, R. P. (1988). On treating the older patient with multiple personality disorder: "Race against time" or "make haste slowly"? *American Journal of Clinical Hypnosis*, 30(4), 257–266. doi:10.1080/00029157.1988.10402748

Kluft, R. P. (1989). Playing for time: Temporizing techniques in the treatment of multiple personality disorder. *American Journal of Clinical Hypnosis*, 32(2), 90–98. doi:10.1080/00029157.1989.10402806

Kluft, R. P. (1992). Paradigm exhaustion and paradigm shift and thinking through the therapeutic impasse. *Psychiatric Annals*, 22(10), 502–508. doi:10.3928/0048-5713-19921001-06

Kluft, R. P. (2011). Reversing rogue trances: Realerting the bewitched, bothered, and bewildered, and recognizing the befuddled. *Newsletter of the American Society of Clinical Hypnosis*, 3–6.

Kluft, R. P. (2012a). Approaches to difficulties in realerting subjects from hypnosis. *American Journal of Clinical Hypnosis*, 55(2), 140–159.

Kluft, R. P. (2012b). Enhancing workshop safety: Learning from colleagues' adverse experiences. *American Journal of Clinical Hypnosis*, 55(1), 85–122.

Kluft, R. P. (2012c). Issues in the detection of those suffering adverse effects in hypnosis training workshops. *American Journal of Clinical Hypnosis*, 54(3), 213–232.

Kluft, R. P. (2013). *Shelter from the storm*. North Charleston, SC: CreateSpace Independent Publishing Platform.

Kluft, R. P. (2016a). *An obituary to die for*. Manuscript submitted for publication.

Kluft, R. P. (2016b). You have to be carefully taught: Dignity considerations in clinical practice, scholarship, and trauma treatment. In S. Levine (Ed.), *Dignity: Psychosocial perspectives* (pp. 141–158). London, UK: Karnac Books.

Kroger, W., & Yapko, M. (2008). *Clinical and experimental hypnosis*. Philadelphia, PA: Lippincott Williams & Wilkins.

Luborsky, L., & Auerbach, A. H. (1969). The symptom-context method. Quantitative studies of symptom formation in psychotherapy. *Journal of the American Psychoanalytic Association*, 17(1), 68–99.

Lynn, S. J., Myers, E., & Mackillop, J. (2000). The systematic study of negative post-hypnotic effects: Research hypnosis, clinical hypnosis, and stage hypnosis. *Contemporary Hypnosis, 17,* 127–131.

MacHovec, F. (1986). *Hypnosis complications: Prevention and risk management.* Springfield, IL: Thomas Books.

Meares, A. (1961). An evaluation of the dangers of medical hypnosis. *American Journal of Clinical Hypnosis, 4*(2), 90–97.

Mott, T. (1992). Untoward effects associated with hypnosis. *Psychological Medicine, 10,* 119–128.

Orne, M. T. (1965). Undesirable effects of hypnosis: The determinants and management. *International Journal of Clinical and Experimental Hypnosis, 13*(4), 226–237. doi:10.1080/00207146508412945

Page, R. A., & Handley, G. W. (1993). The effect of preventive measures in reducing aftereffects to hypnosis. *American Journal of Clinical Hypnosis, 36*(1), 26–37. doi:10.1080/00029157.1993.10403036

Shor, R. E. (1959). Hypnosis and the concept of the generalized reality-orientation. *American Journal of Psychotherapy, 13,* 582–602.

Shor, R., & Orne, M. (1965). *The nature of hypnosis.* New York, NY: Holt, Rinehart, & Winston.

Spiegel, H., & Spiegel, D. (2004). *Trance and treatment.* Washington, DC: American Psychiatric Press.

Strauss, B. S. (1991). The use of a multimodal image, the apple technique, to facilitate clinical hypnosis: A brief communication. *International Journal of Clinical and Experimental Hypnosis, 39*(1), 1–5. doi:10.1080/00207149108409614

Tutkun, H., Yargic, L. I., & Sar, V. (1996). Dissociative identity disorder presenting as hysterical psychosis. *Dissociation, 9,* 244–252.

Wark, D. M. (2006). Alert hypnosis: A review and case report. *American Journal of Clinical Hypnosis, 48*(4), 291–300. doi:10.1080/00029157.2006.10401536

Watkins, J., & Watkins, H. (1997). *Ego states: Theory and therapy.* New York, NY: W. W. Norton.

Research Methods in Medical and Psychological Hypnosis

Steven Jay Lynn and Erik Woody

Research methodology in hypnosis is a complex, multifaceted topic; indeed, entire books have been written in an attempt to cover it (e.g., Sheehan & McConkey, 1982; Sheehan & Perry, 1976). In this brief chapter, we necessarily set out far more limited goals. First, given that the realm of hypnosis is full of startling, counterintuitive, and even "magical" experiences and phenomena, we devote some attention to the potential advantages of trying to cage such phenomena within the framework of rigorous research design. In particular, by referring to some classic experiments in the history of science, we outline major features of effective research design, which apply as fully to hypnosis as to any other domain. Next, we distinguish among three major types of hypnosis research, which require somewhat different handling of these basic design issues. Finally, we discuss a few of the specific design issues that arise in each of these areas of hypnosis research and provide references to literature in which further detail is available.

REAL LIFE VERSUS RESEARCH DESIGN

One of the best known poems in the English language is a sonnet by Robert Frost, in which the poet, faced with the choice between two paths in life, takes the road "less traveled by." Many people think the point of the poem is that this is the better choice; however, the poem actually focuses on the foregone alternative, as is evident in the poem's title, "The Road Not Taken." What the poem is actually about is the haunting sense of regret that one will never find out what would have been different if one had taken the other path.

Research designs set up admittedly artificial circumstances that can overcome this basic limitation of real life. In a good research design, we try multiple "roads"; keep careful, systematic records; and find out what difference the choice makes.

That this strategy offers enormous benefits for our knowledge is already evident in what is generally regarded as the first true experiment with people as subjects, conducted in 1747 on a sailing ship by James Lind, a Royal Navy surgeon. For more than two centuries, scurvy, a disease, had devastated the crews of all long voyages, often killing half or more of the sailors. Although doctors had considerable experience with the disease, they did not know how to treat it. Lind conducted a simple experiment, in which he manipulated one aspect of the diets of six pairs of scurvy victims. He assigned two patients to drink a daily mug of cider, two others to drink a daily mug of vinegar, two others a daily mug of seawater, and so on. Two patients were assigned a daily mug containing the juice of two oranges and a lemon. The results were dramatic and unmistakable: compared with their fellow patients assigned to the other drink conditions, the two citrus drinkers recovered remarkably.

This example illustrates that a good research design can show something important and useful well in advance of being able to guess what the underlying mechanism might be. Indeed, that vitamin C was the causal agent was not discovered until the 20th century. It also illustrates how the essence of a good research design is a well-conceived, clear comparison between two or more things. The ineffective conditions were not just duds; instead, their presence in the design powerfully confirms the specificity of effects. Finally, this example shows that it is the limiting of extraneous differences that makes the comparison of conditions effective. Aside from the daily drink, everything about the sailors' rations was kept the same; and sailors were assigned to conditions, avoiding confounds such as only the healthier sailors selecting some kinds of drinks.

From the early investigation of hypnosis came a seminal development in research design. Specifically, in 1782, the king of France appointed a commission of eminent scientists, led by Benjamin Franklin, to investigate the work of Franz Mesmer, whose cures had been attracting a great deal of public attention. There was really no doubt that Mesmer and his associates produced striking effects in people, as the commission members could readily observe for themselves. Unlike Lind's experiment, in which underlying mechanisms were unknown, in this case there were two competing hypotheses about the mechanism involved in Mesmer's effects, and these are what the commission's work focused on. Mesmer had advanced a theory of animal magnetism, which hypothesized that the effects were produced by a physical fluid possessed by all living organisms, which could be condensed and conducted from one organism to another. In contrast, the commission members' observations of the phenomena suggested to them that the underlying mechanism was purely psychological, or what they termed *imagination*.

Unfortunately, neither proposed mechanism was directly observable, making them frustratingly difficult to distinguish. The strategy eventually adopted by the commission was to block one of the proposed mechanisms and observe what happened to the phenomena obtained. Over a series of experiments, their chief manipulation was blindfolding the subject, which blocked the cues necessary to stimulate the subject's imagination, but not any transfer of physical fluid. These experiments showed consistently that blindfolding completely eliminated the subjects' response, supporting the hypothesis that imagination was the underlying mechanism. In addition, these simple but ingenious experiments had a much wider influence as the first placebo-controlled blind trials (Franklin, 1784/1996; see also Gould, 1991).

The commission's strategy of blocking a hypothesized mechanism illustrates the importance of trying to devise conditions that may eliminate a phenomenon for informative reasons. Ideally, both possible outcomes of such a test are interesting—for example, if the blindfold had turned out to have no effect, the result of that experiment would have disconfirmed the commission's ideals about the role of imagination. There is an art to

adopting such a strategy of attempted disconfirmation, because people, including scientists, tend more naturally to follow a confirmatory strategy, investing their effort in finding additional positive cases.

A further, very important aspect of research design is the opportunity to use special methods of measurement that allow the systematic observation of phenomena that would be difficult to discern otherwise. An intriguing example is Michael Faraday's investigation, in 1853, of the spiritualist phenomenon of table-turning. Small groups of people sitting around a table with their hands resting on its top would find that the table eventually moved on its own, dragging the sitters along with it. The sitters honestly believed that they themselves did not initiate these movements. Faraday devised a simple but ingenious apparatus to record the source of the movements: he placed a series of sheets of cardboard on top of the table, reasoning that the greater degree of slippage would occur on the side from which the movement originated. The results showed clearly that the sitters moved the table, rather than vice versa, even though they were unaware of it (Faraday, 1853; see Hyman, 1999, for further discussion of this experiment).

SUMMARY AND APPLICATION TO HYPNOSIS RESEARCH

Our brief consideration of these classic experiments has raised three key issues in effective research design:

1. The essence of a good research design is a well-conceived, clear comparison of two or more things. Anything we want to study needs to be compared to something else, and the choice about that something else is crucial.
2. It is important to think carefully about conditions that may not "work"—that could eliminate a phenomenon for informative reasons. Often such designs involve blocking a hypothesized mechanism, thus entailing a strategy of attempted disconfirmation of hypotheses (rather than simply generating more positive instances).
3. Another essential aspect of good research design is using appropriate, systematic measurement techniques to capture the phenomena of interest in a sensitive, valid way.

In hypnosis research, the first two issues are often discussed in terms of including appropriate "control groups" in the design. It is important to realize, however, that there is no all-purpose control group in hypnosis research, and the best research often employs control groups that are very ingenious, rather than passive benchmarks. Regarding the third issue, because hypnosis involves fairly unusual and unique phenomena, high-quality hypnosis research depends on an array of specialized measures. Moreover, because hypnosis crucially encompasses changes in subjective experience that cannot be directly observed, hypnosis research raises some challenging measurement problems.

Before discussing these issues more specifically, it is useful to distinguish among three broad types of hypnosis research. Following Reyher (1962), Cox and Bryant (2008) distinguished between intrinsic and instrumental hypnosis research. Intrinsic hypnosis research addresses the underlying nature of the phenomenon of hypnosis, including the social, cognitive, and phenomenological factors that may explain hypnotic responding. In contrast, instrumental hypnosis research involves using hypnosis as an investigative tool to address and better understand other phenomena, such as psychopathological conditions like amnesia, paranoia, conversion disorder, and delusions (Cox & Bryant, 2008). To these two broad types of hypnosis research, we would add research on hypnotherapy, which addresses the viability of hypnosis as a clinical treatment, and neurophysiological research involving hypnosis. We now turn to a brief discussion of issues of research design for each of these major types of research.

INTRINSIC HYPNOSIS RESEARCH

In studying the phenomenon of hypnosis, a major problem that needs to be addressed is the very wide range of individual differences in response to hypnosis, with a substantial minority of participants being comparatively unresponsive (see Chapter 5, "Hypnotizability"). For the purposes of an experiment, this large variability in responses from unselected participants would inflate the within-cell variances, and thus increase the size of the error term, resulting in low statistical power.

However, hypnosis researchers have adopted a design strategy that turns these substantial individual differences from a potential weakness into a strength. Specifically, in almost all intrinsic hypnosis research, the initial step is to administer a standardized hypnosis scale to large numbers of possible participants, and, on the basis of their responses to the hypnotic suggestions on these scales, preselect high-hypnotizable and low-hypnotizable groups for subsequent use in the experiment itself. It is also possible, although much less common, to select out a moderate-hypnotizable group. This strategy not only overcomes the within-cell variance problem, but also provides a low-hypnotizability control group with which to compare the high-hypnotizability group. More specifically, if the phenomenon under study in the experiment is truly hypnotic in nature, then the high-hypnotizability participants should perform quite differently from their low-hypnotizability counterparts. An advantage of including participants in the moderate range of hypnotizability is that it makes it possible to determine whether the highly hypnotizable individuals differ in their behavior from more typical or "average" individuals, allowing a better opportunity to address how the responses of highly hypnotizable participants may be distinguishable from those who score at both the low and mid-range of hypnotic responsiveness.

Several standardized hypnosis scales are in fairly widespread use for preselecting participants for hypnosis experiments, including the *Harvard Group Scale of Hypnotic Susceptibility, Form A* (HGSHS:A; Shor & Orne, 1962), the Stanford Hypnotic Susceptibility Scale, Form C (SHSS:C; Weitzenhoffer & Hilgard, 1962), and the Waterloo-Stanford Group Scale of Hypnotic Susceptibility, Form C (WSGC; Bowers, 1993, 1998). Because group-administered hypnosis scales, like the HGSHS:A and the WSGC, are far more efficient with regard to time, they are more commonly used for preselection than individually administered scales, like the SHSS:C. To make sure the high and low hypnotizability groups are as valid as possible, some researchers pretest on two successive hypnosis scales, such as the HGSHS:A followed by the WSGC, and only use participants for the main experiment if they score consistently high or low on both scales. Further information about how hypnosis scales are used in research is provided in Chapter 5, "Hypnotizability." Although there are occasionally expressions of concern whether this preselection strategy is overused (e.g., Woody, 1997), it has become ubiquitous.

In the main experiment, some participants, both high and low hypnotizable, are administered a hypnotic induction, and there is usually some kind of control condition designed to serve as a contrast, in which participants either get no induction or else some other kind of instructions. The no-induction control group is often called, somewhat loosely, the "waking" condition. To someone not familiar with the hypnosis research literature, it may seem obvious that responses to hypnotic suggestions should be far more readily forthcoming after a hypnotic induction than in waking conditions; however, many empirical studies indicate this is not necessarily true, and the differences obtained can be quite subtle (Kirsch & Lynn, 1995).

An important example of an instructed control group is the so-called real-simulator design in which the simulators, usually low-hypnotizable participants, are told to fake the expected behavior and try to fool the hypnotist into thinking they are truly responding (Orne, 1959). The real-simulator design has been applied to a wide array of hypnotic responses and phenomena, for example, age regression (Orne, 1951, 1959) and the experience of nonvolition (Lynn, Nash, Rhue, Frauman, & Stanley, 1983). When people outside the field of hypnosis first hear of the real-simulator design, they are typically very enthusiastic about it, thinking this is the way to find out once and for all whether hypnosis is "real." However, the finding that hypnotic responses can be faked does not mean that hypnosis does not exist, just as the fact that orgasms can be faked does not mean that orgasms do not exist. The real-simulator design actually answers a much narrower question—namely, whether the information in the experimental situation is sufficient for the participant to know what the expected response would be. Unless the experiment involves deception, the answer to this question is usually yes; however, the simulators tend to overrespond compared with the high-hypnotizable real participants.

Another important example of a control group in hypnosis research is the task-motivational instructions that T. X. Barber and colleagues devised to address the question of whether a special state of consciousness is needed to account for hypnotic phenomena (Barber, 1969; Barber & Calverley,

1964; Spanos, & Chaves, 1974). Participants were instructed that their ability to imagine was being tested; they were strongly urged to cooperate with the experiment by actively imagining the suggested effects and were told that others had been successful in doing so. Based on findings that these instructions often yielded behavior comparable to that following a standard hypnotic induction, Barber argued that hypnotic responses were not particularly unusual and did not require the positing of unusual states of consciousness. Nonetheless, a frequent criticism of Barber's research has been that task-motivational instructions—such as "Everyone passed these tests when they tried" (Barber, 1969, p. 46)—may place greater pressure on participants for compliance than is present in traditional hypnotic inductions and lead some participants to exaggerate their responsiveness to suggestions. More recently, other methods of evoking effects comparable to those of hypnotic inductions have been devised that avoid the high pressure statements contained in task motivational instructions (e.g., Council, Kirsch, Vickery, & Carlson, 1983).

As our discussion of the waking, simulating, and task-motivational control groups indicates, the strengths of any particular control group are often balanced by limitations that constrain the inferences that can be drawn. Hence, in designing control groups—perhaps more aptly labeled "comparison groups"—for hypnosis research, it is important to think carefully about the specific hypotheses underlying the particular study and how the evidence for or against them may be clarified by the choice of control group. An off-the-shelf control group, like the waking condition or the real-simulator design, may not be the optimal choice. For example, a control group in which a hypothesized mechanism is blocked may be much more interesting (e.g., Hargadon, Bowers, & Woody, 1995).

Although there are many other possibilities, a widespread design in intrinsic hypnosis research involves high versus low hypnotizability subject groups crossed with hypnotic-induction versus waking conditions, with the crucial prediction being a statistically significant interaction between these two factors. The specific pattern of such an interaction typically supports the hypothesis that high hypnotizability and a hypnotic induction are jointly necessary to obtain hypnotically suggested responses, particularly if those responses are relatively difficult (e.g., hallucinations). A third, mechanism-blocking factor would be expected to yield a three-way interaction.

Rather than handling the hypnotic-induction and waking conditions as a between-subjects factor, it is alternatively possible to have participants serve as their own controls by running them successively in both conditions. Although this design offers relatively high statistical power and can sometimes be justified (e.g., Bowers & Woody, 1996), its weaknesses need to be acknowledged. If the waking condition comes before the hypnosis condition, participants may show "hold back" effects, in which they suppress their best effort until the hypnosis (Zamansky, Scharf, & Brightbill, 1964). Conversely, if the waking condition comes after the hypnosis condition, participants may inadvertently respond again in a hypnotic way. Finally, if order is counterbalanced, there may be strong and confusing order effects; for example, combining the foregoing two ideas, hypnosis may appear to be more effective than a waking trial only when it comes second.

As an alternative to the mechanism-blocking design used by the Franklin Commission and many other eminent scientists for decades, the technique of mediation analysis has recently become very popular in psychological research (e.g., Hayes, 2013). In this approach, the correlational data generated by a study are used to evaluate hypotheses about underlying mechanisms, in accordance with a line of reasoning developed from path analysis. Although such mediation analysis can sometimes be informative, it is typically open to alternative explanations and hence a far weaker form of inference than experimental blocking of the proposed mechanism (Bullock, Green, & Ha, 2010). Woody (2011) explains the issues involved and shows that it is easy to pass statistical tests of mediation analysis even when there is actually no mediation at all.

Researchers have also conducted correlational studies to ascertain the relation between hypnotic responsiveness and personality traits such as absorption, dissociation, fantasy-proneness, thinness of boundaries, and empathy (see Cardeña & Terhune, 2014). Although the correlations obtained can be quite interesting, it is important to recognize that such constructs typically account for only a surprisingly small proportion of variance in hypnotic responding. Moreover, it is important not to confuse correlation with causation.

In addition to carefully evaluating which control conditions to deploy, it is important for hypnosis researchers to tailor their outcome measures to the theoretical or research question at hand. For example, researchers often include measures of suggestion-related subjective experiences that often accompany hypnotic responses, such as the experience of involuntariness (Polito, Barnier, & Woody, 2013; Polito, Barnier, Woody, & Connors, 2014). More broadly, multidimensional measures of subjective experiences, such as the Phenomenology of Consciousness Inventory (Pekala, 1991), are useful in capturing the variability of subjective experiences that are the hallmark of hypnosis. To obtain a more fine-grained snapshot of the experience of individual hypnotic suggestions, researchers have employed the experiential analysis technique (Sheehan & McConkey, 1982), in which experimenters interview participants based on jointly viewing a video-recording of the hypnotic proceedings.

INSTRUMENTAL HYPNOSIS RESEARCH

Hypnosis has proved to be an invaluable investigative tool for studying puzzling psychological phenomena. For example, researchers have used hypnotic methods instrumentally in order to create temporary laboratory analogs of a variety of clinical disorders and conditions (Connors, Langdon, & Coltheart, 2015; Oakley & Halligan, 2010), including functional blindness (e.g., Bryant & McConkey, 1999), delusions (e.g., Kihlstrom & Hoyt, 1988; Noble & McConkey, 1995), hallucinations (e.g., Szechtman, Woody, Bowers, & Nahmias, 1998), compulsive behavior (Woody et al., 2005), emotional numbing and thought suppression (e.g., Bryant & Kapur, 2006), intrusive memories (Hill, Hung, & Bryant, 2010), and the mirrored-self-misidentification delusion (i.e., the belief that one's reflection in the mirror is a stranger, Connors, Barnier, Langdon, Cox, Polito, & Coltheart, in press).

An excellent example of the use of hypnosis to model a complex psychological phenomenon is the study of functional amnesia. Functional amnesia is arguably one of the most compelling and controversial forms of forgetting, whether seen in a clinical or a forensic context, because it involves an extreme and sudden memory loss typically associated with psychological trauma, rather than with brain damage or disease (Kihlstrom & Schacter, 1995). Functional amnesia involves three major features: (a) a subjectively compelling apparent inability to consciously access autobiographical memories and information (i.e., disrupted explicit memory), (b) a continuing influence of the "forgotten" information on behavior, thought, and action (i.e., a dissociation between implicit and explicit memory), and (c) reversibility of the effect (see Cox & Barnier, 2003). Functional amnesia is a major feature of the poorly understood, and often dramatic, psychological disorders of dissociative fugue, dissociative amnesia, and dissociative identity disorder (Giesbrecht, Lynn, Lilienfeld, & Merckelbach, 2008; Lynn, Lilienfeld, Merckelbach, Giesbrecht, & van der Kloet, 2012), and has, for the past three decades, figured prominently in controversies about repressed and recovered memories (Erdelyi, 2006). The spontaneous, transient, and complex nature of functional amnesia has limited its systematic investigation, making laboratory analogs of the phenomenon appealing.

Researchers have used hypnosis to devise ingenious ways to model functional amnesia in the laboratory to modify memory for events before and during hypnosis. Several investigators have argued that posthypnotic amnesia (PHA) can be used to model functional amnesia (Barnier, 2002; Cox & Barnier, 2003; Kihlstrom, 1980; Kihlstrom & Evans, 1979; Kihlstrom & Schachter, 1995; Mendelsohn, Chalamish, Solomonovich, & Dudai, 2008). In PHA, the hypnotist suggests that, following hypnosis, participants will be unable to recall material until they receive a reversibility cue. Although traditionally this targeted material is learned or experienced during hypnosis, it can also be extended to experiences before hypnosis (Bryant, Barnier, Mallard, & Tibbits, 1999). Typically, for high but not low hypnotizable individuals, PHA leads to disrupted explicit memory, discrepancies between implicit and explicit memory, and reversibility when the hypnotist provides a cue to the participant, such as "Now you can remember everything" (Barnier, 2002). The similarities between functional amnesia and PHA (i.e., impaired explicit memory, a dissociation between explicit and implicit memory, and reversibility) have spurred researchers to use PHA as a

paradigm to model and explore disorders of personal memory.

For example, Barnier (2002) asked high- and low-hypnotizable participants to recall a memory from their first day at high school and their first day at university. Following a hypnotic induction, she provided half of the participants with a PHA suggestion for their first day at high school and the remainder of participants with a parallel suggestion to forget their first day at university. Before she administered the reversibility cue to cancel PHA, she assessed, by way of category generation and social judgment tasks, participants' implicit memory for the events and probed for their explicit recall of the events a second time. Barnier found a dissociation between explicit and implicit measures for high-hypnotizable individuals, but not for low-hypnotizable individuals. For highs, their explicit recall returned to the unimpaired baseline level of lows' recall following the reversibility cue. Accordingly, this research provided a useful method for investigating temporary and reversible forgetting of autobiographical memories.

Although the use of hypnosis to investigate clinical disorders and conditions is an exciting, generative area of research, it is important to keep in mind that there may be important differences between the clinical condition and the analog created via hypnosis in terms of etiology, duration, context of occurrence, and age group in which the condition ("real" or analog) is manifested (Connors, Langdon, & Coltheart, 2015). Woody and Szechtman (2011) pointed out that hypnotic analogs are essentially models, which represent only some aspects of the phenomenon under study but may be invaluable for testing theory by manipulating factors hypothesized to be causal.

RESEARCH ON HYPNOTHERAPY

Qualitative reviews and meta-analytic studies consistently document the potential of hypnosis to play a role in the treatment of a wide variety of psychological and medical conditions, ranging from acute and chronic pain to obesity (e.g., Lynn, Kirsch, & Rhue, 2010). The gold standard of treatment research is the randomized controlled trial in which investigators impose control (i.e., equate over treatments or conditions) over variables such as the age of participants, gender, socioeconomic status, and clinical status across hypnotic and non-hypnotic interventions. The selection criteria for the inclusion and exclusion of participants must be stipulated clearly prior to the inception of the study, and consideration must be given to how dropouts will be handled in the data analyses. The most conservative way to deal with this problem is to consider treatment incompleters as treatment failures. Ideally, hypnotizability should be assessed to ascertain the role of hypnotic responsiveness in treatment outcome. The hypnotic and nonhypnotic interventions should be identical, to the extent possible, with the exception that the procedures in the hypnosis intervention will, minimally, be labeled as "hypnotic" (e.g., relaxation defined as hypnosis versus progressive relaxation), or hypnosis will be added to treatment as usual or to a comparison treatment. A no-treatment or wait-list group is necessary to control for changes in the target condition over time and regression to the mean. Moreover, a group that serves as a placebo control is necessary if researchers wish to account for nonspecific effects such as attention, a positive alliance with the clinician, and positive expectancies.

Researchers are advised to administer well-validated clinical outcome measures; provide reliable checks of practitioner fidelity to the treatment procedures on an ongoing basis; and determine, in advance, what level of symptom change constitutes a treatment "success" or a clinically significant change in symptoms. Potential moderators and mediators of treatment outcome, such as expectancies for success, imagery ability, and degree of relaxation or depth of hypnosis, are worthy of assessment. The research should include an adequate number of participants to afford the statistical power to discern treatment effects. The most compelling demonstration of the success of a hypnotic intervention will contrast its effectiveness with a treatment that has already been shown to be effective based on randomized controlled trials.

Neurophysiological Research Involving Hypnosis

Neurophysiological research is one of the most intriguing and active areas of hypnosis-related inquiry. Researchers have established that hypnotic suggestions can produce impressive changes in brain activation that correspond to those produced by actual perceptual experiences. For example, fMRI studies have confirmed that the effects of suggestion are highly specific and produce changes in brain activity that correspond to the sensory, motor, and cognitive processes targeted by suggestions (see Oakley & Halligan, 2010, for a review). In addition, neurophysiological studies of hypnosis have consistently implicated the anterior cingulate area of the brain as involved in some alterations of consciousness experienced during hypnosis (e.g., Szechtman et al., 1998; see also Jamieson & Woody, 2007).

However, because different areas of the brain typically subserve a variety of functions, it is often difficult to interpret brain imaging studies clearly and relate the findings to theories of hypnosis and various classic issues, such as the debate regarding whether hypnosis is an altered state of consciousness. Because most areas of the brain are active most of the time, it is crucial to compare the hypnotic condition under study to well-conceived control conditions. Interpretation of findings is sometimes also compromised by the fact that the wording of the hypnotic and nonhypnotic suggestions often is quite different, raising questions about whether it is the induction of hypnosis or the wording of the suggestions that is responsible for between-group differences that are obtained. Finally, to draw strong inferences about the role of hypnotic responsiveness in mediating or moderating neurophysiological effects, it is important to include participants in the mid-range of hypnotic responsiveness, which has seldom been done.

CONCLUSION

Although the Franklin Commission succeeded in showing that Mesmer's effects were psychological, it lacked the tools of scientific psychology needed to probe and elucidate them (Kihlstrom, 2002). The last half a century, starting with Weitzenhoffer and Hilgard's (1959) development of standardized hypnotizability scales, has witnessed a tremendous burgeoning of research methods for the scientific study of hypnosis. It is fair to say that experiments involving hypnosis have become some of the most intriguing studies in contemporary psychology. Moreover, work using these methods has amply fulfilled a remark of Charles Deslon, the Mesmer associate with whom the Franklin Commission worked: "The imagination thus directed to the relief of suffering humanity would be a most valuable means in the hands of the medical profession" (Dingfelder, 2010).

REFERENCES

Barber, T. X. (1969). *Hypnosis: A scientific approach.* New York, NY: Van Nostrand Reinhold.

Barber, T. X., & Calverley, D. S. (1964). Toward a theory of "hypnotic" behavior: Effects on suggestibility of defining response to suggestion as easy. *Journal of Abnormal and Social Psychology, 68*(6), 585–592. doi:10.1037/h0046938

Barber, T. X., Spanos, N. P., & Chaves, J. (1974). *Hypnosis, imagination, and human potentialities.* New York, NY: Pergamon Press.

Barnier, A. J. (2002). Posthypnotic amnesia for autobiographical episodes: A laboratory model of functional amnesia? *Psychological Science, 13,* 232–237.

Bowers, K. S. (1993). The Waterloo-Stanford Group C (WSGC) scale of hypnotic susceptibility: Normative and comparative data. *International Journal of Clinical and Experimental Hypnosis, 41,* 35–46.

Bowers, K. S. (1998). Waterloo-Stanford group scale of hypnotic susceptibility, form C: Manual and response booklet. *International Journal of Clinical and Experimental Hypnosis, 46,* 250–268.

Bowers, K. S., & Woody, E. Z. (1996). Hypnotic amnesia and the paradox of intentional forgetting. *Journal of Abnormal Psychology, 105,* 381–390.

Bullock, J. G., Green, D. P., & Ha, S. E. (2010). Yes, but what's the mechanism? (Don't expect an easy answer). *Journal of Personality and Social Psychology, 98,* 550–558. doi:10.1037/a0018933

Bryant, R. A., Barnier, A. J., Mallard, D., & Tibbits, R. (1999). Posthypnotic amnesia for material learned before hypnosis. *International Journal of Clinical and Experimental Hypnosis, 47*(1), 46–64. doi:10.1080/00207149908410022

Bryant, R. A., & Kapur, A. (2006). Hypnotically induced emotional numbing: The roles of hypnosis and hypnotizability. *International Journal of Clinical and Experimental Hypnosis, 54*(3), 281–291.

Bryant, R. A., & McConkey, K. M. (1999). Functional blindness: A construction of cognitive and social influences. *Cognitive Neuropsychiatry, 4*(3), 227–241.

Cardeña, E., & Terhune, D. B. (2014). Hypnotizability, personality traits, and the propensity to experience alterations of consciousness. *Psychology of Consciousness: Theory, Research, and Practice, 1*(3), 292–307.

Connors, M. H., Barnier, A. J., Langdon, R., Cox, R. E., Polito, V., & Coltheart, M. (2014). Delusions in the laboratory: Modeling different pathways to mirrored-self misidentification. *Psychology of Consciousness Theory, Research, and Practice 1,* 184-198. doi:10.1037/css0000001.

Connors, M. H., Langdon, R., & Coltheart, M. (2015). Misidentification delusions. In D. Bhugra, A. Munro, & G. Malhi (Eds.), *Troublesome disguises: Undiagnosed psychiatric syndromes.* Oxford, UK: Wiley.

Council, J., Kirsch, I., Vickery, A. R. & Carlson, D. (1983). "Trance" vs. "skill" hypnotic inductions: The effects of credibility, expectancy, and experimenter modeling. *Journal of Consulting and Clinical Psychology, 51,* 432–440.

Cox, R., & Barnier, A. J. (2003). Posthypnotic amnesia for a first romantic relationship: Forgetting the entire relationship versus forgetting selected events. *Memory, 11,* 307–318.

Cox, R., & Bryant, R. A. (2008). Advances in hypnosis research: Methods, designs and contributions of intrinsic and instrumental hypnosis. In M. R. Nash & A. J. Barnier (Eds.), *The Oxford handbook of hypnosis: Theory, research and practice* (pp. 311–336). Oxford, UK: Oxford University Press. doi:10.1093/oxfordhb/9780198570097.013.0012

Dingfelder, S. F. (2010). The first modern psychology study. *Monitor on Psychology, 41*(7), 30.

Erdelyi, M. (2006). The unified theory of repression. *Behavioral and Brain Sciences, 29,* 499–551.

Faraday, M. (1853). Experimental investigation of table turning. *Atheneum, 1340,* 801–803.

Franklin, B. (1996). Testing the claims of Mesmerism [English translation of *Rapport des commissaires chargés par le Roi, de l'examen du magnétisme animal*]. *Skeptic, 4*(3), 66–109.

Giesbrecht, T., Lynn, S. J., Lilienfeld, S. O., & Merckelbach, H. (2008). Cognitive processes in dissociation: An analysis of core theoretical assumptions. *Psychological Bulletin, 134*(5), 617–647. doi:10.1037/0033-2909.134.5.617

Gould, S. J. (1991). The chain of reason versus the chain of thumbs. In *Bully for Brontosaurus: Reflections in natural history* (pp. 182–197). New York, NY: W. W. Norton.

Hargadon, R., Bowers, K. S., & Woody, E. Z. (1995). Does counter-pain imagery mediate hypnotic analgesia? *Journal of Abnormal Psychology, 104,* 508–516.

Hayes, A. F. (2013). *Introduction to mediation, moderation, and conditional process analysis: A regression-based approach.* New York, NY: Guilford Press.

Hill, Z., Hung, L., & Bryant, R. A. (2010). A hypnotic paradigm for studying intrusive memories. *Journal of Behavior Therapy and Experimental Psychiatry, 41*(4), 433–437. doi:10.1016/j.jbtep.2010.05.001

Hyman, R. (1999). The mischief of ideomotor action. *Scientific Review of Alternative Medicine, 3,* 30–39.

Jamieson, G., & Woody, E. (2007). Dissociated control as a paradigm for cognitive-neuroscience research and theorizing in hypnosis. In G. A. Jamieson (Ed.), *Hypnosis and conscious states: The cognitive-neuroscience perspective* (pp. 111–129). Oxford, UK: Oxford University Press.

Kihlstrom, J. F. (1980). Posthypnotic amnesia for recently learned material: Interactions with "episodic" and "semantic" memory. *Cognitive Psychology, 12*(2), 227–251.

Kihlstrom, J. F. (2002). Mesmer, the Franklin Commission, and hypnosis: A counterfactual essay. *International Journal of Clinical and Experimental Hypnosis, 50*(4), 407–419.

Kihlstrom, J. F., & Evans, F. J. (1979). Memory retrieval processes during posthypnotic amnesia. In J. F. Kihlstrom & F. J. Evans (Eds.), *Functional disorders of memory* (pp. 172–218). Hillsdale, NJ: Lawrence Erlbaum.

Kihlstrom, J. F., & Hoyt, I. (1988). In T. F. Oltmanns (Ed.), *Delusional beliefs: Wiley series on personality processes* (pp. 66–109). Oxford, UK: Wiley.

Kihlstrom, J. F, & Schacter, D. L. (1995). Functional disorders of autobiographical memory. In A. D. Baddelly, B. A. Wilson, & F. N. Watts (Eds.). *Handbook of memory disorders* (pp. 337–365). New York, NY: Wiley.

Kirsch, I., & Lynn, S. J. (1995). The altered state of hypnosis: Changes in the theoretical landscape. *The American Psychologist, 50*(10), 846–858.

Lynn, S. J., Kirsch, I., & Rhue, J. W. (Eds.). (2010). *Handbook of clinical hypnosis*. Washington, DC: American Psychological Association.

Lynn, S. J., Lilienfeld, S. O., Merckelbach, H., Giesbrecht, T., & van der Kloet, D. (2012). Dissociation and dissociative disorders: Challenging conventional wisdom. *Current Directions in Psychological Science, 21*(1), 48–53.

Lynn, S. J., Nash, M. R., Rhue, J., Frauman, D., & Stanley, S. (1983). Hypnosis and the experience of nonvolition. *International Journal of Clinical and Experimental Hypnosis, 31*, 293–308.

Mendelsohn, A., Chalamish, Y., Solomonovich, A., & Dudai, Y. (2008). Mesmerizing memories: Brain substrates of episodic memory suppression in posthypnotic amnesia. *Neuron, 57*, 159–170.

Noble, J., & McConkey, K. M. (1995). Hypnotic sex change: Creating and challenging a delusion in the laboratory. *Journal of Abnormal Psychology, 104*(1), 69.

Oakley, D., & Halligan, P. W. (2010). Psychophysiological foundations of hypnosis and suggestion. In S. J. Lynn, J. W. Rhue, & I. Kirsch (Eds.), *Handbook of clinical hypnosis* (pp. 79–118). Washington, DC: American Psychological Association.

Orne, M. T. (1951). The mechanism of hypnotic age regression: An experimental study. *Journal of Abnormal and Social Psychology, 46*, 213–225.

Orne, M. T. (1959). The nature of hypnosis: Artifact and essence. *Journal of Abnormal and Social Psychology, 58*, 277–299.

Pekala, R. J. (1991). *The Phenomenology of Consciousness Inventory (PCI)*. West Chester, PA: Mid-Atlantic Educational Institute.

Polito, V., Barnier, A. J., & Woody, E. Z. (2013). Developing the sense of agency rating scale (SOARS): An empirical measure of agency disruption in hypnosis. *Consciousness and Cognition, 22*(3), 684–696. doi:10.1016/j.concog.2013.04.003

Polito, V., Barnier, A. J., Woody, E., & Connors, M. J. (2014). Measuring agency across domains of hypnosis. *Psychology of Consciousness: Theory, Research, and Practice, 1*(1), 3–19.

Reyher, J. (1962). A paradigm for determining the clinical relevance of hypnotically induced psychopathology. *Psychological Bulletin, 59*, 344–352.

Sheehan, P. W., & McConkey, K. M. (1982). *Hypnosis and experience: The explanation of phenomena and process*. Hillsdale, NJ: Lawrence Erlbaum.

Sheehan, P. W., & Perry, C. W. (1976). *Methodologies of hypnosis: A critical appraisal of contemporary paradigms of hypnosis*. Hillsdale, NJ: Lawrence Erlbaum.

Shor, R. E., & Orne, E. C. (1962). *Harvard Group Scale of Hypnotic Susceptibility*. Palo Alto, CA: Consulting Psychologists Press.

Szechtman, H., Woody, E., Bowers, K. S., & Nahmias, C. (1998). Where the imaginal appears real: A PET study of auditory hallucinations. *Proceedings of the National Academy of Sciences, 95*, 1956–1960.

Weitzenhoffer, A. M., & Hilgard, E. R. (1959). *Stanford Hypnotic Susceptibility Scale, Forms A and B*. Palo Alto, CA: Consulting Psychologists Press.

Weitzenhoffer, A. M., & Hilgard, E. R. (1962). *Stanford Hypnotic Susceptibility Scale, Form C*. Palo Alto, CA: Consulting Psychologists Press.

Woody, E. Z. (1997). Have the hypnotic susceptibility scales outlived their usefulness? *International Journal of Clinical and Experimental Hypnosis, 45*, 226–238.

Woody, E. Z. (2011). An SEM perspective on evaluating mediation: What every clinical researcher needs to know. *Journal of Experimental Psychopathology, 2*(2), 210–251. doi: 10.5127/jep.010410

Woody, E. Z., Lewis, V., Snider, L., Grant, H., Kamath, M., & Szechtman, H. (2005). Induction of compulsive-like washing by blocking the feeling of knowing: An experimental test of the security-motivation hypothesis of obsessive-compulsive disorder. *Behavioral and Brain Functions, 1*, 11.

Woody, E., & Szechtman, H. (2011). Using hypnosis to develop and test models of psychopathology. *Journal of Mind-Body Regulation, 1*(1).

Zamansky, H. S., Scharf, B., & Brightbill, R. (1964). The effect of expectancy for hypnosis on prehypnotic performance. *Journal of Personality, 32*(2), 236–248.

Index